GUSTAVUS ADOLPHUS

VOLUME TWO

By the same author

GUSTAVUS ADOLPHUS

A History of Sweden 1611–1626 Volume One

GUSTAV II ADOLF
1632

GUSTAVUS ADOLPHUS

A History of Sweden
1611–1632

by

MICHAEL ROBERTS

Professor of Modern History,
The Queen's University, Belfast

VOLUME TWO

1626-1632

LONGMANS

LONGMANS, GREEN AND CO LTD
48 Grosvenor Street, London W.1
Associated companies, branches and representatives throughout the world

First Published 1958
New impressions by photo-lithography 1964 and 1968

Printed in Great Britain by
Lowe & Brydone (Printers) Ltd., London, N.W.10

PREFACE

I SHOULD like to express my gratitude to those who have assisted me in the writing of this volume: to the Librarian of the University Library, Uppsala, for his extraordinary generosity in lending books to me while I was still resident in South Africa; to the staff of the Swedish Institute, in Stockholm and in London; to my friends and colleagues Professor D. Hobart Houghton, Professor G. H. L. Le May, Dr. G. D. Ramsay, Mr. J. C. Beckett, Mr. J. W. Gray and Mr. G. Hammersley for much helpful advice and criticism; and, most of all, to my wife, for many years of forbearance.

M. R.

BELFAST
January 1957

CONTENTS

A*

PLATES

The photograph of the portrait of Wallenstein is by Brogi. All other photographs are copyright Svenska Porträttarkivet Nationalmuseum, Stockholm.

MAPS

The publishers are indebted to Försvarsstaben, Krighistoriska Avdelningen for permission to use maps in *Gustaf II Adolf* in preparing the maps for this book.

NOTE

All dates, including those for documents emanating from countries using the New Style, are given according to the Old Style, which was used in Sweden at this time, and which in the seventeenth century was ten days behind the New Style. The year, however, is taken to begin on 1 January.

CHAPTER I

SWEDISH SOCIETY IN 1611

WHEN Gustav Adolf fell on the field of Lützen in 1632, Sweden was already one of the great powers of Europe. At Westphalia, sixteen years later, Swedish diplomats negotiated as equals with the plenipotentiaries of the Emperor, the King of France and the States General. For two or three generations after that, European statesmen gave to Sweden the attentive consideration due to a great military state, even though its interventions had latterly become only intermittently formidable.

To the men of 1611 this would have seemed, if they could have foreseen it, an astonishing development. And it may well be asked what economic and social basis supported this superstructure of military power. Experience showed, no doubt, that whatever its nature it was in the long run inadequate to imperial responsibilities. Yet it was at least sufficient to establish an empire, if not to maintain it; and this in itself is sufficiently surprising. The Swedes of Gustav Adolf's day, for all their Gothic fantasies, knew well enough the slenderness of their resources; and later generations exalted 'Swedish poverty' into a national characteristic, and almost into a national virtue.[1] Sweden was, no doubt, poor; though no poorer than Scotland, or Norway, or East Elbia. Yet comparison with France, England, the Netherlands, Germany west of the Elbe, and even Denmark, was very much to Sweden's disadvantage. The traveller from Germany or from western Europe noticed this at once; and, if he were acute and sympathetic, discreetly diagnosed Swedish pride as the attempt to compensate for an inferiority in material well-being of which the upper ranks of society, at all events, were frequently conscious.[2] The soil of Sweden yielded no large exportable surplus of agricultural commodities; and the mineral wealth which lay beneath the surface still awaited proper exploitation, for Sweden lacked the capital resources requisite to its development. The middle class was small in numbers, and economically weak; towns were

[1] See, *e.g.*, C. J. L. Almqvist, *Svenska fattigdomens betydelse* (1838), especially p. 20.

[2] S. Hallberg, *Från Sveriges storhetstid. Charles Ogiers dagbok* [cited: Ogier], pp. 19, 57.

few and insignificant; trade for the most part mainly in the hands of foreigners. The standard of life of the peasantry was certainly no lower than in many continental countries; but the aristocracy and the monarchy made but a poor showing when set beside their counterparts in western Europe. The gracelessness and meanness of the houses of the nobility, the modest dimensions and inexpensive architecture of the churches, unfavourably impressed the visitor from abroad. Karl IX found it necessary to warn his nobles not to permit their servants to appear at his coronation in ragged clothes; and even as late as 1633 the regency took good care not to invite representatives of foreign powers to Gustav Adolf's funeral, lest they should see the poverty of the land.[1] It was perhaps symptomatic of the differing standards of living in England and Sweden in the sixteenth century, that whereas in Sweden prunes were highly prized luxuries especially imported for the delectation of the court, in England they were ordinarily supplied free of charge by brothels to their patrons.

Certainly no observer, in the year of Gustav Adolf's accession, could have supposed Sweden capable of the extraordinary efforts of the next three decades. The country seemed to lack the industries, the exports, the navigation by which the sinews of war might be acquired. Nor were these deficiencies offset by an abundant population available for military service. It has been calculated that in Gustav Adolf's time the population of Sweden proper may have numbered 900,000, with perhaps a further 400,000 for Finland.[2] Its distribution was very uneven. In Östergötland and Västergötland, as in the provinces grouped round the great lacustrine system of central Sweden, men lived reasonably close together, and small towns were frequent; while northwards up the coast from Stockholm, and all along the coast of Finland, ran a narrow margin of well-populated country. But the whole of Lappland, the inner parts of Västerbotten and Österbotten, the high forests towards the Norwegian border, and much of the interior of Finland, were unsuited to support any but the most sparsely scattered settlement. And even the more thickly populated districts seemed somewhat desolate to an English eye.[3]

It is difficult to be positive about population-trends in the seven-

[1] M. A. Ohlsson, *Stormaktstidens privatpalats i Stockholm*, p. 15.

[2] S. Sundquist, *Sveriges folkmängd på Gustaf II Adolfs tid*, pp. 122, 182, 279 etc.; *id.*, *Finlands folkmängd och bebyggelse i början av 1600-talet*, p. iii.

[3] G. Westin, *John Durie in Sweden*, p. 6.

teenth century, but it seems likely that in Sweden, as in most European countries except Spain, the numbers were rising slowly.[1] Yet there can be little doubt that Sweden must have felt, more than some other lands, the effect of factors which operated to keep the rate of increase down. From the middle of the sixteenth century the country had been almost continuously at war; and two of these wars—the Seven Years' War of the North and the War of Kalmar—had involved serious devastations of portions of Swedish territory. Mortality from disease was high, for hygienic conditions seem to have been bad, even by the standards of that age: Germans like Samuel Kiechel, Danes like Peder Galt (a prejudiced witness, however) thought Sweden notably unclean. The old town of Stockholm, with its wooden houses jammed together on their little islands, was undoubtedly extremely dirty; and though the strong current of the Mälar carried away much of the refuse, contamination made water a dangerous drink and poisoned the atmosphere along the shore.[2] Artificial sanitation can scarcely be said to have existed, now or for centuries to come: the first underground sewer in Sweden is said to have been laid down in 1864.[3] Pipe-led water supplies were unknown.[4] The smaller provincial towns presented less formidable problems of public health just because they were smaller; but everywhere the tight-packed wooden houses, with stalls and barns and shippons in uncomfortable proximity outside, with windows tight-shut against the cold, afforded fine harbourage for parasites, and intolerable stenches to the fastidious nose. In the country the inns were notoriously bad and dirty.[5] From the point of view of public health it was perhaps no bad thing that, in town and country alike, fires were frequent and destructive.[6]

[1] It has been estimated that in the period 1620-1720 they rose annually by between 2·2 and 2·7 per 1000: B. Boëthius, *Gruvornas, hyttornas och hamrarnas folk*, pp. 11-12. For some general remarks on European population-trends in this period (which seem, however, to be erroneous for Sweden), see G. Franz, *Der dreissigjährige Krieg und das deutsche Volk*, pp. 54-5.

[2] H. Schück, *Stockholm vid 1400-talets slut*, p. 204; Troels Lund, *Hälsobegrepp i Norden*, pp. 281-3, for sanitary conditions in Scandinavia; *ibid.*, pp. 266-271, for epidemics. Steinkallenfels in 1615 thought Swedish conditions better than those in Estonia: A. N. von Steinkallenfels, *Reise in Schweden und Liefland*, pp. 1-4.

[3] *Självstyrelse i svenskt samhällsliv*, p. 153.

[4] Gustav Adolf projected one for Stockholm in 1627: N. Ahnlund, *Från Medeltid och Vasatid*, p. 186.

[5] *Samuel Kiechels resa i Sverige 1586*, p. 352; *cf.* B. Whitelocke, *Journal of the Swedish Embassy*, I. 145, 187; Galt, pp. 12-13.

[6] The first general ordinance about firefighting dates from 1661, but local organizations had long existed: A. Löfgren, *Det svenska tenngjutarehantverkets historia*, I. 319; *cf.* H. Schück, *Stockholm vid 1400-talets slut*, pp. 213-14.

In housing conditions such as these, the Swedish population existed on a diet which in general was more than ample to support life but scarcely well-adapted to build up resistance to disease. Heckscher estimated that the diet of the average Swede in the sixteenth century, when reckoned in calories, compared not unfavourably with that of the average Swede about the year 1913; but it seems probable that his estimate was too high, and in any case the calorific value seems to have declined sharply in the following century.[1] The food was indeed copious, monotonous and sometimes bad, at least for all save the topmost levels of society. The civil servants working in Uppsala castle at the opening of the seventeenth century appear to have subsisted mainly on bread, salt fish and salt meat, and beer.[2] The staple diet for the peasant was porridge, coarse bread and turnips.[3] Ogier was regaled, in quite distinguished company, on 'high meat, turnips and radishes'. Galt complained of perpetual fluxes as a result of the badly cooked and badly preserved food.[4] The inability to feed stock through the winter meant that for nearly half the year no fresh meat was to be had; butter was salt and often rancid; fish was often salted too; and it is probably true to say that at the end of winter a majority of the population must have been in a sub-scorbutic condition. Very little milk was drunk, for it was all turned into butter; very few eggs were eaten; and the peasant was probably short of vitamin C, as well as of vitamins A and D.[5] Bread was reported by Ogier to have been commonly adulterated with wort and fennel [6]; but this at least was preferable to some of the substitutes to which the peasant was driven in bad years, even in central Sweden, and which were almost normal in some of the more infertile districts. In Lappland and northern

[1] E. F. Heckscher, *Svenskt arbete och liv*, pp. 90-2, 149. B. Odén, *Rikets uppbörd och utgift*, p. 338, for correction of Heckscher's estimate, and *cf.* P. Nyström, *Avelgårdsprojektet 1555-6*, pp. 250-1. The later decline in calorific value seems also to have been less than Heckscher supposed: T. Lagerstedt, *Livsmedel och livsmedelproduktion under stormaktstiden*, pp. 4-6. A similar decline occurred in England: J. C. Drummond and A. Wilbraham: *The Englishman's Food*, p. 52; though English standards were clearly much higher than Swedish: *ibid.*, pp. 49-57.

[2] F. Wernstedt, *Ståthållaren Christoffer Wernstedt*, pp. 44-5.

[3] C. Annerstedt, *Om samhällsklasser och levnadssätt*, p. 56.

[4] Ogier, pp. 55, 100. 'I have perpetuos ventris fluxus, salva reverentia, ex cibis male coctis et non satis salsis': Galt, p. 14.

[5] E. F. Heckscher, *Historieuppfattning, materialistisk och annan*, p. 87; H. Forssell, *Anteckningar om Sveriges jordbruksnäring i sextonde seklet*, p. 102; Drummond and Wilbraham, *op. cit.*, pp. 88, 90, 92. Possibly scurvy was kept sub-acute by decoctions of fresh pine-shoots: on this see the somewhat sceptical judgment in Drummond and Wilbraham, p. 320.

[6] Ogier, p. 14.

Norrland we hear of dried fish or fish-roes being used instead of bread; in other parts of Sweden bread might be made, in an emergency, of chaff, bran, turnip- or cabbage-roots, Iceland moss and meal, bones, heather, horse-droppings, or flax-seed. Bark-bread, or bread made from a mixture of bark and meal, was common enough in hard times. It took a practised stomach to digest it; and there were peasants who with pessimistic logic made a practice of eating it every year, so that when the inevitable failure of the harvest arrived their digestion should be conditioned to deal with it. Bark-bread, indeed, was a normal feature of Swedish life for centuries, and was eaten in years of privation as late as the latter half of the nineteenth century.[1] On the other hand, imported luxuries—notably sugar—were beginning to give some variety to the diet of the upper classes; but their effect was probably not important until Kristina's reign.[2]

The deficiencies and monotony of the food were partly atoned for by the strength and variety of the liquor. The ordinary drink, for young and old alike, was beer; which, in view of the state of the water-supply, was no bad thing. Home-brewing of beer was universal, at least in the country: in the towns there were taverns where the thirsty artisan could obtain it. The taverner was bound to indicate to the public whether he sold strong beer or small beer; and a glass suspended outside the door signified the one, a wooden beer-can the other. The strong beer was esteemed rather thick for an English taste; and Galt, who disliked most things Swedish, did not like it either.[3] The taverner might sell only Swedish ale: the vending of imported liquors was reserved to the innkeeper. But this restriction upon the taverner's activities does not seem to have interfered much with his prospects of making a livelihood, if we may judge from the fact that in Jönköping in Gustav Adolf's time there were no less than eighteen taverners to a total of 148 burgesses.[4]

[1] For these substitutes for bread, see N. Keyland, *Svensk allmogeskost*, I. 111-14; L. Levander, *Fattigt folk och tiggare*, pp. 19, 32-4; B. Boëthius, *Ur de stora skogarnas historia*, pp. 36, 67; Steinkallenfels, p. 7; and for examples from the eighteenth and nineteenth centuries, C. von Linné, *Ungdomsresor*, I. 73, 139-40; *Journal av Petrus Laestadius*, II. 101. Substitutes in England seem to have been both less common and less disagreeable: Drummond and Wilbraham, pp. 55, 106.

[2] Apiculture declined after the Reformation, as a result of the suppression of the monasteries (the monks had often been skilled apiarists) and the lessened demand for wax: H. Juhlin-Dannfelt, *Lantbrukets historia*, p. 419.

[3] Whitelocke, II. 115; Galt, pp. 2, 4.

[4] Björkman, II. 150. For the whole subject, see L. Levander, *Landsväg, krog och marknad*, pp. 82-134, 194, 198.

Nevertheless, the Swedes were by no means conservative in their drinking habits, and the innkeeper did plenty of business: the excise of 1612 enumerates twelve sorts of beer and ten of mead,[1] and there were many imported wines, though their use was confined to the wealthier classes. The most famous Swedish drink of a later age, snapps (*brännvin*), was at the beginning of Gustaf Adolf's reign only gradually establishing itself. In the sixteenth century it had been used in the making of gunpowder; as a medicine, supposed especially efficacious against the plague; and by Erik XIV (it is said) as a form of torture; but by the beginning of the seventeenth century it was becoming favourably known as a drink. In 1619 we hear of its use upon festive occasions by the young men of Uppsala. Up to the end of the sixteenth century most of it was imported from France; but during the Russian wars of Johan III the Swedish armies learned the distilling of it for themselves. But it was not until the lesson had been relearned during Gustav Adolf's campaigns in Muscovy that the drink became popular among Swedes at home. *Brännvin* remained expensive until home-distilling became usual; and in this the nobility led the way. Their example was quickly followed; and soon every village had its still. In some cases the liquor was stored, for want of better quarters, in the church, and the parson would supplement his stipend by letting out the distilling-pan to his congregation. In Gustav Adolf's time it was still considered a foreign drink; and his ordinance of 1622 accordingly prohibited its sale by taverners. The prohibition was of small significance. By 1638 the consumption had risen so greatly, as a result of home-distilling, that the government began to think of *brännvin* as a possible source of revenue.[2] Thus Gustav Adolf's reign, among other portentous changes which transformed the face of Sweden, saw the establishment in popular favour of a drink which at times threatened to become almost as important an influence upon society as gin or port in eighteenth-century England. Not, it should be added, that *brännvin* was needed to deflect Sweden from the paths of sobriety: the Swede, like the Englishman and the Dane in that age, had a

[1] A. A. von Stiernman, *Samling utaf . . . Förordningar etc. angående Sweriges Commerce Politie och Oeconomie* [cited: *CPO*], I. 574.

[2] E. Olan, *Svenska brännvinets historia*, pp. 7-21; E. G. Geijer, *Svenska folkets historia*, II. 333 *note* 1; Björkman, *Jönköpings historia*, I. 152-3; N. Keyland, *Svensk allmogeskost*, II. 97. It seems fairly clear, however, that *brännvin* was drunk in Stockholm already by the end of the fifteenth century: H. Schück, *Stockholm vid 1400-talets slut*, pp. 404-6.

formidable reputation for tippling.[1] Drinking and drunkenness were a normal feature of life at every social level; potations were a weapon of diplomacy; drunkenness was essential to hospitality; and intoxication was the sincerest form of flattery. The coming of *brännvin* probably did no more than shorten the road to oblivion; and may thus, perhaps, in its economy of time, be considered an advance towards modernity. Its arrival was coincident with the coming of another social vice—the 'drinking' of tobacco, which begins in Sweden in Gustav Adolf's time: by the end of the reign the university authorities were already showing some concern at its abuse by the undergraduates at 'cornute-ales' and other celebrations.[2]

In such a society the expectation of life was short. Death by violence—in the wars, or in the civil brawls of that proud and hot-tempered generation—accounted for some; under-nourishment, vitamin-deficiency and sheer starvation for many; dirty living and epidemic diseases for many more. The birth-rate was certainly high; but the death-rate, even in the upper ranks of society, was tremendous: two generations later Johan Ekeblad seems to record a death among his friends and acquaintances in almost every other letter. In Gustav Adolf's time Sweden was visited by severe epidemics of plague: they occurred, for instance, every year from 1620 to 1624, being especially mortal in Östergötland and Närke in 1622, and in Stockholm in 1623; and there were other outbreaks in Stockholm in 1629 and 1630.[3] There was little medical skill available to meet them: Mönnichhofen, the German engineer who saved Stockholm from Kristian IV in 1612, and was killed before Gdov in 1614, is reported as praising Sweden 'because it had but

[1] In the sixteenth century one *kanna* of beer (about half a gallon) was considered a reasonable daily allowance, though Johan III's soldiers got four *kannor* apiece: Heckscher, *Historieuppfattning*, p. 86. Compare the English allowance of one gallon *per* man to troops while at sea (C. Falls, *Elizabeth's Irish Wars*, p. 63), or the Dutch provision in 1582 of 500 tuns (=126,000 gallons) for 10,000 men for five days or about 2½ gallons *per* man *per* day: J. W. Wijn, *Het Krijgswezen in den Tijd van Prins Maurits*, p. 383. On Swedish drinking habits see Ogier, pp. 61, 65, 73; Whitelocke, I. 416; K. W. Herdin, *Uppsala på 1600-talet*, I. 71. Gustav Adolf for his wedding ordered over 13,000 quarts of wine and 82,000 quarts of Stralsund and Rostock ale—besides, presumably, Swedish-brewed liquor: Annerstedt, *Om samhällsklasser*, p. 49.

[2] For tobacco, see Herdin, *Uppsala på 1600-talet*, III. 43-4; Keyland, *Svensk allmogeskost*, II. 100 *note* 2; *Johan Ekeblads brev*, I. 293. A duty was imposed on imported tobacco for the first time in 1629: W. Smith, *Studier i svensk tull-administration*, p. 67.

[3] *Axel Oxenstiernas skrifter och brefvexling* [cited: *AOSB*], II. III. 42, 44, 48, 62; *Svenska riksrådets protokoll* [cited: *RRP*], I. 210, 214, 217; II. 34, 39; J. Hallenberg, *Svea Rikes historia under Konung Gustaf Adolf den stores regering*, V. 342-4; Galt, p. 69.

one King, one religion, and one medico, which is a sign of health'.[1] In 1629 John Casimir was pleading with Camerarius to send him a Dutch doctor, since no reputable practitioner was to be had in Kalmar.[2] The barber-surgeons had had a gild since 1571, and its regulations demanded a sojourn abroad; but qualified physicians were rare, and outside a few of the larger towns there were probably none.[3] Gustav Adolf himself was attended by a Scots physician, Dr. James Robertson; but he does not seem to have been remarkable for skill in his profession.[4]

The best protection against epidemics that the age afforded was provided not so much by Dr. Robertson and his brother practitioners as by a sound constitution. But a sound constitution demanded an adequate standard of nutrition; and that, apart from all considerations of vitamin-content, was attainable only if harvests were good. The whole of life, from the apex of society to its base, was indissolubly bound to the soil. The power of the monarchy, the wealth of the aristocracy, the stipends of the clergy and the prosperity of the towns were all as dependent upon the good management of the land and the vagaries of the weather as was the life and well-being of the tax-paying peasant farming his own few acres.[5] Everyone was more or less of a farmer. And not only was it a predominantly rural society: it was also a predominantly peasant society. Probably nine-tenths of the population worked on the land. Thus the harvest-yields directly affected a great majority of the population, and indirectly affected all. Gustav Adolf's reign was a relatively fortunate period in this respect: the harvests were generally from average to good, though there were some bad years in his last decade; and at no time was there a deficiency serious enough to cause such a catastrophic shortage as occurred, for instance, in 1596 and 1597.[6]

[1] Geijer, III. 80.

[2] F. C. von Moser, *Neues patriotisches Archiv für Deutschland,* I. 102-3; *cf.* E. Wrangel, *De betrekkingen tusschen Zweden en de Nederlanden op het gebied van letteren en wetenschap*, p. 294.

[3] Herdin, III. 119; Whitelocke, II. 57. As late as 1732 Linnaeus could write, 'Here in Gävle is the last apothecary's shop as you go north, and the last Provincial Doctor': Linné, *Ungdomsresor*, I. 29.

[4] For Dr. Robertson, see C. Forsstrand, *En Stockholmsläkare under förra hälften av 1600-talet, passim*; Ekeblad, I. 141.

[5] For the correlation of well-being and harvest-yield, see Heckscher, *Svenskt arbete och liv*, p. 107; for the rural nature of the towns, see (*e.g.*) Herdin, III. 132-8; G. Lindgren, *Falbygden vid 1600-talets mitt*, pp. 51, 57 (for Falköping); D. Hannerberg, *Närkes boskapsbestånd på 1620- och 1630-talen*, pp. 97-9 (for Örebro).

[6] T. Söderberg, *Sveriges ekonomiska struktur och utveckling under Gustav Adolf*, p. 51; Hannerberg, *op. cit.*, pp. 18-23.

Much less than half of Sweden's soil was suitable for arable cultivation; and though everywhere the peasant tried to raise some sort of crop, a broad distinction can be made between the areas of grain-surplus and those of grain-deficiency. The southern provinces were predominantly pastoral; and this was true even of the relatively untimbered and fertile Västergötland. These provinces tended to pay their rents in cattle or butter. The central provinces around Lake Mälar, on the other hand, were grain-growing, and tended to pay their rents and taxes in grain. The mining area of the Bergslag—in Värmland, Dalarna and Närke—was a region of grain-deficiency; and so was most of Norrland. The granary of Sweden proper was Östergötland, which in normal years had a large surplus; and this surplus went to supply some of the needs of the areas which could not feed themselves: for Sweden, like England, was in the happy position of having no internal customs barriers. The conquest of Livonia added a particularly rich grain-growing territory to the Swedish dominions.[1]

In the areas of grain-deficiency the emphasis was upon cattle, rather than sheep; though the wool of the local breed provided the farmer's wife with the raw material for the cloth she produced at home.[2] In the far north, besides the cattle, there was hunting and fishing to supplement the peasant's income: seals in the skerries, salmon in the rivers, *strömming* (a small kind of herring) out to sea. Most villages would have their own fishing-rights in the neighbouring streams, and for many the fishing provided the necessary cash income wherewith to pay their taxes.[3]

In the grain-growing areas, as well as in the areas of grain-deficiency, the main crop was still barley, with nearly two-thirds of the total. Wheat accounted for probably not much more than one per cent. of the harvest, and was grown only in the area around Lake Mälar; oats was increasing, especially where three-field cultivation prevailed, but it was esteemed an inferior sort of grain, and was always reckoned for taxation-purposes at half the value of barley and wheat. Rye formed about a third of the crop, and by the middle of the seventeenth century may perhaps have caught up with barley: it

[1] H. Forssell, *Anteckningar om Sveriges jordbruksnäring*, p. 31; E. F. Heckscher, *Sveriges ekonomiska historia*, I. 423; F. Lindberg, *Landshövdingeämbetets äldsta historia*, p. 147; W. Tham, *Lindesberg och Nora genom tiderna*, I. 191.

[2] Ogier, pp. 21, 116; *cf.* Forssell, *op. cit.*, p. 111. For the relative importance of cattle and sheep in a pastoral province, see Hannerberg, *op. cit.*, pp. 51, 53, 55, 103. For wool, S. T. Kjellberg, *Ull och ylle*, pp. 189-92, 607.

[3] Boëthius, *Ur de stora skogarnas historia*, p. 47.

yielded more straw, and in favourable areas cropped almost twice as heavily; and it was especially favoured by those Finnish colonists who began burn-beat cultivation in the clearances they had made in the forests. In any but a bad year, the total yield of grain was adequate to the country's needs, both for brewing and baking, and perhaps left a surplus for export; though for six years of Gustav Adolf's reign export was forbidden.[1]

Agricultural methods and techniques were still much as they had been in the Middle Ages, and much as they would continue for another century or more. Country life remained almost static, and apart from the colonizing efforts of the crown, and the activities of Finnish immigrants (to be described presently), there was little tendency for the area under the plough to increase. To Ogier, the methods employed even in the best grain-growing parts of the country seemed to have a primitiveness such as might have been expected from the first colonizers of the waste, but hardly from an agricultural community with centuries of cultivation behind it.[2] The average village community cultivated its lands on the two- or three-field system, though there were still many which continued to work but a single open-field.[3] The open-field, and sometimes the common meadow too, was allocated among the villagers in strips, in a manner familiar from English examples; though there were plenty of instances—usually where a one-field system prevailed—in which the parcels of land were almost square in shape. Within the area of meadow and arable there were no fences; but a hedge whose proper maintenance was the first of civic duties separated these from the waste. The village community had its own petty court, the court of neighbours, judging cases by local custom, with appeal to the *häradsrätt* as the next instance; and it was this body which enforced uniformity of agricultural practice upon its members and employed the village bailiff to carry out its decisions.

[1] Forssell, *op. cit.*, pp. 17-21; Söderberg, *op. cit.*, p. 49; D. Hannerberg, *Närkes landsbygd*, pp. 238-44; B. Helmfrid, *Tiondelängderna som källa till ett byalags ekonomiska historia*, p. 111; T. Lagerstedt, *Livsmedel och livsmedelproduktion under stormaktstiden*, pp. 8-11; *id.*, *Näringsliv och bygd i Seminghundra härad*, pp. 10, 30.

[2] Ogier, p. 21.

[3] The single-field was both an extensive and an intensive form of agriculture: on the one hand it was worked till it was exhausted, after which cultivation moved to another field; on the other hand the concentration of all available manure upon a single field enabled the land to be used longer than would otherwise have been the case: F. Dovring, *Agrarhistorien*, pp. 36-7; Hannerberg, *Närkes landsbygd*, pp. 179-95; Helmfrid, p. 107; Lagerstedt, *Näringsliv*, pp. 30, 45, 54-7; Juhlin-Dannfelt, p. 403.

Peasant agriculture offered little scope for experiment with new crops or better techniques, for the margin of safety between subsistence and starvation was too narrow to admit the taking of risks. The peasant's rent, or his taxes, took so much (and were designed to take so much) of his production as to leave him just sufficient to live on, in all ordinary years; and though rising prices towards the end of the century, coinciding with a tendency to regard the burdens on the land as fixed and unalterable, modified this situation somewhat in the peasant's favour (at least for a time), he had little prospect of saving, and in a bad year might be in real danger of starvation. The fiscal ideal, repeatedly expressed in royal injunctions, was that each family should have enough land, and no more than enough. The acquisition of additional farms by peasants, and their leasing out to under-tenants, was forbidden: 'peasant must not tax peasant', for an under-tenant, if he paid his rent to his landlord, would have nothing over wherewith to pay his taxes to the crown. So, too, the crown prohibited the splitting-up of farms, since the holders of the several fragments would probably be unable to meet those personal taxes which were levied on a *per capita* basis on all peasant owners. This prohibition was evaded, by various subterfuges, and subdivision did in fact take place, in some parts of the country reaching extreme lengths unusual in England; and where this happened the result was to produce a rural proletariat who eked out an existence by casual labour.[1] But casual labour, however useful at harvest-time, was frowned on by the authorities; and official policy aimed at yearly contracts and an approximate equality of holdings. Thus agriculture was predominantly small-scale subsistence farming within the restrictive framework of village custom, and in such circumstances improvements in cultivation were not to be looked for. The King did indeed take care that the land was not grossly abused; and the peasant who so mismanaged his farm that he could not pay his taxes would find after three years' default that it was declared forfeit. But neither the King nor the nobility, who might have been expected to take the lead in agricultural improvements, were in fact much better in their practice than the peasantry. Gustav Vasa had created special royal farms of unusual size, with a view to feeding his armies, and had concentrated considerable labour-forces upon them; but

[1] For remarkable examples of minute subdivision, see the two maps at the end of Heckscher, *Sveriges ekonomiska historia*, I. And see H. Forssell, *Anteckningar*, pp. 79-84; Lindgren, *Falbygden*, pp. 75-94, 146-52.

they were efficient rather from the point of view of administration than from that of agronomy, and apart from some experiments in sheep-breeding the monarchy did little to set an example. It is possible that the manors (*sätesgårdar*) [1] of the nobility were farmed a little more progressively than were the open-fields, for sometimes they were compact and consolidated units, set apart from the lands of the villagers; but manors, after all, as yet formed only an insignificant fraction of the estates of the nobility. Much noble land consisted of strips intermingled with peasant holdings in the open-fields; and even where this was not so, the noble proprietor preferred to draw rents from his peasants rather than to expand demesne farming.[2]

In those parts of the country where the soil was naturally less fertile or more difficult to work, the return was meagre. In Norrland men were said to be content if they got three good crops in ten years; in parts of Västergötland in 1638 the yield was just over three-fold; and at the end of the seventeenth century the yield from the best land was not more than six-fold, and on the average not more than four-fold. On the richer lands, where crops were grown for food rather than fodder, it was impossible to feed any large number of stock for the six or seven months during which they would be confined to the byres. The few beasts that were not slaughtered in the autumn were fed on dried weeds, or marsh-plants, or leaves, or horse-dung, or in extreme cases on the very straw and bark with which the peasant roofed his cabin; and when spring arrived they were so weak, if they survived, that they had to be carried from the byre to pasture. The shortage of fodder had its effect, in turn, upon the production of food; for the lack of stock meant lack of manure. On the other hand, in many regions which were not grain-producing the forests offered rich grass in the summer months, and the cattle would be driven many miles from the villages to summer-stations deep in the woods, to take advantage of this; while their owners subsisted on stinted allowances of salt butter and sour milk. In such

[1] 'Manor' is to be considered only as a very rough equivalent to *sätesgård*. A *sätesgård* was really a home farm *plus* the farms of the tenants who were bound to do labour-service upon it. There was nothing to correspond to a manorial court.

[2] For the above, see Forssell, *Anteckningar*, pp. 65 *note*, 77-82; Heckscher, I. 118-120, 133-4, 137; B. Boëthius, *Gruvornas, hyttornas och hamrarnas folk*, pp. 13-15, 61-3; G. Thulin, *Om mantalet*, I. 25-30, 40-1; P. Nyström, *Avelgårdsprojektet*, pp. 236-7; Lindgren, *Falbygden*, pp. 24-6, 59, 75; A. Thomson, *Grundskatterna i den politiska diskussionen*, p. 18; Helmfrid, p. 124; Juhlin-Dannfelt, p. 396.

areas the ability to buy grain depended in part upon the ability to produce butter with which to pay for it, and in the brief summer the human population tightened its belt, that the cattle might grow sleek.[1] There were areas, of course, where this precarious balance broke down. Over much of Norrland the peasantry supplemented income by craftwork or domestic industry; or failing that went outside their own district in search of employment. In the south, the peasants of parts of Västergötland became famous all over Sweden, then and long afterwards, as pedlars of textiles and small wooden articles.[2] The ease with which the rising Swedish metallurgical industries recruited an unskilled labour-force in this century is in part explained by the difficulty of winning a livelihood in the upper valleys of Värmland or the forests of Dalarna. In Dalarna, indeed, the pressure of population upon the means of subsistence—aggravated by the extremely minute subdivision of holdings—produced a very special reaction which set its mark upon Swedish life for another couple of centuries. The *dalmas* (as the peasant of Dalarna was called) went out to work at certain definite seasons of the year, during which time his ancestral holding would be managed by his womenfolk,[3] but he took care to return for at least the harvest season. He did not, therefore, like the Västgöta *knalle*, get off the land altogether; but sought, like the Irish haymaker who came over to England while his potatoes were ripening in the garden at home, to make the best of both worlds. The *dalmasar* set off from their villages in marching columns; they were organized, very often, as teams, each with its leader; and they specialized in a certain limited range of employments. They were above all 'navvies', builders' labourers, quarrymen and roadmakers, and as such they played a part in Swedish economic history of considerable importance, even down to the nineteenth century. They went also to the silver-mine at Sala, or to the copper-mines at Falun; they were prepared to do threshing and other agricultural work in districts with richer soils than their own; and many of them earned money carting ore or wood to the

[1] For all this, see Forssell, pp. 35-7, 97-9, 102, 109; Boëthius, *Ur de stora skogarnas historia*, pp. 38-41, 44-9; *id.*, *Skogen och bygden*, pp. 53, 59, 60, 67-8, 161; Heckscher, *Historieuppfattning*, pp. 83-5; Hannerberg, *Närkes landsbygd*, pp. 224-32; Lagerstedt, *Näringsliv*, pp. 15-16, 29.

[2] N. Forssell, *Borås stads historia*, I. 6-11; O. Mannerfelt, *Sjuhäradsbygden före 1622 och Borås stad 1622 1865*, pp. 39-42; Heckscher, *Den ekonomiska innebörden av 1500- och 1600-talets svenska stadsgrundningar*, p. 342.

[3] Sometimes, it seems, to the prejudice of good farming: see a comment by Linnaeus in 1734: Linné, *Ungdomsresor*, II. 161.

furnaces. Domestic industry and peddling, too, were not unknown in Dalarna, especially in the north; but the Dalesmen's characteristic contribution was in the field of heavy unskilled manual labour.[1]

Beyond the boundaries of village cultivation, in Norrland, Dalarna, Värmland, Småland, stretched a vast sea of forest, sporadically islanded by the lonely settlements of a migratory and sometimes shy population; a country where wolves were still a nuisance [2]; a country which was only beginning to be exploited and colonized. The forest was partly the commonage of the villagers, who depended upon the grazing and game and firewood that were to be had in it; and for the rest it was crown property. In its great undulating sweeps of timber the tiny communities that bordered it marked out each its own preserve, whose limits none but the local eye could determine. To-day Sweden's forests are one of the natural assets of the country, and are conserved and safeguarded accordingly; in the seventeenth century they were much more the sign of Sweden's poverty. For the forests grew high, thin and straggling, all encumbered below with brushwood and undergrowth; the trees, too close together, shut out light and air; and in consequence the pasturage which the forest offered was too often much poorer than it ought to have been, and hence enormous areas were needed to provide the villagers with the grazing they required. After uncounted centuries of neglect, the forests of Sweden were choking themselves. To the wealth of the nation they contributed but little. Timber was not yet an important Swedish export, and lumbering was confined to a few coastal towns, where the sea solved the problem of transport. The great timber-exporting country in Gustav Adolf's time was Norway. Pitch and tar were more important, and tar-burning was a typical peasant industry; but even these operations were confined in the main to the maritime belt, and the inland forests

[1] B. Boëthius, *Dalafolkets herrarbete, passim*; *id.*, *Skogen och bygden*, pp. 133-9, 140-52, 154-5; F. Lindberg, *Hantverkarna*, pp. 26-7; B. Beckman, *Dalupproret 1743*, pp. 20-39: *cf.* Bellman's lyric:

. . . och på ängen re'n
Lutad mot en sten
Dalkarln i sin skyffel tar.

(Already in the meadow the Dalesman, leaning against a rock, takes a grip of his shovel.)

[2] *Diarium Gyllenianum*, p. 30; *Johan Ekeblads brev*, I. 266; *Vendels sockens dombok*, p. 88.

were hardly exploited at all.[1] The woods were still, of course, rich in game: in 1581 the peasants of Värmland paid their tithe in elk hides. Yet, from the point of view of game-preservation, as well as from that of improving the economy of the forest, the times were changing, and changing fairly fast. It was Gustav Vasa who first made a real effort to assert—or perhaps to extend—the crown's rights over the forest: he had laid it down that all unoccupied land in northern Sweden belonged to 'God, Ourselves, and the crown of Sweden, and to none other'; and in the seventeenth century, under the influence of the Roman law, the idea began to emerge that the King had a *dominium eminens* over all the forest, while even villages with claims upon the commonage of immemorial antiquity had no more than a *dominium utile*.[2] Gustav Vasa, anxious as always to increase his revenue, had given encouragement to cottagers who were prepared to settle on the waste, in the hope that one day they might thrive sufficiently to be taxed.[3] His successors felt that they could use the forest more advantageously than the local inhabitants did; and Karl IX and Gustav Adolf both acted on that belief. The cutting of beech and oak woods was strictly prohibited; elk was declared royal game; and Gustav Adolf punished any who offended against the law in these respects by transportation to Ingria. The growing demands of industry for fuel for smelting and extraction would soon force the government to face the need for a forest-conservation policy.[4] And one factor conducing to this situation was contributed by the monarchy itself, which had interfered with the ancient economy of the forest by its patronage and encouragement of Finnish colonists.

Emigration from Finland to Sweden had occurred sporadically during the later Middle Ages, mostly into the Mälar district; but such movements of population had not as a rule been either permanent or significant. In the last quarter of the sixteenth century, however, they began to assume some importance. In part they were a spontaneous reaction to the insecurity and lawlessness which

[1] *cf.* Linnaeus: 'The great woods of pine stand deserted and useless, for no one needs the timber, which falls down and rots away. *Quaeritur*, if it were not worth while to make tar and pitch thereof? *R.*, the long haul would not repay the trouble, *dicat judex*': Linné, I. 82.

[2] C. W. U. Kuylenstierna, *Om rekognitionsskogar och under bruk skatteköpta hemman*, pp. 26-31; V. Elgeskog, *Svensk torpbebyggelse från 1500-talet till laga skiftet*, p. 36.

[3] Elgeskog, *op. cit.*, pp. 25-9, 42; Dovring, *Agrarhistorien*, p. 97; Boëthius, *Ur de stora skogarnas historia*, pp. 70-1.

[4] For the forests, see in general Boëthius, *Ur de stora skogarnas historia*; *id.*, *Skogen och bygden*.

marked the history of Finland during Sigismund's reign; in part they were a deliberate policy of colonization instituted by the Swedish authorities, and in particular by Karl IX, who seems to have borrowed the idea from Gustav Vasa. Karl encouraged Finns to come, first to Södermanland and the Bergslag, and later to Värmland; and though the immigration was not significant in Värmland till Gustav Adolf's time, there were already by the end of the century numerous Finns established in all these areas. At the same time a movement of population was in progress across the northern reaches of the Gulf of Bothnia, from Österbotten to Ångermanland, Medelpad, Hälsingland and Gästrikland, and ultimately thence to Norway. The emigration went on steadily until about 1620, when the improvement of conditions in Finland seems to have caused it to slacken; but it continued at least to 1640, and perhaps for twenty years after that. Its effect was to bring to the country a population of some 13,000 or 15,000 Finns, mostly of Finnish rather than of Swedish speech, dispersed throughout the high forests of much of north-central Sweden. But this was only part of a general movement of emigration from Finland, which benefited not only Sweden but also the Swedish overseas possessions of Karelia, Estonia and Livonia, and spread to non-Swedish areas such as Kurland, Prussia, Pomerania and Mecklenburg. It culminated in the participation by Finns in Sweden's solitary attempt to found a colony on the American mainland. The drain on Finland's none-too-numerous population at last alarmed the government; and in 1620 emigration beyond the Swedish dominions was prohibited.[1]

Some of the Finns came to Sweden as agricultural labourers; some as shipwrights or tar-burners; more were attracted to the mining industry, and made a living as charcoal-burners, carters or miners; but the great majority set up for themselves in the forest. They tended to be found most thickly on the southern-facing slopes of the watersheds dividing the river-systems of central Sweden, and in general they chose moraine lands, too stony for the Swedish peasant to work, or lands above the highest marine limit of the post-glacial period, which were ordinarily too distant from the villages. It was here, indeed, that the authorities were most anxious that they should settle, in order that tracts of country previously unworked,

[1] *Samling af Instructioner för högre och lägre Tjenstemän vid Landt-Regeringen i Sverige och Finland* [cited: *SILR*], p. 149; and see J. Hallenberg, *Svea Rikes Historia under Konung Gustaf Adolf den stores regering*, V. 225-6.

or inaccessible, should be put to some profitable use. They brought with them habits of life which had become strange to Sweden; an even lower standard of living than was usual among the Swedish peasantry; their own peculiar folk-lore and superstitions; and their own Finnish speech, to which they clung tenaciously: it survived in Medelpad, for instance, until the 1850's, and in Värmland even until the 1920's. And above all they brought with them an agriculture based upon burn-beat cultivation: in Swedish, *svedjande*.[1] *Svedjande* was not, of course, introduced into Sweden by the Finns; but it had by this time ceased to be widely practised by Swedish farmers. It consisted in making a clearing in the forest and allowing the fallen trees to lie for a year; after which they were burnt as they lay, and rye was sown in the ashes. The result was a splendid crop for two years running, and a luxuriant growth of grass. Ground so cleared and treated did not yield a satisfactory crop for a third year, and the Finn therefore moved on to another part of the forest, cleared another patch, and began again. He made no attempt to remove stumps, and still less stones (an impossible undertaking in the moraine lands), and his plough was a primitive type of fork-plough, which did no more than scratch a furrow between the boulders and the pine-roots. The Finns thus practised a wasteful form of extensive agriculture; and they were encouraged only because nobody in that age could devise any practicable alternative method of putting much of these tracts of country to any equally profitable use. The Finn lived where no man had lived before; if he could be induced to abandon a vagabond existence he might do just well enough to pay his taxes once the six years' respite conceded to him as a colonist had expired; and from the crown's point of view that was a solid, if modest, gain.

Theoretically, these settlements in the forest were not permitted to take place haphazard: the immigrant Finn had to obtain, from the King or his local representative, a certificate in which the site of his intended settlement would be roughly described; and afterwards its boundaries would be viewed and delimited by the *häradsnämnd*.[2] In the sixteenth century this practice seems to have been generally followed. But thereafter the Finns grew lax, and often they estab-

[1] *cf.* the North of England dialect word 'swithering'—*sc.* burning the grass. Magalotti reports that it had at one time been thought that the word *Sverige* was derived from *svedja*, because of the prevalence of the practice there: L. Magalotti, *Sverige under år 1674*, p. 62 and *note* 3.

[2] For the *häradsnämnd*, see Vol. I, p. 316, above.

lished themselves wherever their fancy might lead them, in obliviousness or contempt of ancient commonage-rights. This led to complaints from the Swedish peasantry; but the Finns on their side grumbled that the Swedes would claim commonage at an absurdly great distance from their villages or farms; and often both parties would journey to Stockholm to make representations to the government. Though the *häradsnämnd* usually did fairly by the immigrants, villages might levy blackmail on a Finn lawfully provided with a certificate, and compel him to rent or buy land which was really his already; and instances occurred when villages sold the same rights twice over, so that Gustav Adolf in 1626 was forced to prohibit such sales. There were complaints that the Finns killed far too much game; and many of them never really settled at all. Linguistic differences were another source of friction, and from time to time the authorities in Stockholm adopted an oppressive policy designed to coerce the Finns to abandon their mother-tongue.[1] Gustav Adolf in this respect was an honourable exception; and as long as he was on the throne the Finns were treated with tolerance and sympathy. By the mid-'thirties, however, official circles were beginning to look unfavourably on Finnish immigration, and an ordinance of 1636 prescribed stringent measures against Finns who wandered about the forests without any obvious legitimate employment. The development of the mines had already caused such largely increased demands for fuel that the wasteful *svedjande* had become a nuisance, at all events in Bergslagen; and in 1647 the government, by issuing the Forest Ordinance, at last took steps to safeguard the supply of wood against the immigrants' depredations.[2]

[1] For instance, in 1646 it was ordered that every Finn 'who will not learn Swedish, or go to church, *ting* and *stämma*, or in general show himself obedient to the Authorities and the Clergy, and douce and loving to the Swedes . . . his house shall be burnt up . . . and he be looked upon by every Swede as an outlaw': R. Gothe, *Från trolldomstro till kristendom*, pp. 90-1.

[2] For the Finnish immigration, see E. Falk, *Finnarna i Värmland intill 1600-talets mitt*; Gothe, *op. cit.*; *id.*, *Medelpads Finnmarker*; S. Lönborg, *Finnmarkerna i mellersta Skandinavien*; A. Rydberg, *Finnarna i Värmland*; J. Furuskog, *De värmländska järnbruken*, pp. 96-9; Kuylenstierna, p. 32 *seqq.*; F. Lindberg, *Västerviks historia*, I. 168; Boëthius, *Ur de stora skogarna historia*, pp. 61-6, 72-3. The question as to whether there really was a wood-shortage for the metallurgical industries in Sweden is still debated. It seems likely that considerable concentrations of mines, furnaces and forges in a small area could cause a purely local shortage: apart from the wood consumed for industrial purposes, domestic consumption would then become an appreciable factor, since a household's fuel and fencing requirements are said (perhaps somewhat improbably) to have needed a stretch of woodland of about 5 km. by 2·5 km. for their satisfaction (Juhlin-Dannfelt, p. 420). It seems likely, too, that in at least some

From the Finn on his clearing in the high forest to the ordinary Swedish cottar; from the cottar to the villager; from the villager to the townsman, was a natural and not difficult progression. The village commonage shaded off into the waste, the country faded into the town, without any violent transition: indeed, it has been said that in the sixteenth century town was to be distinguished from country mainly by differing methods of taxation.[1] Stockholm itself, despite its cluttered houses and narrow streets, had still many of the characteristics of an overgrown village. Yet Stockholm was incomparably the most important centre of population, and by its position in the economic life of the country it completely overshadowed all other Swedish towns. Its population in the earlier part of Gustav Adolf's reign may have been about nine thousand, to which perhaps should be added another three thousand more for its suburb of Norrmalm, which at this time ranked as a separate municipality.[2] No other town in Sweden approached these figures; and perhaps none reached the five-thousand mark. It is difficult to construct any list of towns ranged in order of size; but it seems likely that the largest town after Stockholm was Norrköping, and that Gävle, Uppsala, Västerås, Örebro, Arboga and Jönköping were the next most important. In Finland, Åbo and Viborg seem to have been distinctly larger than any others.[3] The total

cases the 'shortage' meant no more than that the cost of hauling timber from more distant woods entailed a prohibitive increase of price: Uhr suggested, for instance, that crown undertakings, which were less concerned to make a profit, felt the 'shortage' less than undertakings in private hands. Uhr found that the wood consumption of eight iron-works in Uppland varied from 97·0 per cent. (for Österby-Gimo) through 34·0 per cent. (Dannemora) and 27·3 per cent. (Leufsta) to 6 per cent. (Hökhuvud) of the estimated yearly growth in the parishes in which they lay. Certainly there can have been no general shortage of wood in Sweden, any more than there was in Norway, where also there were complaints about shortage: J. Schreiner, *Nederland og Norge*, p. 60. But it is clear that there was something like a panic about it in the 1630's, and that in certain areas it led to a dispersion of industry or the separation of furnaces from forges and foundries. See G. Wieslander, *Skogsbristen i Sverige under 1600- och 1700-talen*, pp. 594-647; V. Elgeskog, *Torpläggning*, p. 81; and especially G. Uhr, *Om förhållandet mellan virkestillgång och virkeskonsumtion inom den norduppländska bergshantering under 1600-talets första kvartsekel*, pp. 380-7. For English parallels, see Rhys Jenkins, *op. cit.*, p. 32; E. Straker, *Wealden Iron*, pp. 111-30.

[1] Odén, *Rikets uppbörd och utgift*, pp. 287-8.

[2] Heckscher, I. 384-5; N. Ostman, *Stockholms magistrat och rådhusrätt* (in *Stockholms rådhus och råd*), I. 301-3.

[3] *Svenska riksdagsakter* [cited: *SRDA*], I. 91, gives an assessment for *mantalspenningar*, which provides the basis for an estimate; *Borgareståndets protokoll*, p. 325, gives the official ranking under the *Riksdag* Ordinance of 1617; Heckscher, I. 390, gives a slightly different order; Björkman, *Jönköpings historia*, II. 136, and Hallenberg, V. 137, give lists for 1620 and 1624, based on towns' contributions. But no one list agrees with any other.

population of the towns did not exceed five per cent. of the whole.[1]

Nevertheless, the towns were progressing; and Stockholm, in particular, was rapidly recovering from the decay into which it had fallen at the beginning of the sixteenth century. The recovery, like the original efflorescence, was due in part to trade connexions with north Germany, and especially with Lübeck. From as early as the mid-thirteenth century the German mercantile community had enjoyed special privileges in Stockholm and other Swedish towns. In the later Middle Ages the Hanse had completely dominated Swedish overseas trade; Stockholm was even listed as a Hanseatic town in 1366; the German congregation preserved, and to this day preserves, its identity: in short, Sweden, and especially Stockholm, occupied the position almost of a German colony. It is not surprising, then, that Sweden should have owed to the Germans the introduction of municipal institutions on the continental pattern. From the time of the Town Law of 1350 Swedish town-government was organized in deliberate imitation of German models. Some variations were indeed made to suit local circumstances: the institution of the Common Hall (*allmänna rådstugan*) did something to counterbalance the authority of the *borgmästare* and *råd*, and the influence of the crown was always more powerful than in Germany, if only because in Sweden the towns were so weak[2]; but on the whole Sweden emerged from the Middle Ages with municipal institutions of a German type, which were certainly too elaborate and top-heavy for most of the very modest urban communities to which they were applied. In Stockholm this disproportion was not so striking; but here there was a real danger that the German colony might use the municipal government to obtain control of the town. The Town Law of 1350 had accordingly laid it down that half (and thus by implication not more than half) of the *borgmästare* and council must be Germans, and explicitly reserved the post of town clerk to Swedes. There was a good deal of patriotic resentment of the German predominance; and after the battle of Brunkeberg in 1471 the towns obtained from the victorious Sten Sture a decree that no German henceforward should be admitted to sit on any town council. From this time the position of the Germans began to decline, especially in the reign of Gustav Vasa. Yet there are some signs of a revival of German influence towards the end of the century;

[1] F. Lindberg, *Hantverkare*, p. 7.

[2] For further details of town government, see Vol. I, p. 326 *seqq.*, above.

the Germans in Stockholm meddled in Swedish politics in the 'nineties; and the Charter of 1612 incorporated a demand for the exclusion of foreigners from municipal offices.[1]

The meagreness of urban life, and the insignificance of the urban population, were reflected in the limited development of the gild system. The gild, like the municipality, was an exotic imported from Germany; and it did not greatly flourish on the stony soil of Sweden. The obvious obstacle was the small size of the ordinary Swedish town, which made it unlikely that more than one or two masters of the same handicraft would be pursuing their mystery in the same place. Hence it would be impossible to establish a local gild from mere lack of qualified members; or at best masters of three or four allied crafts would group themselves into a single gild.[2] Moreover, although such trades as that of baker, brewer and butcher could be organized as gilds well enough in Stockholm, it was impossible to force a gild organization upon them in, say, Växjö or Härnösand, since brewing and baking and slaughtering would be done at home in towns as small as these. It was consequently mainly in Stockholm that the gilds took root and flourished.[3] But even in Stockholm the craftsmen were, for the most part, in very modest circumstances: in 1613 there was only one journeyman to every three masters, and only one apprentice to every two.[4] The thin upper layer of urban society was composed mostly of merchants; and though there were already native Swedes of some wealth, the majority of this class was still mainly of foreign origin. Nevertheless, the gilds in Stockholm were of a respectable antiquity: the oldest of them, the tailors' gild, dates from 1356. The German element, as might have been expected, was strong: as late as Gustav Adolf's reign attempts were being made to fix a ratio of three to two between Swedish and German members of the shoemakers' gild of Stockholm, an earlier regulation fixing it at two to one having proved impossible to maintain.[5] The Vasa kings showed themselves benevolent towards the

[1] For the preceding paragraph, see C. T. Odhner, *Bidrag till svenska städernas och borgareståndets historia före 1635*; F. Lindberg, *Fogde, råd och menighet*; N. Ahnlund, *Från medeltid och Vasatid*, pp. 7-33; Ostman, *op. cit.*, I. 7-24; K. Hildebrand, *Stockholms historia*, pp. 64-88; *SRDA*, I. 75.

[2] H. Schück, *Stockholm vid 1400-talets slut*, p. 60.

[3] The lists for Älvsborg's ransom in 1613 gave Stockholm 112 craftsmen, together with 67 on Norrmalm and 52 on Södermalm: Lindberg, *Hantverkare*, p. 48.

[4] T. Söderberg, *Den namnlösa medelklassen*, pp. 63-4.

[5] Lindberg, *Hantverkare*, pp. 120-2. So too in 1620 Stockholm masons fixed the proportion of Swedes to Germans at two to one. And see S. Hansson, *Ur skomakareyrkets historia*, pp. 28-9.

gilds, which accorded well with their general policy of favouring and founding towns; they began to assume the monopoly of issuing valid gild regulations and charters; and they tried to extend the gild system to trades which had not hitherto adopted it. By their large building-operations, by the increasing luxury of their courts, and above all by their efforts to establish or develop industries, they did something to strengthen the position of the craftsman; and their considerable importations of foreign workmen (which before the end of the century had led to a steady trickle of immigrants) brought a marked increase in the number of potential gild members. It is this increase which accounts for the tendency, clearly apparent in the last quarter of the century, to apply the *numerus clausus*, and so limit the number of masters in each gild.[1]

Such developments, however, applied mainly to Stockholm. Except where some new industry was springing into existence—as for instance at Arboga—the Swedish provincial town of the sixteenth century was essentially a market-town. In the later Middle Ages, and throughout the whole of the sixteenth century, markets and fairs had played a part of great political importance in Swedish history, and successive Regents and Kings had taken advantage of the concourse of people to sound or excite public opinion, to enlighten the common man upon royal policy, and to negotiate for the granting of financial aid. After 1600 the rising importance of the *riksdag* deprived the great markets of most of these political functions. Their religious associations had generally vanished with the Reformation. But economically they were still of importance. Most of the more celebrated of them were free markets: that is, markets where stranger could deal directly with stranger without the town's interposing any right of emporium. There were sixteen such free markets in Sweden and Finland, of which Åbo had two, and fourteen other towns one apiece. The most famous of them all was probably the Disting at Uppsala, named in honour of that Queen Disa to whom tradition gave the credit for the settlement of Norrland, and about whom Messenius had written his best-known play.[2] This

[1] For all this, see F. Lindberg, *Hantverkare, passim*; S. Ambrosiani, *Från de svenska skråämbetenas dagar, passim*; N. Ahnlund, *Från medeltid och Vasatid*, pp. 34-67; H. Schück, *Stockholm vid 1400-talets slut*, pp. 67-70; H. Lindström, *Näringsfrihetens utveckling i Sverige*, pp. 2-8; S. Hansson, *Ur skomakareyrkets historia*, pp. 25, 67 *note*. For an example of a thriving sixteenth-century town from which the German element was wholly absent, see F. Lindberg, *Västerviks historia*, I. 97-100.

[2] See Vol. I, p. 506.

market was held early in the New Year, and drew a large concourse of traders from Stockholm and from Norrland. Other celebrated markets were Henriksmässan at Örebro (mainly a market for iron); Mormässan at Västerås; and Samtingen at Strängnäs: all these were important as supplying the mining areas of the Bergslag with the products of the Mälar area, and the imports which reached that area through Stockholm. Götaland specialized in cattle-markets; Larsmässan at Nya Lödöse was famous as a market for fish; and Jönköping's market supplied most of the needs of northern Småland.[1]

These markets were mostly held during the winter months; for it was only in winter, when frost made the soft places firm, and when deep snow smoothed out irregularities of surface and offered easy transit in any direction, that land communications in sixteenth-century Sweden became tolerable or even practicable. At other times the main lines of communication within the country were by water. Mälaren and Hjelmaren (with a little assistance to nature) formed one great water system which linked together most of the main centres of population of Svealand. Lake Väner similarly formed the obvious means of communication between Karlstad and the mining areas to the north of it, on the one hand, and their natural export-routes to the west by way of Brätte (Vänersborg) and Lödöse, on the other; or between either of these and the stock-farming region of Västergötland, with its natural port at Lidköping. Lake Vätter, though less important, linked Vadstena with Hjo, and Närke with Småland; and Gustav Vasa ordered the construction of a harbour at Jönköping, to protect boats from the swell which at times dashes on the beaches of that windy city. Apart from these inland waterways, Sweden has easy and sheltered communications within the skerries which fringe the coast; and between lake and lake, or lake and sea, run short, slow-flowing, navigable rivers, which often—as at Örebro, Karlstad, Borås, Eskilstuna: the list could be prolonged—give to Swedish inland towns a gracious quality which survives even the onslaughts of modern industry.[2] But once the traveller in Karl IX's Sweden deserted the water—unless he were wise enough

[1] For markets, see N. Staf, *Marknad och möte, passim*; Herdin, III. 31-8 (for Distingen).

[2] Of 102 places which in 1916 were ranked as towns, 50 lay on the coast; 22 were linked to the four great lakes or to navigable rivers flowing into them; only 30 were really inland towns: H. Nelson, *Geografiska studier över de svenska städernas och stadslika orternas läge*, pp. 86-91.

to be travelling in winter—he found himself beset with difficulties and hazards. Apart from a few main roads, communications by land were maintained (if at all) by bridle-paths, often of high antiquity and great historical importance, but so inconceivably tortuous that folk-legends grew up to explain how they came to be so circuitous. In the more waterlogged districts a horse might have to pick his way for a score of miles together over the loose logs of a primitive type of causeway. The main roads themselves were winding, steep, stony and encumbered with innumerable gates; and in deep countries such as Östergötland easily degenerated into hollow-ways or mere ditches. Hence both sexes travelled as a rule by saddle-horse, the women often mounted in front of the men. Carriages, intended at first for women only, made their first appearance in Sweden in 1560, when Prince Johan brought one back from England; but they were still extremely rare in 1611: indeed, there were parts of Småland which saw their first wheeled vehicle as late as 1790. Gustav Adolf was complaining in 1619 that over much of Sweden the roads were 'so narrow and stony that they might rather be called bridle-paths than public highways'[1]; and apart from the road between Stockholm and Nyköping there may probably not have been a single road in Sweden passable for wheeled traffic.[2] The route between Västergötland and Närke over Tiveden probably became practicable only in the reign of Karl IX, and the traveller from Älvsborg to Kalmar across country would be lucky if he followed anything better than a cart-track. In outlying provinces—Värmland, Bohuslän, Västerbotten—there were hardly any roads at all; and the great north road round the head of the Gulf of Bothnia was tediously narrow and winding.[3] In these conditions movement was very slow: it took twenty days to get from Kalmar to Stockholm in 1634, and Peder Galt in 1622 found it hard work to cover twelve or fourteen English miles in a day's journey.[4] As to the transport of goods, the alternatives were either the pack-horse or a primitive form of sledge (*bårsläpa*) consisting of two poles whose hinder ends dragged loose upon the ground. The carrier's

[1] Hallenberg, IV. 867.

[2] Ahnlund, *Från medeltid och Vasatid*, p. 190 (but *cf.* Hallenberg, III. 41).

[3] F. F. Carlson, *Sveriges historia under konungarne af pfalziska huset*, II. 70. Nevertheless, Gustav Adolf accomplished some considerable feats of travelling over this road. In 1614, for instance, by organizing relays of horses, he covered as much as seventy miles a day: L. Levander, *Landsväg, krog och marknad*, p. 70.

[4] E. Hildebrand, *Kristina*, p. 77; Galt, p. 1.

waggon was still in the future; and in Gustav Adolf's day no Hobson inspired the youth of Uppsala to epigram.[1]

The difficulties in the way of easy movement, together with the infrequency of towns in certain portions of the country, do something to explain the prevalence of rural trading. When the ways were so bad and so long, men were glad enough to be saved the trouble of going to market themselves, and very ready to buy their salt or their petty luxuries from anybody who would bring these commodities to their doors. Such rural trading (*landsköp*) was, however, quite illegal, and generations of Swedish rulers waged fruitless war against it. The place for trade, they felt, was the town; towns, they were convinced, enriched the state; and if rural trading were permitted, the towns would suffer, their markets would lack buyers and sellers, encouragement would be given to forestalling, the benevolent intentions of a paternal government would be thwarted, and national ruin would ultimately ensue. *Landsköp* of course was not only a Swedish problem: on the continent, and especially in Germany, the authorities took much the same line.[2] The policy, however misconceived, was not (in Sweden at all events) entirely unintelligent or undiscriminating. There was no desire to prevent the countryman from making small purchases of necessities. He might freely sell to his neighbours the produce of a domestic industry which was pursued simply as a side-line and as a supplement to agriculture. For districts exceptionally remote from urban centres, special 'wilderness-markets' (*ödemarksmarknader*) might be permitted. The ancient gild of the Birkarlar existed in fact to practise *landsköp* in the Arctic. Special exceptions were given to the Bergslag, whose mine- and forge-masters were allowed to conduct tommy-shops to supply the needs of their men. From the regions of grain-deficiency, as we have seen, pedlars went out with their packs without interference, the gunsmiths of Hälsingland and the domestic workers of Dalarna in this enjoying the same privileges as the *knallar* of Västergötland. But the government tried to suppress all others who sought to make a living by the practice of retail trade in the country districts, and particularly those who dealt in imported articles such as salt, cloth and spices. Legislation against *landsköp* goes back at least to Magnus

[1] For land communications in general, see Levander, *op. cit.*, pp. 10-74; Försvarsstaben, *Vägar och vägkunskap under trettioåriga krigets sista skede*, pp. 16-17. For some efforts by Gustav Vasa at road-improvement, T. Söderberg, *Stora Kopparberget under medeltiden och Gustav Vasa*, pp. 438-9.

[2] As for instance in Brandenburg: F. L. Carsten, *The Origins of Prussia*, p. 267.

Eriksson's *landslag*, is repeated in Kristoffer's *landslag*, and is especially frequent and drastic under the earlier Vasas. Gustav Vasa remarked on one occasion that it was 'as hard to catch all the wolves that run in the woods' as to lay hands on those that violated these regulations; but if he failed, it was not for want of trying: the number of his edicts against *landsköp* is said to exceed one hundred, and that of 1546 imposed the death-penalty for the third offence. His sons were scarcely less pertinacious, but it cannot be said that they were any more successful. *Landsköp* became a regular profession. Nobles, clergy and townsmen were all as addicted to it as the peasantry were; and despite the savage prescriptions of the law, the sentences imposed upon offenders by the courts seem to have been relatively light.[1] It was partly in an effort to take away at least one of the excuses for *landsköp* that Johan III and Karl IX embarked upon the policy of founding new towns, to act as staples for districts in which *landsköp* had hitherto been especially prevalent. It was a policy which was to be intensified under Gustav Adolf, though with very doubtful success.[2]

Another aspect of the monarchy's attitude to the relationship between town and country, closely connected with that which we have been discussing, was the frequently reiterated prohibition not only of rural trading but also of rural industry. As the towns were to be centres of distribution and exchange, so too they were to be the sole centres of production, and any infringement of their monopoly was to be repressed and punished. Above all, no industry or craft was to be allowed to establish itself within one Swedish mile of any town: here again there is a clear analogy with German custom—indeed, both the idea and the word for it (*bannmil*) were taken over from the German *Bannmeile*. But as with rural trading, so with rural industry, the general rule was mitigated by numerous exceptions. The gild monopoly, as we have seen, could not possibly be maintained for butchers, brewers, bakers and shoemakers: the last, especially, seem to have led an ambulatory existence, going from village to village to do jobbing work as occasion offered. In

[1] Heckscher, I. 128; G. Suolahti, *Finlands prästerskap på 1600- och 1700-talen*, pp. 284-5; J. Ejdestam [etc.], *Bilder ur lanthandelns historia*, pp. 13-19; R. Matz, *Hur bestraffades landsköpet på 1500-talet?*, *passim*.

[2] For *landsköp*, see H. Lindström, *Näringsfrihetens utveckling i Sverige*, pp. 1-2, 9-12; Heckscher, *Det äldre Vasakonungadömets ekonomiska politik och idéer*, pp. 86-91; *id.*, *Våra stadsgrundningars betydelse*, p. 427; B. Steckzén, *Umeå stads historia*, pp. 23, 77; *id.*, *Minneskrift till Piteå stads 300-års jubileum*, pp. 13-17; Levander, *op. cit.*, pp. 139-41; Lindberg, *Hantverkare*, p. 15 *seqq.*

certain parts of the country, particularly in Hälsingland, there was a rich and well-rooted flora of petty weapon-smiths and armourers.[1] The nobles living on their manors maintained a labour-force, part permanent, part temporary, of carpenters, glaziers and other craftsmen, in order to ensure that their higher standard of living should be kept up without the need to have recourse to a possibly distant town. Over such craftsmen they threw the cloak of their protection against the anger and jealousy of the gilds: they *defended* them against interference, and hence such employees were called 'defence-men' (*försvarskarlar*). The defence-men of the nobility were in fact recognized by both government and gilds as a necessary and unavoidable evil, and though both would have liked to control it, neither dreamed of its abolition; but it was an institution obviously capable of abuse, and it was in fact abused: the towns were constantly protesting against its illegitimate extension.[2] In other directions, however, the earlier Vasas made vigorous efforts to constrain Swedish artificers into the framework of their ideal urban system: Karl tried hard to force the country craftsmen of Södermanland to settle in his new town of Tunafors (Eskilstuna)[3]; Johan III founded Hudiksvall in 1582 with the idea of compelling all the gunsmiths and halberd-makers of the surrounding countryside to migrate thither; Gustav Adolf's Borås, as we shall see, was established in the hope of thereby regulating the flourishing domestic industry whose products formed the stock-in-trade of the *knalle*. In 1604 Karl IX proposed drastic legislation to the Norrköping *riksdag*, which would have provided for the forcible removal to the towns of all handicraftsmen without exception. The Estates pointed out the impossibility of carrying out this proposal, and in the end the *riksdag* resolved only that all superfluous craftsmen must flit, the government taking upon itself to determine which these might be. But even this seems to have been quite ineffectual: no machinery was provided for carrying out the law; and the whole problem remained, on Gustav Adolf's accession, very much as it had been for the past half-century.[4]

[1] B. Steckzén, *Om Söderhamns gevärsfaktori i äldre tider*, pp. 17-20.

[2] For *försvarskarlar*, see especially Lindberg, *Hantverkare*, pp. 28-32.

[3] K. Hellberg, *Järnets och smedernas Eskilstuna*, I. 25.

[4] Lindberg, *op. cit.*, pp. 18-25, 101-12; Heckscher, *Det äldre Vasakonungadömets ekonomiska politik*, pp. 86-8, 99; S. Hansson, *Ur skomakareyrkets historia*, p. 36; G. Lindgren, *Falbygden*, p. 61.

In 1611 Sweden's industrial potentialities were just beginning to become apparent. The astute *entrepreneur* from the continent had recently begun to consider investing his capital in Swedish undertakings; the flow of immigrants towards these new opportunities had already set in. It was the mining and metallurgical industries which mainly engaged their attention. Swedish iron and Swedish copper were appearing on the European markets in increasing quantities. They were fit harbingers of Sweden's age of greatness; for upon iron and copper that greatness, in no small degree, was to depend.

Mining, especially mining of iron, was of very ancient date in Sweden, and the men by whom it was practised had long held a peculiar position in Swedish society. The *bergsmän*, as the miners were called, had a status somewhat above that of the peasantry, and it was for long uncertain whether they might not make good their claim to recognition as a distinct Estate. In the fifteenth century they had played a great part in Scandinavian history; but from the time of Gustav Vasa their political influence declined, and the *riksdagsordning* of 1617 marked the end of their aspirations to separate representation in the *riksdag*. The mining districts of Värmland, northern Närke, north-western Västmanland and southern Dalarna had in the Middle Ages been endowed with their own form of local government, with their own courts, their own legal customs, their own royal officials; and these mining areas were known collectively as the Bergslag. The Bergslag had originally been created as distinct administrative units by the crown, in order to safeguard its interest in the mines and ensure an adequate measure of royal control; but throughout the earlier Vasa period these administrative arrangements fell gradually into decay, or were deliberately suppressed, and by 1611 not much of them remained. 'The Bergslag' had already become, what it has since remained, a vague geographical term for the mining districts as a whole, without precise administrative significance.[1]

[1] For a general account of the Bergslag, see F. Seebass, *Bergslagen. Versuch einer kulturgeographischen Beschreibung und Umgrenzung*; M. B. Swederus, *Bidrag till kännedom om Sveriges bergshantering* (1910), pp. 38-41; S. Lindroth, *Gruvbrytning och kopparhantering*, I. 42, 55-6, 152, 158; B. Boëthius, *Gruvornas, hyttornas och hamrarnas folk*, pp. 54-7. There was to be some revival of self-governing institutions, especially at the copper-mines, under Gustav Adolf: *ibid.*, pp. 151-5; T. Söderberg, *Stora Kopparberg under medeltiden och Gustav Vasa*, pp. 254-6. For some English parallels, G. R. Lewis, *The Stannaries*, especially pp. 76-90, 173-4.

Sweden's main mineral resources were iron, copper and silver; and of these iron remained the most important until the very eve of Gustav Adolf's accession.[1] The iron industry in Sweden has a history which goes back at least to the first century B.C., and it was for long based upon ore dredged up in lumps from the bed of lakes, or from marshes. From about the twelfth century, however, true mining began, the ore being won by heating the rock to a high temperature and then suddenly cooling it with water. This process was comparatively effective, though very wasteful of wood, and it was still the only method employed in Gustav Adolf's time: the use of explosives did not come in until the eighteenth century.[2] From ore thus obtained Sweden had long produced a fine-quality iron, famous all over Europe as 'osmund'.[3] In smelting the ore to make osmund a blast was used, produced at quite an early date by water-power; but the blast was too weak to reduce the ore to a really fluid condition, the adsorption of carbon was consequently low, and the iron as a result was very malleable. At some time in the fifteenth century, however, a favourable accident of combustion led to the production of pig-iron. This, as a result of its high carbon content, was brittle, and suitable for casting; but it could also be reheated and partly oxidized to produce malleable iron of the osmund type. About the same time a new and improved type of furnace came in from Germany. In the following century the new pig-iron and the new furnace were combined, to produce osmund by indirect rather than direct process. At this point Gustav Vasa, with his eye ever open for a chance to better the Swedish economy, noticed that Swedish osmund was bought by German merchants at low prices, shipped to

[1] For iron-mining, see also E. F. Heckscher, *Un grand chapitre de l'histoire du fer*; J. Furuskog, *Det svenska järnet genom tiderna*; *id.*, *De värmländska järnbruken*; W. Tham, *Lindesberg och Nora genom tiderna*; Boëthius, *Gruvornas, hyttornas och hamrarnas folk*, pp. 30-211; T. Söderberg, *Bergsmän och brukspatroner i svenskt samhällsliv*; *id.*, *Sveriges ekonomiska struktur och utveckling under Gustav Adolf*, pp. 60-1; H. Carlborg, *Ur osmundsjärnets historia under 1600- och 1700-talen*, pp. 110-27.

[2] Furuskog, *Det svenska järnet genom tiderna*, p. 42: there is a dubious instance of the use of explosives at Falun in 1608: K. E. Forsslund, *Falu gruva och Stora Kopparbergs bergslag*, p. 66. It has been estimated that the consumption of wood at Falun mine in 1610 amounted to about 5 million cubic feet: Lindroth, *Gruvbrytning och kopparhantering*, I. 97-8.

[3] The osmunds were strictly the small, equal-sized pieces (about the size of a match-box) into which the iron was hewn before being packed into casks for export. The name became current for any iron that looked like osmund: thus in England osmund was produced (under that name) and used for making iron wire, especially for wool-combs: H. Hamilton, *The English Brass and Copper Industries to 1800*, p. 38. For a discussion of the origin of the name, see M. Eriksson, *Järnräntor under 1500-talet*, pp. 10-11.

Germany to be hammered into bar-iron, and subsequently sold to Sweden at a large profit. He determined to begin the production of bar-iron in his own country. He imported German workmen; he founded the first big Swedish forges; he encouraged his subjects to imitate his example. The result was a revolution in the Swedish iron industry. Production was gradually turned from osmund to bar-iron, and the new method of smithing ('German smithing', as it was called) obtained a firm foothold. Forge-hammers were set up in parts of the country which had previously been almost uninhabited; Swedish iron-masters were educated in the new techniques; larger and more complex undertakings than ever before arose in considerable numbers: Gustav Vasa in a moment of petulance complained of one of his imported Germans that he built forges 'as big as cathedrals'. Osmund, however, continued to be produced—indeed, it continued to be produced in some districts down to the latter half of the nineteenth century—and it was only slowly that the 'German smithing' and the bar-iron came to equal it in importance: in 1600 the weight of osmund exported was still about double that of bar-iron. By the second decade of the century, however, the export of bar-iron had nearly overtaken osmund, reckoned by weight; and had actually exceeded it in value.[1]

The revolution in the production of iron brought with it the beginnings of a steel industry. In the Middle Ages steel had been manufactured in Sweden under domestic conditions: in the reign of Gustav Vasa production on a larger scale begins at Stålberget in Närke, and later near Säter. The exceptionally high-grade Dannemora ore (known in England, from its port of export, Öregrund, as 'Oreground iron') was especially suitable for the making of steel; and in the latter half of the century production was concentrated in this part of Uppland, and also at Duke Karl's works at Storfors in Värmland.[2]

From a very early date Swedish iron had enjoyed a good reputation; and that reputation was not lessened by the great changes for which Gustav Vasa and his sons were responsible. Karl IX, moreover, instituted an important measure to ensure that no iron should be exported which was flawed or in other respects fell below prescribed standards: in 1604 begins the Swedish system of government

[1] Söderberg, *Sveriges ekonomiska struktur och utveckling*, pp. 26-9. Boëthius (*Gruvornas, hyttornas och hamrarnas folk*, p. 108) has rather less optimistic figures.

[2] C. Sahlin, *Svenskt stål före den stora götstålsprocessens införande*, pp. 27-54; Swederus (1910), p. 89.

testing (*järnvräkeri*), whereby the iron bars were tested for tensile strength by being bent round a bollard in a special government testing-yard in Stockholm.[1] The effective preservation of standards, thus early inaugurated, had a good deal to do with the high prestige of Swedish iron in the seventeenth and eighteenth centuries.

In Gustav Adolf's time, and for a little while afterwards, there was no great differentiation between the worker in the mines and his brother in the forge. The *bergsman* was a miner in the summer, a forgeman in autumn and spring, and a charcoal-burner in the winter. Extraction and manufacture tended thus to be concentrated in the same place; and though from some points of view—notably from that of economy of transport—this was an arrangement which had its advantages, it imposed a drain on the fuel resources of the neighbouring forest, and had ultimately to be modified on that account. The manufactures, like the improvements in the production of iron, owed very much to the enterprise of the monarchy. All the early Vasa kings were keenly interested in developing the manufacture of arms and armour, in order that Sweden might ultimately become independent of foreign supplies; and most of them imported armourers and gunsmiths from abroad to supplement the skill of the local workmen. They had considerable success with this policy. Its most impressive result, at least in the sixteenth century, was probably the manufactories at Arboga, founded by Gustav Vasa in 1551, where all sorts of war material were produced in considerable quantities, together with other useful commodities such as wire.[2] Arboga was not really a 'works'; it was rather a collection of separate master-craftsmen, working close together and to some extent inter-dependently. The crown provided workshops and raw materials; paid wages partly in cash, partly in kind; and allotted specific jobs to specific masters. There was a good deal of specialization and division of labour, much use of water-driven machinery, and something like mass-production to standard patterns, though on a small scale. Nevertheless the masters—of whom there were about twenty in 1550, and more than sixty in 1600—retained their individuality; and the workmen usually combined farming with industry.

Though Arboga was the first and for long the most considerable of these manufactories, it was by no means the only one. Before the

[1] E. W. Dahlgren, *Järnvräkeri och järnstämpling*, for an account of these tests.

[2] For Arboga, see Å. Meyersson, *Vapenindustrierna i Arboga under äldre Vasatiden*, *passim*; Lindberg, *Hantverkare*, pp. 172-4; Boëthius, *Gruvornas, hyttornas och hamrarnas folk*, pp. 99, 183-4.

end of the century there were rolling-mills and turning-lathes at Nyköping, Storfors, Norrahammar and Torshälla; armaments-works of one sort or another at Stockholm, Tunafors and Örebro; while Wira specialized in the production of blades. Cannon were bored at Varmalandsby; and in 1587 an undertaking of the same kind, but destined to be far more famous, was begun at Finspång.[1] But though the total output of these works was not inconsiderable, it by no means sufficed to meet the demands of the home market. Sweden, it is true, seems to have exported cannon-balls to France about 1590,[2] but on the whole was still decidedly an importing country where armaments were concerned. In 1611 Gustav Vasa's goal of self-sufficiency in the materials of war was not within sight. It was to be one of the most important achievements of Gustav Adolf's reign to bring it a long stride nearer; and at times, indeed, almost to attain it.

At the beginning of the seventeenth century copper-mining was approaching iron-mining in importance to the Swedish economy, and had possibly already caught up with it. The centre of the copper industry was the Stora Kopparberg, where a few years later the new town of Falun was to arise.[3] Copper-mining here was almost as ancient as iron-mining: the earliest written reference to the Kopparberg dates from 1288; and it was certainly worked for a century or more before that. In the Middle Ages, and in Vasa times too, it was a co-operative enterprise by a large number of small miners: in 1568 there were 173 of them; in 1580, when prospects were improving, 239. The mine was considered to be the corporate property of the miners of the Bergslag in which it lay; and the *bergsmän*, who were mostly their own masters, possessed so many shares in it apiece. In the fifteenth century they threw dice for the areas to be mined by each, and by the opening of the sixteenth the shares of each man were numerous and scattered, almost after the manner of strips in an open-field. The crown early became an important shareholder; and with the strengthening of the idea of regalian rights

[1] For the history of lathes and rolling-mills, see C. Sahlin, *Valsverk inom den svenska metallurgiska industrien intill början av 1870-talet*.

[2] A. Rebsomen, *Recherches historiques sur les relations commerciales entre la France et la Suède*, p. 24.

[3] For the history of copper-mining, see S. Tunberg, *Stora Kopparbergets historia*; T. Söderberg, *Stora Kopparberget under medeltiden och Gustav Vasa*; K. E. Forsslund, *Falu gruva och Stora Kopparbergs bergslag*; K. E. Hildebrand, *Falu stads historia till år 1687*, I.; S. Lindroth, *Gruvbrytning och kopparhantering*, I-II.

in the sixteenth century it tended to assume a tighter control, and to take a more active part in the business of the Kopparberg. In 1616 the King owned 304 of the total of about 1200 shares, the remainder being divided between four to five hundred small *bergsmän*; but almost two-thirds of the total production came from the royal workings. The share-system, like open-field farming, opposed considerable hindrances to rationalization, technical improvements and large-scale production, and this was perhaps one reason for the comparative failure of Gustav Vasa's attempts to energize the industry in the same way as he had stimulated the mining and manufacture of iron. For the first three-quarters of the sixteenth century, indeed, copper was in a somewhat languishing condition. There were obstinate difficulties about water and falls of rock in the workings. The state of the market offered little incentive to development, for the European supply of copper seems to have been fully equal to the demand, especially after the opening-up of the new copper-mines in Thuringia and Hungary.[1] From the 'sixties and 'seventies the growing preference for bronze cannon did something to improve the demand [2]; and it is said that the fashion—new to Sweden—for covering roofs with copper helped too. But it was not until the 1580's that there was a real turning of the tide. In the years after 1574 the technical difficulties in the mine became for a time less formidable; and the miners were fortunate enough to strike a vein of ore which was both unusually rich and easily accessible.[3] The change in the monetary policy of the Spanish government, which from 1599 began to issue a pure copper vellon currency in enormous quantities,[4] led to a sudden sharp increase in the price of copper after 1600. These developments inaugurated a period of rapid expansion in the Swedish copper industry; and it was further stimulated by the effort required to pay off Älvsborg's ransom.[5] By the middle of Gustav Adolf's reign copper had risen to a position of supreme economic importance: without the Kopparberg, as we shall see, the Swedish victories would scarcely have been possible.

[1] This was felt in England too: see H. Hamilton, *English Brass and Copper Industries*, p. 24, for the unsaleability of copper in 1570.

[2] For the advantages of 'copper' cannon, see below, pp. 230-1.

[3] Lindroth, I. 56-60. Lindroth explicitly rejects the suggestion that the expansion of the 'eighties was the result of a change in the state of the market, or of increased investment in the industry.

[4] E. J. Hamilton, *American Treasure and the Price Revolution in Spain*, pp. 73, 75.

[5] See above, Vol. I, pp. 124-9.

Even in the period before the real efflorescence of the Kopparberg, the copper-mines had given rise to a secondary industry in close association with them. This was the brass industry, first mentioned as early as 1524. It was not until the third quarter of the century, however, that the manufacture of brass really established itself—as a result, it appears, of the arrival in Sweden of a Dutchman named Caspar Johansson. Johansson entered into a contract with Johan III, brought workmen and equipment from the Netherlands, and in 1572 set up the first brass-foundry at Vattholma, near Uppsala. His activities came to an end in 1580, when he was disgraced; but before the end of that decade another brass-works had been established at Högen, which made both castings and wire; and though Johan's projected monster brass-works at Vällinge came to nothing, by the time of Gustav Adolf's accession brass-making had become firmly established, notably at Nyköping (1605) and Skultuna (1607). It was still, however, of minor importance, for though Sweden had abundant copper, there appeared to be little zinc; and the industry was consequently dependent upon importations of calamine from abroad.[1]

The tale of Sweden's mineral resources in 1611 is concluded by the much-prized silver-mine at Sala. The deposits at Sala had been discovered in 1510, and for nearly half a century the mine produced silver in fair quantities. But Sala was no Potosi: by 1570 production had fallen to less than a quarter of what it had been fifty years earlier, and by the close of the century it had become insignificant. Sweden's Indies, as Gustav Adolf was to demonstrate, were located not at Sala but at Falun.[2]

The Swedish mining industry in 1611 was still an industry which was largely in the hands of small-scale producers. The miners were for the most part no better off than the more prosperous of the peasantry; they won the ore by their personal exertions, for the number of hired labourers was still small[3]; and certainly they had no capital resources adequate to the introduction of new techniques and expensive machinery. Some were richer than others, by reason of greater industry or better fortune, and in the co-operative under-

[1] K. Malmsten, *Den svenska mässingsindustriens uppkomst*; *id.*, *En industriplanering under Vasatiden*; S. Erixon, *Skultuna bruks historia*, I. 1-4. Some calamine seems to have been mined near Västervik, but the yield cannot have been large: F. Lindberg, *Västerviks historia*, I. 134.

[2] J. Näsmark, *Sala stad*; Heckscher, *Svenskt arbete och liv*, pp. 59-60.

[3] In the mid-sixteenth century they numbered less than 50 at the Kopparberg: Söderberg, *Stora Kopparberg*, p. 184.

taking at Falun there were larger and smaller shareholders; but none of them could properly be termed a capitalist. And, indeed, not much capital was needed for mining as it was then conducted in Sweden. Techniques were primitive by the standards prevalent in Germany, and would remain so until after Gustav Adolf's time. The miners needed pumps, to cope with the ever-recurrent problem of flooding; and they needed winding gear; but since they were usually unable to pay for such devices, they were content to rely in these matters upon the assistance of the crown, and the crown did not fail them. Gustav Vasa, Karl IX and Gustav Adolf all took a lively personal interest in the mines; and Karl, in particular, seems to have been well acquainted with the practical details of mining. They all believed that the mines might be made to yield a large revenue, and they were all prepared to invest capital in technical improvements. The appropriation of much of the wealth of the church, at the time of the Reformation, had made the monarchy vastly richer than any of its subjects; and it was the monarchy, above all, that supplied the resources for the developments of the sixteenth century. The crown had a large stake in the mine at Falun; many of the richest iron deposits were on crown land; and the *régale* upon the produce of the mines gave the King a direct interest in increasing production. The crown therefore gave the mines all kinds of assistance: it made loans (sometimes, under Gustav Vasa, free of interest); it employed foreign technicians to build and supervise machinery; and it made over to the mines a portion of its revenue, inasmuch as it directed that labour services due to it in the way of carting, tree-felling and so forth should be performed for the benefit of the miners.[1] Without the artificial stimulus of royal aid the mines could scarcely have overcome their difficulties; and Falun, in particular, was indebted to the small staff of German technicians imported by Karl IX for the extraordinary prosperity it enjoyed in the seventeenth century.[2] When Karl IX considered handing over the crown's interests at Falun to the other shareholders, he was dissuaded by the urgent entreaties of the miners; for without the King's help the indispensable engines could not be maintained or replaced.[3]

The backing of successive monarchs was sufficient for the development of the mines; and no great expenditure of capital was

[1] Eriksson, *Järnräntor*, pp. 26-7.
[2] Lindroth, I. 63-6, 101-3, 145, 148; Steinkallenfels, p. 8.
[3] Lindroth, I. 73-8.

required for the production of osmund. But the change from osmund to bar-iron involved heavy outlays, for bar-iron was best produced in large units with heavy hammers.[1] The initiative here, and much of the capital, came once again from the King [2]; as it did also in the setting up of manufactories: among the famous iron-works which owed their origin to Gustav Vasa or his successors were Gimo, Leufsta, Österby, Forsmark, Asphytte and Storfors.[3] The first effective development of Dannemora was the work of Johan III; Karl IX was responsible for the systematic colonization of Värmland in the interests of the expanding iron industry of that area—a famous example of the truth of Geijer's dictum that 'iron opens up the country' ('*järnet bryter bygd*'); and both made use of imported experts, such as the Dutchman Willem van Wijck.

But the tendency towards an increase in the scale of operations, and the need for increased investment, came at a time when the crown was no longer able, as in earlier years, to shoulder the whole cost without much difficulty. After the death of Gustav Vasa, the monarchy was oftener a borrower than a lender. And among those who on occasion advanced money to the King were wealthy members of the high nobility.[4]

In the Middle Ages the nobility had been actively interested in mining. Nobles had possessed shares at Falun; and they had acquired through their tenants interests in the common mines of the Bergslag. By the middle of the sixteenth century, however, they seem to have got rid of these investments almost entirely and to have confined their mining to the iron which was to be found on their own estates.[5] These private mines were never of major importance; but the nobility were nevertheless keenly interested in iron as an article of commerce. They bought up land near the mining districts, and demanded of their tenants that they pay rent in iron. The tenants

[1] Karl IX did indeed encourage the setting up of little forges by small *bergsmän*, but the policy was to be abandoned in the following reign: B. Boëthius and Å. Kromnow, *Jernkontorets historia*, I. 6; Boëthius, *Gruvornas, hyttornas och hamrarnas folk*, pp. 94-5.

[2] *cf.* Henry VIII's importations of founders and finers: Rhys Jenkins, *The Rise and Fall of the Sussex Iron Industry*, p. 17.

[3] E. W. Dahlgren, *De uppländska bruken Österby, Forsmark, Leufsta och Gimo under äldsta tider*, *passim*.

[4] A list of the crown's debts in 1583 totalled 61,700 *daler* borrowed within Sweden, 50,200 borrowed from foreigners, and 70,000 owing to Lübeck. Nevertheless, the royal expenditure on the mines had increased since 1573: Odén, *Rikets uppbörd och utgift*, pp. 394, 398.

[5] Eriksson, *Järnräntor*, pp. 33-4; Söderberg, *Stora Kopparberg*, pp. 71, 151, 177, 192, 206.

obtained the iron by barter against the foodstuffs produced by them, and required by the miners; and the noble landlords by this device saved the trouble and expense of mining and smelting on their own account, and put the burden of transporting the iron from the mining areas upon the shoulders of their tenantry. By these means they concentrated in their own hands a large share of the export trade in iron.[1] Their trading profits on this and other exports furnished them with the means to make loans to impecunious monarchs such as Johan III [2]; and there are signs that before the end of the century they were beginning to invest in forges and manufactories also.[3]

It is clear, moreover, that by 1611 capital had begun to flow into Sweden from foreign merchants and *entrepreneurs*, and increasingly from the Dutch. Already in the 'eighties Willem van Wijck had acquired a lease of the royal mines in Uppland; and the original exploitation of Dannemora, forty years earlier, had been undertaken by a company of which half the members were foreigners.[4] The crown's importation of foreign workmen—for instance, to Arboga, which long remained a foreign colony [5]—soon attracted others who came on speculation, in the hopes of bettering themselves; the trading credit given by foreign merchants often represented an investment in the metallurgical industries; and the day was not distant when foreign capitalists would come in person to Sweden to look after their investments. They would find a land of many opportunities. The *entrepreneur* who leased a mine or a factory from the crown was assured of an abundance of cheap fuel—a consideration of some importance at a time when many of the competing areas on the continent were becoming anxious about their fuel-supply. Ore was copious, rich and easy to mine. There was water in plenty, for power or for transport. There was no difficulty about recruiting labour: peasants from the regions of grain-deficiency, incoming Finns, were reinforced by others who sought the mines or the forges because work in these favoured employments usually exempted a man from military service. At the worst, there were fugitives from justice who claimed the traditional right of asylum in the

[1] Eriksson, *Järnräntor*, pp. 8, 26, 34-7, 63, 82.

[2] Countess Ebba Leijonhufvud lent Johan III no less than 101,200 *daler* at 6 per cent., as well as making loans to Duke Karl: E. Fries, *Svenska adelns familjeliv*, pp. 14-15.

[3] *cf.* Boëthius, *Gruvornas, hyttornas och hamrarnas folk*, p. 110.

[4] *ibid.*, pp. 95-6; Odén, pp. 108-12.

[5] Boëthius, *op. cit.*, p. 163.

Bergslag.[1] Living was cheap and wages were low, by western European standards; for in Sweden the effects of the price revolution, though perceptible, had been delayed. And, not least, the crown was very willing to grant lavish privileges to foreigners who were prepared to be attracted. In the iron industry the foreign element was to play a predominant part: in the copper industry its contribution was perhaps less important, and at no time did the alien capitalists succeed in getting a footing in the corporate activity of the Falun mine. When Gustav Adolf's reign opened, the importation of foreign capital and foreign capitalists was only beginning; but the conditions were already present which were to make it possible for him to harness the wealth and experience of continental financiers to the task of providing Sweden with the economic underpinning indispensable to the country's emergence as a great power.

The expansion of the iron and copper industries left clear marks upon the pattern of Sweden's overseas trade. Until the end of Gustav Vasa's reign, the country—commercially as in other respects—was in a backwater. At the moment when the first joint-stock companies were being formed in England, and when transoceanic markets were beckoning from beyond the horizon, Sweden was a land whose economic development has been compared by her foremost economic historian with that of Carolingian France about the year 1000.[2] Such a country could not be of much consequence in the trade of Europe. In Gustav Vasa's time, in fact, Sweden was little better than a colonial land of north Germany. The liberation of the country from political and financial dependence upon Lübeck, which had been one of the main achievements of Gustav Vasa, had not had as its consequence any disturbance of the virtual monopoly of Swedish commerce enjoyed by the towns of the German Baltic shore. Nor is it certain that Gustav Vasa would have wished it. He had little faith in the business ability of his subjects, and no confidence that they could be trusted to bring back the imports of which Sweden really stood in need, if they were allowed to trade at pleasure, unguided by royal admonitions. A 'passive' trade seemed safer. The foreign merchant should shoulder the risks of importing goods to Sweden; for the advantage in bargaining, the King held, would under this arrangement be with the Swedish purchaser: sooner

[1] Söderberg, *Stora Kopparberg*, pp. 394-9, for this; and for the labour-supply in general, *ibid.*, pp. 428, 431; Boëthius, *Gruvornas, hyttornas och hamrarnas folk*, p. 158.

[2] Heckscher, I. 32.

or later the foreign importer must sell his goods at a reasonable price, or risk not selling them at all, and so lose the money laid out on their freight.[1] Gustav Vasa's object was to obtain the commodities the country required; his restrictions were rather upon exports than upon imports; he had no misgivings about exporting coined money to pay for what he needed (it actually figures in the list of exports): in short, his policy was what Heckscher has termed a policy of provisioning (*försörjningspolitik*).[2] The main channel of trade, both for imports and exports, was through the German merchants; though already by the mid-century the merchants of Antwerp had established themselves as important purveyors of luxuries.[3] Swedish copper, for instance, which was causing Jakob Welser superfluous anxiety in the 'twenties, went to the Low Countries by way of Lübeck or Danzig.[4] The total volume of Swedish trade was small; and except for one or two commodities was scarcely indispensable to the well-being or existence of the nation. In 1559 the main imports were textiles, salt, hops and spices, in that order, and together they accounted for over nine-tenths of the whole.[5] Salt was a vital necessity. Despite various efforts, it had proved impossible to develop a native salt industry [6]: Sweden had no natural salt-pans,

[1] Compare the contemporary attitude of the Scottish burghs: J. Davidson and A. Gray, *The Scottish Staple at Veere*, pp. 47, 67.

[2] For Gustav Vasa's economic ideas, see Heckscher, I. 28-83, 254-65; *id.*, *Det äldre Vasakonungadömets ekonomiska politik och idéer*, *passim*; *id.*, *Historieuppfattning*, p. 90: ('To say that Gustav Vasa was indifferent to Swedish commercial enterprise is to understate the case: he positively disapproved of it'). Some modification of this view is suggested in I. Svalenius, *Gustav Vasa*, pp. 271-3; M. Eriksson, *Järnräntor*, p. 49; and F. Lindberg, *Västerviks historia*, I. 144 ('One of Gustav Vasa's favourite ideas, of course, was to induce Swedish merchants to emancipate themselves from dependence on the Germans, and venture out on their own account to the markets of western Europe').

[3] P. Jeannin, *Les relations économiques des villes de la Baltique au XVIe siècle*, pp. 208, 211.

[4] *ibid.*, p. 205. For the interest of the Fuggers in the possibility of Swedish competition in copper, see G. F. von Pölnitz, *Fugger und Hanse*.

[5] B. Boëthius and E. F. Heckscher, *Svensk handelsstatistik 1637-1737*, p. l, give the following figures: textiles, 35·8 per cent.; spices, 11·8 per cent.; salt, 24·7 per cent.; liquors, 3·9 per cent.; hops, 18·8 per cent.; others, 5·0 per cent.

[6] For salt, see H. Tegengren, *Försök till saltproduktion i Sverige och Finland på 1500-, 1600- och 1700-talen*; E. W. Dahlgren, *Louis de Geer*, I. 324. For an offer by Cecil to sell the secret of English salt-making to Erik XIV, see E. Hughes, *Studies in Administration and Finance*, p. 35. For Scottish exports of salt to Scandinavia, Davidson and Gray, p. 65. As late as Kristina's time Andreas Sparrman could write:

> Om man och kunde Salt at siuda i wårt rijke
> Hwem på nödtorffter all syns wara tå wår lijke?

(Could we but make salt in our country, who then could equal us for all the necessaries of life?): Lagerstedt, *Livsmedel och livsmedelproduktion under stormaktstiden*, p. 14.

and the salt produced by evaporation of Baltic sea-water was not satisfactory. Salt therefore must be imported; from north Germany at first, later from Brouage in the Bay of Biscay, which provided the celebrated 'Bay salt'. During the Seven Years' War of the North, Denmark cut off Sweden's salt supply; and the country suffered severely. For much the same reasons spices were nearly a necessity too. Hops were imported to supplement local resources; but Gustav Vasa was insistent in urging his subjects to establish hop-gardens, and it does in fact seem that the growing of hops became fairly common.[1] But if these three commodities were necessary, or at least highly desirable, a great part of the remainder of Sweden's imports—perhaps nearly half—were luxury goods, designed for the very thin topmost stratum of society who frequented the court.[2]

The exports which paid for these goods were still in 1559 predominantly agricultural produce: just over one-half of the total was provided by butter, hides, grains and timber. Iron (still mainly osmund) was the biggest single item, with between a quarter and a third of the whole; but copper accounted for no more than a twentieth. There were no manufactured articles of any sort.[3]

In the half-century after Gustav Vasa's death this pattern of trade was modified in a number of ways. In the first place, the virtual monopoly of the German merchants suffered invasion; partly by the Dutch, but also (for a time at least) by the Scots. It is true that most of their business seems still to have been confined within the limits of the Baltic; but nevertheless the beginnings are to be seen of an increasing trade with the countries bordering the North Sea and the Atlantic. By the end of the century trade with the Netherlands was of some consequence—not least because Sweden was beginning to prefer 'Bay salt', which came to the Baltic by way of Dutch ports. It was the Dutch, too, who brought to Sweden salted herrings, of which they were now the principal providers. The growth of Älvsborg, and the foundation of Göteborg by Karl IX, are other evidences of the widening of Sweden's commercial interests. In the reign of Karl IX probably not less than a quarter of Sweden's

[1] Heckscher, I. 40.

[2] Some of the cloths, however, may not have been luxury goods: in 1574 the revenues of Johan III included English and 'Bohemian' cloth, paid as tax by the Lapps, who got it from ships going north-about to the White Sea: Odén, p. 274. In 1559 silks, with gold and silver cloth, accounted for 4·3 per cent. of the total imports: Boëthius and Heckscher, p. l. For details of imports of English cloth, see Kjellberg, *Ull och ylle*, pp. 63-70.

[3] Boëthius and Heckscher, p. li.

overseas trade was with countries outside the Baltic.[1] The number of foreign ships calling at Swedish ports was increasing: whereas in 1560 the annual figure stood at something like 350, at the turn of the century it had risen to about 530.[2] There were signs, moreover, that the old policy of a passive trade was being abandoned: in 1600 came an important change in tariff charges, whereby the toll on exports was adjusted so as to give a preference to Swedish merchants.[3] And it is noteworthy that in 1612 the Estate of Burghers was complaining to the government about foreign merchants, and obtaining a restriction upon the duration of their stay; while two years later the Estate delivered a sharply worded protest against the Scots, and requested that they should be excluded from burgage-rights.[4]

There were changes, too, in the main articles of foreign trade: not very significant, perhaps, as regards imports, but very striking as regards exports. As to imports, the predominance of articles of luxury is actually strengthened. In 1613, for instance, textiles, imported liquors and spices make up three-quarters of the total.[5] But the table of exports for the same year shows startling transformations. Imports are no longer paid for with the produce of the meadow and the forest: from the point of view of foreign trade Sweden has become overwhelmingly a mining country. Copper heads the list, with iron not far behind, and together they account for over eighty per cent. of the whole.[6] These figures reflect a real revolution. Nevertheless, though the nature of the exports might have changed, the orientation of Swedish trade had changed much

[1] Heckscher, I. 46.

[2] *ibid.*, I. 43.

[3] C. Danielsson, *1500- och 1600-talens svenska tullpolitik*, pp. 396-400. Even so, Swedes were not exempt from toll, as Danes, Stralsunders and Rostockers were: W. Smith, *Studier i svensk tulladministration*, pp. 32-4; *cf.* Odén, pp. 297-300.

[4] The importance of Scots merchants, remarked on by Heckscher (*op. cit.*, I. 50, 107, 177), is at first sight surprising, and a recent study by Mr. S. G. E. Lythe (*Scottish Trade with the Baltic 1550-1650*) gives little support to the idea that there were strong economic ties between the two countries. But clearly there were some: see, *e.g.*, D. Hj. T. Börjeson, *Stockholms segelsjöfart*, pp. 73-5. In the last quarter of the century numerous Scots are to be found among those who made a profession of *landsköp*: they seem to have been mainly Scottish soldiers of fortune who had enlisted in the Swedish service during the Seven Years' War of the North, and after disbandment had remained in Sweden to pick up a living in this way: T. Söderberg, *Den namnlösa medelklassen*, pp. 57-8. It appears that about 1620 the expression 'schots koopman' was a regular Dutch term for any small merchant, of whatever nationality: see J. Schreiner, *Nederland og Norge 1625-1650*, p. 44 and *note* 2. Is it possible that some of the 'Scots' were really small merchants, and not Scots at all?

[5] Heckscher, I. app. V. table 1. It seems likely that the figures for 1613 are not in all respects normal, for this was a war year; but the general trend is unmistakable.

[6] *ibid.*, I. app. V. table 2.

less. In 1615 almost seventy per cent. of imports came from the four ports of Lübeck, Stralsund, Rostock and Danzig; and the same ports took nearly eighty per cent. of Swedish exports.[1] And the importance of foreign trade to the average man remained small—indeed, it might almost be said that it had grown smaller. The copper and iron that together dominated the list of exports were produced by probably not more than four per cent. of the population. The total value of Sweden's foreign trade was still very trifling: in 1620 it perhaps did not exceed two million *daler*.[2]

In the petty world of Swedish commerce, Stockholm held a position of unrivalled supremacy. Between 1611 and 1622 the average annual value of Stockholm's imports was 354,000 *daler*; while for the next most important port (Norrköping) the figure was 47,000 *daler*. Åbo had 40,000; Viborg, 31,000; Gävle, 30,000; but no other town reached to 20,000.[3] The predominance of the capital was not wholly a consequence of its size, ancient German trading-connexions and advantageous geographical position: in part it was due to artificial stimuli administered by successive monarchs. It had long been a general principle that foreign trade ought to be confined to the ports: the inland towns, it was felt, ought to fetch from the ports the goods which foreign merchants would leave there. This staple policy was designed to benefit all ports equally; but in addition special protection was from time to time given to Stockholm. From as early as the mid-fourteenth century there had existed a restraint of trade known as the Bothnian Staple (*bottniska handelstvånget*), whereby the ports of the Gulf of Bothnia which lay to the north of Stockholm were forbidden to trade southwards of the capital. This meant in fact that they were debarred from export to north Germany, and that their trade in this direction passed into Stockholm's hands. 'The country', said Sten Sture the elder, 'could have no use for so many small towns', whereas the prosperity of Stockholm was esteemed to be in the interests of all. This policy was generally followed throughout the sixteenth century, at all events on paper; though occasionally a King would grant piecemeal concessions to this or that port north of Stockholm, if he happened to be particularly interested in it. The clamour of the Stockholm burghers, however, usually kept the monarchy faithful to the Bothnian Staple, though it

[1] *ibid.*, app. V. tables 4 and 5; *cf.* Boëthius and Heckscher, *Svensk handelsstatistik*, p. liv; Lindberg, *Västerviks historia*, I. 151; Steinkallenfels, p. 2.

[2] T. Söderberg, *Sveriges ekonomiska struktur och utveckling*, p. 106.

[3] *ibid.*, p. 17, table 6.

was rarely able to make sure of its enforcement. In addition, Johan III in 1570 forbade direct import to or export from the ports on the Mälar, such as Västerås, Uppsala and Strängnäs; and Stockholm thus became the staple for this trade also. Karl IX was a strong supporter of the staple policy, and would have liked to push it to extreme limits: in a memorandum of 1595 he advocated the restriction of all foreign trade to the two ports of Stockholm (for the German trade) and Nya Lödöse (for the trade to the west). But if Stockholm were thus to be given a monopoly of the main branch of overseas commerce, it was only logical and equitable that the Stockholm merchants should be excluded from the up-country markets. This was a consequence which Stockholm was not prepared to contemplate; and in the end Karl's plan for canalizing commerce came to nothing: on the contrary, he found himself granting exemptions from the Bothnian Staple to Härnösand, Hudiksvall, Uleåborg and Vasa. But the principle remained. Gustav Adolf would do his best to make it effective; and undoubtedly it contributed something to the dominant position enjoyed by Stockholm in the commerce of the country during his time.[1]

Gustav Vasa's preference for a passive trade, and his striking freedom from any trace of bullionist superstition, become less surprising when they are placed in the economic context of his age. For in sixteenth-century Sweden money as such was of comparatively subordinate importance. The Swedish economy, then and for long afterwards, was far more a natural than a money economy.[2] Gustav Vasa used money for paying his hired soldiers, until after the Dacke rebellion he began to replace them with a national militia; he used money to pay for some of his luxury imports, since the countries from which he purchased them had arrived at a stage of economic development at which they expected cash payment; and he paid some of the wages of some of his employees in coin. But for the most part sixteenth-century Sweden paid its taxes, received its wages, contracted its debts and extorted its interest in goods rather than in money. And this was true even of transactions by no means purely domestic. Gustav Vasa, for instance, discharged his debt to Lübeck in goods, and sometimes in goods of a dangerously perishable nature: at least one instalment was paid in butter. The royal income was

[1] H. G. F. Sundberg, *Den svenska stapelstadsrätten*, pp. 10-31; O. Fyhrvall, *Om det bottniska handelstvånget*, pp. 30-6.

[2] For what follows, see Heckscher, I. 61-91, and app. I and II; *id.*, *Natural and Money Economy from Swedish History in the Sixteenth Century*, *passim*.

extraordinarily various. The accounts for 1573, for instance, show that not more than six per cent. of the revenue was paid in cash: the remainder came in the form of grain, bread, ale, hops, butter, cheese, eggs, meat, pork, fish, live beasts, skins, iron, copper, saltpetre, sulphur, planks, firewood, hay and straw, horses, labour services 'and other commodities'. It is true that revenues in kind were common enough in Denmark; and in parts of Germany some of the domain revenues were still paid in goods; but nowhere was the system so all-pervading as in Sweden, and in no other country was there a special administration created to deal with it.[1] A system of royal warehouses was devised, at first scattered throughout the country at various ports, later concentrated in Stockholm, and in these warehouses the King's butter or fish or iron were stored, until they should be needed for his service, or until the state of the market should be favourable for their sale. Some were disposed of to merchants by way of that compulsory exchange for foreign currency which formed one part of Swedish customs policy.[2] Much perishable revenue, of course, never came to the warehouses at all: it was consumed by the King and his entourage on their perennial progresses round the kingdom; or sold or bartered on the spot for other commodities of which the government stood in need at that particular moment. The agents for these local exchanges were the royal bailiffs, and the King depended upon their skill and fidelity to make the most of the royal income. Thus a great part of the revenue never came into the central treasury (or the King's warehouses), but was utilized for purposes of local government. The workmen employed on building Vadstena or Gripsholm would be paid in the salt fish or butter which had been handed over to the royal bailiff as rent or taxes; and there is reason to suppose that on occasion they might find that the provisions had been over-long in reaching them.[3] The biggest single item in the crown's wages-bill was thus not cash but

[1] Odén, pp. 11, 17, 40, 152-60, 169.

[2] Smith, p. 41; Odén, p. 100; Lindberg, *Västerviks historia*, I. 122-7.

[3] Boëthius, *Skogen och bygden*, p. 131. In 1549 it was discovered that Joakim Bulgrin, in charge of the works at Vadstena, had allowed a consignment of butter to lie undisposed-of for three years, so that it had become 'salt-green'; and, since it was now unsaleable, had distributed it as wages to the workmen who were building the castle. The precise interpretation to be put on this incident is a matter of dispute. For the entertaining controversy (turning partly on the meaning of 'salt-green'), see S. Hedar, *Gustav Vasa och det saltgröna smöret*; B. Boëthius, *Det treåriga Vadstena smöret*; S. Söderlind, *Smöret i Vadstena. Ett diskussionsinlägg.* In this connexion it may perhaps be recalled that '"green" cheese was not, as one might imagine, a variety showing green markings . . . but a very new soft cheese': Drummond and Wilbraham, *The Englishman's Food*, p. 82.

food.[1] The higher civil servants were paid very little in cash: the *ståthållare* or the secretary would receive as his salary the revenues from certain farms, even though his official duties might have nothing to do with that part of the country; and it would fall to him or his agents to make arrangements for realizing or exchanging the perishable portion of them as best he might. The middling ranks of royal employees—handicraftsmen, artists and so forth—seem usually to have been paid partly in money, partly in kind; and Heckscher provides an example which seems to show that this was true for imported experts too.[2] But the lower ranks of the King's service were almost wholly paid in kind: in 1600, when Christoffer Wernstedt was *ståthållare* in Uppsala castle, he had under him a collection of between eighty and ninety government employees and royal workmen; but the total cash expenditure upon them for the whole year amounted to no more than 180 *daler*.[3]

In all this the crown was by no means singular. The same system prevailed throughout the whole of society. The exchange of goods, the satisfaction of needs, proceeded more often than not by barter, at all social levels. If direct barter would not serve, recourse was had to indirect. For example: the men of Dalsland wished to buy fish from their neighbours in Bohuslän, and proposed to pay for it in butter. The men of Bohuslän did not require butter. The butter was therefore taken to Värmland, and there exchanged for iron; and the iron in due course was accepted in payment for the fish.[4] The system was still in full operation in private transactions until well into the seventeenth century. In the Bergslag values were reckoned in iron as well as in money. The men of Gustav Adolf's town of Borås built up a livelihood and a reputation by their expertness in negotiating complex indirect barter transactions.[5] In the seventeenth century Uppsala sold corn to Norrland and took payment in fish, and disposed of the fish to Falun in exchange for copper.[6] The records of local justice in a country parish in Gustav Adolf's time show men paying debts in silver spoons, or belts, or cooking-

[1] Odén, p. 189.

[2] In 1583 Johan III paid Willem van Wijck a wage of 500 *daler*, 2 robes of state, 84 pounds of grain, 1 *skeppund* of hops, 3 *tunnor* of butter, 6 oxen, 18 sheep, 9 pigs, 3 *tunnor* of smoked salmon, 2 *tunnor* of herring, 2 *tunnor* of *strömming*, 1 *tunna* of eels, 1 *skeppund* of dried pike, feed for 5 horses, and clothes for 4 servants: Heckscher, I. 73.

[3] F. Wernstedt, *Ståthållaren Christoffer Wernstedt*, p. 44.

[4] Heckscher, *Svenskt arbete och liv*, p. 42.

[5] Mannerfelt, pp. 39-42.

[6] Herdin, *Uppsala på 1600-talet*, III. 37.

pots, if they happened to be short of coin.[1] The advantageous disposal of revenues in kind was one of the problems of administration which confronted every institution.[2] Nor was the use of goods confined to simple payments in return for other goods received in exchange. There is plenty of evidence that loans could be given, debts contracted, and even interest reckoned and paid, in copper or eggs or oxen, or some other commodity. Even investments could be made in the most unlikely *media*: in 1627 Jakob de la Gardie invested in the Copper Company to the extent of 2000 *tunnor* of oats and 3000 *lod* of silver-gilt plate. Thirty years later Johan Oxenstierna invested in government securities by advancing a loan to the crown 'mostly in meat'.[3]

This obstinate survival of a natural economy until well into the eighteenth century [4] is one of the most striking and singular facts in the economic history of Sweden. An appreciation of it is fundamental to an understanding of the history of Gustav Adolf's reign. For in this respect, at least, he inherited a kingdom which had scarcely progressed at all since his grandfather's day. The cumbrousness, the waste, the complexity of the accounting it entailed might all be endured as long as Sweden's preoccupations were mainly domestic. But they were obviously difficult to reconcile with a vigorous foreign policy, an expanding empire, heavy military commitments overseas—in short, with existence as a great power. Gustav Adolf and his advisers, as we shall see, perceived this; but their efforts to put the revenues of the state on a cash basis, though they went to considerable lengths, were not entirely wise, and were by no means wholly successful: in the late 1660's about thirty per cent. of the revenue was still rendered in goods.[5]

Though coined money played a less prominent part in Swedish life than in the more developed economies of the continent, it was nevertheless in circulation in considerable—and sometimes excessive—quantities; and the currency policy of the monarchy,

[1] *Vendels sockens dombok*, p. 30.

[2] *e.g.* the chapter of Västerås: see B. R. Hall, *Kulturella interiörer från storhetstidens uppryckningsarbete*, p. 61.

[3] Heckscher, I. 637. For small loans in kind by the clergy, see G. Suolahti, *Finlands prästerskap på 1600- och 1700-talen*, p. 282.

[4] The demand to commute commodity-revenue to cash was an issue in the rising of 1743: B. Beckman, *Dalupproret 1743*, pp. 26-7. In Medelpad in the mid-eighteenth century a complex system of barter-equivalents still prevailed, with half a dozen commodities valued in terms of each other: J. Ejdestam [etc.], *Bilder ur lanthandelns historia*, pp. 50-2.

[5] Heckscher, I. 639.

in Sweden as elsewhere, affected the well-being of the lieges. Swedish currency was based upon a parallel standard. On the one hand were the *mark* and its subdivisions,[1] which bore a varying relation to the *mark*-by-weight of silver; on the other was the silver *daler*, which maintained a virtually unaltered silver content, and was supposed to be identical with the Imperial *Joachimsthaler*.[2] The *daler* was first minted in 1534; it was intended to be internationally acceptable; and its use was entirely confined to foreign commerce. Late in the century it became convenient to have a higher unit of account for domestic purposes than the *mark*; and a *daler* was accordingly introduced into the domestic system, first as a unit of account, later as an actual coin, with a value of 4 *marks*. At the same time (in 1593) the 'international' *daler* was renamed the *riksdaler*, though it otherwise remained unaltered. In the first decade of Gustav Adolf's reign the value of the *riksdaler* in Swedish domestic currency stood at 6½ *marks*: thus the *riksdaler* at this time was worth 1⅝ *daler*. In the course of the sixteenth century the *mark* and its subdivisions underwent many vicissitudes. All the earlier Vasas, from Gustav Vasa to Sigismund, debased the currency at one time or another; and under Erik XIV, and twice under Johan III, a chaotic monetary situation developed as the result of severe debasement combined with excessive minting. Karl IX, however, as Regent restored the coinage to its former fineness, and as King maintained it at that level. He left many embarrassing legacies to his successor; but a debased coinage was not one of them.

The period of inflation between 1560 and 1593 of course produced sharp rises in the price of goods. But independently of such temporary phenomena there was a steady rise in prices throughout the second half of the century. It seems, however, that the increase did not become rapid until after 1600. The price-revolution which had been affecting western Europe for half a century took a long time to reach the Swedish backwater; and when its effects did at last become perceptible, they perhaps involved less disturbance than in some other countries.[3] The commodities which entered into Sweden's foreign trade did indeed rise in price on a scale comparable

[1] 8 *penningar* went to 1 *örtug*, 3 *örtug* to 1 *öre*, 8 *öre* to 1 *mark*.

[2] Odén, p. 236.

[3] As A. E. Christensen points out (*Dutch Trade to the Baltic about 1600*, p. 428), there was an excess of exports from the Baltic area which had to be paid for in precious metals, and Spanish treasure flowed in some volume through the Sound. But not much of it, apparently, reached Sweden: see E. F. Heckscher, *Multilateralism, Baltic Trade and the Mercantilists*, pp. 225-7.

with the rise which had occurred elsewhere; but the bulk of the population, which had no interest in any imported article other than salt, did not feel the change very much; and indeed, since fixed incomes were to so large an extent in goods, it was not to be expected that they should.[1]

At the opening of the seventeenth century Swedish society, at least in the eye of the law, was organized into Estates. A man fitted into this or that Estate in virtue of the functions he discharged in society, of the nature of the duties he owed to society, and of the claims he was entitled to make upon society; and his membership of an Estate defined his position and to some extent his rights. And the discharge of a specific function, by a well-defined body of citizens, was apt to induce a tendency to clothe them with duties and rights conformable to it. In 1617 the *riksdagsordning* was to have the effect of fixing the number of Estates at four; and at four they would remain, for two centuries and a half.[2] Nobles, Clergy, Burghers, Peasants did indeed between them comprise the great majority of the population; though there were at all times many who could not be classified in any of these groups, and their numbers were destined always to increase. In the sixteenth century the *bergsmän*, the bailiffs, the officers of the army, all of whom could be considered as occupying a special place in society, and none of whom (except perhaps the last) fitted easily into the four-Estate pattern, had been near to recognition as Estates on their own account. The *riksdagsordning* implied their virtual disfranchisement. And there were others who were in similar case. Agricultural labourers and farm-hands had no place in the Estate of Peasantry, which was confined to those who owned their farms; country merchants, rural manufacturers, apprentices and journeymen were shut out of the Estate of Burghers; the servants of the state, unless they happened to be noble, were unrepresented; and all lived in an awkward social no-man's-land. For the four Estates were sharply self-conscious; and the divisions between them were to become increasingly accentuated. Each had its own appropriate dress; sumptuary legislation sought to

[1] On currency and prices, see Heckscher, I. 207-27. A convenient short guide to coinage, weights and measures is Heckscher, *De svenska penning-, vikt- och måttsystemen*; or (for currency only), *id.*, *Det svenska penningväsendets öden*. A full (and formidable) treatise on weights and measures is L. B. Falkman, *Om mått och vigt i Sverige*.

[2] See above, Vol. I, pp. 289-93.

ensure that the burgher's wife should not seek to follow the fashions of her betters; and until the middle of the seventeenth century the Swedish peasant, like his Russian neighbour, was distinguished by the wearing of a beard.[1]

The various elements within the pattern of society were of very different weight. The Clergy, impoverished and barbarized by the Reformation, and only slowly beginning to recover from that blow; the Burghers, representative of towns which often lacked most of the characteristics of urban society; had behind them neither the wealth and power possessed by the Nobility, nor the Peasantry's mere weight of numbers, and were little able to act as a balancing force between them. The Clergy derived some moral authority from their religious functions; the Burghers at times offered opposition to the pretensions of the first Estate; but politically and socially both were weak. Between them they comprised most of the middle-class elements in society; but their interests were diverse, and their political collaboration uncertain. Sweden, in fact, largely lacked an effective middle class, and in particular lacked those capitalists and lawyers who gave strength to the middle classes in other countries. The gilds, and such merchants as were native Swedes, could not compare with the commercial and manufacturing interests in England; and there was nothing to correspond to the social and political influence exerted by the Inns of Court. There was no gentry class at all. The country's educational institutions were incapable, in 1611, of providing either the practical or the professional training which a rising middle class would have required—except perhaps for those who wished to exchange the poverty of the peasant for the poverty of the parson [2]; and the small, though increasing, class of civil servants still found an expensive tour of foreign universities an almost indispensable prerequisite to a successful career. Thus Swedish society was dominated by the peasants and the nobility; and the great social question concerned the relations between them.

The Estate of Peasantry was by no means a homogeneous body. It was divided into at least three great sections, each of whose position, rights and duties differed considerably from those of the other two. But all had this at least in common: they were free;

[1] T. Söderberg, *Den namnlösa medelklassen*, pp. 50-1; Magalotti, p. 11.

[2] And the burgher class seems to have been indifferent to educational improvements: certainly it took no share in providing educational endowments: T. Söderberg, *Den namnlösa medelklassen*, p. 79.

and it was believed that they had never been anything else but free. There had indeed been slavery in old Scandinavia (it was formally abolished in 1325); but there had never been villeinage or serfdom. The Swedish peasant looked back to a primitive community of more or less equal farmers; and if the days of true equality were very distant, and possibly a little mythical, the freedom was real, and it had always been there. In the course of the Middle Ages, as great blocks of land passed into the hands of the crown or the nobility, many peasants farming upon such lands became in effect the tenants of the one or the other; but this development had never curtailed their liberty nor prejudiced their status in the eye of the law.[1] And when the sixteenth century opened, a majority of the peasants were still, as they had been for centuries, independent yeomen. Nevertheless, there were now three clearly defined categories within the Estate: the peasants of the crown (*kronobönder*); the peasants of the nobility (*frälsebönder*); and the tax-paying peasants, or freeholders (*skattebönder*). By 1560 just under one-third of the land in Sweden proper was in the hands of the crown; about a fifth in the hands of the nobility; and about half in peasant ownership. In Finland at the same time more than nine-tenths of the land was in freeholders' hands. In the interval between 1560 and 1611 there was probably a slight decline in the holdings of the peasants, but it was not such as materially to affect the proportions between the three classes.[2]

The crown-peasants were simply the tenants of the crown, or of the King who wore it. In Gustav Vasa's time the economic and political power of the monarchy had been enormously increased by the plunder of the Reformation; and at the end of his reign the King was 'the biggest private landowner and agriculturist that ever existed in Sweden',[3] with five thousand farms as his personal property, apart from the lands of the crown.[4] After his death, this vast agglomeration was partially dispersed among members of the royal family, and underwent numerous vicissitudes; but Gustav Adolf, especially after the deaths of Johan of Östergötland and Karl Filip, was still a far bigger landowner than any of his subjects. The Vasa

[1] On the idea of a free peasantry, see F. Hedenius, *Anteckningar rörande svenska bondeståndet under Gustaf II Adolfs regering*, pp. 6-7.

[2] Heckscher, *Svenskt arbete och liv*, pp. 40, 88, 151.

[3] Forssell, *Anteckningar*, p. 71.

[4] For a discussion of the nature, administration and method of acquisition of the Vasa family estates, see J. A. Almquist, *Den civila lokalförvaltningen i Sverige*, I. 58-111.

Kings farmed a number of royal manors themselves; but with these exceptions the royal lands were worked by their tenants. The crown-peasants who worked them paid rent; they did a certain number of days of labouring for the crown each year; and they paid a kind of 'fine' (*städja*) at each renewal of their lease. They paid no ordinary taxes; but their rent and obligations corresponded pretty closely with the tax that would have been required of them had they been freehold farmers; and if any extraordinary tax were agreed to by the Estates, they paid it like everybody else. But they had no security of tenure. Their lease might not necessarily be renewed, even though they offered the required fine; and they could be evicted if the King thought proper.

The tax-peasant (*skattebonde*), as his name implied, paid taxes (*skatt*, a tax) instead of rent; but the amount of his obligations differed little from those of the crown-peasant. His legal position, however, was very much better. For he was the owner of his land, and no one could deprive him of it provided he paid his taxes. If, indeed, he neglected to do so for three years, his farm became forfeit; but otherwise his tenure was secure. This security of tenure made the tax-peasant's position seem enviable to many crown-peasants; and in the course of the sixteenth century a tendency grew up for the crown-peasant to make bargains with the crown in order to obtain a similar guarantee. Johan III systematized this by the sale to his tenants of 'birthright', which gave fixity of tenure though it did not confer ownership. All Kings were bound by an obligation not to diminish permanently the possessions of the crown, so that full property could not be conceded; but in practice those who bought 'birthright' were more or less on the same footing as tax-peasants, and were soon classed with them by the treasury.[1]

The *frälsebonde* was the tenant of a noble, to whom he stood in much the same relation as the crown-peasant did to the crown. His rent was supposed to be roughly equivalent to what the tax-peasant paid in ordinary taxes, or the crown-peasant in rent. He held his land on a six years' lease, and when that lease was renewed he paid, as the crown-peasant did, a fine to his landlord. He was exempt from

[1] Kuylenstierna, *Om rekognitionsskogar*, pp. 1-22. They were expressly forbidden to sell their birthright to the nobility, since this would have diminished the crown's revenues; but sale to other peasants was free. The crown reserved the right to redeem. A main motive on the King's side seems to have been the hope that increased security would lead to better use of the land. See J. E. Almquist, *Om ärftlig besittningsrätt till jord före det sjuttonde seklets slut*, pp. 95-116.

all ordinary taxation, and free from any obligation to do labour-services for the King; but he had to do day-work for his noble landlord, and his obligations in this respect were very much at the landlord's discretion, though they usually amounted to something like thirty days in the year. On the other hand, his position was more favourable than that of the crown-peasant in the matter of extraordinary taxation, and other obligations such as *gästning* and *skjutsning*.[1] For all these he was liable at only half the rate applicable to crown- and tax-peasants; and whereas they were organized in groups of ten for purposes of conscription, he was organized in groups of twenty, and was thus only half as likely to be taken for military service. The *frälsebonde* was thus decidedly privileged, in comparison with other peasants; though it may be that his elastic obligations to his landlord offset the lightness of the state's demands upon him. But some *frälsebönder* were more privileged than others. Those whose farms lay within a Swedish mile of a noble's seat (the 'mile of freedom', *frihetsmilen*), and who did day-work there, were in normal times exempt from almost all forms of taxation, ordinary or extraordinary, and from all other public burdens, excepting only the obligation to pay the priest's share of tithe; and the same privileges (and sometimes even wider ones) were enjoyed by those whose farms lay within the fence and paling (*inom rå och rör*) of their landlord's manor. Exemption in one direction, however, may sometimes have implied additional burdens in another; and it is not certain that the *frälsebonde* was materially any better off than other peasants. And he was very much at his landlord's mercy. A noble could evict his tenant without any provocation at any time, provided he repaid him his fine; he could designate him for conscription; he appropriated the crown's share of any fines that the local court might impose upon him; he could administer reasonable personal chastisement. Although it might not be to a landlord's interest to do so, he could undoubtedly, if he chose, treat his peasants extortionately, arbitrarily and cruelly. But if he did so, the peasant had his legal remedy; and in Sweden, if not in Finland, the *häradsrätt* did afford more than a nominal guarantee against illegalities.[2]

The Estate of the Nobility, as is plain from the exceptional position occupied by its peasants, was a highly privileged body.

[1] For *gästning* and *skjutsning*, see above, Vol. I, pp. 115-19.

[2] For a comparison of the position of the *frälsebönder* with that of other peasants, see H. Swenne, *Svenska adelns ekonomiska privilegier*, pp. 100-84, 215-232, 260-314.

And the most characteristic of its privileges—that which marked it off from the rest of the nation—was its exemption from all taxation, save in exceptional circumstances and with its own consent. This freedom from fiscal burdens was called *frälse* (deliverance); the Estate was the *frälsestånd*, its land was *frälsejord*, its peasants *frälsebönder*. The privilege of *frälse* first received statutory confirmation in 1280.[1] It originated in a kind of bargain, which arose out of the needs of the time: in return for exemption from taxation, a man bound himself to do service in person in the King's army on a horse worth at least forty *marks*. This service was known as *rusttjänst*, which may be loosely translated 'knight-service'.[2] At first it was open to anyone, noble or simple, to claim exemption from taxation for his land, provided he did *rusttjänst* in proper form; and as late as the reign of Karl IX the monarchy, in an effort to strengthen the cavalry arm, revived this interpretation of *frälse*.[3] But already by the end of the Middle Ages *frälse* was coming to be considered as a peculiar privilege of the nobility: instead of acquiring *frälse* as the result of doing *rusttjänst*, men did *rusttjänst* because they enjoyed the privilege of *frälse*. It was already forbidden to convert freehold-land (*skattejord*) into *frälsejord*; and the King on his side was prohibited from acquiring *frälsejord*, since it was agreed that the amount of such land ought not to be diminished: in short, the idea had grown up that *frälse* attached to specific pieces of land, and that none but the nobility ought to own them. At the same time, the miscellaneous collection of persons in enjoyment of *frälse* had been gradually transformed into an Estate of the Nobility; nobility and privilege had become hereditary, and entrance to the ranks of the privileged Estate had in practice been restricted to those upon whom the King conferred the patent of a peerage. These developments had important, but contradictory, consequences. If land itself were to be immutably noble, a noble who happened to be too poor to do *rusttjänst* must probably dispose of his land to another member of the Estate, lest the *frälse* character of the land be imperilled. But on the other hand, if nobility were a matter of birth, the failure to perform *rusttjänst* could not annihilate it. Controversy raged round these two points during the sixteenth century, and both awaited a solution at the

[1] For the early history of *frälse*, see C. Öhlander, *Bidrag till de adliga privilegiernas historia*.

[2] For *rusttjänst*, see P. Sörensson, *Adelns rusttjänst och adelsfanans organisation*, and below, pp. 211-3.

[3] See below, p. 197, for Karl IX's *sköldeknektar*.

moment of Gustav Adolf's accession. Another problem of a similar character was that which arose when a member of the nobility (especially a woman) contracted a *mésalliance* with a person of an inferior Estate. If the marriage were recognized, the privileges which attached only to birth would be extended to someone who did not possess the qualification of birth, and the King would lose some of his taxes. If, on the other hand, such marriages were punished by degradation, land which had been *frälse* might become subject to taxation. From the point of view of the nobility this was equally objectionable; and they contended that the rights of their order should be safeguarded by the compulsory transference of the lands of offenders to their next-of-kin. Here too no solution had been reached by 1611.[1]

One change of some importance had occurred in the course of the sixteenth century. In the beginning, the price of *frälse* had been fixed and invariable. A man got exemption for his lands by appearing at the King's host, properly armed and on a horse of the proper value, and it made no difference whether his property were large or small. In 1525, however, came an important innovation. Henceforward *rusttjänst* was to be graded proportionately to the income (or to certain heads of the income)[2] drawn by the noble from his tenants. In calculating this sum, the yield of the nobleman's own manor or home-farm, as well as of the farms lying within its boundaries (*inom rå och rör*), would not be counted. These farms were in any case specially privileged, as we have seen. There was thus a strong temptation to multiply such manors. The noble would declare one of his farms to be a manor (*sätesgård*): that is, he would allege that he effectively farmed it himself; and as a result his *rusttjänst* obligations would be diminished, and more of his peasants would be relieved of obligations to the state—and would consequently be able to render more services and pay more rent to their landlord. Just as the *frihetsmil* proved so elastic in the hands of the nobles that it became a mensurational curiosity,[3] so the growing number of manors tended to turn a privilege into a gross abuse. It was to check this practice that Erik XIV in 1562 limited the number of manors which might be created to three for a count, two for a baron and one for

[1] For much of the above, see especially S. Jägerskiöld, *Förvärv och förlust av frälse*, *passim*.

[2] E. Brännman, *Frälseköp under Gustav II Adolfs regering*, p. 269.

[3] Swenne, pp. 65-77, who gives one instance where exemption was claimed for a farm 26 km. from the manor (*i.e.* more than double the legal distance).

an ordinary noble.[1] The limitation was evaded, for the nobility would establish manors allegedly on behalf of each of their children; and a more effective check on the practice than Erik's legislation was probably the necessity for convincing the jury of the hundred (*häradsnämnd*) that the manor was not a sham, and that it was conducted on a scale conformable to the rank of its owner.[2]

In general, the sixteenth century saw the nobility insisting, more forcibly than ever, on the privilege of birth, and developing a real class-consciousness. This tendency was reinforced by the political struggle between the magnates and the crown, which, latent for most of Gustav Vasa's reign, came into the open in the half-century after his death. One aspect of that struggle was the nobility's repeated endeavours to extort from successive Kings grants of privileges which should formulate, or if the political conjunctures were favourable should extend, the limits of *frälse*. Karl IX, like Erik XIV before him, resisted these demands. He struggled to extract from the nobility military service which should be of real value to the state; he tried to make them useful as a class by compelling their children to learn foreign languages; he tried to induce them to allow their peasants to pay taxes in exchange for the cancellation of the obligation of *rusttjänst*. He was not successful; and when in 1607 he produced a draft of a new version of their privileges, his initiative resulted in a wrangle with the first Estate which lasted for the remainder of his reign, and led to no definite result.[3] Karl's attitude on this question was one of the many grievances entertained by the men who extorted the Charter from Gustav Adolf; and the event proved that the reconciliation of the monarchy with the aristocracy, which was one of Gustav Adolf's major achievements in domestic politics, could be purchased only by further concessions.

The revival of the political ambitions of the nobility, and the reinforcement of their social and economic position, was accompanied and emphasized by another development. This was the crown's habit of giving rewards, conferring pensions, and paying debts, by grants of revenues from specific sources. Such allocations, called

[1] For the creation of manors, see S. Bolin, *Erik XIV och säterifrihetens uppkomst, passim.*

[2] Swenne, pp. 29-32.

[3] N. Edén, *Den svenska centralregeringens utveckling till kollegial organisation*, pp. 25-31; Öhlander, p. 16; W. Tham, *Axel Oxenstierna*, pp. 203-4; *Axel Oxenstiernas skrifter och brefvexling* [cited: *AOSB*], I. 1. 3.

förläning or *beställning*,[1] might have unpleasant repercussions upon the peasants from whom such revenues were drawn. A freehold peasant might find himself paying all his taxes to a nobleman's bailiff; or his neighbour on crown land might find himself doing the like with his rent. When this situation arose, there was some danger, in the case of the tax-peasant, that the noble who took his taxes (and had thus virtually stepped into the crown's place) might fall into the habit of treating him as though he were a *frälsebonde*, might seek to extort more from him than he was bound to pay, or in the worst case might affect to treat his undoubted right of ownership as though it were no better than a temporary possession, and might turn him off his farm.[2] By the beginning of the seventeenth century the free tax-peasant could already perceive a real danger to his liberties. The reign of Gustav Adolf was destined rather to aggravate than to avert that danger.

It was especially acute in cases where the crown repaid a loan or rewarded a service by a donation of revenues 'in perpetual possession'. It is true that for such purposes the crown usually had recourse in the first instance to its own lands, and especially to the Vasa family estates; but donations of tax-revenues were already beginning. Either form of donation, if it had remained unqualified, would have infringed the principle that the King must not permanently diminish the royal revenue; and it was to meet this objection that the *riksdag* at Norrköping in 1604 passed a most important resolution. This laid it down that all such donations and alienations of the crown's revenues were to be restricted to the male line of the recipient, and insisted that the holders of such donations must apply for reconfirmation of them at the beginning of every reign.[3] This last provision was by no means a mere formality[4]; but though the interests of the crown were thus to some extent safeguarded, the provision concerning descent in the male line only gave a new and official impress of hereditability to such donations, and nobles who received them came more and more to regard them

[1] *Förläning* was a grant essentially *to* a person; *beställning* a grant *for* a service. *Förläning* meant a continuous grant of the same revenues; *beställning* a grant of an amount of revenue whose origin might vary from year to year. *Beställning* was a contractual relationship; *förläning* was not.

[2] See, *e.g.*, S. Ljung, *Erik Göransson Tegel*, pp. 61-2.

[3] P. O. von Törne, *Inverkningar av förläningsväsendet på jordbesittningsförhållandena före och efter reduktionen*, pp. 13-16; J. A. Almquist, *Frälsegodsen i Sverige under stormaktstiden*, pp. xii-xiii.

[4] See, *e.g.*, F. Wernstedt, *Ståthållaren Christoffer Wernstedt*, p. 63.

almost as their allodial property. Before 1611, however, such 'Norrköping Resolution estates' were mostly of crown lands: it was not until Gustav Adolf's time that any considerable block of revenues from tax-peasants was thus alienated in perpetual possession.

From whatever source such alienation was made, whether from rents or from taxes, the effect from the crown's point of view was the same. Every alienation diminished the revenue. And every alienation of revenue meant in the long run new extraordinary taxes. The crown, in fact, was already beginning to pay for services or purchase financial accommodation by the disposal of its capital assets. Under Gustav Adolf the process was to be pushed much further, as a matter of deliberate policy. But already it was causing concern: concern to the treasury, and concern to all crown-peasants and tax-peasants. Before the sixteenth century was out, the demand had been raised for a resumption by the crown of these and similar grants: for a *reduktion*, as it was called. It was raised again, pretty sharply, at the first *riksdag* of Gustav Adolf's reign; and thereafter it was never wholly silenced until the great *reduktion* of 1680.[1]

The Swedish nobility was not a numerous class: in 1611 it may have numbered between 400 and 500 families.[2] It was composed of very diverse elements. A clear distinction existed between the great families who filled the important offices of state and the middling provincial aristocracy; and a less well-defined line separated these last from the petty nobility, or *knapar*. The *knapar* were much the most numerous, and may have included anything from one-half to two-thirds of the whole Estate.[3] They lived in poor circumstances; discharged their obligation of *rusttjänst* with difficulty or not at all; were often indistinguishable, except in point of privilege, from the more prosperous of the peasantry; and were regarded by the higher aristocracy as a menace to the solidarity and prestige of the class. It is significant that when the composition of the Estate was finally determined by the *riddarhusordning* of 1626, only 126 families were considered to be qualified for admittance. The provincial nobility, often of ancient lineage, played little part

[1] Hallenberg, II. 727-8; N. Ahnlund, *Ståndsriksdagens utdaning*, pp. 55, 126; J. A. Almquist, *Den civila lokalförvaltningen*, pp. 52-4, 97.

[2] Forssell, *Anteckningar*, p. 65; Eriksson, *Järnräntor*, p. 36; Söderberg, *Den namnlösa medelklassen*, p. 68.

[3] *ibid.*, p. 39; Forssell, *op. cit.*, p. 68.

in national politics, apart from their attendance at a *riksdag*. A single manor, a half-dozen of farms worked by their peasants, was often the sum of their wealth. It was enough for them to be the acknowledged leaders in their respective hundreds; and if they discharged the office of *häradshövding*, the emoluments attached to it were probably not altogether a matter of indifference to them. Very different from these were the high aristocracy, those twenty or thirty families whose names are writ large on every page of Swedish history—the Bielkes, Posses, Bondes, Stures, Sparres, Rynings, Oxenstiernas, Totts, Leijonhufvuds, and others like them. Though the days had gone by when they were a truly inter-Scandinavian aristocracy, there were still Brahes and Gyllenstiernas on either side of the Danish border. They were bound together by an extraordinarily close web of intermarriages, and they were conscious that the time was not so very distant when the Vasas had been but one, and that not the most important, of their close family circle. Traditionally jealous of the crown, self-appointed guardians of the constitution, they had swallowed hereditary monarchy with repugnance, tended to view the resulting constitutional situation as a contractual relationship, and claimed the extension of their privileges as an equivalent owed to them by the dynasty.[1] They pressed their demands and put forward their constitutional arguments with the more effectiveness, since they were—as the provincial nobility were also—very generally learned in the law. The provincial noble functioned as *häradshövding*, the great magnate filled the office of *lagman*; and at the beginning of the seventeenth century the practice of discharging these duties by deputy was only beginning to become usual. In so far as a lawyer class existed in Sweden at all, it was almost identical with the nobility; and the Swedish analogue of Sir Edward Coke is Hogenskild Bielke.[2]

They were thus uniquely qualified to discharge much of the business of government; and they had an almost professional and hereditary interest in it. The earlier Vasas, by their use of imported administrators or low-born native secretaries educated at German universities, violated the aristocracy's vested interests; and it was intelligible that their reply should be a demand for a guarantee of their monopoly of the great offices of state. Service of this kind, or

[1] S. A. Nilsson, *Kampen om de adliga privilegierna 1526-1594*, p. 24.

[2] S. Petrén, *Lagläsarna. Ett bidrag till det svenska domstolsväsendets historia*, pp. 1-22.

failing that in the armed forces, was almost the only career now open to them; for the church was too poor a prospect to attract them any longer.[1] Moreover, the material rewards of state service were especially desirable to them, since payment by *förläning*, and still more by donations, afforded the prospect of increasing their estates, or at all events their landed revenues.

Though in Johan III's time the crown sometimes defaulted on the payment of these rewards, and though the nobility's demand for increased privileges received some colour from the King's occasional attempts to lay increased burdens upon them,[2] the high nobility were by Swedish standards extremely wealthy, and were probably growing wealthier—both absolutely, and relatively to the crown. Constant wars strained the royal resources, and before the sixteenth century ended the monarchy was glad enough to borrow from the aristocracy. Royal revenues were beginning to pass, temporarily at least, into their hands; and the yield of *förläningar* or donations could be much increased by practices of dubious legality. Every extension of the rights of *frälse*, while it curtailed the crown's income, increased—at least potentially—the amount the noble could extract from his peasants. The arbitrary creation of manors offered another easy way of augmenting their income. By the planting of cottars on their estates (*torpläggning*) they provided themselves with a tied labour-force exempt from all other obligations than those owed to the landlord.[3] Their agricultural revenues, in the shape of rents and labour dues, were thus steadily increasing. Their lands were still scattered widely over the country, and many manors were no doubt established with the legitimate object of providing accommodation for them as they ate their way round their properties. But the scattering of estates had other advantages; for it offered the hope that a crop failure in Uppland might be offset by better harvests in Östergötland; and above all it put the aristocracy in a position to tap the trade-routes. Estates near the Småland border were useful for trade to Denmark [4]; estates in Västmanland were handy for the mining areas. The day of the great compact demesne had not yet come; and the absence of any custom of primogeniture among the

[1] Except in Finland, where the nobility seem to have entered the church even in the seventeenth century: Suolahti, pp. 121, 347-9. Compare the analogous situation in Brandenburg: Carsten, p. 154.

[2] Nilsson, *op. cit.*, pp. 29, 53, 59-69.

[3] V. Elgeskog, *Svensk torpbebyggelse*, pp. 32-3, 43. At the same time, they were encroaching on the commons: *ibid.*, p. 33.

[4] S. Carlsson, *Mellan Bolmen och Holaveden*, pp. 27-9.

aristocracy would in any case have militated against such a development.[1]

Not even a large perambulatory establishment, however, could consume the revenues in kind which were rendered by the tenantry of the great nobles. Their wealth depended, as the King's did, essentially on their marketing those revenues advantageously. And hence they were not merely a *rentier* class; they were also most decidedly a trading class. The right to export, free of duty, the produce of their own estates and the revenues they derived from *förläningar* was one of their essential privileges: if they had lacked it, *förläningar*, and hence state service, could have been of no economic benefit to them.[2] They were forbidden to engage in any general commercial activity outside these limits; but there is no doubt that they practised *landsköp*, and the Estate of Burghers had well-grounded grievances about their infringement of the rights and functions of the towns.[3] In the iron-rents many of them contrived to secure from their tenants they had a most valuable export commodity, less perishable than agricultural produce; and their dealings with foreign merchants may well have played a part in attracting capital to Sweden. They succeeded, moreover, in making good their claim to exemption from the *régale* for the iron-mines on their own estates.[4] Many of the wealthiest of them had long owned ships of their own [5]; and one may guess that some of the largest native shipowners in 1611 were to be found among the nobility. In short, the economic prospects looked bright for the higher ranks of the aristocracy; and though their capital resources would not be adequate to financing the industrial developments of Gustav Adolf's reign (for they spent lavishly on imported luxuries, having much cultural leeway to make up), they would at least be in a position to invest something in the King's undertakings and to take advantage of the opportunities for getting yet more land, which the King's financial policy would provide. And since they were prospering at home, and since they were deeply engaged in foreign trade, they had little economic inducement to favour a warlike foreign policy. Estonia or Livonia might indeed bring to some few of them rewards

[1] Countships, however, went by primogeniture: R. Swedlund, *Grev- och friherreskapen*, pp. 24, 53.

[2] Lindberg, *Västerviks historia*, I. 159-67; Nilsson, p. 21; Smith, pp. 35-6.

[3] *Svenska riksdagsakter* [cited: *SRDA*], II. ii. 234.

[4] Nilsson, p. 110.

[5] Börjeson, *Stockholms segelsjöfart*, pp. 72, 81, 90; Lindberg, *op. cit.*, I. 163.

in the way of fresh grants of land; but for most of them war can have had few attractions until the conquest of Germany opened unexpected prospects of plunder.

The nobility was not, of course, a closed caste; but recruitment from below was as yet comparatively infrequent. The new type of civil servant so favoured by the Vasas was not often ennobled before Gustav Adolf's time; the habitual introduction into the nobility of the professional diplomat, the successful soldier, the foreign *entrepreneur* still lay in the future. For the man with nothing to commend him but his brains, a bishopric rather than a peerage was still the proper object of ambition. The church, indeed, still offered the best scope for social mobility, though within a strictly limited range: the son of the burgher or the peasant, if he could contrive a university education, could easily move from his own Estate into one which was generally esteemed more respectable. But even the clergy were to a great extent self-recruiting within their own order.[1] The social ladder which the professions might have offered was as yet non-existent, or almost so. The hereditary principle was still strong all through society, and the baker's son tended to be a baker, the secretary's a secretary, the parson's a parson.[2] The career of arms no doubt afforded a prospect of rising, though in 1611 the great opportunities were yet to come; and the civil service drew its recruits from all the Estates: the great nobles filled the high offices of state; the *knapar* in financial difficulties were ready enough to take jobs as the King's bailiffs; the burgher might hope to better himself as the King's merchant, or might turn his financial training to account in the service of the treasury; while even the peasant could aspire to the ungrateful office of constable (*länsman*).

But entry into the civil service took a man outside the Estate-structure; and the time had not yet come, in 1611, when a sojourn in this constitutional limbo might be regarded as being only a stage on the road to a peerage. Between the Estates themselves the lines were still clear and sharp, and movement across them was exceptional and not very important. It is true that the government's first choice for conscripts fell on peasant lads who had left the land and apprenticed themselves to a craft; but there were so few apprentices in Sweden (only one to every two masters, even in Stockholm, in 1613) that this was a line of social advance which cannot have been

[1] Suolahti, p. 29; Carlsson, *Svensk ståndscirkulation*, pp. 27-8.
[2] Suolahti, pp. 100-1, 120.

open to very many, and it is clear that the authorities viewed it with disapproval. It is true, too, that decayed nobles not infrequently married the daughters of burghers, or even of the better peasants in their neighbourhood, and for a time their families might vanish from the nobility—though often enough their sons or grandsons would recover noble status; but this too met with reprobation, as being a social evil. It was rare for a burgher to become a *bergsman*, or a *bergsman* a burgher. *Frälse* and burgage-right were as a rule mutually exclusive. There was no temptation for the wealthy merchant to set up as a country gentleman and invest in land; since, if he were not ennobled (and none were in 1611), he would hold his land on the same terms as a tax-peasant, and it was consequently unlikely to prove a good investment in the face of the competition of a privileged noble neighbour. And in any case, apart from any economic considerations, his social position in the countryside would have been anomalous and uncomfortable. Nor were there many merchants, even in Stockholm, who could have afforded the purchase of a sizeable estate: the number of those who were rich enough to own more than one house (and house-property was perhaps their most favoured form of long-term investment) was surprisingly few in the sixteenth century. The organization of society into Estates hampered the emergence of a true middle class, for the persons who in other circumstances would have fallen into that social category were distributed among all four Estates, or fell outside the pattern of Estates altogether.[1]

Thus Sweden at the opening of Gustav Adolf's reign was a remarkably stable—it is tempting to write, static—society. But the coming of foreign capital, attracted by the peculiar opportunities for profit which Sweden offered; the organization of the country for war, which was to be one of the achievements of the coming reign; the expansion of the civil service to cope with Oxenstierna's administrative reforms, or govern the conquered provinces, or conduct the new wide-spreading diplomacy that the wars brought with them—all these influences would make profound changes. Economically and socially, the Sweden of 1632 would be very different from the Sweden of 1611.

[1] For all this, see T. Söderberg, *Den namnlösa medelklassen*, pp. 46, 49-50, 69-70, 74, 80.

CHAPTER II

ECONOMIC AND SOCIAL DEVELOPMENTS, 1611-32

(i) *Introductory*

SUCH, then, was Swedish society, such the Swedish economy, when Gustav Adolf came to the throne. Within the two decades of his reign it underwent important alterations. The commercial isolationism of Gustav Vasa finally disappeared; the resources of the country were rapidly developed; new techniques and new manufactures made their appearance; and Sweden began to make up some of the long leeway that had separated her from the states of western Europe. Without some such changes it is difficult to see how the King's foreign policy could have been sustained. The War of Kalmar and the struggle in Muscovy might be waged with the fiscal methods and war potential of Erik XIV or Johan III; but the hostilities of the 'twenties, and still more the tremendous national effort demanded by the intervention in Germany, necessitated new approaches, experiments and reforms. The plight of the treasury in 1611, bad as it was, grew worse rather than better in the seven or eight years that followed. The government was kept going, in the early part of the reign, by taxes felt to be intolerably burdensome, and by hand-to-mouth loans from the Queen-Mother, from the commanders in the field, from native and foreign merchants, from the States General—from anybody, in short, who was prepared to run the risk of lending money to a hard-pressed usurper.[1] The debts thus incurred, and notably those contracted to the Dutch in the course of the payment of Älvsborg's ransom, weighed heavily on the country, and for most of the next decade Gustav Adolf was doing his best to pay them off.[2] The 'twenties brought fresh theatres of war, more extended campaigns, wider commitments and a much increased expenditure. The demands of 1630 were even heavier, and the

[1] For all this, see above, Vol. I, p. 122 *seqq.* For rates of interest on loans, see, *e.g.*, Hallenberg, IV. 875-6; A. Cronholm, *Sveriges historia under Gustaf II Adolphs regering*, III. 460; E. Grill, *Jakob de la Gardie*, pp. 23-4; E. Wendt, *Det svenska licentväsendet i Preussen*, p. 19; *AOSB*, II. I. 98. A rate of 18 per cent. was not uncommon; and in 1631 Oxenstierna raised a loan at $3\frac{1}{2}$ per cent. per month: Heckscher, I. 577.

[2] For this debt, see E. W. Dahlgren, *Louis de Geer*, I. 63-92.

weeks before Breitenfeld were the worst of all. The war budget rose to alarming heights to match the swollen Swedish armies. Those armies, of whom a considerable proportion consisted of hired mercenaries, demanded pay at rates which—for cavalry at least—made them ruinously expensive. And though pay might at a pinch be replaced by plunder, the mercenary regiments exacted a large disbursement of cash, in the form of muster-money, before they would even take the field.[1] The scale of fighting, the size of armies, in the Germany of the Thirty' Years War, was something new in Swedish experience. A mercenary foot regiment cost over 90,000 *riksdaler* a year in muster-money and pay; a single company of mercenary cavalry cost 25,000 *rdr*. Yet Älvsborg's ransom, which had strained Swedish resources to the uttermost, had amounted to no more than a million.[2] In 1623 the ordinary revenue was estimated at 1,420,000 *daler*, and the total revenue at 2,550,000 *daler*, which at the current rate was equivalent to 1,569,000 *rdr*.[3] But by 1632 the ordinary revenue stood at 2,200,000 *daler*, and the total revenue had risen to 6,500,000 *daler*, which was equivalent (since the *daler* had now depreciated against the *riksdaler*) to about 2,031,000 *rdr*.[4]; and the increase in the burden of taxation may well have been rather greater than is suggested by these figures. In 1632 Sweden spent over 156,000 *rdr*. on the navy alone.[5] And in 1630—the year when the financial strain was felt most acutely—the expenditure for military purposes only was more than half a million *daler* in excess of the total income of the state.[6] In these circumstances the country inevitably ran into debt: as early as 1629 Gustav Adolf's total indebtedness exceeded seven million *daler*.[7] It is true that all the

[1] See P. Sörensson, *Ekonomi och krigföring*, pp. 298-9; *Sveriges Krig*, V. 299-300.

[2] I borrow this comparison from Heckscher, I. 270; and see S. Lundgren, *Johan Adler Salvius*, p. 164 *note* 17.

[3] E. Brännman, *Frälseköpen under Gustav II Adolfs regering*, p. 23; *cf*. Cronholm, III. 475.

[4] Brännman, p. 259; *Sveriges Krig*, I. 56.

[5] Kungl. Krigsvetenskaps-Akademiens Handlingar, *Gustaf II Adolf. 300-års minnet*, p. 92.

[6] Sörensson, *op. cit*., pp. 298-9; Heckscher, I. 295. The figures for income, expenditure and debt in R. Klinckowström and J. Mankell, *Arkiv till upplysning om svenska krigens och krigsinrättningarnes historia* [cited: *Arkiv*], III. xl, which suggest higher sums than those given above, seem in fact to be in agreement with them, the discrepancy depending upon differing equations between *daler* and *riksdaler*.

[7] Dahlgren, I. 252. By 1 January 1631 the pay of the Prussian troops was 1,167,000 *rdr*. in arrear, of which 982,000 *rdr*. was never in fact paid: *Arkiv*, III. l.

states who fought in the great war experienced a severe financial crisis [1]; but Sweden was perhaps worse equipped than most other states to meet it. There arose, as never before in the country's history, a sudden, urgent, inescapable demand for cash, and cash in very large quantities: a demand, in fact, for one of the commodities with which Sweden was least well stocked, and for which hitherto there had been less use than elsewhere. And though the position in 1631 and 1632 was to some extent relieved by the French subsidies; and though in Germany, where the art of getting blood from a stone flourished in high perfection, there were better chances than in Poland of shifting the burden of war to other shoulders; still it is clear that the government of Gustav Adolf, which in 1611 had lived very much as Gustav Vasa's government had lived, was faced twenty years later with problems of unprecedented magnitude.

In order to solve these problems, Gustav Adolf and Axel Oxenstierna were driven, from the early 'twenties onwards, to a re-examination of the whole financial system. For the first time, proper estimates, and even a true budget, were prepared. A succession of new taxes was imposed upon the country, which, taken together, amounted to a most formidable burden; and the net of taxation was cast more widely than ever before, infringing in more than one respect the entrenched privileges of *frälse*. By all sorts of devices, King and chancellor strove to turn as much as possible of the state's income into cash and to dispose of its capital assets in order to augment current revenue. Certain expedients, indeed, they were wise enough to eschew. They did not sell offices or peerages; they did not debase the coinage. But the strain of war did lead (as it was bound to do) to the subversion of the old natural economy, and tended to replace it (at least in part) by a money economy. And when it became clear that the new taxes, however onerous, could not supply the soldiers' insatiable demands, the King was forced to make the most vigorous efforts to contrive that as much as possible should be raised from non-Swedish sources—from the lands occupied by his armies, from ships that touched at Swedish-held ports or went upon their lawful occasions up and down a Baltic dominated by the Swedish fleet.

But these direct methods of raising funds would hardly in them-

[1] Compare, *e.g.*, the financial troubles of the League: W. Goetz, *Die Politik Maximilians I von Baiern und seine Verbündeten 1618-1651*, IV. II. 21, 47, 50, 73, 92-3, 179, 223, 256, 259.

selves have paid for the war. The revenue proved sufficiently elastic to cover (more or less) the outgoings only because it was possible for the government to tap a greatly expanded national production, and because the King had at his command improved methods for marketing the country's exports. And for these developments he was mainly indebted to large investments of foreign capital, and to the business ability of a number of foreign financiers who made those investments. Nevertheless, it was not wholly a matter of capital's finding its way to an eligible opportunity: it was in part a matter of deliberate royal policy. Gustav Adolf used every means to attract foreign investors; and when they came to Sweden he succeeded, on the whole, not merely in using them but also in controlling them. True to the tradition of his grandfather, he tried hard to supervise the vital parts of the economy. Production, marketing, consumption—all were to be the object of regulation; each subject of the crown was considered as a cog, functioning in his appointed place in the great machine of state. The labour of the citizen must enrich the state; since in the wealth and power of the state consisted the spiritual as well as the temporal welfare of the subject. Importation of foreign workmen must energize Swedish industries; and where individual enterprise fell short, the King was ready for experiments with trading companies and ventures into state monopoly.

On the whole, his measures were successful in enabling Sweden to meet the demands of the times. By hook or by crook, somehow or other, the armies were satisfied, mutiny was in general avoided, the victories were won. There were miscalculations, mistakes, follies and sharp disappointments, for Gustav Adolf (whatever may have been the case with Oxenstierna) had little insight into economic problems, and lacked his grandfather's grasp of business and his clear if narrow understanding. His energetic and often misconceived efforts to alter the pattern of Swedish life so that the country should be able to meet the new dangers that surrounded it produced, moreover (as might have been expected), results and repercussions which in themselves gave rise to new stresses, disharmonies ominous for the future. Yet the transformation after 1611 was impressive; and in many respects it was the result of action from above. The social and economic development of Sweden under Gustav Adolf, in fact, was in one aspect the result of a mobilization of all the state's resources for war.

(ii) *The Finances of War*

(a) *Taxation*

Some account of the fiscal system as it existed in the first decade of Gustav Adolf's reign has been given already [1] when discussing the constitutional problems connected with the granting of supplies; here it will be sufficient to recall the tendency for casual and extraordinary grants, conceded by the Estates for a specific purpose or a limited period, to become permanent parts of the normal revenue, and so escape from the possibility of parliamentary control. This was a tendency which became more apparent in the years after 1620. It was the result, no doubt, of the practical inconveniences involved in the summoning of 'over-many *herredagar*' [2] and also of the central administration's natural desire to be able to reckon in advance, with reasonable certainty, upon the sources of income which would be likely to be available to it. A good example of this process of regularizing and stereotyping what had formerly been occasional is to be seen in the case of the so-called *landtågsgärd*. *Gärder* were aids which the King was entitled to levy in wartime in virtue of his prerogative. They took the form of demands for specific commodities, usually those of which the fighting forces stood in need. Very often they consisted of food or fodder of various sorts; but a *gärd* of pikestaffs or snowshoes was by no means extraordinary: it might very well be that only by a *gärd* could the required commodity be obtained in sufficiently large quantities.[3] The *landtågsgärd* was originally a *gärd* for a campaign (*landtåg*); but by the middle of Gustav Adolf's reign it had become an aid to provision fortresses or supply local troops. It was imposed anew in 1614, after the conclusion of the War of Kalmar; and in 1617 was granted by the *riksdag* upon a specific basis for one year. Since no war was raging in the country, a grant was constitutionally necessary. It was collected, however, every year thereafter until 1621, though no further grant was made in the interim. In 1621 it was granted again, and once more in 1622. And in 1624 it was voted for the last time. For the last time, because in 1624 the grant was without any time limit. Thus an impost originally (and very recently) considered as

[1] See above, Vol. I, pp. 311-3.
[2] See above, Vol. I, p. 29.
[3] For a typical example of a *gärd*, see *SRDA*, I. 248-50; for the pikestaffs, G. Petri, *Kungl. första Livgrenadjärregementets historia*, I. 144, Brännman, pp. 5-7; for an example late in the reign, N. Ahnlund, *Från medeltid och Vasatid*, p. 194.

an extraordinary levy for war became within a generation a part of the permanent, indisputable, revenues of the crown.[1]

Such methods of expanding the usual revenues did not, however, carry very far, and from the beginning of the 'twenties it was quite apparent that the fiscal arrangements of the country must be revised and supplemented. Something was done to improve the yield of the old 'determinate revenue': in 1615, 1620 and 1621, partial reassessments, and from 1624 a general reassessment for the whole country, brought the burdens upon the land into a closer relationship to the land's fertility and extent; and upon the basis of the new assessment accurate terriers were drawn up for the first time.[2] What was needed, however, was a tax which should be personal, which should be graduated according to ability to pay, and which should provide a really substantial addition to the royal income. Gustav Adolf and Axel Oxenstierna believed that in the Stock-and-Land Tax (*boskapshjälp*) they had found an impost which satisfied all three requirements. It was granted for the first time at an *utskottsmöte*,[3] in 1620, and the consent of the peasantry to its imposition was subsequently obtained by local negotiations. It was a direct tax, calculated upon the number of horses, oxen, cows and other stock, and also upon the number of acres sown with grain. It thus attempted to hold a rough equality between the pastoral and the arable regions of the country. The towns, indeed, came off well; but they were still sufficiently rural for their contributions to be worth having, and until 1627, indeed, they were charged with a lump sum apiece. The Clergy paid (until 1627 likewise) a cash contribution which varied according to the number of their parishioners. The attempt at graduation was not wholly successful, however: the tax is said to have borne more heavily upon the small man than upon the big one, especially as it was to be paid in cash. The original grant was for a period of two years; but in 1622 it was levied again for a further period of two years. In 1624 it was doubled; in 1626 it was re-imposed without the assent of the Estates; at the first *riksdag* of 1627 it was continued for one year, at the second for two, and the rate was still further raised, so that the man who in 1620 had been

[1] For *landtågsgärden*, see N. Ahnlund, *Ståndsriksdagens utdaning*, pp. 133, 533; F. Hedenius, *Anteckningar rörande svenska bondeståndet under Gustaf II Adolfs regering*, p. 26; A. Thomson, *Grundskatterna i den politiska diskussionen, 1809-1866*, pp. 23-4; E. Ingers, *Bonden i svensk historia*, I. 225.

[2] Cronholm, III. 314; Kuylenstierna, p. 43 *note*; Hedenius, pp. 31-2: *cf.* Helmfrid, p. 118.

[3] For this, see above, Vol. I, p. 305.

paying 8 *öre* tax for his horse was now paying $24\frac{1}{2}$ *öre*. It was reimposed in 1629, and again at the *utskottsmöte* of February 1632; and at last, in 1642, it was turned into a fixed cash contribution, assessed upon the average of the previous three years' payments.

So heavy and universal a tax could not fail to be unpopular, and Oxenstierna himself confessed in 1631 that he did not like it.[1] Galt reported to his government in 1622 that peasants were slaughtering stock to escape it; and in 1626 the authorities were a good deal concerned at the extent to which evasions and frauds prevailed. Yet it fulfilled the purpose for which it was instituted. It became one of the staple items of the revenue, and in 1632 brought in as much as half a million *daler*. This figure would not have been attained had it not been for one feature still to be mentioned. The Stock Tax was one of the first taxes really to infringe the concept of *frälse*. At first the *frälsebonde* paid at half the rate of the tax-peasant, and peasants living within the *frihetsmil* or *inom rå och rör* were wholly exempt—an arrangement which was in accordance with the custom for such extraordinary levies. But from 1627 onwards no exemptions were entertained. The *frälsebonde*, as far as this particular tax was concerned, was henceforward on the same footing as the yeoman. The nobles themselves did not pay the tax; but by permitting its imposition upon their peasants *inom rå och rör* they consented in effect to the crown's taking a larger share, and themselves a smaller share, of the limited resources which the *frälsebonde* had at his disposal after his own needs were satisfied.[2]

Of the same wide incidence was another new direct tax, levied in 1628: the so-called Three Marks' Aid. This aid, which was never granted by the Estates, but was assented to locally after negotiations conducted by the various *ståthållare*, was a poll-tax of three *marks*, which fell with equal weight—much as Älvsborg's ransom had done—upon the prosperous yeoman farmer, the *frälsebonde* living *inom rå och rör*, the farmer's boy, the cottar and the pauper. It was extremely unpopular, and in Västergötland and Småland it was at first actually

[1] *AOSB*, I. VI. 321.

[2] For *boskapshjälpen*, see Stiernman, I. 741-3, 751-5; *SILR*, pp. 131-2; *RRP*, I. 33-4, 63, II. 51, 170; *Sveriges riddarskaps och adels riksdagsprotokoll* [cited: *SRARP*], I. 99, 183, 199; *AOSB*, I. I. 453, I. VI. 321, II. IX. 17; Galt, p. 23; Hallenberg, IV. 836-8; D. Hannerberg, *Närkes boskapsbestånd på 1620- och 1630-talen, passim* (an account of the operation of the tax in the province of Närke); Ahnlund, *Ståndsriksdagens utdaning*, p. 153; Hedenius, p. 27; Swenne, p. 139; Thomson, p. 29; Wernstedt, p. 96; H. Holmquist, *Svenska kyrkans historia*, IV, I. 185. For possible antecedents of this form of taxation, see S. Hedar, *Karl IXs förmögenhetsbeskattningar*, pp. 365-9.

refused. It was not a good tax, and it was levied only on a single occasion; but at least—unlike the old *gärder*—it was a contribution in hard money.[1] Other additional direct taxes were the *utskrivnings-hjälp*—a monetary contribution taken instead of an *utskrivning* in 1629-30; and the 'Ship Money' of 1630, when the nobility by another sacrifice of their immunities agreed to pay 50 *daler* for every horse due from them in *rusttjänst*.[2] More important than these in every respect, however, were two indirect taxes, which together marked a financial epoch. These were the Little Toll—so named in contrast to the old Great Toll on exports—and the Mill Toll. Both were introduced in the early 'twenties, the Little Toll in 1622, the Mill Toll in 1625; and their imposition so soon after the appearance of the Stock Tax is an indication of how rapidly the expenditure of the country was bursting from the limits of the old fixed revenues, and of how impossible it had become for the King to obey the behest of the *landslag* and live of his own.

The Little Toll was a duty levied *ad valorem* upon all 'edible, perishable and consumable goods' brought to market in the towns. It was not a very heavy duty—only one thirty-second of the value of the goods—but the universality of its incidence would have made it intolerable if it had been heavier. It was accompanied by a number of edicts establishing excises on brewing, slaughtered meat, and most forms of provisions. It was originally intended, in accordance with the request of the *riksdag* (which granted it only after strong resistance by all four Estates), to be provisional; it provoked pertinacious and sometimes violent opposition, which in one case at least was punished with death, and which led Oxenstierna to advise the government to connive at laxity in collecting it in the smaller towns [3]; but it established itself so securely that it remained in force until as late as 1810. It had considerable success as a means of raising revenue (by the end of the reign it was yielding about 300,000 *daler* a year) [4]; and, once again, it was to be paid in cash. It thus formed another instalment in Gustav Adolf's plan to provide himself with a predictable money income. But, in addition, it linked up with the policy (to be discussed later) of encouraging the

[1] *RRP*, I. 67 *note* 3, 79 *note* 1, 89-90, 108; Swenne, p. 136; Ahnlund, *op. cit.*, p. 176.

[2] Stiernman, I. 815-16; *SRARP*, I. 137; *RRP*, I. 155 *note* 1.

[3] Geijer, III. 44; *AOSB*, I. VI. 501-2.

[4] T. Söderberg, *Sveriges ekonomiska struktur och utveckling under Gustav Adolf*, pp. 109-10.

somewhat rachitic towns to find their feet and stay upon them. For the peasant producer could not defeat the ordinance and safeguard his pocket by disposing of his goods locally: if he did so, he fell into the notorious sin of *landsköp*. He must bring his goods to market, that the flaccid muscles of urban trading be given the opportunity of exercise; and he must pay the Little Toll, that the King might save him harmless from Sigismund and Wallenstein. Nor was that the worst of it. The peasant must pay toll not only upon the goods he had produced himself but also upon those taxes or rents in grain or butter or hides or fish which he was bound in duty to pay to the crown, and which, by the thoughtful provision of the bailiffs, he was instructed to hand over in the neighbouring town. Thus the peasant paid toll on his rent, or paid taxes twice over. He might even find himself mulcted for the hay which he had cut and carted from the royal meadow as part of the labour-services which were legally due from him. And if the toll was thus most burdensome to the peasant, it was not without its inconveniences even to the towns. Those of more modern foundation, or those who for one reason or another found themselves with nothing in the nature of walls remaining, were faced with the labour and expense of constructing a toll-hedge eight ells high, with toll-gates through it at convenient places.

Yet, though the Little Toll was a nuisance to some and an oppression to many, it had one great countervailing merit (besides its merit as a producer of revenue): it was a tax that hit *frälse* and *ofrälse* alike. Not only did the *frälsebonde* pay at the same rate as his yeoman neighbour, but the noble paid at the same rate as the peasant. This is the first tax to override entirely the principle of *frälse*. Gustav Adolf could carry it only by means of a bargain with the first Estate. In return for their assent to his proposals, he granted them a revision of their privileges which conceded much that they had hitherto demanded in vain.[1]

Equally universal in its incidence was the Mill Toll. This tax was first granted by the *utskottsriksdag* of March 1625, but it had been decided on in principle by the *råd* in the previous December, and as early as February 1625 the treasury seems to have been attempting

[1] For the Little Toll, see Stiernman, *CPO*, I. 805-7, 809-34, 862-85, 902-10; *RRP*, II. 102-3; *AOSB*, II. III. 44, II. x. 268; Galt, p. 71; *A. Brahes tidebok*, p. 143; Hallenberg, V. 16; Ahnlund, *Från medeltid och Vasatid*, pp. 193-4; H. L. Rydin, *P.M. angående det svenska skatteväsendets utveckling*, p. 78; Löfgren, I. 214; K. Hellberg, *Järnets och smedernas Eskilstuna*, I. 267-8, and Björkman, *Jönköping*, II. 133, for the inconveniences of the toll-hedge.

to raise loans upon the anticipation of the revenue it was expected to produce.[1] Its purpose was plainly declared to be the maintenance of a standing army; and it was upon the virtues, conveniences and necessity of a standing army that the government spokesmen dwelt when urging it upon the vainly resisting Estates. The Mill Toll levied a tax upon all grain brought to the royal mills for grinding; and by way of making the burden more equitable, extorted 12 *öre* per *tunnan* for wheat (which was eaten only by the upper classes), 8 *öre* for rye and 3 *öre* for barley (which provided—if it were not a bark-bread year—the bread of the lower orders). It was of course ordered that henceforth all grain should be milled only at the royal mills. But from the beginning this proved difficult to enforce. There were not enough royal mills to serve the country; and even if there had been, it was almost impossible to prevent home-grinding with hand-mills. At first, then, hand-mills were tolerated, and their owners were expected to make a return of the amount of grain ground in them. Naturally there were large frauds upon the revenue. At the end of 1627, accordingly, the King changed his policy. All hand-mills were to be prohibited after 1 January 1629; but for the year 1628 owners of hand-mills were to be permitted to retain them in return for a payment of one *mark* for every person on their farms over the age of twelve. At the same time the amount of grain which households of different sizes might reasonably be expected to require was estimated; and henceforward families which brought less than this amount to the royal mills would find themselves under suspicion. Thus an inquisitorial and oppressive system was contemplated, reminiscent of some of the most notorious abuses of the *ancien régime* in France. But when it came to the point, the clerical work and administrative difficulties connected with such a system daunted the government. It was found simpler and cheaper to fall back on a general cash contribution, on the same basis as that laid down for the owners of hand-mills in 1628. The hand-mills remained; the Mill Toll was for a time practically given up; and in its place was put what was in effect another poll-tax, assessed first at the rate of one *mark*, later at four, and last of all at five. It was now known as the Five Marks' Aid; and it continued, much disliked, until 1631. In that year Gustav Adolf, for reasons which are not very clear, ordered its abolition and a reversion to the Mill Toll; but with the additional provision that the toll was now to be paid in silver. This

[1] *Abraham Brahes tidebok*, pp. 157-8.

last stipulation caused universal consternation; for the depreciation of the Swedish copper currency meant that insistence on payment in silver would almost double the rate of the toll. But though the Estates protested (and Oxenstierna himself had his doubts), the *råd* informed them that the King's orders must be obeyed. The restored Mill Toll, however, was not a great success; and though it outlasted Gustav Adolf's lifetime, it was replaced in 1635 by a fixed direct tax, of three marks. In this form it became a part of the ordinary revenues of the crown; and it was not finally abolished until as recently as 1938.[1]

(b) *Alienations of Revenue*

Thus the latter half of Gustav Adolf's reign saw a great number of additional financial burdens placed upon the shoulders of a community which was not very easily able to bear them. The new taxes were mainly taxes on persons and goods, rather than on land; they attempted, in many cases, a rough equity by graduation of incidence; they made considerable inroads into the immunities of the nobles and their peasants; and, one and all, they were payable in coin. But though Gustav Adolf had thus at his disposal a money revenue far greater than that which any previous Swedish sovereign had enjoyed, it was not nearly adequate to his needs. Often it was imperatively necessary to anticipate income. Always taxes were slow in coming in; and always there were considerable arrears outstanding which it might take months or years to collect. When to these circumstances is added the fact that the ordinary revenues of the crown, upon which the King was supposed to exist, were still paid mainly in kind, and the not less important fact that Sweden was still suffering from an inadequate supply of skilled administrators, it is not difficult to divine the solution which presented itself as the way out of all these difficulties. The solution was, of course, to farm out the revenues, or, in urgent cases, to pawn them or sell them.

This was in any case a development which followed naturally enough upon the already existing practice of *förläning*. We have seen already [2] how this method of rewarding services had established

[1] For the Mill Toll, see Stiernman, I. 782-3; Stiernman, *CPO*, I. 951-5, 977-980; *SRARP*, I. 33, 69; *RRP*, I. xxiii, 13-14, 37 *note* 5, 62-3, 109, II. 129, 237; C. G. Styffe, *Konung Gustaf II Adolfs skrifter* [cited: Styffe], pp. 218-19, 311; *AOSB*, I. VI. 321, II. x. 283, 566-7; Hallenberg, V. 346-52; G. Wittrock, *Regering och allmoge under Kristinas egen styrelse*, p. 46.

[2] Above, pp. 55-7; and Vol. I, p. 123.

itself in the course of the preceding century, and how the resolution of the Norrköping *riksdag* of 1604 had defined the terms upon which the crown might make donations of land 'in perpetual possession'. Under Gustav Adolf both types of *förläning*—that which temporarily alienated revenues in order to pay a wage or meet some other financial commitment, and that which rewarded services by a donation in perpetual possession—increased greatly. In 1612 Gustav Adolf, in accordance with the resolution of 1604, confirmed the holders of the so-called 'Norrköping estates' in their possession; and subsequently he did not hesitate to add to the number of alienations of this type. Until the 'twenties, indeed, most of such alienations were of lands in the Baltic provinces, but before the end of the reign they had become very common in Sweden too. At the time of Gustav Adolf's death just under seven per cent. of the ordinary revenue of the crown had been lost by donations, some of them upon terms more favourable than those of Norrköping.[1] *Förläningar* of the more temporary sort in 1632 accounted for just under five per cent. of the ordinary revenues; but at least these revenues were not really lost to the crown: it was merely that they were assigned to specific expenditure without passing through the treasury. *Förläningar* of this type were already common in 1611, and they increased considerably in the financial chaos of the years that followed. By 1613 they had become so numerous, and had been granted in so indiscriminate a fashion, that the crown did not know which revenues had, and which had not, been assigned, and sometimes granted the same twice over; while its failure to control the illegalities and atrocities of the *län*-holders (especially in Finland) was notorious, and was publicly admitted.[2] At the Örebo *riksdag* of 1617 the Burghers complained sharply of the abuses of *förläningar*: it was no wonder, they considered, that new impositions were constantly being levied, for almost all the royal revenue had been granted away. But they got no satisfaction. The *råd* informed them that somehow or other wages must be paid and obligations met, and clearly implied that *förläningar* were unavoidable.[3]

The system of *förläning* by its obvious convenience in relieving an overburdened administration from the necessity for collecting taxes (and pursuing arrears) may probably have encouraged the

[1] S. Clason, *Till reduktionens förhistoria*, pp. 104-5; J. Vasar, *Utvecklingen av böndernas rättsläge i Estland till Karl XI*, pp. 31-2, for Gustav Adolf's donations in Estland, where he gave away almost all the crown lands.

[2] See above, Vol. I, pp. 114-15; *SICF*, p. 25; Hallenberg, II. 734.

[3] *SRDA*, II. 81, 179; *AOSB*, II. x. 30; Hallenberg, IV. 641-2.

King to adopt the equally convenient expedient of farming out the revenues. The first instance in which the experiment was tried seems to date from 1618. In that year Willem de Besche was allowed to appropriate the revenues of Finspång's *län* in return for a fixed annual payment to the crown; while Jakob de la Gardie was similarly allowed to farm the revenues of the *län* of Kexholm and Noteborg. Although the terms of the latter of these agreements, at least, constituted a very bad bargain for the crown, Gustav Adolf seems to have been so impressed by the ease and certainty with which they provided him with an income that he was prepared to go to great lengths to secure these advantages. In 1621 he drew up a memorandum for the government in Stockholm, in which he declared it to be his object to farm out all the revenues of the crown. Tax-farming in Sweden had, indeed, one great advantage which was not present (or not to the same extent) in, for instance, France: it provided the simplest possible solution to the problem of converting a revenue paid in goods into a revenue available in money. There were occasions, even yet, when it was convenient to Gustav Adolf to be paid in butter or tar; but as the theatre of operations fixed itself permanently in Germany, as the number of mercenaries increased, such occasions grew rarer. Gustav Adolf seems to have felt that the old natural economy was out of date, and to have aimed in his policy at replacing it by methods of finance which were deemed more modern. The day of the royal warehouses, he hoped, was over; and the tax-farmer could attend to those petty concerns of marketing in which Gustav Vasa had taken so sharp an interest: his own attention was more than fully occupied by other matters, more worthy of the royal energies. He is said to have remarked that a King's income ought not to consist of fowls, eggs, butter, cloth and such small gear, but of tolls and duties, of the produce of the mines, and of similar revenues.[1] Already by 1624 there had been considerable progress towards increasing the proportion of cash to goods in the revenue of the state: whereas in 1621 only 217,000 *daler* in coin came into the exchequer, by 1624 the amount had risen to 440,000 *daler*, in addition to 516,000 *daler* reserved for military expenditure.[2] To make the new system work easily, however, some standard and universal equivalents must be fixed, so that natural revenue could be assessed in money values without constant disputes between the

[1] F. Lagerroth, *Statsreglering och finansförvaltning i Sverige*, p. 60; and see Brännman, p. 14.

[2] Brännman, p. 24.

King and his tax-farmers. This was effected by the 'royal assessment' (*kronovärdering*) of 1623, which established a tariff which became more or less permanent, and which in consequence became increasingly unfavourable to the crown as the price of commodities rose.

For some years this policy was followed out with tolerable consistency. The ordinary rents and taxes, the Great Toll on exports, the Mill Toll, were all farmed; the Little Toll was on occasion farmed to the towns in which it was collected; in short, in the mid-'twenties the greater part of the revenue was in the hands of the tax-farmers, or, from being granted in *förläning* or pawned to pay off debt, gave the treasury no trouble. The farmers were of the most various kinds. Some were foreign capitalists, to whom the crown was under great obligations, and upon whose aid the King relied in all sorts of matters; some were *ståthållare*; some, former royal bailiffs; some, minor government officers. Mostly they were unpopular; for, like tax-farmers in all ages and countries, they sought to make the maximum profit for themselves. Their extortions and illegalities occupied the attention of the *riksdag* as early as 1624, and again at both of the meetings of 1627; and at the end of the reign the commonalty were clamouring for the abolition of the system, while even the nobles complained of the strictness with which toll was exacted. The farmers of the crown's 'determinate revenues' stepped into the place of the former royal bailiffs, and were naturally enough invested with the coercive powers against defaulters which the bailiffs had wielded; and though they were expressly debarred from occupying judicial office in the area of their farm, their deputies were not. The extent to which they became regular members of the administration can be judged from the fact that on occasion the *landshövding* felt it to be incumbent upon him to communicate to them the decisions of the *hovrätt* upon matters of ecclesiastical discipline. Thus the tax-payer found himself at the mercy of a speculator who was also an *ad hoc* member of the local government.[1]

From the point of view of the crown, moreover, the experiment

[1] For the preceding paragraphs, see Stiernman, I. 770, 794, 803; Galt, p. 28; *AOSB*, II. III. 51; *Vendels sockens dombok*, p. 28; *RRP*, I. 105; Hallenberg, IV. 879-82; Brännman, pp. 8-12; B. Broomé, *Nils Stiernsköld*, pp. 170-2; H. Cnattingius, *Den centrala kyrkostyrelsen*, p. 228; Heckscher, I. 284, 533; Boëthius and Heckscher, p. xvii; Smith, p. 72. As an example of the abuses that could arise may be cited the case of Welshuisen and Paridon von Horn. These foreign capitalists were allowed to farm (among other revenues) the fines paid in the municipal court of Västervik; and they had the impudence to claim the fine which had been imposed upon themselves in consequence of their illegal trading practices: Lindberg, *Västerviks historia*, I. 186.

proved less satisfactory than had been hoped. Apart from the concern which the growing volume of popular discontent must cause to the administration, it was undoubtedly true that some at least of the farmers made excessive profits. Between 1618 and 1628, for instance, Jakob de la Gardie made a direct profit of about 170,000 *daler* on his farm, besides very large indirect gains which might well have been taken into consideration in fixing the amount of the lease.[1] Worst of all, the rapid depreciation of the *daler* and the widening difference between the royal assessment of 1623 and the true value of commodities measured in *daler* was a source of heavy loss. It was this, probably, which led to the reversal of policy which began about 1629. From that date onward the number of farms declined; and though they had by no means all been terminated when Gustav Adolf died, they were much diminished. The system, as regards direct rents and taxes, was finally abolished in 1635.

But already by 1622 the King's necessities had driven him to a more drastic measure than any of those so far considered. This was nothing less than the sale, not only of crown lands but of the determinate revenues in general, irrespective of whether they derived from crown-tenants or tax-paying yeomen. The intention was that such sales should be made primarily to the nobility: the nobility might be expected to be interested in expanding their estates; it was thought that they would have the capital available for the investment; and it was hoped that they would farm the land they bought better than the existing tenants.[2] The land sold, if it were crown land, then became noble land (*frälsejord*), for which *rusttjänst* was due; and the former crown-peasants became *frälsebönder*. If, on the other hand, the revenues sold derived from tax-paying peasants, the land remained the peasants' property; but in almost every other respect they became virtually equated with *frälsebönder*. The anomaly of their position was expressed in the paradoxical terminology later invented to describe them: they were known as *skattefrälsebönder*. The whole transaction was known as *frälseköp*, the purchasing of land into *frälse*.[3] The terms of sale were exceptionally favourable to the purchaser: with the single limitation that the tax-peasant might not be deprived of his right of ownership, the noble who

[1] E. Grill, *Jakob de la Gardie*, pp. 26-36, 46-7, 60-70.
[2] As in fact was often the case: see Helmfrid, p. 125.
[3] For *frälseköp*, see especially Brännman, *passim*; S. Nilsson's review of Brännman in *HT*, 1952; S. Clason, *Till reduktionens förhistoria*, p. 183 *seqq.*; Heckscher, I. 284-7, 300; and *cf.* Carsten, *Origins of Prussia*, p. 98.

invested in *frälseköp* obtained perpetual possession of his purchase with right of free disposal, and with no obligation to seek royal confirmation at the beginning of a new reign. After 1624 the only provision for the crown's right to recover these revenues was the obligation to give the King an opportunity to repurchase at a price acceptable to the purchaser's relatives, should they decide to dispose of the investment outside the family. Financially, too, the terms were attractive. The price of land until 1629, when depreciation made a readjustment necessary, varied between 25 and 33⅓ years' purchase; thereafter it rose for a short while to 50 years' purchase, to return in 1630 to the earlier figure. These prices gave, on paper, the then very modest yield of at most four per cent. on the capital. But, in fact, the true figure might be as much as ten or eleven per cent., and the average was probably more than six per cent.; for though what was being sold was nominally only the 'determinate revenues', in practice a fair proportion of the 'indeterminate revenues' found its way into the pockets of the buyer. For all these reasons the nobility found *frälseköp* an attractive investment; and since Gustav Adolf was very willing to sell, the crown did brisk business, especially in 1626 and 1628. Gustav Adolf, moreover, was prepared to sell even to non-noble persons, illogical though this might appear, provided such persons were approved by him, or in his absence by the government; and more than a dozen such sales took place, among others to Rudbeckius and Paulinus. But the great bulk of sales were to the high nobility, especially to those who occupied positions in the state's service. *Frälseköp* in Sweden proper occurred mainly in Uppland, Södermanland, and parts of Östergötland, Västergötland and Småland; in Finland, in the coastal districts around Björneborg and Åbo; beyond the seas, in Estonia and Livonia (where almost all the lands of the crown were disposed of), and after 1630 to some extent even in Pomerania. Care was always taken not to sell land adjoining royal castles or manors, and sales in the Bergslag were prohibited also.

Gustav Adolf is said to have intended to pursue the policy of *frälseköp* to the utmost limits, and to have contemplated with equanimity the eventual alienation of all the crown's lands in this manner. In 1636 Axel Oxenstierna expressed one aspect of the policy when he said:

His late Majesty disapproved what old King Gustav and other kings did in drawing all under the crown, and thereby impoverishing the subjects of the country, as was done in King Erik's and King Johan's time, when a *riksråd* or a nobleman was forced to live *sordide*, and he who was somewhat openhanded could not depart this life without great obligations and debts. And therefore did he give his subjects lands, and make them rich, so that he was not averse to giving away Småland, Västergötland, and Finland. . . .[1]

It seems also that the King pinned his faith on a compensatory expansion of indirect revenue to offset what he was losing, and looked to an increase in national wealth from an extension of noble estates. However that may be, the process was not really pushed very far in his lifetime, and the financial implications were a good deal less important than used to be thought. The total purchase-money paid for *frälseköp*, including that for the Baltic provinces and Pomerania, did not, according to the most recent estimate, reach 700,000 *riksdaler* in the whole ten years in which such sales were taking place—which is not a very significant sum when compared with the annual subsidy of 400,000 *rdr.* paid by France in terms of the treaty of Bärwalde; and of that 700,000 *rdr.* perhaps one-third went to the extinguishing of the crown's debts to the purchasers. In Sweden and Finland, the revenues alienated in this way amounted to no more than 47,800 *daler*—a sum which was quite inconsiderable. In 1632, when the total ordinary revenue stood at 2,200,000 *daler*, *förläningar* absorbed 119,000 *daler* and donations 163,000 *daler*. So that the King gave away more than three times as much as he actually sold.[2] But though from the financial angle *frälseköp* was thus of minor importance, it was attended by important social consequences, and it reinforced existing social tendencies which were anything but desirable.[3]

Much more innocuous, though equally insignificant financially, was the sale of crown lands to crown-peasants—a practice inaugurated, as we have seen, by Johan III, and now resumed. By making purchases of this sort, the crown-peasant bought himself out of his tenancy and became a tax-paying owner of the land he occupied. And since he had thus bought himself into taxation, the transaction was known as *skatteköp* (tax-purchase).

[1] Clason, p. 141.

[2] Brännman, p. 97 *seqq.*, 107, 258, 260, 386; Clason, pp. 104-5, though these figures are difficult to reconcile with those on pp 227, 229, and Clason's figure for the ordinary revenue is nearly double Brännman's. For the relation between the *riksdaler* and the *daler*, see p. 47, above.

[3] See below, pp. 149-51.

(c) *Income from non-Swedish Sources. The Prussian 'licences'*

This bold fiscal policy—by some qualified as reckless—was in itself, whatever its merits, quite inadequate to meet the mounting cost of war. Soon after the beginning of the Livonian war, an attempt was made to keep the estimates and accounts for war expenditure separate from those for civil purposes, and this separation becomes quite clear-cut by the end of the reign.[1] It is thus possible to get some idea of how the various revenues of the crown were spent. The war estimates reveal plainly how inadequate to the task of paying for the war were the measures we have been examining. Of the new taxes, only one—the Stock Tax—was expected to make any appreciable contribution to the expenses of the Swedish armies; and it formed only a small part of the total: an estimate for the months June to November 1629, for instance, put the contribution of the Stock Tax to the armies at 120,000 *daler*—out of a total war expenditure for this period of over two millions; and a war estimate for Germany, dated October 1630, counted on obtaining from Sweden, by way of taxation of all sorts, 430,000 *riksdaler*—out of a total of 1,463,000 *riksdaler*.[2] The new taxes, it is clear, were spent mainly at home. The proceeds of *frälseköp* were inconsiderable. The armies in the field were paid by other devices than these.

One great source of supply lay in the resources of the enemy and the neutral. It was one of Gustav Adolf's most cherished convictions that war ought to pay for itself; and though he never succeeded in realizing this ideal, he did raise large sums for current war expenses from the countries occupied by his armies—whether from friends and allies who made more or less willing contribution, or from enemies that were held to ransom. Both Prussia and Germany were wealthy countries, and the coastline from Danzig to Königsberg was one of the great trading foci of Europe. Very large sums were screwed out of Prussia by the Swedish forces: in the winter of 1627-28 they collected a revenue of over a million *daler* from the occupied lands—sufficient to cover almost all the expenses of the army[3]; and although the Prussian contribution dropped very much in subsequent years,[4] it remained important. The conquest of Germany, after Breitenfeld, meant the end of the financial crisis

[1] See *Arkiv*, I. 147, 303-13.
[2] E. Wendt, *Det svenska licentväsendet i Preussen*, pp. 108, 192.
[3] *ibid.*, p. 28.
[4] *ibid.*, pp. 72, 96.

which had seemed so formidable in the summer of 1631, and brought with it an impressive reduction in the amounts drawn from Sweden. The French and Dutch subsidies, the contributions of allies, the ransoms paid by captured towns, and the universally prevailing system of living on the country, made the maxim *bellum se ipsum alet* more plausible than ever before. To take two examples only, from many that could be adduced: Erfurt, after its liberation by Swedish troops in October 1631, was forced to contribute to the King's war-chest at the rate of 14,000 *rdr.* a month; while from Munich, after its capitulation in May 1632, a ransom of no less than 300,000 *rdr.* was extorted. The resources of occupied Germany were systematically exploited; revenues which might be annexed were carefully inventoried; territory was methodically allocated between the armies, as quartering- or mustering-areas. As a result of this policy, whereas in 1630 Sweden had contributed over three million *rdr.* to the war, in 1631 the sum had fallen to just under two million; in 1632 it dropped to little more than half a million.[1] In February 1633 Oxenstierna wrote to the *råd*, 'But that Sweden should be at any charges or further expense upon this business I hold for quite out of the question, saving only such moneys as may be expended on the coastline'; and in December 1634 he wrote, with some slight exaggeration, 'We have now, by the space of four years, sent as good as no money out of the kingdom to the German war.'[2] The 'territorial' strategy of the Thirty Years' War, however abhorrent to military purists of a later age, had in the context of the time solid economic arguments behind it, above all for a country such as Sweden.

But it was not only the inhabitants of Germany or Prussia that provided the resources for their deliverance or subjection: one source of income of the highest importance to Gustav Adolf's war finances came from the neutrals of all nations.

In July 1626 Gustav Adolf began to take toll of ships visiting Danzig, and though for a time the toll was dropped in favour of an attempted blockade, it inaugurated a policy which was to lead to revenue on a scale undreamed of by any earlier Swedish monarch.[3] For in July 1627, as a result of political differences with George William of Brandenburg, Gustav Adolf annexed the tolls levied by

[1] *Sveriges Krig*, V. 299; S. Lundgren, *Johan Adler Salvius*, p. 47 *note* 6; *Arkiv till upplysning om svenska krigens . . . historia* [cited: *Arkiv*], III. 150-5.

[2] *AOSB*, I. VIII. 153; Lundgren, *Salvius*, p. 166.

[3] For the Prussian tolls, see Wendt, *passim*.

the Elector at Pillau, and about the same time toll was once more taken in Danzig Roads. The financial possibilities of these customs dues now became clear to Gustav Adolf and Oxenstierna. Urged on by a certain Pieter Spierinck, a Dutch financier who had been appointed to manage the tolls, the King rapidly extended the Swedish customs barrier until it stretched from the Neva to the Vistula. Spierinck was a man of energy and ability, and apparently an honest one too; he received five per cent. of the amount collected, by way of remuneration, and could therefore be relied upon to be zealous; and he had a tribe of brothers as capable as himself, whom he used to manage the various branches of an enterprise which grew increasingly complex. Tolls had existed before, at all the ports covered by the system; but never before had they been administered so efficiently, so incorruptibly—and so oppressively to the merchant.[1] Nominally the toll at Pillau was at the rate of $7\frac{1}{9}$ per cent. *ad valorem*; but by manipulating the valuations, by cheating on the exchanges, and by other devices, the average rate was raised in 1628 to over 9 per cent. at Pillau. Off Danzig it was as high as $14\frac{2}{9}$ per cent. And on top of this the Swedes clapped heavy harbour dues.[2]

The retention of the tolls was one of the great objects of the Swedish diplomats during the negotiations which led to the conclusion of the six years' truce with Poland at Altmark, in 1629. It was a subject upon which it proved altogether impossible to reach an agreement, and in the end the treaty made no mention of the Pillau tolls at all, and referred the Danzig toll to subsequent negotiations between Danzig and Gustav Adolf. But by passing over the question the diplomats virtually decided it in Sweden's favour, for the Pillau tolls were in Sweden's possession, and in Sweden's

[1] See, for instance, the case of James Ross, in *RRP*, I. 120-2.

[2] Sir Thomas Roe, in a Memorandum on the Baltic Trade, written apparently early in 1630, put the Danzig toll at 30 per cent., and that at Pillau and Elbing at 18 per cent. The latter figure, at all events, seems an exaggeration, and the figure for Danzig is incorrect for the time immediately preceding the truce of Altmark. The Memorandum is in the Public Record Office, State Papers Foreign, Poland (S.P. 88) 7/350. I am indebted to Mr. G. D. Ramsay for a transcript of this interesting document, which is not printed by Gardiner. Kristian IV's (perhaps somewhat over-coloured) account of his conversation with Roe in May 1630 gives some idea of how indignant even so steady an admirer of Gustav Adolf was made by the Prussian tolls. Kristian reports Roe as saying 'He [*sc.* Gustav Adolf] may *proponere* what he will, but if he does not do something about it this summer, we shall help to break his neck for him. . . . Why should we pay him toll, when he does not own a foot of land?. . . does he think he may demand toll because he has a few miserable ships lying here and there?': *Christian den Fjerdes Breve*, II. 271-2.

possession they remained until 1635. The negotiations with Danzig, which eventually resulted in the treaty of Tiegenhoff, were also successful: by that treaty the toll at Danzig was fixed at $5\frac{1}{2}$ per cent., of which Danzig was to take 2 per cent. and Sweden the remainder. A further agreement with George William made a similar arrangement for Pillau. But at most of the other ports the whole of the toll remained at Sweden's free disposal.[1] Nevertheless, it was at Danzig and Pillau that the great bulk of customs revenue was to be expected; and it might appear that the agreements subsequent to the truce of Altmark, by limiting the rate of the toll, had somewhat limited the financial prospects. In reality, this was not so. Danzig and Pillau between them tapped one of the main arteries of European commerce. They were a vital link in the economy of much of western Europe, and especially of the Dutch, whose vessels accounted for more than half of all the shipping passing through the Sound. A great proportion of this shipping was directed to the Vistula and the Kurisches Haff: from 1615 to 1628 the average number of foreign ships visiting Danzig each year was in the neighbourhood of 1200.[2] Only very exceptional circumstances could seriously interfere with this traffic; and even a moderate rate of toll could reasonably be expected to bring in a handsome revenue: at the time of the truce of Altmark it was estimated that Sweden stood to gain 600,000 *riksdaler* annually. But Oxenstierna, under whose general control the Prussian tolls fell, had (as Sir Thomas Roe justly suspected) no intention that the rates should be moderate. He was, on the contrary, resolved to maintain them at their old extortionate level, by the old extortionate devices; and in fact traders who came within range of the Swedish customs ended by paying very much more than the figure agreed upon by treaty. On occasion, moreover, Oxenstierna sanctioned the most naked and cynical violations of the agreements: for instance, he raised the export toll on Hungarian copper to five times the stipulated rate, in an effort to preserve a monopoly of the European copper market for Sweden.

The indignation in western Europe at these tactics was great. The Danes, the English (whose Eastland Company was established at Elbing, and enjoyed Gustav Adolf's protection, on account of its readiness to supply his armies with cloth) and above all the Dutch,

[1] The ports at which the rates of toll were limited by treaty were Danzig, Pillau, Memel, Libau, Windau. But toll was also taken at Reval, Riga, Narva, Pernau and Nyen. Wendt, pp. 164-5.

[2] A. Szelagowski, *Der Kampf um die Ostsee*, pp. 26-7.

all felt the burden, and protested. In April 1630 Oxenstierna was suggesting that selected Dutch magnates be bribed, in order to blunt the edge of their countrymen's indignation.[1] But the customs revenue was too valuable for Sweden to take Dutch anger over-tragically; and Gustav Adolf plainly said that it would not be worth his while to sacrifice the Prussian tolls for the sake of the beggarly subsidy which was likely to be the only tangible result of preserving Holland's friendship—and still less for the sake of those expensive embassies which now constituted the staple of Charles I's foreign policy.[2] In any case, as Oxenstierna tartly reminded the Dutch in February 1631, Sweden was only doing what the Dutch did themselves; and though this parallel (like the name 'licences', which Sweden applied to the Prussian tolls in the fallacious hope of putting them upon the same international footing as the Dutch *licenties*) was misleading and inexact, it was good enough for purposes of political controversy.[3] 'I see well enough', wrote Oxenstierna, in January 1631, 'that the licences are maintained only by force and terrorizing; the greater that force is, the better will our affairs go, and the licences will stand whether they be high or low; but if that force be relaxed, then it is all over with the licences, and with our local budget.' [4]

The Spierinck brothers accordingly prosecuted their business without much regard to the letter of the treaties, or to the feelings of the Dutch skippers.[5] And the harvest was rich—even richer after 1629 than before that date. The following table shows the revenue which Oxenstierna estimated would be yielded by the tolls, from 1628 (the first full year) to 1632, compared with the revenue actually received from them [6]:

Year	Estimated revenue (in *riksdaler*)	Actual revenue (in *riksdaler*)
1628	210,000	329,000
1629	460,000	584,000
1630	560,000	361,000
1631	600,000	553,000
1632	660,000	660,000

[1] *AOSB*, I. v. 253.
[2] Wendt, p. 145.
[3] *AOSB*, I. vi. 148-9.
[4] *ibid.*, I. vi. 39: *cf. ibid.*, 139, 271-6, 483.
[5] The instructions to Aert Spierinck are in *AOSB*, I. vi. 225-34.
[6] Wendt, pp. 89, 98, 107, 184-5, 194, 199, 202.

The explanation for the disappointing result in 1630 is to be found in various accidental circumstances, which in that year combined to discourage shipping. There was a severe outbreak of plague in Poland; a dry season so reduced the water-level in the Vistula as to interfere with navigation; and the rumours of an impending Swedish descent upon Germany deterred many, for they feared lest their ships should be commandeered by the Swedes for transports.[1]

The importance of the Prussian tolls to Sweden's war finance is obvious at a glance. They represented a source of income far larger than any other that was available, except (for a time) for that provided by the copper trade. While at the close of the reign the Stock Tax, for instance, produced 500,000 *daler*, the Prussian tolls were producing 600,000 *riksdaler*—a sum equivalent at that time to at least 1,900,000 *daler*.[2] The French subsidies, under the treaty of Bärwalde, amounted to no more than 400,000 *riksdaler* annually; and though they were undoubtedly useful, they did not begin to come in regularly until the period of greatest financial stringency was past. It was not Richelieu's gold that financed Breitenfeld; far more was it the reluctant contributions of Dutch and English skippers, the tribute of the conquered, the plunder of the occupied areas, and the copper-mines of Falun. The Prussian tolls were reserved almost exclusively for the military budget. In February 1628 they were estimated at one-third of it. Except for one brief and unhappy interval,[3] they were paid in good silver coin. They were, in fact, one of the great bases upon which the war rested. And in consequence the unexpected fall in the yield for 1630 was felt as a disaster. For upon the abundant revenue of the tolls Axel Oxenstierna had been counting in order to find the ready money to satisfy the demands of the troops in Prussia, whom it was now proposed to transfer to Pomerania. Without the expectation of such a supply, Oxenstierna would in all probability never have advised the launching of the German expedition in that year. His consequent inability to move troops to Gustav Adolf's aid, in the months after the landing, imposed a check upon the King's progress in north Germany; and the relatively poor incomings for the earlier part of 1631 were in part responsible for the prolonged financial crisis to which only Breitenfeld put an end.

[1] *cf. AOSB*, I. v. 593.

[2] In 1632 1 *riksdaler*=about $3\frac{1}{5}$ *daler*: *Sveriges Krig*, I. 58.

[3] From 16 July 1628 to 17 April 1629, when payment was ordered at Pillau in Swedish copper coinage: Wendt, pp. 86-8.

(d) *Royal Monopolies*

The plan of raising revenue at the expense of the foreigner, which was so successfully pursued in regard to the Prussian tolls, led Gustav Adolf to other ventures, not all of them so fortunate. It led him, for instance, to engage the crown in an 'active' trade on its own account, in an attempt to exploit favourable market conditions within particular trades and industries. The most important example of this, of course, occurred in connexion with the copper industry; but that experiment was so intimately bound up with the King's policy of industrial development that it is best dealt with in the succeeding section. Two other attempts at royal monopolies, however, may shortly be considered here.

The first concerned the salt trade.[1] Sweden, as we have seen, was dependent upon imports of salt to feed her population throughout the winter. In the second decade of Gustav Adolf's reign most of this salt came to Sweden in Dutch ships. It occurred to the King that the trade might equally well be in Swedish hands and the salt be transported in Swedish vessels. Throughout the 'twenties the price of salt was rising; in part, no doubt, owing to increased war risks, though Gustav Adolf, with characteristic suspiciousness, chose to attribute it to the greed of the Dutch merchants. In November 1627, therefore, he proposed to the *råd* that the crown should take the whole salt trade into its own hands, and convert the supplying of salt into a royal monopoly. By way of safeguarding the consumer, the price was to be pegged at 8 *daler* per ton—a somewhat odd safeguard, certainly, since the current price was then between 6 and 7 *daler*. However, the King hoped for considerable profits, which he intended to apply to military purposes. A proclamation of 28 April 1628 accordingly made salt a royal monopoly, and appointed Erik Larsson and Louis de Geer as factors to manage it for the crown.[2] The experiment proved a total failure. The factors had not enough capital at their disposal to buy salt directly from the producers, and were soon forced to buy from Dutch middlemen in Sweden; Larsson and de Geer did not work well together, and both were overburdened with more important concerns; and, worst of all, the price of salt,

[1] For what follows, see Dahlgren, *de Geer*, I. 324 *seqq.*; H. Tegengren, *Försök till saltproduktion i Sverige och Finland*, pp. 101, 106-7; *RRP*, I. 60; Herdin, III. 39; E. Hughes, *Studies in Administration and Finance*, p. 84.

[2] Stiernman, *CPO*, I. 961-3; *Louis de Geers brev och affärshandlingar* [cited: *LDGBAH*], p. 165.

so far from being pegged, rose by leaps and bounds, and continued to rise for the next few years, as the Swedish *daler* depreciated. In 1628 it stood at 16 *daler* a ton; in 1631 it had risen to 28 *daler*. The rise was inevitably accompanied by suffering and discontent among the Swedish population. Of the expected profits—estimated, with singular optimism, at no less than 200,000 *daler* [1]—there was not a trace. It was no surprise, then, that a proclamation of 18 April 1629 should terminate the monopoly, free the salt trade, and impose an import duty of 2 *daler* per ton.[2]

Undeterred by the failure of this experiment, Gustav Adolf attempted in the following year, 1629, to obtain control of the grain exports from the Baltic to western Europe. He hoped to get all the Russian trade into his hands; but in addition he took steps to buy up as much grain as possible in the Baltic provinces and Poland, and exercised a right of pre-emption upon all surplus grain in Sweden. Corn prices were at that time high on the Amsterdam market, and the King looked forward to large profits: the war estimates for 1629 counted on 300,000 *daler* from the Russian grain alone; those for 1631 provided for no less than 360,000 *riksdaler* from the grain trade as a whole.[3] At first these high hopes seemed well-founded, and large gains were undoubtedly made on the harvest of 1629. The Tsar showed himself benevolent, moved perhaps by Gustav Adolf's plea to be allowed to take care of the export of grain to lands suffering hunger as the result of popish oppression(!).[4] But the attempt to canalize the Russian trade through Sweden's Baltic ports failed; and Gustav Adolf had to content himself with minor speculations in grain exported by way of Archangel, where he was hampered by the corruption and insubordination of the Russian local authorities. The attempt to monopolize the Polish grain broke down in 1630 and 1631, for the favourable conditions of 1629-30 were not repeated. Larger supplies than before reached Holland by way of Danzig, and prices fell as quickly as they had risen. Oxenstierna, who was put in charge of the venture on 18 December 1630, struggled in vain to make the profits that had been expected. But the prices he offered were too low, the alternative export-routes too open, the Swedish copper coin-

[1] Wendt, p. 90.

[2] Stiernman, *CPO*, I. 981. The Göteborg merchants, who had been guaranteed exemption from tolls and excises, refused *en masse* to pay the duty, and it took much persuasion to bring them to a better mind: H. Almquist, *Göteborgs historia*, I. 169.

[3] Wendt, pp. 108, 198.

[4] Dahlgren, I. 318.

age too unattractive to sellers. In his exasperation he wrote to his brother, blaming Skytte for sabotaging the operation of the plan in the Baltic provinces. But the charge was unjust, and indeed irrelevant. The grain monopoly fell a victim, not to Skytte's jealousy or slackness but to the laws of supply and demand. In the summer of 1631 Oxenstierna fell back upon a system of licences to export, and the attempt at cornering the trade was quietly abandoned.[1]

(iii) *Industrial Development*

In 1611, though Sweden was still predominantly an agricultural country, the riches of the Bergslag were already of more than local importance. Copper and iron had assumed the leading positions in the list of Swedish exports, and manufactures based upon them were already beginning to establish themselves. The reign of Gustav Adolf witnessed a great acceleration of these tendencies. The government pushed on vigorously with the exploitation of the country's mineral resources; for copper was now a highly vendible commodity, and iron offered the possibility of a large domestic armaments industry. The one brought in a cash income; the other saved a cash outlay. Without the large-scale production of armaments at home, effective intervention in the German war would have been both more difficult and more expensive than it actually was. But it was a matter of great good luck that the needs and intentions of the King happened to agree with the interests of foreign capitalists. The positive attractions of Sweden as a field for investment were in Gustav Adolf's time reinforced by a variety of circumstances which made investment elsewhere more difficult, more hazardous or less remunerative than before. Labour troubles, over-capitalization, difficulties with customs barriers, were operating as a discouragement to *entrepreneurs* in the Low Countries and around Liége; the steady extension of the war in Germany was disrupting trade and industry, and putting out of business some of Sweden's possible competitors.[2] These factors,

[1] For this episode, see *AOSB*, I. IV. 531, I. V. 733, I. VI. 123, 146, 209-18, 258-9, 286, 301, 311, 334, 346, 360, 407, I. VII. 75; *Negotiations of Sir Thomas Roe*, p. 11; Dahlgren, I. 316-18; N. Ahnlund, *Axel Oxenstierna*, p. 589 *seqq.*

[2] J. Yernaux, *La Métallurgie liégeoise et son expansion au XVIIe siècle*, pp. 67-8, 87, 102, 139, 162-5, 167. Yernaux discounts the factor—sometimes adduced in explanation—of religious persecution, and seems to put most weight upon the obstacle to free export imposed by the tariff barriers of neighbouring countries. He gives instances of export of capital and capitalists—closely analogous to that which took place to Sweden—to Spain on the one hand and (in the mid-seventeenth century) to Germany on the other.

coinciding with the lavish inducements which Gustav Adolf was prepared to hold out, sufficed to attract to Sweden not only capital and capitalists but also skilled labour; and without them the King's objectives could hardly have been realized. Gustav Adolf's real contribution to Sweden's economic development was therefore to have seized an opportunity, to have allied himself with the economic forces prevailing at the time and to have harnessed them to his preparations for war.

It was in Gustav Adolf's time that copper first took the lead over iron and established itself in that pre-eminence which it was to hold for more than a generation. Even in 1734, when copper had long lost its premier place, Linnaeus could describe the mine at Falun as 'Sweden's greatest marvel',[1] and a century earlier it was the pride of Oxenstierna and the boast of Gustav Adolf. 'What potentate is there', cried the King, on the occasion of one of his many visits to the Falun mine, 'who has a palace like to that in which we now stand?'[2] And Oxenstierna, in his great Memorial on the copper trade, written in 1630, said: 'Copper is the noblest commodity that the Swedish crown produces and can boast of, wherein also a great part of the crown's welfare stands; and therefore it is most reasonable that we address ourselves to exploit that mine, and to raise and maintain the price of copper, so that the might and riches of our country, and the revenues of the crown, may be strengthened and increased.'[3] And when in 1625 John Casimir reported damage to the workings, the King replied: 'What Your Highness tells me of damage at the Kopparberg has made me very melancholy; for it is there that the strongest sinews of our state may be weakened, which God forfend.'[4] Such utterances are not to be dismissed as mere rhetoric. Copper was indeed the strongest nerve, the most important natural resource, the war-winning commodity, of the nation.

And its place in the economy of Europe became, in Gustav Adolf's time and in the years immediately after his death, scarcely less dominant than that which it occupied in Sweden's own economy. From 1620 to 1632 the annual production of the Falun mine ranged from about 1250 to about 1900 tons; while at the peak year 1650 it reached 3000 tons. These figures may appear small. But in 1630

[1] Linné, *Ungdomsresor*, II. 175.
[2] Swederus (1909), p. 2; *cf.* K.-E. Forsslund, *Falu gruva och Stora Kopparbergs bergslag*, p. 51. Gustav Adolf visited Falun twelve times.
[3] *AOSB*, I. I. 344.
[4] Styffe, p. 372.

the exertions of 4000 workmen at the Keswick mine produced no more than 65 tons of copper wire. In 1650 the total copper production of the whole of Europe was not much more than 3100 tons, and the world production for the same year has been estimated not to have exceeded 6000 tons.[1] Sweden's chief European competitor—Transylvania—was during the Thirty Years' War mostly cut off from her normal market in the Low Countries by the hostilities in central Europe, and the Swedish customs barrier at Danzig and Pillau; the copper-mines of Mansfeld were similarly disabled; and the competition of Japan was only beginning to be felt.[2] Swedish copper, in fact, enjoyed a virtual monopoly of the European market, and the real problem for Gustav Adolf was to ensure that the utmost advantage was extracted from this favourable situation.

Mining techniques showed no important development in this period. German technicians continued to give aid and counsel, and by 1628 they had so far prevailed over the carelessnessor conservatism of the miners as to persuade them at least to discuss the construction of a shaft [3]; but mining practice remained crude and dangerous—as for instance in the habit of robbing the pillars—and the first timbered shaft in Sweden would not be completed until 1639. As the workings became deeper (and by 1624 some of them had reached a depth of 107 metres) [4] there were increasing difficulties, and frequent falls of rock. Rationalization or modernization of procedure was still hampered by the organization of the industry. Falun remained an association of small miners; and even the boom of the first half of the seventeenth century did not alter the position. For the first decade of the reign, indeed, there was some efficient control from above, for the crown retained its large holding of shares, and from 1613 to 1619 took extraordinary measures to stimulate production. The payment of Älvsborg's ransom was effected mainly by the sale of copper, which yielded the *riksdaler* for which Kristian IV had stipulated in the treaty of Knäred. In order to ensure an abundant supply, the King during this period exercised a right of pre-emption over all the copper produced by the mine; and the effect was that the whole copper trade passed for a time into the hands of the crown.[5]

[1] Heckscher, *Historieuppfattning*, pp. 177, 184-5; Söderberg, p. 22; Hamilton, *English Brass and Copper Industry*, p. 99, and *cf. ibid.*, p. 56.
[2] For further discussion of Japanese copper, see below, p. 97 *note* 3.
[3] S. Lindroth, *Gruvbrytning och kopparhantering*, pp. 101, 154, 189-93, 250-9.
[4] Forsslund, p. 61; *cf. RRP*, I. 170.
[5] G. Wittrock, *Svenska handelskompaniet och kopparhandeln*, pp. 2-8.

needed a copper currency; in the spring of 1626 he hoped to make the acceptance of the Swedish coinage one of the conditions for his adhesion to the League of the Hague; in 1627 he tried to force the coinage into circulation by insisting that the Pillau tolls be paid in it; in 1628 he was sounding Bethlen Gabor as to the possibility of a common coinage policy; and in May 1629 he succeeded in imposing Swedish currency upon Stralsund.[1] The areas occupied by Swedish troops were made to take the new copper coins: in the closing stages of the Polish war Livonia and Prussia were deluged with unwanted small change. The same policy was pursued in the larger field presented by the Swedish conquests in Germany. The treaty with Pomerania in July 1630, the treaty with Mecklenburg in February 1632, made express provision for Swedish copper's being current in those states.[2] Gustav Adolf made persistent efforts to induce Nuremberg, Ulm, Strassburg and Frankfort-on-Main to accept it, or at least introduce a copper coinage of their own; and he certainly contemplated forcing it upon the four circles of upper Germany.[3] And even though the Swedish experiences of a copper coinage could hardly be considered encouraging, the urgent need to get rid of the surplus copper led Gustav Adolf to repeat the experiment in Germany in 1632. On 29 January of that year he ordered that the entire produce of Falun should be coined into *Kreutzer*, designed solely for circulation in Germany. Minting began at Säter in March, and Axel Oxenstierna reckoned on pouring half a million *Kreutzer* into Germany before the end of the year. In the event, less than half of this amount actually reached the continent, and it met with no very favourable reception.[4]

But before this final effort, circumstances had forced a suspension of the minting of copper for Sweden. By 1631, even Gustav Adolf had begun to appreciate the connexion between the excessive minting and the rising cost of living. And, what affected him much more, he had come to realize that the coining of copper in these large quantities, so far from raising the price of the crude metal, was actually contributing to depress it. For the depreciation of the copper *daler*, as against the silver *riksdaler*, had now proceeded so far

[1] *Verbaal van Gaspar van Vosbergen*, pp. 129-31; *AOSB*, I. I. IV. 192-3; W. Carlsson, *Gustav Adolf och Stralsund*, pp. 233-4, 245; C. Wibling, *Sveriges förhållande till Siebenbürgen*, pp. 22-3.

[2] *Sveriges traktater*, V. 387, 712.

[3] Wolontis, p. 79; Wittrock, pp. 153-4; F. Bothe, *Gustav Adolfs und seine Kanzlers wirtschaftspolitische Absichten*, pp. 84-7.

[4] Wolontis, p. 78; Bothe, p. 88.

that the coin was actually worth less than its copper content. The result was that purchases of crude or plate copper practically ceased, and Amsterdam supplied its needs by importing coined *daler* in bulk, while the price of uncoined copper fell proportionably. As early as 1629 Skytte told the *råd* that 'In Amsterdam for eight days running they had done nothing but weigh out copper coin which they had stolen away '.[1] It was now plainly absurd to suppose that a continuation of minting would serve its purpose. Since copper was coming on the market in any case in the form of coin, it might much better be let loose upon the market unrefined, and the King might save his minting-costs.

The history of Gustav Adolf's copper policy since the abolition of the company in 1628 had, indeed, been uniformly unfortunate. Deposition availed as little as minting to halt the fall in prices. Refined copper (*gårkoppar*), which had fetched 60 to 63 *riksdaler* at Amsterdam in 1628, fell to 50 *riksdaler* in November 1630, and to less than 44 *riksdaler* six months later.[2] Erik Larsson and Louis de Geer, the joint factors of 1628, each in turn discovered the impossibility of satisfying the King's unreasonable expectations. De Geer soon withdrew; Larsson was not long in following him; and Gustav Adolf turned instead to far-from-disinterested foreign agents, such as Pieter and Elias Trip of Amsterdam, until in January 1631 he fell back once more on Erik Larsson, who added the management of the copper trade to his general responsibility for war finances.[3]

In this chaotic state of affairs it was the miners, as usual, who came off worst. In January 1630, indeed, their fixed price per *skeppund* was raised from 50 *daler* to 65; but this was an alteration much overdue, and by no means compensated them for increased cost of living and payment in depreciated *daler*. But in any case the increase was of doubtful value, for the crown emulated the company in its failure to discharge its debts to the miners promptly. Their distress was such that they were driven on occasion to sell their copper to private persons at less than the legal rate in order to get ready money. Receipts for copper duly delivered and weighed at the government

[1] *RRP*, I. 180; Heckscher, *HU*, pp. 188-9; Wolontis, pp. 72-4; *AOSB*, I. I. 486-8, and *cf. ibid.*, I. VI. 409, 524; II. I. 743; *Arkiv*, II. 378 *seqq.* In 1633 the only way by which Salvius could get rid of *Kreutzers* was by pawning them in Hamburg: Lundgren, *Salvius*, pp. 70-1.

[2] Wolontis, p. 32.

[3] Dahlgren, I. 188-201; Olsen, pp. 49-53; Wittrock, p. 118 *seqq.*; F. Breedevelt van Veen, *Louis de Geer*, pp. 99-100.

weighbridge at Falun began to be accepted as a sort of paper currency; but as early as 1630 there are complaints that the miners lost up to one-third of the value when negotiating these 'notes'. And the close of Gustav Adolf's reign saw a truly scandalous situation, in which the state, whose military successes had in considerable measure depended upon the miners' exertions, was in default on almost two-thirds of the amount due to them.[1]

The last year of Gustav Adolf's life, however, brought a slight turning of the tide. The Amsterdam merchants, who in 1630 had been 'lying in wait with open maw' (to use Oxenstierna's expression) for the large quantities of copper which, they were convinced, Sweden must sooner or later throw upon the market, grew tired of waiting. The stint began to take effect; copper was once more briskly enquired for. Gustav Adolf, after all, had been able to hold out a little longer than his customers, and his policy was able to register at last a modest success. The price of copper in Amsterdam took an upward turn, and this trend was made more pronounced by the brilliant manipulations of the market for which Louis de Geer was responsible.[2] The combined effect of these two factors was to push the price of *gårkoppar* from 45 *riksdaler* to 72 *riksdaler*; and though the rise proved temporary, it enabled Gustav Adolf to die with the illusion that his copper policy had been proved right in the end. It was an illusion which Oxenstierna no longer shared. In his Memorial of 30 April 1630 [3] he had analysed, with remarkable shrewdness, the situation in which the industry found itself; and he had come to the conclusion that the best policy the crown could follow was neither management by a company (which had all the evils of monopoly) nor a royal control of the industry (which subjected the revenues of the crown to the chances of a speculative market), but a free trade, which should yield a revenue in the shape of export dues. The march of events after Gustav Adolf's death did not permit the chancellor to live up to his theories. Yet, though the management of the copper exports proved so baffling and disappointing a venture, the story of Gustav Adolf's difficulties and failures should not be allowed to obscure the all-important fact that the revenue actually yielded by the industry, though so much less

[1] K.-E. Hildebrand, *Falu stads historia*, I. 27-9; *RRP*, II. 43-4, 47; Wittrock, pp. 130-1, 156.

[2] *LDGBAH*, pp. 227, 235-42; Wolontis, pp. 37-8; Dahlgren, I. 204-7; Heckscher, I. 453.

[3] *AOSB*, I. I. 344 *seqq.*

than the King hoped, was essential to the national finances. Even in the darkest days of 1629-31 the King was drawing large sums from copper; and of all the incomes that helped to finance the war, none, except the Prussian tolls, could compare with that derived from the 'Indies' of Falun.

The development of the iron industry in Gustav Adolf's time was less spectacular and dramatic than the story of copper, but it was at least as remarkable, and of much more enduring significance. The great age of the Swedish copper industry was short, and by the end of the seventeenth century it was over; its decline was scarcely less rapid than its rise; and when it fell, it fell for ever. But the history of the iron industry has been one of continuous progress; and if in the eighteenth century circumstances conspired to give it a position in the trade of Europe not much inferior to that which had been enjoyed by copper in the previous age, its future was securely based upon widely scattered fields of ore, which even yet show little sign of being exhausted. And in the history of Sweden's iron industry the reign of Gustav Adolf was in many respects a turning-point. It saw the beginning of important changes in organization; it saw the adoption of new metallurgical techniques; it saw a sharp upward trend in the curve of production. For the first time an iron manufacture on a large scale, conducted mainly by private enterprise, firmly established itself side by side with the extractive and refining branches of the industry, and Sweden's armaments-works were by 1632 capable of dealing with most, if not with all, of the greatly expanded demands made upon them during the German wars. And all these developments—or nearly all of them—were linked with the appearance on the scene of a crowd of foreign capitalists and *entrepreneurs*, Dutch or German for the most part,[1] who brought with them the resources needed to start these new ventures, and who imported the new techniques which contributed to their success, and the skilled workmen to apply them.

The result was a great increase in production, both of iron itself and of manufactured goods, and the development of an export trade which by the end of the reign was, in point of value, little if at all inferior to the export trade in copper. It was no longer, however, a trade such as it had been in the days of Gustav Vasa. The prohibition

[1] But not Jews; Oxenstierna is said to have been anti-Semitic: H. Valentin, *Judarnes historia i Sverige*, pp. 22-5.

upon the export of osmund was still in force; and though in the earlier part of the reign exports of osmund seem still to have been tolerated (probably for fiscal reasons),[1] they were certainly declining. Karl Bonde boasted of having almost annihilated the production of osmund in Värmland; and though export of osmund was not finally stopped until 1636, it was powerfully discouraged.[2] The production of pig-iron and bar-iron, on the contrary, went ahead strongly. The annual output of pig-iron was calculated by Karl Bonde in 1625 to be in the neighbourhood of 50,000 *skeppund*, or 9500 tons.[3] None of this was exported. The staple of export was of course bar-iron; and here the advance was very marked. For the decade 1613-22 the average annual weight of bar-iron exported was about 18,000 *skeppund*, or 2400 tons; by 1625 the figure had more than doubled, and stood at 45,000 *skeppund*, or about 6000 tons.[4] If in addition to this figure is reckoned a considerable export of manufactured iron goods, especially armaments, it is plain that iron was now among Sweden's main sources of wealth. In part these increases were the result of the reduction of possible competition abroad as a consequence of hostilities on the continent; but, in the main, the expansion was caused by positive conditions in Sweden.

The monarchy continued to take great pains to encourage the industry. Gustav Adolf urged systematic prospecting for ore, and specially enjoined this duty upon his Surveyor-General, when that post was created in 1628.[5] He was active in fostering any new mines—as, for instance, those in Dalsland, or that opened at Smålands Taberg in 1617.[6] In 1630 he set up the General Office of Mines (*Generalbergsamt*), in an effort to co-ordinate the administration of the *bergslagen*. To this Office the *bergmästare* were hence-

[1] It is included in a list of customs rates for 1613: Stiernman, *CPO*, I. 577.

[2] Söderberg, p. 60; Heckscher, I. 462; H. Carlborg, *Ur osmundsjärnets historia under 1600- och 1700-talen*, pp. 110-27. In 1642 Oxenstierna told the *råd* that the representatives of Danzig had informed him that in Danzig alone 60 hammers had been put out of work by the prohibition of the export of osmund: Boëthius, *Gruvornas, hyttornas och hamrarnas folk*, pp. 121, 163.

[3] Söderberg, pp. 26-8, 57. J. Furuskog, *De värmlandska järnbruken*, p. 160, gives 31,000 *skeppund* for 1624.

[4] Söderberg, pp. 29, 58; Heckscher, *Un grand chapitre de l'histoire du fer*, p. 234, gives 3060 [metric] tons as the average for 1627-32; and *id.*, *HT* (1923), p. 339, 4060 [metric] tons for 1631-33. Mr. Hammersley informs me, however, that all these quantities must be considered as surprisingly small when compared with contemporary English production.

[5] Swederus (1910), pp. 47-8; J. Waaranen, *Samling af urkunder rörande Finlands historia*, V. 108.

[6] Swederus (1910), pp. 200, 235-8; Cronholm, III. 276; and *cf.* Tham, *Nora och Lindesbergs historia*, p. 172, for the activity of the government's inspectors.

forward to be responsible; and from it, nineteen years later, was to evolve the College of Mines (*Bergskollegium*), an administrative board similar to the previous-existing *Collegia*.[1] Soon after Gustav Adolf's death the Office began to put into operation policies which reflected the changes that had taken place in his lifetime. One such change concerned the smithing side of the industry. The actual winning of the ore from the rock—and, to some extent, the smelting of it—remained under Gustav Adolf much what they had been under Gustav Vasa: the work of groups of independent small-scale miners, forming a quasi-gild, and bound together by little more than common status in society, and common rules for their activities.[2] But the forges were developing in a different direction. There was a strong tendency, which Gustav Adolf's policy did everything to encourage, for the forges to pass out of the hands of small operators into those of financiers, or groups of financiers, with abundant capital at their disposal. Units in this branch of the industry began to grow bigger. The government viewed this development with approval; since the technical advances which were required could be effected only by considerable expenditure, and since the production of bar-iron, and the conversion of bar-iron into manufactured goods such as nails or guns, had much to gain by methods of mass-production. The competition for dwindling fuel-resources was in some areas on the verge of forcing the forge and the manufactory away from the same geographical location as the mine; a social cleavage was opening between the miner and the smelter, on the one hand—who were more and more falling to the status of peasants—and the new class of forge-masters and works-owners (*brukspatroner*), on the other.[3] In Gustav Adolf's time the process was only beginning; but that it was beginning is shown by the celebrated Memorial on the Bergslag drawn up by Karl Bonde in 1625. Since the year 1607, when he had been appointed *ståthållare* of Dalarna and the copper- and iron-*bergslag*, Bonde's long career as a civil servant had been constantly and intimately connected with the mines, and he was destined later to become the first president of the *Bergskollegium*. In 1625 he was commissioned to report on the iron industry, and his report was not

[1] Swederus (1909), p. 27; C. T. Odhner, *Sveriges inre historia under Drottning Christinas förmyndare*, p. 164.

[2] It has been estimated that in 1624 there were 1211 iron-*bergsmän*, 318 furnaces and 608 osmund-smiths: Söderberg, *Bergsmän och brukspatroner*, p. 17.

[3] For all this, see Furuskog, *op. cit.*, pp. 119-22; *id.*, *Svenska järnet genom tiderna*, pp. 71-4; Heckscher, *HU*, pp. 150-4; Swederus (1910), pp. 60, 62-3, 128; Falk, *Finnarne*, p. 267; Söderberg, *Bergsmän och brukspatroner*, pp. 4-5.

only a compendium of every sort of information about it but also pointed the way to policies which he was to put into effect a decade later. Apart from the statistics it contained, the main weight of the report lay in Bonde's contention that the crown must retain its regalian rights in the mines, in order to be able to ensure their proper exploitation; and in his plea for a consistent policy of capital investment in the industry. He realized that the putting of the forges into the hands of *entrepreneurs* of ample resources, and the elimination of small miners, was the best way to eradicate osmund. He foresaw the struggle for fuel, and perceived the obvious consequence that it would be the forges and manufactories, and not the smelters, who would move to fresh quarters.[1]

To the process of transferring the forges to the hands of wealthy capitalists the crown actively contributed. Whereas in the sixteenth century successive sovereigns had led the way to more modern methods by the experiments and innovations carried on in forges and works under royal control, and indeed had very often set up new works with this end in view, under Gustav Adolf the crown to a large extent divested itself of the management of such undertakings. In part, this seems to have been the result of a conviction that private ownership was more efficient—if only because less clogged with red tape [2]—than state ownership; but equally it seems to have been a result of financial straits and a part of the King's fiscal policy. A forge or works would be pawned to a capitalist who advanced a loan; or, especially during the 'twenties, such concerns would be leased to private speculators, in precisely the same way as the other sources of revenue were farmed out, and for the same reasons. And there is little reason to doubt that the policy brought great advantages. It brought, among other things, advances in technique. As regards mining, indeed, iron was as static as copper, and suffered from the same difficulties, which only much later inventions would remove: difficulties with falls of rock, difficulties with water, difficulties in locating the ore. But to the furnaces and forges the foreigner brought workmen more skilled than the native Swede, and processes which produced a better iron than had been possible before. Such, for instance, was the new type of French hearth for smelting, which was built with brick, instead of the more primitive wood-and-earth

[1] B. Boëthius, *Karl Bonde*, pp. 325-32; Tham, *Nora och Lindesbergs historia*, pp. 49-50, 171.

[2] See, for instance, E. W. Dahlgren, *De uppländska bruken Österby, Forsmark och Gimo*, pp. 30, 49-51.

structure which had been used before: it consumed less charcoal, and produced less slag. Such was the introduction from Germany of new methods of making steel. And such was the famous 'Walloon smithing', introduced first to Finspång by Willem de Besche, and later made general in the Uppland forges by Louis de Geer. It did not differ very greatly from 'German smithing' (though it produced much better iron), and its employment was confined mainly to Uppland; but it suited the Uppland ores, and the result—thanks also, perhaps, to the exceptional freedom of those ores from sulphur and phosphorus—was a finer quality of iron than any Swedish forge-master had offered before.[1]

The introduction of new techniques and superior workmen, and the new abundance of capital, had effects which were not confined to the production of better bar-iron. On the contrary, they were accompanied by an efflorescence of manufactures of all sorts; and this was especially notable, as might have been expected, in the armaments industry and in subsidiary industries which ministered to the needs of the army. In 1611 Sweden had but one large concern engaged upon the manufacture of small-arms and armour—the royal 'factory' at Arboga. For the rest, muskets, forks, pikes and bullets were produced in small quantities, and with little uniformity in quality or design, by a host of scattered weapon-smiths, in half a dozen provinces, under the supervision of special 'factors' appointed by the crown. In 1615, for instance, the government allocated contracts to 17 musket-makers of Uppland, each of whom engaged to produce 17 muskets a year.[2] But these native sources of supply were already quite inadequate—except perhaps in the article of pikes—even before the great military expansion of the 'twenties; and Sweden was dependent for much of her war equipment upon imports from Liége, Namur, Solingen or Aachen, which were negotiated through the intermediary of Dutch financiers and agents: thus in 1618, and at other times in the immediately succeeding years, Louis de Geer undertook commissions of this

[1] Heckscher, *Un grand chapitre*, pp. 137-8; *id.*, *HU*, pp. 146-8; *LDGBAH*, p. 89; Swederus (1910), pp. 56-7; C. Sahlin, *Svenskt stål*, pp. 62-4. The distinction between German and Walloon smithing was this: pig-iron was oxidized and its carbon content removed in two stages; in German smithing the same hearth was used for each stage; in Walloon smithing each stage took place in a separate hearth. Walloon smithing doubled the rate of production, at the cost of a much greater wages-bill: Boëthius, *Gruvornas, hyttornas och hamrarnas folk*, pp. 119-21.

[2] *Sveriges Krig*, I. 502. And in 1618 one Peder Andersson of Tortuna was given one *hemman*, with freedom from *utskrivning* for two boys, in return for making yearly 52 muskets properly finished: Dahlgren, I. 94.

nature on Gustav Adolf's behalf.[1] In regard to cannon, indeed, the country was rather better off, and during the first decade of the reign may have come somewhere near to supplying its own still modest requirements: in 1615, for instance, de Geer obtained leave to import guns into the Netherlands from Sweden; and though he found that in fact Sweden had no surplus for export, he would hardly have been at the trouble of making the enquiry if Sweden had herself been a heavy importer.[2]

Nevertheless, the position was far from satisfactory. The arms industry was widely spread, difficult to control and short of capital. And it was becoming increasingly plain that Sweden might expect to be driven back for arms upon her own resources; for as the war in Europe spread, the competition among buyers became keener, and importation became physically more difficult. In many ways, therefore, the best hope might seem to lie in attracting foreign experts to the country. Already in 1617 Anton Monier had arrived in Sweden from Brabant; and in 1619 came the Siegroths, father and son, from Hesse.[3] Both these were great gunsmiths, and the Siegroths were to play no small part in Gustav Adolf's later victories. The de Besche family had been in Sweden since 1595, when Willem arrived from Liége. He was followed by his three brothers, Gillis, Hubert and Gerard—all of them architects who set their mark upon Swedish buildings. Willem was an architect too; but he developed his main interest in the iron and copper industries. In the pursuit of these employments he came into business contact with his compatriot de Geer in 1615; and this led to de Besche's taking a lease of the Finspång works, with de Geer's financial backing, in 1618. Here he introduced Walloon smithing; and hence, it is scarcely too much to say, sprang the remarkable industrial developments of the next decade.[4]

It was in the 'twenties that foreign capital began to be really interested in Sweden as a field for investment; and it was in the 'twenties that the need for accelerating domestic arms production really became urgent. Gustav Adolf's first reaction to the situation was to try to do something to concentrate the country's gunsmiths, in order that their work might be the more easily supervised. In 1620, for instance, he ordered all rural practitioners of the craft to

[1] Dahlgren, I. 49, 96; *LDGBAH*, pp. 12-14, 64-6.
[2] Van Veen, pp. 8, 12; Dahlgren, I. 39.
[3] L. Hammarskiöld, *Artilleriöverstarne von Siegroth*, pp. 8-15.
[4] Wrangel, p. 36 *seqq.*; Dahlgren, I. 26-8.

leave their farms and move into the nearest town, on penalty of abandoning their occupation; and he projected the setting up of central arms factories at Söderhamn, Norrtälje, Örebro, Norrköping and Jönköping.[1] But the order proved impracticable, though it remained an ideal which the King did not abandon. At the same time, however, he embarked upon a deliberate policy of leasing out the undertakings which were in the crown's possession, very often to foreign *entrepreneurs*. Thus Arboga, for instance, was farmed out to Erik Gudmundsson in 1622; and a year later the crown's interests in Nora and Lindesberg were farmed out to Hubert de Besche.[2] Meanwhile, in 1622, a partnership in which Willem de Besche was the leading spirit had concluded with the crown a contract whereby they were given a monopoly of the casting of iron cannon. The contract was renewed in 1625; but in the meantime the monopoly had been infringed by an agreement between Gustav Adolf and Paul Auleander (one of de Besche's own partners) under which the Österby works in Uppland were leased to him, in return for his promise to supply the King with very large quantities of muskets and war equipment, including 400 iron guns. Auleander had neither the organizing skill nor the capital resources to fulfil his engagements, and by 1625 it was plain that his venture must fail.[3] In that year the King tried another experiment. Stimulated by the apparent success of the Swedish Trading Company in managing the copper trade, and urged on by Karl Bonde, he decided to launch an Iron Company, which should be entrusted with the sole management of all Sweden's iron exports, and was to be constituted on the same general plan as the Trading Company. But this was a project which was still-born. The multiplicity of the iron-mines, in contrast with the concentration of copper-mining at Falun, would in any case have made the work of the company a matter of great difficulty, even if it had been successfully floated; and in fact the investing public showed so little confidence in it that by the autumn of 1625 no more than 800 *daler* of capital had been subscribed.[4] In June 1626, therefore, the King fell back on the Swedish Trading Company; and, as

[1] Stiernman, *CPO*, I. 756.

[2] Å. Meyersson, *Vapenindustrierna i Arboga under äldre Vasatiden*, p. 47; Swederus (1910), p. 165.

[3] Dahlgren, I. 116-19; *id.*, *De uppländska bruken*, pp. 71-5; K. Hellberg, *Järnets och smedernas Eskilstuna*, I. 57.

[4] Heckscher, I. 490; Hallenberg, V. 207 *seqq.*; Wittrock, p. 49. There had been earlier moves towards an Iron Company in 1624: Almquist, *Göteborg*, I. 261-6.

we have seen, authorized it to control not only iron exports ('as far as possible') but also the iron manufactories, and especially those working upon armaments. And, once again, an attempt was made to concentrate the weapon-smiths in a few main centres.[1] A month later, Auleander's contract for Österby was taken from him and assigned to Willem de Besche, who thus, with his already existing contract of 1622, secured a real monopoly of the casting of iron cannon.[2]

By 1627 it had become apparent that Gustav Adolf's policy for iron had become somewhat confused. De Besche, now that Auleander was eliminated, had a monopoly of the production of iron guns; but the manufacture of all other sorts of war equipment was disorganized by changes of policy and lack of any really efficient control. The need for armaments was more urgent than ever with the opening of the Prussian front; and the King's characteristic impatience and craving for quick results led him into contradictory commitments. He needed a man of outstanding organizing ability, strong personality and long pocket, able to integrate the whole arms industry and to gear it to production-levels hitherto unattained, and esteemed unattainable. He found the man he needed in Louis de Geer. For years de Geer had moved behind the scenes of Swedish industry; now, at the right moment, he emerged from the wings; and for the remainder of the reign, and for long after it, he held, unchallenged, the centre of the stage.

The family of de Geer came originally from the bishopric of Liége[3]; but in the last decade of the sixteenth century they had moved, probably for economic reasons, to Dordrecht, and it was at Dordrecht that Louis de Geer received his early education. That education was not specifically technical; but certainly he early acquired great knowledge of the technology of the iron industry. He served an apprenticeship to commerce in France, and no doubt obtained useful lights from his father, who was a banker. One of his sisters married Elias, another Jakob Trip; and de Geer was thus closely connected with that important family of capitalists, and indeed for some time had a share in their transactions. In 1614 the Trips, and in 1615 de Geer, moved to Amsterdam; and in Amsterdam de Geer set up for himself as an armaments contractor, banker and

[1] B. Boëthius, *Karl Bonde*, pp. 331-2; Wittrock, p. 80.
[2] Dahlgren, *De uppländska bruken*, pp. 79-82.
[3] For what follows, see Dahlgren, I. *passim*; van Veen, *passim*.

dealer in general merchandise. It was Willem de Besche who first attracted his attention to Sweden; and by 1617 he had begun the long history of his dealings with Gustav Adolf. In the following year Gustav Adolf proposed that he should come over to Sweden with a contingent of workmen, and embark upon the refining of copper [1]; but though nothing came of this suggestion, de Geer's interests were already engaged by his provision of much of the financial backing for de Besche's lease of Finspång.[2] He took a part in facilitating the arrangements in connexion with the States General's loan for the payment of the first instalment of Älvsborg's ransom; and in return was granted an agency for the marketing of copper in the Netherlands. In the early 'twenties he was making loans and advances to the Swedish crown and supplying armaments for the Polish war; and it was no doubt his desire to get some solid security in his hands that led him to participate in the lease of Finspång and other similar arrangements. But he probably perceived, with his sharp eye for an investment, the opportunities for expanding the Swedish iron industry; and he must have been aware that the high quality of the Dannemora ore made it especially suitable for steel. At all events, he continued his association with de Besche; and although—as in the case of Finspång—he did not allow his name to appear, he was a partner in the concern which secured the monopoly of iron guns in 1622. When de Besche took over Auleander's concession in 1626,[3] de Geer—still anonymously—was de Besche's partner in that too. Thus by 1627 he had established himself in a strong position. He was already an international figure. Through de Besche he had the monopoly of the Swedish armaments industry within his grasp, if only the Trading Company could be got out of the way. And Gustav Adolf was very ready for a new experiment.

In April 1627 the monopoly of all arms production in Sweden was given to de Geer and de Besche.[4] De Besche soon faded from the picture, and died in 1629, by no means a wealthy man; and for the following two years de Geer was solely responsible for the armaments industry. The royal factors were subordinated to him; and crown works and private gunsmiths alike produced to his orders. It was his business to ensure that domestic production was accelerated sufficiently to provide Gustav Adolf's armies with their requirements.

[1] Dahlgren, I. 51.
[2] *LDGBAH*, pp. 21-5, for the lease.
[3] *ibid.*, pp. 97-9.
[4] *ibid.*, pp. 131-4, and *cf.* pp. 125-9, 136-8, 169.

He succeeded beyond expectation, meeting demands much in excess of any that might reasonably have been foreseen in 1627. His contract of 27 April 1627 bound him to equip, from Swedish resources, fifteen regiments of foot and 3000 horse; and this undertaking was satisfactorily fulfilled. In 1627 he was already exporting to Holland 400 cannon, manufactured at Finspång, and was receiving orders from France.[1] By 1629 he could recommend that the importation of war material should cease, since Sweden was now effectively self-sufficing.[2] In 1632 his exports of cannon from Nyköping had risen to 910.[3] It seems, indeed, that the number of cannon exported was much in excess of the number supplied to the King; and that it was to the export market that the monopolists mainly looked for their profit on this article.[4] Their most important contribution to the Swedish armies was rather in the matter of small-arms and armour: between November 1629 and the close of 1630, de Geer delivered to Gustav Adolf's armies no less than 20,000 muskets, 13,670 pikes and 4700 suits of cavalry armour; and by 1631 the domestic production of muskets was adequate to satisfy all Sweden's needs.[5] In January of that year Gustav Adolf, made confident, perhaps, by de Geer's apparent ability to comply with all demands that might be put upon him, ordered him to supply arms and equipment for thirty-two foot regiments and 8000 cavalry by the ensuing summer.[6] This order, indeed, was more than Sweden could manage, and in any case Gustav Adolf, gorged with the spoils of victory, later on simply cancelled it; but it provides some indication of the demands which de Geer had to face, and of the confidence which the King had in his administrative and financial talents. His abilities, indeed, were in excess of his scruples: he did not hesitate to bribe the government official whose duty it was to inspect his deliveries; and some at least of the war material he sent out was of very poor quality.[7] In 1630 de Geer quarrelled with Gustav Adolf, and in consequence relinquished his control of the royal factories at Arboga and Jäder; and in 1631 the contract of 1627 was completely annulled. The crown resumed control of its own factories. But de Geer continued to be by far

[1] *LDGBAH*, p. 140; van Veen, p. 84.
[2] *LDGBAH*, p. 117.
[3] Dahlgren, I. 420-1; *Sveriges Krig*, Supp. Vol. II. 249; C. Heijkenskjöld, *Svensk styckegjutning och lodstöpning av järn under perioden 1540-1840*, p. 73.
[4] L. Hammarskiöld, *Ur svenska artilleriets hävder*, pp. 22-7.
[5] Dahlgren, I. 139; *Sveriges Krig*, V. 370.
[6] *Arkiv*, I. 303-5; *LDGBAH*, pp. 203-4.
[7] Dahlgren, I. 146; van Veen, p. 94.

the greatest figure in Swedish economic life. His numerous factories, the diversity of his interests, his far-spreading financial operations, put him in a unique position in Sweden. The list of the undertakings in which he was concerned is indeed a conspectus of Swedish industry as it existed at the close of the reign; for there was scarcely an important branch of it in which he was not engaged.

His prime interest, however, continued to be iron and iron-manufactures, and here his undertakings gradually grouped themselves into three main areas.[1] One of these lay in Södermanland and Östergötland, and included the works at Finspång, Nyköping and Norrköping. Finspång specialized in the heavier type of iron cannon; Nyköping in the small two-pounders. Norrköping, which de Geer made his headquarters and the capital of his industrial empire, had a very large manufacture of miscellaneous war material. The second area lay in the Mälar-Hjelmare region, and included the works at Åker and Skeppsta; the small undertakings of the region of Nora and Lindesberg, which produced such things as shot, grenades, spikes, wire and horse-shoes; and the works at Torshälla, which specialized in making a special kind of iron for nails. The third area lay in the Uppland ironfield, where de Geer had acquired the famous works at Leufsta, Gimo and Österby, the last of which concentrated upon the production of cannon-balls. In addition, he possessed an outlying establishment at Kroppa, in Värmland. The whole represented by far the largest concentration of industry in the hands of any Swedish subject, and probably also the most modern and the best managed.

Iron, however, was by no means de Geer's only concern. The reign of Gustav Adolf, as might have been expected from the great increase in the output at Falun, witnessed a notable expansion of the brass industry. The circumstances of the time conduced to such a development. The great brass-producing region of Europe—the area about Aachen—was suffering from a shortage of raw material; or, rather, was being driven to rely increasingly upon Swedish copper, since supplies from Germany and Transylvania were hard to get. The demand for brass was brisk; and although Sweden was still dependent upon imports of calamine—some of it from the Limburg area [2]—there was a real opportunity for a Swedish brass industry. On general principles, moreover, it was considered preferable to

[1] See, for what follows, Dahlgren, I. 150, 364-411; *LDGBAH*, pp. 194-6.
[2] Yernaux, p. 119.

manufacture, or partly to manufacture, raw materials at home rather than to export them to be worked up abroad, to the profit of the foreigner. And finally it was clear that when Gustav Adolf was concerned to impose a stint upon the copper market the more copper that could be turned into brass at home the better. At the beginning of the reign there were only two brass-works of any consequence in production. One was at Skultuna, where from 1612 Jakob Johansson held a lease of the crown; the other was at Nyköping, where since 1610 Willem de Besche, among other activities, had been making brass.[1] In 1620, however, Gustav Adolf seems to have decided that the brass industry must be energized and organized. He accordingly secured the services of a certain Arnold Toppengiesser, a member of one of the leading families in Aachen, and entrusted him with the task of remodelling Swedish brass production upon German lines. This involved the greater use of machine power in the hammering of sheet brass; and this, of course, demanded capital expenditure. Toppengiesser was at first associated with Johansson in the lease of Skultuna, and was able to improve its production considerably. The King was obviously impressed with the results he obtained, for in 1621 he attempted to reorganize the industry, with Toppengiesser's assistance and under his supervision. The Swedish brass-founders were now to be formed into a gild on the model of that existing in Aachen; Toppengiesser was to have the right to import three of the total of twelve masters; and he was himself to act as alderman of the gild. It is not clear how far these provisions were actually carried out; but it is certain that the King's favour to Toppengiesser continued. In 1623 an agreement was concluded between them for the reviving of the defunct brass-works at Vällinge, and in 1626 Gustav Adolf gave Vällinge to Toppengiesser as a donation. It developed into a factory of the type usual in Aachen, and its main product was brass wire, for which there was a strong demand abroad.[2] About the same period de Geer began to interest himself in brass. In 1620 he acquired an interest in de Besche's Nyköping foundry, and in 1623 they jointly started a brass-works at Danviken, which continued in production until 1630. But it was not until 1627 that brass became one of de Geer's major interests. In that year he founded his brass-works at Norrköping as part of the great complex of undertakings which he was locating there. It

[1] Swederus (1910), pp. 69-74.

[2] K. Malmsten, *En industriplanering under Vasatiden*, pp. 56-88; Hallenberg, V. 230-3.

developed rapidly, and soon became one of the most important of Swedish brass-foundries, and a show-place for foreign visitors, with its fifteen separate furnaces and its fifty-four employees. De Geer accounted it as the most valuable of all his properties. It produced mainly semi-manufactured goods, such as plate brass and brass wire, and it exported very large quantities of them: for the two years 1630-31 exports brought in nearly 246,000 *daler*.[1]

In 1611 Sweden had no textile industry of any consequence. The country's needs were served by the homespun of domestic industry, or by the imported fabrics of western Europe. As the problem of clothing the ever-increasing armies grew more pressing, and as the movement towards something like a uniform began to develop, the lack of any considerable manufactory at home began to be more seriously felt. Attempts were made from time to time to start such manufactories—for instance, at Arboga and Kalmar; and in 1620 a venture was launched at Jönköping by a company which had the backing of the crown. It took some time to find its feet; and the King, attributing its difficulties in part to the inferior quality of Swedish wool, tried on one occasion to mend matters by ordering the slaughtering or castration of all the rams in the neighbourhood. In the end, whether as a result of this measure or not does not appear, it had a moderate success; though it never quite realized the King's expectations.[2] In this field, too, de Geer intervened with characteristic energy. The manufactory which he set up at Norrköping in 1627 made both coarse and fine cloths, in a variety of colours; primarily with a view to supplying the needs of the workmen who were employed in one or other of his various undertakings. The amount produced in 1630 was about 4500 ells; but soon after 1631 the enterprise appears to have been discontinued.[3]

For the rest, it must suffice to mention de Geer's interest in saltpetre, and his lease of Linköping saltpetre-works in 1628; his two rope-walks, one on Norrmalm, the other at Norrköping; his activity as a shipbuilder; his establishment of his own private paper-mill (it was only in Gustav Adolf's reign that paper began to be manufactured in Sweden in any quantity); his tin-works; his early interest in sulphur; his willingness to advance money and to act as a banker

[1] Dahlgren, I. 395-407; Ogier, pp. 24-5.

[2] Kjellberg, *Ull och ylle*, pp. 89-136; Björkman, *Jönköping*, II. 197-206; Heckscher, I. 507-9.

[3] Dahlgren, I. 412-17; Kjellberg, pp. 140-1. Magalotti thought poorly of Swedish cloth: Magalotti, p. 47.

to members of the Swedish nobility in need of such accommodation; and his establishment, in order the more conveniently to supply his workmen with their requirements, of general stores in Stockholm and Norrköping.[1] But of all his various enterprises, it was his iron-works and his cannon-foundries, his forges and his manufactures of small-arms and hardware, that took the imagination of contemporaries; it was these, perhaps, which constituted his greatest contribution to his adopted country; and it was these, certainly, which were recited as chief among his services in his patent of nobility. In 1627, upon his first settling in Sweden, he took Swedish citizenship [2]; largely, it seems, in order to obtain exemption from the Sound Tolls, under the terms of the treaty of Knäred. He never became a Swede in anything save denization; and his ordinary vehicle of communication remained to the end Dutch or French. Yet his settlement in Sweden proved permanent; Leufsta has remained the seat of his family; and more than one of his descendants (including one prime minister) have played a prominent part in Swedish life. It was characteristic of the age that he should have united to exceptional business ability a genuine personal piety: while still a young man he vowed to give a tithe of all his gains to God.[3] To John Durie he seemed 'a paterne of liberality' [4]; and Comenius found in him an enlightened patron. To his workmen he was a considerate employer, ever careful of their interests and concerned for their comfort. In 1632 he had still twenty years of life before him; but he had already laid the foundation of that huge fortune [5] which was to enable him in 1644 to astonish Europe by providing and equipping, from his own resources, a fleet of thirty warships for the service of Sweden.

An achievement of this magnitude would scarcely have been possible had it been based solely upon the resources of the Swedish labour-market. The expansion of industry depended not only upon imports of capital: it depended almost as much upon imports of skilled labour. The brass industry, to take only one example, was virtually created by immigrants. Miners and forgemen, smelters and

[1] *LDGBAH*, p. 171; *RRP*, I. xxx; *Sveriges Krig*, Supp. Vol. II. 282-3 (for saltpetre); *LDGBAH*, pp. 125, 170; Dahlgren, I. 167 (for the rope-walks); S. Ambrosiani, *Papperstillverkning i Sverige intill 1800-talets mitt*, p. 71 (for paper); van Veen, p. 122 (tin); *LDGBAH*, p. 38 (sulphur); van Veen, p. 141 (shops); *ibid.*, p. 140 (cash advances).

[2] *LDGBAH*, p. 139.

[3] H. Holmquist, *Svenska kyrkans historia*, IV. I. 417-18.

[4] G. Westin, *John Durie in Sweden*, p. 2.

[5] He left over 607,000 *riksdaler*: Heckscher, I. 314. His profits on arms were computed at times at 50 per cent.: *RRP*, II. 63.

turners, skilled artisans for every branch of the metallurgical trades, were either spontaneously attracted or deliberately recruited. They came from Austria (as the Geijers did) or from Germany; a few from Scotland or from England; but most of all they came from the old Burgundian lands, with which Sweden seems to have had economic links of long standing.[1] And no employer was more active in bringing foreign workmen to Sweden than Louis de Geer. As early as 1615 he was recruiting copper- and brass-founders for de Besche; and in the following year was seeking to enlist colliers and iron-workers from the country around Liége.[2] When in 1618 he joined de Besche in the leasing of Finspång, the influx of these Walloons grew into a considerable stream: colliers and woodcutters from Sedan, smiths from Liége, mill-builders from Amsterdam, and many miscellaneous artisans of all sorts, were induced to sign a contract and make trial of Sweden.[3] De Geer always said that though he could train Swedes as gun-founders and smiths, he must have Walloons as furnace-masters and smelters; and he also preferred his own countrymen for managerial and clerical positions. Hence wherever de Geer was active a little colony of such men would arise. They came to Sweden on short-term contracts, with free passage there and back provided; and as a rule they left their families behind, at least to begin with. They were enlisted by a regular labour agency, with the full consent of their governments; and usually it was slack trade or unemployment which prompted them to go.[4] In Sweden they were well treated, and indeed highly privileged; for they were exempted for six years from all taxation and all municipal burdens, and they were not liable for conscription.[5]

[1] Yernaux mentions, without giving precise details, that the admissions to burgage-rights at Liége in the period 1565-1607 include a number of Swedes: Yernaux, p. 21.

[2] E. W. Dahlgren, *Ett bidrag till Valloninvandringens historia*, pp. 82-4; *LDGBAH*, pp. 4-10.

[3] *LDGBAH*, pp. 37, 42, 50, 78-80, 89; Westin, *John Durie in Sweden*, pp. 2-3: '. . . you must know that he is a great man in theis parts & in a manner a Lord over all the Minerall trades for Cannon & Copper workes, which in the life of the King he vndertooke to mannage for the good of this Realme, and to this effect he planted many Townes of this Kingdome with strangers, and is a Lord of a great Territory where he setteth strangers a worke for all sorts of Manufactures cheifely in Iron and Copper, & indeed is the head of the plantacon of strangers in theis quarters, & this Crowne hath made vse of him to that effecte that forraigners might be brought hither to populate the Country, & to raise vpp the trades and Mechanicall Workes which in other places are in vse.'

[4] On this, see Yernaux, pp. 67-8, 87, 102, 139.

[5] Dalhgren, *Ett bidrag till Valloninvandringens historia*, pp. 84-95, for the whole question; and see, *e.g.*, *LDGBAH*, pp. 182, 186.

The fact that some of them were Calvinists (as de Geer was) and some Arminians caused a shaking of heads among the straiter Lutherans; but the Charter of 1612 had already safeguarded them from actual persecution, and de Geer made efforts to secure for them the services of ministers of their own persuasion.[1] Between 1620 and 1630 he was responsible for importing at least 275 Walloons, and a rather smaller immigration continued thereafter. Perhaps in all some three hundred families eventually settled in the country.[2] The figure may possibly appear somewhat insignificant, particularly since the communities, small as they were, long remained remarkably resistant to assimilation into the general mass of the population and seem to have been generally unpopular[3]; yet the Walloons had an effect out of all proportion to their numbers. They brought to Sweden the most advanced techniques of their time; and by doing so they laid the basis for that predominance in the iron industry which by the end of the century was to be an accomplished fact.

The industrial developments which we have been considering, notable though they were, were at first relatively limited in range. The industrialization was essentially an industrialization for war. It was concerned mainly with the manufacture of armaments, or with trades such as cloth-making or rope-making which were mostly producing for the armed forces. To this general rule brass was perhaps the only important exception. Though no doubt some such development would have come about, as a consequence of Sweden's attractiveness to the foreign investor, even though the country had been at peace, it is clear that the needs of the forces accelerated the expansion. Yet it would be unjust to the King and his chancellor to suppose that their economic policy was directed solely to the satisfaction of immediate and—one might hope—transitory military needs. Their purpose reached further; and they aimed through the assistance of such men as de Besche and de Geer at the permanent enrichment of the state, the making fruitful of potentialities hitherto

[1] Holmquist, *op. cit.*, IV. 1. 407-8, 412-20; *LDGBAH*, pp. 157, 208.

[2] Heckscher, *Un grand chapitre*, p. 137; Lindberg, *Västerviks historia*, I. 215.

[3] Thus 'Skogekär Bergbo' wrote (perhaps about 1630):

En deel aff them vthstänger
wårt folck aff theras winst
och ther widh swenske dränger
ju brukar aldraminst.

(Some of them shut out our own people from earning a living, and hence small prospect for Swedish lads): E. Källquist, *Thet swenska språketz klagemål*, p. 133. For 'Skogekär Bergbo', see above, Vol. I, pp. 512-13.

lying dormant, the development of a permanent export trade. That Sweden should be self-sufficing in this matter of armaments was an important guarantee of her safety; but Gustav Adolf was also looking for markets for the products of his industries, markets in Europe and beyond. And he was more than willing that his export trade should be carried on in Swedish bottoms.

(iv) *Trade and the Towns*

If in matters political the significance of Gustav Adolf's reign—or at least of one aspect of it—may be summed up in the statement that he brought his country into the main current of European history, something similar is true in regard to economic affairs. The peripheral and primitive position which Sweden had occupied under Gustav Vasa, and which had already begun to be modified in the time of Karl IX, was now for ever abandoned: with Gustav Adolf, Sweden's economic interests became fully European, and his policy in economic matters conformed to the mercantilist patterns of the age. The main concern was no longer the simple securing of the goods the country needed; royal policy was no longer merely a policy of provisioning. For Gustav Adolf, trade was an end in itself, an indispensable (and perhaps the most eligible) source of wealth: 'the welfare of the nation', as he was fond of remarking, 'depends on trade and navigation'. And by 'trade' he meant an active, not a passive, trade; by 'navigation', a commerce conducted for choice in Swedish vessels. Sweden therefore must develop a mercantile marine, and (for this reason among others) a navy to protect it. For foreign trade provided those precious metals, those cash resources, for which the King was always looking; since for the first half of the reign, at all events, there was normally a surplus of exports over imports.[1] Exports, moreover, should comprise as many manufactured or partly manufactured goods as possible, since it was bad business to allow the profits of manufacture to go into the pockets of the foreigner, and sound policy to make the country as independent of imports as might be. The King's task, therefore, must be to ensure by wise regulation that trade flowed along the channels most advantageous to the interests of the state, and that it was managed upon principles which secured the maximum afforcement of the country's economic and political strength. Gustav Adolf's *penchant*

[1] Boëthius and Heckscher, p. xxv.

for regulation, monopoly and state enterprise was by no means shared by Axel Oxenstierna; but even Oxenstierna agreed that it was the business of government to 'steer' trade by tolls and tariffs, and was for encouraging manufactures by clapping high duties upon the export of raw materials.[1]

In some respects Swedish commercial policy and aspirations, and the general pattern of Swedish trade, altered very little in Gustav Adolf's time. The predominance of the north German towns diminished, of course, especially after the imperialist advance upon the Baltic put them more or less in the position of beleaguered garrisons. But the nature of Swedish imports remained much as before: salt was still the only one that concerned the nation at large; though the spread of continental standards of comfort and luxury, which was one of the results of the wars, no doubt stimulated the demand for pure luxury goods: by 1637 textiles accounted for over forty per cent. of imports, and almost a quarter of this went upon silks, or cloth of gold or silver.[2] The historic ambition to control the trade between Russia and the West still survived as an active principle of policy; and indeed it required the extensive Baltic conquests of Gustav Adolf's time to demonstrate the delusion upon which it was built. Short of a Swedish occupation of the entire southern shore of the Baltic, from Lübeck eastwards, and a Swedish conquest of Archangel too, the foreigner would always find a way round the Swedish customs posts. The treaty of Stolbová did indeed lead to the growth in commercial importance of the Neva, as the result of the establishment of the new fort at Nyen, and it settled the old quarrel about the trade to Narva; but it bred controversies between Narva and such recent conquests as Ivangorod, while Reval also competed for the favours of the government.[3] Still, it was from Narva that Gustav Adolf tried to persuade Vosbergen that the Dutch should import their grain; and it was at Narva that des Hayes de Cormenin fixed the staple for Richelieu's projected Baltic-Caspian trade.[4] But little came of these ideas; and not much more of Gustav Adolf's attempts to intervene personally in the Russian grain trade. More important was the change in the nature of Swedish

[1] Boëthius and Heckscher, pp. xxii-xxiii; C. Danielsson, *1500- och 1600-talens svenska tullpolitik*, p. 407.

[2] Boëthius and Heckscher, p. l.

[3] A. Soom, *De ingermanländska städerna och freden i Stolbova*, pp. 34-44; *AOSB*, I. II. 575 *seqq.*, 728, I. V. 203.

[4] Vosbergen, *Verbaal*, p. 120; *AOSB*, II. III. 191; H. Hauser, *La Pensée et l'Action économique de . . . Richelieu*, pp. 111-19.

exports and in the location of the markets to which they were consigned. The expansion of the copper industry was dependent until 1626 upon the existence of a vast market in Spain. The keeping open of the trade to Spain became therefore a major item in commercial policy; and even as late as 1632, when the Spanish government had ceased to buy copper, Gustav Adolf was anxious if possible to avoid an open breach with Madrid. And since trade between the revolted Netherlands and the Spanish ports was forbidden in war-time, a considerable share of these copper exports passed by way of Hamburg, where many Dutch merchants had established themselves with a view to circumventing the ban. Close personal and business ties linked Amsterdam to Hamburg, and extended thence to Stockholm. The earlier importance of Danzig and Lübeck in the export of copper to western Europe came to an end; and Hamburg became not merely the centre of the Swedish intelligence system but a focus of Swedish economic interests.[1]

At the same time new exports rose to importance: manufactured goods such as weapons, hardware and sheet brass; natural products hitherto of subordinate interest such as grain (which seems to have enjoyed a boom in the late 'thirties), timber and, even more markedly, tar.[2] All of these, to an increasing degree, began to go westwards, outside the Baltic, and above all to Holland. The growth of the new Göteborg that arose after 1619 is the visible sign of this changing orientation. For Göteborg's trade was all outside the Baltic; the most important of her markets was Amsterdam; and Dutch skippers settled in Göteborg, as they settled in Hamburg, in order that they might trade freely with Spain, in defiance of the prohibition of the States General.[3] By 1636 the predominance of the Dutch in the trade of Sweden was clearly reflected in the statistics for the Great Toll.[4] The great Dutch merchants, indeed, were somewhat scornful of the unenterprising Swedish traders [5]; but if the cautious natives still sometimes preferred the safety of a passive trade, they no longer

[1] H. Kellenbenz, *Unternehmerkräfte im Hamburger Portugal- und Spanienhandel*, pp. 18, 24, 69, 84-6, 129, 179, 210, 225, 236-7, 339, 348-9.

[2] Boëthius and Heckscher, pp. li, 104-5; *AOSB*, II. III. 84; Almquist, *Göteborg*, I. 249; Lindberg, *Västerviks historia*, I. 157-8, 358.

[3] Almquist, *Göteborg*, I. 230.

[4] Of a total value of goods passing through the customs of 463,000 *daler*, carried by 133 skippers, Holland had 220,000 *daler* and 34 skippers; Lübeck, Kolberg, Elbing, Danzig, Stralsund and Rostock together had 131,000 and 66 (over half of which was Lübeck's share); Scotland, 45,000 and 14; Denmark, 30,000 and 12; England, 29,000 and 4: Börjeson, *Stockholms segelsjöfart*, p. 142.

[5] Lindberg, *Västerviks historia*, I. 380-1.

had government approval for their caution. The development of the mercantile marine was now an object of official policy.[1] Within a few years of Gustav Adolf's death the importance of native commercial enterprise would be recognized by the creation of a Board of Trade (*Kommerskollegium*) on an equal footing with those other *collegia* which had been established by the Form of Government of 1634.

Thus Swedish commerce emerged from the confines of the Baltic. The new trading horizons thus revealed stimulated the King to bolder speculations. The ships which sailed from Göteborg to the west, the trade which was emancipating itself from Hanseatic influences, need not stop short at the Straits of Dover—nor, for that matter, at the Straits of Gibraltar. The Atlantic lay open to the ships of all nations, and there was still plenty of room for a newcomer on the coasts of the American continent. The notion of controlling and organizing trade by means of a monopoly company was familiar enough to Gustav Adolf, and recent history provided him with many examples of companies created to exploit in common a distant market and to bear in common the more than ordinary risks and expenses attendant upon such exploitation. The English and Dutch East India Companies had led the way; and within Scandinavia itself Kristian IV had already followed their example. In 1616 he founded the Danish East India Company upon Dutch models, and at the suggestion of Dutch merchants; in 1625 he followed it up with a West India Company too.[2] Even Karl IX had at one time contemplated the creation of a trading company to Persia.[3] Any concrete proposal for a trading company was therefore likely enough to find a sympathetic hearing by Gustav Adolf, if only because it might appeal to him as a matter of national prestige. And in October 1624 just such a scheme was submitted to him: submitted, moreover, by an acknowledged expert in the subject.

This was the Dutchman Willem Usselincx.[4] Usselincx was born in 1567 at Antwerp; and after spending his early manhood in Portugal, Spain and the Azores, he returned in 1591 to Holland and set up as a merchant. He was a strong Calvinist, a fierce hater of Spain, and a business-man with a keen eye for an opportunity. It was not long before he propounded his idea of a West India Company,

[1] See, *e.g.*, *AOSB*, I. VIII. 91.
[2] J. A. Fridericia, *Danmarks Riges Historie*, pp. 103-4.
[3] Cronholm, III. 464.
[4] For Usselincx, see C. Ligtenberg, *Willem Usselincx*, *passim*.

which should combine privateering against the enemy with legitimate trade. But it was to be something more than a mere speculation: it was to engage in missionary activities, and it was to found colonies of settlement. The Americas were to provide the Netherlands not only with raw materials but with new markets; and the gratitude of pious investors was to be manifest in an annual increment of souls redeemed. His company would have been open to Protestant investors of all nations, and it would have given the ordinary shareholder a larger part in the direction of affairs than, for instance, in the Dutch East India Company. These proposals did not commend themselves to the majority of Usselincx' countrymen, and least of all to the pacifically inclined Oldenbarnevelt. The Dutch (apart from a few empire-builders such as Jan Pieterszoon Coen) were not primarily interested in creating colonial markets, nor did they trouble much about missions. Still less were they anxious to attract foreign investors. Usselincx' ideas met with no success at all until 1618, when the collapse of Oldenbarnevelt's authority gave Usselincx' Gomarist friends a chance of forwarding his schemes. But even then the West India Company which was finally incorporated in 1621 by no means tallied with his ideas; and in any case the capital was not fully subscribed. Usselincx, disillusioned and disgusted, refused the highly paid post which the West India directors offered him, and set off for Danzig, with the idea of establishing himself there as the local agent for Dutch business houses. On his way thither he passed through Göteborg; and there, in a single interview of six hours' duration, he converted Gustav Adolf to the plan which he had failed to realize in Holland. Usselincx was authorized to float a 'General Company for Commerce and Navigation with the Lands of Africa, Asia, America and Magellanica'; and towards the end of 1624 he issued a glowing prospectus,[1] in which were set forth the advantages enjoyed by Sweden in undertaking such a venture, as compared with the Spaniards and Dutch, together with the prediction that profits of 100 per cent. might be considered by no means unlikely. The lands from which the greatest return was expected were apparently Abyssinia and that *Terra Australis* which was supposed to stretch from New Guinea to the Horn, and possibly even onwards to the Cape. Of this important trade, the company's privileges (dated 14 June 1626)[2] gave it the monopoly for twelve years. The company

[1] Stiernman, *CPO*, I. 911-22; *cf. ibid.*, I. 910-11; *AOSB*, I. II. 777.
[2] Stiernman, *CPO*, I. 932-47.

was to obtain preferential treatment in the matter of tariffs; the crown was to receive one-fifth of all precious metals imported, and one-tenth of all the fruit; and Usselincx himself was to have a commission of one-tenth per cent. on all the company's transactions. For the rest, the organization was taken over bodily from Dutch models, without any regard for the very different economic conditions obtaining in Sweden. The company was to have the right to conclude treaties and alliances, but not to make war; though its agents were to be entitled to offer resistance in self-defence, which in practice would probably come to much the same thing.

Energetic measures were taken to persuade investors to come forward with the necessary capital. Gustav Adolf put himself down for 400,000 *daler*, a sum which entitled him, in terms of the company's charter, to nominate four directors. Actually, he nominated only two; but as he omitted to pay for his shares, this was less self-denying than it appeared to be. Queen Kristina, John Casimir and many members of the *riksråd*, the nobility and the army followed the King's example in taking up shares, though they were not usually able to avoid paying for them. Moral suasion of a quite Colbertian nature was applied to members of the aristocracy to induce them to subscribe, and a vigorous effort was made to attract the small investor.[1] Usselincx went on a propaganda tour to the Baltic provinces; and he had high hopes of the investors of Germany, who were finding it increasingly difficult, in the disturbed state of that country, to place their capital to advantage.

But when, in April 1628, Usselincx returned to Sweden, he found that in his absence things had gone ill with his project. Instead of preparing to tap the natural riches of *Terra Australis*, and to supply the teeming markets of Magellanica, the directors had embarked upon petty enterprises of a local nature—trading with Russia; collaborating with de Geer in the running of a rope-walk in Norrköping; dealing in small consignments of butter and tar; and involving themselves in the affairs of a glass-works. 'He who desires to sail to the equator', remarked Usselincx with some point, 'must set his course southwards'[2]; but the directors seem not to have grasped this truth as firmly as Usselincx could have wished. In 1628, indeed, they planned to freight a ship for the West Indies, and

[1] *SRARP*, I. 18; H. Lundin, *Joannes Baazius' kyrkliga reformprogram*, p. 34 *seqq.*; Börjeson, *Stockholms segelsjöfart*, pp. 161-4.

[2] Ligtenberg, p. 125.

they actually signed on a skipper and paid his wages for a whole summer; but somehow the trip never came off. The grand project stuck on the stocks; investment never came up to expectation (too much Swedish capital was already locked up in the Swedish Trading Company); Gustav Adolf, who was genuinely well-disposed to Usselincx' plans, was too distracted by military and political concerns to keep the company's needs in mind or to intervene effectively on its behalf. Usselincx, faced with the prospect of another disheartening fiasco, asked for and at the end of 1628 obtained his release from the King's service; commenting disgustedly to Axel Oxenstierna that he would have done better to apply himself to the flute or the viol, and so at least have ensured his ability to make a livelihood. The company continued for some time after his departure from Sweden in a semi-animate condition, until in May 1630 it was fused with the Ship Company, which had been founded in 1629 to provide ships for the Royal Navy, and which was really only a thinly disguised form of taxation.[1] Its fortunes were not improved when four ships, sent to Spain at the close of 1631 on the express orders of the *råd*, were confiscated by the Spanish authorities by way of reprisal for Gustav Adolf's operations in the Rhineland.[2]

The career of the Southern Company (to give Usselincx' scheme the short title by which it was generally known) thus seemed to be at an end; but the victories of Gustav Adolf in Germany revived its founder's ever-sanguine spirits, and he hastened to re-enter the Swedish service in the hope that the Swedish conquests would open to him those hoards of German capital which, he was still convinced, only awaited an opportunity to pour into his company's cash-boxes. Usselincx obtained the King's leave to beat up for investors in the Empire; and in Stralsund and Stettin he enjoyed a measure of success. In 1632 Oxenstierna gave him letters of recommendation to Frankfort-on-Main; and although both King and chancellor probably found his importunacy at inconvenient moments a great nuisance, they continued to interest themselves in his schemes, and undoubtedly used Sweden's military predominance to put pressure on the German investor.[3] So much so, that one historian

[1] For the Ship Company, see below, Chapter IV; and Stiernman, *CPO*, I. 973-6; Börjeson, pp. 164-73.

[2] Börjeson, p. 175.

[3] The company's privileges were extended on 10 April 1633, and the powers granted to Usselincx were renewed on 1 May of the same year: *AOSB*, I. VIII. 422, 586.

has held that a main reason for Gustav Adolf's intervention in Germany, and a dominating consideration after he got there, was the harnessing of German capital to Usselincx' commercial projects.[1] This is an explanation of the King's career which was not taken very seriously when it was first propounded, and which is generally discredited now; but it has at least the merit of throwing into high relief the strong commercial ambitions of Gustav Adolf, and the chronic Swedish lack of capital, which did so much to throw difficulties in the way of their realization. Yet though the grandiose aims of the Southern Company were never realized, some portion of the seed which Usselincx had sown did, soon after the King's death, germinate and shoot : in 1637 a new company was founded; and four years later Sweden established a colony on the Delaware.[2]

Gustav Adolf was deeply imbued with a sense of the importance of towns to any well-regulated state. As he looked southwards over the Baltic he could observe, at close range, a large constellation of urban communities whose wealth and prosperity made them strong, or brought strength to the rulers of the territories in which they were located. Swedish history—and not least in the sixteenth century—provided evidence of the political power that could be wielded by these trading cities; and even in Gustav Adolf's time they appeared the natural sponsors of every advance in civilization, from new styles in architecture to better brands of beer. The town, then, was conceived as the natural centre of culture, and the natural focus for trade. But to the discharge of such functions the towns of Sweden—with the possible exception of Stockholm—were obviously inadequate. Oxenstierna expressed the concern of the authorities at this state of affairs when he wrote:

It is well ascertained by experience that those lands and kingdoms which are adorned and protected with good and well-regulated towns, are always in greater certainty and security, and less subject to alterations; their inhabitants are in general richer and more prosperous, by reason of the reciprocal traffic and trade which such towns bring with them. . . . With us, unfortunately, as there have hitherto been no good towns, so few can judge more certainly than we of the prejudice which such a state of affairs brings with it; inasmuch as that by reason of it we cannot, when

[1] F. Bothe, *op. cit.*, *passim*; compare Ligtenberg, pp. 148-62.

[2] For the connexion with Usselincx' earlier schemes, and for the whole question, see C. Ward, *Svenskarne vid Delaware*, pp. 23-84.

hard pressed, obtain help and deliverance from the towns, as other nations can; but everything must fall upon the poor peasantry. . . . And so, too, we buy merchandise and manufactures from the general merchants dearer than anywhere else in the whole world, and this only for lack of proper merchants and traders of our own.[1]

The overseas trade of the country—the only trade by which it grew richer—ought therefore to be concentrated in the larger towns and not be deprived by dissipation over the whole country of much of its beneficial effect. If this were done, Sweden's towns might perhaps develop as the towns of the Hanse had developed, with incalculable benefit to the country as a whole. But to ensure that, it would be necessary to take special measures. Swedish citizens must be encouraged to venture upon an active trade; and care must be taken that a large share of the total trade of the nation was retained in Swedish hands. Foreign merchants must be restricted to specific ports, and not suffered to gain a footing in the internal commerce of the country, roaming around, 'year in, year out' [2]; for too many foreign towns were built on Swedish merchandise. In short, the commerce of Sweden must be rationalized, and a clear division made between staple-towns, whose business was to trade with the foreigner, and upland towns, whose business was to retail the imports which the staple-towns received. So too between the various classes of the population. Trade was the privilege (and almost the *raison d'être*) of the burgher; and therefore members of other Estates—of the clergy, for instance, or the nobility—must not be suffered to invade their preserves.

Very early in the reign Gustav Adolf began to take measures along these lines; stimulated, perhaps, by that clause in the treaty of Knäred which established reciprocal free trade between Sweden and Denmark, and which consequently threw wide the doors to the superior resources and greater experience of Danish merchants. At all events, as early as March 1613 he summoned representatives of the towns to a Trade Meeting (*Handelsdag*); and two months later he produced the first draft of an ordinance for regulating the trade of the country.[3] At the *riksdag* which met at Örebro in January

[1] *AOSB*, I. I. 330; *cf.* Heckscher, *Den ekonomiska innebörden av 1500- och 1600-talens svenska stadsgrundningar* (*HT*, 1923) [cited: Heckscher, *HT* (1923)], p. 313; *id.*, *Våra stadsgrundningars betydelse*, p. 428.

[2] 'Nicht anders als ein hauffen circumforanei': *AOSB*, I. II. 236; Oxenstierna to Heinrich Broke, Burgomaster of Lübeck, 24 August 1615.

[3] *SRDA*, I. 278-9, 289-99.

1614 this draft was thoroughly debated; on 10 February it was agreed to by the Estates; and it became law as the Trading Ordinance of 1614.[1]

The Trading Ordinance drew a clear distinction between an active and a passive trade. Henceforth, a passive trade would be permitted only to some thirteen staple-towns named in the Ordinance.[2] To these towns, and to these towns only, might foreign traders henceforth resort: from the upland towns they were to be wholly excluded, and might not even proceed to them to collect their debts.[3] None of these staple-towns, it may be noted, lay north of Gävle. All imports, then, were to be concentrated in the staple-towns; and the inhabitants of the rest of the country must come to the staple-towns to fetch them. For, by an equitable provision, the staple-towns, having been given a privileged position in regard to foreign trade, were to be debarred from trading within the country: their merchants might no longer travel to the inland towns or frequent the inland markets. Gustav Adolf thus effected the clear-cut distinction which his father had proposed in 1595 but which he had never been able to carry out.

The active trade of the country was similarly regulated. The thirteen staple-towns, together with one other in Sweden and four in Finland,[4] were to have the right to export to foreign countries, provided that they did so in their own ships. In addition, four 'Bothnian' towns (Hudiksvall, Härnösand, Uleåborg, Vasa) were given the right to export in their own ships, except that they were forbidden to carry any edible commodity south of Stockholm. This clause was the only mitigation of the old 'Bothnian Staple', which otherwise was maintained in all its rigour. All trade in Norrland was to be confined to these four towns, with Torneå; and they were strictly forbidden to sail to any Swedish or Finnish port south of Stockholm or Åbo; though all Swedish towns were permitted to sail to the Bothnian towns without restriction, provided they did so in their own ships. Finally, the servants of the crown or the nobility were forbidden to engage in trade in any town unless they had become burgesses and bore their share of municipal burdens; and

[1] *SRDA*, I. 425, 431-45, for preliminary discussions; *ibid.*, 445-54, for the Ordinance. And see O. Fyhrvall, *Om det bottniska handelstvånget*, pp. 39-40.

[2] Stockholm, Nya Lödöse, Kalmar, Göteborg, Västervik, Söderköping, Norrköping, Nyköping, Södertälje, Gävle, Åbo, Viborg, Reval.

[3] For abuses connected with debt-collecting expeditions, see K.-E. Hildebrand, *Falu stads historia*, I. 131.

[4] Öregrund; Helsingfors, Borgå, Björneborg, Ekenäs.

it was provided that anyone who had become a burgess of a town might not quit it for another until he had resided in it for six years.

The objects of the Ordinance are plain. Gustav Adolf hoped to ensure the prosperity of the thirteen staple-towns by concentrating foreign trade in them; he hoped to give the upland towns a countervailing advantage by debarring the staple-towns from resorting to them; he intended, by maintaining the Bothnian Staple, to continue the now traditional policy of favouring the capital; and he hoped, by the provisions regarding the use of ships for export, to stimulate the creation of a mercantile marine. It proved, however, impossible to implement this programme in its entirety. The exclusion of Stockholm from the internal market provoked lively protests; for, as Karl IX had found, Stockholm could not live on foreign trade alone. Many of her merchants had previously made a living by acting as underhand intermediaries between foreigners and the Bergslag, and this would now be impossible. The very limited privileges accorded to Hudiksvall and Härnösand aroused the jealousy of the staple-towns, and Stockholm did not hesitate to call these ports 'illicit'.[1] Foreigners, too, complained of the new arrangements, as well they might.[2] By 1616 Gustav Adolf had come to the conclusion that the Ordinance must be modified, in view of the loud objections of his capital; and in that year he began to make minor concessions: in February, Stockholm, Åbo and Björneborg were given the right to attend two free markets a year in Österbotten; and in June Stockholm was accorded permission to attend the annual market of SS. Peter and Paul in Arboga.[3] In the following February the whole question of trade regulations was discussed again at the Örebro *riksdag*,[4] and at the coronation *riksdag* later in the year the government at last came forward with an amended edition of the Ordinance of 1614. It met with strong opposition from the towns, and from the Queen-Mother; and in the end it was forced upon the Estates by a somewhat violent exercise of the royal authority.

The Trading Ordinance of 1617, despite the opposition it encountered, really represents a partial capitulation by the King.[5] The

[1] *Stockholms stads privilegiebref*, pp. 163-5; Ahnlund, *Från medeltid och Vasatid*, p. 180; and *cf.* Stiernman, *CPO*, I. 655-60; *AOSB*, I. II. 172, 205; *SRDA*, I. 285-6.

[2] Cronholm, III. 242; *AOSB*, I. II. 206.

[3] Stiernman, *CPO*, I. 681-2; *Stockholms stads privilegiebref*, pp. 166-7.

[4] *SRDA*, II. 82-3, 218-19, 221-6, 230.

[5] Text in Stiernman, *CPO*, I. 690-704. It seems to have been drafted by Johan Skytte: Brännman, p. 55.

rights of the staple-towns are confirmed and extended; the limitation upon them—the *quid pro quo* to the upland towns—is tacitly dropped, and the concessions of 1616 are confirmed; the Bothnian Staple is more rigorously enforced. Foreigners coming to trade may not stay in the country more than eight weeks in a year. Helsingfors and Borgå are added to the list of staple-towns; and the number of towns permitted to engage in active trade is increased by the addition of these two, together with Raumo and Nystad in Finland, and a number of towns in the newly acquired Baltic provinces; but it is now enacted not only that they must sail in their own ships but also that the crews must be ordinarily resident in the town from which they sail. The limited right of Härnösand, Uleåborg and Vasa to participate in the active trade is now entirely taken away, and of all the Norrland towns only Hudiksvall retains the concessions of 1614.[1] In short, the attempt to compensate the upland towns for the favours extended to the staple-towns is virtually abandoned; and the special position of Stockholm is confirmed. The provisions about native crews may be considered as a reinforcing of a Navigation Act which had been promulgated a few weeks earlier (17 August 1617). By this Act,[2] all Swedish shipowners who should arm their ships with not less than three pair of cannon of a specified type were to pay import duty at one-half, and export duty at one-third, of the normal rate; while all skippers, helmsmen and boatswains who should take up their permanent residence in a Swedish port were to be given six years' exemption from taxation. The object of the Act was not only to encourage the mercantile marine but also to provide a fleet of armed merchantmen which might supplement the Royal Navy in an emergency; and in this it was analogous to the Danish legislation providing for *Defensionsskibe*, or to the Spanish policy of creating *Almirantazgos*. But its most permanent significance is perhaps that it is the first piece of Swedish legislation providing for tariff discrimination in favour of native shipping.[3]

The Trading Ordinance of 1617 was a clear sign that the staple-towns were weaker than Gustav Adolf had hoped three years earlier. Its promulgation, moreover, necessarily involved the government in

[1] Partial concessions were made to Härnösand in 1622 and 1626: Fyhrvall, pp. 43-5.

[2] *Stockholms stads privilegiebref*, pp. 171-3.

[3] Danielsson, p. 404. Börjeson (*op. cit.*, pp. 125-6) is sceptical about the Danish analogy, pointing out that a mere half-dozen cannon was very inadequate armament. He suggests the purpose was rather self-defence against pirates in western waters.

further action. In pursuit of the ideal of a uniform, government-controlled system of trade, the Ordinance had enacted, more stringently than ever, that all trade in Norrland must be confined to the Bothnian towns. But such a provision was in 1617 impossible to enforce. There were no towns in Västerbotten north of Härnösand, and a strict adherence to the Ordinance might have entailed upon the peasantry of the northern parts of this region a journey to market of perhaps a couple of hundred miles. In such conditions *landsköp* was inevitable, as the very existence of the gild of Birkarlar proved. The Ordinance, indeed, had explicitly admitted this, and had promised that new marketing centres in Norrland should be established. Thus the outburst of town-founding which followed after 1620 was in one aspect a consequence of the policy of 1617. In order to carry out a scheme of trade regulation designed to bring real economic strength to a limited number of favoured towns, Gustav Adolf found himself committed to the founding of a shoal of new towns, most of which were predestined throughout their existence to be economically feeble.[1]

In 1618 and 1620, accordingly, expeditions were sent to Norrland to discuss the problem with the inhabitants and to select suitable sites.[2] As a rule, they chose places which were already small centres of population, or places in which a chapel was located.[3] The Birkarlar, faced with suppression, volunteered to flit to Luleå [4]; and there seems to have been a genuine local demand for the revival of a town at or near Umeå [5]; but on the whole the local populations showed no desire for new towns, and strong hostility to them when they appeared. Söderhamn was something of an exception, for it was from the beginning intended as a 'manufactory-town' on the pattern of Arboga, in which the rural weapon-smiths of Hälsingland could be concentrated, for greater ease of supervision by the government factor and greater facility of supplying them with raw materials.[6]

[1] It was hoped, no doubt, that they would also serve as garrison-towns or military depots; but the military motive was entirely secondary: B. Steckzén, *Minneskrift till Piteå stads 300-års jubileum*, p. 26.

[2] B. Steckzén, *Umeå stads historia*, pp. 29-31; *id.*, *Piteå*, p. 31; N. Ahnlund, *Sundsvalls historia*, I. 28, 34.

[3] Luleå and Piteå, for instance, had been chapelries and parishes since the fourteenth century: Ahnlund, *Oljoberget och ladugårdsgärdet*, p. 123. For a discussion of the siting of these Norrland towns, see H. Nelson, *Geografiska studier över de svenska städernas . . . läge*, pp. 24-5, 94-9.

[4] B. Steckzén and H. Wennerström, *Luleå stads historia*, pp. 19-37.

[5] Steckzén, *Umeå*, pp. 31-7.

[6] B. Steckzén, *Om Söderhamns gevärsfaktori i äldre tider*, pp. 20-2.

But Sundsvall, though it soon became a town of the same type, by the migration thither of weapon-smiths from Medelpad who refused to move to Söderhamn, was not originally intended to be anything more than a market-town and a port; and as such—lying as it did half-way between Hudiksvall and Härnösand, and within easy reach of both of them—it was in its origin the most superfluous and unjustifiable of all the new foundations.[1] In addition to these Norrland towns on either side of the Gulf of Bothnia there were some others, founded as a rule to check *landsköp* in districts where it was especially prevalent. Such, perhaps, was Alingsås; such, certainly, was Borås, where the local peasantry agreed to found a town on condition that the right of peddling be reserved to the future burgesses and denied to those who stayed outside. In effect, *landsköp* became hereafter the privilege and monopoly of the inhabitants of Borås, to the great indignation of less-favoured towns in Västergötland; and the burghers were given a direct incentive to maintain the exclusive character of this privilege, by that clause in their charter (1622) which made over to them the goods of all others convicted of *landsköp*. The creation of Borås was thus one more attempt to put a stop to this evil, this time by the ingenious expedient of concentrating it—as other trades were also to be concentrated—in a town. One reason for the special favour shown to Borås may have been the King's desire to encourage the pedlar's trade across the border; for the *knallar* came back from Denmark with their packs stuffed full of *riksdaler*, and of these the King was always in need. Certainly the town's privileges expressly debarred foreigners (by which may be understood Danes) from attending Borås market.[2]

The charters given to these towns of the early 'twenties, and the terms of their foundation, were on the whole very uniform. The inhabitants were granted twelve years' freedom from taxation (six in the case of Umeå); they were allowed to establish a *bannmil* around the town, within which no craft might be exercised, and which usually measured four Swedish miles; and they were given a grant of land from the King. In some instances the land was already owned by free tax-paying peasants, who could not be dispossessed

[1] Ahnlund, *Sundsvalls historia*, I. 40, 43-5, 50-1. One peasant remarked that Sundsvall 'deserved to be burned in Hell, for being founded between Hudiksvall and Härnösand'.

[2] O. Mannerfelt, *Sjuhäradsbygden före 1622 och Borås stad 1622-1865*, is now supplanted by N. Forssell, *Borås stads historia*, I: for the above, see pp. 14, 38-42, 44-6, 60, 68.

without compensation; and in more than one case the crown forgot, or neglected, to provide for this, so that the burden fell upon the struggling municipality.[1] It was a burden which most of them could ill afford to bear. For indeed there was scarce one of them that throve.[2] Luleå in the 1620's had only nine permanent inhabitants, and by 1650 only about thirty-two; while Umeå in 1630 had only forty-three.[3] At Alingsås in 1627 half the population owned cattle, at an average rate of more than eleven beasts per man.[4] In 1635 the *riksråd* was seriously thinking of abolishing Sundsvall, since it 'didn't seem to get on'.[5] Gustav Adolf at the close of his reign described the new towns as 'idle, rotting and tumbledown'; Gabriel Gustafsson Oxenstierna in 1636 called Norrtälje 'little better than a thieves' kitchen'; his brother Axel was no less contemptuous of the new towns in 1639; and in 1633 the *råd* placed foremost upon its list of economic problems for discussion the question of what was to be done in view of the fact that 'our towns in Sweden are all declining'.[6] Nor did the future hold much prospect for them. In 1835 there were complaints in Piteå that 'whole platoons of goats' wandered about the streets; and in 1925 only two of Gustav Adolf's foundations —if we exclude Göteborg, to be noticed presently—were included among the twenty most important Swedish towns, and they were Borås and Sundsvall, which owed their prosperity respectively to the cotton and timber industries, and had each risen to importance only in the nineteenth century.[7] Of the eighteen new towns founded between 1611 and 1654, only six could muster a population of one thousand in 1800.[8] The truth was, that it was a mistake in a country as sparsely populated as Sweden to try to force trade to towns. *Landsköp* was a more natural and more appropriate method for the exchange of goods than recourse to a distant market; and even though the new town might much diminish the distance, the toll-

[1] Steckzén, *Umeå*, pp. 40-6; *id.*, *Piteå*, pp. 32-45; Ahnlund, *Sundsvall*, I, 41, 48, 54; C. M. Kjellberg, *Norrtälje stad 1622-1922*, pp. 9-14; *cf.* Lindberg, *Västerviks historia*, I. 261.

[2] Heckscher, *Våra stadsgrundningars betydelse*, p. 425, where he observes 'A town cannot live on privileges and geographical position'.

[3] Steckzén, *Umeå*, p. 57; Holmquist, *Svenska kyrkans historia*, IV, 1. 201.

[4] Heckscher, *op. cit.*, p. 430.

[5] Ahnlund, *Sundsvall*, I. 81.

[6] S. Loenbom, *Upplysningar i svenska historien*, III. 90-1; Heckscher, *HT* (1923), pp. 324-5, 341.

[7] Heckscher, *Våra stadsgrundningars betydelse*, pp. 429-30. Borås, however, alone of all these towns, made good progress in the early years: N. Forssell, *op. cit.*, I. 94-5; Mannerfelt, p. 39.

[8] Heckscher, *HT* (1923), p. 322.

hedge which surrounded it discouraged the peasant. And in any case he preferred, if it were at all possible, to ship his goods to Stockholm and obtain better prices. The peasant, in fact, resented the compulsion to trade with the new towns; and, having moved in, he had no idea—and no chance—of making a living as the ideal burgess of Gustav Adolf's imagining. He tilled his stony acres, fished for *strömming* or salmon, grazed his herds in the high forests, precisely as before; and was a town-dweller by accident, or by order. Indeed, the government's intention in these new foundations could probably have been realized without the creation of towns at all, or the granting of municipal privileges. It would perhaps have served just as well—or as ill—to prevent *landsköp* if Gustav Adolf had simply appointed market-places at a bridge, or a cross-roads, and ordained that exchange or barter should be carried on there. Perhaps he realized this: at all events, he tried the experiment. In the new privileges which in 1620 were granted to Kalmar, Västervik, Jönköping and Norrköping, it was stated that because of the great distances between urban centres each of these towns should have the right to trade throughout the whole year at certain *köpingar* (market-places) in the surrounding countryside. Jönköping, for instance, was allotted five such places. Anyone wishing to open a shop or to settle at one of these spots must first acquire burgess-rights in the town upon which it was dependent. Peasants might come and trade every day; but all peasants living within two Swedish miles were bound to come in every Saturday, whether they had anything to buy or sell or not. And no craftsman might practise his craft in a *köping* unless with the permission of the gild in the parent town, of which he must have been admitted a member.[1] In spite of the oppressive and absurd compulsory provisions, the experiment may have been a success in such parts of the country as Bergslagen, where it met a real need. But in Gustav Adolf's time it was applied only in a few provinces; and after the introduction of the Little Toll the government preferred, for obvious fiscal reasons, to try once more to force trade to the towns.[2]

Gustav Adolf's town policy was not, however, a record of unredeemed failure. He gave much encouragement to Falun, for instance—a town which arose spontaneously without government

[1] Björkman, *Jönköping*, II. 79, 101; W. Tham, *Lindesbergs och Noras historia*, pp. 198-9; H. Lindström, *Näringsfrihetens utveckling i Sverige*, p. 44.

[2] For some of the difficulties, see Lindberg, *Västervik*, I. 267, 341, 346.

interference—and it was only accident which deferred its incorporation to the following reign.[1] The development of the iron industry led to similar urbanization at Nora and Lindesberg.[2] Gustav Adolf refounded, rebuilt, refortified and removed the town of Jönköping, which had been destroyed during the War of Kalmar; he gave it special concessions which made it unique among upland towns and virtually exempted it from the provisions of the Trading Ordinances; and he endowed it in 1620 with a charter notable for its enlightened sanitary and educational clauses, as well as for a new type of town government.[3] And Jönköping, at least, seems to have made satisfactory progress. But by far the most important of his efforts in this sphere was his foundation of the new Göteborg in 1619.

The establishment of a major port at the estuary of the Göta had been an object of Swedish policy at least since the reign of Erik XIV. Though communications with Stockholm and the Mälar region were bad, and long remained so, the water-route up the river to Brätte and so by Lake Väner to the mining districts of Värmland and Närke was easy, apart from a necessary portage at Trollhättan. And above all, a port on the Göta opened directly on the western seas, and no hostile King of Denmark could close the Sound against its trade, though he might indeed (as the War of Kalmar proved) maintain a blockade of its harbours. Gamla Lödöse and Nya Lödöse had successively, but inadequately, filled the rôle of Sweden's port towards the west; Älvsborg had been constructed as a fortress to defend them. At last, in 1607, Karl IX had founded the new town of Göteborg, on the island of Hisingen. By the most lavish grants of privileges he had sought to attract foreigners to his foundation, and, for preference, Dutchmen; and he had so well succeeded that the first Göteborg was almost wholly a Dutch town, and Dutch had been the tongue in which the municipal business was conducted. But the first Göteborg had perished at the hands of the Danes during the War of Kalmar, and its inhabitants had retired to Nya Lödöse, or left the country. As long as Älvsborg's ransom remained unpaid, and the Göta region in Danish hands, there was nothing to be done; but as soon as the last instalment was

[1] *AOSB*, I. i. 287-93; K.-E. Hildebrand, *Falu stads historia*, I. 17, 61-104; Ahnlund, *Axel Oxenstierna*, p. 219.

[2] Tham, *op. cit.*, pp. 244, 250.

[3] Björkman, *Jönköping*, II. 15-30, 68-76, 79, 88-100, 103; H. G. F. Sundberg, *Den svenska stapelstadsrätten*, p. 43. Kalmar, which had also suffered during the war, was rebuilt too: L. W. Munthe, *Kungl. Fortifikationens historia*, I. 243-52.

accounted for, and Älvsborg handed back by Kristian IV, Gustav Adolf took steps to revive his father's work. In 1619 he personally inspected and approved a new site, this time on the south bank of the river, and here the modern Göteborg grew up. The old settlers were invited to return, and once again efforts were made to bring colonists from the Netherlands. The Dutch formed a committee to bargain with Gustav Adolf, and the terms they demanded were high; but in the end agreement was reached, the settlers began to come over, and the new town received its privileges in July 1621. They were on the model of the earlier charter of 1607, though they did not go so far as that document in giving the town an extraordinary position within the Swedish state. Moreover, many of the conditions most insisted on by the Dutch—as for instance a special form of municipal government and their own system of law—were not, in the sequel, secured. Town government in Göteborg on the whole did not differ widely from that in other Swedish towns; and the ordinary Swedish law ran in the city. Business might now be conducted in Swedish as well as in Dutch. The best sites were to be allotted to those who undertook to build stone houses. The town was given sixteen years' exemption from taxation; all the assets of Nya Lödöse were transferred to it and the citizens of Nya Lödöse forced to remove themselves to Göteborg; it received considerable grants of land in *förläning*, and was allowed to appropriate half the revenue from tolls for the first sixteen years of its existence. Toleration, which was not, however, to extend to public worship, was accorded to Arminians and other foreign protestants.[1]

Thus Göteborg was launched, and upon exceptionally favourable terms. It soon attracted foreigners of various nationalities; and its first town council included, besides ten Dutchmen and seven Swedes, one Scot. The German element soon became important; and among early Scots residents we find the names of Stewart, Maclear, Spalding, Carnegie, Sinclair, Kinnaird, Lindsay, Ogilvie and Hunter.[2] The second Göteborg, in fact, was less overwhelmingly Dutch than the first, and the Swedish element was from the beginning sufficient to prevent its ever becoming, as its predecessor had seemed likely

[1] For Göteborg, see Almquist, *Göteborgs historia*, I. *passim*; *SILR*, p. 131; *AOSB*, I. I. 327-30, I. II. 367, 395; Ahnlund, *Oxenstierna*, p. 227; Holmquist, *Svenska kyrkans historia*, IV. I. 409-11; Lindberg, *Hantverkarna*, pp. 153-4. For some similarities, Davidson and Gray, *The Scottish Staple at Veere*, pp. 164-5, 185.

[2] Almquist, I. 320.

to become, a foreign city on Swedish soil. Its growth was not as rapid as Gustav Adolf had expected: it showed no signs, as he had hoped it would, of displacing Danzig as the great grain-port of the North, and it never became (even after Erik XIV's dream of a Göta canal became a reality) the great centre for the transit trade between east and west. It was some years before it developed a satisfactory harbour. By as late as 1670 its population was probably not much in excess of 4000.[1] Yet it was certainly not a failure like—for instance—Luleå; and quite early its citizens began to develop that connexion with the Värmland mines upon which much of the future prosperity of the city was to be based. They leased the crown's revenues in charcoal; they became shareholders in forges and factories. When in 1624 Gustav Adolf visited Göteborg (and made some useful reforms in its government) he proposed forming a 'Trading Company for Värmland', to be based on Göteborg; and though the ill-fated Iron Company took the place of that project, the idea was sound. So too, perhaps, was the other suggestion made by him at this time, for a wood-exporting company; for Göteborg soon developed an export of masts.[2] At all events, by 1636 the Göteborgers had already obtained a firm footing in the Värmland ironfield; and the next century, which would usher in the great age of Swedish iron, would also bring the efflorescence of its natural port of export.

The importance which Gustav Adolf attached to the part to be played by the towns in the national economy led him, from the very beginning of the reign, to show himself benevolently disposed towards their demands for privileges and ready to protect the burghers against improper competition.[3] And though at times their eternal querulousness caused his patience to snap,[4] he showed a steady concern for their welfare—as, for instance, by his printing of the Town Law in 1618; by his great statute remodelling town government in 1619[5]; by the new privileges which he accorded to a number of towns in 1620 and 1624.[6] And, not least, he took care of their interests by his protection and encouragement of the gilds, who found in him and his ministers allies against interloping craftsmen (*bönhasar*), rural industry, and even (though less consistently)

[1] Heckscher, I. 389.

[2] For these projects, see Almquist, I. 261-6.

[3] *Stockholms stads privilegiebref*, pp. 156, 159, 161.

[4] *e.g.* in February 1617: *SRDA*, II. 52; and *cf.* Lindberg, *Västerviks historia*, I. 141.

[5] For this reform of town government, see above, Vol. I, p. 327 *seqq*.

[6] Jönköping, Kalmar, Västervik, Norrköping, Arboga, in 1620; Sala in 1624.

the defence-men of the nobility. In 1616, for instance, he forbade *bönhasar* shoemakers to practise their craft in the Stockholm suburbs.[1] The statute of 1619 made definite the fees payable on admission as a burgess; and the same law fixed the extent of the *bannmil* at four Swedish miles. In 1620 the government made a strong effort to compel all weapon-smiths to move in from the surrounding country either to Jönköping or to Norrköping [2]; and it actually succeeded in removing the weapon-smiths of Hälsingland to the new town of Söderhamn. In regard to defence-men, indeed, it was forced to proceed with more caution: the right to maintain them was tenaciously defended by the first Estate, and had to be formally conceded in the privileges granted to the nobility in 1617 [3]; while the abuse (much complained of by the towns) whereby nobles installed their servants in their town property, and through them carried on commercial activities, although refusing to pay scot and bear lot,[4] was never really satisfactorily dealt with. Yet, despite the privileges of 1617, something was done to reduce the evil of defence-men; and in this matter the sympathies of the government were certainly with the towns.

This emerged from the reforms of the gild system which began about 1620. In 1620, as we have seen, an effort was made to find a solution to the problem of *landsköp* by the creation of *köpingar*, which were to be dependent colonies of the five towns to which the privileges of 1620 were granted. It very soon occurred to Oxenstierna that the system of *köpingar* might be of value, not only in combating *landsköp* but also as a method of eradicating illicit craftwork and of forcing country craftsmen into town gilds. It was determined, therefore, to experiment with a similar scheme for Stockholm's *län* and Uppland, and to establish *fläckar* (*lit.* 'spots') which would in fact be *köpingar* under another name, as legalized centres for craftsmen. In the following year, partly with a view to implementing this idea, the King appointed a special commission, headed by Gabriel Gustafsson Oxenstierna and Lars Skytte, which was charged with undertaking a general revision of the regulations of the gilds, the correction of abuses in them, the suppression of

[1] S. Hansson, *Ur skomakareyrkets historia*, p. 31.
[2] F. Lindberg, *Hantverkarna*, p. 225; Heckscher, I. 588; *cf. SILR*, p. 136.
[3] For the privileges of the nobility, see below, pp. 156-7.
[4] T. Berg, *Skytte*, p. 6; *LDGBAH*, p. 205, for a complaint against de Geer for not taking burgage in Norrköping, and for 'defending' more hands than he needed for his manufactories; and *cf.* Herdin, *Uppsala på 1600-talet*, I. 103-4.

interloping, and, of course, the selection and establishment of *fläckar*.[1]

The commission of 1621 is a good example of the passion for regularization, for uniformity, and for efficient direction of effort, which both Gustav Adolf and Oxenstierna seem to have felt, and which was so fertile of legislation in the middle years which followed the treaty of Stolbova. And, inasmuch as it was expected to lead to the extinction of interloping and the constraining of all handicrafts into the framework of the gild system, it was also a sign of their remarkable optimism. Nevertheless, the gilds had reached a stage in their development at which some action was probably called for. Karl IX had been a friend of the gilds quite as zealous as his successor ever was, and with his backing they had developed a narrow corporate spirit, and a tendency to exclusivism, which were especially inappropriate in Swedish conditions. The policy of strictly limiting the number of masters (the so-called *numerus clausus*), which Karl IX had actively encouraged, was unwise at a time when the government was striving to encourage manufactures, to strengthen the economic position of the towns and to attract foreign technicians as immigrants. Yet in 1611 no less than half of the craft-gilds in Stockholm had the *numerus clausus*,[2] and even in those that had not, there was a tendency to make mastership too difficult, and in particular too expensive.

This, then, was one of the questions to which the commission turned their attention. In September 1621 they promulgated a set of general regulations for all the gilds (the so-called *Generalembetsskrå*).[3] This laid it down that only six Stockholm gilds should be allowed to apply the *numerus clausus* in future; it reformed other abuses which had made the attainment of mastership difficult; it strengthened the position of the gilds by permitting them for the first time to own gild-halls, and giving them a licence to sell liquor on their premises[4]; it made it difficult for burgesses of a town to be also the defence-men of the nobility, and thus virtually deprived defence-men of burgess-rights; it made regulations for the election of officers in the gilds, for the conditions of apprenticeship and the

[1] Lindberg, *Hantverkarna*, pp. 193-9.

[2] *ibid.*, pp. 124-5, 178-224; H. Lindström, *Näringsfrihetens utveckling i Sverig*, pp. 13-20; and in general S. Ambrosiani, *Från de svenska skråämbetenas dagar*; Hansson, *op. cit.*; Herdin, III.

[3] Stiernman, *CPO*, I. 781-93; and *cf. ibid.*, I. 807-9.

[4] Including *brännvin*.

conduct of journeymen; it established—a novelty for Sweden—the obligation of a journeyman to take the road; and it announced the government's intention to establish *fläckar*. The policy behind these regulations was undoubtedly to extend the gild system as widely as possible, and to secure that as few craftsmen as might be were left outside it. If four masters of one craft existed in one place, they must form a gild; if less than four, they must join the gild which lay nearest to them: thus, for example, the Uppsala skinners would become a kind of colony of the skinners of Stockholm.[1]

These general regulations were followed by the revision and re-issue of the charters of particular gilds: thus the shoemakers and the hatters received new privileges; while a comprehensive charter was given to all the smiths—locksmiths, hammersmiths, spur-makers, gunsmiths, clockmakers, sword-polishers, farriers and others; who, though forming separate gilds, were sufficiently akin to be dealt with in one set of regulations.[2] It was probably the commission's original intention to proceed to a similar revision of the privileges of all the gilds; but this was too protracted an undertaking for them to carry out. But if the work of reform was not carried through in detail, the main principles had at least been laid down, and they continued to govern the gilds for more than a generation, without much modification. After 1622 the gilds were more firmly entrenched in Swedish life than ever. Coming comparatively late to Sweden, they retained their vitality long after the gilds of England had become empty anachronisms: they were still vigorous in the first half of the nineteenth century; and the compulsion upon a craftsman to belong to a gild was not abolished until 1846. For this longevity Gustav Adolf's reforms may claim some of the credit. They could not, indeed, so far prevail over geography as to be successful in eliminating rural industry; they could not realize their aim of forcing all craftsmen into the gilds; but they are a characteristic example of the King's desire to organize the economy of the country into forms which could be easily supervised, controlled and directed; and that desire—like his desire to steer trade to the towns, or direct it through prescribed channels to specific markets—was one more manifestation of his determination to put Sweden upon the same footing as less backward nations, his determination to modernize the country's

[1] Herdin, III. 96.

[2] Hansson, p. 103; Ambrosiani, p. 60 *seqq.*; Stiernman, *CPO*, I. 793-803; and, for the gild reforms in general, Löfgren, I. 14, 55 *seqq.*, 146-7, 159, 206-8, II. 48.

institutions—in economic matters, upon current mercantilist models—his determination that the national energies must be mobilized as efficiently as possible, for the support of that foreign policy which prudence, religion and hard necessity seemed to impose.[1]

Such a mobilization could not be total so long as there were hands that were idle and men who made of poverty a profession. Gustav Adolf believed, as firmly as his contemporaries in England, that the sturdy beggar was a canker in the commonweal, and that the poor must be set on work.[2] Since the Reformation the care of the poor, the sick, the orphan and the tramp had fallen to private charity, or to the state. Gustav Vasa had been careful to make some provision for these people out of the spoils of the Church, and a Hospital Ordinance of 1571 (it formed part of the Church Ordinance of the same year) had attempted a general treatment of the problem—among other provisions by permitting parishes to erect small cottages for the sick and indigent. But, on the whole, the state of the poor had grown worse during the sixteenth century, and continued to grow worse down to the earlier part of Gustav Adolf's reign. The hospitals were made to house not only the aged and infirm, who were received only if they made a contribution sufficient to provide their keep, but also the true paupers, who made no such contribution. They fell increasingly into decay or scandalous mismanagement, and few parishes availed themselves of the permission accorded by the Ordinance of 1571. Sturdy beggars increased in numbers, despite repeated legislation against them, and took refuge on occasion from the action of the authorities by enlisting as defencemen[3]; and the institution of the pass or badge for beggars, by licensing the profession, showed the state's inability to suppress it.[4] Wandering bands of gypsies presented local authorities with a special problem, with which, as a rule, they were quite unable to cope.

The relatively quiet years after 1617 gave Gustav Adolf his first opportunity of addressing himself to the question, and in 1619 he took his first measures. The statute for the towns which was

[1] Masters and journeymen were exempt from conscription: Löfgren, I. 319. It is remarkable that among the peace terms suggested by the *råd* in March 1632 was one which would have made Swedish masters automatically free of German gilds: R. Klinkowström and J. Mankell, *Arkiv till upplysning om svenska krigens och krigsinrättningarnes historia* [cited: *Arkiv*], II. 395.

[2] For the poor, see B. H. Dahlberg, *Bidrag till svenska fattiglagstiftningens historia*; G. Lindstedt, *Översikten af den svenska fattigvårdens historia*; L. Levander, *Fattigt folk och tiggare.*

[3] H. Swenne, *Svenska adelns ekonomiska privilegier*, p. 233.

[4] Levander, *Fattigt folk och tiggare*, p. 149.

promulgated in that year enjoined upon each of them the setting up of a house for children; and in the towns which received their privileges in 1620 this injunction was specially included. The purpose was avowedly to provide hands: the children were to be given a minimum of education, were to be set to learn a trade, and in due time were to be sent out into the world to practise it. This order seems to have been complied with, at all events in Jönköping.[1] But this was to tackle only the fringe of the problem. In the following year, 1620, the King laid before the clergy (it was the same meeting at which he passed his strictures upon the Swedish educational system) enquiries as to a general reform of the administration of the poor.[2] He suggested two main principles: first, the concentration of the poor's hospitals into fewer and larger institutions (in the old hospitals, as he pungently remarked, they had been treated 'worse than dogs'), and secondly the principle that those who were received into the new institutions should be required to pay according to their means. The clergy proved to be as difficult to move in this matter as in regard to education. They disliked the King's proposals, foresaw difficulties, and for their own part suggested merely that henceforward all beggars must be licensed by the bishop of the diocese: they would thus have been subject to a kind of diocesan law of settlement.[3] Despite these discouraging answers, the King proceeded to draft a scheme for the setting up by the crown of a large hospital in each diocese, to hold at least 1000, without prejudice to existing institutions. If the poor could pay, they were to be made to pay; if not, a contribution was to be levied on the town or *härad* in which the hospital was situated.

For the moment, the scheme was allowed to drop; but in the instruction issued in 1621 to the commission on the craft-gilds, Gustav Adolf ordered them to see to the erection of a house for children in Stockholm; and in 1624 steps were taken to make a start on these lines. There were to be 100 children of both sexes, who were to remain in the house for at least three years and be taught to weave and spin. The Master was to import skilled weavers from Germany, at his own cost, to act as instructors. Only in exceptional cases was a child under the age of four years to be taken;

[1] Björkman, II. 104. In 1634, 21 per cent. of the adult population of Jönköping were more or less paupers: *ibid.*, II. 226-7.

[2] P. E. Thyselius, *Handlingar rörande svenska kyrkans och läroverkens historia*, I. 5-6.

[3] *ibid.*, I. 19-27; Hallenberg, IV. 844.

bastards were to receive a more general and less specialized education than legitimate children; the inmates were to be washed once a fortnight; and those with brains were to be allowed to continue their studies, if boys, or were to be given a small marriage portion, if girls. In 1626 a levy was imposed on every parsonage in Sweden of one *tunna* of corn every four years, to support the house; and though the Master mismanaged affairs, so that some of the children escaped and took to begging, the manufacture of cloth was actually begun. But by this time the original purpose of the institution had become obscured. For reasons of economy, the house for children was early combined with a house of correction for vagabonds, and the two were rapidly transformed into a typical house of industry. By the end of the reign the institution was deeply in debt and had become a minor government factory working for the Admiralty (in part at all events), and employing non-pauper labour.[1]

In 1624, however, Gustav Adolf produced a really comprehensive poor law—the first in Swedish history—and, despite the misgivings of the Clergy and the financial fears of the Peasants, he succeeded in getting his scheme adopted by the Estates.[2] This remarkable enactment shows a clear appreciation of the fact that poverty was a complex and not a simple problem, and it outlines a plan of action which, if it could have been carried out, would have given Sweden perhaps the most efficient and humane poor law in Europe. All begging was henceforward to be strictly forbidden. The able-bodied poor, if willing to work, were to be assisted to find employment. Sturdy beggars were to be sent to houses of correction, of which there was to be one in every province. Children were to be put in separate houses, and there to be taught a trade. The parochial almshouses (*käringastugor*) were to be discontinued; and instead the impotent and aged poor were to be sent to one of the projected new hospitals. Instead of the twenty-one ill-conducted hospitals which had formerly existed, there were now to be eleven large hospitals, one for each province, and inmates were to pay according to their means.

This admirable scheme remained on paper during the King's lifetime, and it was never put into effect as a whole.[3] It would have entailed very heavy expenditure on buildings and staff, and the

[1] S. Wieselgren, *Sveriges fängelser och fångvård*, pp. 33-43.

[2] *AOSB*, I. 1. 351-8, or Thyselius, I. 43-51, for the scheme; *ibid.*, I. 51-6, for criticisms of it.

[3] See, for instance, *RRP*, II. 97.

King was not prepared to impose additional burdens upon a country already over-burdened, especially since the scheme obtained only the most lukewarm approval by the Estates. The administration of the poor, therefore, continued much upon the old lines, except perhaps in the towns privileged in 1620; begging and private charity held the field; and of institutional relief the most efficient was probably that which was under the control of a businesslike and humane bishop such as Rudbeckius.[1]

If Sweden's export trade were to be expanded as Gustav Adolf hoped, if the natural wealth of the country were to flow freely to the ports, internal communications must be improved, both by land and by water. Karl IX had seen the importance of this in his day, but the improvements he had actually carried out were of small consequence. Nevertheless, he pointed the road which Gustav Adolf was to follow, and the force of his example was not lost upon his successor. Both the King and his chancellor were interested in the development of water-communications, for it was by water that the heavy metallic exports could most conveniently be transported: Oxenstierna, indeed, is said to have revived the idea of a canal linking the east and west coasts, by way of Lakes Väner and Vätter.[2] At all events, the 1620's were filled with projects for canal-building—projects which were perhaps in their entirety too grandiose for the resources at the King's disposal. In 1620 Gustav Adolf ordered investigations to be made into the possibility of making the Motala river navigable, and so providing a link between Vättern and the Baltic; in 1621 he rebuilt the locks at Lilla Edet on the Göta, which had originally been constructed by his father; and in 1627 he ordered measures to be taken to construct an unbroken water-route between the Kopparberg and Lake Siljan. But his main achievement was to begin, in 1629, the construction of the Hjelmare canal, to connect Lake Hjelmare with Lake Mälar, by way of the Arboga river. This, when completed, did something to provide a good cross-country route from Stockholm to Göteborg, against the possibility of a Danish closure of the Sound.

He was equally active in improving the roads. Work was done on the route to the Bergslag; on the road from Stockholm to

[1] For the Church's share in poor relief, see, for instance, *AOSB*, II. XII. 27, 378; Rudbeckius, *Dagbok*, pp. 62, 74, 229; B. R. Hall, *Kulturella interiörer från Storhetstidens uppryckningsarbete*, pp. 1, 33, 41.

[2] For canals, see C. G. Styffe, *Om Sveriges kanalbyggnader intill medlet af adertonde seklet*, pp. 29-54.

Nyköping; on the road from Vimmerby to Västervik; and on that from Jönköping to Linköping along the eastern side of Lake Vätter.[1] In 1620 the *ståthållare* of Norrland and Österbotten were instructed to see that the roads were kept clear of obstacles, especially those from the Kopparberg and the iron-mining regions to their most convenient ports at Gävle and Hudiksvall; and it was ordered that roads and bridges were to be at least ten ells broad, and if possible were to be stone-paved.[2] Other improvements took place, or new roads were built, between Värmland and the Väner region; between the interior of Småland and Kalmar; and on the great north road round the head of the Gulf of Bothnia, which was reconstructed as far as Piteå. The appointment of Anders Bure as Surveyor-General in 1628 was a further indication of the government's interest in the matter.[3] On the other hand, the roads in the frontier areas towards Denmark and Norway were systematically neglected, in order to make invasion difficult; and nine years after Gustav Adolf's death the government actually declared that it would be best pleased if they should become absolutely impassable.[4]

Associated with this improvement of the roads was the origin of the Swedish postal system. In part it was forced upon the country by the new system of local government which began to be effective about 1620; in part it was made essential by Sweden's closer political contacts with the continent, and especially with Germany. In 1620, therefore, came two developments: on the one hand a foot-post, reserved to the use of the government, and designed to maintain closer touch between the central administration and the *ståthållare*; on the other, the first public post. This latter connected Stockholm with Hamburg and Copenhagen, by way of Markaryd and Helsingör; and though it was operated by couriers who travelled the whole route, and not, as in the Taxis system in Germany, by relays of postmen each covering only a short stretch, it did at least provide relays of horses at proper intervals as far as the Danish border. From 1624 other lines were organized on the same pattern —to Göteborg, Falun, Åbo, Reval and Härnösand. The postal system, however, increased the already intolerable burden of

[1] Cronholm, III. 224; Lindberg, *Västerviks historia*, I. 142.
[2] *SILR*, p. 140.
[3] Instructions in *SICF*, pp. 248-50; E. Vennberg, art. *Anders Bure* in *Svenskt Biografiskt Lexicon*.
[4] C. T. Odhner, *Sveriges inre historia under Drottning Christinas förmyndare*, p. 252.

skjutsning,[1] and it was to relieve the peasants that Axel Oxenstierna eventually carried through the reform of 1636, which provided relays of letter-carriers and proper post-houses, and so really inaugurated the modern Swedish post-office.[2]

(v) *Social Consequences*

The economic developments which we have been considering brought with them far-reaching social consequences: consequences whose real nature was only beginning to be felt in Gustav Adolf's lifetime, but which were to give a new character to the generation which immediately succeeded him. The great adventure in Germany had, indeed, hardly begun when the King fell on the battlefield, and sixteen more years of it lay ahead of those who shouldered the responsibilities he left behind him; yet in 1630 Sweden had for so long been a state at war, the national energies had for so long been harnessed to a military machine, that the German war meant merely the intensification of exertions with which the country was already in a measure familiar. The strain was nevertheless felt severely, both in the drain of manpower and in the weight of taxation. Year after year the King's commissioners came round the country to pick men for the militia; the age-limits for service grew wider; and in the rotas from which men were chosen the upper age-limit was in 1620 abolished altogether, so that one rota is actually said to have included a centenarian.[3] And though some care was taken to choose those of the able-bodied who could best be spared, there must have been many instances in which the running of a farm was made difficult, or appreciably less efficient. The number of deserters in the latter portion of the reign tells its own tale.[4] As early as 1617, of twenty-three peasants on the rota for Tjust hundred, five were taken by the King's sergeants, together with two farm boys and a tramp; and in 1622 it was said they were recruiting mere youths and boys.[5] In Medelpad in 1629 the loss of men through the wars is said to have been so considerable that emigration from the province was forbidden and the incoming Finns were doubly welcome to the

[1] See above, Vol. I, pp. 115-19, for *skjutsning*.

[2] N. Forssell, *Svenska postverkets historia*, pp. 1-40; Odhner, pp. 255-6. The conquests in Germany led to Sweden's taking over the Taxis system in the areas under her control.

[3] B. C:son Barkman, *Gustaf II Adolfs regementsorganisation*, p. 118.

[4] S. Sundquist, *Sveriges folkmängd på Gustav II Adolfs tid*, pp. 273-4.

[5] Cronholm, III. 573.

authorities.[1] But though many other instances of the drain of men could be cited, and though its effects were often locally severe, recent demographical investigation tends to the conclusion that the wastage has been exaggerated; that many or perhaps most of those drawn for the militia did come back; and that the strain upon the country was less intolerable in reality than it appeared to be in the minds of contemporaries.[2]

Yet, after all, a burden is as heavy as it feels; and the Swedes of Gustav Adolf's day felt it to be very heavy. In particular they groaned under the ever-increasing taxation of the 'twenties. And they showed their resentment. They showed it by tumults, riots and petty rebellions: from 1623 onwards there was scarcely a year when some disturbance of a more or less serious character did not take place. In 1623 there was trouble in Dalarna; in 1624 in Småland; in 1626 the peasants of Ulvsund's *län* and Noraberg rioted against the conscription, the taxes and the new copper coinage, and the ringleaders were deported to Ingria. In the same year Reval obstinately refused to levy the Little Toll. In 1627 came a disturbance in Orsa (Dalarna) led by a German tailor of chiliastic leanings: he was impaled at the Kopparberg, and four of his associates were deported to Ingria. In 1628 two *härader* in Västergötland refused to pay taxes, and the peasants of Norra and Södra Möre raised a tumult: every tenth man was deported to Ingria. In 1629 there was more trouble in Dalarna, and again in 1631, when there was resistance to conscription; and in the last year of the reign the Dalesmen were voicing angry complaints against the tyrannous procedures of the tax-gatherers.[3] And it was not only from the peasantry that complaints arose. The burghers protested violently on occasion[4]; and even among the aristocracy there were warnings to be heard. Gabriel Gustafsson Oxenstierna, for instance, was writing to his brother the chancellor in 1628 of the exhaustion of the country, and he painted a still darker picture in a celebrated letter of April 1631.[5] And though Axel Oxenstierna on this occasion took

[1] R. Gothe, *Medelpads Finnmarker*, p. 39.

[2] S. Sundquist, *Finlands folkmängd och bebyggelse i början av 1600-talet*, pp. 19-20.

[3] For all these disturbances, see *AOSB*, II. III. 69, 111-12, 155, 159, 160, 204, 251; Galt, p. 56; *RRP*, I. xvii-xix, 22 and *note* 3, II. 170; *Abraham Brahes tidebok*, pp. 164, 182; Geijer, III. 49; Cronholm, III. 567 *note* 1; E. Ingers, *Bonden i svensk historia*, I. 245; Ahnlund, *Oxenstierna*, p. 262.

[4] See S. Arnoldsson, *Krigspropagandan i Sverige före trettioåriga kriget*, pp. 23-5.

[5] *AOSB*, II. III. 169, 210, 218-21.

the line that the burdens must be borne, however heavy they might be, even he had noted signs of war-weariness two years earlier.[1] In some parts of Sweden, at least, the 'twenties showed a progressive impoverishment which was not all to be ascribed to indifferent harvests.[2] The statisticians of a later age have indeed assured us that the number of farms which were deserted, or incapable of paying tax, was not unduly large, at least in Sweden proper[3]; but this is a consolation which contemporaries do not seem to have appreciated. The King must have his money and his men, despite the audible groans of his lieges; and though he could on occasion be moved to compassion, and permit mitigations in particular cases, in general he was quite relentless. His subjects must exert themselves to the very limit of their capacity: in his own harsh words, '*nec tantum quid debeant, sed quid possint subditi*'.[4]

The peasant's plight, however, was not the result simply of the impoverishment of his material and human resources. The King's new financial techniques exposed him to social and political dangers which were even more disturbing, because more likely to be permanent. The system of tax-farming put him very largely at the mercy of the farmers, for not merely did it encourage extortion, but very often it endowed the farmer with the functions of a royal official. The farmer took the place of the bailiff, and was thus able to interpose in his own person between the aggrieved peasant and the central government, and perhaps to exercise unfair pressure upon the course of justice, if the matter should come to court. Another danger was the practice of paying a part of the wages of the army by assigning to officers the revenues (or a part of them) due from certain farms to the crown—a practice which led quite early to attempts to squeeze the peasant off the farm altogether.[5] Worst of all were the dangers from *förläningar* to the nobility, and from donations and *frälseköp*. If the characteristic sin of the age were indeed, as Baazius asserted,[6] the oppression of the poor by the rich, it was here that it was most apparent and notorious. The tax-peasant whose taxes were assigned or donated to a nobleman found himself in a position in which it might behove him to be constantly

[1] *AOSB*, I. IV. 703; *cf.* I. VI. 320.
[2] D. Hannerberg, *Närkes boskapsbestånd på 1620- och 1630-talen*, *passim*.
[3] Sundquist, *Sveriges folkmängd*, p. 13; but *cf.* Lagerstedt, *Näringsliv*, p. 25.
[4] Ahnlund, *Ståndsriksdagens utdaning*, p. 176.
[5] Stiernman, I. 770-1; *SILR*, p. 166: for later developments, see Wittrock, *Regering och allmoge under Kristinas egen styrelse*, pp. 9, 26.
[6] Lundin, *Baazius*, p. 15.

on his guard against a sustained and insidious attempt to transform him into a *frälsebonde*. The nobleman who bought for cash down the crown's revenues from a group of tax-farms might only too easily succumb to the temptation to better his bargain by endeavouring to annex those services which only the *frälsebonde* was obliged to give to him. The emergence in the sixteenth century of the doctrine that the King was the ultimate owner of all land, while the peasant's right of property was no more than a *dominium utile*, was comparatively innocuous as long as taxes were paid by the peasant direct to the crown. But when the taxes were allocated to a nobleman, or bought by him, there was a very real risk that the purchaser might try to make good the contention that the King had surrendered not only the income but also the *dominium*, and in virtue of this notion might hold himself free to do the very thing which the terms of his *förläning* or his purchase forbade him to do—namely, to deprive the peasant of his birthright.[1] It was unclear, moreover—as it still is—whether the noble had the right to collect from the tax-peasant the indeterminate as well as the determinate revenues, whether he was entitled to claim the labour-services which the crown had exacted, and whether he was justified in taking for himself the amount of any new and extraordinary taxes to which the *riksdag* might assent.[2] In 1647 peasants acquired by de Geer through *frälsekop* would be complaining of 'innumerable' labour-services, 'heavy and unusual' *corvées*.[3] In 1643 *skattefrälsebönder* lamented that nobles deliberately devastated their woodlands, so that they might buy up the birthright of the peasants they thus impoverished and turn their land into *frälsejord*.[4] In 1649 the nobility were accused of establishing cottars 'to the prejudice of the villagers', and of maintaining them by force.[5] But the grievances of the 'forties were no new growth: their roots stretched back to Gustav Adolf's time. Already in 1618 Jasper Matsson Kruus (who had a good

[1] P. von Törne, *Inverkningar av förläningsväsendet på jordbesittningsförhållandena före och efter reduktionen*, pp. 7-12, 61; Brännman, p. 114; *cf.* C. Weibull, *Drottning Christina*, pp. 51-4.

[2] von Törne, pp. 28-37, 41-3; Brännman, pp. 165-7. But see the review of Brännman in *Historisk Tidskrift* (1952) by S. A. Nilsson, especially pp. 41-4, which challenges some of Brännman's conclusions on this point. For some of the methods whereby the nobility tried to retain the crown's indeterminate revenues for themselves, see R. Swedlund, *Grev- och friherreskapen*, p. 220.

[3] G. Wittrock, *Regering och allmoge under Kristinas egen styrelse*, p. 63, and *cf. ibid.*, 188. For a lament in verse, from 1645, R. Gothe, *Medelpads finnmarker*, p. 52.

[4] Elgeskog, p. 107.

[5] Wittrock, *op. cit.*, pp. 109-10; for their motives, Elgeskog, pp. 77-8.

name as a humane landlord) made no distinction in treatment between his old *frälsebönder* and the peasants on the lands which had been donated to him. Very often, it seems, the noble purchasers of taxes asserted and illegally enforced the crown's right of *skattevrak—i.e.* they confiscated the farms of those who were three years in arrear with their taxes; and there are complaints that they demanded excessive sums from tax-peasants in order to drive them into default.[1] As early as 1624 the King granted letters of protection to some peasants in Uppland (former crown-peasants) living on land which had been sold to Gabriel Bengtsson Oxenstierna, in order to safeguard them against his attempts to extort from them heavier dues and services than they had been bound to render to the crown.[2] And in December 1627 a royal 'resolution and declaration' proclaimed that it was illegal to take away the rights of the tax-peasants or drive them from their farms.[3] This was no more than to enunciate a legal commonplace; and it is significant that Gustav Adolf should have felt that it needed to be enunciated. The peasants' best defence against illegalities of this sort lay in the still-vigorous democracy of the hundred-court (*häradsting*). There were, no doubt, not a few instances in which the legal dexterity or covert menaces of the lord were too many for the jurors; and the lord's right to have recourse to the *hovrätt* as a *forum privilegiatum* also gave him an advantage. But there is ample evidence to show that the *häradsting*, even in the more adverse conditions of twenty years later, maintained the rights of the peasantry with remarkable staunchness and success, and that the *hovrätt* upheld their decisions, or gave judgment in first instance, with admirable impartiality.[4]

The dangers to peasant rights were no doubt most in evidence when a noble was anxious to provide himself with a reserve of labour in order to extend demesne farming; and the chorus of complaints about the abuses connected with the setting up of manors (*sätesgårdar*) would suggest that the two things were closely correlated. But this does not seem to have been the case. Where the manor was created with the genuine intention that it should be a family seat, there was very often an increase in demesne farming: strips would be consolidated, by exchange, purchase or eviction; roads would be redrawn; hamlets would disappear from the map. But

[1] von Törne, p. 22; Brännman, p. 164.

[2] Hallenberg, V. 144-5.

[3] von Törne, p. 26; Hedenius, p. 13.

[4] On all this, see H. Munktell, *Till frågan om böndernas ställning vid 1600-talets mitt*, *passim*.

such cases were still comparatively few. The tendency towards a consolidation of noble land into large blocks made only slow headway. Men who invested in *frälseköp* no doubt tried to buy revenues from land adjacent to their own, and in part succeeded; but payment for state service by *förläning* usually implied a scattering of sources of revenue, since the choice of which revenues to hand over was in the hands of the treasury, and not of the recipient; and above all the custom of dividing up the inheritance tended to break down the great estates soon after they were built up. In any case, many manors were farmed by tenants on a share-basis; some were let on lease; and some were wholly bogus, mere tax-dodging devices: the owner would furbish up a derelict building and proclaim it a manor—hence the expression 'to make a manor with half a drum of paint'. In view of these things, the nobility's claim that the transference of land to their control implied better utilization must be treated with some reserve, though it suited the crown to believe it. It seems, moreover, that the creation of great estates was often followed by the replacement of tillage by pastoral farming.[1]

Nevertheless, it has been estimated that by the mid-century perhaps eight per cent. of the farms in Sweden were included in great estates; and it is certain that the peasants looked upon the formation of manors with alarm. They saw ahead of them the terrifying prospect of a degradation of status and a whittling away of rights which would end in reducing them to the hopeless servitude of the peasants of the Baltic provinces. Even in 1624 Peder Galt, despite his living in one of the most vulnerable social glasshouses in Europe, did not hesitate to cast a stone at conditions in Sweden: it was intended, he wrote, to reduce the peasantry to a Livonian level.[2] The conquest of the Baltic provinces familiarized those of the Swedish nobility who were granted estates there with a debased social order which contrasted sharply with the traditional freedom of their native country. Their association with Estonia and Livonia probably dulled their sensibility and heightened their class-feeling, and the German wars must often have hardened them and implanted in them a military arrogance. However that may be, Gustav Adolf's reign paved the way for social conflict and a real struggle of classes.

[1] For the above, see Heckscher, I. 322, 328, 333; von Törne, pp. 62-93; Lagerstedt, *Näringsliv*, pp. 48, 62, 64-70; Elgeskog, pp. 78-9.

[2] Galt, p. 107. For social conditions in the Baltic provinces, see J. Vasar, *Utvecklingen av böndernas rättsläge i Estland*, pp. 25-33; H. Sepp, *Bidrag till Ingermanlands historia under 1600-talet*, pp. 75-7; Brännman, p. 179.

It put the peasantry upon a road which, if pursued, would have led to their enchainment and would have threatened the freeholder with a *servitus*.[1] As early as the *riksdag* of 1634 the Estate of the Peasantry was making violent attacks upon the nobility, demanding a *reduktion*, clamouring for a curtailment of noble privileges, and accusing the aristocracy of planning to reduce them to serfdom or slavery.[2] 'They know', said a spokesman of the peasants in 1650, 'that in other lands the commonalty are slaves; they fear the like fate for themselves, who are nevertheless born a free people.' [3] And Oxenstierna, a moderate on social questions, could say only, 'though they are *glebae adscripti*, yet are they not slaves'.[4] But when the nobleman was allowed to maintain his private prison, when the traditional right of the head of the household to administer correction was transformed into a nobleman's use of the wooden horse, and other Teutonic tortures brought home from the wars, the peasant might well feel that the time had come to stand up for his liberty.[5] Had the trends which grew so marked after 1632 been allowed to develop to their logical conclusion—had the monarchy not intervened, in three successive reigns, to check the evils which had arisen from its own policy—Sweden might have undergone in the seventeenth century a social revolution which perhaps only another revolution could have undone. By 1650 the first Estate would be faced with concerted action against it by the other three, while the crown for its own ends hallooed them to the attack.

There was, it is true, another side to the picture. The power and privileges of the noble were used, in some instances, not to exploit their peasantry but rather to secure their well-being. Per Brahe, whose county of Visingborg, with its 747 farms, covered an area as big as Mecklenburg, was an outstanding example of this sort of benevolent despotism. If he spoke of himself in much the same style as a prince of the Empire would have employed, if he maintained his own guard in his own uniform, if he appointed a council of regency against the contingency of his demise, or to function in his absence, he used his rights and immunities to protect his 'subjects' from military service and other state burdens; he cared

[1] As the Clergy put it in 1650: 'For he who owns the land and the farms rules the country; and thereby is introduced a *servitus*.'

[2] B. Lövgren, *Ståndsstridens uppkomst*, pp. 8-9. It was probably the clash of classes which prevented the Swedish Estates from using the situation created by the alienation of royal revenues to establish full parliamentary control of finance.

[3] Wittrock, *op. cit.*, p. 165.

[4] Quoted in Suolahti, p. 137.

[5] Wittrock, pp. 187, 228, 232.

for their education; he planted the whole countryside with fruit-trees; and in general took so intelligent and kindly an interest in his people that the peasants still remembered him with affection at the end of the eighteenth century: the phrase 'in the count's time' has become a regular proverbial expression, signifying 'in a happy hour'.[1] Such landlords were no doubt a small minority; yet the nobility as a class did not lack defenders, even outside their own order.[2] To many of the clergy—who in this showed themselves good Lutherans—it seemed to be a duty to preach acquiescence in social distinctions, even though they might be deepening to abuses, and to bring the common man to a sense of the God-ordained nature of the institution, not of monarchy only, but of aristocracy too. Elias Terserus, endeavouring to wean the Dalesmen from hostility to the nobility, Paulinus in his *Ethica*, Johannes Matthiae at the critical *riksdag* of 1650, Rudbeckius himself upon occasion, all took the same line.[3] And indeed much could be urged in their favour. If their pretensions were high, so too was their sense of public duty. If they claimed as of right a monopoly of the leading positions in the civil and military service of the crown, they were for long the only class in the country which was trained to fill such positions effectively. Recruitment from below, however much the older families might dislike it, would preserve them from inbreeding and degeneration, and would in the end make of them a real aristocracy of talent—the only ruling aristocracy in modern times, perhaps, which can stand comparison for political ability, addiction to state-service and many-sided capacity with the aristocracy of eighteenth-century England.

What then was the attitude of Gustav Adolf to the nobility's social pretensions? Was it merely financial exigencies that led him to *frälseköp*, and to those other measures which redounded so greatly to their advantage? To some extent the events of 1612 had already provided the answer to these questions. Gustav Adolf had obtained the throne by the grace of Oxenstierna and the nobility, at the price of acquiescing in the terms of the Charter, and upon the clear understanding that he would treat his nobility better than they had

[1] E. Fries, *Svenska adelns familjelif*, I. 90-4; S. Carlsson, *Mellan Bolmen och Holaveden*, p. 56.

[2] For Schering Rosenhane's defence of his fellow-nobles (1650), see Lagerstedt, *Näringsliv*, p. 70.

[3] N. Ahnlund, *Ståndsriksdagens utdaning*, pp. 55, 126; J. A. Almquist, *Den civila lokalförvaltningen*, pp. 52-4; Wittrock, *Regering och allmoge under Kristinas egen styrelse*, p. 169.

been treated by his father. A reconciliation with the first Estate was inevitable if the monarchy were not to expose itself to the danger of a revival of the oligarchic republicanism of Erik Sparre. And in the first few years of the reign the process of 'healing and settling' was indeed carried through with sufficient success to blunt the edge of Sigismund's intrigues and appreciably to reduce the number of aristocratic exiles.

Yet it is clear that Gustav Adolf, unlike his father, had no fear of his nobility: at all events in the latter half of the reign. His personal pre-eminence was so assured, his self-confidence was so great, that he felt himself master of the situation, and remained untroubled by any notion that the nobility might one day again occlude the monarchy. If it had not been so, he could never have contemplated the ultimate transference of all the crown lands into other, and mainly noble, hands; nor would he, perhaps, have framed the Form of Government as he did. And because he did not fear them, he had no hesitation in demanding sacrifices of them. The large infringements of *frälse* which the new taxation after 1620 involved would not have been tolerated by the nobility of an earlier age, nor attempted, perhaps, by any earlier Vasa. From time to time the Estate, as it reluctantly acquiesced in some new imposition, would make requests that their acquiescence should not be regarded as a precedent, and that the King or the *råd* should guarantee that the demands upon them would not be repeated.[1] Such requests were invariably rejected—on occasion with considerable brusqueness. And in one famous instance, when in January 1627 the nobility made a grant upon almost the same conditions as applied to the *ofrälse* Estates, they met with a rebuff which could only have been administered by a King who was supremely sure of himself. The first Estate had accompanied their grant with a resolution in which they prayed that it might not be regarded as a precedent, and had added that they made it 'of their affection and good dispositions' (*av affektion och benägenhet*). But Gustav Adolf was by no means prepared to accept the implication that his subjects were conferring a favour upon him. He replied sharply that he had no need of their affection or good dispositions, but that what they had done had been in virtue of the duty and fidelity which they owed him.[2]

But though the King could use this tone on occasion, his relations

[1] *SRARP*, I. 13, 52, 204; *RRP*, II. 209-11; Stiernman, I. 825-7.
[2] *AOSB*, II. III. 111.

with his nobility were on the whole cordial; and despite the frequent infringement of their fiscal immunities, his reign saw the consolidation, and even the improvement, of their purely social privileges. At the first *riksdag* of the reign, in December 1611 and January 1612, he had granted them a new code of privileges as part of the general constitutional settlement which was to sponge away the record of Karl IX. The privileges of 1612 are therefore in great part concerned with the protection of the nobility against what they considered to be the malpractices of the preceding reign: conviction for treason was not to carry with it corruption of blood; forfeited estates were to go to next-of-kin, and not to the crown; security was given against delations; in capital cases nobles were to be tried by their peers, and so forth. But in addition they gained new advantages: farms *inom rå och rör* were henceforth to be equated with manors for fiscal purposes; better privileges were accorded for farms within the mile of freedom (for instance, in regard to *corvées*); and it was laid down that conscription on farms outside the mile of freedom should be at half the rate obtaining for tax- and crown-peasants. They secured confirmation of their rights to church patronage, of their exemption from customs dues, of their right to maintain a 'reasonable' number of defence-men, and of their right to hunt on their own estates. Though the nobility accepted the position that *frälsejord* might be laid under taxation if its owner were unable to do his *rusttjänst*, they established the converse proposition that tax-land inherited by a nobleman should thereby acquire *frälse*. But even at this exceptionally favourable moment they failed to obtain the assent of the crown to their demand that extraordinary aids should be collected on the crown's behalf by their own bailiffs; and they were equally unsuccessful in a proposal that the poorer members of the Estate might be allowed to club together to provide a single cavalryman.[1]

It became apparent, moreover, that the King was not unaware of the ways in which the nobility strained the privileges which were accorded them. At the end of 1612, Michil Olofsson drew up for Gustav Adolf a draft of a possible limitation of privileges, in consequence of these malpractices.[2] Besides providing a conspectus

[1] For the demands of the nobility, see *SRDA*, I. 102-9; for the text of their privileges, *SRDA*, I. 111-23; for comments, C. Öhlander, *Bidrag till de adliga privilegiernas historia*, pp. 19-29, 62; Swenne, pp. 8-11, 78-85.

[2] *SRDA*, I. 267-75. For a discussion of this, see S. A. Nilsson, *Reaktionen mot systemskiftet 1611*, *passim*.

of current abuses, this draft enunciates very plainly the principle that the crown must reserve the right to resume its grants of land if its favours are abused, and in particular may lay land once more under taxation if its owner does not render proper *rusttjänst*. The draft was never promulgated; and it might perhaps have been dismissed as the last effort of the men of Karl IX's day to stem the new current, if it were not that the King himself revived many of these complaints in 1617. He was especially concerned at the evasion by *frälsebönder* of the obligation of *skjutsning*, and at the abuses resulting from the nobility's privileges in regard to arrest and trial for serious crimes. As to the latter point, the nobility made some necessary concessions, though not till 1619; and two years later Gustav Adolf curtailed another abuse by depriving them of their right to collect fines levied by royal courts on their peasants.[1] But no action was taken upon the burning question of what was to happen when a woman of the nobility married, or committed fornication with, an *ofrälse* man; though both King and nobility had raised this point in 1617.

In 1622, however, it became necessary to strike a bargain with the first Estate. The King was imposing the Little Toll for the first time; he was determined that the nobility and their peasants should pay it; and to purchase their consent he was prepared to acquiesce in some of their proposals. He agreed, therefore, to a lowering of the rate of *rusttjänst*,[2] and conceded the demand he had refused in 1612: henceforward nobles whose estates did not yield revenues equal to the production of half a cavalryman at the standard rate might combine, two by two, to render their service. And henceforward the woman of noble birth who took to loose living was to lose her property (though not, as the Estate had wished, be exiled); the nobleman who committed fornication with his betrothed (a very frequent practice among the lower classes) would find that both he and she were mulcted of two years' income for the benefit of the poor; the same penalty would be enacted for marriage against the will of parents or guardians; and, finally, marriage with a person of *ofrälse* condition would involve forfeiture of landed estate, not to the crown but to next-of-kin.[3]

[1] Styffe, pp. 236-7; *SRDA*, II. 81, 141; J. Schmedemann, *Kongl. Stadgar*, ... [*etc.*] ... *Angående Justitiae och Executions-Ährende*, I. 173-81; Stiernman, *CPO*, I. 688-90; Hallenberg, IV. 568-70, 636-8; Cronholm, III. 542-52; Öhlander, pp. 30-4, 60. For abuses connected with fines, see Hallenberg, II. 863; Waaranen, *Samling*, IV. 125; Öhlander, p. 57.

[2] For a fuller treatment of the question of *rusttjänst*, see below, Chapter III.

[3] Öhlander, p. 35; Swenne, pp. 10-11.

Thus the King obtained the consent of the nobility to a violation of their fiscal immunities by assenting to a tightening-up of the social rules governing the behaviour of the aristocracy. By doing so, he abandoned some claims which the crown had long maintained; but his gain in immediate revenue was far in excess of the income that might be expected from any prospective forfeitures. The nobility, on their side, really made less financial sacrifice than might appear, since they probably recouped themselves (at least in part) from their peasants [1]; while on the other hand they made good the position that *frälse* inhered in land, at the same time as the concession about co-operative *rusttjänst* established their alternative contention that nobility was a matter of birth rather than of service duly performed. The peerage, as we shall see, was becoming more readily accessible from below; but the grant of privileges of 1622 at least ensured that those who reached it should hold themselves aloof from the *ofrälse* world from which they had emerged; it strengthened the corporate spirit of the aristocracy; and by isolating them socially it prepared the way for the political isolation which overtook them in 1650 and 1680. And with this reinforcing of their class-consciousness came, perhaps, a revival of the old feelings of antagonism towards the crown. As long as Gustav Adolf lived, with Axel Oxenstierna as his most intimate adviser, this was not apparent, and possibly it was not consciously felt: the King's personality, the chancellor's authority within his own order, the dangers from abroad, combined to persuade the first Estate to subordinate class-interest to the claims of patriotism.[2] But the debates on the Form of Government revealed its re-emergence; and Axel Oxenstierna himself was later reported to have said that 'now that God, by Gustav Adolf's death, had given them back their liberty, they would not let go of it again in a hurry'.[3] And all the old fear of a hereditary monarchy was to appear when, upon the election of Karl Gustav as heir apparent, Jakob de la Gardie cried out that his mind misgave him 'that we are making slaves of ourselves'.[4]

In Gustav Adolf's time a profound change began to overtake the social structure of the aristocracy. The *Riddarhusordning* [5] had

[1] Brännman, pp. 21 *note* 89, 155; von Törne, p. 41.

[2] See, *e.g.*, Ahnlund, *Oxenstierna*, pp. 418, 452-5.

[3] Lövgren, *Ståndsstridens uppkomst*, p. 27, and *cf.* pp. 10-11. The story comes from Peder Vibe, the Danish Resident.

[4] F. F. Carlson, *Sveriges historia under konungarne af pfalziska huset*, II. 96.

[5] See above, Vol. I, pp. 293-6.

eliminated a large number of families who lacked the material resources to maintain a gentlemanly standard of life; but their disappearance was more than offset by the arrival of a new nobility with no other title to acceptance than a long purse or the favour of the sovereign. The second quarter of the century saw a very large increase in the membership of the *Riddarhus*: between 1626 and 1632 the number of families represented in it rose from 126 to 187. For the first time the peerage was rapidly recruited from below. The successful soldier, even of foreign birth,[1] the diplomat,[2] the civil servant,[3] the merchant or the financier,[4] and even the humble mathematician or medico,[5] might now end his career with a patent of nobility, and a new high-sounding surname. Sweden now offered a career open to talents; a peerage was now the reasonable expectation of any man, whatever his origin, who gave the state distinguished service. The ennoblement of Skytte had led the way. The Oxenstiernas had not liked it, and their jealousy of Skytte long remained a factor in domestic politics [6]; but no one had ventured to show resentment at the promotion of Gustav Adolf's old tutor, and Skytte had married his daughter to a Gyllenstierna, and his brother to a Bååt.[7] But the flood of peerages in the late 'twenties was not welcomed. The rise of Salvius provoked stronger feelings than the rise of Skytte; probably because Skytte's case had been viewed as an exceptional incident, unlikely to be repeated, while that of Salvius showed ominous signs of being typical. Son of the town-clerk of Strängnäs, educated (typically for his generation) first at Uppsala, then abroad, married to a rich goldsmith's widow, Salvius used his opportunities (despite the low rates of pay said to be prevalent in the Swedish service) [8] to build up a great fortune; and in due course became *hovråd*, *riksråd*, and eventually baron, to the intense indignation of many of the old families, who possibly discerned, in careers like his, some danger of a revival of the abhorred 'rule of secretaries'.[9] An

[1] *e.g.* Hamilton, Fleetwood, Ramsay, Douglas.
[2] *e.g.* Anders Svensson, Salvius, Tungel.
[3] *e.g.* Johannes Nicodemi, Mårten Augustinsson.
[4] *e.g.* de Geer, Wewetzer, Erik Larsson, Peder Gudmundsson.
[5] *e.g.* Anders and Olof Bure.
[6] See P. Sondén, *Johan Skytte och Oxenstiernorna*, *passim*.
[7] *AOSB*, II. III. 76, II. III. 200; *Peder Galts Depescher*, p. 97.
[8] *Arkiv*, II. 46. Grubbe wrote to Oxenstierna on 8 September 1630: 'No one, moreover, will serve for the wages we pay, and yet H.M. thinks they are too high.' They were high enough, all the same, for civil servants to invest in crown lands and revenues.
[9] For Salvius, see Lundgren, *Johan Adler Salvius*, *passim*.

impressive proportion of the new creations, moreover, were not Swedes by birth: they were Germans, Dutchmen, Balts or Scots, who had entered Gustav Adolf's service in order to carve out a career: rough soldiers of fortune, some of them, or sharp financiers—not all of them of unimpeachable honesty.[1] Of all the families introduced into the *Riddarhus* since 1626, 42½ per cent. have been of foreign birth; between 1611 and 1680, of 670 new peerages, no less than 360 went to foreigners, 180 to men of burgher origins (whether Swedish or foreign), 190 to civil servants; and it was Gustav Adolf who initiated these developments.[2] By the 1640's the debates of the Nobility had become too polygot for the comprehension of the Burghers and Peasants.

Between the old aristocracy and the new—between the ennobled and those of noble birth—social tension was mounting; and it would reach a climax in the years around 1650. It was, indeed, mitigated to some extent by the emergence of a system of clientelage: Salvius took Axel Oxenstierna as his 'patron', as Grubbe did also.[3] It was mitigated too, perhaps, by the habit of sending the sons of the nobility to the university in the charge of a preceptor or *informator*; for the bonds of friendship between pupil and preceptor might survive, even though the preceptor, assisted by his pupil's favour, made so good a career for himself as eventually to join him in the *Riddarhus*: many of the leading Swedish diplomats of the 'fifties, for instance, were linked by ties of friendship with Erik Oxenstierna because they had all been at Uppsala together.[4] But such mitigations could not remove a fundamental antagonism. And side by side with it was the antagonism between the great magnates and the middling and lesser nobility—an antagonism which was independent of questions of lineage, and which was probably sharpened by the tripartite division of the first Estate, effected by the *Riddarhusordning* of 1626.[5] The handful of counts and barons, the rather larger handful of *råd*-families, looked down on the rest of the nobility, even though they might boast an ancestry of equal or

[1] The case of Abraham Sixt van Sandelier, created a baron by Gustav Adolf, patent subsequently annulled: Swedlund, pp. 120-1.

[2] Heckscher, *Svenskt och utländskt under Sveriges storhetstid*, p. 2; Söderberg, *Den namnlösa medelklassen*, p. 94.

[3] *Arkiv*, II. 313; Lundgren, *Salvius*, pp. 9, 139; *cf.* Söderberg, *op. cit.*, pp. 105-7.

[4] *e.g.* Lars Cantersten, Magnus Dureel, Israel Lagerfelt, Harald Appelboom: E. Fries, *Erik Oxenstierna*, pp. 8, 16.

[5] See, *e.g.*, Erik Oxenstierna's remarks in 1655, in Fries, *op. cit.*, pp. 190-1.

greater antiquity; and it appears as if the arrogance of this group of magnates were tending to increase. Erik Rålamb defied Gustav Adolf himself, when ordered to wait at the King's table [1]; and though *mésalliance* with the lower orders was no longer a burning question, it was significant that controversy shifted to the consequences of a marriage between a count's daughter and a simple nobleman.[2] The aristocracy's attitude to the lower orders appeared in their refusal any longer to send their sons to be educated in the same schools as the sons of their non-noble neighbours [3]; and even so humane and scholarly a person as Oxenstierna could dismiss an academic with the contemptuous remark: 'What is an academic person? A gown, a pair of breeches, and a handful of books.' [4] But the cleavage within the nobility was not only between high and low, or between *parvenu* and aristocrat; it was also a cleavage of generations. The young men of rank had moved fast and far ahead of their fathers, and would no longer be content, as they had been, to 'take a look into the women's quarters, feed the beagles and greyhounds, go a-coursing, set bait for foxes, and traps for wolves, and, if the weather be unfit for these things, sit at home and drink tobacco'.[5] The contrast of generations appears vividly when, for example, the portrait of Karl Karlsson Gyllenhielm is set side by side with that of Herman Wrangel. The one, ruddy, plain, solid and provincial, with his old-fashioned bushy beard and half-rustic, half-nautical air; the other, sallow, curled, elegant, half-Frenchified, half-Italianate, every inch the cosmopolitan aristocrat. The young nobles of the 'thirties and 'forties knew more of the world outside Sweden than their fathers had known, and not only because they explored it at the sword's point. The habit of the Grand Tour was already being formed, and to the men of Kristina's court Italy was something more than the centre of popery, or a former tributary of the Goths. They brought back libraries and pictures from their travels; the most wealthy of them retained their own court-painters; their wives were now usually literate, and well able to negotiate with their agents abroad for the purchase of the latest French fashions. The concentration of government in Stockholm, which was one

[1] *Handskrifter rörande Skandinaviens historia*, VIII. 12-13, for this affair.

[2] Fries, *Svenska adelns familjelif*, I. 110; S. Carlsson, *Ståndscirkulation*, p. 20.

[3] W. Karlson, *Kungligt, adligt, lärt och lekt*, pp. 199-206; W. Sjöstrand, *Grunddragen av den militära undervisningens . . . utvecklingshistoria*, p. 159.

[4] Wittrock, *Regering och allmoge under Kristinas egen styrelse*, p. 216.

[5] *Svenska folket genom tiderna*, IV. 23.

effect of the administrative reforms of the reign, led to a concentration of social life in the capital, and the building of town-residences for those whom government business compelled to live there. There are signs, before the end of Gustav Adolf's reign, of a housing-shortage among such people; and the acquisition—or (a novelty, this) the leasing—of country houses conveniently close to Stockholm became an object of concern to noble families.[1]

They had not yet, perhaps, mastered the art of being comfortable: in 1634 Ogier found their houses chilly and bare; but they were learning fast, and they spent lavishly on luxuries: a generation later the inventory of Ebba Brahe's possessions would give an impressive idea of the magnitude of their expenditure upon furniture, stuffs, jewels and objects of art[2]; and in 1644 the government would find it necessary to issue an ordinance designed to restrain extravagance in dress, entertainment and marriage-portions.[3] Their wealth, reinforced by the plunder of the wars, no doubt continued in part to be invested in trading companies and ships, and still more in land, and was just beginning to be invested in industry; but the bulk of it went upon building, and upon imported luxuries, and they were not seldom financially embarrassed by reckless indulgence in prestige-spending. Sweden would probably have followed at the fringe of the great currents of European fashion and manners, even had the war never been fought. But the war brought the country nearer to the centre of the stream; it made the hectic forcing-house culture of Kristina's court a possibility; it enabled Sweden to produce, in Magnus Gabriel de la Gardie, a nobleman whose real achievement might be summed up, a little unkindly, by saying that he would have excited no remark at the court of Louis XIV.

Yet, though the topmost level of Swedish society was thus in process of acquiring a comparatively high polish, the old ways persisted side by side with the new. Barbaric amusements alternated incongruously, even in Kristina's time, with the new ballets and operas.[4] If the war brought to Sweden the social arts and the polite accomplishments, it brought also other less desirable qualities: the vulgar ostentation of riches, the mentality of the adventurer, and a

[1] For the above, see Fries, *Svenska adelns familjelif*, pp. 29, 30, 40, 82, 86; *id.*, *Erik Oxenstierna*, pp. 23, 27; Sjöstrand, pp. 191-5; Lagerstedt, *Näringsliv*, p. 72; Ahnlund, *Oxenstierna*, p. 541.

[2] W. Karlson, *Ebba Brahes hem, passim.*

[3] Karlson, *Kungligt, adligt, lärt och lekt*, p. 171.

[4] *Johan Ekeblads brev*, I. 42, 59, 61, 66, 73-4.

strain of cruelty and brutality which is perceptible in the age of Kristina and Karl X Gustav. The aristocracy had become militarized; their education was increasingly coloured by training for war [1]; and in the standing army, where perhaps 500 officers' commissions were reserved to them, they found a favoured field for their ambitions.[2] A generation was to return home from Germany which had received its education in the school of the Thirty Years' War, had learned honesty at free-quarters, and morality in the baggage-train; a generation flushed with military success and indurated to the miseries of the rabble. And that generation, if it had ever felt the need to find a scapegoat for sins of which (to do it justice) it was scarcely conscious, might perhaps have claimed Gustav Adolf as its father.

Nevertheless, the material advance was notable, and it was not confined to the nobility. It was to be seen, for instance, in the burghers. Although the leading part in the expansion of Swedish trade during Gustav Adolf's reign had been taken by foreigners, the native merchants had also had their share. They were, moreover, increasingly associated with the foreign incomers in partnerships to farm revenues or lease crown property [3]; and it is clear that they must now have included among their numbers some men of substantial wealth. Although immigrants such as Wewetzer or de Geer were ultimately ennobled, their presence in Sweden raised the social consequence of the burgher class as a whole; and when a native Swedish merchant invested his savings in the purchase or lease of a portion of the King's revenues, when he therefore stepped into the place of the King's bailiffs, discharged their judicial functions, presided at the local *ting*, he made, and was conscious of making, a great social advance.[4] An increasing number of such men contracted marriages with daughters of the nobility; and the improved social position even of those who did not was reflected in a growing tendency to submit themselves to the immortalizing attentions of a portrait-painter.[5] The ordinary craftsman, too, was often a more cultured person than his predecessor of the early years of the century:

[1] Sjöstrand, *op. cit.*, pp. 110, 113, 120, 123, 171 *seqq.*, 240-3, 475.
[2] *ibid.*, 155-6. Oxenstierna estimated the number of posts reserved to the nobility at more than 800, a majority being in the armed forces. On the defects of the younger generation of officers, see Banér's views in B. Steckzén, *Johan Baner*, p. 230.
[3] *e.g.* Lindberg, *Västerviks historia*, I. 179.
[4] *ibid.*, I. 181-2.
[5] Söderberg, *Den namnlösa medelklassen*, pp. 95, 115.

his house was better furnished, and he drank claret instead of ale to his dinner.[1] The inventory of the effects of Göran Jeske, pewterer, who died in 1652 leaving 52,550 *daler*, included an item of 214 *daler* for books.[2] Such persons could call themselves educated men; and clergy and civil servants were glad enough to bind their sons apprentice to them. The government looked to them for moderate investments in its various companies, and probably did in fact attract them. The wealthier merchants were just beginning to put their money into the new forges and iron-works—though the initial capital for such undertakings for some time came from foreigners or (a new feature, this) from the nobility—and for the first time they were showing signs of investing in land: some of the crown revenues sold in *skatteköp* were bought by such persons.[3] But even yet the purchase of land was inconvenient socially and unprofitable economically, unless it were accompanied by ennoblement. Ennoblement, however, was by now far from improbable for the great merchant, especially if he could contrive to become the crown's creditor; for the crown on its side was not averse to discharging its debts to such persons cheaply by throwing in a title as a makeweight against its failure to meet its obligations in full.[4] For the lesser burghers, however, house property in the towns was still the usual placement for their money: investment in land was not yet for them.[5] The burgher class in general as yet had no great desire to exchange a town life for the country; the less so, perhaps, since life in Stockholm was becoming more agreeable. The rebuilding after the great fire of 1625 brought many improvements, and a conscious effort was made to build not only for usefulness but for appearance, and indeed for national prestige. Ogier was still disposed to be contemptuous in 1634, and the only house to win his commendation was—significantly enough—that of the foreign financier Erik Larsson von der Linde; but local poets were already extolling the beauties of Stockholm, and by the time Magalotti wrote his account of Sweden in the 'seventies he could pronounce its buildings to be unmatched outside Italy.[6] The second quarter of the century saw

[1] Löfgren, *Det svenska tenngjutarehantverkets historia*, II. 73; *cf. ibid.*, 50, 63.
[2] *ibid.*, II. 70.
[3] Almquist, *Om ärftlig besittningsrätt till jord*, p. 126.
[4] Söderberg, *op. cit.*, pp. 85, 99, 102.
[5] Löfgren, I. 313-14.
[6] M. A. Ohlsson, *Stormaktstidens privatpalats i Stockholm*, pp. 9, 12, 17-21, 56, 73, 101; *cf. Stockholms stadsprivilegiebref*, pp. 200-1; Ogier, pp. 81, 105-7. Ogier was impressed by the French manners and fashions of von der Linde's daughters.

a rapid growth in the number of Stockholm's inhabitants: from an estimated 10,000 in 1620 they rose to perhaps 40,000 in 1660. The suburbs, and especially Norrmalm, expanded [1]; and the new villas were often provided with gardens. Gardens and gardening had been virtually unknown in Sweden in Karl IX's time: under Kristina they had become a fashion.[2] The establishment of market-gardens close to Stockholm made possible a better supply of green vegetables, and the diet of the burghers probably benefited accordingly: it certainly seems to have improved in one other particular, for by the 'thirties the drinking of milk appears to have become not unusual.[3]

Even the church was better off materially in 1632 than at the beginning of the reign. The parishes had slowly recovered from the financial shock of the Reformation and had once more begun to accumulate property. The Estate of Clergy was able to promise to invest 100,000 *daler* in the Southern Company [4]; individual bishops made sizeable investments too; and a few of them were permitted, and had the means at their disposal, to indulge in *frälsekop*.[5] The average parish priest, it is true, was as poor as he had ever been: indeed, he may well have been poorer; for *frälsebönder* were often lax about paying him his tithe, and the increasing transference of land into noble hands represented a real threat to his income.[6] The arbitrary interventions of noble patrons of benefices spoiled the chances of preferment for many: and the growth of a system of clientelage, whereby the parson took the noble (or even his bailiff) for his 'patron', compromised the independence of others.[7] Between the ordinary parish priest and the great magnates of the ecclesiastical hierarchy there was now a lessening community of interest and a growing antagonism; for the parson shared the hardships of the peasant, and faced similar dangers of social oppression, while the bishops were moving socially towards the first Estate, and would

[1] G. E. Berg, *Boskapsskötsel och jordbruk i det gamla Stockholm*, p. 194.

[2] Juhlin-Dannfelt, p. 408; Lagerstedt, *Livsmedel och livsmedelproduktion*, pp. 19, 43; Karlson, *Kungligt, adligt, lärt och lekt*, p. 220.

[3] In 1636 the Stiernflycht family bought 'several litres' three or four times a week: Lagerstedt, *op. cit.*, pp. 13-14.

[4] Börjeson, *Stockholms segelsjöfart*, pp. 161-4.

[5] It is said that in Finland a good deal of the silver plundered from Germany found its way into clerical hands: Suolahti, p. 321; and in 1634 Paulinus was pleading with Oxenstierna for the assignment of some of it to Strängnäs: *AOSB.* II. XII. 55.

[6] *ibid.*, pp. 228-30.

[7] At all events, in Finland: *ibid.*, pp. 146-51.

soon look forward to the ennoblement of their children as an ordinary occurrence. If at the end of the century thirty per cent. of the clergy are estimated to have been the sons of peasants, only two of the twenty-one bishops came from peasant homes.[1] Within the Clergy, as within the Nobility, a clash between high and low was already discernible in the future; and though the church, as before, offered opportunities for social mobility, the range of upward movement was for the great majority very limited.

Nevertheless, by 1632 Swedish society had become markedly less static than in 1611. And this was especially noticeable in the rise of groups which did not fit into the official categories of society, since they did not belong to any of the four Estates. New opportunities were opening for the emergence of a professional class: most conspicuously, in diplomacy and the civil service. It is in Gustav Adolf's reign that diplomacy becomes a distinct career; and Anders Svensson is the first Swedish professional diplomat.[2] Svensson, indeed, was ultimately ennobled; and diplomacy proved to be one of the most hopeful roads to the peerage. But only a minority of diplomats could expect to reach this eminence: the majority, like the majority of chancery officials, treasury clerks, dockyard superintendents and assessors in the *Svea hovrätt*, would end their days as commoners, though their sons might conceivably be more fortunate than they. The civil service was now, no doubt, a ladder whose upper end rested on the steps of the *Riddarhus*; but it was still more an important agent in the formation of a new middle class. The evolution of a university-trained middle-class civil service, admitted to office after a preliminary examination, was not complete until the eighteenth century, and even at the beginning of the Age of Freedom considerably more than half of university students still entered the church [3]; but the emergence of the civil service as a regular profession may be said to date from Gustav Adolf's reign, and the rewards it offered undoubtedly made it attractive. Boys who would earlier have followed their father's trade, or sought a career in the church, now ate the King's bread, and became neither burghers, nor clergy, nor (unless they were fortunate) nobles. This was true, too, of many who made a career in the army; for it was still possible, during the Thirty Years' War, for the son of a peasant or a

[1] S. Carlsson, *Svensk ståndscirkulation*, pp. 27-8.

[2] E. Hildebrand, *Den svenska diplomatiens organisation i Tyskland under 1600-talet*, *passim*; *Den svenska utrikesförvaltningens historia*, p. 66.

[3] S. Carlsson, *op. cit.*, pp. 50, 65.

burgher to rise to officer's rank, and so to find himself divorced from his social origins yet denied a defined place in society.[1] It was in Gustav Adolf's time, moreover, that the law became organized as a regular profession. The legal reforms of the decade after 1611 broke with Swedish tradition by permitting the employment of advocates [2]; and though conservative prejudice was still strong against them—the draft privileges for Norrmalm in 1624 prohibited them from pleading in the municipal courts on the ground that they fleeced their clients [3]—still by the end of the reign they had made good their footing, and the closing phases of Wivallius' career suggest that they were able to make a reasonable living.[4] But it was not only in regard to advocates that the law became professionalized. The creation of the *hovarätter* ws necessarily followed by the appointment of full-time professional judges. Local justice, and judicial administration, needed trained men. As the nobility fell into the habit of delegating their duties as *lagmän* or *häradshövdingar* to deputies, those deputies (*lagläsare*) emerged as a district branch of the legal profession, and their social standing began to rise.[5] Swedish law was already taught at Uppsala [6]; and soon after the mid-century the university would produce a galaxy of distinguished jurists. And education itself was becoming a profession distinct from the church, though it was still in fact represented at the *riksdag* by the Estate of Clergy, and though the social position of professors was modest, and long remained so.[7]

These people of no particular Estate were very generally rising in the world; and they represented a strong and dynamic element of mobility within the Swedish society. Though they were as yet probably to be reckoned in hundreds rather than in thousands, it would not be long before they became sufficiently numerous to require a collective name; and the term by which they were eventually designated was paradoxical enough, for they were dubbed 'persons of estate' (*ståndspersoner*). Persons of some social standing they certainly were, occupying a middle ground distinctly above the

[1] *ibid.*, p. 22.
[2] See above, Vol. I, p. 337.
[3] *Stockholms stadsprivilegiebref*, pp. 180-200.
[4] See above, Vol. I, p. 502.
[5] S. Petrén, *Lagläsarna. Ett bidrag till det svenska domstolsväsendets historia*, especially pp. 27-32.
[6] See above, Vol. I, p. 341.
[7] In the Table of Ranks of 1714 a professor was equated with a captain in a non-ranking regiment: Carlsson, *Svensk ståndscirkulation*, p. 64.

burghers, and far above the peasants: though they might not yet be noble, they might easily become so; and they felt themselves to be, and were increasingly esteemed to be, gentlemen. They were not by any means recruited only from the professions. The bailiffs and land agents of the nobility accounted for very many of them. The emergence of others was traceable to the new developments in the iron industry. The urban communities which were arising near the mines—at Nora, for instance; or round the copper-mine at Falun—were hybrids between burghers and *bergsmän*; and already there was appearing a class of prosperous independent forge-masters and works-owners, who were not seldom founders of long-lived family businesses. Industrialists of this sort, living often in remote parts of the country and unrepresented in the Estate of Burghers, were a major civilizing influence in the backwoods: without them the Värmland of Gösta Berling, or of Geijer's *Minnen*, would have been an impossibility.

The reign of Gustav Adolf had seen the final emergence of the *riksdag* as a body of four, and no more than four, Estates. Yet before the reign came to an end this clear-cut division was already beginning to be blurred; and the class had already been born whose existence was ultimately to be the real cause of the abandonment of the Estates system. By 1632 men were moving more easily from Estate to Estate than had been possible a generation earlier; the opportunities for advancement were better and more various; and some of the most attractive of them now fell outside the official socio-political pattern. The coming of the foreigners had to some extent cut across the old distinctions: certainly it had helped to establish new standards and create new needs. The war had accelerated social change; it had put a premium on ambition and weakened the barriers against it. The nobles and the bishops, the burghers, the industrialists and the new professional class could all look forward to a future which might well be better than the past. Only the peasants fought doggedly to stand firm against the quickening current of the age.

LOUIS DE GEER

GUSTAV HORN

CHAPTER III

THE ARMY

(i) *The European Background*[1]

For much of the Middle Ages the art of war remained curiously static. The heavy-armed cavalry, which had been the military discovery of the late Empire, continued to be the decisive element in every western European army from the fourth century to the fourteenth. In pitched battles, attack predominated over defence; for the knight, unless he attacked, had no military significance. Mass and impact were more important than missile weapons. Engagements tended to resolve themselves into some hundreds or thousands of simultaneous hand-to-hand encounters; military discipline decayed; and the commander's control of the battlefield was only intermittently effective. Progress in armaments seemed to be limited by the endurance of the horse: neither the inventiveness of the craftsman nor the imagination of the general rose to innovations capable of seriously modifying the stereotyped military pattern. Feudal society had been based on the supremacy of the man-at-arms; and it owed its continued survival to a primitive technology and a petrified tactic.

The first major shock to this venerable vested interest was administered by the English bowmen at Crécy. The English long-bow was by far the most efficient missile weapon so far devised; and it transformed tactics wherever it was employed. The balance tipped in favour of the defensive: the epoch of hand-to-hand fighting drew to a close. Hard on the heels of the long-bowmen came the hand-gunners. Despite the advantages which gunfire conferred upon the besiegers of feudal strongholds, the early firearm was in a tactical point of view as clearly a defensive weapon as the long-bow. The English long-bow tactics had thriven on the rashness of a chivalry which attacked (because it could do no other

[1] For this section, see in general H. Delbrück, *Geschichte der Kriegskunst im Rahmen der politische Geschichte*, IV.; M. Jähns, *Handbuch einer Geschichte des Kriegswesens von der Urzeit bis zur Renaissance*; Sir C. Oman, *The Art of War in the Middle Ages*, I.-II.; *id.*, *The Art of War in the Sixteenth Century*; Generalstaben, *Karl XII på slagfältet*, I.; *id.*, *Sveriges Krig*, I.; O. Laskowski, *Infantry Tactics and Firing Power in XVI Century*; J. Colin, *Les Transformations de la guerre*; L. Tingsten, *Huvuddragen av medeltidens samt nya och nyare tidens krigskonst.*

than attack), and was mown down by an unprecedentedly deadly and concentrated fire before it could press its attack home. French firearms drove the English out of France by similar means—so galling the bowmen that they abandoned their natural waiting game and advanced to an attack which they were ill-equipped to carry out: as, for instance, at Formigny and Castillon.[1] Thus each of the two major military discoveries of the late Middle Ages pointed in the same direction: towards the primacy of firepower and away from the primacy of impact. And this, indeed, was the direction in which the military art was ultimately to evolve.

But the evolution was complicated, and its pace seriously delayed, by the almost accidental emergence of a quite different counter to the supremacy of the man-at-arms—a counter which (as a technical achievement) might easily have been developed at any time during the preceding millennium.[2] This was the celebrated Swiss column. The Swiss column consisted of a large body of men, several thousands strong, grouped into orderly massive rectangles. The size of each rectangle varied, for it was usually about one-third of the total infantry force available. The three outermost ranks of the column were armed with a new weapon—the eighteen-foot pike; and they wore body-armour. They were well protected against cavalry, since their great mass possessed enormous inertia and since the pike was longer than the lance. Inside the columns, behind the pikes, were rank upon rank of halberdiers, designed for the hacking and chopping of hand-to-hand fighting. Outside the columns was a curtain of missile weapons—cross-bows and hand-guns at first, later hand-guns only—apt for skirmishing purposes. But though the Swiss column thus possessed very great defensive strength (since it was equally resistant to attack from front, flank or rear), it had also (in contradistinction to the long-bow and the hand-gun) formidable offensive possibilities. As it moved forward, slowly indeed, but in disciplined unity to the tap of drum, it could steam-roller any defence by sheer mass and momentum, unless that defence were also organized upon the same model.[3] The effect of its impact upon

[1] Oman, *Art of War in the Sixteenth Century*, p. 32.

[2] The Swiss used pikes effectively at Laupen as early as 1339.

[3] The Swiss column is sometimes loosely referred to as a phalanx. The description is misleading: the Swiss attack depended for its success upon mass and shock; that of the phalanx did not. The words of Frederick the Great might be applied to the Swiss attack: 'the whole success of a battle depends on not halting without orders, but advancing in regular and close order against the enemy': R. Günther, *Die Entwicklung der Feuertaktik der Infanterie*, pp. 6-7.

the Burgundian chivalry of Charles the Bold was disintegrating. For the first time for centuries infantry had developed a successful offensive tactic.

The question now was whether the Swiss methods could be successful against the improved missile weapons of the age. Luckily for themselves, the Swiss never came up against English bowmen. Had they done so, the range, rapidity of fire and astonishing penetrative power of the long-bow, together with the slow tempo of the Swiss advance (imposed by the need to keep formation) could not have failed to produce a massacre; and might probably have modified the military history of the next century and a half. The case was very different in regard to firearms. Artillery was as yet scarcely mobile [1]; its rate of fire probably did not exceed three or four rounds an hour; its inaccuracy was virtually unlimited.[2] Confronted with gunfire, the early Swiss columns lay down until the ball had passed them by and then resumed their advance at leisure.[3] Nor were the hand-gunners a serious menace at first. Their weapons were portable only with difficulty, dangerous to their owners, and with a rate of fire scarcely superior to that of the artillery. Once they had discharged their pieces, they were practically defenceless until they had reloaded; and that operation might easily take some minutes. The triumph of the Swiss, in fact, was made possible because the abandonment of the long-bow (and even of the cross-bow) caused a catastrophic reduction in firepower.[4] The armies of the late fifteenth century were bemused by the roar of the cannon, and vainly imagined that its daunting moral effect might offset its inability to hit the largest and most vulnerable human targets ever presented to a gunner. The Swiss themselves presently discarded cross-bows for their skirmishers, and armed them with the arquebus; with unfortunate results. For in order that the arquebusiers might be protected between one round and the next, they had to be drawn closer to the pikes. They were now firmly attached to the columns; and were ranged, two deep, on every side of the pike-square. The

[1] The use of horses to draw artillery seems to have come in with the French invasion of Italy in 1494: Delbrück, IV. 47.

[2] For a discussion of the efficiency of artillery, see below, pp. 228 *seqq.*

[3] Delbrück, IV. 48.

[4] For an interesting estimate of this development in numerical terms, see Laskowski, *op. cit.*, *passim.* Elsewhere Laskowski calculates that the firepower of Casimir Jagiełłon's infantry (armed with the cross-bow) compared with that of the Polish infantry of the mid-sixteenth century (armed with firearms) was as 40:1. Laskowski, *Uwagi na marginesie nowego wydania Zarysu Historji Wojskwośce w Polsce Generała Mariana Kukiela*, p. 36.

column was thus encompassed by a thin envelope of firearms which impeded it either in attack or in defence and had to be removed hastily just before the moment of impact. The momentum of the column (its strongest asset) was thus reduced; and such firepower as the arquebusiers possessed was still further diminished by a battle-order perversely wasteful of manpower: unless the column were actually surrounded, at least half the arquebusiers would be unable to take part in the fighting. That the Swiss in these circumstances should have succeeded in imposing their ascendancy upon Europe is to be ascribed to the novelty of their methods, to their strong *esprit de corps*, to their notorious ferocity,[1] but above all to the inability of their opponents to bring adequate concentrations of fire to bear upon them.

By the second decade of the sixteenth century an answer to the Swiss tactic began to emerge. This consisted in the massing of firearms behind natural or artificial obstacles designed to impede the Swiss advance and disrupt their formation. It worked well: the rate of gunfire was slowly improving, the number of guns was increasing fast; and the Swiss (like the English earlier) could be galled into rash attacks. At Ravenna (1512) artillery for the first time decided a battle; at Marignano (1515) the Swiss suffered severe casualties; at Bicocca (1522) they met with serious disaster.[2] The Swiss predominance came to an end: their military development had been too specialized and one-sided for them to be able to adapt themselves easily to changed conditions.

The Swiss tradition, however, survived, with appropriate modifications, and in other hands. The Landsknechts, created after 1479 by Maximilian I and originally designed by him to be a German national army, were trained and organized on Swiss models, and had latterly stood up well to the Swiss at push of pike. Their campaigns against the Turks (who had excellent artillery) suggested that the pike-blocks would be less vulnerable if they were reduced in size,[3] and revealed that their formation could be disrupted by a resolute cavalry attack on the corners of the squares. Almost contemporaneously, the need for some modification had been perceived by

[1] Delbrück, IV. 79.

[2] Oman, *Sixteenth Century*, pp. 25, 26, 33, 139, 184-5; Delbrück, IV. 88, 101, 103-7, 110.

[3] The old-style Swiss system seems, however, to have reached its logical conclusion in the famous imperial order of battle before Vienna in 1532, when an army of anything between 70,000 and 120,000 men was drawn up in three immense blocks, surrounded by a girdle of shot 20,000 strong: Delbrück, IV. 111.

the Spaniards. By the first decade of the sixteenth century Spain had developed a first-rate infantry (modelled originally on the Landsknechts), and by the time of the peace of Cambrai the Spanish foot had already become the finest fighting force in Europe. Spanish commanders seem to have been concerned at the wastage of man-power involved in the Swiss methods: they made some attempt, for instance, to utilize the men in the centre of the squares by arming them for a time with swords and bucklers and encouraging them to creep forward below the pikes, with a view to taking a more active part in the *mêlée* than was involved in the Swiss method of simply leaning on the man in front.[1] They realized, too, the tactical advantage of having more than three bodies of infantry on the battlefield. In the 1530's, therefore, similar modifications of the Swiss methods took place in Germany and in Spain. The pike-squares became smaller. The proportion of firearms increased; and in consequence the girdle of shot around the square was made five deep instead of two deep. To protect the corners of the rectangles, four little squares of shot were placed at each angle, outside the main body: they came to be known as the 'sleeves'. And finally, in the Spanish system (though not yet in the German) the firepower of the unit was increased by the addition of a 'forlorn hope' of 500 arque-busiers, pushed out as a detached force ahead of the main body. These new-model units were called in Spain *tercios*. The first *tercios* were created in 1534, and for more than a century they ruled the battlefields of Europe, as the Swiss had done before them. Each *tercio* was a tactical unit of a definite size, based (in theory, at least) on an administrative unit (the regiment), also of a definite size; and in these respects it represented a great advance on any-thing that had preceded it. Originally, the *tercio* numbered 3200 men: 1600 pikemen in the middle, 900 musketeers or arquebusiers in the girdle, 50 musketeers in each of the sleeves, and 500 musketeers in the forlorn. In 1584 its size was reduced (for all new *tercios*) to 1500.[2]

[1] *ibid.*, IV. 63; *Karl XII på slagfältet*, I. 95, 104.

[2] For the *tercios*, see Oman, *op. cit.*, pp. 58-61, 579; R. Altamira, *Historia de España*, III. 292-5; J. W. Wijn, *Het Krijgswezen in den Tijd van Prins Maurits*, pp. 424-6; G. B. C:son Barkman, *Gustaf II Adolfs regementsorganisation vid det inhemska infanteriet*, pp. 4-6, 21-4 (with a good diagram). The origin of the name *tercio* is uncertain: it may originally have signified a *third* of the whole army (*cf.* the Swiss column); or it may derive from the fact that it comprised each of the three arms—pikes, arquebuses, muskets: Altamira, III. 294; A. Ballesteros y Beretta, *Historia de España*, IV. 2. 89. Londoño seems to think that the name is connected with the number of men comprising the unit: 'y aunque antiguamente eran tres mil

The *tercio* had many advantages over the Swiss column. It was a less vulnerable target. It utilized manpower more economically. By increasing shot to an equality with pikes, it also increased its firepower. The smaller size of the *tercio* now made it possible to group units in tactical formations; and *tercios* were in fact usually grouped in threes, or in fours if sufficient were available: in the latter case they were drawn up in lozenge-shaped or chequer-board formation, with the rear *tercio* in reserve.[1] Some attempt at more effective combination of arms became possible; for some of the pikemen were now left unarmoured, so that they might move swiftly in support of the shot [2]; and (in theory at all events) each *tercio* had a force of 100 cavalry attached to it.[3] Nevertheless, the disadvantages of the *tercio* remained serious. The wastage of manpower, though less extravagant than in the Swiss system, was still grave: of the 40 ranks of pikemen, only the first five (or at the most six) could effectively use their weapons.[4] The increased depth of the girdle of shot would actually have diminished the firepower of the *tercio* had it not been partially offset by a new technique of firing. This was the countermarch. To execute the countermarch, the front rank of shot discharged their pieces, and doubled outwards to the rear to reload; successive ranks repeated the evolution; and (if the formation were deep enough, and the shot handy with their weapons) by the time the rearmost rank had fired, the original front rank would be ready to give its next volley, the formation would have resumed its original order, and the enemy would have been subjected to a more or less continuous fire.[5] But such a procedure was possible

---

soldados, por lo cual se llamaban Tercio y no Legiones . . .': S. de Londoño, *Discurso sobre la forma de reducir la Disciplina militar a mejor y antiguo Estado*, p. 34. On the other hand, the author of *The Swedish Intelligencer* could write in 1632 (when it was certainly no longer true), '. . . a full tercio (so the Spanish call a Brigade) that is, a whole third part of the Armie, how many soever the Armie be': *The Swedish Intelligencer*, IV. 6-7.

[1] The formation sometimes called the 'Spanish Brigade', but wrongly so; since it was not really a regular higher tactical unit: *cf.* P. Pieri, *La Formazione dottrinale di Raimondo Montecuccoli*, p. 93.

[2] Londoño, *Disciplina militar*, p. 30.

[3] Altamira, III. 294.

[4] Wijn, p. 426. Even Sir James Turner, concerned as he was to defend pikemen against the sneers of Daniel Lupton (who had written, in 1642, that only the first three ranks of pikes 'can do hurt'), did not venture to claim that more than six ranks could effectively participate in the struggle: Turner, *Pallas Armata*, p. 178.

[5] The countermarch is sometimes considered to have been an innovation of Maurice of Orange, who is said to have borrowed it from Aelian (see, *e.g.*, W. Hahlweg, *Die Heeresreform der Oranier und die Antike*, pp. 73-4); but in fact it seems to have been used much earlier than Maurice: training in evolutions of

only to the relatively deep formations of the 'sleeves', and perhaps of the forlorn: of the 900 shot surrounding the pike-square, the great majority would at any given moment be inoperative. The increase in the number of musketeers and arquebusiers, moreover, exacerbated the already formidable difficulty of providing them with adequate protection. In theory, they were supposed to take cover behind the pikes when attacked by hostile cavalry, either by withdrawing to the rear of the pike-square or by taking refuge inside it: some *tercios* were organized as hollow squares to provide for the latter contingency. But it was now no easy matter for the 1600 exposed shot to withdraw to safety behind an equal number of pikes in the face of cavalry advancing at the trot; it was geometrically impossible for all of them to be accommodated within the square; and it was exceedingly dangerous to admit any, since their passage through the ranks might well disrupt the solidity of the pike-hedge at the crucial moment of impact. And if a *tercio* were once breached, or even if the pikes became crossed, and so produced confusion, the *tercio* was lost. No less awkward were the problems presented by the new formation in attack. If the girdle of shot remained attached to the pike-square, the effect of the impact of massed pikes must be dulled, even though the musketeers (as they often did) should use their butts as clubs.[1] If, on the other hand, the shot dispersed shortly before impact, the possibilities of confusion and disorder were considerable. And if in attack the forward elements of the shot detached themselves and advanced to skirmish, they forfeited that protection which it was the whole purpose of the *tercio* formation to provide. The *tercios* did indeed attack on occasion, and with great success; but it is difficult to understand how they did it, unless they adopted the last of these expedients. But, even so, their pace

---

this sort goes back at least to 1516 in Spain (Delbrück, IV. 172), and a form of it may possibly have been employed by the Spaniards at Pavia: J. Alm, *Eldhandvapen*, I. 87. It seems likely, however, that the three classic varieties—the Macedonian, the Lacedaemonian, the Choric—do represent Maurice's imitation of Aelian. The more involved forms of countermarch were essentially training-exercises rather than battle tactics: 'And truly [writes Turner in 1671] I think the hazard were small, if all the three several countermarches were for ever banish'd out of all Armies, except those of our Enemies. It is true, I never saw any of them used in sight of an Enemy, for if they be practis'd then, I am confident, confusion would follow them': *Pallas Armata*, p. 11. But forty years earlier the simpler forms were effective in battle: see *Monro his Expedition with the worthy Scots Regiment*, II. 187-90; though Monro virtually admits that such varieties as 'the Slavonian countermarch' were mere parade-ground manœuvres.

[1] '. . . till they come to Push of Pike, and Buts of Muskets': Monro, II. 186.

in attack was deliberate, and their advance had to be punctuated by halts to enable the rear ranks to close up in order that the solidity of the square might be maintained.[1]

Yet in defence the *tercio* was undeniably effective: attacking infantry were dispersed by the shot; attacking cavalry, after scattering the shot, broke on the pike-hedge, which, because it faced in all directions, could neither be outflanked nor taken in rear. Battle tactics in the middle of the sixteenth century, therefore, tended to be increasingly defensive; commanders relied increasingly upon missile weapons: the change was apparent in the prolonged musket-duel which opened the battle of Cerisole in 1544.[2] But it was precisely in this type of long-distance fighting that the *tercio*, by reason of the way it arranged its shot, was least effective. The *tercio*, in fact, flourished because defence and attack had by this time become equally enfeebled.

Nevertheless, the efficiency of firearms was perceptibly increasing. The advent of the muzzle-loading gun and the supplanting of the breech-loader may have been a doubtful improvement from the point of view of the rate of artillery fire, for the breech-loader had been provided with spare chambers ready charged[3]; but in all other respects it was an advantage. The substitution of iron cannon-balls for stone increased the destructive power of the cannonade, and by enabling calibres to be reduced without loss of effectiveness made possible also a reduction in the weight of the gun. The introduction of horse-drawn artillery by the French contributed much to the success of their Italian campaigns from 1494 onwards. And the first half of the century had seen the first fumblings towards a science of ballistics: the publication of Niccoló Tartaglia's *La Nuova Scientia* at Venice in 1537 provided gunners with a handbook to which they clung pertinaciously until the third quarter of the seventeenth century, in despite of Galileo and Torricelli.[4] The most important improvements, however, occurred in a field entirely neglected by the theorists of ballistics—the field of small-arms. Early in the sixteenth century, the musket began to make its appearance in the armies of the major powers: both sides possessed

[1] Wijn, p. 433.

[2] Günther, p. 3; and see Oman, *op. cit.*, p. 57. A symptom of the same tendency towards the defensive was that the *tercio* abandoned not only the sword but even the essentially offensive halberd, and was now armed uniformly with the pike: O. S. F. Odenrick, *Lantkrigskonstens utveckling*, II. 19.

[3] L. Hammarskiöld, *Ur svenska artilleriets hävder*, p. 4.

[4] A. R. Hall, *Ballistics in the Seventeenth Century*, pp. 33-52.

muskets at Pavia.[1] The musket had the advantage over the arquebus of a slightly greater effective range, but above all of a higher penetrative power, thanks to a heavier ball and a more powerful charge; so that its ball could pierce the stronger armour which had been evolved to meet the threat from the arquebus.[2] The disadvantages were, however, considerable. The musket was much heavier than the arquebus; so heavy , indeed, that it could be aimed only from a fork-rest, which the musketeer carried as part of his equipment. Its recoil was so violent that it had to be fired from the chest rather than from the shoulder; and even so, the interposition of a cushion was often found desirable.[3] Loading was a complicated process, and took much time.[4] Since the musket was a matchlock, the musketeer might be rendered innocuous by a sudden shower; while the glow of the burning match betrayed his approach at night.[5] The consumption of match was enormous, and presented a new problem of supply.[6] But the essential point about the musket was that its cumbrousness neutralized, for a long time to come, the increased firepower provided by its improved penetrative qualities. It was not noticeably more accurate, nor significantly longer ranged, than the arquebus; it was less mobile (it could not be used, as the arquebus could, for skirmishing on horseback); and its firing-rate was lower.[7]

[1] Delbrück, IV. 110.

[2] For the musket, see Alm, *Eldhandvapen*, I. 82, 188-90; C. H. Firth, *Cromwell's Army*, p. 80; *Sv. Krig*, Supp. Vol. II. 110-11.

[3] J. J. Wallhausen, *L'Art militaire pour l'infanterie*, p. 41.

[4] So complicated, that the drill-books of the early seventeenth century were able to devise anything up to 99 words of command for the operation; though in action these were usually reduced to three: Alm, I. 188.

[5] A Swedish soldier in America in the 1650's, confronted with fireflies, exclaimed that the woods were full of musketeers: Alm, I. 192. At the end of the sixteenth century the Dutch invented a tin tube pierced with holes, as a match-protector: *ibid.*, I. 105.

[6] *ibid.*, I. 52; Firth, pp. 83-4.

[7] The rate of fire of the musket is a matter of controversy. Estimates for Gustav Adolf's time vary from 6 rounds in 8 hours (!) to 2 to 3 rounds a minute. The latter must be nearer the truth, or Monro could hardly have written 'hot service, so that a Souldier was not able to handle his musket for fear of burning': Monro, I. 23. Wijn found by experiment that a musket could get off one round every two minutes: *Krijgskundige Aantekening van Johan . . . van Nassau*, p. 11 *note* 1. Yet Montecuccoli reckoned that an allowance of 16 rounds per day was adequate to a musketeer's needs: Montecuccoli, *Mémoires*, p. 58. Since the effective range of the musket was not more than 100 paces, the musketeer could in any case hardly hope to get off more than two rounds at advancing infantry in the time which elapsed between their coming into range and the beginning of the hand-to-hand struggle: *Sv. Krig*, Supp. Vol. II. 110. On the general question, *ibid.*, II. 194; Wijn, p. 149; Laskowski, *Uwagi*, p. 51; Alm, I. 190-1. The use of cartridges would have increased the rate of fire, but the only European ruler to adopt them in this century seems to have been Stephen Bátory: Laskowski, *Uwagi*, p. 49.

It had undeniable advantages over the arquebus when it came to blasting a hole in the side of the *tercio*, and it was for that reason increasingly popular; but until the musket could be made handier, and until a fire-discipline could be evolved which would countervail its deficiencies, the arquebus would not be wholly superseded for skirmishing troops.[1]

The immediate tactical effects of the introduction of the musket were therefore not great. It was far otherwise with the wheel-lock pistol. The wheel-lock motion seems to have been invented in Nuremberg towards the end of the fifteenth century, and the wheel-lock pistol to have made its appearance about 1520.[2] Its importance lay in the possibility which it offered of combining firepower with mobility. In order to disrupt a *tercio* it was first necessary to create a breach in it into which cavalry could penetrate. This perhaps might have been effected by massed horsemen charging at the gallop; but the military experts of the age were not prepared to attempt it. They preferred to rely on firearms; and they were naturally anxious to diminish the range at which those firearms would be used. The solution was obviously to use 'shot on horse-back'. But the mounted arquebusier was a clumsy instrument; his weapon was heavy, and difficult to handle on horseback; and it seems very unlikely that he could discharge it with any accuracy (or, indeed, with safety to himself) if his mount were moving at much more than a walk. But the pistol opened new prospects. Provided the spring did not break, or the wheel get bent, or the pyrites fall out, or the pistol go off prematurely in the rider's jack-boot, it could be fired with either hand even at the gallop. It is true that it was hopelessly outranged both by arquebus and musket, for it was effective against armour only at very short range indeed—perhaps as little as five paces.[3] Nevertheless, resolute pistoleers might hope to ride in to this distance and to blow a gap in the *tercio* into which lancers could subsequently charge. At all events, the pistol was

[1] G. Droysen (*Beiträge zur Geschichte des Militärwesens in Deutschland während der Epoche des dreissigjährigen Krieges*, p. 46) was mistaken in supposing the arquebus to be nearly extinct by 1560: arquebusiers did notable service in the Spanish armies in the Netherlands—for instance, at Mook in 1574 (Wijn, pp. 153, 165-6, 374, 429, 445, 495) and they were still fighting at the opening of the Thirty Years' War, though by this time armed with the carbine: H. Wertheim, *Der toller Halberstädter. Herzog Christian von Braunschweig im pfälzischen Kriege*, I. 90, 115.

[2] Alm, I. 53, 80.

[3] Oman, *op. cit.*, pp. 85-6. Tavannes wrote: 'il faut que la bout [of the pistol] *touche*': Wijn, p. 164. Hahlweg seems alone in his view that the range of the pistol was 50-80 paces: *Die Heeresreform der Oranier und die Antike*, p. 101 *note* 220.

generally adopted, first by light, then by heavy, cavalry: the cuirassiers, the *Reiters*, of the second half of the century, were all pistoleers.

The tactical consequences of the change were unexpected and disconcerting. Heavy cavalry abandoned the attack *en haie*, and began to advance in deep formation.[1] The reason for the change was not in order that a great mass could be concentrated for impact upon the weak spot in the defence; for there was, in fact, no impact. It was rather that commanders hoped by this battle-order to achieve a concentration of fire. With this end in view they evolved the caracole.[2] A squadron of heavy cavalry, six or seven deep upon a front of fourteen or fifteen, would ride to within thirty paces of the enemy; they would then turn right, and simultaneously discharge their left-hand pistols. The manœuvre was then repeated by wheeling about and firing the right-hand pistols. By this time they were supposed to be within ten paces of the enemy. The caracole being now over, 'dann wendet sie sich geschwinde'[3]; as no doubt they were very glad to do. The effect upon the enemy was by no means proportionate to the difficulty of the evolution: the rear ranks stood an excellent chance of hitting their front-rank men, and with commendable prudence usually fired their pistols in the air. It is, indeed, difficult to resist the conclusion that the whole performance was nearly as futile as it was elaborate.[4] This would have mattered less if other cavalry had been at hand to charge into such gaps as the pistoleers might chance to create. But the rise of the pistoleers was accompanied by the eclipse of *l'arme blanche* as a

[1] Deep order seems first to have made its appearance at St. Quentin: Wijn, p. 439.

[2] For the first time either at Dreux (1562) or Sievershausen (1553): Delbrück, IV. 148; Alm, I. 119.

[3] *Sv. Krig*, Supp. Vol. II. 149-51. There seems to have been another form of caracole, which was in fact a countermarch on horseback: see, *e.g.*, *Pallas Armata*, p. 231; Alm, I. 119; Odenrick, II. 49. E. von Frauenholz (*Das Söldnertum in der Zeit des dreissigjährigen Krieges*, I. 60) contends that this was the true caracole, and that it was executed at a range of 200-300 paces (*cf.* Droysen, *Beitr. z. Gesch. d. Militärwesens*, p. 43), since it could not otherwise be performed with safety; and that pistoleers, forced to fire at such short range as to scorch the enemies' faces, were incapable of caracole. But contrast Wijn, pp. 442-3; G. Gualdo-Priorato, *L'Histoire des dernières campagnes . . . de Gustave-Adolphe*, pp. 280-1; and J. J. Wallhausen, *Art militaire à cheval*, pp. 62-3. Whereas Droysen (*Militärwesen*, p. 43) maintained that arquebusiers were expected to be dead shots at 200-300 paces, and to be able to fire at all speeds and from all positions, Wijn (p. 445) more modestly suggests that they fired at 'as much as 40 paces': but *cf.* Priorato, p. 274. The whole subject seems much in need of investigation.

[4] And it must have needed exceptionally level and open country for its execution.

cavalry weapon. The lance fell into disfavour; by the end of the century it had almost disappeared, save in the armies of Spain. Military theorists lamented its disuse, and Spanish commanders in the Netherlands could testify to its impressive performances in attack[1]; but the lance needed careful training, and horsemen of quality, while the pistol made neither of these demands.[2] Thus the pistoleer everywhere gained the ascendant: in the French, German and Dutch armies the lance wholly disappeared; in the Spanish its importance was much reduced.[3] Instead of relying upon the impact of the mass of man and horse, the cavaliers of western Europe were reduced, in battle, to a debilitated popping of pistols, their pace was reined back to (at best) a trot, and although cavalry might still be, on many a field, the chief battle-winning arm, it was so only because the old-style *tercio* was becoming an increasingly passive element in battle. Only in Poland (and perhaps in the armies of Henry IV) did a proper appreciation of the tactical rôle of cavalry survive; and even Poland did not wholly escape the *Reiters* and the mounted arquebusiers.[4]

By the time the Eighty Years' War began, therefore, the developments both of infantry and of cavalry had been such as to discourage the offensive spirit and to put a premium upon caution. Developments in the science of fortification reinforced this trend. The powerful new artillery which the French brought into Italy in 1494 had forced Italian engineers to devise new defensive systems: led by Michele Sanmichele and Antonio de Sangallo the younger, they began to apply the principle that the best defence against siege artillery is artillery. Towns were now surrounded by heavier

[1] As at Mook (1574) and Gembloux (1578)—and (it might be added) against Cromwell's forces on Hispaniola in 1655: Wijn, pp. 429, 496, 498.

[2] *cf.* Montecuccoli, *Mémoires*, pp. 16-17; J. J. Wallhausen, *Art militaire à cheval*, pp. 3-11, 29.

[3] Wijn, pp. 157-62; J. Alm, *Blanka vapen och skyddsvapen*, pp. 138-9. Wallhausen (*op. cit.*, p. 29) writes: 'take away the Lancer's offensive potentialities, and leave him only the defensive, and you have the Cuirassier'.

[4] *Etienne Batory*, p. 385; Laskowski, *Uwagi*, p. 47; M. Kukiel, *Zarys historji wojskowości w Polsce*, p. 54; Weygand, *Histoire de l'Armée française*, p. 123. The great Polish victory at Klušino in 1610 was won because the Polish cavalry charged at the gallop with the sabre at the moment when the opposing *Reiters* had just completed a caracole and were retiring to reload: T. Korzon, *Dzieje wojen i wojskowości w Polsce*, II. 164 *seqq.*; Kukiel, p. 56. In view of the influence of the pistol upon cavalry tactics, it is impossible to agree with Mr. Hall when he writes: 'none of these inventions, however [in regard to small-arms], had the effect of modifying tactics or creating a new scientific interest, since none of them increased the effective range or accuracy of the weapon': Hall, *Ballistics in the Seventeenth Century*, p. 8.

curtain-walls, broken at intervals by blunt-nosed bastions, with small ravelins in between: the whole being designed not only to present the attacker with a nearly impregnable mass of masonry but also as a system of gun-emplacements from which the besieged could bombard the enemy. In the last quarter of the sixteenth century the Italian style of fortification was revised and improved by the Dutch, and particularly by their great engineer Simon Stevin. They made much use of water barriers; they introduced the *faussebraie* as a new defensive firing-line on a lower level than the walls; they made their bastions sharp-angled, to give a better field of fire; they drew their bastions closer together, so that the intervals could now be commanded by small-arms fire; and in the last stages of the Dutch system they threw out hornworks, crownworks and half-moons, to provide a system of interdependent defences in depth.[1]

All these developments—in cavalry, infantry and military engineering—combined to give the defence a clear advantage. In consequence, the last two-thirds of the sixteenth century saw a general petrifaction of the art of war. Battles became increasingly the exception: the wise commander, careful of his '*Reputatie*', avoided an engagement if he could.[2] The strength of the new defences protracted sieges to enormous lengths; while the size of the garrisons required to man such defences made it appear hazardous to leave strong places untaken in one's rear. Whole campaigns were devoted merely to siege-warfare; and the gaining of a victory was prized mainly because it permitted an undisturbed application to the real business of siege-operations. A war of movement, a deep invasion, became very difficult; strategy (in so far as strategic thinking existed at all)[3] aimed not so much at the annihilation of the opposing army as at the occupation of territory. Even so, it failed to push matters to a logical conclusion: the strategy of annihilation

[1] E. Ericsson, *Olof Hansson Örnehufvud och svenska fortifikationsväsendet*, pp. 22-4; Wijn, pp. 254-75, 310-11; J. U. Nef, *War and Human Progress*, pp. 51-2. By the end of the century the Italian style had penetrated to Poland (Kukiel, p. 55), and by the beginning of the next the Dutch style had reached the Baltic: when the Poles besieged Pernau in 1609, it was defended by 'fortelmi niderlandskiemi': Korzon, II. 150.

[2] *e.g.* E. von Frauenholz, *Lazarus von Schwendi. Der erste deutsche Verkünder der allgemeinen Wehrpflicht*, pp. 201, 230; Monro, II. 57, 204. 'Nowadays', wrote Henri de Rohan, 'one fights more like a fox than like a lion, and war consists far more in sieges than in battles'—which he thought fit only for Turks and Persians: Frauenholz, *Das Söldnertum in der Zeit des dreissigjährigen Krieges*, I. 49.

[3] The numerous military textbooks of this period, as of the next, are virtually silent on strategical questions: Lazarus von Schwendi is a possible exception. See, on this question, Wijn, pp. 520 *seqq.*, 540-1.

by exhaustion (*Ermattungsstrategie*) had to wait for the concluding period of the Thirty Years' War before it found really practised exponents. On the battlefield, the concentration on increasing fire-power involved heavy sacrifices of speed and mobility; it involved also an increase in the weight of defensive armour, which in turn slowed up operations.[1] Though there were already signs that battle-groups were tending to be smaller, no tactical unit had yet been devised which would be flexible in the hands of a skilled commander; the proper use of reserves was still almost impossible; the problem of the combination of arms had been tackled clumsily and tentatively, if it had been tackled at all [2]; the prevailing deep formations, and the preference for firearms as against the lance or the bow, reflected the ascendancy of brute untrained mass over the skilled individual fighter. In short, tactics had withered, strategy had atrophied; and the men of the sixteenth century took refuge in firearms whose proper use they were still unable to compass, as an all-too-simple answer to their military difficulties. A military reformer was needed; and in the last decade of the century a constellation of reformers made its tardy appearance.

The military reforms which are usually associated with the name of Maurice of Orange (but which in fact owed quite as much to his cousins William Louis and John of Nassau) were in a sense the product of the Renaissance.[3] Though they were in part imposed and conditioned by hard experience in the field, and though they owed something to recent improvements in the Spanish system, they were based essentially upon the maxims of the great military theorists of antiquity; and above all upon Vegetius, Aelian and Leo VI. The Middle Ages had never quite forgotten Vegetius; and both Vegetius and Aelian were among the very early printed books. In the sixteenth century numerous editions of these and other classical military writers were published, both in the original and in translation. The military theorists of the age rediscovered the virtues of the Roman legion, became familiar once more with cohort and maniple, and

[1] The cuirassier's armour in its simplest form weighed about 24·2 kg.: *Sv. Krig*, Supp. Vol. II. 16-18; *cf.* Firth, p. 112.

[2] As Pieri remarks, their combination of pikes and muskets was still 'incerta, inequale, aleatoria': P. Pieri, *La formazione dottrinale di Raimondo Montecuccoli*, p. 93.

[3] For Maurice's reforms see, in general, *Krijgskundige Aantekening van Johan . . . van Nassau* [*ed.* J. W. Wijn], *passim*; W. Hahlweg, *Die Heeresreform der Oranier und die Antike*; J. W. Wijn, *op. cit.*; G. B. C:son Barkman, *Gustaf Adolfs regementsorganisation*, pp. 7-9, 31-8; Oman, pp. 568-72.

were able to expound the principles of linear tactics. Doctrinaire amateurs such as Machiavelli drew heavily on Vegetius [1]; and Lazarus von Schwendi in turn drew heavily on Machiavelli.[2] Francis I and Henry II both embarked on attempts to reconstitute the legion as a tactical unit; though in each case the attempt ended in a fiasco.[3] But it was left to the princes of the house of Orange to do something more than theorize upon a classical basis; and it was a Dutch savant, Justus Lipsius, who provided, in his *De militia Romana* (1595), the most uncompromising championship of Stoic ideals and Roman military methods, and the most emphatic assertion of the superiority of ancient to modern methods of fighting.[4] Maurice and his cousins, from their study of classical authors and their reading of Lipsius, imbibed fresh ideas about the proper utilization of manpower, the combination of different types of arms, the advantage of smaller tactical units and of linear formations, and the necessity and nature of infantry training. From the war-games they played with lead soldiers they slowly elicited the solutions to the difficulties which lay in the way of putting their ideas into practice. In the years after 1589 they inaugurated a real revolution.

The Maurician reforms meant, first, a better use of manpower. Formations became shallower, especially for the pikemen, whose depth was reduced to ten, and later to five men—about the maximum, as we have seen, that could effectively participate in combat. The pike-square became an elongated oblong, five deep on a front of fifty. It also divested itself of its absurd cummerbund of musketeers: the shot were now stationed in platoons of forty men each, ranged three and three on either side of the pike-hedge, facing the enemy

[1] For a convenient estimate of Machiavelli as a military writer, see *Makers of Modern Strategy* [*ed.* E. J. Earle]; but *cf.* Oman's severe judgment (*On the Writing of History*, p. 159): 'Machiavelli, a civilian steeped in Ancient History, presumed to philosophize on the art of war, but got hopelessly wrong: he backed the wrong horse in almost every one of his recommendations. He thought that firearms were going to continue negligible, that the day of cavalry in battle was quite over, and that infantry was going to continue in very large units, using neither pike nor arquebus, but short weapons for close combat like the sword of the ancient Roman legionary. His forecasts were hopelessly erroneous.' Sir James Turner was equally trenchant: 'Machiavelli . . . presents the world with a Milice of his own, the birth of his own brain, a hodg podg of some of the Ancient, and some of the Modern Militia, with a mixture of many of his own inventions': *Pallas Armata*, p. 161; and *cf. ibid.*, p. 116.

[2] E. von Frauenholz, *Lazarus von Schwendi*, pp. 16-17.

[3] Oman, p. 45; Turner, *Pallas Armata*, pp. 29-30, 164.

[4] Much to Sir James Turner's indignation: *Pallas Armata*, p. 353. For the importance of Lipsius, see G. Oestreich, *Der römische Stoizismus und die oranische Heeresreform*, *passim*.

in column of fours.[1] Shot and pikes were still linked together integrally in one unit; but the shot no longer got under the pikemen's feet, and the pike-squares no longer prevented half the shot from executing an orderly countermarch.

Secondly, the tactical unit was greatly reduced in size. The battalion, with 250 pikes, 240 shot and an extra 60 for a forlorn, numbered 550 men; and was intended to correspond to the Roman cohort.[2] Its size, and above all its shape (it covered a front of 258 paces and had a maximum depth of ten men), made some form of linear battle-order inescapable. And in fact the battalions, brigaded in groups of six, were drawn up to form three distinct lines of battle, arranged after the mode of *triplex acies* in *quincunx* pattern. Whether tactical units higher or lower than the battalion may have existed seems uncertain, for the confusion of terminology is considerable. Some attempt, however, seems to have been made to establish an identity between the half-regiment of three companies (the administrative unit) and the battalion; but it does not appear that the number of companies in the regiment, or the number of men in the company, was ever constant, and the attempt was a failure.[3] In other respects, however, the battalion and the triple line registered a marked advance. The new system was much more manœuvrable than the old *tercio*: if tactical combinations were to be attempted, the *tercio* was a very intractable instrument. A Spanish army of 12,000 men would have four tactical units; a Dutch army of the same strength would have twenty-four.[4] The Spanish system could provide a reserve only by refusing one whole *tercio*. This was too extravagant; and such a reserve could interfere only at one point in the battle, since to split it up would be to destroy its whole character as a fighting organization. In short, the Spanish system lacked tactical small change, and could meet an urgent demand for ninepence only by tendering a five-pound note. But in the Dutch

[1] The longer front of pikes, moreover, made it easier for the shot to take cove behind them, though this was *not* the main purpose of the reform.

[2] Note that Maurice did not, as is often stated, increase the proportion of shot. The object was not so much greater firepower as a better use of manpower: Wijn, pp. 173-80, 467.

[3] Barkman, p. 38; contrast Wijn, p. 437, and Frauenholz, *Söldnertum*, I. 46. Even on the supposition that Wijn is thinking of the administrative unit, while Barkman is considering the tactical unit, it appears quite impossible to reconcile either their figures, or their terminology, or their diagrams: Barkman, pp. 33-8; Wijn, pp. 476-9. G. Petri, *Det Kungl. första livgrenadjärregementets historia*, I. 317, offers an explanation which is irreconcilable with either. I have followed Barkman.

[4] I borrow this striking illustration from Barkman, p. 8.

system one or more battalions of the third line could quickly and easily be manœuvred into position to support any point that seemed to be threatened. On the other hand, unless they learned to form front to a flank, the lines of battalions were far more vulnerable to encircling movements by cavalry on the wings than the old *tercio* had been; and it is not clear that they ever did learn it.

These major reforms were supported by others, hardly less important, in almost every branch of the military art. Maurice was a great innovator in siege warfare. His massive barrages against a strictly limited objective enabled him greatly to quicken the pace of siege operations, and marked an epoch in poliorcetics. He did much to standardize Dutch artillery, both as to calibres and as to quality. He was a dabbler in new weapons of horrific character, with names to correspond, such as those *saucisses de guerre* which for a moment engaged his attention [1]; and by his use of the newly invented field-glass, and his patronage of the military map-makers, he showed his appreciation of the applications of science to war. His use of field-fortifications, and his insistence that soldiers should do their own digging, look forward to Gustav Adolf; and so too do the strict discipline of his armies and the Articles of War which he caused to be promulgated.[2]

Two preconditions were essential to the success of these reforms. The first was that the Dutch armies should be paid well, and above all paid punctually. Only a well-paid army could be induced to undergo that radical disturbance of its ingrained military conservatism which the new methods involved. Maurice succeeded in convincing the States of the need for this reform; and the Dutch armies were the most regularly paid in Europe.[3] The second condition was an efficient system of training and drill. The *tercios* had not needed much of either: they may have been wasteful of manpower, but at least they economized on training. But for the new formations drill was indispensable. Maurice was a first-rate trainer of infantry; and his reforms were accompanied by a sudden recognition of the fundamental importance and significance of drill.

[1] Wijn, pp. 223-4. Other devices included gas-shells, and a steel saw, with silencer attachment, for fixing to the gates of towns besieged by the Dutch armies.

[2] For all this, see Wijn, pp. 319 (maps), 320-8 (science), 81-103 (discipline), 254-89 (sieges and field-fortifications), 186, 214-42 (artillery), 386-8 (baggage-train); F. L. Robertson, *The Evolution of Naval Armament*, p. 90; Hahlweg, pp. 132-4; Sir G. N. Clark, *The Seventeenth Century*, pp. 112-13.

[3] Though not (on paper) the best: the Dutch month was longer than others: Wertheim, I. 87.

And in this, more directly than anywhere else, the men of the new Dutch school drew upon the classics. Aelian was their master here: from him they derived their evolutions, from him they translated, often quite literally, their words of command—learning for the first time to make them short and precise, and not forgetting his injunction to put the operative word last. How new the whole subject was to them may be seen from those elaborate and highly confusing paragraphs in which the authors of their drill-books explain exactly what is meant by such an order as 'Right turn'.[1] But Maurice's contemporaries flung themselves into drill with all the passionate ardour of those who have seen a great light. Indeed, there was some danger that the whole art of war might be viewed exclusively from the angle of the parade-ground, and that facility in 'embattling by the square root' might be esteemed the pinnacle of martial virtue.[2] Yet the drilling itself was a reform of enormous and far-reaching importance. It strengthened discipline. It marked the beginning of a process (still continuing) whereby the soldier was raised from the primitive level of the pikeman in the middle of the *tercio* to that of a professional who was also more or less of a technician[3]; but paradoxically it also marked the beginning of a process which was to turn him, for a couple of centuries, into the passive instrument of other wills than his own. By necessitating a much more numerous, and much better educated, body of officers and N.C.O.s than any previous army of modern times had required, it provided new careers and new prospects for many, and had important social implications.

Nevertheless, for all its merits, the new Dutch system had serious weaknesses. The most important of these was its failure to reform cavalry tactics—a failure possibly to be ascribed to the fact that the Romans themselves used cavalry (at least until the late Empire) more as mobile shot than as shock troops.[4] The cavalry, in Maurice's battle-line, was indeed not more than five deep, but it was left to caracole according to the prevailing vicious fashion, and the lance was formally banished from the Dutch armies in 1597.[5] No attempt was made to tackle the problem of combining horse and foot, nor

[1] For all this, see Hahlweg, pp. 25-98, 103, 110-16; Wijn, pp. 138-40, 430; *cf.* J. J. Wallhausen, *L'Art militaire pour l'infanterie*, p. 65 *seqq.*

[2] For embattling by the square root, see Turner, *Pallas Armata*, pp. 266-8.

[3] 'A Souldier without letters', says Monro, 'is like a ship without a Rudder, or like a bird without feathers': Monro, II. 196.

[4] F. E. Adcock, *The Roman Art of War*, p. 25.

[5] Wijn, p. 45, and see *ibid.*, pp. 42-7, 452-3, 514; Oman, p. 548; *Sv. Krig*, I. 84.

any in the direction of combining light artillery with either.[1] The linear formation, with all its advantages, was liable to become rigid; the battalion proved in the event too small a tactical unit for independent life; and above all, the Maurician tactic turned out to be no less defensive in character than that which it aspired to supersede. This may possibly not have been Maurice's intention: indeed, the champions of the new system claimed as one of its merits its offensive spirit.[2] But in fact it was scarcely used offensively by Maurice at all. Turnhout was a mere encounter, Nieuwpoort represents a comparatively early stage of the new methods: in neither case, at all events, was there any attempt to revive the offensive rôle of the pike. Thereafter Maurice fought no more pitched battles. His strategy was to the full as cautious as that of any of his contemporaries (it was, in fact, much more orthodox and unenterprising than Spinola's),[3] and he looked upon a battle as the last resort of a commander rather than as the logical object of warfare. He waged war, it has been said, as though he were playing chess; and his constant concern was to limit the risk.[4] The feudal chivalry or the Swiss column, with all their crudity, had at least possessed the aggressive temperament.

Yet it is clear that the Dutch reforms forced tacticians all over Europe to reconsider their principles; and to contemporaries they seemed to transform the art of war. If at the beginning of Elizabeth's reign the younger Granvelle could declare that 'the art of war is now such that men be fain to learn anew at every two-years' end',[5] the pace of change seemed even more rapid forty years later. Protestant Europe, in general, was converted to the Dutch methods, which seemed to pay such handsome dividends against Spain; and the Protestant princes of Germany sent their noblemen to receive a military education—the first systematic military education of modern times—at that famous military academy, presided over by Jakob von Wallhausen, which John of Nassau established at Siegen.[6] In

[1] John of Nassau was not oblivious of these things; but nothing practical was done: Wijn, p. 214.

[2] Thus van Reydt wrote in 1633: 'Hy [William Louis] begost van dien tydt aen met aller yver ende ernste sich te bereden tot een offensyf oorlogh. . . .': Hahlweg, p. 130.

[3] After 1604 Spinola broke all the rules by trading on the fact that the Dutch commanders considered the fighting of a battle as a sign of poor generalship, and by conducting his operations without bothering much about sieges: Wijn, pp. 540-1.

[4] See the dictum of William Louis, quoted in *Krigsvetenskaps Akademiens Handlingar* (1932), pp. 36-7.

[5] J. U. Nef, *War and Economic Progress* (*Ec. Hist. Rev.*, XII.), p. 15.

[6] Wijn, p. 74; W. Sjöstrand, *Grunddragen av den militära undervisningens uppkomst- och utvecklingshistoria i Sverige till år 1792*, pp. 16-18.

England, military authors championed the reformed tactics; in Denmark, Kristian IV employed them in his war with the Emperor. In Germany, princes such as Maurice the Learned of Hesse evolved their own variations of them.[1] Brandenburg used them in the Cleves-Jülich war. Frederick V and Christian of Brunswick lost battle after battle against the imperialists on principles which they certainly believed to be Dutch.[2]

Catholic Europe viewed the reforms with more scepticism. It did not seem to Tilly or Spinola that the case for the superior effectiveness of Maurice's methods was made out. Nieuwpoort was scarcely evidence one way or the other; and between Nieuwpoort and the death of Maurice in 1625 the Dutch contrived to avoid a major engagement. The performances of the German Protestants in the early years of the Thirty Years' War were hardly calculated to establish the inferiority of the old order. Nevertheless, the Spanish school of tacticians was not above learning from the enemy.[3] It may be that theorists such as Basta showed themselves more ready to make changes than were the commanders in the field[4]; yet by the time Gustav Adolf landed in Germany the *tercio* had been considerably modified. Its numbers were reduced, and might now be as low as 1000 men; and it tended to lose in depth and gain in frontage. The girdle of musketeers was sometimes dispensed with; and the sleeves, now much strengthened, were made broader too. Smaller *tercios*, and more of them, were increasingly aligned in *quincunx* formation, so that to the casual eye the battle-order on the imperialist side might on occasion appear not so very dissimilar from the battle-order of their opponents.[5]

In short, when Gustav Adolf appeared upon the battlefields of Europe, the controversies provoked by the reforms of Maurice and his collaborators were still undecided; and the process of reform which had been begun in the Netherlands was still incomplete. Maurice had failed to see—or at least had failed to pursue—the logical consequences of his new methods. The old order was challenged, but it was not yet overthrown; the full implications and potentialities of the new were still undeveloped. Gustav Adolf, with

[1] M. Lenz, *Landgraf Moritz von Hessen* (*Kleine historische Schriften*, II.)' pp. 128-33; Hahlweg, pp. 148-52.

[2] Barkman, pp. 39-40; Hahlweg, pp. 141-80.

[3] Barkman, pp. 44-8.

[4] As a contemporary commentator observed: 'Si discute alla romana, ma si continua a combattere alla tedesca': Pieri, p. 95.

[5] See, for instance, Verdugo's formation of 1590: Wijn, pp. 427, 432-3; Barkman, pp. 12 *note*, 51-2; Jähns, pp. 1209-10.

a firmer hand, a wider strategic vision, a more trenchant mind (and an extra generation's experience), was to take Maurice's methods, apply them, add to them and improve them, and in doing so was to impose upon the art of war a pattern which it retained almost unmodified until the advent of the revolutionary armies of France.

(ii) *The Swedish Background*

The heavy-armed cavalry of the Middle Ages had never gained a secure foothold in Scandinavia.[1] The topography of the peninsula—its vast forests, extensive mosses and innumerable lakes—had presented obstacles which made it an unsuitable terrain for cavalry operations; and its social structure had never been such as to ensure the subordination of all classes of society to the maintenance of a martial aristocracy. Here, more than anywhere else in Europe, the primitive Germanic military tradition had persisted; and the invader who ventured into the Swedish forests was met by a *levée en masse* of the population, fighting mainly on foot, and grouped, if the country were open, in large irregular masses. Though the nobility owed service on horseback (*rusttjänst*) in return for their fiscal immunity, they formed only an inconsiderable portion of the army. Essentially, the mediaeval Swedish army, like the Swiss, was a peasant army, and its weapons were simple and inexpensive—the bow, the cross-bow, the spear, the billhook and the pole-axe.[2] The *landslag* laid it down that no man was to be compelled to take service beyond the frontiers without his own consent; but it also made explicit the obligation to serve without pay in defence of the country. The Swedish peasant soldiers were adept in the use of natural advantages, and relied largely on *bråtar* [3] to hold up an invader.

[1] For this section see, in general, *Sv. Krig*, I.; Petri, *op. cit.*; G. B. Barkman, *Svea Livgardets Historia*, I.; *Karl XII på slagfältet*, I.; Generalstaben, *Axtorna*.

[2] For the armament of the late-mediaeval Swedish army, see Alm, *Blanka vapen och skyddsvapen*, pp. 128-9; *Sv. Krig*, I. 61; Petri, I. 29. The bow was still in use in Dalarna in the mid-seventeenth century (F. F. Carlson, *Sveriges Historia under konungarne af det pfalziska huset*, II. 42); but firearms seem to have become common among the peasantry in Gustav Vasa's time (Alm, *Eldhandvapen*, I. 126).

[3] A *bråte* was a combined ambush and booby-trap, constructed in the forest. When the enemy fell into the ambush he found himself blocked by felled trees in front, and assailed in flank and rear. His difficulties were increased by the fact that the trees surrounding the position had been partially sawn through, and were now brought crashing down on his head. A schematic sketch is given opposite *Karl XII på slagfältet*, I. 118. The device was common to other forest-clad countries: it was used by the Bohemians during the Thirty Years' War; and in Finland during the Lappo troubles, as late as 1932: P. M. Hebbe, *Svenskarna i Böhmen och Mähren. Studier i tjeckiska folktradition och litteratur*, p. 187.

Fighting on their own ground, mobile, resourceful, and masters of guerrilla, they were as difficult to conquer as the Welsh at the time of the Edwardian invasions; and many a Danish inroad came to grief in Småland or on the Holaveden. At Haraker in 1464 the peasant levies were able to defeat a regular Danish army of the continental type in pitched battle. But the mediaeval Swedish infantryman lacked the discipline of the Swiss, nor was he armed with the modern battle-winning weapon, the pike; and when, at the beginning of the 1520's, Gustav Vasa was struggling to eject the Danes from Sweden, these defects made themselves severely felt. The Danish professional army, trained in the new techniques of continental warfare, could be defeated, in the long run, only by forces that had received a similar training. Gustav Vasa was therefore driven to employ German mercenaries. They were expensive, but they were necessary if Sweden were to win her independence; and at least they had the advantage that they were not likely to hamstring foreign policy by insisting on a constitutional right to decline service outside Sweden's borders.

During the crisis of the war of liberation, moreover, the King had found it necessary, in order to keep his armies up to strength, to make the great innovation of paying his subjects to defend themselves. When the war was over, he found it inadvisable to disperse his army altogether. The disturbed state of the country, and the danger of a revival of Denmark's plans for a Scandinavian union, compelled him to maintain a nucleus of troops upon which he could rely. As between a paid force of Swedes and a paid body of mercenaries, the choice—on military grounds, at least—was not difficult: Gustav Vasa dismissed his subjects to their homes and retained the professionals. It was with foreign mercenaries that he intervened in the Counts' War in 1534; it was with foreign mercenaries that he suppressed the dangerous revolt of Nils Dacke in 1543. But if a Danish invasion had once again threatened Sweden's existence, the old Swedish army would have sprung into life once more; the summons *man ur hus* would have gone out; and from every farm and homestead the Swedish yeomanry would have assembled to repel the attack. As late as 1543 Gustav Vasa could draw up his army in the three roughly organized groups of the primitive Germanic host.[1] Despite the mercenaries, the real army in an emergency was still what it had always been: a peasant army,

[1] Petri, I. 60.

light-armed, fighting on foot, strong in archers and formidable with the billhook at close quarters in broken country.

And, as it happened, Gustav Vasa was by no means satisfied with the conduct of his mercenaries during the Dacke revolt. They had proved insubordinate; they had committed outrages on the civil population. They were also extremely expensive. By 1544 he was coming to the conclusion that a mercenary army was a wasteful and unreliable institution. It occurred to him that an equally satisfactory result might possibly be had more cheaply by training native Swedes in the methods of continental warfare. At the Västerås *riksdag* of 1544 he persuaded the Estates to allow him to try the experiment. Some of the mercenaries were retained to train the new levies; the rest were disbanded; and the King began the formation of a new army, paid, permanent, disciplined and recruited (at first) by voluntary enlistment. And this was the first truly national standing army of modern times.

It was not long before certain disadvantages began to appear. The rate of enlistment was slow. The voluntary principle had soon to be abandoned. A new feature entered into Swedish life with the beginnings of conscription (*utskrivning*).[1] The peasants resented this as a thing unprecedented in peace-time, and at first it was thought advisable to admit many exceptions; but *utskrivning* had come to stay. By the end of the century the population had become reconciled to it, and grumbled at it only as they grumbled at the taxes or the *corvées*—as an evil necessarily incidental to the maintenance of government.[2] Secondly, it was found inconvenient to keep the whole army in being all the time. Some of the soldiers were therefore permitted to return to their farms in peace-time (which saved their keep and necessitated only the payment of a very small yearly retaining-fee); some were billeted in the towns or on the country clergy; and the rest—and these were the only ones who could be said to be on full pay—were employed in guarding the royal castles. Thirdly, the new army was still very inadequately equipped, despite its mercenary drill-sergeants. It consisted very largely of infantry armed with cross-bows or arquebuses. There was little attempt to introduce the new armoured pikemen, deemed so essential on the continent. The ageing King grudged the expense, and he had

[1] For a description of methods of *utskrivning*, see below, pp. 209-10.

[2] The once turbulent border province of Småland was made to provide the kernel of the new army: *cf.* the Highlands after the 'forty-five: *Sv. Krig*, I. 24.

been impressed with the ineffectiveness of this type of soldier in Dacke's rebellion: in the forest regions of Småland, where the revolt took place, the bullets and arrows of the rebels had done great execution upon the lumbering mercenary pikes. Gustav Vasa was ready enough for military experiment when he felt that the results were likely to justify it: he imported gun-founders and artillerists from Germany, established a cannon-foundry in Stockholm, encouraged the construction of what appears to have been a primitive armoured fighting vehicle, and has, in short, every title to be regarded as the founder of the Swedish artillery.[1] But he seems to have persuaded himself that pikes were a needless extravagance. Fortunately the heir to the throne, Erik, had other ideas. In the 'fifties Sweden became involved in war with Russia, and Erik foresaw the approach of another struggle with Denmark. What was good enough for Småland would not suffice for the open fields of Skåne: where cavalry could operate freely, shot must have the protection of pikes. Erik therefore induced his father to rearm the infantry with pikes; he began a remodelling of the administrative and tactical units; and before the old King died considerable progress had been made. It might reasonably have been expected that when the next Danish war broke out there would be Swedish *tercios* to bar the way to the Jutish cavalry.

But, disregarded by continental contemporaries, unnoticed by subsequent historians, the Swedish army was entering upon a period of development which led not to the *tercio* but in precisely the opposite direction. The accession of Erik was the signal for an experiment in tactics which might have become famous if Erik had lived as long, and occupied as central a position in European affairs, as did Maurice of Orange. Among the many interests which engaged Erik's extraordinarily versatile genius, the theory of war took a leading place. He was familiar with the works of Caesar and of Vegetius (a Swedish translation of Vegetius' *Epitome* had appeared early in Gustav Vasa's reign), and he seems also to have been influenced by the theorizings of Machiavelli. He aspired to re-create the Roman legion, and in particular to restore to infantry its offensive character. He perceived that the military methods of his time were unsatisfactory, because they endeavoured to exploit the peculiar advantages of musket and pike simultaneously, and succeeded only in cramping the style of both. It seemed to him that it should not

[1] L. Hammarskiöld, *Ur svenska artilleriets hävder*, pp. 8-10, 13, 71-81.

be impossible to devise a tactical form which should liberate the two arms from the fetters which they imposed upon each other. The military traditions of his country enabled him to appreciate the devastating effect of well-directed fire at close range. From the Swiss he learnt the offensive potentialities of the pike. From his studies of ancient history he imbibed an appreciation of the mobility and flexibility of the Roman cohort. He was the very first commander in Europe to translate into practice those principles of antique warfare to which so many military theorists of the age paid an unfruitful homage. Thirty years before Maurice of Orange, he reached much the same answer to some of the great tactical problems of the day. The instrument of Erik's new system was to be the *fänika* or battalion of 525 men. It was to be divided into five *kvarter* of 105 men. Three of these *kvarter* were to be placed in the front line, grouped to form a single tactical unit: this unit was to comprise a block of pikes, fifteen square,[1] flanked on either side by two columns of musketeers, fifteen deep upon a front of three. The other two *kvarter*, who were mainly equipped with firearms, but stiffened by forty pikemen, were to form the forlorn hope; but in contrast with the plan of the *tercio* they were placed behind the front line, and could thus be used either as skirmishers or as reserve. The battalions were ranged side by side in two lines: Erik was thus the first commander since the coming of firearms consciously to develop linear tactics. The battalion was both an administrative and a tactical unit: four or five of them formed a regiment, or, as Erik liked to call it, a legion.[2] Thus in many respects Erik anticipated the work of Maurice. But he went further. He insisted that the pike, properly supported by musketeers, was an offensive weapon. He used the countermarch offensively, to provide something like a creeping barrage of small-arms fire. He exploited the increased manœuvrability which was the result of his linear formation to execute outflanking movements with his infantry. In regard to cavalry, his work was less important, and its results less happy; but at least he appeared to be familiar with the most recent continental practice: in the very year after the battle of Dreux he adopted the caracole.[3]

[1] More precisely, 171 pikemen and 54 halberdiers.

[2] The clearest account of Erik's system, with a diagram, is in Barkman, *Regementsorganisation*, pp. 65-7.

[3] There may have been some direct influence from France, through Frenchmen in Erik's service: E. Zeeh, *L'Influence française sur les méthodes de guerre en Suède du XVIe au XVIIe siècle*, pp. 19-21.

Against the Danish army in 1565 Erik's new model infantry brilliantly justified itself at the bloody battle of Axtorna; and had his cavalry been of the same quality Axtorna might have been remembered as a landmark in the history of tactics. Erik boldly broke away from the military traditions of his country; but in doing so he resisted the temptation to follow blindly the models in vogue overseas. His reign was too short, his military activity too remote from the main current of European affairs, for his achievements to attract observation abroad; and even in his own country he met with stubborn opposition. Those curious contradictions of character which ruined his political career affected even his military reforms; his arrogance forbade him personally to supervise his system in action on the battlefield, because the Danish commanders were not his equal in rank; and his habit of absenting himself from the front line as soon as fighting was in prospect provoked unkind remark among his troops. The Seven Years' War of the North was upon him before he was ready for it, and it is difficult to recast an army in war-time. And thus it fell out that Erik's experiments perished with him; and one of the most original military thinkers of the sixteenth century has been forgotten until our own day.[1]

Johan III took little interest in military affairs. The army gave him to understand that it had had enough of royal experiments, and demanded that Erik's reforms be abandoned. His political position, as a usurper, was such that he could not afford to ignore these demands. The nobles gained fresh privileges; the Estates received a Charter; and the private soldier was allowed (in the middle of the Danish war) to throw aside his heavy modern equipment and return to the armaments and tactics of 'good King Gösta'. No further explanation need be sought for the disastrous peace of Stettin.[2] Throughout the reign the army continued to decline in efficiency. Its successes against the Russians are to be ascribed in part to the leadership of Pontus de la Gardie, but mainly to the still more inept tactics of the Muscovite armies. It was a war of positions and sieges, and this concealed the inability of the Swedish troops to fight pitched battles against good cavalry. The last decade of the century saw Sweden too occupied with internal strife to think of military reform. It was

[1] Neither Oman nor Delbrück mentions Erik XIV.

[2] So pronounced was the army's aversion to heavy equipment that in 1575 twenty targes were handed over by the armoury to the royal kitchens for use as pot-lids: Alm, *Blanka vapen och skyddsvapen*, p. 238.

not until the accession of Karl IX that the problem was again taken up in earnest.[1]

Karl IX found the Swedish armies little more advanced than they had been in 1550. The work of Erik XIV was almost forgotten. No enemy with modern equipment or a modern tactic had attacked the country since 1570, and the army was now quite unfitted to deal with a resolute invader. Karl did at least realize this. It was his misfortune that he had himself no talent for soldiering, nor even much ability as a military organizer. He did his best. Confronted successively by wars with Poland, Russia and Denmark, he sought to modernize his army according to the precepts of foreign experts. In 1601 he was fortunate enough to secure the services of the leading theorist of the Netherlands school, John of Nassau; to whom it fell, by a singular irony, to attempt to indoctrinate the Swedish armies with principles which had first been applied by a Swedish King.[2]

John of Nassau had a task difficult to the point of impossibility. He was asked to revolutionize the tactical system of an army which was entirely lacking either in the organization, or the weapons, or the training necessary for the purpose. It was also small in numbers, and Karl had great difficulty in increasing it. *Utskrivning* was unpopular, the general opinion being that the army was large enough: the *riksdag* of 1600 even suggested its reduction. Nine thousand men were conscripted in 1601, but by 1604 the King was reduced to filling the gaps in the ranks by the expensive hiring of mercenaries. From 1605 to 1611 a return was made to *utskrivning*; but the results never came up to expectation, since the system was vitiated by inefficiencies both at the centre and at the periphery. Too much was left to ill-controlled local authorities, and attempts by the central government to establish permanent military representatives in the provinces did not much mend matters. The lack of any administrative unit above the *fänika* was a nuisance: how great a nuisance can be realized if we imagine no mediate instance between the War Office and the battalion. Conscription was not only inefficient, it was tardy: in 1611 the conscripts did not make their appearance until the end of April.[3]

Still more deplorable was the backwardness of the army in the matter of armaments. The laxity of Johan and Sigismund had

[1] Petri, I. 201; *Sv. Krig*, I. 76; *ibid.*, Supp. Vol. II. 19.
[2] Petri, I. 309, 316.
[3] *ibid.*, I. 305-6, 354; E. Hornborg, *Gustav Adolf*, p. 79; Barkman, *op. cit.*, pp. 71, 115; *Sv. Krig*, I. 96.

permitted the infantry to discard pikes and body-armour almost entirely. Their favourite weapon was now the arquebus, fitted with wheel- or matchlock: they had not even been equipped with the musket, though that weapon had almost superseded the arquebus on the continent, except for skirmishers. Thus the foot, virtually unprotected by pikes, was at the mercy of any enterprising cavalry commander. Certainly the Swedish cavalry was in no case to protect it. For the horsemen, like their fellows in the infantry, had drooped under the weight of their armaments.[1] They had flung aside both the cuirass and the lance, and had become, one and all, ill-protected pistoleers. It was cheaper, it was more comfortable, and anything seemed to be good enough to beat the Russians. Less skill was needed in riding, less training for the horses. Karl IX bitterly observed that all that his cavalry was good for was to plague peasants.[2] For both arms retribution was preparing. The Polish horsemen, unequalled in Europe, and unperverted by the caracole, were soon to prove their ability to face fantastic odds against their Swedish opponents, and to drive them from the field with a charge at the gallop; and when that had happened, the fate of the Swedish foot was not enviable. Karl did see that danger; and even before 1605 he was doing his best to reintroduce the pike for infantry and the sword for cavalry. But against the passive resistance of his army even his strong will and imperious temper were unable to prevail. It was not easy, moreover, to obtain all the pikes and swords required at short notice; and those who were issued with them as often as not refused to exercise themselves in their use.[3]

In these circumstances it is no wonder that John of Nassau went home in disgust after only a year with the Swedish army.[4] But before he went he had made a start in converting it to the new Dutch system, and his successors in the command (Karl especially)

[1] Alm, *Blanka vapen och skyddsvapen*, pp. 242-4; Petri, I. 308-9; *Sv. Krig*, Supp. Vol. II. 19. Karl's experiences were by no means unique. In most European armies pikemen were giving trouble to their commanders by refusing to wear the prescribed armour; and military writers lamented the tendency to cut short the pike for convenience' sake. Cavalry armour was getting lighter too. As the penetrative power of the musket increased, the armour needed to give protection against it was becoming so heavy that neither man nor horse could easily bear it: Wijn, p. 138; Odenrick, II. 19, 34; Monro, II. 191. It is noteworthy that Monro, champion of the pike as he was, selected as 'the most honourable of all weapons, and my choice in the day of battell', not the pike, but the half-pike: Monro, II. 192.

[2] Alm, *Eldhandvapen*, I. 156.

[3] Petri, I. 339.

[4] *ibid.*, I. 331.

attempted to carry on his work. Since war was actually raging, the change was largely a matter of improvisations and short-cuts: for success, it would have needed a period of peace and a thorough reorganization of the army's peace-time administration and training. As it was, the officers were sceptical of the new methods, and the soldiers were sulky and slack in practising manœuvres. Moreover, until complete rearmament had been carried through, the Swedish commanders were taking great risks in applying a system of tactics for which they were not properly equipped. The result was the appalling disaster of Kirkholm in 1605, when the Polish general Chodkiewicz defeated a Swedish force nearly four times the size of his own and actually killed almost thrice as many Swedes as the total number of Polish troops engaged. The battle was lost, partly because the Swedes fell into a simple booby-trap of the type employed by William the Conqueror at Hastings, partly because they lacked the ability to manœuvre quickly to meet an emergency, and partly because they were desperately short of pikes. When the Polish cavalry had swept the Swedish pistoleers from the field, the battle ended in a massacre of foot similar to that which closed the battle of Marston Moor, but even more sanguinary.[1] Karl's reaction to Kirkholm was to offer all sorts of inducements to men who would be prepared to train as pikemen: their farms were to be for ever free of tax, they were to have special pay and quarters, they were even to be allowed to sport a coat of arms. The inducements proved inadequate: the *sköldeknektar* (as they were called) remained an insignificant handful.[2]

The War of Kalmar revealed how meagre was the result of Karl's efforts. Despite heavy purchases of modern arms and equipment, despite continued efforts to improve organization, the Swedish army in 1611 was in no condition to meet the Danes in pitched battle upon equal terms. The Poles had just reinforced the lessons of Kirkholm by crushing de la Gardie at Klušino. Morale was low. Karl had more or less committed the country to the adoption of something like the new Dutch tactics; but he had been quite unable to provide the necessary preconditions upon which success depended. There were no stable tactical or administrative units; no adequate

[1] There are accounts of Kirkholm (not easy to reconcile in all details) in Petri, I. 345-51; Korzon, II. 144-6; Kukiel, pp. 59-62; C. Bennedich, *Ur det gamla Gardets öden*, pp. 37-9; but the best is now in Barkman, *Svea livgardets historia*, I. 530-43.

[2] Petri, I. 353.

system of training; no really competent staff. The administration of the army, both at the centre and the circumference, was defective, where it was not non-existent. The system of recruitment was slow and unsatisfactory. The country was largely dependent upon importations for the rearmament which had been undertaken. A King of no ordinary measure was needed, if Sweden were ever to become a respectable military power: a King who should be at once a tactician capable of grasping and applying the principles of Maurice, and an administrator able to enforce obedience to his will.

(iii) *Gustav Adolf's Administrative Reforms*

(a) *Recruitment: Pay: Organization*

The education of Gustav Adolf had from an early stage included instruction in the principles of the military art. Under Skytte's guidance he had been made familiar with those classical authors—Livy, Aelian, Frontinus, Vegetius, Polybius—who had provided the theoretical basis for Maurice's reforms; and he seems also to have read the more recent exponents of their doctrines, such as Machiavelli and Justus Lipsius. At the same time he learned something of the methods of the Spanish school, and is said to have acquired that facility in drawing up an army in the shape of 'the Quadrate or Square, the Wedg, the *Tenaille* or Tongs, the Saw and the Globe' to which contemporaries devoted such innumerable pages of their textbooks, but which they took good care to forget upon the battlefield.[1] He certainly learned some mathematics, and ever afterwards insisted on its practical value to the soldier; and Skytte seems also to have insisted upon his familiarizing himself with such mechanical and engineering devices as a soldier might expect to have to use. But Skytte's knowledge of war was purely theoretical; and for practical instruction or training Gustav Adolf had to look elsewhere. He got astonishingly little of it. We hear of his meeting Dodo von Inn- und Knyphausen in 1607; and in 1608 he was certainly given two months' intensive instruction by Johan de la Gardie, then on leave from the Russian theatre of war. His tutor, Otto Helmer von Mörner, may also have helped him, for von Mörner had been in the Dutch service.

[1] Turner, *Pallas Armata*, p. 112; Barkman, *Gustaf Adolfs regementsorganisation*, p. 69. C. Falls (*Elizabeth's Irish Wars*, p. 43) reproduces these formations from Barnaby Rich's *A Pathway to Military Practice*, and seems to imply that they were actually used in battle.

But at the time of Gustav Adolf's accession his military education was at best sketchy.[1]

It was supplemented, perhaps, by a meeting with John of Nassau at Heidelberg in 1620, when long conversations on the art of war are said to have taken place[2]; but on the whole Gustav Adolf might fairly claim to be in this respect mostly self-educated. No military textbook by a Swedish author existed before the end of the reign, nor any Swedish translation of a modern military author before 1626; and no training was available in Sweden such as was soon to be had at Kristian IV's academy at Sorø.[3] Indeed, few contemporaries shared John of Nassau's belief in the value of an education of this sort: a knowledge of the elements of drill, the ability to maintain discipline, practical experience in the field, and above all mere length of service, were popularly supposed to be all that a general required in the way of education. Gustav Adolf did not share this view. Though his formal training had been short and scanty, he acknowledged his debt to it and recommended diligent study to all military aspirants. To learn by practical experience, he held, was to learn the slow way, and not perhaps the safest way.[4] He would have agreed with Turner, that 'It is a pity, and sometimes a matter of sport, to hear men glory that they are old soldiers, who have never either learned, or have forgot, what belongs to their profession, and so upon the matter prove themselves to be old fools'; and with Monro, that 'It is not time, or number of yeares that makes a brave soldier, but the continuall meditation of exercise and practice.'[5] Among the list of military virtues which Gustav Adolf expected in a commander—a list which no doubt reflects the neo-Stoicism of Lipsius—were not merely *virtus*, caution, authority and fortune, but also science.[6]

Nevertheless, it is clear that much of the King's skill as a commander was in fact acquired by practical experience in the field. Such education as he had predisposed him to the Dutch school of

[1] For Gustav Adolf's military education, see *Karl XII på slagfältet*, I. 75, 119-20; Barkman, pp. 69-73; E. Wrangel, *De Betrekkingen tusschen Zweden en de Nederlanden op het Gebied van Letteren en Wetenschap*, p. 56.

[2] Barkman, pp. 92-3.

[3] Sjöstrand, *Grunddragen av den militära undervisningens . . . utvecklingshistoria*, pp. 41, 44, 47, 52, 56, 59, 201, 207-9. Sorø was founded in 1623: K. C. Rockstroh, *Udviklingen af den nationale Haer i Danmark i det 17. og 18. Aarhundrede*, I. 48.

[4] Styffe, pp. 65-7; Sjöstrand, pp. 100-1.

[5] *Pallas Armata*, p. 210; Monro, II. 175, 196; and *cf.* Sjöstrand, pp. 16-18, 78-80.

[6] Generalstaben, *Gustaf II Adolf*, p. 74. For the neo-Stoicism of Lipsius, and its effects on soldiering, see G. Oestreich, *op. cit.*, *passim.*

fighting, and most of the military men with whom he came into contact belonged to that school [1]; but the application of their doctrines to the special circumstances of warfare in Skåne, Ingria or Livonia had to be made on the spot. Gustav Adolf's early wars presented very differing military problems, offering between them a wide variety of experience; and the King did not fail to profit by it. By the time he landed in Germany he had acquired a technical mastery of nearly all aspects of generalship. On this point contemporaries are emphatic and unanimous. Apart from all questions of tactical brilliance or strategic insight, Gustav Adolf had a thorough knowledge of every side of the commander's daily work. Spanheim praises him as a drillmaster and trainer [2]; Monro observes that he was so skilful in embattling an army that he might have acted as his own major-general.[3] He was certainly an expert gunner.[4] He was famous throughout Europe for his skill in constructing earthworks and field-fortifications [5]: Radziwiłł complained in 1622 that he could not cope with an enemy 'who like a mole fights under ground, and who being weaker in cavalry protects himself against it by trenches and bastions' [6]. He had mastered—and indeed improved on—the fashionable art of castrametation.[7] He had a wonderful eye for country, and was esteemed especially expert at 'recognoscing'.[8] And though his sieges were few, they proved him thoroughly versed in the latest Netherlands assault-techniques.[9] In short, he seems to have made himself familiar with every branch of his business, for (as Monro remarks) 'he thought nothing well done that he did not himself'.[10]

In a memorandum written about 1619 Gustav Adolf laid down

[1] Wrangel, p. 7; Barkman, p. 74, quoting Axel Oxenstierna.

[2] *Sv. Krig*, Supp. Vol. II. 99.

[3] Monro, II. 31.

[4] Hammarskiöld, *Ur svenska artilleriets hävder*, p. 200.

[5] N. Ahnlund, *Axel Oxenstierna*, p. 253; *Sv. Krig*, Supp. Vol. II. 404-5; Monro, II. 127; Ericsson, *Olof Hansson Örnehufvud*, p. 20. For the high standards he set in this matter, see the story in Monro, II. 38-9.

[6] X. Liske, *Öfversikt af den polska litteraturen med särskilt afseende på den svenska historien*, p. 360.

[7] H. Hamilton, *Krigsmaktens och krigskonstens tillstånd i Sverige under konung Gustaf II Adolfs regering*, p. 389; Wrangel, p. 7; Monro, II. 209, which presumably reflects Gustav Adolf's practice.

[8] 'In point of recognoscing His Majesties judgement was wonderfull. . . .': Monro, II. 92. For Gustav Adolf's interest in maps, see Försvarsstaben, *Vägar och vägkunskap i Mellaneuropa under trettioåriga krigets sista skede*, pp. 41-2.

[9] For Gustav Adolf's interest in the science of fortification, see L. W. Munthe, *Kungl. Fortifikationens historia*, I. 214-16.

[10] Monro, II. 21.

the preconditions for the existence of a satisfactory army. It must have a proper recruiting system; its units must be properly organized; it must be strictly mustered, to prevent frauds; and it must be straitly disciplined.[1] None of these preconditions existed in Sweden upon his accession; and quite early in the reign he addressed himself to the work of introducing them.

The first problem was the basic one of manpower. And at once the question arose as to the relative merits of a conscript and a mercenary army. The Swedish foot was provided mainly by *utskrivning*; the Swedish cavalry partly by native volunteers, partly by *rusttjänst*. But both cavalry and infantry had latterly been supplemented by hired troops, and the performance of the native levies in the War of Kalmar had not been impressive. The advantages and disadvantages of the mercenary and the conscript were at this period a matter of general debate among military men. The case for a national army had been strongly put by Machiavelli, influenced no doubt by the example of the farmer-soldier of the early Roman republic; and from Machiavelli the idea had passed to Lazarus von Schwendi, who in his *Kurtzer Begriff eines gantzen Kriegswesens* (1578) had urged the creation of a German national army, part volunteer, part conscript, on the grounds of patriotism, economy and administrative convenience.[2] At the turn of the century various rulers had made experiments in this direction, especially in Germany. Local militias had been raised (usually of infantry only) under the name of *Landesdefension* or *Defensionswerk*, with the aim of supplementing, and in some cases of eventually replacing, the old mercenary armies. Maurice of Hesse had been prominent in this movement; and he was followed by the rulers of the Palatinate, Wolfenbüttel and electoral Saxony, but above all by Maximilian of Bavaria, whose *Landesdefension*, initiated in 1596, was much the most considerable of all these attempts.[3] Outside Germany, national militias of ancient lineage survived here and there—moribund in England, vigorous

[1] Styffe, p. 5.

[2] E. von Frauenholz, *Lazarus von Schwendi*, pp. 16-21. Von Schwendi wrote: '. . . im grundt is das sicherist und beste sich seiner underthanen zum Krieg, sowiel man immer gelegenheit und mittel darzu gehaben mag, fürnemlich zu gebrauchen, und sy bewert zumachen, in ain Austailung, aufbott und ordnung zu bringen, und zum Krieg anzufüeren. Dann die frembden besolden leutt, sein shier nimmer so trew, gehorsamb und so fertig, als die Underthanen, und kosten viel mehr aufzubringen und zu erhalten': *ibid.*, p. 205.

[3] For this, see E. von Frauenholz, *Die Landesdefension in der Zeit des dreissigjährigen Krieges*, *passim*; Lenz, II. 128-31; Wertheim, I. 67-75; Droysen, *Militärwesen*, pp. 5-7.

and highly effective in Poland.[1] In Denmark, arrangements closely resembling the Swedish *utskrivning* existed side by side with an army which was mainly professional.[2]

The contrast, it should be emphasized, was felt to be not so much between native and foreign troops as between conscripts and mercenaries; and there were many who thought that Spain had found the right solution. For the Spanish army was predominantly a mercenary army (the conscripts being mostly malefactors, very prone to desertion), but at the same time it was also a predominantly national army. Most of the mercenaries were in fact Spanish volunteers, and many of them were *hidalgos.* They were employed on long-term contracts, unlike most foreign mercenaries; and this, together with their national pride, gave to the Spanish armies greater solidity than was possessed by the casual aggregations of professionals, hired for the season, which made up a great part of the armies of most other states.[3] It certainly appeared to be true that the national militia, or the national conscript army, was inferior as a rule to the army of mercenaries, whether of the Spanish type or not. The German experiments with militias all failed most ignominiously. The idea of training successive batches of raw peasants in the countermarch did not appeal to drill-sergeants when practised mercenaries were to be had for the hiring.[4] Conscription required considerable administrative machinery, if it were to work well; and because fresh drafts tended to be made only at annual intervals, it was difficult to keep units up to strength. Those for whom the example of antiquity had weight could reflect that even the Romans abandoned the notion of a citizen militia after the battle of Actium.[5] Kristian IV (despite the urgings of an economically minded Council) was always sceptical about *utskrivning*: 'worse than beasts', he called his conscripts; and he disliked putting modern weapons in the hands of a peasantry which had every reason to feel discontented.[6] The crisis of his German war forced him to forget his fears; but though the performance of his conscripts was considered not unsatisfactory, their opponents had a poor opinion

[1] For England, see Cruickshank, *Elizabeth's Army*, pp. 6-8, 10; for Poland, Laskowski, *Uwagi*, pp. 38-9; Kukiel, p. 45.

[2] Rockstroh, I. 4-38; T. Mathisen, *Fra bondeoppbud til legdshaer, passim.*

[3] Altamira, III. 289-93; Wijn, p. 57.

[4] As was said of the Württemberg militia, 'des malheureux arrachés à leurs familles font toûjours de mauvais soldats': Priorato, p. 184.

[5] T. Parker, *The Roman Legions*, p. 76.

[6] Rockstroh, I. 65.

of them.[1] But perhaps the weightiest testimony of all against the conscript army was the experience of the Dutch: the great reforms of Maurice were carried through (and contemporaries believed that they could only have been carried through) by an army of punctually paid mercenaries.[2]

On the other hand, there was no disguising the fact that the mercenary army was subject to inconveniences and disadvantages of its own. The most obvious and unavoidable of these was the expense. This might not have mattered so much if armies had remained small. But armies were getting steadily larger: at the beginning of the Thirty Years' War an army of 20,000 was considered large; in 1627 Wallenstein had 100,000; in the autumn of 1631 Gustav Adolf had 130,000.[3] Moreover, a considerable proportion of them—and an increasingly large proportion—would be cavalry; and cavalry, even though the very heaviest types were now declining, was terribly costly.[4] The waging of warfare by mercenary armies was becoming possible only to large or wealthy states—hence the attempts at *Landesdefension* by small ones—and the example of Spain might suggest that there were limits to the burdens which even large and wealthy states could bear. It was, no doubt, some partial offset that the mercenary colonel had now to make himself responsible for the heavy capital outlay on horses, arms and equipment; but colonels made allowance—very handsome allowance—for this in the terms of their contract, as the men did in their (at least nominal) rates of wages. And it was in any case a question whether an arrangement which left to the *entrepreneur* the provision of arms and equipment, and so precluded any standardization in these matters, was in the interests of military efficiency.[5]

Again, the mercenary army (apart perhaps from the Spanish)

[1] Rockstroh, I. 83; H. Hallwich, *Fünf Bücher Geschichte Wallensteins*, II. 183, quoting Aldringen.

[2] Though Johan of Nassau himself was not so sure: *Krijgskundige Aantekening van Johan van Nassau*, pp. iv, x.

[3] Frauenholz, *Söldnertum*, I. 36-7; *Sv. Krig*, V. 27-8.

[4] In England in the 1590's it cost about £30 to provide and equip a cavalryman: Falls, *op. cit.*, p. 53.

[5] Wijn, pp. 10-13; Droysen, *Militärwesen*, p. 90; Wertheim, I. 83: 'the summit of a Landsknecht's desires was to have extra stockings [over and above those issued to him] of scarlet cloth, laced with real gold cord'. It is curious that Wallenstein, usually so progressive a reformer, should have preferred to leave this matter of armament to his colonels—no doubt from economic motives: in February 1632 he wrote to Aldringen, 'Wasz der herr vor die waffen geben wirdt, dz zihe er derjenigen comp. wiederumb ab, welche es bekommen werden; dan man musz den brauch, nicht lassen auffkommen, dz man den Obristen die Waffen schaffet': H. Hallwich, *Briefe und Akten zur Geschichte Wallensteins*, II. 225-6.

lacked those reserves of morale which arise from patriotic feeling. The men followed the standard, and had no hesitation in changing sides once the standard was lost: superstitious, connoisseurs of military excellence, they tended to rally to the general who had Fortune and Reputation on his side.[1] Their colonels regarded war as a business, the raising of troops as an investment: to be given the right to levy a regiment was a lucrative mark of royal favour.[2] The men, of whom a good proportion would, ideally, be old soldiers (old soldiers were put in the front rank of pikes and were paid double), were bound to one another by fixed rules and conventions: they had all the ceremoniousness of a gild, and all a trade union's prickly insistence upon its rights.[3] They were very delicate to handle; their usual reaction to what they conceived almost as an industrial dispute was to mutiny; they had in many cases their own systems of internal discipline; and there were certain things—for instance, heavy manual labour such as digging—which they were not prepared to do. Colonels of mercenary regiments notoriously cheated by drawing pay for non-existent soldiers; personation at musters was a normal occurrence; and the legalized addition to the colonel's emoluments of what may be regarded perhaps as a cost-of-living allowance, in the form of the admission of so many passevolants or dead-pays[4] on the rolls, was simply a sign of their employer's inability to eradicate the abuse. The shortness of their hiring-contracts (as a rule not more than six months) made the planning of any long-term operations difficult and the execution of any protracted scheme of training practically impossible. The short contracts, moreover, added to the financial burden, for a lump sum had to be paid down upon the

[1] P. Sörensson, *Krisen vid de svenska arméerna i Tyskland efter Banérs död*, p. 17; *cf.* Turner: 'I had swallowed, without chewing, in Germanie, a very dangerous maxime, which was, that soe we serve our master honestlie, it is no matter what master we serve': *Memoirs*, p. 14.

[2] *cf. The Swedish Intelligencer*, I. 117: '. . . in reward of which service and some others, the Emperor makes him a Colonell, granting him commission to raise two new Regiments'. Aldringen began life as a lackey, and ended as a Field-Marshal; Leslie returned to Scotland in 1638 a rich man: examples could be multiplied: M. von Boehn, *Wallenstein*, p. 90; C. Sanford Terry, *Alexander Leslie*, p. 10.

[3] Wertheim, I. 121-7; Droysen, *Militärwesen*, pp. 23, 28-31, where he writes: 'so erkennen wir . . . bei dem Militärwesen jener Zeit einen durchaus zünftigen Charakter. Das Verhältnis der Befehlhaber zu den gemeinen Knechten ist das des Meisters zu den Gesellen. In weitschweifigen Formalitäten, stereotypen Phrasen, die sie begleiten, bleibt das Kriegshandwerk hinter keinem der übrigen zünftischen Gewerben zurück.'

[4] *Arkiv till upplysning om svenska krigens . . . historia*, III. lv-lx, 282-3; Droysen, *Militärwesen*, p. 27. For a discussion of dead-pays, see Wijn, p. 119.

conclusion of each new contract, and a month's pay was due on first mustering. Hence the innovation of Maurice, who continued to pay his mercenaries throughout the winter, even though there were no operations in progress, in preference to facing the heavy outlay of disbandment and rehiring—an arrangement which materially assisted his training of his men in the new methods of warfare.

There was thus something to be said against both conscript and mercenary armies, and it does not appear that Gustav Adolf had at first any decided preference for conscripts; indeed, at some time fairly early in the reign he made a note of his reasons for preferring mercenaries: they fought better, because they were volunteers; they avoided a drain on the nation's manpower; they were experienced and trained men; and they had a better reputation in the field ('*et bella constant fama*').[1] But he soon learned to rate the military qualities of his subjects more highly: there was nothing wrong with their spirit, he wrote, provided they were well led. No soldiers could excel them in forest warfare; and they formed first-rate material for the navy.[2] By 1622 the Danish envoy Peder Galt was commenting acidly on the King's overweening confidence in his Swedish troops.[3] And in the following year the King dilated on their excellences for the benefit of Maurice of Orange, in language which could hardly have gone much further in enthusiastic commendation.[4] By 1629 he was warning the *råd* that '*exteri milites* are faithless, dangerous, and expensive'.[5]

But whatever his view of the question, Gustav Adolf was always forced by circumstances to supplement native by hired troops. Sometimes their numbers were few—in 1617 he was able to entertain all the foreign officers at one dinner-party[6]; often they were very many. To begin with, they were drawn, for choice, from England and Scotland[7]; many names famous in later Swedish history

[1] Styffe, p. 61. [2] *ibid.*, pp. 4-6.

[3] '*Mirum, quantum* king of Sweden *confidat in pedite, equite et navibus suis, adeo ut et omnibus se in illis superiorem credat*': *Peder Galts Depescher*, p. 22.

[4] 'Pedites hi non mercede conducti, aut propter periculorum ignorationem data in cauponis fide collecti, sed certo judicio ac delectu habito, e rustica plebe conscripti, integri aetate, sueti laboribus, ferendis oneribus, tolerando frigori, aestui, inediae, vigiliis, nullis adsueti delitiis, et qui parvo contenti sunt vivere. Plerique non ignari rei communis nauticae artis fabricandi, obsequio erga superiores prompti, nec mandata ulla recusantes, disciplinae militaris observantissimi; faciles ad discendum militaria exercitia, validis corporibus; et si res tulerit, ac recte fuerint ducti, mortis malorumque contemptores': *AOSB*, I. II. 594 *note*.

[5] *RRP*, I. 219. [6] *Abraham Brahes tidebok*, p. 95.

[7] Oxenstierna wrote of the English and Scots recruits in February 1630: 'they are good fellows, easier to deal with than others tend to be': *AOSB*, I. v. 109.

established themselves on Scandinavian soil at this period by way of service in Scottish regiments—as Hamilton, Douglas, Sinclair, Ramsay, Fleetwood, Colquhoun; later, especially after 1631, they were mainly German. The proportion of foreign mercenaries in the Swedish armies showed a steady increase, which became rapid after Breitenfeld. Sweden could not supply more than a small and decreasing fraction of the men needed for Gustav Adolf's ever-expanding area of operations in Germany; the easing of the financial strain after Breitenfeld made it possible to hire more troops than ever before, and about the same time the muster-money demanded seems to have dropped sharply [1]; and in any case Gustav Adolf came more and more to pursue a deliberate policy of avoiding the sacrifice of Swedish lives. If the Swedish regiments were kept intact, he remarked on one occasion, Sweden would still be safe, even if 'not a bone' of the mercenary force should return from the campaign.[2] Swedish troops were more and more employed on garrison duty (in some cases because they were too raw to be put into the field without further training), or stationed in those vital coastal areas of Pomerania which Gustav Adolf considered it to be essential to safeguard, and which he therefore entrusted to troops upon whose fidelity he could rely.[3] There were some, indeed, who considered that the Swedish soldier was no match for the German in the field, and was more liable to fall sick; but the justice of this contention is disputed.[4] At all events it is a fact that the percentage of Swedes in the Swedish army declined steeply. Except at the very beginning of the German campaign they rarely formed a half of it; at Breitenfeld barely a quarter. In February-March 1632, of 140,000 men under Gustav Adolf's command, only 13,000 were Swedes and only one brigade was wholly Swedish.[5] After Gustav Adolf's death, Axel Oxenstierna followed the policy of putting the burden of the war on the shoulders of Germany, and this policy was applied to the provision of manpower as well as of other military necessities.[6] As Germany became exhausted, and Sweden's financial

[1] *Arkiv*, III. lxiv; Droysen, *Militärwesen*, pp. 14-15. The drop occurred *before* Breitenfeld.

[2] *Sv. Krig*, III. 191.

[3] *ibid.*, IV. 227, V. 365; *SRARP*, I. 217.

[4] P. Sörensson, *Krisen*, p. 15; *id.*, *Fältherrar, härorganisation och krigföring under trettioåriga krigets senare skede. En orientering*, p. 143; contrast F. Pira's review of the former of these in *HT* (1933).

[5] P. Sörensson, *Ekonomi och krigföring under Gustaf Adolfs tyska fälttåg*, p. 298; *Sv. Krig*, V. 298; Petri, II. 154.

[6] *AOSB*, I. VIII. 162, 610.

resources (for this and other reasons) contracted, armies diminished greatly in size and fell to the level of 1620, or below it. At the battle of Wittstock in 1636, Banér had only 16,000 men, and of these perhaps one-third were native Swedes.[1] Nevertheless, occasional *utskrivningar* still provided reinforcements from home, and as late as 1646 no less than 6630 men were levied for despatch to Germany.[2]

Gustav Adolf could not foresee these developments. In the early years of the reign it was obvious that Sweden could not afford the financial burden of large mercenary forces; and for that reason, apart from any personal preference for the one or the other, he must make every effort to improve and reorganize the system of *utskrivning* which he had inherited from his grandfather.

In the half-century before Gustav Adolf's accession the procedure for *utskrivning* had gradually taken shape. It had become customary to appoint a mixed commission to do the work, drawn half from military, half from civil, officials. Under Johan III there had been initiated the system of *löftesmän*, whereby every man liable to military service had someone responsible for him, so that if he deserted, his guarantor could be called on to pay a fine or find a substitute. It was already customary to include in the register of conscriptable material all those between the ages of 15 and 50, though it was the general rule to take only those between the ages of 20 and 40. By 1611, in fact, the main outlines had been established: what was lacking was efficient administration and continuity of policy.[3] Gustav Adolf made little alteration in the system for some years after his accession, though he was certainly conscious of the need for some reform.[4] The question was complicated by the semi-independent position of the two royal duchies, and by the fact that Älvsborg and its dependent *härader* were still in pawn to Denmark.[5] In 1617, however, the upper age-limit for inclusion in the registers was raised from 50 to 60; and in 1620 Gustav Adolf drew up new and elaborate regulations which laid down fixed principles for *utskrivning*, established rules for the conduct of the commissioners, and, in general,

[1] L. Tingsten, *Fältmarskalkarna Johan Banér och Lennart Torstensson såsom härförare*, pp. 63-75; *Det svenska svärdet*, p. 112. Torstensson had no more than 15,000 at the opening of the campaign of 1642: S. Lundgren, *Johan Adler Salvius*, p. 201.

[2] Försvarsstaben, *Från Femern och Jankow till Westfaliska Freden*, pp. 78, 80.

[3] Barkman, pp. 107-12; *Sv. Krig*, II. 133.

[4] See, *e.g.*, *AOSB*, I. II. 370, where Oxenstierna speaks of the need for peace so that the militia may be reformed.

[5] See above, Vol. I, pp. 122-38.

put the whole system for the first time upon a solid and satisfactory basis.[1] The upper age-limit was now abolished altogether, so that all males over 15 were eligible for inclusion in the lists. At the same time the limits 18 to 40 were fixed for those actually to be conscripted, though in practice the range was slightly wider.[2] The significance of abolishing the upper age-limit becomes clear in the light of the procedure which the commissioners employed. The conscriptable persons (with certain exceptions to be noticed presently) were organized into groups of ten—the *rotar*—and when the annual conscription was held each *rota* had to supply, as a rule, one man suitable for service—*i.e.* one man between the ages of 18 and 40.[3] By including in the *rotar* old men who were incapable of service the effect was obtained of a much more rigorous conscription of those of strictly military age. Those members of the *rota* who were not conscripted were expected (in practice, forced) to contribute each the sum of 18 *daler* (the so-called *rotepenningar*) to fit out the conscript.[4] The *utskrivning* was done by a commission, heralded by royal proclamations read from the pulpit by the clergy. The commission comprised the military officer in charge of the recruiting district, the *landshövding* or *ståthållare*, and the *lagman*; assisted by inferior military officers, the *häradshövding*, the hundred-jury, the local bailiff, the priest, and some others. Upon the arrival of the commissioners, they were met with the revised lists of eligibles, drawn up by the local priest and his vestrymen (*sexmän*), and scrutinized by the *häradshövding*. All inhabitants were bound to assemble to meet the commissioners; and men who absented themselves, together with travelling pedlars and craftsmen 'on the road', were chosen to serve without further ado or enquiry. The *rotar* being made up, and exemptions verified, the commission repaired to the local assembly-hall (*tingstugan*). Each *rota* then filed in, and the most likely looking candidate was haled off, soon to be mustered and drafted to his unit.[5] Until 1627 it was possible for a *rota* to hire a substitute, but in that year the practice was forbidden because it impoverished the *rota* and made its members incapable of paying their ordinary dues and taxes.[6] It was, however, possible for a whole

[1] Styffe, p. 6 *seqq.*
[2] *Sv. Krig*, II. 133-4.
[3] The *rota*-system was in existence in Stockholm already at the close of the fifteenth century: Schück, *Stockholm vid 1400-talets slut*, p. 384 *seqq.*
[4] H. Swenne, *Svenska adelns ekonomiska privilegier 1612-1651*, p. 221; Petri, II. 20.
[5] Styffe, pp. 14-25; Barkman, pp. 116-20.
[6] Barkman, p. 117.

district to contract out of the national conscription: thus Dalarna concluded an agreement with the King in 1621 whereby the inhabitants were exempted in return for maintaining a standing force of 1400 foot; and this example was later followed by other provinces.[1] The anxiety of the government to avoid the appearance of anything like martial law in all these proceedings, and in any arising from them, is noteworthy: the presence of the *lagman* ensured that the ordinary law of the land should not be flouted in the *tingstuga*[2]; and the King took especial pains to see that the trial of deserters took place before the civil authorities, with the military in the rôle of public prosecutor, 'since [he wrote] in all legal process it is unreasonable that one man should be both accuser and judge'.[3]

The commissioners were given explicit instructions as to the type of man to be preferred in choosing conscripts. Apart from absentees, who were taken irrespective of their occupation, the favourite selections were 'redundant' craftsmen, journeymen, and young peasant boys. The King preferred them to be persons of some little property, for if they had money they would be well nourished, and it is easier to fight on a good constitution than on a bad one. Journeymen craftsmen were approved of because they were considered to be 'usually peasant lads who from a light and wilful temper have shown no stomach for farming and have therefore learnt a craft'. The 'scum of the earth', on the other hand, was viewed with disfavour, and accepted only with reluctance and to fill gaps.[4] Various classes of persons were altogether exempt: those who had a son already serving; the only sons of widows; workers in the armaments industry or in the mines—hence an annual exodus to seek temporary employment in these sheltered industries; priests, bailiffs, N.C.O.s' personal servants.[5] And, most important of all, the nobility. The nobles themselves, as bound to do service on horseback (*rusttjänst*), were exempt altogether. So too were their personal servants; and special privileges were granted to their peasants. Until 1627 *frälsebönder* were grouped in *rotar* of 20 instead of 10; and they paid

[1] *Handlingar rörande Skandinaviens historia*, XXXV. 210-16.

[2] See, for instance, *AOSB*, I. II. 319.

[3] Styffe, p. 46.

[4] *ibid.*, pp. 37, 40: contrast the familiar complaint of Barnaby Rich: 'We disburden the prison of thieves, we rob the taverns and alehouses of tosspots and ruffians, we scour both town and country of rogues and vagabonds': quoted in Falls, *op. cit.*, pp. 45-6.

[5] Styffe, p. 29. Additional exemptions (including fox- and bird-catchers and saltpetre-men) were included in the instructions for 1631: *Arkiv*, III. 248-54.

only half as much in *rotepenningar*, and only half as much towards the commissioners' travelling expenses, as did the other peasants. One important countervailing disadvantage was that the noble had the right to name any of his peasants, at his pleasure, to serve as a conscript. In the last few years of the reign, however, these noble privileges were somewhat curtailed. After 1626 the national emergency induced the nobility to take an ampler share of the nation's burdens, both in regard to taxation (as for instance the Stock Tax) and in regard to *utskrivning*. In January 1627 it was agreed that the peasants of the nobility, like the crown-peasants and tax-paying peasants, should be grouped in *rotar* of 10, and that this should apply even to those living within the *frihetsmil*, and *inom rå och rör*.[1] The nobility urged that this should not be taken as a precedent; but Gustav Adolf refused to give any pledge on that score, and they did not insist. Another modification to the system came in 1630, when the *rotepenningar* were ordered to be paid direct to the treasury, whose officers in return issued the conscripts with cloth and equipment.[2] In this year, indeed, the peasants escaped an extra *utskrivning* only by paying a special tax (the *utskrivningshjälp*) in place of it; but they were also forced to pay the normal *rotepenningar*, although no conscripts had actually been taken.[3] The constant need for fresh drafts was by this time leading the *råd* to scrutinize exemptions more carefully, as the clergy found to their cost in 1629 and 1631.[4] The drain of men was indeed serious. In 1626 about 8000 men were levied; 13,500 in 1627; 15,500 asked for in 1628, though less than 11,000 were actually raised; 8000 in 1629; 9000 in 1630, though the King had hoped for 13,000.[5] Not all those that were conscripted were in practice drafted for service; and it is said that in Gustav Adolf's time the number actually taken in Finland was not much more than half the number conscripted.[6] But, even so, it was a heavy burden for the country to bear.[7] By the end of the reign there were complaints from all classes, and even from the provincial authorities; there were occasional clashes between soldiers and peasantry; farms were abandoned for lack of labour; there were numerous desertions by conscripts who took to the woods, especially

[1] Swenne, pp. 224-5. For the meaning of these terms, see above, pp. 52.
[2] *Sv. Krig*, Supp. Vol. II. 122.
[3] Swenne, p. 221; *Arkiv*, I. 63, 155-6, 409-11.
[4] *RRP*, I. 166, II. 98, 100.
[5] *Sv. Krig*, II. 244-5, 320-1, 388-9, 394, 505, III. 223-5.
[6] E. Hornborg, *Gustav Adolf*, pp. 85-6.
[7] As Gustav Adolf himself realized: *Arkiv*, I. 192.

in Finland.[1] The *råd* had promised that there should be no *utskrivning* in 1631, since there had been five in the last four years; but they could not keep their promise, and the complaints were renewed more vehemently than ever.[2] But though there was considerable murmuring and discontent, there was little open resistance. The flow of reinforcements continued to come in at a fairly satisfactory rate. The King's object was attained: *utskrivning* had been made to work, and the conscript army was kept up to strength.

The reform of the methods of *utskrivning* affected only the infantry; for no part of the cavalry was raised by conscription. In Gustav Adolf's time, as in that of his predecessors, the Swedish cavalry consisted either of foreign mercenaries or of native volunteers, or of the horsemen provided by the nobility by way of *rusttjänst*. The institution of *rusttjänst*, which dated from the close of the thirteenth century, consisted in the obligation to provide one or more properly equipped heavy cavalryman for service in the King's host; and it was in return for this service that the nobles enjoyed their *frälse*.[3] Since Gustav Vasa's time the number of horsemen required of each noble had been graduated according to his assessed income; and both Gustav Vasa and Erik XIV had been strict in exacting their due. But in this respect, as in some others, the accession of Johan III marked the victory of the aristocracy over the monarchy. By the privileges which Johan granted to the nobility in 1569, *rusttjänst* was fixed at the rate of one horseman for every 400 marks' hereditary income (the previous figure had been 300 marks), and the number of days' service outside the country which the King could require without pay was restricted to 14. This easing of the burden of *rusttjänst* was followed under Karl IX by the virtual breakdown of the whole institution. Relations between the monarchy and the nobility were as bad as possible, and the nobility revenged itself on the King by refusing to discharge its obligations. It was in vain that Karl proposed that the crown should forgo *rusttjänst* altogether in return for the sacrifice by the nobility of some of the fiscal exemptions of their peasantry; it was in vain that he inflicted (though it is very doubtful if he collected) a

[1] Already in 1620 it was reported from Finland that soldiers had prosecuted a search for deserters in such fashion that the inhabitants 'told the *ståthållare* to his face that there have been rebellions for less': Hornborg, p. 97.

[2] *Sv. Krig*, V. 351, 359; *RRP*, II. 79, 95, 101, 113, 209-11; *AOSB*, II. IX. 33.

[3] For *rusttjänst*, see P. Sörensson, *Adelns rusttjänst och adelsfanans organisation*, *passim.*

swingeing fine upon a notorious recalcitrant.[1] The nobility, though they insisted doggedly on their privileges, would not provide the *quid pro quo*; and Karl was in no position to proceed to extremities against them.

Still less could Gustav Adolf venture upon severity during the War of Kalmar. In the first years of the reign the crown's just claims were flagrantly ignored, and the King was fain to bear it with what patience he could muster. Though Sten Leijonhufvud owed 24 horsemen for only a portion of his estates, in May 1612 the total force produced by the *rusttjänst* of the entire nobility did not exceed 20 horse.[2] In the privileges which Gustav Adolf granted to the first Estate in 1612, as in the revised version of 1617, the terms accorded in 1569 were reaffirmed—except only that this time there was no mention of foreign service at all. Gustav Adolf did his best to bring the nobles to a sense of their duty; but he had only moderate success. The evasions and excuses continued: even Axel Oxenstierna on one occasion obtained the remission of *rusttjänst* for some of his Livonian domains, on the curious ground that the country was at war.[3] Some 200 horse made their appearance in 1623, some 250 in 1625. In 1622 the King was forced to make further concessions as the price of the nobility's consent to their participation in the payment of the Little Toll: the rate of contribution was now fixed at one man for every 500 marks' income.[4] In 1626, it is true, a new *rusttjänst* ordinance was promulgated which regulated more exactly the conditions of service and ordered that fines for delinquency be paid to the building-fund for the *Riddarhus* [5]; but it seems to have made little difference. There was some anxiety in aristocratic circles lest the King should really mean what he said; Jakob de la Gardie's bailiff, and even Jakob de la Gardie himself, were sharply reprimanded because his *rusttjänst* was ill-performed [6]; the *råd* was instructed to keep an eye on the nobility, and did from time to time issue orders that something should be done [7]; but in fact matters

[1] Hallenberg, I. 409-10.

[2] Sörensson, *op. cit.*, p. 220; *SRDA*, I. 231.

[3] Ahnlund, *Axel Oxenstierna*, p. 318. For other examples of evasion, see, *e.g.*, *AOSB*, I. II. 158; Cronholm, III. 541.

[4] But note that *rusttjänst* was due on lands bought in *frälseköp*: Brännman, pp. 153, 173-4; and of course the value of money had fallen since 1569.

[5] C. Öhlander, *Bidrag till de adliga privilegiernas historia*, p. 36; Swenne, p. 11; N. Edén, *Den svenska centralregeringens utveckling till kollegial organisation*, p. 147.

[6] Hallenberg, V. 451; *AOSB*, I. III. 320; *cf. AOSB*, II. x. 73.

[7] *RRP*, I. xxix, xxxix, 69, II. 46.

went on very much as before. In 1630 the number of men raised by *rusttjänst* was only 375.[1]

Rusttjänst was not quite dead—we hear of it as late as 1643 [2]—but plainly it was unenforceable on any strict basis. Gustav Adolf's relations with the nobility, unlike his father's, were good; the nobles showed, by sacrifices of their immunities and by personal service, that they were anything but impermeable to patriotic appeals; but neither the King nor the emergency could induce them to discharge this obligation honestly. That Gustav Adolf, in an effort to maintain *rusttjänst*, should have expended efforts so disproportionate to the result obtained, is perhaps to be explained by his reluctance to see an undoubted right of the crown go by default; but also by the urgent need of well-equipped cavalry and the high cost of hiring foreigners. For the *rusttjänst* horsemen were, by Swedish standards, heavy cavalry; and they were the only heavy cavalry which Sweden provided.

The great proportion of the force raised from native resources was in fact light cavalry—light, at least, in regard to armour if not as to weapons—and it was furnished entirely by voluntary enlistment. At the beginning of the 1620's the available strength seems to have been in the region of 2500; but the numbers increased considerably in the latter half of the decade, and by the spring of 1630 reached a figure not far short of 8000.[3] In 1626 the *råd*, in an access of patriotic devotion, offered to provide and fit out an entire cavalry regiment without cost to the crown.[4] There seems to have been no difficulty about recruiting; and the quality of men enlisted was good: there were very few desertions from the cavalry.[5] The Swedish horses were small (they rarely stood more than 12 hands), but they proved sturdy and serviceable; and though Sweden had no great tradition of cavalry fighting, the volunteers ended by being fully a match for the best troops that Pappenheim could bring against them. The Finnish horse, in particular—*agmen horribile haccapelitorum*—acquired a formidable reputation.[6]

[1] Generalstaben, *Gustaf II Adolf*, p. 206. Contrast Treitschke's absurd statement that 'jeder Edelmann, der in Kriegzeiten daheim blieb, den Kehricht zu hüten, verlor seine Kronlehen' (Treitschke, *Gustaf Adolf und Deutschlands Freiheit*, p. 9): this probably reflects a misunderstanding of Hallenberg, V. 451.

[2] C. T. Odhner, *Sveriges inre historia under drottning Christinas förmyndare*, pp. 122, 208.

[3] *Sv. Krig*, I. 109, III. 282-3.

[4] *AOSB*, II. III. 98.

[5] N. Belfrage, *Erik Soop och västgöta ryttare*, p. 22.

[6] A. Korhonen, *Om finska rytteriet under Gustaf II Adolf*, pp. 242-3. The hakkapelites got their name from their war-cry, 'hakka päälle!'—'fall on!'

It would have been in vain that Gustav Adolf reformed the methods of recruitment if he had not at the same time paid a proper attention to the problem of pay. Only if his armies were regularly paid could they be maintained in discipline; and without discipline there could be no training. Three-quarters of a century earlier, Gustav Vasa had been disposed to make a merit of paying his conscripts; but in Gustav Adolf's time the victim of *utskrivning*, bound to serve for twenty years or until he reached the age of fifty,[1] felt entitled to a proper reward. Gustav Adolf was well aware of the need to assure to his conscripts a steady wage.[2] It was out of the question, in the early years of the reign, that he should disburse the large sums in cash which Maurice had at his disposal; but the techniques already in use for the payment of civil servants, miscellaneous creditors and speculative *entrepreneurs* could be applied well enough to the army. Payments could be decentralized as far as possible, and as far as possible they could be in kind; and the treasury could be relieved (it was hoped) of a good deal of accounting.

The method which was evolved was to pay the army directly out of the land-revenues. Officers were usually given a farm free of tax, in addition to their wages.[3] When an officer had a farm allotted to him (usually, though not always, on one of the crown estates), he simply collected as his pay the rent which would otherwise have been paid to the crown, leaving the original crown-tenant in possession; or, alternatively, he could take the farm and work it himself, rent-free. If, however, he were allotted a tax-paying homestead (*skatte-hemman*), this latter option was denied him, for the peasant-occupier was not a tenant but an owner, and not arbitrarily to be evicted. In such a case the officer collected from the owner the amount due to him, and the owner deducted this from the tax he owed to the government. If the rent from a royal farm were greater than the pay due, the officer had a proportionately smaller amount allotted to him in the way of allowances in kind. If the rent were less than the pay, the treasury paid him a supplementary allowance in cash. From the point of view of the treasury there was a standard, notional, farm of given size and productivity, which was the unit for the assessment of rent and taxes. This fiscal idea was the *hemman*, or

[1] Styffe, p. 59.
[2] *ibid.*, p. 42.
[3] Petri, I. 420-1 for pay-arrangements early in the reign; II. 16 for rates of pay for various ranks for 1621.

homestead; and a farm might from the treasury's point of view be reckoned as a whole *hemman*, or it might be a fraction of a *hemman*. The peace-time yearly wage of the infantry private, apart from an allowance in clothes, seems to have been assessed for most of the reign at one-eighth of a *hemman*. The ordinary foot-soldier, if he had a farm of his own, was therefore allowed to deduct a sum equivalent to the amount due from one-eighth of a *hemman* from the money he owed in rent to the crown or in taxes to the treasury. If he did not own a farm himself (as was the ordinary case), he would be billeted on one, and the farmer would deduct from his rent or taxes a like amount, and pay it over to the soldier, who was bound to help his host with the work of the farm in return for his board and lodging: the owner of one *hemman* might thus distribute the greater part of his tax-payments among soldiers billeted upon him.[1]

This system of planting every soldier on a farm, or at least of ensuring that every soldier had a farmer responsible for his maintenance, was a great assistance to the treasury: the army's finances were decentralized, much book-keeping was saved, less coin was needed. It prepared the way for the more fully developed methods of Karl XI's *indelningsverk*. It had reference, however, only to peace-time: in war-time two different methods of payment were used. If the army were engaged in a war of movement, or in active operations against the enemy, the soldiers were paid a monthly wage in cash—at all events, in theory. If, on the other hand, the troops were engaged in garrison duty or other tasks in the rear, they received—again in theory—a smaller cash allowance, under the name of *läning*, and in addition supplementary allowances in kind.[2]

The method of payment of the cavalry was similar, though the rates were much higher than for the foot: the trooper was rewarded, when not on active service, with the tenure, or the revenues, of one whole *hemman*, or an equivalent abatement of his taxes, and his allowances and pay in war-time were at a proportionately higher rate; so that it was reckoned that man for man the native cavalry

[1] *Arkiv*, III. lx-lxii. 'The manner of maintaining their militia forces', wrote Whitelocke in 1654, 'was said to be this:—A horseman was quartered in the house of a boor, or husbandman; if the man will work himself and his horse with the boor, to help him in his husbandry, then the boor gives the man and his horse . . . their meat, and the boor will give the man perhaps some small sum of money besides. . . . In like manner it is for the foot-soldiers': Whitelocke, *Embassy*, II. 136-7.

[2] *Arkiv*, III. lxii. These arrangements were by no means regularly adhered to: there were years when it was all *läning* and no pay for certain units, or one month's pay and eleven months' *läning*. Note that *läning* was of slightly different significance for foreign mercenary troops: see below, p. 217.

were about nine times as expensive as the infantry.[1] Moreover, the cavalryman, in addition to his *hemman*, obtained exemption from *gästning*, *skjutsning*, Stock Tax and *utskrivning*, for himself, his family and his personal servants. When he became too old for the service, if he lived so long, he was usually given a farm free of tax as a pension. And on active service *läning* and pay were, for the cavalry, equal in amount.[2] It was no wonder that there was a steady supply of volunteers. Indeed, these advantages did not merely attract recruits; they also allured others who by age, sex or family ties were themselves incapacitated from serving. Hence arose the practice of fitting-out (*rustning*), whereby anybody, male or female, who fitted out a cavalryman with the expensive equipment he required, and succeeded in inducing him to serve, could occupy the *hemman* allotted to him, and enjoy the benefits and privileges that went with it. In such case the man who actually served was called the *sventjänare*.[3] Often he was the brother, son or son-in-law of the person who paid for his *rustning*; and acquisitive and business-like women frequently invested in *sventjänare*. A considerable proportion—perhaps a quarter—of the native cavalry consisted of *sventjänare* in 1630. It became a matter for complaint that officers already serving fitted out troopers in order to obtain more and better farms for themselves.

There were, indeed, certain serious inconveniences attendant upon this method of payment, despite its advantages. To pay a large army in this way, a very great number of farms was required: in 1618, for instance, some 1600 officers and men of Östergötland received 329 *hemman* between them. And these were the infantry; cavalry needed far more: in 1624 no less than 441 *hemman* were assigned to the Västgöta regiment alone.[4] When the cavalry force began to be expanded in the mid-'twenties, the resources of crown lands began to run short. Another disadvantage of the system was the unfairness with which farms were allotted by the military authorities: in 1624 the peasants demanded that all allotments should

[1] A greater or less discrepancy was common to all armies: Wijn, p. 124; Firth, pp. 186-7, 39-40: 'A trooper was a capitalist in a small way . . . his pay was three times that of a foot-soldier.'

[2] For all this, see Belfrage, p. 19 *seqq.*; *Sv. Krig*, Supp. Vol. II. 118; *Arkiv*, III. lxiii.

[3] Belfrage, p. 21; *cf.* Firth, p. 243: 'Persons well affected to the parliament undertook to provide a horse and man to serve in Essex's army. If they provided the horse only, they were paid one and fourpence a day; if the rider also, two and sixpence.' And on *sventjänare*, *cf.* E. Ingers, *Bonden i svensk historia*, I. 234.

[4] Belfrage, p. 34.

be made in future by the *ståthållare*, and that compensation be given for damage and abuse of the land. It was alleged that unscrupulous military tenants, and especially those who held the farm in virtue of having fitted out a *sventjänare*, would suck the farm dry in a couple of years and then get another allotted to them; and if they should happen to be killed in battle, their widows (who could keep the farm for one year after their widowhood) were even worse. Thus the careful husbandry of years might be undone by the indifference, ignorance or rapacity of a predatory militia.[1] It was to meet this situation that a new war tax, the Mill Toll, was imposed in 1625; for the declared purpose of the tax was to permit the payment of conscripts in cash. In actual fact, it seems to have made little difference. The allocation of *hemman* continued, and twenty-two years later it was provoking much the same kind of complaint.[2]

The government was not so easily able to meet its obligations towards the mercenaries whom it was compelled to hire. As a member of the *råd* observed many years later, 'the Swedes are better troops to pay; they content themselves with *commis* and suchlike, but the Germans will have their money'.[3] An immediate and inevitable outlay, if mercenaries were to be secured at all, was the muster-money, which till 1630 was at the rate of 8 *rdr.* a head for infantrymen.[4] Once this initial payment was made, however, the Swedish government, like every other government, hoped that its mercenaries would fight on credit. All governments during the Thirty Years' War enlisted far more mercenaries than they could afford to pay regularly, and trusted to the chapter of accidents—a victory, a lucrative sack, extortion from the civilian population—to extricate them from their financial difficulties. In theory, Gustav Adolf's mercenaries were paid each month half their full wages, together with *läning* in lieu of the remainder [5]; but in fact they usually received only *läning*, although this was much less satisfactory for mercenaries than for conscripts. *Läning*, explains the author of *The Swedish Discipline* (writing, of course, from the mercenary's point of view),

. . . is *Lending*, in the paiement of the soldiours meanes, for which this is

[1] Petri, II. 54-5.
[2] G. Wittrock, *Regering och allmoge under Kristinas egen styrelse*, p. 67.
[3] S. Lundgren, *Salvius*, p. 165 *note* 2, quoting *RRP*, XIV. 268, for 1650. *Commis*: truck payment, often in the form of cloth: Wijn, p. 121.
[4] *Arkiv*, III. lxiv: the price dropped in 1631 to 6 *rdr.*, and then to 4.
[5] *ibid.*, lxiv-v.

the Kings order. Wheras so much is due to them at the months end; the King deviding the month into 13 [*sic*: *recte* 3] equall parts; vpon the first, eleuenth, and one and twentieth day of the moneth, payes them a third part of their meanes before-hand as it were: which is called *Lendings*.[1]

It was, in fact, a system of ten-day advances against the time when the government should feel itself strong enough to risk a 'full pay'—an occasion occurring in theory every fourth month, but too often deferred to that perilous moment of 'thanking off' (as Monro calls it, in his teutonized English), when the commander would be compelled to reveal the precise extent to which he proposed to cheat his soldiers of their reward. For *läning*, even if paid in cash, did little more than provide the soldier with subsistence: it was only at a full pay that he could hope to realize a profit and receive what in Sweden was called his 'right deserts'. The embarrassment experienced by governments unable to meet their obligations at such times was among the arguments advanced by contemporaries in favour of a national standing army.[2] Meanwhile, pending a full pay, the best hope for the mercenary soldier was that his general should organize for him a satisfactory system of 'quarter'; which in Gustav Adolf's army (at all events in the later months in Germany) probably implied, as it did in Wallenstein's, the exaction from the inhabitants of the district occupied by the army not only of shelter, food, forage, salt, fuel and light, but also of heavy monetary contributions—heavy enough, in the case of some of Wallenstein's troops, to provide the entire pay of the troops.[3]

Gustav Adolf's mercenaries, in fact, were paid—or left unpaid—on the same basis as those of other monarchs and commanders; and were certainly not less troublesome. And the colonels who raised them made their profit in much the same way as elsewhere. The armies of Gustav Adolf were no more exempt than were the armies of Richelieu from the evil of passevolants: no less than fourteen of them to each infantry company, as Monro carefully informs us.[4]

[1] *The Swedish Discipline*, p. 79; *cf.* Wijn, pp. 18, 121; Cruickshank, p. 93.

[2] Frauenholz, *Söldnertum*, I. 22.

[3] Sörensson, *Ekonomi och krigföring*, p. 304; M. Ritter, *Das Kontributionssystem Wallensteins*, pp. 225-49, for an analysis of his methods.

[4] Monro, II. 183. Passevolants in this sense were designed to be a kind of perquisite or cost-of-living allowance to the captain. But they also existed in the Swedish army, unofficially, in the sense that later became common: thus Grubbe wrote to the King in September 1632: 'Nowadays a great abuse has taken root among soldiers, to run from one army to the other—indeed sometimes from one company to the other', and since mercenaries were in short supply 'not many new men are recruited, but the same ones, who desert from other regiments, so that

It was to require more than one generation of military reformers to eradicate this abuse.

The reforms in the system of recruiting went hand in hand with a reorganization of the army's tactical and administrative units; for that reorganization, among other things, involved the allocation of definite recruiting areas to each of the new regiments; and, conversely, the maintenance of units at more or less fixed strengths could be achieved only if the system of *utskrivning* were functioning properly.[1] In 1611 the *fänika* was still the highest tactical and administrative unit for the foot; for though 'regiments' existed whose companies were supposed to be recruited from specific areas, their composition was so loose and the regiments so variable in size that they might as well not have existed at all. Gustav Adolf clearly realized that the best basis for an effective war-time army was a sound peace-time administration; but until the peace of Stolbova he was too fully occupied in the field to give the problem much thought. The hired regiment of 1613 and the conscript regiments of 1615 were no great improvement on what had preceded them; though a step forward was taken in 1616, when certain *härader* were assigned to each *fänika* as recruiting-areas.[2]

With the end of the Russian war in 1617, the King was at last able to give the matter more attention. His first task was to decide on his tactical unit; for his administrative units must be designed in such a way that they could be formed easily into whatever tactical unit was determined upon. The old confusion of 'companies' and *fänikor* of varying strengths must be ended. Soon after 1617 he made his decision.[3] The new tactical unit was to be the squadron. It was to consist of 408 men, *plus* officers and N.C.O.s. It was to be made up of a central block of pikes 216 strong, arranged six deep, and flanked by two wings of musketeers, each containing 96 men, also six deep. In addition, there was to be attached to each squadron an additional body of 96 musketeers, known as 'attached' or

many do no other service than to help new recruiters to fill up their numbers, and exhaust the countryside at the muster-places': *Arkiv*, II. 585-6. Turner, writing forty years later, recollected only 10 passevolants to each Swedish foot company in Gustav Adolf's time: *Pallas Armata*, p. 197. Droysen gives the number as only two or three: *Militärwesen*, p. 28. But at least by Turner's time the word 'lending' had fallen into disuse: Turner did not know what it meant: *op. cit.*, p. 199.

[1] Petri, II. 20; *Sv. Krig*, I. 108.

[2] Barkman, pp. 76-7; Petri, I. 418.

[3] For what follows, see Barkman, pp. 80-182; Petri, II. 6-12, 39-46, 60-1, 70-1, 81, 83, 105-7.

'commanded' (*kommenderade*) musketeers. The squadron was split into various subdivisions, corresponding roughly to the subdivisions of a modern company.[1] Gustav Adolf seems to have been well satisfied with the squadron: at all events, its size and composition were not altered for the rest of the reign. It was indeed (as we shall see) found necessary later to lump three or four squadrons together to form a brigade, since the squadron was found in practice to be unable to discharge all the duties that were laid upon it; but the constitution of the squadron itself remained unchanged. The attached musketeers were in practice frequently used for outpost duty, for reconnaissance and for collaboration with cavalry, so that their presence with the squadron could as a rule be assumed only if the army were drawn up to give battle *en règle*, and not always then. It is clear that the squadron looks back, on the one hand, to Erik XIV's *fänika* (compare the attached musketeers with Erik's forlorn hope), and on the other to Maurice's battalion. It was, however, considerably smaller than either, and the proportion of pikes to musketeers (if we exclude the attached musketeers) was distinctly *higher* (and not, as is often stated, lower) in the squadron than in the Dutch battalion (216 to 192, as against 250 to 240). Like the battalion, it was in one aspect designed to be the instrument of a defensive tactic—the necessary result of the inexperience of the Swedish troops and the weakness at this time of the mounted arm; but like the *fänika* it later showed itself capable of markedly offensive action through co-operation with cavalry and artillery, and through mutual support of muskets and pikes. The squadron, in fact, proved itself eminently adaptable. There was not much similarity between Gustav Adolf's styles of fighting in 1621 and 1631; but the squadron appeared to be equally suited to either.

Meanwhile the organization for providing the administrative basis for the army had been worked out: it was apparently done by Axel Oxenstierna sometime in 1616.[2] The country was to be divided into eight recruiting areas, two in Finland, six in Sweden,

[1] The 216 pikes were split into two divisions of 108: each division had six corporalships of 18 men (3×6); each corporalship three files of 6 men. The 192 musketeers were also split into two divisions of 96: each division contained two platoons of 48; each platoon had two corporalships of 24 (4×6); each corporalship four files of 6. The 96 attached musketeers were organized like the musketeers of the main body. The squadron had 4 captains, 4 lieutenants, 4 ensigns, 8 sergeants, 12 pike corporals, 4 *furirer*, 16 drummers and pipers—*i.e.* 52 officers and N.C.O.s in addition to the 408. The attached musketeers had 8 N.C.O.s.

[2] *AOSB*, I. I. 366; Petri, I. 418.

though of these six two—the duchies of Östergötland and Södermanland—fell for the present under the control of their respective dukes. Each of these areas comprised two or three provinces, and each was to raise one 'provincial regiment' (*landsregiment*) of about 3000 men. This regiment was to be organized into companies of 272 (of whom 252 were to be in the ranks): there would thus be 12 companies to a regiment. The company itself was subdivided into three 'quarters' (another reminiscence of Erik XIV) and six subquarters (*underkvarter*). Each *underkvarter* had 18 pikes and 24 muskets, and was thus equivalent to one corporalship of pikes and one corporalship of muskets in the squadron. Thus two companies provided the personnel for one squadron, and in addition furnished the overplus of musketeers needed for the squadron's attached musketeers.[1] And each regiment would provide six squadrons. There seems to have been some idea of grouping squadrons into bunches of six to form a higher tactical unit—no doubt in imitation of the Dutch brigade—but for the present this notion was not pursued.

In this, its first form, the provincial regiment never really got into working order. When, in 1621, its structure was revised, there were only four regiments which had the full twelve companies. The mobilization against Poland had tested Oxenstierna's system, and it had not come out of the test very well.[2] There had been delays; there had been confusion. While it was felt that the general principles of the system remained valid, it was decided that the size of the company must be reduced. In 1621, therefore, the strength of the company was fixed at 148, or, if we reckon only those in the ranks, at 126—just half the old figure.[3] In order to provide a squadron and its attached musketeers, four companies would now be needed instead of two. At the same time a step was taken in the direction of a new higher tactical unit, by associating two squadrons to form a 'field-regiment' (*fältregiment*)—a development which recalls the Dutch double-battalion.[4] There now existed two types of regiment side by side: the provincial regiment, an administrative,

[1] The squadron comprised 408 men plus 96 attached musketeers, *i.e.* 504 in all; one company (excluding officers and N.C.O.s) contained 252 men.

[2] *Krigsvetenskaps Akademiens Handlingar* (1932), p. 14.

[3] The new quarter corresponded to the old *underkvarter*. Note that while the old company had 20 officers and N.C.O.s to 252 men, the new had 22 officers to 126 men. For a description of reorganization in Västergötland, see E. Bensow, *Kungl. Skaraborgs regementes historia*, I. 249-50; for the process in Östergötland, B. Steckzén, *Johan Baner*, pp. 76-7.

[4] Thus in 1624 Patrick Ruthven writes of 'the eight companies which have formed my regiment': *AOSB*, II. IX. 355.

peace-time organization; and the field-regiment, a tactical, war-time organization. It remained only to be decided what numerical relation they were to bear to each other. If the provincial regiment remained of a size to provide six squadrons, it was plain that it would also provide three field-regiments. But it was felt that since the number of companies in the provincial regiment had now been raised from 12 to 24, the colonel should be given increased staff. This was done; and at the same time the provincial regiment was subdivided for administrative purposes into three field-regiments. Thus the tactical and administrative hierarchies had at last fused at the top, since the field-regiment was now common to each. For a time the size of the provincial regiment was reduced to equal only two field-regiments; but by 1624 it had been found possible once more to make the provincial regiment furnish three field-regiments of eight companies each. As the field-regiment became better established, the importance of the provincial regiment declined, and already by 1624 men were beginning to speak of the field-regiment simply as 'the regiment', adding sometimes 'of eight companies'. By the end of the decade the provincial regiment had ceased to have any real significance. Its work was done: it had provided the *cadres* round which the army in the field was built. The field-regiment had taken its place, and the administrative and tactical aspects were now one. The great expansion of the army at which the King aimed after 1626 was reckoned in field-regiments.[1] But the field-regiment preserved the territorial basis of the old provincial regiment, for each field-regiment was drawn from one particular province or *län*.[2] The administrative work of the colonel of the former provincial regiment was thrust back on the reluctant civil authority—the *landshövding* or *ståthållare*. From about 1628, moreover, a development which arose out of the Polish war drove the final nail into the coffin of the provincial regiment. This was the emergence of a new higher tactical unit, the brigade. The brigade was a combat-group of three, and later of four, squadrons (*i.e.* of two field-regiments).[3] A provincial regiment containing three field-regiments was clearly ill-adapted for conversion into brigades.[4] By the close of the reign,

[1] He hoped for 27; by 1626, 24 had been raised.

[2] It was not always possible to adhere to this, since a unit that had sustained heavy losses might receive drafts from other districts: *Sv. Krig*, III. 227-9.

[3] For a discussion of brigade tactics, see below, pp. 250 *seqq*, 270.

[4] It is true that in the German campaigns the brigades were more usually formed of 3 squadrons (1½ field-regiments); but by that time the provincial regiment had disappeared: *Krigsvetenskaps Ak. H.* (1932), pp. 26-7.

therefore, the field-regiment had established itself as the only regiment; and some, at least, of the original field-regiments have survived to our own day in continuous life.[1]

The native cavalry, like the infantry, suffered at the beginning of the reign from lack of clearly defined and well-considered tactical and administrative units. But in their case the difficulty was less serious than with the foot, since the existing organization, loose and imprecise as it was, did contrive that the tactical and administrative units should be identical. Originally this unit was the banner (*fana*); but by the beginning of the 1620's this term was giving way to that of *kompani*, the strength of each company being about 125 horse, with attendant baggage animals. By 1623 Gustav Adolf had decided to allot to the cavalry, as to the infantry, specified recruiting areas. They were not identical with the areas allotted to provincial regiments, for the more northerly provinces could hardly be expected to produce horsemen; but the eight most southerly provinces in Sweden and Finland were each asked to be responsible for one squadron of horse. The squadron of cavalry was to consist for the time being of three companies of 125 each; but it was hoped to make the squadron the basis of a future system of cavalry regiments, and from the beginning some of the squadron-commanders were given the rank of colonel (*överste*). For the present, the numbers were small, and until nearly the end of the Polish war it was possible to retain the company as the normal tactical and administrative unit. After the theatre of operations shifted to Prussia the demand for cavalry increased, and from about 1626 it was not unusual for the squadron to number four or even five companies. The design of the cavalry regiment of eight companies (or two squadrons) was already beginning to take shape; and in 1628 the union of Erik Soop's two Västgöta squadrons marked the foundation of the first Swedish cavalry regiment. In 1630 the whole force of native cavalry (except that from Finland) was similarly organized into regiments.[2]

The work of administrative reform was completed by the creation of definite units and a fixed establishment for the artillery. The

[1] See, however, G. Nordström, *Régiments Jaune, Bleu, Vert, Rouge et Blanc de l'ancienne Armée suèdoise, passim.*

[2] For the above account, see Belfrage, pp. 18, 26, 28, 36, 46, 59; *Sv. Krig*, II. 136-8, 398, III. 263; Generalstaben, *Gustaf II Adolf*, p. 124. The Swedish cavalry company and regiment were of about the normal size. It is surprising to find that in England, by about 1600, the cavalry regiment 'was established as a *tactical* unit' (my italics): Cruickshank, pp. 38-9: contrast Wertheim, I. 75-7, for Germany.

Swedish artillery, as we have seen, dates from Gustav Vasa; and already in Erik XIV's time it had been provided with a central office of control (*arkli*) presided over by an officer of high rank (the *tygmästare* or *arklimästare*) who was responsible not only for gun-founding and the custody of the royal arsenals but also for the artillery in the field.[1] This arrangement continued until Gustav Adolf's accession, when the office of *arklimästare* was split in two and remained divided until 1617. In that year, however, a new office of superior rank was created, that of *rikstygmästare* (corresponding roughly to that of Master-General of the Ordnance), and given to a member of the *råd*, Gabriel Bengtsson Oxenstierna; while one of the previous *arklimästare* was continued in office as *fälttygmästare*—*i.e.* officer in command of the artillery in the field—though he was now subordinate to the *rikstygmästare*.[2] In 1618 the command in the field, though under a different title, was given to Anton Monier (later to be better known as an *entrepreneur* and industrialist), whose appointment continued the tradition, which had prevailed since Gustav Vasa's time, of importing the technical experts in the artillery from abroad.[3]

Hitherto the artillery had not been organized into permanent units; but under the influence, perhaps, of the impression produced by the excellent performance of the gunners at the siege of Riga, Gustav Adolf proceeded in 1623 to put it on a more solid military footing. In that year D. F. von Siegroth (son of the famous gun-founder) was given command of a newly created artillery company; and this company was the first regular artillery unit in the Swedish army.[4] In the years that followed, the artillery expanded; and by 1629 six companies had been formed. They were now brought together to form the first artillery regiment; and the command was given to a twenty-seven-year-old officer, Lennart Torstensson, who was soon to make a reputation as the greatest artillery general of his generation. The new artillery regiment comprised four companies of gunners, one company of 'fireworks' (*i.e.* bombs, grenades, petards and other explosive devices) and one of sappers: one of the gunner companies (and it was much the largest) was exclusively for the service of those 'regiment-pieces'[5] which were to contribute so

[1] Hammarskiöld, *Ur svenska artilleriets hävder* [cited: *USAH*], pp. 8-86; *Sv. Krig*, I. 97.
[2] Hammarskiöld, *USAH*, pp. 125-8.
[3] *ibid.*, pp. 71, 129: *cf.* Hallenberg, I. 300.
[4] Hammarskiöld, *USAH*, p. 142; *Sv. Krig*, Supp. Vol. II. 288-90.
[5] For these, see below, pp. 232-3.

much to Gustav Adolf's success in Germany. By thus organizing the artillery as a distinct branch of the army, Gustav Adolf improved upon the practice of the Emperor and the League.[1] The reform was accompanied by an increase in the number of native Swedes serving with the artillery and a corresponding decrease in the number of mercenary troops; so that by the end of the Thirty Years' War the artillery was perhaps more truly national than any other branch of the service.[2]

(b) *Armaments and Supply*

Among the most obvious and urgent tasks confronting Gustav Adolf on his accession was the rearming of his forces with modern weapons. And this applied with especial force to the infantry. In the absence of any effective cavalry, the foot must be armed with pikes if it were to have a chance of surviving the charges of the Polish horsemen; and it must have muskets if it were to be able to develop a firepower equal to that of continental armies. The task had been beyond the strength of Karl IX: Gustav Adolf seems to have accomplished it without any observable friction; though the change was not made all at once.

It was characteristic of the backwardness of Sweden in military matters that the first really serious and successful attempt to establish the pike as the normal infantry weapon (if we discount Erik XIV's brief experiment) came at a time when its merits were already becoming a matter of controversy among military writers. Even such champions of the pike as Monro write of its virtues in a tone which is almost defiant, as though they felt the need to justify their preference.[3] That this should have been so is to be explained by the increasing relegation of pikemen to a purely defensive part in battle: more and more they were coming to be considered merely as the indispensable stiffening without which musketeers could not be secure; hence Grimmelshausen's remark that a pikeman never hurt anybody who was not foolish enough to impale himself upon his weapon.[4] But Gustav Adolf, like Erik XIV before him, had

[1] *Sv. Krig*, Supp. Vol. II. 295, 380-1; Sjöstrand, pp. 377-8.
[2] Hammarskiöld, *Gustaf II Adolfs artilleri*, p. 85.
[3] Monro, II. 37, 191: *cf. Pallas Armata*, pp. 178-86.
[4] Alm, *Blanka vapen och skyddsvapen*, p. 144; Frauenholz, *Söldnertum*, I. 38-9.

other ideas of the pike's potentialities, though it took many years before he was in a position to develop them fully. He had no idea of economizing on pikemen: on the contrary, he rather increased than diminished the proportion of pikemen to musketeers.[1] Very early in the reign he began the rearming of his foot: not merely were they made to trail the pike, but they were also made (if they were pikemen) to wear armour—pot, gorget, back-and-breast, tassets.[2] It is by no means clear how the King overcame the passive resistance which had defeated the efforts of Karl IX; but it is clear that he did overcome it. And as the men in the ranks were armed with the pike, so their officers were armed with the partisan.[3] The King even made some small improvements upon current practice. In 1616 the pike was slightly shortened. As a result of experiences in the Polish war, the foremost part of the pike-shaft was sheathed with iron, so that attackers could not hew it off with their swords.[4] Between 1626 and 1628 a special type of pike, which seems to have been a Swedish invention, was in use in Prussia: it was in effect a half-pike, with the butt-end sharpened so that it could be either driven into the ground or fitted in rows into balks lying before the pikeman's feet, and would thus form an additional obstacle to attacking cavalry. Such pikes were called swine-feathers [5]; and though they had but a short life (at least in the Swedish armies), they seem to have impressed contemporaries: Sir James Turner, for instance, was moved, even at an interval of some forty years, to almost lyrical reminiscence:

When the infantry by several Regiments or Brigades are drawn up in Battel, and the Pikes and those Stakes fixed in the ground, they make a

[1] Laskowski is entirely in error when he writes: 'In the reforms of Gustav Adolf was manifested a decided tendency to diminish the number of pikes in relation to that of the musketeers, and even to their complete elimination and a uniform arming of the whole infantry': *Uwagi*, p. 51. But Kristian IV seems to have had some such idea: Rockstroh, I. 3.

[2] Alm, *Blanka vapen*, p. 140; *Sv. Krig*, Supp. Vol. II. 90. As late as 1624 not all pikemen had got their armour: Petri, II. 47. In this matter of armour, again, Sweden was decidedly late: within a decade of Gustav Adolf's death the buff-coat was beginning to oust it.

[3] On the partisan, see H. Seitz, *Bardisanen som svenskt drabant- och befälsvapen, passim.*

[4] *Sv. Krig*, Supp. Vol. II. 88.

[5] *ibid.*, II. 112-13; Alm, *Blanka vapen*, p. 136. Swine-feathers were used by Scottish (but not by English) armies during the Civil War: Firth, p. 92. It is probably to them that Alexander Leslie was referring when he wrote in May 1639 of some 3000 'sw fetheris' being in preparation, and not (as Sanford Terry thought) to 'Swedish spring-locks': C. Sanford Terry, *Alexander Leslie*, p. 65 *note* 4; and *cf. ibid.*, p. 180.

delightful show, representing a Wood, the Pikes resembling the tall trees, the Stakes the Shrubs.[1]

As to firearms, Gustav Adolf's reign saw the definitive victory of musket over arquebus as the Swedish infantry weapon. The type preferred was the matchlock, as less liable to mechanical failures; but each squadron would probably have a sprinkling of wheel-locks, for use at night, when it was desirable not to betray the presence of troops by the glow of their matches.[2] Gustav Adolf effected improvements in the musket also. It was made appreciably lighter; but not (as is so often stated [3]) so much lighter that the fork was dispensed with: the fork continued to be used in Swedish armies at least till the time of Karl X Gustav. He seems, also, to have done something to standardize the charge of powder; though it is uncertain whether (as is sometimes supposed) he introduced the paper cartridge for muskets.[4] But he did secure a much greater uniformity of calibre than obtained in either the Dutch or the imperialist armies.[5] He does not, however, seem to have followed the example of his ally William of Hesse-Cassel, who armed some of his units with rifled muskets.[6] On the whole, his reforms of the musket were less radical than has been imagined; but they were nevertheless quite sufficient to play an important part in the superiority of firepower which became so evident at Breitenfeld. Swedish musketeers, like those in other armies at this date, wore no armour.[7]

Not much need be said as to the equipment of the cavalry. Gustav Adolf never seems to have considered arming them with the lance. They were given pistols, as were cavalry elsewhere; but

[1] *Pallas Armata*, p. 170.

[2] Alm, *Eldhandvapen*, I. 160-8; Odenrick, II. 25.

[3] *e.g.* Priorato, p. 273; Delbrück, IV. 202; K. Deuticke, *Die Schlacht bei Lützen*, p. 70; B. Liddell Hart, *Great Captains Unveiled*, p. 114; *Führertum* (*ed.* von Cochenhausen), p. 108. The misunderstanding possibly arises from Gustav Adolf's abolition of swine-feathers after 1628; for the swine-feather had a little hook at the forward end which could be used as a musket-rest: Alm, *Blanka vapen*, p. 142.

[4] *Sv. Krig*, Supp. Vol. II. 92-8, 100-3; Petri, II. 107; Barkman, p. 14 *note* 6; Alm, *Eldhandvapen*, I. 174-5, 186.

[5] *Sv. Krig*, Supp. Vol. II. 141; Wijn, p. 133.

[6] Rifling was considered justified only for sporting purposes: those using rifled weapons in war were usually shot without quarter if taken prisoner, since they were employed mainly as sharpshooters for picking off officers: Alm, *Eldhandvapen*, I. 176; Jähns, p. 1205. For William of Hesse, see C. ffoulkes, in Introduction to Gaya, *Traité des armes*, p. xv.

[7] Odenrick, II. 44.

they were also given swords, and it was intended that they should use them. But if they thus carried the weapons of the cuirassier, they did not (at least if they were native cavalry) carry the cuirassier's weight of armour, possibly because the small Swedish horses could not bear it.[1] Gustav Adolf's reform of cavalry, however, was not so much a matter of different arms as of a different way of using them.

The position in regard to artillery was quite otherwise. Here the reign saw constant experiment, and, in the end, the production of new weapons of very great importance, not only for Sweden but for the whole military history of western Europe. In 1611 the artillery stood upon a rather different footing from either infantry or cavalry. It was still, in the mediaeval sense of the word at least, very much a 'mystery'. The patron of artillerists was St. Barbara [2]; and they had certainly need of all her protective care. Empirical in its methods, incalculable in its results, the artillery of the sixteenth century had mainly been useful at very short range—as, for instance, at Ravenna in 1512. Yet the guns of that age, imperfect as they were, demanded of those that served them a knowledge and a technique quite out of the compass of the pikeman or the pistoleer. Hence gunnery remained a craft; and those who practised it had something of the jealous corporative spirit that frowns upon outsiders. The science of ballistics was still in a primitive stage; and the gunners dealt in approximations of the most generous sort. Range-finding was both slow and inaccurate [3]; and when the range had at length been determined, the required elevation was obtained by the crude expedient of hammering in larger or smaller wedges between the barrel and its bed. It was extremely difficult to make satisfactory practice upon targets lying higher than the gun. It was still generally believed that the range of the piece varied directly as the length of the barrel; and this was one of the factors which hindered a reduction in weight and

[1] As Hornborg suggests: Hornborg, *Gustav Adolf*, p. 82.

[2] Wijn, p. 48.

[3] Odenrick, II. 19-21, for methods of range-finding. Estimates of the ranges of sixteenth- and seventeenth-century guns vary so much that it is difficult to attach much value to them. But it seems that 720 metres is a liberal estimate for heavy guns; and 650-700 for a 24-pounder: *Sv. Krig*, Supp. Vol. II. 191-207, 258, 329-32. See also T. Jakobsson, *Über die Schussweiten der schwedischen Artillerie der Gustaf Adolfs-Zeit*, pp. 418-19; *Krigsvetenskaps Akademiens Handl.* (1932), p. 30. The estimates in Frauenholz, *Söldnertum*, I. 41, seem far too high. Imperialist artillery was quite ineffective at Werben at a range of about 1000 metres: *Sv. Krig*, IV. 392; and it was not until the enemy had planted batteries within 40 paces of the walls that Monro considered the range too close for comfort: Monro, II. 9.

a consequent increase in mobility.[1] The rate of fire was still extraordinarily slow [2]; and even improved techniques of loading could not do much to accelerate it, for it was necessary to allow the black smoke from the crude powder to clear away before firing again, and in any case the barrel had usually to be cooled (with vinegar, for choice, or perhaps with milk) after only a few rounds.[3] If, abandoning the notion of rapid fire as Utopian, the gunner aspired at least to accuracy, his task was no easier. He could not be sure that the charge was identical for each round—and indeed, since one way of varying the range was to vary the strength of the charge, he probably did not desire that it should be so. It was this objection that delayed the adoption of cartridges wired to the ball.[4] He could not be sure that his powder was of constant composition, or properly corned. If he had the misfortune to have to do with iron guns, he might have to reckon either with a rusty barrel or with too much windage between barrel and shot. The usual rule was that the windage should not exceed one twenty-first of the calibre; but it was generally held that special allowance should be made for iron guns, since they rusted so easily. It was esteemed a sharp stroke of policy to have your guns with calibre rather larger than those of your enemy: you could then use his cannon-balls, while he could not use yours.[5] The life of a gun was very short: according to some authorities not more than thirty rounds. The life of a gun-team was not much longer. For the lighter pieces, each horse in the team of six or nine had to draw about 280 kilograms: it is no wonder that the mortality *per annum* was estimated at from twenty to thirty per

[1] Hammarskiöld, *USAH*, p. 93 (for high-lying targets); Wijn, p. 202 (for relation of barrel-length and range): even Turner in 1671 believed this: *Pallas Armata*, p. 175.

[2] Once again estimates vary, and no clear-cut conclusion seems possible as to rates of firing: See *Sv. Krig*, Supp. Vol. II. 185-8. Odenrick (II. 28) reckoned 8 rounds an hour for a 24-pounder, and 20 for a good regiment-piece; Wijn (p. 199) 8-10 for some unspecified field-gun; Turner (*Pallas Armata*, pp. 193, 196) from 8 for a whole cannon to 15 for a 3-pounder. At Lützen, Wallenstein's 24 guns got off 1298 rounds in perhaps 6 hours—an average of about 9 an hour. John of Nassau in the 'nineties reckoned that no gun in any case would be called on to fire more than 4-5 rounds in the course of a battle: Wijn, p. 214.

[3] ffoulkes, *ap.* Gaya, p. xxii; *Sv. Krig*, Supp. Vol. II. 186-7.

[4] Another objection was that on account of the honeycomb and flaws in the metal of the gun 'you shall scant get the cartridge home unto the bottom of the piece': Robertson, *Evolution of Naval Armament*, p. 79.

[5] *Sv. Krig*, Supp. Vol. II. 333, 336-7. In England, throughout the sixteenth century, windage was fixed at a quarter of an inch, irrespective of the calibre of the gun: Robertson, p. 76. In Maurice's armies, soldiers who retrieved enemy balls were rewarded: Wijn, p. 295.

cent. The biggest guns (48-pounders) needed from 33 to 39 horses; and where horses were not easily obtainable the peasantry had to be co-opted *en masse*.[1] Though the consumption of ammunition was anything but heavy, the ammunition-train was formidable: for the Livonian campaign of 1625 Gustav Adolf's 36 guns needed 220 waggons and 1116 horses; for the German campaign of 1630 his 72 guns needed something over 100 waggons and 1000 horses. The marked disparity between the two sets of figures is perhaps as good an example as could be got of the effect of the King's reforms upon the Swedish artillery.

Gustav Adolf inherited from his father some sixteen distinct types of cannon. The old confusion of calibres and nomenclature had indeed been a little diminished by Erik XIV, and by the end of the century approximate uniformity of calibre had been established within each type. Karl IX had reduced the weight by shortening the barrel. But much remained to be done. The classification of types was not so simple or so convenient as, for instance, in France, where they had lately been reduced to no more than six; and the weight of pieces of all types was still excessive. There were, broadly, two main classes of guns: the siege-guns (*murbräckor*), graded in multiples or fractions of the *kartog*; and the field-artillery, which included all sizes of *slangor*, falconets, *stenbyssor*, *vagnborgsstycken*, *potthundar*, *mickhackar*, and many others equally fancifully named.[2] A separate branch was formed by the 'fireworks'—mortars which hurled (among other things) fire-balls and bombs. The heavy guns were always of 'copper': that is, of gunmetal, an alloy of 12 or 13 parts of copper to one part of English tin, with a dash of bellmetal added. Gunmetal was preferred because it did not rust; it could be recast; it had a higher tensile strength; it did not burst so easily, and when it did, it merely cracked, instead of hurling jagged pieces in all directions, to the imperilment of bystanders. To be safe, an iron barrel had to be much thicker than a 'copper' one. For big guns, therefore, iron was out of the question. On the other hand, 'copper' guns were said to have a shorter life, to bend at the muzzle, to burn out at th vent, and to lose their tin-content and become spongy.[3] There was a growing tendency to make some of the smaller field-pieces of iron, if only because iron was very much

[1] *Sv. Krig*, Supp. Vol. II. 262-3, 353; and see Hammarskiöld, *USAH*, p. 146.
[2] *Sv. Krig*, Supp. Vol. II. 25, 35-9, 76-81, 165; Robertson, p. 75.
[3] Robertson, pp. 69, 83-4.

cheaper: in the time of Karl IX the price-ratio in Sweden was 80:6.[1] But since Sweden had huge deposits of copper, and a flourishing copper industry, this consideration did not weigh very heavily.[2] Shot was made of cast-iron, except for siege-pieces, which had to be provided with hand-forged shot, since cast shot tended to splinter when fired at stone walls.[3] In all these matters Sweden was perhaps less backward in relation to the continent than was the case in regard to infantry and cavalry; and was certainly much better off than Denmark, who, having no mineral resources, could not afford copper and had to make do with iron. In Germany the confusion of types was even worse than in Sweden, despite the efforts of Maximilian I and Charles V. In no part of Europe was there a really effective field-artillery, because in no part of Europe was there as yet a field-artillery that was satisfactorily mobile.

In laying down a policy for his gun-founders, Gustav Adolf seems, from an early stage of the reign, to have kept in view certain ultimate tactical objectives. These may be defined as the extraction from foot, horse and guns of the utmost of the advantages inherent in each; and the welding of all three into a unified whole, of which the parts should be interdependent, collaborating, flexible; solid and unflinching in defence, and in attack capable of that concentration of force which was beyond the abilities either of the Spanish or of the Dutch school. For the guns, that meant above all increased mobility, which in its turn meant decreased weight. Firepower depends not so much on firing often as on firing often at the right place; and the field-artillery of the pre-Gustavian era, planted four-square in front of the battle-line, taken, retaken and abandoned half a dozen times in the course of an engagement as the tide of battle rolled back and forth, was not in a position to make the best of such firepower as it possessed. But an artillery that could be rapidly brought into play at the point required, an artillery leavened and emancipated, would be an artillery that could give the best of which the gunners and the guns were capable.

The King began by systematizing the classification of his guns, abandoning the old names and substituting a gradation according

[1] *Sv. Krig*, Supp. Vol. II. 39-40, 171.

[2] On the relative merits of 'copper' and iron, see Odenrick, II. 33; Turner, *Pallas Armata*, p. 189 (he thought copper guns burst *more* easily than iron); Hammarskiöld, *USAH*, p. 7; *id.*, *Om svenskt artilleri i äldre tider*, p. 40; *Sv. Krig*, Supp. Vol. II. 184, 235.

[3] *ibid.*, II. 54.

to the weight of the projectile (as, for instance, 24-pounders, 12-pounders or 6-pounders)—a system which was first adumbrated by Maurice and which lasted as long as cannon-balls. The massive *murbräckor* were altogether abandoned, and the 24-pounder became the army's heaviest weapon. By 1630 this process had been carried so far that the artillery had been reduced to three main types—the 24-pounder, 12-pounder and 3-pounder. At the same time, by standardizing and improving the quality of powder it became possible to reduce the thickness of the barrel without fear of accident. Guns were rebored, to ensure greater uniformity of calibre. Successful attempts were made to reduce the weight of the piece by still further shortening the barrel. By relegating iron guns as far as possible to fortresses, breastworks and ships, the King ensured that the armies in the field should be equipped almost exclusively with the lighter 'copper' guns.[1] He was continually encouraging his workmen to produce new types of lighter pieces, and personally supervised their testing on the proving-ground outside Stockholm.[2] By 1623 real progress was being made. A gun-founder of skill, von Siegroth, was beginning to produce pieces, cast by a secret process, which were decidedly lighter than anything else of their type. A new light 6-pounder stimulated the King to further efforts. The result was Melkior Wurmbrandt's famous 3-pounder, known to history as 'Gustavus Adolphus's leather gun'. In this weapon an extremely thin 'copper' barrel was bound round with rope and mastic, and the whole covered with a sheath of hard leather. It was not quite a new invention: it had been known at Zürich in 1623, and Kristian IV of Denmark had caused a similar gun to be constructed; but Gustav Adolf was the first commander to make extensive use of it. But its career with the Swedish armies lasted for no more than two years (1627-29), and at the end of that time it was supplanted by a much superior weapon. Its significance has, in fact, been greatly exaggerated by historians: it is best considered as the most successful of the many experiments which were to lead to the 'regiment-piece' (*regementsstycke*). The leather gun had sacrificed everything to mobility: for fear of splitting the barrel it had to be provided with special powder and a much reduced charge, with resulting loss of muzzle-velocity and range; but even so it was much too

[1] Hammarskiöld, *USAH*, pp. 31-4, 128, 147-8; *id.*, *Gustaf II Adolfs artilleri*, pp. 69-71; *Sv. Krig*, Supp. Vol. II. 42, 169-70, 216, 296.

[2] See the description in N. Ahnlund, *Gustav Adolf the Great*, pp. 116-17.

fragile.[1] The regiment-piece avoided most of these drawbacks. Essentially it was similar to the leather gun: in spite of the fact that the barrel was now all-metal, the total weight was about the same. Both were 3-pounders; both, thanks to an improved type of gun-carriage, could be drawn by a single horse with ease, or if necessary could be manhandled by two or three men. The capacity of the regiment-piece for rapid fire was greatly heightened, however, by the introduction in conjunction with it of the artillery cartridge—a testimony to the improved workmanship of the gun-founders—the charge being wired to the shot for convenience and speed of loading. The range of the piece was probably about 300 metres [2]; and the usual shot was canister or grape.

The regiment-piece was one of the decisive factors in Gustav Adolf's success in Germany. He took over eighty of these guns with him in 1630, and many more followed. They revolutionized the rôle of artillery in battle; for one platoon in every infantry squadron now had one of these pieces assigned to it, and was thereby enabled to play much the same tactical part as a section equipped with an automatic weapon in a modern army. Nowhere is the close connexion between the King's tactical conceptions and the armaments with which he provided himself more apparent. The regiment-piece gave Sweden an immense advantage; for neither Denmark nor the Catholic powers could at first show any weapon to compare with it. Kristian IV's interesting experiments ran aground on the shallows of his own character [3]; Tilly was fast rutted in the old style of

[1] Hammarskiöld, *Gustaf II Adolfs artilleri*, pp. 71-2; *id.*, *USAH*, pp. 147-50; *Sv. Krig*, II. 138-9; Supp. Vol. II. 180-2, 235-41. Hammarskiöld differs from Odenrick (*op. cit.*, II. 29) and from the author of this section of *Sv. Krig*, Supp. Vol. II: they contend that the leather gun overheated after 10 rounds, as a result of the bad conductivity of the sheathing; Hammarskiöld, on the contrary, writes that 'round after round could be fired without intermission and without cooling or cleaning'. The fault of the gun, in his view, was its fragility (*USAH*, p. 148). Hammarskiöld makes it clear that the system of thin barrels and leather sheathing was applied experimentally to the 24-pounder and 6-pounder also, as well as to the famous 3-pounder (*ibid.*, p. 147). The leather gun made a considerable sensation in military circles: even in 1631, when it was no longer in use, the imperialist defenders of Frankfurt-on-Oder shouted from the walls, 'What you Strumbling- [*sc. strömming*, Baltic herring] eaters, haue you eaten vp all your Leather-gunnes for hunger?': *The Swedish Intelligencer*, I. 89. The Scots used leather guns in 1640, but they are said to have lasted only one day: Terry, *Leslie*, pp. 116, 121 *note* 1; Firth, pp. 156-7. Frauenholz (*Söldnertum*, I. 41) makes the unintelligible comment that the leather guns were 'mehr Improvizationen für Bauernaufgebote gewesen'.

[2] *Sv. Krig*, Supp. Vol. II. 191-207, 223, 253, 296; Hammarskiöld, *USAH*, pp. 33-4, 150; *id.*, *Om svenskt artilleri . . .*, p. 45.

[3] *Sv. Krig*, Supp. Vol. II. 304-13.

fighting. But Wallenstein saw the new possibilities. He was not too conservative to take a leaf out of his adversary's book; and during his second generalship he deployed his marvellous administrative talents to create a new artillery park, with trained horses and drivers, and with specially constructed light guns for use with infantry. Even so, his 6-pounders needed four horses to haul them.[1] Throughout the period 1630-32, therefore, Sweden had the upper hand as regards artillery. Gustav Adolf's 24-pounder, for instance, was reduced in weight until it was considerably lighter than that of the imperialists, and could easily be dragged overland by horses instead of being mainly dependent upon water transport. The number of guns, moreover, was as a rule greater, both absolutely and relatively, on the Swedish side: at the beginning of the German campaign it reached the remarkable figure of 9·4 per thousand men.[2] And a generation later Sir James Turner could write, as it seems with justice: 'The *Swedish* Trains of Artillery since their first footing in *Germany* have had the reputation to be the most exactly composed, and conducted by the most experimented Artists, of any in *Christendom*.' [3]

The rearming of the infantry with pike and musket, the creation of a really effective field-artillery, could hardly have been carried out so successfully if Gustav Adolf had not been able to supply his requirements from domestic sources. The mineral resources of the country, and the expansion of the metallurgical industries throughout the reign, gave Sweden in this matter a great advantage over her enemies. Weapons could be produced at home more cheaply than they could be imported, and possibly more cheaply than they could be manufactured abroad; and the rearmament of the forces was in consequence effected with less strain to the finances than might have been expected. It is true that at the beginning of the reign it was

[1] *ibid.*, II. 315-18, 321, 383-5. At Lützen the Swedes had ten 24-pounders, ten 12-pounders, and about forty light guns, nearly all of them 3-pounders; Wallenstein had nine 24-pounders, two 16-pounders, two 14-pounders, four 12-pounders, one 7-pounder, and two 6-pounders to each regiment: Hammarskiöld, *USAH*, p. 193. After 1632, Swedish guns tended to grow slightly heavier again: too much had been sacrificed to mobility.

[2] *Sv. Krig*, Supp. Vol. II. 207. Napoleon considered 4 per thousand to be a good number to aim at; in the Boer War the British had 2·5 per thousand, the Boers had 1·25 per thousand: J. Colin, *Les Transformations de la guerre*, pp. 23, 43. At Nuremberg in August 1632 Gustav Adolf concentrated no less than 169 guns against Wallenstein: they included 33 24-pounders and 102 3-pounders: Hammarskiöld, *USAH*, p. 182: *id.*, *Gustaf II Adolfs artilleri*, p. 81, makes the number 175.

[3] *Pallas Armata*, p. 194.

still necessary to import small-arms and armour; but by the end of it Sweden was fully self-supporting in these articles.[1] The various *entrepreneurs* to whom Gustav Adolf entrusted the direction of the iron industry were likewise able to supply the King's demand for iron guns: indeed, their profits from guns came mainly from exporting surplus stock to other countries.[2] The 'copper' guns were made at the royal factories on Norrmalm, or at Nyköping, Kalmar or (after 1630) at the Kopparberg.[3] Indeed, apart from a single mortar imported from Germany in 1616, there is no record of any piece of artillery's being imported into the country during the whole course of the reign.[4] Gustav Adolf could venture into Germany with the knowledge that the Swedish armaments industry was fully able to provide for the army he took with him. It seems unlikely, however, that the vastly increased forces under the King's command in 1632 were all equipped and armed from Sweden: most of them were mercenaries who would bring their own weapons with them when they joined the Swedish colours. Steps were taken, moreover, to organize arms production in Germany, and thus save transport; and in the later stages of the Thirty Years' War much of the war material required by Banér and Torstensson was manufactured to Swedish orders in the workshops of the occupied areas.[5]

In the matter of gunpowder the position was not so satisfactory. Despite Gustav Adolf's improvement of existing saltpetre-works, and his foundation of new ones, the country was unable to produce all the saltpetre that was needed. The saltpetre-man was as active and unpopular a figure in the Sweden of Gustav Adolf as in the England of James I. Since 1583, indeed, churches and churchyards had been exempt from his prospecting activities; but such of the peasantry as kept cattle or horses—which meant almost all of them—could not escape his visitations. But not all his digging could fill the gap between production and consumption; nor could de Geer, who was given a lease of the Linköping powder-mills in 1627, do much to improve matters. In spite of the fact that the steady rise in the price

[1] See above, p. 113; and *Sv. Krig*, Supp. Vol. II. 128-9.

[2] See above, p. 113; and Hammarskiöld, *USAH*, p. 27. D. Norrman, *Gustav Adolfs politik mot Ryssland och Polen under tyska kriget*, pp. 15, 112, for exports to Russia.

[3] Hammarskiöld, *USAH*, pp. 16-21, 154; Hamilton, *Krigsmaktens och krigskonstens tillstånd*, p. 280.

[4] *Sv. Krig*, Supp. Vol. II. 184.

[5] Hammarskiöld, *USAH*, p. 21; Försvarsstaben, *Från Femern och Jankow*, p. 69.

of saltpetre was an incentive to develop the native industry, Sweden in 1630 was producing only about half the gunpowder required. There seems reason to believe, however, that the situation was appreciably better in 1632 than in 1611; and the same applies to that other military necessity, match, for the manufacture of which the King took measures by the setting up of rope-walks.[1]

There was one other item in the soldier's equipment to which Gustav Adolf gave some attention: his clothes. Gustav Adolf's career fell in a transitional period in the history of military costume: the days of full armour were passing, but the era of uniforms had not yet arrived. As long as a considerable proportion of an army was clad in armour, there was no point in providing uniforms for it; and even had armour been cast aside, the mercenary's easy habit of changing sides by enlisting overnight under the standard of the victor might have made uniforms more confusing than distinctive. The usual practice, therefore, was for each side to select a token before battle—a white armband, a green branch in the hat—so that in the *mêlée* it might be possible to distinguish friend from foe: the Habsburg armies for many years wore a red cord for this purpose, and Swedish troops for that reason had a standing instruction to avoid red tokens.[2] Nevertheless, in many European armies the beginnings of something like a uniform had already appeared. In part this was almost accidental, the consequence of an issue of cloth from the same bale to a whole unit; in part it was deliberate.[3] Some of the soldiers of Mansfeld, and of George William of Brandenburg, can be said to have worn real uniforms; and both Maximilian of Bavaria and Kristian IV of Denmark made serious attempts at clothing their soldiers upon a distinctive standard pattern.[4] Wallen-

[1] *Arkiv*, I. 113; *Sv. Krig*, Supp. Vol. II. 68; *cf.* Wijn, p. 230; Hamilton, pp. 239-40. For shortage of saltpetre, powder and match in April 1632, see *RRP*, II. 165. For artillery supplies in general, Hammarskiöld, *USAH*, p. 154. For local supplies of sulphur, *Sv. Krig*, V. 372.

[2] Frauenholz, *Söldnertum*, I. 40; Priorato, p. 151.

[3] The English armies offered examples of both cases: Cruickshank, pp. 71-2; Falls, p. 54; Oman, p. 385. No uniforms existed on either side at the beginning of the Civil War: Firth, pp. 232-4.

[4] Frauenholz, *Söldnertum*, I. 41-2; Wertheim, I. 94; *Sv. Krig*, Supp. Vol. II. 393-403; Rockstroh, I. 18, 52-3; Hallenberg, IV. 817 (for Denmark); Knötel-Sieg, *Handbuch der Uniformkunde*, pp. 1, 5, 149, 193, 247, 311, 341, 354, for the authors' estimate of the dates of introduction of uniform into the armies of the leading European countries. It is noteworthy that in general they consider that there were no true uniforms before about the middle of the century. Wertheim, on the contrary, writing of Germany in the early 1620's, says: 'Die Uniformierung war im Allgemeinen bei den Armeen durchgeführt, und zwar waren durchgängig die Röcke in den Fähnlein eines Regiments gleich. . . .': Wertheim, I. 94.

stein's lifeguard had a uniform; and so had other small picked bodies of men elsewhere, particularly if they were used frequently upon ceremonial occasions. The armies of Maurice, however, seem to have had nothing that can be called a uniform, and neither had Spinola's; while the French armies had to wait for Le Tellier, if not for Louvois, before they obtained theirs.[1]

Since Gustav Vasa's time it had been customary in Sweden that the conscripts should be fitted out with clothes by the other members of their *rota*. Thereafter the government took care to keep them out of rags by issuing them with cloth as part of their wages.[2] Neither the rustic garments produced by the *rota* nor the government's imported cloth (which might vary in hue at every issue) was calculated to give to the conscript levies a smart and soldierlike appearance; and Gustav Adolf presently became conscious that his troops presented a somewhat motley and boorish aspect. In 1621, therefore, he ordered that 'since many will judge contemptuously of the infantry for its clothes' sake, and since thereafter derogatory words may be disseminated in foreign countries concerning the whole army, in the King and country's despite, therefore shall newly conscripted foot-soldiers be enjoined . . . to provide themselves with proper clothes instead of their long smocks and peasant attire, wherewith less consideration ought to be had of the material itself, than that the clothes shall be well made'.[3] In the following year he improved on this by ordering that every regiment, or at least every company, should be uniformly clothed. The order was not generally enforced; but already in 1620 the Östergötland regiment adopted its colours of red and gold; in 1621 the dress of the Västergötland regiment was standardized, and 200 tailors were corralled to make uniforms for it to prescribed patterns; in 1625 the King's lifeguards were given what was probably a ceremonial dress of black and gold; and in the same year the tailors of Uppland were summoned to Stockholm to work on government contracts. In 1626 and 1627 the King elaborated a plan for a central clothing depot for the army. Clothes for the troops were to be in constant production by a large permanent establishment of tailors; they were to be cut in two standard sizes only (two-thirds of them in the large size, one-third in the small); and they were to be either blue with red facings,

[1] Wijn, p. 369; L. André, *Michel Le Tellier et Louvois*, pp. 350, 354.
[2] *Sv. Krig*, Supp. Vol. II. 80-4.
[3] Hamilton, p. 73.

or in some similar contrasting combination of colours. Cloth was to be supplied by Swedish textile manufactures.[1] In 1630 he tried to suppress one source of diversity by ordering that in future the *rotar* should give the conscript money instead of cloth, and leave the clothing of him to the government.[2]

These details make it plain that Gustav Adolf did aim at putting the native army, at least, into uniform. He seems in the main to have been moved by a desire that his troops should present a smart appearance: there is no evidence one way or the other as to whether his efforts were inspired by any genuinely military motive. And it is doubtful whether his plans had much success. It is not certain whether the central clothing depot ever began production, or assembled its army of tailors and cutters, or indeed ever existed at all. Swedish regiments were certainly known by various colours—the Blue Regiment, the Yellow Regiment, and so forth [3]; but they seem to have been named for the colour of their standards rather than for the colour of their coats.[4] There is no indication that the Swedish armies in Germany were so readily identifiable that they were able to dispense with tokens in battle: on the contrary.[5] And it is certainly true that in the closing years of the war the government had reverted to the old system (if it had ever departed from it) of issuing the troops with cloth and leaving it to the individual soldier to have the material made up to suit his fancy.[6]

(c) *Training and Discipline*

Among the fragmentary writings of Gustav Adolf which have been preserved is one in which he sets out his ideas as to the duties of the soldier and the qualities which a commander is entitled to expect to find in him. And he sums up in these words: '*Summa*, I expect of him, under the article "Virtue", that he shall be of good life and conversation, diligent in ordering, laborious in performance, valorous in danger, various in his capacities, and swift in execution.' [7]

[1] For the above, Petri, II. 14; Bensow, I. 251; *Sv. Krig*, Supp. Vol. II. 385-92.

[2] *Sv. Krig*, III. 256. But the so-called 'little war aid' levied in this year was a levy of furs, shoes, shirts and stockings for the troops: *ibid.*, V. 372.

[3] *e.g.* I. Hoppe, *Geschichte des ersten schwedisch-polnischen Krieges*, p. 147, and elsewhere, refers to them as 'Die Blauröckel'.

[4] G. Nordström, *Regiments Jaune, Bleu, Vert, Rouge et Blanc de l'ancienne Armée suèdoise*, pp. 343-5.

[5] The Swedes wore green branches as a token at Breitenfeld: *The Swedish Intelligencer*, I. 122; Monro, II. 64.

[6] Försvarsstaben, *Från Femern och Jankow*, p. 76.

[7] Styffe, p. 64.

Such men, as he probably realized, are not born but made; and he devoted considerable thought to making them.

The means he used were training and discipline. As he was Maurice's heir in the field of tactics, so he was his pupil in regard to training. New, unfamiliar and often cumbrous weapons, new tactical units, a new style of fighting, demanded as a precondition for success intensive drilling of the individual soldier and careful exercises by smaller and larger bodies of troops. From the time when the King's military reforms began to get under way—that is, from about the beginning of the 'twenties—he never relaxed the training of his troops. Conscripts, after levying, were drafted in batches to the lifeguards, which served as a training battalion and supplied instructors. Mercenaries were drilled *rota* by *rota* under the *rota*-master, with the help of old soldiers versed in Swedish methods. Basic training took about a fortnight. Musketeers were especially drilled in loading; all, whether musketeers or pikes, were trained to manœuvre to tap of drum; and all were trained to know, as the very fundamental of discipline, their places in the ranks.[1] Drill and exercises of this sort were going on constantly, as occasion offered: the army was never allowed to be idle. A few instances may stand for many. As soon as the truce with Poland was concluded in 1622, Banér's regiment was put through a course of training.[2] During the Prussian campaign of 1628, advantage was taken of delays in the advance upon Graudenz to exercise the army in taking up formation, strengthening field-fortifications, and the orderly establishment of bivouacs.[3] Large-scale manœuvres were held outside Stockholm while the army was waiting for transports and breezes to take it to Germany in 1630.[4] On the day before Breitenfeld, and in the camp at Nuremberg, the troops were practised in the kind of fighting which was expected on the morrow.[5] In short, no commander until that time, not Maurice himself, took so much care to prepare his army for its task; and it was because so many individual soldiers and so many units had been thoroughly familiarized with the part they were to play in battle that the Swedish squadrons could show such resilience, initiative and resource in a

[1] *Sv. Krig*, II. 324, V. 307; Sjöstrand, p. 481.
[2] G. Björlin, *Johan Banér*, I. 51.
[3] *Sv. Krig*, III. 415.
[4] *Krigsvetenskaps Akademiens Handlingar* (1932), pp. 31-2; Monro, II. 2; and *cf. Peder Galts Depescher*, p. 32.
[5] *Sv. Krig*, IV. 450; Monro, II. 141.

crisis—as they did, for instance, at Breitenfeld. Perhaps only the personal authority of a commander who was also a sovereign could have achieved such a result: at all events, it appears that training became less thorough after Lützen.[1]

The narrative of Monro has familiarized posterity with the system of discipline that prevailed in the Swedish armies in Gustav Adolf's time; and William Watts's *The Swedish Discipline* made his Articles of War accessible to the contemporary English reader. From the beginning, the armies of Gustav Adolf have enjoyed in Protestant historiography a reputation for good conduct. To some extent the reputation is deserved. But the Swedish armies were in reality by no means so uniformly well-behaved as has been alleged, nor was Gustav Adolf himself so notable an innovator in the sphere of military discipline as has been supposed.

The Articles of War which Axel Oxenstierna read to the army assembled on Årsta Meadow in 1621 (and which every regimental commander read to his troops once a month thereafter) were indeed in some respects new; but they were based on familiar continental models, and they had had many forerunners in Sweden.[2] Their origins may be sought in the regulations made by mediaeval Swedish rulers for the conduct of their personal bodyguards; then in the code of discipline for the navy put out by Gustav Vasa in 1535; in the same monarch's Articles of War of 1545; and in similar Articles issued by his successors, and notably by Erik XIV. They borrow something from the code of Ferdinand of Hungary (1526), something from the famous code of Maximilian II (1570), something from the code of Maurice.[3] The Articles of 1621 were prepared in draft by Gustav Adolf himself, and subsequently revised by Axel Oxenstierna; and the presence of numerous transcripts of continental codes in the archives in Stockholm makes it clear that they took care to familiarize themselves with the systems in use abroad. Yet in certain important respects the Articles of 1621 differ from other codes of military law of that age. They were, in the first place, designed primarily for a national conscript army. They laid down the

[1] Turner, *Pallas Armata*, p. 210.

[2] The text is in J. Schmedeman, *Kungl. Stadgar, Förordningar, Bref och Resolutioner*, p. 15 *seqq.*; English version in *The Swedish Discipline*, p. 39 *seqq.*; Gustav Adolf's draft in Styffe, p. 243 *seqq.*

[3] For their provenance, see A. Gierow, *Bidrag till det svenska militärkyrkoväsendets historia*, pp. 21-79; O. Brusiin, *Gustav II Adolfs krigsartiklar*, *passim*; Frauenholz, *Söldnertum*, I. 5-6, 23-7. For Swedish military discipline in general, Hamilton, pp. 9-36.

soldier's duties—including (be it noted) his duty to dig when ordered to do so—and the punishment for neglect of those duties; but they entirely lacked provisions defining the obligations of the commander to his soldiers.[1] Gustav Adolf's Articles of War were orders: they were not the terms of an agreement between contracting parties. They made no provision, as was usual in the case of Landsknechts, for N.C.O.s to be associated as assessors with the judges at a court-martial. In the case of moral and religious offences, it was the chaplain, in the Swedish Articles, who appeared as plaintiff. The Articles were much superior to those of Maurice, for instance in clarity and orderliness of arrangement.[2] Above all, they applied the same principles which had underlain the creation of *Svea hovrätt*, and established a hierarchy of military jurisdiction: inferior court-martial, presided over by the colonel; superior court-martial, presided over by the Marshal; final appeal to the King: a system which gained added solidity with the creation of a permanent *krigsrätt* in Stockholm in 1630.[3]

Apart from these aspects, the Articles did not much differ from other Articles. Punishments were severe, and at times ferocious—the death penalty was imposed for something over forty offences; but they were less draconian, and more carefully graduated, than in the Articles of Maurice.[4] The use of decimation is possibly to be considered a peculiarly Swedish characteristic; as the punishment of running the gauntlet certainly was.[5] There has been a disposition, both among contemporaries and among historians, to lay stress upon the religious provisions of the code; but it is easy to exaggerate the singularity of the Swedish armies in this respect. It is true that prayers were held twice a day and a sermon delivered once a week. Each company, as well as each regiment, had its chaplain, drawn from the same province as the men; and the appointment of these chaplains remained in the hands of the ecclesiastical, rather than of

[1] Droysen, *Militärwesen*, p. 23; *cf.* J. Paul, *Gustaf Adolf*, II. 42; Generalstaben, *Gustaf II Adolf*, p. 111.

[2] Wijn, p. 104.

[3] Steckzén, *Krigskollegii historia*, p. 48; K. Grönfors, *Ur det svenska militära rättegångsväsendets historia*, pp. 208-43; Brusiin, *op. cit.*, pp. 386-8. By Turner's time this arrangement of military-judicial instances seemed to him to be normal: *Pallas Armata*, pp. 295-6. The contention of Brusiin and Grönfors that this system of superimposed instances was unique for its day seems to require modification in the light of Wijn, pp. 91-2.

[4] Brusiin, p. 383.

[5] Monro, I. 45. The point about the gauntlet was that, since it was inflicted by a man's comrades, it did not degrade him, as other punishment did: *Pallas Armata*, p. 349.

the military, authorities.[1] The Articles prescribed heavy penalties for swearing, blasphemy, sacrilege and moral offences; they forbade the sale of liquor during church hours, and tried to compel church attendance; they had penalties for the chaplain who appeared at prayers drunk. No loose women were permitted in the Swedish camp; and the establishment of a Swedish regiment made no provision for a *Hurenweibel*.[2] Duelling was sternly forbidden. But most, if not all, of these things could be matched from the history of other European armies of the period: in the early Huguenot armies, for instance, very similar moral sanctions were in force [3]; Leicester's code of 1585 foreshadows Gustav Adolf's at point after point [4]; every company in the *tercio* was supplied with a *capellán*—Londoño (who attached the greatest importance to proper religious ministrations) considered that ideally every army ought to be equipped with a bishop [5]; and the religious exercises of Gustav Adolf's godly army are quite eclipsed by the prodigies of devotion attributed to the forces of Chodkiewicz.[6]

Nevertheless, Gustav Adolf's soldiers had—for some time at least—a good reputation, and certainly a good opinion of themselves. 'Such as were birds of the Divell's hatching,' writes Monro, 'all such were banished from the Army, that was led by Pious and religious *Gustavus* of never dying memory.' [7] Their good behaviour was commented on (by a friendly observer) soon after their first coming into Germany; and at Greiffenhagen, and later at Kreuznach, they distinguished themselves by their self-control and obedience to orders in the moment of victory.[8] From Nuremberg it was reported that 'their conversation was wont to be of God and His mercies; and though they might be bemused by the juice of the grape, there was heard from them no ill language, nor was there marked any looseness or unseemliness in their behaviour'.[9]

[1] On the religious organization of the Swedish armies, see Hj. Holmquist, *Svenska kyrkans historia*, IV. 1. 396-400; Petri, II. 21-2; Gierow, pp. 102-39. Roman Catholic mercenaries were dependent upon casual encounters with a priest; as at Munich, where five priests were kept constantly busy on Sundays and feast-days in hearing their confessions: J. Baur, *Die Kapuziner under die schwedische Generalität im dreissigjährigen Kriege*, p. 9.

[2] Many wives (even of noblemen) accompanied their husbands to the wars, as Banér's did: Steckzén, *Johan Banér*, p. 93.

[3] Oman, p. 400.

[4] Cruickshank, pp. 144-51.

[5] Altamira, III. 293; Wijn, pp. 366-7.

[6] T. Korzon, *Dzieje wojen i wojskowości w Polsce*, II. 143.

[7] Monro, II. 19.

[8] *Sv. Krig*, III. 400-1, V. 281; *The Swedish Intelligencer*, I. 71.

[9] Generalstaben, *Gustaf II Adolf*, p. 315.

But, as Coligny remarked on one occasion, 'Young hermits may become old devils'; and though there is abundant evidence that Gustav Adolf and his officers did their best to maintain the high standards which Monro remembered, the event proved that not even native Swedes, and still less the mercenaries in the Swedish service, could resist the temptation to plunder and excesses, when plunder and excesses were the most promising alternatives to severe privation. The deterioration set in as early as the autumn of 1630, and was directly caused by the King's inability to pay his troops; and it was not halted by the improved economic situation after Breitenfeld, since by now the army was preponderantly composed of hard-bitten German professionals.[1] The Swedes, indeed, seem to have maintained a noticeably better standard of behaviour for some time thereafter: in May 1632 Jakob Wagner noted that at Augsburg the conscripts were much better disciplined than the mercenaries.[2] It may well be that there continued to be a perceptible difference between the conduct of Swedish and German troops (though there are plenty of instances of excesses by Swedish soldiery before ever they set foot in Germany)[3]; but in considering the effectiveness of Gustav Adolf's discipline the distinction is irrelevant. Whether through lack of money to pay his armies, or as a result of the employment of mercenaries, the King was in fact unable, however good his intentions, to enforce his Articles of War in such a way as to protect the civilian population of Germany. In March 1631 Teuffel complains that his troops are committing 'unheard-off excesses'[4]; in April Gustav Adolf was unable to save Frankfurt-on-Oder—a Protestant town—from being savagely sacked. At the end of the year the Brunswick lands were terribly ravaged by the armies of Banér and William of Weimar[5]; Göttingen was plundered in February 1632[6]; and all that winter there were complaints of the behaviour of the King's German troops in Thuringia.[7] Monro

[1] It was difficult to control mercenary regiments, since they dealt with all disciplinary matters internally: *Arkiv*, III. lix-lx.

[2] *Die Chronik des Jakob Wagners über die schwedischen Okkupation in Augsburg*, p. 19.

[3] See, for instance, Hallenberg, V. 429; *AOSB*, I. IV. 128, 138, II. IX. 47, 78; *Sv. Krig*, II. 501. Bennedich remarks that the discipline of the Swedish armies 'was never what we like to imagine it to have been': C. Bennedich, *Ur det gamla Gardets öden*, p. 83.

[4] *AOSB*, II. IX. 568; *cf. Arkiv*, II. 45-6.

[5] W. Huschke, *Herzog Wilhelm von Weimar als Statthalter Gustav Adolfs in Thüringen*, p. 30.

[6] *ibid.*, p. 32.

[7] *ibid.*, p. 12.

himself has no illusions about what happened at Donauwörth [1]; and as the armies advanced into Bavaria in the spring of 1632 the King, for more or less valid military reasons, permitted his soldiers to harry and burn without check, provoking Pappenheim to reprisals in Weimar some months later.[2] The breakdown of discipline was so serious by the autumn of 1632 that it was among the main reasons which prompted Gustav Adolf to summon the Swabian, Franconian and Rhenish circles to a meeting at Ulm.[3] And for a succinct compendium of the atrocities committed by the troops under Swedish command the interested enquirer could not do better than turn to the patent issued by Axel Oxenstierna in February 1633.[4]

Gustav Adolf vacillated a little in his reaction to this state of affairs. There were moments when the pressure of military necessity forced him to harden his heart. To complaints from John George in February 1632 he answered that 'war is war, and soldiers are not novices'.[5] But on the whole he continued to struggle for a humaner form of warfare. At Mainz in 1632 he caused to be printed a German version of the Articles of 1621, with additions and modifications designed to tighten up discipline, and to make the code more conformable to the altered circumstances.[6] When George William of Brandenburg in July 1632 asked what he should do with some Swedish officers who had committed outrages, the King impatiently replied, 'Has my brother-in-law no gallows in his country, or is he short of timber?' [7] And at Nuremberg he addressed the troops in a speech of comprehensive commination which was long remembered.[8]

The effects were small. In much of Germany, and all of Bohemia, the Swede and the Turk and the devil had much the same

[1] Monro, II. 114.

[2] Huschke, p. 81; *Sv. Krig*, VI. 30-1, 352.

[3] G. Irmer, *Die Verhandlungen Schwedens und seiner Verbündeten mit Wallenstein und dem Kaiser*, I. 284-6.

[4] *AOSB*, I. VIII. 202-7.

[5] K. G. Helbig, *Gustav Adolf und die Kurfürsten von Sachsen und Brandenburg*, p. 70; *cf.* Styffe, p. 548. Compare Wallenstein's sardonic comment: 'Wollen sie Krieg führen und menagieren, dem Reiche Gusto und nicht Disgusto durch die Einquartierungen geben, so suchen sie sich unsern Herrgott zum General und nicht mich': Hallwich, *Geschichte Wallensteins*, I. 442.

[6] L. Frohnhäuser, *Gustav Adolf und die Schweden in Mainz und am Rhein*, pp. 135-44; *The Swedish Discipline*, pp. 69-73; *Sv. Krig*, V. 300-7.

[7] K. Spannagel, *Konrad von Burgsdorff*, p. 35.

[8] Printed in Paul, III. 124-5 *note* 19. For the King's difficulties in regard to discipline, see, *e.g.*, *Arkiv*, I. 395; Droysen, *Schriftstücke von Gustav Adolf* [cited: *Schriftstücke*], pp. 123, 140-4, 197, 223; *Handlingar rörande Skandinaviens historia*, XXV. 109-11; *Sverges traktater*, V. 647-8; *AOSB*, I. VII. 59; and *cf.* the comments in Priorato, pp. 223, 328.

reputation. The later stages of the war produced folk-songs and folk-legends in Bohemia in which the Swede appeared in a variety of horrific guises: Czech children were sung to sleep with a lullaby which recommended earnest prayer, since Oxenstierna would be coming in the morning; 'szwed' passed into the Czech language as a word for a criminal or ragged fellow; and the legend of the 'Swedish drink' frightened even those little boys who did not believe in Oxenstierna.[1]

It was a melancholy ending to Gustav Adolf's attempt to create a godly army. Yet the attempt had by no means been wholly in vain. For, in the first place, whatever the outrages committed upon the civil population, the internal discipline remained on the whole good: Tilly, for instance, was deeply impressed by the willingness of Gustav Adolf's troops to fight to the last man at Neu-Brandenburg.[2] In the second place, however great the fall from grace in the later years of the war, there had been a time when the Swedish army had been in truth a godly army. And the ideals of Gustav Adolf's Articles were not forgotten; the chaplains did not cease their ministrations; and serious-minded men such as Monro, men who believed that truth and righteousness lay all on one side 'in this old Quarrell', could idealize the army as they had known it in the King's lifetime, precisely because there was a solid basis of reality beneath their fantasy. Gustav Adolf had provided the Protestant world with the idea of a Protestant army, with a standard of military virtue against which to measure, with a tradition of piety which never died in the hearts of those Scottish soldiers of fortune whom the King's personality had ennobled into warriors for truth. They took back the idea, the standard, the tradition to their native country; and they infused them into the army of the Covenant. And when that army succumbed at last to the genius of Cromwell, its leaders (if they had been honest with themselves) might have recognized in the victor an adept of the same school as themselves, who united in his own person (as they had failed to do) the military and the moral heritage of the Swedish King.

(iv) *Gustav Adolf's Tactical Reforms*

The great reforms which have been outlined above were not the work of a mere administrator concerned with efficiency for its own

[1] P. M. Hebbe, *Svenskarna i Böhmen och Mähren*, pp. 90-4.

[2] K. Wittich, *Magdeburg, Gustav Adolf und Tilly*, p. 278; *cf.* Delbrück, IV. 205.

sake: they were, and were intended by their author to be, the preliminaries to a new style of fighting. They were designed by a general for practical application in the field. But as the reorganization of the army was not to be accomplished in a moment, so the new tactics to which it led did not spring suddenly into existence, but evolved slowly over a whole decade. The King experimented on the battlefield as at the war office; though for many years the imperfection of the instrument at his disposal necessarily restricted his range. The goal of his reforms must early have been formulated in his mind; the methods by which he sought to attain it changed under the influence of practical experience and with the ripening of his own genius. The ideal tactic is that which combines hitting-power, mobility and defensive strength: every age has sought to approximate to this ideal. From the point of view of tactics, military history can be viewed as a succession of oscillations back and forth, in which the emphasis is laid now on one, now on another of these elements, to the prejudice of the other two. There have been relatively few tacticians who have cultivated all three with equal success. Gustav Adolf was perhaps one of them. Within the limits imposed by the circumstances of the age, he eventually evolved a tactic solid in defence and incisive in attack, and capable of a mobility which astonished his enemies.

About the year 1620, when Gustav Adolf was beginning his military reforms, there were, as we have seen, two main schools of tactics, two main methods of drawing up an army for battle. The Spanish school still depended upon the mass effects obtained by the *tercio*; though the *tercios* had now been diminished in size, and were commonly ranged in groups of three, in arrowhead formation, or sometimes in groups of four, diamond-wise, the fourth *tercio* in such a case acting as a reserve. The Dutch school, based on the much smaller unit of the battalion, favoured a rigidly linear order of battle. Neither was ideally suited to the warfare of the new age. Military fashions had changed a little since the days of the Netherlands revolt; and the commanders of the earlier period of the Thirty Years' War were less chary of battle than Parma and Maurice had been. And apart from the cavalry actions which completed the discomfiture of a wavering or beaten foe, battles were now decided mainly by long-range weapons—by pistol and carbine, musket and cannon. Firepower was the secret of victory. In these circumstances the complementary defects of the Dutch and Spanish systems became more obvious than ever. The Dutch lines developed a creditable intensity of fire, but could not roll forward easily to the attack. The *tercio* could crash into action, though at a foot-pace, but its depth and imperfect manœuvrability (even in its more modern, streamlined, version) diminished its firepower. And on both sides the cavalry was still prancing and curvetting in the wasteful intricacies of the caracole.

The War of Kalmar and the Russian war undoubtedly taught Gustav Adolf some valuable lessons. From the War of Kalmar he learned the value of field-fortifications. From the Russian war he obtained dear-bought experience of siege-operations. From both he learned the techniques of devastation.[1] But neither was particularly relevant to the norms of battle on the continent. It was not until after the resumption of the struggle with Poland that Gustav Adolf's tactics really began to evolve upon independent lines. It was the Polish war, undoubtedly, that convinced him of the viciousness of current cavalry tactics. The Polish horsemen had retained a true type of cavalry fighting long after the troopers of the west had reduced themselves to blazing away ineffectively with pistols. They did, no doubt, carry and use the pistol, but their characteristic weapons were the lance and the sabre; and the pistol was fired only as a preliminary to the charge at a gallop. From experience in Poland, Gustav Adolf drew the inference that a new cavalry tactic must be devised and a new cavalry trained to use it; and the further inference that a better-disciplined infantry must be given the means to develop a fire so hot that even if their cavalry were defeated, musketeers and pikemen together would be able to escape annihilation.[2]

The 'twenties, therefore, saw developments along three lines. the intensification of firepower, the combination of arms and the improvement of the cavalry. The battle of Wallhof, in January 1626, gave some indication of the direction in which Gustav Adolf was proceeding.[3] At Wallhof the advanced guard of cavalry was given added striking-power by having a body of 1000 musketeers attached

[1] *Sv. Krig*, I. 570-2; Barkman, *Gustaf II Adolfs regementsorganisation*, p. 71; *Krigsvetenskaps Akademiens Handlingar* (1932), pp. 38-9; *Kampen om Østersjøn*, p. 101.

[2] It was asserted by J. Staszewski (*Baltic Countries*, II. (1936) 278) that Gustav Adolf was influenced not only in cavalry tactics but also in infantry tactics by the reforms of Stephen Bátory. The most recent (co-operative) work on Bátory gives no support to this view: *Etienne Batory*, p. 385.

[3] For Wallhof, see *Sv. Krig*, II. 224-35.

to it; the Swedish army displayed a rapidity in deploying from column into line which was unusual at this period, and the battle was decided by the action of strong detachments of musketeers on either wing, who took advantage of the wooded terrain to execute a turning movement which forced the enemy to retreat through a bottle-neck in disorder.[1] At Mewe,[2] in September 1626, the Swedish infantry was able to drive off Polish cavalry by musket-fire, and followed this up by storming a steep escarpment in the face of a numerically superior enemy and blasting the Poles from the field by superiority of fire-discipline. The combats at Dirschau,[3] on 7 and 8 August 1627, mark another important advance. Hitherto Gustav Adolf, in the well-grounded conviction that the Polish horsemen would prove better than his own, had avoided cavalry engagements—as he did, for instance, at Mewe.[4] But by 1627 his reorganization of the cavalry had proceeded so far that he was anxious to test his work. The result of the fighting at Dirschau made it apparent that the Swedish horse could now meet the Poles on more or less equal terms. Dirschau, moreover, presented other significant features. Once again musketeers were attached to the cavalry, to assist their attack. It was at Dirschau that Wurmbrandt's leather guns appeared in action for the first time, two of them being attached to each infantry squadron. And, finally, it was at Dirschau that the squadrons were for the first time drawn up in battle-groups of three—an arrangement from which was soon derived the new higher tactical unit of the brigade.

Until 1627, Gustav Adolf's orders of battle had been typically defensive, for they had been conditioned by his unwillingness to take risks in the face of the enemy's superior cavalry. They were derived from the Dutch school, for they were clearly linear in type. Those that have been preserved reek of the textbook, and might almost be taken for caricatures, so unlikely does it appear that they can ever have been of practical use. They were highly complex and geometrical in plan, and indeed resemble nothing so much as fanciful

[1] Contrast Colin's remark (*Les Transformations de la guerre*, p. 92) that an enveloping movement by foot on the wings was too difficult for a seventeenth-century general to attempt.

[2] For Mewe, see *Sv. Krig*, II. 283-96.

[3] For Dirschau, see *Sv. Krig*, II. 354-65; but contrast Kukiel, p. 65.

[4] As Konopczyński remarked (*Dzieje Polski Nowożytnej*, I. 270), 'The Kirkholm reputation of the hussars still so discouraged the pursuer that he did not attempt to use his advantage in the open field'.

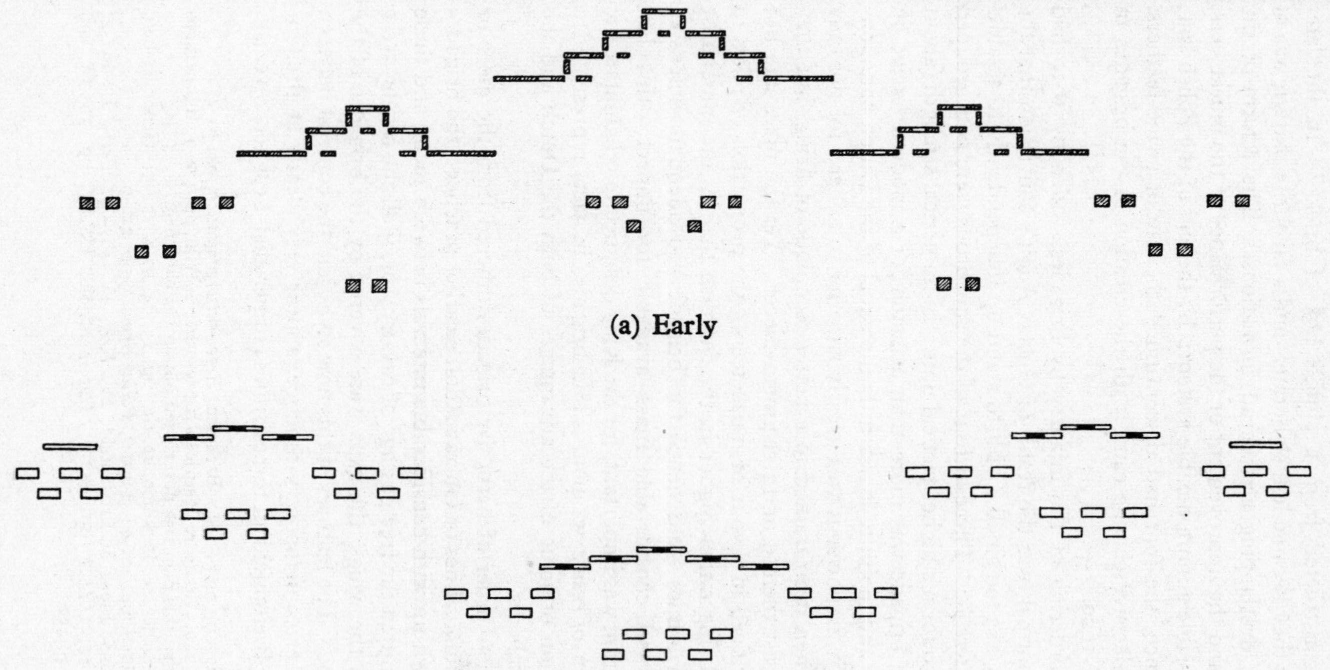

SWEDISH ORDERS OF BATTLE UNDER GUSTAV ADOLF

designs constructed from a child's box of bricks.[1] In the later 'twenties they became less elaborate; and a favourite pattern was of flattened, overlapping arrowhead formations.[2] The reform of the cavalry, and the improvement of the performance of the musketeers, made possible a more flexible system: by the end of the Polish war, for instance, the foot had discontinued the use of swine-feathers. But the decisive change came with the creation of the brigades in 1628 and 1629.

The ordering of the infantry by brigades, which by 1630 had become normal, was the result of Gustav Adolf's conviction that the squadron was too small a unit to stand up independently to assaults from the *tercios*.[3] Three or four of the squadrons were now grouped together to form a higher tactical unit. In numerical strength (about 2000) the brigade was more than a match for a modern *tercio*; in flexibility and mobility it was fully the equal of the Dutch battalion-group. In firepower it was greatly superior to either; for not only had the men been trained in a better technique of firing, but they had to assist them 9 or 12 regiment-pieces. Yet the pikes had not been sacrificed in favour of musketeers—the proportion of pikes to muskets being rather higher in the Swedish than in the imperialist or Dutch armies—and hence the brigade had adequate defensive strength and considerable mass available for impact: this last consideration was important, for the King designed to rehabilitate the pike as an *offensive* weapon. The brigade, in fact, represented a combination of some of the advantages of both the Dutch and the Spanish schools.

The new order of battle by brigades differed from the more or less continuous lines of Gustav Adolf's earlier practice: the brigades were drawn up with considerable intervals between them, and these gaps permitted the free passage of cavalry; or, if all the cavalry were placed on the wings, the gaps were covered by the brigades of the second line. The features of this new style, and the contrast between it and other contemporary practice, appear very clearly at Breitenfeld.[4] At Breitenfeld all three armies (Imperialist-Leaguer, Swedish,

[1] See diagram on p. 249. Barkman, *Regementsorganisation*, pp. 81-4.

[2] See p. 249. Compare Maurice's battle-order in Wijn, pp. 478-9: it is perhaps significant that this plan was never tried out on the battlefield.

[3] For brigades, see Barkman, *op. cit.*, pp. 13, 74, 97-8, 102-5; Generalstaben, *Gustaf II Adolf*, pp. 401-2; Turner, *Pallas Armata*, pp. 228-9.

[4] For dispositions at Breitenfeld, *Sv. Krig*, IV. 487-94; Petri, II. 131-2; Generalstaben, *G II A*, pp. 281-4; Hammarskiöld, *USAH*, pp. 163-6; and diagram on p. 252.

Saxon) placed their infantry in the centre, and flanked it with cavalry wings. There, however, the similarity stopped. The Swedish army, unlike the other two, was drawn up in two distinct lines. In the centre were the four infantry brigades, each with six regiment-pieces, each composed of three squadrons, and each at most six deep.[1] On the right wing were 4100 horse; on the left, 2300. Interspersed between the cavalry squadrons were strong detachments of musketeers, four on each wing; so that the right wing had 1200 of them, the left 800. These troops were provided, partly by the 'commanded' musketeers of the second-line infantry, partly from Banér's German regiment, which was composed exclusively of musketeers.[2] There was ample space between the foot brigades of the centre for the squadrons of reserve cavalry to pass through. In front, in the centre, 12 heavy guns were drawn up in one large battery. Behind the right wing was a reserve of three squadrons of cavalry, for it was on this wing that the King meant to make his main effort. The second line was similar to the first: cavalry wings (the right being once again the stronger) and an infantry centre of three brigades of three squadrons apiece, each brigade being provided, as in the first line, with six regiment-pieces. Behind the centre of the first line was a substantial reserve of cavalry and infantry; behind the centre of the second a small reserve of cavalry.

The Saxon army, which adjoined the Swedes on their left so as to form a continuous front, was ordered upon sharply contrasting principles. Both the infantry centre and the cavalry wings were arranged in pyramidal formation, with the apex pointing at the enemy—a transitional form not dissimilar from those which Gustav Adolf had at one time employed. There was but one line, and apparently no reserve. The Saxon foot provided a good illustration of the advantages of Gustav Adolf's regimental organization, for it was arranged in clumps of 1000 men, and since the Saxon regiments were not of any fixed or constant size, they had to be split up to form these 'battalions'—in contrast to the Swedish system, where administrative and tactical units were by now coincidental.

The battle-order of Tilly represented the latest phase of the

[1] Musketeers were six deep; but shortage of pikes had made it necessary to reduce their depth to five. The use of the four-squadron brigade was perhaps considered unnecessary in view of the fact that between the first and second lines, in the centre, was a reserve of mixed cavalry and infantry.

[2] Gustav Adolf did not raise regiments of musketeers from choice, but because it was already becoming difficult to get enough pikemen.

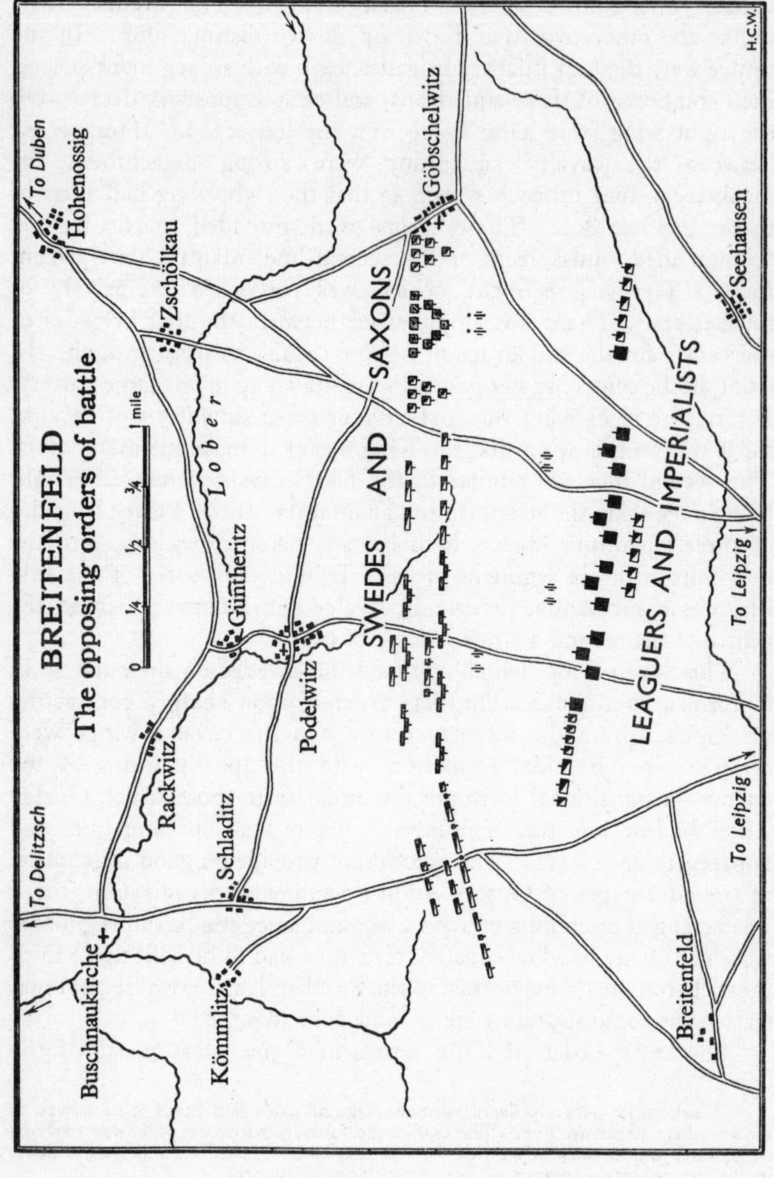
BREITENFELD
The opposing orders of battle
0 ¼ ½ ¾ 1 mile
To Duben
Hohenossig
Zschölkau
Göbschelwitz
Seehausen
Lober
Güntheritz
Podelwitz
Rackwitz
Schladitz
To Delitzsch
Buschnaukirche
Kömmlitz
SWEDES AND SAXONS
LEAGUERS AND IMPERIALISTS
To Leipzig
To Leipzig
Breitenfeld
H.C.W.

Spanish school. The two wings were composed exclusively of cavalry; the guns were all concentrated in the middle; and the centre itself was composed of four groups of three *tercios* apiece, with one spare *tercio* over on either flank. Each *tercio* had musketeers before it and on its flanks; but there were now no musketeers to its rear, and the 'sleeves' were wholly absent.[1] The *tercios* numbered about 1500 apiece, and were probably 30 deep on a front of 50. As they were drawn up at the beginning of the battle, the twelve *tercios* had something of the appearance of a line. But this was an illusion, for there was no real attempt at linear order; there was no real second line at all; and the only support for the *tercios* was provided by a strong body of cavalry placed to the rear of the centre. Nor were the groups of *tercios* in any sense higher tactical units, as were the Swedish brigades. There was nothing to correspond to the regiment-pieces, and no attempt to combine musketeers with cavalry. The Swedish battle-order, indeed, appeared as something quite different from anything that had been seen on a German battlefield before; and it was no wonder that the Saxon allies viewed it with undisguised astonishment.[2]

By the time the battle of Lützen was fought, these innovations had ceased to be a Swedish monopoly.[3] Gustav Adolf's victories had compelled a reconsideration of the Spanish system; and Wallenstein, who kept an open mind on military, as on religious, matters, had begun to apply the methods of his adversary. It was not possible for him to carry through a complete alteration until his troops had been trained in the new system; but he did introduce improvements based on Swedish practice. At Lützen he provided his infantry—or at least a part of them—with a light field-gun copied from the Swedish regiment-piece; he stiffened his cavalry wings with small detachments of musketeers[4]; and he threw forward an advance party of musketeers in the manner of the Swedish 'commanded' musketeers, to hold the highway and ditch that ran across his front.

[1] Priorato (pp. 287-8) remarks that the lateral extension of the 'sleeves', which had become frequent in the later phases of the Spanish system, led to their being too far from the pikes to give them effective aid against cavalry, and that this led in Montecuccoli's time to their reduction to a front of 20.

[2] *Sv. Krig*, IV. 448.

[3] As Fleetwood wrote, 'The enimies army was ordered like ours': G. Fleetwood, *Letter from George Fleetwood to his Father*, p. 6; J. Seidler, *Untersuchungen über die Schlacht bei Lützen*, pp. 33-40; *Sv. Krig*, VI. 414-20; G. Wittrock, *Die Schlacht bei Lützen*, p. 49; Kungl. Liv-Rustkammaren, *Gustav II Adolf vid Lützen*, p. 18; Generalstaben, *G II A*, pp. 387-8.

[4] Only about 15 to each wing, however.

He reduced the depth of his cavalry squadrons to six and that of his infantry to ten. He drew up his army in two (or possibly three) distinct lines,[1] with a small cavalry reserve behind the first line—a formation entirely at variance with his previous practice. And, evidently impressed by the mobility and firepower of the Swedish brigade, he reduced the size and increased the frontage of his infantry battalions and grouped them (in the first line at all events) in threes—two to the front; one, covering the gap, to the rear.[2] The second line, like the first, comprised cavalry wings and an infantry centre.

The Swedish dispositions at Lützen [3] were in the main a repetition of those which had been used at Breitenfeld. The army was ordered in two lines of almost equal strength; each line having six cavalry squadrons on each wing and six brigades of foot in the centre. 'Commanded' musketeers were interspersed between the cavalry of the first line in five detachments of 200 each on either wing—a much stronger force than Wallenstein had provided. One important modification was the allocation of two regiment-pieces to each of these ten musketeer detachments, so that each cavalry wing in the front line had ten of these guns at its disposal. Another was the thinning of the depth of the cavalry squadrons from six to three—apparently a deliberate innovation, and not prompted (as was the similar reduction in the depth of pikes from six to four) by a shortage of manpower. The infantry reserve behind the first line, and the cavalry reserve behind the second, were somewhat smaller than at Breitenfeld. Lastly, both sides divided their heavy artillery: the imperialists into two main batteries—one of them well out on their right wing; the Swedes into four batteries of five guns each.

The new style of battle-line at Breitenfeld and Lützen had been evolved by Gustav Adolf in order to enable him to exploit, as well as the circumstances of the time permitted, the potentialities at his disposal; and it proved to be mobile, strong in defence and surprisingly effective in attack. Its success depended on a proper utilization of the qualities of each arm and on an unprecedented skill in combining one arm with another; and these things in their turn had been made possible by a lengthy period of training, which

[1] The point is disputed.

[2] This may reflect the influence of Basta.

[3] *Sv. Krig*, VI. 425-6; Generalstaben, *G II A*, pp. 390-2; Kungl. Liv-Rustkammaren, *Gustav II Adolf vid Lützen*, p. 20; Hammarskiöld, *USAH*, p. 195.

improved and in some cases revolutionized the fighting methods of every part of the army.

Despite the predominance of firearms, it remained true even at this period that missile weapons alone could not bring victory: they could shake and perhaps demoralize an enemy, but for the final stroke the impact of close fighting was required. Cavalry, therefore, even the debilitated cavalry of this caracoling age, was essential as a battle-winner. Gustav Adolf fully appreciated this[1]; but he saw no reason why his horsemen should be as ineffective and denatured as contemporary military fashion prescribed. His aim was to make better use of the impact of cavalry in the earlier stages of an engagement; and his experience in Poland had suggested how this might be done. The native Swedish cavalry, which was mostly of the cuirassier type, inasmuch as it was armed with pistols and sabre, was at first very inferior to its continental adversaries. It was imperfectly armoured; it often lacked one of the prescribed pair of pistols, and the other was often a bad one; and it was mounted on horses which, though hardy, were usually small.[2] It was equally unfitted, therefore, to deal with a Polish lancer or a German pistoleer. Gustav Adolf did something to improve the standard of equipment; but he diminished, rather than increased, the weight of armour, for it was important not to sacrifice freedom of movement for the sake of defensive strength. Before the end of the Polish war the native cavalry had learnt to meet Koniecpolski's cuirassiers with confidence; and in Germany the Swedish, and especially the Finnish, horse was clearly superior to any mercenary cavalry. At Burgstall they scattered Tilly's horsemen[3]; at Breitenfeld they proved more than a match for Pappenheim himself—though Pappenheim too had served his apprenticeship in the Polish school.[4]

Gustav Adolf's cavalry tactics were based on a return to *l'arme*

[1] See, for instance, his letter to Oxenstierna of 18 March 1630, where he writes that it will be essential to take a strong force of cavalry to Germany, since pitched battles are to be expected: *ASOB*, II. I. 570.

[2] *Krigsvetenskaps Akademiens Handlingar* (1932), pp. 30-1; Alm, *Blanka vapen*, pp. 244-6; *Sv. Krig*, Supp. Vol. II. 118-21. It had one other disadvantage, which Gustav Adolf did not succeed in eliminating: it was not trained to negotiate ditches, dykes and other obstacles: this was to hamper it severely at Lützen (*AOSB*, II. VI. 38; *Sv. Krig*, VI. 431; Priorato, p. 219): hence perhaps Fleetwood's comment on Lützen: '. . . had not our foote stood like a wall, there had not a man of us come off alyve, they being certen twyce our number, and our horse did but poorly' (Fleetwood, p. 9).

[3] For Burgstall, see *Dagbok förd i det svenska fältkansliet*, p. 21; *Sv. Krig*, IV. 385.

[4] Laskowski, *Uwagi*, pp. 48-9.

blanche. The caracole was wholly abandoned [1]; and with it, formations in depth. Swedish cavalry was drawn up, at the close of Gustav Adolf's career, in only three ranks. In attack, the first rank only was permitted to fire its pistols (and even then only one pistol of the pair); and firing was forbidden until they could see the whites of the enemy's eyes. The second and third ranks kept their pistols charged, against an emergency; but their real weapon was the sabre: the pistolling was little more than a gesture towards current military convention. After the first rank had fired, the attack was pressed home at the gallop.[2] These methods proved highly effective against a caracoling enemy; but against resolute cavalry, or solid infantry, they required the supplement of additional missile support. Gustav Adolf met this requirement, from an early stage in the German war, by the device of combining cavalry with musketeers. This was the object of the groups of 'commanded' musketeers which were placed between the cavalry squadrons or attached to cavalry units sent out to skirmish. Their function was, by pouring a volley into the enemy's ranks, to provide an opening into which cavalry might charge. After they had fired, the horsemen would fall on; during the ensuing *mêlée* the musketeers would employ themselves in the complex business of reloading; and by the time the cavalry rode back from their attack, the musketeers would be ready with another volley, to cover their retreat, or provide them with another objective. Monro tells us how it was done at Breitenfeld:

the Horsemen on both wings charged furiously one another, our Horsemen with a resolution, abiding unloosing a Pistoll, till the enemy had discharged first, and then at a neere distance our Musketiers meeting them with a *Salve*; then our horsemen discharged their Pistolls, and then charged through them with swords; and at their returne the Musketiers were ready again to give the second *Salve* of Musket amongst them.[3]

The process was thus an alternation of charge and discharge. The fire support made available to cavalry was very much greater than

[1] At all events by the native cavalry; though Monro (II. 98) mentions the Rhinegrave Otto's cavalry caracoling in defence. Monro, however, sometimes seems to use 'caracole' to mean something like a cavalry sweep, *e.g.*, 'to divert the enemie from him, his Majestie did make a caracole with the halfe of his Army towards *Swede* [*sc.* Schwedt]' (*ibid.*, II. 23; and *cf.* II. 31). The Swedes attributed the defeat of Solms's cavalry in January 1632 to his using the caracole (*Sv. Krig*, V. 463); and the imperialists' defeat at Burgstall to the same cause (*Dagbok*, p. 21).

[2] So *Sv. Krig*, Supp. Vol. II. 118-21. At Lützen special orders were given not to fire until the enemy had done so: *ibid.*, VI. 433.

[3] Monro, II. 65: for other examples, see *ibid.*, 31, 51, 55.

was provided in any other contemporary army; and at Lützen it was formidably increased by the provision of regiment-pieces in addition to the musketeers.

There were, however, disadvantages. By tying his cavalry to musketeers and gunners, Gustav Adolf was forced to make heavy sacrifices of pace and momentum; for, except for the last fifty yards or so, the horsemen were restricted to a foot-pace if they were not to lose touch with their supporting fire. This was undeniably a serious drawback. Gustav Adolf's reform of cavalry tactics was, in fact, an attempt to make the best of two worlds: he tried to give to his mounted arm the advantages which were so obvious in the Polish school, and at the same time to endow it with the resources of mobile shot which contemporary commanders prized so highly. The result was a half-measure, a compromise, which was really unsatisfactory.[1] Yet, imperfect as it was, it was so much better than prevailing practice in Germany that it was successful; and, being successful, was imitated: already at the Alte Feste the cavalry of Wallenstein abandoned the caracole, and the great onslaughts of Piccolomini at Lützen, which so nearly turned the scale in the imperialists' favour, were something very different from the performances of the pistoleers of an earlier age.[2]

The devising of an improved method of fighting for the infantry presented similar, though less insoluble, problems. Once again it was a question of finding a satisfactory form for the combination of firepower with *l'arme blanche*. In the Dutch armies, a more efficient use of firearms, which was the result of the adoption of a linear order, had been purchased at the cost of sacrificing the infantry's ability to fight offensively, for though the shallow formations of Maurice's pikemen were sufficiently solid to offer protection to the musketeers, they lacked the mass which made the attack of a *tercio* formidable. Gustav Adolf was not prepared to forgo the advantages of linear order and diminished depth: his infantry stood six deep, against Maurice's ten, for he held that in deeper formations the rear ranks would not hear the word of command—a consideration which, significantly enough, had not weighed much with earlier tacticians.[3]

[1] As Polish military historians are not slow to point out: thus Kukiel: 'This was not yet the Polish tactics, but it was a step forward under their powerful influence' (*op. cit.*, p. 65); or the less charitable comment of Laskowski: 'it was but a timid compromise between tactics based on firearms, and the tactic of the cavalry charge' (*Uwagi*, p. 48).

[2] Kungl. Liv-Rustkammaren, *Gustav II Adolf vid Lützen*, p. 31; *Sv. Krig*, VI. 216.

[3] *Sv. Krig*, V. 308.

But at the same time he wished to restore to his infantry the possibility of effective attack. As in the case of the cavalry, he found the answer to his problem in the better organization of fire and in the combination of arms.

At first the Swedish musketeers practised a form of the countermarch, except only that two ranks fired simultaneously, whereas in the normal countermarch only one rank fired at a time. It was characteristic of the King that the evolution was designed to be used in such a way that the men always gained ground instead of remaining in the same place. Thus Monro writes:

> . . . to [*sc.* two] Rancks, having made readie alike, they advance ten paces before the bodie, being led up by an Officer that stands in even Front with them. . . . The second Rancke being close to the backe of the foremost, both gives fire alike, priming and casting about their Muskets they charge againe where they stand, till the other two Rancks advance before them, and give fire after the same manner, till the whole Troop hath discharged, and so to beginne againe as before, after the order of the through-countermarch; ever advancing to an enemie, never turning backe without death, or victorie.[1]

This form of countermarch implied greater speed in reloading than contemporaries thought practicable; or alternatively it implied covering action by pikes to protect the musketeers while they were recharging their pieces. It was clearly the latter alternative upon which Gustav Adolf relied; for soon after the opening of the German war he pushed the intensification of fire a stage further, by his introduction of the salvo as a normal practice in musketry.[2] The salvo, as its name implied, was originally a volley fired in salute; its use on the battlefield had been confined to special emergencies, since after discharging it all those who fired would for some minutes be virtually defenceless. Earlier commanders had aimed at the maintenance of continuous fire by the device of the countermarch: Gustav Adolf, on the contrary, aimed at missile shock as the preliminary to fighting at close quarters; and the salvo was designed to secure it. For the salvo, three ranks fired simultaneously, either countermarch-wise or by doubling the ranks so that the depth of the platoon was in effect reduced from six to three. A variety of schemes of fire thus became possible: ranks 1, 2 and 3 might fire a salvo

[1] Monro, II. 190.

[2] The salvo was used at least as early as Werben: 'putting a hedge betwixt us and the enemy, we advanced till we were in even line with him, and then giving a *Salve* amongst them, incontinent we made the enemy retire': *ibid.*, 54.

alternately with ranks 4, 5 and 6; or there might be salvos from alternate platoons or divisions, each with doubled ranks; or all six ranks of one or more entire platoons might fire simultaneously.[1] *The Swedish Intelligencer* describes how the Scots brigade used it at Breitenfeld:

> The Scots presently ordering themselues in seuerall small battagliaes, about 6 or 700 in a body, presently now double their ranckes, making their files then but 3 deepe, the discipline of the Kinge of Sweden been neuer to march aboue 6 deepe. This done, the foremost ranke falling on their knees; the second stooping forward; and the third ranke standing right vp, and all giuing fire together.[2]

Whereas the countermarch in its simple form had produced perhaps 24 volleys from each rank within the space of an hour, the salvo concentrated the effect into one or two tremendous discharges. As Sir James Turner put it:

> . . . you pour as much lead into your enemies bosom at one time as you do the other way at two [or six] severall times, and thereby you do them more mischief, you quail, daunt, and astonish them three times more, for one long and continuated crack of thunder is more terrible and dreadful to mortals than ten interrupted and severall ones.[3]

And the effect was immensely increased when the salvo was combined with rounds from the regiment-pieces which were now attached to the foot brigades and which, it is important to remember, were sufficiently light to be moved in ordinary circumstances by two men.

This development necessarily demanded as its corollary a strong force of pikes, to cover the musketeers in the interval between salvos; and this in itself would provide sufficient explanation for the higher proportion of pikemen in Gustav Adolf's army than in the armies either of the Dutch or Spanish schools: it was because he was short of pikemen at Lützen that the losses of the Swedish foot in that battle were so heavy.[4] But he designed the pike—and in this he differed from all contemporary commanders of the Dutch school—to be something more than a defensive weapon. For infantry, as for cavalry, the salvo was conceived as the preparation for victory rather than as itself the battle-winner: the decisive blow would come at close quarters. The charge of the horsemen was paralleled

1 Barkman, *Regementsorganisation*, p. 98; *Sv. Krig*, IV. 514-15.
2 *The Swedish Intelligencer*, I. 124.
3 Turner, *Pallas Armata*, p. 237.
4 *Krigsvetenskaps Akademiens Handlingar* (1932), p. 62.

in the infantry by the push of pike; the pikemen were to thrust into the gaps in the enemy's ranks which the salvo had produced; they were to safeguard the musketeers as they reloaded by offensive action rather than by standing fast as a wall behind which the shot could take cover. One main reason for the failure at the Alte Feste was that the ground did not permit pike attacks. For the last time—and at the very moment when the old pike tactics of the *tercio* were finally outmoded—the pike was treated as a battle-winning weapon; and one of Gustav Adolf's constant anxieties in Germany was to secure sufficient pikemen to preserve the balance of arms which his tactics required.[1]

Similar principles governed his handling of artillery. He aimed at using his guns to obtain the maximum intensity of fire at the point where it was needed, rather than a general, dispersed cannonade; he wished them to provide the closest possible collaboration with other arms; and as a result he concentrated more and more upon increasing their mobility, even at some sacrifice of weight of shot. Before Gustav Adolf's time it was very rare for the heavy guns to be moved once they had taken up their place on the battlefield, and the gunners had therefore to stick it out in exposed positions, or abandon their guns: the loss or capture of artillery was a common criterion for deciding which side had been victorious. Breitenfeld was the last occasion in Gustav Adolf's lifetime when both sides placed their guns thus in the centre of the battle-line. The decreased weight and increased manœuvrability of the Swedish ordnance became obvious at Lützen: in the course of that battle the Swedish gunners moved their pieces more than once to give support to other arms at crucial moments [2]; and Wallenstein obviously sited one of his batteries in the hope of providing a cross-fire throughout the engagement.[3] The way was already clear, at the time of the King's death, for the emancipation of the artillery and for the remarkable feats of mobility achieved by Torstensson's artillerists at Jankow.[4] But it is not in regard to field-guns that Gustav Adolf's main contribution in this

[1] Generalstaben, *G II A*, p. 392. The shortage was felt as early as June 1631: Droysen, *Schriftstücke von Gustaf Adolf, zumeist an evangelische Fürsten Deutschlands*, p. 133; and *cf. ibid.*, p. 171. It was not, as Turner suggested (*Pallas Armata*, p. 177), the result of the King's rapid marches after Breitenfeld.

[2] Hammarskiöld, *USAH*, p. 195.

[3] *Sv. Krig*, Supp. Vol. II. 260. Maurice had attempted this at Nieuwpoort, however: Oman, p. 596.

[4] For Jankow, see Försvarsstaben, *Slaget vid Jankow 1645, passim*; L. Tingsten, *Fältmarskalkarna Johan Banér och Lennart Torstensson*, pp. 268-79.

sphere is to be sought. His most important achievement lay rather in the perfecting of the light regimental gun, which could be sent anywhere, attached either to infantry or cavalry, and used on all occasions—even for skirmishing and reconnaissance.[1]

In other respects than these it does not appear that Gustav Adolf introduced any important innovations in artillery practice, despite his contemporary reputation as a gunner. He did indeed fire salvos from his batteries at Riga and Nuremberg, which was unusual at the time; and his intense concentrations of fire upon the defences of Demmin, Frankfurt-on-Oder, Landsberg, Marienberg and Kreuznach, which enabled him to capture these places so expeditiously, has been considered something unique for the period.[2] But in these matters he seems to have been anticipated by Maurice: in creeping barrages, mass fire, co-operation between guns and storm-troops, he had little to teach the Dutch. In the field he undoubtedly handled his guns with excellent effect, notably at the passage of the Lech in April 1632, when, under Torstensson's command, three batteries of 72 guns maintained an intense barrage which forced the enemy to take cover, while a fourth battery of 18 guns swept the approaches to the actual crossing-place. And there seems reason to believe that the Swedish gunners were superior to their opponents: at Breitenfeld they are said, on Gustav Adolf's testimony, to have fired three rounds to the imperialists' one [3]; and Pappenheim attributed to them a major part in deciding the issue of the battle.[4]

The essential contributions of Gustav Adolf to tactics, then, were his restoration, both to cavalry and infantry, of the capacity for the offensive; his intensification of the firepower of all arms as a necessary preliminary for such action; his insistence upon mobility; and his success in solving the problem of the satisfactory combination of the different arms of the service. To these should be added one other, which was almost a precondition for all the rest, and at least as important for the future: his ability to develop, in the small units of his battle-line, a spirit of self-reliance and initiative, both

[1] To take a single example: on 29 July 1631 Gustav Adolf personally led a reconnaissance against Tilly's forces and took with him six of these light regiment-pieces: before his time such a combination of arms would hardly have been possible: *Sv. Krig*, IV. 395; *cf.* Monro, II. 55.

[2] Monro, II. 211; Priorato, p. 323; Hammarskiöld, *USAH*, pp. 136-42, 161; *Sv. Krig*, IV. 48, 131-42, V. 333, Supp. Vol. II. 258. But see the comments in L. W. Munthe, *Kongl. Fortifikationens historia*, I. 340.

[3] *AOSB*, II. I. 741.

[4] S. Riezler, *Geschichte Bayerns*, V. 387; and *cf.* Monro's concurrent judgment: *op. cit.*, II. 68.

in his officers (so markedly more numerous than in any other army) and in his men. Almost all these characteristics were displayed at Breitenfeld; and a short account of that battle may serve as an example of how the new Swedish tactics worked in practice.[1]

At Breitenfeld it was Tilly who attacked. After the preliminary cannonadings, the action began with the advance of the *tercios* against the centre of the allied line. As they drew near it, however, they made a right-incline, so that the impact of their attack fell wholly upon the Saxon army, which was drawn up on the Swedish left. At the same time cavalry fights were developing on either wing, but especially on the imperialist left, where Pappenheim was in command. Tilly's plan seems to have been to crush Gustav Adolf between two flanking movements—a device which he had used with success at Wimpffen in 1622. Gustav Adolf, on his side, aimed at outflanking Tilly's army on its left wing and rolling it up from that side; for Tilly's line of retreat led out of his left flank. The cavalry action on the Swedish right and the imperialist left became therefore a duel between Gustav Adolf and Pappenheim, each endeavouring to outflank the other. The right was the stronger of the Swedish wings; and Pappenheim found to his dismay that, thanks to the ease with which it could be reinforced as required, it seemed to be capable of apparently indefinite prolongation. The more he drew to his left in an effort to turn the King's flank, the further the Swedish right was extended. Moreover, the combination of musketeers, cavalry and regiment-pieces presented him with a new problem, which he was unable to master; and his furious assaults were beaten back repeatedly, with considerable loss. Far different was the course of events upon the other wing. There the cavalry of the League had swept the Saxon horse from the field, and the *tercios* had lumbered slowly but relentlessly through the Saxon foot to their accustomed triumph. With some few inconsiderable exceptions, the whole Saxon army was broken, scattered or chased from the field; and soon Tilly's veterans were raising the shout of 'Victoria!'

The position of the Swedish left wing, which had adjoined the Saxon army, now appeared critical. Here Gustav Horn had some 4000 men under his command. When the Saxons fled, he found the

[1] The best account of Breitenfeld (which, unlike Lützen, is a relatively uncontroversial battle) is in *Sv. Krig*, IV.

great bulk of Tilly's infantry (about 20,000 strong), with some 2500 horse, bearing down upon his exposed flank. The whole Swedish army was in imminent danger of being rolled up from the left. Horn met the situation with a manœuvre which astonished his adversaries: he formed front to his flank. The carrying out of this evolution in an orderly manner in the heat of battle appears to be new in modern warfare; and it was made possible by the nature of Gustav Adolf's order of battle, and by the training and discipline of his army. Neither Erik XIV, nor Maurice, nor Tilly employed a tactical formation or a tactical unit which would have made such an evolution possible. Horn was able, moreover, to obtain reinforcements without confusion from his reserves, from the second line, and from the other wing. Some little time, however, necessarily elapsed before they could arrive, and meanwhile he stood in great peril of being overwhelmed. Acting on his own initiative, he met the situation by attacking the enemy with every man at his disposal. The *tercios* were still in some confusion after their rout of the Saxons: Tilly's steam-roller had not quite been brought round to the new line of advance. Given a quarter of an hour's breathing-space, they would have made mincemeat of the Swedish left; but a quarter of an hour was not vouchsafed to them. Horn's cavalry, musketeers and regiment-pieces crashed into them before they had recovered themselves, and were soon supplemented by most of the pikemen and musketeers of the second line. The new tactics of salvo and charge were now employed in attack, with terrible effect. After desperate fighting the *tercios* were driven backwards and inwards in increasing disorder: their very numbers had now become a fatal handicap, for they became so tightly packed together that the pikemen could not use their weapons effectively. And now at last Gustav Adolf, using the same tactics on the other wing, had driven Pappenheim from the field by a combination of musket salvos and cavalry charges, and the Swedish right, sweeping round in an arc, wheeled inwards to capture the guns that had been planted by Tilly in the centre of his position. These guns were now turned upon the chaos of the reeling *tercios*. When night fell, the invincible Tilly was a wounded fugitive, and the army of the League was totally overthrown. The result was the more remarkable in that the whole of the centre of the Swedish front line—that is, the great majority of the Swedish infantry—had stood fast throughout the day, forming a link between the two wings but otherwise taking no part whatever in the engagement. Tilly had been defeated by little more than half of the Swedish army.[1]

Breitenfeld was, from the Swedish point of view, a defensive battle (though it was won because the new tactics were offensive in spirit); and it has been questioned whether Gustav Adolf's methods were equally applicable to an engagement in which the initial assault must come from the Swedish side.[2] The fight at the Alte Feste is irrelevant in this connexion, since local conditions prevented the employment of pikes and guns as Gustav Adolf preferred to employ them; and the passage of the Lech, though a remarkable demonstration of the fighting qualities of the Swedish soldier and the excellence of the Swedish gunnery, presented little scope for the new system. But Lützen provided an answer to any doubters. Against resistance much more formidable—and more formidable precisely because it was based on Swedish models [3]—and despite the handicap imposed by shortage of pikes, the Swedish army was able at last to beat Wallenstein out of his carefully chosen position and to end the day unchallenged master of the field.

It is indeed unlikely that Gustav Adolf would have remained content with a tactic which was not at least as apt to attack as to defence, for as a commander he was strongly imbued with the offensive spirit. The general tendency in the age of the Thirty Years' War, as we have seen, was away from the cautious siege-warfare of the Netherlands revolt and towards a more enterprising and vigorous form of campaigning [4]: Tilly in his earlier years was famous—as Pappenheim was later to be—as a fiery commander who was ready to seize any good opportunity to engage. But no general of that age

[1] *cf.* Delbrück's judgment: 'Was Cannä für Hannibal ist, das ist die Schlacht bei Breitenfeld für Gustav Adolf: der Sieg der Kunst über die wohl in hohem Masse vorhandene, aber zu plumpe militärischen Tuchtigkeit': Delbrück, *op. cit.*, IV. 206.

[2] Notably by Bennedich: 'His brigades became moving fortresses, excellent in defence, but too complicated for use in a powerful attack' (*cf.* Chemnitz, I. 475); and again: 'For the first time [at Lützen] Gustav Adolf's brigades were led to an attack in the open field, and, as far as we know, for the last time also. They did not stand the test; their offensive power was too little': C. Bennedich, *Ur det gamla Gardets öden*, pp. 4-5, 84. But see the strictures of Barkman, *Gustav II Adolfs militära gärning i den krigsvetenskapliga litteraturens belysning*, pp. 270, 294-5.

[3] It seems likely that Wallenstein employed the salvo: he had certainly done so at the Alte Feste: K. Spannagel, *Konrad von Burgsdorff*, pp. 41-2; Barkman, *op. cit.*, p. 272; and imperialist narratives lay stress on the intimate collaboration of their infantry and cavalry: Kungl. Liv-Rustkammaren, *Gustav II Adolf vid Lützen*, p. 26.

[4] For some remarks on the reasons for this development, see Generalstaben, *G II A*, p. 402.

went as far in tactical audacity as Gustav Adolf—at all events after Breitenfeld. In part this was simply a question of temperament. The King was notorious for the recklessness with which he exposed himself; and his preference for doing everything himself, rather than delegate duties to his subordinates, frequently put him in danger. His habit of personal reconnaissance was pushed to fantastic lengths, as exemplified by his crossing of the Rhine at Oppenheim to inspect the Spanish positions, by his solitary boat-trip up the Elbe from Tangermünde, or by his famous conversation with an enemy sentry near Rain.[1] He stormed, sword in hand, at the head of an assault-column during the attack on Frankfurt-on-Oder. Not content to be commander-in-chief, he was driven by his ardent and impetuous nature to be in turn sergeant-major, engineer, gunner and cuirassier; and there is no doubt that he derived a real satisfaction from personal participation in the *mêlée*. But his readiness to seek battle was something more than an aspect of his character: it arose also from his belief that the total victory with which he hoped to terminate the German war could not be won without the destruction of the enemy's forces on the battlefield. It is possible that he underrated the annihilating effect of mere manœuvre—the disintegration of his army after the Alte Feste was certainly a shock to him, and it seems to have modified his ideas—yet he was himself a skilful practitioner of this form of warfare. Before Breitenfeld his resources were so small that he could not venture to risk them in battle needlessly, and he had thus at times to try to effect his object by less direct means; but after Breitenfeld, when his supplies were reasonably secure, when his armies were swollen with fresh recruits, when (above all) he had realized the superiority of his troops and his methods to any that he was likely to encounter—then he constantly sought battle and was prepared to run great risks to bring the enemy to action.

He had to fight, of course, within the framework of the circumstances of his time. There was little opportunity for a tactician in the Thirty Years' War to use (for instance) the weapon of surprise; for surprise at that time was a matter of accident rather than of design, the result of the difficulty of obtaining speedy and accurate information. The Swedish intelligence-service in Germany was organized with considerable efficiency, but it ceased to function properly when Gustav Adolf and his armies moved south into regions

[1] *Sv. Krig*, V. 100, 512; *Dagbok*, p. 20.

whose population was predominantly Roman Catholic.[1] In the summer and autumn of 1632 Gustav Adolf and Wallenstein moved their armies about south and central Germany under the influence of false reports and rumours, and wasted much energy in providing against contingencies which better information would have eliminated from their calculations; and even when they did come up against each other they were capable of forming very erroneous ideas of their adversaries' proceedings. Surprise was made difficult, too, by the formal nature of contemporary battle. Armies rarely attacked unexpectedly: it was considered too risky. The elaborate ordering of troops which was held to be necessary before a major engagement took time and thought; and armies were slow in deploying. Great importance was attached to the selection of a position: to have the sun behind you, and the prevailing wind in the enemy's face, was a great advantage in those days before smokeless powder. Both at Breitenfeld and at Lützen Gustav Adolf was allowed to march his forces on to a battlefield previously selected by his enemy without any attempt at interference. The risk of 'disarray', of losing the choice of ground, was esteemed too great to be taken.[2]

It was not easy, moreover, to force battle upon an enemy who had determined to decline it, as Gustav Adolf found at Nuremberg. Withdrawal to the shelter of a fortified town, or behind a river barrier, was usually sufficient to discourage attack; and in open country field-fortifications of sufficient strength to deter an adversary could be thrown up in a couple of days.[3] Gustav Adolf himself was an acknowledged master of the spade, and at Marienburg, Schwedt, Werben, Nuremberg and Naumburg he constructed great entrenched camps which extorted the admiration of his contemporaries and effectively baffled his enemies.

Yet he was more willing than any other commander of his time to seek battle in circumstances which made a regular and formal engagement impossible. By 1632 he was prepared to take risks which no other general of his age would have taken. The crossing of the Rhine was considered a daring operation; the crossing of the

[1] *Den svenska utrikesförvaltningens historia*, pp. 92-3; Generalstaben, *G II A*, pp. 215-18; K. Wittich, *Magdeburg, Gustav Adolf und Tilly*, p. 270; *cf.* Monro's notion of military intelligence as consisting in the having 'some secret friend with the enemy', or the getting hold of 'a subtill Boore': Monro, II. 201.

[2] The parliamentarian order of battle for Naseby, for instance, was drawn up six days before the battle: Firth, p. 62.

[3] *Krigsvetenskaps Akademiens Handlingar* (1932), pp. 36-7; P. Sörensson, *Fältherrar, härorganisation och krigföring*, pp. 146-7.

Lech, in the face of a powerful army, well supplied with guns, was so unorthodox a venture as to be scarcely credible. The attack on the Alte Feste provoked less astonishment, for men were growing habituated to the King's methods; but it is probable that none of his contemporaries would have attempted it, nor any other army have brought it so near to success. Not merely did he attempt a frontal assault upon a long-prepared and strongly defended position but he chose to attack it upon a front which was steep, broken and wooded, where the ordinary methods of fighting, as inculcated by the Swedish discipline, availed little: brigade formations could not be maintained, pikes could hardly be used at all. Moreover, the attack was launched simultaneously by two separate battle-groups, who approached their objective from different directions with only the minimum of liaison possible between them.[1]

But if there was in Gustav Adolf something of the *bravura* of a Karl XII or a Peterborough—a capacity for brilliant improvisation which was lacking, for instance, in Wallenstein—he was none the less a remarkably solid and methodical strategist. His advance into Germany proceeded slowly, because he was never willing to take a step forward before he was sure of his foothold; and Magdeburg was lost because he was not prepared to violate this principle to the hazard of his army. Throughout the German war he took pains to ensure that his base-areas, as they were successively pushed forward further and further into Germany, were properly organized and firmly linked together. Until Breitenfeld, undoubtedly, the keynote of his strategy was caution.[2] But quite early he had evolved the plan of encircling Austria from the west and south-west, and so cutting the Emperor's hope of reinforcement from Brussels or Madrid—a testimony to his grasp of the fact that victory could not yield its full effects unless it led to the extrusion of the enemy from his base areas —and in 1632 he adhered to this strategy with extraordinary hardihood, in the face of powerful attempts to distract him. Those attempts were in the end successful; but it is remarkable that he should have coolly ignored them for so long. As a strategist, in fact,

[1] *cf.* Banér's daring manœuvre at Wittstock.

[2] It was this, no doubt, which provoked Clausewitz's verdict: 'Ein kühner Invasions- und Schlachtenfeldherr war Gustav Adolf überall nicht . . . er liebte mehr den künstlichen manövrirenden, systematischen Krieg'; and again, 'Kurz war er ein gelehrter Feldherr voller vorsichtiger Kombinationen': Clausewitz, *Strategische Beleuchtung mehrerer Feldzüge*, pp. 29, 47. Ranke saw more clearly when he wrote: 'Wallenstein war ein podagrischer Stratege, der König ein General von rüstiger Beweglichkeit': *Wallenstein*, p. 195.

he might be censured by a hostile critic for being too cautious before Breitenfeld and too rash thereafter. His calculation of risks was not always just, nor his judgment impeccable; and he relied overmuch on diversions, which too often failed to divert. Yet there is nothing in the history of warfare before his time which can compare, for magnitude and boldness of conception, with his plan for that co-ordinated advance on Vienna which, he was convinced, would end the war. If for a time Wallenstein was able to wrest the initiative from his hands, that was because Wallenstein's military and political problems and responsibilities were very much less complex than his own. It is probably true to say that while on the whole the importance of Gustav Adolf's contributions to tactics has been generally acknowledged, his merits as a strategist have been underrated.

Gustav Adolf's achievements were so striking, and the effect of his reforms so far-reaching, that it is easy to exaggerate his originality; and it may be that Swedish military historians have at times succumbed to the temptation to do so. In some respects his work had been anticipated by the Spanish school: the *tercio* had its own recruiting area, as Gustav Adolf's regiment had; and in the Spanish as in the Swedish army the tactical and administrative units coincided.[1] As a military administrator Wallenstein was at least Gustav Adolf's equal, and probably his superior; and Kristian IV was not far behind.[2] In training and drill Gustav Adolf built on foundations laid by Maurice and his cousins. The national army, and the system of *utskrivning*, had parallels in Denmark and Norway.[3] It was Maurice who first practised *l'ordre mince*,[4] Maurice who first reversed the current trend towards diminishing the proportion of pikes to muskets, Maurice who began the systematic training in firing by ranks.[5] There is some evidence that Wallenstein shared Gustav Adolf's estimate of the tactical rôle of the pikeman.[6] The

[1] Wertheim, I. 88; Wijn, p. 32.

[2] *Sv. Krig*, Supp. Vol. II. 404.

[3] Rockstroh, I. 19; T. Mathisen, *Fra Bondeoppbud til Legdshaer*, p. 30 *seqq.*

[4] Koniecpolski, too, is said to have reduced the depth of his infantry to six or seven: Laskowski, *Uwagi*, p. 50.

[5] Wijn, p. 430.

[6] On 16/26 March 1632 Wallenstein addressed a circular to all his colonels which included the following passage: 'Demnach bei den Teutschen Regimentern der üblen brauch [Dudík printed 'Völkerbrauch': I have adopted the MS. emendation written by Hallwich in the margin of his copy] eingerissen, dass die Piquen der schlechtesten Mannschaft, so sie nicht zu gebrauchen wissen, vnd wann sie nur dieselben auf den achseln tragen khönnen, es alles woll aussgerichtet zu

cavalry charge had survived in the west under the auspices of Henry IV; and John of Nassau had denounced the caracole.[1] Stephen Bátory is said to have introduced musket-cartridges [2]; and both the Spanish and the Dutch school devoted much attention to the production of a really light and mobile gun.[3] The attachment of cavalry to infantry had been attempted by the *tercios*, and the *piqueros desarmados* were designed to facilitate the collaboration between them.[4] Gustav Adolf's real contribution was not that he devised a military organization and a method of fighting that were wholly new; it was rather that he appropriated, with judicious eclecticism, those tendencies and developments in the military art which offered possibilities of progress; and, having appropriated them, developed and transformed them. In his hand the sound but only partially effective ideas of others were for the first time fully realized, and became potent. His work embraced, as no other man's did, a dozen separate improvements from a variety of sources, so that he was able to combine all that was best in contemporary practice while discarding the weaknesses that had vitiated the methods of the rival schools. He advanced, not along this or that narrow and specialized channel, but upon a broad front which covered everything from recruiting to military mathematics, from battle tactics to field-chaplains, from strategy to drill. But though in many of his reforms he had been anticipated, however ineffectively and tentatively, by others, he was no mere borrower: his ideas may not have been wholly original, but very often he reached his conclusions by applying the lessons of experience and the basic principles of war rather than by direct imitation. The military art was in a stage at which it was not surprising if more than one commander should hit upon the same device for solving problems that were common to them all. But none other of them was able to bridge the gap between idea and realization with his certainty and success. In him is

---

sein vermeinen, gegeben werden, vndt aber auss vhrsachen, dass, wen ein Regiment zu Fuess mit des feindts regiment serriret, die Musqueten gar wenig, die Pikhen aber den meisten effect thuen, wesswegen denn billich den tapferisten vnd besten Knechten die Pikhen geben werden . . .': B. Dudík, *Waldsteins Correspondenz*, II. 7.

[1] Oman, pp. 466-7; Frauenholz, I. 60.

[2] Laskowski, *Uwagi*, p. 49.

[3] Wijn, p. 214 *seqq.* (for John of Nassau); Turner, *Pallas Armata*, p. 192 (for Spinola).

[4] Londoño, p. 30; Altamira, III. 294. The French armies of the sixteenth century frequently *mixed* cavalry and shot; but it does not appear that they combined them: Weygand, p. 108; Oman, p. 405; Turner, *Pallas Armata*, p. 271.

incarnate the military revolution which began in the middle of the sixteenth century and was completed in the armies of Louis XIV. It was he, rather than Maurice, who ensured the triumph of the linear order, he who best solved the puzzle of combining arms, he whose vast enterprises produced the first great upward leap in the size of armies. While Maurice and Tilly appear as figures cramped and crippled by one-sided developments, Gustav Adolf is beautifully balanced and free.

There was no immediate future, as it proved, for the massive architecture of his strategy: the later stages of the war were unpropitious to such plans. Germany could no longer support the huge armies required to carry them out, and commanders had to do the best they could with forces of moderate size. The indecisiveness of battle became in these conditions more marked than ever, and the brilliant victories of Banér, Torstensson and Wrangel were usually void of strategic significance. But in regard to tactics Gustav Adolf's influence was profound, and his legacy lasted long. Linear order held the field for centuries; and Rocroi, won by Swedish methods, finally endorsed the verdict of Breitenfeld.[1] The Swedish discipline became the model for the training of troops; the Swedish organization of firepower and the Swedish combination of arms won general acceptance.[2] A light regimental artillery became universal; and the mobility of the Swedish field-guns remained unexcelled until the days of Frederick's horse-artillery. The rehabilitation of cavalry which Gustav Adolf had begun was completed with the furious charges of Condé and Turenne.[3] And the administrative improvements which he had sponsored achieved a European reputation through the belated imitations of Le Tellier and Louvois.

In some other respects his innovations failed to hold their ground. He had carried the diminution of the weight of his artillery too far: increased mobility had involved sacrifice of effectiveness, and soon after his death it was found expedient to cast guns rather heavier than in his lifetime.[4] Again, the brigade did not long survive as a higher tactical unit: after 1632 it was abandoned in favour of the

[1] Weygand, p. 131; *cf.* Turner, *Pallas Armata*, pp. 215, 234.
[2] C. S. Terry, *Alexander Leslie*, pp. 154, 208, 234, 241, for some Scottish examples; Weygand, pp. 151-3; E. Zeeh, *L'Influence française sur les méthodes de guerre en Suède*, pp. 22-3.
[3] Weygand, p. 153.
[4] Hammarskiöld, *USAH*, p. 34.

regiment of two squadrons.[1] The change may have been one of the consequences of the contraction of the size of armies, and particularly of the decline of the pike, which set in once more in the later stages of the war. For Gustav Adolf was not able to convince his contemporaries of the pike's offensive potentialities: largely, it seems, because of the increasing difficulty of obtaining mercenaries willing to wield this cumbrous weapon, or to bear the body-armour that usually went with it; and also, perhaps, because pikemen were traditionally paid higher wages than the shot.[2] The result was what might have been expected. The offensive rôle of infantry became more difficult to sustain; linear tactics stiffened into rigidity; battles came more and more to be decided by cavalry actions on the wings, while the mass of the foot confined their participation to sanguinary musketry-duels. Gustav Adolf's combination of musket and pike was forgotten. But the invention of the bayonet at the end of the century was proof of the soundness of his ideas.

Gustav Adolf left behind him a great school of young soldiers, trained by him for command—Banér and Torstensson, Gustav Horn and Bernard of Weimar; and he is the military ancestor of Montecuccoli, Cromwell and Turenne. His influence on European warfare can be ranked with that of Frederick and Napoleon. Genius and character combined to make him a great soldier; and Napoleon showed his wonted penetration when he included Gustav Adolf among the small band of commanders—only seven in all—upon whom he bestowed the hard-won accolade of his respect.[3]

[1] Barkman, *Regementsorganisation*, p. 199; *id.*, *Gustav II Adolfs militära gärning*, pp. 274-5.

[2] Turner wrote: 'though after *Gustavus Adolphus* King of *Sweden* entred *Germany*, Squadrons and Batallions of Pikes were to be seen in all Regiments and Brigades of both Parties, and that Pikemen were still accounted the Body of the Infantry, yet after his Victory at *Leipsick* over the Imperial forces under *Tilly*, the Kings Marches were so quick in pursuance of his successes . . . and the retreats also of other Armies from him, were so speedy, that first the Pikemens defensive Arms were cast away, and after them the Pike itself, insomuch that all who hereafter were levied and enrolled, called for Muskets. But notwithstanding this, when new Regiments were levied after that great King's death, Colonels and Captains were ever order'd to levy and arm Pikemen proportionably to the Musquetiers; yet after they had endur'd some fatigue, the Pike was again cast away, and no Soldiers but Musquetiers were to be seen': *Pallas Armata*, p. 177. But see, too, p. 260, *note* 1, above.

[3] *Krigsvetenskaps Akademiens Handlingar* (1932), p. 71; Jugannière, *Une Révolution dans la tactique au XVIIe siècle*, p. 77.

CHAPTER IV

THE NAVY

THE achievements of the Swedish armies under Gustav Adolf were of so remarkable a character, the effects of the King's military reforms were of such general importance, that it is not surprising that they should have overshadowed the more modest services of the navy. From 1613 to 1632 there was but one naval engagement of any consequence, and in that the Swedes were defeated. The history of the fleet during the reign can therefore show nothing to compare with the victories in Germany; and in the sphere of naval tactics Sweden, so far from leading the way, followed at some distance behind the maritime powers of the west.[1]

Yet when all this has been conceded, it remains true that a strong navy, at least as much as an efficient army, was an essential pre-condition for Sweden's emergence as a great power. Sweden became great by the extension of her control of the eastern and southern shores of the Baltic: the Swedish empire was essentially a maritime empire. If it were to survive even for a decade, the Baltic must be made an ally rather than an enemy, a bridge rather than a barrier. The water that divided Sweden from the overseas possessions might be narrow,[2] but it was broad enough to be a fatal obstacle if the convoy-routes were left unprotected, if privateers could prey upon commerce, if the sea-keeping were allowed to become lax. Hence it was found necessary to maintain naval stations at strategic points over the whole length of the Baltic coastline—at Kalmar and Stockholm, Åbo and Viborg, Kexholm, Riga and Elbing; hence Swedish warships could be found everywhere from Wismar to Reval, from Barösund to the Vistula; and hence it was that the maintenance of a navy strong in numbers, and at least the equal of any possible rival

[1] There are two good recent accounts of the navy in this period: the co-operative work *Svenska flottans historia*, I., and *Sv. Krig*, Supp. Vol. I. This chapter draws largely upon them both. Older general works, still useful, are A. Zettersten, *Svenska flottans historia*, I.; G. Unger, *Illustrerad svensk sjökrigs-historia*, I.; A. Munthe, *Sjömaktens inflytande på Sveriges historia*, I. A general history of naval wars in the Baltic is E. Hornborg, *Kampen om Östersjön*. A good modern history of naval architecture and naval tactics for Europe as a whole is much wanted.

[2] No point in the Baltic is more than 67 sea-miles from land.

as an efficient fighting force, remained a constant preoccupation of Gustav Adolf and his advisers.

The first and most obvious threat to Sweden's security at sea came from Denmark, which saw in Swedish pretensions in the Baltic a usurpation of Danish rights and a denial of claims to *dominium* which in law rested upon the contention that the Sound was to be considered as a river flowing through Danish land, and which in fact depended upon the ability of the Danish fleet to enforce them. From the point of view of naval operations, Denmark occupied an extremely favourable strategic position. From bases on either side of the Sound the Danish navy could operate freely, either in the Baltic or in the Kattegat, upon the inner lines. A highly defensible obstacle—the narrows of the Sound—could block any attempt by Sweden to unite the west-coast fleet, based on Älvsborg or Göteborg, with the Baltic fleet based on Kalmar or Älvsnabben. Sweden was therefore faced with the fact that two of her main naval bases could easily have their sea-communications interrupted. In times of danger she was constrained to divide her forces—just as France, for instance, was compelled by Spain's command of the Straits to maintain a navy of the Ponant and a navy of the Levant. Moreover, the arrangement was especially disadvantageous, since Göteborg was not at this period very readily accessible from Stockholm. This was equally true, as far as land-communications went, of Kalmar; but Kalmar could be reached from Stockholm without difficulty by vessels coasting within the skerries, whereas Göteborg might in war-time be cut off from the Baltic altogether.

To this superior strategic position Denmark could add a population not less apt to maritime enterprise, and resources for the support of a fleet much beyond those which Gustav Adolf could command, at all events during the early part of the reign. The Danish navy was financed by the Sound Tolls paid by passing merchantmen: Kristian IV could boast that his magnificent fleet had not cost his subjects a *daler*. Thus freed from financial anxieties, he could give rein to his enthusiasm for all things nautical, could import shipwrights from Scotland, England or Holland to build for him warships of the most modern design, and could create a fleet powerful enough to give him effective command of the sea during the War of Kalmar.[1]

[1] J. A. Fridericia, *Danmarks Riges Historie*, IV. 117; *Sv. Krig*, Supp. Vol. I. 52-5. For Kristian's Scottish shipwrights—Mr. Balfour and Mr. Sinclair—see Monro, I. 87.

The course of that war was sufficient demonstration to Gustav Adolf and his chancellor of the vital importance of sea power to Sweden.[1] Had Karl IX's fleet been better officered, better prepared, better built and more numerous, there need have been no question of submitting to the crushing burden of Älvsborg's ransom. Kalmar and Älvsborg had fallen largely because the Swedish sea-captains could not or would not dispute the Danish command of the sea. The Danish fleet had consistently covered the right flank of the advance northwards up the eastern coast; it had enabled Kristian twice to conquer Öland; it had made possible damaging raids by landing-parties as far north as Söderköping. Indeed, it might easily have been used, in the closing months of the war, to land an invading army of sufficient strength to capture Stockholm itself. In addition, Kristian's navy had maintained a loose blockade of Sweden; Danish privateers had harried merchantmen plying between Swedish and Hanseatic ports; while a North Sea squadron had virtually isolated Sweden from western Europe.

The manifold dangers of naval weakness, thus ominously made plain, were no new thing to Swedish statesmen. Half a century earlier, Erik XIV had thoroughly grasped the necessity for a strong fleet. The Seven Years' War of the North had been a naval war even more than a war on land; and, at least until Erik's throne began to totter, it had been a war in which the Swedish navy won great victories. Swedish naval historians see in the period of Klas Horn's command a golden age, when Sweden was master of the Baltic and the Danish flag was swept from the sea. In spite of the hard terms of the peace of Stettin, the war really registered the defeat of Fredrik II's attempt to restore the old Scandinavian Union; and the main credit for defeating it must be given to Erik and his admirals. The War of Kalmar proved only too clearly, however, that if the fleet were neglected the attempt might be renewed. And even if Danish kings were to abandon the hope of reversing the verdict of 1523, they could still use the command of the sea to inflict serious material damage. Sweden was almost wholly dependent upon the Atlantic coasts for supplies of salt; and salt was a necessity of life. A superior Danish fleet could cut off this supply. Again, the development of Swedish power in the Baltic would scarcely have been possible without the

[1] Ahnlund indeed suggested that Gustav Adolf deliberately took the Danish fleet as his model: Ahnlund, *Svensk östersjöpolitik under det tidigare 1600-talet*, p. 15.

fuller exploitation of the country's mineral resources and an increased export-trade, notably in copper. But almost all Sweden's exports went by sea; and whether the merchantmen were bound for the north German ports or for the open waters of the west, they were equally vulnerable to Danish attack. The idea of commerce-protection as a function of the royal navy was indeed mostly foreign to the admiralties of the early seventeenth century, for merchantmen were expected to be able to protect themselves; but it was plain that Sweden's economic expansion would make desirable the development of the mercantile marine. Here Denmark once again provided an object-lesson; for Kristian IV had encouraged the building of armed merchantmen (the so-called *Defensionsskib*) by paying subsidies to owners who equipped their ships so as to fit them for incorporation into the royal navy in war-time. Sooner or later it seemed likely that Sweden would be driven to take some analogous measure.[1]

The danger from the Danish navy receded with the redemption of Älvsborg and the subsequent improvement of relations between the two countries; but it was never forgotten, and towards the end of his life Gustav Adolf was taking precautions against the outbreak of another naval war with his old enemy. In the meantime, fresh causes for anxiety had appeared, first in the attempts of Sigismund III to create a Polish fleet and later in the designs of Wallenstein and the Habsburg plans for establishing control over the Baltic.[2] To meet the double threat from Copenhagen and Wismar it might be necessary to maintain a fleet upon something like a 'two-power standard'.

The naval preparations of Sigismund may be considered to be the consequence of the truce of Deulinie, which closed to him the overland approach to Sweden through Russia. He had, indeed, been bound by his coronation charter, the Pacta Henriciana, to build a fleet for the Republic[3]; but this was an article which his political enemies among the Polish nobility showed no anxiety to enforce.[4] He set about his attempt to create a navy with great constancy of purpose and an inexhaustible patience; and by dint of persistent endeavour over a number of years he did at last obtain a squadron based on Danzig, which, though small, was quite big enough to cause concern in Stockholm. Sigismund was well aware that the main

[1] See above, pp. 131.

[2] See below, p. 317 *seqq.*

[3] J. Czołowski, *Marynarka w Polsce*, p. 99; A. Szelągowski, *Der Kampf um die Ostsee*, p. 87.

[4] Wł. Konopczyński, *Dzieje polski nowożytnej*, I. 269; Czołowski, p. 120.

immediate obstacle to his restoration was the Swedish navy. Without the command of the sea, he dared not risk even the comparatively short passage from Danzig to Kalmar. He needed a clear path for the passing of large bodies of troops across the water. For as long as Sweden had a fleet in being, that path was barred. Hence his attempts to build up a fleet which could brush Gustav Adolf's ships aside; hence his willingness to transfer to Wallenstein the forces which he had collected in the Vistula ports. If by a junction with the nascent imperial navy a concentration of force could be effected strong enough to scatter the Swedish commanders, Sigismund was not prepared to stickle upon a point of dignity.[1] Thus the danger from Poland was renewed, in more menacing shape, in the Spanish-imperialist designs upon the Baltic. In this situation the navy was Sweden's first line of defence: it was one of the cardinal maxims of Gustav Adolf's foreign policy that it is better to engage the enemy on his doorstep than wait to receive him on your own. Thus the navy played much the same part in the war with Poland as the navy of Drake in England's struggle with Spain. Gustav Adolf was not, indeed, called upon to meet an Armada; but his seamen kept watch on the ports of Poland and Mecklenburg with the same sense of the importance of their task as inspired those Elizabethan captains who thrust enquiring noses into Cadiz Bay. There was the same feeling at home of imminent national peril. And, as we shall see, there were achievements in the maintenance of blockading and patrol activity which even the Elizabethans never accomplished.

As the navy was the chief bastion in home-defence, so it was the springboard in attack, setting down Gustav Adolf's armies at the Düna mouth, at Pillau or at Peenemünde. It was the navy which made possible the retention of Stralsund, the last bridgehead on the north German coast. It was the navy which provided Gustav Adolf with the strategic initiative in launching his attack on Germany in 1630, since it enabled him to choose for himself the area in which he would engage the enemy, who was thus from the beginning compelled to conform to the plans of the invader. And when the landing had been made and the lodgment effected, and when it became necessary to broaden the base on the sea-coast before proceeding to a deeper penetration, it was again the navy which offered the easiest solution to the problem.

[1] He did insist, however, that the Polish squadron be kept distinct from that of the imperialists.

Without the effective command of the sea, in short, both the Polish and the German wars would have been inconceivable. Both wars were fought, to begin with at all events, at the end of a long line of communications. The sea-routes to the battlefields must be patrolled; troops must be transported; food, fodder and military stores moved in bulk. The task thus imposed upon the navy was heavy; and it says something for Gustav Adolf's captains that it should have been successfully discharged. If they had faltered or fumbled, if they had been unskilful or negligent, then all was upon the hazard. This was very well understood by the King. For a man who spent so much of his life in soldiering, Gustav Adolf had a remarkable grasp not merely of the intelligent use of the fleet in combination with other arms but also of the broad principles of naval strategy. If he was inclined to enjoin caution upon his captains, that was only because he was anxious to avoid the needless weakening, by rash engagements against odds, of a fleet upon which everything depended. He believed in keeping the enemy pinned down in his ports. He was the only king of Sweden ever to command a fleet at sea; and he astonished his seamen by the accuracy and range of his information upon the technical details of working and fighting a ship.[1] His sailing instructions were full and precise. He was insistent and urgent in pressing on his building programme.[2] And he went out of his way on one occasion to express his sense of the superior importance of the services of his sailors as compared with those of his soldiers, and to promise them a correspondingly better reward.[3] Oxenstierna, though he lacked his master's acquaintance with the *minutiae* of the mariner's profession, was no less convinced of the need for Sweden to be strong at sea: thus on 8 January 1631 he wrote to Gustav Adolf: 'It seems to me that it is essential that Your Majesty should above all things labour to create a powerful fleet at sea; a fleet of good ships, and most especially a fleet very numerous, so that you may be master of every nook and cranny of the Baltic; and, further, that all sailors, and all that is used aboard ship, be before all else well maintained, and meetly and handsomely provided, so that the crews may be kept both in spirits and in health; even though this should mean the having a regiment or two the less on land.'[4] And when after the King's death the responsibility for

[1] See the classic description in *Johan Hands dagbok*, p. 6; and *cf.* Styffe, pp. 532, 534.

[2] See, *e.g.*, *AOSB*, II. I. 29, 168, 300; *Arkiv*, I. 310.

[3] *Sv. Krig*, Supp. Vol. I. 196.

[4] *AOSB*, I. VI. 37.

Sweden's safety passed into his hands, he summed up his views in the remark: 'In the fleet (under God) stands the safety and prosperity of our fatherland.'[1] Nor were the other advisers of the King indifferent to the navy's welfare: at the beginning of the reign the *råd* referred to 'the fleet, upon which the whole welfare of the realm do seem to hang'; at the end of it the same body drew up a rota of its members, so that all took turns to inspect the Stockholm shipyards; while in 1625 they dipped deep into their purses in order to defray at their own charges the expense of building a warship for the King's service.[2]

What, then, were the achievements of Gustav Adolf's navy? what its duties? and how did it discharge them? For officers and crews it was no doubt an unrewarding service, lacking the stimulus of battle or the hope of glory; monotonous, rigorous and unhealthy; and without much prospect of prize-money to act as incentive. A service not without danger, however, in those uncharted, unbuoyed and unlighted waters,[3] where good harbours were few, rough seas frequent and fogs liable to occur at all seasons. The reefs and skerries of Scandinavia were not more dangerous than the lee shores of Kurland and Livonia, as appeared from the disaster of September 1625, when no less than ten of the King's ships were driven to destruction on the rocks of Domesnäs. Yet though the annals of the navy in this period do not, perhaps, make exhilarating reading, they record much devoted service, and they show more variety of experience than might at first sight appear.

There was, in the first place, the duty of direct collaboration with the armies. This began very early in the reign, for it was of some importance during the campaigns in Russia. Thus Nöteborg was blockaded from the sea side by the squadron of light craft which the Swedes had formed after the capture of Kexholm; Ivangorod was similarly blockaded by a squadron based on Narva; and the Swedish redoubt on the Neva was guarded by shallow-draught vessels

[1] *AOSB*, I. VIII. 89. And in the autumn of 1631 the imperial councillors minuted that a lost battle did not hurt the Swedes, since their command of the sea ensured their retention of the ports: H. Hallwich, *Briefe und Akten zur Geschichte Wallensteins*, I. 561.

[2] Munthe, *Sjömaktens inflytande*, I. 261; *RRP*, I. 71.

[3] Charts were still rare in the Baltic; lighting and buoying only just beginning. Navigational aids were much inferior to those in the west: as late as 1578 a ship might have no compass; and nautical instruments such as the Jacob's Staff or Davis's quadrant were still unusual: *Sv. Krig*, Supp. Vol. I. 46-7; *Svenska flottans historia*, I. 381-94.

(*pråmar*) from Viborg. The harassing activity of the Russians compelled the King to create and maintain an inland squadron on Lake Ladoga, and a kind of naval guerrilla warfare developed on the lakes and rivers of north-east Russia. Without a naval detachment to keep open Novgorod's water-communications by way of the Volchov and Ladoga, it would not have been easy for de la Gardie to keep his hold upon the town. At a later stage in the campaign similar craft were used upon Lake Peipus, in connexion with the operations against Gdov. Had such support not been available, the task of maintaining the army, in a country devastated by both sides, and served only by bottomless muddy tracks, would have been appreciably more difficult.

The experience thus gained of the value of naval assistance was repeatedly drawn upon in Gustav Adolf's later campaigns. The struggle with Poland, fought out at first in the Düna valley and later in the delta of the Vistula and around the Frisches Haff, offered opportunities similar to those in Russia. It is true that the navy played but a small part in the Kurland expedition of 1617-18; for though Gyllenstierna was instructed to give every assistance to the land forces, the main body of the fleet was ordered home as soon as the Düna redoubt had fallen; and there is no doubt that Stiernsköld thereafter felt the lack of naval support. But from the time of the renewal of the war in 1621, the fleet was frequently used to assist the land operations. It played a considerable part in the capture of Riga, and afterwards the ships of shallower draught were constantly used in conjunction with land campaigns in the valleys of the Düna, the Aa and the Schwed. The sailors of Gustav Adolf thus re-discovered the old Viking river-routes; and the crews of the *lodjor* bent to the oar, under the command of King Berik's lineal descendant, as once their forefathers had forced their longships upstream on their journey to the rapids, the portages, Kiev and Miklagård.

The same methods were employed in Prussia, though the Vistula proved shallower than the Düna, and ordinary galleys could no longer be used. But it was the fleet that forced a declaration of neutrality from Königsberg by a threat of bombardment; it was the fleet that captured Putzig—the best harbour on the southern shore of the Baltic—in July 1626; and it was the fleet that kept the Frisches Haff clear of intruding Polish privateers who might threaten communications between Pillau and Elbing. And when Gustav Adolf at last landed in Germany, he found the fleet of the utmost assistance in the opening phases of the campaign. It was his command of the Stettiner Haff, for instance, which enabled him to enforce the capitulation of Bogislaw XIV without dangerous loss of time; for instead of crossing from Wollin to the mainland at Anklam, where imperialist troops were waiting to bar his way, he was able to embark 9000 men and sail directly to Stettin, thus taking Bogislaw by surprise and depriving him of the possibility of resistance. And though the bulk of the fleet now returned to home waters, a squadron was left behind, stationed at Stralsund, which Gustav Adolf destined for a part in forthcoming operations. When towards the end of 1630 the moment arrived for extending his somewhat restricted bridgehead in Pomerania, he planned to use the fleet as a moving base for an invasion of Mecklenburg; and only persistent contrary winds prevented the execution of this design. The Stralsund squadron, nevertheless, gave useful assistance to the land forces on more than one subsequent occasion. Its blockade of Kolberg and Greifswald contributed to the capture of those places; and it gave important aid to Tott in his attack upon Warnemünde. And, finally, by occupying the island of Poel, the fleet was able to make its blockade of Wismar fully effective and so prepare the way for the capitulation of 12 January 1632.

Gustav Adolf's policy of fighting his enemies on their own territory, though it had everything to be said for it strategically and politically, necessarily put a strain upon the navy. His expeditionary forces had mostly to be transported and convoyed across the Baltic: only a small proportion of them reached the scene of operations by the land-route over the Karelian isthmus. Once arrived on foreign soil, they were to a considerable extent dependent upon the fleet for munitions, remounts, provisions, money and reinforcements. The initial delivery of the expedition to the point selected for landing was often an operation of considerable magnitude: thus for the attack on Riga in 1621 the navy carried 14,000 soldiers in 106 transports, with an escort of 52 warships. The invasion of Prussia in 1626 demanded very similar provision: once again 14,000 troops were embarked—on this occasion upon 81 transports—while the escorting fleet consisted of 29 men-of-war, together with one pinnace, 24 galleys and 6 *strussar*. The galleys and the *strussar* were shallow-draught boats able to negotiate the waters of the Frisches Haff, and when the fleet reached Pillau the troops were transhipped to them for the final stage of their journey to Passarge. All previous exertions were, however, surpassed in the organization of the armada which carried Gustav Adolf to Peenemünde in 1630. On this occasion the arrangements were complicated by the fact that besides the main body of troops which was to embark in the Stockholm archipelago, other contingents were to be sent off simultaneously from Norrköping, Söderköping, Västervik and Kalmar, besides further bodies to be ferried from Finland, the Baltic provinces, Prussia and Stralsund. The whole operation demanded administrative ability of a high order if the landing-forces were to arrive on the scene at approximately the same time; and there was danger that if the arrangements broke down the army might arrive in driblets and be beaten piecemeal. Moreover, provision had to be made for the fleet to be met off Rügen by light landing-craft from Stralsund, in order to facilitate speedy disembarkation. It says much for the efficiency of the Swedish admiralty that these elaborate arrangements functioned almost without a hitch. A fleet of about 100 transports took on board some 15,000 men at Älvsnabben; 25 royal ships, 4 armed merchantmen and innumerable light craft accompanied them. Within a few days of their arrival most of the other contingents had been safely delivered at the landing-place. It was an achievement to which it is not easy to recall a parallel in the seventeenth century.

Hardly less remarkable were the performances of the navy in observing and blockading enemy ports. It will be recollected that as early as 1615 Gustav Adolf's uneasiness at reports of Polish naval preparations had led him to despatch a reconnoitring expedition to Danzig.[1] When the war with Poland was resumed in earnest in 1621, the need for such observation of enemy preparations was felt to be urgent. Thus in May 1623 a preliminary reconnaissance of Danzig was made, to be followed in June by a large-scale demonstration commanded by the King in person. A fleet of twenty ships, carrying two regiments of soldiers, sailed to Danzig roads, with the idea of constraining Danzig to a promise of neutrality and an undertaking not to permit Sigismund to use the port as a base for the invasion of Sweden. The Polish fleet, which had been a danger almost wholly imaginary in 1615, had latterly begun to acquire some substance. As early as 1617, twenty ships for the Polish service were ready at Dunkirk, though fortunately for Sweden they never reached the Baltic. In 1621 Sigismund took into his pay a Scottish shipwright, James Murray, and once more began to build ships on his

[1] See above, Vol. I, p. 218.

own account; and by 1622 the first of them was ready in Danzig.[1] Ships were bought from England, or were confiscated from merchants; and twelve more were said to be building in Flanders. At the time of Gustav Adolf's demonstration in 1623, Sigismund had three warships, some commandeered merchantmen, and from 50 to 80 *lodjor* at his disposal. This was a force which could not be ignored; and when the Swedish fleet retired from Danzig, ten ships were left behind to prevent the Poles from coming out. They were soon withdrawn; but they mark the beginnings of a Swedish blockade of the south Baltic ports which grew increasingly effective in the next six or seven years.

For Sigismund did not interrupt his building programme. Six ships were launched between 1624 and 1626; and when Danzig, for fear of complications with Sweden, became increasingly inhospitable to Polish vessels, their base was transferred to Putzig.[2] By the autumn of 1626 seven ships were almost ready; a year later the number of vessels in actual service had risen to ten; and in the spring of 1628 to twelve, with fifteen more fitting out. Two of these were destroyed in June 1628 by an attack from the land as they lay in the Vistula; but Sigismund's persevering efforts were obviously yielding some result at last.

In the summer of 1626 Gustav Adolf sent two scouting expeditions to the Vistula, which returned with reports more reassuring than the facts actually warranted; but in the following year the transference of the theatre of operations to Prussia, and the consequent necessity of protecting the line of communications to Sweden from molestation by Polish forces, determined him to attempt a systematic blockade of Danzig. At first it was enforced only during the campaigning season, or from April-May to October, after which the ships returned to their bases. Their departure, however, was the signal for Sigismund's fleet to come out of hiding and take to the high seas. In late autumn and early spring the Poles maintained an extensive privateering activity over much of the southern Baltic. Their object was to cut off the supply of provisions and munitions from abroad and thus to starve the Swedish armies out.[3] Since it might well happen that Gustav Adolf's ships might be ice-bound in their ports long after English or Dutch ships had put to sea in

[1] Czołowski, pp. 115-18.
[2] *ibid.*, p. 119.
[3] E. Wendt, *Svenska örlogsflottan och handelsbeskattningen i Preussen*, p. 46.

the spring, Sigismund's Danzig squadron often made good prizes before the laggard blockading force arrived in May. The King was therefore anxious to keep his ships on the Danzig station as late as possible in the year. In 1626 the blockade was called off in October; in 1627 not until mid-November. On this occasion there occurred the only important naval engagement of the reign. Nils Stiernsköld, the admiral in command, was on the point of returning to his base when on 18 November Sigismund's fleet, under its Danish commander Arend Dickman,[1] made a sudden sortie from Danzig under cover of mist and caught the Swedish squadron unprepared. The odds were against Stiernsköld, who had but six ships to Dickman's ten; and of these six four were scarcely engaged at all, and fled with all speed back to Älvsnabben. In consequence, Stiernsköld's ship, *Tigern*, together with her consort, *Solen*, was attacked in overwhelming strength. Stiernsköld was killed, his ship captured, and *Solen* was blown up by her crew when further resistance was obviously hopeless.[2] The defeat came at an awkward moment, when the transport home of troops was still in progress; and it revealed that the new Polish navy was not to be trifled with. Its effect on Gustav Adolf was to strengthen him in his determination to maintain the blockade to an even later date in the following year.

There were already additional arguments of great weight for making the blockade more effective; for it was in 1627 that Gustav Adolf and Oxenstierna hit upon the plan of financing the war from the tolls levied upon merchants trading to Poland. In 1627 the navy began to enforce the collection of toll at Pillau. The blockade now became a means to compel foreign merchantmen to land their cargoes at Pillau instead of at Danzig. In the following years, as the yield of the tolls became more and more an indispensable constituent of Swedish war finance, a system of coastal patrols was developed, extending from Kolberg on the one hand to Libau and Windau on the other, so that a considerable section of the fleet found itself converted into a gigantic coastguard service.[3] It was testing work for ships and crews, especially when it was protracted until late autumn or early winter. It was a service, however, to which the

[1] Czołowski makes him a Lübecker: Czołowski, p. 125.

[2] *AOSB*, I. I. 119, II. I. 367-8; Czołowski, pp. 136-47; B. Broomé, *En polsk relation om sjöslaget utanför Danzig 1627, passim.* It seems to have been rare to blow up one's ship at this period; though there is a Dutch instance from 1606: J. C. de Jonge, *Het Nederlandsche Zeewezen*, I. 205.

[3] See above, pp. 82-4.

King attached the greatest importance, as may be seen from an incident which occurred in November 1628. The main blockading squadron had sailed for home waters on 25 October, leaving Henrik Fleming with four ships to maintain the watch until further orders. Fleming, misled by false information, left his station to go on a wild-goose chase after Polish ships which were said to have slipped out of the Vistula. He failed to find them; and as his crews were discontented, and much reduced by sickness, he returned to Sweden. The King received him with a severe reprimand, and, late as the season was, ordered him back at the end of November to his post.[1]

The trials of Fleming's detachment, pitching drearily in the choppy seas off Danzig in a Baltic November, were equalled or exceeded by others of Gustav Adolf's blockading forces. During the winter of 1629-30, for instance, two ships actually remained on the watch outside Danzig until January. And the record of the detachments under Erik Ryning's command, which were sent to patrol the Mecklenburg coast from 1629 to 1632, is not less remarkable. In the autumn of 1627 Wallenstein had captured Wismar, and had proceeded to turn it into a base for the projected Spanish-imperialist fleet which was to give the Habsburgs the mastery of the Baltic. His attempts to get ships from the Hanse towns met with little success, and he had no better fortune with the Infanta Isabella; but in the spring of 1629 he obtained an important reinforcement in the shape of nine ships of the Polish navy, which slipped out of Danzig in the course of the winter and made their way to Wismar. Their escape made it possible to reduce the strength of the Swedish forces off the Prussian coast, but on the other hand made imperative the patrolling of the stretch between Stralsund and Lübeck.[2] This duty was entrusted to a squadron of nine ships under Erik Ryning, which maintained an almost continuous blockade throughout the winter of 1629-30, effectively countered the efforts of the superior imperialist forces to get to sea, and kept Wismar sealed up until Gustav Adolf's armies finally captured the town in 1632.

These were very notable performances. The Baltic is at all times a stormy and treacherous sea, and especially so in winter. The crews suffered severely from dysentery and scurvy and cold. The work was tedious and hard, and must have presented serious problems of discipline to the commanders. In severe weather there was danger

[1] *Sv. Krig*, Supp. Vol. I. 189.
[2] *AOSB*, II. i. 501; *RRP*, I. 158 *note* 4; *Sv. Krig*, Supp. Vol. I. 59-62.

from ice, and at all seasons the risk of fog. The ships were kept out for months at a time without relief, and often returned to port more or less unseaworthy. In such conditions it was no ordinary test of endurance and seamanship to keep the seas until December or January. Indeed, it was a feat which perhaps no other navy of the period would have attempted.[1]

The Swedish navy has thus some title to be proud of its achievements under Gustav Adolf. But no devotion to duty would have availed had the fleet been starved of ships; no resolution could have redressed the balance had the men who manned them been constantly exposed to the maladministration of incompetent shore establishments. The navy of Karl IX could never have maintained the blockade of Wismar. The Nils Stiernsköld who died gloriously fighting against odds in Danzig roads was a very different officer from the Nils Stiernsköld of the Kalmar war. The precision of organization which took Gustav Adolf's armies over to Peenemünde was quite beyond the capacity of the officials who in 1611 and 1612 vainly laboured to secure a concentration of the scattered and insubordinate detachments of the Baltic fleet.[2] The Gustav Adolf of the sixteen-twenties would have known how to deal with any squadron which dared to behave as the Älvsborg squadron did in 1612.

Karl IX had bequeathed to his son a navy which seemed sunk in lethargy, riddled with peculation and incompetent in its command. The responsibility for this state of affairs did not lie with the King, who throughout his reign had done his best to put matters upon a better footing. It had been impossible, however, to compensate for the derelictions of the two previous reigns: the fleet which Gustav Vasa had created, which Erik XIV had brought to so high a pitch of excellence, had under Johan III dwindled in numbers and catastrophically declined in efficiency—largely, as it seems, because

[1] 'When we read that the Elizabethan great-ships were regarded as unfit to leave harbour in winter, and listen to Ralegh and Monson boasting how they kept the sea till autumn, the Tudor navy seems to recede into something primitive and unformed. Yet for another hundred years its endurance was hardly increased, and even on the eve of the eighteenth century Sir Cloudesley Shovel, a sailor born and bred, could roundly assert that an admiral who kept his fleet out after October deserved to be shot': J. S. Corbett, *The Successors of Drake*, p. 437. Yet there was plenty of naval activity in winter—in the Narrow Seas—during the first Dutch war.

[2] For the chaotic state of the navy in 1611-12 see, *e.g.*, Hallenberg, I. 171 *note* (b), 403, II. 825; S. Ljung, *Erik Göransson Tegel*, p. 37; *Sv. Krig*, Supp. Vol. I. 81, 90-1, 107-8, 110.

after 1570 Johan's main enemy had been Russia, which did not possess a fleet at all. When Johan died, the navy was in so poor a condition that it could not be trusted to provide a seaworthy ship to bring over Sigismund for his coronation, and Dutch vessels had to be hired for the purpose.[1] In the years of civil war at the close of the century conditions deteriorated still further, and when Karl finally emerged as the victor he found the fleet in a sorry condition. It must be conceded that he tackled the problem with energy; and to a certain extent he did effect an improvement. As far as mere numbers went, he increased the fleet, by building and purchase, from about 45 to about 110 units; but many of these were light craft of no great importance in war. Only about one-third of them were armed with even medium artillery, and there were but two heavy guns (36-pounders) in the whole fleet. Had the Swedish fleet ever engaged the Danes in battle during the War of Kalmar, they would have found themselves out-gunned and out-sailed, and it would probably have gone hard with them. Perhaps Karl's commanders were aware of this.

Such, then, was the far from encouraging picture presented by the navy in 1611. If it were ever to be an effective force it would require to be re-formed, rebuilt, reorganized and purged of unsatisfactory officials. And that is precisely what Gustav Adolf attempted to do.

In regard to building, Sweden's requirements differed considerably from those of—for instance—England or France. The mesh of archipelagos which fringes the coast of Sweden and Finland demands ships of special design—light, shallow-draughted, long in relation to their beam, and preferably equipped with oars, at least as an auxiliary means of propulsion; since the narrow channels and innumerable islands make navigation a matter of difficulty to a sailing-vessel. It was early recognized—by Gustav Vasa, for instance—that Sweden really needed two distinct fleets: one, a fleet of light craft to operate within the skerries; the other, a high-seas fleet capable of riding out the storms and breasting the heavy seas of the open Baltic. During the War of Kalmar there is a clear distinction made between the 'Little Fleet', which coasted up and down the skerries, or ferried troops over to Öland, and the Grand Fleet, which made more extended (but equally ineffective) cruises to the German coast. And since the campaigns of the armies, in

[1] Czołowski, p. 102.

Russia, Livonia, Prussia and Pomerania, were for the most part fought in regions where the geographical features made the use of shallow-draught vessels possible, it is not surprising that such vessels should have been laid down more or less steadily throughout the reign. These little ships went under a variety of names—*bojort*, *båt*, *esping*, *flöjt*, *galeja*, *håp*, *krejare*, *jakt*, *lodja*, *pråm*, *skuta*, *struss*, *skärbåt*—and it is difficult, and perhaps profitless, to try to distinguish them.[1] One feature was common to all, namely that they were all equipped with oars as well as sails. Their size varied considerably: an *esping* seems to have been little bigger than a ship's boat or wherry; a *flöjt*, on the other hand, was a moderate-sized freighter, presumably corresponding to a Dutch *fluit*. There was wide variation within the limits of a single type. Thus a *galeja* (galley) might range in length from 40 to 60 feet, and in beam from 5 to 13. Still more indefinite was the *lodja*. The *lodja* was a type of craft imported from Russia, where it had been used for centuries for inland navigation. It was undecked, moderately capacious, with one or two masts, carrying a normal complement of from two to six men, and armed with a couple of light cannon. In 1607, however, we hear of the construction of *lodjor* of twelve banks of oars, big enough to take a hundred men and provisions for two months, yet capable of being dragged ten kilometres overland. *Strussar*, similarly, show considerable variation in size: the largest attained a length of 70 feet and carried a crew of ten. All these types were in regular service in Gustav Adolf's time; but the most useful seem to have been *lodjor*, *strussar* and *galejor*, and it was these which were turned out by the shipyards in the greatest numbers. After the close of the Russian war *lodjor* seem no longer to have been much employed as fighting ships; but they retained their importance as transport and supply-ships, and as landing-craft.[2] As Gustav Adolf moved inland from Pomerania their usefulness declined, and the King, who on more than one occasion during the 'twenties had shown his anxiety that they should be available in adequate numbers,[3] decided to concentrate upon building only big ships: little ships, he now considered, were simply good timber spoiled.[4] Nevertheless, at the close of the reign

[1] Compare, on the confusion of nomenclature, B. Hagedorn, *Die Entwicklung der wichtigsten Schiffstypen bis ins 19. Jahrhundert*, pp. 7-9.

[2] For instance, in 1630: *cf. Arkiv*, I. 135. In March 1632 Gustav Adolf ordered the creation of a fleet of small boats to patrol the Elbe: *ibid.*, I. 566.

[3] *e.g. AOSB*, II. I. 168, 300.

[4] *Arkiv*, I. 562-5.

the light craft still formed almost as large a proportion of the fleet as in 1611.

The revival of Sweden as a naval power, however, required more than the launching of shoals of *lodjor* and *prâmar*. The renaissance of the navy under Gustav Adolf depended in the first place upon the energy with which he kept the high-seas fleet up to strength. Karl IX had left behind him a fleet of some 110 ships; but of these only 30, with 20 pinnaces, were sailing-vessels. Many of them were quite new. By 1613, when the war with Denmark ended, the total number of units afloat had fallen to between 50 and 60, in spite of great building activity; and the numbers continued to fall until 1616, when they sank below 50. From this point there was a steady recovery; the first considerable ship built since 1613—*Harboviks Lejon*—was launched in 1615; *Riksnyckeln*, of 250 *läster*,[1] in 1616; and *Rikskronan*, of 350, in 1618. Thereafter the number rises until the end of 1624, when the fleet had 90 units: the period between 1621 and 1624—which coincides with the beginning of Klas Fleming's work at the admiralty—sees the greatest shipbuilding activity of any portion of the reign since 1613. In 1625, however, came the Domesnäs disaster, with the loss of ten ships, and this was followed soon after by the accidental loss of three more; so that the curve falls sharply for some years. It rises again in the last four years of the reign; and if ships laid down in 1632 but not completed at the time of the King's death be included, together with the relics of the Polish fleet captured at Wismar, then the figure at the end of the reign was in the neighbourhood of 90. There was thus an apparent decrease of about 20 since 1611; but this was probably more than offset by the increase in the average tonnage. There is little doubt that the navy of 1632 was heavier, more modern in design and more formidable than the navy of twenty years earlier.

Until 1618 the crown undertook the building of ships upon its own account; but in that year it began to let out the work to contractors, the first of these being the Dutchmen Paridon van Horn and Christiaan Welshuisen. The work was executed, however, by crown workmen, and was subject to governmental control. In 1620 a new contractor, Anton Monier, made his appearance, and in the years that followed did a good deal of work for the navy. Fitting and rigging was also let out on contract; indeed, by a very undesirable arrangement it was from 1615 a monopoly of Admiral Rickard

[1] Eight *läster* was probably roughly equivalent to thirteen English tons.

Clerck.[1] The contract system no doubt relieved an overworked administration of some labour; but it does not seem to have been reliable or efficient, and on occasion the contractors became lax for want of proper supervision.[2] In 1628 all contracts were cancelled, and the work was once again undertaken by the admiralty.

In addition to the building programme, efforts were made to strengthen the fleet by other means. Thus in 1612 Gustav Adolf concluded an agreement with Paridon van Horn for the hiring of 15 ships and 60 *bojorter*; but the treaty of Knäred was signed before they could be delivered, and the agreement lapsed. In 1624 Salvius was instructed to try to persuade a couple of well-armed Hamburg merchantmen to bring salt to Sweden from Portugal, the intention being to commandeer them for the navy when they arrived. In 1628 ships were bought from Holland and Lübeck, through the agency of Louis de Geer; and in the following year, through James Spens, from England; and Monier and Paridon van Horn also negotiated purchases abroad. And even as late as March 1632 Salvius was ordered to do his best to induce ten to twenty freebooters to take service with Sweden.[3] But these expedients were not of great importance, and the development of the navy depended really upon the number of vessels that came off the stocks.

The period of greatest activity in the shipyards—the years immediately after 1620—coincides with the rise of the influence of Klas Fleming.[4] In 1620 Karl Karlsson Gyllenhielm was placed in charge of the navy, with Fleming as his chief assistant. Gyllenhielm had had some earlier naval experience, but he was already somewhat infirm, and the main burden of business fell upon his subordinate. Fleming's career, like that of so many other sea-commanders, had hitherto been purely military, and he had virtually no knowledge of naval affairs when he took office. He soon turned himself into an expert; and in the next ten years he became one of the greatest naval administrators in Swedish history. He saw active service in command of the blockading squadron off Danzig, and thus acquired some practical insight into the needs of the service; and eventually, after a long and distinguished career, he was killed in action against

[1] Hallenberg, III. 342; A. Munthe, *Svenska sjöhjältar*, V. 20; Zettersten, I. 357; Lindberg, *Västerviks historia*, I. 390 *seqq.*; *cf. RRP*, I. 28 *note* 5.

[2] *AOSB*, II. I. 303; *Svenska flottans historia*, I. 312.

[3] For these transactions, see *RRP*, I. 79 *note* 6; *AOSB*, I. IV. 584; Lundgren, *Salvius*, p. 14; E. Wendt, *Amiralitetskollegiets historia*, I. 18; *Arkiv*, I. 573.

[4] There is a biography of Klas Fleming in A. Munthe, *Svenska sjöhjältar*, V.

the Danish navy in 1644. Fleming did more than any man to ensure the ascendancy of Sweden on the sea. At times the King was sharply critical of his administration; but the defects he censured seem to have arisen from the undue amount of work which was placed on Fleming's shoulders: between 1629 and 1631, for instance, besides being responsible for naval affairs, he filled the leading post in the treasury. Fleming, indeed, may stand with Axel Oxenstierna and Karl Bonde as the type of the aristocratic civil servant; and his work for the navy may not unfitly be compared with the achievements of Samuel Pepys. Between 1620 and 1630 sixteen great-ships were built under his supervision. The amount of money expended on the fleet steadily rose: in 1616 it had stood at 72,776 *daler*; in 1632 it reached 483,277 *daler*.[1] The Danish ambassador Peder Galt, who had once drawn a highly imaginative picture of the King of Sweden weeping over his deserted wharves, soon changed his tone, and by 1624 was showing intelligible concern over the progress of Fleming's fleet.[2]

The Domesnäs catastrophe, however, produced a situation which could not be remedied by ordinary measures. Six weeks after the event, three members of the *råd*, Axel Oxenstierna, Svante Banér and Jakob de la Gardie, sent an appeal to their colleagues to subscribe to a fund for replacing the lost ships; and each of the three promised to contribute the substantial sum of 2000 *daler*.[3] At the same time Gustav Adolf commandeered eight or ten merchantmen in Riga. These expedients proving inadequate to the emergency, the government at the end of 1628 hit upon another plan. In a proposition to a meeting of delegates from the towns, which assembled at Stockholm in January 1629, Gustav Adolf suggested the formation of a 'Ship Company'. The towns were to combine to form a company, which should provide and maintain sixteen [4] armed merchantmen, which were to be at the disposal of the royal navy in case of need. They would be allowed to fell oak for building them in the crown forest, free of charge; and for such time as the ships were in the royal service the King would pay interest on the company's capital. The towns accepted these proposals; but in the sequel they showed considerable reluctance to implement them. Some were backward in making their contributions; others tried to buy ships from abroad.

[1] E. A. Spens, *Flottan under Konung Gustaf II Adolfs regering*, pp. 91-2.
[2] *Peder Galts Depescher*, pp. 91, 111. [3] *AOSB*, I. III. 212.
[4] The King originally suggested forty: Styffe, p. 313; *RRP*, I. 162-4.

The King found it necessary to expostulate in strong terms in December 1629, and the towns apologized for their remissness.[1] However, by the close of the reign twelve of these 'Company Ships' were serving with the navy, and though the number fell short of expectations, it was a valuable reinforcement. It also afforded the King a good ground for approaching the nobility with a request for similar exertions. In June 1629, accordingly, the first Estate agreed to contribute (for this occasion only) the somewhat meagre sum of 50 *daler* for every horse owed by them in *rusttjänst*, and further recommended that the moneys they had subscribed to the Southern Company should be diverted to the fitting out of more ships.[2]

By such means as these, supplementing the exertions of Klas Fleming and his coadjutors, the navy recovered from the state of weakness into which it had fallen in 1625. At the end of the reign the shipyards were more active than ever; and the situation so far improved in the years after 1629 that by the spring of 1631 Gustav Adolf and Oxenstierna could discuss, with an optimism which turned out to be ill-founded, the formation of a separate fleet based on the ports of Prussia.[3]

What, then, was the composition of Gustav Adolf's sailing fleet? Into what classes of vessels was it divided, and what were their distinctive features? And how did Swedish ship-design in this age compare with contemporary practice abroad? It is extraordinarily difficult to give a precise answer to any of these questions; largely because not a single contemporary drawing of a Swedish ship seems to have been preserved. Nevertheless, it is possible to hazard some tentative conclusions on the basis of the information available. It seems clear, for instance, that in the evolution of naval types Sweden in the sixteenth century conformed broadly to the course of development in western Europe, though possibly lagging somewhat behind Spain and Portugal on the one hand and England and Holland on the other. As in the case of light craft, it is difficult now to grasp the real distinction between types, and the general looseness in the use of nomenclature makes any attempt to do so fruitless; but still it is fairly clear that Sweden had progressed from the mediaeval cog to the caravel, and from the caravel to something not very dissimilar

[1] A. A. von Stiernman, *Alla riksdagars och möthens . . . beslut*, I. 816-18; *AOSB*, I. IV. 584; *RRP*, II. 33.

[2] *Svenska riddarskaps och adels riksdagsprotokoll* [cited: *SRARP*], I. 120-1; *RRP*, I. 155 *note* 1; *Arkiv*, I. 41; *Sv. Krig*, III. 259-61; Börjeson, *Stockholms segelsjöfart*, pp. 164-73; and see above, p. 126.

[3] *AOSB*, I. VI. 195, II. I. 689.

to the galleon. Gustav Vasa's fleet, for instance, boasted as its chief glory the *Göta Ark*, known to contemporaries and to posterity as a caravel. She was a big ship of 400-450 *läster* burden (650-730 tons)—bigger than the average caravel in the west [1]—and was considered to be among the largest vessels of her time; but she was considerably inferior in size to Henry VIII's *Great Harry*, and there are some indications that she may have approximated to a galleon in type: her length, for instance, was 3·2 beams, which suggests a galleon. Erik XIV's *Mars* is said to have been even bigger, but precise details are lacking; and it is always possible that these large ships may have been designed (as *Great Harry* was) more for the glory and prestige of the monarch than upon any very definite plan of naval warfare. Certainly there is but little relation to be perceived, then or for some time afterwards, between size and tactical use.

Both *Göta Ark* and *Mars* had high fore- and after-castles and a well-marked waist; though it is recorded of Gustav Vasa that on at least one occasion he caused the high upperworks of a ship to be dismantled or reduced. *Mars* may perhaps have resembled more the ships of the next century, if we may credit the tradition which ascribes to Erik the introduction of the tumblehome into Swedish ship-design. It seems at all events certain that Erik's ships were extraordinarily stable: it was said that all the guns aboard could be dragged to one side of the ship and there discharged without risk of her heeling over at a dangerous angle. There are signs in Erik's time of a specifically Swedish technique of shipbuilding, unknown elsewhere: thus Erik is said to have armoured his ships along the waterline by providing them with a double hull at this point, and filling the intervening cavity with iron-ore.[2] But if there really was a distinctively Swedish school of naval architecture, it was probably soon obscured or modified by the foreign shipwrights who were increasingly imported from the Netherlands, England or Scotland.

By the end of the sixteenth century the purely sailing-ships of the royal navy were clearly distinguished, in nomenclature and function, from the hybrid types which tried to make the best of both oars and sails. A new sailing type also emerged about this time. This was the pinnace, which thus made its appearance in the Swedish navy a full half-century after its adoption in England. The pinnace was

[1] Hagedorn, p. 70.

[2] *Samuel Kiechels resa i Sverige*, p. 339. But for some possible Spanish parallels (rather later, however) see M. Lewis, *The Navy of Britain*, pp. 133-4.

designed to be auxiliary to the regular men-of-war; it was lighter, a faster sailer and specially useful for reconnaissance work. At first it was of very small dimensions: in Karl IX's time it measured only 40 feet in length, though this was later to increase. But though so small, pinnaces were always grouped with 'ships', and never with 'craft'; for like the 'ships' they were not vessels of free movement, since they lacked oars. It is indicative of the confusion of nomenclature that smaller vessels might be called 'ships' or 'pinnaces' indifferently. The confusion may possibly be connected with the new fashion (which came in about 1600) for fitting 'ships' with three masts instead of four (omitting the bonaventura mizzen), and thus obliterating one of the most obvious distinctions between 'ships' and 'pinnaces'.

In Gustav Adolf's reign, probably about the year 1616, a new classification for sailing-ships in the navy was laid down, on the basis of their complement: 'royal ships' (*royalskepp*) were those with a crew of 200; 'proper warships' (*lagom örlogsskepp*) those with a crew of 60. In 1621 this latter category was subdivided into 'warships' and 'lesser warships', and the minimum figure for the crew of a royal ship was reduced to 93. In each case pinnaces were placed in a separate category. The size of ships in each of the three classes of 1621 was reckoned to be 200-450 *läster*, 120-200 *läster* and 100-150 *läster* respectively; while pinnaces might be of 60·to 80. The classification is very similar to that laid down by Lionel Cranfield's commission on the Royal Navy in 1618 [1]: there the categories were 'ships royal', 'great-ships', 'middling ships' and 'small ships', with pinnaces once again in a class by themselves. There is, however, one striking difference: in each case the English ships were heavier. Thus an English 'ship royal' was defined as being over 800 tons; a Swedish *royalskepp* had a maximum of 730 tons. At the other end of the scale a Swedish pinnace had a maximum burthen of 130 tons; while the English pinnace was defined as being not more than 300 tons. But the most important difference between Gustav Adolf's navy and that of James I seems to have lain not so much in the size of the ships as in their design. At the beginning of the century a Swedish warship is said to have had a length of two and a half beams, and thus to have corresponded with the Elizabethan great-ship. From about the end of the 'seventies, however, the tendency of English shipwrights had been to build rather longer and narrower,

[1] J. S. Corbett, *England in the Mediterranean*, I. 68-9.

and the new ships of the Armada programme had usually a length of three and a third beams—that is, they were built more on the lines of a true galleon than their predecessors had been. But at this point the English shipwrights called a halt; and though there were subsequently many changes in fashion, it is broadly true to say that the galleon-specification continued to be a sort of pivot upon which English design oscillated, now leaning a little to one side, now to the other, but never varying very far from the norm.[1] Far different was the case with Swedish shipwrights. After having clung to the great-ship dimensions rather longer than their English colleagues, they seem to have followed western fashions, but to have wildly exaggerated them. Gustav Adolf's reign shows this tendency very clearly. In 1618 a ship was launched with a length of 3·7 beams; in 1625 an official specification provided for a length of 4 beams; while in the opinion of some historians the warships launched in the mid-'twenties reached the extraordinary length of 5 beams—a figure which did not differ widely from the proportions of a galley. Since armament remained unaltered, or was even increased, and since the spread of canvas was certainly not reduced, it is hardly surprising that the ships of the new type proved unweatherly and crank. The inevitable result came in 1628, when *Vasa* turned turtle on her trials, in fair weather and smooth water, with considerable loss of life.[2] Fortunately this warning was heeded, and by 1630 the length had been reduced to the more reasonable figure of 3·3 beams.

For the rest, there is not much precise information to be had about the design of Gustav Adolf's ships. It is clear that foreign shipwrights were imported, especially from Holland, and it is said that naval architecture was influenced by Dutch models. On the other hand, it seems that high poops and even forecastles were not unusual all through the reign, which does not suggest Dutch influence. There is nothing to indicate that the Swedish navy had any of the new 'race-built' ships of which *Revenge* was the classic type in the Elizabethan navy—ships with flush decks, low freeboard, and lying 'low and snug in the water, like a galleass'; yet this was the style of building favoured by Dutch shipwrights in the first

[1] F. L. Robertson, *The Evolution of Naval Armament*, pp. 6-32; Corbett, *Successors of Drake*, pp. 422-3; Lewis, pp. 81-3.

[2] *RRP*, I. 103. By 1653 the reaction had gone so far that Whitelocke could describe *Hercules* as 'fitter for a defence in fight than for an assailant or for fleetness, more bulky than nimble, much unlike our English frigates': Whitelocke, *Journal of the Swedish Embassy*, I. 166.

decades of the century.[1] It does not seem legitimate to infer that the prevailing practice in the Baltic was more backward and conservative than in the west, for it is known that vessels of Kristian IV's navy, for instance, excited the admiration of English experts when he visited London in 1606. It might be easier to offer conjectural explanations if reliable information were available about Swedish battle tactics in this period; but this too is involved in too much obscurity for any firm conclusions to be possible.

In armament the navy of Gustav Adolf could show some advance upon that of his predecessors. In the sixteenth century the efficiency of the fleet had been appreciably reduced by the confusion of types and calibres which was then normal. Not merely would cannon of different sizes, designed for different purposes, lie side by side on the gun-deck, but there was no consistency in the arming of any particular ship.[2] With the approach of winter, the ship would be laid up and dismantled; and before spring came round her guns might have been commandeered for the army, or for one of the King's castles, so that when in the following season she once more put to sea, she might well be of much less value as a fighting unit than in the previous year. Karl IX had done his best to standardize naval armament, but though he had reduced the range of types carried, much still remained to be done. Gustav Adolf continued these efforts, with better success. The heaviest types of cannon were now discarded, as were also the last of the dangerous light breech-loaders, and the bigger ships began to be armed almost exclusively with culverins, *slangor* and falconets. By the mid-'twenties these old names were abandoned for a more modern classification based on the weight of the shot, and henceforward the three predominant types were 24-pounders, 12-pounders and 6-pounders. The number of guns carried certainly tended to fall: Gustav Adolf's *Göta Ark* (the second ship of that name), which was among the biggest in the fleet and is said to have compared with any warship afloat, carried 70 guns, whereas in Erik XIV's time ships of 90 or even 100 guns were not uncommon. On the other hand, there is no doubt that Gustav Adolf's ships developed greater firepower than their predecessors; the reduction in the number of guns depending on the discarding of the lighter and less effective types.

[1] Corbett, *Successors of Drake*, p. 422; de Jonge, I. 271-3.

[2] This confusion persisted in the Dutch navy until well into the seventeenth century: de Jonge, I. 271-3.

Nevertheless, it is plain that the Swedish navy, compared with the Danish, was seriously undergunned; and it is doubtful whether this inferiority was really offset by the alleged superiority of Swedish gunpowder. It is probable, too, that the guns were undermanned—as they certainly were, for instance, in the navy of Elizabeth. Guns could still be either of iron or of 'copper'; but the use of iron guns was declining, and by the end of the reign the policy was to make them all of copper, if only in order to help to use up the copper output at home and keep it off the international market until prices should improve.[1] The bigger ships had guns ranged in two tiers; but in the absence of ships' drawings it is impossible to determine whether they were genuine two-deckers or not.[2]

Gustav Adolf's reign saw important advances in the manning of the fleet, both as regards officers and ratings. Until his time there had really been no regular and permanent ranks in the navy, for there had been no corps of officers in constant employment. The title of admiral or captain was conferred on an individual for a single campaign, and lapsed when that campaign was over. And, equally, there had been no fixed rates of pay, for there had been no regular budget for the navy. It might therefore happen that one captain would be paid much less than another, without any valid reason. Gustav Adolf reformed this unsatisfactory state of affairs. From 1614 dates the first real naval establishment; for in that year the sixteen best captains were retained as ordinary captains in the permanent employ of the crown. The number rose to thirty before the end of the reign; but even this proved inadequate, and from time to time 'extraordinary' captains were recruited from abroad. In 1620 the rank of lieutenant was established; and in the same year five vice-admirals were appointed, each to be in command of a squadron. In 1628 the new rank of major was created, intermediate between that of vice-admiral and that of captain. There was always some difficulty in obtaining satisfactory Swedish recruits for commissioned ranks in the navy, for the service was considered less honourable than the army, and the pay was inferior; and in other respects the army seemed to offer better prospects.[3] A considerable

[1] *Arkiv*, I. 304, 541. For proportions of iron guns to copper, see Zettersten, I. 378-9.

[2] *Prince Royal* (1610) was the first English two-decker; *Sovereign of the Seas* (1637) the first English three-decker: Lewis, p. 85. At the battle of the Downs, only the Dutch flagship was a true two-decker: de Jonge, I. 279; *cf.* Robertson, *Evolution of Naval Armament*, p. 16.

[3] Zettersten, I. 36; Munthe, *Sjömaktens inflytande*, I. 264-5; Spens, pp. 86-9.

proportion of naval officers therefore was recruited from abroad, and especially from Holland. The Swedish officers were usually, though not invariably, nobles; though at least two ratings—Lars Bubb and Lars Matsson—worked their way up in Gustav Adolf's time to the command of a ship, and later ended their careers as admirals and members of the peerage.[1] Something like a normal establishment was laid down also for petty-officers; though petty-officers, in contradistinction to officers, were as a rule employed only on a yearly contract. By the end of the reign the usual complement was a mate and second-mate, boatswain and boatswain's-mate, with a *konstapel* (earlier called *arklimästare*) as gunnery-officer. And whereas in Karl's time there had frequently been half a dozen helmsmen on each ship, the number under Gustav Adolf was reduced to one (or, in the case of royal ships, two), which possibly simplified navigation.[2]

Gustav Vasa had created the Swedish navy before his country had acquired much of a mercantile marine; with the result that from the beginning there had been difficulty about finding qualified crews. It was a difficulty which persisted under Gustav Adolf. From time to time attempts were made to supplement the local resources of manpower by importations of sailors from abroad; but though some were undoubtedly brought in, this was too expensive a method to be practised on a large scale.[3] From time to time, too, the pressing of seamen was ordered. But the main resource, for the navy as for the army, was *utskrivning*. It was hoped, by turning over the drafts from coastal areas to the navy, to ensure that some at least of the conscripts should be men with sea experience; and conscripts from the towns were also assigned to the navy, presumably because so many towns lay on the coast. By the beginning of the 'twenties, however, the government was finding recruitment by *utskrivning* unsatisfactory. There was considerable loss by desertion; and the filling of the gaps thus created—or of those not less serious gaps which were the result of epidemics—could not be undertaken immediately, since any fresh *utskrivning* needed the consent of the Estates, and must consequently await the next meeting of the *riksdag*. *Utskrivning* was in any case very unpopular, and any practicable alternative would probably be preferred to it. Such an alternative had been devised for the army: already in 1621 Dalarna had concluded an agreement with the King whereby the province

[1] Zettersten, I. 90. [2] *ibid.*, I. 107.

[3] See, *e.g.*, *SRDA*, II. 165; *AOSB*, I. vi. 30, 307, 338, II. i. 727.

undertook to provide a fixed and constant number of men for service in the army, making good any wastage as it occurred, and in return was exempted from the ordinary *utskrivning*. In 1623 this system was applied, in Finland, Åland and parts of Uppland, to recruitment for the navy; and in 1624 it was accepted by the towns. Six companies of sailors (nominally 2400 men) were to be raised and maintained by these means. Each sailor was to be quartered on a peasant or townsman during the winter, was to work for him in return for board and lodging, and by him was to be paid a yearly wage of 18 *daler*, this amount being deducted from the amount his host would otherwise have paid in taxes. The companies were to be kept permanently up to strength. The government would thus secure a guaranteed manpower-income, and would avoid a great deal of administrative work.

In practice, the scheme did not at first work out very well. Peasants who had already paid their taxes in full for the current year were understandably reluctant to pay a further 18 *daler*, and in Finland many of the sailors quartered on farms seem to have been kept on starvation rations. There were difficulties about replacements, so that the government was forced to violate its undertaking and raise fresh recruits by *utskrivning*. There were many complaints about the quality of the men provided: the Danish agent Peder Galt remarked on one occasion that 'they make sailors of men who are too small to be soldiers',[1] and Klas Fleming complained that they sent him cripples and rogues. By 1627 the scheme had more or less broken down. At the beginning of 1629, however, another attempt was made with the towns. It proved no more successful; and by the close of 1632 the towns had been forced to agree to another *utskrivning*, from whose operation Stockholm alone was excepted. It was not until 1635 that the new plan—famous in Swedish history for more than two centuries as *ständigt båtsmanshåll*—was at length really launched.[2] It had failed under Gustav Adolf, partly because

[1] Galt, p. 13.

[2] For *ständigt båtsmanshåll*, see O. Törnbom, *Båtsmanshållets uppkomst*, *passim*. The manning of galleys raises questions which seem to be unanswered. Though hard labour in the galleys seems to have been a punishment for criminals (Geijer, III. 69), it does not appear that such persons formed the only, or the main, element in their crews. Were they provided by ordinary *utskrivning*? Were the rowers specially selected? Was the pay higher? The subject seems at present obscure, and one may well envy the confidence of a modern naval historian who, after stating that galleys could not have existed in the Baltic, continues, 'Où trouver des forçats dans la mer Baltique? . . . Où razzier les populations paisibles sur ces côtes désertes et inhospitalières?': R. La Bruyère, *Maillé-Brézé*, p. 97.

the central administration of the navy was still rudimentary and understaffed; partly, it seems, because the rates of pay were discouragingly low: at the close of the reign Klas Fleming was doing his best to have them increased.[1]

Discipline in the navy had been very lax during the War of Kalmar, and one of the great needs of the service was an improvement in this respect. On the whole, conditions seem to have changed for the better by 1632, though Klas Fleming could still refer to the officers in general as 'a lot of trash'.[2] Punishments were severe: the death penalty was frequently imposed, and such punishments as keel-hauling, running the gauntlet, ducking, or setting a defaulter to work in the anchor-smithy, were very common. Gustav Adolf on one occasion attributed the difficulty of getting recruits for the navy to 'their cruel officers' faithless conduct'.[3] Life aboard ship was very hard: the crew slept on deck, without bunks or hammocks, till 1676. Food was bad, though usually plentiful; crews suffered greatly from cold; and pneumonia, scurvy, dysentery and eye-afflictions were common. Even in Klas Fleming's time the seaman could be needlessly sacrificed to sheer administrative muddle, as a grisly instance from 1623 proves.[4] Disease was so serious in the blockading squadrons that special arrangements had to be made for the crews to convalesce in the healthy climate of Öland.[5] Some comfort the government did indeed devise by the institution of barber-surgeons in the 'twenties, and by the provision of religious consolation, dispensed by chaplains, and forcibly administered as part of the ordinary routine; but neither the one nor the other much diminished the mortality on board.[6]

At the beginning of the sixteenth century there was virtually no central administration for the navy. Admirals were appointed for specific tasks, and had no permanent title or fixed employment. Naval affairs in general fell within the purview of the treasury, which controlled expenditure. The only permanent official was really the King himself. In 1602, however, Karl IX established the office of High Admiral (*riksamiral*), and invested Axel Ryning with it. But

[1] Törnbom, p. 57; *cf.* Munthe, *Svenska sjöhjältar,* V. 27-8.
[2] Törnbom, p. 57.
[3] *AOSB*, II. I. 731.
[4] *Svenska flottans historia*, I. 357; *cf.* Törnbom, p. 50.
[5] Zettersten, I. 182.
[6] *ibid.*, I. 178. But soon after 1632 there were only three or four surgeons in the whole fleet: C. T. Odhner, *Sveriges inre historia under Drottning Christinas förmyndare,* p. 223.

it was still far more an honorific title than an efficient office. Ryning was freely employed on other work, and exercised little control over the navy. The efficient official was his second-in-command, the vice-admiral, to whom was added (from 1606) a port-admiral (*holmamiral*) charged especially with the supervision of the shipyards and shore establishments at Stockholm. In 1612 Ryning was succeeded as *riksamiral* by Göran Gyllenstierna, who held the office until his death in 1618; and in 1615 the offices of under-admiral and port-admiral were combined in the person of Nils Bielkenstierna. It was in this period that the notion of an 'admiralty', as a standing central government for the navy, first emerged: the term is first employed in 1618. It was not, however, until 1620 that real progress was made. In that year Karl Karlsson Gyllenhielm was made *riksamiral*, with Klas Fleming as his right-hand man, and it is to their exertions that Sweden is indebted for the establishment of the admiralty as one of the great offices of government in 1634. From 1625 Fleming united the offices of vice-admiral and port-admiral; but since both he and Gyllenhielm were often at sea, the administration not infrequently lacked a responsible head. In 1630, therefore, Erik Ryning was appointed as an additional vice-admiral, and in 1631 the post of port-admiral was revived as a separate appointment. Erik Ryning, however, was constantly engaged on the blockade of Wismar; and in fact it was Fleming who bore the responsibility and took the decisions. His position in the treasury much facilitated naval finance, and he had only to be absent for a short while before the admiralty got into difficulties with the holders of the purse-strings.[1] In the course of the 'twenties the office acquired a secretary and an accountant, and in 1631 it established a court-martial in Stockholm, under the charge of a port-admiral. As long as Gustav Adolf lived, however, the final step to a regular 'collegial' organization was not taken. This was probably merely accidental, for the suggestion had been under discussion for some years. At all events. the admiralty received its definitive establishment by the Form of Government of 1634, which constituted it as one of the *Collegia*, and provided that it should consist of the *riksamiral*, two admirals or councillors (preferably men with experience at sea), and four vice-admirals or ship's captains, of whom

[1] Fleming repeatedly pledged his own credit to ensure that the navy should get what it required, and by 1631 stood to lose not less than 50,000 *daler*: Munthe, *Svenska sjöhjältar*, V. 26.

the port-admiral or port-captain should always be one. Thus for the navy, as for other branches of the state's service, the trend of development under Gustav Adolf reached in the *Regeringsform* its logical conclusion.[1]

It remains to consider how far the Swedish navy in this era conformed to the developments in naval tactics which had been so important in the history of the western maritime powers during the previous half-century. The period between the opening and the close of the sixteenth century had seen a revolution in naval warfare. The old predominance of the galleys had been ended for good, at all events in Atlantic waters: Spinola's disastrous experience in the Channel in 1603 really marks the end of the attempt to resist the tide of progress. The old 'scientific' naval battles, with their geometrical military formations and their tactics based on the effort to ram the adversary, had vanished. Manœuvrability and precision were sacrificed to firepower and sea-endurance. The triumph of the sailing-ship, however, came gradually: as late as Lepanto the future seemed to lie with hybrids such as the galleass, which appeared to combine the advantages of both forms of propulsion. But the defeat of the Armada marked an epoch in naval history: henceforward sea-fights would be decided by weight of metal combined with sailing qualities. The hand-to-hand struggle on the enemy's deck, the concentration of fire upon the rigging, so as to disable, as a preliminary to boarding, were no longer essential to victory; and with these developments came a change in naval architecture of which the Elizabethan 'race-built' ships may be taken as the most advanced representatives.

These changes are mirrored but obscurely in Sweden's naval history. It comes perhaps as no surprise that Erik XIV, alone of the earlier Vasas, should be credited in some quarters with a grasp of the new principles; for Erik was, after all, a many-sided genius. The claim advanced for him is that he exploited the broadside and rejected boarding twenty years before the Armada; but it seems doubtful whether the claim can be fully substantiated.[2] It is true that he reduced the number of soldiers carried in his warships, so that the proportion was now 35-40 soldiers to 60-65 sailors[3]; but

[1] E. Wendt, *Amiralitetskollegiets historia*, I. 8-36; N. Edén, *Den svenska centralregeringens utveckling*, pp. 283-4, 289-95.

[2] Hornborg, *Kampen om Östersjön*, pp. 131-7.

[3] *Sv. Krig*, Supp. Vol. I. 7.

it is not clear that he ever laid it down as a principle that his commanders should not attempt to board: it was rather that he concentrated on devices for making boarding more difficult and dangerous for the enemy. He is credited, with more certainty, with introducing a battle tactic based on groups of three ships; but there is no doubt that this was a formation borrowed from the Danes. But if Erik was indeed a tactical innovator, the lessons that he taught were forgotten for half a century; and there is little trace of the new spirit in the navy of Karl IX.

Gustav Adolf's navy—like that, for instance, of Richelieu—comprised both sailing-ships and oared vessels. But unlike Richelieu's admiral Maillé-Brézé, Gustav Adolf's commanders never attempted to combine the two tactically.[1] The 'skerry fleet' was kept quite distinct from the high-seas fleet, and no attempt was made to treat the galleys as a sort of naval cavalry. In the Baltic, it is true, the galley's rôle as a battle-winner was not yet quite played out; but in Gustav Adolf's time it had fallen temporarily out of use in battle on the open sea.

Apart from such general observations as these, comment on Gustav Adolf's naval tactics is hampered by lack of material; for it is difficult to base conclusions on a single minor engagement, supplemented by orders which were not carried out, and a handful of sailing instructions. On the whole, however, the conclusion that emerges is that in this field the King was behind his contemporaries in England. Boarding had been ordered by Karl IX in the Kalmar war, and boarding was certainly the aim of the incompetent manœuvres of Captain Jon Planting in May 1627, when he vainly tried to intercept five Polish ships which were slipping back to Danzig from Kolberg. Stiernsköld, no doubt, sought to avoid being boarded by Dickman in November 1627, and Peter Blume was successful in preventing it off Wismar three years later [2]; but there is nothing to suggest that the Swedish commanders would have neglected a favourable opportunity themselves to board the enemy. The Armada tactics were essentially defensive tactics; they depended for their success—as the old English long-bow tactics did—upon the obstinate aggressiveness and stupidity of the foe. When the galleons ceased to try to board, and consequently ceased to be battered to bits at the waterline, naval warfare became what it has

[1] *cf.* La Bruyère, *Maillé-Brézé*, pp. 142, 221.
[2] *Arkiv*, I. 715, II. 130-1.

mainly continued to be ever since—an artillery duel conducted under severe handicaps. It is true that Gustav Adolf's fleet was better armed than Karl IX's; but it is no less true that it was not as well armed as Kristian IV's—which would hardly have been the case if Gustav Adolf had grasped the decisive importance of artillery. It is perhaps significant that in his time the proportion of soldiers to sailors aboard ship rose to 50:45.[1] There is no reason to suppose that his warships had abandoned those high 'castles' which had no other justification than purely military considerations. And indeed the instructions to Henrik Fleming in 1628 make it fairly clear that the main object of the gunners was to damage the enemy's rigging, so that having been thus immobilized he might be boarded: only if boarding was for one reason or another impossible was fire to be directed against his hull.[2] In view of this, it cannot be held to be of any significance that Swedish captains were urged to aim at close action, in order that their artillery might take full effect. The only example of a broadside during Gustav Adolf's naval wars seems to come from the Polish rather than the Swedish side.[3] And as late as 1644, in the great battle of Femern, Swedish tactics certainly aimed at boarding.[4] It would require the example of the first Dutch war to convert the leading naval powers to the new English method of 'plenty of room and a stand-off fight'.[5] On the other hand, it is claimed for Gustav Adolf that he was an innovator in that he divided his fleet into detachments of various sizes upon various occasions, to each of which was allotted a specific tactical rôle in the event of battle. But his claim to originality in this must be adjudged doubtful; and in any case such dispositions, had they been put to the test, would have been vitiated, in that age of primitive signals, by

[1] *Sv. Krig*, Supp. Vol. I. 19. Examples of the proportion of soldiers to sailors in the English navy are:

1558 (*Victory*) . . .	100 : 268
1603 (*Triumph*) . .	120 : 340
1624 (*Speedwell*) . .	0 : 100, plus 64 seaman-gunners:

Lewis, p. 292. Klas Fleming in 1633 protested against the excess of soldiers over sailors: Zettersten, I. 140.

[2] *Sv. Krig*, Supp. Vol. I. 266-7.

[3] At Oliva, the Polish *King David* 'machte die Stücke klar . . . gab dem Pellican die gantze seite vom Schiff, und schoss alle Stücke zugleich in ihn loss, dass man eigentlich hören konnte, wie die Schiffe knasterten, und die Leute darinnen lamentirten': Broomé, *En polsk relation*, p. 103.

[4] *Det svenska svärdet*, pp. 148-57.

[5] Robertson, *Evolution of Naval Armament*, p. 8; *cf. ibid.*, p. 21. The Dutch used a broadside, however, at Gibraltar in 1607: de Jonge, I. 208.

the impossibility of preventing a naval engagement from degenerating into a confused *mêlée*.

The importance of Gustav Adolf's reign in the history of the Swedish navy, therefore, is not to be sought in any tactical innovations, nor in any revolutionary progress in design. It lies rather in the establishment of a stronger and more efficient organization; in the recognition of the vital importance of the navy to the welfare of the country; in hard training provided by the maintenance of the blockade; and in the new spirit which was infused into all branches of the service. A decade after Gustav Adolf's death the navy was to wipe out the humiliations of 1611-13. That it was able to do so is to be ascribed very largely to the tonic effect of the personal interest of the monarch and to the remarkable exertions of Klas Fleming.

CHAPTER V

FROM THE LANDING AT PILLAU TO THE DANISH ALLIANCE

(i) *The Background to the Prussian Expedition*

By the close of the year 1625 the attempts which had been making since the autumn of 1624 to form a comprehensive Protestant league had palpably failed. No general Protestant front had emerged to support the rash enterprise of the King of Denmark; no effective resistance had been opposed to the armies of the League and the condottiering levies of Wallenstein. Sweden had gone her own road; Bethlen Gabor had been left out; and the Hague congress, which, it had been expected, would provide the occasion for a great rally of the friends of the evangelical cause, had been little better than a rump. Kristian IV, disillusioned even before he had begun serious operations, was already complaining that his allies and instigators were singularly unpunctual in the payment of promised subsidies.[1] The notion that the oppressed Protestants of Germany would make all haste to flock to the Danish standards had proved itself to be no more than a notion: John George of Saxony in January 1626 roughly rejected an invitation to join the grand alliance, and threatened to appear openly for the imperialists should the Lower Saxon Circle fail to come to a satisfactory understanding with the Emperor[2]; George of Brunswick-Lüneburg had already abandoned the Protestant side and was busy raising an army for Wallenstein, in the hope of imperial favour for his designs upon the territories of his cousins; while towards the close of 1625 the Hanseatic towns—which had neither forgotten nor forgiven King Kristian's dynastic

[1] Vosbergen, p. 171 *seqq.*; *Christian IVs Brev*, I. 472: *cf.* Hist. MSS. Comm., *Rutland*, I. 476 (Feb. 1626), where Henry Manners writes to Sir George Manners: 'It is likewise fearde the Kinge of Denmarke will presently, if he have not allredy, dissolve his army, for breach of covenants from hence both for men and money.'

[2] In December 1625 the Infanta was writing to Philip IV that John George was to mediate a peace between Spain and the Netherlands: *Correspondance de la Cour de l'Espagne sur les affaires des Pays-Bas au XVIIe siècle* (*ed.* H. Lonchay, J. Cuvelier, J. Lefèvre) [cited: Lonchay], II. 241.

and economic ambitions in north Germany—ostentatiously expressed their devotion to the *Reich*.[1]

In the west, the Dutch were heavily engaged with the armies of Spinola. The death of Maurice and the loss of Breda had made

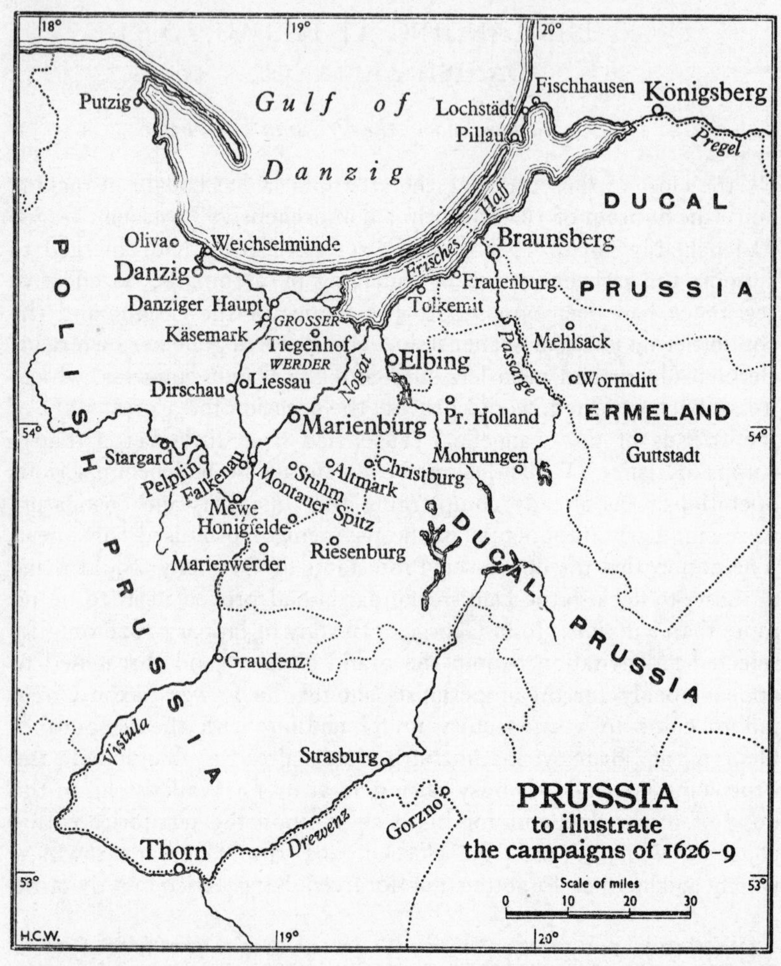

1625 a black year for them: for the present they could give no hope of military aid, and Kristian might count himself fortunate if they

[1] H. Hallwich, *Fünf Bücher Wallensteins Geschichte*, I. 275, 311, 360-3; Ranke, *Wallenstein*, p. 40.

paid their promised subsidies in good time. England was in little better case. Buckingham, in unwonted accord with the popular leaders in the Commons, had rushed into a Spanish war which he had neither the resources to sustain nor the talents to win. A sour and suspicious parliament would soon be clamouring for an explanation of the failure at Cadiz, and was unlikely to grant the King the means to meet his financial commitments to Denmark. The French marriage, which had been Buckingham's tit-for-tat to Olivares, was bringing its own crop of difficulties; and already Richelieu was complaining that the terms of the marriage-treaty were not being kept. There was increasing friction between London and Paris; and that was one reason, at least, why France had declined to become a party to the league of the Hague.

The quarrel about Henrietta Maria's personal devotions came most inopportunely for Richelieu, and aggravated a situation already sufficiently difficult. Throughout 1625 he had been confronted simultaneously with two major problems. On the one hand he had committed himself in Italy to a reoccupation of the Valtelline; while on the other he had been called upon to deal with a serious Huguenot revolt.[1] If France were to be of any assistance to the Protestants of Germany, she must free herself from at least one of these embarrassments. It was not possible for Richelieu to decide his line of action in advance: upon the seriousness of the threat from the Huguenots, upon the development of the military situation in Italy (and in Germany too) his policy must be dependent; his hand must be free to make concessions to either enemy, as the advantage of the moment might dictate. It was for that reason that he had evaded the offers of alliance against Spain, which England had pressed upon him early in the year.[2] France's interest was still peace; her chief need still was time to recover; she was still a power very much on the defensive. For a localized and limited objective such as the Valtelline, where the rewards of success were high and tempting, Richelieu was prepared to risk a war; but he was not anxious to commit himself to hostilities, or even to auxiliary action, in Germany. His important memorandum on policy, written in

[1] In December 1624/January 1625 Soubise carried out his celebrated *coup* against the French naval squadron at Blavet, and held the seas until his defeat by Montmorency in September: G. Hanotaux, *Richelieu*, III. 45-6, 53, 55. John Casimir wrote to Camerarius (17 May 1625): 'Ist zu erbarmen, dass Soubise *hoc rerum statu* hat moviren wollen': Moser, *Neues Patriotisches Archiv*, I. 49.

[2] Hanotaux, III. 32-3.

May 1625, sounded the note of caution over and over again [1]; the support which he half-promised for the Bellin plan was expressly stipulated to be secret, and to be financial only [2]; and by November he had come to a position in which he made even monetary aid contingent upon similar contributions by England, Sweden, Denmark and the Dutch, and upon their severally and collectively undertaking effective military action.[3] In these circumstances it was natural that England, who desperately needed French money to supplement her own unpaid subsidies to Denmark, should have tried to mediate between Louis XIII and his revolted Protestant subjects. But Charles's attempts at mediation, though well-intentioned, were of so tactless a nature as to increase the acrimony of Anglo-French relations.[4] Early in 1626 Richelieu did indeed make proposals to England whereby France should contribute to the efforts of the Hague allies by means of a diversionary campaign in Italy. It is not certain that the offer was seriously intended; but if so it was quickly wrecked by the crotchety intractability of Charles I, and no more was heard of it. Richelieu was still inclined to think that the league of the Hague should be supported, as the best means of preventing the subjection of the Germanies to Spain; but the memorandum which he submitted to the King in February 1626 shows how far he still was from a just appreciation of the factors controlling the politics of northern Europe, for that memorandum assumed an identity of interest and policy between Kristian IV and Gustav Adolf, and reckoned on the support of the Hanse towns for Denmark.[5] And the event was to show that Richelieu's policy of doling out an Elizabethan minimum of support to the Protestant interest was based on a miscalculation too.[6]

Before this became plain, however, the internal troubles of France had once more forced French foreign policy out of its course. In March 1626 Richelieu saw himself compelled to make a peace with Spain at Monçon, whereby he deserted his allies of the league of Avignon and in effect sacrificed his recent gains in the Valtelline; and for the next few months France made a show of appeasing her

[1] Avenel, II. 77-84.

[2] G. W. Vreede, *Inleiding tot eene geschiedenis der Nederlandsche Diplomatie* [cited: Vreede, *ND*], I. App. pp. 78-81.

[3] Avenel, II. 148-9.

[4] Gardiner, VI. 38-55; Hanotaux, III. 94-9.

[5] Avenel, II. 198 *seqq.*; Gardiner, VI. 87-90.

[6] G. Fagniez, *Richelieu et l'Allemagne*, p. 23.

old enemy.[1] As an effective support for the Protestant front Richelieu had always been uncertain; and he might now—at all events for the present—be left out of the reckoning altogether.

The original begetter of the evangelical league—the Elector George William of Brandenburg—had long since disowned his progeny. It was not that he had altered his opinions; it was rather that the changing circumstances of Germany were now dictating a more colourless line of conduct. The electorate's defences were in a desperate condition; the imperial armies were much nearer than they had been in the summer of 1624. In July 1625 the imperial emissary Karl Hannibal von Dohna so thoroughly frightened the Elector that he dropped all active participation in the plans of the league.[2] His spirits were in any case somewhat damped by Gustav Adolf's refusal to swallow his bait, and by the ostentatious disapproval of his political mentor, John George of Saxony. And hence he had sent no representative to the Hague congress.[3]

Yet at the very moment when George William was thus going about on the imperialist tack he was engaged in bringing to a conclusion a negotiation which was certainly not viewed with favour at Vienna, and which is perhaps to be considered as the sole remnant of an earlier and more courageous phase of his policy. This was a project for a marriage treaty and a political alliance with Bethlen Gabor, the Prince of Transylvania. Bethlen Gabor had been ruling Transylvania since 1613. He was a not unfamiliar type of ambitious barbarian, unscrupulous, ruthless, able after his fashion, with a veneer of civilization and a strong superficial piety.[4] His political programme, conditioned by his geographical position, was essentially simple: he aimed at playing off Vienna against Constantinople, and at acquiring additional territory for himself in the resulting confusion. He was thus driven to a policy of expedients, *volte-faces*, and nimble perfidies. He had, perhaps, a certain weakness for grandiose projects and large combinations; but this was offset by the cheerfulness with which he accepted a half-loaf, and by a personal attention to the *minutiae* of politics which was the result of an oriental love of

[1] W. Mommsen, *Kardinal Richelieu*, p. 31; Hanotaux, III. 56; H. Günter, *Die Habsburger Liga*, pp. 22-3.

[2] *Sv. Krig*, II. 239; N. Ahnlund, *Gustaf II Adolfs första preussiska fälttåg . . .* (*Hist. Tidskr.* (1918)), p. 77 [cited: Ahnlund, *HT* (1918)].

[3] Ritter, III. 311-12.

[4] He had read through his Bible twenty-six times: Ranke, *Wallenstein*, pp. 51-2. The record, however, seems to have been held by George of Baden-Durlach, with fifty-eight times: Ritter, III. 153.

intrigue for its own sake.[1] At all events, he pursued his tactics with considerable success for a decade and a half, and eventually died without Vienna's really having had leisure to settle the long score against him. The most recent of his border wars had taken place in 1623, when he had violated the peace of Nikolsburg (concluded in January 1622) and invaded Habsburg Hungary. The moment proved ill-chosen; for 1623 was the year of Stadtlohn, and Ferdinand proved stronger than he had expected. Bethlen had accordingly accepted an armistice, and converted it into a peace (on the Nikolsburg terms) in May 1624. And in token of contrition, or with a view to putting the screw on the Porte, he had intimated his willingness to accept a Habsburg princess as his consort. Vienna received the suggestion with incredulity, indignation and contempt [2]; but the news that it had been made caused a flutter at the court of the exiled King of Bohemia. Another wife must certainly be found for Bethlen if he were to be retained within the Protestant political system. It was now that Madeleine von Farensbach (sister to the egregious Wolmar, and a lady-in-waiting to the Queen of Bohemia) put forward the name of Catherine of Brandenburg, the sister of George William, and consequently the sister-in-law of Gustav Adolf.[3] The suggestion was a good one; for Bethlen had already shown some desire to come to a political understanding with Sweden.[4] He lost no time, therefore, in sending his physician upon a visit of reconnaissance to Berlin; and about the same time renewed his attempt to make contact with Gustav Adolf. Unluckily, his envoy, Dr. Quaedt, was arrested on Polish territory and cast into prison; for it was discovered that he was intriguing to place his master on the throne of Poland, and was already in touch with Leszczyński and other Polish malcontents.[5] Dr. Quaedt remained for some months incarcerate, and the attempt to concert measures with Gustav Adolf had for the moment to be postponed. The marriage negotiations with Brandenburg, on the other hand, made good progress. George William, in his timidity, felt it incumbent upon him to take the Emperor's opinion on the

[1] D. Angyal, *Gabriel Bethlen*, pp. 19-28, 55, 72-80; Ranke, *op. cit.*, pp. 51-2; C. Wibling, *Sveriges förhållande till Siebenbürgen*, pp. 4-6. Sir Thomas Roe once said of Bethlen that he was capable of tearing off his own shirt if he supposed that it suspected his intentions: Angyal, p. 72.

[2] Angyal, pp. 49-55.

[3] *ibid.*, pp. 58-9; Ahnlund, *Storhetstidens gryning*, pp. 100-1.

[4] Ahnlund, *Gustaf II Adolf och tyska kriget* (*HT* (1917)) [cited: Ahnlund, *HT* (1917)], p. 250 *note* 1.

[5] Angyal, pp. 69-70; Konopczyński, I. 269.

project; but Ferdinand coldly professed his indifference, and the Elector accordingly continued the negotiations with the active encouragement of Sweden and the Dutch.[1]

Meanwhile other enemies of Habsburg had been angling for Bethlen's alliance. In January 1625 Richelieu sent an envoy to him; in the summer Paul Strassburg left for Transylvania as the emissary of Frederick V; and soon afterwards Bethlen opened negotiations in Constantinople with the ambassadors of England, France and Venice.[2] In the autumn Dr. Quaedt, now enlarged, began to be active in the north: in October he interviewed Kristian IV, who in his turn despatched an envoy to Transylvania. In September Bethlen took the precaution of getting the Sultan's leave to ally with the western powers if he should wish to do so—despite the Porte's renewal of the treaty of Zsitva-Tőrők some months earlier.[3] In short, it appeared as though Bethlen was to be drawn into the Anglo-Danish coalition, and that at any moment his troops might take the familiar road to Vienna.

This development, however, did not occur. No firm arrangement was reached between Kristian and his backers, on the one hand, and Bethlen Gabor on the other. The Prince of Transylvania failed to become a member of the Hague alliance; and the only solid result of all this diplomatic activity was the offensive and defensive alliance between Bethlen and George William concluded in December 1625; and the marriage with Catherine, which at last took place in March 1626.

To Gustav Adolf, as he surveyed the European scene at the close of 1625, the situation did not appear to call for any immediate or radical revision of the decision he had taken six months earlier. He still considered that the terms which the western powers had offered to him were such as he could not safely accept. His objections to the strategy which they had proposed remained undiminished.[4] If a general Protestant league could have been created, with suitable guarantees of financial support and military effectiveness, he might have been prepared to embark upon a campaign in Germany, with the restoration of Frederick V to his dominions as one of its objectives. Failing such a league, he still held that the best contribution Sweden could make to the Protestant cause was to continue to hammer the

[1] *AOSB*, I. III. 6, 8, 66, 166-7; Vosbergen, pp. 151-63.
[2] Angyal, pp. 56-7; Ranke, p. 83.
[3] Angyal, pp. 59, 61; Ritter, III. 314.
[4] See Vol. I, pp. 244-5, above.

Polish armies, and to reserve any intervention in Germany for the eventuality that Kristian and his allies might come to grief. For the sake of Protestantism everywhere he must wish the Danes well in their undertaking; but if things went badly for them, he was ready to come to their assistance next summer. And he made little effort to disguise his feeling that things might not improbably go badly for them.[1] In the meantime, he went his own way without much caring about the jealousy of Kristian or the clumsy advances of Buckingham. By February 1626 he and Oxenstierna had made up their minds that, whatever the Hague allies might do, the war with Poland must go on; and some time in the course of the spring they took the decision to transfer the main theatre of operations to Prussia.[2]

The idea of a campaign in Prussia was not a new one. As early as July 1620 the *råd* had approved in principle a scheme for aiding Brandenburg against Poland by means of an expeditionary force to the Vistula[3]; and in March 1624 Hans George von Arnim had pressed upon Gustav Adolf a plan for seizing Putzig by a *coup de main*.[4] In the course of the discussions concerning a Protestant League, Gustav Adolf had frankly told Bellin that he preferred an advance through Cassubia upon Silesia to the suggested line of operations along the Oder[5]; and from Sweden's point of view a descent in the neighbourhood of Danzig offered much better advantages than a landing at Stettin or Kolberg or some other Pomeranian port. For Danzig was a pistol pointed at the heart of Sweden: the naval base from which, above all others, a Polish fleet might best launch an invasion.[6] Danzig itself, however, had already demonstrated its strength and its ability to defy Swedish threats; and if a move were to be made to Prussia some less intractable port of disembarkation would be necessary, at all events to begin with. Already in August 1625 Oxenstierna's thoughts had turned to Memel, in the first place as a base for a campaign to take Lithuania in flank and rear; and before the end of the year Gustav Adolf seems

[1] *AOSB*, I. III. 54-6, 226; Styffe, pp. 373, 461.
[2] Ahnlund, *Oxenstierna*, pp. 327-9; Ahnlund, *HT* (1918), p. 86.
[3] Ahnlund, *HT* (1917), p. 250.
[4] Cronholm, I. 431 *note* 1; G. Irmer, *Hans Georg von Arnim*, p. 38.
[5] *Sv. Krig*, II. 172-3.
[6] *AOSB*, I. III. 71. As early as 1617 Sticke, the Dutch agent in Berlin, had pointed out the great importance of Danzig to Sigismund for 'recuperatie der Croon Sweden, Dominatie *in Mari Balthico*, ende bevorderinge van syne geimagineerde septentrionalische Monarchia': G. W. Vreede, *Nederland en Zweden*, p. 136.

to have broached the subject with the Elector of Brandenburg.[1] George William naturally refused to entertain the suggestion that Memel should be put in Swedish hands[2]; but about the new year both Gustav Adolf and Oxenstierna were pressing it upon their correspondents at Berlin.[3] In a letter to von Götzen of 5 January 1626 Oxenstierna drew a horrific picture of the danger of the Elector, with the armies of Wallenstein 'diverting themselves in your front hall'; he asserted that it would be easy for Gustav Adolf to stand on the defensive in Livonia and concentrate on the rescue of Brandenburg, provided that he were given warning in good time, and facilities for landing at Stettin or Stralsund; and he suggested that George William might avoid the wrath of his Polish overlord if it were arranged that Memel should capitulate after a sham siege.[4] Already, therefore, even before the victory at Wallhof, the plan of campaign for 1626 was taking shape in the minds of the King and his chancellor; and on 30 December Gustav Adolf was ordering Oxenstierna to see to it that there should be a good supply of landing- and river-craft, and to arrange for the transfer of the Älvsborg squadron to the Baltic.[5]

For the moment, the question of a port of landing was allowed to drop, and Gustav Adolf turned his attention to the search for possible allies. There were three princes who might conveniently assist Sweden by a direct attack on Poland: George William of Brandenburg, the Tsar and Bethlen Gabor. Of these, George William was out of the question: he was miserably afraid of offending Poland, he was in no condition to fight, and his dearest wish was to be left in peace. Some attempt was made on the Tsar: an embassy was decided on as early as December 1625, and left for Moscow in the following February; but though it was well received, it had no

[1] *AOSB*, I. III. 136 *note*; Ahnlund, *Oxenstierna*, p. 313; Ahnlund, *HT* (1918), p. 79.

[2] *AOSB*, I. III. 292, II. I. 295.

[3] Or, alternatively, the handing over of a port in Pomerania: *AOSB*, I. III. 298.

[4] *AOSB*, I. III. 296: 'Caesar nunc tenet, eiecto d:no Administratore, archiepiscopatum Magdeburgensem, Halberstadensem et Hildesiensem; Saxonia Inferior vel paret vel atteritur armis Ligistrarum; Marchiae in propinquo est Walsteinius, et diversatur in vestibulo vestro; Pomeraniam Bavarus jam deglutiit et devorabit brevi (nisi se quis obiiciat serio) obtentu juris, munitus authoritate imperatoria et pellectus spe magnae praedae nec minori facilitate peragendi, si spectes proprias illius et amicorum vires ac vicinitatum Poloni. Et vos dubitatis, quo tandem consilia Ligistrarum ac Poloni evasura sint, haecque vos solos impune habituros creditis? Primine, postremi, an medii sitis quos communes hostes abripiant, perinde esse existimo'; and *cf.* a similar letter to Bellin, *AOSB*, I. III. 300.

[5] *ibid.*, II. I. 300; Ahnlund, *HT* (1918), p. 79.

success.[1] There remained Bethlen Gabor; and here the prospects might seem more hopeful. A convenient pretext for an embassy was provided by Bethlen's marriage[2]; and in March Filip Sadler was sent to Transylvania, ostensibly as the bearer of Gustav Adolf's congratulations to his new brother-in-law, really to propose an alliance and a joint campaign against Poland. But here too the outcome was disappointing. Bethlen Gabor, with his eye on the Polish crown, was not disposed to wage war on the Republic; though he was willing enough to attack the Habsburgs. He spoke hopefully of a general Protestant league; and (more practically) of collaborating with Sweden in an invasion of Silesia. The news of Bethlen's attitude did not reach Gustav Adolf until June, by which time his preparations for a campaign in Prussia were virtually complete; but even had he received the information earlier, it is not very likely that it would have induced him to modify his plans.

Sweden could therefore look forward to no direct aid in her Prussian war. There still remained, indeed, the interested friendship of the Hague allies, and the expected invitation to Gustav Adolf to join them. The offer came at last through Camerarius, who saw Gustav Adolf at Uppsala in March; but Camerarius was unprovided with full powers, and Gustav Adolf refused to listen to him.[3] In May he ordered Spens, his agent in England, to break off negotiations with Conway.[4] The Hague allies, in short, proved as incapable of deflecting him from his purpose in 1626 as in 1625.

Kristian IV, meanwhile, had not been able to balance the failure of his friends' diplomacy by any solid military successes. He missed a possible opportunity of defeating the armies of Tilly and Wallenstein in detail, and on 15 May suffered a severe setback when Wallenstein surprised Mansfeld's army at Dessau Bridge, and defeated and captured its commander, Knyphausen.[5] It is possible that only the imperialists' nervousness about an impending Swedish descent upon the coast of Pomerania prevented Wallenstein from

[1] *AOSB*, II. I. 291, I. III. 336; Ahnlund, *HT* (1918), p. 102.

[2] Styffe, p. 515; *AOSB*, I. I. 525-8; Angyal, p. 63; Wibling, pp. 13-15; T. Westrin, *Filip Sadlers beskickning till Siebenbürgen*, pp. 169-75.

[3] Hallenberg, V. 437-8; Ahnlund, *HT* (1918), p. 90. Buckingham projected another appeal to Gustav Adolf, with Anstruther (of all choices) as envoy; but Camerarius dissuaded him.

[4] *AOSB*, I. III. 315-17. Camerarius reported to Rusdorf that Gustav Adolf was wounded because Charles I preferred to support Kristian IV, and because he was prepared to squander money on Mansfeld rather than on Sweden: Söltl, *Der Religionskrieg in Deutschland*, III. 213.

[5] Hallwich, I. 352.

fully exploiting this victory [1]; but in any case a wedge had been driven between Kristian and his most important coadjutor, and Mansfeld found himself forced south-eastward to Silesia, with the dubious aid of Bethlen Gabor as the best hope of escaping from an awkward predicament. The armies of the Emperor and the League moved slowly northwards: Wallenstein occupied Magdeburg and Halberstadt, evicting the Hohenzollern administrator Christian William; the Dukes of Mecklenburg showed signs of political repentance; Bogislaw XIV of Pomerania, on the one hand urged by Brandenburg to defend his frontiers, and on the other pressed by the imperialists to accept their proffered aid, hovered dispiritedly between rival policies, and speculated gloomily as to what he should do if Gustav Adolf should drop anchor one morning in the Stettiner Haff.[2] In May the Emperor felt strong enough to suggest a *Deputationstag* to consider the possibility of peace; and John George of Saxony, who had latterly positively been encouraging imperialist recruiting in his territories, intimated that he would be willing to attend it.[3]

Thus in the early summer of 1626 the political and military situation in Germany was such as to give Gustav Adolf cause for anxiety; and that anxiety was not allayed by the news that filtered through of the efforts which were being made by Olivares to form a Habsburg league and of the alarming designs upon the Baltic which were bound up with the project. The idea of a Habsburg league seems to have originated in Madrid as early as the middle of 1624; and a year later Olivares was urging a general alliance to defend the Empire, in which might be included not only Bavaria, Poland and Lorraine, but also John George and other moderate Lutherans, and even Kristian IV. Such a league was designed, naturally enough, to serve the interests of Spain. It was hoped that there might be assistance provided against the Dutch; and Olivares spoke vaguely of blowing the ecclesiastical discontents of Scotland into a flame. In June 1625 invitations were issued to a congress to be held in Brussels, and instructions were drawn up for a special envoy who should explain the views of Spain to interested parties in Germany. The English attack on Cadiz, however, caused a postponement of this programme; and John George, under the influence of his court

[1] So Ahnlund, *Kring Gustav Adolf*, p. 165; but *cf*. Hallwich, I. 358-9.
[2] M. Bär, *Die Politik Pommerns während des dreissigjährigen Krieges*, pp. 2-5.
[3] Hallwich, I. 365, 418.

chaplain Hoë von Hoënegg, for once allowed feelings of confessional solidarity to prevail over devotion to the house of Habsburg, and declined to concern himself in the business. But in May 1626 the congress duly met in Brussels to consider Spain's proposals; and Protestant Europe (not least Gustav Adolf) awaited the issue with some degree of nervousness.[1]

The sessions at Brussels were protracted for some months; but at an early stage it became apparent that there was little hope of such a league as Olivares had imagined to himself. Bavaria declined to interest herself in Spain's war against the Dutch; and even Ferdinand refused to pledge himself to continue fighting until a port on the Baltic had been secured.[2] This last point had been especially urged by Spain, for it was an essential preliminary to the realization of a far-reaching plan for Habsburg predominance in the north. This plan was parallel to, though independent of, the scheme for a Habsburg league; and it was to attain considerable importance in the next few years. It was not by any means a new idea: indeed, its history went back to the previous century.[3] In part it was the outcome of Spain's struggle with the Dutch, whose vitally important Baltic trade Spain hoped to cripple; but it was also bound up with imperial pretensions to sovereignty over the Baltic Sea, which had been asserted from time to time quite independently of Spanish interests. In its most recent manifestation the idea had originated in Madrid, where Olivares and the imperial envoy Ludwig von Schwarzenberg had hatched a scheme (which looked back to a similar project of the 1590's) for a Spanish-German trading company, to be based on two ports in East Friesland, and to be designed to capture the carrying-trade of the Dutch. Spain had latterly been improving her mercantile defences by the foundation of an association of armed merchant-men (*almirantazgo*); and was now proposing to establish new *almirantazgos* for Belgium and the German coast. Vienna was favourably disposed, provided the goodwill of the Hanse were obtained. This might be expected to present no difficulty, in view of the pains taken by Ferdinand to humour their susceptibilities. In the early months of 1626 the plan began to take

[1] H. Günter, *Die Habsburger-Liga*, pp. 5-11, 12; Fagniez, *Richelieu et l'Allemagne*, pp. 20-1.

[2] Olivares also insisted that Maximilian hand back all the Lower Palatinate to Spain: Lonchay, II. 265.

[3] J. Paul, *Die nordische Politik der Habsburger vor dem dreissigjährigen Kriege*, *passim*; J. A. Fridericia, *Danmarks ydre politiske Historie* [cited: Fridericia, *YPH*], pp. 10-11; Hallenberg, I. 103-4; A. Szelągowski, pp. 43, 129-30.

shape, and an emissary was sent to Poland with large and specious promises (non-committally received by Sigismund) which were designed to enlist the master of the Vistula against the Dutch.[1]

Such, then, was the plan put forward by Olivares to the Brussels congress: a Habsburg economic *imperium* was to be established in central Europe with the aid of the Hanse; the trade of the Baltic was to be monopolized by the same combination; and a Habsburg-Hanseatic fleet was to wrest the mastery of the sea from the Protestant powers. Naturally an indispensable preliminary was a Baltic port in Habsburg hands. The refusal of Ferdinand to pledge himself not to lay down his arms until such a port was obtained, even more than the hostility of Bavaria to the whole scheme, was fatal to its chances at Brussels. Olivares, somewhat damped by its reception, and seduced by the hope of French friendship skilfully dangled before him by Richelieu, forbore to press the question. The cold fit was on him; and at the end of June he was offering Kristian IV something not far removed from benevolent mediation.[2] Nevertheless, Spain's designs on the Baltic remained a vague menace in the background; and they reinforced the alarm with which Gustav Adolf watched the approach of Wallenstein's armies to the southern borders of Mecklenburg and Pomerania. Sweden's economic interests forbade a quarrel with Spain, as long as a quarrel could be avoided; but if the Spanish fleet were joined to the Polish, if a Baltic port should become a Spanish naval base, then the pretensions of the Emperor to the sovereignty of the sea would have some teeth put in them, and a Polish invasion would draw a long stride nearer. Wallenstein and Tilly, after all, were land animals, and even if they lined the shores of Pomerania with their garrisons they must perforce give Sweden some months' or years' breathing-space before they could build a fleet to ferry their legions over; but a Spanish Armada in Stettin or Stralsund would mean danger imminent and deadly—not to the cause of Protestantism only but to the very existence of Sweden. It might still be that the efforts of Kristian IV and his broken-winded coalition might avail to hold the coastline on the landward side; and as long as Denmark was undefeated she might close the Baltic to the navy of Spain, as she

[1] Lonchay, II. 247, 250, 261; A. Gindely, *Die maritimen Pläne der Habsburger*, pp. 2-9; O. Schmitz, *Die maritime Politik der Habsburger*, pp. 12, 15, 23-31, 36; H. C. Messow, *Die Hansestädte und die Habsburgische Ostseepolitik*, pp. 11-14, 22-3; J. Corbett, *England in the Mediterranean*, I. 128, 131-2.

[2] Günter, pp. 13-20; *Christian IVs Breve*, II. 27.

already safeguarded it from the Dunkirk privateers [1]; but it is none the less true that the first emergence of the Habsburg maritime plans in the spring and summer of 1626 was an added reason to Gustav Adolf for transporting the main theatre of war from the Düna to the Vistula—to an area from which he might hope to control Danzig and be within striking distance of Pomerania.

For the opening of this new scene he needed, as he had so often pointed out, a secure port of disembarkation. And that port, it was already plain, must be provided by his brother-in-law of Brandenburg. As to which port it should be, the greatest uncertainty long prevailed on both sides of the Baltic; and Gustav Adolf's enemies spent the spring in anxious speculation. Sigismund III guessed Pillau; George William—naturally enough—feared for Memel, and he did what he could with his limited resources to strengthen the defences of both places. Ever since 1623 the Emperor had been fearing a Swedish expedition to Germany; and in the early months of 1626 Wallenstein was bombarded with reports of Gustav Adolf's appearance in Pomerania, or even in Mecklenburg.[2] In reality, the King was still hesitating. He was increasingly uneasy at the attitude of Brandenburg, for it was becoming more and more apparent that imperialist influences were getting the upper hand at Berlin. In May, Adam von Schwarzenberg returned to Brandenburg from his mission to Bethlen Gabor, and on his way home had an interview with Karl Hannibal von Dohna which seems to have been decisive for his future policy.[3] Schwarzenberg was already a Roman Catholic: he left the meeting with Dohna a convinced imperialist, believing that the only hope of safety for the electorate lay in a steady adherence to the house of Habsburg. The return of Schwarzenberg, coming hard on the heels of Mansfeld's disaster at Dessau, effectively cured George William of any lingering fancies of an evangelical coalition; and in a desperate effort to avert a Swedish landing in Prussia he had already despatched a special emissary, in the person of Samuel von Winterfeld, to persuade Gustav Adolf to betake himself elsewhere.

Winterfeld's embassy was the last hope of that party among the Elector's advisers which was hostile to Schwarzenberg and his

[1] G. W. Kernkamp, *De sleutels van de Sont*, pp. 12-13; *cf.* Gardiner, V. 32.

[2] Ahnlund, *HT* (1917), p. 265 *note* 2; Ahnlund, *HT* (1918), pp. 79, 91-2, 103-7; P. Simson, *Danzig und Gustaf Adolf*, p. 8; Hallwich, I. 340; W. Carlsson, *Gustav II Adolf och Stralsund*, p. 11.

[3] R. Koser, *Geschichte der brandenburgischen Politik*, pp. 409-10.

imperialist policy,[1] and which still hoped for cordial relations with Sweden. On this latter account it had the blessing of Kristian IV. The proposal which Winterfeld was commissioned to make was that Gustav Adolf should land his forces either at Wismar or (as Kristian preferred) at Kammin, and should strike inland either up the Oder or the Elbe, as circumstances might dictate. In such a case Kristian would hand over Mansfeld's mercenaries, together with the French subsidies needed to pay them. Unfortunately, while Winterfeld was still on the road to Sweden, Wallenstein's defeat of Mansfeld invalidated at least a part of this plan; and in any case, as Oxenstierna was later to remark, it was only too apparent that Winterfeld '*turbato potius, quam firmato consilio Brandenburgicae aulae ablegatus*'.[2] He was not even furnished with full powers; he travelled incognito and not as the official representative of the Elector; his instructions enjoined upon him extreme caution; and the suggestion of a landing at Wismar had never been submitted to Adolf Frederick of Mecklenburg for his approval.[3] The prospects of a successful outcome to the mission were small from the beginning.

Winterfeld found the Swedish court at Strängnäs, where Gustav Adolf was attending the interment of his mother; and he had scarcely arrived, and had not yet seen the King, when he fell seriously ill. Oxenstierna visited him on his sick-bed; but the chancellor's conversation was not encouraging to an invalid: he showed little interest in Winterfeld's mission, and rumbled darkly that things had come to that pass 'dass es biegen oder brechen musste'. And indeed, while the unhappy Winterfeld lay ill in his uncomfortable quarters, the final decision had been taken. At a meeting of the *råd* in Strängnäs on 19 May the King's resolution to transfer the war to Prussia was formally approved.[4] Ten days later, Winterfeld had his audience with the King in Stockholm. Gustav Adolf delivered a broadside on the folly and feebleness of Brandenburg's policy. He informed the envoy that though he had for the present no notion of making a campaign in Germany, he was resolved to move the seat of the Polish war as near to the German border as he could, so that he might be in a position to give assistance if it should be required. And since George William would not give him the facilities he needed at Memel, he must hand over Pillau to a Swedish

[1] Ahnlund, *HT* (1918), pp. 92-5; Irmer, pp. 50-1.
[2] *AOSB*, I. III. 325.
[3] Ahnlund, *HT* (1918), pp. 93-5.
[4] Styffe, p. 295; *Abraham Brahes tidebok*, p. 162.

garrison. It was in vain that Winterfeld pointed out that a campaign in Prussia would have little effect on Wallenstein and Tilly, whose main theatre of operations lay on the Elbe. It was in vain that he prophesied that the imperialist forces would press on to the conquest of Jutland and would at last make themselves masters of the Sound. Gustav Adolf professed himself sceptical; and in a second interview with Oxenstierna on 6 June Winterfeld was forced to listen to another comprehensive commination of his master's policy, or lack of policy.

There was, no doubt, something to be said for Winterfeld's contention. If Gustav Adolf were now to seize Pillau in defiance of the Elector, might he not equally well seize Wismar in defiance of the Duke? If he were seriously concerned for the Protestant cause, could it be denied that a campaign in Mecklenburg was more likely to aid that cause—and aid it at the point where aid was most needed—than a campaign in Prussia? To these arguments the King might reply that as long as he had a war with Sigismund in progress his hands were not free. That war could not be terminated by his unilateral action: it took two to make a peace. As long as there was no peace he could not allow his attention to be distracted: if he did so, he might one day find a Polish armada in the Swedish skerries. Despite the fight at Dessau Bridge, the forces of Kristian IV were still considerable, and his main army intact; and if the Hague allies did their duty, the position in Germany should at least be held firm: there was not at this time any reason to expect the collapse which in fact followed upon the disaster at Lutter. In the meantime, Gustav Adolf was taking the best means he could think of to disembarrass himself of the Polish complication by bringing the severest pressure to bear upon the economic life of the Republic; and he was still sufficiently close at hand to exercise some influence upon the course of military operations in Germany. For his purposes Pillau was probably the most suitable landing-place that could be selected. Danzig and Königsberg seemed too formidable; Memel was too far to the east; Kolberg and Libau were more excentric still, and their harbours were poor. Putzig, indeed, had a superb harbour: behind the Hela peninsula whole armadas might ride securely in the bight.[1] But Putzig was on the wrong side of the Vistula, and any advance southward from it would be threatened in flank from Danzig. If only George William, and his neighbours the

[1] A. Szelągowski, *Der Kampf um die Ostsee*, pp. 46-7.

Dukes of Pomerania and Mecklenburg, would cast aside hesitation and identify themselves wholeheartedly with Sweden, the Polish war might be ended expeditiously, the Habsburg-Polish plans for Baltic domination be stifled at birth, the advance of the imperialists be checked or slowed down, and the foundation be laid for a north German league strong enough to hold its own against the Emperor without the dangerous assistance of Denmark.

It was considerations such as these that determined the King's line of action in May 1626. Winterfeld's mission was viewed by both King and chancellor with intelligible suspicion. In spite of his protests, the Brandenburg envoy was kept in virtual isolation; he was not allowed to communicate with his government; he was not informed of Gustav Adolf's intended attack upon Pillau until the King had actually embarked; and he was not permitted to return home (where he met with a very cold reception) [1] until the invasion-fleet had put to sea. These extraordinary measures were only part of an elaborate system of security which was rigorously applied by the government in the weeks before the expedition started. A special pledge of secrecy was given by the members of the *råd* who attended at Strängnäs on 19 May; the *ståthållare* who forwarded transports to the great concentration outside Stockholm were kept in ignorance of their eventual destination; and southbound merchantmen were detained in Swedish harbours lest they carry news of military preparations to the enemy.[2] These precautions were remarkably successful, and the first certain intimation of Gustav Adolf's intentions which his adversaries received was his landing on Prussian soil.

By the end of May all was ready. A force of 14,000 men was embarked in a great fleet of 125 vessels [3]; on 23 June they weighed anchor; and before a blusterous but favourable breeze the whole armada steered its course for Prussia.

(ii) *The Campaign of 1626: Mewe*

And thus they came to a land rich in natural resources, and made richer still by the commercial activity which was borne upon its arterial rivers; a land well able to support an impecunious army;

[1] Ahnlund, *HT* (1918), pp. 107-8.
[2] Ahnlund, *Oxenstierna*, pp. 333-4; B. Steckzén, *Johan Banér*, p. 84.
[3] *Sv. Krig*, Supp. Vol. I. 161.

a land which might be milked of its riches by tolls and customs dues; a land easy of access to the invader; a land, finally, which after a century of peace was wholly unprepared to receive them.[1] As the foremost ships dropped anchor off the sandy spit on which the town of Pillau lay, they found to oppose them a few hundred troops inadequately protected by half-finished earthworks, and three armed merchantmen hired by the Elector from Danzig, upon whose captains lay the responsibility of ensuring that no vessel hostile to the King of Poland should penetrate into the shallow waters of the Frisches Haff. Neither the Elector nor his suzerain had taken any effective precautions: Königsberg itself was not as strong as could have been expected; while the other towns to the south of the Haff—Braunsberg, Frauenburg, Elbing, Marienburg—had garrisons inadequate to a protracted defence. Of a field-army in the neighbourhood there was as yet no trace, apart from a force of 1500 men recently despatched by Sigismund to Ermeland. The strategic surprise was complete; Prussia was for the moment virtually defenceless.[2]

Gustav Adolf wasted no time in preliminaries. The commandant at Pillau was given three hours in which to decide whether he would admit the Swedish fleet into the Haff, and soon afterwards a detachment of troops was put on shore to secure the town. The commander in Königsberg, arriving in haste to parley, was assailed with demands for a clear statement as to whether Brandenburg would be friend or foe; and though he succeeded in deferring a decision on the matter of Königsberg's neutrality, he was forced to agree to a Swedish occupation of Pillau. The entry to the Haff being thus secured, Gustav Adolf left the conduct of negotiations in the hands of Filip Sadler, installed three regiments in Pillau, and continued on his way. He had taken care to provide himself with shallow-draught vessels suitable for navigation in the Haff; and in these he sailed straight to the mouth of the Passarge. His plan was to effect a landing in the neighbourhood of Braunsberg, capture that city and move with all speed upon the Vistula. Once astride the Vistula, he would build up a defensive base along the southern shore of the Haff covering the mouths of the Passarge and the Nogat, and thus effectually cut off the grain-growing areas of Poland from their

[1] I. Hoppe, *Geschichte des ersten schwedisch-polnischen Krieges in Preussen*, p. 49.

[2] For details of military operations, see *Sv. Krig*, II.; G. Petri, *Kungl. första Livgrenadjärregementets historia*, II.; C. Bennedich, *Ur det gamla Gardets öden*.

natural export-routes. His position at Pillau would enable him to block the exit from the Pregel. His severance of the Vistula route would inflict heavy damage on his old adversary Danzig. Thus his strategy was based not only on military considerations but on a conscious determination to avail himself of economic weapons.[1]

The absence of all serious resistance made the execution of this plan a matter of little difficulty. The landing near the Passarge took place without molestation on 29 June; on 30 June Braunsberg was taken, after a short defence. Following Tilly's evil precedent at Heidelberg, the King ordered the library of the Jesuit seminary to be sent home to Sweden: it was the first of a long succession of such consignments. Thus the centre of *émigré* conspiracy, the training school of the Counter-Reformation, passed into Gustav Adolf's hands; and a strong garrison of 550 men gave some security that it should not easily escape from them. From Braunsberg detachments were sent out to the south, to guard the left flank of the army from any Polish forces which might be lodged in the upper valley of the Passarge. No such forces were encountered; but the towns of Mehlsack and Guttstadt were laid under forced contribution, and Wormditt was occupied as a bastion on that side. Gustav Adolf now moved to Frauenburg, which he occupied without opposition on 1 July[2]; and thence on the same day to Tolkemit. His next objective was Elbing. Elbing was a city of some importance, and as a trading centre was second only to its rival Danzig. Here the Eastland Company had established their factory,[3] and here Gustav Adolf intended to fix the administrative and military centre of his Prussian conquests. Elbing had made some half-hearted gestures of self-defence; but the electoral commandant, Fabian Dohna, had no intention of offering serious resistance, and the persuasions of the King were sufficient to convert the vacillating burghers.[4] On 5 July Elbing surrendered and received a garrison whose strength (1300 men) indicated the importance Gustav Adolf attached to its retention.

[1] *AOSB*, II. 1. 307 *seqq.* for Gustav Adolf's account of the opening of the campaign.

[2] While the Swedes were holding a thanksgiving service in the cathedral, most of the town was destroyed by enemy arson: *Per Brahes tänkebok*, p. 10.

[3] They later gave Gustav Adolf a substantial loan: H. Almquist, *Svenska folkets historia*, p. 452. For the Eastland Company in Elbing, see A. Szelągowski and N. S. B. Gras, *The Eastland Company in Prussia*, *passim.*

[4] *Sv. Krig*, II. 267-8; Ahnlund, *HT* (1918), p. 108 *note* 2; F. Weber, *Dietrich von Falkenberg*, pp. 25-7.

A Swedish governor, Bengt Oxenstierna, was installed [1]; and before many weeks had passed Elbing had taken an oath to hold Gustav Adolf and his heirs as established by the Norrköping succession-pact for their rightful Kings and lords, and to be true and faithful subjects of the Swedish crown.[2] They were to prove less pliable in matters ecclesiastical, it is true [3]; but they seemed by their action to have reconciled themselves to permanent incorporation into the Swedish realm. If Elbing were thus to go the way of Riga and Reval, was Prussia, perhaps, to follow Livonia and Estonia and become an integral part of the monarchy? It certainly looked like it.

These developments, however, lay some distance ahead; the immediate problem after the taking of Elbing was whether to strike without delay directly at Danzig, or whether to prepare the way for a siege by cutting her communications with the interior. It seems possible that if Gustav Adolf had had a larger force at his disposal he could now have carried Danzig by assault; but he still cherished the hope of coming to terms with the city, and in any case the delay in the arrival of reinforcements, the need to protect his line of communications with Pillau, and the numerous detachments from the main body for purposes of garrisoning or of reconnaissance, had left him with a field-army too small for a direct attack. He turned without delay, therefore, to the other alternative. Marienburg, the old headquarters of the Grand-Master of the Teutonic Knights, was so weakly garrisoned that its formidable defences were useless: it fell on 8 July. Gustav Adolf had now straddled the Nogat and reached the Vistula. In order to close the river to traffic a bridge-head on the western bank was required. The spot selected was the little town of Dirschau, which was occupied on 17 July; and here the King built a bridge of boats across the river, while two detachments were thrown out to establish advanced positions at Mewe and Stargard.

With the establishment of a lodgment on the further shore of the Vistula Gustav Adolf had completed the strategic design with which he had begun the campaign. He commanded all the river-routes, from the Pregel to the Vistula: not a boat could enter the Frisches Haff without his leave, nor a quarter of grain be exported from Poland by the usual channels. For the moment the King's im-

[1] S. Loenbom, *Anecdoter*, II. 20. For Bengt Oxenstierna ('Traveller-Bengt'), see S. Hedin, *Resare-Bengt*, *passim*, and p. 480.

[2] Hoppe, p. 91.

[3] *ibid.*, p. 136.

mediate concern must be the consolidation of what he had won and the pressing on of defence works at Pillau, Braunsberg and Elbing, and above all at the critical point at Danziger Haupt, where in the angle between two arms of the Vistula a strong fortified position was under construction, as a muzzle to Danzig.[1] More than this he could not undertake, until the laggard reinforcements should arrive. In the meantime, there were plenty of problems of diplomacy to engage his attention.

George William of Brandenburg had received the news of the landing with deep indignation. If this, he exclaimed bitterly, was what he had to expect from his friends, what interest could he have in supporting the common cause? Better follow Schwarzenberg's advice and turn imperialist: as long as the Emperor remained Emperor, George William and his son might then at least be sure of the electorate.[2] But it was of the essence of the Elector's unhappy position that his support would not make very much difference to either side: whether Brandenburg were friend or foe, the Swedish armies would violate the neutrality of Prussia, as the imperialists violated the neutrality of the Mark. Gustav Adolf, indeed, would have preferred to remain on good terms with his brother-in-law: when he found that the customs revenue at Pillau belonged to the Elector, and not (as he had supposed) to the Polish crown, he ordered his agent to refrain from appropriating it.[3] But if George William should turn surly, the ties of relationship would not prevent Gustav Adolf from dealing ruthlessly with him. This became obvious at a very early stage from his treatment of the Elector's Prussian subjects. The Prussians, and especially the citizens of Königsberg, found themselves in an intolerable position: the Elector was far away in the Mark; the Swedes were knocking imperiously at their door, demanding a declaration of neutrality which might, if they gave it, compromise them with their sovereign, and compromise their sovereign with his feudal overlord the King of Poland. They did their very best to play for time—at Pillau first, then at Königsberg, and finally at Tolkemit, where their delegates had a stormy two-hours' interview with Gustav Adolf on 3 July. Their objections were swept aside on a flood of pungent oratory. Let them join with Sweden, and the King would defend them

[1] Orders for works at Pillau in *AOSB*, II. I. 313.
[2] G. Droysen, *Gustav Adolf*, I. 282.
[3] E. Wendt, *Det svenska licentväsendet i Preussen*, pp. 36-7.

against Poland or the Devil himself. If they refused, they must expect to be harried from the fortresses he proposed to build in Elbing and Pillau, and at the last they would see the Swedish warships in their harbour, and would answer plainly to his question [1]: '*Vinco aut vincor, vos maculabimini*'. After an interval to digest this, the delegates met the King again on 11 July at Liessau, and virtually agreed to his demands: the duchy declared itself neutral pending instructions from George William, while Königsberg declared itself neutral without any reservation. And with that, for the moment, Gustav Adolf professed himself content.[2]

He would have been much better pleased if he could have obtained such a declaration from Danzig. Gustav Adolf never seems to have had much confidence in his ability to capture Danzig as he had captured Riga, and from the opening of the campaign he seems to have aimed rather at neutralizing the city. He did not choose his methods with much tact. He began, indeed, on 27 June, with an offer which was not unreasonable: if Danzig would provide Sweden with supplies at moderate rates, her neutrality should be respected, her trade left free, her citizens protected from plunder and her roadstead exempt from tolls. But on the very next day, long before any reply to this offer could be made, he issued a rasping proclamation in which he accused Danzig of un-neutral conduct, announced his intention of levying toll forthwith on ships putting into the port, and forbade the payment of toll to the agents either of Danzig or of Sigismund. On 3 July thirteen Swedish warships under Karl Karlsson Gyllenhielm took up their stations in the roadstead. Opinion in Danzig was divided as to the best course to pursue, for the town was ill-prepared for a siege, and the garrison (apart from the burgher militia) did not much exceed 1000. The lower orders were bellicose; the richer classes more cautious. Danzig therefore delayed her answer, in hopes of news of the approach of a Polish army. At length, however, on 16 July, the burghers made an offer which in substance gave Gustav Adolf all he could reasonably expect. Danzig would pledge herself to refrain from military or naval preparations against Sweden, to disarm any Polish ships in the port, to send away any Polish artillery and to supply both sides with provisions at reasonable rates. In return, she asked only for a guarantee against hostile actions and the removal of the blockading fleet. Gustav

[1] Hoppe, pp. 59-68; Droysen, I. 280; Paul, II. 57.
[2] Hoppe, p. 80.

Adolf would have done well to accept these terms. Instead, he haggled; put forward a demand for the disbandment of all troops in the town; insisted on acceptance of these terms within eight days. Unluckily for him, there arrived in Danzig on 17 July the Castellan of Kulm, bringing good news of Sigismund's preparations, and exhortations to stand fast. The Swedish troops had already angered the Danzigers by unauthorized acts of plunder; the Swedish blockade was already drawn tight; the Swedish capture of Putzig on 19 July threatened Danzig from the north-west, while the fortifications at Danziger Haupt menaced the city from the east. The Danzigers' blood was up. On 2 August it was their turn to deliver an ultimatum; on 4 August Gustav Adolf formally declared war on the burghers.[1] It was a deplorable error. The King's hectoring style of negotiation had driven him to a breach which he had not really desired and which he might probably have avoided; and the result was really a serious diplomatic defeat: in later years Axel Oxenstierna was wont to say that it was the resistance of Danzig which had interposed the greatest hindrance to the full realization of the King's plans in Prussia.[2] And hostilities against Danzig did not merely cramp his military operations up the Vistula: they compromised the position at sea; and they led inevitably to unpleasantness with the maritime powers of the west.

To the champions of the Protestant cause, Gustav Adolf's landing at Pillau had come as an unpleasant shock. At a moment when Kristian IV's campaign in Germany was showing little promise of success, the only other power to whom they could turn for solid aid was once more committed to excentric operations. The Dukes of Mecklenberg, in a sudden panic at the approach of Wallenstein, had thought better of their earlier determination, and in July had actually offered Gustav Adolf a guaranteed landing-place at Wismar. It was too late, at all events for this year; and the King could only urge in reply, as he had urged so often before, the formation of a north-German league independent of Denmark: 'but it seems [he added sourly] *me surdis fabulum narrare*'.[3]

Kristian IV was no less concerned at the new development; for he believed (correctly, as it turned out) that it would make any collaboration between Gustav Adolf and Bethlen Gabor very difficult.

[1] Simson, pp. 9-17; Weber, p. 29. Oxenstierna continued to hope for a peaceful settlement: see his letter of 31 August, *AOSB*, I. III. 351.

[2] Ahnlund, *Weichselmynningen i svensk historia*, p. 10.

[3] Styffe, pp. 464-5; *Sv. Krig*, II. 131.

On 25 July he sent Jørgen Sefeldt on a mission to Gustav Adolf, with a proposal that part of the Swedish forces should be diverted to a joint advance upon Franconia and Bavaria. It was a proposal which the existing military situation made it difficult, if not impossible, to accept. But in order to clarify the situation and provide a touchstone of Kristian's co-operative zeal, Gustav Adolf made a counter-proposal. Would Kristian conclude a defensive and offensive alliance, to be restricted to the two of them alone, and to be directed against 'the whole Popish League', including Poland?[1] It immediately became apparent that he would not. Not even military disaster could make such terms palatable to him.

Military disaster had, indeed, already overtaken him. On 17 August the imperialist armies overwhelmed the Danes in the bloody battle of Lutter[2]; and immediately the whole position in Germany, which hitherto had seemed relatively stable, became fluid once more. By the end of the month the defections from the Protestant league had begun, led by Frederick Ulric of Brunswick-Wolfenbüttel (Gustav Adolf's brother-in-law), and followed shortly by the Gottorp Dukes[3]; and by mid-September Camerarius was writing to Rusdorf that it was all over with them in Germany.[4] In England there was voluble consternation; in France, Richelieu met the situation with a feeble diplomatic offensive upon Bavaria.[5] The Dutch, whose mercantile susceptibilities had been so outraged by the Swedish blockade of Danzig that they had been ready to cheer a rumour of a Polish victory, recovered consciousness of their evangelical mission and hastily despatched an envoy to Copenhagen to offer assistance.[6]

In the general collapse of the Protestant front, the only hope now appeared to be in Prussia and in Transylvania, with Bethlen Gabor and Gustav Adolf; and it became more than ever a matter of common concern that some sort of co-operation between them

[1] Styffe, pp. 286-90; *Christian IVs Breve*, II. 33-40; Ahnlund, *HT* (1918), p. 111.

[2] The Danes lost 8000 dead, and all their guns: Hallwich, I. 545; see P. Engelstoft, *Christian IVs Tidsalder*, pp. 253-4, for the causes of the disaster.

[3] Hallenberg, IV. 894-5; Hallwich, I. 615; Ritter, III. 338.

[4] 'Was aber soll ich von Deutschland sagen? Es ist dahin—dahin!': Söltl, *Der Religionskrieg in Deutschland*, III. 216. Camerarius put the main blame on England, and remarked that he had not expected so soon to regret James I: *ibid.*, 215.

[5] Gardiner, V. 140; J. Baur, *Philipp von Sötern*, I. 127; Fagniez, *Le Père Joseph et Richelieu*, I. 267-71.

[6] Schybergson, *Sveriges och Hollands diplomatiska förbindelser*, pp. lxxvi-lxxvii.

should be arranged. Gustav Adolf for his part was not unwilling. He had striven hard to convince the Transylvanian envoy of the superior merits of a campaign in Prussia as a prelude to a combined assault on the hereditary dominions of the Habsburgs; but Bethlen remained sceptical, and was disposed to resent Gustav Adolf's presence in Poland. The remnants of Mansfeld's army were making their way south-eastward, and eventually reached the Transylvanian border at the end of August; and it was with them, rather than with Gustav Adolf, that Bethlen intended to act. Early in August he declared war on Ferdinand.[1] But Mansfeld proved a broken reed; the news of Lutter made it plain to Bethlen that this time his luck was out; and though his armies gave a good account of themselves against Wallenstein, he found it expedient to conclude an armistice on 1 October. Two months later he converted it into a peace, on the old Nikolsburg terms.[2]

As for Gustav Adolf, he sat still in his camp at Dirschau throughout the month of August, waiting for reinforcements from Livonia. He was still willing to entertain the notion of a diversionary campaign against Silesia, if only the necessary preconditions were fulfilled. At the capture of Marienburg there had fallen into his hands a Russian named Rubtsov, and Gustav Adolf had sent him to the Tsar, in the hope of inducing a Muscovite attack on Poland which would give the Swedish forces leisure for a sally to the south-west. True, the recalcitrance of Danzig now made a Silesian diversion much more risky than it would have been had Danzig remained neutral; but if England or Holland would provide him with 6000 horse and 50,000 *rdr.*, he would engage to traverse the intervening country without difficulty. He put this proposition to the Dutch; and the Dutch dealt with it by referring it to Charles I—a line of action which, in Charles's then notorious financial straits, could only be construed as an uncivil refusal. And with that the oft-reiterated project for a Silesian diversion received its interment, at least for the present.[3]

The tidings of the landing at Pillau reached Warsaw on 1 July and caused the greatest excitement. The King and his advisers were certainly not unprepared for the news; but the Polish nobility, which had hitherto shown little interest in Sigismund's contest with

[1] Incited, it seems, by Camerarius: F. H. Schubert, *Ludwig Camerarius*, p. 363.

[2] Angyal, pp. 64-7; Hallwich, I. 559-65, 608-9; Wibling, pp. 17-19.

[3] Ahnlund, *HT* (1918), pp. 108-10, 114-15.

Gustav Adolf, were shocked into a realization of the fact that the welfare of the dynasty might possibly be identical with that of the Republic. For the first time the war came forcibly home to them. Upon the free export of their corn depended their economic existence, and the threat to their pockets served to remind them that their King was not the only enemy of the true patriot, nor *aurea libertas* merely an affair of internal politics. Whether they liked it or not, the war had become their concern; and they accordingly made fewer difficulties about providing some sort of an army, even though they were content for the present to allow Sigismund the privilege of paying for it out of his private resources.

The most pressing military necessity, from the Polish point of view, was to come to the assistance of Danzig; to encourage the burghers in their fidelity; and to draw off Gustav Adolf's forces by a move down the Vistula. On 1 August, therefore, Sigismund left Warsaw with a force of some 5000 men and began to concentrate at Graudenz. By the end of August he had collected an army of close on 8000 foot and 4000 cavalry; and although no one on the Polish side (Sigismund not excepted) appeared very ambitious to command this force, it was so much more numerous than the army of Gustav Adolf at Dirschau that the opportunity could not be neglected. By 9 September the Poles had moved northward, and were investing, with the whole of their forces, the little town of Mewe, which formed the most southerly outpost of the Swedish position, and was held by some 140 men under the command of the Scottish Captain Kinnemond. The defences of Mewe were even weaker than the garrison, and it seemed impossible that the town should hold out for long. But unfortunately for Sigismund, his artillery was relying upon second-hand cannon-balls, and these proved too big for the barrels of his guns [1]; so that for fourteen days he lay outside Mewe without making any perceptible impression upon it.[2]

To find the Polish army in the open field and destroy it there—this was the natural conclusion of Gustav Adolf's movements since his landing; and even had he not felt the obligation to rescue Kinnemond he would probably have seized the opportunity for a battle. His army was, indeed, much inferior in numbers to Sigismund's: he had some 6300 foot and only 1200 cavalry. Nevertheless, he moved up the river to Falkenau; and here he threw a bridge

[1] T. Korzon, *Dzieje wojen i wojskowosci w Polsce*, II. 238.

[2] For the strategic object of Sigismund's siege of Mewe, see Simson, p. 21.

across the Vistula to the Grosser Werder. Sending Banér across it, he possessed himself of the strong defensive position in the angle formed by the divergence of the Vistula and the Nogat; and here, at the Montauer Spitz, he was later to build up one of the key-points in the defensive system which guarded the delta. With a view to obtaining more accurate information about the strength of the enemy he now determined on a reconnaissance in force. Leaving the bulk of his force in camp at Falkenau, he set out on 12 September with 2000 men to probe the Polish position. The result was the first battle of Mewe. If the Poles had shown more skill and resolution, this might easily have been a serious Swedish disaster. For Gustav Adolf and his small force soon found themselves penned with their backs to the Vistula; with their only line of retreat—to their right flank—in danger of being cut; and with the Polish army in vastly superior force in a position which Gustav Adolf was too weak to assail, commanding the low river-meadows in which the Swedish force was manœuvring. With a little determination Sigismund might probably have captured Gustav Adolf on this occasion. As it was, the steadiness of the Swedes, their skill in manœuvre and their speed combined to save the day, and Gustav Adolf got back to his camp with a good idea of the task that confronted him.

In the course of the following week the King received substantial reinforcements,[1] which brought his numbers up to some 10,000 foot; and with these on 19 September he moved to the relief of Mewe. His weakness in cavalry, and the still-surviving memories of Kirkholm, led him to avoid any type of engagement which would give the Poles a chance to exploit their superiority in that arm; and the action which developed on 21 September resolved itself into an attempt to storm the heights occupied by the Poles. The assault was made with a picked force of some 3000 foot, supported by artillery, who fought their way up parallel ravines to the plateau overlooking the river and maintained themselves there in spite of strenuous efforts to dislodge them. The bulk of the forces on either side was not engaged at all. Nevertheless, this limited action and partial success was pregnant with future triumph, for it was won by the intimate combination of musketeers, pikemen and gunners, by the spirit of initiative shown by individual units and their commanders, and by the superior morale of the Swedish forces. And though no general battle developed, the engagement attained its

[1] *AOSB*, I. III. 354.

object. Sigismund drew off westward to Pelplin, abandoning the siege of Mewe, and Gustav Adolf entered the town in triumph.[1]

The victory at Mewe might reasonably have been expected to inaugurate a vigorous offensive against the main Polish army. There was everything to be said for attempting a decisive stroke immediately, before Sigismund should be reinforced by the troops which Koniecpolski was gathering together in the neighbourhood of Thorn. For some reason that is not apparent, the opportunity was missed. No attempt was made to follow up the victory. Gustav Adolf retired tamely to his camp at Falkenau, where he presently fell ill; and early in October he crossed over into the Grosser Werder by his new bridge and prepared to go into winter quarters. Johan Banér was put in command of the crucial position at Danziger Haupt; Axel Oxenstierna was established in Elbing as governor-general of the occupied territory with very extensive powers [2]; and Gustav Adolf hastened back to Stockholm. From the Swedish point of view, the campaign of 1626 was over; and if it finished somewhat lamely, it had undeniably brought great advantages. There could be no doubt that no previous campaign had inflicted such material damage on Poland [3]; and never before had the superiority of the Swedish soldier been so apparent. A broad base for future operations had been obtained, and defensive works had already made it passably secure. Oxenstierna entertained the highest hopes of the effect upon Poland of the stoppage of the corn-trade: the Poles (to use his own expression) were 'in the bag' [4]; with only a little more effort Sweden would be able to impose a glorious peace; and they might all look forward soon to sitting, 'if not under a fig-tree, at least under our lindens and oaks, and minding our affairs in peace'.[5] It seemed that Gustav Adolf might safely go home in the expectation of a quiet winter.

(iii) *Winter Quarters, 1626-27*

But the winter proved anything but quiet. Koniecpolski, the new Polish commander, was a man of giant physique, immense energy

[1] For the battles of Mewe, see *AOSB*, I. III. 353-4; Loenbom, I. 48 *seqq.*; *Sv. Krig*, II. 280-96; Petri, II. 65-7; Bennedich, pp. 64-6.
[2] Ahnlund, *Oxenstierna*, p. 415.
[3] *AOSB*, I. III. 354.
[4] 'Då haffue vij nu fått fienden så i säcken att han moste på sijdstone tiggia freden': *AOSB*, I. III. 384.
[5] *AOSB*, I. III. 385.

and considerable military talent, and he had no intention of allowing Banér and Oxenstierna to take their ease in winter quarters unmolested. From November to April he kept up a continuous hammering at the Swedish positions. Oxenstierna's instructions had ordered him to concentrate his troops in quarters, to take no undue risk merely in order to defend the Grosser Werder, but to put strong garrisons in the towns, and at all costs to hold Pillau, Dirschau, Elbing and Danziger Haupt.[1] Even this, however, proved unexpectedly difficult. A surprise attack was made on Pillau in November. An attempt was made to cut off Elbing's supplies in March. The smaller towns, such as Mehlsack and Christburg, were endangered by the Polish sympathies of their inhabitants. Over the whole of the central area occupied by the Swedes the swift-moving Polish cavalry carried out destructive raids, so that there was scarcely a village in the Grosser Werder which was not reduced to ashes. Wormditt, the Swedish bastion on the upper Passarge, was lost in November, after only three days' siege; and far to the west Putzig, which had been captured in the previous July, was closely invested, and eventually capitulated after a heroic defence towards the end of March 1627.[2] No less serious was the loss of control of the sea. Until the end of October Danzig had been blockaded both by sea and by land; but with the approach of winter the Swedish squadron in the roads was withdrawn. Its place was immediately taken by Danziger and Polish privateers, who swept the Baltic unchallenged until the belated melting of the coastal ice permitted the Swedish fleet to put to sea again in the following spring.[3] Thus for nearly six months Gustav Adolf's forces in Prussia were cut off from supplies and reinforcements. And this was the more serious because the severity of the winter, the systematic devastations of the enemy and the crampedness of the quarters played havoc with the efficiency of the Swedish army. In January 1627 their spirit was still said to be high [4]; but in the months that followed they suffered severely from epidemics in their inadequate and insanitary cantonments; and there was constant difficulty about paying the troops.[5] The final misfortune of the winter came in 1627, when a detachment of

[1] *AOSB*, II. I. 316 *seqq.*
[2] For these episodes, see *AOSB*, II. IX. 402, I. III. 468, II. IX. 41, 64, II. IX. 53, I. III. 432, 513, II. IX. 74.
[3] *Sv. Krig*, Supp. Vol. I. 167-70.
[4] A. Korhonen, *Om finska rytteriet under Gustaf II Adolf*, pp. 247-8.
[5] *AOSB*, I. III. 400, II. IX. 85.

mercenaries, recruited in north Germany to reinforce the army of Prussia, was compelled by Koniecpolski to capitulate at Hammerstein, after a bold attempt to make its way to Oxenstierna overland.[1]

If the military situation during the winter months was gloomy, the diplomatic picture was not much brighter. In the latter half of October the usual negotiations for a truce had been opened; and, as usual, had stuck fast almost immediately. The Poles were prepared to permit Gustav Adolf to retain Sweden for his lifetime, provided that the reversion should fall to Sigismund and his heirs, and that in the meantime Sweden should pay an annual tribute; while the Swedes favoured a truce for Sigismund's lifetime on a basis of *uti possidetis*, or failing that a truce for a term of years.[2] But the attitude of each side was stiff: the Poles, more than ever before, had made Sigismund's cause their own; while the Swedes were already beginning to frame their terms with a view not only to the settlement of the dynastic dispute but also to the general international situation. This is apparent from the debate in the *riksråd* on 23 November 1626. A discussion then took place upon the question whether it was expedient to purchase a real peace (as against a mere truce) by the retrocession of the conquered areas in Prussia. No decision was recorded, but the arguments against the suggestion are interesting. It was urged 'that H.M. feared that it might be *pax non pax*, on the pattern of *Hispani contra Belgium* and *Galli contra Neapolin*', since it was well known that Papists kept faith only so long as it suited them; that the conquered areas were too useful to Sweden, and too dangerous in enemy hands, to be surrendered; that to subject Protestants once again to the Popish yoke would cause 'an aching conscience'; that a truce was preferable to a peace, since it might be had without cessions of territory; that any cessions would encourage Sweden's jealous neighbours; that '*gentes generosae* are not wont to restore so easily *juste occupata*'; and, finally, that 'whereas Sweden is by the acquisition of these lands mightily enlarged, she would thereby [*i.e.* by handing them back] be constricted again and lose her revenue and reputation'.[3] These arguments make

[1] *AOSB*, I. III. 528-31; *Sv. Krig*, II. 305-9; Bär, pp. 13-15; Rudel, *Die Lage Pommerns vom Beginn des dreissigjährigen Krieges bis zum Eintreffen Gustav Adolfs*, p. 72 *seqq*.

[2] For these negotiations, see, *e.g.*, *AOSB*, I. III. 370, 373, 379, II. I. 325, II. VIII. 9, II. IX. 56.

[3] *RRP*, I. 35-6.

it plain that a new chapter in Swedish policy is opening. Hitherto the main obstacles to an arrangement have been the dynastic difficulty and the mutual suspicion of the two parties. But to these are now added other grounds: the moral obligation not to hand over once-redeemed Protestants to Popish darkness and oppression, the argument of 'reputation', the argument of financial expediency. Could Sweden expand her armies without the tolls she was levying at the mouths of the Prussian rivers? Dared she risk the restoration of Polish control—and hence perhaps of imperial and ultimately of Spanish control—in the ports of the Vistula delta? In the altered circumstances of the close of 1626, did she desire a peace at all, if it must be bought on such terms? These novel questions, this new attitude, were not induced by a sudden access of bellicosity, by the intoxication of victory, by an abruptly emergent political or economic imperialism. They were the consequences of the crumbling of Danish resistance in Germany, of the alarming tidings of Spanish designs upon the Baltic, of the feeling, strengthening slowly to a conviction, that Sweden must sooner or later find herself involved in the war against the Emperor and the League. A settlement which might have been perfectly satisfactory in the limited field of Swedish-Polish relations might well be dangerous when considered in the wider context of Sweden's attitude to the general European problem. Side by side with the particular interests of the Swedish Vasas there would run henceforward considerations of general Protestant strategy. From this time onward Gustav Adolf fights and negotiates with one eye on Germany.[1]

Whatever Gustav Adolf's feelings about the desirability of purchasing peace with Poland, there is no doubt that he would have been glad of any reasonable accommodation with Danzig. But no such accommodation, it appeared, was to be had. The Danzigers had already asked the Hanse to mediate[2]; and Gustav Adolf tried to induce the Dutch to do so. But the Dutch were indignant at the blockade of the Vistula: some 57 per cent. of all the ships passing through the Sound are said to have been bound to or from Danzig in a normal year, and it was not unusual for more than half the Dutch

[1] In December 1626 the Infanta Isabella reported an approach by Erik Larsson von der Linde. Larsson had indicated that Gustav Adolf would be glad of imperial or Spanish mediation to settle the dispute with Poland. It seems likely that this was merely a manœuvre to propitiate Spain, in hope of facilitating the sale of copper: Lonchay, II. 295 and *note* 2, 297-8.

[2] Simson, p. 30.

ships trading to the Baltic to make Danzig their first port of call.[1] In November 1626 a development occurred which rammed home the lesson that Gustav Adolf would have done well to permit the city to retain its neutrality; for in that month Sigismund paid a visit to Danzig and was cordially received by the burghers. His object was to establish a naval base. The loss of Putzig in July had deprived him of the yards in which the first ships of his new navy had been built; and he now asked leave to transfer his building operations to the wharves of Danzig. His request was agreed to; and in the course of the winter Gabriel Posse took up his residence as head of a special commission charged with the duty of pressing on the construction of a fleet.[2] And this news came at a moment when it was rumoured that Spain had promised Poland a subsidy of three million gulden, and the aid of the Spanish navy.[3]

As the long winter drew to a close and the opening of the campaigning season approached, Gustav Adolf renewed his negotiations with Kristian IV. The battle of Lutter had not made him any less suspicious of Kristian's goodwill, nor did it dispose him to engage himself any more readily than before in enterprises which discommended themselves to his judgment; but the elimination of any possibility of a Danish hegemony in north Germany at least removed one complication. And Gustav Adolf acknowledged that the gravity of Denmark's position obliged him to make another effort to reach agreement with his neighbour, if any firm agreement were to be had. In December 1626, therefore, he sent Rasche to Copenhagen to renew the offer of a defensive and offensive alliance, on much the same terms as he had suggested in August. But Kristian, on his side, was suspicious too: the crisis of 1624, the uncooperativeness of Gustav Adolf in 1625 and 1626, were still too fresh in his recollection for it to be otherwise. He was already wishing himself well out of his German commitments: even before the battle of Lutter he had put out peace-feelers to the Infanta[4];

[1] Szelągowski, pp. 26-7; Wendt, p. 27. Oxenstierna tried to minimize the interruption of trade caused by the blockade. He contended that merchants could equally well do their business at Stettin: *AOSB*, I. III. 467. There seems no doubt that corn was in fact exported by alternative routes: see *AOSB*, I. III. 406. When de Geer came to Sweden early in 1627 he tried, in vain, to persuade the King to abandon the blockade of Danzig. Gustav Adolf replied, 'I have taken the water from them; I would take the air if I could': F. Breedevelt van Veen, *Louis de Geer*, p. 79; Ahnlund, *Kring Gustav Adolf*, p. 192.

[2] Simson, p. 23; Messow, pp. 59-61; Wendt, p. 47; *Sv. Krig*, Supp. Vol. I. 56 *seqq.*

[3] *AOSB*, I. III. 406.

[4] Lonchay, II. 279, 284.

and his council was urging him to accept the mediation of John George.[1] His response to this new overture was therefore limited to an offer to hand over Mansfeld's army in Silesia, so that Gustav Adolf might attack the Habsburg hereditary domains—an offer which was largely discounted by the virtual extinction of Mansfeld's army as an effective fighting force. Nevertheless, Gustav Adolf did not abandon the negotiation. In March 1627 Jonas Bureus, the Swedish agent in Denmark, was instructed to seek an interview with Kristian. Bureus met the Danish council on 21 April, and, while rejecting the idea of co-operation with Mansfeld, again offered an alliance, on condition that it was limited to Sweden and Denmark alone. Some excuses were made for Sweden's attack upon Danzig, and the hope was expressed that Kristian would continue to resist Wallenstein's advance to the Baltic. On 4 May Kristian informed Bureus of his intention to continue the struggle; and two days later Bureus presented him with more detailed proposals for a treaty. But once again Gustav Adolf was demanding an alliance directed against all Roman Catholic enemies; and once again Kristian refused these terms, since his existing commitments bound him to friendship with at least one Catholic power, namely France.[2] Kristian had no intention of allowing Gustav Adolf to drag him into war with Poland. He still hoped against hope for effective support from the maritime powers, and he was not prepared to compromise that prospect by associating himself with the campaign in Prussia, or participate in the odium attaching to Gustav Adolf's blockade of the Vistula.

The negotiations therefore stranded. Kristian and Gustav Adolf turned their attention to preparations for the campaign of 1627, each in his own field, and each without giving much heed to the other. And in May Gustav Adolf sailed once more for Pillau with substantial reinforcements, and a determination to moderate to a more sober level the transports of the Poles and imperialists over the capitulation of Hammerstein.

(iv) *The Campaign of 1627: Dirschau*

Gustav Adolf landed at Pillau on 8 May 1627, and was confronted immediately with a crisis in his relations with his brother-in-law of Brandenburg. The events of the autumn of 1626 had put George

[1] Kr. Erslev, *Aktstykker og Oplysninger til Rigsraadets og Staendermødernes Historie i Kristian IVs Tid* [cited: Erslev], II. 22-4.

[2] *Christian IVs Breve*, II. 78-9 and *note* 1; Erslev, II. 119-20.

William in an exceptionally awkward predicament. Compromised on the one hand by Gustav Adolf's use of the port of Pillau and the presence of Swedish troops in East Prussia, he found himself exposed on the other to the threat of invasion by the armies of Wallenstein and Tilly, who had long resented his professed 'neutrality' in the Danish war. After Lutter, Tilly had no scruples about violating Brandenburg territory, while the Danes in their turn showed equally little consideration for the Elector's feelings. At the end of October the troops of the League began to settle themselves in the Altmark, and soon afterwards Wallenstein moved his forces into the district round Crossen. For one desperate moment George William, in his irritation, thought of openly allying himself with Gustav Adolf. But the Swedes treated him so roughly in Prussia, and the danger from Tilly and Wallenstein was so close, that he was soon persuaded by Schwarzenberg to remain true to the Emperor. And it was on Schwarzenberg's advice that George William, in January 1627, transferred his court to Königsberg, leaving a weak, divided and ill-instructed regency behind him in Berlin. Schwarzenberg hoped that the Elector's presence in Prussia might convince Sigismund that he was not Gustav Adolf's accomplice, or might at least efface the unfortunate impression produced in Warsaw by the refusal of the Prussian *Landtag*, at its meeting in December, to recognize its obligations 'as a limb of the Polish crown'. Nevertheless, George William still clung to his neutrality; and when Koniecpolski, meeting him at Marienwerder in transit to Königsberg, asked him to place his armed forces at Sigismund's disposal, he was given a clear refusal.[1]

In the months that followed, however, the policy of neutrality began to break down, as relations with the Swedish authorities in Prussia deteriorated. All requests for the evacuation of Pillau were rejected; and the Elector retaliated by prohibiting intercourse with places occupied by the Swedish forces. Oxenstierna retorted by forbidding trade with Königsberg, whose attitude had long been ambiguous; and in April 1627 the municipal authorities found themselves constrained to accept the conditions which he dictated to them. The irritation of the Elector was strongly excited by the news that the Swedish reinforcements which capitulated at Hammarstein had violated Brandenburg territory while on the march thither.

[1] *AOSB*, I. III. 403, 412, 416, 420, 446, 457, 462; Hoppe, pp. 123, 143; J. Gebauer, *Kurbrandenburg in der Krisis des Jahres 1627*, pp. 2-29.

By mid-April it was commonly reported that he had become wholly Polish in sympathy. He was said to be concentrating troops near Königsberg and to be contemplating an attack on Pillau; and about this time he began to fortify Fischhausen and Lochstädt.[1] Early in May Karl Hannibal von Dohna made his appearance in Königsberg, conjured up like some genie at Schwarzenberg's urgent summons: the time was ripe, Schwarzenberg considered, to bind the Elector irrevocably to the imperialist cause[2] And indeed George William offered little resistance to the warnings and blandishments of the imperial emissary. Exasperated by Swedish exigence, haunted by fear lest he might share the fate of Frederick V, George William reached an agreement with Dohna on 12 May, whereby he undertook to support the transfer of the Palatine electorate to Maximilian for his lifetime, promised eternal devotion and fidelity to the Emperor, and agreed to acquiesce in whatever measures should conduce to 'the general peace and union of the Empire'. All Brandenburg was to be thrown open to Wallenstein's troops save the major fortresses and the towns of residence; and the regency at Berlin was transferred to the hands of George William's more 'reliable' cousin, the Margrave Sigismund. In short, the very court which had launched the Bellin plan in 1624 had cravenly abandoned the Protestant cause; and for this service George William was rewarded by the Emperor (as a mark of special favour) with 'das Predikät und Ehrenwort: Durchläuchtig'. It was even rumoured in Vienna that George William might turn Roman Catholic.[3]

Thus at the moment of Gustav Adolf's arrival the Elector was consummating his political nuptials with Dohna; and had his policy been backed by adequate resources the Swedish armies might well have found themselves in awkward straits. Gustav Adolf was well aware that the Elector's policy was tortuous and two-faced; but he does not seem to have known how deeply he had committed himself to the imperialists: his theory was that any act of hostility on the Elector's part would be at best half-hearted, and undertaken only in order to safeguard his Prussian fief from confiscation.[4] In his view, the situation could be met by a combination of threats of vengeance and exhortations to play the man; and these were the tactics he

[1] *AOSB*, I. III. 492, 495, 499, 502, 509-12, 525, II. IX. 407; Gebauer, pp. 30-41.
[2] Hoppe, p. 168.
[3] Gebauer, pp. 70-82, 85, 100-1; Irmer, p. 55; Ritter, III. 342; Hallwich, II. 100-1; *Sv. Krig*, II. 313-14; Koser, p. 413.
[4] Droysen, I. 301; Gebauer, p. 39.

adopted in his interview with the two emissaries from the Elector who met him soon after his landing. In the circumstances, they appeared to suffice. Three days after concluding the agreement with Dohna, George William reached a temporary settlement with Gustav Adolf at Lochstädt. The Elector promised that for the next four months (until Michaelmas) he would not concentrate troops, nor fortify Lochstädt, nor attack Pillau; while the King undertook to withdraw his troops from the Elector's Prussian dominions during the same period, except for such as were necessary to defend Pillau and to keep open his line of communication with that port.[1]

The news of the Lochstädt agreement did much to discredit George William in the eyes of his new imperialist friends: Wallenstein had never trusted him, and now felt that his suspicions had been confirmed.[2] And it was not long before Gustav Adolf was equally disillusioned. For the Elector was bound by his obligations to the crown of Poland to provide a fixed number of men for the Polish service, as well as to maintain a number of warships in the port of Pillau in case of need. Having lost Pillau to the Swedes, George William found himself unable to discharge his obligation in full, and by way of compensation added an extra 700 men to his ordinary contingent of 500. Early in July this contingent set out to join the Polish forces. At Mohrungen they found their road barred by a Swedish detachment which had been sent to intercept them, and after little more than a token resistance they nearly all went over to the enemy and enlisted in the Swedish service. Gustav Adolf unkindly suggested to the discomfited Elector that he should take better care of his army another time; George William, in his chagrin, openly declared his sympathy with Poland; and Oxenstierna took advantage of the intermezzo to appropriate the revenue from tolls levied at Pillau.[3] But neither side really desired a rupture; and on 6 August another agreement was patched up, whereby each engaged not to interfere with trade; the neutrality of Königsberg was to be respected; and the Elector undertook to refrain from raising any more troops.[4] Thus

[1] *AOSB*, I. III. 549; *Sverges traktater*, V. 331; Wendt, p. 50; *Sv. Krig*, II. 329-31; Ahnlund, *Oxenstierna*, p. 431; *id.*, *Kring Gustav Adolf*, pp. 101-10.

[2] Hallwich, II. 106, 117.

[3] *AOSB*, I. III. 582, 605; Hoppe, pp. 187, 190; *Sv. Krig*, II. 349-52; Koser, pp. 415-17. The appropriation of the Pillau tolls was at first intended only as political blackmail, not as a permanent arrangement: Ahnlund, *Oxenstierna*, p. 436.

[4] *Sv. Krig*, II. 352. The agreement was renewed in October, with some additional provisions to enable the Elector to fulfil his obligations to Poland: *Sverges traktater*, V. 333.

George William was constrained not to make a nuisance of himself, Gustav Adolf went off with the Pillau tolls in his pocket (an important gain), and the Swedish base was secured for that season from any danger from the Elector.

It proved less easy to secure it from the attacks of the Poles. Gustav Adolf had made unusual efforts to strengthen his forces in Prussia: an *utskrivning* in the spring had yielded the unprecedented figure of 13,000 recruits; but of these, 6000 had been left behind in Sweden to guard against emergencies.[1] Still, the King had sailed from Älvsnabben on 4 May with no less than 7000 men, and re-inforcements continued to arrive all through the summer—mostly mercenaries from Scotland. Gustav Adolf had also brought with him some 30 new guns (more than half of them siege-guns) in addition to the new 6-pounders, and the 'leather guns' which made their first appearance at the close of the campaign. In June he had rather more than 21,000 men at his disposal; but not less than 8500 of these were assigned to garrison duties, and although the King still had a field force more numerous than any which Koniecpolski could bring against him, he probably had no great hopes of striking a decisive blow this year.[2] And, indeed, not only did he never really succeed in wresting the strategic initiative from the hands of the enemy, but there were moments when even the security of his base area seemed seriously threatened. Koniecpolski had established himself with his main body south-west of Dirschau, while a smaller Polish force under Kazanowski lay in Ermeland near Wormditt. It was Koniecpolski's aim to storm Danziger Haupt, which blocked the navigation of the Vistula and threatened Danzig; while Kazanowski hoped by an advance down the Passarge to capture Braunsberg or Elbing, and so cut the Swedish base in two and sever the vital line of communication which led from Pillau to Dirschau. Fortunately for Gustav Adolf, the Polish commanders timed their threats to fall alternately rather than simultaneously, and it was thus possible to beat them off *seriatim*; but they kept him rushing from one face of his beach-head perimeter to the other, and thus effectively prevented his undertaking any operations of importance.

Koniecpolski's attack on Danziger Haupt was the first to develop. From his position at Käsemark on the left bank of the Vistula the Polish commander was harassing the defenders and preparing an assault. Gustav Adolf might have crossed to the left bank at Dirschau

[1] *Sv. Krig*, II. 320-1, 327.

[2] *ibid.*, II. 326-7, 333, 335.

unmolested, but he felt that he had no time to spare for such a *détour*. He therefore marched his troops straight to the Vistula at a point almost opposite to Käsemark; and on the night of 22-23 May launched a hazardous attack across the river in flat-bottomed boats. It might well have succeeded; but the usual mishap in the dark caused confusion in the crossing, and when the King intervened to restore order the boat in which he was sitting came under heavy fire, he himself was wounded and forced to retire, and the action was accordingly broken off.[1] The King soon recovered, and Danziger Haupt was reinforced and made safe; but there was no disguising that the affair at Käsemark had been a failure. Before it could be retrieved, Gustav Adolf had to hurry off to the Passarge sector, where at the beginning of June Kazanowski carried out a long-prepared swoop on Braunsberg. Gustav Adolf arrived just in time to save the town from capture; but he failed to come up with Kazanowski's force, which got clear away.[2] And while he was on his way to Braunsberg he was overtaken by news of an attack upon Mewe, at the extreme south-western angle of his position. Misled, perhaps, by the resistance offered by Mewe in 1626, he decided to ignore this threat and make another attempt upon Käsemark. This time he was successful: Käsemark was taken on 4 July; and by its capture the garrison of Danzig was forced back to the main defences of the city and deprived of a rich supply area, while Gustav Adolf obtained an important new bridgehead on the left bank of the Vistula. This gain, however, was offset by the fall of Mewe on the previous day (the garrison appears to have exhausted its ammunition); for Koniecpolski's army was now free to advance northward and so prevent the King from using his victory at Käsemark for an attack on Danzig.

In mid-July the movements of George William's contingent called Gustav Adolf away once more to the east; but after the capitulation at Mohrungen he turned again to the Vistula and established himself at Dirschau. Here on 7 and 8 August were fought two battles of some importance. The first was a purely cavalry affair, and ended in a Swedish victory; the second was a general action, and would almost certainly have resulted in a major Swedish success had not Gustav Adolf at a critical moment been seriously

[1] *AOSB*, I. I. 107-9, I. III. 550-1, II. III. 118; *RRP*, I. 42; *Sv. Krig*, II. 335-44.

[2] *Sv. Krig*, I. 345.

wounded by a musket-ball in the neck and shoulder.[1] As at Käsemark, the King's wound led to the termination of the engagement. The chance of crushing Koniecpolski before his expected reinforcements arrived was lost, and the only apparent consequences of the battles were a stiffness in the King's fingers which lasted for the rest of his life, a tenderness around his shoulder which made him unable to endure body-armour henceforward, and a poem *Sur la blessure du Roy de Suède* from the pen of one of the Dutch diplomats who had been witnesses of the action.[2] But though the battles of Dirschau thus decided nothing, they were of considerable significance. They marked a stage in the military regeneration of Sweden. At Mewe in 1626 the new Swedish foot had proved its superiority; at Dirschau the new Swedish cavalry covered itself with glory. The action of 7 August had been provoked by the King in order to test the quality of his horse. They had come well out of it: the Polish cavalry—hitherto accounted the finest in Europe—had been unequivocally worsted; the memory of Kirkholm had been exorcised at last. Further, the battles of Dirschau revealed the rapid maturing of Gustav Adolf as a tactician, the development of a new style of fighting, the success of the King's recent administrative reforms. But one thing, at least, was still lacking, as the fiascos of Käsemark and the second day at Dirschau showed—a school of commanders trained in the King's methods, who could be relied upon to carry out his plans in his absence. The military history of the German war would show how well this want had been supplied in the few years that intervened between Dirschau and Breitenfeld.

After the battles of Dirschau both sides subsided into comparative passivity. The Poles were occupied with negotiations for peace under Dutch mediation; Gustav Adolf felt that he lacked the numerical strength for a decisive stroke, and in any case he was increasingly worried by the news from Germany, and anxious, perhaps, to conserve his forces for a real emergency. But before the campaign came to an end he made a successful move upon Wormditt, the base from which the Poles had harassed the Passarge front during the preceding months. The state of the roads made the use of siege-guns impossible, and accordingly the King for the first time used his newly invented 'leather guns', though they were by no means

[1] *AOSB*, I. I. 109-11, I. III. 612 *seqq.*; *Sv. Krig*, II. 354-69; N. Belfrage, *Erik Soop och Västgöta Ryttare*, p. 51.

[2] Hoppe, p. 207; E. Wrangel, *De Betrekkingen tusschen Zweden en de Nederlanden*, p. 6.

intended for operations of this sort. Nevertheless, the attack was vigorously pressed, and on 1 October Wormditt fell into Swedish hands. A fortnight later Gustav Adolf left for home. Axel Oxenstierna remained as governor and commander-in-chief, with Thurn as field-marshal, and Johan Banér in command at Haupt.[1]

On the whole, the campaign had been a disappointment. Polish resistance was stronger than ever. Economic warfare had not shown the expected results. And the Polish negotiators bated not a whit of their claims and pretensions. This emerged clearly enough from the fruitless efforts of the Dutch to arrange either a peace or at least a protracted truce. Their mediation had been undertaken upon the earnest representations of Danzig, seconded by the pressure of the Dutch mercantile community; and the mediators themselves had experienced in their own persons a practical demonstration of the inconveniences to which shipping was exposed, for the Swedish admiral on patrol had refused to allow them to land at Danzig and had insisted on their going round by Pillau. They had arrived towards the end of May; and all that summer and autumn they passed back and forth between the combatants in an endeavour to find some ground of agreement. When they began to weary of their thankless task, Danzig renewed entreaties to them to persevere; and in November George William, whose desire for peace at least equalled their own, came forward to associate himself with them in the work of mediation. After negotiations of infinite tedium they at length compassed a congress at Riesenburg in January 1628, and another at Honigfeld in February; while throughout the winter desultory armistices were prolonged from week to week. But the congresses proved barren; the Dutchmen quarrelled with the Brandenburgers on points of precedence; the mediators could make no progress; and at last, in March 1628, Oxenstierna cut short the proceedings by declaring that Sweden did not consider any truce for less than fifteen months worth the trouble of negotiation. Before the end of the month the Dutch envoys had taken their departure; and their going marked the increasing coolness between Gustav Adolf and his old allies.[2]

[1] *Sv. Krig*, II. 365-9; *AOSB*, I. I. 118.

[2] *AOSB*, I. 120-204, I. III. 547, 556, 568, 595-8, 601, 623, 627, I. IV. 7, 11, 45, 57-66, 68, II. I. 390; X. Liske, *Öfversigt af den polska litteraturen med särskilt afseende på den svenska historien*, pp. 379-93; Styffe, p. 308; J. H. Siccama, *Schetz van de diplomatieke Betrekkinge tusschen Nederland en Brandenburg*, pp. 90-3; *Sv. Krig*, II. 376-80, 385.

These negotiations, vain as they were, have nevertheless some interest, if only for the instructive contrast which they present to the equally vain negotiations of 1626. In 1626, in the first flush of initial success in Poland, the Swedes had taken a high line; the *råd*, as we have seen, had tended to the view that the new conquests must be retained in any permanent settlement; and the terms of Elbing's capitulation had reinforced the impression that part at least of Prussia was to be incorporated into the Swedish realm. But now Oxenstierna was more moderate. In return for a truce of thirty years he professed his willingness to retrocede all conquests from Poland, and even to abandon the lucrative revenue from tolls, if in exchange the Poles would recognize Gustav Adolf's right to Estonia, defray his war expenses, grant religious toleration and restore ancient privileges to the retroceded provinces, and pledge themselves to extort a renunciation of the Swedish throne from the next elected King. But as the Swedes abated their demands the Poles stiffened theirs, insisting now upon total abandonment of the Swedish conquests and the succession of the Polish Vasas after Gustav Adolf's death. The key to the altered situation lies in Germany. As Gustav Adolf himself observed, the Poles were 'so blown up' by the successes of the imperialists that they would not accept reasonable terms, much less propose them. The collapse of Denmark, which made a quick settlement with Poland imperative, made it also impossible.

(v) *The Consequences of the Danish Collapse*

After six months' respite, during which Kristian IV had in vain tried to obtain peace on acceptable conditions, the imperialist advance was resumed in the summer of 1627. In mid-July Tilly crossed the Elbe and invaded Lauenburg. In August the Danes sustained a severe defeat at Bernstein, and by the end of the month the imperialists had penetrated into Holstein. Kristian IV had not succeeded in restoring the morale or the efficiency of his armies in the interval since the close of the previous campaign, and under these renewed blows all real resistance broke down. The Danish forces disintegrated; by the end of September the Emperor's troops had reached the Limfjord, and were already contemplating leaping the water to the islands. Wolmar von Farensbach was interesting

Wallenstein in a plan for invasion by flat-bottomed boats; and in imperialist circles there were rumours that the Danish nobility was thinking of deposing Kristian, and might even be willing to put Ferdinand in his place. The council at Copenhagen washed their hands of the whole affair: they took the line that this was a private quarrel between Kristian IV and the Emperor; they protested that Denmark was not to be considered as a belligerent; and they refused Kristian's suggestion that they should take it upon themselves to write to Wallenstein for terms.[1] Tilly thought the war was over, and was talking of giving aid to the Spaniards and the Poles; while Wallenstein proclaimed to his correspondents his anxiety to be off upon a crusade which should for ever put an end to the danger from Islam.[2]

The Danish catastrophe involved grave political and military consequences which touched Sweden nearly. One by one the bastions upon whose resistance Gustav Adolf had relied went down; the rout of Denmark was followed by the conquest of Mecklenburg, the conquest of Mecklenburg by the occupation of Pomerania. In Mecklenburg the Danish armies were driven back step by step until their solitary foothold was the island of Poel; and even this had to be relinquished in December. Adolf Frederick and his brother were driven into exile, and by a refinement of malice were forbidden to leave their wives behind them.[3] The port of Wismar, which had refused to allow Adolf Frederick to put a garrison in it, was forced to accept an imperialist garrison in October. After Mecklenburg, it was the turn of Pomerania. Bogislaw XIV, unlike Adolf Frederick, had always been at pains to show his loyalty to the Emperor, and very recently had received from him the assurance that imperial troops would not be quartered in his duchies save in the direst necessity. That necessity was now deemed to have arisen. Wallenstein and his master had sniffed the sea-breezes, and no scruples would deter them now. Their object had become the full control of the whole German Baltic coastline: 'There are twenty-eight ports in Pomerania,' said Wallenstein, 'and we must put garrisons in them all.' Wolgast and

[1] Erslev, II. 44, 54-6. They relented in November, and agreed to address an appeal to John George: *ibid.*, 61. For a vivid picture of the desperate state of affairs in Denmark, see *ibid.*, 72-5.

[2] Hallwich, I. 692, II. 58, 76-7, 149, 164, 183, 201, 220-4; Engelstoft, pp. 255-259; Droysen, I. 294-5; Ahnlund, *Gustaf Adolf inför tyska kriget*, p. 25; Ahnlund, *Storhetstidens gryning*, p. 111; *AOSB*, II. III. 127, 130; *RRP*, I. 55.

[3] Ranke, p. 86; Irmer, p. 67; Messow, pp. 25-7; W. Carlsson, *Gustaf Adolf och Stralsund*, p. 23.

Stettin, indeed, bought themselves off, as Rostock had done earlier; but Arnim held the island of Rügen, and in November Wallenstein imposed upon Bogislaw the humiliating capitulation of Franzburg, which placed Pomerania effectively under imperial control.[1] By the end of 1627 the imperialists held the whole north German coastline from the Oder to the Dollart, with the exception of a handful of towns (Stettin, Stralsund, Rostock, Lübeck, Hamburg, Bremen were the most important) which retained a precarious independence and professed neutrality, and a still smaller handful (Stade, Glückstadt, Krempe) which held out for Denmark. Ranged in a great arc which extended from the north of Jutland to the Stettiner Haff were some 100,000 men, half surrounding the Danish islands, ready to invade them, wanting only the opportunity and the means of transport. A few more practicable harbours in Pomerania or Mecklenburg, a fleet scraped together from the terrorized Hanse, and reinforced, perhaps, by Spanish and Polish contingents, and the jump across to Sjaelland would be easy. And thence it was a short step to Hälsingborg and Malmö. The Sound might then be shut, Dutch commerce dealt a crippling blow, Sweden's strategic imports interfered with. In a more distant perspective lay visions of the Polish Vasas restored to Stockholm and the whole Scandinavian north regained for Rome. But for the implementing even of the most modest of these plans the indispensable prerequisites were good harbours and a strong fleet. Wallenstein might perhaps provide the harbours; but what agency could create in a hurry a fleet powerful enough to defy the combined navies of the Protestant powers? It was in an attempt to provide a solution to this difficulty that the Emperor and his allies recurred with increased energy to the plans for a Habsburg fleet, which Olivares had adumbrated at the Brussels conference in 1626.

The Spanish designs on the Baltic, which had received a temporary setback at the Brussels conference, had revived somewhat upon the news of the battle of Lutter. The Infanta Isabella had already written to Wallenstein urging him to proceed without delay to the seizure of a Baltic port; and at the close of 1626 Aytona had been sent from Madrid to reinforce the effect of this letter. He had succeeded in inducing Wallenstein to promise that after concluding his campaign against Bethlen Gabor he would erect two forts on

[1] Carlsson, pp. 21-6; Irmer, pp. 68-73; Messow, pp. 27-9; Rudel, *Die Lage Pommerns . . . 1620-1630*, pp. 89-96.

the lower Elbe, and so cut off the Dutch from access to Hamburg.[1] It does not seem, however, that he implemented this promise; and the initiative in the months that followed passed—ominously enough—to Poland. In January 1627 the Queen of Poland had appealed to the Infanta Isabella to send twelve Dunkirkers to the Baltic to reinforce the nascent Polish navy. Gabriel Posse's efforts were beginning to bear fruit, and the little squadron in Danzig was now ready to put to sea. Would Spain provide an admiral? The combined force (it was suggested) might begin by capturing Helsingör and Älvsborg, which could then be handed over to Spain, and might proceed to secure the conquest of Sweden for Sigismund. The response of Philip IV to this appeal was prompt and generous: towards the end of April he replied, promising a fleet of twenty-four sail, and suggesting Sigismund's eldest son, Władysław, as its commander. This squadron was to prey upon Dutch merchantmen and 'otros enemigos mios'. Since it might be difficult to pass such a force through the Sound, Philip suggested that it would be a better plan to build or hire the vessels within the Baltic; and with this end in view one Gabriel de Roy was sent to negotiate with the Hanse, while D'Auchy started on a long-postponed mission to Danzig and Warsaw.[2] At the same time the project was revived in Vienna; and in order to disarm the usual German suspicion of Spain, the nominal command and ownership of the projected Baltic fleet was made over to Ferdinand, since Sigismund was unwilling for Władysław to accept it. The base originally intended was Danzig, or failing that Putzig; but Ferdinand was doubtful whether Danzig could be trusted, and it was possibly the same doubt that prompted Sigismund and Władysław to pay another visit to the city in August 1627. At all events the Emperor and Wallenstein seem soon to have favoured some harbour lying further west; and this was certainly one of the motives behind their anxiety to possess themselves of the Pomeranian and Mecklenburg ports. Wallenstein was as impressed as Philip IV had been with the difficulty of introducing a Spanish squadron into the Baltic, and made the characteristically bold suggestion that if Spain would maintain a force in the North Sea, access to the Baltic should be provided for it through a canal across the isthmus at Kiel. In the meantime he put pressure on Lübeck

[1] Lonchay, III. 271; Gindely, p. 9; Schmitz, p. 32; Messow, p. 15; Carlsson, pp. 14-15.

[2] Lonchay, III. 303, 307, 326, 346, 356; Gindely, pp. 8-10; Schmitz, p. 36 *seqq.*; Günter, pp. 24-6; Ahnlund, *Gustaf Adolf inför tyska kriget*, pp. 9-10.

and Wismar, and from each of them extracted imprecise and unwilling promises to provide ships in 1628.[1]

If, then, a fleet were to be created within the Baltic, without direct Spanish aid, the assistance or connivance of the Hanseatic towns would be indispensable; and here, it was hoped, the other half of Olivares' design would prove an effective bait. The creation of a great German-Spanish trading association, endowed with a monopoly of the trade between central Europe and the Peninsula, and protecting its commerce by *almirantazgos*, would enrich the Hanse, inflict loss on the Dutch and perhaps lead to a unified economic system for the whole *Reich*. Above all, it would provide a reserve of armed merchantmen upon which the commander of the imperial fleet might draw. The prospects for such an arrangement seemed by no means unpromising. Apart from the obvious menace of the powerful imperial armies, the towns had other motives for acquiescence. They had a long-standing dislike of Kristian IV's ambition in north Germany, and they had more recent and immediate grievances in the behaviour of the Danish troops and the high-handed actions of the Danish fleet. Gabriel de Roy sought to cultivate these dispositions; and when he moved on to Danzig two further imperial envoys (Ludwig von Schwarzenberg and Dr. Wenzel) appeared at Lübeck to reinforce such impression as he might have made.

The Hanse towns, however, proved unexpectedly resistant. They disliked Spain for her maltreatment of their merchants; and they took leave to doubt whether the Emperor's proposals did in fact proceed (as he protested) from mere 'paternal solicitude'. Lübeck was suspicious; Danzig would take no step without consulting Lübeck. In the background, Swedish and Danish agents warned the towns not to step into the imperial trap. A meeting of the Wendish towns in December 1627 postponed any consideration of the question until the following year. The quarterings of imperial troops in the states of the littoral had made a painful impression on them: 'the Emperor', as Wenzel regretfully constated, 'had not a friend in north Germany'. And when the full *Hansetag* met in February 1628, the towns took refuge in those devices of procrastination for which the structure of the Hanseatic League offered such eminent opportunities. The hectoring tactics of Wallenstein, and the able propaganda of the Swedish agent Rasche, confirmed their worst fears; the triumphant defence of Stralsund gave them

[1] Messow, pp. 16-18; Schmitz, p. 44; Gindely, pp. 12-13; Simson, p. 35.

courage; and in September 1628 they finally declined all participation in the proposed trading company.[1]

Thus the attempt to induce the Hanse to sail under the house-flag of Habsburg eventually came to naught, as it was bound to do if the towns kept their spirits up. But in the autumn of 1627 such an outcome appeared anything but inevitable. To Gustav Adolf it seemed that Wallenstein's immense successes on land might enable him to revolutionize the balance of power at sea. In Wismar he had already a tolerable harbour at his disposal; and it seemed likely that he would have another shortly, in Stralsund. He was known to be determined to create a war fleet, and it was reasonable to suppose that such a fleet would act in conjunction with the force which Sigismund and Gabriel Posse were building up at Danzig. The Polish navy was still small, no doubt; but the defeat of Nils Stiernsköld's squadron on 17 November 1627 proved that it could no longer be dismissed as negligible.[2] It was a gloomy omen for the future. Sweden could not afford to lose the ships; she could not afford to lose the tolls which her squadron had been extorting. Coming at a moment when the Habsburg plans for Baltic supremacy were taking shape, when it seemed possible that the shipping of the Hanse might be placed at Wallenstein's disposal, the battle off Oliva forced upon Gustav Adolf the reconsideration of his attitude towards the German problem, and at the same time made inevitable a new and more serious approach to Denmark.

It was probably not until Gustav Adolf's arrival at Kalmar in October 1627, on his way home from the summer campaign, that the full gravity of Denmark's position was borne in upon him; for it was only then that he heard the news of the total evacuation of Jutland, of the attempts of the imperialists to effect a lodgment on Fyn, and of the apparent collapse of the Danish morale. Nevertheless, it is clear that ever since the autumn of 1626 the King and his chancellor had been watching, with mounting anxiety, the course of affairs in Germany.[3] Gustav Adolf's decision in 1626 to transfer the war to Prussia and to leave Kristian to deal with the German situation had been based on two assumptions: first, that a campaign

[1] Messow, pp. 32-47, 68-74, 84-7; Gindely, pp. 14-20, 25; Ahnlund, *Gustaf Adolf inför tyska kriget*, pp. 25-6, 51; Hallwich, II. 274-6; Carlsson, pp. 18-19; Ritter, III. 379.

[2] For this, see pp. 283, above.

[3] *AOSB*, II. I. 357 and *note*, and *cf.* II. III. 139, II. IX. 409; *SRARP*, I. 24-32; Ahnlund, *Oxenstierna*, p. 451.

in the Vistula valley would constrain Sigismund to make peace—or at worst a long truce—within a reasonably short time; and secondly, that Denmark and her allies would be able to continue fighting until his own hands were free to aid them. Neither of these assumptions proved correct, though each was reasonable enough at the time it was made. The defences of Protestantism had fallen one after the other with a rapidity that no one could have foreseen; the resistance of Poland had proved unexpectedly tough. Gustav Adolf found himself confronted with what seemed to him to be imminent danger from Wallenstein at a moment when he still had his hands more than full with Koniecpolski—precisely the situation, in fact, which his policy had been calculated to avoid. And it now became a question whether he ought not to forestall the threat from Wallenstein by timely aid to those that were still in a position to make a fight for it. Upon Adolf Frederick even good words were wasted (though Gustav Adolf was not sparing of exhortation) [1]; but towns such as Wismar and Rostock might perhaps defy the conqueror if given a clear promise of assistance. As early as May 1627 Gustav Adolf was offering to send troops to defend them; and in the autumn a regiment was waiting at Kalmar to sail for Wismar. But before it could embark came news that Wismar had opened her gates to an imperialist garrison.[2]

Already then, a year before the expedition to Stralsund, Gustav Adolf had brought himself to the point of actively preparing for intervention in Germany. For he recognized it as a vital Swedish interest to prevent the establishment of an imperial naval base and invasion-port in such a place as Wismar. The question remained, however, as to whether in the altered circumstances the war with Poland ought not to be abandoned: would it be possible to maintain the struggle simultaneously in Pomerania and in Prussia? There were certainly some who doubted it: at the end of August Gabriel Gustafsson Oxenstierna was suggesting withdrawal from Poland [3]; and, as we have seen, the Swedish negotiators were at this time offering remarkably reasonable terms for a long truce.

The transference of the Swedish military effort to Germany was naturally the last thing that Wallenstein wanted. His object was to keep Denmark and Sweden apart; and throughout the autumn he

[1] Styffe, pp. 468-9.
[2] Ahnlund, *Gustaf Adolf inför tyska kriget*, pp. 17, 20-1; Carlsson, p. 36.
[3] *AOSB*, II. III. 131.

engaged, through his agents Arnim and Farensbach, in complicated diplomatic manœuvres designed to effect this object. On the one hand, Kristian IV was entertained with the prospect of being made imperial admiral; on the other, Gustav Adolf was tempted with the offer of a partition of Kristian's dominions. Wallenstein offered Sweden an alliance against Denmark, a mediated peace with Poland, and either Norway or Denmark itself as an imperial fief. The negotiations appear to have been taken seriously by at least some observers: at the end of the year Maximilian of Bavaria was certainly under the impression that Gustav Adolf was ready to join the Emperor in return for a share in the spoils. But the principals had no faith in each other; and neither Oxenstierna nor Wallenstein really believed in the possibility of an alliance against Denmark. It required no great stock of Protestant virtue in Gustav Adolf to elude Wallenstein's proposals. And even had the King been simply the ambitious conqueror of certain historians' imagining, the advantages to be gained by acceptance were so dubious, the good faith of the negotiator so suspect, that he could hardly have closed with the offer.[1]

At the beginning of November 1627 Gustav Adolf reached Stockholm, and in a letter to Axel Oxenstierna dated 6 November he plainly faced the fact that it was unlikely that he could avoid being drawn into the German war sooner or later.[2] He ordered Oxenstierna to send three regiments back to Kalmar, to be ready against any sudden emergency; he concentrated small craft at Stockholm ready for despatch to the aid of Denmark if they should be needed.[3] On 18 November he outlined a plan for the division of the Swedish forces into three armies, of which one (of fifteen regiments of foot and thirty-four companies of horse) was to be stationed in Sweden to act as a reserve for the defence of Denmark.[4] And on 13 December he opened the second *riksdag* to be summoned in this critical year, with a speech and a *Proposition* in which the international situation was painted in hues more sombre than ever before. There was the usual emphatic disclaimer of responsibility for the Polish war, the usual demand—now more urgent than ever—for further exertions in the raising of men and money; but in addition the Estates were plainly warned of the gravity of the situation and the

[1] *AOSB*, I. III. 634; Hallwich, II. 246-7, 335, 338-9, 356; Ahnlund, *Gustaf Adolf inför tyska kriget*, pp. 29-30; *id.*, *Oxenstierna*, pp. 460-2; Droysen, I. 305.

[2] *AOSB*, II. I. 356 *seqq.*

[3] *ibid.*, II. I. 357-8.

[4] *ibid.*, II. I. 363.

danger of invasion: 'As one wave follows another, so the popish league comes closer and closer to us. They have violently subjugated a great part of Denmark, whence we must apprehend that they may press on into our borders, if they be not in good time powerfully opposed.'[1] To meet this situation, the King asked the Estates to appoint a secret committee to discuss foreign policy, since he considered it undesirable that matters of such delicacy should be debated in the full *riksdag*. The Estates complied with his request; the first secret committee was constituted; and on 12 January 1628 Gustav Adolf expounded the situation to them in all its bearings, and asked their advice on three principal points. Should they wait for an imperialist attack behind their own frontiers, or seek to forestall it by waging war in the enemy's territory? Should they assist Kristian IV to defend himself? Was there any need for further consultation of the *riksdag*, in view of the fact that 'an open war between this country and the Emperor seems very possible'? The committee's reply was unambiguous and decisive: they recorded their opinion that the notion of neutrality in the present situation in Germany was a mere delusion; and they gave it as their view that the Emperor had already given ample cause for war by his encouragement of Sigismund, and by his 'open conspiracy to deprive us of all trade and navigation, and (which is worst of all) of the sovereignty of the Baltic, which from time immemorial has attached and appertained to the Swedish crown'. They emphatically endorsed the policy of fighting their enemies abroad rather than at home; they pronounced in favour of aid to Denmark; and they expressed the opinion that no further consultation with the *riksdag* was required before acting on these recommendations.[2]

The answer of the secret committee marked an epoch in the history of the reign. Intervention in Germany was already virtually approved by the representatives of the nation. Whether intervention was indeed to take place—the mode, the place, the time for carrying it out—all this was remitted to the King's judgment. The *riksdag*, through the secret committee, had given the King authority to go forward, and it was now for him to decide whether he would avail himself of it. Before the final decision was taken which would send the Swedish armada to Peenemünde there would be many hesitations,

[1] Styffe, pp. 305, 627; *SRARP*, I. 49, 73-6; Carlsson, pp. 36-7; Ahnlund, *Ståndsriksdagens utdaning*, p. 174.
[2] Stiernman, I. 806-10.

and some apparent turning back; the judgment of King and chancellor upon the course expedient to pursue would not always coincide; the King would seek to spread the burden of decision by further consultations with his *råd*; there would be moments when he would experience qualms of misgiving, and even unease of conscience; but from 12 January 1628 Gustav Adolf could proceed with the certainty that if the worst came to the worst, if Sweden must plunge into the incalculable adventure of a German war, his people were forewarned, approving, likeminded with himself. They had faced the situation, surveyed its implications, and taken their decision. Two years later, when Gustav Adolf at last deemed the moment to be propitious, that decision was put into force without further ado; and no voice was raised to suggest that the King had stampeded the country into a struggle which it would have preferred (or would have been able) to avoid. There would be grumbling, there would be disturbances, provoked by the drain of men and the oppression of the taxes; but the King and the clergy between them had so far convinced the nation of the reality of the peril that for so long as Gustav Adolf lived there would be no real opposition to the war.

The logical corollary to the reply of the secret committee was an alliance with Denmark. Ever since the imperialist invasion of Jutland in August 1627 Kristian IV had shown himself disposed to resume the negotiations which had failed in the preceding March and July. On 12 September 1627 he wrote to Gustav Adolf from Glückstadt to ask for aid from the Swedish navy in blockading the north German ports and so preventing an invasion of the Danish islands. Gustav Adolf made no reply until his return to Sweden in mid-October, and by that time, as he pointed out, the season was too far advanced for any major naval operations. But he informed Kristian of Wallenstein's insidious offers, and he promised to send an embassy to Copenhagen to discuss the prospects of common action.[1] It seems that Gustav Adolf delayed committing himself to any specific plan, partly because he wanted fuller and more authentic information as to how far the demoralization of Denmark had gone, and partly because he still nursed the hope that some effectual aid might come from Denmark's western allies. That hope, however, had now become desperate indeed. England was at war

[1] *Christian IVs Breve*, II. 116; Erslev, II. 33, 53, 83-4; *AOSB*, II. I. 352-5; Ahnlund, *Gustaf Adolf inför tyska kriget*, pp. 36-9.

with France and Spain; and Charles I's contribution to the Protestant cause was limited to the despatch of four regiments of poor quality to Stade; the offer to Kristian (in lieu of subsidy) of a jewel alleged to be worth £100,000, which proved to be unpawnable; and the making of Gustav Adolf a Knight of the Garter.[1]

In November two Danish envoys were sent over to Stockholm; and with them began protracted negotiations which did not reach a final settlement until April 1628. The discussions were not over-cordial.[2] On the Swedish side, indeed, there was something like a Scandinavian community of feeling with Denmark, and in later years Oxenstierna was to recall this as one of the few moments when a real *rapprochement* with Denmark had been possible [3]; but Kristian IV, humiliated and sore at his defeats, jealous of Gustav Adolf's successes, was difficult to deal with. Though circumstances had forced him to appeal to his old enemy, he was determined not to surrender the control of his forces. His agents asked for money, powder, ships and men; but they had no notion of Gustav Adolf's having any say in the use to which such reinforcements should be put. Nor was Kristian prepared, in the hour of disaster, to enlarge his commitments by embracing Sweden's quarrel with Poland. He was willing, if forced to it, to prohibit the passage through the Sound of contraband of war destined for Polish ports; but further than that he would not go. Above all, no concession must be made which might prejudice Denmark's claims to *dominium maris*. In his view, the right policy for Sweden was to patch up a peace with Poland and strike southward to Silesia in collaboration with an offensive from Transylvania by Bethlen Gabor. But such a plan ignored recent developments in eastern Europe. The Sultan was deeply involved in a holy war against the Shiites, and in September 1627 had concluded with the Emperor the treaty of Szön, whereby the treaty of Gyarmath was extended for a further twenty-five years. This left Bethlen Gabor isolated; and he was too wary to provoke the Emperor at a moment when no help was to be expected from the Porte in case of emergency.[4] But if a Silesian diversion was thus out

[1] Gardiner, V. 152-3, 160, 164-6 etc.: for repercussions on Franco-Dutch relations, see A. Waddington, *La République des Provinces-Unies, la France et les Pays-Bas*, I. 76-81. For the investiture with the Garter, Hoppe, p. 209; *AOSB*, I. I. 116-17, 623-4.

[2] For the discussions, see Ahnlund, *Gustaf Adolf inför tyska kriget*, pp. 44-8; Carlsson, pp. 38-41; Erslev, II. 105-6, 120-1; Droysen, I. 318-19; Weibull, p. 33; Fridericia, *YPH*, pp. 34-5.

[3] Fridericia, *YPH*, p. 34.

[4] Ranke, p. 67.

of the question, the alternatives put forward by Gustav Adolf were such as Kristian's pride forbade him to accept. He could not, even at this perilous moment, agree to a joint army under Gustav Adolf's command—especially since it was proposed that two-thirds of it should be provided by Sweden, and all of it be paid by Denmark. Nor could he accede to the suggestion that Swedish troops should take up winter quarters on Danish soil.

These jealousies and suspicions ensured that no comprehensive plan of action such as Gustav Adolf desired would emerge from the negotiations. Yet something at least was effected. For on 4 January 1628 the diplomats concluded, and on 28 April Kristian IV at last ratified, a treaty whereby Sweden and Denmark entered into an alliance for three years.[1] Sweden promised to place eight ships at Denmark's disposal; Denmark undertook to stop the passage of any ships sailing to Danzig. It was not much, perhaps; and in the sequel it became even less, for Gustav Adolf sent the eight ships to Stralsund instead of to Copenhagen, and from the outset Kristian strove to sabotage the alliance by a separate peace with the Emperor. Nevertheless, the treaty was significant. The overmastering tide of events had swept the two bitter rivals into a position in which they stood shoulder to shoulder, fighting to ward off a common danger. The attempt of Wallenstein to divide them had, for the moment, failed. The purely Scandinavian contest for *dominium maris* had been laid aside, at least for the present; and Gustav Adolf and Kristian had bound themselves in an alliance. It was an alliance concluded in no warmth of feeling, no spirit of confidence, no agreement upon methods to be pursued or objects to be striven for. They did not trust each other one inch. The bond that bound them was a common fear; and each recognized that the destruction of one would involve the ruin of the other. Kristian IV, especially, swallowed necessity with a wry face; and when a year later another and less arduous road to safety should present itself, he would not hesitate to take it and leave his ally in the lurch. Yet in spite of everything the treaty of April 1628 was a memorable one; for, if it did nothing else, at least it saved Stralsund.

[1] *Sverges traktater*, V. 337-42: *cf. AOSB*, II. I. 376, 386; Erslev, II. 168.

CHAPTER VI

FROM STRALSUND TO PEENEMÜNDE

(i) *Stralsund*

THE conclusion of the Swedish-Danish alliance implied a check to the political intrigues of Wallenstein and a challenge to his military measures. The attempt to divide the Scandinavian states had, apparently, failed; the attempt to establish imperial control over the southern Baltic shore would, it seemed, meet with the united resistance of Kristian IV and Gustav Adolf. Wallenstein, however, made no immediate change in his plans or his proceedings. By the spring of 1628 he was in full possession of Mecklenburg, installed in the room of the exiled Dukes,[1] and he had every intention of holding fast to the duchy. But in his new capacity as north German prince he began to look more favourably upon the possibility of peace—especially with Denmark, from whose territory Mecklenburg was most readily accessible to attack. Ferdinand II might talk of the permanent retention of Slesvig and Holstein for the Habsburgs [2]; but his general was increasingly disposed to consider their restoration upon payment of an indemnity; and his allies of the League were very unwilling to carry on the fight against Denmark after Kristian's armies had been driven beyond the limits of the *Reich*.[3] Peace—if it were to be had on reasonable terms—was already the goal of Kristian IV's policy. Disillusioned by the false promises of the western powers, disheartened by military defeats, enervated by the pacifism of his council and the complaints of his people, his chief wish was to escape from the whole miserable imbroglio on any tolerable

[1] Patent promulgated 1 February 1628: F. Förster, *Albrechts von Wallenstein . . . ungedruckte, eigenhändige vertrauliche Briefe*, I. 291-5; H. Hallwich, *Fünf Bücher Geschichte Wallensteins*, II. 381. Adolf Frederick asked Gustav Adolf to intercede for him with the Emperor; but Gustav Adolf refused: 'Ich aber sorge, man wird uns beide auslachen und desto mehr böses zufugen': Ahnlund, *Gustaf Adolf inför tyska kriget*, p. 53. Wallenstein's being given the duchy meant that Brandenburg lost her old claims to the reversion: R. Koser, *Geschichte der brandenburgischen Politik bis zum Westfälischen Frieden*, p. 417.

[2] In December 1627 he was offering to sell Slesvig and Holstein to Spain: S. Riezler, *Geschichte Baierns*, V. 335.

[3] [*ed.*] W. Goetz: *Die Politik Maximilians I von Baiern und seine Verbündeten*, IV. II. 14, 16-17 *note* 3; Förster, I. 320-1, 334, 403.

conditions. Sooner or later, then, it was likely that Wallenstein and Kristian would come to terms. The Swedish alliance was for Kristian a *pis aller*, and its dissolution was predicable from the hour of its conception.

Nevertheless, for as long as Kristian's counterscarp in north Germany was assailed, he must continue the fight. And if Wallenstein's possession of Mecklenburg from one point of view made peace more probable, his proceedings as the Emperor's commander made it less so. His occupation of Wismar, his nomination in April 1628 as 'General of the Oceanic and Baltic Seas', his obvious ambition to command the imperial fleet, contradicted his irenical leanings and crusading fantasies, and made the threat of Habsburg naval expansion in the north more explicit than ever before.[1] In 1628 the threat became mainly imperialist, rather than Spanish, for Spain this year was heavily engaged in the Netherlands, and in the autumn suffered a major disaster when Piet Hein captured the Plate fleet[2]; but whether imperialist or Spanish, the Habsburg navy was taking shape in Wismar. Wismar, however, soon proved unsatisfactory as a naval base; and it was for that reason, among others, that Wallenstein came to the fateful resolution to besiege and capture the port of Stralsund.[3]

Stralsund was a member of the Hanseatic League, and in virtue of her wealth, and of an exceptionally favourable geographical position (which made capture exceedingly difficult), had long assumed an independent, and sometimes a defiant, attitude towards her lords, the Dukes of Pomerania. It was Stralsund's ambition to become an imperial free city, and some of the burghers were not without hope that the prevailing confusion in Germany might present an opportunity for realizing that ambition. As in so many German towns at this epoch, there was a sharp antagonism between the municipal aristocracy, as represented by the council, and the mass of the burghers; and this antagonism was incorporate in the persons of the burgomaster, Dr. Lambert Steinwich, and the popular leader,

[1] In the spring of 1628 he was asking the Infanta to send him 15 Dunkirkers; but Isabella considered that the passage of the Sound would be too risky: Lonchay, II. 389.

[2] The Spanish agent, Gabriel de Roy, was extremely unpopular: Wallenstein called him 'ein bestia von Schwarzenberg angesteckt': H. Messow, *Die Hansestädte und die habsburgische Ostseepolitik*, p. 62. For Wallenstein's interest in the fleet, see Förster, I. 129, 163.

[3] Messow, pp. 77-8; O. Schmitz, *Die maritime Politik der Habsburger in den Jahren 1625-1628*, p. 60; A. Gindely, *Die maritimen Pläne der Habsburger* [etc.], pp. 22-4.

Josquinus von Gosen. Steinwich, with the ultimate goal of *Reichsunmittelbarkeit* always before his eyes, was inclined to political caution; von Gosen, with no burden of municipal responsibility, could afford to indulge a violently Protestant and anti-imperial sentiment. But apart from these questions of tactics, Stralsund was strongly Lutheran; and relations with Sweden, both economic [1] and political, had long been exceedingly close. As early as April 1625 Gustav Adolf had offered to send help to the burghers if they should need it; in 1627 he had despatched Dietrich von Falkenberg to advise them about their fortifications; and though the defence of Stralsund had not been specifically mentioned during the negotiations for an alliance with Denmark, it had undoubtedly been implicit in them.[2]

Stralsund had managed to get herself excepted from the treaty between Bogislaw XIV and the Emperor, which threw open Pomerania to the imperial troops; but the town council was under no illusions of security, and since the autumn of 1627 had been conserving and increasing supplies against a possible emergency. But the store of powder was low, the supply of trained soldiers and modern artillery inadequate, and the fortifications on the landward side, despite recent modernization, by no means satisfactory.[3] In February 1628 the long-expected emergency came, when Arnim occupied the isle of Dänholm, which commanded Stralsund's harbour. The council, conscious of the inadequacy of its preparations, on 11 February 1628 concluded with Arnim the treaty of Greifswald, whereby Stralsund pledged herself to pay Arnim 30,000 *Reichsthaler*, and permitted the occupation of Dänholm; but this was merely a device to gain time. Immediately after the signing of the treaty, Steinwich addressed simultaneous appeals for help to Kristian IV and to Gustav Adolf.[4]

Gustav Adolf replied on 28 February with a message of encouragement, and shortly afterwards sent Kristoffer Ludvig Rasche to Stralsund, with instructions to incite the burghers to resistance and

[1] Stralsund enjoyed a specially favoured position in regard to Swedish customs dues: T. S. Dillner, *Studier rörande Finlands handel under tidsrymden 1570-1622*, I. 80-1, 159.

[2] F. Adler, *Die Belagerung Stralsunds 1628*, pp. 110-12; W. Carlsson, *Gustaf Adolf och Stralsund*, pp. 26-8, 34-5; J. Paul, *Gustaf Adolf*, II. 90, 106.

[3] *Sv. Krig*, III. 54, 70; *cf.* Vosbergen's judgment in 1625: *Verbaal van de Ambassade van Gaspar van Vosbergen*, pp. 150-1.

[4] Ahnlund, *Gustaf Adolf inför tyska kriget*, pp. 49-51; G. Irmer, *Hans Georg von Arnim*, p. 77.

promise them aid. Simultaneously he instructed Count Philip Reinhold von Solms (who had for some time been in the Danish service, but was on the point of exchanging it for the Swedish)[1] to discuss the possibility of conjoint action with Denmark.[2] Kristian IV, for his part, despatched an agent to Stralsund in March, and another in April; but the burghers were nervous of entrusting themselves to the protection of Denmark alone, and the tactlessness of the first of Kristian's emissaries made a bad impression on them.[3] The eviction of Arnim from Dänholm on 5 April precipitated imperialist counter-measures which really inaugurated the regular siege of the town; but even in these circumstances Stralsund could resolve on 9 April not to accept any foreign garrison. The burghers still set their hope upon the sister-towns of the Hanse: not until experience had proved how little was to be expected from that quarter,[4] and not until the military position was desperate, would they go back on this resolution. They knew well that it would be easier to summon foreign aid than to dismiss it.

To Gustav Adolf, discussing the problem of Stralsund in a letter to Oxenstierna on 31 March, the desirability of sending assistance to the defenders was by no means clear. He saw the advantages plainly enough: Wallenstein would be diverted from possible interference in Poland; Denmark would be strengthened to resist; the town would be a useful base for the Swedish navy. If no help were offered, Stralsund might surrender in despair. But on the other hand an expedition to deliver it might well require a large and expensive army; the forces retained for the defence of Sweden proper might in consequence be dangerously reduced; and it must always be doubtful whether relief by foreign troops would really be welcome. Nothing, at all events, could be done without Denmark; and, for the present, it might be sufficient to leave the rendering of assistance to Stralsund's Hanseatic neighbours.[5] Thus Gustav Adolf, like Steinwich, set his hope upon the Hanse; and between them they came very near to losing the town. And though Stralsund

[1] *AOSB*, II. I. 386.

[2] *Sv. Krig*, III. 79; Carlsson, pp. 33-4, 42.

[3] Carlsson, pp. 46-7.

[4] *Sv. Krig*, III. 56; Carlsson, p. 44. Envoys from Stralsund, Lübeck, Bremen, Hamburg and Brunswick were sent in April to intercede with the Emperor. They had a private interview with Wallenstein at Prague, when he burst out: 'Ihr Bestien! was wollt ihr euch dem Kaiser widersetzen! seid Rebellen!': Paul, II. 95. Otherwise the Hanse's only contribution was a loan of 15,000 *Reichsthaler*, and even it was not paid to Stralsund until after the siege.

[5] *AOSB*, II. I. 387-9; *cf.* Ahnlund, *Gustaf Adolf inför tyska kriget*, p. 55.

was not quite the 'last Protestant bastion' of popular historiography, its loss would undoubtedly have had awkward repercussions, both in a naval point of view and from the moral effect upon the anti-imperialists of Germany.

Yet for Gustav Adolf, as for Steinwich, the miscalculation was both explicable and pardonable. Steinwich was clinging to the hope of independence; Gustav Adolf was distracted by conflicting claims upon his attention. The implication of any considerable aid to Stralsund was pretty plain: sooner or later—and probably sooner—Sweden would find herself entangled in the civil wars of Germany. Gustav Adolf had no great wish to be involved in them—at least, not for the present; certainly not till the war in Poland was safely over. He recognized, however, that it was already highly probable that Sweden would be drawn into the conflict: if not by intervention at Stralsund, then as a result of her assistance to Denmark, or even as a consequence of imperialist succours to King Sigismund, of which there were already rumours not altogether without foundation.[1] He had shown how pessimistically he viewed the prospects for 1628 by his unprecedentedly heavy demands for recruits: the figure for the *utskrivning* for this year was fixed at 15,500, and in fact something over 10,000 fresh troops were actually raised. In the disposition of his forces for 1628, moreover, he planned to leave no less than 14,000 men in Sweden to serve as an army of reserve, which should be ready to rush to the aid of a tottering Denmark, or defend Sweden from actual invasion.[2] The danger, in fact, was felt to be very near: in April Gustav Adolf was seriously alarmed by a false report of an imperialist conquest of Fyn; and Oxenstierna wrote that when he thought of the state of Denmark it 'made his hair stand on end'.[3] Yet even in this critical situation the armies in Prussia must be maintained, if ever the dreary struggle were to be brought to a conclusion; and in the spring of 1628 the claims of the Polish theatre were reinforced by unexpectedly bad news from Livonia.

Since the battle of Wallhof in January 1626, Livonia had been a field of operations of subordinate importance. The fighting had been punctuated by frequent armistices, and Swedish strategy had concentrated mainly on holding the advantages already won. The

[1] Förster, I. 124-6; Ahnlund, *Axel Oxenstierna*, p. 484; and *cf. AOSB*, II. I. 395 *seqq.*

[2] *Sv. Krig*, II. 388-9, 394.

[3] 'Så att migh väl offta håren stå till ända, när jagh på Danmark tänker': *AOSB*, I. IV. 124.

Swedish commander, Jakob de la Gardie, was sluggish and unenterprising, and was further disqualified for his post by his strong conviction that the war was not worth fighting, and ought to be terminated as soon as possible. In these circumstances the Swedes slowly lost ground in 1626 and 1627. The defensive quadrilateral which Gustav Adolf had built up was invaded; and suddenly, in the late winter and early spring of 1628, just at the moment when Gustav Adolf was laying his plans for the forthcoming campaign, Swedish resistance collapsed. For a time it seemed doubtful whether even Riga could be held; the total eviction of Swedish forces from Livonia seemed imminent; the fruits of all Gustav Adolf's exertions from 1621 to 1626 appeared likely to be lost.[1]

In these circumstances it was no wonder that Gustav Adolf should have felt that the most urgent task confronting him was to relieve the pressure upon Livonia. In a long letter to Oxenstierna on 1 April 1628 the King announced his intention of going over in person with an army of 4000 men: he would rendezvous in Kurland and Samogitia, and would hope to conquer those provinces, and perhaps Lithuania too. He would thus be able, as he put it, to 'link up *littora maris Baltici*', and so provide himself with a secure entry to, and line of retreat from, the theatre of operations. To the various objections which had been raised to this plan by members of the *råd*, Gustav Adolf had cogent replies: Sweden herself could now hardly be in any danger, protected as she was by an army of 14,000 men, by the Danish fleet of 40 ships, with the Swedish fleet to second it; and as to the expense, 'if we cannot say, *bellum se ipsum alet*, then I see no good outcome to all the work we have set our hand to'. With reasonable fortune, he should be able to complete the Livonian campaign in time to go to Prussia this year, if need be raising an army '*à la* Wallenstein' [2] to fight the imperialists there. For the Polish war must go on, whatever the danger to Stralsund. A truce would mean no diminution of Sweden's burdens; for an army no less in size would have to be kept on foot in Prussia, against the possibility of imperialist intervention. It was no longer possible, indeed, to draw a clear line between Sweden's Polish quarrel and the struggle of German Protestantism:

[1] *Sv. Krig*, II. 457, 459, 466, 470, 474, 479-80; E. Grill, *Jakob de la Gardie*, pp. 84-5; E. Hornborg, *Gustav II Adolf*, p. 39, quotes the Finnish proverb about de la Gardie: 'Lähtee suvi, lähtee talvi, vaan ei lähde laiska Jaakko' ('Summer goes, winter goes, but lazy Jakob goes not').

[2] 'på Wallenstenischt viss'.

things are come to this pass, that all the wars that are waged in Europe are commingled and become one, as is shown by the actions of the Papists in Germany, and the help given by the Spaniards to Rochelle, and last summer against us in Prussia, as well as by sundry consultations holden at the Emperor's court, where, as it is certainly reported, it was resolved to press on, by the occupation of these Scandinavian lands, to that tyranny over body and soul which they lust after. . . .

To meet this design, to repel this tyranny, Sweden must fight; and she must for choice fight in Polish Prussia, for no country offered better facilities as a battleground, being open, extensive, fruitful, and impotent to resist.[1]

Within a week of the date upon which this letter was written, news came that the situation in Livonia had taken a turn for the better. De la Gardie had been replaced as commander-in-chief by Gustav Horn; and Horn had infused a new vigour into the defence of the province. By the end of March all serious danger was over. By mid-April Gustav Adolf had virtually abandoned the idea of going to Livonia.[2] Axel Oxenstierna, for his part, had never favoured it. The chancellor was for another campaign on the Vistula, to be directed this time against Weichselmünde, or Graudenz, or possibly even against George William's town of Königsberg. Gustav Adolf on the whole agreed with him; and on 4 May 1628 he embarked once again for Prussia. But at the very moment of embarkation came a letter from Karl Karlsson Gyllenhielm, the admiral on the Danzig station, containing most disagreeable tidings. Stralsund, it appeared, was in grave danger; supplies of powder were nearly exhausted; the prospects of continued resistance were dubious. Gyllenhielm had intercepted a certain Schacht, sent by Stralsund on a fruitless errand to beg powder of Danzig; and from him had learned of the critical state of the town's defences.[3] And thus, just as the campaign in Prussia was due to begin, Gustav Adolf was confronted with a situation which might well throw all his calculations into confusion and make the contemplated blow at Graudenz appear a strategic irrelevancy.

The King's reaction to the news was prompt. He sent off a special agent, Bönhart, with a message of encouragement; and forwarded a consignment of gunpowder, with an irritated enquiry

[1] *AOSB*, II. I. 395-400.
[2] *ibid.*, II. I. 401-5.
[3] Carlsson, pp. 49-54; *Sv. Krig*, II. 405.

as to why they had not applied to him for it in the first place. He had hardly landed in Prussia before Bönhart returned (30 May) accompanied by envoys from Stralsund who begged him for the loan of 600 men. The crisis at Stralsund had indeed come far earlier than Gustav Adolf had expected; and the situation had already, from the Swedish point of view, been compromised. For Stralsund in this emergency had broken her resolution not to admit a foreign garrison, and on 22 May had appealed for troops to Kristian IV. Kristian had wasted no time in sending aid; and on 25 and 28 May the arrival of contingents of Danish troops had saved the town, at least for the present.[1] If the evil of a foreign garrison must be endured, Stralsund would certainly have preferred a Swedish to a Danish; but Kristian was close at hand and had no other obvious commitments, while Gustav Adolf was distant and likely to be engaged on two fronts. He proved, moreover, to be more cautious than his ally; and also more exacting. For though he did indeed send the 600 men, under Rosladin and Duvall, and though he directed to Stralsund the eight warships which by his treaty with Kristian he was bound to place at Denmark's disposal, he also sent with them a diplomat, Filip Sadler, charged to negotiate an alliance with Stralsund; and Sadler's instructions laid it down that the alliance must be concluded before a man or a musket was landed to aid the defenders.[2] Only if there seemed a real danger of the town's falling was he empowered to waive this condition. On 20 June Rosladin and Sadler arrived off Stralsund; and immediately opened negotiations. On 23 June these negotiations were successfully completed, and the troops were landed, proceeding almost immediately from the ships to the firing-line.[3] On the same day Wallenstein came to Anklam to direct the siege, and, as he hoped, to grace the triumph of his army with his presence. His arrival was followed by heavy onslaughts, especially on the 24th, and from the 27th to the 29th, when the position seemed almost hopeless: Rosladin was severely wounded (he died on 5 August), Duvall was taken, and the town council prepared to negotiate for a capitulation.[4] But once again the situation was retrieved. Rosladin from his death-bed persuaded the burghers to

[1] Carlsson, pp. 58-60.

[2] *Sv. Krig*, II. 407; Carlsson, pp. 55-8.

[3] E. Ericsson, *Rosladin och Stralsunds belägring 1628*, p. 222; Carlsson, p. 62. A classic first-hand account of the course of the siege is in Robert Monro, *Monro His Expedition with the Worthy Scots Regiment*, I. 62-79.

[4] Ericsson, *Rosladin*, pp. 228-9; *AOSB*, I. IV. 195.

reject the council's arrangements to admit a Pomeranian garrison; on 2 July 400 Danish troops arrived, in the nick of time; between 5 and 7 July heavy rains damped the ardour of the besiegers; and finally, on 9 July, the Danish commander Holck appeared, with McSpynie's Scottish regiment, 1100 strong.[1] This last event was the real turning-point. On 15 July Wallenstein retired sullenly to Güstrow, leaving to Arnim the odium of breaking off the siege; on 22 July the imperialists began to withdraw; by the end of the month the siege had been definitively abandoned, thanks not least to the appearance of a Danish fleet of 100 sail off Rügen—the prelude to Kristian's unhappy campaign on Usedom in August. The main body of Swedish auxiliaries, under Alexander Leslie, did not arrive until 17 July.[2]

Thus Stralsund was saved; the best available naval base in those parts was denied to Wallenstein; and a magnificent port of entry made over to either of the Scandinavian powers if—or when—one of them should decide to intervene actively in Germany. To this result both allies had contributed. But the main, the decisive, contribution had not been Swedish. When Wallenstein drew off there were far more Danish than Swedish soldiers in the town. If the credit for the deliverance of Stralsund must be assigned to any one man, it must be given not to Gustav Adolf but to Kristian IV.

The rescue of Stralsund brought with it new and delicate problems. Inside the town the situation was anomalous and explosive. Two deliverers maintained two garrisons, each on bad terms with the other; and the labourer who had arrived at the eleventh hour not merely claimed equal status with his colleague who had put in a more timeous appearance but actually enjoyed a superior position. Sweden had a treaty with Stralsund as the price of her aid: Denmark had not. It was clear that the situation could not be left to fester: the position must be regularized and tidied up, if only to avoid unnecessary strains upon the Swedish-Danish alliance. Gustav Adolf, at all events, still wished to keep that alliance alive, although as early as the beginning of August he was foreseeing the possibility of its early dissolution. Moreover, from the point of view of military efficiency (and no man could safely assume

[1] Ericsson, *Rosladin*, p. 231; Irmer, p. 91; Carlsson, pp. 73-8; *Sv. Krig*, III. 91-7. The capitulation with Arnim and the preceding negotiations in Förster, I. 365-9.

[2] Carlsson, pp. 84-8. For Leslie's early career, see C. Sanford Terry, *Alexander Leslie*, pp. 17-19.

that Wallenstein might not make a second attempt), a single auxiliary force under a single command was much to be preferred to the existing arrangements. On 4 August, therefore, Gustav Adolf despatched Axel Oxenstierna on a mission intended to put an end to these ambiguities: he was to go to Stralsund and inform the council that they must make a choice between Sweden and Denmark. As far as Gustav Adolf was concerned, it was a matter of indifference to him which they chose: his concern was essentially that Stralsund should be kept safe, without prejudice to his good relations with his ally.[1]

On 22 August Oxenstierna arrived in Stralsund. He was shocked at the weakness of the fortifications, and informed the burghers that had he known how inadequate they were, he would never have risked a night within the walls. Despite this unpromising beginning, the negotiations progressed rapidly, and Oxenstierna had little difficulty in bringing the council to a favourable decision.[2] If they must choose between Denmark and Sweden, they could hardly fail to choose Sweden, since (apart from all other considerations) Sweden, unlike Denmark, was not formally at war with the Emperor, and by accepting Swedish aid they were not putting themselves in the position of inviting into Germany the enemies of the *Reich*.[3] Armed with this decision, Oxenstierna went on his way to Copenhagen, and on 5 September was successful in inducing Kristian IV to agree to a unified command at Stralsund in Swedish hands.[4] Kristian consented to withdraw all Danish troops except for one detachment of 300 men.[5] It proved in the sequel not entirely easy to implement these agreements, for the Danes raised claims for expenses and compensation as a pretext for delaying their departure. Holck, the Danish commander, did not quit Stralsund until the end of December; and the last of the Danish garrison did not go until April 1629.[6]

[1] *AOSB*, II. I. 407-20; Carlsson, pp. 140-6; Ahnlund, *Gustaf Adolf inför tyska kriget*, pp. 59-60.

[2] *AOSB*, I. I. 531-5, II. I. 425-6; Carlsson, pp. 151-3; Ahnlund, *Oxenstierna*, pp. 495-6.

[3] *AOSB*, I. IV. 235. It was just during these days at Stralsund, indeed, that Oxenstierna took the opportunity to renew conversations with Wallenstein's agent. There was probably little sincerity on the chancellor's side, as there certainly was none on Wallenstein's; and Oxenstierna's other commitments forbade him to protract them: Förster, I. 346, 387, 398; Ahnlund, *Oxenstierna*, pp. 496-8.

[4] *Sverges traktater*, V. 345; Carlsson, pp. 160-4.

[5] *AOSB*, I. IV. 218, 227, 232; for Danish counter-demands (which Oxenstierna was not empowered to grant), see Erslev, II. 169-70.

[6] Carlsson, pp. 192-7. 216.

What then was Sweden's position in Stralsund, now that Denmark had been elbowed out? In what relationship did the town stand to the Swedish crown? There is no doubt that from the beginning the rulers of Stralsund accepted Swedish aid with reluctance, and felt considerable nervousness as to its possible political consequences. In particular, they feared what they called a Swedish *patrocinium*. In the terms which Gustav Adolf formulated on 30 May as the price of his aid, he demanded a defensive alliance which should last for the duration of the war and include other members of the Hanse. The treaty which Sadler actually concluded with Stralsund on 23 June was more or less conformable to this: the alliance was to be for twenty years (an earlier demand for an 'eternal' alliance was not pressed); it was to be defensive in character, and was to include the Hanse; and Stralsund's privileges and independent status were expressly guaranteed.[1] Gustav Adolf showed himself gracious to the Stralsunders, in contrast with the brusque manner of Kristian IV; the Swedish commander in Stralsund, by a special agreement, was subject in some respects to the control of the council (as Holck was not)[2]; and, in general, Stralsund felt somewhat relieved, and was disposed to hope that Gustav Adolf had no ulterior designs upon them. But in August their confidence was somewhat shaken. Gustav Adolf now refused to sanction Sadler's treaty, and revoked the ratification which he had already given on 22 July. Conditions in Stralsund after the siege were not reassuring (Sadler informed the King that what the town really needed was a good Swedish governor), and Gustav Adolf was coming to feel that he must be free to use Stralsund as an offensive base and not merely as a defensive outpost.[3] Further negotiations as to the terms of the alliance were now necessary; and in the last week of August envoys from Stralsund arrived in Gustav Adolf's camp at Graudenz,[4] and entered upon extended conversations with Johan Adler Salvius, who conducted the talks on Gustav Adolf's behalf. They made it clear that, failing *Reichsunmittelbarkeit*, Stralsund would prefer her relations to the Duke of Pomerania not to be compromised; they reiterated their desire for a purely defensive alliance; and though they were indeed

[1] *Sverges traktater*, V. 342-5; Carlsson, p. 62; Paul, II. 105.
[2] Carlsson, pp. 71-2.
[3] *ibid.*, pp. 70-1, 91: as Gabriel Gustavsson Oxenstierna later remarked, Stralsund was a place 'quo . . . nullibi melior invenire potest, unde bellum in superiorem Germaniam transferri possit': *RRP*, I. 123.
[4] Carlsson, pp. 96-101.

willing to concede to Gustav Adolf a *patrocinium*, it must be a '*patrocinium solo nomine*'. Salvius, on his side, made proposals which the council could hardly fail to find extravagant and outrageous: he suggested that they should swear fidelity to Gustav Adolf instead of to Bogislaw XIV; that Gustav Adolf should appoint the magistracy in Stralsund; that appeal from Stralsund's municipal courts should lie to *Svea hovrätt* in Stockholm; and that Swedish coin should be current in the town: in short, he proposed a '*subjectio realis*'. In return, he promised a 'royal succour' next spring, and adequate defence (at Sweden's expense) in the interim.[1]

There was no reconciling points of view so divergent, and for the moment Salvius allowed his demands to drop; but the military convention of 29 August, and the treaty of 2 September, gave the King some part, at least, of what he was wanting. By these agreements the Swedish commander in Stralsund was given a measure of authority over all troops in the town, whether Swedish or not; and Stralsund bound herself not to make peace with the Emperor except with Sweden's consent and participation.[2] By a subsequent treaty of 27 September that regiment of the Stralsund garrison which was paid by the town was bound to swear fidelity to Gustav Adolf, just as though it had been a unit of the Swedish army.

On these terms, then (which satisfied neither party), Stralsund became Gustav Adolf's first German ally; and Alexander Leslie, left in charge of the garrison, Gustav Adolf's first commander in Germany: indeed, he came not far short of being his first *ståthållare* there.[3] The number of Swedish-paid troops gradually increased: at the end of 1628 there were some 3000; a year later, 3350; in June 1630, 5700.[4] Leslie kept up a steady pressure on the burghers to improve their fortifications.[5] The population of the town was predominantly in favour of the Swedish alliance (which indeed brought some mercantile benefits), though the old ambitions towards independence were by no means forgotten; but Gustav Adolf would

[1] Carlsson, pp. 102-21; Paul, II. 111.

[2] *AOSB*, I. IV. 214-18; Ahnlund, *Oxenstierna*, pp. 495-6; Carlsson, pp. 125-30.

[3] See his complaints about his inadequate pay: *AOSB*, II. IX. 421. Monro's comment was characteristic: '. . . it faring then with *Trailesound*, as with *Sara*; she became fruitfull when she could not believe it, and they became flourishing having gotten a *Scots* Governour to protect them, whom they looked not for, which was a good *Omen* unto them, to get a Governour of the Nation, that was never conquered . . .': Monro, I. 77.

[4] Carlsson, p. 240; *Sv. Krig*, III. 111.

[5] *AOSB*, II. IX. 416-20.

have liked more severity—even '*exilio aut morte*'—against anti-Swedish elements.[1] Swedish coin began to circulate, including the depreciated Swedish copper.[2] Yet Gustav Adolf could not feel that the position was satisfactory: the imperfect and indeterminate nature of Swedish control appeared to him anomalous, and he would have been glad to change it so that it should rest upon some such basis as Salvius had outlined at Graudenz. Stralsund was deeply in his debt, from a purely financial point of view, and there seemed in 1629 little prospect that she would be able to discharge her obligations. In September 1629, therefore, the King ordered Sten Bielke to do what he could to prepare the way for the eventual incorporation of Stralsund into the Swedish dominions, and at the same time indicated that he would be happy to obtain the subjection of Stettin too.[3] In November he warned Stralsund not to enter into any negotiations with the Hanse without first consulting him.[4] In the discussions in the *råd* from 4 to 6 May 1630, Gustav Adolf insisted (in opposition to some of his advisers) that even though the imperialists should evacuate Mecklenburg and Pomerania (the former a sufficiently improbable contingency), Stralsund, and if possible Wismar also, must be retained by Sweden as *assecuratio* against a recurrence of the danger which had so narrowly been averted in 1628.[5]

Thus the independence of Stralsund was gradually whittled away; Steinwich's dreams of autonomy vanished in the battle-smoke; and for close on two centuries the city experienced not the least happy portion of her history as an integral part of the Swedish realm. When Karl XII returned from Turkey, it was to find Stralsund the sole defiant remnant of his Baltic empire; and a century later Gustav IV Adolf would experience within her walls a loyalty and affection which were denied him in his fatherland.

Gustav Adolf's relations with Stralsund are of especial interest; for they form the prototype of his relations with many of his later allies in Germany. Under the compulsion of immediate peril the two parties enter into an alliance; but the very nature of the military situation, the inescapable considerations of military security, turn the alliance before very long into at least a temporary subjection to

[1] Carlsson, pp. 248-9.
[2] *ibid.*, pp. 233-4, 245.
[3] *ibid.*, pp. 251-2; Ahnlund, *Gustaf Adolf inför tyska kriget*, p. 276.
[4] Carlsson, p. 250.
[5] *RRP*, II. 1-5; Ahnlund, *op. cit.*, p. 373.

Sweden: a right to garrison transforms itself into a title of authority which cannot in the immediate future be abandoned; and military logic converts a temporary and benevolent occupation into an *assecuratio* which assumes the dimensions of a vital interest of state.[1]

(ii) *The Consequences of Stralsund*

The intervention at Stralsund brought Gustav Adolf closer to decisions of the utmost gravity. It was still conceivable that he should dissociate himself from the general struggle in Germany: the easy-going international code of the day made it quite possible for him to remain the mere auxiliary of the Stralsunders, or even of Kristian IV, without necessarily proceeding to an open breach with their enemies. If Sweden were to stand strictly on the defensive, were to venture into Germany no further than the outermost ring of Stralsund's defences, then the convenient fiction of neutrality could probably be maintained. But if Stralsund were to become the base for offensive operations against Wallenstein or Tilly, then war with Emperor and League was probably inevitable. A German war had already been sanctioned in principle at the beginning of 1628; but that decision had only given approval in advance, should such a war become necessary. It was by no means clear, on the morrow of Stralsund's deliverance, that it had become necessary yet.[2] To a very considerable degree the burden of decision, the initiative in policy, now lay with Sweden. It would depend, very probably, upon Gustav Adolf's plan of campaign for 1629 whether the latent quarrel with the Emperor should pass at last into open war.

There is every reason to suppose that Gustav Adolf, if he had thought it practicable, would have preferred to maintain at least a formal and ostensible neutrality. If for no other reason, then because in 1628 the temper of his people was giving him cause for anxiety.

[1] In February 1638 Oxenstierna told the *råd* that there was no ground for the suspicion (not unreasonably entertained by the burghers of Stralsund) that Sweden desired to annex the town: 'which neither his late Majesty nor the now reigning sovereign ever thought of, since their Majesties sought nothing other than that the Emperor might not get a foothold in the harbour there. . . . Nor is it profitable to the crown of Sweden to keep Stralsund alone, but rather the garrison is a burden': *RRP*, VII. 151. But whatever the intention, the final effect was the same.

[2] Though Gustav Adolf had said, as early as May 1628, when he decided to aid Stralsund, 'Nos vero cum hoc modo bello eorum immissi jam simus': Carlsson, p. 56 *note* 1.

The financial strain of the war was already perceptible; the burden of taxation had been growing steadily. The *utskrivningar* were of unprecedented severity; and the volume of complaint was increasing. In the summer of 1628 discontent came to a head. In June, just after the King's departure for Poland, serious disorders broke out in Småland and spread thence to Östergötland. The peasants complained of the *utskrivning* and refused to pay the Three Marks' Aid. By August the position was so serious that John Casimir (who no later than May had been assuring Oxenstierna that the situation at home was good) was forced to go down himself to Kalmar and to hold up the departure of Lars Kagg's troops until mid-October that they might be available for the restoration of order. A special agitator, or government propaganda-chief, was sent to the disturbed areas to calm them down, or rather to divert their ebullience into more patriotic and evangelical channels.[1]

Nevertheless, Gustav Adolf had made up his mind that, whatever the state of popular opinion, an extraordinary military effort would be required for 1629. In mid-November alternative army estimates for the following year were drawn up. The more conservative of them, based on the assumption that the war would be fought only in Prussia and Livonia, called for an army of over 41,000 men; the more lavish pitched the requirements as high as 56,000, and of these no less than 20,000 would be based on Stralsund.[2] Thus Gustav Adolf was weighing the possibility of offensive action in north Germany, though as yet he had not clearly made up his mind about it. It was a question upon which the King and his chancellor did not at present see eye to eye. To Oxenstierna, writing from Elbing, with Polish problems thick-encompassing about him, it seemed that the old policy, steadily pursued since 1621, was still the best. Better finish with Poland before running into new embroilments of incalculable scope. It might be true that Wallenstein had publicly declared Gustav Adolf to be his enemy [3]; open war with the Emperor might sooner or later be inevitable; but it was obviously to Sweden's interest to avoid it as long as possible, and Oxenstierna was more sanguine than his master that it could be deferred for a little while

[1] *AOSB*, II. III. 169, II. X. 543, 547-8; S. Arnoldsson, *Krigspropagandan i Sverige före trettioåriga kriget*, p. 17.

[2] *AOSB*, II. I. 441-2.

[3] As Maximilian wrote to the Elector of Mainz (17 October 1628): 'Wallenstein lässt den Kg. Schweden öffentlich als Feind ausrufen—so provoziert man neue Feinde, ehe man mit den alten fertig ist. Ob man dadurch zum Frieden kommt?': Goetz, IV. II. 152.

longer. The Poles, he was confident, were weakening: another campaign might finish them off. His counsel, then, was to stand on the defensive in Stralsund and concentrate every effort on an offensive in Poland. The converse policy, he pointed out, would mean a larger army, since many garrisons would be needed in Prussia, even for a defensive campaign, whereas the defensive in Germany demanded but one—the garrison of Stralsund. The imperialists would heavily outnumber any army Gustav Adolf might be able to put in the field in Pomerania. Admittedly the absence of any positive Swedish effort in Germany might discourage the surviving Protestant powers there; but that, in his view, was a risk which must be taken.[1]

Twelve months earlier, Gustav Adolf might probably have found these arguments unanswerable: in December 1628 he was not so sure. Faced with this difficult decision, he had recourse to his usual policy of spreading the responsibility. The matter was laid before the *råd*. In a series of meetings between 15 December 1628 and 8 January 1629 the problem was put to them by the King in person, and argued out in all its bearings.[2] Gustav Adolf himself opened the discussion. He began by reviewing the state of Sweden's relations with the Emperor, and argued that the responsibility for the existing tension did not lie with him. Sweden, he claimed, had given no provocation: at Stralsund he had done no more than assist in thwarting the unauthorized designs of one of the Emperor's unruly generals [3]—an action by no means comparable (as the Emperor contended) with Charles I's assistance to La Rochelle. But though Sweden had thus given no cause for a breach, the imperialists had been gratuitously provocative. They had assisted Sweden's enemies in Poland; they had entered into a conspiracy to deprive Sweden of her trade and navigation; they had infringed Sweden's *dominium maris* by the creation of an imperial navy and the appointment of Wallenstein to command it. Moreover, Sweden had grievances more general, and more serious, than any of these: the tyranny of the Emperor to the Protestants of Germany, the general Popish design

[1] *AOSB*, I. IV. 269-81, 282-8; Ahnlund, *Oxenstierna*, pp. 518-22.

[2] For what follows, see *RRP*, I. 123-5; *Abraham Brahes tidebok*, p. 175; *Arkiv*, I. 20-4; *AOSB*, II. I. 445-50; Ahnlund, *Öfverläggningar i riksrådet om tyska kriget 1628-1629* [cited: Ahnlund, *HT* (1914)], pp. 109-19; *id.*, *Gustaf Adolf inför tyska kriget*, pp. 104-12.

[3] Gustav Adolf had some grounds for this contention, for Ferdinand II had actually forbidden Wallenstein to prosecute the siege: Hallwich, II. 489, 500. Tilly disapproved of it: S. Riezler, *Geschichte Baierns*, V. 337.

for the subjection of heretics, the Habsburg ambition to set up a 'universal monarchy'.[1]

The King then asked the advice of the *råd* upon three closely connected questions. First, should they make an attempt to keep the peace with the Emperor? Secondly, assuming this to be impossible, should they meet the imperialists at home or in Germany? And lastly, supposing they preferred to fight abroad, should they carry on operations in Germany offensively or defensively? To one at least of these questions only one answer was really possible: no member of the *råd* could really be expected to opt for fighting the imperialists on Swedish rather than on German soil.[2] The *råd* accordingly resolved on 15 December that Stralsund must be safeguarded for the future from falling into the Emperor's hands (and, equally, from falling under a Danish *patrocinium*); that if Sweden became involved in war in consequence, such a war should be waged in Germany rather than in Sweden; and that the decision upon whether a war against the Emperor be conducted offensively or defensively should be left to Gustav Adolf. By Christmas they had progressed to the opinion that a war with the Emperor was inevitable; on 2 January they discussed the possibility of mediation by a third power or the sending of an embassy direct to Vienna, and on the King's recommendation rejected both; and finally, on 8 January 1629, they came to the resolution towards which Gustav Adolf had been gradually manœuvring them for the past month: they decided to wage war on Ferdinand II, to wage it in Germany, and to wage it offensively. From this moment a Swedish invasion of Germany was a question only of time and opportunity: that it occurred in 1630 rather than in 1629 was a mere accident.

What, then, were the arguments which Gustav Adolf employed to draw his *råd* along with him to this fateful decision? And what were the reasons which so prevailed with him as to induce him to

[1] Compare the views of a Bavarian agent on imperialist designs (29 January 1629): 'Utuntur belli suasores specioso praetextu. Danum opprimendum, fretum Suntianum occupandum, frumentatione polonica commerciisque Batavos prohibendos, religionem septentrionibus inferendam, imperio quietem non fore, nisi obtento baltici maris dominatur. Haec Caesar sincere, alii pro affectu quisque suo. Impugnare aperte ista foederati non audent, alii ne domus austriacae incrementa suspecta habere videantur, ideoque ipsi in suspicionem veniant': Goetz, IV. II. 240.

[2] This was, indeed, a hoary old dilemma: it had been used by Gustav Vasa as justification for interfering in the Counts' War, and he in his turn had probably borrowed it from Vegetius: G. Petri, *Kungl. första Livgrenadjärregimentets historia*, I. 67. For the present instance, *cf. AOSB*, I. I. 138; Styffe, p. 221.

abandon that policy to which he had hitherto been so constant, and of which Axel Oxenstierna was still the champion—the policy of disposing of Poland before engaging in a new commitment? In part they were grounded upon the effect produced by Swedish policy abroad: intervention in Germany would encourage the Protestant party there; it would gratify England, Bethlen Gabor and the Dutch; while if Sweden refrained from intervention, her prestige with the Hanse would diminish. In part they were based upon consideration of the military position in Germany: intervention would keep the imperialists at a decent distance from Denmark and prevent the prosecution of their naval projects; while the landing of 6000 men in Stralsund would make an effect out of all proportion to their numbers, since the numerical superiority of the imperialists was offset by their need to disperse their forces in innumerable garrisons. And in part they were the result of the King's estimate of probable developments in the war against Sigismund III: a blow by Sweden in Germany would prevent interference by Wallenstein in Prussia. And this was the more necessary, since Poland and Prussia were so stripped of all necessities of life that the arrival of an additional army would inevitably entail the withdrawal of the Swedish forces.[1] And finally, Gustav Adolf believed he discerned the possibility of a useful diversionary campaign based on Stralsund —a limited offensive up the Oder—which, without committing many troops, might occupy considerable forces of the enemy, might deter Wallenstein from meddling on the Vistula, and perhaps might distract Koniecpolski too.

From this argumentation it emerges that Gustav Adolf had radically altered his opinions since the spring of 1628. Then, he had contended that the best place to fight the imperialists, if and when they must be fought, was Prussia, and that this was one reason (among many others) for continuing to campaign there; now, his object was to keep the imperialists out of Prussia, to fight them in Pomerania, and by so doing to divert their attention from the Vistula. But the offensive strategy which he now induced the *råd* to endorse was to be an offensive of limited scope, subordinated to the main immediate aim, which was still, as before, victory in Poland. The offensive in Germany was by no means to imply the putting of the Vistula war into cold storage, as the opening of the Prussian campaign

[1] This, it is pertinent to note, is in flat contradiction to the line of argument developed by Gustav Adolf only nine months earlier. See above, p. 363.

had meant the putting of the Düna war into cold storage. The successful termination of the war in Poland had indeed become more urgent than ever. If the imperialists were to move troops to Prussia, the chances of bringing the struggle to a conclusion would recede into the distance. And if the old policy of fighting the imperialists only in Poland were persisted in, Sweden might also find that a second imperialist attack on Stralsund was successful; or might find Stralsund the only oasis in a desert of political and religious servitude. Security for Sweden now meant security for Stralsund; it was no longer to be won at Graudenz or Danziger Haupt. A real security might probably involve a Swedish occupation, not only of Stralsund (and of Wismar and Stettin too) but of considerable tracts of country in northern Germany. For, after all, could Scandinavian Protestantism ever safely disarm while Protestant Germany was at the mercy of the oppressor? Such questions as yet lay in the future; but one thing was clear already: the Swedish troops in Stralsund must be something more than a garrison. In the opening days of 1629 King and ministers had reached the conviction that they must send to Stralsund what would in effect be an expeditionary force. The rôle of such a force would be, first, to facilitate, by effective diversions, the termination of the dynastic war in Poland; and afterwards to form the advance party of the army of liberation which, by bringing freedom to the states of north Germany, would also bring repose to the perturbed peoples of Scandinavia.

Since this was to be the line Gustav Adolf was to follow, Swedish diplomacy was called on for a renewed effort. Apart from the alliance with Stralsund and the fast-waning friendship of Denmark, Sweden was still in the isolated position which she had freely chosen in 1625 and 1626. Hitherto, attempts to end that isolation had come mainly from the outside world; but now Gustav Adolf himself took the initiative, and the winter of 1628-29 saw a sudden burst of activity by his agents. For a campaign of this sort the prospects were, perhaps, more favourable than they had been for some time. The outbreak of the war of succession in Mantua and Montferrat not merely distracted the attention of Ferdinand II from Germany, Poland and the Netherlands, but was to occupy the energies of a considerable part of his armies, and at the same time offered the prospect of friendship and co-operation with the anti-Habsburg powers which were involved in it. The Mantuan crisis, for instance, had the effect of preserving the Dutch from an imperialist onslaught which Wallenstein (though not the League) [1] would have been very glad to deliver; and in consequence 1628 was a good year for Frederick Henry, on land as well as at sea. England was still immeshed in simultaneous wars against France and Spain; but the assassination of Buckingham removed one of the main obstacles to a settlement with France; the fall of La Rochelle in October 1628 deprived the war of any assignable motive; and peace with France was by the end of the year a question only of time: it was concluded, at Susa, in April 1629. At the same time, England's interest in Baltic questions was reviving: just before Buckingham's assassination there was talk of sending a British fleet to the Baltic to ensure that the Protestant powers should be masters of that sea [2]; and in the following year the mission of Sir Thomas Roe would demonstrate that the party of Protestant solidarity in London had by no means given up the struggle. Most important of all, Richelieu was now moving towards a foreign policy more positive and confident than had hitherto been possible for him. With the Dutch, indeed, France's relations were something less than cordial, mainly owing, as it seems, to Richelieu's arrogant and dictatorial tone towards them; but their interests ran too plainly along similar lines for either to desire a real breach.[3] The feigned friendship with Spain, which had successfully prevented the conclusion of a Habsburg league in 1626, had now served its purpose; and Richelieu was chafing at the delay before La Rochelle, and burning to take up the cudgels for Nevers in Mantua. The fall of La Rochelle was immediately followed by preparations for the invasion of Italy: the ending of Huguenot rebellion meant that France once more became eligible as an ally for all Protestant powers who had a quarrel with Habsburg.

[1] Goetz, IV. II. 18, 94.

[2] Gardiner, V. 345-6; J. S. Corbett, *England in the Mediterranean*, I. 141. In the last months of Buckingham's life he was drawing closer to Gustav Adolf than ever before. On 8 May 1628 he concluded an extraordinary private treaty with Sweden, whereby Gustav Adolf bound himself to support Buckingham in a fantastic venture in which he was interested just then. Buckingham had in his possession secret information about an exceedingly rich gold-mine, discovered by Raleigh, in one of the West Indian islands. His scheme was to conquer this island and establish himself there as an independent sovereign. Gustav Adolf pledged himself to recognize Buckingham as a sovereign prince; to decline any treaty with Spain or the Emperor prejudicial to Buckingham's new kingdom; and to send, on request, 6 ships and 4000 men to defend it against any attacker; in return, Buckingham and his successors for ever would pay Sweden one-tenth of the produce of the mine: A. Rydfors, *De diplomatiska förbindelserna mellan Sverige och England*, pp. 110-12.

[3] A. Waddington, *La République des Provinces-Unies, la France, et les Pays-Bas espagnoles de 1630 à 1650*, I. 76-81.

It was in this light, certainly, that Gustav Adolf regarded the capitulation—not as another in the long series of Protestant disasters but rather as a victory for authority over rebellion, which might well free the strength of France for the service of the evangelical cause.[1]

In this more auspicious conjuncture of affairs Gustav Adolf launched his diplomatic offensive. In the early months of 1629 James Spens was sent to England, Dietrich von Falkenberg to the Netherlands and Dr. Zobel to France. All of them were charged, in the first instance, to try to raise recruits in the countries to which they were sent. Their success was varied, and in general considerably less than Gustav Adolf had hoped, for the mercenary market was tight in 1629, and few troops were to be had.[2] Spens and Falkenberg, however, had additional tasks imposed upon them. Spens was to try to obtain support from England in cash, to the extent of 400,000 *rdr.* a year, and to raise once more the question of a general evangelical alliance; Falkenberg, in collaboration with Camerarius, was to attempt to revive the Swedish-Dutch alliance of 1614 (it was to expire in April) and to broaden its basis by the inclusion of other suitably disposed powers. In addition, Spens was instructed to offer mediation in the Franco-English war, and to suggest a French invasion of Italy. As to the last two points, his mission proved supererogatory, for Richelieu had crossed the Alps before he arrived in England, and the peace of Susa was completed before he could take a hand in it. But even in regard to the other items in his instructions his efforts led to no result. England did indeed listen to him with sympathy: the return of Roe from Constantinople at the end of 1628 had done something to counterbalance the passivity of Mr. Secretary Weston, for Roe had a keen sense of the importance of the Baltic to British interests, and he dreamed of joint action by Gustav Adolf and Bethlen Gabor.[3] But not even Roe's enthusiasm could push England into fresh engagements now, at a moment when Charles and his parliament were

[1] L. Weibull, *De diplomatiska förbindelserna mellan Sverige och Frankrike 1629-1631* [cited: L. Weibull, *DF*], p. 11; Ahnlund, *Gustaf Adolf inför tyska kriget*, p. 117. Contrast Droysen's curiously obtuse comment: *Gustaf Adolf*, I. 352-3.

[2] F. Weber, *Dietrich von Falkenberg*, pp. 48-55; Rydfors, p. 120; *Sv. Krig*, II. 506, III. 235 *seqq.*

[3] *Letters relating to the Mission of Sir Thomas Roe to Gustavus Adolphus* [cited: Roe], pp. 2-4, where he calls the Baltic 'the Indyes of the materials of shipping'; Rydfors, pp. 116-18; Styffe, p. 535; F. H. Schubert, *Ludwig Camerarius*, pp. 367-8.

approaching a final rupture.[1] And the efforts of Roe and Spens to incite the Venetian ambassador to persuade his government to promise financial aid had no better fortune. The Seignory was friendly, for the Republic felt herself imperilled by the prospect of a Habsburg victory in Mantua, but the ambassador in London did not feel justified in pledging his government.[2] Camerarius and Falkenberg did no better in the Netherlands. The Dutch were as resentful as ever of the Swedish tolls at Danzig and Pillau; they were not very interested in a general alliance, which would be of only problematical value to them; and their reaction to Swedish approaches was distinctly cool.[3]

While these overtures were being made to the western powers, another emissary of Gustav Adolf had been making a diplomatic round trip of Europe, with the ultimate object of renewing contact with Bethlen Gabor. An embassy to Transylvania had been planned as long ago as November 1627, and had actually been sent off in the summer of 1628, when Paul Strassburg left Sweden for Bethlen Gabor's court.[4] He had found Bethlen left rather high and dry by the peace between the Emperor and the Porte, for it had cut him off (on paper at least) from the hope of Turkish aid; but he still aspired to the fiefs of Moldavia and Wallachia, and he was more active than ever in promoting agitations designed to facilitate his succession to the Polish crown—though he tried hard to keep this dark from Strassburg. In these circumstances Strassburg made little progress; and accordingly in November 1628 Gustav Adolf determined to second his efforts by the despatch of another envoy. The man selected for this task was none other than Wolmar von Farensbach, who since 1627 had turned his coat and reconciled himself with Sweden. It was thought that the part played by Madeleine von Farensbach in promoting Bethlen Gabor's marriage [5] might make her brother an acceptable personage in Transylvania.

[1] Zobel, unappreciative of these difficulties, referred to Charles I as '*rege anglo stomachobundo*': Paul, II. 123 *note*.

[2] J. Bühring, *Venedig, Gustav Adolf und Rohan*, pp. 1, 44-9; Roe, p. 5.

[3] Carlsson, pp. 26-7; Rydfors, pp. 115-21; M. G. Schybergson, *Sveriges och Hollands diplomatiska förbindelser*, pp. lxxxvii-xcix; *RRP*, I. 132 *note* 1; Ahnlund, *Gustaf Adolf inför tyska kriget*, p. 187: Schubert, *Camerarius*, pp. 357-9. The instructions for Camerarius are printed in Söltl, III. 271-4: it is noteworthy that Gustav Adolf demanded that he should be considered as '*Haupt*' of the alliance for the duration of hostilities, and have the '*Directorium*' of military operations.

[4] His mission had economic as well as political objectives: he was to try to persuade Bethlen to co-operate in keeping up the price of copper: C. Wibling, *Sveriges förhållande till Siebenbürgen*, p. 23.

[5] See above, p. 310.

Farensbach went first to The Hague, where he met Roe on his return journey from Turkey; and Roe perhaps painted the benevolent dispositions of Bethlen Gabor in somewhat too rosy colours. Thence he went to Switzerland, with orders to get in touch with the Protestant cantons; and from Switzerland he crossed into Italy, visiting Mantua and Venice. In Venice he was well received, and the Seignory put guides and galleys at his disposal.[1] He eventually arrived in Transylvania in May 1629. In some respects he found the situation favourable: the Porte had recently had successes against the Persians, and felt more at leisure to give some attention to European affairs. But the attitude of the Transylvanian magnates was not encouraging; the Roman Catholic minority among them had been heartened by the Emperor's victories; and, worst of all, Bethlen Gabor's wife, the Brandenburg princess Catherine, upon whom Gustav Adolf had hoped to be able to rely, had been converted to Roman Catholicism, and now used her influence against Sweden. Bethlen Gabor himself was so preoccupied with his designs on Poland that he had little interest for any other project—and had indeed come to look upon Gustav Adolf as a possible rival for the Polish crown. Strassburg and Farensbach could not agree; and Farensbach, alleging in justification that Gustav Adolf had given him inadequate support, shortly afterwards returned to his imperialist allegiance. Bethlen Gabor himself died on 15 November 1629, at the age of 49, and the internal affairs of Transylvania became for a time confused.[2]

The apparent results of Farensbach's embassy were therefore *nil*. Yet that embassy was itself a sign that Gustav Adolf was gradually being drawn into the European vortex. Apart from Farensbach's visits to the Protestant cantons, and to Venice, he had made a special point of establishing contact with George Frederick of Baden, then living in exile at Geneva, and had urged him to use his influence to stir up Strassburg, Ulm and Nuremberg to do something for the Protestant cause. About the same time Gustav Adolf was in touch with Julius Frederick of Württemberg. These contacts represent the first tentative attempts since 1623 to create a Swedish party in Germany.[3] And beyond the boundaries of Germany, in the far

[1] Bühring, pp. 40-1.

[2] For the missions to Bethlen Gabor, see *AOSB*, I. IV. 724, II. III. 185; Angyal, pp. 70-2; L. Weibull, *DF*, p. 9; Wibling, pp. 20-37; Ahnlund, *Storhetstidens gryning*, p. 124; Wł. Konopczyński, *Dzieje polski nowożytnej*, I. 278.

[3] B. Boëthius, *Filip Sadlers beskickning 1629-1630*, p. 212.

east and south-east of Europe, Gustav Adolf was already beginning the search for possible auxiliaries: it was now that he first contemplated the sending of an embassy to the Tatars of the Crimea; it was now that the ground was prepared for the first permanent Swedish Resident at Moscow, whose appointment dates from 1631; it was now that Gustav Adolf obtained that access to the Russian grain-market which was to be so important to him in the next year or two.[1]

(iii) *The Loss of Denmark*

In the letter of 30 November 1628 in which Oxenstierna expounded to the *riksråd* his view of the course to be followed by Swedish policy, he had alluded to the advantages to Sweden of the Danish alliance. 'Denmark', he had written, 'I hold at this time, and for so long as she continues to make head against the Emperor, for nothing other than a bastion for Sweden, and the Danish fleet and army as the unpaid servants of my country.'[2] But now the bastion was crumbling, and the servants would serve no longer.

By the close of 1628 both Kristian IV and Wallenstein were obviously ready for peace. Wallenstein was anxious to have his hands free for action in Italy, where he had private schemes for his own advantage; he may possibly have been sincere in his loudly professed desire to be off on a crusade against Constantinople; and he was certainly increasingly nervous of the possibility of Swedish intervention in Germany. From his fastnesses on the Baltic shore he watched, as under the compulsion of some powerful fascination, every move of the King of Sweden. As Erik Ryning's squadron cruised off his coast, blockading his infant navy in its ports, his hatred of Gustav Adolf grew hotter; but it was a hatred strongly tempered by admiration, and not without an alloy of fear. Wallenstein maintained Johann Kepler in his service as his private astrologer; and each of them wasted a good deal of time calculating Gustav Adolf's nativity, and drawing the appropriate inferences.[3] In comparison with the baleful Northern Lights which dazzled Wallenstein

[1] Ahnlund, *Storhetstidens gryning*, pp. 120-1; *id.*, *Gustaf Adolf inför tyska kriget*, p. 312; V. Giterman, *Geschichte Russlands*, I. 475-6. Sweden had been in contact with the Crimean Tatars before, in 1581 and 1592: G. Jarring, *Gustaf II Adolf och Tatarerna på Krim*, p. 306.

[2] *AOSB*, I. IV. 279.

[3] *cf.* Wallenstein's letter to Arnim, 21 May 1628, thanking him for sending the date of Gustav Adolf's birthday: Förster, I. 338.

from Stockholm, the feebler luminary of Copenhagen now held little interest for him. The Danish war was no longer important. He gave no support to Pappenheim's schemes for an invasion of the Danish islands in 1629. Visions of a Habsburg domination of the Baltic, to be secured by a conquest of the Sound, might tempt von Strahlendorf and attract Ferdinand; but Wallenstein had other matters to think of.[1] As for Kristian IV, he fought only for as long as there was no prospect of a tolerable peace. He was jealous of Gustav Adolf, who had supplanted him at Stralsund, and relations were not improved by Kristian's levying toll off Ruden upon vessels proceeding to Stralsund.[2] The meeting of the Hanse in September 1628 had urged him to make peace. His own subjects were clamouring for it. For the international and religious consequences he cared little—or at least he put such considerations behind him.

By the end of November 1628 Wallenstein had induced Tilly to agree that negotiations should be begun, and it was soon decided that the peace conference should take place at Lübeck, and that it should open on 6 January 1629.[3] Kristian IV, on his side, made no difficulty; and the first formal session was duly held, with fewer preliminary delays than might have been expected, on 22 January. Wallenstein and Tilly were both represented by commissioners, but the negotiations were really managed by Wallenstein from Güstrow.

To this conference Sweden, as Denmark's ally, had some right to expect an invitation. No such invitation was forthcoming. If Denmark were resolved on peace, Gustav Adolf would have preferred that Sweden should be asked to act as mediator. No suggestion of Swedish mediation was ever made. Both Wallenstein and Kristian were determined to exclude the possibility of Swedish interference [4]; and Kristian's instructions to his representatives, by omitting any mention of Stralsund and by avoiding the question of *dominium maris*, were perhaps designed to deprive Sweden of any *locus standi*.[5]

[1] Ahnlund, *Kring Gustav Adolf*, pp. 171-2, 175, 179; Förster, I. 398; Hallwich, II. 454, 527; Fridericia, *YPH*, p. 31 *note* 4; Ahnlund, *Gustaf Adolf inför tyska kriget*, pp. 64-5, 69-71, 81-2. Wallenstein seems to have suborned an agent to murder Gustav Adolf about this time: *ibid.*, pp. 95-7.

[2] *Christian IVs Breve*, II. 188; Carlsson, *Gustaf Adolf och Stralsund*, pp. 235-6. To Swedish complaints Kristian retorted that he was only doing what Gustav Adolf was doing off Danzig.

[3] For the negotiations, see E. Wilmanns, *Der Lübecker Friede*, *passim*.

[4] Wallenstein wrote: 'Ihre Majestät sollen nur mit Dänemark und keinem Andern traktieren, denn sie kommen nicht, zu komponieren, sondern zu turbieren': Hallwich, II. 544.

[5] Fridericia, *YPH*, p. 38.

Nevertheless, Gustav Adolf determined at least to make an effort to obtain access to the meetings. Karl Banér, Johan Adler Salvius and Johan Sparre were appointed Swedish commissioners, and the negotiators at Lübeck were informed that Sweden desired admission to the conference, as being concerned with the fate of Stralsund. The commissioners were provided with instructions to seek a comprehensive settlement for north Germany, to which Sweden, as well as Denmark, might be a party. Sweden would demand that the troops of the Emperor and League evacuate both the Saxon Circles; that all new fortifications on the North Sea or Baltic be demolished; that the ports be free, and no warships be maintained there. Denmark was to regain her lost possessions, but in return Kristian was to disband his forces. All princes within the Saxon Circles, and the Counts of East Friesland and Oldenburg, were to recover their lands as they had held them before the war: those who had been adjudged guilty of offences against the Emperor were to be mulcted of a fine, and in the case of the Dukes of Mecklenburg Sweden would stand guarantee for its payment. Sweden for her part would evacuate Stralsund, provided the town were guaranteed its former rights and were paid an indemnity for the damage it had sustained at imperialist hands.[1]

These were conditions which had no chance of acceptance. It was the moment when the cause of Ferdinand II stood at its zenith; when the Emperor in the plenitude of power regained was on the eve of proceeding to the promulgation of the Edict of Restitution; when the total victory of the Catholic cause in north Germany seemed assured. Yet it does not follow, because such terms were unacceptable, that they were drawn up to be rejected. They were a statement of what Gustav Adolf now conceived to be necessary if Sweden's security were to be a reality for the future. No mention was made of the Palatinate, of Bohemia, of the fate of Protestantism in south Germany. From Gustav Adolf's point of view the proposals were severely practical: they represented a considered goal of policy; or, in another aspect, they represented the price for his abstention from interference in Germany. But whatever their nature, the Swedish conditions never came before the conference. Gustav Adolf's commissioners were refused a safe-conduct through Denmark. When a Swedish agent presented himself at Lübeck in

[1] Ahnlund, *Gustaf Adolf inför tyska kriget*, pp. 127-31; on which also the following paragraphs are mainly based.

February, the imperial commissioners declined to admit him. And when in March Sweden tried at least to obtain admission for the representatives of Stralsund, Wallenstein retorted that he would shoot any Stralsunder who might fall into his hands.[1] The only resource which remained was an appeal to public opinion; and in April Gustav Adolf, with the assent of the *råd*, put out an appeal to the Electors in which his grievances against the Emperor were recited at large; and followed it up with a separate letter to the Elector of Saxony, in which stress was laid upon their common Lutheranism, and help was offered, if he should need it. Both the appeal and the letter were propaganda-pieces; and both fell remarkably flat.[2]

Meanwhile the Danish and imperial negotiators had made a start. The prospects of agreement at first appeared far from encouraging. The imperialists began with demands which would have utterly ruined Denmark: they required the cession of the Danish portions of Slesvig and Holstein, the handing over of Jutland to Saxony (in exchange for which John George was to evacuate Lusatia, which he had been occupying as a pledge since 1621), the renunciation of all dynastic ambitions upon the north German bishoprics, the closing of the Sound to enemies of Habsburg, and the payment of a large war indemnity. Extravagant as these demands were, the terms proposed by Denmark were scarcely less high-pitched. The Danish commissioners required the evacuation and restoration of all Danish territory, with an indemnity for damage; a guarantee of safety for the Protestants of the Lower Saxon Circle, and an amnesty for those who had taken up arms against the Emperor.[3] It was no wonder, therefore, that the negotiations at Lübeck should soon have stuck fast, with little apparent hope of removing the deadlock. Kristian IV, however, had foreseen this situation. His demands had been made exorbitant in the first instance in the hope of saving Holstein, or at least Jutland; and he had prepared effective measures to persuade Wallenstein to adopt a more conciliatory attitude.

[1] Ahnlund, *op. cit.*, pp. 141, 145, 160-1. Leheusen, the Swedish agent who tried to obtain admission to the conference, told Ogier that the snub then inflicted so rankled with Gustav Adolf that it was among the factors that decided him to intervene in Germany: Ogier, pp. 98-9.

[2] *Arkiv*, I. 33-7; B. F. von Chemnitz, *Königlichen Schwedischen in Teutschland geführten Krieg*, I. 12-14; *cf.* Lundorp, *Acta Publica*, III. 49-50; Ahnlund, *op. cit.*, p. 178; *Sv. Krig*, III. 150-1.

[3] Ahnlund, *op. cit.*, pp. 137-8; Fridericia, *YPH*, pp. 39-43.

Early in January, Kristian had issued an invitation to Gustav Adolf to meet him on the frontier for personal conversations. The place suggested was Ulvsbäck; the date, 20 February. Gustav Adolf accepted this invitation. It seemed to offer him a chance—probably the only chance that now remained—to keep Kristian true to the alliance, to influence the negotiations at Lübeck and possibly even to bring about their failure. On 20 February, therefore, they met at Ulvsbäck parsonage. Gustav Adolf took with him Jakob de la Gardie, Per Banér, Johan Sparre and Gabriel Gustafsson Oxenstierna, who has left a famous description of the occasion; Kristian was accompanied by members of his council. Gustav Adolf began by asking whether Kristian had any information about the progress of the imperial navy, and followed this by an enquiry as to how the negotiations at Lübeck were progressing: Kristian answered that there did not seem to be much chance of peace. Discussion then turned on the best method of dealing with the menace of Wallenstein's fleet. Kristian contended that the easiest way was to burn the ships in their ports; Gustav Adolf urged that the only certain method was to capture the ports themselves. Gustav Adolf next made concrete proposals. He suggested that Denmark should follow an agreed policy at the Lübeck negotiations and formulate conditions of peace in consultation with Sweden; and when Kristian objected that he had already presented his peace terms to the Emperor, and could not alter them now, Gustav Adolf produced alternative proposals for carrying on the war. He was ready to bring 'a stately army' to Germany, to act as director of a joint force, to supply three-quarters of the men and defray three-quarters of their cost. Kristian professed some scepticism as to whether Gustav Adolf could make good these offers, and added that in any case he could himself make no further military effort. The only help he wanted from Sweden was two or three ships: not that he really needed them, but '*ad augendam famam*'—*i.e.* to impress the imperial negotiators at Lübeck. Gustav Adolf then touched, not over-modestly, on his own exertions for the Protestant interest, not omitting the bullet in his shoulder (which Kristian was allowed to feel), and protested his readiness to lay down his life for the common cause. To a question from Gustav Adolf as to what Denmark relied upon for her safety, Kristian answered, 'On God'; but Gustav Adolf retorted by urging that God helps those that help themselves. Pressed further on this point, Kristian confessed that he had no hope of the western powers (which, all things considered, is not surprising), but alluded vaguely to the possibility of a diversion to be produced by the Turks, or the Saxons, or the Bavarians, or by revolts of the conquered populations. At this point lunch was taken. 'Little was eaten,' reported Gustav Adolf, 'but we made up for it by drinking quantities of bad wine, which had perhaps been frozen.' This indiscreet dietary did not improve their tempers. When Kristian once again coldly refused all co-operation, Gustav Adolf in exasperation turned to the Danish councillors who were present and addressed to them a '*monitum valde pungens*'; at which Kristian understandably appeared 'somewhat irritated'. He now sharply asked Gustav Adolf 'what business Y.R.H. has in Germany, and whether you have any real ground for complaint against the Emperor'. Gustav Adolf changed colour, took a step or two forward, burst out with 'Is that a question worth asking?' and proceeded to the familiar catalogue of his grievances, to which Kristian answered not a word.[1]

With that the meeting came to a stormy end. Gustav Adolf's verdict on the affair was '*summa, parturiunt montes, nascitur ridiculus mus*', and he conjectured that Kristian must have been drunk when he issued the invitation.[2] Kristian, on the other hand, reported that 'The meeting went well, thank God, so that we parted friends'.[3] It would have been more accurate to say that they did not part in open enmity; but it was undoubtedly true that from the point of view of Kristian's immediate advantage the meeting had been all that he designed it to be. It impressed Europe. It impressed the imperial negotiators at Lübeck. It gave to the uninitiated just that appearance of Scandinavian solidarity which Kristian needed if he were to extort reasonable peace terms from Wallenstein. It probably made the peace of Lübeck possible. But it had other consequences which were less favourable to Denmark in the long run. The fiasco at Ulvsbäck meant that when Gustav Adolf intervened in Germany—and Kristian can now have had no doubt that such an intervention was coming—he would intervene alone. If Sweden were beaten, Denmark would escape immediate involvement in the catastrophe; but her position as the guardian of the Baltic narrows would be more untenable than ever, her natural ally against imperial naval pre-

[1] *Riksrådet Gabriel Gustafsson Oxenstjernas berättelse, passim*; *AOSB*, II. I. 463-4, II. III. 173-4; Ahnlund, *Gustaf Adolf inför tyska kriget*, pp. 149-52; P. Engelstoft, *Christian IVs Tidsalder*, pp. 262-4.

[2] *AOSB*, II. I. 464.

[3] *Christian IVs Breve*, II. 178-81; *cf.* Erslev, II. 217-18 *note* 6.

tensions would be gone, and a triumphant Habsburg would scarcely be likely to leave her long in the enjoyment of an independent policy. But if Gustav Adolf were successful in Germany, the case would be little better. A Swedish *patrocinium* of north Germany would put the mastery of the Baltic into Gustav Adolf's hands, it would deprive Denmark of the leadership of the Protestant north, and it would set a bar quite as effective as imperial conquest to the dynastic ambitions of the house of Oldenburg upon the north German bishoprics. Kristian, indeed, could not afford to see Gustav Adolf successful; and from the moment that he forced him to follow his own line in Germany, the logic of events, reinforcing the animosities of the past, edged him into covert or overt hostility to his over-mighty neighbour. Had the alliance been maintained, had Kristian participated, on anything like a footing of equality, in the German venture, Gustav Adolf would have been to some extent 'grouped', and the danger to Denmark would have been less. By the attitude Kristian adopted at Ulvsbäck, he relieved Gustav Adolf of the necessity for taking any sort of account of Denmark's feelings and interests, and enabled him to point to Kristian as a renegade from the Protestant cause. It may be admitted that it would have been difficult, even to impossibility, for Kristian to turn his back at this juncture upon the chance of peace; but it is none the less true that the meeting at Ulvsbäck seriously affected the future history of his country. It registered another step downwards from the position of primacy in the north which Denmark had indisputably enjoyed in 1613. And it completed Gustav Adolf's disillusionment with Kristian IV.

For the moment, however, the effect was all that could be desired: even in February Wallenstein had been pressing concessions upon the Emperor; in March, determined that there should be peace, he began secret negotiations behind the back of his delegates to the Lübeck conference. Early in April he and Tilly sent a joint representation to the Emperor urging in the most emphatic terms the absolute necessity of moderation, so that peace with Denmark might be made before the expected blow was delivered from Sweden.[1] And now, at the eleventh hour, those powers whose delusive promises of aid had done so much to disillusion Kristian with the evangelical cause, awoke to the danger of the loss of Denmark. England despatched Sir Thomas Roe to persuade Kristian to continue the

[1] Goetz, IV. II. 352; Wilmanns, p. 48 *seqq.*; Hallwich, II. 541-2, 550; Fridericia, *YPH*, pp. 47-9; Droysen, I. 361-2.

war; the Dutch suddenly became fertile of promises of increased financial support; and in April there arrived in Denmark, by way of Munich, Richelieu's agent Hercule de Charnacé, charged, among his other commissions, to induce Kristian to make a separate peace with Bavaria and the League.[1] This was an idea which would have commanded some support among members of the League if it had been made a year earlier. At this moment, however, Maximilian was distrustful of France; for there were persistent rumours of a French invasion of the Rhineland, to support the restoration of Frederick V. Richelieu's plan of reconciling Maximilian and Kristian, on lines so strikingly anticipatory of the treaty of Bärwalde,[2] therefore came to nothing.[3] But whatever its reception in Munich, the time had gone by for its favourable consideration in Copenhagen. It was now too late. Kristian had made up his mind to conclude; the terms which Wallenstein was offering were too attractive for a beaten and humiliated monarch to decline; peace was as good as made. On 27 May Wallenstein and Tilly ratified the peace of Lübeck; on 7 June the treaty was made public.[4]

It proved to be astonishingly moderate. Kristian renounced, for himself and his sons, all pretensions upon the north German bishoprics; he promised to abstain in future from all meddling in German affairs; and he resigned his office as captain-general of the Lower Saxon Circle: at a stroke a dozen years of Danish foreign policy were swept away. But on the other hand he paid no indemnity; and the imperialists evacuated all their purely Danish conquests: not a foot of Danish territory was sacrificed. Urban VIII condemned it as a scandalous peace; Kristian, with no thought now for the Palatinate or even Mecklenburg, wrote complacently to Adolf Frederick that 'he had no ground for complaint', and even had the effrontery to strike a medal in honour of 'the final victory of the good

[1] Roe, p. 5; Fridericia, *YPH*, pp. 53-6. There seems little to be said for Gardiner's suggestion (Roe, p. 6) that it was the dissolution of parliament on 10 March that frightened Kristian into making peace.

[2] Among the terms Richelieu proposed were the following: 'Le armi dell' uno rispettino li estati dell' altro in maniera che s'astenghino d'usar atti di hostilita in prejudicio di detti loro stati, e piacendo a Baviera questo, il re di Francia si promette, che il re di Danimarca lo gradira e dara parola al re di Francia d'osservarlo, dando il duca di Baviera una simile parola a S. Mta di non offender Danimarca in [*sic*] congiungere le sue arme con chi assalisse li stati del detto re di Danimarca.' Further, 'Re di Francia s'impieghera con Inghilterra et Danimarca *et lor collegati* [my italics], che non offendino Baviera ne li stati gia posseduti dal Palatino': Goetz, IV. II. 408-10.

[3] Goetz, IV. II. 99, 143, 221, 318, 323, 332, 402, 414, 434, 439; Riezler, V. 355-7.

[4] Wilmanns, p. 71.

old cause'.[1] Of *dominium maris* there was no mention: Kristian tacitly maintained his claims; but already on 24 April Ferdinand had appointed Gabriel de Roy as imperial commissary-general, to push on the building of the fleet. As to Kristian's ally, Gustav Adolf might, if he notified his intention within three months, become a party to the treaty—a privilege which was indeed open to Denmark's former backers in the west, as also to Spain, Poland and the League.[2]

The Protestant world was deeply disturbed by the peace of Lübeck; and Vosbergen, discussing the situation with Roe in July, 'spake doubtfully and fearfully of some secrett articles'.[3] There were no secret articles; but the published treaty was bad enough. It meant the final breakdown of the Anglo-Palatine plans for a Protestant league. It meant, in fact, the end of one phase of the great war, and the opening of another.

Upon Gustav Adolf its apparent effect was less than might have been expected: partly, no doubt, because he had foreseen the outcome. When informed of the treaty, he merely replied that he would be glad of Kristian's good offices in seeking a settlement with the Emperor; and Kristian, on his side, responded with a vague offer of mediation.[4] Gustav Adolf did not want a breach with Denmark, least of all now; and whatever his private feelings, he contrived to keep the tone of his communications with Copenhagen reasonably cordial. The only obvious consequence of the peace of Lübeck in Sweden was in fact a resolution of the *riksdag*, on 29 June, whereby the Estates in effect ratified the *råd*-resolutions of December and January, and, by approving the terms which Gustav Adolf had intended to propose at Lübeck, associated themselves definitively with his conception of security.[5] But the *riksdag* on this occasion met in the King's absence; for on 21 May 1629 Gustav Adolf had landed at Pillau for the last of his campaigns in Poland.

(iv) *The End of the Polish War: the Truce of Altmark*

At the close of 1627, and in the spring of 1628, Axel Oxenstierna had been optimistic about the military prospects in Poland. His

[1] Fridericia, *YPH*, p. 106; *id.*, *Danmarks Riges Historie*, p. 209; *cf.* Erslev, II. 187-90.

[2] Fridericia, *YPH*, pp. 106-7, 110; Ritter, III. 412-13; *Sv. Krig*, III. 50. So much for Frederick V's plea to Kristian to include him in the peace: Goetz, IV. II. 344.

[3] Roe, p. 32.

[4] Fridericia, *YPH*, pp. 119-20; Styffe, p. 604.

[5] Stiernman, I. 814; *SRARP*, I. 95.

plans for the campaign of 1628, as we have seen, envisaged either an attack on Weichselmünde or an advance against Graudenz, whereby Sweden would provide herself with a new supply area to supplement the exhausted resources of the delta, and would, incidentally, cut the main line of communication overland between Warsaw and Danzig.[1] When Gustav Adolf landed in May 1628 he approved these suggestions, and the campaign of 1628 resolved itself in fact into an unsuccessful attempt to carry the second of them into execution. The lack of success was due, in the first instance, to the weather. The early summer was exceptionally wet, all major operations became impossible, and the army suffered greatly from the flooding of its quarters: Per Brahe in after years vividly remembered how the water kept creeping up his bed-posts.[2] But an offensive must have been delayed in any case, for the new levies came over but slowly. Until August, no action of any consequence occurred, apart from a sudden dash upon the Vistula by Gustav Adolf, which resulted in the destruction of a number of Polish warships lying in the river between Danzig and Weichselmünde.

In August the weather cleared up, and Gustav Adolf with an army of 15,000 men (including no less than 6000 cavalry) moved south to seek out Koniecpolski, who with a force of 10,000 men was encamped around Mewe. On their way they occupied Marienwerder, which belonged to George William of Brandenburg, and this did not improve Gustav Adolf's relations with his brother-in-law. The real object of the campaign that followed was to destroy Koniecpolski's army; but it was an object which never came within sight of attainment. Gustav Adolf pushed on to Graudenz, from Graudenz to the Drewenz, and thence to Strasburg (which he took); but Koniecpolski gave him no real chance of battle. He stood behind his earthworks at Graudenz and refused to come out; he declined to be lured into the open by diversionary attacks on his communications with Mewe; he devastated the country so that the Swedish armies could not live upon it. On 29 September Gustav Adolf was forced to begin the retreat from Strasburg; and it proved disastrous. Nearly 5000 men were lost by desertion or casualties; Baudissin was surprised, beaten and wounded by a detachment of Polish cavalry; the complete destruction of the army was averted only by the speed of the Swedish withdrawal. When in mid-October Gustav

[1] *Sv. Krig*, II. 405-6.
[2] *Svea Rikes Drotset Grefve Per Brahes tänkebok*, p. 20.

Adolf went into winter quarters around Preussisch-Holland, veterans of thirty years' standing said that they had never seen an army in such a state. Axel Oxenstierna might boast about Sweden's now being able to defy the Poles in open country, but the plain truth was that Gustav Adolf had been outgeneralled, and the campaign had been a fiasco.[1]

The chancellor, left behind at Elbing when Gustav Adolf returned to Sweden, passed a winter which put a severe strain upon even his ordinarily equanimous temperament. He felt himself neglected by the King, he considered that the difficulties he had to contend with were not appreciated by the home government, and he suspected that Skytte was intriguing against him. To his brother he complained that never in his life had he been so overburdened with work and so harassed by anxieties.[2] Not least among them was the enterprise of the Polish commanders, whose plundering raids deprived the Swedes of supplies and menaced them in their winter quarters. It was in an effort to check these raids, and also with the idea of relieving the isolated Swedish outpost at Strasburg, that Oxenstierna at the end of January 1629 ordered Herman Wrangel to march south, in the hope of catching and destroying the Polish forces under Potocki. Wrangel chased his enemy for three days before coming up with him at Gorzno. Here on 2 February was fought one of the biggest battles of this war. It resulted in a complete victory for the Swedes: some 500 prisoners were taken, and the Polish casualties were numerous.[3] Wrangel immediately pressed on in the hope of taking Thorn; but though he succeeded in mastering the outworks, it was soon clear that he had little chance of capturing the town itself. With Polish reinforcements coming up fast, the best he could do was to relieve Strasburg and hurry back to the delta before any misfortune overtook his little army.[4]

The battle of Gorzno was thus barren of any serious military consequences; but in other respects it had results of some importance. It made a strong impression upon contemporaries, re-establishing the prestige of Swedish arms, which had been somewhat dimmed by the unsuccessful campaign of 1628; and it persuaded the Poles to

[1] For this campaign, see *Sv. Krig*, II. 411-32; Petri, II. 85-90; Hoppe, p. 251 *seqq.*; T. Korzon, *Dzieje wojen i wojskowośce w Polsce*, II. 245 *seqq.*

[2] *AOSB*, I. IV. 335, II. VI. 38, II. IX. 136; Ahnlund, *Oxenstierna*, pp. 533-6.

[3] *AOSB*, I. IV. 359-75, II. IX. 137-40, 142; *Sv. Krig*, II. 439-50.

[4] The Poles struck a medal to commemorate Thorn's deliverance.

agree to an armistice.[1] Negotiations for a cessation of hostilities had been in progress for much of the winter, and at one time they seemed to have made some progress: Sigismund showed himself so far conciliatory as to accord Gustav Adolf, in the powers which he gave to his negotiators, the style of King of Sweden, which certainly represented an important concession. Oxenstierna, however, never had much faith in the Poles' sincerity,[2] and his scepticism was confirmed when they refused to agree to the Swedish proposal for an armistice till 31 May 1629. But the battle of Gorzno made the Poles change their tune: on 8 March they accepted the Swedish suggestions; and for nearly three months there was a truce upon the Vistula.[3] When next hostilities were resumed, the long-expected imperialist intervention in Poland was an accomplished fact.

During the abortive negotiations of the winter, Ferdinand II had asked Sigismund III to try to obtain his inclusion in any truce between Sweden and Poland.[4] This rather unexpected request was a measure of the anxiety with which the Emperor was now beginning to regard the situation in the Baltic and in north Germany. He feared a Swedish landing in force at Stralsund; he feared a possible Swedish campaign up the Oder, which might bring Gustav Adolf's armies to the Habsburg province of Silesia.[5] But if a stable truce, in which Ferdinand was included, proved unattainable, the alternative, from the imperialists' point of view, was force. They were as anxious to keep the Polish war alive as Gustav Adolf was to wind it up, and for the same reasons; and if negotiations failed, they must try armed intervention. The idea was by no means a new one. In the summer of 1626 the Poles had themselves refused Wallenstein's proffered aid. In the spring of 1627 Wallenstein had written that whatever happened Sigismund must not be left in the lurch; and in April of that year the imperialist general Adolf of Holstein transferred himself to the Polish service. An imperialist contingent had fought at Dirschau. A year later there were strong rumours of concentrations on Brandenburg territory, supposed to be destined for service in

[1] *cf. AOSB*, II. IX. 145-6, 762-3.

[2] Nor much opinion of their intelligence: he wrote to his brother on 4 January 1629: 'In many things the Polack must be handled like a child. There are plenty of peasants in Sweden who have a great deal more sense than some of the starosts and voyvodes in Poland': Ahnlund, *Oxenstierna*, p. 460.

[3] For these negotiations, see *AOSB*, I. IV. 293, 308, 310, 312, 322, 389, 393, 397, 409, 418, II. I. 428-36, 455.

[4] Gindely, p. 35.

[5] Ahnlund, *Gustaf Adolf inför tyska kriget*, p. 166: *cf.* the similar fears of the League: Goetz, II. IV. 187-8, 428, 438.

Poland.[1] Yet the Poles themselves viewed the prospect of Habsburg aid with distaste and alarm. They feared that a strong army might give the King a chance to clip the wings of *aurea libertas*. They feared that Wallenstein, as the price of his help, might demand west Prussia for the *Reich*.[2]

The news of Gorzno forced them to stifle their fears and put their prejudices in their pockets. Negotiations with Wallenstein had in fact been in progress since September 1628: they were now brought to a point; and the *sejm* at last agreed to admit imperialist auxiliaries, to the number of 10,000. Wallenstein wasted no time. In April he sent an army of 12,000 under Arnim to the Polish border, with instructions to penetrate some days' march into Poland before announcing their arrival. He knew the repugnance with which the Poles accepted his aid; and he wished to present them with a *fait accompli* before they could change their minds. His precaution proved justified. The arrival of Arnim and his men unloosed a medley of recriminations and accusations. The *sejm* denied that they had given permission to bring in 10,000 men: the maximum, they said, was 6000; they blamed Sigismund for conspiring with Wallenstein against their liberties; Sigismund, who disliked Arnim as a former Swedish officer, upbraided him for advancing into the country without leave; the representatives of the *sejm* demanded that he should quit Poland forthwith. It was only after heated exchanges that a convention was agreed upon between the Republic and the imperial commander; and it proved sufficiently galling to Arnim. His army was not to be admitted to quarters in any Polish town, but was to camp in open country; an oath of fidelity to the King and Republic of Poland was exacted from his men; and though he retained the independent command of his troops, he recognized Sigismund as his commander-in-chief.[3] In short, the imperialist intervention began in the worst possible circumstances, with relations already strained to breaking-point. Arnim was already complaining bitterly to Wallenstein; and almost from the start of the campaign was on the verge of resigning his command.

[1] *AOSB*, I. IV. 143; Baur, *Philipp von Sötern*, I. 105; Ahnlund, *op. cit.*, pp. 23-4; *id.*, *Oxenstierna*, pp. 439, 481.

[2] Konopczyński, I. 274; Paul, II. 71: a Polish commissioner at George William's court refused to drink the Emperor's health, saying, 'Quid mihi cum Caesare? Ego sum minister et amans Reipublicae. Odi Caesarem': *ibid.*, II. 117.

[3] *Sv. Krig*, II. 452; Irmer, pp. 105-6; Ahnlund, *Gustaf Adolf inför tyska kriget*, pp. 195-6.

The Polish-Habsburg conjunction on land had been preceded by a union of their forces at sea. The relief of Stralsund had finally shattered whatever prospect there might have been of aid from the Hanse for the Habsburg fleet, and the imperial commissioners had accordingly been thrown back upon their own resources. By the close of 1628 they had in the harbour of Wismar a dozen or so of warships, more or less fit to take to the high seas if Erik Ryning would let them out; manned by pressed and reluctant crews; and under the command of Count Philip of Mansfeld. Efforts were now made to induce Sigismund to send his own little navy from Danzig to Wismar. Madrid pointed out that though each squadron was comparatively impotent, taken singly, there was some chance of doing something if they were united. After much persuasion Sigismund at last capitulated to these arguments: early in the new year of 1629 his ships crept out of the Vistula; and at the beginning of February seven of them came safely to port in Wismar.[1]

The arrival of Arnim in Prussia threw Gustav Adolf's plans for 1629 entirely out of gear. The offensive from Stralsund became impossible, and the King's presence became imperative not on the Oder but on the Vistula. Wallenstein had achieved his object: the German campaign was deferred until 1630. In the spring of 1629 Gustav Adolf had been moving gradually to the view that the offensive in Germany, which he had now quite decided on for this summer, must be the main and not merely the subordinate effort. This certainly was his plan if a long truce with Poland could be obtained. In the early spring he was hoping to invade Germany in June; but the comparative failure of his recruiting agents in the west, and the growing likelihood of Wallenstein's sending troops to Poland, caused him to modify this programme. On 18 April he held a meeting of the *råd*, in order to associate them with his policy. They dutifully advised him not to purchase a truce with Poland by extravagant concessions, and he in return informed them that he had now decided to defer the campaign in Germany until the autumn.[2]

[1] A. Czołowski, *Marynarka w Polsce: Szkic historyczny*, pp. 151-2; Messow, pp. 77-8; *Sv. Krig*, Supp. Vol. I. 61-2. Sigismund's decision was taken as early as August 1628. He regretted it later, for Kristian IV's fleet retaliated by privateering against Danzig shipping. But it was then too late.

[2] *AOSB*, I. IV. 282-8, II. I. 458-62; *Sv. Krig*, II. 513, III. 142-4; Ahnlund, *HT* (1914), p. 120; *id.*, *Öfverläggningar i riksrådet April 1629* (*HT* (1915)), pp. 94-6.

At the same meeting they approved an instruction for Sten Bielke, who at this time was sent on a mission to Wallenstein which, as Gustav Adolf frankly avowed, was intended, by its offers of peace or truce, to serve as a useful propaganda-point.[1]

The news of Arnim's arrival in Poland upset all these calculations. Oxenstierna's lamentations and forebodings were now seen to have been by no means excessive or alarmist. The King at once left for Prussia; and on 21 May landed unexpectedly at Pillau for the campaign which, he was resolved, must be the last of the Polish war. He found his army, as usual after the winter, reduced by sickness and much in need of reinforcement. Of the total of some 23,000 men at his disposal, moreover, more than 9000 were distributed in garrison duty; and he was thus left with no more than 14,000 available to meet the 26,000 of Koniecpolski and Arnim. In these circumstances the only hope of any major success was to throw himself upon Arnim before he effected a junction with the Poles, and to trust to the notorious ill-feeling between them to prevent Koniecpolski's coming to Arnim's aid. This plan formed the basis of Gustav Adolf's operations early in June, when he marched in the direction of Graudenz in the hope of catching Arnim isolated. But Arnim eluded him; and Gustav Adolf found it wiser to withdraw, first to Marienwerder, and then to Marienburg. The Poles and imperialists, who had temporarily patched up their differences, now effected their junction; and on the road from Marienwerder to Marienburg they came up with Gustav Adolf's rearguard at Honigfelde, and there inflicted upon him the severest defeat Sweden had sustained at Polish hands since the battle of Kirkholm. Gustav Adolf himself was in great danger, and it was only with much difficulty that the Swedish column disengaged itself.[2]

The defeat at Honigfelde drove the King back on the defences of the delta; and until the end of July he was waging a purely defensive warfare. On the one flank of the Swedish position Arnim battered away at the Montauer Spitz; on the other the main Polish army assailed the great fortified camp which Gustav Adolf had constructed

[1] *RRP*, I. 127: 'Scopus hujus missionis est, ut vel pacem obtineamus, si velit, vel inducias, ut paremus nos commodius, et ut subditi videant pacificum animum nostrum ac tanto obsequiosiores ad sui protectionem [sint]; ut satisfaciamus et justificemus nos toti mundo; ut justificemus nos Ducibus Germaniae.'

[2] *Sv. Krig*, II, 517, 520-40; Petri, II. 96-7; Korzon II. 252-5; Hoppe, p. 413; C. Bennedich, *Ur det gamla Gardets öden*, pp. 74-5, for a criticism of the campaign.

around Marienburg. The Swedish defences held good. After a crisis at the beginning of July the danger to the Montauer Spitz gradually faded, for Arnim had no heart for the work. He was deeply disturbed, as a loyal Brandenburger, by Polish designs against Königsberg (in which he declined to collaborate),[1] and his resignation from the imperial service was already decided on. At Marienburg, on the other wing, Gustav Adolf's field-fortifications proved too much for Sigismund and Koniecpolski, though they made major attacks against them in mid-July. By the beginning of August the Polish offensive had petered out on both wings; Gustav Adolf's hold on the delta was secure; and Sweden stood, in the late summer of 1629, very much where she had stood three years earlier. As far as military operations went, the war was over.[2] Already, at Altmark, the diplomats were battling towards an agreed settlement.

The initiative came from France. As France's struggle with the Habsburgs in Italy developed, Richelieu became increasingly anxious to disengage Gustav Adolf from the Polish war that he might be free to play the part of French instrument and pensioner which had been somewhat naïvely designed for him; while Father Joseph, for his part, hoped that if the war could be stopped Poland might be enlisted in his favourite project of a crusade. Hence the final item in Charnacé's instructions, which Father Joseph drew up in January, was a charge to mediate a truce or peace in the Swedo-Polish war. Hitherto, Charnacé's mission had not been marked by much success: in Germany, in Denmark, his exhortations had achieved nothing at all. He was to redeem his embassy from failure, and to inaugurate his protracted diplomatic connexion with Gustav Adolf, in the negotiations which were now to begin.[3]

Charnacé arrived in Marienburg on 1 July, and at once began efforts to arrange a conference. His reception at the hands of the Poles was ungracious. It is true that the Polish nobility was by this time anxious for peace, for trade on the Vistula was suffering severely; and the heavy expense of Arnim's auxiliary corps was already felt as an intolerable burden.[4] But they had not invited French media-

[1] *cf. AOSB*, II. 1. 493, 499; Hoppe, p. 403; Irmer, p. 115.

[2] *Sv. Krig*, II. 543-4, 548-9; Irmer, pp. 108-9, 112, 115.

[3] For the earlier phases of Charnacé's embassy, see G. Fagniez, *Le Père Joseph et Richelieu*, I. 275-8; L. Weibull, *DF*, pp. 12-14.

[4] D. Norrman, *Gustav Adolfs politik mot Ryssland och Polen under tyska kriget*, pp. 18-19.

tion; and they could not forget that there was already another French ambassador in the north whose language and policy by no means squared with Charnacé's. This was Charnacé's rival Des Hayes de Cormenin, who had been sent by Richelieu to negotiate with Denmark and Russia with a view to obtaining for France the monopoly of the Caspian trade by way of Narva, and a reduction of the Sound tolls upon it. Des Hayes was no friend to Poland, and among other projects he was trying to forward was the idea of an alliance between Michael Romanov and Bethlen Gabor, directed against Sigismund.[1] It was natural that the Poles should at first be suspicious of French sincerity. Gustav Adolf on his side was not much more forthcoming when Charnacé had his first audience on 17 July.[2] Sweden certainly needed a cessation of arms in Poland; but the King was not prepared to buy it upon any terms. For a peace—which would of course imply the renunciation by Sigismund of his family's claims upon Sweden—Gustav Adolf would probably have felt himself obliged to surrender all his conquests. For a long truce he would be willing to sacrifice the more outlying of his acquisitions, provided the river-mouths remained in his hands. But in reality he did not want a peace at this particular juncture. A stable truce would suit him far better. A peace would mean the loss of the Prussian coastal areas, and this in turn the loss of the tolls levied upon commerce by the Swedish authorities. Without those tolls it would be difficult to raise the money to pay the mercenaries already in the Swedish service, and almost impossible to defray the cost of the German expedition of next year. The financial situation was such that Sweden could not at the moment afford a peace.

Charnacé soon seems to have appreciated this fact, and to have concentrated his attention upon obtaining a truce. Even so, it proved uphill work. The commissioners appointed on each side met for the first time on 30 July, midway between the two camps at Marienburg; but their respective terms seemed quite irreconcilable. The Poles demanded, as the price of a long truce, the retrocession of all Swedish conquests in Prussia except Pillau; the Swedes offered to hand back only Strasburg, Wormditt, Guttstadt, Mehlsack and Dirschau—the

[1] A. Tongas, *L'Ambassadeur Louis Deshayes de Cormenin*, pp. 73-87; H. Hauser, *La Pensée et l'action économique . . . de Richelieu*, pp. 111-19; M. Cichocki, *Medjacja Francji w rozejmie altmarskim*, p. 165.

[2] Richelieu, *Mémoires*, II. 67-72.

most distant and indefensible outposts of their position. From the ensuing deadlock Charnacé was rescued by the offer of Brandenburg to associate herself with France in the work of mediation. George William was as anxious for a settlement as either of the belligerents could possibly be, having felt all the inconveniences and dangers of being, as Roe put it, 'a grayne of corne betweene two millstones, brused to make bread for others'.[1] Charnacé accepted the offer; and the joint mediators interviewed Gustav Adolf on 11 August, in the hope of finding him more compliant. They made no impression; and this time it seemed that negotiations must be at an end. The Brandenburgers, however, now suggested a compromise. They proposed that Sweden should hand over Marienburg, Danziger Haupt and the Grosser Werder, not to the King of Poland but in sequestration to the Elector, who should retain them for the duration of the truce and hand them back to Sweden if no definitive peace had been concluded when the truce ran out. In exchange, and as a guarantee for Brandenburg's restoration of the sequestrated lands at the proper time, Sweden should be allowed to occupy the electoral towns of Pillau, Fischhausen, Lochstädt and Memel, with the districts adjoining them, and should be permitted to continue the levying of toll.

This scheme had much to commend it to all parties. As early as 21 August it was accepted in principle by Sigismund, and it appeared likely to form the basis of a speedy settlement. But in fact the truce of Altmark was not signed for another month; and the main cause of this delay was probably the arrival of yet another mediator, in the person of Sir Thomas Roe. Roe had been sent out on much the same sort of diplomatic tour as Charnacé, and had arrived in Gustav Adolf's camp by way of The Hague, Copenhagen and Königsberg.[2] His first contacts with the Swedes were unpromising. When his credentials were examined, it was found that they did not give Gustav Adolf all the titles to which he laid claim, 'especially that of Potentissimo, though [as Roe remarked] there were enough for any Christian King'[3]; and Gustav Adolf, highly incensed,

[1] Roe, p. 40. For Brandenburg's earlier troubles, see, *e.g.*, *AOSB*, I. IV. 136, 252; Hoppe, p. 354.

[2] For the earlier phases of Roe's mission, see Roe, pp. 10-22; Fridericia, *YPH*, pp. 111-17; Rydfors, p. 127 *seqq.*

[3] Roe, pp. 35-7; *AOSB*, I. IV. 590, 594. This was a point that seems to have rankled with Roe: he was still indignant about it in a conversation with Kristian IV in May 1630. Kristian suggested that a proper title for Gustav Adolf might be '*fortissimum omnium stultorum in toto mundo*': *Christian IVs Breve*, II. 272.

refused to see him for nearly a fortnight. Even worse, Roe proved to be charged to mediate a peace rather than a truce, and his insistence on this point was a source of great annoyance to the Swedes. Inevitably, he looked jealously on Charnacé, whom he described as an 'enterloping French ambassador'; and the Poles considered (what Roe certainly did not intend) that he was a friend to Poland.[1] On the whole, his arrival was more of a hindrance than a help: the Brandenburger Hoppe considered that it spoilt everything.[2] Roe, however, was too honest, too amiable, too able, too obviously an admirer of Gustav Adolf and too sincere in his devotion to the interests of Protestantism to be *persona non grata* for long; and Oxenstierna adroitly directed his energies into the negotiation of a separate treaty between Sweden and Danzig, in the concluding of which he did very good service.

Early in September Gustav Adolf had a meeting with George William at Fischhausen,[3] and on 13 September the Swedish and Polish commissioners resumed their negotiations at Altmark. Both sides had by this time come to the conclusion that the scheme of sequestration by Brandenburg had better be accepted; and on 16 September the truce of Altmark was signed.[4] It embodied the proposals originally made by the electoral mediators for a Brandenburg sequestration; it guaranteed to the Roman Catholics the right to the use of one church in Braunsberg and three in the district under Swedish control; it conceded to the Swedes *e silentio* the right of collecting toll at Pillau and Memel, and remitted to a separate treaty with Danzig the question of the toll collected there. Sweden kept her conquests in Livonia, except Mitau, which was restored to Duke Frederick of Kurland. The truce was to run for six years. On 6 November the treaty of Fischhausen, between Sweden and Branden-

[1] Konopczyński, I. 276.

[2] Hoppe, p. 451: his rubric at this point runs: 'Der englische Gesandte zerstöret die Tractaten'. And see the tart comments in Richelieu, *Mémoires*, II. 73.

[3] Gustav Adolf irritated the Elector by giving him good advice, and particularly by his warnings against Schwarzenberg. As it happened, such warnings were less justified at this moment than usual, for Schwarzenberg was temporarily under the influence of the French envoy Marcheville, and was advocating reliance upon France, rather than upon the Emperor: Gindely, pp. 49-50.

[4] Text in *Sverges traktater*, V. 347-56; a map in *AOSB*, I. IV, at end. For the negotiations in general, see H. Brulin, *Stilleståndet i Altmark*, *passim*; Cichocki, *passim*; Gindely, pp. 46-53; *Sv. Krig*, II. 555-64; *AOSB*, I. IV. 569, 579, 610, 632, 645, 657, 721, I. V. 21, II. I. 512; Roe, pp. 37-8; Ogier, p. 88, for a story of difficulties about precedence.

burg, delimited the sequestered districts [1]; on 18 February 1630 the treaty of Tiegenhof—which was mainly the work of Roe—made peace with Danzig, fixed the rate of toll to be collected there at $5\frac{1}{2}$ per cent., and divided it in the proportion of 2 per cent. to Danzig and 3·5 per cent. to Sweden.[2] And finally a treaty with Kurland on 29 March 1630 secured to Sweden the tolls at the ports of Libau and Windau.[3]

The long war with Poland, which had lasted now for nearly thirty years, was over, at least for the time; and Sweden had come out of it better than the recent run of the fighting might have made probable. True, Sigismund's line had not renounced their pretensions on the throne of Sweden; but they had now little chance of making them good. Sigismund's fleet was bottled up in Wismar; Sigismund himself was known to be approaching his end, and when he died it would be strange if Gustav Adolf could not contrive confusion in Poland. The truce of Deulinie was running out, moreover, and after 1631 Poland was likely to have her hands full with another Russian war. Meanwhile, Sweden controlled the Frisches Haff and the Kurisches Haff; Elbing, Braunsberg and Pillau were in her possession; Memel was hers in pledge for the sequestered areas. Of all the rivers of Prussia, only the Danzig arm of the Vistula did not flow through territory in Swedish occupation, and here the treaty of Tiegenhof gave Gustav Adolf the effective check provided by the lion's share of the customs dues. The right to levy toll was indeed, from the Swedish point of view, the most valuable aspect of the truce. The aim both of Roe and of Charnacé throughout their negotiations had been to make it possible for Sweden to intervene in Germany; but the mere cessation of fighting in Poland would hardly by itself have secured this object. It is just possible that Gustav Adolf might have compassed the German expedition without the aid of the revenues from the Prussian tolls, but it is by no means probable. The Swedish territorial gains in Prussia were more of a liability than an asset, since it took troops to garrison them. The essential gain which Gustav Adolf made at Altmark was financial.

[1] *Sverges traktater*, V. 358-66; *AOSB*, I. IV. 663-71, I. V. 45, 170-81.

[2] *Sverges traktater*, V. 367-75; Roe, pp. 45-6; *AOSB*, I. IV. 618, I. V. 18; Wendt, p. 131; and see above, pp. 82-3. Danzig by this treaty promised not to fit out or build warships, or to permit building or fitting out, in her harbour: Oxenstierna had failed to get this inserted in the treaty of Altmark.

[3] *Sverges traktater*, V. 375-7, 379-80; *AOSB*, I. V. 47; Paul, II. 140.

(v) *From Decision to Action*

The negotiators at Altmark were yet upon the final stages of their labours when Gustav Adolf quitted the pest-ridden camp [1] and hurried back to Stockholm. He was sure by this time that the Polish war was over; and there was no point in lingering for the concluding formalities: his task must now be to set in train the preparations for the great venture which had been implicit in the French mediation, so that he might be ready to move into Pomerania in good time next year. But as the irrevocable acts drew nearer, as the Polish preoccupation which had stood in their way was removed, the difficulties and dangers of the new course of policy appeared larger than before, and doubts which had been many times resolved arose again, more insistently. Was the war in Germany really inevitable? The King himself had said so, often enough; he had twice argued the case to his *råd*, and twice convinced them; and it was not three months since a *riksdag*, held perforce in his absence, had by its resolution endorsed his arguments and reinforced the *råd's* decision. Yet, as the formidable nature of the enterprise grew more apparent the closer he approached it, the tho ght would recur that possibly it might be worth while to renew the attempt at negotiation. Sweden had been excluded from the Lübeck conference, certainly; Sten Bielke's mission to Wallenstein seemed to prove that Gustav Adolf's terms were utterly unacceptable to the imperialists; but there was plenty of evidence to show that Wallenstein, at least, was afraid of a Swedish landing. There was growing tension between Wallenstein and the League; the difficulties of carrying the Edict of Restitution into effect were becoming ever more apparent; the preoccupation of the Emperor with the Mantuan war was obvious. Was it not conceivable that some substantial concession could be obtained by bargaining? Let it be assumed, however, that war with the imperialists could not be avoided—that the arguments with which Gustav Adolf had convinced himself, his chancellor and his *råd* were in fact good: did it follow that it might not be better that such a war should be deferred? Was it certain that the best terrain on which

[1] 'We treate from one army to another, now lodged in one, now in the other, in the field of Golgotha; the plague is so hott in both that I never saw such a mortalitye in Turky, India, nor I thinke can be in Cairo, the seat of the plague, for the number. All the countrye is dispeopled; in 80 English mile not a house to sleepe safe in; no inhabitants except a few poore weomen and children *vertendo stercorarium* to find a corne of wheate': Roe, p. 37.

to fight it was Pomerania? Prussia, indeed, now that the truce of Altmark was signed, was out of the question; and no man would wish to fight it in Sweden. But was there not perhaps something to be said for fighting it in Denmark? Doubts and speculations such as these seem to have beset the King constantly during the whole period which lies between his return from Prussia in September 1629 and that day early in June 1630 when his armada finally put out from Älvsnabben. They were doubts and hesitations not unnatural to a man in his situation. The German war, if it came, might well determine the fate of his country for generations to come. If it were embarked upon, and were to end ill—if he found no allies in Germany or outside it; if it led to military disaster—how heavy his responsibility should the verdict of posterity prove to be that war had after all been avoidable! The warning of Lutter, the recent humiliation of Kristian IV, must have been strong upon him. He felt the need to be reassured that he was not wantonly gambling with the destinies of Sweden; the need for yet another careful examination by his advisers of his analysis of the European situation; the need, finally, for absolution in advance, in case the wheel of fortune should turn to his disadvantage. And so, though the preparations for war go steadily on, though the mercenaries are enlisted, the *utskrivningar* carried through, though the transports are slowly collected, and the diplomatic preliminaries at no time pretermitted, Swedish policy moves feverishly and fitfully from this project to that expedient; now seeking allies for war, now making genuine offers of peace; now confident and aggressive, now cautious and almost despairing, as the mind of the King is affected by the news that reaches him from Germany, from Prussia or from Denmark.

On the morrow of the truce of Altmark three lines of action were certainly open to him. One of them was represented by the presence in his camp of the French and English ministers. An English alliance seemed within the bounds of possibility: Roe had given him much encouragement, and was very anxious to persuade his government to secure Gustav Adolf's services while they were still to be had. A French alliance had actually been offered. The terms, it is true, had been unsatisfactory, the subsidies tendered inadequate, and France's proposed share in the joint effort had been vague and meagre; but the offer would certainly be renewed.[1] There would be no need, it seemed, for Gustav Adolf

[1] L. Weibull, *DF*, pp. 15-16.

to land in Germany without an ally. Another possibility derived from that clause in the peace of Lübeck which permitted the adhesion of Sweden within three months of the conclusion of the treaty. The three months had, indeed, elapsed; but Kristian IV would probably be only too ready to use his good offices to bring about an accommodation with the Emperor. If Gustav Adolf should change his mind and prefer peace, the road to it was still open. And lastly, he might use the mediation of Denmark to defer war until an apter moment, to entertain the Emperor with negotiations never intended to reach a result, and to frighten the enemies of Habsburg into promises of adequate aid.

Confronted with this choice, Gustav Adolf nerved himself for the decision by yet another fortifying dose of advice from his *råd*. In October the members gathered in Uppsala (the plague was raging in Stockholm); and here on 27 October and the succeeding days the old ground was gone over afresh. As at the *råd*-meeting of a year ago, the debate was conducted almost on the lines of an academic disputation; and now, as then, Johan Skytte was put up to play the part of Faculty Opponent. His arguments against an invasion of Germany were not, perhaps, very impressive; but the King himself had already confuted in advance all the best points on that side, and little was left for Skytte to say. Only one new point was made in favour of invasion: Gustav Adolf pointed out that the cost of the war would be much diminished if Sweden were to control the Pomeranian coast and were thus able to levy toll there. And for the first time he spoke of the need to take Rügen. The resolution of the *råd* was taken on 3 November. It was unanimous for war, even Skytte concurring.[1] Gustav Adolf was moved; and he wound up the meeting in a speech which moved his hearers:

That I have laid these things before you has its cause in this: not that I have myself doubted that the offensive is the better part, but that you might now have liberty to speak your minds to the contrary, and the less liberty hereafter to dispute whether I have done right or no. . . . And as I hope that this measure shall conduce to the welfare *patriae*, so I hope too, that if it prove not so, no man will impute it to me for a fault. For I have no other intention herein than *patriae utilitatem*. What tribulation I am like to have of it, I foresee right well: the difficulty that, for lack of means, we are not able to please everybody, *unde* discontent,

[1] For these debates, see *RRP*, I. 218-26; Ahnlund, *Gustaf Adolf inför tyska kriget*, pp. 234, 256-8, 260; *cf. AOSB*, II. I. 519, 523.

ill-will, disturbance. Next, the lack of means itself. *Dubius eventus belli, unde nullam vanam gloriam spero; exemplum habeo a Rege Daniae*, in what *incommoda domestica et externa ceciderit*. The voice of slander, ever ready to tax this man with that offence, and that man with this; and so no *gloria* to be expected. *Satur sum gloriae, ut ampliorem non petam. Ergo* I expect that you should not say of me that I look to *vanam gloriam*, or to any other cause than *solam utilitatem et securitatem patriae*; and however it may happen, you shall put the best construction on it, to young and old, that all subjects may cordially embrace the good cause. And I exhort you so to carry it that either you or your children see it brought to a good end; which God grant us. For myself I perceive that I need look for no rest, until I find it in the rest eternal.[1]

Nothing, one would have thought, could be more final and conclusive. Yet within a week Gustav Adolf was off on another tack, and had laid before the *råd* proposals barely reconcilable with those endorsed on 3 November. Soon after that meeting he had received from Kristian IV a letter enquiring whether he could be of any service as intermediary between Sweden and the Emperor. As Gustav Adolf fell to considering what answer should be sent to this letter, all the old suspicion of the 'Jute' came uppermost once more. What security could he look to on that side if he became involved in war in Germany? Was it not the part of wisdom, then, to present Denmark with a demand for a guarantee? Sweden might signify to Denmark her willingness to negotiate with the Emperor, but if Danish assurances proved unsatisfactory, was not the first priority possibly a preventive war against Kristian IV? Would it not perhaps be most expedient to fight the imperialists in Denmark rather than in Pomerania or Mecklenburg? Denmark might profess to be neutral; but could Sweden, out of regard for her own safety, admit the possibility of neutrality, or tolerate the existence of neutrals at her gates? The *råd*, to whom these points were referred on 10 November, were by no means anxious for a war with Denmark; but they did agree to send an embassy to Kristian to demand guarantees, and there is no doubt that the presentation of such a demand might easily have led to war, despite the anxiety of the Danish council to steer clear of trouble.[2] Fortunately, more moderate counsels eventually prevailed. The embassy was cancelled, and the reply to Kristian was made by letter. It proved to be not an ultimatum but an intimation that Sweden would be ready to treat with the Emperor,

[1] *RRP*, I. 228-9. [2] Erslev, II. 200-1.

and a suggestion that a conference to settle their differences be held in Danzig on 1 April 1630.[1] Two days later, on 12 November, Gustav Adolf decided to prepare the way for these negotiations by sending Per Brahe, as the bearer of an official Swedish *apologia*, on a special mission to Vienna.[2]

Brahe's instructions were subsequently revoked, and his embassy never took place; but the idea of the Danzig conference remained, and both sides took it seriously. The advantages of such a conference, from Sweden's point of view, were obvious. If the Emperor were willing to accept Sweden's terms, or something approaching them, Gustav Adolf would be glad enough to call off his invasion. In any case, it was his strong conviction that the best time to negotiate with an enemy was when you were actually fighting him: military successes, he found, were persuasive arguments.[3] If the conference broke down, it would at least have established the machinery for discussion; and it would be useful to have such machinery available, even though hostilities might continue. It would, moreover, keep the Emperor in uncertainty about Gustav Adolf's real intentions, and possibly lead him to neglect his preparations. And if the worst came to the worst, it would provide Sweden with the means of getting out of the German war if circumstances should prevent the carrying into execution of the Uppsala resolutions of 3 November—a contingency which at times appeared by no means improbable.

Meanwhile, it was proper to proceed upon the assumption that the campaign in Germany would take place. Throughout the winter and spring preparations were pressed forward; and, as Roe drily observed, it was a fair assumption that these recruitments were 'certeynely not pour faire la monstre nor to conquer the North Pole'.[4] There was great diplomatic activity. Swedish agents were busy all over Germany, making contact with the disaffected or oppressed princes, with imperial cities who felt themselves menaced, with all, in short, who might reasonably be expected to rally to a Swedish landing. Already Dietrich von Falkenberg was in touch with Bernard of Saxe-Weimar, and possibly also with his brother William[5]; and in November Count Philip von Solms was commissioned to get

[1] *RRP*, I. 229 *seqq.*; Fridericia, *YPH*, pp. 130-5; Ahnlund, *op. cit.*, pp. 261-6.
[2] *Per Brahes tänkebok*, pp. 22-3; Ahnlund, *op. cit.*, p. 267; *id.*, *HT* (1914), p. 109 *note* 1.
[3] *cf. AOSB*, II. III. 190.
[4] Roe, p. 52.
[5] Ahnlund, *Gustaf Adolf inför tyska kriget*, p. 297.

into touch with William of Hesse-Cassel and George of Hesse-Darmstadt.[1] Anders Svensson was ordered in December to try to influence Lübeck and the Hanse to ally with Sweden, and at the same time was instructed to call on Gustav Adolf's uncle, Archbishop John Frederick of Bremen, whom the operation of the Edict of Restitution had reduced to the position of being virtually a prisoner in his own diocese.[2] In October, a special agent was sent to encourage the Mecklenburg Dukes.[3] In January Andreas Kochticz, a Bohemian refugee in Sweden, was despatched to prepare the way for a rising in his own country.[4] More important than these individual efforts were the great diplomatic reconnaissances of Kristoffer Ludvig Rasche and Filip Sadler. Rasche's tour arose out of the arrival in Sweden of Christian William, the dispossessed Administrator of Magdeburg. Christian William, who had nothing to lose, bombarded Gustav Adolf with the most grandiose plans for impracticable enterprises, military and diplomatic; and at the end of October the King suggested, by way of giving him harmless employment for the winter, that he should undertake a mission to the Protestant Swiss cantons and the oppressed princes of south Germany. Rasche was deputed to accompany him as the King's representative and to see that he committed no indiscretions. Their start was delayed; and before they got away Christian William, who did not greatly fancy being shepherded round Switzerland by Rasche, had suggested instead that he go to his old diocese of Magdeburg to find out whether anything could be done there. During the summer of 1629 Magdeburg had successfully survived investment by Wallenstein; the spirit of the citizens was high; and a majority looked hopefully to Sweden for deliverance, and was even prepared to pay for it by welcoming back Christian William. In view of all this, Gustav Adolf agreed to the change of plan, though he warned the Administrator to be careful. But though the original mission of Christian William was thus cancelled, that of Rasche remained; and in December he set out on it. At Lübeck he gave assistance to Anders Svensson in his negotiations with the Hanse and Adolf Frederick of Mecklenburg; at Lüneberg he had conversations with Duke George.[5] Thence he went to south Germany and Switzerland,

[1] *ibid.*, p. 296.
[2] *ibid.*, pp. 270, 288.
[3] *ibid.*, pp. 280, 285.
[4] *ibid.*, p. 311.
[5] Rasche had already sounded him in May 1628: *ibid.*, p. 122.

where he embarked upon a series of diplomatic soundings which kept him away from Sweden until far into 1630.[1]

At the same time Filip Sadler was engaged on a tour of a similar nature. He too was to make for Switzerland, taking on his way certain of the more important Protestant courts of Germany, and was to return by way of Italy and France, so that Sweden might have reliable information about the Mantuan war and France's real part in it. On the way he was to deliver to suitable recipients letters explaining Swedish policy, and was in conversation to take especial pains to justify Gustav Adolf's decision to invade Germany next year. Sadler arrived at Lübeck early in December, and by the new year had reached Dresden. Here occurred a highly significant meeting with the Elector John George. John George received him courteously; but he proved quite unresponsive when Sadler urged the need for solidarity among Lutherans. For political reasons of his own he was not sorry just at this moment to receive a Swedish envoy, by way of a hint to the Emperor to be reasonable; but at heart he was too patriotic a German not to abhor the idea of foreign intervention. On 11 January 1630 he told Sadler plainly that if Gustav Adolf landed in Germany the Elector of Saxony would be found doing his duty by the Emperor's side. Thus the attitude of Saxony was made perfectly clear in good time. Gustav Adolf may later have found John George disappointing, exasperating, even treacherous; but he could not complain that he had not received fair warning.[2]

Compared with this episode, the rest of Sadler's trip was of minor importance. He called at Nuremberg, Ulm and Stuttgart, and had talks with leading citizens in each place. He probably met the Dukes of Württemberg.[3] Everywhere he found strong Protestant feeling, much sympathy for Sweden, but a firm refusal to take any positive steps. Until the position of the Emperor and the League had been shaken by a great defeat, the odds were too desperate for a spontaneous Protestant rising. As to the Swiss, their internal dissensions made them an unpromising field. The immediate results of Sadler's mission were thus negligible. Yet it made a considerable political sensation, not least in the imperialist camp. It came to the Protestants of the south as a ray of light through the political murk that encompassed them. The popular imagination

[1] *ibid.*, pp. 291-5.

[2] B. Boëthius, *Filip Sadlers beskickning, passim*; Ahnlund, *op. cit.*, pp. 232-3, 304-9.

[3] Roe, p. 62.

already looked to Gustav Adolf as the coming saviour of Protestantism; and mystics and astrologers, seers, neurotics, fanatics and charlatans combined to give unprecedented vogue to the old story of the Lion of the North. Already, as Wallenstein complained, the Germans awaited Gustav Adolf as the Jews their Messiah—not the princes, perhaps, who foresaw that rescuers can be exigent and that gratitude is a poor ground for friendship, but certainly their peoples, whom the princes, by reason of their weakness or folly, were no longer able to protect against an international mercenary soldiery and a revengeful alien church.[1] Swedish propaganda was already active—had been so, indeed, since the emergence of the Habsburg naval threat in 1627-28, and still more so since the relief of Stralsund. Sadler's journey showed that the Lion of the North was not indifferent to the woes of Germany, and the hopes of the vanquished were animated proportionably.

Meanwhile Charnacé, his work at Altmark being successfully completed, had followed his quarry to Sweden. It was his business to enlist Gustav Adolf as Richelieu's pensioner, and though his instructions bound him too tightly for his comfort, and though he at first lacked the powers requisite for treating with Sweden upon any satisfactory basis, he stuck to his task with much pertinacity (having no doubt been indoctrinated with Richelieu's views on the virtue of continuous negotiation),[2] and was in the end unlucky to leave Sweden empty-handed. For both sides desired the alliance. But Richelieu tried to buy Gustav Adolf too cheap; and Gustav Adolf on his side was not prepared so to bind himself as to lose control over his own destinies. At Altmark, and during the December negotiations, he had made considerable demands: France was to provide a North Sea fleet, to be placed at Sweden's disposal, and Gustav Adolf was to have the *Directorium foederis* in Germany, the North Sea and the Baltic. He was insistent that there should be a real equality of status between the allies: France was to be pledged not to make peace in Italy for so long as war continued in Germany; or, if she did so, was herself to throw an army across the Rhine. If these capital points were conceded, Sweden might be willing to do without

[1] *cf.* the remarks of the burgomaster of Stettin, as reported by Fegraeus (6 September 1629): Adlersparre, III. 123.

[2] 'J'ose dire hardiment que négocier sans cesse, ouvertement ou secrètement, en tous lieux, encore même qu'on n'en reçoive pas un fruit présent et que celui que l'on peut attendre à l'avenir ne soit pas apparent, est chose du tout nécessaire pour le bien des États': *Testament politique de Richelieu*, p. 347.

subsidies altogether.[1] Richelieu, on his side, was anxious to fit Gustav Adolf into his policy of building up a 'third party' in Germany, of which the nucleus should be the Catholic, but anti-imperial, Bavaria. French agents had now been wooing Maximilian for some years, and their prospects of making a real impression on him were beginning to brighten, as the breach between Wallenstein and the League became more apparent. Richelieu was not prepared to sacrifice this ripening fruit of his diplomacy for the sake of Gustav Adolf's assistance; but he believed that he could induce Gustav Adolf to accept Bavaria as an ally, or at least could constrain him to promise not to molest Maximilian in his possessions or electoral dignity. This proved in the end to be a delusion; and its effect was to vitiate much of Richelieu's diplomacy for the succeeding three years.[2]

The negotiations with France dragged on throughout the winter and early spring, in various places and through various agents; and more than once they were broken off. By the beginning of March 1630 Gustav Adolf had been driven to very serious modifications of his original attitude: he consented to the limitation of the alliance to six years, to a reduction of the subsidy to the rate of 300,000 *rdr.* a year, even to the recognition of the neutrality of the League. In return, Richelieu had scarcely advanced at all to meet the Swedish demands. The draft treaty was already drawn up, success appeared to be assured, when at the last moment the King changed his mind, and upon a quite trivial point broke off the discussions.[3] He probably felt that he had been too compliant; and he was almost certainly right. As he wrote to Oxenstierna on 17 March, it was scarcely a good bargain to put himself so wholly at Louis XIII's '*nutum et arbitrium*' for the sake of 'three *tunnor* of gold'.[4] Oxenstierna agreed with him: he did not at all relish the notion of a French alliance, and he was by no means sorry that the negotiations had broken down.[5] Swedish policy in Germany was not really

[1] *AOSB*, I. I. 536; L. Weibull, *DF*, pp. 15-25; Riezler, V. 267, 281, 283-4.

[2] Any such arrangement was of course anathema to Camerarius; and Camerarius seems to have exerted considerable influence upon Swedish policy at this time: Schubert, *Camerarius*, pp. 369-75.

[3] They were renewed again in April, but with no success: L. Weibull, *DF*, p. 55; Adlersparre, III. 181.

[4] *AOSB*, II. I. 567, 573. For the negotiations in general, see L. Weibull, *DF*, pp. 27-44; Richelieu, *Mémoires*, II. 298-303; Fagniez, I. 561 *seqq.*; *AOSB*, I. I. 537, I. V. 255; *Arkiv*, I. 104-5.

[5] Ahnlund, *Oxenstierna*, p. 566. In 1636 Oxenstierna had not forgotten his resentment: he told members of the *råd* 'how France through Charnacé lured his late Majesty into the war, and afterwards sat and manœuvred matters to her advantage in Germany, by favour of our arms . . .'; *RRP*, VI. 746.

coincidental with French, and no treaty which had the effect of subordinating the one to the other could be durable: the French alliance on these terms (to take a single instance) would nullify in advance any advantage Sweden might hope to extract from the Danzig conference. It would be better on all accounts to restrain the impulse to buy an ally on any terms, for the future might well bring a better bid. Charnacé accordingly went his ways; and nine months later the treaty of Bärwalde proved Gustav Adolf's judgment to be sound. He did not then get all he had asked for in December 1629; but he got more than was offered in March 1630.

Nevertheless, the breakdown of the negotiations with France meant that Gustav Adolf must plunge into the German adventure without any other ally than the city of Stralsund. In Germany his agents had cast bread upon the waters, but the moment of its returning was not yet. No German state dared yet to declare itself in his favour; many looked forward to his arrival with distaste, some with hostility, none with the confident hope of the devotees of the cult of the Lion of the North. Those most nearly concerned still hoped, in the spring of 1630, that a Swedish landing might be averted; and Bogislaw of Pomerania, and George William of Brandenburg, made attempts at mediation which their imperialist friends and oppressors were not backward to encourage.[1] They had no success. The determination to invade had been taken, and was not to be shaken by appeals or arguments. Oxenstierna told Roe quite openly in January of the forthcoming campaign.[2] Yet there were times, all through the first half of 1630, when King and chancellor came near to despair, when the pressure of difficulties seemed likely to prevail over their resolution, and when they were driven to think for a moment of alternative lines of action. Since the truce of Altmark, Oxenstierna had been grappling desperately with the problem of the German mercenary cavalry in the Swedish service. Their wages were much in arrear, and there seemed little hope of paying them. Until these arrears were discharged it would be impossible to disband them; and as long as they remained embodied in Prussia they continued to pile up the state's indebtedness to no purpose. The only hope of dealing with them was to offer fresh employment. This the German war would certainly provide; but the awkward question remained how to transport them to Germany,

[1] *AOSB*, I. v. 87-9, 103; Hallwich, *Briefe und Akten*, I. 17-19; Bär, p. 254.
[2] Roe, pp. 61-3.

and (still awkwarder) how to content them in the meantime. The German cavalry, in fact, were a nightmare to Oxenstierna. Towards the end of December the situation was so critical that Gustav Adolf almost resigned himself to abandoning any idea of a campaign in Germany as utterly impracticable; and the correspondence between King and chancellor took on an unwonted note of depression, of bafflement, almost of desperation. In mid-January Gustav Adolf was writing of the 'inextricable labyrinth of difficulties' which confronted him; in March the problem of the unpaid cavalry had become so acute that he intimated that unless Oxenstierna could give a satisfactory report from Prussia, the expedition could not be proceeded with.[1] Not until April could the chancellor write that he saw some prospect of a satisfactory arrangement with these turbulent creditors.[2]

There were other difficulties, too, which at one time also came near to causing the postponement, if not the cancellation, of the expedition; and the most important of these was the policy of Denmark. Kristian IV, though he had assumed the part of mediator between Sweden and the imperialists, had never really appreciated the nature of the issues that divided them. For the fate of German Protestantism he had now little interest to spare, and he showed complete incomprehension of Gustav Adolf's desire to obtain political security for the Baltic by some arrangement ensuring an adequate bastion on the southern shore of that sea. For him the question was a quarrel about Stralsund, and perhaps also about Mecklenburg; and he would accept any plausible arrangement, oblivious of whether it could be upset again as soon as his back was turned.[3] He had a deep—and intelligible—suspicion of Gustav Adolf. He believed him to be aiming at the mastery of the Baltic. He believed that this German expedition was designed from the start to lead to large annexations of territory.[4] He resented Swedish interference in north German politics. In this frame of mind he was ready enough for an intrigue with his former enemies. At the beginning of 1630 he was offering to lend himself to the mercantile and naval schemes of the Habsburgs, and negotiations were afoot with Gabriel de Roy for

[1] *AOSB*, I. v. 158-66, 170-81, 289-306, II. I. 544, 553-9; *Arkiv*, I. 79-85, 103-5.
[2] *AOSB*, I. v. 251.
[3] Adlersparre, III. 154: report of Fegraeus, 21 January 1630.
[4] *ibid.*, 166, 200. Compare the observation of Kristian's council, in their memorial of 8 June 1630: 'we live in a manner of speaking by his [Gustav Adolf's] grace, and are incapable of withstanding him': Erslev, II. 236.

making Kristian's port of Glückstadt the staple-town for the trade from Germany to Spain.[1] This was a gratuitous provocation to Hamburg, and it was immediately resented. More sinister, from the Swedish point of view, were Kristian's intrigues about Rügen. Rügen had for long been a Danish fief, and was still ecclesiastically subject to the bishop of Roskilde; and for some years Kristian had been thinking of reasserting his authority over it. At the time of the siege of Stralsund it had passed into imperialist hands, and at the beginning of 1630 was still occupied by Wallenstein's troops. Its capture would obviously be among the first objects of any Swedish invasion of Germany; and it was unlikely that Wallenstein would be able to retain his hold on it for very long. It was therefore to the interest both of Kristian and of Wallenstein that the island should pass into Danish hands in exchange for a suitable *quid pro quo*; and negotiations on these lines (in which Bogislaw of Pomerania was also involved) were proceeding at the close of 1629.[2]

Early in the new year news of these intrigues reached Sten Bielke in Stralsund. He promptly informed Gustav Adolf; and in the following month his warning was confirmed by George William of Brandenburg.[3] The possession of Rügen would give Sweden a landing-place and a base more commodious than Stralsund; and in any case the island could not be left in dubious or unfriendly hands. Gustav Adolf had long realized that he must take it; but he had warned Alexander Leslie that he was to make no move until he could be certain not merely of capturing but also of holding it. Now he could delay no longer. At the end of March Swedish forces from Stralsund landed on Rügen, and in the course of the next two months gradually overran it, until on 20 June the last of the imperialist garrisons was evicted.[4] The Swedish occupation of north Germany had begun.

The crisis over Rügen, however, had brought relations with Denmark once more to a state of tension. Kristian IV, apparently under the influence of a momentary panic lest Sweden and the Emperor should reach agreement at his expense, had already on 21 March suggested to his council the expediency of a preventive war

[1] Fridericia, *YPH*, pp. 151-2; H. Kellenbenz, *Unternehmerkräfte in Hamburger Portugal- und Spanienhandel*, p. 29.

[2] Fridericia, *YPH*, pp. 138-42; *AOSB*, I. v. 254, II. i. 568.

[3] *AOSB*, I. v. 145; *cf.* Roe, p. 75; Ahnlund, *Gustaf Adolf inför tyska kriget*, p. 320.

[4] *Arkiv*, I. 93-4; *Sv. Krig*, III. 111-14; Carlsson, *Gustaf Adolf och Stralsund*, pp. 262-3.

to stop Gustav Adolf while there was yet time, or alternatively had proposed that Denmark should offer to shut the Sound to Swedish ships in exchange for Wallenstein's restoration of Mecklenburg to its rightful owners; but the council had been horrified at such extravagances, and nothing had come of them.[1] Now, in April, the fear of Danish intrigues led Gustav Adolf to make a similar suggestion. As in the preceding autumn, he allowed himself to entertain the idea of presenting Kristian with a demand for a guarantee of real neutrality. If it should be refused, he would 'immediately, *integris viribus*', throw his armies against Denmark. A war with Denmark now was easy, for it was still possible to compromise with the imperialists at Danzig; but a stab in the back from beyond the Sound, while Sweden was deeply committed in Germany, might be a serious matter.[2] The King's nerves were on edge; and he took the affair more seriously than it warranted. Oxenstierna, with his solider and more phlegmatic temperament, declined to panic. He told the King plainly that he thought the demand for a guarantee to be impolitic and a war with Denmark unnecessary at present (though he conceded that it might become necessary later); and he recapitulated with the utmost energy all the reasons which made it essential that Sweden should concentrate upon the German expedition.[3] His advice prevailed; and once more the idea of an attack on Denmark was abandoned—or at least postponed. To this decision the follies of Danish foreign policy may have contributed. Kristian's aggressive attitude had already involved him in a war with Hamburg over the levying of toll in the Elbe, and Sweden could feel that in these circumstances his potentialities for mischief were restricted. Gustav Adolf confined himself, therefore, to giving diplomatic support to Hamburg, and instructed Anders Svensson to incite the burghers to ask for Swedish aid.[4] When at the end of May he made his final dispositions for the defence of Sweden in his absence, he did indeed provide for the contingency of a Danish attack; but it was clear that he did not esteem the danger to be very formidable.[5]

In the meantime, the slow preparations for the Danzig congress

[1] *Christian IVs Breve*, II. 254-8; Fridericia, *YPH*, pp. 143-6; Erslev, II. 225-7.
[2] *AOSB*, II. I. 579-81.
[3] *ibid.*, I. v. 295-9.
[4] *ibid.*, I. v. 419, II. I. 613, II. IX. 769; Adlersparre, III. 188-92; *RRP*, II. 5-7; *Arkiv*, II. 13; Fridericia, *YPH*, pp. 147-58.
[5] *RRP*, I. xli-xlvi, II. 7; *Arkiv*, I. 136-8; *Sv. Krig*, III. 192.

had not been intermitted. Both sides hoped something of the negotiations, though neither, perhaps, had much faith in the possibility of a long-continued peace. The imperialists were anxious to gain time until they had mastered their difficulties in Italy; Ferdinand for a moment played with the idea of getting himself included in the truce of Altmark; and he was even prepared to promise the evacuation of Pomerania, provided Sweden withdrew from Stralsund and offered guarantees against any further hostile action.[1] Sir Thomas Roe on the basis of conversations with Oxenstierna at the end of January concluded that Gustav Adolf 'resolves to make a peace'.[2] Oxenstierna was franker and more cynical in his correspondence with the King: the purpose of the congress, he wrote, was 'to *abusere* the enemy and keep him on a string, as he us', and to 'encourage the Emperor against France'; and the aim of Swedish diplomacy must be to spin out the negotiations.[3] There was some confusion (possibly deliberately created by Kristian IV) about the date the congress was to begin; and when Karl Hannibal von Dohna arrived in Danzig early in April, he found no Swedish commissioners to meet him, and no sign of their coming.[4] Even the Danish mediators had not made their appearance. The Swedish commissioners did not receive their instructions until the end of April; the final decision in Stockholm upon Sweden's terms was not made until the beginning of May; and the procrastinatory techniques of Oxenstierna contrived to prevent any business being done for several weeks thereafter.[5] The negotiations had made no progress at all when Gustav Adolf's army landed in Germany. Yet up to the very last moment there was always a possibility that they might become serious; for up to the very last moment there was a chance that Gustav Adolf's difficulties might prove too many for him and that the whole expedition might have to be cancelled or postponed. In May there were disquieting rumours that the imperialists might once again make a diversionary attack on Sweden's possessions in Poland; and as late as 2 June Gustav Adolf, depressed by the difficulty

[1] Dohna wrote to Torquato Conti that not much was to be expected of Danish mediation, because of '*odium nationis*': Fridericia, *YPH*, p. 165 *note* 3; Ahnlund, *Gustaf Adolf inför tyska kriget*, pp. 327-8.

[2] Roe, pp. 65-6; *cf.* Bär, p. 253.

[3] *AOSB*, I. v. 253, II. I. 581. Yet in April Anders Svensson was ordered to urge the Hanse to send delegates to Danzig 'because if any safe and honourable peace for them in Germany is to be made, it must be made now, or it will never be made at all': *Arkiv*, II. 13.

[4] Hallwich, *Briefe und Akten*, I. 7, 10, 27-9.

[5] Ahnlund, *op. cit.*, pp. 330, 376, 382; *id.*, *Oxenstierna*, pp. 573-81.

of mustering his troops and the 'faithlessness' of some of their officers, was writing to Oxenstierna to suggest that it might be better to patch up a peace.[1]

But these were the transitory qualms of a harassed man, overwhelmed with work, and burdened, it can hardly be doubted, by an overmastering sense of responsibility before a tremendous moment. They had no effect upon the work of preparation for the campaign, which had been going on steadily throughout the winter and spring. And indeed, the forward state of Sweden's military measures was not the least of the reasons why the campaign could not be avoided. The large bodies of troops that had been raised or hired had to be used somewhere, since they could not be kept in idleness in Sweden. The German mercenary cavalry would be content with a payment on account of wages only if they were assured of continued employment, and for very pressing reasons that employment must take place in an area which was not too distant from Prussia.[2]

In the autumn of 1629, when the plans for the German expedition were drawn up, it was decided that Sweden in 1630 would need an army of 75,000 men. Of these, no less than 22,000 would be reserved for home defence. The expeditionary force to Pomerania, it was hoped, would number just under 30,000. At the time this estimate was drawn up, the total on the Swedish muster-rolls, in all theatres and services, did not exceed 45,000. For 1630, then, another 30,000 men would have to be raised somehow. It was not to be expected that any very large proportion of them could be provided by *utskrivning*. The *riksdag* of 1629 had granted an *utskrivning* for the next two years, and for the first time the nobility had consented that their peasantry should be reckoned on the same basis as the *ofrälse*; but there were already signs that the manpower-income of the country was becoming less resilient. The government did not expect to raise more than 13,000 men by this means, and in the event the yield was not much more than 9000.[3]

They were driven back, therefore, upon the recruiting of mercenaries. The time was propitious: the ending of the Polish, Danish and English wars threw many soldiers out of employment. On the whole, the Swedish agents did very well. Among their more satisfactory bargains were a commission to the Marquis of Hamilton

[1] *AOSB*, I. v. 333-42, II. i. 609, 612; Ahnlund, *Gustaf Adolf inför tyska kriget*, p. 380.
[2] *Arkiv*, I. 174-6.
[3] *Sv. Krig*, III. 185-9, 217, 223-5; Petri, II. 100.

to raise an army,[1] and, on a smaller scale, the enlistment of Lord Reay's regiment, which had served Kristian IV with distinction in Germany, and was to find immortality in the narrative of Robert Monro. Despite the disappointing yield of the Prussian tolls,[2] and despite the harassing difficulties about the German cavalry in Prussia, the King in April and May 1630 was sufficiently optimistic to increase the size of his German army in his calculations from 30,000 to 46,000, of which no less than 11,000 were to be cavalry—a sign that he contemplated an offensive campaign; while at the same time the estimated total was raised to 85,000. These estimates were in excess of what could actually be achieved; but at the beginning of June there were 72,500 men under his command, of whom some 38,000 were native Swedes.[3]

Meanwhile, on 14 May, the King had met the three upper Estates in Stockholm. There was no need, after the resolution of the secret committee in 1628, to seek their sanction for what he was about to do. They were not summoned to advise him. The purpose of their meeting was rather that they might hear his explanations; that through them the nation might learn why the war, foreseen these two years and more, had at last come upon them; that the King might show that his hands were clean and his conscience clear; and that (more specifically) he might obtain their approval for the peace terms which he was offering to the Emperor at Danzig. Long ago, in Gustav Adolf's boyhood, his tutor Skytte had taught him the expediency of a ruler's appealing to his subjects in 'an elegant oration' before leading them to war.[4] Perhaps the King recalled that early lesson now. At all events, he used the opportunity to take leave of his people. In a speech of noble eloquence he addressed to the *råd*, to each of the three Estates, and to the absent peasantry, an appropriate message of farewell.[5] As literature, the oration takes its place among the masterpieces of Swedish eloquence; as politics, it is the crowning moment of the reign, the public consummation of the union of King and people. And it is extraordinarily characteristic of Gustav Adolf's mind. His valediction to the nobility, for instance, invoked the memories of the old Goths, and incited his hearers to emulate them. The clergy were reminded that they had the power

[1] Hist. MSS. Comm., *Hamilton*, p. 47; J. Rushworth, *Historical Collections*, I. II. 53. [2] See above, pp. 84-5.

[3] *Sv. Krig*, III. 207-8, 264, 398; *cf*. Hist. MSS. Comm., *Various*, V. 133.

[4] *Valda aktstycken till svenska undervisningsväsendets historia*, p. 21.

[5] *SRARP*, I. 139-42, 146-8; Styffe, pp. 628-33; Stiernman, I. 820.

to 'turn and twist the hearts of men', and adjured to use it for the public interest; and were warned—with a side glance at Rudbeckius, no doubt—to be on their guard against the sin of pride. The economic policy of the reign crystallized into a few lapidary sentences to the burghers, for whom his wishes were 'that your small cabins may become great houses of stone, your little boats great ships and merchantmen, and that the oil in your cruse fail not'. And the very accents of Gustav Vasa echoed again in his parting benediction to the peasantry—the peasantry, upon whom the main burden of this new war would inevitably fall: 'As for the commonalty, my wish for them is, that their meadows may be green with grass, their fields bear an hundredfold, so that their barns may be full; and that they may so increase and multiply in all plenteousness, that with gladness and without sighing they may perform the duties and obligations that lie upon them.' To each Estate its function, from each its proper service. And from the King himself the highest service and the greatest sacrifice. 'And as it is wont to be, that the pitcher is borne so oft to the well that it breaks at last, so may it befall even with me, who have now in so many occasions and perils been forced to shed and pour out my blood for the welfare of the Swedish realm—yet hitherto by the gracious protection of God without forfeit of my life —and must shed it again at the last. . . .' He had, perhaps, a strain of the Vasa morbidity. But as he took his leave of them, at that meeting on 19 May 1630, he seems to have felt that this time it would be a farewell for ever. '. . . And so now, before I leave you, I would commend you all, my Swedish subjects and Estates here present (and those absent too), in soul, life and welfare, to the most gracious protection of Almighty God, desiring that we, after this miserable and painful life, may by God's will meet again in the heavenly Kingdom of eternity, and in God find life and gladness.' His arguments for crossing into Germany might seem a curious compound of political necessity, national prestige and confessional zeal; but for him at least the sense of mission was strong.

The expedition had originally been planned to sail on 1 May; but the negotiations at Danzig, and the difficulties with the German cavalry, had combined to delay it. By the middle of the month, however, troops were concentrated round Stockholm ready for embarkation, and foreign and native regiments alike were being exercised in Gustav Adolf's new style of tactics. On 26 May the embarkation of the troops began; and by the end of the month it had been completed, at least for the troops around the capital. Other contingents were supposed to be sent off simultaneously from Norrköping, Söderköping, Västervik and Kalmar, as well as from Finland, the Baltic provinces and Prussia. It proved impossible, however, to find shipping for them all: the Stockholm *échelons* alone required about a hundred vessels for their transportation.[1] In the end the number of men Gustav Adolf took with him to Germany at his first landing did not exceed 14,000, of whom less than 3000 were cavalry.[2] This disappointing figure was in part attributable to very numerous desertions—over 4000 among the newly raised Swedish foot [3]—and it was this that partly accounted for Gustav Adolf's fit of pessimism at the beginning of June. He had other anxieties too. The army had no sooner embarked than the winds turned contrary; and for nearly three weeks his transports lay at anchor, until it seemed that there might be insuperable difficulties about provisions.[4] At last on 17 June the wind changed, the ships at Älvsnabben lifted anchor, and the great armada set sail for Rügen. Off Öland they were met by news that the island was already in Leslie's hands. They accordingly altered course for Usedom; and there they made their landfall. On 26 June, in a violent thunder-storm, the landing-parties went ashore at Peenemünde.[5]

It was exactly a hundred years since the Confession of Augsburg had been presented to Charles V.

(vi) *The Object of the Expedition*

As the news of the King's landing spread through Germany and Europe, contemporaries speculated upon the objects at which he aimed and the motives which impelled him. The three ecclesiastical Electors, for instance, considered that the real purpose of the invasion was the restoration of the dispossessed Mecklenburg Dukes; or at least believed that if they were restored to their duchies Gustav Adolf would make no difficulty about returning home.[6] Sir Thomas Roe, torn between admiration for the man and suspicion of the states-

[1] *Sv. Krig*, Supp. Vol. I. 209-10. [2] *ibid.*, III. 363-4.
[3] *ibid.*, 231. [4] *RRP*, II. 11-12; *Arkiv*, I. 159-66.
[5] *Dagbok förd i det svenska fältkansliet* [cited: *Dagbok*], p. 14; *Sv. Krig*, III. 398-404.
[6] J. Baur, *Philipp von Sötern*, I. 195. The Spanish envoy at Regensburg made the naïve but characteristic suggestion that the whole difficulty might be settled by a marriage between Kristina and Władysław: Günter, p. 52.

man, inclined to see in Gustav Adolf, now the destined saviour of Protestantism, now the cunning and ambitious exponent of an aggressive foreign policy; and was always ready to believe that he could be persuaded by suitable concessions to 'goe home and gett children, to make war that way against the posterity of the King of Poland'.[1] Kristian IV had no doubt that the expedition concealed a bid for *dominium maris*, and aimed at a Swedish annexation of Pomerania.[2] And the average Protestant abroad, knowing little of high politics, probably agreed with the Swedish trumpeter Theet, who knew very well (for the army padres had told him) that Gustav Adolf went over to Germany to defend the cause of true religion.[3] Since that day, historians have debated the matter at intervals; but they have not been much more successful than contemporaries in arriving at an agreed conclusion. Was it religion or politics, idealism or ambition, that drove him on?

To Gustav Adolf's contemporaries the question would have seemed improperly framed. It was not their habit to keep politics and religion in watertight compartments, either in action or in thought. If they laid greater emphasis for a moment on the one, they did not thereby exclude the other. It is easy to find statements which seem to put the whole venture upon a basis of political calculation: thus on 27 October 1629 Gustav Adolf stated flatly to the *råd* that the prime cause of war was imperial designs upon Sweden and the Baltic.[4] Yet on 3 February 1633 Oxenstierna wrote to Salvius (whom it would have been quite purposeless to try to mislead) that the King's aim had been 'first and foremost to liberate these and all his co-religionists and relatives in the Empire from the popish yoke'.[5] The two statements were but different aspects of the same thing. Gustav Adolf was neither the ideal Protestant Hero of nineteenth-century Swedish historiography nor the *Realpolitiker* of Droysen. He was compounded of both these elements, and hence different from either. The synthesis of religion and politics, incarnate in him, was well conveyed by Oxenstierna when in 1637 he told the *råd* that religion

was not our *principalis scopus*. His late Majesty had other large causes of war. True it is, that religion ought not to be propagated *armis*, but its

[1] Roe, pp. 49-50, 59, 61-3, 69. [2] Adlersparre, III. 200.

[3] Loenbom, *Historiskt Archivum*, I. 32.

[4] 'Principalis causa belli inter nos et Caesarem est, quod is vult Sueciam et mare Balticum occupare': *RRP*, I. 224-5; *cf. ibid.*, VIII. 454.

[5] *AOSB*, I. VIII. 131.

arma are rather *spiritualia*, as *preces* and *lacrymae*; but the true *principalis scopus* is, that *regnum Sueciae* and *consortes religionis nostrae* may remain in security, and be in their *esse* preserved, *tam in statu ecclesiastico quam politico*. It is therefore in this case not so much a matter of religion, but rather of *status publicus*, wherein also religion is comprehended.[1]

Religion was still a fundamental of life, and therefore of politics; it formed an essential element in the state's welfare, in the liberty and happiness of the individual: it was indeed comprised, along with worldly and temporal considerations, in that *status publicus* to which Oxenstierna alluded. Of all the national rights and liberties which might be threatened by developments south of the Baltic, none was more precious than that right of spiritual self-determination which had been the gain of the Reformation. It is futile to deny the importance of the religious motive in shaping Gustav Adolf's policy. In this respect he was no more a mere *Realpolitiker* than Father Joseph was. The whole course of his policy, from the early 'twenties onwards, demonstrated his concern for the evangelical cause; and his willingness to postpone his own more national quarrels to the claims of that cause—provided he were not asked to adventure Sweden's resources upon an obviously unsound bottom—was manifested more than once.

Nevertheless, it is clear that a policy based on a synthesis of this sort may be distorted, consciously or unconsciously, into a policy of political aggression, and religious conviction be harnessed to the daemon of a conqueror. And it has been suggested, for instance, that the King's object was really the creation of a great empire of Scandinavia; and an observation once let fall by Oxenstierna is adduced as ground for this view. It might have been thought that the record of Swedish policy between 1626 and 1629 was sufficient refutation of this notion; but in any case the evidence upon which it rests turns out upon inspection to be imaginary. Oxenstierna never made the remark attributed to him: what he did say was that if Gustav Adolf had followed his advice he might have become arbiter of the north—a very different matter.[2] Nor is it necessary to attach too much importance to the story, told to the *råd* at third hand in November 1635, that from the beginning Gustav Adolf intended 'an *imperium Macedonicum*' in Germany, and a permanent

[1] *RRP*, VII. 53.

[2] This story was accepted by Droysen (*Gustaf Adolf*, II. 666). It was finally exploded by Ahnlund: see Ahnlund, '*Kejsardömet Skandinavien*', *passim*.

diminution of the power of the Emperor.[1] There is not much more substance, either, in the contention that the underlying motive in Swedish policy was economic. It has been argued that Gustav Adolf's object was to establish a control of the mouths of all the rivers flowing into the Baltic, and of all the main ports upon that sea, in order to enrich himself by the levying of tolls, as Kristian IV was enriching himself by the tolls at the Sound; or that this was simply an extension of the old Swedish policy of trying to control the trade between Muscovy and the west; or that the expedition to Germany was merely a means to obtain a vent for Swedish copper, or to find capital resources for Usselincx' commercial enterprises.[2] Now it is true that Gustav Adolf more than once alleged imperial interference with Swedish trade and navigation as one of his grievances against the Emperor; but in so far as this was seriously meant, it was but another aspect of the purely political necessity for the liberation of the Baltic coast from the threat of Habsburg domination. If Gustav Adolf really put the control of the Russia trade high among his list of objectives after 1617, it has left relatively little trace in his intimate correspondence with Oxenstierna. It is, no doubt, quite true that in the two years before 1630 the King had learnt the value—the indispensability—of the Prussian tolls to the Swedish war budget. It is also true that he adduced the prospect of imposing tolls on the German rivers as one of the arguments in favour of intervention.[3] And there is no doubt—as his negotiations with Pomerania, Brandenburg, Mecklenburg and the imperial cities show—that he would have been glad to find a vent for Swedish copper in Germany. But these were considerations relatively new: the line of policy which led Gustav Adolf to Peenemünde had begun to be apparent long before most of them were heard of. Nor can this interpretation be squared with the King's willingness to abstain from action in Germany if the Habsburgs would withdraw from the coastlands, and if the Germans themselves could provide adequate security against their returning. The economic advantages which he undoubtedly sought in Germany were not ends in themselves: they were means to other ends—ends religious, ends political—and a recognition of

[1] *RRP*, V. 298.

[2] For the economic interpretations, see F. Bothe, *Gustav Adolfs und seine Kanzlers wirtschaftspolitischen Absichten*, *passim*; and *cf.* A. Attman, *Freden i Stolbova 1617. En aspekt*, *passim*.

[3] *RRP*, I. 225. But in 1650 Oxenstierna explicitly asserted that this was not the motive of the invasion: *RRP*, XIV. 472.

the importance of economic factors does little to advance the enquiry into the nature of his real designs.

Yet it is true that there are indications that for some years before 1630 Gustav Adolf was contemplating more or less permanent annexations on the southern shore of the Baltic. The terms of the surrender of Elbing in 1626; the remarks in the *råd*, at the close of the same year, on the inexpediency of retroceding *juste occupata*; the history of Sweden's relations with Stralsund; the increasing disposition to regard not only Stralsund but also Wismar as necessary to Sweden's safety—all seem to point in this direction. Certain of the King's expressions in the *råd*-debates of 1629, moreover, might be made to bear a very extended interpretation. In discussing the prospects of a war in Germany he had said, '*Si vincimus, in nostra potestate erit facere quod placuerit*' [1]; and, some months later, '*Si rex victor, illi* [the German princes] *praeda erunt*'.[2] Among the motives for intervention in Germany which he urged in October 1629 was '*ob spes plures, si in Germania possimus* advance somewhat' [3]; and to Oxenstierna, after detailing the arguments for the expedition, he added, 'To say nothing of other great hopes we may look to, if God bless the design.' [4] It would be possible to contend that behind these dubious phrases lay a programme of aggression. Yet in regard to each of them other explanations are possible. The King's remark about making the German princes his booty is now generally accepted as a mere debating answer thrown out in the heat of a lively discussion; and the same may well be true of the somewhat similar remark that preceded it. As to the *spes plures*, it seems most natural to suppose that Gustav Adolf was referring to the prospect of liberating not only the states of the Baltic coastline and of the two Saxon Circles but the states of south Germany also: it might not appear a very hopeful prospect for the present; but (as he told the *råd* in May 1630), it might well become possible in the future.[5]

Something can be collected concerning the King's intentions from the proposals for a settlement of Germany which he or Oxenstierna put forward in the eighteen months before the landing. In May 1629, for instance, in a letter to John George, Gustav Adolf laid down as essential conditions of peace the restoration of the Mecklenburg Dukes, and the evacuation by the imperial armies of the Baltic seaboard and the Lower Saxon Circle: in return for this he was prepared

[1] *RRP*, I. 128. [2] *RRP*, I. 222. [3] *RRP*, I. 224.
[4] *AOSB*, II. I. 544. [5] *RRP*, II. 3.

to abandon Stralsund.[1] Of upper Germany, of the Palatinate, there was as yet no word; and even so interested a party as Roe could not reproach him for the omission.[2] But at Altmark, when the King talked with Charnacé, he produced a set of *Conditiones finales* which went much further: all imperial fortifications on the seaboard—and in the Grisons too—were to be dismantled; Stralsund was to be compensated for damage incurred during the siege; the territorial arrangements of 1618 were to be restored for the whole of Germany; and the imperial armies were to be withdrawn from the Empire.[3] Thus Frederick V, for instance, would be restored to the Palatinate; though not to Bohemia.[4] This extended programme was perhaps put forward in order to attract the support of England and France (though the restoration of Frederick would scarcely commend itself to Richelieu, whose policy was to court Maximilian), and the point about the Grisons duly appears in the treaty of Bärwalde. It may be doubted whether the King believed it practicable; or possibly he had realized the strength of French objections to parts of it: at all events, at the time of the discussions at Uppsala in October 1629 he had fallen back upon a programme which aimed at the liberation only of north Germany.[5] And to this he remained constant until the end of April 1630: evacuation of the coastlands and the Lower Saxon Circle by the imperialists, with a Swedish evacuation of Stralsund in exchange. But in the instructions for Oxenstierna for the Danzig congress, dated 30 April 1630, there appeared an important modification: Gustav Adolf himself added the qualification that the evacuation of Stralsund was not to take place until it could be effected without risk.[6] In the critical *råd*-debates of 4-6 May this line was pushed a step further: it was then resolved that Stralsund must be retained, even if the Emperor accepted Sweden's terms, and Wismar must be acquired and held, because 'we cannot be secure if we hand back anything which we cannot immediately retake'.[7] A week later the King was reproving Oxenstierna for omitting from his draft peace terms 'the most important thing of all—*assecuratio*'. By this term he meant territorial security for the imperialists' discharge of their undertakings; and this could be

[1] Gindely, p. 40.
[2] 'I thinke no man can convince me with reason why he should marry our quarrell for charitye and without dower': Roe, p. 7.
[3] *AOSB*, I. I. 536-7; L. Weibull, *DF*, p. 16 *seqq.*
[4] Schubert, *Camerarius*, p. 374.
[5] *RRP*, I. 218-26.
[6] *AOSB*, II. I. 595.
[7] *RRP*, II. 1-4.

provided, he considered, only by the retention of Stralsund 'or anything else we can lay our hands on'.[1] But it is clear that the security he desired was still limited to north Germany: on the eve of the invasion he had no great hope of a general settlement for Germany as a whole upon the basis of a return to 1618, still less a plan of his own for territorial or constitutional alterations within the Empire. And in so far as he hoped at this time for compensations for the injuries he had received, or indemnification for his war expenses—for *satisfactio*, as it was later to be termed—his ideas did not as yet take the form of territorial annexations.

Since the end of 1628 Gustav Adolf had from time to time put out statements of his grievances against the Emperor. The document known as *Appellatio ad Caesarem*, the letters to the Protestant Electors, the manifesto to the Regensburg meeting, were widely disseminated throughout Europe, and were obviously designed to influence public opinion.[2] In part they were mere propaganda; and complaints of different kinds and varying weight were heaped up without much regard to logic or consistency, in order that the total effect might be as massive as possible. But the purpose of these documents was not only to justify Swedish policy to the world. They were meant also to justify it to Gustav Adolf himself. As an attentive reader of Grotius, he knew well what latitude was permitted to him who waged a 'just' war; and it was essential to prove that this war fell into that category. Grotius had laid it down that danger imminent and certain alone could justify the violation of neutrality [3]; and since that was what Gustav Adolf had it in contemplation to do, there must be no doubt about the danger. On broad grounds he might feel convinced that he was justified; but there were times when he wondered whether his arguments would seem equally cogent to others. If he took and kept Wismar, for instance, would it not be 'iniquitous' thus to deprive the Dukes of Mecklenburg of one of their towns? [4] If he hung on to Stralsund after the imperialist

[1] *AOSB*, II. I. 603.

[2] *ibid.*, I. I. 528-31; *Arkiv*, I. 33-7; B. P. von Chemnitz, *Königlichen Schwedischen in Teutschland geführten Kriegs*, I. 7-9; M. C. Lundorp, *Acta publica*, III. 42-8; *The Swedish Intelligencer*, I. 42-3.

[3] 'Prima igitur causa justi belli est injuria nondum facta, quae petit aut corpus, aut rem': *Hugonis Grotii De Jure Belli ac Pacis Libri Tres*, II. I. 2 §3; and again: 'Hinc colligere est, quomodo ei, qui bellum pium gerit, liceat locum occupare, qui situs sit in solo pacato: nimirum si non imaginarium, sed certum sit periculum, ne hostis eum locum invadat, et inde irreparabilia damna det': *ibid.*, II. II. 10.

[4] *RRP*, II. 3-4. Jakob de la Gardie replied: 'Regem posse quidem occupare illorum dominia, sed non dominum fieri'.

threat had gone, would not that be a breach of treaty obligations? Would it not seem as though he had gone to Germany for no other purpose but to 'amplify his realm'? [1] It was not enough for him to feel that he had been in the right; he must be reassured that the public thought so too. As late as December 1630 he could address to the *råd* a long interrogatory, in which he rehearsed once more the familiar story of his injuries at the Emperor's hands, and appealed to them for an opinion as to whether they did not constitute a justification for his actions from the standpoint of international law. Gustav Adolf, indeed, had too tender a conscience to be a wholly convincing Goth.

Certainly he believed that the war which was beginning was essentially defensive in character: a war for the safety of Sweden, and equally a war to save the surviving remnant of German Protestantism. And he was above all concerned to ensure that he should not have this work to do twice over. He had at this moment no ally save Stralsund; he was beset by doubts and uncertainties; he was utterly unable to foresee the progress of events in Germany after he should have landed. He was, in short, in no position to hatch, nor was the *råd* likely to have endorsed, a grandiose scheme of conquest. Beyond the most general and vague notions, he cannot have had much idea what he should do when once the German campaign should have begun.[2] He was going to Germany, not with any wild idea of overturning the constitution of the Empire, or of placing himself in the room of Caesar, nor even (on a more modest scale) of reconstituting the old Protestant Union under Swedish patronage; but with the intention of pushing Wallenstein's troops away from the coast, and somehow contriving that they should not come back. How that was to be done, he did not precisely know: perhaps by a shorter or longer Swedish occupation of the endangered areas, perhaps by a system of alliances; but first, and most essential of all, by military power. The indispensable prerequisite to any stable settlement was the eviction of the imperial armies from the

[1] *RRP*, II. 2.

[2] As Oxenstierna wrote, in January 1633, 'Sei ins gemein gewesen, des feindes *conatus* zu brechen, dessen vorhaben, und was er durch die Ostseh thuen wollen, bekant. Haben also ihre maj. die meinung gehabet, ihr reich und die Ostsehe zu versichern und die bedrengte lande zu liberiren, hernach weiter zu gehen, oder zu stutzen, nachdem es sich schickete; hetten anfangs so weit zu kommen, nicht vermeinet . . . *momenta temporum* weren allezeit das fundament gewesen': G. Irmer, *Die Verhandlungen Schwedens und seiner Verbündeten mit Wallenstein und dem Kaiser* [cited: Irmer, *VS*], II. 26.

coastlands and the infliction upon them of defeats severe enough to deprive them of the power of further mischief. No political system was likely to be worth the building until a real victory was won: the aim of diplomacy, for as far ahead as he or Oxenstierna could see, must be to obtain military co-operation, military alliances, military security. The immediate object was limited to north Germany. As to whether north Germany could be esteemed safe so long as the south was in bondage, he did not at this stage enquire too closely. The search for security would later take him into paths he certainly had not yet dreamed of, would commit him to ventures which in May 1630 he would probably have rejected out of hand as chimerical; but these thorns were as yet concealed. As his newly landed soldiers fell to digging themselves in under the eye of their commander, the prospects, though hazardous, did not seem too complex, nor the immediate goal impossibly distant. The methods to be employed to reach it might still be uncertain; but the goal itself stood clear. It was never to be quite as clear again.

CHAPTER VII

FROM PEENEMÜNDE TO THE FALL OF MAGDEBURG

(i) *Europe in the Summer of 1630*

THE arrival of Gustav Adolf and his army upon the shores of Pomerania made less impression in Europe than might perhaps have been expected. His coming had been so long foretold, and so long delayed, that the news came as no surprise to anyone. Moreover, Europe was just then particularly preoccupied with other concerns, some of them of high interest and complexity. The skies of Protestant Germany might grow lurid with embattled armies contending in the clouds; the godly might be edified and encouraged by the vaticinations of feeble-witted virgins; but, on the whole, the rulers of Europe were at this moment thinking of other things.[1]

This was true even of France, although France had devoted more attention to the business of getting Gustav Adolf into action in Germany than any other foreign power. Richelieu, with the peace of Alais safely made, and the Huguenots (as it was to turn out) finally subdued and pacified, had since 1629 felt free to pursue a more active and less cautious foreign policy; and the first-fruits of it had been the intervention in Italy on behalf of Charles of Nevers's claims upon Mantua. With the support of Urban VIII and of Venice (whose armed forces provided a conveniently innocuous sphere of action for the troublesome Rohan),[2] France was waging an even struggle with Spain in north Italy. Savoy was constrained to abandon the Spanish alliance, and Pinerolo was taken in March 1630; but these

[1] Of general works dealing with the military and political history of the period 1630-32, by far the best is now *Sveriges Krig*, which devotes no less than four large volumes (III.-VI.) to Gustav Adolf's German campaigns. This work supersedes all others, and the military narrative that follows is mainly based on it. Of books in languages other than Swedish, the best and most recent is J. Paul, *Gustaf Adolf*, II.-III. Though now somewhat out of date in places, M. Ritter, *Deutsche Geschichte im Zeitalter der Gegenreformation und des dreissigjährigen Krieges*, III., is still worth reading; and so (with the same reservations) is K. Wittich, *Magdeburg, Gustav Adolf und Tilly*. Shorter narratives of military operations are Generalstaben, *Gustaf II Adolf*, and L. Tingsten, *Gustav II Adolfs politik och krigföring i Tyskland 1630-1632*; to which may be added G. Petri, *Kungl. Första Livgrenadjärregementets historia*, I.-II. (and numerous other regimental histories), G. Björlin, *Johan Banér*, I.

[2] J. Bühring, *Venedig, Gustav Adolf und Rohan*, pp. 67-8, 77-8.

successes were balanced by the imperialists' capture of Mantua soon after Gustav Adolf landed in Germany. A strong Spanish army looked likely to be successful at the siege of Casale; and the support of Ferdinand II and Wallenstein might well in the long run be sufficient to decide the issue in favour of Spain.

The imperialists appeared in Italy only as auxiliaries, and between the Emperor and the Most Christian King there was as yet no formal breach of the peace. But Richelieu redoubled his efforts to cause trouble for the Habsburgs in Germany. In 1629 and 1630 he made several attempts to detach Maximilian of Bavaria from the Emperor: in October 1629 he even produced a draft treaty of alliance, though for the moment nothing came of it.[1] His emissaries were at work among the ecclesiastical Electors: the Elector of Trier, alarmed by Spanish claims to a protectorate over his see, became a French pensioner early in 1630 [2]; and the Elector of Cologne was also said to be not unaffected by French persuasions. Encouragement was given to the idea that Maximilian might be the next King of the Romans; and Charnacé expended some time in trying to persuade George William of Brandenburg to promise his vote.[3] French agents exacerbated Protestant resentment at the Edict of Restitution, and incited the members of the League to make a stand against Wallenstein. On the western border of the *Reich* this undeclared war upon the Emperor for a time seemed likely to develop into an open conflict: in the spring of 1630 a direct clash in Lorraine appeared almost inevitable. Early in 1629 Richelieu had formulated his Rhine policy in a famous memorandum, laying it down that France must seek, not so much to conquer and annex the lands to the east of her existing frontier, but rather to control observation-posts upon the river from which she could discern in good time any impending danger from Germany.[4] Nevertheless, the imperialist sympathies of Duke Charles of Lorraine, and the need to distract the Emperor's efforts from north Italy, led Richelieu to contemplate an invasion of Lorraine in 1629; and the flight of Gaston of Orleans to the Duke's court, later in that year, was a warning of trouble to come.[5] Early in 1630, moreover, the Emperor did what Richelieu

[1] B. Baustaedt, *Richelieu und Deutschland*, pp. 34-5; Ritter, III. 452.

[2] J. Baur, *Philipp von Sötern*, I. 142-4, 152, 178-9; W. Mommsen, *Kardinal Richelieu. Seine Politik im Elsass und in Lothringen*, p. 44.

[3] Roe, pp. 41-4.

[4] Avenel, III. 181 *seqq.*; Baustaedt, p. 39; W. Mommsen, *Richelieu als Staatsman*, p. 235 *seqq.*

[5] Hanotaux, III. 226; Mommsen, *Kardinal Richelieu*, p. 59.

should have done in 1629: he sent his troops into the diocese of Metz, putting garrisons in Vic and Moyenvic.[1] The imperialists were across the Rhine in force. In alliance with a great French feudatory (for Charles of Lorraine was also Duke of Bar), and possibly even with the heir apparent, they constituted a serious threat to Richelieu's position.

It was no wonder if in these circumstances the Cardinal took care to improve relations with the Dutch. In June 1630 an alliance was concluded between France and the States General, in terms of which France was to grant a subsidy of one million *livres* a year for the next seven years, the Dutch pledging themselves in return not to make peace with Spain without France's knowledge.[2] This treaty put an end (at least for a time) to negotiations for a truce or peace between Spain and the Dutch, which had been going on intermittently ever since the siege of 's Hertogenbosch in 1629.[3] But if Richelieu thus ensured that the struggle in the Low Countries should continue, the treaty of 1630 offered no prospect of Dutch aid for his designs in Germany. There had been a moment, indeed, in the latter part of 1629, when it had appeared possible that the Dutch would become seriously entangled in the quarrels of the Empire. Wallenstein's fruitless attempt to save 's Hertogenbosch for Spain [4] had provoked, by way of retaliation, a Dutch invasion of north-west Germany. Their troops were active in Jülich, Mark and Cleves; a strong Dutch garrison held the fortress of Wesel. The Emperor feared Dutch 'practices' with the Hanse.[5] Zealous evangelical spirits such as Juliana of Hesse saw in these developments the possibility of a Dutch alliance with the Protestant states of north Germany, and perhaps with Sweden also [6]; but such ideas evoked no sympathy in Frederick Henry of Orange. Frederick Henry was for neutrality in Germany, if possible; he was prepared to extricate himself on reasonable terms from his commitments in the Rhineland (and in fact evacuated his troops, by agreement, in the summer of 1631); and if he must take

[1] R. Keller, *Die Friedensverhandlungen zwischen Frankreich und dem Kaiser auf dem Regensburger Kurfürstentag 1630*, p. 23; Mommsen, *Kardinal Richelieu*, pp. 36-8; Baur, I. 184-5.

[2] A. Waddington, *La République des Provinces-Unies, la France et les Pays-Bas espagnoles de 1630 à 1650*, I. 125; Ritter, III. 442.

[3] They had been prompted, on the Dutch side, by the desire to end the ravages of the Dunkirk privateers, and by the exhaustion of Dutch finances: Waddington, I. 65-9; A. van der Essen, *Le Cardinal-Infant*, p. 27.

[4] He sent no less than 11,000 men to its relief.

[5] Baur, I. 156; Koser, p. 422; *Sv. Krig*, III. 289.

[6] Ahnlund, *Gustaf Adolf inför tyska kriget*, p. 298.

up an attitude to German problems, would have preferred to support an effort at German Protestant self-help rather than the armed intervention of Sweden.[1] At the beginning of 1630 he was trying, as so many before and after him were to try, to induce John George to put himself at the head of a movement of resistance. Towards Sweden his attitude was non-committal at best, and at worst cold: the Dutch were suffering from the Prussian tolls. The attempts which Gustav Adolf had been making, ever since March 1629, to renew the alliance of 1614 (it expired in April 1629) made no headway at all. The States General, on the contrary, showed a disquieting tendency to be friends with Denmark: so much so, that in the spring of 1630 Kristian IV, in a burst of enthusiasm which proved premature, announced to his Council that the alliance was as good as made.[2]

In this, however, he was much mistaken. It was not so much that, with characteristic instability, Kristian was simultaneously negotiating with Gabriel de Roy and the Habsburgs; it was rather that by midsummer he had proved himself in Dutch eyes to be no more tender of mercantile feelings than Gustav Adolf himself. His foolish quarrel with Hamburg angered them; and by his levying of toll, both at the Elbe mouth and off Ruden, he flouted their most delicate susceptibilities. Recognizing at last that he had run himself into a diplomatic *impasse*, Kristian in June broke off negotiations with the States General, and resigned himself for the time being to pursuing no more than two incompatible policies at once.[3]

The only result, indeed, of Kristian's political ventures was to arouse general distrust. Gustav Adolf and Axel Oxenstierna had no faith in his sincerity as a mediator at the Danzig conference; while Kristian on his side was understandably irritated by the tone and pretensions of the proclamation which Gustav Adolf caused to be drawn up while in transit to Germany.[4] In the months before the launching of the expedition a rupture with Denmark had more than once seemed imminent; and Gustav Adolf began his Pomeranian campaign against a familiar background of rumours of Danish naval

[1] *ibid.*, p. 355; Droysen, II. 54 *note* 4, 55.

[2] Ahnlund, *Gustaf Adolf inför tyska kriget*, pp. 273, 357; *Christian IVs Breve*, II. 266; Fridericia, *YPH*, pp. 120, 158-60; A. Gindely, *Die maritimen Pläne der Habsburger*, p. 40; B. Boëthius, *Svenskarne i de nedersachsiska och westfaliska kustländerna* [cited: Boëthius, *NSK*], p. 10.

[3] Fridericia, *YPH*, pp. 122-7, 162, 172-5.

[4] S. Lundgren, *Johan Adler Salvius*, p. 26.

preparations.[1] But on the other hand Kristian's relations with the imperialists were not much more cordial. The operation of the Edict of Restitution seemed to put a final bar to any revival of his policy of collecting north German bishoprics; he had steadily refused to recognize Wallenstein as Duke of Mecklenburg, since the dispossessed Dukes were his near relations; and in the quarrel with Hamburg the Emperor, to Kristian's surprise and chagrin, found it politic to espouse the cause of the imperial city.[2]

While Charles I's 'dear Unkle of Denmark' was thus making nonsense of his foreign policy, Charles himself could scarcely be said to have a foreign policy at all. Sir Thomas Roe grew increasingly depressed at England's failure to enrol Gustav Adolf under the Palatine's standard, and at the absence of any sort of instructions from home.[3] Charles was indeed prepared in the interests of his sister to permit—or encourage—recruiting for the King of Sweden's armies; but the days were past when England could afford even to make the gestures of leadership; and the evangelical cause seemed to have gone with the parliament into cold storage. The foolish war with France was already over; for some months Rubens had been in London negotiating for a settlement with Spain; and by June 1630 Olivares's diplomacy had induced Cottington to sign the peace which Charles finally ratified in November.[4]

Apart from side-issues such as this, Olivares was in 1630 devoting himself, as usual, to the pursuit of that elusive political quarry, a Habsburg league; and was inclined to hope that the Italian war might help him to secure it. Spain had foreseen the Mantuan crisis; and though the death of Vincent II found Olivares without a policy, his mind was made up for him by the Spanish commander on the spot.[5] Spain stood to gain very much by intervention. If she could instal her candidate in Mantua, and in the process annex Casale to the Milanese, she would consolidate her command of the route from Barcelona to Vienna, reinforce her domination of Italy (the more necessary now that there was, in the person of Urban VIII, a hostile Pope), and cut off France from her ally Venice. Olivares appealed

[1] *AOSB*, I. v. 365, 369, 373-4, 390, 396, 440, 445, 451; *Arkiv*, II. 29; Fridericia, *YPH*, pp. 170-1.

[2] Fridericia, *YPH*, pp. 123-7, 173-5.

[3] Roe, pp. 80, 83.

[4] van der Essen, p. 41.

[5] M. F. Alvárez, *Gonzalo Fernández de Cordóba y la Guerra de Sucesión de Mantua y del Monferrato*, pp. 41-6, 56-9; H. Günter, *Die Habsburger-Liga*, pp. 31-2.

successfully for the support of Ferdinand II in Mantua; he dangled Italian dukedoms before the imperial generals; he gave solid backing to Wallenstein against the increasing pressure of his enemies in Germany.[1] Spanish policy now aimed at a reconstruction of the Roman Catholic party in the *Reich* round the person of the Emperor: the leadership of Bavaria was to be terminated, and the old League dissolved. Philip IV especially resented the League's indifference to his war with the Dutch. He was prepared, indeed, to make an effort to propitiate Bavaria sufficiently to prevent Maximilian from coming to terms with France; and with this end in view had at last recognized the Bavarian electorate in July 1629.[2] But on the whole Spain and Bavaria were on bad terms, each encouraging the rivals of the other and contriving obstacles to each other's policies. It was not difficult for the princes of the League, with Maximilian at their head, to represent themselves (as in Charles V's time) not only as the champions of constitutionalism but as the defenders of Germany against a sinister Spanish influence at Vienna, and—still worse—a hispaniolized general with an alien professional army.

The eviction of Denmark and the imperialist triumph had brought no peace to Germany. The conquerors were dividing against themselves; the conquered grew increasingly desperate. The military victory of the Emperor had been followed by a religious retribution designed to tip the political balance still further in his favour. In March 1629 the Edict of Restitution inaugurated a territorial readjustment which in north Germany amounted to a major upheaval. The ecclesiastical reservation was now to be a law of the Empire; church lands henceforth were to be inalienable; the Calvinists were formally excluded from the religious peace. The Archduke Leopold William and Duke Francis William of Bavaria were successively intruded into those north German bishoprics once regarded by John George or Kristian IV as the natural refuges of their younger sons. Protestant clergy were expelled from Augsburg; and in Württemberg, whose able chancellor Dr. Löffler was looked on as the soul of the Protestant resistance, imperial troops were quartered to ensure that the Church should regain her own.[3] It was a revolution; and not the less so because such a change legally required the consent of

[1] R. Quazza, *Preponderanze straniere*, pp. 163-70; Hallwich, II. 556; Ranke, *Wallenstein*, p. 132; Baur, I. 156-8.

[2] Günter, pp. 38, 56; Waddington, I. 83.

[3] G. Egelhaaf, *Gustav Adolf und die deutsche Reichsstädte*, pp. 230-40; T. chott, *Württemberg und Gustav Adolf*, p. 348; Ritter, III. 432-3.

the Diet, and not merely (as had been the case) the *fiat* of the Emperor. Even Catholic princes deprecated these unconstitutional methods,[1] though on religious grounds they might be prepared to connive at them. As to the Protestants, they appeared to have neither the means nor the heart for resistance.

Yet even in this deplorable situation the number of German rulers who were prepared to welcome Gustav Adolf's coming was few; and still fewer the number of those ready to assist him. His preliminary propaganda, his attempts to induce some German power to invite him to intervene, met with no response.[2] Some princes were impotent in exile—as for instance Adolf Frederick and John Albert of Mecklenburg, or Gustav Adolf's uncle, John Frederick of Bremen,[3] all of whom were to be found gloomily contemplating the wreck of their fortunes from behind the walls of Lübeck. Some were paralysed by their isolation: there could be little hope of early succour for Württemberg, or Baden, or the Protestant cities of south Germany. Some had hitherto contrived to escape the storm, and hoped to continue to do so: the great Hanseatic cities of Hamburg and Lübeck continued their obstinate (and profitable) neutrality; and a meeting of the Hanse, which had been called to decide on a reply to Gustav Adolf's offers of the spring of 1630, was prudently postponed, and never in fact foregathered.[4] Oldenburg and East Friesland were occupied by foreign or imperial troops, and anxious only to be rid of them.[5] This was also the case of Pomerania and Brandenburg. Pomerania's position was exceptionally difficult. Duke Bogislaw XIV was the last of his line; and by a succession pact his country would pass on his death to the Hohenzollerns of Brandenburg. He desired, therefore, to keep on good terms with George William. He also desired to keep on good terms with George William's brother-in-law, Gustav Adolf; not only because Pomerania was the obvious starting-point for a Swedish invasion,

[1] As the Elector of Trier, *e.g.*, did: Baur, I. 152.

[2] *Arkiv*, II. 13; *AOSB*, II. i. 550; Generalstaben, *Gustaf II Adolf*, p. 218.

[3] John Frederick of Holstein-Gottorp was brother of Gustav Adolf's mother, Kristina. He was Bishop of Lübeck as well as of Bremen. On him, see G. Droysen, *Die niedersächsischen Kreisstände während des schwedischen-deutschen Krieges 1631 und 1632*, pp. 18-19.

[4] Boëthius, *NSK*, pp. 12-13, 18-19, 24; Ahnlund, *Gustaf Adolf inför tyska kriget*, p. 340.

[5] Boëthius, *op. cit.*, p. 65 *seqq.*; S. F. Hammarstrand, *Bidrag till historien om Konung Gustaf II Adolfs deltagande i trettioårige kriget* [cited: Hammarstrand, *Bidrag*], pp. 44-6. The imperial troops were not withdrawn till the spring of 1631: *ibid.*, p. 48 *note* 1.

but also because of the profitable trading connexion of the Pomeranian ports with Sweden, and the consequent pro-Swedish feeling of their inhabitants.[1] On the other hand, the Duke was notoriously loyal to the Emperor, and had in the past received many assurances that imperial troops would be imposed on his country only in case of extreme necessity. Yet Pomerania was now filled with Wallenstein's garrisons; and the Duke entirely lacked the power, though he did not lack the will, to escape from his predicament. But even in this deplorable situation Bogislaw felt that he had more to fear than to hope from a Swedish landing.

The position of George William of Brandenburg was little better; and the policy of timid acquiescence which he had recently followed, on Schwarzenberg's advice,[2] had done nothing to propitiate Wallenstein: his mild protests at the excesses of the imperial soldiery had been most roughly received.[3] As a Calvinist, he was especially threatened by the Edict of Restitution. Perhaps it was this fact which produced, at the beginning of 1630, the first signs of a change in the Elector's policy. The influence of Schwarzenberg began to wane [4]; and his place was increasingly taken by Levin von Knesebeck, and by Hans Georg von Arnim—now in temporary retirement after his resignation from the imperial service. Both these men favoured a more resolute attitude towards the Emperor. Each believed that German Protestantism could still effect its own deliverance without foreign intervention. Despite present miseries, George William agreed with his neighbour Bogislaw in fearing that the coming of the Swedes might bring worse; but if they did come, he hoped that the invasion could be used to induce Ferdinand II to be more reasonable, and thus to make any alliance with Sweden against the Emperor unnecessary. It is in Berlin, quite as much as in Dresden, that we may see the germ of that 'third party' which was later to be so important, and was eventually to conclude the peace of Prague.[5]

Yet if the policy of Arnim and von Knesebeck were to have any

[1] M.Bär, *Die Politik Pommerns während des dreissigjährigen Krieges*, pp. 5, 63.

[2] *cf.* John Casimir's comment to Camerarius in June or July 1629: '. . . und ist ja die Blindheit des guten Churfürsten zu Brandenburg zu bedauren, der die Gäste selbsten zu sich ins Land bittet . . . dann es ja eine Blindheit über alle Blindheit ist': Moser, *NPA*, I. 89.

[3] Ahnlund, *Gustaf Adolf inför tyska kriget*, pp. 300-1.

[4] R. Koser, *Geschichte der brandenburgischen Politik bis zum westfälischen Frieden von 1648*, p. 424; R. Armstedt, *Die schwedische Heiratsplan des Grossen Kurfürsten*, p. 7.

[5] G. Irmer, *Hans Georg von Arnim*, p. 116.

chance of success it must certainly secure the support of the Elector of Saxony; and George William, like so many others in and out of Germany, was to waste much time in the next two years in looking vainly to John George for a lead. John George stood to lose much by Restitution. He was threatened in his sees of Merseburg, Meissen and Naumburg; and he saw his son August's coadjutorship to Magdeburg set aside in favour of a Habsburg. His strong constitutional sense was outraged by the arbitrary manner of the Edict's promulgation; and he was not much mollified by Ferdinand's assurance that it should be applied against him (as a special favour) only after due process of law.[1] Yet he clung obstinately to his loyalty and his neutrality; abhorring foreign intervention in German quarrels, and persuading himself that somehow he could continue to avoid the fate of his neighbours and keep the electorate clear of imperial troops. John George was patriotic and on the whole honest; but he was averse to thought, self-deluding, thoroughly selfish, and so jealous of political or religious initiative in others as to be in a high degree contra-suggestible. He was not prepared to face a new civil war in Germany until he was actually attacked; but he was very ready to exhort suffering Lutherans to cultivate the Christian virtue of patience, provided he could himself escape molestation. He was as deaf to the appeals of Frederick Henry or William V of Hesse-Cassel as to the immoral attractions of French gold[2]; and he had a well-grounded distrust of rash adventurers such as Christian William of Brandenburg. Since the middle of 1629 Gustav Adolf had been bombarding the Elector with letters justifying his conduct, explaining his motives and exhorting to political solidarity.[3] John George's usual reaction had been to take refuge in a bleak silence; but he had made at least one unambiguous declaration of hostility.[4] Of all the Protestant princes of Germany he was perhaps the least likely to welcome Gustav Adolf's arrival, or to co-operate with him thereafter; for in Gustav Adolf he saw not merely a fomenter of civil strife, an inciter to unconstitutional opposition, and a foreigner: he saw also in him what was worse than all—a rival. Yet it was with John George above all that Gustav

[1] Ritter, III. 429, 436-7.

[2] K. G. Helbig, *Gustav Adolf und die Kurfürsten von Sachsen und Brandenburg 1630-1632*, pp. 8, 24.

[3] *ibid.*, pp. 4-9; G. Droysen, *Schriftstücke von Gustaf Adolf zumeist an evangelische Fürsten Deutschlands* [cited: *Schriftstücke*], pp. 1-15.

[4] See above, p. 406.

Adolf was doomed by the nature of the case to co-operate if ever he were to form a strong Swedish party in Germany.

For the moment, nevertheless, the best hope for Gustav Adolf might seem to lie not in electoral Saxony but in that region to the west and north-west of it which was dominated by the ducal houses of Saxe-Weimar, Brunswick-Lüneburg and Hesse-Cassel; for all of these had looked forward to his coming, all were now in dire peril, and two of them (Brunswick-Lüneburg and Hesse-Cassel) were involved in dynastic disputes with imperialist branches of their families. Duke William of Weimar, and still more his younger brother Bernard, had already shown interest in Gustav Adolf (Bernard had been in touch with Falkenberg in Holland), and both were champions of a more vertebrate Protestant policy. William V of Hesse-Cassel, who had recently succeeded upon the abdication of his illustrious father Maurice, was to prove himself the most radical of all the German princes, and had probably fewer scruples than any about ignoring the constitutional proprieties when dealing with the Emperor. George of Lüneburg had been in active imperial service till 1629, but was said to have quitted it on the day of Gustav Adolf's landing, in the hopes of enlisting under him; and his elder brother Christian was reputed favourable to Gustav Adolf too.[1] Apart from these, there was the dubious asset of the independent enterprise of the Administrator of Magdeburg, Christian William, who in June 1630 had still to make good his large promises; and the potential aid of some of the great imperial cities—whenever it should be safe to grant it. But of actual assistance there was none. Gustav Adolf entered Germany without a single ally apart from Stralsund.

Nevertheless, there were many aspects of the German situation which were decidedly encouraging. And above all, the obvious and widening breach between Wallenstein and the League. For some time now—and more especially since February 1628, when the electorate had been made hereditary in Maximilian's line—the League had been striving for peace in Germany. Bavaria and her allies had no intention of getting involved in the quarrels of Spain with France and the Dutch[2]; and their tendency to listen to

[1] For Weimar, Hesse-Cassel and Lüneburg, see J. Kretzschmar, *Der Heilbronner Bund*, I. 25-42; *id.*, *Gustav Adolfs Pläne und Ziele in Deutschland*, pp. 4-9; Boëthius, *NSK*, pp. 47-8, 63; Ahnlund, *Gustaf Adolf inför tyska kriget*, pp. 414-415; W. Struck, *Das Bündnis Wilhelms von Weimar mit Gustaf Adolf*, pp. 22-6; C. von Rommel, *Geschichte von Hessen*, VIII. 49-87.

[2] Goetz, IV. II. 18, 94.

wandering French diplomats was a sign of this. They were quite opposed to any idea of a Habsburg league. And they were disposed to be casual or indifferent to the danger from Sweden, holding it to be an entanglement into which Ferdinand had drifted because of Wallenstein's attack on Stralsund, and out of which he might be left to extricate himself.[1] The League was groaning under the burden of its own armaments; its members were defaulting with their contributions (Maximilian secretly making them good out of his own pocket)[2]; and their most urgent wish just now was for a large reduction in their own forces, and a still larger in Wallenstein's.[3] Upon Wallenstein's exactions they blamed (rather unfairly) not only the continuing unrest within the Empire but also a good share of their own difficulties. In reality, they hated Wallenstein both on personal and political grounds. He had condemned the Edict of Restitution[4]; his army was full of Protestants, and he himself had promised the Estates of his new duchy of Mecklenburg to preserve Protestantism in the country[5]; he had dangerous family ties with notorious Bohemian exiles such as Trčka[6]; he had been guilty of sharp and taxing speeches about the Electors in general and Maximilian in particular.[7] A campaign of slander was launched against him: he was accused of aiming at the disarming of the League[8] (perhaps a not improbable charge), at an electoral hat, even at the imperial crown.[9] But essentially they resolved to destroy Wallenstein because they feared in him the architect of imperial despotism and the enemy of those anarchical notions which they were in the habit of referring to as the liberties of Germany.

Their opportunity came at the electoral meeting which opened

[1] *Sv. Krig*, III. 302.

[2] Wittich, *Magdeburg, Gustav Adolf und Tilly*, p. 239. In December 1628 Maximilian even had the effrontery to ask for monetary aid from Spain: Goetz, IV. II. 196-7.

[3] Goetz, IV. II. 65-6; Ahnlund, *Gustaf Adolf inför tyska kriget*, pp. 251-2.

[4] Hallwich, II. 568.

[5] Ranke, *Wallenstein*, p. 124.

[6] A. Gaedeke, *Wallensteins Verhandlung mit den Schweden und Sachsen 1631-1634*, pp. 9-10.

[7] 'Er wolle den Kurfürsten mores lehren; sie müssten von den Kaiser, der Kaiser nit von ihnen abhängen'; again: 'Ich bin gewohnt, dem Haus Österreich zu dienen und nicht von der bayrischen Servitut mich strapazieren zu lassen. . . . Der Herr Tilly ist der bayrischen Kommissäre Sklave. . . . Wegen der Patienz, so er mit diesen Hundsföttern haben muss, wird er bei Gott coronam martyrii erlangen, der gute Alte': Pfister, *Kurfürst Maximilian I von Bayern*, pp. 240, 248; Riezler, V. 325-33.

[8] Goetz, IV. II. 435.

[9] Hallwich, II. 470; Baur, I. 72.

at Regensburg less than a fortnight after Gustav Adolf's landing. Against the remonstrances of the Protestant Electors [1] the League did indeed maintain a solid front with the Emperor—Ferdinand is said to have declared that sooner than modify the Edict of Restitution he would go in his bare shirt, and lose wife and child, crown and sceptre [2]—but once that confessional duty was discharged they set themselves with success to thwart the imperial designs. The Protestant Estates had no need to halloo on the pack of Wallenstein's enemies; and even Richelieu modestly disclaimed for France's representatives the merit of his fall.[3] By 3 August Ferdinand had succumbed to the pressure brought to bear upon him: on that day he conceded Wallenstein's dismissal; and two imperial councillors were sent to seek out the general at his headquarters, to break the news as gently as they might.

The fall of Wallenstein cleared the way for measures to ease the burdens of the *Reich*—which had, indeed, been the ostensible purpose of the attack upon him. It was agreed that the armies of the Emperor and his allies were to be drastically reduced, the one to 40,000 men, the other to 20,000.[4] But when it came to the point, the League declined to lower their forces to that figure; and in the end the reduction was never very significant. As to measures to regularize the payment of troops and stop the soldiery from living at free quarters, the best thing they could do, after months of wrangling, was to resolve that henceforth contributions for their maintenance should be voted directly by the Diet or by the assemblies of the Circles. This in effect meant that the troops would probably not be paid at all.[5] The result of the League's compassion for the woes of Germany was thus to leave the imperialist armies on a less satisfactory financial basis than before, to make it necessary for them to live by extortion, and, by removing Wallenstein, to deprive them of the only man whose organizing genius might conceivably have mitigated the ill-effects of this state of affairs.

The Emperor, thus vanquished in the matter of Wallenstein, suffered another rebuff when the Electors peremptorily refused to

[1] John George and George William did not attend in person. For John George's demands, see Lundorp, III. 89.

[2] Wittich, *op. cit.*, p. 247.

[3] *Testament politique de Richelieu*, p. 117; Helbig, p. 22.

[4] *Sv. Krig*, III. 366-7; A. Ernstberger, *Wallensteins Heeressabotage und die breitenfelder Schlacht*, p. 45.

[5] Ritter, III. 454-6; *cf. The Swedish Intelligencer*, I. 21.

listen to the suggestion that his eldest son be elected King of the Romans. It is possible that on this latter point the negotiators whom Richelieu sent to Regensburg may have done something to stiffen the resistance of the Electors; though in general their importance has been much exaggerated by admirers of the Cardinal.[1] But, if so, Ferdinand seemed to have his revenge upon France in the settlement of the Mantuan question. For by the treaty signed early in October the Emperor, in exchange for yielding Mantua to Nevers, extorted from Brûlart and Father Joseph a pledge that France would give no aid or countenance to rebels against imperial authority or their allies. He thus debarred France from making mischief in Germany (and, possibly, from assisting Gustav Adolf) at the same time as he liberated the imperial armies in Italy for use north of the Alps. But Ferdinand was ever unlucky. It soon proved that Brûlart had exceeded his instructions (which had confined him to a peace in Italy only); the treaty was promptly disavowed by Richelieu; and when, in March 1631, peace was finally made at Cherasco, Ferdinand found himself in the undeserved position of making all the sacrifices and getting nothing in return.[2]

The negotiators at Regensburg had been so preoccupied with their domestic quarrels on the one hand, and with the affairs of Italy on the other, that they had had little time or attention to spare for Gustav Adolf. Representatives of Pomerania had appeared at Regensburg to ask the aid of the Empire in resisting invasion[3]; but the only response was to despatch on 3 August (the very day when Wallenstein's dismissal was decided) a letter from all the Electors to the King of Sweden, in which they controverted his arguments, denied the reality of his grounds for war and invited him to withdraw.[4] The Emperor, for his part, would probably not have been sorry to patch up a settlement with Gustav Adolf; and possibly Maximilian and his friends had moments when they almost feared that he might do so.[5] But one thing was clear enough: the League, by its reckless animosity against Wallenstein and its historic fears of imperial power, had itself created a situation far more favourable to

[1] Mommsen, *Kardinal Richelieu*, p. 39; *cf.* Fagniez, *Le Père Joseph et Richelieu*, I. 523-30.

[2] Avenel, III. 949-52; Fagniez, I. 492-507; Hanotaux, III. 270-89, 418; A. Leman, *Urbain VIII*, pp. 22-42; Keller, pp. 22, 53 *seqq.*; Mommsen, *op. cit.*, pp. 40-1, 43; Ritter, III. 460.

[3] Lundorp, III. 48-9.

[4] Printed in *Sverges traktater*, V. 820-2; Gustav Adolf's reply, *ibid.*, 822-6.

[5] Fagniez, I. 513; *cf. Sv. Krig*, III. 302.

Sweden's prospects in Germany than at any time before. They had resolved to cut down the imperial armies; they had done their best to deprive them of proper financial support. They had removed from his command the only soldier of genius whom Gustav Adolf might have to meet; and for months after his dismissal they had delayed, by their purblind disputes, the appointment of a commander to succeed him. It was only in November, and then at Ferdinand's earnest solicitation, that the command-in-chief was at last accepted by the reluctant Tilly.[1] A rift had appeared in the forces arrayed against Sweden, and into that rift France was busily engaged in trying to drive a wedge. In the first six months of Gustav Adolf's campaign in Germany, although a view of the Protestant camp was scarcely inspiriting, the political conjunctions were much less adverse than Gustav Adolf could have foreseen.

(ii) *The Opening Campaign, June 1630-January 1631*

If in June 1630 the impending meeting at Regensburg promised distraction to the politics of Gustav Adolf's enemies, the military opposition which awaited him was by the same token less formidable than might have been expected. The exhaustion of north Germany, the divided counsels of the Roman Catholic leaders, and above all the drain of the Mantuan war, reduced the forces arrayed against him to manageable proportions.[2] By the close of 1629 some 36,000 imperialists were serving in Italy; by the middle of 1630 their number had risen to 55,000. Wallenstein himself, underrating the danger in the north, moved his headquarters to Memmingen in May, and on the eve of his dismissal was contemplating going to Italy in person. Apart from an imperial army in north-west Germany, estimated on paper at 15,000 men, the only force in the Emperor's service available to meet the Swedish invasion was the army of Conti, nominally of the respectable strength of 53,000 men, but in reality numbering probably not more than 30,000 effectives. It was not that Wallenstein had neglected the danger-spot in Pomerania: from the spring of 1630 to the time of his dismissal he had striven to send Conti reinforcements and to raise new recruits.

[1] Riezler, V. 361-3; Wittich, p. 238. By way of complicating his position, he was bound to keep the imperial and League armies separate. Some imperialists, at least, had serious doubts as to Tilly's capacity: B. Dudík, *Waldsteins Correspondenz*, I. 54.

[2] For what follows, see *Sv. Krig*, III. 344-8.

But the calls upon available forces were many; recruiting had been discouraged in the spring of 1630 by an Emperor anxious to avoid irritating his allies unduly; and 30,000 in the end was as much as could be compassed at the critical point.[1] The difficulty of feeding so large an army necessarily prevented their being grouped in one area, and hence it happened that they were scattered thinly in garrisons over the whole maritime strip from Mecklenburg to the borders of Polish Prussia. The possibilities for swift concentration were, moreover, diminished by the fact that the Oder cut the imperialists' position in two, and was capable (unless frozen) of being an awkward barrier. The imperialist garrisons were strongest in Wismar, Rostock, Greifswald and Kolberg, any one of which might conceivably be among Gustav Adolf's objectives; and two striking-forces were assembled some little way inland from the coast. The larger of these forces lay around Gartz and Greifenhagen, twin positions on either bank of the Oder some way above Stettin: they constituted, offensively, a threat to Stettin; and, defensively, a barrier to a Swedish advance up the Oder against Habsburg Silesia. The smaller force was disposed in and around Anklam and Stolpe, and was designed to hinder free movement parallel to the coast, and especially to check any advance from Stralsund upon Stettin. Attempts to induce Bogislaw to admit an imperialist garrison into his capital had proved unavailing, and Wallenstein had apparently shrunk from coercion lest Stettin prove another Stralsund: it was a serious miscalculation.[2] Morale, discipline and supply in the imperial armies left a good deal to be desired, but were by no means so decayed as has been asserted—at all events, as long as Wallenstein continued in the command.[3] The prospects of reinforcements were not bright.

The armies of the League lay to the west of the Elbe, dispersed—even more widely than Conti's—over the Lower Saxon Circle, Westphalia and the upper Rhine. Their dispositions were entirely defensive; they had long been inactive; and it would take weeks or months to bring them into effective operation. Between them and Conti lay something of a vacuum; and it was not without significance for the future that the diocese of Magdeburg was at this time virtually denuded of troops.[4]

[1] See Wallenstein's remarks, quoted in Wittich, p. 220; and *cf.* B. Dudík, *Waldsteins Correspondenz*, I. 8.

[2] Bär, pp. 255-8.

[3] *cf.* Wittich, pp. 224-31, and Ritter, III. 472, with *Sv. Krig*, III. 330.

[4] *Sv. Krig*, III. 316-78, for the above account.

Gustav Adolf's intelligence service had served him well. Before his arrival he had obtained a picture of the enemies' dispositions which accorded (for that age) surprisingly well with the facts.[1] And the conclusion to be drawn from the information available to him was, that provided he could carry out his plans for a rapid concentration of troops in the theatre of operations, and especially if he could transport his cavalry quickly from Prussia, he ought to be able without much difficulty to establish a practicable bridgehead in Pomerania. Thereafter his campaign must aim in the first place at expelling Conti's force from the Baltic littoral, from Kolberg to Lübeck: this was, by definition, the prime object of the expedition. But if the imperialists were to be denied the possibility of returning, it must aim further at inflicting upon the enemy serious defeat in battle, at destroying those armies which might otherwise be in a position to 'infest' Pomerania and Mecklenburg in future. Difficulties of transport and supply would probably dictate the line of any major advance into the interior; and it was clear from the beginning that if such an advance took place it must, for the sake of the heavy artillery, be either up the Oder (which would enable early pressure to be put upon the Emperor's hereditary lands) or by way of the Spree and the Havel to the Elbe (which would put Gustav Adolf into touch with the most promising area for raising potential allies). And since military strength might as much depend upon political developments as political success upon military victories, it might well be that considerations of diplomacy would play their part in determining strategy. But for the present, at all events, the choice need not be made. The first task was to get a secure foothold.

Peenemünde lies at the extreme north-west tip of the straggling island of Usedom, which with its companion island of Wollin forms a sort of breakwater at the wide mouth of the Oder and encloses the broad and shallow waters of the Stettiner Haff. It had originally been intended, as we have seen, to go ashore on Rügen: the change of destination was for the better. A landing on Usedom brought Gustav Adolf within striking distance of Stettin, which must be one of his earliest objectives in any case; it turned the imperialist position on the Peene between Stolpe and Anklam; and it made it possible to operate at a very early stage upon both banks of the

[1] *cf.* the two maps in *Sv. Krig*, III. 204-5 and 340-1.

Oder. For Usedom and Wollin, separated from each other and from the mainland to east and west only by very narrow channels, formed an island-bridge across the mouth of the Oder by which Gustav Adolf could move troops across the river freely. His command of the sea, reinforced by the shallow-draught craft which he had ordered up from Stralsund, enabled him to use the Stettiner Haff as a highway; and the absence of any but the most trifling resistance on the islands (which the imperialists never seem to have intended seriously to defend) permitted his operations to get away to a flying start.[1] By the end of the first week of July Usedom and Wollin were firmly in his possession, and Kammin (on the mainland east of Wollin) had been occupied without resistance. The possibility was now open for operations either in western or eastern Pomerania. The first move, however, must be upon Stettin, for Gustav Adolf could not afford to see it in Conti's hands, and was well aware that it might easily fall to a sudden assault. Its possession was necessary as the first measure to expand his base and to increase the area from which he could draw supplies; and it was highly desirable as a spearhead directed against the main imperialist position at Gartz and Greifenhagen. Bogislaw XIV tried hard to preserve its neutrality; but the appeals which he directed to Gustav Adolf on 8 and 9 July had no effect. On 10 July the King shipped 10,000 men in flat-bottomed boats from Caseburg across the Haff, and appeared unexpectedly on the Duke's doorstep. The citizens of Stettin waved a welcome from the walls, while Gustav Adolf spoke kindly but firmly to Bogislaw outside them. And since (as he pointed out) the fortifications were in no state to defy a serious attack, a capitulation followed the same day.[2] A garrison of Swedes was installed (Bogislaw stipulated for no German mercenaries); negotiations for an alliance were set on foot; and the work of providing Stettin with effective fortifications was put in hand without delay.

There is some reason to suppose that if Gustav Adolf had now made an attack upon Gartz he would have taken the imperialists by surprise, and might possibly have captured that position. His strength on landing had amounted to some 10,400 foot, 2750 horse and 81 three-pounders; and he had been joined in the first week of July by an additional 4000 infantry from the Stralsund garrison.

[1] Grubbe's description of the landing in *Arkiv*, I. 696-8; *cf. ibid.*, I. 173-4, II. 21; *AOSB*, II. 1. 617; *Dagbok*, pp. 13-14.

[2] *AOSB*, II. 1. 620; *Arkiv*, I. 698-700; *Dagbok*, p. 14; *The Swedish Intelligencer*, I. 50-1; Bär, p. 270.

Of these, he had about 10,000 at his disposal in Stettin.[1] Conti had some 12,000 men spread out between Gartz and Anklam, and might have found it difficult to concentrate them quickly against a sudden attack. But the opportunity, if it was an opportunity, was deliberately neglected. Gustav Adolf was no more anxious than any other general of his day to attack the enemy in prepared positions if any alternative offered; and the imperialists at Gartz were well protected. It was in any case too early for a thrust inland. There would be plenty of time to win battles when the expected reinforcements should have arrived. For the moment, Gustav Adolf commanded only a small expeditionary force, by no means corresponding to his expectations. In many of the units a high proportion of the men were raw recruits. He could not afford to hazard his small force in a major engagement. What he needed was a firm control of an extended strip of coastline and a penetration in some depth, so that his ports should have adequate protection and his cavalry room for foraging. Stettin itself was still an advanced post jabbed into the enemy's territory, threatening to cut his positions on the Oder in two, and urgently in need of consolidation and support in flank. The occupation of Stettin, therefore, was followed not by an immediate attack on Gartz but by a series of minor operations to east and west designed to give a really secure base in Pomerania. It might be slow, but it was sure; and for the present, at least, there was no external pressure to be quick.

The first blow was struck to the east. On 12 July the Swedes took Damm; on the following day they took Stargard. On 4 August they pushed towards Kolberg, capturing Greifenberg and Treptow.[2] Gustav Adolf's intention was to attack Conti in eastern Pomerania from two sides; and Oxenstierna was instructed to send in troops from Prussia, to take possession of Stolp [3] and Rügenwalde. But this plan had in part been anticipated; for Robert Monro, wrecked with a detachment of reinforcements on its way from Prussia to Stettin, had occupied these places already.[4] The effect of these and similar operations was that by the middle of August the coast east of the Oder was clear of imperial troops, with the single exception

[1] But probably not all his guns: some seem not to have been landed until late in July: *cf.* Hammarskiöld, *USAH*, pp. 156, 158.

[2] Treptow on the Rega; not to be confused with Treptow on the Tollense, near the Mecklenburg border.

[3] Stolp on the Stolpe; not to be confused with Stolpe on the Peene.

[4] Monro, II. 5.

of Kolberg, where a sizeable garrison retained possession of the port for the time being.

Expansion to the west proved much more difficult: partly because here the imperialists were in stronger force; partly on account of the nature of the country, which was woody, marshy and intersected by rivers. Between Stettin and Stralsund the valleys of the Uecker and the Peene presented obstacles to easy movement. Roads crossed the Uecker at Pasewalk, or near its mouth at Ueckermünde, and then converged upon the bridge over the Peene at Anklam. Gustav Adolf resolved first to clear the more northerly of these routes. On 21 July he simultaneously occupied the crossings at Ueckermünde and Anklam; and two days later he safeguarded the Stralsund-Stettin road from an attack in flank by the capture of Wolgast. But the route to Stralsund was not yet open, for beyond Anklam lay Greifswald, and here a strong imperialist garrison barred the way, and continued to bar it for some months to come, so that Gustav Adolf remained dependent upon his command of the sea for communications between his two main base areas. The alternative route from Stettin to Anklam by way of Pasewalk was not tackled till 3 September, when a detachment of Swedish troops occupied Pasewalk: too small a detachment, as soon appeared; for on 7 September the imperialists, whose communications westwards from Gartz would be jeopardized if Pasewalk were to remain in Swedish hands, retook the position and levelled the town to the ground. It was one of the rare occasions when Gustav Adolf fell into the error of sending a boy on a man's errand.[1]

Nevertheless, by the end of August Gustav Adolf might consider his foothold in Pomerania reasonably secure, provided reinforcements and supplies did not fail him. But it was just here that the prospects appeared most dubious. The troops arrived in Pomerania from their various ports of embarkation with exasperating slowness: by mid-September the total available force did not exceed 26,000. And as the conquest of a base proceeded, the field-army was increasingly bled to provide garrisons, so that it was doubtful if at any given moment as much as two-thirds of the army would be disposable for battle.[2] The King had hardly set foot in Germany before he began

[1] See Gustav Horn's criticism of the King in *AOSB*, II. VIII. 17-18.

[2] At the beginning of September Gustav Adolf had 11,000 men in garrisons, 4000 at Wolgast and on Usedom, and 11,000 concentrated round Stettin: *Sv. Krig*, III. 448. Wittich was mistaken in supposing that Gustav Adolf '[illegible] had 40,000 men at his disposal: Wittich, p. 213.

to worry the government at home to expedite the reinforcements, and for the next five months his correspondence with Axel Oxenstierna in Prussia was much concerned with this topic. The problem of paying the Prussian cavalry was succeeded by the problem of moving them. The best way would have been by sea; but Oxenstierna could not obtain sufficient shipping. Movement by land was difficult, since the King of Poland naturally objected to the passage of large bodies of troops through his territories. In the end, no better solution could be found than to send them overland in detachments small enough for them not to be a terror to the peaceful Polish peasantry. But it took time to arrive at this conclusion, and time before the whole body of them could be brought to the theatre of operations in driblets. It was not until full six months after the landing that Gustav Adolf began to have an army of the size and constitution contemplated in his original plan of campaign [1]; and the lack of cavalry, in particular, was a severe handicap. It is noteworthy that not until a considerable body of the Prussian horse had arrived did Gustav Adolf venture upon his first important offensive action.

In the meantime, the supply position was so serious that any additional troops might even have been an embarrassment. Pomerania had been reduced to utter destitution by imperialist garrisons as early as January 1629,[2] and the situation had probably not much improved since then. But at the beginning of the campaign —at all events before the Swedish army had acquired a sizeable base area to batten on—the provisioning of the forces necessarily came from overseas. Unfortunately, as Gustav Adolf immediately complained, it came in inadequate quantities.[3] Until relations with Pomerania were put upon a footing such that the duchy undertook to provide supplies, they had to be bought for cash—the Swedes in these early days avoiding frank extortion if possible. But there was a chronic shortage of cash; and Gustav Adolf was reduced to raising small short-term loans in Hamburg or Stralsund. He had the usual impatience of the man of action with the difficulties of the administrator, and he wrote in terms of bitter reproach to the exchequer

[1] See, *e.g.*, *AOSB*, I. v. 383, 515, 565, 567, 574, II. I. 617, II. IX. 550, 553; Ahnlund, *Oxenstierna*, pp. 583-4.

[2] Wallenstein then reported: 'die Soldaten allbereits in der Insel Rügen Hunde und Katzen essen, die Bauern aus Not und Desperation sich selbst ins Meer stürzen': Hallwich, II. 260.

[3] *Arkiv*, I. 167.

officials at home. He clamoured for money, for powder, for shovels, for match, for lead; he protested that at home they seemed to have forgotten all about him.[1] The consequences were ruinous, both from the point of view of military efficiency and from that of the comfort of the inhabitants of Pomerania. 'The disorder is greater,' wrote Lars Grubbe on 8 September, 'and the military discipline less, than in the armies of Mansfeld. . . . Popular feeling in the country has undergone a great alteration. And this comes mainly from *licentia militari, conniventibus, imo male agentibus officialibus plaerisque*, so that the ravaging is worse than if we were in an enemy country.' And this at a time when Pomerania was estimated by Grubbe to have already contributed 200,000 *rdr.* to the maintenance of the army.[2]

In these circumstances the modest scope of Gustav Adolf's military operations, at a period when the animosities of Regensburg had gone far to disorganize the opposition, becomes explicable. The imperialist army was indeed in as bad a state as his own; Conti was sick, and his troops sicker; reinforcements were not coming in; no successor to Wallenstein had yet been appointed. The opportunity was obvious, as Grubbe himself observed[3]; but Gustav Adolf was in no case to seize it. But at the end of July there occurred an event which seemed to make some major military effort imperative: on 26 July Christian William arrived safely in Magdeburg,[4] and on 1 August the city concluded an alliance with Sweden.[5] At once the strategic perspectives shifted. Till this moment the natural expectation had been that Gustav Adolf, as soon as he was strong enough, would evict Conti from the Gartz position and begin that campaign up the Oder which he had so often contemplated in the previous six or seven years. But the revolt of Magdeburg opened the prospect of further risings of the discontented and oppressed in north-west Germany, and particularly of Weimar and Hesse; its position on the Elbe gave the King an alternative river line along which to advance. If he were not to wage the war single-handed, he must take his allies where he found them, even if the first of them happened to be of the unsatisfactory quality of Christian William; and above all he must not fail to stand by them. Magdeburg was, no doubt, difficult to

[1] *Arkiv*, I. 204; Styffe, p. 390; *RRP*, II. 35; *Sv. Krig*, III. 438-40.
[2] *Arkiv*, II. 45-6; *cf. ibid.*, 50-1.
[3] *ibid.*, II. 54-6.
[4] *ibid.*, II. 27, for his letter to Gustav Adolf; *ibid.*, 31.
[5] For the background to the alliance, see Droysen, *Gustav Adolf*, II. 104-25.

come at: the neutral territories of Brandenburg and Saxony lay in the road; and even if a right of way over them could be obtained, and even if his own army had been stronger than it actually was, a direct advance south-westward upon the Elbe was at present impossible: as the imperial commander Schauenburg was later to point out, such an advance would have been crushed between Conti's forces in the east and Pappenheim's army of the League advancing from the west.[1] Even by the standards of seventeenth-century warfare, when lines of communication did not give commanders overmuch concern, Gustav Adolf could not plunge into central Germany and cut himself off from his one source of supply and only line of retreat to Sweden, leaving the coastal base weakly held. But something must be done. The news from Magdeburg had scarcely arrived before the King, in letters of 14 and 16 August, wrote to Christian William and to Magdeburg, promising aid—and promising it, moreover, 'forthwith'[2]; on 16 August he issued a general patent to Dietrich von Falkenberg, appointing him his legate and empowering him to raise armies, and sent him off armed with this to render such assistance to Magdeburg as he could[3]; and on the following day he wrote to Oxenstierna outlining the wider prospects which seemed now to open. His aim now, he wrote, would be to occupy the rich cornlands of Magdeburg, Meissen, Anhalt and Mansfeld, to secure the line of the Elbe, to distract the enemy's forces, to give the 'Malcontents' breathing-space to rally to rebellion, 'and thus, to conclude, to touch off a rocket of universal rebellion throughout Germany'.[4] It was unfortunate (he continued) that the Prussian cavalry had not yet arrived: if he had had them with the army he might already have cleared all Pomerania of the enemy, and have been in a position to move them somewhat nearer to those fat ecclesiastical lands to whose plunder they had so long been looking forward.[5]

The King's imagination had taken fire at the events in Magdeburg; and his sanguine temper led him to reckon on a general

[1] *Sv. Krig*, III. 496: such a plan, he considered, would have been 'unbedachtsamb und kindisch'.

[2] 'Darzue sich dan E: Ld: getröstlich zuuorlassen vnd vnsern realen entsaz mit ersten zuuerwarten': S. F. Hammarstrand, *Bidrag*, p. 113; *cf. ibid.*, pp. 112-18.

[3] *Schriftstücke*, p. 192 (full powers for Falkenberg). He did not arrive till 19 October: *Arkiv*, II. 67-8.

[4] *AOSB*, II. I. 635; and *cf.* his letter of 22 January 1631 to John Casimir: Styffe, p. 390 *seqq.*

[5] *AOSB*, II. I. 635-6.

movement of Protestant resistance. But his judgment as a commander remained unaffected; the policy of cautious consolidation and small commitments hitherto pursued was not abandoned; no unnecessary risks were to be taken. Bogislaw XIV, now an ally, pressed him to undertake an attack on Gartz, which lay uncomfortably close to Stettin. Gustav Adolf put him off with excuses. Already he had decided what his next move should be. His intention was a campaign in Mecklenburg.

There were sound arguments for a thrust in this direction. Gustav Adolf himself pointed out that it would give him more commodious winter quarters; that by capturing Rostock and Wismar (as he hoped to do) he would improve his command of the coast—and, incidentally, finally dispose of the Habsburg fleet; and that the expedition would help to relieve pressure on Magdeburg and put him in a better position to bring help to the town.[1] Proceeding by way of Mecklenburg, he might hope to circumvent the imperialists' positions and reach the Elbe by the easiest route. The restoration of the Mecklenburg Dukes would be a first-rate political success; and it might reasonably be hoped that as a consequence Hamburg and Lübeck would take a more positive attitude. And, finally, he would be well placed in Mecklenburg to keep an eye on Kristian IV if he should be disposed to give trouble.[2] A blow at Gartz, on the other hand, might—if it were completely successful, and Conti's army were destroyed—make possible a direct advance on Magdeburg. But a half-success would not be enough; a failure would be serious; Conti's army was growing weaker every day from sickness and privation, and might well be left to itself for a little while longer.

It was decided, then, to march against Mecklenburg. The intention was that the invasion should coincide with risings by the local population—one in Rostock, where the main body of imperialists (some 5400) was concentrated under the command of Savelli; one in the countryside. Falkenberg was very active in inciting the Mecklenburgers to action; but he could get no support from Adolf Frederick, the citizens of Rostock preferred to await the issue, and in the end the only leader to come forward was Francis

[1] *AOSB*, II. I. 638; or, as he put it to Christian William, 'also *per obliquum* wass vnss *per directum ex causis novis emergentibus* vnmüglich gefallen, durch die hilffliche hand Gottes, effectuiren möchten': Hammarstrand, *Bidrag*, p. 118.

[2] For the debate on the Mecklenburg campaign, see *Sv. Krig*, III. 451-5; C. von Clausewitz, *Strategische Beleuchtung mehrerer Feldzüge*, pp. 12-14; Tingsten, p. 4; Boëthius, *NSK*, pp. 39-41; *Dagbok*, p. 15.

Charles of Lauenburg, who agreed to seize Ratzeburg and make it the centre of insurrection. Apart from these political disappointments, there were other difficulties. An advance upon Rostock from Stralsund would have to force the difficult and swampy valleys of the Trebel or the Recknitz and might well be held up there. But Gustav Adolf could not afford to risk prolonged delays lest Conti pluck up courage for a blow at Stettin in his absence. The best chance, he decided, would be to avoid the land-route altogether and transport his army direct by sea from Stralsund. But whether he went by sea or land, the failure of reinforcements to arrive would mean that he must start with far fewer men than he had intended to take; and this in turn would jeopardize the success of the venture.

Nevertheless, the attempt was made. By 15 September the fleet was assembled at Stralsund. The wind was then westerly; and it continued to blow from that quarter without abatement for the next week. By 22 September Gustav Adolf felt he could wait no longer. The naval expedition was abandoned, and he decided to attack Mecklenburg by land, in the hope that the expected insurrections would make his progress easier. He would advance parallel to the coast, using the fleet as a moving base. But once again his plans were put out of gear. The force at his disposal was not the 12,000 men on which he had counted, but a mere 4000 foot and 1450 horse, and it proved too weak to deal with Savelli and capture Rostock; the insurrection in Rostock did not take place; and the insurrection of Francis Charles was mismanaged. He rose, indeed, on 25 September; but instead of seizing Ratzeburg immediately, as had been agreed, he moved first on the Elbe. This move alarmed the League, and soon brought Pappenheim down on him with overwhelming force. Pappenheim caught him while he was besieging the castle at Ratzeburg, and there scattered his little army.[1] Gustav Adolf meanwhile had taken Dammgarten, forced the Recknitz by a manœuvre which foreshadows the passing of the Lech, and on 25 September stormed Ribnitz. But that was as far as he could safely go; and indeed it was fortunate for him that Pappenheim returned to his base after disposing of Francis Charles: a combined attack by Pappenheim and Savelli might have produced a serious reverse. As it was, Gustav Adolf made his way back to Stralsund, leaving a garrison in Ribnitz. The Mecklenburg expedition had been something of a fiasco.

Yet it was from Ribnitz, in these somewhat disheartening circum-

[1] Boëthius, *NSK*, pp. 48-53.

stances,[1] that Gustav Adolf on 1 October drafted for Oxenstierna his grandiose plans for the campaign of 1631. The letter shows extraordinary optimism. Not merely did he assume that all the local difficulties would by then have been overcome, but he proposed to engage in hostilities on the vastest scale along a front which was to extend from the Weser to the Polish frontier. He expected to recruit, by the spring of next year, the enormous number of 80,000 fresh troops, additional to the forces he was counting on already. His intention was to form them into five distinct armies: one, based on Stralsund, under his own command, to enlarge the base area and push the enemy back in western Pomerania; a second, under Horn, to operate from eastern Pomerania against Silesia and (incidentally) to ensure the 'devotion' of Brandenburg. In these tasks it was to be assisted by a third army, also based on eastern Pomerania, under Teuffel. A fourth was to be raised by Christian William, and was to move from Magdeburg up the Elbe; while the fifth was to be formed of those mercenaries whom Hamilton was engaged in recruiting in England and Scotland. In general, the first four armies were to conduct a vast concentric operation against the Habsburg hereditary dominions, while the fifth was to contain the army of the League; or, as Oxenstierna later put it, the two outermost armies would distract the enemy, while the three inner ones engaged him. The whole was a strategic conception of Napoleonic breadth and grandeur: its principal defect was that it lacked a Napoleonic administration behind it. As Oxenstierna was careful to point out, finance would be a limiting factor; the essentials must be provided for first; and those essentials were the King's own army, Horn's army of the Oder, and the garrisons. The chancellor's warning was pertinent: by January 1631 the number of fresh troops that Sweden had been able to raise was not 80,000 but something over 6000. And it certainly sheds a somewhat startling light upon Gustav Adolf's notions as to what the position in the diocese of Magdeburg really was, that he should have supposed it probable that Christian William would be allowed to take the offensive in the following spring with an army of 11,000 men.[2]

The attempt to find a way round to the Elbe through Mecklenburg having for the moment failed, Gustav Adolf fell back on

[1] *cf.* his complaints to John Casimir: Styffe, p. 390.

[2] *AOSB*, II. I. 648-51; Oxenstierna's comments in *AOSB*, I. v. 646, 667; *cf. ibid.*, II. IX. 784; *Sv. Krig*, III. 524-9, and map, p. 526; B. Boëthius, *Några Gustav Adolfs-forskningens problem*, pp. 227-8.

Bogislaw's alternative: the pressure on Magdeburg should be relieved by a pitched battle, and Conti should be driven out of Gartz and Greifenhagen.[1] But for this he must wait until he could build up sufficient strength to be sure of success—must wait, therefore, until the Prussian cavalry, trickling slowly across the Polish border, had been incorporated into the main army.[2] As it turned out, he was forced to wait till Christmas Eve. In the interim, early in November, Conti, who was shortly to be transferred to Italy, celebrated his impending departure by an attempt to relieve the blockaded garrison in Kolberg. The relieving force was intercepted by Horn, who as he pursued them got himself involved in a confused skirmish in a thick fog which ended in a sharp check for the Swedes.[3]

By the first week of December Gustav Adolf had begun the concentration of troops on the east bank of the Oder, in the area around Damm.[4] On 21 December 2200 cavalry arrived overland from Prussia; and at the same time reinforcements reached him from Stralsund by the island-bridge. He had now at his disposal some 6800 foot and nearly 6000 cavalry; and though the foot was barely half as strong as he had intended, he decided to wait no longer. The imperialists at Gartz and Greifenhagen were scattered in winter quarters, harassed by sickness and depressed in morale.[5] On Christmas Eve Gustav Adolf advanced on Greifenhagen; on Christmas Day, after morning prayers and a sermon, his artillery began the assault, seconded by supporting fire from river craft under Leslie. The imperialists were taken by surprise. Before darkness fell the Swedes had stormed into the town; though much of the garrison escaped over the Oder under cover of a spirited rearguard. On the following day Gustav Adolf pressed on across the river to Gartz. At his approach the imperialists were seized with panic, fired the town and destroyed their stores, and withdrew 'in consternation' in the direction of Angermünde, where they were met by long-promised reinforcements from Tilly. Thence they fell back at the new year on Frankfurt. The Swedes followed up the victory by chasing an imperialist detachment into Landsberg and pursuing another as far as Küstrin. Küstrin, guarding the passage of the Warthe, lay within the electorate of Brandenburg; and Gustav Adolf wrote to George William demanding that his pursuing cavalry be

[1] *AOSB*, II. I. 660 *seqq.*; *cf. Arkiv*, I. 241, 248.
[2] *AOSB*, I. V. 592, 621-2, 632, 703, II. I. 653, II. IX. 783 etc.
[3] Hist. MSS. Comm., *Hamilton*, p. 71, for account of this engagement.
[4] *Arkiv*, I. 267. [5] *AOSB*, II. VIII. 22; Styffe, p. 392; Wittich, p. 257.

given free passage. But the commandant at Küstrin had other orders: he let the beaten imperialists through and closed his gates in face of their pursuers.[1] And with that—apart from an ineffectual assault upon Landsberg—the Gartz operation came to an end.[2]

It was Gustav Adolf's first major success on German soil; and his propaganda did not fail to make the most of it.[3] And indeed it had been a vigorous and well-managed affair. It administered a sharp shock to imperialist morale: even Tilly confessed himself 'a good deal taken aback'.[4] It split their position east of the Elbe in two. It helped to free Gustav Adolf's flank and rear for a possible future move in the direction of Magdeburg, and at the same time removed the imperialist threat to Stettin. Gustav Adolf could take up his headquarters at Bärwalde and devote himself for a little to the higglings of diplomacy, in the consciousness that the period of preparation was nearly over. He had now, as he wrote to John Casimir, a 'good foothold and *sedem belli*' [5]; and a wider prospect was soon to unfold itself.[6]

(iii) *Negotiations and Alliances, June 1630-January 1631*

Before ever Gustav Adolf set foot in Pomerania he had been well aware that the task of saving German Protestantism—and therefore of ensuring Sweden's safety—could hardly be carried through without the co-operation of the German Protestant princes themselves. He had tried to incite them to issue an invitation to him to come to their aid. No such invitation had been forthcoming. He was faced upon arrival, therefore, with the political task of constructing a new Protestant front. How it was to be organized, what means were to be employed to give solidity to that rabble of disheartened,

[1] See *Schriftstücke*, pp. 88-94.

[2] Grubbe's relation in *Arkiv*, I. 717; Salvius's in *ibid.*, II. 154-6.

[3] See, *e.g.*, his letters to John George and George William: *Schriftstücke*, pp. 17, 88.

[4] Wittich, p. 314; and *cf.* Hist. MSS. Comm., *Hamilton Supplementary*, pp. 11-12, and Wallenstein's views in B. Dudík, *Waldstein von seiner Enthebung bis zur abermaligen Uebernahme des Armee-Ober-Commando*, p. 24.

[5] Styffe, p. 391; *AOSB*, II. i. 676.

[6] For military appreciations of Gustav Adolf's first period in Germany, see *Kungl. Krigsvetenskaps-Akademiens Handlingar, Gustaf II Adolf. 300-års minnet* (1932), p. 48 ('a brilliant alternation of attacks upon positions, swift offensive thrusts against inferior forces, diversions, and positional defence . . .'); B. Steckzén, *Johan Baner*, p. 115; von Cochenhausen, *Führertum*, p. 103 (quoting Napoleon). For Gustav Adolf's appreciation of the position at the beginning of 1631, *Arkiv*, I. 315-18.

feeble, mutually jealous and mainly selfish rulers, by what devices such an alliance could be made more durable and effective than the old Evangelical Union, of lamentable memory—all this was as yet undecided. But it was clear that Sweden could not for an indefinite period sustain the fight alone; and though gratitude might be an unreliable factor in politics, Gustav Adolf might hope that enlightened self-interest would supply its place, as a motive to induce the princes to align themselves with their deliverer. Allies, at all events, he must have; and above all he must aim at enlisting the two most powerful (or least weak) of the Protestant states—the electorates of Saxony and Brandenburg.

It soon became clear, however, that John George had been further alienated by the Swedish invasion [1]; while even a prince as politically shipwrecked as George William viewed Gustav Adolf's lifebelts with suspicion. Within a week or two of the landing there arrived in the Swedish camp at Oderburg one of George William's privy councillors, Dr. Bergmann, who had been sent off in the first place to persuade Gustav Adolf to stay at home, and who now applied himself to the task of trying to induce him to return there. On 11 and 12 July he had two long audiences with the King, in the course of which Gustav Adolf took the opportunity to make his position clear. He had not come to Germany, he said, from mere lust for conquest: 'I seek not my own in this work, and look to no other *lucrum* than *securitatem mei Regni*'. He had come, not to fight the Emperor, but his unruly servants; not to overthrow the constitution of the *Reich*, but to preserve it, and to deliver the German Estates from 'the fearful tyranny and oppression of thieves and robbers'. Did the Protestant princes still suppose that they could amend their situation by prayers and entreaties and negotiations? 'For God's sake consider a little, and for once adopt *mascula consilia*.' The fate of Bogislaw, who had given no provocation to the imperialists, but had been concerned only to 'drink his half-pint in peace and quiet',[2] should be a warning to them all. '*Qui se fait brébis, le loup le mange*.' Neutrality was no longer possible: the struggle was between God and the Devil, '*tertium non dabitur*'. If George William felt himself unable to defend his electorate, let him put Küstrin into Swedish hands; let the Protestants unite to restore the

[1] John George's reaction to the news of the landing had been to write to the Emperor, urgently counselling him to suspend the Edict of Restitution: Helbig, p. 20; *cf.* H. Knapp, *Matthias Hoë von Hoënegg*, pp. 34-5.

[2] 'sondern nur sein Bierchen in Ruhe getrunken'.

evicted princes; and let them take Gustav Adolf as their protector ('*tutor*'). George William had a claim upon the inheritance to Pomerania: Gustav Adolf would defend that claim; but only on condition that Brandenburg concluded an alliance with him. For himself, he had crossed the Rubicon, and could not now go back until he had obtained the security he sought. But the security must be real—not mere 'paper and ink', but 'something solid in hand': '*Manus meae oculatae sunt, credunt quod vident*'.[1]

This sharp warning to Brandenburg was given further point by the terms of the treaty of alliance with Pomerania, which was under negotiation at the time of Bergmann's visit, and was finally concluded on 25 August.[2] With the Swedish occupation of Stettin, alliance became the only alternative to a hostile military occupation, and Bogislaw was as eager as Gustav Adolf to agree upon a treaty. On the whole, he obtained very good terms. The alliance was indeed to be 'eternal', but it was to be renewable every ten years; it was defensive only; it was expressly stated to be directed not against the Emperor but against the 'harriers of the land'; and it was in no way to infringe Pomerania's integrity, independence, or position and obligations as a member of the *Reich*. Neither party would conclude a separate peace; and Bogislaw bound himself not to enter into any other alliance nor to alienate Rügen—which Kristian IV was suspected of wishing to buy from him—without Gustav Adolf's consent. The alliance was to be open to other states who might wish to join it. The areas occupied by Swedish troops were to be restored in full, without indemnity, at the end of the war. The special position of Stralsund in relation to Sweden was, however, expressly reserved. There was to be free trade between Pomerania and Sweden, and Swedish copper coin was to pass current in Pomerania—but only at its proper exchange value. By separate conventions Gustav Adolf was given the position of supreme 'Director' of the armed forces of the allies, which were to be at his 'absolute disposal' for the duration of the war; Pomerania was to pay, 'once for all', a contribution of 200,000 *rdr.*; and the Swedish toll system was to be extended to Pomeranian ports, with a share in the proceeds to Bogislaw.[3] The Pomeranian negotiators had successfully resisted

[1] G. Droysen, *Brandenburgische Audienzen bei Gustaf Adolf*, pp. 1-23, which supersedes Helbig, pp. 12-17.

[2] The treaty was antedated 10 July, the date of the first draft.

[3] *Sverges traktater*, V. 380-8, 395-404. An earlier Swedish draft in Bär, p. 263 *seqq.*

demands for recognition of a Swedish protectorate, and for the currency of Swedish copper at its nominal value.

The Pomeranian alliance was thus a real treaty (admittedly between a strong power and a weak one) and not a dictated instrument [1]; and Axel Oxenstierna later expressed the view that it had been so generous to Pomerania that it might well attract other allies.[2] Gustav Adolf seems to have made a genuine effort to ensure that his troops should do nothing to infringe Bogislaw's regalian rights.[3] But he made it clear, too, that the safety of his army was the first consideration; and in the sequel he was not able to prevent outrage upon the Pomeranian population.[4] In a speech to the Pomeranian Estates at Stettin on 22 August he had already tried to discount such incidents in advance: if a few villages should chance to go up in flames, he said, it was no great matter. Such mishaps were inevitable in war-time; and when the enemy had been driven away it would be easy enough to rebuild them.[5] And in a typical burst of choler he added, 'And in any case *arma nostra* are in *urbe vestra*: *jure belli* you are my property!' [6] Thus, for the first time on German soil, Gustav Adolf invoked *jus belli*: not, on this occasion, with any serious notion of exacting all that it gave him in international law, but by way of a reminder of how far his rights could have extended had he chosen to press them. It was a warning which many a German prince would be forced to listen to within the next two years.

The Pomeranian negotiators, then, had done well to secure such tolerable terms. And they had won a notable success in refusing to accept a clause which bore directly on the prospective Brandenburg succession, and which has still to be mentioned. This clause (clause 14), which was expressed as a personal reservation of Gustav Adolf, and not as an article agreed upon by both parties to the treaty, laid it down that if Bogislaw should die without male heirs before the Elector of Brandenburg had ratified and confirmed the present treaty, and had also given real aid in the liberation of Pomerania;

[1] As even Kretzschmar conceded: J. Kretzschmar, *Der Heilbronner Bund*, I. 13.
[2] *AOSB*, I. VI. 44-5.
[3] *Arkiv*, I. 209; Bär, p. 285.
[4] *Arkiv*, 213, 316; *AOSB*, I. VI. 44, 159; and see above, p. 446.
[5] Bär, p. 276.
[6] *ibid.*, p. 278: 'Ich habe Stettin in Henden, den Herzog, die fürstlichen Rete, den Rat, und Ihr wollet noch an dem Feind hangen?' Compare Oxenstierna's statement to the *råd*, 9 April 1638, when he said, 'We had a *jus belli* inasmuch as his late Majesty recovered the country from the Emperor's armies, which *jus* his Majesty transformed into a *jus foederis*, simply with the purpose of keeping the Pomeranian Estates in a good humour': *RRP*, VII. 187.

or if any other claimant should dispute Brandenburg's pretension to the succession to Pomerania; then the Swedish crown would take Bogislaw's dominions '*in sequestratione* and *clientelari protectione*' until the right to the succession had been established, until Sweden had been compensated (without cost to Pomerania) for her war expenses, and until the eventual successor had confirmed and ratified the treaty.

Clause 14 had one plain and obvious purpose: to constrain George William of Brandenburg to adhere to the Swedish-Pomeranian alliance—indeed, one of the Swedish negotiators went so far as to say, in an unguarded moment, that this was the fundamental purpose of the treaty.[1] Bogislaw might die any day; and it was known that Bavaria had a claim to the succession. It was not enough, then, to make sure of Bogislaw: it was necessary also to secure that Pomerania, in whatever hands, should be politically reliable. And as a first instalment Gustav Adolf was attempting to blackmail George William into becoming his ally.[2]

For the moment the attempt failed. John George was urging George William to be stout in resisting pressure from Sweden; and a meeting of the Brandenburg Estates early in August took the same line. Arnim, in particular, advocated the policy of creating a 'third party' in Germany, in close collaboration with John George; and it was at his suggestion that the two Electors met at Zabeltitz at the end of the month. George William asked John George to help him to maintain his neutrality, to assist him in garrisoning his fortresses and to support his forlorn attempts at mediation. John George, though as usual declining to accept anybody else's suggestion, came to Zabeltitz in a mood of irritation which for once made him ready for action. He had just received Ferdinand's reply to an embassy which he had despatched in May, and it had proved more than disappointing. The Emperor had flatly refused to make any concession to Saxony in regard to the Edict of Restitution, and had expressed the confident hope that John George would provide him with troops and munitions to be used against Gustav Adolf. To this John George replied by informing Ferdinand that he intended to summon a Protestant Convention to Leipzig to discuss the

[1] Bär, p. 272.

[2] For discussion of the treaty in general, see Bär, pp. 75-84; W. Struck, *Gustav Adolf und die schwedische Satisfaktion*, pp. 350-3; Kretzschmar, *Gustav Adolfs Pläne und Ziele*, pp. 159-63; Paul, II. 115, 170-4; *Sv. Krig*, III. 421-4; H. Hjärne, *Gustaf Adolf*, p. 91.

situation. This was good news for George William. Here, it might seem, was the nucleus of a third party under Saxon leadership which might intervene with effect between the Emperor and the King of Sweden. At Zabeltitz, therefore, George William proposed that they should arm, so that their intervention might have some real weight. But John George was not to be stampeded. All he intended for the present was a Protestant demonstration. The Emperor should be frightened, should be persuaded to be reasonable, so that there should be neither need nor excuse for any German ruler to ally himself with Sweden: further than that he would not go.[1]

In this attitude John George was not shaken by a remarkable offer from Gustav Adolf, which was secretly conveyed to him through Arnim at the beginning of September. By this it appeared that Gustav Adolf was prepared to withdraw from Germany altogether if John George, on his side, would guarantee the safety of north Germany. John George unhesitatingly refused. And not surprisingly; for the security of north Germany, as Gustav Adolf understood it, could have been achieved only by military measures which it was the whole aim of Saxon policy to avoid.[2]

A month later, in mid-October, George William, who had been much disappointed at the meagre results of the Zabeltitz meeting, sent his minister Leuchtmar on a secret mission to Gustav Adolf. Leuchtmar brought the Elector's excuses for doing nothing; and, like Bergmann earlier, he had a somewhat stormy interview. Gustav Adolf now plainly told him that, failing an alliance, George William should not have the succession to Pomerania. But he added that if the Elector would join him now it might be possible to put him in possession of his inheritance immediately (and thus scotch the Bavarian claim), since Bogislaw might probably be induced to accept a decent maintenance for the rest of his life. Leuchtmar had no powers, and George William no courage, to close with this offer; and though the population of Brandenburg was reported to be friendly to Sweden,[3] the Elector clung to his precarious and uncomfortable seat on the fence.[4]

Meanwhile John George had been giving the German Protestants

[1] W. Struck, *Das Bündnis Wilhelms von Weimar mit Gustaf Adolf*, pp. 41-7; Helbig, p. 24; Koser, pp. 425-6; Hammarstrand, *Bidrag*, pp. 34-5, 37; Droysen, II. 220-3, 229-30; Ritter, III. 461; *Sv. Krig*, III. 519-22.

[2] *Sv. Krig*, III. 521.

[3] *AOSB*, II. ix. 552.

[4] Ahnlund, *Gustaf Adolf inför tyska kriget*, p. 420; *Sv. Krig*, III. 530-1.

just sufficient encouragement to induce men like William of Weimar to look to him as a still-possible leader. The Weimar Dukes were concerned at the lack of cordiality between the Elector and Gustav Adolf; and it was at the suggestion of one of their agents that Gustav Adolf on 14 September empowered Dietrich von Falkenberg, as part of his commission in north Germany, to get into touch with John George once more. The approach was made through William of Weimar himself, early in November. This time Gustav Adolf suggested the formation of a league, with himself and John George as the leading members, to be directed against disturbers of the peace in Germany. Sweden, on the one side, and John George with his friends on the other, should each maintain an army of 40,000 men. If this were done, Sweden would at the close of the war restore all territory at present occupied by her, and all that might be occupied hereafter. Gustav Adolf thus proposed to share the labour of safeguarding north Germany with Saxony, upon a basis of absolute equality. To this offer John George seems to have made no reply at all.[1]

By this time John George had become aware that the mere threat to call a Protestant Convention to Leipzig was not enough to induce the Emperor to change his policy. The Protestant princes had for some time been clamouring for the calling together of a *Kompositionstag*, to be attended by both Roman Catholics and Protestants, in order to discuss the question of Restitution. Upon receiving John George's letter announcing the intention to summon a Convention, Ferdinand adroitly overtrumped him by acceding to the demand for a *Kompositionstag*, which was to be held at Frankfort-on-the-Main early in the new year. This disconcerted John George; and on 21 December he met George William once more at Annaburg, to discuss what to do now. This time the Brandenburg delegates were able to carry their point. At Zabeltitz they had been enthusiastically in favour of the Convention; they saw in it the best hope for the creation of a third party; and they now succeeded in persuading John George to stick to it. On 29 December the two Electors sent out invitations to 160 Protestant princes and cities to meet at Leipzig on 6 February 1631. The policy of the third party was to be given a fair trial.[2]

While Saxony and Brandenburg clung to their middle courses,

[1] B. Boëthius, *Filip Reinhart von Solms och Gustaf Adolf före Leipzigkonventet*, p. 116; Ahnlund, *op. cit.*, pp. 419-20; Helbig, p. 28; *Sv. Krig*, III. 535-7.

[2] Koser, p. 427; Wittich, pp. 593-4; Boëthius, *Solms och Gustaf Adolf*, p. 117; Struck, *Das Bündnis Wilhelms von Weimar*, pp. 52-61.

Hesse-Cassel had been making advances in the direction of Sweden. Immediately before Gustav Adolf's landing, the Hessian councillor Dr. Wolf had had a meeting with Falkenberg in Hamburg, and had there been strongly advised to ally with Sweden in good time, while preferential terms were still to be had. At a Hesse family meeting held at Rothenburg at the end of July, however, it was resolved merely to lay their grievances before Gustav Adolf and ask him not to make peace until they should be redressed; any open breach with the Emperor being in the meantime to be avoided. Dr. Wolf was now sent to the Swedish headquarters, and there, after considerable discussion, collaborated in drawing up a provisional alliance (known as the *Eventualkonföderation*) which he took back to Hesse for consideration: it is dated 11 November. Gustav Adolf himself ratified it as a treaty; but Hesse-Cassel, when it came to the point, decided not to risk it, particularly as William of Weimar was unwilling to join on these terms. Both Hesse-Cassel and Weimar, in fact, were awaiting the outcome of the Leipzig Convention before taking any definite step.[1]

Nevertheless, the *Eventualkonföderation* is a document of considerable interest and importance.[2] Unlike the Pomeranian alliance, this was to be an offensive league, aimed explicitly at the Emperor, the League 'and our common enemies'. Hesse-Cassel was to raise an army, and Gustav Adolf promised to send assistance—though the treaty was careful to add (warned perhaps by the difficulty of aiding Magdeburg) 'if possible'—and it was explicitly provided that Gustav Adolf should not be bound to a literal fulfilment of this obligation if his own army would be seriously imperilled thereby. Gustav Adolf took Hesse-Cassel under his 'care and protection'. Swedish troops were to have the right of entry to the lands and fortresses of Hesse, and to maintenance while on Hessian territory. A common war chest was to be established. By an especially important clause Gustav Adolf reserved to himself the 'absolute *directorium*' of the alliance in all cases, and by another entitled himself '*caput* of this confederation'; though it was laid down that he might delegate the command in Hesse to a deputy, to be chosen in consultation with Landgrave William, and to be bound to swear obedience to him as well as to Gustav Adolf. It was expressly declared (in two places)

[1] *Sv. Krig*, III. 540-4; Rommel, VIII. 88-98; Struck, *op. cit.*, pp. 22-39; Ritter, III. 469.

[2] Text in *Sverges traktater*, V. 491-504.

that the rights and liberties of the Landgrave in his dominions were not to be impaired by the operation of the treaty. Any territory conquered by Sweden in the prosecution of the alliance was to remain Swedish. The alliance was to take precedence over all other engagements, and was not to be terminated without the consent of both parties. Its duration was defined as 'until we have achieved our aims'; and its object as the restoration of freedom of conscience, the defence of the liberties of Germany, the preservation of the imperial constitution and 'the safety and welfare of Sweden'.

It is plain that we have here to deal with a very different document from the treaty with Pomerania. It represents, undoubtedly, Gustav Adolf's idea at this time of what an alliance with an inland German state ought to be. Pomerania had declined to admit Gustav Adolf as 'protector'. That omission is here formidably repaired. Hesse-Cassel is to be in his 'protection'; Gustav Adolf is to be '*caput confoederationis*'; to have the 'absolute *directorium*' of their joint forces. William V is to be committed to Gustav Adolf's war aims; he is to bind himself to fight for Sweden's 'safety and welfare'—however those concepts might happen to be defined; and the alliance is to continue 'until we have achieved our aims'—whatever they might happen to be. It is scarcely surprising that historians such as Kretzschmar, who have considered Gustav Adolf as a conqueror aiming from the beginning at a Swedish empire in Germany, should have seen in the *Eventualkonföderation* evidence of the emergence of a plan to dominate German Protestantism, and the first serious attempt to subvert the old fabric of the Empire [1]; while even Struck pronounced that 'this was no alliance *inter pares*, but a military convention, whereby Hesse, despite all reservations, would have surrendered her sovereignty for the duration of the agreement'.[2]

The *Eventualkonföderation* undoubtedly marks a stage in the crystallization of Gustav Adolf's ideas about Germany, but if it is looked at in relation to his German diplomacy as a whole in the first six months after the landing it becomes more intelligible, and a good deal less sinister. During the difficult and at times critical months which followed the launching of the invasion, the King's first and overriding consideration was military advantage for the present, and military security for the future. His position was not such that he was likely to indulge in wide-ranging political plans. He needed,

[1] Kretzschmar, *Der Heilbronner Bund*, I. 33.
[2] Struck, *op. cit.*, p. 35.

first, to secure his base. The treaty with Pomerania safeguarded his control of the essential minimum of territory. There is no real justification for supposing that it was deliberately framed with a view to the permanent incorporation of Pomerania into the Swedish realm.[1] The King's own reservation in regard to Brandenburg (in clause 14) need not, and indeed should not, bear that construction. That clause was designed, as we have seen, to exert pressure on George William to join him. But it was also a necessary safeguard in case George William should refuse to join him. For if Bogislaw were to die within the next month or two, and exchange his 'half-pint' for the nectar of a better world, Gustav Adolf could not afford to see Pomerania in the hands of a successor who was at best neutral ('*tertium non dabitur!*'): not, certainly, for the duration of the war; and possibly not after it.

But if the German expedition were to come to anything, the time was not distant when Gustav Adolf's armies would spread beyond the narrow confines of his beach-head. Security was not a question merely of Pomerania, but of all those north German areas from which an assault upon the coast could be delivered. It was unlikely that Sweden would be able to conquer these territories without allies, and some areas (*e.g.* Saxony and Brandenburg) Gustav Adolf hoped not to have to conquer; or, alternatively, a succession of major Swedish victories would probably bring allies in their train. In either event, Gustav Adolf would be faced with the problem of framing alliances. What was to be their nature? Gustav Adolf saw only two possibilities. Either they would be alliances upon a basis of equality; or they would be alliances in which Sweden dictated the terms. Since his foremost concern was military security, he had no *a priori* preference for the one sort or the other: it was a choice which would depend upon the military power (and political reliability) of the ally. If John George, for instance, were to make a real military effort, Gustav Adolf was ready for an alliance on terms of full parity, as his offer of November showed; and he was even prepared (in September) to leave the task of securing the hinterland entirely to a Saxon-led coalition—if he were satisfied of its adequacy to conduct the fight. On the other hand, the case was very different if the ally were to be Mecklenburg, or Hesse-Cassel, or even Brandenburg. Sweden could not take the risk of allowing any real voice in the conduct of

[1] As Kretzschmar does: *Gustav Adolfs Pläne und Ziele*, pp. 159-63. Contrast B. Boëthius, *Nyare undersökningar rörande Gustaf II Adolfs planer i Tyskland*, pp. 71-4.

military operations to states so weak in a military point of view, and so feeble (as to Mecklenburg and Brandenburg at least) in a political.[1] Gustav Adolf had been watching the performances of the German Protestants these ten years; and their military record was not such as to inspire any statesman to adventure his country's army in consort with them, unless they were straitly bound. Was he to give Hesse-Cassel or Brandenburg greater confidence in 1630 than he had been willing to accord to Denmark in 1624 and 1625, or to France and the Dutch in 1629? Then, as now, he had insisted that he should be '*caput*', 'director'; not from dark political design, but as a measure of military prudence. Neutrality was not possible to the smaller states; it was not possible to Brandenburg, as George William's melancholy experiences, both in Germany and in Poland, clearly proved. Gustav Adolf spoke no more than the truth, however unpalatably he phrased it, when he said as much to Dr. Bergmann. Six years' experience of his brother-in-law's politics cannot have given him much disposition to take any chances with George William. And as to the dispossessed princes—John Frederick of Bremen, Adolf Frederick and John Albert of Mecklenburg were the ones he had in mind—what would their restoration avail if they lacked the means to maintain themselves? The suggestion that they should put their fortresses in Gustav Adolf's hands, and accept him as their '*tutor*', might be politically disagreeable, but militarily it was common sense.[2]

Behind these immediate military considerations, however, there was already emerging a political programme; the programme of *assecuratio*. *Assecuratio* came to mean the carrying out of territorial changes—mainly by cessions to Sweden—of such a kind as to provide Sweden with the political security she was seeking after the war was over: it was, in fact, an aspect of long-range military precaution. There are hints of it to be seen here and there in the negotiations of these first six months. Gustav Adolf had already, before sailing, convinced himself that it would not be safe to evacuate Stralsund in the foreseeable future[3]; hence the provision in the Pomeranian treaty safeguarding his existing arrangement. He would have liked a similar arrangement for Wismar. The idea of *assecuratio* lay behind those clauses in the *Eventualkonföderation* which provided for the

[1] *cf.* Oxenstierna's view (12 January 1631) on the indispensable minimum for alliances with such states: *AOSB*, I. VI. 45.

[2] *cf.* B. Boëthius, *Nyare undersökningar*, pp. 75-6.

[3] See above, p. 422.

prosecution of the war 'until our aims are achieved', and the definition of one of the purposes of the alliance as Sweden's 'safety and welfare'. And it inspired the clause (in the same treaty) ensuring that Sweden's military conquests should remain in her possession: they could be exchanged at a peace conference for territory more necessary to Sweden's strategic defence. *Assecuratio* was still quite vague and indefinite; a thing desirable in itself, though its implementation might well depend upon the run of the fighting. It was not yet in the forefront of Gustav Adolf's policy, for that policy did not as yet contemplate the transference of Pomerania to Sweden—the most obvious *assecuratio* of all. But it was already in the background—it had, indeed, been present *in nuce* since at least 1628; and it was to assume major importance in the last two years of Gustav Adolf's life.

Side by side with *assecuratio*, moreover, was appearing the complementary idea of *satisfactio*. *Satisfactio* meant, successively, the indemnity to be extracted from the defeated imperialists, the reward to be paid by emancipated Protestantism for the Swedish deliverance, the compensation to Sweden for the unheard-of national effort which the war had exacted. It might take the form of a monetary payment, or of a cession of territory (and hence of revenues). As the German war proceeded, Gustav Adolf came to think that a cash indemnity would be an inadequate recompense; and *satisfactio* came more and more to take the form of territorial claims additional to *assecuratio*. The idea of monetary compensation appears in the Pomeranian treaty in the shape of the extension of the toll system to Pomeranian ports; the idea of territorial compensation appears perhaps in the *Eventualkonföderation*, side by side with *assecuratio*, as among the objects included in the expression 'Sweden's welfare'.[1]

It would be erroneous to see in all this the evidences of a long-matured plan of conquest. It was not a question—at least not in the minds of Gustav Adolf and Axel Oxenstierna—of prosecuting a deliberate policy of aggressive imperialism, either political or economic. They were not uninfluenced by arguments from international law as to their country's rights *jure belli*, and they were to found very extensive pretensions on this ground in the years that followed. But they had no notion of setting about the construction

[1] Wolf reported that 'Der Conquestionsgüter halber haben sich I. K. M. bedingt, dass sie keinen einzigen Menschen ohne Ursache zu beleidigen oder dessen Rechte und Hoheiten zu schälern begehren': Rommel, VIII. 98 *note* 114.

of a Swedish empire in Germany, and their war aims remained very much what they had been upon the eve of departure. Gustav Adolf, it is true, in his letter to Ferdinand II at the end of October 1630 so far enlarged his programme for a settlement as to demand the restoration of the *status quo ante bellum* not only in north but in south Germany [1]; but some such declaration on Gustav Adolf's behalf was a necessity sooner or later if ever he were to have a hope of enlisting allies in the south. There is no evidence to suggest that he entertained any design at this stage either against the imperial constitution or upon the imperial crown.[2] On the contrary, great care was taken in both the Hessian and Pomeranian treaties not to interfere with imperial obligations. Members of the Empire were no doubt being incited to revolt; but this was a strain to which the imperial constitution had often been subjected, and Gustav Adolf was inclined to justify rebellion on the ground that the Emperor had in fact broken the original contract between ruler and people. It was clear, no doubt, that the evangelical Estates stood in need of political reorganization; and probably any new Protestant coalition must have an effective *caput*; but it was by no means certain, as yet, that John George could not supply these requirements, given sufficient prodding; and everything suggests that Gustav Adolf would have been very willing for him to do so. In short, a variety of means still seemed to be available for realizing the programme with which he had come to Germany, and the King preserved an open mind on the point. The programme itself remained the same: to remove the danger to Sweden away from the Baltic shore, to prevent its recurring within the foreseeable future, to bring restitution to the oppressed Protestants of Germany: no more than that. But it was enough, in all conscience.

It might even have proved too much without the long purse of France. Since the negotiations for a treaty of alliance between France and Sweden had broken down in the spring of 1630 Richelieu had not ceased his efforts to renew them. And Gustav Adolf, on his side, had sent Lars Nilsson Tungel to Paris even before Charnacé and Fegraeus finally abandoned their conversations at Helsingör. Gustav Adolf had hardly established himself in Pomerania before

[1] *AOSB*, II. I. 653-5; *Arkiv*, II. 167-71; *RRP*, II. 54.

[2] Contrast Kretzschmar, *Der Heilbronner Bund*, I. 5-6. Charnacé had dangled this bait before Gustav Adolf in vain, in March and July 1630: L. Weibull, *DF*, pp. 31, 58.

Charnacé descended upon him at Stettin [1]; and there, at the end of July, the old ground was gone over afresh. The points upon which agreement seemed to be impossible were three. First, the question of precedence: Gustav Adolf was not prepared to allow Louis XIII to be named in the treaty before himself. This, in view of the importance which contemporaries attached to such questions, was a serious obstacle. Secondly, the amount of subsidy France was to pay: the best French offer in July was 400,000 *rdr.* in the event of France's making peace in Italy; otherwise less. Thirdly, the French demand that Sweden should guarantee the neutrality of Bavaria and the League. This Gustav Adolf now absolutely refused, unless his guarantee were accompanied by a corresponding promise from Maximilian. Gustav Adolf's interviews with Charnacé were tempestuous; and any hope of agreement was shattered by Tungel's report on his embassy to France, which arrived while negotiations were proceeding. Tungel had eventually caught up with Richelieu and Louis XIII at St. Jean de Maurienne, where he arrived immediately after the conclusion of an agreement between France and Venice, binding Venice to contribute one-third of any subsidy which France might pay to Sweden in 1630 to a limit of 400,000 *livres.* Richelieu seems to have taken the line that all that now remained to be done could be done by Charnacé; and to have conveyed to Tungel that his embassy was superfluous. At all events, Tungel felt himself to have been treated with discourtesy, and said as much in his report to Gustav Adolf. He went further: he alleged that Charnacé was really empowered to offer more than 400,000 *rdr.*, and had falsely asserted that figure to be the maximum. Gustav Adolf believed this allegation, though, as it happened, it was incorrect. He lost his temper, broke off the negotiations, and refused even to give Charnacé the safe-conduct he had requested.[2] Charnacé, never popular with Gustav Adolf or Axel Oxenstierna, was henceforth regarded by them as a 'jesuitical' personage, in whom no faith could be reposed.[3]

The French ambassador, thus dismissed in disgrace, proceeded by way of Lübeck (where he spent some time upon the hopeless endeavour of reconciling Hamburg with Kristian IV) to Berlin, which he reached in September. There he engaged in an extra-

[1] *Dagbok*, p. 14.

[2] *Arkiv*, I. 704; Weibull, *DF*, pp. 46-52; *id.*, *Gustaf Adolf och Richelieu*, pp. 92-3; Fagniez, I. 565.

[3] *AOSB*, I. v. 521; *Arkiv*, I. 704, II. 26.

ordinary negotiation, whose object was to induce George William and John George to recognize Maximilian's Palatine electorate and to promise *not* to ally with Sweden. Charnacé assured them that if they followed this line the Edict of Restitution would be revoked. George William was interested; John George was not. It was a French intrigue; it lacked that earthy contact with reality on which he flattered himself; he would have none of it. But it was as well for Gustav Adolf's peace of mind that this curious piece of French statesmanship remained hidden from him.[1]

Despite the eccentric proposals at Berlin, Richelieu had already made up his mind that concessions must be made to Sweden. The news of Father Joseph's unlucky Italian treaty at Regensburg only made him the more anxious for a settlement: Gustav Adolf must not be given time to feel that France, by thus making a peace which debarred her from assisting the Emperor's enemies, was abandoning the hope of a Swedish alliance. Charnacé was therefore sent stringent instructions to bring the negotiations to a successful termination. He came to Gustav Adolf's headquarters at Bärwalde at the new year; and at Bärwalde, on 13 January 1631, the treaty between France and Sweden was at last concluded.[2]

The treaty of Bärwalde [3] declared the object of the two Kings to be the defence in common of themselves and their friends, the security of the Baltic and of the Ocean, and the restitution of the oppressed estates of the Empire; to which end it was agreed that all newly constructed imperial fortresses in north Germany '*uel in Rhetia*' (*sc.* the Grisons) must be demolished. Gustav Adolf bound himself to maintain an army of 30,000 foot and 6000 horse in Germany; Louis XIII to pay 400,000 *rdr.* a year, and 120,000 *rdr.* for the year 1630. Gustav Adolf undertook to conform to the law of the Empire in regard to religion in any territories he might conquer (by which was meant that the religion of their lawful ruler would be suffered to continue), and explicitly to tolerate Roman Catholic worship in places where it was already practised. Neither side would enter into negotiations for peace without the other. The alliance was to be valid until 1 March 1636, and was to be open to other princes who might wish to join it. Gustav Adolf was mentioned first in the Swedish copy of the treaty, Louis XIII in

[1] *Sv. Krig*, III. 522; Droysen, II. 247; Weibull, *DF*, p. 63 *note* 2; Koser, pp. 426-7; Richelieu, *Mémoires*, II. 306; Avenel, III. 900.

[2] Fagniez, I. 567; Weibull, *DF*, pp. 60-70.

[3] *Sverges traktater*, V. 438-40.

the French. As to Bavaria and the League, the treaty itself stated generally that they were to be treated as neutrals if they themselves observed neutrality. But in a separate guarantee given by Gustav Adolf on 15 January [1] this provision was made more stringent and specific. Gustav Adolf promised to observe neutrality towards them 'in as far as' they 'sincerely' observed it, 'omnique aduersus Nos *Nostrosque amicos ac foederatos* hostilitatis apertae *vel clandestinae* genere abstinuerint, et in *nulla aduersus Nos hostilia decreta* consenserint' [2] ; and this guarantee was handed to Charnacé only when he had given to Gustav Adolf a written undertaking that it would not be delivered to Maximilian until Louis XIII had received from him a reciprocal assurance.[3]

The mere recital of these terms makes it clear that the treaty of Bärwalde represents a major reverse for Richelieu's foreign policy. The Cardinal had, no doubt, carried his point in certain unessential matters: on the amount of the subsidy Gustav Adolf had in the end contented himself with the sum he had rejected at Stettin; and the inclusion of the Grisons, and the guarantee of Roman Catholicism, could be considered satisfactory to Richelieu too. But on the vital point—Sweden's relations with Bavaria—the French discomfiture had been complete. It had been, and was to continue to be, the aim of Richelieu's policy to foster a party in Germany which, under the banner of German liberties and with the backing of France, should curb the dangerously revived power of the house of Habsburg. He was not without hope of joining Bavaria with Protestant powers such as Saxony in support of a policy of this nature. While France recovered from her dangerous condition of debility, the tactics of Henry II were to be recurred to, with another treaty of Chambord as their outcome, if all went well: the German princes should fight the battle France was as yet too weak to risk. The military aid which France for the present declined to give should be provided by Gustav Adolf. The Swedish armies were to be enlisted in Richelieu's quarrel; the subsidy treaty he would conclude with Gustav Adolf should be framed in such a way as to ensure that the King's military genius subserved French policy. Sweden was not to be permitted, above all, to drive Bavaria back into the imperialist camp by engaging in hostilities with the army of the League. The only links that bound Bavaria to the Emperor were the ties of common Catholicism and the fear of losing the electorate in the event of a Protestant revival.

[1] *ibid.*, 441-2. [2] My italics. [3] *Sverges traktater*, V. 442.

Richelieu intended to take care that Roman Catholic interests were not jeopardized, and he would allay Maximilian's nervousness by persuading France's Protestant clients to recognize Bavaria's right to the Palatinate. In these matters, he hoped, the King of Sweden could be induced to toe the line if his own interests were looked after.[1] For Richelieu needed both Gustav Adolf and Maximilian. He needed the Swedish sword immediately; but he needed the friendship of Bavaria permanently.

The upshot of the negotiations at Bärwalde was to make this programme impossible. The treaty left the future of the Palatinate an open question. So far from securing France against a conflict between Gustav Adolf and Maximilian, it went a long way towards making that conflict inevitable. For Gustav Adolf's undertaking to respect Bavaria's neutrality fell away if Maximilian attacked—not the Swedish army only (which perhaps he might have contrived to avoid), but Sweden's allies—for instance, Magdeburg, which Tilly was already investing; and even Sweden's friends—for instance, Hesse-Cassel. And this was true even though no open, but only clandestine, hostilities occurred. Since Gustav Adolf gave the guarantee, it must be supposed that he would be the judge of what constituted clandestine hostility. Again, the guarantee became void if Bavaria 'consented to hostile decrees against us'—if Maximilian took part, for instance, as a member of the Diet, in the promulgation of a proclamation against the Swedish invasion. It is astonishing that Richelieu, who had been so quick to disavow Father Joseph's Regensburg treaty, should have ratified the treaty of Bärwalde. That the treaty caused him uneasiness, and was recognized by Gustav Adolf as a political success, is shown by Richelieu's chagrin when Gustav Adolf took care to give it the widest possible publicity.[2] It may be that the very moderate success of the Swedish arms since the landing, and the obvious financial difficulties of Gustav Adolf, persuaded Richelieu that the subsidy would be a bridle upon him; and it seems likely that he misconceived Gustav Adolf's character and misinterpreted Swedish policy. At all events, from this moment Richelieu's German policy collapsed. In January 1631 he lost

[1] Grubbe reported to Salvius in [?] March 1631 that Charnacé 'has given us to understand *non oblique* that *Bavarus* is conspiring against the House of Austria; but he has his eye on H.M., and fears to lose the Palatinate': *Arkiv*, II. 223.

[2] Priorato wrote: 'Au camp & dans les villes conquises on alluma des feux pendant trois jours, on ne voyait partout que tables dressées & servies avec moins de délicatesse que d'abondance, & Gustave fit tirer le canon trois nuits de suite': Priorato, p. 37.

control of the situation; and he did not begin to recover it until Gustav Adolf was dead. His money helped to tide the King over the worst of his difficulties; but it ceased to be of major importance as the conquest of Germany got under way; and it never had the slightest effect upon the trend of military operations or the evolution of Gustav Adolf's policies.[1]

(iv) *From Gartz to Frankfurt*

At the moment when Gustav Adolf advanced upon Gartz, Tilly was already contemplating a visit to the Oder front. Schauenburg's army must be strengthened, paid and reorganized, so that the road to Silesia might be well barred; Kolberg must if possible be relieved; the imperial position in Mecklenburg and western Pomerania must be reinforced. The news of the exploit against Gartz, therefore, served only to hasten the implementation of a resolve which had already been taken. On 2 January 1631 Tilly set out from Halberstadt with three regiments of foot and one of horse; and by a notable feat of marching[2] reached Frankfurt—where the wrecks of Schauenburg's army were now gathered—on 14 January. And now for the first time in Germany Gustav Adolf was faced with an antagonist of his own calibre. For the next four or five months the military operations would assume the nature of a duel between them, move and countermove, thrust and riposte, as each strove to seize the initiative and compel the other to conform to the pattern of operations he wished to impose: a protracted struggle of cumulant excitement, watched by Germany in an atmosphere whose tension at last grew almost intolerable, as it became apparent that upon the issue of that duel the fate of Magdeburg would depend.[3]

Since the early autumn the revolt of Magdeburg had assumed a growing importance in the military calculations of either side. From the beginning Gustav Adolf had undertaken a clear obligation towards

[1] For discussion of the significance of Bärwalde, see *Sv. Krig*, III. 548-51; Weibull, *DF*, pp. 66-70; Fagniez, I. 559; Hanotaux, III. 428; E. Falk, *Sverige och Frankrike*, pp. 11-12; Pagés, pp. 144-5; Ritter, III. 479-80. The account in Richelieu, *Mémoires*, II. 339-41, is confused and misleading. Baustaedt's judgment (p. 32) is extraordinary: 'Der französische Standpunkt hatte in Bärwalde gesiegt, Gustaf Adolf sollte . . . seine Waffen nur gegen dem Kaiser richten.' For Urban VIII's (very hostile) reactions, see Leman, p. 3.

[2] He covered something like 200 miles in ten days.

[3] The following narrative is based on *Sv. Krig*, IV; Tingsten; *id.*, *Några data angående Gustav II Adolfs basering och operations-planer i Tyskland, 1630-1632*; Wittich; Boëthius, *NSK*; Monro.

the city. It was with his blessing and through his agents that the burghers had been induced to oppose the Emperor; his trusted officer, Dietrich von Falkenberg, led their defence; his word was pledged, not once but many times, to come to their aid. Honour and policy alike bound him to make good his promise. If Magdeburg were successful in her defiance; if the King were to appear before her walls with 'a royal deliverance'[1]; then the whole of the Protestant north-west would be encouraged to rise against the League, and Gustav Adolf would find allies and to spare for the prosecution of his designs. The five-army plan posited an advance up Oder, Elbe and Weser: Magdeburg, astride the Elbe, would give Gustav Adolf a grip on that river and open the way to Bremen and the Weser valley, where Hamilton's tardy army was expected to make its landfall. A success in this area would counteract Danish intrigues, and at the same time put strong pressure on the greatest German neutral, John George of Saxony. In short, every consideration of grand strategy combined to dictate the relief of Magdeburg as the cardinal object to be pursued.

There is no reason to suppose that Gustav Adolf was oblivious of these considerations; but his freedom of action was by no means absolute. The obviously desirable was not always the obviously practicable; and there were certain limiting factors which he could never afford to ignore. He could not, in the early months of 1631, risk a serious defeat: if this army were destroyed, Sweden could hardly compass its replacement in Germany. He could not, therefore, make a lunge at Magdeburg unless he could be certain of the security of his line of retreat; otherwise a reverse might become a disaster, a retreat might spell annihilation. And, finally, the political advantages of succouring Magdeburg might well be nullified if, in order to relieve it, he was led into violent measures against the most important German Protestant states.

The military position in the early months of 1631 gave actuality to these abstract considerations. Gustav Adolf was short of troops. He had enough to beat Schauenburg at Gartz; he had not enough for a move on Magdeburg. As he wrote to Falkenberg in February, Magdeburg could be delivered only by 'an extraordinary force'—a view, incidentally, in which Falkenberg himself concurred.[2] Once,

[1] This was almost a military technical term: *cf.* Sir James Turner: 'In such an Army as passeth under the name of an Army Royal (which some think should consist of eighteen thousand Foot, and six thousand Horse) . . .': Turner, *Pallas Armata*, p. 194.

[2] *Arkiv*, I. 340-1.

and once only during this period, he had a numerical superiority over Tilly; but on that occasion the necessary concentration was achieved only by stripping Pomerania almost bare; and that could not be safely done for the probable duration of an expedition to Magdeburg. He expected reinforcements, and in large numbers. They did not arrive before Magdeburg fell. In the meantime, his field-army was bled, as all armies in this period were bled, to provide garrisons, whose numbers increased with the expansion of the area of occupation. Moreover, the state of such troops as he had was dubious and at times bad. He could not feed them; he could not pay them.[1] If the army were to be kept together at all, it might seem that an extension of the area upon which it could live was more urgently necessary even than the relief of Magdeburg. Absence of pay forced commanders to dip into their own pockets[2]; drove the troops to grave excesses in friendly Pomerania[3]; and seriously affected the reliability of the foreign mercenary cavalry in particular. And without the cavalry he could hardly risk a pitched battle. Even if these difficulties were to be surmounted, purely strategic considerations dictated abstention from any hasty move to the south-west. From Rostock, Greifswald and Demmin, the imperialists could threaten the right flank of such an advance; from Landsberg and Frankfurt they impended over his left flank and rear, and threatened the heart of the Swedish position at Stettin. And as long as Küstrin and Spandau, guarding the passes of the Warthe and the Havel, remained in the feeble hands of George William of Brandenburg, the King could not feel his line of retreat to be secure. Again, his easiest and best route to Magdeburg must lie through the territory of George William and John George, towards the Elbe bridge at Dessau. From February to April the German Protestants were met in conference at Leipzig: was it in these circumstances prudent to take violent measures against the Electors, and so play into John George's hands and strengthen his contention that Gustav Adolf's expedition was the foray of an alien bandit? Or was it not better, perhaps, to impress the assembled princes by vigorous military action in politically unexceptionable directions? At all events, it was certain that politics could not be wholly left out of the strategical reckoning. And finally, and most important of all, until April there

[1] *ibid.*, 315-19.
[2] N. Belfrage, *Erik Soop och Västgöta ryttare*, pp. 77-8.
[3] Contrast the good intentions of *Arkiv*, I. 209, 213, with the reality of *AOSB*, I. VI. 159, and *Arkiv*, I. 316.

was no reason to suppose Magdeburg to be in any serious danger.[1] The delaying actions of Falkenberg; the fact that the imperialist investing force (at least to begin with) was far too small to venture a storm; the distractions of Tilly, and not least those provided by Gustav Adolf himself—made the siege, for many months, no more than a not very effective blockade. From Gustav Adolf's point of view, it had the very great advantage of tying up imperialist troops which would otherwise have been used against himself, and of committing Tilly to a plan of campaign which might not easily be reconcilable with the action required to counter Gustav Adolf's initiatives. As long as the defenders of Magdeburg were giving a good account of themselves, the siege was a positive advantage to Gustav Adolf. He could not know, for even Falkenberg did not discover it until the first days of May, of that catastrophic shortage of powder which in the end crippled the defence.[2] One main explanation of why Gustav Adolf did not, between January and April 1631, take effective steps to relieve Magdeburg is that all the information at his disposal indicated that for some time to come Magdeburg would not need to be relieved. In the long run, no doubt, supplies would give out; but before then Gustav Adolf was confident that he would be able to deliver the city. Only a great concentration of force, it seemed, would make a storm possible; and Gustav Adolf had every reason to suppose that his own activities would prevent such a concentration from taking place. In the meantime, there was nothing to be said in favour of the policy, advocated by Knyphausen, of 'pushing on to the Elbe and risking a black eye'[3]: it would be neither helpful, nor magnificent, nor war.

Though Gustav Adolf's position was by no means easy, the contradictory claims of prudence and honour were thus (at least for the moment) reconcilable. Tilly, on the other hand, was torn between obligations and policies which were scarcely reconcilable at all. Gustav Adolf had made good his bridgehead; and it was improbable that he could now be evicted from it. The remaining outposts of

[1] See, *e.g.*, Grubbe's optimistic account of 28 March 1631, in *Arkiv*, I. 725-6.

[2] *Sv. Krig*, IV. 245.

[3] On 5 November 1630 Knyphausen advised him, 'zu Erhaltung des zu Magdeburg, fast aus sonderlicher Direction Gottes, angesponnenen und weit angelegten Aufstandes, nicht wohl andere Resolution zu nehmen sey, als den Elbestrom zu suchen und um dessen Erreichung ein blaues Auge zu wagen': *Arkiv*, II. 101. But on 16 November even Knyphausen conceded that the move must be deferred for the present: *ibid.*, 116.

imperialist resistance in Pomerania—Kolberg, Greifswald—were increasingly difficult to come at, and were perhaps no longer worth the effort to relieve. The expectation was that Gustav Adolf would, and indeed must, seek to enlarge his base. Such an enlargement might be either southwards up the Oder, or westwards through Mecklenburg towards the Elbe: Gustav Adolf had already made thrusts in both directions. Had Tilly been the servant of the League only, he would have been able to write off the Oder as the Emperor's private affair; had he been merely imperial generalissimo, he would have concentrated all his efforts on preventing an advance into Silesia. Unfortunately for him, he served in both capacities, and was thus committed to equally vigorous measures in Mecklenburg and in the Neumark. He was, moreover, deeply involved at Magdeburg, and could abandon the siege only with disastrous loss of political prestige and (as an immediate consequence) military security. His three main theatres of war—Magdeburg, Mecklenburg, Neumark—were widely scattered: any unified control of them was virtually impossible. He was increasingly nervous about the impending advent of Hamilton's army. He feared, with justice, a Protestant revolt in Hesse. He was bound, as Gustav Adolf was bound, to consider the effect of military operations upon the Leipzig meeting. The neutrality of John George added to the difficulty of maintaining contact with the Oder front, and for months permitted the easy victualling of Magdeburg. The forces Tilly commanded were in poor condition; and Schauenburg's, in particular, was so demoralized and ill-provided as to give him the gravest concern.[1] Like Gustav Adolf, he expected reinforcements: the armies of Italy were on their way home. But they did not begin to reach Germany until February or March.[2] In any case, it was very doubtful whether he could push the siege of Magdeburg to a successful conclusion and still have adequate forces available to prevent Gustav Adolf from bursting out of his bridgehead in one direction or another. Gustav Adolf had, to a very marked degree, the advantage of the inner lines;

[1] Tilly wrote in January: 'Sollte man mir wider alle meine feste Hoffnung die so oft erbetene Hilfe nicht zukommen lassen, so habe ich die Zuversicht, man werde über mein vielseitiges, treues und untertäniges Bitten eine Schuld oder Verantwortung mir nicht beimessen. . . . Die Gefahr, die Not, die Armut wächst nicht nur täglich, sondern stündlich und augenblicklich. . . . Darum ist mit Hin- und Zurückschreiben, mit Mahnen, Flehen, Vertrösten, noch viel weniger mit dem Ausschreiben von Zusammenkünften und Beratungen der Sache nicht gedient; es muss ihr schleunigst durch die Tat geholfen werden.' Pfister, p. 265; *cf.* Wittich, pp. 341-2.

[2] Ritter, III. 485.

Tilly was repeatedly in the position of having to run round the perimeter to meet a sortie at an unexpected point.[1]

Such was the situation, such the general considerations, which produced the campaigns of the early months of 1631. Each commander had in his hand a card on which, he hoped, his adversary must follow suit; each was conscious of his own, and of his adversary's, political and moral obligations. Gustav Adolf believed that Tilly could not stand idly by and see a Swedish invasion of the Habsburg hereditary lands; Tilly was sure that Magdeburg, sooner or later, must be a magnet to draw Gustav Adolf—perhaps to his destruction. At first, the trumps were in Gustav Adolf's hand: the danger to Silesia seemed more imminent than the danger to Magdeburg. And Tilly himself, almost until the fall of the city, was beset by doubts as to whether he had not better cut his losses and break up the siege. Till April, then, the balance of advantage lay with the King; and the initiative was mainly on his side. He was able by a series of peripheral thrusts to keep Tilly running from Magdeburg to the Oder, from the Oder to the Havel, from the Havel to the Peene. In the course of these operations, in which as a rule Gustav Adolf dictated the conditions, he might hope to catch Tilly at a disadvantage and inflict a serious reverse upon him. From Magdeburg's point of view, Gustav Adolf was assisting the defenders, pending a direct advance to relieve them, by diversions. Clausewitz once laid it down that diversions, to be sound, must draw off more of the enemy than the number of troops required to execute them.[2] In this case the criterion does not apply. Provided Gustav Adolf by his diversions drew off sufficient forces from Magdeburg to make any vigorous prosecution of the siege impossible, his operations had attained their end. And in fact they did so, on every occasion save one. Against this strategy Tilly's reply was at first ineffective. It consisted in sticking to the siege, in spite of distractions, however feeble for the moment the besieging forces might be, in the hope that sooner or later the pressure on Magdeburg would force Gustav Adolf to fight a battle which he was not ready to fight; and probably no one was more pessimistic about the chances of this strategy than Tilly himself. Not until the sudden deterioration of the position in Magdeburg in April and May did it come near to being effective.

[1] As he quite well realized: Riezler, V. 372.

[2] Tingsten, *Gustav Adolfs basering*, p. 324 *note* 2.

In the second half of January, Tilly established himself around Frankfurt-on-Oder. His army was scattered in winter quarters; his energies mainly directed to making Schauenburg's beaten troops into a reasonably efficient force. Gustav Adolf's attack on Gartz had forestalled his designs in eastern Pomerania, driven a deep wedge up the Oder and cut off Schauenburg's force from easy contact with Savelli's detachments on the Mecklenburg border. With something over 14,000 men at Frankfurt, and another 3700 at Landsberg, Tilly was not short of troops; but their condition was not such as to encourage enterprise, at least for the present. If Gustav Adolf should wish to take the initiative, there was not much that Tilly could do to stop him.

Gustav Adolf had his own difficulties in the matter of pay, provisions and discipline; but he did not propose to let the opportunity slip. He could put some 12,000-13,000 men into the field, apart from garrison troops; he was not minded as yet to go into winter quarters; and he believed that he could effect something useful to himself and embarrassing to his enemy. He decided to make a second expedition to Mecklenburg. The plan was to attack the water barrier at the southern end, by way of Neu-Brandenburg, Malchin and Treptow, and thus to turn the right flank of the defences of Mecklenburg and roll them up; thereafter to take the important strategic centre, Demmin [1]; and then complete the conquest of the water barrier by the capture of the only pass through it, at Tribsees. The way to Mecklenburg would then be open; the outposts of the Swedish littoral position would have been pushed well to the south; the imperialist garrison in Greifswald would be cut off from hope of relief. Tilly might feel called upon to intervene to save Demmin; but Gustav Adolf would have the start of him by several days, and it was to be hoped that Tilly would find he had had his marching-exercise to no purpose: in any event, Gustav Adolf would probably have a force about equal to his adversary's. There was, of course, a risk that while he was absent in Mecklenburg Tilly might throw himself upon Horn, who was to be left with 6000 men to cover the approaches to Stettin; but that was a risk which Gustav Adolf was prepared to take.

The first Mecklenburg expedition had been one of those affairs where nothing goes right; the second was one of those affairs where

[1] On the situation of Demmin, see Försvarsstaben, *Vägar och vägkunskap i trettioåriga krigets sista skede*, p. 51.

nothing goes wrong. It started on 29 January, and was completed, with the capture of Tribsees, on 17 February. In the interval the Swedes took Neu-Brandenburg, Malchin, Treptow and Loitz [1]; effected a junction with Knyphausen, coming in with a force from Stralsund; undertook and successfully carried through a regular siege of Demmin, whose exceptional natural defences of water and swamp were partly neutralized by very severe weather; and forced Savelli and some 1800 men, who had taken refuge in Demmin castle, to capitulate. The musket-balls might strike down the King's companions, the ice might give way beneath the formidable burden of that already bulky frame, but this time luck was on Gustav Adolf's side. The King, rejecting proffered aid, extricated himself from the swamp, not without paternal scoldings from a froward Scot; the musket-balls found other lodgment than the royal person.[2] Tilly, moreover, did just as the King had hoped. He made no attack upon Horn, but moved south-west to Havelberg, to bar (as Horn conjectured) a Swedish advance upon Magdeburg. In reality, he was rising to Gustav Adolf's bait, unwilling to stand by inactive while the Swedes conquered Mecklenburg. But he moved too late: on 21 February, as he was on the march from Brandenburg to Neu-Ruppin, he was met by the news of the fall of Demmin. Three days later, the imperialist garrison in Kolberg capitulated, rightly deeming that they had now small chance of relief. The second Mecklenburg expedition had thus been completely successful; the risks had been justly estimated; Tilly had been induced to run about Brandenburg in pursuit of Gustav Adolf; the base area had been notably strengthened, and Swedish power brought appreciably nearer the Elbe. When Gustav Adolf went into winter quarters at the end of February, he might feel that he had won the first round. The troops, as he wrote to Oxenstierna, were in need of rest: when the summer weather set in, he had hopes of taking Rostock and Wismar, and so reaching the Elbe that way.[3]

Tilly, however, was by no means done with. He had been too late to save Demmin [4]; but he seems to have made up his mind that the situation required that he should bring Gustav Adolf to battle

[1] Monro said of the garrison of Loitz that they were 'silly simple *Italians*, and without courage, the poorest Officers that ever I looked on, and unworthy the name of Souldiers': Monro, II. 15.

[2] For these episodes, see Monro, II. 20-1, who is indeed the best authority for the expedition: *Dagbok*, pp. 16-17.

[3] *AOSB*, II. I. 692.

[4] His indignant comments on Savelli's feeble defence are in Droysen, II. 268.

if possible. In the last days of February he moved north from Neu-Ruppin to look for him, with an army of 13,000 men.[1] It was not until 2 March that he received information that the Swedish army had gone into winter quarters. He found himself now in a position not only to deliver an attack upon one of Gustav Adolf's garrisons but to effect some measure of surprise. Gustav Adolf, it is true, was by this time aware that he was stirring; but the King was at first disposed to believe that Tilly's object was merely to create annoyance and prevent the Swedes from settling comfortably into their quarters.[2] A swift attack by Tilly would certainly have caught Gustav Adolf off his guard. Tilly, however, moved somewhat ponderously forward; and it was not until 5 March that it became clear that his blow would be directed against Neu-Brandenburg.

Neu-Brandenburg was a small country town, weakly fortified, and in part protected by marshes. It was held by a force of 750 men, under the command of General Dodo zu Inn- und Knyphausen; who had at his disposal, by way of artillery, only three light regimental guns. Nevertheless, the town formed an important element in Gustav Adolf's defensive system[3]; and Knyphausen had been instructed to hold out to the last ('äussersterMacht'),[4] Gustav Adolf promising him—as late as 2 March—that he would come to his assistance if he were attacked.[5] Knyphausen very properly considered that this instruction overrode the general obligation upon a commander to 'conserve' his troops in circumstances where further resistance could do no good; and since he also took an over-sanguine view of Neu-Brandenburg's defensive potentialities, he rejected all offers of an honourable capitulation.[6] Tilly therefore stormed the place on 9 March; Knyphausen surrendered after a most valiant defence; and some 250 of the garrison were slaughtered by the victors.[7]

The futile heroism of Knyphausen, and the massacre of so many

[1] Including 2000 League troops: so much for Richelieu's treaty of Bärwalde.

[2] *AOSB*, II. VIII. 35; *cf. Arkiv*, I. 364, 379-80, 721.

[3] See his instructions to Banér, as early as 18 and 19 February, for coming to its assistance if it should be attacked: *Arkiv*, I. 342, 346-7.

[4] *ibid.*, I. 353.

[5] *ibid.*, I. 364.

[6] Knyphausen was afterwards censured by Horn and Monro for refusing quarter; but the King, at least, seems to have approved: *Arkiv*, I. 387-8; Monro, II. 28; *Sv. Krig*, IV. 79-81; C. Sattler, *Reichsfreiherr Dodo zu Innhausen und Knyphausen*, pp. 278-96.

[7] Not all, as was generally believed by the Swedes at the time. About 500 prisoners were taken (*Sv. Krig*, IV. 78): contrast Horn's lurid account in *AOSB*, II. VIII. 34. But Grubbe knew the real facts as early as 16 March: *Arkiv*, I. 723.

of the garrison, were the outcome of pure mischance. For on 7 March Gustav Adolf wrote to Knyphausen cancelling the order to resist to the last, and advising him if hard pressed to accept quarter.[1] The letter, however, was intercepted by the enemy, and never reached Neu-Brandenburg. But though this clears Gustav Adolf of the charge that he callously left Knyphausen to his fate, it also makes necessary some explanation of what Gustav Adolf was doing to meet the new situation. In point of fact, Gustav Adolf had been making extraordinary efforts. The news of Tilly's impending attack reached him on 2 March. He at once resolved to concentrate for battle. Urgent messages were sent to Horn, to Banér, to Baudissin, ordering them to rally on Pasewalk.[2] By truly remarkable exertions, a force of more than 19,000 men was collected in this area within five days. To meet them, Tilly had now less than 12,000, and in cavalry in particular (the battle-winning arm) he was markedly inferior to Gustav Adolf (5100 against 8100). On 7 March, then, the day upon which the King sent his last message to Knyphausen, Gustav Adolf had achieved a decided superiority at the critical place and time. To do so he had practically denuded eastern Pomerania of troops. Everything seemed prepared for a pitched battle: Tilly's foray against Neu-Brandenburg seemed likely to terminate in a disastrous defeat.

At this interesting moment Gustav Adolf hesitated, faltered and was lost. He called a council of war. He found many of his senior officers opposed to risking a battle. They professed to be doubtful about the reliability of their cavalry; and they are said to have been impressed by Tilly's glorious reputation as a commander. They succeeded in converting the King to their views.[3] The battle was called off; Knyphausen was given leave to accept quarter; Neu-Brandenburg was to be saved (if saved at all) by—a diversion.

It is difficult not to feel that Gustav Adolf here missed his best chance before Breitenfeld of striking a heavy blow at his enemy. He was quite accurately informed as to the size of Tilly's army; he was fully aware, therefore, of his own great superiority.[4] He possibly did not know (though it was indeed the case) that Tilly was as nervous of his own cavalry as the Swedish generals were of theirs.[5]

[1] *Arkiv*, I. 375, II. 200.
[2] *ibid.*, I. 371, II. 186-7.
[3] Horn's account of this in *AOSB*, II. VIII. 33, 36; *Arkiv*, II. 199-200; *cf.* P. Sörensson, *Ekonomi och krigföring*, p. 305.
[4] *Arkiv*, I. 358.
[5] *Sv. Krig*, IV. 71, 88.

But in any case experience must have taught him that, failing pay, the best remedy for indiscipline and discontent was a victory. The defeat of Tilly at this juncture would have not merely solved Gustav Adolf's local and temporary problems, it would have ensured the deliverance of Magdeburg and left him free to crush either Pappenheim or Schauenburg, at his choice. The decision to avoid battle on 7 March was one of the most conspicuous blunders of Gustav Adolf's military career.

The diversion, no doubt, was well enough planned and executed. While Horn was left in position on the Peene, Banér moved to Angermünde, and Gustav Adolf himself occupied Schwedt, establishing there a fortified camp guarding a crossing of the Oder higher up the river than any so far in his possession.[1] Thence Baudissin with a strong force of cavalry was sent westwards to threaten Tilly's communications with Magdeburg. Thus Gustav Adolf could simultaneously exert pressure on Schauenburg and upon Tilly's flank and rear; and Tilly's army at Neu-Brandenburg was menaced on three sides. But the aim of a diversion is, after all, to divert; and this diversion notably failed to effect it.[2] Tilly stormed Neu-Brandenburg without heeding Gustav Adolf's elaborate dispositions, for the excellent reason that he was in ignorance of what Gustav Adolf was doing[3]; and thereafter vanished for some days beyond the ken of the Swedish intelligence. It was not until 20 March, after an interval marked by a chaos of orders and counter-orders to the Swedish commanders, that it became clear that he had withdrawn from the bag the King had held open for him, and was heading for Magdeburg. He returned, indeed, in pessimistic mood[4]: the Neu-Brandenburg venture had led nowhere; Gustav Adolf, he thought, was trying to wear him out by avoiding battle[5]; the valour of Knyphausen's resistance seemed to him ominous and impressive; and he was already uneasy at the possibility of another Swedish blow on the Oder. Had he known the facts, he would have congratulated himself on emerging with a whole skin from an extremely hazardous predicament. But this time, at least, it was Gustav Adolf who had lost the round.

[1] *Arkiv*, I. 392.

[2] Tingsten, *Gustav Adolfs basering*, p. 324; but contrast Paul, II. 191 *note* 1.

[3] Wittich, p. 415; *cf.* Droysen, II. 279.

[4] *Sv. Krig*, IV. 100.

[5] As Pappenheim put it, 'durch verschiedene Diversionen hin und wieder herumgeführt und liber abgemattet werden, als dass er mit ihr aperto campo kämpfen wollte': Wittich, pp. 408-9.

To the uninitiated observer, certainly, the affair of Neu-Brandenburg appeared damaging to Gustav Adolf's prestige. The Rhenish members of the League, affecting to consider it a great victory, took the opportunity to withhold their contributions, and Maximilian had once more to make good the shortfall from his own pocket.[1] Gustav Adolf, for his part, was well aware of the political necessity for a swift counterstroke. The wavering Protestants at Leipzig must not be left too long under the impression of Neu-Brandenburg. And in any case, it was clear that Tilly must be provided without delay with a new and irresistible diversion if the position at Magdeburg were not to become desperate.

Until the last week of March there had really been no cause for immediate anxiety about Magdeburg. The forces blockading it were still inadequate for a vigorous siege; Tilly was still distracted between his various responsibilities and commitments; until 6 April not a single enemy ball fell inside the town proper.[2] But soon after the conclusion of the operations round Neu-Brandenburg Tilly seems to have faced the question as to what his future policy was to be; and at a council of war held in Brandenburg on 24 March he made his final decision. The siege was to be pushed on with energy; the capture of the town was henceforth to be the immediate military objective.[3] This decision inaugurated the final struggle for the city, and heralded the last phase in the long duel between Tilly and Gustav Adolf. It was followed by swift successes for the imperialists. The first serious attack on the defences proper came on 29 March; by 1 April many of the outworks had fallen; the supply-route by way of neutral Saxony was cut off; and Falkenberg was writing to Gustav Adolf doubting his ability to hold out beyond Easter, which in 1631 fell on 10 April.[4]

Even before the news of these sudden disasters reached Gustav Adolf it had become clear to him that Tilly had returned with his army to the Elbe; and the implications for Magdeburg were plain enough. For the first time the siege was to have the benefit of Tilly's undivided attention. Gustav Adolf, though he habitually overestimated Magdeburg's capacity for resistance, was not slow to realize that he must lose no time in producing a diversion which Tilly would be unable to ignore.[5] Such a diversion had indeed been preparing

[1] A. Ernstberger, *Wallensteins Heeressabotage*, p. 63.
[2] *Sv. Krig*, IV. 201-3, 214.
[3] Wittich, pp. 418-19; *cf.* Horn's comment, 26 April: *AOSB*, II. VIII. 44-5.
[4] *Sv. Krig*, IV. 211-13.
[5] Hammarstrand, *Bidrag*, p. 80.

from as early as the middle of March, when Gustav Adolf established himself at Schwedt. It was to take the form of another offensive against Schauenburg; and the objective this time was to be Frankfurt. Even before the danger to Magdeburg became acute there were strong arguments in favour of such a move: if ever Gustav Adolf was to move to the Elbe, he must make certain of safety in his rear; Schauenburg's army was in process of reinforcing, and it was better to attack it while that process was incomplete; and, finally, a move on Frankfurt was not so excentric geographically to the Magdeburg theatre as might at first appear. Now that Magdeburg was in danger, only a stroke at the Emperor's most sensitive spot—Silesia—was likely to avail to drag Tilly from his quarry.

The attack was mounted with the minimum of delay. By 27 March the concentrations at Schwedt were completed; by 2 April the Swedish army was outside the walls of Frankfurt; by nightfall on Palm Sunday, 3 April, the town was in Gustav Adolf's hands. Wasting no time upon opening a breach, he had prepared for a sudden assault by a short and violent bombardment on a selected point in the weak defences, and the valour of his soldiers (and not least of Monro's Scots) had given him the victory.[1] With the exception of the imperialist cavalry, which got away in good time, the army of Schauenburg and Tiefenbach was virtually put out of action. The storming of this Protestant town was followed by deplorable excesses, not merely upon the imperialist soldiery (who were massacred in revenge for what the Swedes mistakenly believed to have occurred at Neu-Brandenburg) but also upon the persons and property of the burghers.[2] The King did his best to put an end to these outrages; but the military conventions of the age permitted three hours' plundering of a city taken by assault, and his authority did not avail to prevent a breakdown of discipline which, if temporary, was almost complete.[3]

The storming of Frankfurt produced something like a panic in

[1] Monro, II. 30-8; *Arkiv*, I. 728-30; *Dagbok*, pp. 18-19.

[2] 'When any Imperialist cryed *Quarter*; *New Brandenburg* cries the other, and knocks him downe': *The Swedish Intelligencer*, I. 90. The *Rathhaus* was stripped bare, the University plundered of its 'seals, ornaments and maces': Gustav Adolf made restitution afterwards: Wittich, pp. 447-50 and *note*.

[3] Monro, II. 34: 'I did never see Officers lesse obeyed, and respected, than here for a time, till the hight of the market was past: and well I know, some Regiments had not one man with their Colours, till the fury was past, and some Colours were lost the whole night, till they were restored the next day, such disorder was amongst us, all occasioned through covetousnesse, the roote of all evill and dishonesty.'

the councils of Ferdinand II[1]: the fortifications of Vienna and Prague were hastily put in order; the Emperor and the League each set about raising fresh troops; and Catholics and Protestants alike tended to assume that the victory would be followed by an invasion of the Habsburg lands.[2] But such a move would have exposed the Swedish base to attacks from Tilly and would have taken Gustav Adolf still further away from Magdeburg.[3] For his present purpose it would be enough if the Frankfurt operation gave Falkenberg a breathing-space and freed Gustav Adolf of anxiety about the Oder, against the moment when he should be ready to move to the Elbe. Up to a point, the operation was successful in both these respects. That Gustav Adolf confidently counted on attracting Tilly's attention is shown by his placing the whole of his cavalry, during the attack on Frankfurt, as a defensive screen far to the west, to cover him from surprise on that side. And he was perfectly correct in his calculation. On 31 March Tilly received the news of Gustav Adolf's move up the Oder. He at once suspended operations against Magdeburg and hurried to Brandenburg to organize counter-measures; and he would certainly have marched for Frankfurt if he had not been met by news that the city had already fallen. But even as late as 8 April he was so concerned at the danger in the east that he was seriously considering abandoning the siege and moving the major portion of his army to Silesia.[4] From Magdeburg's point of view, the only mistake about the Frankfurt diversion was that it was too brilliantly conducted. Had Gustav Adolf proceeded to besiege the place according to the textbooks, had he taken two weeks instead of two days over the business, the diversion of Tilly would have been effective. As it was, Falkenberg obtained an invaluable respite of about a fortnight, without which his resistance could scarcely have been prolonged into May.

The sequel to the taking of Frankfurt provided a good example of the difficulty of pursuing a sound strategy in the absence of reliable information. For two weeks after 3 April Gustav Adolf remained under the impression that Tilly was actually on the march

[1] As Questenberg wrote to Wallenstein on 13 April, 'Jtzt haists: helff, helff, und non est, qui exaudiat': Hallwich, *Briefe und Akten*, I. 345.

[2] Dudík, pp. 84-5; Wittich, p. 477; Hist. MSS. Comm., *Hamilton*, for Salvius's report to Hamilton. For Tilly's alarm, Droysen, II. 287 and *note* 4; for Pappenheim's caustic comments, Dudík, pp. 70-1.

[3] See the discussion in Wittich, pp. 454-6; *Sv. Krig*, IV. 143, 158; and Tingsten, *Gustav Adolfs politik och krigföring*, p. 61.

[4] Wittich, pp. 439-41; *Sv. Krig*, IV. 213.

against him. While awaiting his arrival, he occupied himself with the capture of Landsberg, which might be considered the logical corollary to the taking of Frankfurt.[1] And because he expected Tilly's coming, he took too small a force, and hence took too long about it.[2] The fortnight which Frankfurt had gained for Magdeburg was frittered away on the capture of a town whose possession, however desirable, was by no means essential. And meanwhile the King deluded himself with the most exaggerated expectations of the improvement in the situation at Magdeburg as the result of the Frankfurt diversion.[3]

It was not long before he was disabused. Letters from Magdeburg which reached him on 22 April contained such grave news that it was immediately apparent that he must take prompt and vigorous action if he wished to save the town. He had at his disposal at this juncture a field-army of about 18,000 men. His cavalry was still unpaid (it had not shared in the plunder of Frankfurt), and its morale was uncertain.[4] Around Magdeburg, Tilly and Pappenheim had by now concentrated over 32,000 men. If it came to a fight, the odds would be heavily against Gustav Adolf. He was, indeed, expecting reinforcements in the near future; but it was now doubtful whether Magdeburg's resistance could be maintained till their arrival.[5] Yet it was now difficult to devise any other means to help Falkenberg than by a direct advance, with the risk of a battle at the end of it. In the last ten days of April Gustav Adolf came to the conclusion that that risk must be taken.[6] But in the way of an advance to the Elbe there were still two formidable obstacles: the absence of a safe line of retreat, lacking control of the fortresses of Küstrin and Spandau; and the ambiguous attitude of John George of Saxony.

(v) *The Leipzig Convention*

Throughout the late winter and early spring, while Gustav Adolf and Tilly were struggling for the initiative, and the defenders of

[1] *AOSB*, I. VI. 270.

[2] See his letter to Banér, 10 April: *Arkiv*, I. 420.

[3] *Arkiv*, I. 421-2, where the King writes to Falkenberg on 17 April, conjecturing that there cannot be more than 4000 men outside Magdeburg, and suggesting that Falkenberg has therefore the chance 'Euch selben in etwas Rath zu schaffen, bis der Allerhöchste Mittel zum roial Entsatts geben möchte'.

[4] *AOSB*, II. I. 715, II. VIII. 45.

[5] Generalstaben, *Gustaf II Adolf*, p. 259; *cf. Arkiv*, II. 181, 203, 246.

[6] Already on 19 April Baudissin was informing Oxenstierna that the King would probably march for Magdeburg: *AOSB*, II. IX. 787.

Magdeburg awaited with growing uneasiness the long-deferred hour of their deliverance, the Protestant Estates of north Germany had been in conference at Leipzig. Fourteen princes had attended in person, twenty-six princes or cities had sent representatives; and although the King of Denmark, and the Dukes of Holstein, Oldenburg, East Friesland and Pomerania [1] failed to put in an appearance—to say nothing of the uncomfortable absence of any representatives from Magdeburg—it was the biggest gathering of Protestant Estates that Germany had seen since the demise of the Union.[2] The proceedings opened on 6 February with a sermon from Hoë von Hoënegg, the influential Saxon court-chaplain, upon a text from Psalm 83, verses 1-2 [3]; and continued four days later with a Proposition from John George which imperfectly concealed its vacuity in a dense cloud of verbiage.[4] Five days earlier the Emperor had issued a menacing rescript forbidding the Protestant Estates to arm.[5]

From the outset it was clear that the Convention would have difficulty in agreeing upon a policy; and it was early decided that resolutions should not be taken by a majority vote, but that each member should be free to accede to, or decline, any proposition that was laid before the assembly.[6] By this procedure John George would avoid the possibility of finding himself steadily outvoted. The risk of such an issue was by no means imaginary, for most of the princes came to Leipzig with the conviction that the only hope of safety lay in the adoption of much more resolute measures than John George had been willing to contemplate in the past. Prominent among this active party was William of Weimar; and with him were associated such men as John Frederick of Bremen, the Mecklenburg Dukes, and Löffler, the able representative of the regent of Württemberg.[7] Some of this party were already hopelessly compromised in the eyes of the Emperor, while others believed that a bold front was necessary to save their lands from plunder by the imperialist armies. William of Weimar considered that a strong Protestant league, independent of Gustav Adolf, had a chance of constraining Ferdinand to abate

[1] Bogislaw could not get a safe-conduct from Tilly.

[2] For the Leipzig Convention in general, see W. Struck, *Das Bündnis Wilhelms von Weimar mit Gustaf Adolf*, pp. 61-94; B. Boëthius, *NSK*, p. 105 *seqq.*; Helbig, pp. 34-40; Ritter, III. 480-3; Rommel, VIII. 105 *seqq.*

[3] H. Knapp, *Hoë von Hoënegg*, p. 38.

[4] Lundorp, III. 130.

[5] *ibid.*, 131.

[6] Struck, *Das Bündnis Wilhelms von Weimar*, p. 73.

[7] For Löffler, see Schott, p. 349.

the pressure of his soldiery, and perhaps even of inducing him to abandon the Edict of Restitution. The attempt, he felt, was worth making; but if it failed, he was prepared to accept the logical consequences and proceed to an alliance between his projected league and the Swedish crown. This policy was not without support within the circle of John George's advisers: Christopher Charles von Brandenstein, one of his councillors, and perhaps also Hoë von Hoënegg, were sympathetic.[1] In the course of the meetings it won further adherents, notably William's brother Bernard, and William V of Hesse; and it was ardently supported by Philip Reinhard von Solms, who attended in the double capacity of representative of the Wetterau Counts and agent of Gustav Adolf. The Weimar policy thus aimed at the creation of a real third party, benevolently inclined to Sweden but (for the present, at all events) uncompromised by any alliance with the invader.

This had for some months been the policy of George William of Brandenburg, and of George William's political mentor, Arnim; but there are signs that the Elector was beginning to doubt whether it was a practicable policy any longer. With Tilly on the Havel, and Gustav Adolf on the lower Oder, an attitude of independence became increasingly difficult to maintain. Of the two representatives whom George William sent to Leipzig, Knesebeck was perhaps still disposed to neutrality, if it could be had; but Götzen already perceived that the position was no longer tenable, and was ready for a secret understanding with Sweden.[2]

Nevertheless, though George William might begin to despair of it, any third party would not lack for leaders. One aspirant to the position was Kristian IV of Denmark. It is true that he had not appeared at Leipzig; but in the course of February he began a negotiation for the marriage of his son Kristian to a daughter of John George (the betrothal actually took place in April), and he coupled this with a proposal for the creation of a joint army and the cementing of a new Protestant union from which Gustav Adolf was to be specifically excluded [3]—an idea, incidentally, which Arnim had already put forward in January.[4] But despite the success of his efforts

[1] *Sv. Krig*, IV. 166; B. Boëthius, *Filip Reinhart von Solms och Gustaf Adolf före Leipzigkonventet*, pp. 119-21; Knapp, p. 38.

[2] Koser, pp. 428-9.

[3] Fridericia, *YPH*, pp. 182-6; Boëthius, *NSK*, pp. 77-8; *Christian IVs Breve*, II. 324-8.

[4] Irmer, *Arnim*, p. 126.

on the matrimonial side, on the political Kristian had little chance. A third party led by Denmark made no appeal to John George; and Kristian's obvious dynastic ambitions were not calculated to commend his leadership to the estates of the Lower Saxon Circle. Still less prospect had the fumbling efforts of France. Melchior de Lisle, whom Father Joseph despatched to the Leipzig Convention, was indeed a Protestant, and the policy he was to urge upon the meeting was one to which *a priori* no exception could be taken, since a reconciliation with the Roman Catholic Electors at the expense of the Emperor, and a readiness to attend the forthcoming *Kompositionstag*, were both lines of action acceptable to the majority of the members.[1] But no one was prepared for a middle party under French patronage; and John George, who did not love the French, was merely irritated by Richelieu's meddling.

And upon John George, it was clear, everything depended. The plans of Solms and the Weimar Dukes, the suggestions of Götzen, all centred on him: without Saxony, a real third party was nearly impossible. It seemed for a moment not unlikely that he might allow himself to be persuaded. Hoë von Hoënegg, a strong imperialist until 1628, had since then been moving rapidly towards a more actively evangelical policy, and his influence with the Elector was considerable. He had urged John George to make use of the Swedish landing to extort concessions from Vienna; he had helped to keep him constant to his determination to hold the Leipzig Convention; and in January had told him that if the Edict of Restitution were not revoked it would be his duty as a Lutheran to fight the Emperor.[2] John George, moreover, ought to have been under no illusions as to Ferdinand's goodwill towards him, or as to his determination to maintain the religious revolution, for he had access to the secrets of imperial policy through a spy in Pappenheim's camp.[3] But neither the knowledge of imperial designs thus acquired, nor the adjurations of his religious adviser, availed to make him change his policy. For him the Convention was designed to be simply a gesture to impress the Emperor, a warning that the evangelical party could still offer resistance if pushed to the wall. He believed that the gesture might well be effective, at least as far as his own dominions were concerned; and if he could ensure the electorate's immunity from the extortions of the imperial armies, and obtain some reasonable guarantee that the Edict of Restitution would

[1] Fagniez, I. 570-2. [2] Knapp, pp. 30-8. [3] Wittich, pp. 332, 335.

not be enforced against Saxon secularizations, he might probably be brought to endure with Christian resignation the ruin of his less adroit neighbours. For him the third party was not yet intended to be a military reality: it was a phantom, rather, conjured up to chill the blood of the imperial commanders. Still less was he willing to assent to the idea that any league that might be born at Leipzig should enter into alliance with Sweden, or put itself under Gustav Adolf's direction. Rather than permit that, he would even assume the semblance of leadership himself. He did not believe that the best road to peace lay through the kindling of yet another civil war; he was too good a patriot not to resent the prolongation of Germany's agony by the infusion of fresh blood—especially if it were foreign; and his narrow territorialism did not seem to him in any way to conflict with the broader interests of religion and the *Reich*: the success of his skilful policy and judicious management would rather provide an instructive example to men of unriper judgment. Strong in an electorate rich and unspoiled by war; able, if given time, to raise a respectable army; he had some confidence in his ability to manage his own affairs and little imaginative sympathy for the intolerable dilemma of his brother-Elector at Berlin.

It was thus not probable that the deliberations at Leipzig would result in any very trenchant action. On the theological front, it is true, surprising harmony prevailed. Hoë and his Lutheran colleagues showed themselves unwontedly compliant to the Calvinist divines who attended the meeting; and so large a measure of doctrinal agreement was attained that the report of it brought John Durie hurrying across the Channel to attend the consummation of the union.[1] But on the political side there was less progress. The Emperor was indeed informed, with many polite explanations, that the Protestant Estates proposed to defy his ban upon their preparations [2]; but beyond this, agreement did not go. Götzen tried hard to obtain support for a fixed plan and common action to raise troops; he pleaded urgently for some aid to Magdeburg; and on 8 March he proposed a solid league, to be directed against the Emperor's evil counsellors, the exactions of the imperial armies and the execution of the Edict of Restitution. The league would have observed a benevolent neutrality towards Gustav Adolf; with the proviso (obviously inserted to safeguard Brandenburg) that any member who should be constrained to a Swedish alliance should not thereby

[1] Batten, *Dury*, pp. 27-8.

[2] Hammarstrand, *Bidrag*, pp. 72-7.

forfeit membership. But neither the persuasions of Götzen nor the busy caballing of William of Weimar and his friends could move John George very far. When at last (on 31 March) he gave a final answer to the suggestions that had been made to him, it proved a sharp disappointment to those who had hoped for a strong lead from Saxony. John George was willing to agree that the Protestant Estates assembled at Leipzig should, between them, raise an army of 40,000 men, and that immediately; he was prepared to assume at least the nominal direction of the enterprise; but he went far to ensuring the ineffectiveness of these steps by referring recruiting and finance to the management of the individual Circles (each of which would appoint its own Captain-General), and by setting up a directing and coordinating committee which would meet only when he chose to summon it (and thus probably would not meet at all). The final resolution of the Convention added to these provisions a sentimental (but unrealistic) appeal to the Roman Catholic Estates, a piece of constitutional argumentation, and renewed assurance that any military preparations would be purely defensive [1]; but such rhetorical flourishes were unlikely to make much effect upon Tilly. On 2 April the Convention ended; and if some of the participants departed rather the worse for John George's beery hospitality, they no doubt echoed the sentiment of a fellow-sufferer when he remarked '*Quid non patimur propter regnum Christi?*'.[2] There had, indeed, been more of high living than of plain thinking at Leipzig.

The attitude of Gustav Adolf to the Convention had from the beginning been friendly. Upon the publication of John George's invitation he had decided to send Martin Chemnitz to represent him, and soon after the opening of the conference he appointed Solms to act with him on Sweden's behalf. In January Salvius was writing that the raising of an independent army by the members of the Convention could be of benefit only to Sweden [3]; and Gustav Adolf early let it be known that he would welcome the formation of an independent Protestant league, and would be prepared to ally with it, even though it were not under his absolute direction; though he characteristically coupled this with stipulations as to his right to pass and repass at strategic points.[4] Solms put a proposal of this sort to the meeting on 21 February, much to John George's disquiet.

[1] Lundorp, III. 145-7.
[2] Helbig, p. 40.
[3] Boëthius, *NSK*, p. 127 *note* 2.
[4] Droysen, *Gustaf Adolf*, II. 294-5.

But when it became clear that such a scheme would meet with objections, the Swedish representatives tactfully forbore to press it; and Gustav Adolf's attitude to John George, officially at all events, remained conciliatory. Reports reaching the King from Leipzig were by no means discouraging; and as late as 28 March Grubbe could comment optimistically on the prospects.[1]

Thereafter, however, the news grew less reassuring. On 29 March Teuffel was reporting that Arnim had returned to Berlin disillusioned with the Convention[2]; and though Chemnitz (who seems to have been taken in by John George) gave far too rosy an account of the doings at Leipzig,[3] the arrival of Götzen put a different complexion upon them. Götzen, who had been sent to Gustav Adolf by George William, met the King on 16 April, between Frankfurt and Landsberg.[4] His report made it quite plain that there was to be no Swedish directory of the Leipzig levies; it revealed the enfeebling decentralization of defensive measures; and it convinced Gustav Adolf that no effective independent league was likely to emerge as a result of them.[5] This last was the most serious aspect of the situation. From Gustav Adolf's point of view, the worst consequence of the Leipzig resolution was not that it barred the way to his military direction, but rather that it made any solid Protestant league highly improbable; and consequently offered an opportunity to Tilly and Pappenheim to scatter the newly raised troops severally, Circle by Circle. It was no wonder that Roman Catholic publicists made a mock of the Convention.[6] And Gustav Adolf must have begun to understand that this result was in fact the result at which John George's policy had been aiming. The upshot of the Leipzig Convention, moreover, though a political success for the Elector of Saxony, was a political disaster for the Elector of Brandenburg. George William had failed to carry his policy; and, having failed, was left naked between the impending swords of Tilly and Gustav

[1] *Arkiv*, I. 726. [2] *AOSB*, II. IX. 567.

[3] *Arkiv*, I. 736; Wittich, p. 621; Hammarstrand, *Bidrag*, p. 78 *note* 1.

[4] J. Kretzschmar, *Die Allianzverhandlungen Gustav Adolfs mit Kurbrandenburg im Mai und Juni 1631*, pp. 3-4; Wittich, p. 621.

[5] *cf.* Horn's report to Oxenstierna, 26 April 1631, *Arkiv*, II. 246-8.

[6] Koser, p. 427, cites a current pasquinade:

Ach die armen lutherischen Hündlein
Halten zu Leipzig ein Conventlein.
Wer war dabei?
Anderthalb Fürstlein.
Was wollten sie machen?
Ein klein Krieglein?

Adolf. There was no longer any political reason to deter the King from attempting to constrain Brandenburg to comply with his requirements; and the long-standing military reasons were now to be given added urgency by the alarming news from Magdeburg.

(vi) *The Fall of Magdeburg*

Already by the spring of 1631 Gustav Adolf had come to the conclusion that if any advance to the relief of Magdeburg were to be made, it must be preceded by some arrangement which would secure his line of retreat to the coast. The two positions which he believed to be essential for this purpose were Küstrin and Spandau; and both lay within the territories of the Elector of Brandenburg. The fate of Magdeburg, therefore, depended not only upon the political benevolence of John George but also upon the military co-operativeness of George William.

Gustav Adolf had raised the question of the garrisoning of Küstrin as early as July 1630 in his talks with Dr. Bergman; and he raised it again at the beginning of January 1631, as a result of the behaviour of the commandant in giving passage to imperialist fugitives from Gartz while denying it to the Swedes who were pursuing them. In an interview with Götzen he had then made it plain that he was demanding not merely free pass and repass but the right to garrison the fortress with his own troops.[1] But the attitude of the Elector at that time had been intransigent; and for the moment Gustav Adolf had not pressed the question. He was prepared to await the outcome of the discussions at Leipzig, in the hope that the emergence of a resolute Protestant confederacy, allied with Sweden, would make the Elector more compliant, or perhaps even render the occupation of Küstrin unnecessary.[2]

But in the next few months George William showed little sign of being disposed to appear openly for Sweden; and in discussions with Brandenburg envoys in February and March Gustav Adolf twice tried to frighten him by bullying tactics, and by threats of excluding him from the Pomeranian succession.[3] It does not seem likely that these threats were seriously meant. Gustav Adolf would have been quite content to see George William succeed to Bogislaw's

[1] Droysen, *Gustaf Adolf*, II. 251-3; *Sv. Krig*, III. 530-1, 538.
[2] *ibid.*, *loc. cit.*; but *cf. AOSB*, II. IX. 786.
[3] Droysen, *Brandenburgische Audienzen bei Gustaf Adolf*, pp. 32-3; Boëthius, *NSK*, p. 3.

duchy, provided he could be induced to promise military co-operation: matters had not yet reached the point at which he felt bound to contemplate the annexation of Pomerania to Sweden. If George William would agree to enter, as Bogislaw had entered, into long-term security arrangements, Gustav Adolf would be ready enough to accept him as a partner on much the same terms.[1]

This emerged clearly from the negotiations begun towards the end of April. As the danger to Magdeburg grew more acute, the question of Küstrin and Spandau became of immediate importance. Gustav Adolf may have been encouraged to hope that it might be settled as he desired, by a report from one of his agents to the Leipzig Convention, to the effect that George William would shortly be sending him a request for the installation of a Swedish garrison in Berlin.[2] George William had, after all, got rid of Schwarzenberg; and Gustav Adolf had already sent him a tactful message of congratulation upon his 'heroic conduct' at Leipzig.[3] But when Götzen arrived at the Swedish camp on 16 April any illusions the King may have entertained were quickly dispelled. Götzen brought proposals from the Elector which were quite unacceptable. In return for a Swedish guarantee of his succession to Pomerania, George William offered collaboration only within the terms of the Leipzig resolution; a defensive alliance which was not to be directed against the Emperor; the ratification of the Swedish-Pomeranian treaty, but not of the vital military convention that was appended to it; and the right only of pass and repass through Küstrin and Spandau.[4] This meant, in effect, that any troops that the Elector might raise would be independent of Gustav Adolf's control, and might be withheld at a critical moment in order to avoid a clash with imperial forces; and it meant, too, that the security offered at Küstrin and Spandau would be inadequate, 'since' (as Gustav Horn put it) '*voluntas hominis* is *ambulatoria*'.[5] In short, the Elector was not prepared to fight himself, was not prepared to help others to fight, and above all was not willing to concede that absolute *directorium* which the King felt to be required by the emergency. If this was the best that he could offer, if he was so insensible of his duty to the evangelical

[1] *AOSB*, II. I. 713.
[2] Hammarstrand, *Bidrag*, p. 78 *note* 1, 87; *Arkiv*, I. 737.
[3] Droysen, *Schriftstücke*, pp. 97, 102; *id.*, *Gustaf Adolf*, II. 341 *note* 1.
[4] J. Kretzschmar, *Die Allianzverhandlungen Gustav Adolfs mit Kurbrandenburg im Mai und Juni 1631* [cited: *Allianzverhandlungen*], pp. 3-4; *id.*, *Gustav Adolfs Pläne und Ziele in Deutschland*, p. 164; Wittich, pp. 625-7.
[5] *AOSB*, II. VIII. 44.

cause at a time when it might seem that every day was precious, then Gustav Adolf must recall him to his duty and compel him to better his offer, by the exercise of judicious pressure or if need be by force. Evangelical public opinion, it might be hoped, would know how to judge between the would-be deliverer of Magdeburg and the particularist politician whose private interests were impeding that deliverance. At all events, Gustav Adolf could waste no more time on the diplomatic *convenances*.

On 29 April the Swedish army broke up from Frankfurt and marched for Berlin. By 1 May they had reached Köpenick, a dozen miles or so to the south-east of it. George William could make no military resistance: Berlin contained only a handful of troops. But he could still fight obstinately with diplomatic weapons. He sent out to parley; and at his request Horn and Steinberg were despatched to Berlin to discuss the projected alliance. The time had passed for the negotiation of long-term arrangements of the Pomeranian pattern: what Gustav Adolf needed now was immediate (even if only temporary) control of Brandenburg's military installations and resources. The envoys were therefore instructed to stipulate for a treaty on the model of the Hessian *Eventualkonföderation*—a treaty, that is to say, which would secure to Gustav Adolf the absolute *directorium*. But they were not to allow themselves to be bogged down in general discussions: the essential point to secure was the immediate garrisoning of Küstrin and Spandau by Swedish troops.[1] To this procedure George William would not agree. In his view these points of detail must be preceded by the general settlement; and on 2 May he made his amended proposal for an alliance.[2] It went some way to meeting Gustav Adolf's demands. It offered him the command in chief within the electorate, together with a vague prospect of the general direction of such future Protestant league as might take shape as a result of the recent decisions in Leipzig; the admission of Swedish troops to all electoral fortresses except Spandau and Küstrin; and a monthly contribution of 20,000 *rdr*. for as long as the Elector should be unable to provide adequate garrisons for them. In return, George William asked a full guarantee of his right of succession in Pomerania. Gustav Adolf was not satisfied with this. Since the Elector had conceded so much to pressure, it was reasonable to suppose that another turn of the screw might extort a complete

[1] Kretzschmar, *Allianzverhandlungen*, pp. 9-11.
[2] *ibid.*, *loc. cit.*; *id.*, *Gustav Adolfs Pläne und Ziele*, p. 185.

surrender. He demanded an interview with his brother-in-law; and on 3 May advanced at the head of a small force upon Berlin. George William, unable to resist, took refuge behind a barrier of petticoats: collecting all his available female relations, he drove out with them to meet the King. In these circumstances, the meeting was necessarily polite; and Gustav Adolf courteously escorted the *cortège* back to Berlin. There the negotiations continued. Gustav Adolf demanded the *directorium* without qualification; he asked 25,000 *rdr.* a month instead of 20,000; and ratification of all the Pomeranian agreements. He offered to evacuate Brandenburg and leave George William to his fate; but he would not quit Pomerania until the Elector should have paid his war expenses, and he proposed to retain Stralsund and Rügen as security for them.[1] George William rejected these terms without hesitation. At last, on 4 May, after a painful crisis, they agreed upon a compromise.[2] The matter of the alliance was by common consent shelved: the passive resistance of the Elector had been successful. On the crucial question of Spandau and Küstrin, it was agreed that Spandau should be garrisoned at once by Swedish troops; while the Brandenburg commandant at Küstrin was to be placed under Horn's orders, with instructions to admit Swedish troops to the citadel in case of emergency. But Spandau was to remain in Swedish hands only until Magdeburg was relieved, or until the need for safeguarding the King's line of retreat from Magdeburg no longer remained.[3]

Four days of hard bargaining had thus given Gustav Adolf some sort of guarantee against a possible defection by the Elector should the Magdeburg expedition take an ill turn. But he had extorted neither a Pomeranian nor a Hessian treaty, neither a permanent alliance nor a temporary subjection. Still, it was an agreement of a sort, and he must make the best of it. On 5 May the army advanced to Spandau; on 6 May to Potsdam. Reconnaissance parties were pushed out as far as the Elbe.[4] But at Potsdam the advance halted. The quickest way to relieve Falkenberg, now that the bridge at Magdeburg was down, was by Dessau, or failing that by Wittenberg. Either route ran across the territory of electoral Saxony. It now

[1] Kretzschmar, *Allianzverhandlungen*, pp. 11-15; Wittich, p. 628; Paul, II. 198; *Arkiv*, I. 427-9, 737-9; *AOSB*, II. I. 720; Koser, pp. 442-3.

[2] *Sverges traktater*, V. 449-54.

[3] Wittich, p. 628.

[4] *AOSB*, II. I. 720; Belfrage, *Erik Soop och Västgöta ryttare*, p. 83; Wittich, p. 487.

rested with John George, therefore, to decide whether Gustav Adolf should reach Magdeburg in time. And perhaps it also rested with him to decide whether, if he did arrive in time, he could escape defeat. The Swedes at Potsdam had barely half the numbers of the imperialists at Magdeburg, and such army as they had was in a semi-demoralized condition for lack of pay.[1] Only if a strong Saxon contingent were available, and if supplies could be got from the still-unravaged electorate, would there be much hope of victory outside Magdeburg. Upon John George, in short, the whole issue now seemed to depend.

John George had never looked upon the Magdeburg revolt with any favour. It was rebellion against a lawful authority, and (what was worse) rebellion suborned by a foreign power. With that power the burghers had concluded an alliance. The movement was led by the ex-Administrator, Christian William, whose character he distrusted and whose claims on Magdeburg he denied. The disturbance in Magdeburg, moreover, brought active hostilities to John George's borders; and the fact that a strip of Saxon territory ran almost up to the walls of the town, though it facilitated the provisioning of the defenders, presented vexing problems to a conscientious neutral. John George's policy towards Magdeburg was, first, to do nothing himself to assist the burghers; and secondly, to prevent anyone else from doing anything. As early as mid-March Arnim had warned him that Gustav Adolf might be unable to make good his promise of relief[2]; by the end of April he was fully aware that the defence might collapse in the immediate future; and he also knew that his loyal neutrality got him no credit with the Emperor.[3] But he was not on that account to be induced to change his policy. Gustav Adolf had been directing appeals to him for nearly a month: two urgent letters of 22 and 23 April had pleaded with him to give the Swedish army pass and repass to Dessau, to make provisions available, and if possible to give active aid.[4] On 6 May the King wrote to John George announcing the conclusion of his agreement with

[1] Lars Grubbe wrote to Oxenstierna about 11 May: 'And indeed I can give no adequate idea of our miserable condition. The foot are fifteen pays in arrear, and both officers and men mighty discontented, so that I never heard such grumbling, both public and private. The foot desert by thousands, and some 600 have gone off in this camp alone. The cavalry do as they list: it is not safe to ride a mile outside the camp. They plunder the land to the bare bones, provoking complaints and curses fit to make you shudder. There is no money here, and none hoped for, until your Grace arrive': *Sv. Krig*, IV. 228.

[2] Hammarstrand, *Bidrag*, p. 77; Helbig, p. 39.

[3] *ibid.*, p. 41.

[4] *Schriftstücke*, pp. 22-5; Styffe, pp. 608-9.

Brandenburg.[1] On the following day he sent the Elector's own *Stallmeister*, Taube, and Hans George von Arnim, who was soon to enter Saxon service, to try to persuade him.[2] From all quarters of evangelical Germany, even from Berlin, John George was subjected to more or less of moral pressure to induce him to give way.

For four agonizing days Gustav Adolf and his army remained idle near Potsdam, awaiting the Elector's response to these appeals. The feeling of frustration, the sense of precious time slipping away, must have made it a period of painful excitement: even the arrangements with George William seemed to hang fire, and it needed an explicit appeal from Gustav Adolf on 11 May before he completed all the formalities.[3] At last, on the evening of that same 11 May, at a moment when Gustav Adolf in despair was making preparations for an immediate march upon Dessau, with or without Saxon permission, John George's reply came in. It proved to be a flat rejection of all appeals for co-operation: he even evaded, on a pretext insultingly transparent, an invitation to a personal meeting with Gustav Adolf.[4]

The King's acknowledgment of this crushing missive was more temperately phrased than might have been expected. The door of negotiation was carefully left open. Gustav Adolf did not disguise his opinion that John George's answer had made a successful advance virtually out of the question.[5] Nevertheless, though the direct route was now closed to him, though he saw himself deprived of those Saxon auxiliaries on which he had counted, he was resolved to go on: with his own forces, he announced, he would march for the Elbe by way of the Havel valley. It was a desperate resolve, taken perhaps on the spur of the moment, borne upon a tide of bitterness, anger, chagrin and (who knows?) remorse: as clear an intimation of a military judgment temporarily in abeyance as was the ultimatum which he simultaneously hurled at the head of George William: either the Elector must conclude an alliance of the type of the *Eventualkonföderation*, or Gustav Adolf would withdraw from Brandenburg and leave him to his fate.[6] Before George William had had time to draw up his answer, and while yet Gustav Adolf's messenger was making his way to Dresden, came the news that radically transformed the situation. Magdeburg had fallen: fallen

[1] *Schriftstücke*, p. 27. [2] *ibid.*, pp. 28-9, 200-2.
[3] *ibid.*, pp. 106-8; *cf. Arkiv*, I. 429-30, 436.
[4] For all this, see *Arkiv*, I. 739-41; Kretzschmar, *Allianzverhandlungen*, pp. 15-16; Wittich, pp. 631-6. [5] *Schriftstücke*, p. 32.
[6] *ibid.*, pp. 109-10; Kretzschmar, *op. cit.*, pp. 17-19.

on 10 May, just as John George was concocting his last reply to Gustav Adolf. Falkenberg was slain, Christian William a prisoner, a great portion of the city—by accident, probably—laid in ashes, and the appalling total of 20,000 persons killed in the sack or consumed in the conflagration. For a full fortnight the Elbe was choked with the corpses of the victims.[1] From the duel with Gustav Adolf Tilly had at last emerged the victor; and the spoils of victory had turned to ashes in his hand.

Within a few weeks of the catastrophe, Gustav Adolf had caused to be published a justification of his conduct, wherein he sought to transfer the blame for the *débâcle* to other shoulders[2]; and from that day to this his actions have been the subject of a controversy hardly less lively than that parallel controversy (happily outside the scope of this book) concerning the responsibility for the burning of the city. Must the blame for the loss of Magdeburg be laid principally at Gustav Adolf's door?[3] Could he have done more than he did to save it? The arguments for an affirmative answer to these questions are both numerous and weighty. It is common ground that he must bear the main responsibility for the original revolt: it was the renown of the King of Sweden, not the battered reputation of Christian William, that inspired the Magdeburg mob to constrain the city fathers to the decisive step. Gustav Adolf encouraged Christian William's venture from calculations of military and political advantage; and Magdeburg, by attracting the attention of his enemies, handsomely performed the part he had allotted to it. Without Magdeburg, his path in north Germany would have been much harder. From the beginning, moreover, he had been lavish in promises of assistance, of 'early', of 'immediate', aid, of a 'royal deliverance'; promises the most explicit and ample, promises which imposed on him a moral obligation which he could not honestly ignore. He proceeded to ignore them (it is contended) for more than eight months, paltering with excuses, trading on Magdeburg's constancy, while he collected useful (but by no means indispensable) military trophies elsewhere. It was not as though opportunities for

[1] For the fall of Magdeburg, see, in general, Wittich; *Sv. Krig*, IV; F. Weber, *Dietrich von Falkenberg*; for responsibility for the fire, H. Teitge, *Die Frage nach dem Urheber der Zerstörung Magdeburgs 1631, passim*; Weber, p. 185 *seqq.*

[2] *Kurtzer aber gegrundeter Bericht | Warumb die Königl. | Mayst. zu Schweden | der Stadt Magdeburg nicht | secundiren können*; *cf. The Swedish Intelligencer*, I. 100-2.

[3] *e.g.* Wittich, p. 494: 'Die erste Schuld fällt auf dem König unmittelbar.'

an expedition to Magdeburg were lacking. As early as November 1630 Knyphausen had told him that he ought to move at once on the Elbe and risk a black eye. Two months later, after the success of the Gartz operation, the King wasted time and dissipated strength in a fruitless attack upon Landsberg, at a moment when the imperialists were in confusion and when, as Pappenheim wrote,[1] an advance on Magdeburg would have placed them in the greatest difficulty. And can it be doubted that if he had brought Tilly to battle after Neu-Brandenburg, in March, with the numerical odds very greatly in his favour, he ought to have been able to beat him, and, having beaten him, to force the abandonment of the siege? Instead, he took refuge in ingenious manœuvres; and tried to disguise his failure from himself and from the world by talking largely of 'diversions'—though indeed none of them diverted for long, and one at least did not divert at all. Even as late as April he expended nearly three weeks after the capture of Frankfurt in irrelevant and inept operations against Landsberg—three weeks which might have been used to constrain George William and bring the Swedish forces to the Elbe. But this dallying might appear almost innocent when compared with the waste of time in negotiating with Brandenburg. What were the issues between them? First, the nature of the security to be offered for the Elector's good faith: as to this, it is contended that Gustav Adolf was over-suspicious; that the military power of Brandenburg was negligible in any case; and that in such an emergency the King ought to have been willing to take a reasonable risk. Next, whether George William should contribute 20,000 or 25,000 *rdr.* a month to the common cause: an issue so trivial as to make comment superfluous. Thirdly, and most fundamentally, whether George William should retain some measure of sovereign independence, or subject himself meekly to Gustav Adolf's *directorium absolutum*. Gustav Adolf, in fact, was using Magdeburg's agony to blackmail the Elector into far-reaching military and political concessions whose ultimate purpose was

[1] 'Und kann gewiss vors Erste dem getreuen Gott nit genugsam gedankt werden, dass der König seine in Händen gehabte Victorie nicht verfolgt und über die Oder gepassiert. Denn er in demselben Zeit zugleich entweder die kaiserliche Armee unordentlich zerstreut . . . oder den Herrn Tilly in einem offenen flachen Land um Treuenbrietzen mit nur drei Regimenten zu Fuss ohne—nennenswerth—Reiterei und ohne Stücke oder aber mich allhin diesseits von Magdeburg mit fünf Compagnien zu Fuss und acht Compagnien Pferden antreffen, und, welchen er von uns nur gewollt . . . erwählen, aufheben und ruiniren hätten können': Wittich, p. 319.

probably the retention of Pomerania for Sweden after the close of hostilities.[1] While Magdeburg was at the last gasp, Gustav Adolf was playing at politics. And when it was all over, with a cold-blooded selfishness [2] which is singularly odious he threw the blame for the tragedy not only on George William and John George but upon the defenders of Magdeburg themselves, accusing them of incompetence, carelessness, lack of energy, even treachery.

Such is the indictment; and it is undeniably a formidable one. Yet to most, if not quite to all, of these arguments and facts a more or less satisfactory reply or explanation is available. It is true, no doubt, that Gustav Adolf incited Magdeburg to rebel, and made promises of aid afterwards; but it is generally agreed that the citizens were misled, not by Gustav Adolf nor even by Christian William, but by the unauthorized expectations held out by Dr. Stallman.[3] Stallman was admittedly the King's agent, and the responsibility for making a bad choice falls on him; but the King was not responsible for the trickery and deception whereby Stallman provoked the rising. As to the promises, Gustav Adolf was fully aware of his responsibility; and he had good reason to believe, at the time that he made them, that they could be implemented. It was the breakdown of financial supplies, the quite unexpectedly slow growth in the size of his armies, that put it out of his power to keep his word. It is noteworthy, moreover, that from February 1631 he was careful to explain that a promise of immediate assistance must be interpreted in the context of the existing military situation: he must not be held to a literal keeping of his word at the price of the ruin of his army, or not Magdeburg only, but the Protestant cause as a whole, would go down to disaster.[4] On the eve of landing upon the shores of a hostile, because enslaved, Germany, Gustav Adolf had sought to stimulate the activity of what in current parlance might be called groups of partisans. Soon after his arrival, this effort was

[1] This is Kretzschmar's line of argument: *Allianzverhandlungen, passim.*

[2] The phrase is Ritter's: 'mit der kalten Selbstsucht des Eroberers [er] die Schuld auf die protestantischen Kurfürsten und vor allem auf die unglücklichen Magdeburger wälzte, auf ihren Geiz, ihre Mattherzigkeit, und das ungestörte Treiben der Verräter': Ritter, III. 492.

[3] Wittich, pp. 516-20, 529, 531-2, 536, 548-9, 552; *id., Dietrich von Falkenberg*, p. 72 *seqq.*; Droysen, *Gustaf Adolf*, II. 177.

[4] *e.g. Arkiv*, I. 295-7, 340-1, 399-400, where Gustav Adolf writes to the *Rath* (20-27 March): 'Mittlerweile haben Wir zu Euch, als discreten und weltweisen Leuten, die gnädigste Zuversicht, Ihr werdet solche Unsere Parole nach die Möglichkeit und nicht so schlecht aufnehmen und deuten, dass Wir wider alle Raison gleichsam hineinplatzen, und damit zugleich Uns und Euch auf einmal in Grunde ruinieren sollten. . . .'

successful in Magdeburg. That the example was not imitated elsewhere in north-west Germany was one of Gustav Adolf's disappointments: it was also an important factor in his inability to come to Magdeburg's assistance. Like all belligerents who foment such partisan activity, Gustav Adolf started with an honest intention to rescue his allies. Like almost all of them, he found in the end that circumstances were too strong for him. It would certainly ill become an English historian, mindful of La Rochelle, Catalonia, La Vendée—to take no other examples—to profess surprise or indulge in moral indignation at such an outcome.

This line of defence breaks down, however, if it can be shown that in actual fact circumstances did afford the King opportunities to redeem his pledges. What of the missed chances and the inexplicable delays? One general answer to this problem lies in the incontrovertible fact that Magdeburg was in no serious danger until the end of March; was not known by Gustav Adolf to be in serious danger until about 21 April; and was eventually lost mainly owing to the sudden exhaustion of the supply of powder, which came upon Falkenberg himself as a shattering surprise at the beginning of May and which could not possibly have been foreseen by Gustav Adolf.[1] For the most part of the nine months of Magdeburg's defiance the question was not between risking the Swedish army and losing Magdeburg: there appeared no reason to suppose either alternative necessary or imminent. All that was required was to ensure that the imperialists were not given the chance to mount a real siege; and, pending the arrival of the new armies Gustav Adolf was expecting, the ideal method of doing this was by diversions. Why risk a battle unnecessarily, in possibly adverse circumstances? Why interrupt that methodical building-up of a base of operations which the King rightly considered to be the fundamental precondition for the grand concentric strategy designed for the summer of 1631? To dash for Magdeburg in November 1630, as Knyphausen suggested, was not only unsound: it was supererogatory. It may well be that, as Pappenheim suggested, Gustav Adolf could have relieved Magdeburg in January, though it must have appeared very improbable to a Swedish eye; but it is much less certain that he would have been able safely to maintain himself there, and Magdeburg might have shortly been once more besieged. Any solid transference of the seat

[1] Though Falkenberg had been anxious about powder (and had told the King so) as early as 25 February: *Arkiv*, II. 181; but *cf. ibid.*, I. 725 *seqq.*

of war from the Oder to the Elbe involved as a desirable and perhaps necessary precondition the conquest of Mecklenburg and the command of the Havel. When in January 1631 Gustav Adolf instead of marching on Magdeburg undertook his second expedition to Mecklenburg, he was not only making an effective diversion: he was also preparing that extension of his base to the west without which Magdeburg could hardly be brought within the sphere of permanent Swedish military control. As to the dallying with Landsberg in April, we have seen that this was the result of the King's ignorance of Tilly's return to Magdeburg, and of his belief that the imperial commander was in fact advancing to attack him.[1] In fact, the only real military opportunity occurred in the days after 7 March, when the King avoided a battle with Tilly at Neu-Brandenburg. By that time Mecklenburg was half-conquered and little more was needed to overrun it; and a victory over Tilly might well have opened the possibility for the firm establishment of a *sedes belli* on the lower Elbe. It might also have done something to provide the King with the reinforcements he was needing, and even to pay them—as the experience of Breitenfeld was to show. But the decisive numerical superiority which he commanded on 7 March was never achieved again. Thenceforward, until Magdeburg fell, Gustav Adolf's forces were always inferior, and usually very greatly inferior, to the imperialist army he would have to meet.

In regard to the negotiations with George William, it may at once be conceded that Gustav Adolf was trying to turn the situation to his political advantage; or, more precisely, was trying to extract from it long-term, as well as short-term, guarantees of military security. But he was not advancing any new principle, nor making new demands: if it was blackmail, the danger to Magdeburg at least had not put the price up. It was, moreover, at George William's insistence that the discussions were diverted from a concentration upon the single immediate issue of Küstrin and Spandau, and allowed to entangle themselves in the general question of an alliance. And as to Küstrin and Spandau, it is worth recording that Clausewitz considered Gustav Adolf's demands to be 'moderate'.[2] They were in any case the continuation of negotiations begun before Magdeburg's crisis became acute: if discussion were broken off now, either Gustav Adolf must risk his army or he must violently coerce Brandenburg—and the latter course would be highly objectionable on

[1] See above, p. 483. [2] Clausewitz, *Strategische Beleuchtung*, pp. 27-8.

political grounds. It is true that after George William made his proposals of 3 May the difference between what Gustav Adolf asked and what he was offered can be (though probably wrongly) considered insignificant. But these proposals did not delay the conclusion of an agreement by more than twenty-four hours. And it can scarcely be contended that George William offered acceptable terms *before* 3 May. The whole course of negotiations with Brandenburg, after their resumption in April, covered little more than a fortnight; the final struggle barely a day. The delay was thus not great. And in any event Gustav Adolf knew, or thought that he knew, that a rescue expedition would be almost impossible without John George's help. The appeals to John George began on 22 April; his final refusal was dated 10 May—by which time the agreement with George William was six days old and Magdeburg was in flames.[1]

Gustav Adolf's reaction to John George's refusal was to prepare for an advance down the Havel, and he might well have carried out this plan if he had not been forestalled by the news of Magdeburg's fall. Was such an enterprise as desperate as it would appear to be? Might not the King have been able to make a demonstration which should be sufficiently threatening to draw off Tilly from Magdeburg but sufficiently agile to enable him to avoid being caught up in a battle which he must certainly lose? And if so, might not such a demonstration have been made at any time after 4 May, without waiting for John George's reply? It is pertinent in this connexion to remember how pessimistic Tilly was about his prospects at Magdeburg: up to the very eve of the storm he was wavering between Pappenheim's policy of finishing with Magdeburg at all costs and his own inclination to cut his losses and be gone.[2] Pappenheim, moreover, had always contended that Magdeburg must be the bait to attract Gustav Adolf to an unequal battle. If, then, the Swedish army crossed the Elbe, might it not be expected that both Tilly and Pappenheim would concur, from different motives, in suspending the siege and seeking to bring on an engagement? To this it may be answered that Gustav Adolf could not know of Tilly's doubts about the siege: the natural assumption was that Tilly would decline to be drawn until Gustav Adolf put himself in a position where his defeat was probable. Alternatively, if Tilly in fact came after him, it was

[1] For views contrary to those presented here, see Kretzschmar, *Allianzverhandlungen, passim*; Tingsten, p. 76 *seqq.*; Paul, II. 197; Koser, p. 433.

[2] Wittich, pp. 211, 489-91; *Sv. Krig*, IV. 146-7; Weber, p. 138.

by no means certain that he could avoid battle, in which case he might find himself with his back to the Elbe and no very easy means of recrossing it. In any case, it seems unlikely that a demonstration in force, moving by way of the Havel, could have reached Magdeburg in time. By the beginning of May, in fact, the military position was such that Tilly could not be stopped from taking Magdeburg if once he made up his mind to it. And if John George had made a different choice, if he had thrown in his lot with Gustav Adolf at any time after receiving the King's letter of 22 April, it is unlikely that the position would have been much altered. For John George's army was still in the making, and the reinforcements he could bring would not have been important.[1] The effect of his adhesion would have been to open the way to a Swedish advance upon Magdeburg which could hardly have failed to be disastrous. John George's obstinacy cannot be blamed for the loss of Magdeburg; but it may perhaps be credited with the preservation of the Swedish army.

Finally, there remains the question of Gustav Adolf's attempt to put the blame for what happened upon the Electors, and in particular upon the Magdeburgers themselves.[2] In regard to John George and George William, the attacks, though not altogether fair, were understandable and pardonable.[3] In regard to Magdeburg, they were in part the result of ignorance of the original divisions of opinion within the city, in part the consequence of Falkenberg's reports of the difficulty of enforcing his authority, in part the reaction of an irritable and over-sanguine temperament to a prolonged strain followed by a crushing disappointment. No doubt Gustav Adolf had also urgent political reasons for exculpating himself. But whatever the explanation, it was a sorry business, revealing on the King's part a grievous lack of magnanimity and imagination. It may indeed be said that the only really discreditable aspect of Gustav Adolf's relations with Magdeburg was his response to the news of its immolation.

[1] *Sv. Krig*, IV. 240.

[2] Weber, pp. 150, 193-7; Wittich, pp. 536-52; *Kurtzer aber gegründeter Bericht, passim*; *Arkiv*, I. 741-2, where Grubbe in a letter to John Casimir gives a typical specimen of opinion in the Swedish camp. A month later Grubbe more or less withdrew the charge of actual treachery, but maintained his severe censure on the conduct of the defenders: *ibid.*, I. 750-6. Salvius was equally condemnatory on 18 May: *ibid.*, II. 256-9.

[3] Wittich, pp. 581, 641; Paul, II. 194; *Arkiv*, I. 739-41, 750-6: Gustav Adolf told George William early in May: 'Am jüngsten Gericht werdet Ihr Evangelischen angeklagt werden, da Ihr nichts bei dem Evangelio habt thun wollen; es wird Euch wohl auch hier vergolten werden. Denn ist Magdeburg weg, und ich ziehe zurück, so seht Ihr zu, was es Euch gehen wird': Irmer, *Hans Georg von Arnim*, p. 129. And *cf. AOSB*, I. VI. 347.

CHAPTER VIII

FROM MAGDEBURG TO MAINZ

(i) *After Magdeburg*

THE failure of Gustav Adolf to relieve Magdeburg undoubtedly dealt a heavy blow to his prestige. Despite the omens and the portents, and in the face of Paracelsus's prophecies, the Eagle had been too strong for the Lion after all. To Gustav Adolf, as indeed to all who were ignorant of Tilly's difficulties, the catastrophe seemed to put the Swedish army in a perilous and perhaps untenable position. Yet, in a political sense, the crisis was not without its compensations. Though some of the Protestant Estates took fright at the news from Magdeburg, others were stimulated to more resolute measures; and all must acknowledge the consequences of their tepid policies at Leipzig. The Swedish propaganda soon began to repair the momentary damage to the King's reputation; and men proved ready enough to take these explanations for truth and transfer the blame from Swedish to Saxon shoulders.

Within the first six months after the landing at Peenemünde, Gustav Adolf had formed his ideas as to the kinds of treaty he desired to make with the princes of Germany. The first sort, of which the alliance with Pomerania was as yet the only example, was intended to provide a permanent security system for the coastlands. The second, of which the still-unratified *Eventualkonföderation* was intended to be the prototype, was designed to give him full control of the military resources of his ally for the duration of hostilities only; and it was considered to be applicable primarily to those states in the interior of Germany whose remoteness from the Baltic made them of less permanent strategic importance to Sweden.[1] These categories, however, were not exhaustive: other arrangements, more favourable to his allies, were conceivable if warranted by circumstances. He had more than once made it plain that better terms might be conceded to a solidly organized Protestant league, even though it were independent of his control; and a shrewd appreciation of this

[1] See Oxenstierna's letter to Gustav Adolf of 12 January 1631, where the distinction between the types is clearly drawn: *AOSB*, I. VI. 43-6.

fact had led George William of Brandenburg to strive for the creation of an evangelical *bloc*, and avoid, for as long as possible, a direct negotiation with Sweden. There can be little doubt that Gustav Adolf hoped that any league of this sort would have the Elector of Saxony at its head. To John George, indeed, he had twice made magnanimous offers,[1] and even after the Leipzig Convention and the disaster at Magdeburg he might be prepared to renew them. For, in a military point of view, the Saxon alliance would be worth all the rest.

The outcome of the Leipzig discussions, however, had thrown strong doubts upon the practicability of this policy in the future. At the Swedish headquarters there was a general feeling of disillusionment; and that feeling was strengthened by the experiences of the first weeks of May.[2] The Leipzig alliance was a poor thing at best, and at worst a heartless fraud. The organization by Circles vitiated it as a military league, while politically it opened the way to the intrigues of Kristian IV, who as Duke of Holstein tried hard to secure the choice of one of his sons to command the forces of the Lower Saxon Circle. John George's failure to assume the effective direction at Leipzig, and the sudden danger to Magdeburg, had forced Gustav Adolf, in his relations with Brandenburg, to fall back upon his original alliance-patterns; and the Elector had been pressed to accept a treaty, first of the Pomeranian, and then of the Hessian type. But though George William contrived to evade either, the negotiations probably played their part in crystallizing the King's ideas. For it was at the height of the crisis over Magdeburg (perhaps about 11 May) that he caused his secretary, Dr. Steinberg, to commit to paper the first general formulation of Swedish policy in Germany since the *råd*-debates of the previous summer.

This document, which is known as the *Norma futurarum actionum*, laid down two objectives.[3] The first was defined as the setting up of 'a new evangelical Chief'—and for that position Gustav Adolf was no doubt the only candidate contemplated; the second, as the creation of a new league under the direction of the Chief and of the evangelical Estates. For effecting these aims the *Norma* posited certain preconditions: the general direction of operations must be in the Chief's hands; the allies must be bound to him *jure clientelari*;

[1] In September and November 1630: see above, pp. 457-8.

[2] *Arkiv*, I. 429-30, II. 256-9; *AOSB*, I. vi. 342.

[3] The text is printed by B. Boëthius in *Historisk tidskrift*, XXXI. 201-4.

they must place their fortresses at his disposal, contribute an agreed quota in men and money, afford his armies free passage and supplies, open their cities to him, and bind themselves not to make a separate peace. And since these terms might well prove difficult to obtain, the *Norma* suggested that allies be won by generous promises and by moderation of behaviour. They should be assured, for instance, that their former liberties would be respected, and their strong places returned to them at the end of the war; and great care must be taken to avoid offending their susceptibilities by word or deed.[1] The league, it was suggested, might have its own 'council of war and state', which would be permanently attached to Gustav Adolf; and it would be the function of this council to take decisions on policy, though it would not be allowed to interfere in the King's execution of its decisions.[2] The estates of Germany were to be recruited for this league one by one; since experience had made plain that it would be a waste of time to hope for any alternative procedure.[3] Every effort was to be made to induce George William to join the association, as being 'undoubtedly *reliquis fax et tuba*', and in particular as offering a line of approach to John George; and with this end in view all possible measures were to be taken to dissipate his 'preconceived suspicions'. Upon John George it would be necessary to keep a watchful eye; and it might even become expedient at last to transfer the *sedes belli* to Saxon territory, by way of bringing him to a better mind. And finally, the *Norma* suggested that in the event of the two Electors' proving complaisant in other respects, concessions might be made to them in the matter of refunding Sweden's war expenses—though such concessions (it was carefully explained) were not to extend to Sweden's claims upon Pomerania.

The *Norma* marked a decisive change in Gustav Adolf's German policy. For the first time since the landing he deliberately planned the creation of a league of German princes, with himself as its head. To this step he was driven not by any desire to arrogate to himself a position of political predominance in Germany, but by the need to provide some cohesive principle to bind together and make effective

[1] 'quod Euangelicos in sinistrarum suspicionum pelagus altius immergat'.

[2] 'Duo enim sunt in bello consideranda, ratio recte gerendi, ratio recte exequendi. Prior animae, posterior corpori similis videtur, quoad illam S.R.M. nihil decerneret citra commune consilium, quoad hanc eidem libera esset manus.'

[3] '. . . quod consilia immer tagk und keine nacht, quod executionem aber immer nacht und kein tagk . . .'

the straggling military efforts of the lesser Protestant states. Without such a co-ordination those efforts would hardly escape disaster. And the result of the Leipzig meeting had shown that the only other man in Germany with the necessary authority and military strength to stand forth as a leader—John George—was determined not to accept that position. Gustav Adolf realized that his league was unlikely to take shape immediately; and the *Norma* foresaw its construction by a process of gradual accretion. One by one the members would be recruited. Each would be bound by the Hessian conditions of military subjection; and this no doubt implied, for as long as it lasted, a measure of political subordination. But there was nothing in the *Norma* to suggest any design that this relationship should continue after the end of the war. The 'new evangelical Chief' would be a military leader, self-appointed to the discharge of a specific military task: by no means a permanent patron or controller. And even within the sphere of strategy Gustav Adolf was ready, it seemed, for some dilution of his authority. The 'special council of war and state' would give all members of the alliance something like equipollence in determining the general plan of campaign, even though they would be debarred from the kind of interference practised by the Dutch field-deputies, and even though their military resources would be wholly under the King's *directorium*. The idea had been foreshadowed already in April, in Gustav Adolf's suggestion to Götzen for a *consilium formatum* with a constitution based on that of the United Netherlands [1]; and it was to appear again, eighteen months later, in the plan for a *corpus evangelicorum*.

But though the weaker states were thus to be provided with a nucleus around which they might gather, it was still uncertain how far such a solution was applicable to the two Protestant Electors. Militarily, indeed, there was not much to choose between George William and John Frederick of Bremen except that the Brandenburg fortresses were of vital concern to Gustav Adolf; but politically George William was in a key position. He had been the most important champion of the idea of a third party; and he had perhaps a better chance than anybody else of influencing the policy of John George. Though Gustav Adolf's distrust of John George was now profound, it was still of the first importance to secure him; but the day had now passed when the King would be willing—as, indeed, he

[1] Kretzschmar, *Gustav Adolfs Pläne und Ziele in Deutschland*, p. 168; *Sv. Krig*, IV. 177.

had earlier been anxious—to see John George as the head of a league of German princes. The new evangelical Chief, for as long as the war should last, was to be the King of Sweden; the Elector of Saxony was to be deposed from that position of primacy in the evangelical world which he had enjoyed for so long; and Gustav Adolf had come to see—what John George had seen long ago—that Sweden and Saxony, even if force of circumstance should ultimately concuss them into an alliance, would henceforward inevitably be rivals.[1]

In the weeks immediately after the fall of Magdeburg the prospect of carrying out the programme of the *Norma* appeared by no means promising. Indeed, almost before the ink was dry on Steinberg's draft the King was forced to water down its principles in order to secure the assistance of Weimar and Hesse. William of Weimar and the Landgrave had both been disgusted by the outcome of the discussions at Leipzig; and immediately after the close of that meeting they had begun to take action on their own account. William of Hesse sent an agent to Gustav Adolf to inform him that he hoped to join Sweden later, as soon as he had raised troops under cover of the Leipzig resolution; and on 5 April he notified Tilly that he did not propose to continue to pay contributions to the imperialists, and intended to form an army of his own. Three days later, on 8 April, Bernard of Saxe-Weimar negotiated with Chemnitz and Solms the compact of Reichardsbrünn, whereby he and his brother, in return for financial assistance, agreed to raise troops on Sweden's behalf, and William of Weimar promised to command them. By the treaties of Cassel, of 22 and 23 April, the Landgrave associated himself with this arrangement, and all three agreed on the terms upon which they were prepared to accept the Swedish alliance. Those terms, though they were indeed based upon the *Eventualkonföderation*, fell short of it in many important respects. They provided for the inclusion of other leading Protestant states in the alliance—Württemberg, Baden, Brandenburg, and even the Dutch were mentioned—in an obvious effort to revive the Brandenburg policy of balancing Swedish predominance by constraining Gustav Adolf to ally not with individual states but with a league; and they made it plain that though the allies would recognize the King's position

[1] For discussion of the significance of the *Norma*, see B. Boëthius, *Nyare undersökningar rörande Gustaf II Adolfs planer i Tyskland* (*HT* (1908)), pp. 77-83; *id.*, *Salvius i den nedersaxiska kretsen maj-dec. 1631* (*HT* (1910)), pp. 162-3; Kretzschmar, *op. cit.*, p. 168 *seqq.*; Paul, II. 212.

as generalissimo, they intended to maintain a real independence of command over their own forces on all occasions when Gustav Adolf was not actually present with their armies.

The envoys of the allies of Cassel did not leave for the Swedish headquarters until 3 May, and did not reach them until just after the arrival of the news of the fall of Magdeburg. At this dark moment, when the military situation was obscure, and the attitude of Brandenburg highly dubious, Gustav Adolf could not afford to reject such proposals as they brought, even though they by no means squared with the ideals of the *Norma*. No record of the negotiations appears to have survived; but it seems that Gustav Adolf felt obliged to make concessions. He promised pensions to Hesse and Weimar in the event of their losing their lands; and he recognized William of Weimar as commander of any troops that he might raise upon his own account, though at the same time he granted him a patent as general in the Swedish service But by this time William was in process of changing his mind. The news of Magdeburg had put him in a panic. He suspended his military preparations, and began to importune John George with requests for his protection. They were very ill received: John George advised him to be less provocative in future. He now made up his mind that he had better drop the Swedish alliance; and he urged the Landgrave, who was imperturbably continuing his recruiting, at least to confine himself to the defensive. Gustav Adolf's favourable reply to his emissaries came too late to restore his nerve: at the beginning of June he hastily took refuge in John George's dominions, leaving his wife behind him. His troops were disbanded, his alliance with Sweden renounced: the fiasco was complete.[1]

Meanwhile, there remained the difficult problem of Gustav Adolf's relations with George William. The fall of Magdeburg had made a fresh settlement necessary, not only because in the worsened military situation the King could less than ever afford to take risks about his line of retreat, but specifically because the basis of the agreement of 4 May had now been removed. Spandau had been placed in Swedish hands for the duration of the Magdeburg campaign; and now that that campaign had reached its lamentable end, the fortress must be restored to the Elector. Gustav Adolf lost no time in

[1] For this episode, see W. Struck, *Das Bündnis Wilhelms von Weimar mit Gustaf Adolf*, pp. 95-123; *Sv. Krig*, IV. 288-91; Boëthius, *NSK*, pp. 129-31; Chemnitz, I. 162-3; W. Huschke, *Wilhelm von Weimar als Statthalter Gustav Adolfs*, p. 2 *seqq.*

reopening negotiations. On 12 May, on the eve of the arrival of the news from Magdeburg, he had addressed to von Pfuel a memorandum which was in fact the first of a succession of ultimata. He offered Brandenburg an alliance 'after the Hessian pattern'; and threatened, if George William should refuse it, to remove his troops from Spandau, and 'safeguard himself by other means'.[1]

So began a protracted and many-faceted crisis which was not resolved until 12 June. The immediate cause of dispute was now, as before, the future of Spandau and Küstrin; and it seems likely that George William would have been willing to accept some temporary arrangement similar to that which had now lapsed, since his own ability to defend Spandau, if it were seriously attacked, was highly dubious, and since the departure of the Swedish forces would leave him helpless before the armies of Tilly. But Gustav Adolf was now demanding the unconditional handing-over of Spandau, the imposition upon the electoral garrison in Küstrin of an oath to fight against 'the present *and future*' enemies of Sweden (among whom, as the Elector rightly felt, John George might well be included), and even for a moment the admission of a Swedish garrison into Berlin.[2] George William rejected this last demand out of hand, remarking that he would rather die than consent to it.[3] He was, indeed, torn between fear of what would happen to him if Gustav Adolf carried out his threat to leave him to his fate, and a rising irritation at his brother-in-law's dictatorial tone, and the grievous burden of the Swedish soldiery encamped in the electorate. By this time Gustav Adolf was insisting on the division of Brandenburg into regular quartering areas, with a monthly assessment upon each[4]; and in the first days of June George William refused these demands in a passionate (but somewhat ill-advised) letter, in which he complained of the 'insolences' of the Swedish troops, and pronounced the King's army to be 'intolerable, and of no service to the common cause'.[5] Gustav Adolf, who in a characteristic letter to the Electress had compared himself with Jacob serving Laban

[1] *Schriftstücke*, pp. 109-10; Kretzschmar, *Brandenburgische Audienzen*, pp. 15-16.

[2] Chemnitz, I. 166; *Schriftstücke*, pp. 112-14, 128; Kretzschmar, *Allianzverhandlungen*, pp. 22, 35-8.

[3] Kretzschmar, *op. cit.*, p. 22. He even consulted his council about taking Saxon garrisons into his fortresses, and about a possible alliance with Denmark: *Sv. Krig*, IV. 325.

[4] Kretzschmar, *op. cit.*, pp. 22-3.

[5] *Schriftstücke*, pp. 115-24.

without receiving the reward to which he was entitled,[1] replied hotly; and in the course of his answer touched on two other aspects of the dispute: the right of Sweden to some compensation for war expenses and the future of Pomerania. If George William persisted in his unfriendly attitude, he could have no legitimate ground for complaint if Gustav Adolf were to retain in his possession, not only the '*jure belli* occupied and conquered duchy of Pomerania' but also such portions of the electorate as were already in his hands, or might pass into his hands hereafter. George William, he complained, was leaving to him all the expense and danger of defending Pomerania, and was then claiming quietly to succeed Bogislaw in Stettin. The door to a Hohenzollern succession, however, was still open: all that he demanded was 'a few inconsiderable places on the Baltic' by way of security for his expenses; and even this demand might be moderated or entirely abandoned at a general peace. And apart from these 'inconsiderable places' he was ready, in return for a binding assurance of friendship, and a 'quite reasonable payment of some of his expenses', to hand over Pomerania to the Elector.[2]

This letter is of some interest as indicating the development of the King's ideas about possible territorial acquisitions in Germany. There is still no clear-cut decision to retain the whole of Pomerania; but the ports are now thought of not only as *assecuratio* but also as *satisfactio*; and the idea that Sweden is entitled to compensation, not only at the expense of the enemy but also of the liberated, emerges more plainly than ever before. Pomerania, however, was not the central issue in the crisis of May-June 1631; and neither Gustav Adolf's final ultimatum of 9 June, nor the treaty that brought the diplomatic struggle to an end, contains any allusion to it. That ultimatum demanded Spandau unconditionally, a binding oath upon the garrison of Küstrin, a proper quartering system for Brandenburg, with a total monthly contribution of 30,000 *rdr.*, and the prohibition of any raising of troops by the Elector.[3] The real issue, in fact, was Gustav Adolf's claim to an absolute *directorium*, his demand that George William should accept the Hessian conditions, his attempt to apply the principles of the *Norma*. All minor points, as Grubbe observed, could be compromised; but on the military subordination

[1] *Schriftstücke*, p. 203 *seqq.*; *cf. Sv. Krig*, IV. 324, for correction of the date of this letter from 3 July to 3 June.

[2] *Schriftstücke*, pp. 115-26.

[3] *ibid.*, p. 128; Kretzschmar, *Allianzverhandlungen*, pp. 35-8.

or independence of the Elector no compromise was possible.[1] George William, for his part, clung to his liberty with admirable coolness and courage, and he stubbornly maintained that it was not merely his right but also his duty, under the terms of the Leipzig resolution, to raise troops of his own.[2]

On 10 June Gustav Adolf's patience at last gave way. His garrison was withdrawn from Spandau in the early hours; and in the course of the morning he advanced, for the second time within five weeks, to attack his brother-in-law in Berlin. As on the earlier occasion, the women of the electoral family came out to bar his passage. This time the King was ready for them. He gave them lunch; and the advance continued. 'The sight of an Army, is a very fierce argument, 'tis a very preuailing *Logicke*'[3]; and since further resistance was plainly impossible, George William made as if to surrender. Accompanied by Arnim, and by members of his council, he emerged from his capital; and—mindful, as a good Lutheran, of the biblical injunction—proceeded to agree with his adversary quickly, whiles he was in the way with him. In the evening the reconciled pair went by boat to the electoral pavilion outside the walls, and there partook of dinner in unruffled harmony and good fellowship. The King was in high spirits, and four times gave the toast of the Elector. And on the following morning, in a somewhat less festive spirit, the treaty was signed.[4]

It was in many respects a surprising document.[5] Spandau was put at Gustav Adolf's disposal for the duration of the war only; and the Swedish troops were to have the right of pass and repass by (but not through) Küstrin, together with the right to be admitted to the citadel in case of extreme need. Brandenburg was to be divided into ten quartering areas, each of which was to pay a contribution of 3000 *rdr.* a month. George William retained the right to raise a limited number of troops upon his own account, provided that he did not interfere with Gustav Adolf's own recruiting or poach mercenaries

[1] See Grubbe's plain statement: *Arkiv*, I. 743. But *cf.* Arnim's very different opinion, Kretzschmar, *op. cit.*, p. 39.

[2] He alleged many other objections too: as Grubbe wrote, with significant impatience, 'Objections also still made of *jura imperii fundamentalia*, die Erbverbruederung, and other such stuff, *hoc perverso Rom. Imperii Statu*, mighty absurd': *Arkiv*, I. 743.

[3] *The Swedish Intelligencer*, I. 95.

[4] For the whole episode, see, in addition to the authorities cited, Grubbe's narratives in *Arkiv*, I. 744-50; Wittich, pp. 695-7; Chemnitz, I. 163-73; Droysen, II. 341-54; Paul, II. 206-7.

[5] Text in *Sverges traktater*, V. 457-60.

from him. And that was all. There was no alliance; no unconditional handing-over of Spandau; no oath imposed upon the Küstrin garrison binding them to fight the present and future enemies of Sweden; no absolute *directorium* for Gustav Adolf; no mention of the Pomeranian difficulty. As in the case of William of Weimar, the programme of the *Norma* was tacitly abandoned; but this time it was abandoned after the King had made every effort to impose it. In its silences, as well as in its positive provisions, the treaty of 11 June represented a diplomatic check for Gustav Adolf. The passive resistance of the feeble had worn down the impetuous violence of the strong; and the true state of the case was not disguised either by the ceremonial belching of the royal ordnance or by the sympathetic echoes provided by the electoral guests.[1]

This result, so meagre as to be almost humiliating, is nevertheless intelligible enough. The explanation has been sought by some historians in the scheme for a marriage between the electoral prince and Gustav Adolf's daughter; and it has been suggested that the prospect of a dynastic union made the King willing to content himself with terms which would otherwise have been unacceptable.[2] It is certainly true that Gustav Adolf had put forward the idea of such a match early in January; and it has been assumed (without much evidence) that the matter must have been talked over with George William on 10 June. But there is nothing to show that the project had at this time passed beyond the stage of general mooting discussion; and the later history of the scheme does not suggest that Gustav Adolf was at any time willing to sacrifice Swedish interests to carry it through.[3] Nor is there anything to show that the Elector's reception of the proposal (if indeed it was seriously discussed in Berlin) was sufficiently encouraging to induce Gustav Adolf to make important concessions.[4] It seems much more probable that Gustav Adolf realized, on 10 June, that he could obtain his demands only by actual violence, and perhaps only by making the Elector his prisoner—and even in that event George

[1] Contrast the very different judgment of Ritter, *op. cit.*, III. 493; as also of *Sv. Krig*, IV. 231, where it is described as 'in a military aspect a more or less complete success for Gustav Adolf'.

[2] So Kretzschmar, *op. cit.*, pp. 38-41; and more recently Paul, II. 198 *note* 2.

[3] See below, pp. 646-9. There is much virtue in Droysen's cautious phrasing: 'Damals soll, wie erzählt wird, auch die Rede davon sein . . .': Droysen, II. 353. For the early history of the marriage negotiations, see R. Schulze, *Das Projekt der Vermählung Friedrich Wilhelms von Brandenburg mit Christina von Schweden*, p. 2 *seqq*.

[4] As Kretzschmar himself admitted: *Der Heilbronner Bund*, I. 16.

William's stubbornness was such that he might well continue recalcitrant. Gustav Adolf had hoped to frighten the Elector into capitulation: when the attempt failed, he did not dare to proceed to extremities. And, indeed, he could not afford to do so. One important item in the policy of the *Norma* was to use George William as an intermediary with John George. At a moment when the political outlook was anything but bright—William of Weimar had just denounced his lately concluded alliance—it was poor tactics to alienate, by ruthless treatment of George William, such possible allies as remained. On 7 June, moreover, Gustav Adolf had received from Arnim a warning which seems to have made some impression on him. Arnim had told him that a policy of violence towards Brandenburg would make a bad impression in Germany: the Protestant princes would suspect that Gustav Adolf coveted the electorate for himself. The King admitted, in reply, that 'That would not be so very absurd: people who did not know his intentions might easily think so'.[1] Three days later he made a last attempt to bully the Elector. His bluff was called; and he had no real alternative to accepting the best terms that George William was prepared to grant.

(ii) *Werben*

The fall of Magdeburg, however gratifying it might be to Pappenheim as proof of the soundness of his judgment,[2] brought to Tilly no relief from his difficulties. It was all very well for Urban VIII to hail the event as '*aeterna monumenta divinae clementiae*',[3] but the destruction of the city made the quartering of any large garrison impossible, and the devastation of the surrounding countryside presented problems of supply even to a small one. For some time to come Magdeburg would be virtually indefensible; and its retention in imperialist hands would involve the stationing of a considerable body of troops within call, and might thus impose a real restriction upon Tilly's freedom of movement. But it was clear that the major portion of the imperialist armies must move, with no long delay, to a better-stocked countryside; and the immediate problem for Tilly was to decide where to go. It might have seemed natural to exploit the triumph which had just been won in order to press on against Gustav

[1] Kretzschmar, *Allianzverhandlungen*, p. 32.

[2] Tilly had dismissed Pappenheim's contention that Magdeburg could easily be taken as 'pure imagination': Riezler, V. 372.

[3] Riezler, V. 376 *note* 1.

Adolf while the moral effect of Magdeburg was still strong, and to bring him to battle on Brandenburg soil while he was still without allies. This, certainly, is what the King feared. But from Tilly's point of view there were weighty arguments against such a course. He had, it seems, an exaggerated idea of the strength of the Swedish forces. Neither he, nor any other commander of that age, had any confidence in his ability to force battle upon an adversary who should persist in declining it. And, most important of all, the region beyond the Elbe and the Havel into which an advance against Gustav Adolf would take him was known to be a region already stripped bare of the means of supporting an army.[1] Further to the west, along the lower course of the Elbe, conditions were better [2]; and from the commissariat's point of view Tilly could quite well have advanced by way of Dömitz (still held by the imperialists) across the Elbe into Mecklenburg. Such a move would have relieved the isolated forces of Virmond and Perusi and threatened the right flank and rear of the Swedish position in the Mark of Brandenburg. But this, too, was a move which Tilly could not risk, for it would have taken him far from his expected reinforcements, and it would have left a clear field to the alarming preparations upon which, in defiance of the Emperor's prohibition,[3] the Leipzig allies were openly engaged.

Those preparations, scattered and unorganized though they were, nevertheless caused Tilly serious concern. The recruiting activities of John George, in particular, appeared ominous; and if Tilly had been able to follow his inclinations he would probably have moved his troops into Saxony as early as May or June. But it happened that the Emperor was at this juncture engaged in efforts to win back John George by diplomatic means; and Tilly was expressly prohibited from making any move in this direction.[4] To the south-west, again, there were alarming signs of future trouble in the activities of the Landgrave; and all over central Germany petty states were making petty efforts which, contemptible in themselves, needed only a unified direction to make them considerable. The Franconian Estates, meeting at Nuremberg, the Suabian,

[1] As even Pappenheim conceded: 'Den König zu suchen, hätten wir durch ein ganz ödes land reisen und diese gute Armee sehr schwächen und verderben müssen': Wittich, p. 677. Droysen's censures on Tilly's inactivity after Magdeburg (II. 362 *seqq.*) seem too harsh: for a criticism of them, see *Sv. Krig*, IV.

[2] *Arkiv*, I. 461.

[3] Chemnitz, I. 179-80.

[4] *Sv. Krig*, IV. 268, 279-81; and see below, pp. 529.

meeting at Esslingen, agreed to raise the contingents for which they had covenanted at Leipzig. Ulm and Strassburg refused further contributions to the imperial armies. In the far south-west, Württemberg and Baden were beginning to levy troops in terms of the Leipzig resolution, and for Tilly it was especially serious that they should have pledged themselves at Leipzig not to give free passage to imperial troops returning from Italy. For in Italy the peace was as good as made [1]; and it was to the now-liberated Italian armies that Tilly looked most hopefully for his much-needed reinforcements.[2] In the weeks immediately after the fall of Magdeburg, Tilly felt that he might at any moment be confronted with something like a general movement of resistance in central Germany. These potential rebels were not yet the allies of Sweden; but if John George should leave them in the lurch they might be driven to become so. Tilly's best policy, then, may well have been (as Pappenheim wished) [3] to turn against the Leipzig allies, and especially against Hesse and Weimar, and coerce them into submission in good time. In the event, he finally decided on a half-measure. On 24 May, leaving 5000 foot and 700 horse in and around Magdeburg to keep an eye on Gustav Adolf, he moved, not south-west against Hesse, but south into Thuringia; his object being to secure his grip upon those defiles through the Thuringian forest by which any reinforcements must probably reach him. And it was this move that put William of Weimar into a panic and prompted his hasty defection from the Swedish alliance.

With the fall of Magdeburg, Gustav Adolf's military position had at once become highly precarious. He had no longer any security of tenure in Spandau or Küstrin; the desperate state of his supplies could be helped only by a quartering agreement with Brandenburg, which so far had eluded him; the danger of an early attack by Tilly appeared great. If it came, he might well find himself

[1] The first agreement at Cherasco was signed on 27 March, the final peace on 9 June: *Sv. Krig*, IV. 298. For the movement of resistance, see *The Swedish Intelligencer*, I. 31-3; T. Schott, *Württemberg und Gustav Adolf*, pp. 350-1; Ritter, III. 485.

[2] Ferdinand also recalled four regiments from Flanders about this time: Droysen, II. 364.

[3] Wittich, p. 676; Droysen, II. 363 and *note* 1. Pappenheim wrote to Wallenstein on 6 July: 'So ist doch diese gute Zeit durch andere considerationes, dass Wir Vnss nit mehr Feinde machen sollen, dass Wir die verhoffte Friedens tractaten dardurch steckhen möchten, dass von Kay. Mt. kein expresser Beuelch dar seye, verabsaumbt worden': Dudík, p. 102.

driven back upon his original coastal base.[1] The advanced post at Potsdam seemed obviously untenable; and the best hope of resistance to lie in consolidating a position along the right-angled front formed by the Spree and the upper Havel, which would cover him against attacks from the south or west. But the key to this position was Spandau, which lay at its hinge; and its effective defence might well require that he should also hold Berlin. There were thus immediate, as well as long-term, military considerations behind the demands which Gustav Adolf presented to the Elector.

By the end of May, however, it began to be clear that no immediate attack was to be expected, and Gustav Adolf decided that he could risk a more advanced defensive position. He determined to make good his grip upon the lower Havel, from Spandau towards its confluence with the Elbe, and if possible to establish a foothold on the Elbe too. If he could do this, he would extend his supply area, threaten imperialist communications with Mecklenburg, and put himself in a better position to lend a hand to any movement of resistance in north-west Germany. It was of some importance that he should be close enough to the Lower Saxon Circle to give weight to the diplomatic campaign which Salvius was there conducting [2]; and it was also very desirable that he should be within reach of the Weser-mouth, where Hamilton's English army was expected to make its landfall; for Hamilton might well require—and had indeed been promised—assistance upon arrival.[3]

As a preliminary to any move upon the Elbe, however, something must be done to complete the clearing of the coastal area. Since the fall of Kolberg, the imperialists' hold on the Pomeranian coastline had been reduced to the town of Greifswald, where Perusi, now wholly cut off, conducted an enterprising if unhopeful defence; but further west Virmond was still well established in Mecklenburg, with a sizeable army of some 9000-10,000 men, and was able to menace any advance on the lower Elbe in flank and rear. It is true that Tott was observing him, with an army somewhat smaller in numbers; but at the end of May there was an alarm that Virmond

[1] See his significant letter to Horn of 17 May, ordering him to make defensive arrangements on the Oder: *Arkiv*, I. 439. His nervousness was increased by the news that Tiefenbach's army in Silesia was being reinforced: Chemnitz, I. 161.

[2] Boëthius, *NSK*, p. 148.

[3] For the history of Hamilton's army, see Hist. MSS. Comm., *Hamilton*, pp. 47, 70-4; Hist. MSS. Comm., *Hamilton Supplementary*, pp. 12-13, 16-18; *Arkiv*, I. 264-5, II. 158-9, 294-7; *AOSB*, I. vi. 53, II. ix. 427-30; *Schriftstücke*, pp. 208-9; Sanford Terry, *Alexander Leslie*, pp. 22-7.

was about to attack,[1] and Tott was given the major share of such reinforcements as were arriving. Some effort to put the position in this area upon a sounder basis was therefore desirable; and no sooner had the treaty with George William been concluded than Gustav Adolf hurried to Stettin. He was met by the news that Perusi had been killed in a sortie, and that Greifswald had at last surrendered.[2] Tott and Karl Banér were now free to begin the invasion of Mecklenburg; John Albert and Albert Frederick could apply themselves to the organization of risings in their favour, in the expectation that this time adequate military support for them would be available. The recovery of Mecklenburg accordingly began. Tott formed the siege of Rostock; Adolf Frederick, on 19 July, took Schwerin by storm; by the beginning of August the imperialists' hold on Mecklenburg had been virtually reduced to Rostock, Wismar and their immediate environs; and on 6 September Rostock capitulated to Tott. The Mecklenburg Dukes, whose expulsion had formed so heavy an item in the account against Wallenstein and the Emperor, were solemnly reinstated in their duchies. All Germany might see that the high tide of imperialist triumph was upon the ebb: the submerged political landscape was beginning once more to appear above the waters.[3]

The news of the fall of Greifswald convinced Gustav Adolf that he had no need to devote his personal attention to Mecklenburg. On 23 June he was back at Spandau; and on the same day he announced his determination to advance on the Elbe.[4] He was by no means too soon. Since the middle of the month the imperialist dispositions had been modified. Tilly himself remained for the moment in Thuringia, with 17,000 men; but the army at Magdeburg had been strongly reinforced, and Pappenheim, who had been sent to command it, had now nearly 13,000 men at his disposal. He had an outpost east of the Elbe at Burg; he was constructing a bridge of boats at Tangermünde; and he was contemplating the seizure of Havelberg, with the idea of establishing a bridgehead on the northern shore of the Havel. Gustav Adolf now moved his main force to the lower Havel and set about fortifying a line of towns (Rathenow, Brandenburg, Fehrbellin, Spandau) to form a barrier to any

[1] *Arkiv*, II. 262.

[2] *ibid.*, II. 276; Chemnitz, I. 175.

[3] For the Mecklenburg campaign, see Chemnitz, I. 189-91; *Sv. Krig*, IV. 350-9; Droysen, II. 374; Boëthius, *NSK*, pp. 166-83.

[4] *Arkiv*, I. 454.

imperialist thrust beyond the river. The Swedish base was thus extended to the south-west; and this new base area was to be defended, as the coastal base already was, by a well-planned chain of fortified positions. At the same time he began to send out offensive cavalry patrols towards the west.[1] And on 28 June he himself broke up from Brandenburg; and taking 2000 'commanded' musketeers and all his cavalry, marched by way of Jerichow for the Elbe. Slipping between the imperialist positions at Werben and Burg, he reached the river opposite Tangermünde. The exceptionally dry summer made it possible for his infantry to ford the Elbe[2]; the imperialists were taken by surprise; and Tangermünde fell to the Swedes, with little opposition, on 2 July.

The capture of Tangermünde implied a sharp change in the military situation. Gustav Adolf was now across the Elbe in force; Pappenheim withdrew his outposts on the eastern bank; a rich supply area was laid open to the Swedish armies[3]; the initiative had passed once more into the King's hands. And the first great step had been taken into central Germany, away from that coastal belt which had hitherto been deep enough to accommodate his campaigning: it was at Jerichow that the Swedes marched off the maps which they had brought from Sweden[4]—a detail significant for the light it sheds on the depth of penetration foreseen in 1630.

In the first week of July Gustav Adolf was considering how best to use the opportunity which his swift movement had given him. He was conscious of an obligation to do something to distract Tilly's attention from Hesse; and he considered either an advance upon Magdeburg, which would draw Tilly northwards, or a strong cavalry raid into Silesia, which might divert his attention to the east.[5] It soon appeared that Tilly was too close to him for either to be practicable. He decided, therefore, upon a rapid concentration of available forces, so that he might be able to offer battle when the imperialists should approach. Most of the foot had been left behind to work on the fortifications which were feverishly building on the

[1] Chemnitz, I. 176.

[2] They crossed the Elbe, as Monro remembered, by wading 'where never one was seene to passe with Cannon before': Monro, II. 49.

[3] It was urgently needed. Even on 16 July Gustav Adolf wrote from Werben to Oxenstierna that he was 'abandoned by all our servants [at home], and able to carry on the war only *ex rapto*, to the damage and annoyance of all our friends', and referred to the 'intolerable plundering and robberies' of his troops: *AOSB*, II. 1. 734; and *cf. Arkiv*, I. 454.

[4] *Arkiv*, I. 461.

[5] *ibid.*, I. 470, 473-5, 759.

Havel line[1]; but Banér was now ordered to seize Havelberg[2] (he took it by storm on 12 July), and all other troops that could be spared were called to the Elbe. Tangermünde, however, was not entirely suitable as a rendezvous. Gustav Adolf needed a strong defensive position behind which his incoming troops could gather, and Tangermünde did not fulfil this requirement. It was also uncomfortably near to Magdeburg. On 10 July, therefore, he decided to move north to Werben.[3]

Werben lies on the western bank of the Elbe, opposite to the point at which the Havel falls into it. The Elbe here makes a semicircular bend to the west, and the town of Werben stands within it. Across this extensive arc Gustav Adolf now drew a chord of defensive works, with Werben itself as a strong-point in the centre; and behind these defences he established in the level water-meadows—conveniently drained of their ordinary marshiness by the long drought—a great camp, connected to the eastern bank of the Elbe by a bridge of boats. Strategically the position was admirable, since it commanded both Elbe and Havel, and left great freedom for operations in any direction. As an example of field-fortification, it won the admiration of contemporaries, and not least of Tilly.[4] Tactically it was not without its anxieties, since a single bridge was the sole available line of retreat.[5]

Within the perimeter at Werben Gustav Adolf rapidly collected a considerable army. Heavy reinforcements were taken from Tott in Mecklenburg and from Horn on the Oder; the defence line from Havelberg to Küstrin was stripped to the danger-point; George William was explicitly warned that his left flank was being exposed to any enemy who should care to risk a raid, and advised to shut himself in his fortresses.[6] By 20 July Gustav Adolf had 15,000 men at Werben, including 6000 cavalry; and he had no less than 150 guns.[7] Within a further ten days, he hoped, his strength would have risen to 24,000. He was anxious to fight Tilly; and he was anxious to fight him soon, before the reinforcements from the army of Italy

[1] *Dagbok förd i det svenska fältkansliet*, p. 20.

[2] *Arkiv*, I. 463; *Dagbok*, p. 20.

[3] He had been considering this move as early as 5 July: *Arkiv*, I. 464.

[4] *Sv. Krig*, IV. 382.

[5] See the comments on the prevailing fondness for defensive positions of this type (*cf.* the Swedish position at Marienburg) in Wijn, *Het Krijgswezen in de Tijd van Prins Maurits*, p. 405; and for an example of consequent disaster (Jemmingen, 1568), *ibid.*, p. 490.

[6] *Schriftstücke*, p. 134 *seqq.*

[7] This figure includes, of course, light regiment-pieces.

should have arrived [1]; for he already knew that the Italian levies had crushed the incipient resistance of south-west Germany,[2] and that some of them, at least, were now on their way north. But before the Swedish concentration was complete Tilly was upon him.

The news of Gustav Adolf's swoop on Tangermünde galvanized Tilly into action. For nearly a month he had been passive in Thuringia, uncertain where to turn, and prepared for trouble from all quarters. The King's initiative forced him north, to cover Magdeburg. Pappenheim was summoned to join him; and by 20 July their junction had been effected. Tidings of Tilly's approach reached the King on 14 July; and two days later he led a strong force of cavalry in the direction of Wolmirstedt—partly, as it seems, to reconnoitre, partly to give his horsemen an opportunity of matching themselves against the imperialist cavalry. At Burgstall and Angern, on 18 July, they succeeded in surprising the enemy; to such good effect that three imperialist regiments were scattered in rout.[3] The action had a tonic influence on the morale of the Swedish horse, and it was heavily publicized by Gustav Adolf's propaganda [4]; but its most immediate value was that it provided prisoners from whom the King learned with certainty that Tilly intended to attack Werben: it had earlier seemed possible that he might strike at the Havel, or even thrust past the Swedish position and drive into Mecklenburg.[5] The imperialist army was for the moment somewhat larger than the Swedish; and Tilly, too, was anxious for battle. But the aspect of the Werben position, when at last he came in sight of it, was sufficient to cool even Pappenheim's impetuosity. Tilly's march had not been quick enough to catch the Swedes with their breastworks half-finished; for 'where he did but march with his Army in the day time, we with spades and shovells, wrought our selves night and day in the ground, so that, before his coming, we had put ourselves out of danger of his Cannon'.[6] It is possible that Gustav Adolf, confronted by such defences, might have ventured an assault; but certainly no other general of that age would have risked it. The fighting of 27 and 28 July, therefore, resolved itself into reciprocal cannonading, sorties in strength and fierce skirmishing outside the Werben perimeter. The King had every motive for encouraging Tilly to remain,

[1] *Arkiv*, I. 478, 481.
[2] *Schriftstücke*, p. 135.
[3] Chemnitz, I. 185.
[4] *Sv. Krig*, IV. 385 *note* 1.
[5] Generalstaben, *Gustaf II Adolf*, pp. 266-8; Boëthius, *NSK*, p. 168.
[6] Monro, II. 49.

for he expected by the end of the month to be in sufficiently superior strength to risk a general engagement. But Tilly soon decided that there was nothing to be effected at Werben; and in any case he was in difficulties with his supplies. On 29 July he withdrew his forces and returned to Tangermünde, there to await reinforcements; and near Tangermünde for the moment he remained, a potential threat to the Swedish defences on the lower Havel.[1]

The actions at Werben constituted a considerable military success. In the first direct encounter with the ever-victorious Tilly—the commander (so his soldiers believed) especially favoured by fortune—Gustav Adolf had decidedly come off best. The event greatly heartened his army; and it enhanced his own confidence: he would not in future listen, as he had listened at Pasewalk, to councils of war urging caution in the face of Tilly's redoubtable experience. The damage to his reputation sustained at Magdeburg was fully repaired; and in a military aspect Werben was not, as Magdeburg had been, a barren victory. Wallenstein, maliciously observing from his retirement the difficulties of his successor, had no doubt of the significance of what had happened; and he told the Saxon chamberlain Lebzelter that in Gustav Adolf the Emperor had provoked the most dangerous enemy he had yet encountered.[2]

Nor were the advantages that flowed from Werben wholly military; for the discomfiture of Tilly lent impetus to certain political trends which had already begun to be apparent. In May and June there is no doubt that the men who were at the heart of Swedish policy—the King, Oxenstierna, Lars Grubbe—were all disillusioned and cynical about the German Protestant princes. In mid-June Grubbe was suggesting that the King, after establishing an advanced defence-line along the Elbe, might well withdraw to Sweden, leaving a token-force under a subordinate.[3] A week later, he wrote:

From all this one can easily judge the counsels of the German princes, namely that they still try to be neutral; but yet seek by recruiting soldiers (and thanks to the nearness and assistance of His Majesty's army) to recover their liberty. And when they shall have attained that, it is pretty

[1] For Werben, see *Arkiv*, II. 297-300; *AOSB*, II. I. 737; Monro, II. 50-8; Chemnitz, I. 186-8; *Sv. Krig*, IV. 295-7, V. 331.

[2] Hallwich, *Wallenstein und Arnim*, p. 149.

[3] *Arkiv*, II. 280; and on 23 July Gustav Adolf wrote to George William threatening to withdraw to Stettin and leave him to his fate unless he was more punctual with his contributions; Bär, p. 287.

clear that they will make all speed to be rid of him. And since His Majesty's intent goes no further than to a restoration of public liberty, so I think that if he can get proper satisfaction for his great outlay, he may well rest content with that.[1]

The King's feelings were similar: he told the *råd*, on 2 July, that the Protestants of Germany 'are no further disposed towards us than that they may be maintained by us against the Emperor, and that they may put themselves under the protection of our arms for the recovery of their former freedom; after which they will be ready, one and all, to drive us away with violence and ingratitude'.[2] And Oxenstierna from his Prussian outpost wrote scornfully that from Brandenburg and Saxony nothing better was to be expected. But with his usual acuteness he added the conjecture that this '*motus universalis Germaniae*' could hardly fail to make a considerable change in the position.[3] He was quite right. The Leipzig allies, whose uncoordinated efforts were menaced with suppression, began now to look to Sweden for succour; and here and there in Germany the patient labours of Swedish diplomacy showed signs at last of paying a modest dividend. Gustav Adolf, whatever his mental reservations, was not disposed to refuse it.

In the Lower Saxon Circle, Salvius had been working intermittently for the past year to bring members to some useful resolution.[4] Until May 1631 Gustav Adolf would have been willing, for the sake of effective aid, to enter into an alliance with the Circle as a whole, or with some league formed out of its members; since the area was of great importance to him as opening up a line of advance along the Weser, and as the intended field of operations for Hamilton's army when at last it should arrive. He had been ready, therefore, to conclude upon terms which would leave a large measure of independence to his allies; and he had even been prepared, at a pinch, to acquiesce in the choice of Kristian IV as captain of the forces of the Circle. Swedish policy towards Denmark had been outwardly conciliatory since the summer of 1630. Gustav Adolf had no desire to be involved in trouble with his neighbour at a time when the bulk of Sweden's forces was fully engaged in Germany. Nevertheless, Kristian's attitude had more than once caused great anxiety; and both the King and Oxenstierna had long been in a state of

[1] *Arkiv*, I. 755. [2] *ibid.*, I. 456. [3] *AOSB*, I. VI. 342.

[4] For a very detailed account of Swedish diplomacy in the Circle at this time, see Boëthius, *NSK*, pp. 10-140; and Lundgren, *Salvius*, p. 27 *seqq.*

simmering alarm about Danish naval preparations, Danish claims to Rügen, Danish designs upon Kolberg, Danish tolls off Ruden, Danish intrigues with Tilly, Wallenstein and the Tsar. Despite the financial weakness of Denmark and the strong pacifism of Kristian's council, Oxenstierna considered another war to be sooner or later inevitable; though he felt (as did the *råd* and the secret committee, both of whom were consulted) that nothing should be done to precipitate it.[1] The need to avoid giving provocation to Denmark had made Salvius's task in the Lower Saxon Circle one of difficulty and delicacy; for Kristian was at odds with his neighbour, Frederick III of Holstein-Gottorp; he was the irreconcilable enemy of John Frederick of Bremen, whose see he coveted for one of his sons; his greed for the bishopric of Schwerin complicated his relations with the Dukes of Mecklenburg; while his aggression upon Hamburg had driven that city to look for protection to the Emperor.

With the drawing up of the *Norma*, however, Swedish policy in the Circle began to change, though it took Salvius some little time to bring his actions into conformity with the new course.[2] The aim now was no longer an alliance with the Circle as a whole, but rather a series of treaties with individual members of it; it was no longer supposed that the Circle might be left to effect its liberation by its own efforts; and less care was taken of Kristian's feelings. As early as 6 May Gustav Adolf had reached an understanding with John Albert of Mecklenburg, who promised on behalf of himself and his brother to enter into an alliance of the type of the *Eventualkonföderation*, and accepted a military command which virtually put him in the position of a Swedish general, and a general of somewhat inferior rank at that.[3] The signing of a treaty was indeed deferred for the present, for Adolf Frederick still hoped to enter the Swedish alliance as member of a wider league; but in practice the Dukes were now bound to Gustav Adolf. The first treaty in the spirit of the *Norma* to be actually concluded was that with John Frederick of Bremen, signed on 23 July.[4] John Frederick had been clamouring for it since

[1] The danger from Denmark occupies much space in the correspondence of the period: see *AOSB*, I. VI. 26-40, 72, 89, 140, 286, II. I. 686, 689, 709; Adlersparre, III. 220-2, 258-9, 267, 269; *Arkiv*, I. 188, 313, 409, 456-7, II. 29, 208-12; Stiernman, I. 828 *seqq.*; *RRP*, II. 55; Fridericia, *YPH*, 177-9, 190-8; Boëthius, *NSK*, pp. 11, 26-9, 78-87, 98, 100; Erslev, II. 271-2.

[2] Grubbe wrote to Salvius on 5 May 1631: 'De directorio [of the Circle] nemo . . . ex iis, qui Lipsiae fuerunt, S.R.M:ti quicquam tribuere dignati sunt. Aliis igitur artibus horum hominum ambitiosa temeritas erit corrigenda': Boëthius, *HT* (1911), pp. 161-2; *id.*, *NSK*, p. 141 *seqq.*

[3] Boëthius, *NSK*, pp. 62-3.

[4] *Sverges traktater*, V. 463-73.

mid-March. He now accepted Swedish protection; and in return placed his military resources entirely at the King's disposal, the supreme command in Bremen being to be exercised by a deputy of Gustav Adolf's appointing. The alliance was to be for the duration of hostilities only; it was to take precedence over all other treaties (though John Frederick reserved his obligations under the Leipzig resolution and as a member of the Circle); possible disputes between the parties were to be decided by arbitration; and though Gustav Adolf's right to occupied enemy lands as a security for his war expenses was safeguarded, the treaty gave him no ground for claims on this score against his ally. Finally, in order to ensure the continuance of the alliance in the event of John Frederick's death, it was provided that the treaty was also to be subscribed by the Estates of the diocese. Except for the last proviso, the Bremen treaty was in every respect the sort of instrument which the *Norma* had envisaged, and of which the *Eventualkonföderation* had been the original blueprint.[1]

Gustav Adolf would have been glad of an alliance of this type with one or other of the members of the house of Welf. The Welfs were at this time divided into two main branches: the senior line, of Brunswick-Wolfenbüttel, represented now by the elderly and childless Duke Frederick Ulric; and the junior line, of Lüneburg-Celle, with Duke Christian at its head. Christian was unmarried; but his younger brother George was married and had children, and George was heir-presumptive to the whole Welf inheritance, and the hope of his family. The Wolfenbüttel branch had taken an actively Protestant part in the earlier years of the war, and Frederick Ulric had suffered for his aid to Kristian IV; but his cousins in Celle had been moderate imperialists, and George had until very recently been serving in the imperialist armies. On the day Gustav Adolf landed, however, he resigned his commission, and since then he had shown a desire to take service with Sweden, provided he could be given an assurance that he would not be required to bear arms against the Emperor. Gustav Adolf could give no such assurance; but he issued a commission for George which was held in suspense until he should choose to take it up.[2]

When, therefore, on 29 May Gustav Adolf ordered Salvius to

[1] Boëthius, *NSK*, pp. 91-2, 150-2; Ritter, III. 494; Droysen, *Die niedersächsische Kreisstände während des schwedisch-deutschen Krieges*, pp. 18-19.

[2] Kretzschmar, *Gustav Adolfs Pläne und Ziele*, pp. 1-10; Boëthius, *NSK*, pp. 110, 123.

make an exploratory visit to Wolfenbüttel and Celle, he could count on at least one sympathizer among the Welfs. Nevertheless, Salvius had but poor success. Frederick Ulric was in no position to risk the anger of the imperialists; while Christian of Celle pleaded his prior commitments under the Leipzig resolution and complained with justifiable acerbity of the intolerable excesses of Gustav Adolf's German troops in the country west of the Elbe.[1] He did, however, send an emissary to see Gustav Adolf at Werben, charged *inter alia* to support the plea of Anton Günther of Oldenburg for a Swedish recognition of his neutrality.[2] The Emperor had already recognized it; and Gustav Adolf, though he had earlier been reluctant to do so, since Hamilton might wish to land on Oldenburg territory, was now prepared to offer a somewhat ambiguous guarantee (which he afterwards attempted to evade) in view of the fact that the treaty with John Frederick of Bremen was thought to have secured a safe port of disembarkation for the English army.[3] But this concession had little effect on Christian of Celle; and the utmost his envoy was prepared to offer was an exiguous monetary contribution to the Swedish war-chest.[4] Gustav Adolf did not decline it. But the day was not far distant when the Welfs would find themselves confronted with Swedish demands of a very different order.

Meanwhile the Leipzig allies of south Germany had met with disaster. As the imperial troops under Fürstenberg debouched from the Alpine passes the defiance of the Protestant Estates broke against a force that was too strong for them. Memmingen and Kempten submitted on 7 June; Julius Frederick of Württemberg on 1 July; Ulm eleven days later. They renounced the Leipzig resolution, disbanded their troops and opened their lands as quarters to the imperialists.[5] Hesse and Weimar, menaced by Tilly's Thuringian army, could give no help; and though Solms sent off a column, resistance collapsed before it could reach Württemberg. The moral was not lost upon the Estates of Franconia: their meeting at Nuremberg, summoned to organize resistance, ended by granting a heavy contribution to the Emperor.[6]

Amid the general collapse, two or three Protestant leaders con-

[1] Kretzschmar, *op. cit.*, pp. 10-12; Boëthius, *NSK*, p. 165.

[2] *Dagbok*, pp. 22-3.

[3] *Sverges traktater*, V. 473-6. The Oldenburg question had been under discussion for the last six months or more: *AOSB*, I. vi. 47; Boëthius, *NSK*, pp. 66-75.

[4] 1800 *rdr.* a month: Kretzschmar, *op. cit.*, p. 13.

[5] Chemnitz, I. 181-3.

[6] *Sv. Krig*, IV. 293-305; Schott, pp. 350-1.

trived to keep their courage. One was Solms, active as ever in the Swedish interest. Another was Bernard of Weimar; and a third was William of Hesse. Bernard had tried in vain to keep his brother constant to his engagements and steadfast in the Swedish alliance; and when it was clear that his leadership could no longer be reckoned on, Bernard boldly took his own line and hastened to Gustav Adolf at Werben. He arrived in time to distinguish himself in the fighting, and was presently appointed to a Swedish command; so beginning an association with Sweden which was to outlast the King's lifetime.[1]

William of Hesse had doggedly persisted in his policy, despite the fall of Magdeburg, the defection of William of Weimar and the crushing of resistance in south Germany. For a time, in June, it had seemed impossible that his small army should escape destruction. Tilly lay on the south-east border of Hesse, preparing to overrun it; and no help seemed likely. To a blunt enquiry as to whether he intended to stand by the resolution of Leipzig, John George returned a shuffling and evasive answer.[2] The Landgrave did not change his measures. And at the last moment came deliverance. Gustav Adolf's stroke at Tangermünde forced Tilly to defer a reckoning with Hesse; only a small corps of imperialists was left to keep an eye on the situation; and this corps the Landgrave promptly attacked and dispersed. His victory laid bare Tilly's precarious line of communications: the passes of the Thuringian forest were no longer safe for imperialist waggons; money to pay Tilly's troops could get no further north than Würzburg.[3] And since William V had now irrevocably committed himself, he did not hesitate to draw the logical deduction: at the end of July, after a last interview with John George, he made his way to Gustav Adolf; and on 12 August, at Werben, the Hessian-Swedish treaty of alliance was concluded.[4]

The Hessian alliance, like the alliance with Bremen, was framed in the spirit of the *Norma*, for it was based (as the *Norma* too was based) on the *Eventualkonföderation* of 1630. It was to endure until the aims of the allies were attained, and in the meantime was to be 'fixed and indissoluble'; it gave to Gustav Adolf the absolute directory, and put the Landgrave's military resources entirely at his disposal; and it bound Gustav Adolf to continue the war until Hesse had been restored to the limits of 1618. The Landgrave, on his side,

[1] *Dagbok*, p. 22; Chemnitz, I. 187.
[2] Helbig, p. 50; Rommel, VIII. 116 *note* 138, 118, 123.
[3] *Sv. Krig*, IV. 311.
[4] *Sverges traktater*, V. 476-90; *Dagbok*, p. 23; Rommel, VIII. 124 *seqq*.

promised to maintain 10,000 men and to fight in defence of any non-Hessian lands which Gustav Adolf might conquer, until Sweden had been given a satisfactory war indemnity in place of them. Gustav Adolf was given the right to appoint a deputy to command the Hessian troops in his absence; but it was laid down in the treaty that that deputy should be William himself—a tactful circumvention of one of the less acceptable points of the *Eventualkonföderation*. The Landgrave, however, accepted an appointment to command troops to be raised for Sweden in the Rhenish Circles [1]; and thus became, like John Albert of Mecklenburg and Bernard of Weimar, the military subordinate of the Swedish King. Each party was to send a qualified representative to the other, to maintain liaison between them; a common war-chest was to be established; and neither side was to make claims for compensation against the other. For the next three months the alliance was to be open to other states who might wish to join it, on the same terms. Finally, a special paragraph declared that the League had violated the promises given on its behalf by the French ambassador at Bärwalde, and was now to be held as an open enemy.[2] It was a plain warning to Richelieu that Gustav Adolf did not propose to dance to French piping.

The Hessian treaty gave Gustav Adolf his first important ally in central Germany. And not the first only, but the most undaunted, the most loyal and, on the whole, the ablest. William V joined the Swedes without reservations or qualifications. Duty to the Emperor, respect for the imperial constitution, weighed less with him than with any other German ruler of standing. The descendant of Philip of Hesse was not afraid of revolution, nor was he prepared to balk at the consequences to which the logic of events might lead him. His political audacity, his military gifts and his unwavering fidelity were to make him the chief bulwark of the Swedish system in Germany. Yet he was, after all, in territory and military resources a German prince only of the second rank. Gustav Adolf might with reason look upon the alliance with the Landgrave as the pattern of what such a treaty should be [3]; but it remained as true as ever that he might

[1] And Gustav Adolf gave him 'eine starcke Post Geldes', so that he might recruit them: Chemnitz, I. 198.

[2] An almost identical paragraph had been included already in the Bremen treaty: *Sverges traktater*, V. 467.

[3] '. . . gleichsamb eine Richtschnur vnd *regul* gewesen, nach deren Massgebung die andern [*sc.* alliances] alle abgefasset und eingerichtet worden': Chemnitz, I. 194.

be prepared to swallow terms much less favourable to Sweden if by doing so he could enlist the aid of John George. As the regiments from Italy made their way north in ever-increasing numbers, Gustav Adolf needed large reinforcements if he were to be able to meet Tilly in battle and so prevent an imperialist concentration for the destruction of Hesse. Additional numbers, on the scale he required, could come only from Saxony. John George's attitude would decide, in all probability, the fate of the Landgrave; and it might well decide whether the advanced Swedish position on the Elbe could be maintained, or whether Gustav Adolf must fall back again upon the bastion of Pomerania.

(iii) *Breitenfeld*

In the weeks that intervened between the sack of Magdeburg and the skirmishes at Werben, John George's political system crumbled away. If ever he had been sincere in his support of the idea of a third party, it was now plain that such a policy was bankrupt. Its leading supporters had been driven into other courses: Bernard and the Landgrave had thrown themselves into the arms of Sweden, the Mecklenburg Dukes were in process of restoration by Swedish aid, George William had been constrained to an understanding with his brother-in-law, William of Weimar was a temporarily discredited fugitive. The Leipzig allies in south and central Germany had been terrorized into submission. Any chance of using the third party as an instrument for purely Saxon ends had vanished, and none now looked to John George as a potential saviour of the evangelical cause. The Elector was isolated; a great part of the odium of Magdeburg had been transferred to him; and there could be less hope than ever of inducing Ferdinand, by a military demonstration, to temper his measures in Saxony's favour.

It might well seem reasonable, in this situation, for the Elector to conclude that the best course now open to him was to follow Hesse's example and throw in his lot with Gustav Adolf. But John George tried hard to avoid drawing this conclusion. Neutrality might still be possible if he could raise an army quickly enough, and in sufficient strength, to discourage imperialist aggression. It was true that the good faith of the Emperor appeared, in the light of the information provided by John George's intelligence, to be more than dubious; but a policy of prudence and firmness might still conceivably avert a breach. An alliance with Sweden, on the other hand, would be a blow to John George's self-esteem, it would be a violation of his principles, it would make certain a war with the Emperor—a war in which he would play second fiddle on the Protestant side, a war in which his still-unravaged lands would be devoted to plunder. Nor was there much ground, if the experience of Brandenburg and Pomerania were any criterion, to hope for generous or considerate treatment from a Swedish ally.

When Magdeburg fell, an imperial agent had already been for some time in Leipzig, trying by good words and vague promises to wean the Elector from his allies.[1] The interviews were friendly; and the news from Magdeburg only made John George the more anxious to avoid offence. He would not stop his recruiting, which (as he explained over and over again) was purely defensive in object; but he acceded very readily to a suggestion that he should attempt to mediate between Tilly and Gustav Adolf.[2] But when he approached Tilly early in June, he found imperial policy speaking in harsher accents. Tilly, already harassed and depressed by the signs of revolt in Hesse, was alarmed and angry at John George's military preparations and chagrined at the apparent unwillingness of Vienna to take a strong line about them. In an interview with the Saxon envoys on 10 June he spoke in tones of unmistakable menace.[3] For years, he told them, the Protestants had held the whip hand in Germany: now it was the Catholics' turn. The peace of Augsburg had never been regarded by the Emperor as anything more than an interim arrangement; and the opportunity for its revision had at last arrived. And if John George were really anxious for good relations with the Emperor, let him renounce his secularized lands voluntarily, before they were taken from him by force. Such language was premature, and outran the Emperor's desires; for just a week earlier he had despatched a letter to Tilly ordering him to treat the Elector with consideration: Ferdinand still hoped that persuasion might induce John George to disarm.[4] But this letter did not reach headquarters until 27 June; and in the meantime it is reasonable to suppose that Tilly's threats must have given the Elector a severe shock. Six weeks later, on 23 July, at the moment when the united forces of Tilly and Pappenheim were beginning their advance against Werben,

[1] Droysen, II. 375-6.
[2] Chemnitz, I. 183.
[3] Wittich, pp. 688-92; Helbig, p. 49; Droysen, II. 378; *Sv. Krig*, IV. 274-5.
[4] *Sv. Krig*, IV. 279.

Tilly reinforced the impression: he sent to John George a sharp demand for the disbandment of his levies.[1] The Elector, in a reply dated 6 August, suggested that Tilly should send representatives to discuss the position. But this was a mere device to gain time; for already by the beginning of August John George seems to have decided that a conflict could hardly be avoided. That the imperialists should have evicted the Mecklenburg Dukes was a deplorable and arbitrary exercise of the prerogative; that Pomerania and Brandenburg should be gutted by Wallenstein's soldiery was deeply regrettable; but that Saxony should be deprived of the plunder of the Reformation was utterly intolerable. Rather than endure that, he would even collaborate with Gustav Adolf.

On 7 August—that is, on the morrow of his offer to Tilly to negotiate—John George sent Vitzthum to Gustav Adolf at Werben.[2] He was instructed to ask what measures the King proposed to take if Tilly should move across the Havel and threaten Berlin; and he was to make a definite and noteworthy offer: if Gustav Adolf, in that event, would undertake to deal with Tilly, John George would hold the Thuringian passes and prevent Fürstenberg's forces from coming up from the south. Gustav Adolf was probably surprised by this proposal: his last letter to Arnim (written on 5 July, upon a rumour that Tilly had already invaded Saxony) had contained a somewhat unhopeful adjuration to stand fast, or at the worst to see that the Saxon troops had a chance to take service in the Swedish army.[3] Vitzthum's mission, in fact, marked a decisive change in the Elector's policy; and no one was better qualified to appreciate that than Gustav Adolf. But if it was now clear that imperialist pressure was doing what Swedish argument had failed to do, that was no reason to acquiesce in so vague and undigested a scheme of common action as that which was now presented to him. Vitzthum was sent back on 10 August with an intimation that any military collaboration must be based upon a settled plan and be preceded by some formal agreement; and that it would be well if the King could meet the Elector for an exchange of views.[4] Gustav Adolf rightly deduced that the circumstances which had led John George to depart so far from his previous line of policy would in the end force him to seek the Swedish alliance; and an alliance he meant to have, if he

[1] Droysen, II. 390-1.
[2] *Sv. Krig*, IV. 426-7; Droysen, II. 390.
[3] *Schriftstücke*, pp. 206-8.
[4] *Dagbok*, p. 23; Helbig, p. 51; *Sv. Krig*, IV. 428-9.

could get it. But John George, despite his lively fears of imperial designs, still hoped to meet them without tying himself irrevocably to Sweden: a casual and temporary co-operation, a quick victory, a settlement with the Emperor which would protect him from the Edict of Restitution, and then neutrality—or even collaboration with all good Germans to pack the Swedes back to Sweden: this was the kind of programme which John George in his more sanguine moments proposed to himself.[1]

The event proved otherwise than he had imagined it. On 13 July Ferdinand had at last yielded to Tilly's argument that resolute measures were necessary with Saxony. On that day he wrote to him, leaving it to his discretion to take such action as he should think appropriate in order to bring the Elector and the Landgrave to obedience.[2] This letter reached Tilly shortly before the middle of August; and on 14 August he sent off a virtual ultimatum to John George, demanding the stopping of recruiting and the transfer of the troops already raised to the imperial armies.[3] On 17 August Vitzthum reported to John George the result of his mission to Werben; on 19 August Tilly's ultimatum arrived. It seems likely that it was prompted by reports of Vitzthum's visit to Gustav Adolf; and it is probable too that John George may have got wind of the Emperor's letter, and was thus not entirely taken by surprise. Tilly, in fact, felt himself forced to take action against the Elector in order to forestall his probable junction with Gustav Adolf; while John George was driven to closer association with Sweden than he desired, in order to protect himself against an invasion which seemed to be impending. But if on 14 August Tilly made up his mind that a campaign in Saxony was probable—and in view of his acute shortage of supplies it would certainly not be unwelcome [4]—his best chance of success was already passing. From his position at Tangermünde it would have been possible for him in the early days of August to

[1] It is noteworthy that as late as 18 August Kristian IV remained very sceptical as to the prospect of a Swedish-Saxon alliance: *Christian IVs Breve*, II. 353-4.

[2] Lundorp, III. 204-8; *Sv. Krig*, IV. 407; Paul, II. 219 and *note* 1. Droysen's awkward habit of dating documents of Protestant origin Old Style, and those of Catholic origin New Style, makes his treatment of this period particularly confusing, and seems even to have confused himself: on the same page he seems to date the Emperor's letter as 13 May and (in a note) 23 June: Droysen, II. 378 and *note* 1.

[3] Wittich, pp. 726, 735; Droysen, II. 391.

[4] Ernstberger contended that Wallenstein deliberately sabotaged Tilly's position by ensuring that supplies from his duchy of Mecklenburg should not reach him, and so forced him into an attack on Saxony in order to save his army: A. Ernstberger, *Wallensteins Heeressabotage und die Breitenfelder Schlacht*, *passim*; *cf.* Clausewitz, pp. 39-44; Wittich, p. 745; Paul, III. 10.

move rapidly southwards, cross the Saale at Halle, thrust himself between Gustav Adolf and John George, and so dispose of the Saxons before their recruiting was complete. No sooner had he sent his ultimatum than he did in fact leave Tangermünde; and a week later (on 21 August) he effected his junction with Fürstenberg's reinforcements at Eisleben.[1] But already on 14 August Gustav Adolf had transferred his headquarters to Brandenburg[2]; and at Brandenburg he was within easy distance of Wittenberg. If Tilly attacked the Elector, Swedish aid would probably arrive in time.

John George's reaction to Tilly's ultimatum was to send back Vitzthum to Gustav Adolf with a renewed and more urgent appeal for help. Vitzthum reached Brandenburg on 20 August.[3] He reported Tilly's threats, and the negotiations then going on at Merseburg; but though he asked for speedy assistance, he had nothing to say about an alliance.[4] It was now clear to Gustav Adolf that a breach between Tilly and the Elector might be expected within a matter of days, and he at once took steps to put himself in a position to be able to intervene effectively. Taking all available cavalry with him, he left Brandenburg the same day by the Wittenberg road; and shortly afterwards ordered a general concentration upon Coswig. At the same time he advised John George to withdraw his troops (at that time assembling round Leipzig) behind the Mulde to Torgau. These movements made a junction of the Swedish and Saxon armies secure, and spoiled Tilly's chance of destroying each of them separately.

Meanwhile, on 21 August, John George replied to the imperialist envoys with a flat rejection of Tilly's demands.[5] On 22 August his answer reached Tilly, who at once began to prepare to attack: on this day he moved his headquarters forward to Halle. On the 23rd John George, on Arnim's representations, accepted Gustav Adolf's advice and withdrew his forces to Torgau; and two days later the imperialist troops were over the border and devastating the country around Halle. But even yet the breach was not made irrevocable:

[1] *Sv. Krig*, IV. 413. Chemnitz, however, makes Tilly stay at Tangermünde only till 11 August: Chemnitz, I. 188.

[2] *Dagbok*, p. 23.

[3] *Arkiv*, II. 302.

[4] *Sv. Krig*, IV. 431-2; *Arkiv*, II. 302; *AOSB*, II. vi. 62-3. Droysen's statement that John George asked for an alliance (*op. cit.*, II. 391) is contradicted by *Arkiv*, II. 302, which is the only evidence he adduces in support of it.

[5] Lundorp, III. 208-10.

on 28 August, though by this time Tilly had captured Merseburg, his ambassadors returned with a last appeal to the Elector. It was in vain: John George refused to allow his troops to be used against the Swedes; and he called one of the ambassadors opprobrious names at dinner.[1] On 29 August Swedish troops entered Wittenberg, amid great demonstrations of enthusiasm from the members of the university[2]; on 30 August George William of Brandenburg arrived in the Swedish camp, with a view, no doubt, of offering his good offices in order to a settlement[3]; and on the 31st came the Elector's final appeal for aid. But even at this moment of extreme peril, when Tilly stood before the gates of Leipzig, John George could not bring himself to mention an alliance, nor did he offer Gustav Adolf any sort of security for the future.[4]

Gustav Adolf repaired the omission. From Wittenberg he sent Dr. Steinberg to the Elector, bearing a draft agreement and an invitation to him to subscribe it. But John George was not prepared to sign it as it stood; and the text which Steinberg took back from Torgau was modified in certain important particulars from the original version. John George was willing to accept the King's absolute direction only for such operations as should be agreed upon between them; for the rest, he would pledge himself only to conform to Swedish directions 'as far as possible'; and he demanded that Gustav Adolf in return should bind himself not to infringe his territorial sovereignty. Gustav Adolf's reply to this was to require that officers in the Saxon army should swear obedience to himself. But if he were prepared to swallow John George's reservations (as by this time he was, since a junction of the armies had become urgently necessary), it was futile to stickle for the oath of obedience: not only Arnim, but also Salvius and Steinberg, advised him to waive it. At last he gave way; and on 2 September an exchange of notes concluded the Saxon alliance.[5]

It was an agreement extorted by necessity, and it was repugnant to the feelings of both the contracting parties. John George had been forced to abandon his hope of getting Swedish help without

[1] *Dagbok*, pp. 24-5; Lundorp, III. 210-11.

[2] *Dagbok*, p. 25.

[3] *ibid.*, *loc. cit.* His arrival was followed by another roystering dinner, punctuated by the shooting off of great ordnance.

[4] *ibid.*, *loc. cit.*

[5] *ibid.*, pp. 25-6. Text of the notes in *Sverges traktater*, V. 513-16. For the concluding phases of John George's dealings with Tilly, see Chemnitz, I. 198-203; *AOSB*, I. vi. 464.

entangling himself in Swedish politics; Gustav Adolf found himself with an ally over whom his control was by no means assured. The position was even worse than in regard to Brandenburg: with George William there was as yet no real alliance at all; but at least Gustav Adolf had practical control of the electorate, and George William's military weakness gave good grounds for supposing that he would retain it. But John George had an army of some size, and in Arnim a commander of some talent; and the terms of the treaty reserved to him an undefined, and therefore dangerous, measure of military independence. The duration of the alliance was stated to be 'as long as the danger from the enemy shall continue'—an expression capable of more than one interpretation in the future. John George, moreover, took care that his agreement should be with Gustav Adolf only; and five years later he was able to deny, with truth, that it bound him in any way to Gustav Adolf's heirs and successors. Each party was (from his own point of view) rightly suspicious of the political designs of the other; and Gustav Adolf almost from the beginning seems to have doubted the Elector's good faith. Yet upon this miserable and insecure basis his German policy was henceforth condemned to be founded; for the Saxon alliance, once obtained, could not with safety be abandoned.

The military situation, however, left no leisure for second thoughts. On 3 September Gustav Adolf crossed the Elbe at Wittenberg; on the next night he camped at Düben, where George William and John George joined him; and here on 5 September the junction of the two armies took place—the spruce accoutrements of the Saxons contrasting sharply with the grimy aspect of the Swedish veterans.[1] On that day, while Leipzig was capitulating to Tilly, the allies held a council of war to decide upon their strategy. Gustav Adolf had privately decided to fight; but since defeat would entail an imperialist occupation of much of Saxony, and the possible forfeiture of two electorates, he felt bound to offer John George the alternative of a diversion, which might draw off Tilly without a battle. Nor was he averse to insuring himself against recriminations afterwards, if the fight should go against them, by placing the

[1] The Saxon army, says Monro, 'for pleasing the eye, was the most complete little Armie, for personages of men, comely statures, well armed, and well arraide, that ever mine eyes did looke on, whose Officers did all looke, as if they were going in their best Apparell and Armes to be painted; where nothing was defective the eye could behold'; whereas the Swedes, 'having lyen over-night on a parcell of plowd ground, they were so dusty, they looked out like Kitchin-servants, with their uncleanely rags': Monro, II. 61-2.

responsibility for engaging the enemy upon the Elector's shoulders. But John George and George William did not hesitate. They would have none of diversions; and Gustav Adolf was able to begin his connexion with Saxony by a show of graceful acquiescence.[1]

Tilly was not averse to battle. In the open country to the north of Leipzig, where the slow swells of ground scarcely break the monotony of the plain, he took up his position at Breitenfeld and awaited attack. The field was of his own choosing, apt for the lumbering movements of the *tercios* and the lavish arabesques of his caracoling heavy cavalry. With Fürstenberg's newly arrived army of 11,000 he could put a force of 35,000 men into the battle; and his 12,000 horse had in Pappenheim the best cavalry commander in Germany. Fugger's corps, indeed, was not with him; but it was doing good service in containing the Landgrave. More serious was the failure of Aldringen's army to arrive in time: when Breitenfeld was fought, it still lay well to the south, beyond Jena.

To meet his adversary Gustav Adolf had his own army, 24,000 strong, and the army of the Elector, which numbered about 18,000; and had thus, at the beginning of the engagement, a considerable numerical superiority.[2] He had, indeed, been more successful than Tilly in concentrating his forces at the vital point. It is true that no less than 13,500 men were locked up in garrisons, and if the day went ill the fortresses they manned would cover his withdrawal to the coast. But Tott was left with but a weak army to complete the cleaning-up of Mecklenburg; and in Silesia a force of no more than 6400 must brave it out against imperialists twice as numerous. The commander here was Hamilton; for when the English army at last arrived, it made its landfall not in the Weser, as ordered, but in Pomerania; and was now perishing of epidemics and unaccustomed food in the Oder valley.

As the lark begunne to peepe, the seventh of September 1631, having stood all night in battaile a mile from Tillies Armie, the Trumpets sound to horse, the Drummes calling to March . . . we begunne the morning

[1] *Arkiv*, I. 492-5; *Dagbok*, pp. 26-7; *AOSB*, II. I. 739. The publication of the *Dagbok* has put an end to the earlier debate on Gustav Adolf's motives at the Düben conference (as, *e.g.*, in Wittich, p. 761; Irmer, *Arnim*, p. 140); the relevant passage runs: 'Weijl aber Ih. M. für Ihre person zur Bataille der Zeit begierig gewesen, ist ohne Zweiffel dieses also discuriert worden, damit Sie die Gemuether, und wie sie recht gesinnet sondieren vnd erfahren möchten.'

[2] For these and all other statistics, *Sv. Krig*, IV. 454-73, replaces all earlier authorities.

with offering our Soules and bodies, as living sacrifices to God . . . which done by us all, we marched forwards in God's name;

—forwards, to a day that was to be glorious for Scotland, and a long memory for Robert Monro, who thus recalled its beginning.[1] In full view of the enemy the allies deployed for battle, unmolested; for Tilly was not minded to lose the advantage of orderly formation by premature attack. They took up their positions, Swedes on the right, Saxons on the left, two self-contained armies ordered differently, each after its own system; over against them Tilly's men, ranged in a single deep dark [2] line of eighteen massive *tercios*, with cavalry on either wing. The heavy guns made hot practice, employing the time that remained before the clash of the armies should make further firing impossible. It was nearly two o'clock [3]; a fine day of warm autumn sunshine, the fields all parched by the drought, the wind strong from the south, and the dust-devils eddying before it. On Tilly's left wing Pappenheim advanced to the attack. The *tercios* of the centre began to roll forward. The battle had begun which was to decide the fate of central Germany.

There followed five hours of desperate fighting [4]: Pappenheim's onslaughts repelled, renewed and repelled, again and again; the Saxon army scattered by the *tercios* and driven from the field in rout, with John George and his lifeguards comfortably in the lead of the fugitives [5]; Horn's inspired counter-attack against overwhelming odds; the change of wind to the west, to match the sudden veering of fortune and blind the eyes of Tilly's hard-pressed infantry; then Swedish victory on both wings, the loss of Tilly's heavy guns, the bloody ruin of the *tercios*—their utter annihilation averted only by discipline, valour and night; and over all the inspissated murk of dust and powder-smoke, through which Gustav Adolf peered myopically, imaginative genius supplying what was wanting in optical precision. As the pursuit died away in the dark, and the Swedes bivouacked on the battlefield, and Gustav Adolf went frugally to rest,[6] there was no doubt of the victory; but only the

[1] Monro, II. 63.
[2] They had the sun (and the wind) at their backs.
[3] Chemnitz, I. 211.
[4] For a fuller discussion of tactical questions, see above, pp. 250-3, 262-3.
[5] *AOSB*, II. I. 739 *seqq.*; N. Belfrage, *Erik Soop och Västgöta ryttare*, p. 91.
[6] *Dagbok*, p. 28: 'Den Abend hatten Ihr. M. für Ihrn. grossen Travail ein schlechte Malzeit, in dem ein Capitain von Oberst Winckels Regiment Derselben Brod vnd ein kaltes Hun gabe, darzu Sie Wasser trincken muessen, biss endlich Wein kame.'

morning revealed its magnitude: 7600 imperialists dead upon the field; 6000 prisoners (all foot); 3000 fled away to Leipzig, to capitulate later; those slain in the pursuit or despatched by vengeful peasants, uncounted and uncountable; the whole of the imperialist artillery taken, and 120 standards to grace the Riddarholm church; Tilly himself wounded, a fugitive in Halle. All in all, the casualties in Tilly's army may have amounted to 20,000 men; on the Swedish side to 2100, and those were more than made good by the great numbers of captured imperialists who took service in the King's army. It was the hand of God, the fulfilment of the prophecies, the harbinger of the new age of Gothic greatness. No wonder that Salvius, when he sat down to write an account of that miraculous day for the members of the *råd* at home, found his exultation run away with him and penned that famous passage which (it is perhaps not fanciful to think) sounds as a jubilant fanfare to announce the arrival of Sweden as a great power:

> Ragged, tattered and dirty were our men (from the continual labours of this last year) besides the glittering, gilded and plume-decked imperialists. Our Swedish and Finnish nags looked but puny, next their great German chargers. Our peasant lads made no brave show upon the field, when set against the hawk-nosed and mustachio'd veterans of Tilly. Yet were they mindful how that with victories continual they had made near the whole circuit of the Baltic Sea, driven the Muscovite into the innermost deeps of Sarmatia, and to the Polack prescribed laws. And as for all these same cullions whom they were now to meet in open field, had they not bundled them out already—not from one or two, but from all the strong places that were in Rügen, Pomerania, the most of Mecklenburg, and the whole Mark of Brandenburg? Wherefore they had the less reason to think twice about oppugning them now, when they had no wall to their defence, but were girt only by a little breastplate of iron about their bodies. And thereupon they fell to, and basted the enemy's hide so briskly, that at last he had no choice but yield.[1]

The victory resounded throughout Europe. In England, the enthusiasm was general; in Poland, Swedish prestige rose with a bound[2]; in Moscow, the news was received with the ringing of bells, thanksgiving services and salutes[3]; and the jubilant Protestants of Germany added a topical verse to Luther's hymn.[4] Ferdinand II

[1] *Arkiv*, II. 308.
[2] *AOSB*, I. VI. 490-1.
[3] D. Norrman, *Gustav Adolfs politik mot Ryssland och Polen*, p. 78.
[4] Paul, II. 225, prints it.

contemplated flight to Graz, or even to Italy, and appealed (in vain) to Urban VIII for sympathy and aid [1]; and the agitation for the recall of Wallenstein was powerfully reinforced.[2] And Richelieu might now begin to ask himself whether he had not taken an overdose of 'poison' into his delicate diplomatic system when he ratified the treaty of Bärwalde.[3] For, as the Infanta reminded Philip IV, the disaster might well force Maximilian into a closer collaboration with Habsburg, and cure him—at least for a time—of his morbid inclinations towards France.[4]

(iv) *From Breitenfeld to Mainz*

On the morrow of the battle of Breitenfeld the imperialist commanders fled north-west, Tilly to Halle, Pappenheim to Merseburg; and in this area they tried to rally the wrecks of their army. But Gustav Adolf took up the pursuit vigorously, leaving John George to enforce the surrender of Leipzig, and Tilly was chased from Halle before he could make a stand. His troops were demoralized, his artillery all gone: the only hope for him was to move west beyond the Weser, to a region where numerous imperial garrisons might provide him with troops and guns. By 14 September, 8000 foot and 5000 cavalry had come in to his standards. He lost no time in putting the Weser between himself and his pursuers; and in the Brunswick country began to reorganize his army as best he could.[5]

In the meantime, the Swedish forces concentrated around Halle; and at Halle, between 14 and 16 September, was held a great council of war to discuss the future conduct of the campaign. John George, with the memory of the Saxon flight at Breitenfeld still painfully fresh, received the King's invitation to the meeting with some embarrassment; but a tactful message from Gustav Adolf made all smooth, and it was not long before the Elector, in an access of un-

[1] Leman, *Urbain VIII*, pp. 37, 43; Ritter, III. 523; Dudík, p. 124.

[2] Priorato, p. 86.

[3] Father Joseph had written to Richelieu of Gustav Adolf (August 1630): 'Il faut se servir de ces choses ainsi que de venins, dont le peu sert de contrepoison et le trop tue': Fagniez, I. 566.

[4] Lonchay, II. 591. It had at first been reported in Madrid that Tilly had been victorious and that Gustav Adolf was his prisoner: Günter, *Der Habsburg-Liga*, p. 63 *note* 11. Philip IV could at least console himself by reflecting that he had urgently warned the Emperor against breaking with John George, even if it were necessary to abandon the Edict of Restitution in order to retain his friendship: *ibid.*, p. 90.

[5] *Sv. Krig*, V. 1-5.

wonted enthusiasm, was making bibulous offers to assist in putting his new ally on the imperial throne.[1]

The immediate point to be decided at Halle was the line to be taken by the allied offensive—or rather, offensives; since neither Gustav Adolf nor John George showed any desire to continue joint operations. Three possible choices seemed to present themselves. They might resume the pursuit of Tilly and complete in Westphalia the work begun at Breitenfeld; they might march straight on Vienna, by way of the Oder or the Bohemian passes; or they might move through Thuringia and Franconia along the *Pfaffengasse* ('Priests' Alley')[2] to the Main and the Rhine. And, assuming that two of these lines were chosen (one for each of the allies), there came the further question as to which of the two was to fall to the share of each. They succeeded without much trouble in eliminating one possibility: the continued pursuit of Tilly was rejected, as likely to inflict damage on the lands of the Protestant princes.[3] The only remaining issue, therefore, was whether Gustav Adolf or John George should be entrusted with the advance towards the Rhine. John George would certainly have preferred this right wing of the allied front to be in his own hands; but Gustav Adolf seems to have been determined to keep it for himself. In the circumstances, it is not remarkable that the King should have had his way. The conference therefore resolved that Arnim and the Saxons should try to obtain a firm foothold in Silesia, while Gustav Adolf and his army should at once move to Thuringia. There they would establish themselves securely; and later would resume the advance on Franconia, relieve the pressure on the Protestants of upper Germany, ravage the *Pfaffengasse*, and offer battle to Tilly if he should venture to intervene.[4]

This decision has given rise to a sharp controversy among historians, and was criticized even by contemporaries. Gustav Horn and Axel Oxenstierna both regarded the move on the Rhine as a mistake; and so too did Arnim, though for different reasons.[5] And

[1] *Arkiv*, II. 309-10.

[2] The *Pfaffengasse* was properly the name applied to the road from Halle to Frankfort: *Vägar och vägkunskap*, p. 48 *note* 5.

[3] Chemnitz, I. 216.

[4] *ibid.*, I. 217: 'da selbst einen rechten *stat* formieren; . . . Folgends nacher Francken seine *marche* nehmen, denen Protestierenden in OberLande Lufft machen, vnd die Pfaffen Gasse heimsuchen; auch dem General Tilly, dafern er es zuverwehren vnterstünde, das Haubt bieten'.

[5] *RRP*, VI. 633, XIV. 115; *Sv. Krig*, V. 20-1; Irmer, *Die Verhandlungen Schwedens . . . mit Wallenstein und dem Kaiser* [cited: Irmer, *VS*], I. 81; Geijer, *Svenska folkets historia*, III. 189; Ahnlund, *Oxenstierna*, p. 610.

Clausewitz, though he conceded that the course Gustav Adolf took might be politically the right one, lent his great authority to the view that strictly military considerations prescribed an immediate thrust at Vienna.[1] Those who defend the King's strategy, moreover, differ in the grounds they advance for their opinion: some [2] contend that his judgment was swayed mainly or wholly by military factors, and was on military grounds correct; others [3] place the main emphasis on political considerations, and seem at times doubtful whether, if political factors are ignored, the decision can be considered sound.

It is certainly true that there were attractive arguments in favour of a Swedish offensive against the Habsburg hereditary lands. Although the Emperor began to recruit feverishly as soon as the news of Breitenfeld reached him, there would have been little organized resistance to be expected in the weeks immediately after the battle apart from Tiefenbach's unimpressive army on the Oder.[4] The Protestants of Bohemia were already in touch with their exiles, and would presumably have assisted the Swedes; while the Saxons had long been committed to championing the evangelical cause in Silesia. It was at least possible that Gustav Adolf, if he had advanced quickly, might have taken Vienna as easily as Arnim was later to capture Prague. The Oder line had long been the route by which he had planned an attack upon the house of Habsburg; it led naturally out of his main base; and a move to the Rhine might well be considered excentric: certainly a march from Mainz to Vienna would be likely to meet with serious hazards. In a political point of view, moreover, Gustav Adolf's presence on the Rhine would bring with it complications with France and England (and this perhaps was Oxenstierna's main objection to it), and might well, as Isabella hoped, throw Bavaria back into the Emperor's arms.[5]

On the other hand, it is very doubtful whether the fall of Vienna (if indeed Gustav Adolf had been able to take it) would have been

[1] Clausewitz, p. 47; but see too pp. 94-5.

[2] G. B. Barkman, *Gustav II Adolfs militära gärning i den krigsvetenskapliga litteraturens belysning*, p. 271; *id.*, *Gustaf II Adolf såsom härorganisatör och fältherre*, pp. 55-62; B. Boëthius, *Några Gustav Adolfs-problem*, pp. 225-7; *Sv. Krig*, V. 8-25; Petri, II. 143-4.

[3] P. Sörensson, *Ekonomi och krigföring under Gustaf II Adolfs tyska fälttåg*, pp. 309-15; L. Tingsten, *Gustav Adolfs politik och krigföring i Tyskland*, pp. 90-1; *id.*, *Några data angående Gustav II Adolfs basering och operationsplaner i Tyskland*, pp. 330-3.

[4] Tingsten, *Några data . . .*, p. 329.

[5] Contrast Söltl, III. 291, where it is suggested that one motive for going to the Rhine may have been the hope of an alliance with England and the Dutch, on the basis of the restoration of Frederick V.

decisive either militarily or politically: if history went for anything, the Habsburgs were uncommonly resilient. And the later stages of the Thirty Years' War showed only too clearly how easily an audacious penetration of enemy territory could culminate, expend its force upon a military vacuum and collapse into a retreat which was sometimes disastrous. A campaign against the Habsburg lands, moreover, would isolate Gustav Adolf from his most reliable allies and take him far from the best recruiting areas. The road to Vienna was bad, and mountainous, and long; and the facilities for water-transport (upon which the availability of big guns partly depended) much inferior to those provided by the valley of the Main.[1] The real military objective, in any case, was not Vienna; for since 1630 the main burden of the enemy's exertions had been borne by Bavaria. And already Gustav Adolf seems to have formulated a grandiose strategy of which the move to the Rhine was a necessary part. The Swedish base area, once confined to the littoral of Pomerania, had latterly been advanced to the Elbe and the Havel, and it had been consolidated by intensive work on the fortifications of the towns which guarded the Havel crossings. The time had now come for another move forward—to Franconia first, and then to the Rhineland; which in its turn would be solidly integrated with the older areas of Swedish control. Thereafter the King would hope to extend his base southwards until it reached to the Protestant areas which were only awaiting his approach to throw off the imperialist yoke. From Württemberg and Baden, it seemed, it ought not to be difficult to shut the Alpine passes against further reinforcements for the Emperor from Italy or Spain; just as possession of the Rhineland would block the way to aid from Brussels or Lorraine. Once this situation was established, Gustav Adolf would be favourably placed for rolling up the whole left flank of the enemy position, and Vienna would be reached at last by an advance from the west over a prostrate Bavaria. Much of this must as yet have been vague in outline; but already it is possible to discern the general contours of a strategy which allotted to John George the part of an anchor or pivot upon which Gustav Adolf could swing, in a vast right-handed sweep, severing successively the enemy's contacts with foreign sources of supply, depriving him one by one of those subjected parts of Germany from which he drew provisions to feed, revenue to pay and recruits to man his armies, until at last the resources of all Germany save

[1] L. Hammarskiöld, *Ur svenska artilleriets hävder*, p. 169.

Bavaria and Austria should be at the King's disposal, and numerically overwhelming forces should deliver the *coup de grâce*.[1]

The execution of a plan of this magnitude could not be entrusted to the inexperienced and unreliable Saxon army, nor could its leadership be made over to the politically dubious hands of John George and Arnim. The right wing of the advance was the positive wing; and it was the wing which was most likely to run into trouble. If Tilly should reconstitute his army, his counter-stroke would fall upon the forces making for Mainz: those forces, therefore, must be Swedish, and they must be under Gustav Adolf's command. It might well be, indeed, that before the Swedish columns reached the Rhine, Tilly would have made a junction with the armies of Spain or Lorraine. But in any event Gustav Adolf calculated that a move to the south-west would force Tilly to quit the Lower Saxon Circle and bring him hurrying back for the defence of Bavaria. The advance towards the Rhine was thus designed not merely as part of a long-range strategy but also as a typical diversion which would liberate Brunswick without a battle and rid the Landgrave of the threat to his dominions. Unlike a move on Vienna, therefore, it would consolidate the Swedish position across the whole breadth of northern Germany; and deliver Mecklenburg from the menace of a sudden thrust across the lower Elbe. And finally it would open up, as the Viennese alternative certainly would not, a highly eligible recruiting area—a military consideration of some moment, in view of Gustav Adolf's expansive plans for next year.

There were thus many arguments of a purely military character in favour of the decision reached at Halle. But it could be contended that the plan had also important political advantages. The alliance with John George had meant the defeat, at least for the moment, of the idea of a middle party in Germany: Gustav Adolf was intelligibly anxious to avoid creating conditions favourable to its revival. The victory at Breitenfeld had proclaimed the passing of the leadership of the evangelical cause from Saxon to Swedish hands; and the King would tolerate no revision of that verdict. If the Protestants of south Germany were (as they appeared to be) on the eve of liberation, their deliverance must not be at the hands of the Elector. The policy of Halle was certainly, in one aspect, a policy designed to shut John

[1] For this, see L. Tingsten, *Några data . . .*, pp. 322-38; *Sv. Krig*, V. 22 and *note* 4, 23, 31, 282-4, 314, 330-8, VI. 7, 16, 33-4, 179, 259; G. B. Barkman, *Gustaf II Adolf såsom härorganisatör och fältherre*, p. 61.

George out of Germany, to thrust him into activity in areas where no significant political advantage was to be reaped by the invader, to embroil him still deeper in those direct hostilities with the Emperor which he had always sought to avoid, and so to make his political dependence on Sweden the more secure. And it may well be that Gustav Adolf was not averse to forestalling any political designs which Richelieu might be entertaining in the Rhineland.[1]

The conclusion that emerges from these considerations is that there was ample military justification for preferring the *Pfaffengasse* to the defiles of the Bohemian forest; and since political advantages pointed the same way, it is perhaps unprofitable to try to evaluate the relative importance of the one as compared with the other. It is true that the surviving evidence alludes exclusively to military considerations; but it seems unrealistic to suppose that the King was oblivious of the political issues involved.[2] All this presupposes, however, that in practice the choice lay simply between Vienna and Mainz. But there was in fact a third possibility. Is it really feasible to dismiss so easily the suggestion that the proper course for Gustav Adolf after Breitenfeld was to press on with the pursuit beyond Halle, keep hard on Tilly's heels, cut off his stragglers, prevent his rallying anywhere, and not relax until the wrecks of his army were ruined beyond the possibility of reconstruction?[3] In the days after Breitenfeld Gustav Adolf (it is difficult to avoid the conclusion) failed to exploit to the utmost a real opportunity to push home his advantage, and so to put Tilly's army out of action for good and all. At this moment the true military objective was neither Vienna, nor Munich, nor Mainz: it was Tilly's army; and it might seem to be a prime consideration to ensure that an army on the run should not be given time to recover its breath. A move to the north-west would have had other advantages: it would have tended to consolidate a Swedish base to the west of the Elbe, and so safeguard Gustav Adolf against imperialist attacks by way of Dömitz in the direction of the

[1] These arguments represent the line taken by Ritter, III. 503; Tingsten, *Gustav Adolfs politik och krigföring*, pp. 90-1; *id.*, *Några data*, pp. 330-3; Sörensson, *op. cit.*, pp. 309-15; Droysen, II. 426. Wibling suggested that Gustav Adolf may have been influenced by the diminished prospects of aid from Transylvania: C. Wibling, *Sveriges förhållande till Siebenbürgen*, p. 47; and Droysen attributed great weight to the King's hopes of action against Vienna by Wallenstein: Droysen, II. 427. Bothe, of course, saw in the advance to the Rhine a move in Gustav Adolf's plans for the economic domination of Germany: *Gustav Adolfs und seine Kanzlers wirtschaftspolitische Absichten auf Deutschland*, p. 104.

[2] This more or less represents Paul's point of view: Paul, III. 9-10.

[3] C. Bennedich, *Ur det gamla Gardets öden*, pp. 79-80, takes this line.

Baltic ports; and it would have delivered the Welfs from the burden, and the Landgrave from the fear, of enemy occupation.[1] And in the sequel (it may be argued) the failure to deal firmly with the Lower Saxon Circle at the most favourable moment that was ever to occur proved infinitely deplorable. Tilly, left in peace to re-form his army, had by mid-October collected a force so formidable that Gustav Adolf believed himself almost on the verge of disaster [2]; while the Lower Saxon Circle remained for the rest of his life something of a 'Spanish ulcer',[3] which his subordinates (partly by their incapacity, partly by the King's fault) proved unable to cure, and to which Gustav Adolf had no leisure to attend. Until this area was firmly under control, the Swedish position between the Saale and the Main was always in danger of being cut in two. The opportunity to concentrate attention on Westphalia and the Lower Saxon Circle presented itself in September 1631. It was missed; and it did not recur. Arnim, whose main aim was the restoration of peace to Germany, expressed the view—almost immediately after Breitenfeld—that the shortest road to peace lay through a Swedish advance against Tilly, and the prevention of any rallying of his army; and at the end of the year, when experience seemed to have justified him, he complained with great bitterness that Gustav Adolf had ignored his advice in this matter.[4] Wallenstein is said to have been of the same opinion.[5] And it appears, indeed, that the King was not unaware of his opportunity: he told a Weimar councillor on 11 September that he intended before turning southwards to follow Tilly to Halberstadt and Aschersleben 'because he is still weak' [6]; and on 18 September he ordered Banér to send a cavalry detachment to take Halberstadt, since he was informed that Tilly was in the neighbourhood 'in great disorder'.[7] The condition of Tilly's troops was such that they could hardly have made a stand: the army's war-

[1] The Landgrave was hurt and alarmed at the Halle decision, and appealed urgently for help: *AOSB*, II. VIII. 54; Rommel, VIII. 150-5; Droysen, II. 450 *note* 3.

[2] See below, p. 552.

[3] Steinberg once truly remarked, 'Solange der König die Weser und den niedersächsischen Kreis zwischen Weser und Elbe nicht purgiert, laboriert er am Podagra': Kretzschmar, *Gustav Adolfs Pläne und Ziele*, p. 14.

[4] *Sv. Krig*, V. 18; Irmer, *VS*, I. 81-2: Tungel reported on 26 December that Arnim had replied to Swedish reproaches about his conduct of operations by saying 'that he could never have foreseen or believed that H.M. would allow Tilly so long *haleine* and *loisir* to think about Bohemia. If H.M. had followed hard after Tilly there would not have been any emergency in Bohemia. But since H.M. has rather been pleased to seek his own advantage, than to pursue Tilly', he (Arnim) has had to make shift as best he could.

[5] Droysen, II. 421.

[6] *Sv. Krig*, V. 11-12; *cf.* Tingsten, *Några data*, p. 333.

[7] Droysen, II. 428.

chest had been lost, with most of its baggage, and a great part of the troops were without weapons.[1] It is contended, indeed, by those who defend the decision at Halle, that these scattered groups did not form a solid military objective, that a pursuit of them would have been 'a blow in the air'. This is a tenable argument; but it cannot be held simultaneously with the view (also put forward by the King's defenders) that any advance north-westwards would have driven Tilly to collect his forces, and so have brought Gustav Adolf up against an enemy of superior strength.[2] Tilly collected his forces in any case, and to such purpose that the King found himself threatened with superior numbers soon enough. Indeed, the gravamen of the charge against the King really lies in the fact that he knew Tilly's weakness and disorganization after the battle, but yet assumed that by some inevitable process he would succeed in producing another army of formidable dimensions: the main justification given for the Halle decision was the need for Gustav Adolf to take the right wing in order to oppose effective resistance to Tilly's attacks.[3] The recovery of the imperialists was accepted as a foregone conclusion; and nothing positive was done to prevent it.

It is, no doubt, true that a relentless pursuit and a full exploitation of victory were foreign to contemporary military fashions [4]; but this argument, though it may explain the King's decision, can scarcely justify it. It is true, too, that to clear the Weser valley of the imperialists would have taken time and trouble, since they held a number of fortified places in this region. But in view of its great importance, and of the trouble it was to cause in the future, we may

[1] Droysen, II. 450 *note* 2, for quotations from reports by Tilly.

[2] Barkman, *Gustaf Adolf såsom härorganisatör*, p. 58; *Sv. Krig*, V. 7, 20; *cf.* Tingsten, *Några data*, p. 328.

[3] *e.g.* Salvius's letter to the *råd*, 24 October 1631 (*Arkiv*, II. 310): 'Since H.M. army and *praesentia* is needed where the greatest danger appears, namely in the Empire [*sc.* as against Bohemia] where Tilly, Altringer, Fugger, Merode, Ossa, Pfaltzburg collected themselves together again, since this is the *Totalwerk* and the other but a particular (which however will follow the *totum*) . . .' But it was precisely in the Brunswick lands that Tilly and his generals 'collected themselves together again', no man molesting them! And *cf.* Chemnitz's impercipient remark that Tilly had retired to the Weser, 'where by drawing together the troops of Aldringer and Fugger he might easily collect a strong *corpo* again', and hence be a danger to the right flank of the advance (Chemnitz, I. 216). And Oxenstierna in 1636 recalled that Gustav Adolf had justified himself by saying 'that since Tilly after the battle near Leipzig went off towards Brunswick, and the Duke of Lorraine afterwards joined him with 10,000 men, he was bound to follow him, for had he [Gustav Adolf] gone towards the hereditary lands, then the whole enemy forces had fallen upon the Elector of Saxony' (*RRP*, VI. 633). But neither before nor after Tilly's junction with Lorraine did Gustav Adolf 'follow' him.

[4] Tingsten, *Gustav Adolfs politik och krigföring*, pp. 129-30 *note*.

perhaps be pardoned for thinking that the time would not have been ill-bestowed. It is said that Tilly hoped that the King would follow him, and that he had his plans to elude him if he did so [1]; but it is difficult to believe that Tilly was in a condition to form any very subtle plan in the week after Breitenfeld. And certainly not much weight can be attached to the official explanation of why the pursuit was abandoned: the inhabitants of Pomerania and Brandenburg might well have made sardonic comments on Gustav Adolf's professed anxiety to spare the lands of Protestant princes; and the future lot of the Brunswick duchies would probably have been a good deal more tolerable if the imperialists had been definitively evicted now. And as to the suggestion that a campaign in the Weser valley would have left the enemy a free hand to raise fresh forces in the south, it is clear that the Halle decision left them no less free. For, as Gustav Adolf made quite plain in a letter of 17 September to Oxenstierna, his original intention was to go into winter quarters in Thuringia: the advance to the Rhine was to be deferred until next year. The rich bishoprics of Franconia would be forced to make contribution in the meanwhile—they would, to use the King's phrase, be 'infested' [2]—but the main Swedish position until spring was intended to bar the Thuringian passes and to form a bridge between John George on the one hand and the Landgrave on the other.[3] If this determination could have been adhered to, some of the more serious consequences of the failure to pursue Tilly might well have been avoided. Gustav Adolf would have been in no danger of finding Tilly cutting across his line of advance with a superior army (as was to happen in October); and the diversion which was to free Brunswick and Hesse would have been successful without the grave risk to Gustav Adolf which, in the event, it actually entailed. Moreover, it is even probable that the Lower Saxon Circle might have been effectively cleared of the enemy in the course of the winter, since the King at Erfurt would have been sufficiently close to the

[1] Petri, II. 144; Tingsten, *Några data*, p. 328; and *cf. Sv. Krig*, V. 63, where it is stated that Tilly *feared* that Gustav Adolf might attack him and was desperately anxious to concentrate quickly.

[2] *cf.* Chemnitz's 'die Pfaffengasse heimsuchen'.

[3] *AOSB*, II. I. 746: 'We are proceeding in person with the army to Thuringia, to utilize whatever may still be available there, arranging matters so, that we may take up our winter quarters there, having Hesse, Meissen and electoral Saxony around us, and by God's grace shall apply ourselves to infesting sundry bishoprics in Franconia and to bringing them into contribution, and so make ourselves so strong in numbers this winter that we may be *bastant* at the beginning of spring.' And *cf.* the letter of Camerarius, in Söltl, III. 304.

scene of operations to supervise his subordinates (and to give them orders relevant to the actual, rather than to the imagined, military position), and since his own immunity from danger would have relieved him from the necessity of calling on his generals for reinforcements, and so ruining their operations just when they seemed on the point of being successful. To go into winter quarters around Erfurt, in fact, would have been an acceptable second-best; and it would have represented a continuation of that cautious and methodical strategy which had hitherto characterized all his operations in Germany. But events proved that it was almost impossible to stick to a plan of this sort. In order to make sure that the diversion which was to liberate north-west Germany should be effective, Gustav Adolf was driven to undertake operations which led him deep into Franconia; the very success of his diversion exposed him to undue risks; and in the sequel he was forced to fix his front line not on the Thuringian passes but on the Main.

All this was not foreseen when, on 17 September, the Swedish army broke up from Halle and moved off in the direction of Erfurt.[1] Erfurt was a part of the dominions of the Elector of Mainz. It lay at the centre of a network of roads, and in particular at the intersection of important north-south and east-west routes; and it was a position of the utmost strategic and political importance.[2] Its citizens were mainly Protestant; but they were anxious to avert a Swedish occupation if possible, and sent representatives to parley with the King. They were told that neutrality would not be tolerated. And while the town council was still trying to make up its mind what to do, William of Weimar (who had joined Gustav Adolf again soon after Breitenfeld) cut short their hesitations by getting inside the gates with a detachment of cavalry and occupying the city for Sweden.[3] Gustav Adolf entered Erfurt on 22 September. An oath of fidelity to Sweden for the duration of the war was imposed upon the burghers; the fortifications were taken in hand; a garrison of 1500 men was installed; and Erfurt became—what it was to remain for some years—one of the bastions of the Swedish position in Germany.

[1] For the Franconian campaign, see Monro, II. 78 *seqq.*; and Grubbe's narratives in *Arkiv*, I. 767-71.

[2] *Vägar och vägkunskap*, p. 51, for the importance of Erfurt.

[3] For William's *coup*, see Monro, II. 76. For Gustav Adolf in Erfurt, W. Huschke, *Wilhelm von Weimar als Statthalter Gustav Adolfs*, p. 7; J. Bierehe, *Gustav Adolf in Erfurt*, pp. 4-8. For the agreements with Erfurt, *Sverges traktater*, V. 530-4, 552-3.

The King was now free to 'infest' Franconia, and, if possible, to divert Tilly from an attack upon Hesse. But before he moved forward he made proper arrangements to safeguard his rear. Banér was ordered to concentrate troops around Calbe: he was to try to take Magdeburg, and was also to hold himself in readiness to send aid to John George if he should need it; Tott was to move across the lower Elbe into the Lower Saxon Circle as soon as he had completed the reduction of the Mecklenburg ports; and both were to make large levies of recruits.[1] William of Weimar, with whom (as with his brother) an alliance was now concluded, was appointed governor-general of Thuringia, with orders to form a third army in the country around Erfurt.[2] And for the main body too, under the King's command, many new regiments were to be raised. Plainly, Gustav Adolf did not underestimate the task that still lay before him.

On 26 September the King marched out of Erfurt with 23,000 men and headed southwards for Franconia. They traversed the Thuringian forest in two columns moving by parallel roads, Gustav Adolf on the left, Horn on the right, and virtually no resistance was encountered: Königshofen, the strongest fortress in the bishopric of Würzburg, capitulated without a fight on 30 September; Schweinfurt opened its gates two days later; and Gustav Adolf had reached the upper Main. It was by no means certain that he would be able to stay there. By the end of September he had received news that Aldringen and Fugger were on their way to join Tilly; and soon afterwards he was informed that Charles of Lorraine was moving in the same direction.[3] The King could do nothing to interfere with these junctions. If, therefore, his diversion were successful, he might find himself in presence of an imperialist army considerably larger than his own; and if it were not, he might well be forced to return to assist Banér and the Landgrave. In either event he needed reinforcements: on 4 October he appealed to John George to lend him a thousand men.[4] Meanwhile, until the situation became clearer, he continued his advance.

On the morning of 4 October a Swedish trumpeter summoned Würzburg to open its gates. The bishop had fled betimes, and was well on his way to Frankfort, where his sudden arrival brought to an end the desultory wranglings of the *Kompositionstag* which had been

[1] *Schriftstücke*, pp. 39, 148.
[2] *Sverges traktater*, V. 535-50; Huschke, pp. 3-4, 23.
[3] *Sv. Krig*, V. 48, 55-6.
[4] *Schriftstücke*, p. 43.

in session there since August [1]; and it was left to 'Father *Ogleby*, Abbot of the *Scots* Cloyster', to arrange the capitulation.[2] The town council paid 80,000 *rdr.* to escape the plundering of the city; and Gustav Adolf entered Würzburg on the following morning. Three days later, the episcopal castle of Marienberg, on the other side of the river, was taken by storm in a brilliant feat of arms. The atrocities of the sack of Magdeburg were here in part avenged and emulated; and a fabulous booty enriched the army, the King, and ultimately the university library at Uppsala.[3]

Gustav Adolf remained in Würzburg for nearly a month. He was busy, among other concerns, with the organization of the newly occupied areas. Northern Franconia was for the moment a lordless land; and if it were to make proper contribution to the Swedish armies it must be provided with a machinery of administration. A new civil government for Franconia was accordingly set up, manned to a great extent by the old officials, but bound now to Gustav Adolf by oaths of fidelity; and Solms was installed as governor of Franconia for the time being. Religious houses were taken over and their property administered by the government; an exchequer was organized, and a military administration; and the rewarding of the King's supporters by donations began. It was not intended by these arrangements that Franconia should become a permanent Swedish possession; but it was very clear that Gustav Adolf was now committed to the occupation of the valley of the Main.[4]

The King was also occupied, during this lull in operations, with matters of politics. He had already issued, from Magdeburg, a proclamation to the Franconians in which he represented himself as the champion of the oppressed Protestants of central Germany [5]; and he now launched at the heads of the three ecclesiastical Electors an ultimatum which he can scarcely have expected them to accept.[6] The bishop of Bamberg, who had remained in his diocese, sent a

[1] For the *Kompositionstag*, see Lundorp, III. 215; *Schriftstücke*, pp. 144-6; Helbig, p. 58; Fagniez, *Le Père Joseph et Richelieu*, I. 578; Ritter, III. 506. Even John George had called it 'eine Komödie und lauter Spiegelfechterei': Riezler, V. 383.

[2] Monro, II. 79.

[3] Priorato, p. 101; Paul, III. 25. A good narrative of the storm in Monro, *loc. cit.*; and see C. G. Scharold, *Geschichte der kön. schwedischen und herzogl. sachsen-weimarischen Zwischenregierung im eroberten Fürstbisthume Würzburg i. J. 1631-4*, I. 8-31.

[4] For the reorganization of Franconia, see Droysen, II. 444-9: Monro, II. 85.

[5] *Sv. Krig*, V. 54.

[6] L. Frohnhäuser, *Gustav Adolf und die Schweden in Mainz und am Rhein*, p. 19; J. Baur, *Philipp von Sötern*, I. 219.

representative to Würzburg to negotiate, in the hope (which turned out to be well-founded) that if he could spin out the discussions the approach of Tilly would eventually distract the King's attention. On the Protestant side there was much coming and going: George of Lüneberg-Celle arrived to take up his long-deferred commission; delegates came from Württemberg, offering excuses for their earlier collapse and promises of aid for the future; a treaty was concluded with the Estates of Franconia, with provisions for further separate treaties with Ansbach and Bayreuth, and with the city of Nuremberg.[1] Soon after Breitenfeld Martin Chemnitz and Max von Rehlingen had been sent by Gustav Adolf to Franconia, to rally support there among the Protestant Estates; and they had addressed themselves in particular to the Hohenzollern Margrave Christian of Bayreuth, and to Nuremberg. Neither had found it easy to take a decided step, for there were imperialist troops in their neighbourhood; but the rapid advance of the King's armies, and the threats and persuasions which his agents addressed to them, at last made up their minds for them, and at Würzburg they declared themselves ready to ally with Sweden.[2]

Meanwhile, Gustav Adolf's diversion was having its effect upon Tilly. In the weeks that had elapsed since Breitenfeld, Tilly, having been left entirely to his own devices, had made a remarkable recovery. The wrecks of his army had been retrieved and regrouped; the imperialist-held fortresses of the Weser valley had provided him with fresh artillery; Aldringen and Fugger had been allowed to bring their armies to a rendezvous near Fulda; and by the end of the first week of October his concentration was complete. He had now some 25,000 men at his disposal, and he proposed to use them to chastise Hesse.[3] The Landgrave could not hope to meet Tilly in the field, and was driven to take refuge in his strongholds of Cassel and Ziegenhain. To Gustav Adolf he sent urgent appeals for succour.[4] But the King refused to listen to him: it would not be long, he was confident, before his diversion disburdened Hesse of Tilly's army.

These calculations proved perfectly correct. Gustav Adolf's

[1] *Sverges traktater,* V. 557-61. For the negotiations at Würzburg, see *Arkiv,* I. 767-8.

[2] For the mission of Chemnitz and Rehlingen, see Droysen, II. 440-3; G. Egelhaaf, *Gustav Adolf und die deutsche Reichsstädte,* pp. 245-9; S. Donaubauer, *Nürnberg um die Mitte des dreissigjährigen Krieges,* pp. 1-43.

[3] For Tilly's recovery, see *Sv. Krig,* V. 65-71.

[4] *Sv. Krig,* V. 65; Rommel, VIII. 155-61.

invasion of Franconia, with its threat to Tilly's communications with Bavaria, could no longer be ignored. Maximilian, with his usual tact and good sense, had left the future conduct of operations entirely to Tilly's discretion; and a council of war at Tilly's headquarters now discussed what was to be done. There was some suggestion that they should try to save Würzburg; but in the end the policy of Pappenheim and Fugger was adopted, and it was decided to effect a junction with Charles of Lorraine, and thereafter to seek battle. On 9 October Tilly's army left Fulda; on 14 October it reached the Main at Aschaffenburg; and there, soon afterwards, Lorraine and his army came in. Tilly had now between 40,000 and 45,000 men under his command, with 26 guns; and though they were in many respects pitiably ill-provided, and though morale was far from high, they were nevertheless a numerically imposing force. They crossed the Main, marched on Miltenberg, and continued south-easterly to Tauberbischoffsheim, which they occupied on 25 October. They were now a bare day's march from Gustav Adolf at Würzburg, and a major engagement seemed imminent. 'Here also', as Monro observes,[1] 'we see Generall *Tillie*, though beaten at *Leipsigh*, in lesse then five weekes time, he drawes together againe a strong Army, with Fifty thousand men,[2] and lies downes [*sic*] within three miles of his Majesties Army. . . .' Monro makes no further comment: for him, as for Gustav Adolf, this untimely resurrection was apparently considered in the light of an unfortunate natural phenomenon, as independent of the King's control as a sudden thunderstorm or a sharp shower of hail. If indeed Gustav Adolf had refrained from pursuing Tilly after Breitenfeld because he did not wish to dissipate his forces in chasing fragmentary remnants which offered no solid military target, he was now provided with an objective as tangible as could be desired. But though Tilly for a moment entertained the idea of giving battle, Gustav Adolf certainly did not. He felt himself unequal to the enemy, and tried hastily to concentrate reinforcements at Würzburg, calling upon the Landgrave, upon Banér, upon William of Weimar, for assistance.[3] He called in vain: Banér and the Landgrave were too far away; Weimar's army was as yet only in process of formation. To John George, on 26 October, he wrote complaining petulantly of the

[1] Monro, II. 82.
[2] This was the King's estimate: *Schriftstücke*, p. 46.
[3] *Arkiv*, I. 510; *Sv. Krig*, V. 78.

paucity of aid he received from German princes who still alleged their obligations under the Leipzig resolution as a pretext for declining to help him, and threatening the Elector with the prospect of a retreat which would expose his lands to the enemy. He would not have ventured so far, he added, if he had foreseen that he would be thus hamstrung '*in medio victoriae cursu*'.[1] But it was neither legitimate nor generous to blame John George. The crisis which now threatened Gustav Adolf was of his own making, and he was fortunate to get out of it with a whole skin.

From the information that reached the Swedish headquarters at Würzburg, it appeared that the place immediately threatened by Tilly was Ochsenfurt. The news was alarming; and on 26 October, in evident agitation, the King set out from Würzburg with a small force, in the hope of getting there before Tilly's blow should fall. Marching at a great pace, he arrived in the small hours of the morning of the 27th; inspected the fortifications; and conducted a personal reconnaissance of the surrounding countryside. The defences were strengthened with anxious haste; infantry reinforcements arrived on the 28th, the bulk of the cavalry on the 31st. But the expected attack did not occur. Tilly's activity round Ochsenfurt had been a mere demonstration; for he had after all decided against offering battle. Maximilian had ordered him to take no risks; and in view of the state of his army Tilly was very ready to obey. On 28 October he marched off to Rothenburg on the Tauber; took Windsheim on 1 November, and Ansbach on the 7th; and began to think about the possibility of an attempt on Nuremberg. The crisis thus passed as quickly as it had arisen. But it had revealed very clearly the risk that Gustav Adolf had been taking in Franconia. His forces were not adequate to the enterprise to which he had committed himself. For the moment he had lost, not merely the initiative but also, it seems, his nerve.[2] The comment of Monro tells its own tale:

To speake truth, all the time I did follow his Majestie on occasions, being neere three yeeres, I did never see His Majestie so much troubled in minde and resolution, as at this time in *Oxenford*, not knowing himselfe what to resolve, the enemie being behind him and before him; able to pursue *Wurtzburg*, and *Oxenford* alike; and to my minde if he had, he might have carried both at that time; for our Armie was not only

[1] *Schriftstücke*, pp. 46-52.

[2] Droysen was very wide of the mark when he wrote, of Tilly's movements: 'Der König kümmerte sich wenig um diese Bewegungen eines Feindes, dessen Unfähigkeit er kennen gelernt hatte': Droysen, II. 451.

scattered and dispersed; but also we were weake, and, which was worse, we were all of us discontented; being too much toyled with marching, working and watching, without any pay or gaines for honest men.[1]

The departure of Tilly, however, changed the situation. There was no longer any argument for going into winter quarters around Erfurt. Apart from the now-isolated imperialist garrisons, the Lower Saxon Circle was cleared of the enemy, and it might seem a mere question of time before they were forced to capitulate, as the remaining garrisons in Mecklenburg were obviously destined to do. The enemy's main army was now in southern Franconia, and Gustav Adolf could not leave the lands north of the Main as a military vacuum. And since the southerly limit of effective Swedish occupation must now be pushed forward to the Main, it was reasonable to complete the seizure of the river line to its natural limit at the confluence of the Main and the Rhine. Already on 1 November a Swedish detachment had taken Hanau. On the following day Gustav Adolf learned that Tilly had decamped; and he decided at once to move westwards towards Frankfort.[2] Rhine and Main were to be conjoined in a unified defensive position which should protect him throughout the winter from attack, whether from Bavaria on the one hand or Lorraine on the other. Banér and Tott and William of Weimar were to hold the Thuringian passes and complete the subjugation of the Lower Saxon Circle; the Landgrave was interrupted (in a fashion soon to become mortifyingly familiar to him) in the middle of a successful little campaign of his own, by an order to bring his forces to join the main army[3]; and Horn was left at Würzburg with some 7000 men to hold the middle reaches of the river and make such progress as he could to the south of it. The main army under the King's command would by this arrangement number 13,000-14,000 men, and the Landgrave, it was calculated, would bring in 7000 more.

The decision to move to the Rhine was a bold one; and it reflects a tendency, now increasingly apparent, to abandon the cautious and methodical strategy which had marked the first twelve months of the

[1] Monro, II. 86; *cf. Sv. Krig*, V. 72-4, 77-81. Gustav Adolf wrote to George William on 2 November, pointing out that at Breitenfeld (contrary to what might be supposed) 'dasz hauptwerckh nit gehoben, noch desz feindes macht genzlich gebrochen, sondern er viel mehr hierdurch irritirt [!] . . .'; and adding, 'wir numehr *in praecipito* stehen': *Schriftstücke*, p. 149 *seqq.*

[2] *Arkiv*, I. 510; *Handlingar rörande Skandinaviens historia*, XXV. 112 *seqq.*

[3] *Sv. Krig*, V. 87-91.

German war, and to run calculated, and often considerable, risks. Horn's position at Würzburg was certainly hazardous. If Tilly should turn northwards against him, he was in great danger of being overwhelmed. But the risk was deliberately taken; and although on 8 November Gustav Adolf had already some reason to think that Tilly might try to cut off Horn from William of Weimar by a move against Schweinfurt, the decision to advance to the Rhine was not rescinded. Gustav Adolf had accurately estimated his adversary's anxiety to recuperate in winter quarters.

Nevertheless, the 'conjunction of Rhine and Main' had all sorts of serious implications. It meant, first of all, increased difficulties and delays in communication between the King and the government in Stockholm. Gustav Adolf was vanishing into the heart of Europe, Oxenstierna was already bidden to follow him, and the *råd* would be left more and more to its own devices. It meant also a very great extension of the whole scale of operations: from the narrow Pomeranian beach-head the war was now broadened to include all central Germany between the middle Oder and the middle Rhine, with the prospect of still wider extensions to follow. Already seven armies were operating in this region—the army of the Oder, John George's forces in Lusatia and Bohemia, the armies of Tott, Banér, William of Weimar and the Landgrave, and the main army under the King himself. All of them were now to be moved in obedience to plans of operations of ever vaster scope; and the problem of co-ordinating their activities became more and more formidable, if indeed it had not already become insoluble. Behind this immense curving front, as it was gradually pressed forward, more and more of Germany must be organized to ensure security of communications, regularity of contributions in money and supplies, a free flow of recruits. An administrative system must be devised for the occupied territory; finances, postal services, justice, ecclesiastical affairs, must all be taken in hand and put in order. And just as the mounting scale of military activities made necessary intensive recruiting, to provide armies of a magnitude scarcely seen before in western Europe, and certainly undreamed-of by Gustav Adolf at the outset of the war, so too the civil arrangements for occupied Germany demanded a strong corps of administrators. Sweden could provide neither the one nor the other from native resources. The King would need thousands of German mercenaries, scores of German secretaries, officials and diplomats. German princes and princelings as military commanders or civil governors, if the enterprise were to be carried to a successful conclusion.[1] And these new involvements coincided with an increase in the complexity of diplomatic problems. When Gustav Adolf marched for Mainz, he was heading away from John George, and every additional mile between them made it more difficult to ensure that the Elector maintained a line of policy—both military and diplomatic—consonant with that of his ally. In this situation it became more than ever necessary that the other Protestant Estates of north Germany—and especially those whose lands lay in areas where Gustav Adolf's long line of communications might be vulnerable—should be attached to Sweden by the strongest and most binding links. Again, the whole future trend of operations, directed as they were towards the gradual absorption of south Germany into the area of temporary Swedish control, and the ultimate capture of Vienna, was in itself a political programme: it implied the denial of the possibility of a compromise peace, the determination to aim at nothing less than total victory, the acceptance of the argument that the safety of Sweden and the liberation—not merely of north Germany but of all Germany—were indissolubly connected. Once on the Rhine, moreover, it might be difficult to avoid a clash with the Spanish troops in that area, with consequences which might well be grave. And it was quite certain that Richelieu would view with alarm any encroachment by Sweden upon a sphere of influence which he had long desired to reserve exclusively for France.[2] In November 1631 Gustav Adolf moved out of the relatively simple world of Baltic concerns and plunged into a dark labyrinth where difficulties of every sort proliferated and new insidious dangers lay in the path; where the forces engaged were bigger, and the problems on a grander scale, than any that he had handled before. It was possible, it was even probable, that he might reach the centre of that labyrinth, and stand victor in Vienna (and further than that his vision as yet did not go), but the question remained how he was to get out of it again. It was a question

[1] For further discussion of these questions, see below, p. 620 *seqq.*

[2] The Papal Nuncio wrote from Paris to the Cardinal-Nephew, on 13/23 November 1631, alluding to Gustav Adolf's march: 'i progressi del quale caminano cos celleri che appena l'occhio sopra la carta di cosmographia può seguirli. Qui se ne parla constupore e se ne vede con gelosia, et forse pare che questi grandi progressi denigrino le glorie della Francia. . . . Quello che importa è, che il male supera ogni remedio, la Francia non potendo più useare pretesi contro Suetia, perchè è troppo vicino a questo regno et troppo potente': Leman, *Urbain VIII*, p. 63 *note* 1.

which was destined to occupy the most arduous years of Oxenstierna's career.

These lengthening shadows were perhaps scarcely observed in November 1631. The army advanced down the valley of the Main on either side of the river (the artillery went by water), unopposed, unmenaced, triumphant; and the memory of those golden days stirred Monro to unwontedly lyrical prose. They moved, he writes,

> through fertill soyles and pleasant countries, their marches being more like to a Kingly progresse, then to warres, being in a fat land, as this was, abounding in all things, except peace: they had plenty of corne, wine, fruite, gold, silver, Iewells, and of all sort of riches could be thought of, on this River of the *Maine*, where the Townes and pleasant Flects [1] lie by the water, not distant, in many places, half an *English* mile from one another; being one of the pleasantest parts, and wholesomest for ayre that I did see in all *Germany*. . . .[2]

On 17 November they entered Frankfort, the first foreign army to do so since the foundation of the Holy Roman Empire—Gustav Adolf 'on a black Spanish charger, in a scarlet cloak with silver embroidery'.[3] Their next objective was Mainz; but before they could pursue it they were halted by a loud cry of alarm to their rear. Tilly had arrived before Nuremberg on 19 November, had been refused admission or contributions, and for a day or two had made half-hearted motions as though to coerce the city to submission. Nuremberg had by this time a garrison of 5000 men, in part raised under Gustav Adolf's commission; and they skirmished with spirit in the meadows outside the walls. But with the fate of Magdeburg still fresh in recollection, they sent urgent appeals to the King for succour; and Gustav Adolf, who had as good cause to remember Magdeburg as they, did not hesitate. On 26 November he announced his determination to make for Nuremberg at once, and to relieve it at all hazards.[4] Three days later, as he was about to set out from Frankfort on this errand, he was met by news that the danger was over: Tilly had abandoned the enterprise. Eleven thousand men under Gallas were now by the Emperor's order detached from the main body and sent into Bohemia in an effort to halt Arnim's

[1] Swedish *fläckar*, rural market-places, hamlets.

[2] Monro, II. 89; *cf.* Frohnhäuser, p. 5.

[3] Fryxell, *Handlingar*, p. 37. The King entertained George of Hesse-Darmstadt to dinner, and at table 'narrated the battle of Leipzig from beginning to end' to this somewhat ill-chosen auditor.

[4] *Schriftstücke*, p. 166; Styffe, p. 396; Frohnhäuser, pp. 34-5.

advance; Charles of Lorraine and his army turned about and made their way deviously homeward[1]; Pappenheim, disgusted at his leader's caution, had already taken an early opportunity to seek an independent command for himself; and Tilly, with a much-diminished and somewhat demoralized force, went into winter quarters in the country round Nördlingen.[2]

The King was now free to turn his attention to Mainz; and the prospect appeared by no means inviting. The city, which lies on the left bank of the Rhine, was well-provisioned and strongly fortified[3]; and there were plenty of Spanish troops in the neighbourhood to provide it with a garrison. The Main had been made unnavigable, so that there would be difficulties about siege artillery; and without it a direct assault across the Rhine was hardly to be thought of. Gustav Adolf decided, therefore, to move south up the right bank of the river in the direction of Heidelberg, with a view to liberating this part of the Palatinate. Before he had gone far, he came upon a redoubt which the Spanish garrison of Oppenheim had established on the eastern shore as a bridgehead for further operations; and in the immediate neighbourhood he also hit upon a spot at which a convenient island in the stream made a crossing feasible. He determined to engage the redoubt and effect the crossing. On 6 December, with only three companions, the King explored the further shore in a characteristically daring personal reconnaissance; and on the following day, with the assistance of some sunken boats providentially discovered, the army was thrown across the Rhine in an operation which was a model for all such undertakings.[4] Oppenheim capitulated on 8 December, and its castle was stormed; the garrison of Worms, impressed by these successes, evacuated the town; and on 10 December, 'in cruell tempestuous weather for frost and snow',[5] the Swedish forces turned north for Mainz. On the following day they appeared before its walls. The Elector's appeal to the Spaniards for aid had produced but a meagre response; and the 1000 men they sent him brought the total garrison to not much more than double that number. The Elector himself was not among them. Correctly assessing the chances of resistance, he had fled on

[1] Schott, *Württemberg und Gustav Adolf*, pp. 362-4.

[2] Riezler, V. 383. Gustav Adolf was jubilant: 'I account this victory, and the not being constrained at this time to deliver that place, not inferior to the battle of Leipzig': Frohnhäuser, p. 37.

[3] *ibid.*, p. 21 *seqq.*, for the operations against Mainz.

[4] *ibid.*, 75, 84-6, 92; *Sv. Krig*, V. 99-103.

[5] Monro, II. 94.

the day that Oppenheim fell, to join the bishops of Würzburg and Worms in the comparative security of Cologne. Gustav Adolf wasted no time on preparations for a regular siege. On 12 December he was ready to storm the city. The defenders, however, had no desire to try their fortune; and on the same day Mainz capitulated to the Swedish demands.[1]

So ended this astonishing campaign, which impressed itself upon the imaginations of contemporaries much as did the Italian campaign of the young Buonaparte. In three months the forces of Emperor and League had been shattered in battle, hustled out of north Germany and driven back to seek recruitment in their own countries. The King appeared irresistible; and if Breitenfeld had left any in doubt as to the quality of his army, Marienberg and Oppenheim must have sufficed to dispel it. The liberation of the Protestant south seemed to be but a matter of time; the evangelical cause might look forward to 1632 as the year appointed for its final triumph. With the resources of half Germany to draw upon, with vast armies recruiting for next year, the King might hope that he had seen an end of difficulties about pay and reinforcements. As he kept his Christmas in Mainz, the sun shone full upon him; and his servants were tempted to think that for him no goal was unattainable.

Yet it was but winter sunlight after all; and in the shadows the air was sharp enough. Though Gustav Adolf himself took the Spanish danger lightly, the government at home was of another opinion.[2] In the middle distance lay the menace of Wallenstein's political and military resurrection. The King's relations with the German Protestant princes were uneasy, largely undefined and pregnant with future trouble. The long line of communications from the Rhine to the Baltic ports was all too open to attack. Much would depend on how far the position in north-west Germany could be made secure before next year's campaigning began. And it was an evil presage that at the very time when Gustav Adolf crowned his triumphs with the taking of Mainz, Pappenheim should have arrived in the Lower Saxon Circle to begin those brilliant operations which were to do so much to upset the King's calculations.

For the moment, however, military considerations must take second place to diplomacy. The main task of the winter must be to

[1] Frohnhäuser, pp. 28, 46-7, 100-1; *Sv. Krig*, V. 106-7.
[2] See below, p. 576.

attempt to adjust the political situation to conform to the new military realities. For months Gustav Adolf had been pressing his chancellor to make haste to join him in Germany [1]; and now that the Swedish armies sat astride the Rhine it was more necessary than ever that Oxenstierna's phlegm should temper his master's choler in the conduct of negotiations. When the chancellor at last arrived at Mainz, towards the end of January 1632, he came none too soon; for the tangles and tensions of politics were demanding a cool head and a practised and professional hand.

[1] The King had sent for him as early as April but local difficulties delayed him: *AOSB*, I. VI. 247, 323, 336, 363, 368, 513, 536 *seqq.*

CHAPTER IX

GUSTAV ADOLF AND EUROPE, 1631-32

(i) *The East*

Gustav Adolf might well have hesitated to establish himself in the Rhineland for the winter, and his Christmas festivities might well have been less brilliant, if he had not been able to feel reasonably secure about the position in the east. The truce of Altmark had made intervention in Germany possible; and only the assurance of its continuance permitted the King to break away from his Baltic base and indulge in the hopes and hazards of a campaign in central Europe. If the Protestants of Franconia and Suabia were to be liberated, if the danger to the evangelical religion everywhere were to be permanently removed, and the twin roots of evil grubbed up in Munich and Vienna, there must be no renewal of complications on the Vistula. That consideration alone is sufficient to explain why, through all the preoccupations of the German war, Gustav Adolf never ceased to think of Poland. Should the Poles denounce the truce, or should their rearmament make it appear probable that they might be preparing to denounce it, the war in Germany would have to be waged (at best) on strictly defensive lines in Pomerania, or even (at worst) abandoned altogether. For Poland was the national enemy of thirty years' standing; Sigismund was the inexorable dynastic rival. The most imminent threat of invasion had come from the Vistula, and the Polish navy had in its time caused more alarm, and inflicted more damage, than all Wallenstein's preparations had been able to compass. If a resurgent Poland were to overrun Livonia and recover Riga, Estonia and Karelia would be endangered, the gains not only of Altmark but of Stolbova might be jeopardized, and the fruits of twenty years of dogged struggle might be lost. And, finally, without the revenues from the Prussian licences neither the German war, nor perhaps any other, could be carried on upon the scale to which the King had now become habituated.

There were thus good reasons for Gustav Adolf's constant vigilance about developments within the Republic; and though he certainly exaggerated the dangers to be feared, his anxiety was intelligible enough. He was, however, fortunate in having means at his disposal for ensuring the continued quiescence of his enemy. Those means were of two kinds: either he might incite Poland's neighbours to attack her, and so weaken and distract her forces; or he might by intrigue in the Republic produce an internal instability or confusion which would make an aggressive foreign policy impracticable. Both means were tried; though the event was to prove that they were not equally efficacious.[1]

Poland at the beginning of the 'thirties was ringed round with potential enemies. The death of Bethlen Gabor in 1629 had, indeed, removed one dangerous aspirant to the Polish throne, and the confusion that followed gave the Poles a breathing-space on that frontier; but it was always possible that Swedish diplomacy might incite Bethlen's successor to attack them. It was barely ten years since the last great war with the Turks; and if the Sultan could disengage himself from entanglements in Asia it was not unreasonable to expect a resumption of that struggle. The Tatars of the Crimea lived in a state of perennial border warfare with their Polish neighbours to the north, and at the end of 1629 their raids had assumed formidable proportions. It was likely enough that they would seize the opportunity of Poland's weakness to renew their forays. But the most imminent and the most serious danger came from Muscovy. The truce of Deulinie was to expire at midsummer 1632, and everything seemed to show that the Russians intended to resume the war. Michael, or at least his father Filaret, was determined to recover Smoleńsk, and the White Russian borderlands lost in 1618; and the Romanov dynasty could not feel itself secure as long as Władysław continued to use the title of Tsar.

In these circumstances it was an obvious Swedish policy to cultivate good relations with Moscow, to supply the Russians with war material and military experts, and to exacerbate their resentments against the Poles. This policy was formulated by Gustav Adolf as early as 1626[2]; and it was steadily pursued. In January 1629 Anton Monier had been sent to Moscow to urge the Tsar to take up arms as soon as the truce ran out; in December he had returned there with offers to sell Swedish munitions. On both occasions he was very well received. The Russians were prepared for the moment to forget

[1] C. Wejle, *Sveriges politik mot Polen, 1630-1635*, has now been superseded by D. Norrman, *Gustav Adolfs politik mot Ryssland och Polen, 1630-1632*, for this period. The following account is based largely on Norrman.

[2] *AOSB*, I. III. 337-9.

Stolbova in return for Swedish assistance, and they were willing to make considerable concessions to obtain it: Monier's request for leave to buy grain and saltpetre for Sweden was granted without delay.[1] Thus Gustav Adolf's Russian policy brought him not only political benefits but commercial advantages; and the concession granted to Monier provided the starting-point for those attempts to secure a monopoly of the Russian grain trade from which the King expected such lucrative returns.

It was perhaps the prospect of a similar combination of political and financial gains that led Gustav Adolf to embark upon another venture of some importance. In November 1630 he had an interview at Stralsund with an errant Frenchman named Jacques Roussel, who had insinuated himself into the Swedish service by attaching himself to Paul Strassburg in Transylvania in the previous year. Roussel's knowledge of eastern Europe was extensive, and Strassburg had sent him to Constantinople, where he had done useful service. He had returned to the north by way of Moscow; and from Moscow he brought the suggestion that Gustav Adolf should make himself responsible for the raising of a mercenary army in Germany on the Tsar's behalf, which could be used on the expiry of the truce to attack Poland from the west simultaneously with a Russian invasion from the east. Gustav Adolf would hire the troops and provide officers, muster-places and armaments; Russia would foot the bill.[2] The proposal made a double appeal to the King. In the first place, he welcomed any measure which would conduce to the outbreak of a Russo-Polish war; for such a war would not only immobilize the Poles: it would also distract the Tsar's attention from Narva and Nyen. In the second place, the enterprise promised to be extremely profitable. No one had better reason than Gustav Adolf to know the huge gains made by those military *entrepreneurs* who raised mercenary regiments. He was now invited to act in the capacity of recruiting colonel, and on a very large scale; and he may well have calculated on extracting from the Russians (who seem not to have been conversant with the current market rates) subsidies which would yield him a handsome profit. It has been estimated, indeed, that if the plan had been carried through, the King's gains would have been about 127,000 *rdr.* a month, or more than twice as much as he drew from the Prussian licences.[3] On the other hand, there

[1] Norrman, pp. 10-17. [2] On Roussel, see Norrman, p. 32 *seqq.*
[3] *Arkiv*, I. 787; Norrman, pp. 143-9.

was an element of risk in the business. It was arguable that the raising of such an army would constitute a violation of the truce of Altmark. Gustav Adolf had no wish to break that treaty; the last thing he desired was to give the Poles a pretext for hostilities. Oxenstierna, though he remarked that it was 'a singular God's providence in the constitution of this world that the Grand Duke has such respects to your Majesty, and is so willing in everything',[1] was reluctant to trust providence too far. He warned the King that the scheme was very likely to involve Sweden in war with Poland, and he seems to have had misgivings as to the morality, as well as to the expediency, of the venture.[2] But Gustav Adolf was not to be deterred. On 23 November 1630 he instructed Monier to return to Moscow with an offer of co-operation in raising troops in Germany; in March 1631 he appointed Jakob Möller the first permanent Swedish agent in Moscow; and on 21 June he wrote to the Tsar giving leave for Alexander Leslie[3] to raise 5000 men in north Germany for the Russian service.[4] The Tsar was by this time hoping for a Swedish alliance; and in January 1632 he informed Möller that he accepted Gustav Adolf's offer to levy an army in Germany, and that the numbers he should require would be 10,000 foot and 2000 horse. Correspondence between Moscow and south Germany was slow; and it was not until the latter half of April that the King received the Tsar's letter. He replied in June, enthusiastically welcoming the Russian decision.[5] A strong Russian commission set out for Germany to discuss the details of recruiting; and in October the Tsar began operations against Smoleńsk. But the operations had made little progress, and the commission had got no further than the Neva, when the news of Gustav Adolf's death put an end to the idea of assaulting Poland on two fronts.

Nevertheless, Gustav Adolf's Russian policy had in appearance been a success. The goodwill of Moscow had been won, at least for the moment, and with it important advantages. The recruiting scheme, if he had lived to operate it, would have yielded him a handsome revenue. The Russian attack on Poland might no doubt have come about in any case; but Gustav Adolf had certainly helped to make it certain. The indispensable precondition for Sweden's continuance as the leading power in the Baltic was the prevention

[1] *AOSB*, I. VI. 123. [2] *ibid.*, I. VI. 492. [3] Alexander Leslie the younger.
[4] *AOSB*, I. VI. 51-2, II. I. 738-9; Norrman, pp. 48-51, 64-73; *The Swedish Intelligencer*, I. 32-3. [5] His letter is in *Sverges traktater*, V. 783-6.

of a reconciliation and coalition between potential rivals. By securing the friendship of the Tsar, Gustav Adolf was blocking the plans of Kristian IV, who was also a suitor for it [1]; by encouraging the Tsar to attack the Poles, he was insuring Sweden against a Slavonic front such as had more than once seemed a possibility in the past. Yet, if he had lived some years longer, if the German army for service against Poland had indeed been raised, he might well have found himself faced by a situation which he had not bargained for. The Russo-Polish war might have merged into the grand conflict in Germany, and Sweden might have been committed once again to fighting the imperialists on the Vistula; for the Habsburgs could hardly see Poland destroyed without an attempt at rescue. If, on the other hand, Poland had collapsed under the attack from east and west, Gustav Adolf might have been compelled, as Karl X Gustav was compelled twenty years later, to intervene in order to prevent a Russian conquest. Gustav Adolf's Russian policy, in fact, was sound only if the struggle between Russia and Poland were indecisive and protracted. In 1632 all the probabilities were against this. The almost incredible military weakness and unpreparedness of Poland [2]; the country's obvious desire for peace; the internal factions which convulsed it; the suspicion of Sigismund's dynastic plans, which had so long sabotaged the best-meant efforts in the national cause; the improvements, in arms and training, in the Russian troops, and their vastly superior numbers—all these things seemed to presage a catastrophe for Poland. Gustav Adolf could not foresee the military talents and gifts of leadership of Władysław IV. Like many Swedish commanders after him (and like the Poles themselves), he despised and underrated the Russians. Taught by Koniecpolski, he had considerable respect for the military qualities of the Poles. But he had an erroneous idea of their military preparedness, and of their willingness to fight. Skytte and Oxenstierna—though Oxenstierna, to be sure, was as suspicious of the Poles as any man could be—sent in repeated reports of the absence of preparations, of the apathetic quiet of the country, of its military weakness.[3] They seem to have made no effect upon Gustav Adolf.

[1] Fridericia, *YPH*, I. 196-8.

[2] In January 1631 the Polish army consisted of 1000 dragoons on the Podolian border: Norrman, p. 42.

[3] *e.g.* *AOSB*, I. VI. 179, 205, 221, 269. But Oxenstierna characteristically added, on one occasion, 'but what kind of secret designs are hatching in Poland at the moment can better be imagined than assessed': *AOSB*, I. VI. 387.

It appears, then, that his intrigue with the Muscovite was based upon an unsound evaluation of forces. And it is difficult to resist the conclusion that his second line of operations—the weakening of Poland by the fomenting of internal broils—was vitiated from the start by miscalculations of a similar nature.

Since the mid-'twenties, Swedish efforts to sow dissension in Poland had been directed towards winning the adherence of the leading Dissidents, and in particular of Christopher Radziwiłł, the great Protestant magnate of Lithuania.[1] The truce of Altmark caused no interruption of this policy. From Radziwiłł's point of view there was much to be said for maintaining contacts with Sweden. Gustav Adolf was better able to give assistance to the Polish Protestants than (for instance) George William of Brandenburg, who was the only other likely saviour; and it might well be that such assistance would shortly become necessary. It was obvious that Sigismund III could not live much longer; and Radziwiłł—like Raphael Leszczyński in Poland proper—hoped to use an interregnum to recover something of that equality of religious rights which the Protestants had enjoyed before Sigismund's accession.

It was the prospect of an interregnum that produced a new development in Sweden's Polish policy. This was nothing less than the putting forward of Gustav Adolf as a candidate for the Polish throne. The idea goes back at least to the beginning of 1629, when Oxenstierna mentioned it as a possible counter-move to the pretensions which Bethlen Gabor was at that time advancing [2]; but it first became an official policy in April 1630, when Gustav Adolf wrote to Oxenstierna ordering him to prepare the way for his candidature. He was to try to secure the support of Danzig and Thorn; and was to enter into correspondence with Radziwiłł and Leszczyński. Even though nothing should come of these initiatives, the King considered that the manœuvre would have been justified if it provoked faction and disturbances in Poland.[3]

It is not easy to form an opinion as to how far Gustav Adolf soberly contemplated another union of the Swedish and Polish crowns in his own person. The date of this order, so shortly before the sailing of the expedition to Germany, might make it seem unlikely that he can have desired so serious a complication of his plans.

[1] See above, Vol. I, pp. 164-6, 205-15, 252-3.
[2] *AOSB*, I. IV. 341-2.
[3] *ibid.*, II. I. 582; *cf. ibid.*, I. V. 304.

Yet at that time it was still possible that the negotiations with the Emperor might avert a war; and if Ferdinand II himself should be a candidate (as Oxenstierna feared)[1] there was something to be said for providing the Poles with an alternative: Gustav Adolf habitually underrated the Polish aversion to foreigners. But on the whole it seems probable that he did not at this stage intend anything beyond the stirring up of trouble in the Republic. Even so, Oxenstierna was not enthusiastic: in acknowledging his master's order he drily assured him that he would forward his candidature 'as time and opportunity may offer'.[2]

Opportunity first presented itself with the arrival of Roussel in Pomerania; and it was Gustav Adolf who seized it. The King was under no illusions as to Roussel's steadiness and discretion; but the Frenchman seemed to be well informed about Polish politics, and he did not lack for zeal. Gustav Adolf decided to risk employing him; and at the end of November 1630 gave him a general commission to make contact with the Polish magnates, and if possible to influence the *sejm* on his behalf. Roussel accordingly made his way to Riga, where Skytte found him something of an embarrassment; and at Riga began to prepare a propaganda-offensive upon Poland. The choice of such an agent is perhaps an indication that the King did not pitch his expectations very high.

This impression is reinforced by the events of the following spring. In February 1631 there occurred an important meeting of the *sejm*. Its main business was to consider, at Sigismund's behest, the question of the succession. Sigismund would have liked the crown to be declared hereditary; or, failing that, an election *rege vivente*. The diet disappointed him on both counts. It refused to alter the existing procedure, and declined to discuss the claim of any candidate until a vacancy should actually have occurred. Oxenstierna and Skytte both had agents at the diet, and these agents were able to get into touch with Polish leaders[3]; but it was clear, in view of the diet's decision, that any attempt to canvass for Gustav Adolf was premature, and Oxenstierna did not fail to point this out in his letters to the King.[4] Gustav Adolf's reply, on 22 April, explicitly disavowed any serious desire for the crown: 'there is no need to do

[1] *AOSB*, I. v. 322.
[2] *ibid.*, I. v. 304.
[3] *cf.* Gustav Adolf's instructions to Oxenstierna, 6 January 1631: *AOSB*, II. I. 677 *seqq.*; and *ibid.*, I. vi. 78 *seqq.*
[4] *ibid.*, I. vi. 178-9, 195.

anything more in the business, being indeed but a matter indifferent'.[1]

In this posture affairs remained for the better part of a year. In the spring of 1632, however, the *sejm* was summoned to meet again. Roussel, who had hitherto effected little (his attempt to incite the Zaporozhian Cossacks to revolt had ended in fiasco),[2] took the opportunity to commit a series of disastrous indiscretions. To the dietines in February, to the diet in March, he addressed circular letters in a variety of tongues, in which he urged that the only hope for Poland lay in a personal union with Sweden. The letters were objectionable not only as to matter but also as to manner; for they were so boastfully and provocatively phrased as to offend every Polish susceptibility. They were universally regarded as a gross impertinence; and they made the emergence of any genuinely pro-Swedish party in Poland extremely improbable.[3]

An obstacle not less formidable was presented by the personality of Sigismund's eldest son, Władysław, who by this time was coming to be recognized as the most likely successor to his father. Władysław had a high admiration for his cousin Gustav Adolf, and was anxious to arrange a meeting with him; and he hoped that it might be possible to negotiate a lasting peace with Sweden, and even to form an alliance against the Muscovite, as in the days of Johan III and Bátory. But he had no intention of renouncing either his Swedish or his Russian title if he could help it—he would have been glad, indeed, to abandon the crown of Poland in exchange for that of Sweden—and he was determined to maintain his rights with energy. He was in close touch with Wallenstein and the Habsburgs; and his trip to Karlsbad in May caused Oxenstierna to speculate anxiously upon what might be afoot.[4] In the spring of 1632 he was deep in plans for raising an army to serve with the Emperor in Germany; for Sigismund was expected to accept an invitation to join the new Habsburg league.[5] Władysław, however, was no Catholic zealot; and it was his indifference to religious issues that commended him to the Dissidents, who hoped for equal rights if he were elected to the throne. But, indeed, the prince's brilliant and attractive qualities made him popular with all parties in Poland, save

[1] *ibid.*, II. I. 710. [2] *ibid.*, II. X. 322; *cf.* Norrman, pp. 88-9.
[3] Norrman, pp. 100-1.
[4] *AOSB*, I. VI. 365, 435, 437; Hallwich, *Briefe und Akten*, II. 159-60, 500; Norrman, p. 59.
[5] Norrman, p. 104.

with those Catholic extremists who wished for a monarch who should be the tool of the church. Gustav Adolf was unlucky, perhaps, to find so exceptionally strong a candidate in the field; for it was certainly the prospect of Władysław's election which nullified Swedish attempts to exploit the Dissidents.

Sigismund III died on 20 April 1632: a sincere, single-minded, high-hearted man; intelligent, richly gifted, and a friend to all the arts; a true son of his parents. It was his misfortune to win few friends in either his native or his adopted country; and the retrospective rancour of the historians of both has left to posterity a portrait of him which does much less than justice to a character which was devoid neither of attractiveness nor of nobility. A month after his death, Radziwiłł wrote to Gustav Adolf putting his services at the King's disposal. He declared himself willing to support his candidature, if it were seriously intended; but he attached certain conditions: Poland must be safeguarded from Russian attack—a matter which especially interested Radziwiłł, since an invasion would fall first on Lithuania; a decent provision for Sigismund's five sons must be guaranteed; and Radziwiłł himself must be given a substantial loan. If, however, Gustav Adolf should not intend to press his claims, then Radziwiłł would support the election of Władysław and work for a firm peace between the two countries.[1]

This letter did not reach Gustav Adolf until July. In the meantime, he had already despatched Nicodemi and Bielke to Poland, in order that they might be present at the election-diet. Their orders ran on familiar lines: they were to foment dissension in the Republic, and to prevent the election of any of Sigismund's sons.[2] There is not much indication here that Gustav Adolf entertained any exaggerated hopes of his own chances. But Radziwiłł's letter was more explicit and encouraging than anything so far received out of Poland; and if Gustav Adolf really desired to be elected, the best chance would probably lie in agreeing to his terms. Despite Oxenstierna's obvious disapproval, the King did not hesitate. Radziwiłł was informed that all his conditions would be accepted; and steps were taken to pay him the money he required. To Oxenstierna Gustav Adolf cynically observed that these promises must be construed 'conditionally'—conditionally, that is, upon his finding it practicable or convenient to fulfil them.[3]

[1] Norrman, pp. 161-7. [2] *AOSB*, I. vii. 525-6; Norrman, pp. 191-2.
[3] *AOSB*, I. vii. 495-8, II. i. 823, 838, II. x. 335.

In the event, his answer, whether sincere or not, had no effect upon the course of affairs in Poland. Long before it arrived, the issue had been virtually decided. From the moment of the vacancy, in fact, Radziwiłł had made up his mind to support Władysław. His negotiations with Gustav Adolf, like his negotiations with George William, had no other purpose but to secure foreign support if it should be necessary to appeal to arms during the interregnum in order to obtain satisfactory terms for the Dissidents. Provided his religion were secure from oppression, he had no intention of disturbing the peace of the Republic. Far from allowing himself to be used as the tool of Swedish policy, he aspired rather to make Gustav Adolf the instrument of his own. He was more than ready to lead a Protestant faction; but a Swedish faction had no particular interest for him. As long as Sigismund lived, the grievances of the Dissidents made possible the combination of Radziwiłł's aims with Swedish designs; but the prospect of Władysław's accession destroyed this working alliance. And even if Gustav Adolf had stood forth as a candidate in real earnest, it is difficult to believe that Radziwiłł would not have preferred Władysław. When Nicodemi and Bielke arrived in Poland, the Dissident nobility came to them, not to promise support for Gustav Adolf but to enlist his backing for Władysław's cause. George William of Brandenburg, whom Gustav Adolf had once counted on to 'put in a word on his behalf',[1] now plainly declared himself of the same party. On 14 October 1632 Władysław completed the wreck of Swedish policy by signing a document in which he promised the Dissidents far-reaching religious liberties.[2] The news of a Russian invasion of Lithuania persuaded the Poles to forgo for once the pleasures of a protracted interregnum or a disputed election. On 29 October Władysław was unanimously chosen King of Poland. It is true that he had been forced, before his election, to give a secret promise to renounce his claims to the throne of Sweden[3]; but Gustav Adolf remained ignorant of this engagement, and in any case Władysław did not honour it in the future. It is true, too, that one of Władysław's first actions was to write a friendly letter to his cousin; but before it was despatched Gustav Adolf was dead.

Gustav Adolf's Polish policy since 1630 had failed completely. If indeed he coveted the throne, the defeat of his candidature could hardly have been more ignominious. If, on the other hand, he had

[1] *ibid.*, II. I. 767. [2] Norrman, p. 263. [3] *ibid.*, pp. 281-7.

no other object than to disturb and weaken the Republic, he had failed to achieve it. Poland was weak indeed in 1632—weaker, certainly, than Gustav Adolf imagined—but the weakness arose from the pacificism of exhaustion, and Swedish intrigues had no part in producing it. Poland's revival under Władysław provides ample retrospective justification for Gustav Adolf's attempts to exclude him from the throne; but it provides, too, a measure of the magnitude of his failure. Gustav Adolf underestimated Polish patriotism; he overestimated the separatist tendencies of men like Radziwiłł. He hesitated and fumbled; he chose his agents unwisely. But in the last resort he failed, not by reason of his mistakes but because the circumstances of the moment in Poland made any success almost impossible. He dared not commit himself too deeply; and anything less than a whole-hearted effort could not succeed. The result was a personal triumph for Władysław.

The King's schemes for harassing the Poles by foreign war had been directed mainly to securing the intervention of Muscovy. It would, however, have been a possible line of action to induce similar attacks by the Sultan, and by his vassals the Khan of the Crimean Tatars and the Prince of Transylvania. This line was not pursued. Each of them, indeed, was a factor in the King's calculations; but he considered that any aid they could give him would be more usefully directed against the Habsburgs: the Russians, he hoped, would give the Poles enough to do.

Gustav Adolf's first contact with the Turks occurred in 1629, when Paul Strassburg, at that time in Transylvania, sent Roussel and the Marquis de Talleyrand (another Frenchman of the same kidney) to Constantinople to plead the cause of Sweden. The Dutch envoy, Cornelis Haga, was still at his post there, and it was thanks to his assistance that the Pasha Cahimarchus was induced to send to Gustav Adolf a letter offering the friendship of the Porte.[1] No immediate effect came of this; but both Gustav Adolf and Oxenstierna were encouraged to hope that the Sultan might launch an attack upon the Austrian lands.[2] In this, however, they were deluding themselves. The Ottoman Empire was passing through a period of internal

[1] The Greek patriarch also favoured the Swedish cause, possibly influenced by the idea which prevailed among some of his church that Gustav Adolf might liberate the Greeks from the Turkish yoke: A. Boëthius, *Romanus Nicephori och Gustaf Adolf*, pp. 299-303.

[2] *AOSB*, I. vi. 404, II. i. 656; *Arkiv*, I. 237.

instability, and its energies were fully engaged by a long-drawn war with Persia. Yet the goodwill of the Sultan was worth having, if only to ensure that he should not forbid his vassals to side with Sweden; and it was with the object of securing his support in Transylvania that Gustav Adolf now ordered Strassburg himself to visit Constantinople.[1] He arrived there in June 1632, at a moment when Sweden's military reputation stood at its zenith; and though he brought with him none of the presents demanded by custom, he was magnificently received. He made the most of the propitious moment, and for the benefit of the Capudan Pasha traced upon a globe the limits of the Swedish realm—fixing them, with pardonable licence, to include everything from Lappland to Alsace.[2] But though the Porte exerted a benevolent influence in Transylvania, and perhaps in the Crimea too, and though the Pasha of Ofen (no doubt on instructions from Constantinople) offered to put his forces at Gustav Adolf's disposal,[3] it was soon apparent that the Turks were not likely for the present to involve themselves in central Europe.

The Khan of the Crimea, Djanbek Geraj, had not thought it necessary to wait for his suzerain's approval before getting in touch with Sweden. News of Swedish preparations may possibly have reached him by way of Moscow: it is at all events certain that the initiative was his own. In January 1630 an embassy of nine arrived in Stockholm bearing letters in the Tatar tongue which no one could read. Interpreters were somehow discovered, and on 8 January the leader of the mission had audience in Uppsala. He offered to send 40,000 men to attack either Poland or the Habsburgs, at Gustav Adolf's choice. In view of the very recent conclusion of the truce of Altmark, the King expressed a preference for the latter of these alternatives; and having entertained his guests royally at Västerås, dismissed them with gifts. He also resolved to explore the Crimean possibilities a little further. In December 1630, Benjamin Baron—yet another of those French experts on eastern Europe who tended to gravitate to the Swedish court—set out for Bakhtchi-Seraj with an offer of 150,000 *rdr.* in subsidies in return for help against the Emperor. He was given a most cordial welcome. In 1632 he returned, bringing with him another Tatar embassy and fresh proposals from the Khan. The Sultan, it seemed, had issued

[1] *AOSB*, II. I. 719.

[2] C. Wibling, *Sveriges förhållande till Siebenbürgen*, pp. 50-2; H. Almquist, *Svenska folkets historia*, pp. 586-7.

[3] Hallwich, *Briefe und Akten*, III. 138-9.

imperative commands to the Khan to supply 30,000 men forthwith for service against the Persians; but there would still be a force of 30,000 available for use against the Emperor, provided Gustav Adolf could guarantee its free transit through Transylvania. The Tatars reached Stockholm in May. Their money was almost exhausted, their clothes were in rags, their appearance decidedly disreputable. The *råd* looked dubiously at them; but at last decided to forward them to the King. With their wardrobes refurbished at Sweden's expense, they proceeded to Germany in search of Gustav Adolf. They never found him. After kicking their heels all winter at Erfurt, they were eventually sent home in 1633 with a polite refusal of their offers. Sweden, it was explained, was not in a position to guarantee a safe passage through Transylvania. It was the answer which Gustav Adolf himself would have been obliged to make, if ever they had caught up with him.[1]

Transylvania, indeed, was the only one of this trio of states from which any aid could reasonably be expected. Bethlen Gabor had no doubt proved an unreliable ally in the 'twenties; but Transylvania was at all events a Protestant country directly menaced by the Habsburgs; and it was possible that its new ruler might prove stauncher than Bethlen. The death of that prince, however, had been followed by a period of confusion. Bethlen's widow, Catherine of Brandenburg, whom he had designed to be his successor, threw away whatever chances she may have had (and she had some, for the Sultan supported her) by the indiscretions of her private life and her foolish vacillations between the Catholic and Protestant factions in the country. The control of Transylvania passed first to Bethlen's brother Stephen, and then, at the close of 1630, to George Rákóczy. Catherine appealed to her brother the Elector of Brandenburg, and to her brother-in-law the King of Sweden; and though neither retained any illusions as to her political and personal reliability, it was felt that for the sake of the family something should be done to see that she was honourably provided for.[2] And it was also desirable that good relations should be established with Rákóczy, in case he should prove to be firmly established in Transylvania. The

[1] G. Jarring, *Gustaf II Adolf och tatarerna på Krim*, pp. 306-7; *RRP*, II. 167; *AOSB*, II. x. 329; *Dagbok*, p. 55. The court of Vienna was well informed of these intrigues, but seems not to have been unduly concerned: Hallwich, *Briefe und Akten*, I. 559, II. 190, 599-601, 728, 766-8.

[2] A. Szilágyi, *Georg Rákóczy I im dreissigjährigen Kriege*, pp. iii-xiii, 3-12; Wibling, pp. 39-43, 48-9; *AOSB*, I. vi. 163-6; *Arkiv*, I. 143; Droysen, *Gustaf Adolf*, II. 69.

obvious choice for this difficult and self-contradictory mission was Paul Strassburg; and at the end of April 1631 he was duly instructed to proceed to Weissenburg. He was to find out what had really been happening in the country; he was to try to discover whether Catherine had really turned Roman Catholic, and to get some sort of settlement for her; and he was to take cautious soundings as to Rákóczy's political views, and, if they proved favourable, push him into war with the Emperor.[1]

Strassburg's departure was delayed for six months by his illness; and it was only in February 1632 that he reached Transylvania. He found Rákóczy well disposed, and ready enough to quarrel with the Habsburgs. He professed, however, to be unable to risk a declaration of war without the sanction of the Sultan; and accordingly Strassburg, when he left Transylvania for Constantinople in March, undertook to do his best to obtain it. In his absence, Rákóczy himself began negotiations directly with Gustav Adolf, whose advance into Germany had now made him more accessible. It immediately became apparent that Rákóczy was not prepared to take any positive steps without the most ample guarantees. He was a shrewd, cunning and ambitious politician; and he had no idea of exposing himself merely in response to Gustav Adolf's vague exhortations. In June 1632 a Transylvanian envoy, Bonczidai, reached Gustav Adolf's camp, and more solid negotiations began. Bonczidai demanded that the Swedes should detach a corps to co-operate with Rákóczy; he demanded an alliance not with Sweden only but with a Protestant league; and in return for the promise of an army of 60,000 men he asked for 400,000 *rdr.* in subsidies, and the right to retain all his conquests: Tungel tartly commented to Salvius that Rákóczy seemed to be singularly like his predecessor.[2]

These terms were quite unacceptable. Gustav Adolf had no troops to spare to assist Rákóczy, nor money to subsidize him to that extent; and as to the Protestant league, he was only too well aware that no such body existed, and was in any case determined that Rákóczy should acknowledge his right to the absolute direction of military affairs. Bonczidai was plainly told that Rákóczy's terms were too stiff, and that he had better make use of an exceptionally favourable opportunity before it passed. The negotiations thereupon came

[1] Szilágyi, pp. 16-29.

[2] G. Irmer, *Die Verhandlungen Schwedens und seiner Verbündeten mit Wallenstein und dem Kaiser* [Irmer, *VS*], I. 262; *AOSB*, I. VII. 277; Szilágyi, pp. xix-xxi; *Sv. Krig*, V. 234-5.

to an end. Rákóczy had for a moment hoped to take advantage of Swedish successes to make cheap and safe territorial gains; Gustav Adolf had hoped to tempt Rákóczy into a political speculation on the strength of general assurances and Protestant principles. Neither had much grasp of the circumstances which limited the freedom of action of the other, and each had a hard-headed determination not to be cheated. By evading an alliance each at least avoided disappointment.[1]

Thus, of all Gustav Adolf's negotiations in eastern Europe not one had any measure of success, except for that which aimed at exploiting the Muscovites' desire for revenge. The intrigues with the Dissidents came to nothing; the embassy to the Turks did no more than nourish delusive hopes in apocalyptically-minded Greeks; and all the comings and goings of seedy Frenchmen and lousy Tatars served only to prepare those shallow and sandy foundations whereon Karl X and Karl XII were one day to raise such insubstantial political edifices.

By the autumn of 1632 it had become very clear that no second front against the Habsburgs was likely to be opened in the East.

(ii) *The West*

(a) *France, Spain and the League*

The appearance of the Swedish armies on the left bank of the Rhine brought with it a real danger of a war with Spain. At Mainz and Oppenheim Gustav Adolf had been confronted with Spanish troops; and he had not hesitated to attack them. There were plenty of Spanish units in the Lower Palatinate, and the operations of the winter made it clear that the King was not prepared to consider them as neutral. Relations with Spain were ostensibly correct; and Gustav Adolf could not know that as early as 5 June 1631 the Spanish council of state had decided in principle upon a war with Sweden.[2] But both the King and Oxenstierna were aware that Spain had been offered serious provocation, and that peace or war might well depend upon the readiness of Philip IV to ignore the challenge. Oxenstierna had heard a report of the capture of Mainz

[1] Already in August 1632 Rákóczy had sent pacific assurances to Vienna, and the imperial advisers did not expect trouble: Hallwich, *Briefe und Akten*, II. 767-8, III. 25. For Gustav Adolf's scepticism about Transylvanian aid, *ibid.*, II. 349.

[2] Günter, *Die Habsburger-Liga*, p. 78.

at Stettin: and he had at once written to the *råd* warning them of the possible consequences, and urging them to put the west-coast defences in order against any attack from Dunkirk.[1] The King himself, on 31 December, sent home a characteristic request for the opinion of the *råd* upon the situation: was war inevitable? was it desirable? was it better to take the initiative, or to allow the break to come from the Spanish side? Spain, after all, was a useful counterpoise to France. But on the other hand the Spanish armies were in the Palatinate; and no peace for Germany could be safe or satisfactory which did not include among its provisions the restoration of Frederick V to his hereditary dominions.[2]

The danger was perhaps even greater than Gustav Adolf supposed; for just at this time Spanish policy seems to have been aiming at turning the middle Rhine into a major theatre of war. Spanish agents were influential at the court of Charles IV of Lorraine, who was deep in intrigues with Marie de' Medici and Gaston of Orleans. The bitter enmity of Spain and Bavaria,[3] the obvious Spanish desire to break down the Bavarian-controlled League, the improvement of Anglo-Spanish relations since the peace of 1630—all led Spanish statesmen to recur to the old idea of a Habsburg league: a league to which this time they hoped to attract, as peripheral allies, Charles I, Kristian IV and even Frederick V.[4] Among the cardinal points in this programme was the establishment in the Palatinate of a powerful Spanish force, which should assume the protection of the ecclesiastical Electors, provide support for Charles IV, and possibly even restore the eldest son of Frederick V, if satisfactory guarantees could be obtained. And on 4 February 1632 the Spanish ambassador in Vienna did in fact sign a treaty which would have laid the foundations of such a Habsburg league. The court of Madrid subsequently declined to ratify it, on the ground that it lacked a definite point against France and the Dutch; but in fact co-operation between Madrid and Vienna became closer than for some time previously.[5]

[1] *AOSB*, I. vi. 570.

[2] *Arkiv*, I. 541-5.

[3] Philip IV was at this time writing that 'el mundo tiene hoi al Duque [*sic*] de Baviera por el enemigo mayor de la casa de Austria': Gardiner, *The Personal Government of Charles I*, I. 220 and *note* 1; and *cf.* G. Mecenseffy, *Habsburger im 17. Jahrhundert*, pp. 22-3; Günter, pp. 115-16.

[4] Lonchay, II. 604.

[5] Günter, pp. 79-80, 99, 103, 105, 107; van der Essen, *Le Cardinal Infant*, pp. 100-1. At the new year, 1632, Philip IV rejected an offer to murder Gustav Adolf for 30,000 Hungarian ducats (Günter, p. 120); and *cf.*, for the Spanish reaction to Gustav Adolf's successes, Lonchay, II. 611-15.

The object of Spain, then, seemed at the close of 1631 to be to engage France in an area where imperialist aid was to be expected, and where Richelieu would be unable to evade a conflict: in January 1632 the Spanish council took a formal resolution (which later had to be cancelled) to declare war on France.[1]

Nevertheless, a breach with Sweden, even in these circumstances, was not inevitable; since both sides could represent themselves as mere auxiliaries to their respective allies. And on the Swedish side (despite some loose remarks by Gustav Adolf) a breach was certainly not desired. In the *råd* discussions of 11 and 13 April 1632 the sense of the meeting was against a rupture [2]; and in the formal advice to the King of 30 April they recommended the avoidance of any hasty decision. A war with Spain would involve commitments of unforeseeable extent, which Sweden probably lacked the resources to meet; there was danger of Danish intervention—and of Polish also, once the truce ran out—and no reliance to be placed on England.[3] And they might have added that Spain was too important a buyer—or at least a potential buyer—of Swedish copper for a war to be lightly risked. Gustav Adolf, in fact, did not risk it. From Augsburg, on 23 May 1632, he wrote to the *råd* ordering them to organize a shipping company at Göteborg for preying on Spanish commerce, on the principles established by Queen Elizabeth [4]; but in reality nothing significant was done. Military operations against Spanish armies on the Rhine and Moselle were not followed by a declaration of war. In December 1632 the *råd* was still debating the Spanish question, and had come no nearer to a positive policy.[5]

The tension with Spain was nevertheless a factor of importance in Sweden's relations with France. The peace of Cherasco, on 9 June 1631, and the vulgar swindle which put Pinerolo into French hands in October,[6] gave Richelieu the security he sought in Italy, and enabled him to turn his attention to the problem of France's

[1] Leman, p. 101.

[2] *RRP*, II. 154-63.

[3] *Arkiv*, II. 436-42; *cf. ibid.*, II. 423. The Swedish naval preparations against possible attack on the west coast are described in E. Zeeh, *Gustav II Adolf och den svenska västkustens försvar*, pp. 19-22.

[4] *AOSB*, II. 1. 802-3: the reference to Elizabeth's methods is Gustav Adolf's own.

[5] *RRP*, II. 243, 245.

[6] Flassan, *Histoire de la Diplomatie française*, II. 460 *seqq.*; Leman, *Urbain VIII*, pp. 25-35. Even Bichi, the papal nuncio in Paris, wrote that 'Questo punto di Pinerolo . . . e delicatissimo e scabroso': *ibid.*, p. 57 *note*. Any reaction by Ferdinand II was inhibited by the grave military situation after Breitenfeld, and by the discouragement of Olivares.

eastern frontier, which was henceforward to occupy the premier place in his diplomacy. Ferdinand II, indeed, held that France was still debarred from intervention in Germany by the provisions of Father Joseph's Regensburg treaty, which the peace of Cherasco had modified only in regard to Mantua[1]; but nobody paid much attention to this argument. From Richelieu's point of view it was high time for France to assert herself beyond the Rhine. It was by now very plain that the treaty of Bärwalde had wholly failed to make Gustav Adolf a French mercenary; and it was extremely doubtful how far Richelieu would be able to exercise any restraining influence upon him. It was therefore necessary for France to fall back upon her complementary policy of patronizing a middle party—a party which, it was hoped, could be deployed against the Habsburgs in the name of the liberties of Germany, and against the Swedes as the alien exploiters of German misery. Very soon after the signature of the treaty of Bärwalde this policy had been resumed: a French envoy, de Lisle, had been sent to the Leipzig Convention, another had been present at the *Kompositionstag* at Frankfort; and attempts had been made under French auspices to induce the two assemblies to make contact.[2] Nothing much came of this; but in the summer of 1631 Richelieu was able to congratulate himself on realizing the long-cherished project of a Bavarian alliance. The treaty of Fontainebleau, concluded on 20 May, was the product of Maximilian's fear of Gustav Adolf, and of his nervousness of the Spanish influences which he supposed to be dominant in Vienna; and it was facilitated by the untiring anti-Habsburg diplomacy of the agents of Urban VIII.[3] It bound Maximilian to France for eight years in a defensive alliance; it guaranteed the electoral dignity to the whole of the Bavarian line of Wittelsbach; it pledged each party to defend the possessions, 'inherited or acquired', of the other; and it was to be kept secret. Its value, to either party, was extremely small. Simultaneously with the signature of the treaty, Bavaria appealed to France for protection against a possible Swedish attack; only to be told that, since Maximilian was the aggressor, the *casus foederis* did not arise.[4] By the treaty of Bärwalde, Richelieu had tried to

[1] Leman, p. 7.

[2] Fagniez, I. 570-3; Baustaedt, p. 35.

[3] Flassan, II. 455 *seqq.*; Hallwich, *Briefe und Akten*, I. 379-81; Riezler, *Geschichte Baierns*, V. 379-81; Mommsen, p. 44; Pagès, *La Guerre de Trente Ans*, pp. 142-3; Quazza, pp. 185-6; Günter, p. 64; Paul, III. 70. On papal policy, Leman, pp. 3, 11, 15, 17.

[4] Fagniez, I. 575-6.

neutralize Bavaria as against Gustav Adolf. He now admitted that the basis of Bärwalde had been destroyed by Maximilian's actions; but at the same time concluded with him a treaty which protected the Elector against every attack save that with which he was in fact threatened. Maximilian had no illusions as to the altruism of French policy.[1] He entered into the treaty of Fontainebleau as a form of insurance. The ink was scarcely dry upon it before he was made aware that he had thrown away his premium. The loss, as it happened, was not serious; for Maximilian had been very careful to hedge around his promises with specific conditions. The treaty was not to prejudice his oath to the Emperor or his obligations to the Empire, 'as far as the law of nature allows'. And to secure himself against misunderstandings in Vienna, he took care to violate the pledge of secrecy and confide the terms of the alliance to Ferdinand II.[2] Thus the treaty of Fontainebleau, which did nothing to prevent that clash between Sweden and Bavaria which Richelieu was so anxious to avert, also did nothing to split Maximilian from his Habsburg ally; while it left the way open (if Maximilian honoured his imperial obligations) for Bavarian resistance to any French advance into Alsace.

In July St. Etienne was sent upon another mission to John George and to Maximilian, to urge them to stand together under French protection.[3] He had no success, either with the one or with the other; and when he went on to press neutrality on the ecclesiastical Electors, not even Trier, the most Francophil of them all, was willing to listen to him.[4] Any prospects which such efforts may have had seemed to be shattered by John George's alliance with Sweden, by the battle of Breitenfeld, and by the Swedish advance to the Main. St. Etienne in Munich, and de Lisle in Leipzig, laboured to prevent the breach between Saxony and Bavaria from becoming irremediable; but they made little headway.[5] Richelieu therefore was driven to reformulate his policy. In October he despatched Charnacé to Maximilian. Charnacé was charged with the task of extending the treaty of Fontainebleau to include all members of the League, while at the same time deleting those reservations (as to fidelity to the Emperor) which had helped to make the original treaty nugatory. And he was also to make another attempt to repair the failure at Bärwalde, by

[1] Riezler, V. 366.
[2] Hallwich, *Briefe und Akten*, I. 458.
[3] Ritter, III. 517-18.
[4] Baur, *Philipp von Sötern*, I. 199.
[5] *Sv. Krig*, V. 237.

inducing Maximilian to agree to the idea of opening negotiations with Gustav Adolf for the neutrality of Bavaria and the League: French aid, it was explained, would be available against the Emperor if Maximilian were attacked by him in consequence of such an arrangement.[1]

Charnacé's mission was the opening move in a policy which engaged much of Richelieu's attention for the next six or seven months: a policy to which he continued to cling long after its hopelessness ought to have been apparent. Its main recommendation, from Richelieu's point of view, was that it provided some sort of a substitute for direct French participation in the war. But before it was well launched, events forced the Cardinal to commit himself in a region which was of such importance to France that he felt bound to take trenchant action.

The political position in Lorraine, and in the three bishoprics of Metz, Toul and Verdun, was from the French point of view thoroughly unsatisfactory. For some time Richelieu had been made nervous by the presence of imperialist troops in Vic and Moyenvic. His representatives at Regensburg had tried in vain to secure the withdrawal of these troops; and one reason for his disavowal of Father Joseph's treaty had been that that treaty seemed to leave open the future not only of Vic and Moyenvic but of the three bishoprics also.[2] In 1625 the Cardinal had attempted to secure a more precise definition of French rights in this area by the setting up of a commission to investigate recent 'alienations' from the lands and dependencies of the three bishoprics. The report that emerged was a curious anticipation of the tactics and arguments of the *Réunions* of 1680; and it was a main cause for Charles IV's hostility to France. For most of the alleged alienations were now Lorraine territory; and they included not only such controversial items as the abbacy of Gorze but also places such as Marsal, which Charles (and everyone else) had hitherto considered to be incontrovertibly Lorraine territory.[3] Charles had acquired the duchy of Lorraine in 1624 in right of his wife, Nicole, and had been duly recognized by the Emperor; but Louis XIII had refused to recognize him as Duke

[1] Avenel, IV. 208; Fagniez, I. 580-1; *cf.* Hallwich, *Briefe und Akten*, I. 522-5, 582, 586.

[2] G. Zeller, *La Réunion de Metz à la France*, II. 240-1; Keller, *Die Friedensverhandlungen zwischen Frankreich und dem Kaiser auf dem Regensburger Kurfürstentag*, p. 23; Baur, I. 184-5; Mommsen, pp. 36, 38, 59, 84.

[3] Zeller, II. 230-5.

of Bar, which was a French fief, linked to Lorraine by a personal union. In the face of provocations such as these, it was no wonder that Charles should have become a warm supporter of the Habsburgs[1] and a notorious focus of anti-French intrigue. The Cardinal's domestic enemies looked to Lorraine for aid and comfort; and early in 1631 Gaston of Orleans—for the second time—fled from France to seek refuge at Charles's court at Nancy.[2] Lorraine became a base from which the party of Gaston and the Queen Mother might launch an invasion which should reverse the verdict of the Day of Dupes and overthrow the minister. In June 1631 Charles concluded an agreement with the Emperor for the raising of troops, ostensibly for service against Gustav Adolf. Richelieu strongly suspected that they would be used to support the intrigues of Gaston.[3] In September, therefore, he sent Charles a sharp warning, and threatened him with invasion unless these troops were moved away from the French frontier. The effect was doubly satisfactory; for not only did Charles remove his troops, but he removed them (in response to an appeal from Munich) to join Tilly in Franconia, and so did something to restore the balance of military power in Germany in the weeks after Breitenfeld.[4] For the moment Gaston was checkmated; and Charles gave comprehensive assurances of good conduct. But in October it was deemed expedient for Louis XIII to move with a considerable army to the eastern frontier.[5]

Matters might have rested there until Gaston had screwed up enough courage for his next perfidy, had it not been for the appearance of the Swedish armies on the Rhine. Gustav Adolf's rapid progress on the left bank suggested the disturbing possibility that Lorraine might be overrun not by French but by Swedish troops: Charles IV had given Gustav Adolf ample cause for war. This was a prospect which Richelieu could not but view with uneasiness. There was danger, too, that Gustav Adolf might take the initiative in evicting the imperialists from Moyenvic, which they had recently fortified, and so jeopardize French control of the bishopric of Metz.[6] Louis

[1] It was said that he aspired to the electorate of Saxony or of Brandenburg: Baur, I. 205.

[2] Hanotaux, III. 340-1; Mommsen, p. 60; Gardiner, I. 225-8: he had fled to Lorraine earlier, in the autumn of 1629.

[3] Ritter, III. 519.

[4] Avenel, IV. 187 and *note* 1, 188 and *note* 1; Mommsen, pp. 62-3; Hallwich, *Briefe und Akten*, I. 500.

[5] Avenel, *loc. cit.*

[6] Hallwich, *Briefe und Akten*, II. 48-9.

XIII considered action by France to be urgently necessary. On 30 November, therefore, the Duke de la Force was ordered to form the siege of Moyenvic[1]; and on 17 December it capitulated. In the course of the siege de la Force succeeded in intercepting a letter from Charles which still further compromised him in French eyes; for in it he promised the imperialist commander to do his best to prevent Moyenvic from falling into the hands of Louis XIII.[2] The French intervention had brought him hurrying home to Nancy after a sojourn with his uncle Maximilian at Munich; but his arrival in Lorraine coincided with the news of the fall of Moyenvic, and in any case he had no army to hand. He had no choice, then, but to submit, at least for the moment. He accordingly hastened to Louis XIII's camp at Metz, full of facile penitence and glib assurances; and on 27 December Richelieu imposed upon him the treaty of Vic.[3] The Duke promised to preserve good relations with France, and as an earnest of his sincerity handed over his fortress of Marsal for the next three years; and by a significant provision undertook to give military aid and transit facilities to French troops if France should intervene on behalf of the Roman Catholics of Germany. Thus, if Richelieu should be driven in desperation to take the field against Gustav Adolf, he would be able, he hoped, to count upon Charles as his ally. The Cardinal was very pleased with himself over the treaty of Vic.[4] He would have been a little less cock-a-hoop had he realized the falseness of Charles, or had he foreseen that Gaston, before many weeks were out, would be negotiating at Vienna through his accredited agent Des Hayes de Cormenin.[5] The Lorraine affair was by no means over.

[1] 'Sa majesté estant résolue d'une façon ou d'autre d'avoir ceste place, et principalement à ceste heure qu'elle a advis des extraordinaires progrez que faict le roy de Suède, lequel a desjà passé le Rhin': Avenel, IV. 213.

[2] See Ernest Montecuccoli's account of Charles's plans, in Dudík, *Waldsteins Correspondenz*, I. 12.

[3] Zeller, II. 246; Avenel, IV. 237 *note* 2; Mommsen, pp. 88-90; E. Falk *Sverige och Frankrike*, p. 16.

[4] Avenel, IV. 243: 'Après avoir pris Moyenvic par force, réduict mons[r] de Lorraine à la raison, et receu Marsal pour gage et seureté de sa foy, garenty la religion en Allemaigne, sauvé la ligue Catholique, l'avoir unie à la France contre la maison d'Autriche. . . .'

[5] *ibid.*, IV. 241 *note*; Richelieu, *Mémoires*, II. 414; Tongas, *Des Hayes de Cormenin*, p. 97 *seqq*. Des Hayes arrived in Vienna in January. His instructions were to negotiate with (among others) 'the King of Hungary': this was not, as Tongas supposes (p. 101), Bethlen Gabor, but Ferdinand III. Bethlen had died in 1629, as Tongas himself points out; and even Gaston is likely to have been aware of his demise. See Hallwich, *Briefe und Akten*, II. 82, 213, 235, for evidence of Charles's double-dealing.

Nevertheless, Richelieu might for the moment feel that the situation on the Moselle had been brought under control. Gustav Adolf had been forestalled. It was far otherwise on the middle Rhine, and in Germany. Somehow or other, he must save his intended sally-ports from falling into Swedish hands; and above all he must rescue Maximilian and the League from the ruin that was now impending over them, for upon their political survival the French system in Germany mainly depended. The ambivalence of his policy, as between Sweden and Bavaria, made it undesirable and dangerous to effect Maximilian's deliverance by military action; and the domestic situation made him anxious to avoid war even for the sake of the Rhine crossings. Diplomacy, then, was the only resource; and the objectives towards which diplomacy must be directed were two. First, to induce Gustav Adolf to admit the neutrality of Bavaria and the League; and secondly, by cajolery or threats, to push the Swedish armies back to the right bank of the Rhine, and induce them to stay there. Thus the Cardinal, who had failed to make Gustav Adolf jump through the hoops when he was weak, was now to embark upon an unpromising attempt to cozen him into doing so when he was strong.

He began upon the matter of neutrality; and the opening of his campaign brought him some success. Philip von Sötern, the Elector of Trier, had for some time shown French proclivities; and the occupation of his electorate and his capital by Spanish troops in 1630 had reinforced this trend. Of all the members of the League, he was the most likely to lend himself to Richelieu's designs. To him, therefore, was sent a French envoy, at the end of November; who so influenced the Elector that on 11 December he put himself and his electorate under French protection. In return, Saludie was sent to Ehrenbreitstein (where the Elector had taken refuge) with an offer to arrange for Trier's neutrality. The offer was enthusiastically accepted; von Sötern remarking that Saludie came like an angel from heaven.[1] Trier was important not only in a political but also in a strategic point of view; for Coblenz, and the great fortress of Ehrenbreitstein which stood opposite to it on the eastern shore of the Rhine, lay within the electoral dominions; while another Rhine passage of importance—that at Philipsburg—belonged to von Sötern in his capacity of bishop of Speyer. Richelieu hoped that the Elector might be induced to put Coblenz into French hands [2]; and though

[1] Baur, I. 221.

[2] Avenel, IV. 251-4.

for the moment he was disappointed in this, von Sötern did at least invite the French to occupy Philipsburg.[1]

Meanwhile, Charnacé, reinforced by St. Etienne, had arrived in Munich on 21 November.[2] His business was to persuade Maximilian to open negotiations with Gustav Adolf for the neutrality of the League; and the tactic he adopted was to try to stampede him into a decision. He offered promises and inducements: if Gustav Adolf violated any agreement for neutrality, France would aid Maximilian with 15,000 foot and 2000 horse; if neutrality could only be agreed on, Gustav Adolf would certainly be willing to consider a general peace. He also offered threats: if Maximilian should refuse to be neutral, France would join with Sweden.[3] Maximilian found it very difficult to make up his mind. There was no time to consult the League as a whole; and though he did consult his brother, the Elector of Cologne, he got little satisfaction of his consultation. Maximilian was a loyal, if somewhat exigent, ally; and he shrank from deserting Ferdinand at this crisis. He foresaw that the neutralization of the territories of the League would throw the whole burden of war upon the Habsburg hereditary lands. But the military situation was dark; and when he turned to Tilly and Aldringen for an expert assessment of the prospects he found them gloomy in the extreme: Tilly, it seemed, was 'quite perplexed, . . . *in consiliis* quite irresolute'.[4] At last, after prolonged agonizing, Maximilian agreed to formulate his terms; and on 14 December he delivered them to Charnacé. They were sufficiently stiff: there must be full restitution of the lands of the League now in possession of the enemy; Maximilian's right to both Palatinates, and to the electorate, must be conceded; and the imperialist troops at present scattered over Germany must be guaranteed a free retreat to the Habsburg hereditary lands. The acceptance of these terms was to be a condition precedent for Bavaria's neutrality.[5]

Such terms meant that Charnacé's mission had failed. It was scarcely to be expected that Gustav Adolf would look at them. So far from effectively detaching Maximilian from Ferdinand II, the negotiations had made it plain that he deserted his ally with

[1] For this episode, see Droysen, II. 479; Baur, I. 220-1; Mommsen, pp. 134-5.

[2] Riezler, V. 394.

[3] *Sv. Krig*, V. 237.

[4] Riezler, V. 395-6. For the extremely gloomy view of the military situation on the imperialist side, see Hallwich, *Briefe und Akten*, I. 667-9, 688-9, II. 16, 38, 39-40, 54-5.

[5] Droysen, II. 479; L. Weibull, *DF*, pp. 97-8; *Sv. Krig*, V. 238.

reluctance, and under sharp prickings of conscience.[1] It was no consolation, from the French point of view, that Maximilian should have suggested—and indeed urged—that the French should occupy Mannheim; for Mannheim lay east of the Rhine, and for the French presented risks and difficulty.[2] There was some doubt, too, how far other members of the League would be prepared to conform to Maximilian's terms. A meeting of the less important members, at Ingolstadt on 25 December, was induced without much difficulty to endorse his policy [3]; but the Elector of Cologne was following a line of his own, and infuriated Maximilian by informing him that he proposed to wait and see what the prospects of a general peace really were before committing himself.[4] The pressure of events, however, was soon to become too strong even for the Elector of Cologne. The Elector of Mainz, and the bishops of Würzburg, Worms and Osnabrück, had all taken refuge in the city of Cologne; and at a meeting with the Elector on 31 December they decided, despite the urgent warnings of Spain, to accept the idea of neutrality, and to send the bishop of Würzburg to Metz (where by this time Louis XIII and Richelieu had established themselves) to announce their decision and enlist the support of France.[5]

By the end of 1631, then, the League had more or less fallen in with Richelieu's wishes. With Gustav Adolf the Cardinal had made much less progress. His first move had been to send Melchior de Lisle on a special mission to Mainz, apparently with the idea of testing the King's temper. De Lisle was to remonstrate with him for his attack on the League, as being a breach of the treaty of Bärwalde; and he was to demand that he recognize the neutrality of Bavaria and her allies.[6] The response was ominous: Gustav Adolf

[1] Maximilian kept the Emperor informed of what he was doing; tried to argue that it would redound to the Emperor's advantage; and urged that Louis XIII would in any case be a properer mediator than George of Hesse-Darmstadt. He did not know (he admitted) what the French designs were; but he had an impression that Louis XIII coveted a position on the Rhine!: Riezler, V. 398; Hallwich, *Briefe und Akten*, II. 23-4.

[2] Riezler, V. 394-8; Baur, I. 225; Avenel, IV. 251 *seqq.* Mannheim soon afterwards fell into Swedish hands.

[3] It was significant that the meeting, in an effort to reconcile the desirable with the necessary, resolved to seek mediation 'in conjunction with the Emperor': Droysen, II. 481-2.

[4] Droysen, II. 479; *Sv. Krig*, V. 238. For his appeal to Spain for aid, see Lonchay, II. 598.

[5] Hallwich, *Briefe und Akten*, II. 61-4, 241-50; Baur, I. 227-8; Droysen, II. 480.

[6] *Arkiv*, I. 775 *seqq.*; Frohnhäuser, p. 112; Droysen, II. 482-3; L. Weibull, *DF*, p. 97.

intimated that he would be willing enough to grant neutrality provided the League ceased hostilities, withdrew its forces from the Emperor's armies, disbanded all its troops and transferred them to the service of France. Thus reinforced (he observed), France would be able to attack Burgundy, Luxemburg, Flanders and perhaps Italy.[1] And in order to make sure that the sting in the tail of this answer should not fail to make its effect, Gustav Horn [2] was sent to Metz on 24 December with instructions to repeat it. He was to say other disagreeable things also; as that Gustav Adolf could have a peace in Germany whenever he chose—which would mean that disbanded Swedish mercenaries would reinforce the Habsburg armies against France. And he was to suggest, 'as it were in jest', that Louis XIII might well aspire to the Empire himself, and Richelieu to the Papacy.[3] This last sally, as it happened, stirred an already vibrant string: the political gossips at the French court were just at this time canvassing the possibility of Louis' election as King of the Romans.[4]

Any faint possibility that France might intervene actively on the lines suggested by Gustav Adolf, or that Richelieu's diplomacy might be given a cutting edge by the use of military force, was effectively disposed of by the decision of the French council on 27 December. At that meeting Richelieu succeeded in defeating a proposal for an immediate invasion of Alsace, on the valid ground that it would alienate France's friends in Germany.[5] The debate is of interest as revealing the extraordinary inability of French statesmen to form a correct idea of what Gustav Adolf might reasonably be expected to do. It was urged, for instance, that if France were to attempt to ally with the Emperor against Sweden, and Gustav Adolf were to get wind of it, he might himself join Ferdinand, turn against France and condemn her to 'eternal war'; or, again, that if France were to remain purely passive, Gustav Adolf would crush the Roman Catholics of Germany, 'occupy the passes of the Rhine and the Grisons, carry his arms to Italy to overthrow the Papacy, and destroy Roman Catholicism everywhere'. The policy of supporting the German Catholics, of infiltrating peacefully towards the Rhine, was endorsed, among other reasons, because 'this would divert the King

[1] Falk, p. 16 *seqq.*; Droysen, II. 483.
[2] Gustav Horn the younger, not the field-marshal.
[3] Falk, pp. 16-17; *Sv. Krig*, V. 239.
[4] Hanotaux, III. 429.
[5] Papal diplomacy was also opposed to such a course: Leman, p. 102. The decision did not prevent Richelieu from threatening the Archduke Leopold with invasion a few days later: *ibid.*, p. 89.

of Sweden from his Italian venture; for if the King turned south, the French army could cut his communications in Germany, and his line of retreat'.[1] Such arguments make it clear that Richelieu, in his relations with his ally, was fumbling for a policy in the dark. That France should ally with the Emperor in order to check the advance of Sweden was perhaps conceivable; that Richelieu should suppose Gustav Adolf capable of it argues astonishing ignorance. It is possible that Gustav Adolf's remarks to de Lisle, as to his ability to get a peace in Germany at any time, may have provided an explanation, though hardly a basis, for these fantasies. But to talk of the King of Sweden's 'Italian venture' would certainly have excited (if he had known of it) the well-attested risibility of that monarch. Richelieu had indeed a policy, of a sort; but he could not hope to carry it into effect without sacrificing his alliance with Sweden; he could not count on splitting Bavaria from the Habsburgs without binding himself to support Maximilian in arms; and a breach with Sweden, and military aid to Bavaria, would almost certainly lead to further Swedish advances west of the Rhine. His only chance, perhaps, of inducing Gustav Adolf to conform to his wishes was an immediate declaration of war against the Habsburgs; and this he had made up his mind not to risk for the present. Without the backing of effective force, Richelieu was only preparing humiliation for himself and his country; and in no long time humiliation duly followed.

On 30 December Charnacé arrived in Mainz with Maximilian's terms for neutrality, and forthwith laid them before the King. They were at once rejected. Like Maximilian, Gustav Adolf foresaw that the neutralization of the lands of the League would transfer the burden of war elsewhere; and mainly, he feared, to the lands of the Protestant princes. The rich Catholic territories of central Germany were almost essential to the maintenance of the war upon the increased scale which he contemplated for 1632. Therefore, as he at once made plain to Charnacé, the restitution of the Swedish conquests must wait for the general peace. Moreover, as a condition precedent to the granting of neutrality he would require the total disarming of the League. It was in vain that Charnacé hinted at French military aid in return for Bavarian neutrality: Richelieu's naïve hope that Gustav Adolf might be induced to move off in the direction of Vienna in return for vague promises of French action

[1] For these debates, see Hanotaux, III. 431; Fagniez, I. 585; Pagès, p. 160.

on the Rhine was at once shattered. A second interview, on 2 January, came to an abrupt conclusion when the King, losing his temper, told Charnacé that sooner than grant neutrality on the terms that France was pressing upon him, he 'would put the whole affair into the hands of Spain, and make a universal peace; whereat Charnacé appeared tolerably perplexed'.[1]

Four days later, on 6 January, yet another French ambassador arrived at Gustav Adolf's court. This was the Marquis de Brézé, Richelieu's brother-in-law; and the choice of so distinguished a personage was obviously designed to give weight to Charnacé's negotiations. With Brézé's arrival, the issue of neutrality for the moment gave way to the second element in Richelieu's policy—the attempt to edge Gustav Adolf away from the Rhine. This was a desperate enterprise indeed. Brézé had the unenviable task of suggesting to Gustav Adolf that he should hand over his conquests west of the Rhine—including the great base he was constructing at Mainz—either to the ecclesiastical Electors or to France; and in support of this proposal he advanced the claim that these regions had been French since the days of Dagobert.[2] It was not, perhaps, an argument to carry much weight with one who claimed to be the legitimate successor of Magog, Ubbe, Berik and Alarik.[3] And when he suggested that Gustav Adolf should compensate himself by annexations in north Germany, he drew upon himself the angry retort, 'I am come as *protector*, not as *proditor*, *Germaniae*'.[4] Arguments failing, the two ambassadors fell back on threats: the King of France, they hinted, was ready to march with an army of 40,000 men. This was a crass psychological blunder. 'Your King,' retorted Gustav Adolf heatedly, 'has no need of so many men in order to beat me. Had it depended on mere numbers, it had not been I who beat the Emperor, but he me. Let your king go where he will; but let him have a care not to cross the path of my armies, or he may look for a *rencontre* with me.'[5] And there, for the moment, they left it.

[1] *Arkiv*, I. 775 *seqq.*, for these interviews.

[2] Richelieu, *Mémoires*, II. 362 *seqq.*; L. Weibull, *DF*, pp. 98-9; Pagès, pp. 158-9; Fagniez, I. 589.

[3] This kind of 'historical' argument was one of Richelieu's regular diplomatic weapons: R. von Albertini, *Das politische Denken in Frankreich zur Zeit Richelieus*, pp. 147-9, 153.

[4] L. Weibull, *DF*, pp. 98-9.

[5] Droysen, II. 487; Weibull, *loc. cit.*; *Sv. Krig*, V. 240. Mommsen (*op. cit.*, p. 133) follows Fagniez (*op. cit.*, I. 585 *note* 2) in making Gustav Adolf at this interview offer the left bank of the Rhine to France in return for military aid.

Gustav Adolf was soon ready with a more careful and explicit statement of his conditions for neutrality; and these he presented to the ambassadors on 9 January. He made three concessions. He was prepared to allow the League an army of 12,000 men—provided it was kept dispersed; he abandoned the demand for the immediate restoration of the whole of Germany to the territorial arrangements of 1618, and insisted on this only for the Lower Saxon Circle; and he was willing to concede a truce of fourteen days, so that the French might have time to coerce the League into acceptance of his conditions. His terms were certainly stringent. The League was to give no open or secret aid to the Habsburgs; their troops were to be withdrawn from all their conquests; Maximilian must content himself with the Upper Palatinate only, pending an agreement with Frederick V. In return, Gustav Adolf, after acceptance of his conditions, would restore the lands he had taken from the Electors of Cologne and Trier—except for Speyer; he would retain his other conquests until a general peace; and he would refrain from attacking the League in any lands as yet unoccupied by his troops—though from this assurance Bamberg was specifically excepted. The truce was not to apply to sieges and blockades already undertaken by Swedish troops. All Protestant princes and Estates of Germany were to be considered 'in so far as they desire it' as standing under Swedish protection. England and France were to be invited to mediate between Maximilian and Frederick V. And, finally, France must guarantee the good faith of the League; and must also guarantee the ultimate restitution to all German Protestants of their territorial possessions as they had existed in 1618, if an agreement on neutrality should be concluded.[1]

Brézé, as was to be expected, refused to subscribe to these terms. But now it was Gustav Adolf's turn to threaten. The truce terms were presented to the ambassadors as an ultimatum; and the King is said to have cried, 'Sign, then; or get you gone and tell your King to take again the road by which he came to Germany.' [2] And after some protests they did sign; and the truce began on the following day.[3]

That they should have signed, and (still more) that they should

[1] *Arkiv*, I. 778-9; Droysen, II. 489-90; *Sv. Krig*, V. 240-1.

[2] Frohnhäuser, p. 112.

[3] The French guarantee, however, excepted the places held by Maximilian 'in *utroque* Pallatinatu': *Sverges traktater*, V. 649-50; Gustav Adolf to Horn, 10 January 1632, *Schriftstücke*, pp. 212-13.

not have been disavowed, is the measure of France's impotence. For this was no ordinary diplomatic defeat; it was a capitulation. Richelieu had now undertaken to press upon his clients terms which only desperation could make tolerable; he had shouldered a contingent obligation to intervene in Germany to restore the *status quo ante bellum*; and by consenting to Gustav Adolf's stipulations about the Palatinate he had violated his engagements under the treaty of Fontainebleau, and broken faith with Maximilian. If neutrality came about on this basis, Richelieu's Catholic allies in Germany would be useless to him, while his Swedish ally would be raised far beyond the possibility of influence or control by France. The instructions and memoranda drawn up by the Cardinal at this period reveal clearly enough a sense of having lost all command of the situation. On 9 January, in fresh instructions to Brézé, he proposed another set of solutions for the problem of the lands west of the Rhine—all of them obviously unacceptable to the King [1]; he ordered Brézé to try to induce the Elector of Cologne to cede Dinan; he was ready to allow Gustav Adolf to retain the Lower Palatinate until the conclusion of a general peace, since Frederick V would be incapable of defending it.[2] A memorandum of 11 January, after laying it down that the time had come to set limits to the progress of Sweden, reached the illogical conclusion that France must for the present pursue a policy of caution.[3] Another, of 22 January, suggested the keeping of a large army on the eastern frontier, but simultaneously advised against the invasion of Alsace, and urged the preservation of peace (at least for the present) with both Gustav Adolf and the Emperor.[4] And, finally, the instructions transmitted to Charnacé on 27 January were of an astonishing flaccidity [5]: Charnacé was to avoid provocative language, and to give no pretext for a rupture; he was to implore Gustav Adolf to refer the whole matter to a general peace conference ('*le roy le luy demand à sa prière*'); he was to try to persuade Gustav Adolf, by any arguments that might occur to him (clearly Richelieu could think of none) to refrain from taking Breisach. And if Gustav Adolf should enquire

[1] Gustav Adolf was either to restore all his conquests from the League; or to put them into French hands; or to agree in principle to restore such as should be determined on at a general conference; the bishops meanwhile being allowed to exercise spiritual authority. Or two other alternatives, equally far-fetched.

[2] Avenel, IV. 251 *seqq.*

[3] Pagès, pp. 161-2.

[4] *ibid.*, p. 163.

[5] Avenel, IV. 256 *seqq.*

why France remained militarily inert, he was to reply that 'it is not the custom in France to begin campaigns before spring'. To such fatuous equivocations was the Cardinal now reduced.

However, he did his best to persuade his German *protégés* to follow the line he had chalked out for them. Their appeals for French support were rejected; and pressure was brought to bear upon them to comply.[1] Not without success: on 21 January Cologne signified to France his acceptance of the Swedish terms—though with reservations which Oxenstierna deemed 'jesuitical'; and Trier had already given an unreserved adhesion.[2] Maximilian, though he continued to struggle for better conditions, seemed likely to follow suit: as late as 19 January he saw little hope of escape; as late as 27 January Aldringen was reckoning on Bavarian neutrality; and Wallenstein took the precaution of calling in all imperialist units serving with the League armies.[3] The prospects looked so good that Brézé had no difficulty in getting Gustav Adolf to agree to the prolongation of the armistice for an additional week.

At this juncture, however, there fell into Swedish hands a letter from Maximilian to Pappenheim, which made it plain that Pappenheim was ordered not to allow the armistice to interrupt his operations in the Lower Saxon Circle.[4] Now Gustav Adolf had certainly considered that the withdrawal of Pappenheim from this region was a condition of the armistice [5]; and Swedish propaganda made much of the incorrigible faithlessness of the papists. Unfortunately, it does not appear that the cessation of arms had been respected by the Swedes either: Horn's activity in Franconia is difficult to justify.[6] But at least the order to Pappenheim revealed the true feelings of Maximilian. Maximilian had never meant to accept neutrality if he could help it; he had latterly been at pains to convince Wallenstein and the Emperor of this; and at the end of January he began to gather his forces for the blow which Tilly was to strike against Horn a month later.[7] Oxenstierna later remarked that Maximilian had 'betrayed' France [8]; but in truth France had betrayed herself, for

[1] *AOSB*, I. VII. 17; Fagniez, I. 583, 589; Baustaedt, p. 54.

[2] *Sverges traktater*, V. 650-5; Baur, I. 228.

[3] Riezler, V. 400-1; Hallwich, *Briefe und Akten*, II. 146; Oxenstierna confidently expected Maximilian's acceptance: *AOSB*, I. VII. 17.

[4] Chemnitz, I. 278; *cf.* Hallwich, *Briefe und Akten*, II. 134, 136.

[5] *Schriftstücke*, pp. 212-13.

[6] *Sv. Krig*, V. 462.

[7] *ibid.*, 472, 475-6, 479, 482; Droysen, II. 490-5; B. Dudík, *Waldstein von seiner Enthebung bis zur abermaligen Uebernahme des Armee-ober-Commando*, p. 294; Hallwich, *Briefe und Akten*, II. 153, 182-3, 205-6.

[8] *AOSB*, I. VII. 65.

from the moment of Charnacé's visit to Munich in the previous autumn Richelieu had been well enough informed of the Elector's feelings. Maximilian was still prepared to go through the forms of negotiating, in the hope of gaining time; but he neither expected nor desired an agreement. And in these sentiments Gustav Adolf was now inclined to concur.

When, therefore, Charnacé and Brézé once more had audience with the King (on 18 February), they were subjected to a painful interview. They found him '*si aigre, que si nous eussions voulu rompre et luy déclarer la guerre nous l'eussions fait avec facilité*'. And when they told him that representatives of the ecclesiastical Electors might be expected shortly, he replied only that '*c'étaient des coquins et des traîtres*', and if they ventured into his camp he would hang them.[1] No wonder if, in the wreck of their diplomacy, Charnacé and Brézé sought a face-saving escape from their difficulties in pressing for a general peace.[2]

Gustav Adolf started for his last campaign on 3 March. He was not without hope that it might produce in the League a more accommodating temper. If he could win another major victory over Tilly, there might well be a better harvest to be garnered from negotiation. For the moment, Oxenstierna was ordered to protract the talks with the League members, pending a military decision.[3] In France he had now no faith at all. He reckoned with the possibility of French intervention against him; and he recommended the chancellor to get rid of the French ambassadors, 'the sooner the better'.[4] For spinning out negotiations, Oxenstierna had few superiors, even in the seventeenth century; and the representatives of Maximilian, Cologne, and Trier, who came to him in March, would no doubt have been driven to the limits of exasperation by his tactics had they not at an early stage discovered a providential lack of consonance between their several instructions. This was pretext enough for the envoys of Bavaria and Cologne to take their departure on 27 March.[5] They did not return. And with their going the last vestiges of Richelieu's plan for running Bavaria and Sweden in double harness vanished too. Bavarian neutrality, as Oxenstierna remarked, was 'sunk'.[6]

[1] Pagès, p. 165. [2] *Arkiv*, II. 364. [3] *AOSB*, II. I. 761.
[4] *ibid.*, II. 771-2. [5] *ibid.*, I. VII. 65, 103, 218.
[6] The negotiations, he wrote to the *råd* on 19 April, 'föll i brunnen' (*lit.* fell into the well): *AOSB*, I. VII. 218.

But the envoy of Trier, shrewder than his colleagues, remained. He had something solid to offer, for the French had still not occupied Philipsburg; he was the particular friend of France; he had a sharp eye to his own advantage; and he did not despair of a separate arrangement. Gustav Adolf was willing to bargain with him. He would have been glad enough to have Philipsburg and Ehrenbreitstein in his own hands, in return for according neutrality; but he was prepared, if need be, to see them placed in the hands of France.[1] If Richelieu were to obtain them, he would first of all have to evict their Spanish garrisons, and the doing so might perhaps bring France to that open breach with Spain which he desired. And Richelieu was, in fact, able to persuade the Elector to ratify the arrangement concluded between them in December.[2] Thereafter the French ambassadors succeeded without much difficulty in mediating between Trier and Sweden; so that on 12 April a treaty was signed whereby Gustav Adolf recognized the neutrality of the electorate, agreed that Philipsburg and Ehrenbreitstein be occupied by French troops, and for himself acquired the right to occupy Speyer—a useful measure of insurance against French double-dealing in Philipsburg.[3] On 26 May Ehrenbreitstein admitted a French force; and when on 22 June Gustav Horn captured Coblenz, he handed over that place also to the French, against guarantees of free passage across the river to the Swedish armies.[4] In August French troops evicted the Spaniards from Trier itself. But when Gustav Adolf fell at Lützen, they had still failed to overcome the resistance of Philipsburg's dogged garrison.

Thus Richelieu, with Gustav Adolf's acquiescence, did not emerge quite empty-handed from the diplomatic struggles of the winter. His success in Trier, moreover, was accompanied by a simultaneous victory in Lorraine. Charles IV had never meant to observe the treaty of Vic. It had been nullified in advance by his consent, three days before its signature, to the marriage of his sister Margaret to Gaston of Orleans.[5] The news of this agreement did not reach the French government for some months; but already in February Oxenstierna was warning Richelieu that Charles was

[1] *AOSB*, II. I. 762, 781.

[2] Baur, I. 236-7; Mommsen, p. 135.

[3] *Sverges traktater*, V. 734-44; *AOSB*, I. VII. 183 *seqq.*, 218.

[4] Avenel, IV. 319-22; *AOSB*, I. VII. 287, 378, 409, 446, 451, 475, 500, II. I. 790-1, 796, 870; Hallwich, *Briefe und Akten*, II. 497; *cf. Sverges traktater*, V. 773-82.

[5] Avenel, IV. 250 *note* 1; Mommsen, p. 94.

making mischief.[1] The Cardinal prepared a leisurely vengeance, dissimulating his indignation until his arrangements were complete. On 30 May he sent Charles a final warning [2]; and on the same day Charnacé concluded with Oxenstierna a convention whereby it was agreed to adopt a common policy towards Lorraine. Louis XIII undertook to bring the Duke to reason, and to prevent his engaging for the future in measures inimical to Sweden. If in consequence France were attacked by Spain or the Emperor, Sweden would give military assistance.[3] Early in June the French forces moved into Lorraine; and on 16 June Charles was compelled to sign the treaty of Liverdun, whereby the treaty of Vic was confirmed, and France obtained, by way of additional security, the towns of Stenay and Jametz.[4]

Richelieu's success in Trier and Lorraine was real enough (among other things, the collapse of Charles made it easy to deal with Gaston); but it could not offset the ruin of his policy in Germany. Indeed, the independent line taken by Trier dealt the final blow to the League, which it had so long been Richelieu's aim to support: the spring of 1632 saw its final extinction. With the rest of its former members, and conspicuously with Maximilian, France was now discredited; and the Elector turned in his isolation more than ever to Vienna for aid, as Spanish statesmen had hoped that he would. Gustav Adolf, on the other hand, had little to regret in his handling of relations with France. He had, indeed, failed to involve Richelieu in war with the Habsburgs; but France's commitments in Trier and Lorraine might do that for him shortly. His main concern throughout had been military rather than political: if

[1] *AOSB*, I. vii. 20; Avenel, IV. 269-78.

[2] Avenel, IV. 271-4, 275, 303; Mommsen, p. 95.

[3] *Sverges traktater*, V. 767-70; *AOSB*, I. vii. 401-4, II. i. 814. Charnacé seems also to have offered an alliance more explicitly directed against Spain: in a letter of 5 June (now apparently lost) Oxenstierna asked the King whether he should sign such a treaty; and the King replied on 9 June expressing surprise that he should have thought it necessary to enquire, since a breach with Spain seemed probable: *AOSB*, II. i. 808-9. In the spring of 1632 Spain had virtually decided on an attack on France in Alsace: the orders for it were cancelled only in June: Lonchay, II. 617, 627. Navaz' discussions with Richelieu in April about peace (Avenel, IV. 278-82) were probably insincere on both sides. No additional Franco-Swedish alliance seems to have been concluded, however. It is significant that Gustav Adolf welcomed Richelieu's move into Lorraine as offering some assurance that France would be unable, for a little while at least, to turn her arms against himself.

[4] Hanotaux, III. 362-3. The French invasion was accompanied by propaganda which made the point that Charles IV's policy hindered France from giving aid to the Roman Catholics of Germany: Mommsen, p. 96.

he were to advance upon Munich and Vienna in 1632 he must have security for his right flank and rear—that is, he must be assured of a firm grip upon the middle Rhine. To hand over Mainz to France, to evacuate the left bank, in return for mere promises, would have been stupid; and threats he felt himself strong enough to contemn. It was a matter of indifference to him whether France established a foothold on the Rhine or not, provided his military interests there were not jeopardized. If the French had given a firm assurance that they would at once engage the Habsburg armies in this area, if they had openly joined forces with Sweden (as the Spaniards feared they would),[1] he might have been ready enough to quit Alsace: he did not need Richelieu's cajolings to direct him towards the Austrian hereditary lands. But failing such an assurance, he must create a solid base on the Rhine, big enough to provide him with recruits and supplies, firm enough to interpose a barrier to the flow of men or money from Brussels to Vienna. And to effect this, he must enlarge the area under Swedish control. He could not risk a nominally neutral Bavaria which should stand with forces intact ready to fall upon him at a favourable moment, as he strove to coerce Ferdinand II into making peace; nor could he tolerate the restoration of the rich ecclesiastical lands of central Germany, which he hoped to exploit to his advantage, as long as the war continued. He had no desire to pick a quarrel with France; on the contrary: he was too well aware of the value of French subsidies. Indeed, it was a cardinal point of his policy that a breach with France was to be avoided.[2] But he seems to have divined that Richelieu was acting on the same principle [3] and to have skilfully exploited the advantage which that knowledge gave him. The confusion and feebleness of French diplomacy [4] made it easy for him to impose his will; and the tactlessness of the French envoys presented him with opportunities (which he would have been wiser to decline) to deploy a brutality of language which reinforced the French feeling that they had to do

[1] Isabella to Philip IV, 8 December 1631: Lonchay, II. 598.

[2] Vitzthum on 27 December reported Gustav Adolf as saying that 'die einzige Consideration wäre nur, dass man Frankreich nicht zum Feinde machte': G. Droysen, *Die Verhandlungen über den Universalfrieden im Winter 1631/2* [cited: Droysen, *Universalfrieden*], p. 215; and Oxenstierna made the same point to Einsiedel on 6 February: *ibid.*, p. 231.

[3] Kuttner reported to Maximilian on 4 January that in no case would France break with Sweden: Riezler, V. 400.

[4] *cf.* de Lisle's extraordinary attempt, in March 1632, to interest William V in the idea of a peace by suggesting that Urban VIII was planning a new Council of Trent, to which Protestants would be invited: Rommel, VIII. 180.

with a Gothic savage, insensible to the pre-eminent importance of France's having everything exactly as she chose. It was a trait which he inherited from his father and his grandfather. But it grew more marked in the last year of his life; and it was difficult for contemporaries not to see in it the arrogance of the conqueror. The Franco-Swedish alliance still stood, in the summer of 1632, and no doubt now remained as to the dominant partner in it; but there was henceforth scarcely even the pretence of friendship.

(b) *The Dutch and the Swiss*

On either flank of the long western frontier of Germany, outside the *Reich* but still closely linked to it, lay the composite republics of the United Netherlands and the Swiss Confederation. Neither had as yet been drawn into the German wars; and each was equally anxious to escape involvement. The Swiss clung to their neutrality, and the peace and prosperity of their country presented a startling contrast to the misery and devastation that prevailed just across their border [1]; the Dutch had their own war to wage, and throve on it exceedingly. Yet the Swiss were brought to the very brink of the abyss by their inevitable interest in the control of the Alpine passes, through which Spanish reinforcements could most easily be sent to Austria; while the issue of the struggle in the Netherlands was of concern to the whole of Europe. In both areas French diplomacy had long been active—so active that statesmen in Paris were prone to regard each republic as almost a French client. The coming of Gustav Adolf to the Rhine, therefore, the advance of his armies north and south along the river, added a sudden and unwelcome complication to the politics of the Cantons and the States General; and produced in France some apprehension lest Swedish influence, backed by Swedish armies, might threaten or supplant the traditional ascendancy of France.

As concerned the Dutch, Richelieu had really little to fear. It is true that the outbreak of hostilities between the Swedish and Spanish forces in the Rhineland had an immediate effect upon the military situation in the Netherlands, and certainly gave assistance to Frederick Henry.[2] But since the failure in the spring of 1630 of Camerarius's attempt to renew or replace the Swedish-Dutch alliance

[1] The contrast is well described in Grimmelshausen, *Simplicissimus*, Book V. ch. 1.

[2] Blok, IV. 313.

of 1614,[1] relations between the two countries had not been intimate. The Dutch wished Gustav Adolf well in his German enterprise; but they gave him no immediate support, either in men or money. It was not until May 1631 that the States General resolved to accord him a subsidy of 50,000 gulden a month, and then only for three months [2]; and though in December they signed a treaty with Sweden whereby the subvention was to be continued for a further two months, they made it clear that they could send no troops to Germany,[3] and in the sequel they proved far from punctual in the payment even of these meagre contributions. They were, however, sufficiently impressed by Gustav Adolf's successes, and sufficiently exacerbated by Kristian IV's manipulations of the Sound Tolls, to be proof against advances from Denmark: when Kristian approached them with a view to an alliance, they replied by suggesting a general league, to include both Denmark and Sweden.[4] But there was, nevertheless, a certain reserve in the Dutch attitude; and it was from time to time apparent that they were not without sympathy for the idea of a third party in Germany, and would certainly prefer that Gustav Adolf should as far as possible be 'grouped'. They patronized Frederick V; they renewed their alliance with Brandenburg.[5] In England, indeed, they rightly had little confidence, and would have had even less could they have known the plans which Charles I was revolving: Hamilton's agents found them decidedly unfriendly.[6]

The natural collaborator in Dutch policy towards Sweden was, in fact, France. In June 1630 the Franco-Dutch alliance had been renewed for a further period of seven years, and Richelieu (as he told the Spanish secretary Navaz in April 1632) regarded its maintenance as a fundamental point in French policy.[7] For each party, the natural enemy was Spain; and each was prepared to look with benevolence on princes hostile to Spain, whatever their religion. The Dutch, therefore, sympathized with Richelieu's encouragement

[1] For this, see Schybergson, *Sveriges diplomatiska förbindelser med Holländerna*, pp. lxxxvii-c. [2] *Sv. Krig*, III. 545; *Sverges traktater*, V. 454-6.

[3] *Sverges traktater*, V. 601-3. Gustav Adolf was still hoping for a renewal of the old alliance: Söltl, III. 222.

[4] Fridericia, *YPH*, I. 203-4; *Sv. Krig*, V. 250; J. Schreiner, *Nederland og Norge 1625-1650*, pp. 51-3, for Dutch attempts to mediate in September 1631 between Kristian IV and Hamburg.

[5] 2 April 1632: J. Hora Siccama, *Schets van de diplomatieke Betrekkinge tusschen Nederland en Brandenburg*, p. 106; Waddington, I. 116.

[6] Hist. MSS. Comm., *Hamilton Supplementary*, pp. 14-15; *ibid.*, *Hamilton*, p. 70. [7] Avenel, IV. 280; Waddington, I. 125.

of Maximilian and the League, and themselves kept on good terms with them. They would have been glad enough to see Richelieu's plan for the neutralizing of these princes succeed; but when it failed, their object must be, as France's was, to induce Gustav Adolf to direct his main attack upon the Habsburgs, and to restrain him from kicking over the traces of the French alliance.[1] With this end in view, the States General despatched special embassies to Gustav Adolf and to Richelieu early in 1632. Vosbergen, who went to France, was instructed to press for arrears of subsidy and a French attack on Flanders; but the main point of his mission was to urge closer co-operation between France and Sweden. Richelieu was benevolent; but he was so little able to control Swedish policy that the best reply he could make to Vosbergen was to suggest a grand alliance, to comprise France, Sweden, England, the Dutch and the leading members of the League.[2] This was a political castle in the air, not unattractive to the Dutch, perhaps, but by no means the answer Vosbergen could have wished. When he took his departure in May, he returned empty-handed.

Nor was the embassy of Cornelis Pauw to Gustav Adolf more successful. Pauw's instructions ordered him to emphasize the community of purpose between the wars each was waging, to urge the maintenance of unbroken solidarity with France, and to counsel moderation in the internal affairs of Germany. In March 1632 he had his audience with Gustav Adolf: it was not an agreeable experience. As to the main objects of his mission he achieved little; and Gustav Adolf took the opportunity to launch intemperate complaints about the behaviour of the Dutch: the troops they paid off, he contended, were at once enlisted in the imperialist armies, so that Dutch parsimony reinforced Sweden's enemies; while the failure of the States General to send him any armed assistance had been mainly responsible for his inability to take Cologne.[3] Pauw departed, somewhat damped; and though Frederick Henry later sent conciliatory messages, Dutch-Swedish relations continued to be less than entirely cordial. There was no question of renewing

[1] Waddington, I. 117.
[2] *ibid.*, I. 118, 129, 381-92; *Sv. Krig*, V. 252-3.
[3] Waddington, I. 118; *Sv. Krig*, V. 251-2. Gustav Adolf had sent Bengt Oxenstierna on a special mission to the Dutch at the close of 1631, with instructions to sound their reactions to the Swedish advance to the Rhine. It proved equally unfruitful (S. Hedin, *Resare-Bengt*, p. 486). For Gustav Adolf's concern about the disbandment of Dutch troops, see his letter to Camerarius of 7 July 1631, in Söltl, III. 222.

the alliance of 1614. The Dutch and German wars proceeded parallel to one another, as before. And France, rather than Sweden, remained the chosen friend of the republic.

Until very recently, the Swiss Cantons, unlike the Dutch, had remained on the outermost verge of Sweden's political interests and diplomatic activity. It was only when intervention in Germany seemed imminent that Gustav Adolf began to devote attention to the politics of the Confederation. In 1629 Farensbach had called at Zürich and Geneva on his way to Transylvania; and a year later Filip Sadler had come to Switzerland with exhortations to solidarity against the house of Habsburg. Farensbach had effected nothing; and the sharply polemical tone of Sadler's message not only alienated the Catholic Cantons but even alarmed the Protestants, who felt that they could not risk provoking the Emperor at a moment when he had large forces just over the border. Nevertheless, Sadler did succeed in making contact with the more militant wing of the Swiss Protestants; he recruited a useful agent for Sweden in the person of the exiled Palatine officer Hans George von Peblis; and after he had departed, Peblis succeeded in gradually transforming the Protestant extremists into a pro-Swedish faction.[1]

At this stage, and for some time afterwards, Gustav Adolf's interest in Switzerland was restricted to the question of the control of the Alpine passes; and in this Swedish policy coincided with French. It was in an effort to secure the Valtelline that Gustav Adolf sent Kristoffer Ludvig Rasche to Venice in 1631, with offers of an alliance. Venice had agreed, under French pressure, to be responsible for one-third of the subsidy to be paid by France to Sweden, and in the Mantuan war had been France's firm ally.[2] But in July 1631, when Rasche arrived, the Seignory was irritated by Richelieu's apparent indifference to Venice's interests at Cherasco, and anxious only to evade further entanglement in French projects. Venice was nearly bankrupt; within a decade she had lost half her population by plague; and she neither wished nor needed a Swedish alliance. Richelieu's attempts to persuade the Seignory had no effect; and Rasche left Venice with nothing to show for his visit.[3]

[1] L. Haas, *Schwedens Politik gegenüber der Eidgenossenschaft während des dreissigjährigen Krieges*, pp. 83-96; F. Fäh, *Gustav Adolf und die Eidgenossen*, pp. 5-8; *Utrikesförvaltningens historia*, p. 104.

[2] J. Bühring, *Venedig, Gustav Adolf und Rohan*, pp. 1-17, 54-65.

[3] *ibid.*, pp. 87-94, 133, 161, 189-203.

This failure may have inspired Richelieu to take more direct action to secure the passes. In October 1631 he ordered Rohan, who was still in the Venetian service, to proceed at once to the Grisons. His object was to assist the Grisons to recover the Valtelline, which had been neutralized but not restored to them by the terms of the peace of Cherasco. Rohan, to whom Venice gave a grudging leave of absence, was enthusiastically received by the Grisons, and was elected their general; and it seemed for a moment as though the Valtelline might at last pass to Protestant control. Richelieu, however, neglected to follow up this initiative. Preoccupied with the problems of Bavaria and Lorraine, he had no attention to spare for Rohan, nor money either. The attack on the Valtelline was forbidden, at all events for the present.[1]

Meanwhile, Gustav Adolf, having arrived at Mainz, was looking at Switzerland at rather closer range than in the past. Seen from this distance, the country appeared to him not simply as the key to the passes but as a providentially unravaged area from which troops and supplies might possibly be extracted. And when, in December 1631, Rasche arrived in Switzerland from Venice, his instructions were mainly framed to that end. Soon after his arrival he had an opportunity of opening his business to the general diet of the Confederation. Rasche was a person of truculent and overweening temper, excessively prickly about his dignity, and impetuous in his proceedings: '*gran professore d'una estraordinaria stravaganza*', the Venetian Resident reported.[2] He addressed the diet in the same orotund and 'megalogothic' style [3] which he had employed to the Seignory [4]; and with as little effect. The Swedes and the Swiss, he told them, were the oldest nations in the world. Each (confusingly enough) originated from the other. Therefore they ought to be bound by an alliance; and an alliance, in fact, was what he was commissioned to offer them. The diet took time to consider this proposal; and Rasche occupied the interval by visiting Catholic Lucerne, where he uttered menacing warnings to all enemies of the Protestant cause. It was not altogether surprising, perhaps, that the diet at its meeting in February should have sent him a civil refusal: even Berne and Zürich had ventured only to urge further consideration of the offer.[5]

[1] *ibid.*, pp. 221-9; D. Veraguth, *Herzog Rohan und seine Mission in Graubünden und im Veltlin*, pp. 18-28.

[2] Haas, p. 105 *note* 66.

[3] For megalogothicism, see above, Vol. I, p. 509 *seqq.*

[4] Bühring, pp. 190-1, for his speech in Venice.

[5] Haas, pp. 99-104; Fäh, pp. 9-18.

Rasche did not leave Switzerland. In March he received fresh letters of credence from Gustav Adolf, directed this time to the Protestant Cantons only; and with them he began a fresh negotiation. His demands now were explicit, and they were far-reaching: Gustav Adolf asked aid in men and money, the assignment of muster-places for his recruits, the prohibition of recruiting by powers hostile to Sweden, and a close alliance. The towns considered these terms impossible. They drew up an answer which was intended to be tactful, but which in fact infuriated Rasche by reason of stylistic inadvertencies. Rasche now took the line which Gustav Adolf had taken to George William of Brandenburg in 1630: neutrality was inadmissible in principle and impossible in practice.[1] A sardonic comment on this doctrine was provided by the King's letter of 17 April to the Thirteen Cantons, in which he alluded to rumours that the Duke of Feria was to bring Spanish troops through the passes, and demanded that the Swiss should take steps to enforce respect for their neutrality.[2] It is true that he simultaneously asked leave of the Protestant Cantons to raise 24 companies within their borders—a request which they were able to reject on the ground that their neutrality would be compromised if they accepted it.[3] For Gustav Adolf, it is clear, Swiss neutrality meant a neutrality benevolent to Sweden, and would be tolerated only on that understanding. Rasche had, indeed, to acquiesce in the final rejection of his demands by the Protestant Cantons in April, and in August left Switzerland an embittered man[4]; but Gustav Adolf continued to hope that he might be able to involve the Swiss in his war. The Protestant Cantons, though their attitude was formally correct, did in fact connive at recruiting for Sweden within their territory; and the King seems to have thought that with judicious pressure they might be persuaded to appear openly on his side. As late as October 1632 he was trying to induce them to agree to a definition of neutrality, to be embodied in a treaty, which would have made them effectively the clients of Sweden.[5]

These developments were viewed with concern by almost every-

[1] Haas, pp. 105-6.

[2] The letter is printed in *Sverges traktater*, V. 756-7.

[3] Haas, p. 109; Fäh, pp. 38-9, 43-5. He had earlier asked Peblis to request Zürich to divert the imperialists' attention while he formed an army round Berne: Haas, p. 99.

[4] *ibid.*, pp. 107-10.

[5] *ibid.*, p. 113 and *note* 93. The passes were effectually closed to the imperialists in the summer of 1632: Hallwich, *Briefe und Akten*, II. 734.

body interested in Switzerland. The English Resident, Oliver Fleming, who on the instructions of his government was pursuing a peculiarly unrealistic and impracticable policy which no Swiss would even consider—Fleming had some sympathy for Swedish aims, if only because they clashed with French [1]; but France, Spain, the Emperor and the Pope were almost equally alarmed. On 6 May a full meeting of the Swiss diet took place at Baden, with the prime object of considering the dangers arising from Gustav Adolf's letter of 17 April. An envoy from the Emperor attended; France was represented by Rohan; and Spain and the Nuncio were active behind the scenes. On the necessity for keeping the Swedes out of Switzerland even Habsburg and Bourbon could agree.[2] Rohan was ordered to plead for a renewal of the old ties of friendship between France and the Confederation, and to urge the need for excluding all foreigners from Swiss soil; and at the same time France made some effort to act as mediator in the struggle between Catholic and Protestant Cantons, which at this time threatened to degenerate into civil war.

Thus Gustav Adolf's policy in Switzerland in the end brought him into conflict with his French ally; and his later dealings with Rohan, with their implicit threat of a Swedish descent upon Italy, only added to Richelieu's disquiet.[3] The King had no long-range plans or formed design in this area, whether for Switzerland, the passes, or the peninsula; but his obvious intention to exploit momentary advantages to the uttermost, until no part of central Europe seemed safe from his interference, and his heavy-handed treatment of the feelings of other states where military needs were concerned, alarmed and angered Richelieu, and was already alienating neutral and even friendly opinion.

(c) *Denmark and England*

Even Kristian IV, it is said, could not forbear to celebrate the news of Breitenfeld with *feux de joie*.[4] But this Protestant blaze was soon put out. The old matters of quarrel remained, and Breitenfeld served but to aggravate them. Sweden and Denmark were still rivals for the leadership of the Protestant world, despite the recent

[1] Haas, p. 111 and *note* 85.
[2] The Confederation's letter to Gustav Adolf, assuring him of their neutrality, is in *Sverges traktater*, V. 754-5; Veraguth, p. 30.
[3] See below, p. 711; and Veraguth, p. 31; Hallwich, *Briefe und Akten*, II. 758.
[4] Fridericia, *YPH*, I. 211.

slump in Denmark's reputation; and from Moscow to The Hague Danish diplomats strove to detach the powers from friendship with Sweden and bring them into an arrangement with Kristian IV.[1] Danish warships still lay off Ruden, taking toll of merchantmen, and the irritation caused by this proceeding was just not sufficient for any state to proceed to a breach upon it.[2] The Sound Tolls went up (to meet the expenses of rebuilding Kronborg, destroyed by fire in 1629) or down (in response to energetic Dutch protests) in a manner very disturbing to trade[3]; but Sweden remained unaffected by these vacillations, except in so far as Kristian's alienation of his mercantile friends in the west tended to rally them to Gustav Adolf. In the Lower Saxon Circle the grim struggle between Danish and Swedish influences continued. Kristian IV had not for a moment abandoned his hope of recovering the lost bishoprics of north Germany for his sons; and if there were a prospect of obtaining them cheaply he would be equally willing to strike a bargain with Gustav Adolf or with Ferdinand II. His policy was opportunist, impulsive, short-viewed in its choice of means; and it was liable to lead him into situations to which war might seem to be the only outcome. Kristian did not desire war, at least not at present; but he greatly coveted objects which only a victorious war could assure to him. But his country was in no condition to risk a conflict; and the Danish council's realization of this was an important factor in keeping the peace.[4]

In the weeks immediately after Breitenfeld the Estates of the Lower Saxon Circle held two meetings in Hamburg, to decide upon their policy towards the war. The questions at issue were, the size of the army to be raised by the Circle; the choice of a commander for it; and the relationship which both were to bear to the Swedish forces. Kristian hoped to bring the troops effectively under his own control by securing the appointment of his son, Prince Ulrik, as captain-general of the Circle; Salvius exerted himself to defeat this project, and to persuade the Circle to put their forces under Tott; while many of the Estates preferred a middle line, which would leave their army some measure of independence.[5] Kristian's

[1] For Kristian's negotiations with the Tsar, *ibid.*, 196-8; with the Dutch, *ibid.*, 198-200.

[2] See Gustav Adolf's recommendations to Pomerania, 23 September 1632: Bär, p. 291.

[3] C. E. Hill, *The Danish Sound Dues and the Command of the Baltic*, pp. 102-6; Erslev, II. 329-30, 332-3.

[4] See, *e.g.*, the council's warning of 16 January 1631: Erslev, II. 271-2.

[5] Boëthius, *NSK*, pp. 242-51; Fridericia, *YPH*, I. 216-17.

representatives at Hamburg were urging that the first task of the new army should be to liberate Bremen and Mecklenburg—obviously in the hope of forestalling a Swedish liberation of these controversial areas.[1] Gustav Adolf, following the proceedings as best he could at a distance, became uneasy at the trend of the discussions. On 26 November he instructed Salvius to make a protest which was edged with a familiar threat: if Kristian persisted in his attempts to secure the choice of Ulrik and so disturbed Gustav Adolf's 'absolute directory of this war', he would make peace with the Emperor 'somehow', and leave Kristian to do the best he could. If Kristian continued to raise troops, Salvius was to try to induce Bremen and Brunswick-Lüneburg to forbid recruiting in their territories; and if the numbers raised should exceed 2000, Tott was to prepare to quarter himself in Holstein.[2] But even before these instructions were written, the Circle had reached a decision. On 10 November they resolved that their army should remain a separate force, though it would collaborate with Tott's army in case of need; and they repelled Kristian's efforts on behalf of Prince Ulrik. They also gave it as their opinion that Sweden was entitled to retain, as *satisfactio*, only those territories which had been conquered from Catholic princes. It was a last brave attempt by the Estates of the Circle to retain a measure of independence. As regarded Sweden, the attempt proved vain; but it was at least successful in thwarting the plans of Denmark.

Soon after the battle of Breitenfeld Gustav Adolf gave an audience to a Danish emissary, Oynhausen, who had been sent by Kristian to Germany upon a variety of commissions.[3] To Gustav Adolf Oynhausen suggested a marriage between Ulrik and Kristina, probably with the idea of forestalling any plans for a Brandenburg match. But the King gave a smooth refusal; and Oynhausen proceeded on his way to negotiations which were possibly more seriously intended. His destination was Prague; and here on 5 October 1631 he had an important interview with Wallenstein. For some time past Wallenstein and Kristian had been discussing the possibility of the sale of certain portions of Wallenstein's duchy of Mecklenburg to Denmark.[4] The scope of the talks was now widened to include the bishoprics of Bremen and Verden. Wallen-

[1] Boëthius, *NSK*, pp. 221.
[2] *Arkiv*, I. 519-20.
[3] For Oynhausen's mission, Fridericia, *YPH*, I. 212-15.
[4] Förster, II. 158, 160-4.

stein was urging the Emperor to secure the friendship of Kristian by consenting to their inclusion in the bargain; the more so since both dioceses (like Mecklenburg) appeared very likely to fall into Swedish hands in the near future. Ferdinand II, however, was not to be induced to abandon the claims of the Archduke Leopold so easily; and scrupled (to the vigorously phrased disgust of Wallenstein) [1] to allow the lands of the Church to return to Protestant hands. The bargain therefore fell through; though Wallenstein characteristically incited Kristian to seize the bishoprics at once while the Emperor was unable to prevent it.

Simultaneously a negotiation of a similar kind had been opened in north Germany. Maximilian of Bavaria, concurring for once with Wallenstein's policies, was most anxious for the friendship of Denmark; and, like Wallenstein, was prepared to buy it by the cession to Kristian of places which the imperialist forces had little hope of retaining. In October he asked Rainach and Camargo to make contact with the Danish commandant in Glückstadt, with this end in view; and soon afterwards negotiations began at Trachtersheim. Kristian IV was keenly interested; he was not without hope of acquiring the towns of Stade and Bremen by these means; and he did in fact, by a convention of 8 February 1632, obtain the right to garrison Freiburg.[2]

Thus in the autumn and winter Kristian was actively engaged in trafficking with Gustav Adolf's enemies. There were even rumours of negotiations with the privateers of Dunkirk. At the same time he was making passes at the political virtue of one of Sweden's most important friends: at the end of 1631 a Danish envoy was sent to John George, in order to persuade him to make peace. The envoy complained bitterly, '*inter pocula*', of the paucity of support given to his master in 1626, as compared with that now available to Gustav Adolf; but neither his complaints nor his persuasions had much effect. For the moment John George was constant to the Swedish alliance.[3]

Nevertheless, it was scarcely surprising that Gustav Adolf should have felt uneasy at Kristian's busy intrigues. In the Lower Saxon

[1] Irmer, *VS*, I. 47-51, for this interview. Wallenstein remarked that the imperialists 'vielmehr auf der pfaffen geschwetz, als auf die conservation ihrer kaiserlichen reputation achteten'.

[2] Fridericia, *YPH*, I. 219-20; Boëthius, *NSK*, p. 308. For Vienna's resentment of this initiative, and Maximilian's deprecatory reply, see Hallwich, *Briefe und Akten*, I. 600, 628-9.

[3] Irmer, *VS*, I. 86, 91.

Circle military precautions were taken: Swedish forces surrounded Stade; John Frederick of Bremen, professing to believe that Freiburg was still in imperialist hands, attacked it, and evicted the Danish garrison.[1] And Gustav Adolf took advantage of a visit by Baudissin to Holstein upon private business to convey a serious warning to Kristian. Baudissin was to demand that Kristian should either openly ally himself with Gustav Adolf; or allow his contingent to the Lower Saxon army to join the Swedish forces, and recognize Gustav Adolf as director of the Circle; or adopt an attitude of complete political passivity. If he chose the last of these options, Gustav Adolf was prepared to give countenance to his sons' pretensions to Bremen and Verden.[2] It was very nearly an ultimatum; and the precautionary measures ordered on the Swedish side make it clear that Gustav Adolf took into account the possibility that it might lead to war.[3] Kristian's position was difficult: to accept would have been a greater humiliation than he was prepared to face; to refuse might entail disaster. After consultation with his council he at last decided to do neither, but to make a serious effort at mediation in Germany.

He had already (on 20 February) ordered Fredrik Gynther to make the somewhat naïve proposal that Gustav Adolf should evacuate the Lower Saxon Circle, provided that the imperialists did the same [4]; and he now made simultaneous tenders of good offices to both sides. On 18 March he wrote to the Emperor; and on the same day he instructed Thott and Sehested to proceed to the Swedish headquarters. They had audience of Gustav Adolf at Ingolstadt on 22 April; and informed him that though Kristian could not accept any of his options, he was anxious to do what he could to bring about a peace. They were courteously received; but their offer was decisively declined, and they were informed that Kristian might hope to recover the bishoprics only if his sons would consent to be attached to Gustav Adolf by those ties of friendship and gratitude which bound the other German princes whom he had restored to their dominions—in other words, only if they would consent to be Swedish clients.[5]

[1] Boëthius, *NSK*, p. 311.
[2] Fridericia, *YPH*, I. 224-5; Boëthius, *NSK*, p. 320.
[3] *Arkiv*, I. 570-3; *AOSB*, I. VII. 76, II. I. 773; *RRP*, II. 143; Boëthius, *NSK*, pp. 312-15.
[4] *Christian IVs Breve*, III. 2.
[5] Fridericia, *YPH*, I. 233; Erslev, II. 360-1; Hallwich, *Briefe und Akten*, II. 381, 660-1.

While the Danish ambassadors had been making their way to the King, the situation in the Lower Saxon Circle had become tenser than ever. On 31 March Gustav Adolf was seriously thinking of abandoning his campaign to the Danube and marching for Holstein [1]; on 4 April Kristian laid before his council plans for strengthening Denmark's defences [2]; on 9 April Pappenheim drove off the Swedish forces blockading Stade and occupied it himself. He was under no illusions as to his chances of keeping it for long; and it therefore became his object to reach an agreement with Kristian whereby he might hand over the town to a Danish garrison. Negotiations were opened; and this time the imperialists made no scruple to bait the hook with Bremen and Verden.[3] They could afford to do so; for in the explosive atmosphere which prevailed in the Lower Saxon Circle at the time a Danish acceptance of Pappenheim's proposals could scarcely fail to cause a rupture with Sweden. Pappenheim came very near to effecting a master-stroke of policy: on 30 April Tott was writing to Oxenstierna that war with Denmark seemed inevitable.[4] At the last moment it was averted. In his anxiety to make certain of success, Pappenheim seems to have overreached himself by demanding, as a condition of the agreement, that Kristian should at once break with Sweden. If the agreement had been concluded, the demand would have probably proved superfluous; but it served to open Kristian's eyes to the risks he was running. On 2 May he abruptly stopped the negotiations; on 8 May Pappenheim evacuated Stade; and the peace was saved.[5]

It was the last serious crisis in the long history of strained relations which stretched back throughout the reign to the War of Kalmar. Since 1611 the problem of Denmark had never been far from the King's thoughts, and always a factor influencing his policy. For the remaining months of his life, as the complexities of German affairs increased with fearful swiftness about him, he was able to view the position in the north with more indifference. There was an alarm again in July, and another in September [6]; and Oxenstierna, at all events, felt that sooner or later Sweden would need to renew the struggle with 'the Jute'; but when that time should come they

[1] *AOSB*, II. I. 775-6.
[2] *Christian IVs Breve*, III. 10.
[3] Fridericia, *YPH*, I. 230-1.
[4] *AOSB*, II. IX. 705.
[5] Fridericia, *YPH*, I. 231-3.
[6] *Arkiv*, II. 522-3; *RRP*, II. 189.

could face the prospect with some confidence. In the crisis of the spring of 1632 provisional orders had been sent to Tott to invade Jutland from the south with every man at his disposal[1]; in December and February the first attempts had been made to draw Frederick III of Holstein-Gottorp into a Swedish alliance; and in June 1632 Frederick abandoned his neutrality and concluded a draft treaty with Gustav Adolf.[2] The strategy which was to lead to Brömsebro had already been devised; the Gottorp alliance, which was to poison Swedish-Danish relations from Karl X Gustav to Karl XII, was already discernible in the distance; a dynasty of wars was already engendering.

If in regard to Denmark the main preoccupation of Swedish policy was to exclude Kristian IV from north Germany, in regard to England the objective was the exact opposite. Though neither Gustav Adolf nor Oxenstierna had many illusions about Charles I and his ministers, they clung to the hope of committing England to full-scale intervention on the continent.[3] By 1630, however, that hope had become faint indeed. Charles was, perhaps, more generously anxious to do something for the Palatines than James I had latterly been; but his circumstances after the dissolution of 1629 made a major war unthinkable. The peace with France was followed in 1630 by peace with Spain; and Charles fell back on his father's tactics of trying to secure the restoration of Frederick V by diplomatic bargaining with the Habsburgs. He lent himself, at least for a time, to a plan whereby England should constrain the Dutch to accept mediation in their quarrel with Spain; while Philip IV, in return for these services, would bring pressure to bear in Vienna for the restoration of some member of the Palatine house. With this end in view, Anstruther was sent to Vienna in the spring of 1631, to second the persuasions of Madrid. He soon found that Spanish professions were not borne out by Spanish actions. Although it was no doubt true that Olivares had rather see Frederick V in the Lower Palatinate than Maximilian of Bavaria, there seemed reasonable prospects of the military control of the area passing into Spanish hands; and if the Spanish troops were to evacuate the fortresses they occupied, Spain would expect a more substantial equivalent than

[1] *Arkiv*, I. 586-8.
[2] *AOSB*, II. IX. 792; Fridericia, *YPH*, I. 218; Boëthius, *NSK*, pp. 356-8.
[3] *AOSB*, I. VI. 30, 53; *cf. ibid.*, 395.

simple mediation in the Netherlands. Olivares, in fact, was now demanding as the price of the Palatinate an English declaration of war upon the Dutch. Whatever Charles I's opinions upon the morality or wisdom of such a policy might be, it was plain enough that he could not afford it; and the plan was accordingly abandoned.[1]

The disappointment was the less severe because by the autumn of 1631 it was already very doubtful whether co-operation with Spain was not an outmoded policy. The battle of Breitenfeld suggested the reflection that if the Palatinate were to be recovered by inducing some other power to do the work in return for services of minimal value, the right quarter to which to address such proposals was Sweden, rather than Spain. Charles had no difficulty in re-adjusting his tactics. His habit of keeping two irreconcilable foreign policies in being simultaneously did at least insure him against being discommoded by changes in the fortunes of war. Since 1629 he had taken care to maintain good relations with Gustav Adolf, at comparatively small cost to himself. He had, in particular, permitted the Marquis of Hamilton to raise 6000 men in Britain for the Swedish armies, and he had made money available to him to facilitate his musters. Hamilton's army served a double purpose: it demonstrated Charles's loyalty to the Protestant cause; and it was a useful hint to the Habsburgs that England's goodwill might be worth conserving. Every sort of difficulty and misfortune, it is true, appeared to dog Hamilton's enterprise: it proved difficult to raise the men, and a great part of those eventually obtained were of bad quality; the treachery of Farensbach, whom Gustav Adolf had unwisely detailed to assist with the levies, imperilled the whole enterprise; Hamilton himself was menaced by court intrigues and the preposterous accusations of his enemy Lord Ochiltree.[2] The force eventually landed in Pomerania rather than in the Weser—largely because Gustav Adolf had been unable to fulfil his promise to provide a strong detachment to cover the landing; and within a few months of setting foot on German soil it had been reduced by the ravages of disease to a handful of companies. Hamilton, ordered after Breitenfeld to subordinate

[1] Gardiner, *Personal Government of Charles I*, I. 208-16, 231, 236; Green, *Elizabeth of Bohemia*, pp. 272-3, 281 *note* 6; Mathew, *Age of Charles I*, pp. 30-4.

[2] For the antecedents of the Hamilton expedition, see Hist. MSS. Comm., *Hamilton*, pp. 47, 70-3; *Hamilton Supplementary*, pp. 12-13, 16-18; *Arkiv*, I. 264-5, II. 294-7; *Schriftstücke*, pp. 208-9; *AOSB*, II. IX. 427-30; Burnet, *Memoires of the . . . Dukes of Hamilton*, pp. 5-15; *De svenska ätterna Hamilton*, pp. 64-7; Gardiner, *op. cit.*, I. 223-4. For Farensbach, see above, Vol. I, pp. 160-1, 163-6; and *cf.* Oxenstierna's drastic comment, *Arkiv*, II. 159.

himself to Arnim, considered that the terms of his agreement with Gustav Adolf had been broken (since he had been promised an independent command) and became a man with a grievance; and his ill-humour was not allayed by his later association with the over-cautious Banér.[1] As a contribution to Anglo-Swedish amity, in fact, the Hamilton army was of very doubtful value. Yet it had certainly alarmed the imperialists—at all events before it arrived; its presence on the Oder may possibly have affected Tilly's strategy before Breitenfeld [2]; and Charles I was not disposed to lose any opportunity to remind Gustav Adolf that he had actually paid money towards it.

In the autumn of 1631, then, Charles despatched Sir Henry Vane to Germany, that he might sound Gustav Adolf about the Palatinate and 'enter into a league with the King of Sweden upon emergent occasions'.[3] The choice of envoy was characteristic: Vane was a 'Spaniard'—that is, an isolationist; and, unlike Sir Thomas Roe, he could be trusted not to allow Protestant enthusiasm to inveigle England into rash commitments. After a brief visit to Denmark (he did not succeed in meeting Kristian IV) Vane caught up with Gustav Adolf at Würzburg early in November, and accompanied him on his triumphant progress to Mainz. He found the King ready enough to discuss the question of the Palatinate. But though Gustav Adolf invited Hamilton, by way of a graceful and propitiatory gesture, to act as a kind of umpire in the negotiation,[4] the terms he propounded on 9 November were stiffer than Vane had expected. He was willing to restore Frederick to Bohemia, the Palatinate and the electoral dignity, but only in return for a very substantial equivalent. Charles must undertake to pay and maintain, for the duration of the war, two regiments of horse and eight of foot; he must agree to resist any attempt by the Spanish navy to invade Sweden; and there must be a formal alliance for a term of years to be agreed upon between them. Most ominous of all: Gustav Adolf must have the absolute control, not only of the conduct of the war but also of the making of the peace, subject to a vague obligation to consult the wishes of England.[5]

These were terms which Vane had neither the desire nor the

[1] Hist. MSS. Comm., *Hamilton*, pp. 74, 78; Burnet, pp. 16-19; *De svenska ätterna Hamilton*, pp. 70-4: C. S. Terry, *Alexander Leslie*, pp. 22-7. Oxenstierna later blamed Hamilton for the dissolution of the army; 'which through want of knowledge in the Marquis in military affairs, and of care to provide for them, perished': Whitelocke, *Embassy*, I. 313.

[2] Burnet, p. 16.

[3] J. Rushworth, *Historical Collections*, I. II. 107, 129-30.

[4] Hist. MSS. Comm., *Hamilton*, p. 74.

[5] *ibid.*, p. 74.

power to accept; and the negotiations made no progress for the next two months. When they were resumed at Frankfort in January it was under auspices still more unfavourable. On 9 January Gustav Adolf had forced Charnacé to accept his terms for the neutrality of Bavaria and the League. Those terms contained no guarantee of the restoration of the Palatinate: they provided only that England and France should mediate jointly between Frederick and Maximilian. It seemed that Gustav Adolf was prepared to betray the Protestant cause in exchange for Richelieu's desertion of Bavaria. The restoration of the Palatinate had certainly been among Swedish objectives at the time of Gustav Adolf's landing in Germany, and had been specifically mentioned on more than one occasion.[1] In the treaty of Bärwalde, indeed, the phraseology had been made quite general, and the Palatinate had nowhere been referred to explicitly; but there is no reason to suppose that Gustav Adolf deliberately abandoned the cause of Frederick, either then or in the months that followed. The avoidance of any allusion to the Palatinate at Bärwalde made the treaty easier for Richelieu to swallow with a good grace: it did not indicate that Gustav Adolf was throwing over Frederick's cause for the sake of courting Maximilian.[2] But the situation was very different now. If France succeeded in forcing the Swedish truce terms upon her friends, south Germany would be at Gustav Adolf's feet, Swedish influence would be paramount upon the Rhine, the doom of the Austrian Habsburgs would be virtually assured. If Gustav Adolf had insisted, in his terms to Charnacé, on the full restitution of the Palatine lands, he might well have strained French compliance too far. When once the truce was accepted, the weight of Sweden would be sufficient to ensure a decision favourable to Frederick. And in a broader view the gains at stake in the truce were so large, the benefits to evangelical Germany so manifest, that Frederick's claims might well be postponed.

When, therefore, Vane pressed for a pledge to restore the Elector, he was answered that for the moment Gustav Adolf could not bind himself to fight Maximilian. But he was prepared either to restore the Spanish-held lands, and negotiate with Richelieu and Maximilian for those held by Bavaria; or, failing this, he would restore Frederick by arms to the whole of his inheritance in return

[1] Schubert, *Ludwig Camerarius*, pp. 374-5.

[2] Contrast Schubert, *op. cit.*, p. 379, where he writes: 'es war offensichtlich, dass Gustav Adolf in den folgenden Monaten [*i.e.* after Bärwalde] die französische Rücksichtsnahme auf Bayern in manchem teilte'.

for 12,000 men, a defensive alliance against Spain and a subsidy of £25,000 a month.[1] In short, if Gustav Adolf were to renounce the great advantages which the truce would bring him, he must have compensation of a solidity, and on a scale, far beyond England's ability to provide.

The breakdown of the negotiations for a truce made any discussion of these terms superfluous; but the painful impression they produced was not easily effaced. In February 1632 Frederick V quitted his retreat in the Netherlands and presented himself (with the aid of a loan from the Dutch) at Gustav Adolf's court. He was received with royal honours; and Gustav Adolf took occasion to snub George of Hesse-Darmstadt at table for failing to address Frederick in the style proper to a reigning monarch.[2] But though there was much cordiality, though the ceremonial banquets were unusually festive and protracted, though Gustav Adolf professed himself much pleased with the modesty of Frederick's demeanour, the King of Bohemia soon discovered that the King of Sweden had no intention of putting him in immediate or unconditional possession of his lost dominions; and that the King of England's ambassador was negotiating about the Palatinate behind his back.[3] Even though the war with Bavaria was now once more in full flame, and a Swedish conquest of the whole of the Palatinate a probability in the near future, the altered situation made little difference, it seemed, to Frederick's immediate prospects. And the reason for this state of affairs was not difficult to find. It had been put bluntly by Richelieu when he wrote that 'the frivolity and feebleness of the Palatine must make one apprehend that if he had it [*sc.* the Palatinate] in his hands at this moment he would lose it or misuse it'.[4] Gustav Adolf had to consider not only the rights and wrongs of the Palatine question but also the general military and political strategy of the evangelical cause as a whole. A settlement which satisfied Frederick, but weakened the Protestant position in the remainder of Germany, would be a pledge too dearly redeemed. If Germany had been secure against a renewed Habsburg or Catholic offensive, it might have been possible to contemplate the immediate return of Frederick to the electorate. But it was hardly possible now. Gustav Adolf's plans for the next campaigning season involved an advance upon Vienna by way of Bavaria. It was essential to them that his main forward

[1] Rushworth, I. II. 130-2. [2] Irmer, *VS*, I. 123; Frohnhäuser, p. 109 *seqq.*
[3] Green, *Elizabeth*, p. 285; Frohnhäuser, p. 83. [4] Avenel, IV. 254.

base on the middle Rhine should be firmly held; essential that he be able to feel secure against attack on his right flank and rear. Time's revenges, and the satisfying spectacle of historic wrongs tardily set right, must wait for the hour when the military situation should permit such luxuries. And in any case the peculiar position of Frederick, by reason of his close kinship to the ruler of a major power, must not be permitted to break the solidarity of Protestant action in Germany. If the shipwrecked Palatine wished to be rescued, he must obey the directions of his rescuer or be stunned into temporary insensibility; if he aspired to add himself to the evangelical army, he must resign himself to marching in step. There was no place for new recruits with ideas of their own—it was difficult enough to manage John George; nor was there much of a welcome for any ally whose actions might be influenced by the dubious wisdoms of Charles I and his council.

In March 1632 negotiations began again. Gustav Adolf had started his campaign; and it was Oxenstierna who now had to deal with Vane. At the same time, he was conducting a parallel negotiation with Frederick. Neither the one nor the other produced an agreement. With Vane, Oxenstierna's initial difficulty was the size of the subsidy to be paid by England, and the difficulty of securing its regular remittance. On Gustav Adolf's instructions, he gave way on this point, and agreed to accept Vane's final offer of 40,000 *rdr.* a month.[1] But fresh difficulties immediately arose. As soon as the financial question had been settled, Vane raised objections to the Swedish proposal that England should give naval aid in the event of an attack from Dunkirk. Oxenstierna asked only that England should participate as an auxiliary; but Vane refused to agree to anything that might compromise Charles with Madrid. Yet it was unfair of the chancellor to lay the blame on Vane for raising new obstacles, for on the Swedish side, too, a new demand had been presented which Vane felt equally unable to accept: a demand for freedom of worship for Lutherans in the restored Palatinate lands. Nor could Vane, in any event, have admitted the Swedish claim to a 'directory' over the terms of peace.[2]

[1] It was in any case more than Gustav Adolf had asked of Charles I in 1629: the figure then was 400,000 *rdr.* a year: A. Rydfors, *De diplomatiska förbindelserna mellan Sverige och England*, p. 121.

[2] For these negotiations, see *AOSB*, I. VII. 66 *seqq.*, 103, 218, II. I. 760-1, 771-2, 776, 781; *Sv. Krig*, V. 248-9; *cf.* Oxenstierna's comment to Whitelocke: Whitelocke, *Embassy*, I. 301.

The negotiations with Frederick V stranded upon reefs of a similar formation.[1] Frederick objected to a provision whereby any strong place in his dominions, taken or to be taken by the Swedish forces, might remain in their hands for the duration of the war, if Gustav Adolf should judge it militarily desirable to keep it. Equally obnoxious was the same provision as had been put into the draft treaty for Vane concerning the rights of Lutherans in the Palatinate. Most alarming of all was a clause whereby Frederick, 'like the rest of the princes', should acknowledge Gustav Adolf's absolute directory, and 'not depend upon any other king, prince, body or state, but only upon His Majesty'.[2] This clause certainly suggested to contemporaries that Gustav Adolf was trying to place Frederick in some position of feudal subordination; and their view has been accepted by many subsequent historians.[3] It seems, however, to be a mistaken view. If Gustav Adolf had wished to break the tie which bound Frederick to the Emperor, or to fix him as a vassal of the Swedish crown, he would surely have used a more explicit formula than this. The clause is concerned with military rather than with legal relationships; and it seems to be designed to secure that Frederick should be a disciplined, obedient and (if possible) grateful member of Gustav Adolf's military and political league.[4] Frederick was to avow that Gustav Adolf was his protector and deliverer; and by renouncing all dependence on any other 'king, prince, body or state' he was to be debarred from taking an independent line as the *protégé* of Charles I, or of the Dutch—or even of the King of France, who had patronized a Palatine Elector before, and might well do so again. All that Gustav Adolf demanded of Frederick, once peace

[1] *AOSB*, I. VII. 69-71.

[2] 'Ut hoc [*sc.* the restoration of Frederick] cum ratione et spe aliqua tentetur, totius belli directio maneat in potestate S:ae R:ae M:tis, ejusque absolutum directorium rex Bohemiae more reliquorum principum agnoscat, nec ab alio rege, principe, corpore vel statu quam sola S:a R:a M:te dependeat.' The phrasing is equally vague in Oxenstierna's Swedish paraphrase: ('. . . aff ingen annan ähn Kong. M:tt allena dependerar . . .'). Note that Gustav Adolf did not claim from Frederick (as from Vane) the absolute directory of the peace: he was concerned to shut out English meddling in German affairs; but Frederick would not be in a position to make difficulties about the peace terms.

[3] Rushworth, I. II. 166, where it is stated that Frederick is to hold his lands 'as a donation of the King of Sweden'; *cf.* Schubert, *Camerarius*, p. 378: 'geradezu ein Lehnsverhältnis zur schwedischen Krone sollte der Winterkönig eingehen'; or Gindely, *Friedrich V*, p. 41: 'in eine weit abhängigere Lage . . . als die war, in der er als Reichsfürst zum Kaiser gestanden war'; and Kretzschmar, *Gustav Adolfs Pläne und Ziele*, 170. The explanation in *Sv. Krig* (V. 249), that the real purpose of the clause was simply to reserve any Swedish claims until the final peace settlement, seems scarcely adequate.

[4] *cf.* his negotiations with Mecklenburg, and with the Welfs, below, pp. 636-7.

should be made, was a 'firm and inviolable friendship'. Once the war was over, his lands and fortresses would be restored to him in full. It may probably be true that Gustav Adolf intended to insist that the Palatine should be a member of his projected Protestant league after the war[1]: such a league could not lack the leading Calvinist state in Germany. But the immediate problem was to ensure that an alliance with the Palatine did not bring military weakness rather than strength, and to make certain that Frederick should not lend himself to be a tool for the ambiguous policies of his brother-in-law.

The negotiations which Oxenstierna was conducting accordingly broke down. Vane and Frederick betook themselves to headquarters, following the King in his marchings and counter-marchings through Germany, importuning him for an audience at moments more or less inappropriate, and seeking to move him from a line of conduct to which he had every intention of adhering. Frederick enjoyed his brief hour of triumph, in recompense for long years of disappointment, when he accompanied Gustav Adolf upon his entry into Munich; and his pathetic optimism continued intermittently to assert itself[2]; but for the most part it was all hopelessness and disillusion. Vane, perhaps, had never hoped very much of his mission. He had a violent quarrel with Gustav Adolf in Munich; Hamilton was resentful at the King's refusal to permit him to raise fresh troops in Germany, and so make possible his resumption of an independent command; and both Hamilton and Vane were offended by the brusqueness with which they were treated: Hamilton had already commented adversely on 'the excessif ambision and intollerable pryd of the King of Sueden'.[3] English goodwill declined markedly under the influence of their despatches; and Charles and his ministers received with coolness the tidings of the continued triumphs of 'the Dragon King'.[4] In June the choice of Windebank rather than Roe for the vacant secretaryship gave a clear indication that British foreign policy would continue to be 'Spanish'. By July

[1] Ahnlund, *Oxenstierna*, pp. 665-6.

[2] Rushworth, I. II. 171-2, 175; Hist. MSS. Comm., *Hamilton Supplementary*, p. 22.

[3] Hist. MSS. Comm., *Hamilton*, p. 78; *cf.* Burnet, pp. 17-24.

[4] *CSP Domestic*, 1631-33, p. 179, for the Dragon King, a name coined by the Earl of Carlisle; *ibid.*, p. 293, for Sir Tobie Mathew on Gustav Adolf's 'covetousness and arrogancy and inordinate ambition'; *ibid.*, pp. 322-3, for the indifference of the court; and *ibid.*, p. 401, for the concern of Sir Thomas Roe at these developments.

Vane was refusing to consider an alliance at all, and was prepared to offer only subsidies for an undefined period—which meant, as Gustav Adolf rightly suspected, subsidies for one month only.[1] By this time the King had come to the conclusion that it would be better to defer any treaty with England until after he had reached a satisfactory arrangement with Frederick.[2] At the beginning of August Charles sent Hamilton and Vane letters of recall; soon afterwards Vane quitted the King's camp and made his way to Strassburg. Gustav Adolf hoped that Hamilton, upon his arrival in London, might open Charles's eyes to the impracticability of Vane as a negotiator, and bring the English to a better mind; but in the meantime the negotiations were at a stand.[3]

Frederick proved as intractable as Vane. By September both he and Gustav Adolf were heartily weary of each other's company, and Frederick asked and obtained the King's leave to move to the Palatinate. But before he went, at Neustadt-on-Aisch, he was handed a new draft of an alliance, which differed in some important respects from that which had been debated in February.[4] There were the same provisions for Swedish control of the military resources of the electorate, the same requirement that Frederick should not 'depend' on any other prince, the same demand for a firm and inviolable friendship after the war. But the provisions regarding toleration for Lutherans were made more explicit, with far-reaching demands for educational and religious autonomy. In addition, Frederick was to be bound to acknowledge the *beneficium* he had obtained—an expression heavily laden with ominous overtones [5]; and it was provided that he was to be restored only to those lands which incontestably belonged to the Palatinate before the outbreak of war, and in regard to which no litigation was pending.[6]

Frederick was deeply indignant at these terms; and on 22 September he addressed to the King a protest of unwonted sharpness.[7] Gustav Adolf's reply was delayed, no doubt by military

[1] Gardiner, I. 238-9.

[2] Hist. MSS. Comm., *Hamilton Supplementary*, p. 22.

[3] *ibid.*, pp. 24-5; Rushworth, I. II. 167-9, 170-4; *AOSB*, II. I. 851; Irmer, *VS*, I. 280 *note* I.

[4] Printed in Moser, *Patriotisches Archiv*, VI. 179-84.

[5] '. . . agnoscens acceptum beneficium, renovet, firmet & uberius declaret haec pacta, ac simul hujus belli onere liberatus in posterum alat in exercitu Regis certam partem exemplo reliquorum Principum, prout convenerit'.

[6] '. . . quae sine controversia ac lite pertinuerunt ante hosce motus Germanicos ad Electoralem Palatinatum, ceteris reservatis amicabili compositioni aut legitimae decisioni, cum hac cessione S.R. Maj. nemini praejudicari velit'.

[7] Moser, VI. 176-9.

preoccupations, until 28 October.[1] He professed himself astonished and hurt by Frederick's reactions; and protested that there was 'not the least syllable' in the proposed terms which could be considered as prejudicing his rights: even James I (he added) could not have raised any objection. On the question of toleration for Lutherans, indeed, Gustav Adolf would make no concession; but *beneficium*, it now appeared, meant no more than 'benefit'[2]; and the reservation of the claims of others to Frederick's lands referred only to private rights: there was no intention of suggesting any doubt as to Frederick's title to his hereditary dominions. From which it may perhaps be inferred, *e silentio*, that there was no intention either of restoring him to Bohemia.[3] And, finally, any return to the basis of discussions established in February was impossible, since those discussions had been conducted upon the supposition of English aid, and it was now clear that this would not be forthcoming.

Thus, on the eve of Lützen negotiations with the Palatine had reached a dead end. Gustav Adolf accepted their failure with indifference; and Oxenstierna added a sharp comment to the effect that Frederick did not seem to realize his own impotence.[4] Neither King nor chancellor was in a hurry to conclude a permanent treaty. Gustav Adolf needed the Palatine lands to supply him with subsistence, recruits and muster-places; and he needed them as a solid pivot upon which his armies could swing south-east to the Danube. But he did not need English aid sufficiently to induce him to pay England's price, or to blind him to the grave risk of founding any calculation, military or political, upon the promises of the English government; and he did not need Frederick V at all. The Palatine should obtain his own again, no doubt—when it was safe for him to have it; the Lutherans must certainly be tolerated; the Palatinate must be drawn permanently into the orbit of the new evangelical league he was evolving; but in the meantime he held the electorate in his grip, and he had no idea of relinquishing it for the present. For the moment, Frederick was an importunate nuisance, whom it was tempting to bully—much as he had tried to bully George William

[1] Moser, VI. 185-90.

[2] '. . . E.L. Vns für Ihren Benefactorem erkhennen, die zugestellte Lande von niemandt anderst als Vns recognosciren, darüber Vns Ihrer bestendigen Trew vnd Holdschaft, auch einer solchen Freundschaft versichern, Welches durch keinerley Respect vnd Absehen auf Fremde oder Bündniss mit jemandt andern wandelbahr gemacht werden khönne.'

[3] But see below, p. 751.

[4] *Arkiv*, II. 618.

of Brandenburg. But for all that he should have his hereditary lands restored to him in due course: on 31 December 1631 Gustav Adolf had written to the *råd* that 'unless all our co-religionists in Germany, and particularly the King of Bohemia, be restored to the Palatinate, we cannot see how a secure peace is to be obtained'; and early in 1633 Oxenstierna reported that at the time of the battle of Lützen Gustav Adolf had already made up his mind to restore it—and indeed on 4 April 1633 the treaty of restitution was actually signed.[1] But, as Oxenstierna remarked in 1638, Sweden had not entered the German war simply for the sake of the Palatinate, but for 'liberation and security *sui status et vindictam injuriae Caesareanae*'.[2] And by September 1632 a better acquaintance with Frederick, and a better appreciation of the military difficulties, may well have made Gustav Adolf chary of pledging himself to the restoration of the Palatines to Bohemia. Gustav Adolf resented the pressure of England; he resented England's jealousy of himself: 'when H.M. had gotten so far that he was able to restore the Palatine, it annoyed [England and France] that they had to ask it as a favour of H.M.'.[3] In his dealings with Vane and Frederick, as in his dealings with Charnacé and Brézé, Gustav Adolf's political realism was inexorable. But from the standpoint of those who had to negotiate with him it was not only inexorable: it was insufferable. The calculated prolixity and procrastination of Oxenstierna at least did something to provide an emollient to the rasping logic of Swedish policy; but the King's hot temper, exacerbated by the crises of the summer, his contempt for his German allies, his suspicion of their fidelity, his bitter realization of his own political isolation, bred a trenchancy of speech and rudeness of manner which seemed to the diplomats to spring—and perhaps in part they did spring—from the pride of victory. He was himself conscious of the danger: he strove earnestly to practise a Christian humility, to give to God the glory, to remember that his life was in God's hand and himself as grass that is cut down. But inherited temperament was too strong for the precepts of religion. The Vasa pride, the Vasa talent for making enemies with the tongue, the Vasa misanthropy, could no more be suppressed—even in this,

[1] *ibid.*, II. 541-4; Irmer, *VS*, II. 30; *AOSB*, I. VIII. 479-85; *cf. AOSB*, I. VIII. 40; Helbig, pp. 78-80, where John George is asked whether he has any objection to Frederick's restoration; Irmer, *VS*, I. 139-40, where Oxenstierna insists that the Palatine vote must be Protestant, and the exiles restored in the Palatinate and Bohemia.

[2] *RRP*, VII. 307.

[3] *RRP*, VI. 504.

the least atrabilious and least morbid of them all—than could those volcanic outbursts of choler which he afterwards so sincerely regretted. The course of events laid great temptations upon him; and perhaps it was impossible that a man of his character should not succumb to them. The triumphs of 1631 and 1632 brought with them as many dangers as they dispelled. And of these dangers not the least was that the King should lose the sense of moderation; and in the search for the logical, the desirable, and even the right, should forget the virtues of compromise.

CHAPTER X

GUSTAV ADOLF AND GERMANY

(i) *The Organization of Germany*

It was in the autumn and winter of 1631 that Gustav Adolf began seriously to take in hand the organization of Germany. It was a task unforeseen in 1630, and undertaken from necessity rather than from choice; and though much of the work was done by civilians, and concerned purely civil matters, it was essentially a military operation.

The advance to the Rhine had brought under Swedish control large areas of north and central Germany. Some territories had been recovered for their former owners; others were conquests from the enemy and at the disposal of the victor; all were to be defended against an imperialist counter-attack. A string of Swedish garrisons stretched back through Franconia to the Mark and the coastal base; and their payment, supply and reinforcement—and, not less, their relations with the civilian population—presented a multitude of problems to the commander-in-chief and his field-chancery. As the King's armies grew larger, the organization of supply grew constantly more complex; and as the number of separate armies increased, so too did the delicate problem of allocating recruiting and supply areas between them, and ensuring that one general did not poach upon another's preserves. If the recruiting drive of the winter should yield the results which Gustav Adolf hoped and expected, these problems would become enormously more difficult. War must sustain war; but the King rightly believed that a planned and controlled exploitation, carried through by authorized officials, had a better chance of meeting his needs (besides being less provocative to public opinion) than the haphazard plundering and competitive marauding of individual units. The campaign of 1632 could be waged only if every resource of the areas occupied and to be occupied were utilized as economically and efficiently as possible. To burn the villages, torture the peasants and drive the population to the deep forests was not merely repugnant on grounds of humanity; it was a reckless living upon capital.

Better in every way to use the existing civil administrations, or where necessary make new ones; to collect tribute in the guise of taxes; to enlist the aid of the local authorities in the reservation of muster-places. Wallenstein had seen this too; though he had not always been able to manage matters as he would have wished. Thus the Swedish exploitation of Germany, in Gustav Adolf's lifetime at least, was intended to be founded, not upon atrocities and terrorism, but upon a careful calculation of capacity to pay, and upon the principles of rough justice. It was stringent; it was even pitiless; but it aspired to be fair.[1] Atrocities occurred, certainly, and in numbers which made the King very angry [2]; but the government did its best to prevent them, and it did not hesitate to impose exemplary punishment upon such offenders as it could catch.

Gustav Adolf, then, found himself forced to create a military administration for occupied Germany, and to integrate the civil administration into it as best he could.[3] It was a task for which he was not equipped. The clerical and administrative resources to do it simply did not exist on an adequate scale at the Swedish head-quarters. On a handful of secretaries and diplomats—Grubbe, Nicodemi, Sadler, Salvius and the rest—pressed an enormous mass of miscellaneous business; and on the King himself a still more oppressive burden of decision, on all points, military and civil. Until Oxenstierna joined him in January 1632 he was without any collaborator with whom he could work on terms of intimate confidence. There was no one of his assistants of sufficient standing or sufficient experience to take decisions without reference to him; and even Oxenstierna sometimes erred on the side of caution in this respect. Gustav Adolf, in fact, was for a time fighting a campaign, acting as chief of general staff and minister of war, and governing an occupied country, very nearly single-handed. He was dealing with problems of Napoleonic variety without any of the Napoleonic machinery. Like Napoleon, he was harassed by the personal jealousies of his marshals; like Napoleon, he left them the minimum

[1] See, *e.g.*, *AOSB*, I. VI. 566-7, where Oxenstierna discusses how much may reasonably be extorted from Pomerania.

[2] How far the reality was from the King's intentions may be seen from the accounts of Swedish atrocities in, *e.g.*, Franconia and the Lower Saxon Circle. For Franconia, see C. G. Scharold, *Geschichte der kön. schwedischen und herzögl. sachsen-weimarischen Zwischenregierung im eroberten Fürstbisthume Würzburg i. J. 1631-1634*, I. 39, 41, 46-7, 65-7, 129 *seqq.*; for the Lower Saxon Circle, see, *e.g.*, Trana's letter to Oxenstierna of 9 April 1632, in *Arkiv*, II. 410-13.

[3] A modern study of Swedish administration in Germany is a *desideratum*.

of initiative. If at times during the last year of his life Gustav Adolf makes mistakes, if he wounds allies and alienates friends by tactlessness, bullying or violent explosions of anger, a partial explanation is perhaps that he was a man driven to the limits of endurance by a crushing weight of responsibility and work. The complexities of 1632 had come upon him by a gradual development, as one military move followed logically upon the last; and each new situation brought its improvised solution. He had little leisure to elaborate his plans, whether military or political: he had a clear notion of how best to meet the needs of the moment, and he had ideas as to the future which were probably always rather vague and general. A political and military objective had been easy enough to define at Stockholm in 1630; at Mainz, eighteen months later, it was much more difficult. In 1632 Gustav Adolf's main concern was to carry on the war. Politically and militarily he lived from hand to mouth: time enough when the Habsburgs were disposed of to settle finally with the weary perversities of Germany.

In the meantime, by successive improvisations and devices, something like a regular government was created for the occupied territories. It centred on Mainz, where it took shape during the winter and spring of 1632. To the war chancery was added a standing council, a judicial authority (largely concerned with military discipline) and an exchequer.[1] Their constitution and functions were still in need of definition in October 1632, when Oxenstierna drew up an instruction to himself touching these matters [2]; and they did not assume the firm contours of their counterparts in Sweden until 1633.[3] But a beginning was made. In the financial field, as was to be expected, this rudimentary government was especially well developed. At its head stood a grand treasurer (*storskattmästare*); its agents collected what had once been the Emperor's tolls; it promulgated books of rates; it required proper accounts of revenues received: it organized a regular Domesday of the occupied lands.[4] The auditor-general and quartermaster-general were kept busy making inventories of the country's resources, and erecting magazines for the collection of provisions and armaments [5]; and commissioners

[1] Frohnhäuser, p. 121.

[2] *AOSB*, II. I. 857 *seqq.* An earlier arrangement, never put into effect, in *ibid.*, II. I. 808.

[3] See, for instance, the Exchequer Ordinances for the electorate of Mainz and for Swabia: *AOSB*, I. VIII. 393, 748.

[4] *AOSB*, I. VII. 143, 282 *seqq.*, 298, 313-15, 354, 357-8, I. VIII 109, II. I. 753, 768.

[5] *ibid.*, I. VII. 126, 270 *seqq.*; Scharold, I. 49, 124 *seqq.*

saw to it that the local authorities handed over the contributions which had been imposed upon them. Specific revenues were appropriated to the payment of the Queen's civil list during her stay in Germany.[1] A real attempt was made to transfer to Germany the methodical and economical administrative habits which the Swedish war office had evolved, and which had contributed not a little to the efficiency of the Swedish armies. The maintenance or improvement of communications was taken in hand; the Thurn-Taxis postal system was placed under Swedish control; the printing-presses of Mainz and Frankfort were set to supplement the flow of Swedish propaganda; and a highly organized news and intelligence service was gradually created.[2]

Local government was under the control of governors (*ståthållare*) appointed to take charge of this or that Circle or district, or set over an important city, as Johan Sparre was in Mainz. Thus George Frederick von Hohenlohe was *generalståthållare* in the Swabian Circle, his brother Kraft in the Franconian, the Rhinegrave Otto in the two Rhenish Circles, Louis of Anhalt in the dioceses of Magdeburg and Halberstadt, George Louis von Löwenstein in Erfurt.[3] Their business was to keep the old civil administration in operation, to see to it that the contributions were promptly paid, and to ensure that local differences did not put obstacles in the way of the conduct of the war. Side by side with them were Swedish agents—such as Salvius in the Lower Saxon Circle—with special powers or commissions; or military commanders installed as Residents in particular towns, as Alexander Erskine was in Erfurt.[4]

One of their duties was to see to it that Lutherans were given proper facilities for the exercise of their religion, even in districts formerly Catholic or Calvinist. In Magdeburg and Halberstadt the Lutheran church was thoroughly reorganized, and a special Church Ordinance on the Swedish model was drawn up under the supervision of Johannes Botvidi.[5] But the Catholics, to their undisguised surprise, were nowhere actively persecuted, though they were frequently dispossessed of their churches, and sometimes heavily

[1] *AOSB*, I. VII. 253.
[2] *Vägar och vägkunskap under trettioåriga krigets senare skede*, p. 75; *Sv. Krig*, Supp. Vol. I., for Swedish intelligence services.
[3] *Schriftstücke*, p. 223; *AOSB*, I. VII. 23, 73, 342, 530, I. VIII. 507, 580; *Sverges traktater*, V. 528.
[4] *AOSB*, I. VII. 323. For a full account of Swedish administration in the diocese of Würzburg, see Scharold, I. 59-65, 90, 143-6, 159-79.
[5] Holmquist, *Den svenska kyrkans historia*, IV. I. 453-4.

mulcted; the Jesuits in particular being treated with severity.[1] The tolerance which Gustav Adolf showed to Catholicism, his frank curiosity as to its doctrine and ritual, his ability—to be strikingly demonstrated in Munich—to get upon terms of easy and cordial intercourse even with Jesuits, made a deep impression on contemporaries, and have appeared to some historians to be strangely at variance with the furious anti-papalism of his earlier years—as exemplified, for instance, in the Statute of Örebro. But the inconsistency is superficial only. The violence of his hostility to the Roman church was born of fear: when he stood victor in Erfurt or Mainz, when he entered in triumph the political capital of the shattered League, he could forget the alarms of Örebro, or the fumbling intrigues of Bähr and Anthelius.

The personnel of the emergent administration in Germany was, of necessity, largely German. Sweden had too much difficulty in staffing her domestic civil service with competent administrators to have any reserve adequate to these new demands. German recruits, however, proved easy to obtain: just as ambitious Protestant princes sought the command of a regiment in the King's service, so men like Steinberg, or Wolf, or Sadler, were only too ready to exchange their former employment for a position in the Swedish administration and the honourable title of *hovråd*—as Camerarius had done before them, and as Grotius was to do later. The Swedish service in Germany, whether civil or military, offered the career open to talents; and men were not slow to enlist in it. The relationship with a foreign employer into which they thereby entered caused no difficulty in the case of the average civilian. But the position of a German territorial prince was more dubious. By accepting a Swedish commission he became Gustav Adolf's subordinate, bound to him by a military oath, and subject if necessary to his disciplinary action. His military obligations might easily abridge his princely rights; and they clashed with his duty to Emperor and *Reich*. As the Swedish armies grew bigger, as more and more German princes and nobles entered the King's employment, an increasingly anomalous position arose, and no real solution to it was possible.

[1] Priorato, p. 111; Frohnhäuser, pp. 128-34, 144; Huschke, pp. 7, 75; Paul, III. 34-5; *AOSB*, I. VII. 316; J. B. Baur, *Die Kapuziner und die schwedische Generalität im dreissigjährigen Kriege*, pp. 5-11; L. Schaedel, *Gustav Adolf von Schweden in München*, pp. 122-5; *Die Chronik des Jakob Wagner*, pp. 12-21. But for the contrast between the King's principles and his subordinates' practice, see Scharold, I. 36-7, 44, 52, 68-88, 159-83. There seems, moreover, to have been some persecution of the Jews: *AOSB*, I. VII. 57; Scharold, I. 132.

William of Weimar, for instance, could be reconciled to his subordinate status only by being given the titular post of second-in-command, for which his military talents by no means qualified him.[1] Even landless princes such as Bernard of Weimar and George of Lüneburg were difficult subordinates, and sometimes impossible colleagues for the Swedish generals who had to work with them.[2] The German princes and nobles could not altogether be treated as though they were in the same position as Swedish subjects. Oxenstierna complained bitterly that nothing gave him more trouble than 'these many grand gentlemen', whose handling demanded unremitting tact[3]; and a lesser man such as Salvius had often a hard time of it with them. But, as Oxenstierna admitted with a sigh, it was a *necessarium malum*, and they must make the best of it. It was not surprising, perhaps, that Swedish civil servants on the one side, and some German princes on the other, should have seen in the assumption of the imperial crown by Gustav Adolf an easy way out of these difficulties.[4]

Problems of a similar kind arose from the distribution of the spoils of war. As the conquest of central Germany had proceeded, Gustav Adolf had used the confiscated ecclesiastical lands to reward his own men, or to attach his German generals more firmly to his cause. The process, begun in Thuringia and Franconia, was continued in south Germany; and in Württemberg, for instance, lands which had been restored to the Catholic church as recently as 1630, in virtue of the Edict of Restitution, were given away as soon as they fell into Swedish hands.[5] In May 1633 Oxenstierna told the *råd* that donations had been so numerous that a great part of the Swedish conquests had passed out of the King's hands by the date of his death; and that the German allies and officers had in consequence become demoralized, since they had come to think more about the prospects of a donation than of the common cause. Donations, however (as Oxenstierna admitted), were almost unavoidable; for the King could not keep all these lands in his own

[1] Huschke, pp. 24, 45-50; *Schriftstücke*, p. 179.

[2] Oxenstierna was given 'absolute command' over Bernard of Weimar and Christian of Birkenfeld in order to prevent their quarrelling: Ahnlund, *Oxenstierna*, p. 672.

[3] *AOSB*, I. vii. 486.

[4] Salvius, for instance, wrote to Grubbe on 12 October 1631: '*Si res regi Sveciae bene cesserint tum omnes principes non solum foederatos* but also *subditos habebit*, and consequently *omnes portus*': Boëthius, *NSK*, p. 207.

[5] T. Schott, *Württemberg und Gustav Adolf*, pp. 381-2.

control, and by giving them away he was able to discharge his indebtedness in the matter of arrears of pay.[1] The important question was, rather, upon what terms the donations were made. As Oxenstierna explained, the King was always careful to reserve his *jus superioritatis*, and his right to levy contributions.[2] Sometimes he went much further: when William of Hesse-Cassel was presented with the dioceses of Fulda, Corvey, Paderborn and Münster, it was provided that in the event of his line becoming extinct his subjects in these territories would then owe allegiance to the crown of Sweden.[3] And in the donation for Louis Philip of Simmern it was laid down that he should accept Swedish garrisons, tolerate Lutheranism (Louis Philip was a Calvinist) and 'recognize' Gustav Adolf for his '*beneficium*'.[4] Terms such as these undoubtedly suggested a feudal relationship. But it is questionable whether the suggestion was seriously intended.[5] What Gustav Adolf was concerned to secure was the liberty to draw freely upon the resources of the donated lands, the effective military control of them, and if possible the political reliability of the recipients. The holder of a donation must 'depend' upon him for that donation, just as Frederick V must 'depend' on him for the restored Palatinate: that is, he must do as he was told—for the duration of the war, at all events. It was not to be tolerated that a successful general who had been rewarded by a grant of church lands should deprive his benefactor of such assistance as

[1] *AOSB*, I. VIII. 673-83: *ibid.*, 751-825, has a selection of 85 such gifts made in the King's lifetime; and *cf. ibid.*, I. IX. 34, for Bernard's donation. For donations in Franconia, see Scharold, I. 37-9, 89-90, 112-24.

[2] *AOSB*, I. VIII. 673 *seqq.*; *cf. ibid.*, 638.

[3] *ibid.*, I. VIII. 644, 647.

[4] *ibid.*, I. VII. 95-6. The word may, however, have been used in its general, non-technical sense; as it probably was, for instance, in the alliance with Mecklenburg of 29 February 1632: *Sverges traktater*, V. 706; see below, p. 637 *note* 1; and above, pp. 615-6.

[5] See the further discussion below, pp. 638-42; and *cf.* Paul's comment (*op. cit.*, III. 29): 'Eine Loslösung der von Gustav Adolf verschenkten Ländereien aus dem deutschen Reichsverbande oder etwa gar ihre Angliederung an das Königreich Schweden ist zu keiner Zeit in Frage gekommen, auch nicht, als er späterhin dazu überging, sich den Lehnseid schwören zu lassen. Es war das nur die damals noch durchaus übliche staatsrechtliche Form bei Übertragung grösserer Ländergebiete und wurde von Gustaf Adolf angewandt, um sich gewisse Rechte zu sichern und die betreffenden Herren seinen Plänen, die ja zuletzt ganz offen auf einen dauernden Zusammenschluss der evangelischen Stände gingen, gefügig zu machen'. So too with the donations to William of Hesse: he took them 'ohne einigen Respect gegen den Kaiser und in der Eigenschaft eines ganz und gar nicht unterworfenen, sondern allerdings freien und franken Fürsten und der Krone Schweden freien Alliirten und Conföderirten'; but he did so only until 'es im Römischen Reich . . . einen versicherten Frieden und eine andere Verfassung geben würde': Rommel, *Geschichte von Hessen*, VIII. 184.

those lands could provide. Yet the impression remained, in the minds of many contemporaries, that Gustav Adolf aimed at annexing to himself the imperial prerogatives, and at giving a real meaning to all those antique feudal rights which the Emperor had latterly been scarcely able in practice to enforce. The replacing of Ferdinand by Gustav Adolf might indeed do much to regularize a situation which was becoming unpleasantly complex; but the princes might well ask themselves what would become of the precious liberties of the German nation if the Vasa ousted the Habsburg. Wallenstein and the Edict had been bad; a 'Macedonian domination' might well be worse.

(ii) *The Welfs and Mecklenburg*

The doubts thus provoked by the terms of some of the donations were strengthened by the much more serious question of the relationship between the King and his prospective allies. As Gustav Adolf's military power began to sprawl over Germany, as the increase in the area of conquest diluted that power's concentration, the need for a tight control over the German princes became even greater than before. Not even Breitenfeld had succeeded in producing that general Protestant league under Swedish direction which had been the objective of the *Norma futurarum actionum.* Gustav Adolf was still proceeding by the method of accretion: one state after another was to be added to Sweden's list of allies, each by its separate treaty, and all bound together only by the cement of Swedish direction. In the summer and autumn of 1631 a succession of treaties, more or less upon the Hessian model, was designed to bring in a number of princes in this way: a draft agreement had been signed with John Albert of Mecklenburg in May; a treaty with John Frederick of Bremen in June; in July Salvius was instructed to proceed to a definitive treaty with the Mecklenburg Dukes; in August the final agreement with William V of Hesse-Cassel was signed; in September an alliance was concluded with the Princes of Anhalt.[1] But neither of the Mecklenburg drafts received the King's approval; and as the autumn advanced it seems that he began to think that arrangements of the Hessian type were no longer adequate to his needs. There were certain areas of such crucial strategic importance that only a much more stringent control could guarantee

[1] *Sverges traktater*, V. 463-73 (Bremen); 476-90 (Hesse-Cassel); 524-8 (Anhalt).

the safety of his operations. One such area was the Baltic coastland; another was the region of the middle Weser.[1] He must be sure of Mecklenburg; he must be sure of the duchies of the Welfs. Pomerania, he was beginning to feel, must remain permanently in his hands. And, as luck would have it, in each of these cases he had to deal with powerless princes upon whom, it was tempting to think, it would be easy to impose his will. For a time, then, Gustav Adolf tries to cut loose from the Hessian pattern of alliances and to impose upon the Mecklenburg Dukes, and upon the Welfs, terms more drastic than he had ever demanded before or was ever to demand again. In this he failed. And the attempt cost him dear; for out of it arose the progressive alienation of the German Protestant princes from the cause of their deliverer.

The Welfs, it will be remembered,[2] were divided into two lines: the senior, of Brunswick-Wolfenbüttel, and the junior, of Lüneburg-Celle. The childless Duke Frederick Ulric was the head of the Wolfenbüttel branch; while Duke Christian, who was unmarried, ruled in Celle. Neither of these princes had as yet committed himself in regard to Sweden: in the autumn of 1631 the forces of Tilly were still in occupation of almost the whole of the Welf duchies. Christian's brother George, however, who was heir-presumptive to the whole Welf inheritance,[3] was for the present a landless prince, and as such could afford to take rather greater political risks. In October 1631, therefore, he at last accepted the commission in the Swedish service which had been made out for him in the previous year.[4]

The first approach to the Welfs from the Swedish side, as we have seen, was made in May 1631, when Salvius was sent to Celle to propose an alliance. Christian had then evaded the offer, alleging prior obligations under the Leipzig resolution; but had consented in August to make a modest contribution to the Swedish war-chest.[5] Towards the end of November, Salvius made another and more successful attempt, as a result of which a treaty of alliance was concluded on 6 December.[6] It was a typical example of the Hessian-style alliance,

[1] L. Tingsten, *Gustav II Adolfs politik och krigföring i Tyskland*, p. 113.

[2] For the domestic circumstances of the Welfs, see Kretzschmar, *Gustaf Adolfs Pläne und Ziele*, pp. 1-8.

[3] He was, in fact, the ancestor of the Hanoverians.

[4] His patent is in *Sverges traktater*, V. 557-8; Kretzschmar, *op. cit.*, pp. 14-18; Droysen, *Die niedersächsischen Kreisstände während des schwedisch-deutschen Krieges*, p. 5 *seqq.*

[5] Kretzschmar, *op. cit.*, pp. 11-13.

[6] *Sverges traktater*, V. 588-99.

except for two provisions. One recalled the treaty with Pomerania, since it provided for a renewal of the alliance every ten years; the other pledged the parties to assist each other in the event of any attack (without limitation of time) which might be considered to be a consequence of the treaty. Both, therefore, suggested a more permanent commitment, not necessarily restricted to the duration of the present war, than was usual in treaties of the Hessian pattern. But the most notable feature of the treaty with Lüneburg-Celle was that Gustav Adolf refused to ratify it. And it is clear that his refusal arose from his hope of obtaining much more far-reaching concessions, not only from Christian but also from his cousin Frederick Ulric.

Discussions with Frederick Ulric had begun in October, and had been conducted in Halle, under the auspices of the King's *ståthållare*, Louis of Anhalt. On 28 November agreement had been reached upon the terms of a treaty which is known as the Halle Compact.[1] It contained all the usual 'Hessian' provisions, including a guarantee against infringement of the Duke's territorial rights, a Swedish *directorium* for the duration of the war, and a prohibition upon other alliances without Gustav Adolf's consent. But it contained also some new stipulations. Any former imperial revenues in the lands to be recovered were to be paid to Gustav Adolf. Frederick Ulric was to be bound to assist him 'hereafter'—an expression which might be thought ominously vague. And clause 14 provided that the Duke should 'gratefully recognize' Gustav Adolf, in his capacity as 'Supreme Head of the evangelical Electors, Princes, and Estates of the German Nation', for all the Brunswick and Hildesheim lands, as they should be recovered—excepting only those to which the Lüneburg line might have a claim by feudal law and family agreements. Now the Wolfenbüttel line had for many years been in possession of the secularized bishopric of Hildesheim, until deprived of it by a judgment of the Imperial Chamber of Justice in 1629; and they also considered themselves to have rights to three districts (*Ämter*) which—in their contention—were attached to Hildesheim. The securing of the *Ämter* was one of Frederick Ulric's objects in entering into this negotiation. It was in every way unfortunate that Gustav Adolf had already committed himself to promising them to George of Lüneburg; but by the Halle Compact this promise was implicitly revoked in favour of the Wolfenbüttel line. Both Welf lines were therefore concerned to know the precise interpretation to

[1] *Sverges traktater*, V. 691-7.

be placed on clause 14. What did 'recognition' mean? and what exactly were the lands for which it was to be given? The Swedish diplomats at Halle returned a reassuring answer to these enquiries. Recognition was to apply only to Hildesheim and the *Ämter*; and any suggestion of vassalage was explicitly disavowed. All that was required, it seemed, was that Frederick Ulric should recognize Gustav Adolf 'out of gratitude', and '*titulo protectionis vel advocatiae*'.[1] But even if this answer (vague enough, indeed) were acceptable to Frederick Ulric, it could not remove the anxieties of his Lüneburg cousins. Not only was George coolly deprived of his *Ämter* but he was even robbed of his chance of inheriting them after Frederick Ulric's death; for the Compact provided that both Hildesheim and the *Ämter* should be given to Frederick Ulric and the heirs of his body—not to his heirs at law. When Frederick Ulric should die, not the *Ämter* only but the whole Hildesheim diocese would pass away from the Welfs and presumably revert to Gustav Adolf, as the donor.

The Halle Compact, however, was not acceptable even to Frederick Ulric. On his instructions, negotiations were resumed in Frankfort on 20 December with Louis of Anhalt; and some concessions—notably in regard to the hereditary rights of the Lüneburg line—were made on the Swedish side. But now came a trenchant intervention from Gustav Adolf himself. He refused to approve the new draft; he refused to ratify even the Halle Compact—precisely as he had refused to ratify the treaty with Lüneburg. And on 1 January 1632 Filip Sadler presented to the Wolfenbüttel delegates the draft of a treaty drawn in the most startling terms.[2] By this draft Frederick Ulric was to place himself under the King's protection; and in return was promised the restoration of his hereditary lands, and of the diocese of Hildesheim. As to the *Ämter*, Gustav Adolf undertook only to 'consider means' for conquering them if they should prove to be really the lawful appendages of Hildesheim; and should they in fact be recovered, to give them to Frederick Ulric and his heirs 'as princely fiefs'. In return, Frederick Ulric was to accept Gustav Adolf's *directorium* and place his fortresses and military installations at the King's disposal. But if he should die before the end of the war, and the Lüneburg line should

[1] Kretzschmar, *Gustav Adolfs Pläne und Ziele*, pp. 31-3.

[2] Text, with Brunswick amendments, printed in Kretzschmar, *op. cit.*, pp. 247-77.

succeed to his territories, these fortresses were to be returned to them only on condition that the new Duke should ratify this alliance, and should not meanwhile have 'forfeited' his claims by joining the imperialists.[1] And it was further required that the Estates of the various Welf lands should pledge themselves not to do homage to any ruler who failed to confirm this treaty.[2] The alliance with Sweden was to be binding on the Duke and his successors 'for ever'; they were to 'look to' [3] Gustav Adolf alone, now and in the future; and they were to conclude no alliance (whether repugnant to the treaty or not, apparently) without his consent. They were to pledge themselves not to make peace until Gustav Adolf had been assured of an 'acceptable, sufficient, royal satisfaction'. And in sign of gratitude for these benefits, Frederick Ulric was to recognize Gustav Adolf and the crown of Sweden for both Hildesheim and the *Ämter*—though only for himself and his heirs-male.[4] Finally, the Swedish military dictatorship, and the stipulated Brunswick contingents to the Swedish army, were not merely to continue to the end of the war, but were to persist in 'wars arising out of this one'—an expression which, liberally construed, might well have bound Frederick Ulric to the Swedish war chariot until the peace of Nystad.

The Wolfenbüttel delegates rejected this draft without hesitation. To them it seemed to involve an intolerable interference with the rights and privileges of their master. It meant the end of the independence of the Welfs for longer than anyone could foresee. It meant, they thought, the tearing away of Brunswick from the body

[1] 'Sich solcher Lande und Sachen nicht verlustig gemacht haben': Kretzschmar, p. 259. Compare the attempt to put pressure on Brandenburg by threatening to debar the Elector from the reversion to Pomerania.

[2] There had been a precedent for this in the treaty with John Frederick of Bremen, which had included a clause requiring the assent of the Estates to the treaty: *Sverges traktater*, V. 467.

[3] 'auf sie allein unser Absehen haben': Kretzschmar, p. 261.

[4] Kretzschmar (p. 47) held that Gustav Adolf claimed recognition for the whole body of the Welf hereditary lands; but he was probably mistaken: see the review by C. H. H[allendorf] in *Historisk tidskrift*, XXIV (1904), pp. 45-8, and Boëthius, *NSK*, p. 274 *note* 2. The crucial passage runs: 'So wollen wir zu mehrer Bezeigung unserer Dankwürdigkeit uns, unsere Fürstentümber, Graf- und Herrschaften, Land und Leute nicht allein dem königlichen Schutz bestermassen, wie obstehet, ergeben, sondern auch, sobald wir zu wirklicher Possession solcher Land und Güter wiedergelangen und respective kommen, dieselbe mit ihren Hoch-, Frei-, und Gerechtigkeiten, auch allen Pertinenzien für uns und unsere Leibeserben von SKW und dero Erben und Successorn an der Kron Schweden gebührendermassen zu Lehen empfangen und rekognoszieren . . .' It is clear from the general tenor of the preceding sentences of the clause that 'wiedergelangen' refers to Hildesheim (and not to the hereditary lands, as Kretzschmar thought), and 'kommen' to the *Ämter*. Text in Kretzschmar, pp. 263-4.

of the Empire. They suspected that it might cover a design to turn the whole Welf inheritance into a fief of the Swedish crown. They were ready, they were even anxious, for an alliance with Gustav Adolf; but it must be an alliance '*jure foederis et societatis*, and not *per modum dependentiae*'.[1]

Their firm stand had its effect. Gustav Adolf postponed further negotiations until Oxenstierna should have arrived at headquarters; and the chancellor, when he resumed the discussions in February, discreetly withdrew from the advanced position which the King had rushed forward to occupy. The final draft, which became the treaty of 5 February 1632, was a much more moderate document than its predecessor, though even so it represented a considerable advance upon treaties of the ordinary Hessian type.[2] Gustav Adolf took Frederick Ulric into his protection, and promised to use every effort to restore him to his lands—including Hildesheim and the *Ämter*; Frederick Ulric recognized Gustav Adolf as 'supreme Head and Director *titulo protectionis vel advocatiae*' for the Hildesheim lands alone; and his princely rights and privileges were twice declared to be unprejudiced by anything contained in the treaty.[3] Disputes as to interpretation were to be submitted to arbitration. Frederick Ulric was no longer restrained from making alliances which were not repugnant to the treaty. But though it was provided that a joint council of war should be set up, and remain in being for so long as hostilities continued in Brunswick, it was also provided that the King's absolute direction could be delegated to one of his generals. Moreover, the ominous clause as to 'wars arising out of this one' was retained: Frederick Ulric's contributions in men and money were to extend to such wars; and only at their conclusion would Gustav Adolf hand back the Duke's fortresses. And Frederick Ulric's successors would not recover them even then, unless they had in the meantime ratified the treaty.

The pattern of the negotiations with Brunswick—rejection by the King of an agreed draft; diplomatic crisis in January, with vastly enlarged Swedish demands; a slight softening of terms thereafter—was repeated, with minor variations, in the case of the Mecklenburg

[1] Kretzschmar, p. 46.
[2] *Sverges traktater*, V. 670-88.
[3] It is not quite true, as Kretzschmar asserted (*op. cit.*, p. 44), that Sadler's draft had pointedly omitted all declarations of this sort: see the conclusion of clause I. 7 of the draft: *ibid.*, pp. 256-7.

Dukes. There was, however, one fundamental difference. Although in June Gustav Adolf had still been ready to negotiate with Mecklenburg for an alliance of the Hessian type,[1] he had soon altered his opinion; and even before Breitenfeld had made up his mind that a treaty valid only for the duration of the war would be inadequate security in the case of a state with a Baltic coastline. Any alliance with Mecklenburg must have some element of permanence, and it must therefore be after the Pomeranian, rather than the Hessian, model. And in the interests of the Swedish navy, and to ensure to Gustav Adolf a safe embarkation if the worst should happen, he must have one or more of the Mecklenburg ports in his hands.[2] The agreement which John Albert had concluded in May was therefore left unratified (his brother, Adolf Frederick, had in any case not subscribed to it), and early in August Steinberg was sent to the Dukes with a draft treaty which came to them as an unpleasant shock.[3] Like the Pomeranian alliance, it was to be 'eternal', the intention being to renew it every ten years; but in all other respects it was much harsher than the agreement which Gustav Adolf had imposed upon Bogislaw XIV. Wismar was to remain in Swedish possession after its recovery, as a pledge for the King's war expenses; Sweden was to have the right to collect tolls on the rivers and at the harbours of the duchy; a free-trade clause opened the way for depreciated Swedish copper coin; the Dukes were to make no treaties of any sort during the war without Gustav Adolf's leave; and the alliance was to take precedence over all other obligations. The Dukes refused these terms; and in the course of negotiations with Salvius later in August succeeded in extracting some concessions from him. Their efforts did them no good; for on 17 September, at Halle, Gustav Adolf drew up, and himself signed, a treaty even more alarming than his original draft.[4] The word *clientela*, to which the Dukes had taken particular exception, was indeed omitted; but the intended relationship was adequately conveyed by the words *protectio* and *tutela*. All Salvius's concessions were now cancelled. Gustav Adolf was now arguing that he was

[1] *Sverges traktater*, V. 715-16; *Arkiv*, I. 464 *seqq.*

[2] See the motivation in the final treaty with Mecklenburg of 29 February 1632, in clause VII: *ibid.*, V. 709; and Oxenstierna's remarks, *AOSB*, I. VI. 572-3.

[3] For a close analysis of these negotiations, see Boëthius, *NSK*, pp. 62, 167-203; *cf.* Kretzschmar, pp. 187-90; Paul, III. 58-61.

[4] Salvius was sent with it to Adolf Frederick at Rostock: his instructions are in *Arkiv*, I. 497; text of draft in *Sverges traktater*, V. 717.

entitled, by the laws of war, to retain *all* occupied areas, until 'at least' his war costs had been paid.[1] He did not, however, propose to do so; but he would keep Wismar and Warnemünde (not Wismar only, as in the previous draft) until such time as he should have reached agreement about the ownership of these places—not with the Dukes, but with the Empire.[2]

While Adolf Frederick was concocting a counter to these demands Gustav Adolf went off to his campaign in Franconia, and the reconquest of Mecklenburg proceeded. By the beginning of November the fall of Wismar appeared to be only a matter of time: on 16 November the defenders were granted an armistice of four weeks, at the expiry of which they were to surrender, if not previously relieved.[3] The question as to who was to garrison the place once it had capitulated suddenly became urgent. Gustav Adolf was resolved to keep it in his own hands; Adolf Frederick was understandably anxious to prevent the Swedes from getting a foothold, for he had good reason to fear that once they were in it would not be easy to get them out again. Gustav Adolf had been profoundly irritated by Adolf Frederick's rejection of the alliance that had been proposed to him. No German prince had been in a more hopeless position in 1630; of none could it more truly be said that he owed his restoration entirely to the efforts of others. Very recent history had shown that he was incapable of maintaining his independence against imperialist attack. His port of Wismar had been the base for Wallenstein's fleet: it could not be suffered to revert to the Duke's keeping until all had been made safe in Germany—and perhaps not even then. The resistance of the Mecklenburg Dukes seemed to Gustav Adolf to be flagrant ingratitude: one more of those petty obstacles which selfish particularism threw under the feet of Germany's deliverer. As the future of Wismar hung in the balance, his patience suddenly gave way. At least he would make sure of Wismar, whatever the consequences. On 20 December he despatched an angry letter to Banér, ordering him to prevent Adolf Frederick from occupying the port, if necessary by force, and to allow his army to plunder the

[1] 'donec belli saltem nostri sumptus nobis refunderentur': *ibid.*, V. 719.

[2] *ibid.*, *loc. cit.*: 'donec de ijs plenius nobis cum imperio Romano convenerit'; see Boëthius, *NSK*, p. 185 *note* 2.

[3] Boëthius, *NSK*, pp. 187-95. Wismar capitulated on 12 January 1632. The Mecklenburg commander was allowed to assume command in the town only in the name of Gustav Adolf: *Arkiv*, II. 355-6.

inhabitants of the duchies.[1] It is true that second thoughts convinced him of the unwisdom of such crude violence: the letter was recalled before it reached its destination. But when on 30 December Adolf Frederick arrived at headquarters to plead his cause, he found the King quite intractable. Mecklenburg was Swedish, he contended, by right of conquest: if Adolf Frederick wanted his lands back again, he must consent to recognize Gustav Adolf for them. This Adolf Frederick refused to do; and the discussions reached a deadlock at once.[2]

The arrival of Oxenstierna set the talks going again; but it did not at first lead to any softening of the Swedish terms. Gustav Adolf on 27 January did indeed offer to renounce his *jus belli*, but only on the impossible condition that Mecklenburg should cut itself off from the Empire and assume the status of an independent state.[3] The proposals put forward at Halle, which Adolf Frederick had considered so oppressive, were now no longer regarded even as adequate on the Swedish side.[4] It was not until 3 March that the Duke was presented with conditions which he could bring himself to accept.[5] They were extremely onerous: more onerous than those which he had previously rejected out of hand; but the stark alternatives between which he had to choose were now—as Oxenstierna made clear—alliance on the best terms Sweden could be persuaded to grant, or a Swedish occupation on no terms at all.

The Mecklenburg alliance (antedated to 29 February) was thus a dictated settlement.[6] It was 'eternal', being renewable at every change of ruler in either state; it took precedence over all other obligations upon the Dukes [7]; it put Wismar and Warnemünde in Swedish possession for the duration of the war; and it gave Sweden the absolute direction of the alliance. The duchies were to admit

[1] *Arkiv*, I. 534-5; *cf.* the letter to Salvius of 5 November 1631 (*ibid.*, I. 506-7), and Oxenstierna's indignant comment to Erik Andersson Trana on the terms of the capitulation of Rostock, of which he remarks that the Dukes 'have taken more care of their own interest and advantage than of the King's safety': *AOSB*, I. VI. 572. Gustav Adolf seems to have feared Danish intrigues in Mecklenburg: Boëthius, *Salvius i den nedersaxiska kretsen maj-december 1631*, p. 177.

[2] Boëthius, *NSK*, pp. 196-7. For the negotiations from December onwards, see the report of Johann Cothmann, printed in Kretzschmar, *op. cit.*, pp. 316-62.

[3] Boëthius, *op. cit.*, p. 197. Adolf Frederick got wind of such an idea (no doubt from Salvius) as early as the winter of 1630-31: *ibid.*, p. 54.

[4] *Arkiv*, II. 364.

[5] Oxenstierna foresaw his capitulation as early as 17 February: *AOSB*, I. VII. 24. See, on his share in the negotiations, Ahnlund, *Oxenstierna*, p. 653.

[6] *Sverges traktater*, V. 704-14.

[7] 'Neque adversus haec ulla exceptio valeat antiquorum seu novorum pactorum, foederum aut nexuum homagij': *ibid.*, 713.

Swedish copper currency at its face value; Gustav Adolf was to have the right to collect tolls.[1] The Dukes were bound to render military aid, in this war and all wars arising out of it with all their forces, in other wars according to their ability. Yet Adolf Frederick's stubborn resistance had not been wholly in vain. The claim for recognition had been dropped. Membership of the Empire was specifically retained. Adolf Frederick might hope that his acceptance of Gustav Adolf's terms had barred the way to any further claims grounded upon mere occupation. The wording of the treaty undoubtedly left a loophole for such claims; but Oxenstierna assured the Duke that there was no intention of pressing them against Mecklenburg, and with that assurance he had perforce to be content.[2]

The history of the negotiations with Mecklenburg and the Welfs marks a stage in the evolution of Gustav Adolf's policies in Germany. The comparative moderation which had characterized the Pomeranian treaty, the *Norma*, and even (despite the violence of the pressure applied) the interim arrangements with Brandenburg, was now thrown aside. In the autumn and early winter of 1631 Gustav Adolf put forward claims which the German Protestants could only regard as outrageous. This development was the King's personal policy. Sadler and Steinberg, Salvius and Louis of Anhalt were its instruments, not its originators; and the latter pair found to their chagrin that the King's exigence outran the instructions upon which they had based their diplomacy. The reason for this relatively sudden change of temper, this swift raising of the level of Swedish demands, can only be conjectured. It may be that the dramatic improvement in the military position after Breitenfeld led Gustav Adolf to think that he could now afford to take such measures as seemed to him to be necessary, without regard to the feelings of those with whom he had to act; though it is to be noted that the first example of the new spirit is provided in Steinberg's draft treaty for Mecklenburg, which dates from early August. It may be that he was moved to more trenchant action by his growing feeling of disillusionment with, and contempt for, the German princes with whom he was yoked. The resistance of Brandenburg,

[1] *cf. AOSB*, I. VII. 135 *seqq.* Rostock petitioned the King against the taking of toll, but received a very firm refusal, coupled with an assurance that the town might rely on Gustav Adolf's *patrocinium*: *ibid.*, I. VII. 173-4. Soon after, a book of rates was issued for Mecklenburg: *ibid.*, I. VII. 203 *seqq.*

[2] *Sverges traktater*, V. 706; Kretzschmar, pp. 191-2; Boëthius, *NSK*, p. 199; and see below, p. 642 *note* 1.

the tergiversations of William of Weimar, the tardy and grudging friendship of John George, the constant intrigues in the Lower Saxon Circle, the maddening sweet reasonableness of George of Hesse-Darmstadt—they seemed all to be symptoms of an ambivalence of attitude which to him was almost criminal. 'They wagge as the bush doth, resolving ever to quit their best friend in adversity', wrote Monro of the German princes [1]; and Oxenstierna expressed the general Swedish impression when he wrote:

> When I consider the differing designs of the Circles in general, and of each Estate and town in particular, and the *consilia media* that they follow, and how they are more ready to conceive a jealousy of this or that one of Y.M.'s projects, and to run into opposing counsels, rather than that they shall conform themselves to Y.M.'s laudable designs; and albeit now and then they may do so in words, after the manner of diplomacy, yet are they not serious in it, and imagine to themselves naught else but how always to contrive a clause through which they may slip out of their promises—then I perceive that so long as Y.M. plays this game and acts the suitor, the terms will always turn to your disadvantage, since they, as *homines otiosi* with naught else to do but think on such things, know well how to avail themselves of the like practices to *adstringere* Y.M. and raise a multitude of *actiones* and *praetensiones*, to Y.M.'s small profit.[2]

The tendency of the princes, when negotiating, to try to reserve their duty to the Empire, or their commitments to the Leipzig resolution, or their complicated family compacts, appeared as a pretext to shift the burden and the risk of action to other shoulders than their own. The impatience of Swedish diplomats confronted with these delaying tactics was given characteristic expression by Lars Grubbe, in the course of the negotiations with Brandenburg in May 1631, when he noted: 'Objection still made on grounds of *jura imperii fundamentalia*, *die Erbverbrüderung*, and other such stuff, mighty absurd.' [3] To Gustav Adolf it seemed worse than absurd: it seemed to be calculated ingratitude. It was his misfortune to suffer from the delusion that gratitude ought to be a factor in politics. He did not realize how dangerous to friendship is the conferring of an immense boon that can never be requited. His own proceedings went far to make the liberated princes unmindful of what he had done for them; and the last year of his life was certainly embittered by a sullen resentment at their lack of proper appreciation of his services. This

[1] Monro, II. 44. [2] *AOSB*, I. VI. 556-7. [3] *Arkiv*, I. 173.

feeling lay behind the formularies of the various draft treaties with Frederick Ulric: again and again the text specifies that the Duke accepts this or that obligation 'from thankfulness'. And the same phrases appear in the final treaty with Mecklenburg.[1] It is as though the King were grimly resolved to extort, by the most ruthless diplomatic pressure, the expression of a sentiment which was no longer spontaneous.

Since, then, he could not count on gratitude, and since the self-interest of the princes appeared to be anything but enlightened, the links by which he was to bind them to him must be made more massive than before. There is no doubt, now, that the connexion with Sweden is to be at least semi-permanent. The Mecklenburg treaty is 'eternal'; and the various provisions about '*bella e hoc bello enata*' in the Brunswick treaty foreshadow a period of dependence which might easily prove extremely protracted. The insertion of such provisions is understandable enough: they guaranteed to Gustav Adolf the assistance of his ally in the event of an attack by Poland, or Spain, or even France; they secured him against a Habsburg revival after the peace. But they were too elastic to be accepted willingly by any ally. From Gustav Adolf's point of view they were an advance towards the creation of a Protestant league which should remain in being after the war, as a kind of security-police for Germany, a Concert of Central Europe to safeguard the peace against further assaults from the revolutionary power which had deprived an Elector of his rights, and set Wallenstein in Adolf Frederick's place. And his own relationship to this evangelical concert was made more explicit than ever before: as the Brunswick treaty made clear, he was to be recognized as supreme head of the organization.

What this title was to imply, what rights it was to convey—these things were left uncertain, and perhaps the King himself could not at this stage have given them a precise definition. But they were not the less alarming for being vague. The course of these negotiations had certainly suggested that the most dangerous revolutionary, from the German point of view, might be Gustav Adolf rather than Ferdinand II. His claims to 'recognition' shocked and frightened the princes, for they seemed to imply a design to usurp the Emperor's

[1] 'Promittimus . . . Nos acceptum beneficium grato animo semper reputaturos atque agnituros esse' (§ II); 'Nos Duces Megapolenses [obstringimur] ad subsidium, operam fidelem et constantem gratitudinem' (§ III): *Sverges traktater*, V. 706-7.

place, or to disrupt altogether the old framework of the Empire. Had he not suggested, to Adolf Frederick, the radical step of cutting Mecklenburg loose from the Germanic body? Though the apparent attempt to impose upon the Welf hereditary lands, and all the Mecklenburg duchies, a position of vassalage to the Swedish crown had indeed been dropped, they could not forget that something of the sort had been tried (despite soothing Swedish expostulations to the contrary); and the terms on which the Hildesheim lands were to be donated—*titulo protectionis vel advocatiae*—had an uncomfortably feudal ring. Nor was it reassuring to remember the King's insistence upon clauses by which the alliance with Sweden was to override all other obligations, even to the Empire.

To Gustav Adolf these alarms were either unintelligible or, in so far as they were intelligible, of no great account. His attitude to the Empire was neither reverent nor iconoclastic: it was indifferent. He found its constitutional complexities irritating at times, but he was prepared to accept it as a going concern, and use it if it could be made useful. Mecklenburg, indeed, was a special case: an outwork to Sweden, about which he could afford to take no chances. It was conceivable, geographically, that the duchies should be a Swedish fief, as Ösel had once been a Danish; and Salvius had been urging this solution as early as the winter of 1630.[1] It was also conceivable (at least to the King) that Mecklenburg should be separated from the *Reich*—freed, that is, from those moral and constitutional inhibitions which had paralysed so many German states in the past, to Sweden's imperilment—and should enter into a close and permanent political arrangement with Sweden. But these were only possible solutions. Since the Dukes reacted so strongly against them, he was content to drop them, provided he obtained an alliance which gave him the full security that he sought. As to the Brunswick lands—and as to the other lands away from the sea—the situation was rather different. It is unlikely that he thought of any of them as permanent fiefs of the Swedish crown; and Frederick Ulric's suspicion that he wished to make the Welfs his vassals for their hereditary domains was unjustified, though not in the circumstances unnatural. But conquered or reconquered ecclesiastical lands were another matter. To donate them to his allies on terms which left the Emperor's feudal superiority unchallenged seemed absurd. As long as the war lasted, there was no point in admitting, even tacitly, the imperial rights (for instance)

[1] Boëthius, *NSK*, pp. 54, 257.

to river tolls; and a great deal to be said for diverting such revenues to Gustav Adolf's pocket.[1] And since in Germany there could be no land without a lord, it seemed logical, at least in the meanwhile, to step into the Emperor's shoes. How it would be at the peace was a different question, which as yet he had not seriously tackled: if Sweden herself became a member of the Empire—for example, as holder of Pomerania (a possibility which he was just coming to consider)—then it might be that these ecclesiastical lands would become mediate, rather than immediate, fiefs of the Empire. But this was but one solution among many: for the moment he was concerned only to make reasonably satisfactory interim arrangements. And neither for Brunswick nor for Mecklenburg was recognition the essential point in his programme. The demands he made, the rights he claimed, were not the consequence of the imposition of a feudal or quasi-feudal relationship; they were based partly on a *jus belli* as yet held rather *in terrorem* than thoroughly applied, but mainly upon a Swedish protectorate which arose naturally from the military situation, and about which, for the present at least, there could be no argument.

Gustav Adolf was able to proceed on these lines with the more confidence because he felt himself to be solidly based on the best contemporary opinions on international law. Grotius's *De jure Belli ac Pacis* had appeared in 1625, and it was well known to Gustav Adolf —who is said, indeed, to have carried a copy about with him on his campaigns. However that may be, the great treatise certainly provided ample justification for his proceedings in Germany. For Grotius had laid it down that the conquest of a territory—always provided that it were solidly secured, and not merely a transitory occupation—conveyed a title not only to the land but also to the incorporeal rights of the evicted party.[2] It could therefore be argued with propriety that Gustav Adolf, when he took possession of the ecclesiastical lands of his enemies, acquired all those feudal superiorities which had formerly pertained to the Emperor, and was entitled to give away these lands by donations in which his *jus superioritatis* was expressly acknowledged. And in virtue of this doctrine he was also entitled to grant the Hildesheim lands to the Welfs on a feudal,

[1] Bothe was even disposed to see behind such provisions a deliberate plan to obtain economic control of the great trade-routes of Germany: F. Bothe, *Gustav Adolfs und seine Kanzlers wirtschaftspolitische Absichten*, pp. 100-1.

[2] *Hugonis Grotii de jure Belli ac Pacis Libri Tres*, III. VI. 4 § 1, 5, 7 § 1, III. VII. 4, III. VIII. 4 § 2, III. XX. 12 § 2.

or quasi-feudal, tenure. But this was not all. For Grotius also taught that the question as to whether the vanquished had really a right to the lands of which he was deprived was irrelevant to the validity of the rights of the victor.[1] Gustav Adolf could therefore claim that the lands of friends and allies, recently in enemy possession but now liberated by him, were also at his disposal *jure belli*. This was the basis of his demand that Adolf Frederick and his brother should recognize him for Mecklenburg, and it could be applied with equal force (and equal benefit to Sweden) to Pomerania too.[2] And if it were objected—as the Wolfenbüttel delegates did object—that the terms which he presented to them were an intolerable infringement of the liberties of the weaker party, Gustav Adolf could quote Grotius's opinion that even very unequal alliances are not necessarily to be held to have this effect. Grotius specifically admitted, as legitimate, alliances in which one party is bound to preserve the authority of the other, '*ad quod genus referenda sunt jura quaedam eorum, quae nunc vocantur protectionis, advocatiae . . .*': such allies, he adds, are '*sub patrocinio, non sub ditione*'.[3] Indeed, the provision for arbitration, normally included in alliances of the Hessian type, and included also in the Brunswick treaty, seemed to Grotius to be one of the characteristic marks of an equal alliance.[4]

The authority of Grotius, therefore, provided new and weighty arguments both for *satisfactio* and for *assecuratio*. Not that the old demand for *satisfactio* as a recompense for Sweden's expenditure of men and money in the common cause was abandoned: Gustav Adolf lost no opportunity of pressing his claims on this ground. The Welfs were bound to fight until an adequate compensation should have been made; Wismar and Warnemünde were to be Swedish as pledges for a future indemnity. But in the draft of the Mecklenburg

[1] Grotius, III. VI. 7 § 1: but see also Grotius's restriction in *ibid.*, III. XIII. 1 § 1.

[2] Gustav Adolf to Salvius, 17 December 1631, where he asserts his *jus belli* to Pomerania, Mecklenburg, the dioceses of Magdeburg and Halberstadt 'and several other evangelical places which we, with the greatest labour and expense, have liberated from the hand and violence of the enemy': *Arkiv*, I. 530-2, the date corrected from 20 to 17 December in *Sverges traktater*, V. 582-3.

[3] Grotius, I. III. 21 §§ 1-3.

[4] *ibid.*, I. III. 21 § 6; but see too his caution in 21 § 10. Richelieu's remarks on unequal alliances may be cited in this connexion: 'Bien que ce soit un dire commun que quiconque a la force a d'ordinaire la raison, il est vrai toutefois que de deux puissances inégales, jointes par un traité, la plus grande court risque d'être plus abandonnée que l'autre. La raison en est évidente: La réputation est si importante à un grand prince qu'on ne sauroit proposer aucun avantage, qui puisse compenser la perte qu'il feroit, s'il manquoit aux engagements de sa parole et de sa foi': Richelieu, *Testament politique*, pp. 354-5.

treaty drawn at Halle in September the King was careful to insert the word '*saltem*': they were to be pledges 'at least' until his indemnity had been paid [1]; and he did not hesitate to point out that *jure belli* the whole of Mecklenburg was his to claim. *Satisfactio*, on this broader interpretation, might mean the satisfaction given to the victorious injured party, to be assessed as much on moral as on material grounds. So too with *assecuratio*: the rights which Grotius gave him might conceivably be used to constrain the princes whose lands he had recovered into membership of a tight-knit league which should provide Sweden with effective security; or they might be used to place in Gustav Adolf's hands large areas of inland Germany which could be used for bargaining at a peace conference. In either event it was plain that the concepts of *satisfactio* and *assecuratio* were beginning to alter. *Assecuratio* no longer meant merely the securing of Swedish influence on the maritime states, but rather a programme, as yet not clearly defined, for some sort of police-force or permanent bastion much further south. *Satisfactio* no longer meant a mere indemnity, but rather territorial gains on the Baltic. The old *assecuratio* was becoming the new *satisfactio*, and a new *assecuratio* was emerging.[2]

These developments came rapidly, partly because the military situation was so swiftly transformed in Sweden's favour; partly because the King's hot and impetuous temper led him to rush with indiscreet precipitancy towards a solution which seemed to him to be logical, but which it would have been wiser not to disclose so frankly. Gustav Adolf was no diplomat; and it was a misfortune for him that at this critical moment of the German war he was in personal charge of his foreign policy. As in his relations with foreign powers, so in his dealings with the German princes, he frightened and alienated by his intemperance, his impatience with delay, his insensitiveness to others' feelings, and an inherited inability to suffer fools gladly. Oxenstierna's suspicion of the goodwill of the princes was at least as great as his own; but Oxenstierna's famous phlegm could retard negotiation to a pace at which change seemed less formidable, and could veil the naked assertion of power in a seemly fog of German subordinate clauses. That the Brunswick and Mecklenburg negotiations did at length result in treaties is to be

[1] 'donec belli saltem nostri sumptus nobis refunderentur': *Sverges traktater*, V. 719.

[2] B. Boëthius, *Salvius i den nedersaxisksa kretsen*, pp. 188-90.

attributed more, perhaps, to his emollient tactics than to any real alteration in the Swedish point of view. It was in vain that Adolf Frederick tried to secure a reformulation of that ambiguous sentence which opened the way to further Swedish claims: the chancellor gave him good words, but the very simple change of phrasing was not made.[1] As to Frederick Ulric, though he signed the treaty himself, he quite failed to induce Gustav Adolf to do so. His agents pestered Oxenstierna in vain; they pursued Gustav Adolf across Germany, and received excuses which they can scarcely have regarded as other than frivolous.[2] It was not until November 1633, a year after the King's death, when circumstances had greatly altered, that the Brunswick treaty was ratified on the Swedish side.[3]

(iii) *Brandenburg*

The sharp advance in Gustav Adolf's claims on the Baltic coastlands, as revealed in the negotiations with Mecklenburg, necessarily affected Sweden's relations with Brandenburg also. The crisis of May and June 1631 had centred round Gustav Adolf's demand for an 'absolute direction' of Brandenburg's military resources: the question of Pomerania had at that time been subordinate. Gustav Adolf had wished to constrain George William into an alliance of the Hesse type, for in the critical military situation of the early summer the overriding consideration had been military security for the moment rather than long-term political strategy. With the passing of the crisis, and the improvement in the military position which began at Werben and was made definitive at Breitenfeld, a reconsideration of policy became necessary. The arrangements of May and June had been something less than an alliance, and it was obviously desirable to supplement them. The impression produced upon the Elector by the Swedish victories might perhaps make him more ready to accept 'Hessian' terms; and he had already offered to conclude a 'Pomeranian' alliance—provided the military conventions were omitted.[4] He was, indeed, as resentful as ever of Swedish

[1] The Dukes were restored '[salva] actione nobis . . . regnoque Sveciae adversus singulos pluresve imperii status ex hoc bello enata competente': they tried in vain to replace 'singulos pluresve' by 'alios': *Sverges traktater*, V. 706.

[2] Sadler told the delegates that Gustav Adolf was too busy to sign it: it would take him six weeks to read it: Kretzschmar, p. 102; and *ibid.*, pp. 91-103, for the whole episode. Ahnlund considers that the treaty of 5 February was 'not entirely serious' on the Swedish side: *Oxenstierna*, p. 653.

[3] Kretzschmar, p. 103 *note* 4.

[4] See above, p. 491.

exactions, and with good cause; for on 31 August 1631 he had been forced to sign an agreement whereby his monthly contribution was raised, for the next three months, from 30,000 *rdr.* to 40,250 *rdr.*[1] But it was explained that this was a temporary measure only, pending the time when the Swedish armies should be able to batten on the rich ecclesiastical lands of Franconia; and by mid-September that prospect had become reasonably bright.

On 17 September, then, Salvius received instructions which empowered him, among many other tasks, to negotiate an alliance with Brandenburg.[2] As was to be expected, he was to propose a treaty which should combine the features of the Hessian and Pomeranian agreements: it was to be 'eternal'; and it was to give Gustav Adolf the absolute directory: a treaty, in fact, very similar to that afterwards concluded with Christian of Lüneburg in December. But it was the negotiations already in progress with Mecklenburg that were responsible for some further points in his instructions: Salvius was to obtain George William's assent to a Swedish occupation of the Pomeranian coast '*donec plenius nobis cum imperio* [not, as might have been expected, with Brandenburg] *convenerit*'; he was to secure free trade between the two countries, the acceptance by Brandenburg of Swedish copper currency, and the right of Sweden to levy toll on Brandenburg and Pomeranian harbours and rivers; and he was bidden, in view of recent reactions of Adolf Frederick, to avoid or moderate such expressions as '*jus clientelae*, *tutelae*, *avocatiae*, *patrocinij*'. From all of which two conclusions may be drawn: first, that Gustav Adolf was thinking of a permanent occupation of the coastlands (in Pomerania and Mecklenburg alike), to be confirmed by agreement with the Emperor at a peace; and secondly, that he attached less importance to words than to facts. To which may be added the observation that the projected alliance with Brandenburg, and the later treaty with Lüneburg-Celle, represent the first attempt to establish a permanent connexion (as against an alliance for the duration of the war) with non-maritime German states.[3]

These proposals aroused no enthusiasm in George William. His

[1] *Sverges traktater*, V. 507-10; Kretzschmar, *Die Allianzverhandlungen Gustav Adolfs mit Kurbrandenburg*, pp. 41-2.

[2] For the following paragraphs, see B. Boëthius, *Aktstycken rörande Salvius' underhandlingar med Brandenburg*, pp. 127-45.

[3] See the discussion in B. Boëthius, *Nyare undersökningar rörande Gustaf II Adolfs planer i Tyskland*, pp. 83-6.

policy, now as before, was to evade allying singly with Gustav Adolf. If only he could organize a league of Protestant princes, he might be able to talk with the Swedes on more nearly equal terms: already in August he had tried to induce John George to agree upon a common front with this end in view. But John George had been as unhelpful as ever; and George William was driven to those evasions and subterfuges which are the necessary weapons of the weak. He would prefer (he explained) a negotiation with a Protestant league; he was willing to consider a separate treaty; he could not act without consulting John George; he would discuss it later; or—since Salvius could not stay for an answer—he would discuss it when Salvius returned to Berlin.[1]

Salvius therefore went his ways, to negotiations in the Lower Saxon Circle which proved almost as inconclusive as this one and a good deal more complex; and the Brandenburg alliance was once again deferred. Gustav Adolf noted with dissatisfaction the Elector's efforts to increase his army, and pointedly suggested that the additional manpower might have been more usefully employed in reinforcing a victorious army of proved efficiency[2]; Oxenstierna, looking in at Berlin on his way from Elbing to Frankfort, registered a strong if imprecise impression that the Elector was playing a double game.[3] But this intelligence perhaps alarmed the King less than might have been expected. For already in September he had cast a lure before the Elector; and he was now waiting, not without hope, for the fish to rise to his bait.

The fly which was to catch George William was, of course, the suggestion of a marriage between the Electoral Prince and Kristina. The Brandenburg council began to discuss it at the time of Salvius's visit[4]; and it is reasonable to suppose that Salvius had been charged with some verbal communication to the Elector. It was the first time that Gustav Adolf had made the idea a serious factor in his policy. And the reason for his adoption of it now is plain, and was in fact plainly stated by Oxenstierna in a report to the *råd* in February 1633.[5] Gustav Adolf proposed the match because he had come to the conclusion that he must retain in his hands after the

[1] See Salvius's report, in *Sverges traktater*, V. 510-13, completed in Boëthius, *Aktstycken rörande Salvius' underhandlingar*, pp. 144-5; and *Arkiv*, II. 311.
[2] *Schriftstücke*, p. 155.
[3] *AOSB*, I. VII. 6.
[4] Kretzschmar, *Gustav Adolfs Pläne und Ziele*, p. 204.
[5] *AOSB*, I. VIII. 167.

end of the war not only *oram maritimam*, but the whole of Pomerania. In February 1632 he informed John George of his wish to annex the duchy[1]; in March the *råd* in Stockholm urged it as a necessary provision in any peace settlement, and suggested compensation for George William.[2] And it has been suggested that the setting up of the Magdeburg-Halberstadt military government, immediately after Breitenfeld, is an indication that even as early as September Gustav Adolf was looking upon these lands as possible compensation for Brandenburg.[3] But if he were thus to deprive the Hohenzollerns of their reversionary rights to Pomerania, more substantial inducements than these would be required. The compensation he now proposed was his daughter's hand. In September, indeed, the extent of his designs upon Pomerania did not emerge; but it was implicit in the marriage scheme that Brandenburg should withdraw opposition to his plans for north Germany. The Elector and his councillors thought the price high—too high. Gustav Adolf might still have one or more sons; even if he did not, the Prince would be no more than Consort in Sweden; and there would be complications with George William's feudal overlord, the King of Poland.

When, therefore, in February 1632 the Elector sent Götzen and Leuchtmar to Gustav Adolf to discuss the matter of the alliance, he gave them no instructions on this point. Gustav Adolf, however, raised it at once.[4] In their first audience on 15 February, and on subsequent occasions, he pressed the idea of the marriage upon them as the ideal method of cementing the alliance; and urged the immediate sending of the Prince to receive his training in war and religion at the Swedish court. The Queen, understandably interested in so intimate a family match, made one of her rare incursions into politics to second her husband. In March, after Gustav Adolf's departure for the Danube, Oxenstierna gave the Brandenburg envoys a more precise outline of what was intended. Should Gustav Adolf die without heirs-male (a contingency which he himself now seems to have regarded as probable), the Prince was to inherit the Swedish crown: though each country would retain its own laws and customs, Sweden and Brandenburg were to be linked in a personal

[1] Boëthius, *NSK*, p. 3.
[2] *RRP*, II. 143-8.
[3] Struck, *Gustav Adolf und die schwedische Satisfaktion*, p. 481.
[4] For what follows, see R. Schulze, *Das Projekt der Vermählung Friedrich Wilhelms von Brandenburg mit Christina von Schweden*, pp. 2-5; Ahnlund, *Oxenstierna*, pp. 658-61; Kretzschmar, *Gustav Adolfs Pläne und Ziele*, pp. 207-14.

union and the closest of alliances—as Gustav Adolf put it, they would 'form together one *corpus* and depend [1] on one head'. If a son were born to the King, the Electoral Prince would be allotted 'all my *jus belli* out here in Germany', while Livonia and Prussia remained attached to the Swedish crown. These German territories, it was suggested, should be ruled by Kristina and her husband much as Isabella and Albert ruled the Spanish Netherlands.[2] And if Gustav Adolf had more sons than one, the Electoral Prince would be given preference before the younger sons in the distribution of the German conquests. But it was an essential condition that the Prince be brought up as a Swede in Sweden; and it was no less essential that he be educated as a Lutheran.[3]

To Götzen, at least, this proposal made an immediate appeal. He did not believe that Gustav Adolf was likely to have any more children, and it seemed to him that an acceptance of the Swedish plan would in due time make Brandenburg the greatest power in the North and the unquestioned leader of Protestant Germany. George William was less sanguine. For him, the requirement that the Prince should change his religion was a serious obstacle; and past experience had perhaps disposed him to look with suspicion on any proposal from Gustav Adolf. He was prepared, however, to consider the scheme; and he suggested that the religious problem might be tackled radically by the summoning of a conference of divines to seek a basis of doctrinal agreement between the Lutheran and Reformed churches. He wrote to Oxenstierna in this sense, and asked for information about Swedish ritual and church-government. To this letter Oxenstierna seems to have made no reply.[4]

The chancellor's own attitude towards the marriage was, indeed, non-committal. It was even non-cooperative. He obeyed his instructions; but he showed an unusual lack of zeal. He was careful not to commit Gustav Adolf's terms to paper. He evaded George

[1] Compare the use of this word in the demands upon Frederick V: see above, p. 613. For a similar use in regard to Magdeburg, see the King's letter to E. A. Trana, 18 March 1632: *Arkiv*, I. 577.

[2] Kretzschmar (*op. cit.*, pp. 212-13) argued that this implied that they would be detached from the Empire and become mere outlying provinces of Sweden. It seems doubtful whether Gustav Adolf meant his example to be an exact parallel: his letter to Oxenstierna on the subject is not a draft treaty or a pattern constitution, but a quite short and generally phrased communication; and his later insistence that Pomerania should be held by Sweden as an imperial fief makes it unlikely that he would have wished to forgo the possibility of using the imperial machinery in Sweden's interests.

[3] *AOSB*, I. VIII. 168. II. I. 766-7,

[4] Schulze, pp. 5-10.

William's questions about the Swedish church. When Gustav Adolf invited him to formulate his ideas in a memorandum, he pointedly neglected to comply.[1] After Gustav Adolf's death he was indeed candid enough to confess to the *råd* that they might be hard put to it to find a more eligible match for Kristina [2]; but it is clear that he never looked upon it with much favour. And for this there may have been a personal rather than a political explanation. For in the course of the interviews at Frankfort with Götzen and Leuchtmar, Maria Eleonora had said that if her brother were to reject this offer she would marry Kristina to Oxenstierna's son Erik. In this she may well have been serious: at all events, such a marriage remained a political possibility, rumoured from time to time, discussed intermittently in whispers by the chancellor's ill-wishers, until in 1648 Axel Oxenstierna found it expedient to put an end to the talk by finding another bride for his son.[3]

However that may be, it was certainly true that George William showed no undue precipitation in embracing the brilliant prospects which were thus offered to his house. Stockholm, it appeared, was not worth the *Augustana*. He did not turn the offer down; but to make its acceptance dependent upon a successful pursuit of the notorious will-o'-the-wisp of a reconciliation among Protestants was scarcely very encouraging. Gustav Adolf knew only too well from past experience the difficulty of pinning down the Elector; and he felt bitterly that George William's elaborate deliberation was merely a device to gain time—that it was, indeed, tantamount to a refusal.[4] His chagrin was given free expression in his remarks to the Nuremberg delegates in June.[5] When at the beginning of September he drew up his draft for the post-war settlement of Germany, there was no mention of the Brandenburg marriage: Sweden was to take Pomerania for herself, as an imperial fief,[6] the Elector receiving Magdeburg and Halberstadt in exchange. And when about the same time Konrad von Burgsdorff, the Brandenburg envoy, took his leave of the King, Gustav Adolf savagely told him that he would not allow Pomerania to fall into the Elector's hands, even though he might have to fight for a century to keep it.[7]

[1] Ahnlund, *Oxenstierna*, pp. 658-61. [2] *AOSB*, I. VIII. 168.

[3] Ahnlund, *Oxenstierna*, p. 660; E. Fries, *Erik Oxenstierna*, pp. 46-54, 321.

[4] Kretzschmar saw in Gustav Adolf's attitude evidence that he had never sincerely desired the match.

[5] Breyer, p. 229.

[6] Ahnlund, *Oxenstierna*, pp. 701-2; *AOSB*, I. I. 541.

[7] K. Spannagel, *Konrad von Burgsdorff*, p. 382.

Gustav Adolf may well have been mistaken about the sincerity of his brother-in-law. Oxenstierna, at least, bore testimony to the fact that the prospect of the marriage had served to attach Brandenburg with unwonted firmness to the Swedish cause.[1] But though this was a consequence of the plan, it was not therefore the motive that inspired it. The match was not proposed simply as a bait; its prime object was not to drive a wedge between Brandenburg and Saxony.[2] That Gustav Adolf should have turned away from the project in the last months of his life is no proof that it was not seriously meant in February 1632. From the Swedish point of view the scheme had strong arguments in its favour. It settled the dangerous controversy over the Pomeranian inheritance in a manner which amply assured Sweden's safety. It offered to Sweden, no less than to Brandenburg, a notable increase of power; and in 1632 it seemed unlikely that the tail would wag the dog. And it provided some sort of solution to the problem of the Swedish succession. It is impossible that the King and his servants should not have had that problem constantly at the back of their minds: at any moment a stray shot might confront the country with a major constitutional and dynastic crisis. The Brandenburg marriage was one possible means of insurance against that accident. It was not the only one: when George William's irritating caution had caused Gustav Adolf to lose patience, he drew up, in consultation with Oxenstierna, the constitutional scheme which formed the basis of the Form of Government of 1634. And on one view of Oxenstierna's policy it is natural enough that he should have preferred the prospect of a girl ruler to the prospect of a Brandenburg prince who was not over-far from his majority. As to Gustav Adolf, it may well be that if he had lived he would have returned to the idea of the marriage—provided that George William had complied doucely with his demands. His change of mind arose, on the one hand, from his impatience and his suspiciousness of his brother-in-law's honesty; and on the other from those pressing anxieties about the succession which made some sort of arrangement for the future a matter of urgency to him. But

[1] *AOSB*, I. VIII. 168.

[2] As Kretzschmar contended (*op. cit.*, p. 214). Apart from such arguments, Kretzschmar adduced a remark of Maria Eleonora to Gabriel Gustavsson Oxenstierna in 1633, to the effect that the marriage had not been seriously intended. But at the time the remark was made she was strongly pressing the acceptance of a Danish proposal that Kristina should marry Kristian IV's son, Ulrik, and she had every reason therefore to minimize the seriousness of the approach to Brandenburg: see *AOSB*, I. VIII. 291-302.

whatever line he followed, Pomerania was now to be his. The qualms of 1630 were finally dispelled, the territorial *satisfactio* determined on; and the good Duke Bogislaw might devote himself to his tankard without concerning himself further in the matter.[1]

(iv) *The Imperial Cities*

It is possible to discern in the closing weeks of 1631 the ending of one phase of Gustav Adolf's German policy and the opening of another. Hitherto, he had been greatly concerned to bind the princes to him by regular alliances, usually of the Hessian pattern, though latterly with Pomeranian characteristics. But as 1631 gave place to 1632 this anxiety to make formal alliances appeared to diminish. On the contrary, he began to refuse ratification to agreements made by his servants on his behalf. The treaties made with Christian of Lüneburg, the Counts of the Wetterau, Christian of Bayreuth, and even with William of Weimar,[2] were all left incomplete because the King withheld his sanction; and the draft treaty with Württemberg (concluded in March 1632) remained a draft, without binding force.[3] The terms of these agreements no longer satisfied him; their limitation to the duration of the war no longer seemed to him to be adequate. To give aid to Sweden while the war lasted, to pool the resources of Protestant Germany under Gustav Adolf's direction and control—this was so obvious a matter of good sense and sound policy that only the blind or the treacherous would decline it. But the teaching of experience, and the obligations which victory brought with it, suggested the desirability of a more durable form of connexion between the German states and their deliverer. The fortune of battle had presented him with an opportunity, which might well prove unique, for devising a settlement of Germany which should safeguard, for the foreseeable future, both German Protestantism and Swedish interests. Six months earlier, when his position was still precarious, the Hessian-type alliance had seemed the natural resource. Now, he might feel reasonably confident of his ability to defeat the enemy (though much still remained to do);

[1] As, indeed, he did; to such good purpose that he died in 1637.

[2] Huschke, *Wilhelm von Weimar*, p. 23: the draft treaty in *Sverges traktater*, V. 535 *seqq.*

[3] *Sverges traktater*, V. 637-44: in effect Württemberg behaved as though the treaty had been signed: *ibid.*, 643-4; *AOSB*, I. VII. 363; T. Schott, *Württemberg und Gustav Adolf*, pp. 359, 388-9.

and though the moment for considering a peace settlement might still be distant, he was conscious that the existing pattern of alliances provided no real basis on which to build. The remoter objective of the *Norma*—the creation of a permanent Protestant league under Swedish patronage—was now becoming a possibility: he must not prejudice the prospect by piling up treaties which were irrelevant to that objective (since they were limited in duration) and which would need to be replaced or remodelled if it were to be attained.

Since this was so, he neglected to consummate alliances all but completed, to the confusion of his diplomatists and the chagrin of those who negotiated with them. And in some cases he tried, by bluster and bullying, to extort alliances more to his liking. With the Welfs he failed; and, having failed, he characteristically evaded ratifying the terms he had been forced to accept. With Mecklenburg, on the whole, he succeeded; and the alliance was duly ratified. But it was the last alliance of any importance to be concluded with a German state. In 1632 Gustav Adolf whenever possible avoided formal alliances. He proceeded, for choice, by way of *ad hoc* conventions, by simple interchange of notes, leaving the field clear for whatever political system might be necessary or practicable in the future. His ideas of what that system might be were still nebulous; though they were beginning to solidify rapidly under the pressure of victory. But for the moment, at least, it seemed better to enter into as few binding and limiting commitments as possible. This was Oxenstierna's policy; and it was he, perhaps, who first suggested it to the King, in a letter of 9 December 1631.[1] And one element in it, common to King and chancellor, was provided by their irritation at German recalcitrance to Swedish demands, and their ingrained suspicion of the slipperiness and selfishness of the princes. But to the general principle of avoiding alliances there was one major exception. For, however uncertain Gustav Adolf might be about Sweden's future line in central and south Germany, he had already made up his mind about the north-east. Pomerania and the ports must be part of his *satisfactio*. And consequently the alliance with Mecklenburg was completed; and every effort was made to settle the Pomeranian question by an alliance with Brandenburg.

The new style of Swedish diplomacy was displayed in Gustav Adolf's negotiations with the Imperial Cities. For a variety of reasons the King was anxious to enlist their support. Many of them

[1] *AOSB*, I. vi. 556-7.

were traditional strongholds of Protestantism, which even in the high tide of the Counter-Revolution had contrived to maintain their religious and political independence. Though their fortifications, as a rule, were somewhat old-fashioned, they were of sufficient strength to withstand a siege of moderate duration, and this gave them great strategic importance. They were the natural places for the location of stores and magazines; and Gustav Adolf was already determined to use them for that purpose. Some of them were the obvious centres upon which the administration of Swedish-occupied Germany might be based. The exceptionally stringent terms imposed upon Frankfort,[1] the requirement that Erfurt swear fidelity 'at least' until the end of the war,[2] probably reflect the King's determination to use them as administrative and military capitals. And Nuremberg and Strassburg, Ulm and Augsburg were all of obvious strategic and logistical importance.

The active support of the cities was also desired on economic grounds. To Gustav Adolf, accustomed as he was to the modest scale of Swedish urban life, the cities of Germany seemed much richer than they were; and he tended to overrate by a considerable margin their capacity to contribute to the common cause. Nor was he inclined to pay much attention to the connexion between their ability to pay and the immunity of their traditional trade-routes from interruption. He required from them money, or men, or supplies and munitions; and he was prepared to make short, strictly limited agreements with towns that would provide them. He did so, for instance, with Lübeck, and Brunswick, and Bremen, and Hamburg[3]: Hamburg paid 150,000 *rdr.* to be left alone, and extorted the King's promise to respect her trade with Spain. Frankfort was not so fortunate: though she did indeed obtain a guarantee that her fair would not be interfered with, the most important of her commercial ties were with Spain and Austria; and while the city was in Swedish hands this business declined, and Frankfort with it.[4]

Nevertheless, the urban communities of Germany looked

[1] *Sverges traktater*, V. 584-7; G. Egelhaaf, *Gustav Adolf und die deutsche Reichsstädte*, pp. 409-10; *Sv. Krig*, V. 193-4.

[2] *Sverges traktater*, V. 530-4: the phrase appears in the note handed by Gustav Adolf to Erfurt, but in that which Erfurt handed to him the text runs merely 'as long as' the war lasts.

[3] *ibid.*, V. 574-8 (Hamburg, 26 November 1631); 604-7 (Brunswick, 6 February 1632); 663-8 (Lübeck, 19 January 1632); 722-6 (Bremen, 23 March 1632). On the relative wealth of Hamburg and Lübeck, and their aid to Gustav Adolf, see S. Lundgren, *Salvius*, p. 32.

[4] Lonchay, II. 622 (Isabella to Philip IV, 1 May 1632); Breyer, p. 223.

impressively wealthy to a Swedish eye; and even Usselincx came to Germany in the hope of there raising the capital he needed for his Southern Company.[1] And Gustav Adolf for some time entertained the curious delusion that the wealth of the German cities qualified them to serve as the natural dumping-grounds for depreciated or unsaleable Swedish copper. It became a leading point in his policy to include in the agreements he made with them a clause similar to that which he had forced upon the Dukes of Mecklenburg, whereby the towns should undertake to admit Swedish copper coinage at its face value. These attempts met with solid opposition from the burghers, who were as well qualified to appreciate the dangers of depreciated currency as any set of men in Europe; and in every instance the Swedish demand was rejected. The townsmen of central and, still more, of south Germany were well enough disposed to the Protestant Hero; but for heroic measures, when it came to finance, they had no taste at all. Also, they were frightened of sharing the fate of Magdeburg, and anxious if possible not to break off their trading connexions with the Habsburg lands.[2] For the sake of religion they hoped that Gustav Adolf might win; for the sake of trade they wished he would be quick about it. And on every ground of prudence they hoped to make their support of the Swedish cause as little compromising as possible.

Nuremberg provides a good example of this. In October 1631 the Regent of Württemberg had approached Ansbach, Bayreuth and Nuremberg with a proposal to negotiate jointly with Gustav Adolf.[3] The Nurembergers contrived to evade this suggestion; but shortly afterwards a threatening letter from the King (possibly intended as an ostensible letter, to safeguard them against imperial vengeance)[4] had induced the burghers to lend him a substantial sum of money, and to send envoys to discuss an alliance. On 23 October they had participated, with the representatives of Bayreuth, in the conclusion of a subsidy treaty which Gustav Adolf later declined to ratify.[5] On this occasion Sweden had offered an alliance; but the offer had not

[1] F. Bothe, *Gustav Adolfs . . . wirtschaftspolitische Absichten*, p. 108 *seqq.*, and above, p. 126.

[2] Nuremberg, for instance, tried to limit her aid to Gustav Adolf to operations against the League, and wished to include the Emperor in any agreement: S. Donaubauer, *Nürnberg um die Mitte des dreissigjährigen Krieges*, p. 120.

[3] For Nuremberg, see Donaubauer, *passim*; Egelhaaf, pp. 245-9; Schott, p. 361; *Sv. Krig*, V. 187 *seqq.*

[4] Gustav Adolf used this device with Württemberg also: Schott, pp. 361, 373.

[5] *Sverges traktater*, V. 558-61.

been taken up. Relations with Gustav Adolf continued to be uncomfortable: he was dissatisfied and suspicious; they were fearful of committing themselves, and at odds with the representative whom Gustav Adolf had sent to them. The momentary threat from Tilly in December did something to nerve their resolution, and provoked a reassuringly swift reaction from the King; but when he sought to improve the occasion by urging them to admit the Swedish copper coinage, the council returned a firm refusal. They were prepared to listen to him when he urged them to strengthen their walls; but they were deaf to entreaties to undermine their economy.

By this time it appeared unlikely that they would be able for long to resist Swedish pressure for a convention. If it must be made, there was something to be said for making it in conjunction with other cities similarly circumstanced; and Nuremberg accordingly hoped for a common front with Frankfort, Ulm and Strassburg.[1] This, as it happened, was the arrangement which Gustav Adolf would have preferred. An opportunity presented itself early in 1632. On 6 February representatives of the four cities met together in Heilbronn; and to this meeting Gustav Adolf sent envoys with proposals to lay before the delegates. He suggested that Sweden should conclude a convention with the four towns jointly; he asked them to levy an excise for the benefit of his war-chest; and he urged them to accept the Swedish copper coinage. Not one of these proposals was agreed to. That for a joint convention was ruled out because neither Ulm nor Strassburg had provided their delegates with powers covering an arrangement of this sort. The excise and the copper coinage were rejected unanimously; nor would they even consent to accept Swedish copper for coining at their own mints. Ulm was warmly Swedish; Frankfort was in Gustav Adolf's grip; Nuremberg was at least friendly; but all were firm. Their main concern, indeed, was to impress on the Swedish representatives their hope that the imperial and ecclesiastical lands lying within their jurisdiction should be handed over to them, and not given away by Gustav Adolf to his generals or clients. In this, as the sequel revealed, they were successful. But from Gustav Adolf's point of view the Heilbronn meeting was a flat failure.[2]

[1] *ibid.*, 748-9.

[2] For the Heilbronn meeting, see *Arkiv*, II. 362-3; Egelhaaf, pp. 412-19; Paul, III. 62-6; K. Jacob, *Strassburgische Politik vom Austritt aus der Union bis zum Bündniss mit Schweden*, p. 138. Vane's report of 9 August gives a good idea of the impression made upon foreign opinion by these negotiations: Rushworth, I. II. 168.

The King was therefore driven back upon separate negotiations. Frankfort had been dealt with already [1]; but on 13 February 1632 a military convention was concluded with Ulm, which accepted Patrick Ruthven as its commandant, promised assistance to Sweden in this war and in others arising from it, and in return was given the revenues from Roman Catholic property within its territories.[2] On 30 March a similar convention was signed with Nuremberg: the city agreed to give Gustav Adolf 100,000 *rdr.*, and received the possessions of the Teutonic Order in exchange.[3] Despite this agreement, however, relations continued uneasy, for Gustav Adolf considered that Nuremberg was not doing enough to bring her fellow-members of the Franconian Circle to similar terms; and there were some stormy passages in April. It was not until his second visit to the city, in June, that the final notes were exchanged which defined the terms upon which the parties were to collaborate.[4] Strassburg's position was perhaps the most difficult of all, for she was wedged in between France and the Habsburg lands in Alsace; and all through the 'twenties she had pursued a timorous policy of appeasement. By the end of 1631, however, the burghers were beginning to realize that neutrality was no longer possible; and they welcomed Gustav Adolf's victories not only for the sake of Protestantism but as providing them with an escape from the necessity of choosing between Ferdinand II and Louis XIII. Yet the tradition of neutrality died hard; and it was not until 28 May 1632 that Nicodemi succeeded in inducing the burghers to enter into an agreement with Sweden. By the terms of this agreement the town promised to 'act as becomes a true evangelical patriot and ally'—that is, to defend itself against Gustav Adolf's enemies, and abstain from negotiation with them; it acknowledged Gustav Adolf as its protector, and promised assistance for the duration of the war; it gave pass and repass to Swedish troops over the strategically important crossing of the Rhine which it controlled; and it agreed to accept a Swedish garrison in case of emergency. Gustav Adolf, on his side, undertook not only to respect Strassburg's rights as an immediate vassal of the Emperor (a promise which was incorporated into all these agreements with Imperial Cities) but

[1] By the treaty of 1 December 1631: *Sverges traktater*, V. 584-7.

[2] *ibid.*, 698-703; Egelhaaf, pp. 419-20. On Ulm's previous relations with Sweden, J. Endriss, *Ulms Beziehungen zu Gustav Adolf*, p. 13.

[3] *Sv. Krig*, V. 222-3: this is not printed in *Sverges traktater*, V.

[4] *Sverges traktater*, V. 745-9: the treaty was antedated to 14 April.

also to do nothing to prejudice the town's good relations with France.[1]

The agreement with Strassburg was yet another diplomatic defeat for Richelieu, who had done his best to prevent it [2]; but it could not disguise the fact that Gustav Adolf had failed in his plan to make of the great cities of south Germany a solid unified block upon which a larger political superstructure might later be raised. Nevertheless, the idea was not abandoned; and at Nuremberg in June the King's language to the city fathers showed that he was still looking at it, a trifle wistfully perhaps, as a possibility for the future.[3]

(v) *The Project for a General Peace. Gustav Adolf defines his Objectives.*

On 26 September 1631 there was held in Frankfort a meeting between representatives of Hesse-Darmstadt and Mainz. Its purpose was to consider measures for the re-establishment of a general peace; and its sponsor was the Landgrave George of Hesse-Darmstadt.[4] George was a well-meaning young man of twenty-six. Straitly Lutheran, and staunchly imperialist, he had married a daughter of John George, and had been suitably distressed by the breach between the Emperor and his father-in-law. He tried hard to be a good ruler to his subjects; and he saw clearly enough that the best service he could do them was to free them from the burdens and threats of the contending armies.[5] He was on the worst of terms with his cousin William V of Hesse-Cassel, part of whose paternal inheritance he had contrived to acquire by sharp practice [6]; and he had every reason to be apprehensive if William and his Swedish ally should march in his direction. He had, moreover, all John George's

[1] *ibid.*, 760-7; Jacob, *op. cit.*, pp. 12, 40-1, 47, 96-112, 119, 128-46; Egelhaaf, pp. 427-8; and see *AOSB*, II. 1. 768-9; *Arkiv*, II. 367-9, where Gustav Adolf instructs Nicodemi not to insist on Strassburg's pledging aid for '*bella e hoc bello enata*' if they resist the suggestion (as in fact they did).

[2] W. Mommsen, *Kardinal Richelieu. Seine Politik im Elsass und in Lothringen*, pp. 140-1.

[3] C. W. F. Breyer, *Beyträge zur Geschichte des dreissigjährigen Krieges*, p. 221.

[4] Irmer, *VS*, I. 4-8, for the minutes of the meeting; G. Droysen, *Die Verhandlungen über den Universalfrieden im Winter 1631/32* [cited: Droysen, *Universalfrieden*], pp. 144-252, for a general account of these negotiations; *Arkiv*, I. 770-2, for Grubbe's report of them.

[5] As early as September 1630 John George had thought of him as a possible mediator: Helbig, *Gustav Adolf und die Kurfürsten von Sachsen und Brandenburg*, p. 27.

[6] Rommel, VIII. 30-2.

dislike of foreign invaders who assailed the authority of the Emperor. He was consequently strongly anti-Swedish; and one main reason for his anxiety to end the war was in order to rid Germany of the foreigner. He therefore proposed to the Elector of Mainz that a conference be summoned to discuss not a religious settlement but a profane peace. He hoped by these tactics to reconcile John George with the Emperor and to drive a wedge between him and Gustav Adolf.[1] Since it was essential to his plans that the Elector should attend the conference, he pitched upon Mühlhausen as a suitable place to hold it; and he suggested that the Archduke Leopold and the Count Palatine Wolfgang William (for the Catholics), with himself and Christian William of Brandenburg-Culmbach (for the Protestants), should act as mediators. On 12 October he sent letters with these proposals to John George and to the Emperor.[2]

The Emperor gave them a good reception. Already on 9 October he was reported to be ready for a reconciliation with Saxony[3]; and he now proceeded to consult a panel of theologians as to whether George's invitation might without sin be entertained. Their opinion was strongly in favour of it: indeed, they went so far as to advise him that he might if necessary suppress or suspend the Edict of Restitution.[4] On 5 November, therefore, he sent a cordial acceptance.[5]

John George's reactions were more mixed. He would, of course, have been happy to be reconciled to the Emperor, upon satisfactory conditions; and before September was out Arnim had already urged him to make peace quickly, while the fortunes of war were still in his favour.[6] But he had committed himself to an alliance with Gustav Adolf which precluded him from making a separate peace, and for the present, at all events, he was determined loyally to observe his obligations. George's proposals had made it clear that he intended to exclude Gustav Adolf from direct participation in the negotiations: the congress was to be a strictly German affair. In his simple-minded way George had expressed the hope that John George would be able to bring to the conference 'a contingent guarantee from the King of Sweden . . . by which he would undertake, after the reconciliation

[1] Irmer, *VS*, I. 36-7.
[2] *ibid.*, 16-18, 19-24.
[3] *ibid.*, 8-10.
[4] Leman, *Urbain VIII*, p. 83: the papal nuncio in Paris also urged Richelieu to support the plan: *ibid.*, p. 60.
[5] Irmer, *VS*, I. 51-3.
[6] Droysen, *Universalfrieden*, pp. 161-2.

of the evangelical princes with the Emperor and League, peaceably to quit the soil of Germany'.[1] On that point John George had no illusions: it was impossible, he replied, that Gustav Adolf, 'who now maintains so mighty an army *in visceribus Imperii*', should acquiesce in an arrangement made without his participation.[2]

The Landgrave was in the meantime finding this out for himself. On 14 October his envoy, Dietrich Barthold von Plessen, arrived at the Swedish camp at Würzburg. His mission had a double purpose.[3] In the first place he was to try to extract from the King a recognition of Hesse-Darmstadt's neutrality and an undertaking that the Landgrave's dominions should not be burdened with contributions to the Swedish armies; and in the second he was to inform Gustav Adolf of the plan for a peace conference. Von Plessen had a most uncomfortable interview.[4] When he began by deploring what he described, in a remarkable euphemism, as the 'prevailing irregularities' in Germany, and asserted his master's desire to remain neutral, Gustav Adolf waved him aside: he could not, he said, consider George either as a friend or as a co-religionist, but rather as a hypocrite and an enemy; let him look to himself, or 'he would be after him'. But if the Landgrave would abandon his papist friends, and hand over his fortresses, some arrangement might be possible: '*nunquam sera est ad bonos mores via*'. There was point, nevertheless, in von Plessen's reply: 'We cannot all', he said, 'take up arms; some few must be left over, to talk and act for peace': it was God, he added mildly, that gave the victory; and no doubt He could take it away again. This brought them to the second point in von Plessen's mission; and he proceeded to produce his master's proposals for a conference. But to them the King made no reply.

Von Plessen's report of his reception alarmed the Landgrave. On 26 October he wrote to Gustav Adolf, begging that any attack on him might be postponed until he had had a chance to consult his agnates and his Estates. He added further details about his peace conference, and with singular lack of tact enquired whether Sweden would be content to be represented by the Protestant Electors.[5] On 2 November the King acknowledged this letter.[6] The only purpose of the war, he informed him, was to obtain a solid peace; but he

[1] Irmer, *VS*, I. 19-24.
[2] Droysen, *Universalfrieden*, p. 164.
[3] His instructions are in Irmer, *VS*, I. 10-15.
[4] His relation is in Irmer, *VS*, I. 28-35.
[5] Irmer, *VS*, I. 39-44. [6] *ibid.*, 53-5.

doubted whether the imperialists were yet prepared to make one. As to George's proposals, he could say nothing until he had consulted with Brandenburg and Saxony. Meanwhile, the Swedish advance continued. The King had already informed the Landgrave that he intended to march through his dominions, and had demanded the surrender of his strongholds.[1] Rüsselsheim, in particular, was of importance to him, since it commanded the main road from Frankfort to Mainz. George's agitated protests and appeals were unavailing: on 19 November Gustav Adolf imposed upon him the treaty of Höchst.[2] Nevertheless, it was a treaty of quite unprecedented lenience. The Landgrave, alone of all German princes, was allowed—for the time being—to be neutral; Rüsselsheim was to be handed over, indeed, but 'only *ad tempus*'[3]; the Swedish armies were to be ordered to spare Darmstadt from contribution and quartering—a provision which was a sharp disappointment to William V, who had been looking forward to quartering his forces on the lands of his cousin.[4]

The reason for this mild treatment seems to be that Gustav Adolf was prepared to give George special privileges for as long as his efforts at mediation had some prospect of success. He had at once written to John George and George William to elicit their reaction to the Landgrave's proposals; and he had refused to commit himself until their answers were in his hands.[5] There was, no doubt, much that was objectionable to him in George's suggestions: Mühlhausen was unacceptable as a meeting-place on military grounds; and he took special exception to being treated merely as an appendage to the negotiations. He was not prepared to allow his friends and his enemies to settle upon terms in his absence, and then to be confronted with an agreed scheme to which his adhesion would be invited. Also, he must have some assurance that the projected conference would deal seriously with the matter of his *satisfactio*. But despite these doubts and reservations, despite a strong scepticism as to the sincerity of Roman Catholics in general, and of the imperialists in particular, he did not simply dismiss the proposal out of hand. On

[1] Irmer, *VS*, I. 46-7.

[2] *Sverges traktater*, V. 566-72; Frohnhäuser, pp. 14-16.

[3] In a subsequent note of 22 November, however, Gustav Adolf defined this to mean 'for the duration of the present war': *Sverges traktater*, V. 573.

[4] Irmer, *VS*, I. 61-2. The promise was kept, more or less, till April 1632; but by May it had become impossible to deny William V any longer: *AOSB*, I. VII. 92, 99, 193-4, 197, 269, II. VII. 341-2, 345.

[5] *Schriftstücke*, pp. 244-6; Irmer, *VS*, I. 65-8.

14 December he communicated it to the *råd* at home, with a request for their opinion; and added the comment that the affair had advanced to the point at which a regular peace conference might probably be expected.[1]

It was on 7 November that Gustav Adolf wrote to John George asking him to send an envoy with whom he could discuss George's proposals; but for weeks no word came back from Dresden. It was not until 4 February that Kurt von Einsiedel arrived in Frankfort as the Elector's special emissary.[2] This delay did not arise from any lack of interest in the project: on the contrary, the Swedish agent at John George's court considered that the Elector and his ministers scarcely thought of anything else,[3] and in Holland it was rumoured that John George was on the point of making peace.[4] In reality, he was finding it difficult to make up his mind what to do. On the one hand, Arnim was pressing peace upon him in the name of Germany; on the other, Hoë von Hoënegg was urging him to continue the fight in the name of the evangelical cause.[5] In this dilemma he resolved to take counsel with his cousin of Berlin; and George William was invited to a meeting at Torgau to discuss the whole question.[6] The Torgau conference did not begin until 7 February, two days after Einsiedel had his first audience with Gustav Adolf; but it affected the fate of Einsiedel's mission. For, on the one hand, it led John George to give him non-committal instructions; and on the other, the news that it was pending excited Gustav Adolf's resentment and suspicion. The long delay in replying to his request for an envoy had angered him already; he was nervous about Arnim's intrigues with Wallenstein,[7] and annoyed at John George's dallyings with Denmark; and when he found that Einsiedel's instructions did not cover the points which he was especially anxious to discuss he allowed his pent-up irritation to find vent in a furious outburst. He complained, in the first place, that the Elector was reprehensibly slack about keeping in touch with him: he, after all, had been

[1] *Arkiv*, I. 529.

[2] Droysen, *Universalfrieden*, pp. 216-22.

[3] Tungel reported on 7 January that 'they are more concerned to distil from their brainpans how the negotiation may be continued, than to think about arming themselves or warding off the visible danger that hangs over them': Irmer, *VS*, I. 97-100.

[4] Irmer, *Arnim*, p. 163.

[5] Knapp, *Hoë von Hoënegg*, pp. 40-1.

[6] For the Torgau conference, see Droysen, *Universalfrieden*, p. 234; Helbig, pp. 67-8; Knapp, p. 42; Irmer, *VS*, I. 145; *Sv. Krig*, V. 122-3.

[7] For this, see below, pp. 682-3.

punctilious in informing John George about his own doings.[1] 'What sort of an alliance is it, what sort of correspondence, when I must pick up such information from merchants, or from the gazettes!'[2] But this was a small point in comparison with the affront of the Torgau conference. That the two Electors should discuss peace terms together, without even troubling themselves to ascertain what Sweden's claims might be, was utterly intolerable. They would make peace, would they, without ensuring that their deliverer obtained a reasonable recompense for blood and treasure poured out on their behalf! So much for the hope of *satisfactio*. This was 'German faith', this princely gratitude, this the loyalty of allies! 'Laughing bitterly', he remarked that 'he saw very well, that the services he had performed were not to be credited with the importance which really attached to them.'[3]

On the following day Einsiedel saw Oxenstierna. Oxenstierna was at least in command of his temper, but he pointed out the Elector did not seem to have appreciated the need for concerting a common line of action before rushing into a negotiation; and he repeated, though more moderately, the King's complaint that his interests were being neglected.[4] The former objection, as it happened, was at least exaggerated; for at Torgau one of the main difficulties had been George William's insistence that some sort of machinery be set up in order to ensure that the allies should present a solid front at the proposed conference. But whether exaggerated or not, the Swedish resentments were sufficient to destroy, at any rate for the present, Landgrave George's chances of appearing as the Arch-Pacificator of the Holy Roman Empire.[5]

It was Einsiedel's impression that Gustav Adolf did not consider that the time was ripe for making peace. And in this Einsiedel was probably correct. Certainly the armistice terms which the King outlined to Hesse-Darmstadt in January were such that he can scarcely have expected the imperialists to accept them, and were even more severe than those he put forward for Maximilian and the League. He demanded not only that they should withdraw their

[1] *e.g.* about the neutrality negotiations with France.

[2] Droysen, *Universalfrieden*, p. 248.

[3] *ibid.*, pp. 222-7.

[4] *ibid.*, pp. 228-32.

[5] Gustav Adolf, in a more genial moment, had nicknamed him 'des heiligen römischen Reiches Erzfriedstifter'.

troops from all positions on the Elbe and the Weser, and from the Lower Saxon Circle, but also that he should be left in undisturbed possession of the dioceses of Mainz, Würzburg and Bamberg: the Emperor was to be penned back into southern Germany.[1] And Einsiedel was certainly right in thinking that the King hoped for further military successes before embarking upon serious negotiations. On 10 February he informed the Landgrave George that 'My victories are not at present on such a scale as to make it possible to constrain the Catholics to a sure peace. The stage has indeed been reached where it is possible to treat with them *aequis armis*. But they have still kingdoms whose power is unbroken, as for instance Spain, whence they may expect an ample succour.'[2] As he told the Hesse-Darmstadt delegates in March, he could not be unmindful of God's punishment of Saul, who suffered Agag to live; nor could he forget how Hannibal threw away his chances after Cannae. The Protestants were not yet sufficiently united among themselves to enter a peace conference; and his own status among them in any negotiations was still to be determined. And, in the last resort, who could trust the Catholics to keep faith with heretics?[3] His deep-ingrained, unreasoning fear of Catholic duplicity, inherited from his father, reinforced by stories of St. Bartholomew imbibed in youth, confirmed by the troubled decade of conspiracy after his accession—this was not peculiar to him alone: it was shared by many Protestants of that age, and not least by Oxenstierna.[4] But it was a real obstacle to peace, and indeed might seem logically to make any peace impossible.

Nevertheless, though Gustav Adolf in the early months of 1632 was still unwilling to treat, the intervention of Hesse-Darmstadt forced him to think more precisely about the terms upon which a settlement might be acceptable; and forced him therefore to formulate to himself more clearly the sort of arrangements for Germany which might ensure that any peace should be durable. The plan of a permanent Protestant league, first adumbrated to Leuchtmar in the autumn of 1630, sketched again in the *Norma* as an objective to be aimed at, now began to take final shape: a league which should

[1] Droysen, *op. cit.*, p. 232; Irmer, *VS*, I. 109.
[2] Droysen, *op. cit.*, p. 243.
[3] Irmer, *VS*, I. 136-9.
[4] See, for instance, his letter to Gustav Adolf of 2 November 1630 (*AOSB*, I. v. 666), and his remarks to the Hesse-Darmstadt envoys, 22 October 1632 (Irmer, *VS*, I. 286-90).

not only win the war but save the peace. In the existing condition of Germany, it seemed to him, such an organization would be viable only if it were directed by a strong hand; it would serve its purpose only if its policies were guided by a power exempt from—because superior to—the petty jealousies of the German princes; and it would be effective only if it possessed real military strength. The conclusion was inescapable. The Protestant league must take Sweden for its patron, its arbiter and its champion. Gustav Adolf had drawn this conclusion before the end of 1631; and in December he put his ideas to William V—who was chosen as his confidant, no doubt, because he was the most radical and the most reliable of all the princes. The King added another suggestion. The league must maintain a standing army; and the imperialists must be disarmed at the peace.[1] The reactions of William V and his advisers to these ideas were all that could have been hoped: indeed, they were positively enthusiastic. On their own account they now proposed that Sweden should be given whatever Gustav Adolf might choose to ask as *satisfactio*, and that the most important strategic points in Germany should be provided with Swedish garrisons.[2] Thus encouraged, Gustav Adolf began to think of the implications of his proposals. In March 1632 he and Oxenstierna were telling the Hesse-Darmstadt delegates that Sweden must hold Pomerania as an imperial fief; that Maximilian must be deprived of his electorate; and that the electoral college must be reorganized so as to ensure that there should be if possible four, or at least three, Protestant Electors.[3] But now a disagreeable speculation suggested itself. It occurred to him to wonder whether a Protestant standing army, and the disarmament of the Catholics, would really afford the security he needed. Even if the peace treaties were to enforce disarmament, was there any guarantee that the Catholics would stay disarmed? It would be so easy for the Emperor, under the cloak of discharging his imperial duties, to find an opportunity for rearming![4] This was a line of thought which could lead to only two conclusions: either that no peace with the Emperor was possible at all; or that another Emperor—perhaps a Protestant?—must be found. Gustav Adolf did not proceed to either conclusion. But that such misgivings should have assailed him is an indication of his increasing preoccupation with the problem of guarantees. And it is certain

[1] Irmer, *VS*, I. 71-7.
[2] *ibid.*, *loc. cit.* and 125-33.
[3] *ibid.*, 136-9.
[4] *ibid.*, 138.

that he was coming round to the view that post-war security might be difficult to get if the internal arrangements of Germany were simply to revert to the basis of 1618. Arnim heard with indignation stories of how the King had told Einsiedel that he would make peace only as director of the Protestant forces, Elector of Mainz and Head of the evangelical Estates; and of how he had said that the old imperial constitution, with its ties of feudal obligation, must be rendered null and void.[1] If this were really the programme, who could say what might not be 'necessary' in the way of *satisfactio* and *assecuratio*?

In reality, Gustav Adolf had as yet by no means settled in his own mind what the programme must be. In the heat of indignation, in temperamental audiences such as those with Einsiedel, in unbuttoned table-talk at Frankfort, a shower of incandescent ideas was scattered broadcast under the hammer-blows of his conversation. The effect upon bystanders was sensational and even painful; the permanent importance sometimes small. He may, for an instant, have toyed with the notion of becoming Elector of Mainz—Oxenstierna was to do so later—as one means of ensuring a Protestant majority in the electoral college. Yet it was but a notion, among many; no more serious, perhaps, than his threat to retire to Sweden and leave the evangelical party to fend for itself.[2] He was by no means the only man on the Protestant side to contemplate some reorganization of the Empire. Even John George, most conservative of politicians, was brought to admit to the Swedish ambassador in March that 'he saw that fate, and the particular providence of God, had now brought matters so far, that the *imperium* must be cast in another mould', and that 'they should take the old constitution of the Empire, extract from it whatever was good and suited to the present conjunctions, and use that, rejecting the remainder as lumber'.[3] William of Hesse had been more specific: in reply to Gustav Adolf's enquiries about Landgrave George's peace plan, he had declared that any peace treaty must provide for the exclusion of the spiritual Electors from participation in imperial elections, and their replacement by lay princes; the revocation of the Edict of Restitution; the restoration to lay hands of all ecclesiastical lands secularized, whether before or after the Peace of Passau; full liberty to secularize in future, and the abrogation of the Ecclesiastical Reservation; equality of representa-

[1] Irmer, *Arnim*, p. 170.

[2] This was thrown out in table-talk as late as February 1632: Droysen, *Universalfrieden*, p. 245.

[3] Irmer, *VS*, I. 161.

tion for Protestants and Catholics in the *Reichskammergericht*; full toleration for Protestants in Catholic territories; heavy indemnities for war damage, to be paid by the League; and the expulsion of the Jesuits, and of the Spanish troops, from German soil.[1] It was the old revolutionary programme of the Palatine party, sharpened by adversity and barbed with the spirit of revenge.

In these domestic German controversies Gustav Adolf had little direct concern, except that he was determined to hold the balance down so firmly on the side of the Protestants that it should never again be tilted against them. His objective was simple enough: what baffled him was not ends but means. His fear of being cheated in the end, his chronic suspicion of his adversary's good faith, was betraying him into the grievous error of thinking that the only permanent solution was total victory. He was coming to believe that no alliance could be lasting unless it put his ally into a position of subjection; that no league could be effective unless its members were Swedish puppets; that no settlement could be acceptable unless it were buttressed at every corner by Jesuit-proof—and fool-proof—guarantees; almost that no one was to be trusted in Germany save himself and his men. Up to a point, he was right. But it does not seem to have occurred to him that his ruthless determination to save the Protestants from themselves might so turn the hearts of the princes as to weaken, rather than strengthen, the barriers he was trying to build up. He did not realize that just as they had resented the pressure he applied to them in order to be able to carry on the war, so they would resent the pressure he applied to them in order to make sure of getting a satisfactory peace. True, it was their war, and their peace, as much as his; and if they were disposed to lie down under servitude, he must force them to be free; but he might have remembered that compulsory emancipation is an operation which is better sweetened with tact. He did not perceive that an equitable settlement might

[1] Irmer, *VS*, I. 125-33. That such demands were not isolated instances appears from a document of uncertain provenance, headed *Postulata Evangelicorum*, printed in Hallwich, *Briefe und Akten*, II. 366-7. This demanded the revocation of the Edict; a return to the territorial limits of 1619; a reform of the *Reichskammergericht* and the *Reichshofrat*; three to four Protestant electorates; the restoration of the Palatinate, Mecklenburg and Bohemia; Sweden to be an Estate of the Empire for Pomerania—Brandenburg receiving Magdeburg and Saxony Halberstadt; indemnity for Gustav Adolf, and confirmation of his donations. And it added, 'Die assecuratio solle denn effect unnd würcklichkhaitt haben, dz mann nit nur 10, 20 Jahr, sonnder vort unnd vorth sicher sein möge, nit allein gegen teutsche, erbare, aufrichtige cathol. Stendte, sonndern auch gegen perfidos unnd fridtbrüchige.'

stand longer than a dictated peace. The *råd* at home saw this. When they met in March to debate Gustav Adolf's request for their advice, they included in their recommendation many of the King's own war aims: the full restoration of Germany to the position of 1618, Pomerania and Wismar for Sweden, a Protestant league still linked to Sweden after the war.[1] But their discussions showed a sense of the danger of pursuing logic too far. Some of them were doubtful of the wisdom, or the practicability, of total victory: as Gabriel Gustafsson Oxenstierna put it, '*Illa pax aut aequa erit, aut iniqua. Si aequa*, it may be enduring; *sin iniqua*, and if it is concluded upon conditions which are not to be borne, *tunc nulla securitas sperari potest, nisi devictis in solidum hostibus*[2] . . . War begets war; and so comes *bellum in perpetuum*.'[3] The restoration of the persecuted and evicted Protestants of Germany; a fair return for Sweden's sacrifices; a reasonable measure of security—that was all that most of them wanted. The clerk summed up a general discussion in these words:

> And when the Protestants are thus able more or less to hold the balance against the Catholics, it is to be presumed (under God) that the war has reached its object. But should the war be further extended, it is to be feared that our friends may become our enemies, and—some *invidia*, some *taedio belli*—may enterprise that which may conduce to the prejudice not of us only but of all our fellow-Protestants, and thus make our situation worse than before.[4]

The *råd*, it is clear, were not political perfectionists: Gustav Adolf, perhaps, was. They were not condemned to deal with the German princes, as he was; but they were obliged to deal with the Swedish people. Remote from the fervid cauldron of Germany, they judged, more coolly than was possible to the King, that the hour was at hand when the essential object of the German war could be considered accomplished. What was the Valtelline to them?

For three months, from the beginning of March to the end of May, there was no significant development in the King's attitude to the problem of settling Germany. His attention was absorbed by his first campaign to the Danube. But the threat to Saxony, which led him to turn once more northwards, and his growing concern about

[1] *Arkiv*, II. 391-6.
[2] *RRP*, II. 144.
[3] *RRP*, II. 145.
[4] *RRP*, II. 147.

the reliability of John George as an ally, led him to send to the Elector's court a special envoy of unusual distinction, in the person of the Palsgrave August. The purpose of his mission was to try to secure a common line of action upon the question of peace, and to put before the Elector Gustav Adolf's views as to the bases upon which it could safely be concluded. August's instructions were dated 1 June, at Donauwörth.[1] A week later, Gustav Adolf was in Nuremberg; and here, on 9 and 10 June, four interviews with representatives of the city took place. At the first and last, Sadler and Chemnitz spoke on the King's behalf; and at the two others, Gustav Adolf himself addressed the delegates.[2] Meanwhile, August's arrival at Dresden was followed by lengthy discussions with the Elector's council, conducted on the Swedish side mainly by Dr. Löffler, who had been borrowed from Württemberg to reinforce Gustav Adolf's diplomatic corps.[3] From August's instructions, and from the discussions at Nuremberg and in Dresden, it is possible to obtain a synoptic view of Gustav Adolf's plans at a moment when they had at last crystallized into what was probably their final form.[4] There was little, perhaps, that was wholly new or unexpected; but for the first time the problem was discussed in all its bearings, and much that had hitherto only been implied became clear and explicit.

Peace, he told the Nurembergers, was certainly his object. No man had better reason to desire it than himself, who had been at the wars now from his youth up, and was become old and ailing in the service. But what sort of a peace? The imperialists would offer restitution, toleration, anything: a peace treaty was but a scrap of paper, and what availed paper against cannon? Negotiate, by all means—but '*sub clypeo*'; make peace if possible—but not without guarantees. To be safe now, and secure hereafter, two things were essential: there must be a *corpus bellicum* to conduct the war, and a *corpus politicum* to preserve the peace.

By a *corpus bellicum* Gustav Adolf meant an integrated military alliance, with a standing army to which all members contributed. The chequered pattern of alliances which had hitherto been made to serve must be replaced by a unified military league, with a single

[1] They are printed in Irmer, *VS*, I. 199-208.

[2] C. W. F. Breyer, *Beyträge zur Geschichte des dreissigjährigen Krieges, passim*, for these interviews.

[3] The journal of the embassy is in Irmer, *VS*, I. 209 *seqq*.

[4] For his momentary deviation into other solutions, under pressure of circumstances, see below, pp. 748 *seqq*.

head and a fixed organization. There would be a standing council of war, presumably representing all members; but there could of course be only one '*capo*'. The obvious candidate was Gustav Adolf himself. But he professed, at least, to consider alternative choices as possible: John George, for instance, or William of Hesse. George William of Brandenburg he specifically ruled out; partly from a feeling of resentment at his attitude over Pomerania and the marriage (the feeling emerged very plainly at Nuremberg), but also, perhaps, from a well-grounded belief in the Elector's incapacity for command. The *corpus bellicum*, at all events, was represented as being not necessarily under Swedish control. But it is doubtful how far this was seriously intended; and it may be assumed that what he wanted was a regular Protestant standing army under his own command. Experience with mercenary forces in Germany had no doubt taught him the military and financial advantages of such an arrangement.

Side by side with this body would stand the *corpus politicum*, or *corpus evangelicorum*. In one aspect it was simply a necessary extension of it. The military league would be confronted with decisions not only on matters of strategy but also on questions of politics; and it must necessarily have a political organization to deal with them. But its more important and more permanent function would be to act as a species of Metternichian fire-brigade, trained to smell the first whiff of smoke, and equipped either to extinguish the flames of political arson or to dowse the reeking censer of revolutionary Catholicism. It was his hope that all the Protestant estates of Germany would be members of this body; and he would have liked the great Imperial Cities to lead the way. But he made it clear that adhesion would be voluntary: members would be allies, not clients; they would be linked together by compacts freely negotiated. At Nuremberg he pointed, vaguely enough, to the United Netherlands as a possible model. And he made it equally clear that he regarded a league of this sort as no less essential than the *corpus bellicum*: when the Nuremberg delegates saw Sadler and Chemnitz for the second time, and presented a memorandum in which they supported the formation of a military league but said nothing of a *corpus politicum*, they were sharply taken to task. There was no suggestion that the leadership in this post-war league should be entrusted to John George or William V. Palsgrave August was charged to ask John George bluntly whether he would support Gustav Adolf as director of such a league; if not, the alternative was to 'content' him and allow him to retire from Germany altogether. As long as Sweden remained the leading Protestant participant in the German war, Gustav Adolf claimed the direction of the political league: the right man to command the fire-brigade was clearly he who had, almost single-handed, extinguished the preceding conflagration.

But, whether the King were serious in his alternative or no, it became a question as to what would, in fact, 'content' him. What were now his demands for Sweden? What did Sadler and Chemnitz mean when they spoke at Nuremberg of 'reasonable satisfaction'? One thing at least was certain: a cash indemnity would no longer be considered enough. A report had reached Gustav Adolf that George William had suggested at Torgau that Sweden might perhaps be induced to accept a money payment by way of compensation. Both at Dresden and at Nuremberg this suggestion was vigorously repudiated: Gustav Adolf was no mercenary, to be paid off at the end of the campaign. As he told the Nurembergers, he was arguing not '*ex jure civili*' but from the law of nations; and he now explicitly avowed that he based his claims upon Grotius. The extent of those claims appeared startlingly in the instructions for Palsgrave August. The states of Germany, in the King's view, could be divided into six classes: first, those Protestant states which in 1630 had been wholly in enemy occupation, had been subsequently liberated by Sweden and were now *jure belli* Swedish—for instance, Mecklenburg; secondly, those Protestant states where the prince's authority had been merely nominal until the arrival of the Swedish forces—for instance, Pomerania; thirdly, those Protestant states which had been 'in spirit hostile'—for instance, Brandenburg (Gustav Adolf had not forgotten Küstrin, and now alleged that George William's obstinacy on that occasion cost him 5000 men); fourthly, independent Protestant princes deeply indebted to Sweden for assistance—for instance, John George or William V; fifthly, states that had favoured or aided the enemy—by which he may have intended Hesse-Darmstadt; and sixthly, open enemies, whose conquered territories were declared to belong to the Swedish crown '*cum jure supremo*' and 'with all the rights that their former possessors had'. Against all these classes except the fourth (from which, presumably, he expected only gratitude) he had claims which were good in international law. But it was by no means his intention to prosecute these claims relentlessly and by force. Pomerania, as he frankly told the Nuremberg delegates, he meant to keep as an imperial fief (in this contradicting Sadler and Chemnitz, who had indicated that Pomerania and Mecklenburg might be fully restored in return for 'recognition' of Gustav Adolf): he could not risk another General of the Oceanic and Baltic Seas. The conquered ecclesiastical lands, it seems, were for the present to remain in his hands as bargaining-counters against the negotiation of peace. For the rest, it appears that he intended to maintain, at least in principle, his title to those *jura superioritatis* which he had won by the sword. How far he would press these rights, and whether he would assert them permanently, or merely for the duration of the war—this does not emerge very clearly. It is probable that he was prepared to enforce them in order to constrain the princes to effective contributions to the war effort, and in order to be able to appropriate former imperial revenues to the maintenance of his armies. If, as seems likely, he valued these rights mainly for the financial resources they gave him, and for the possibilities of military exploitation they afforded, there was the less reason to be concerned about them after the peace. Yet if the *corpus politicum* were to be under his direction, it would be at least convenient to retain this hold upon its members; and though none might be constrained to join that *corpus*, these *jura superioritatis* might well provide a means of persuasion for use against Laodiceans. For the *corpus politicum*, after all, was the new *assecuratio*, the form in which one of Sweden's original objects in entering the war was now to be realized, and as such it would be well to take no chances about it. Meanwhile, the mere enumeration of the six classes might bring the princes to a sense of the realities of the situation; and a realization of the extent of the claims which Gustav Adolf was entitled to make might serve to prompt them to better efforts. If drastic action against allies and fellow-Protestants could thus be avoided, that would be all to the good.

All parties in these discussions were conscious of the fact that Gustav Adolf's programme might at some points be difficult to square with the existing pattern of imperial institutions; and all were concerned to minimize its impact upon the old constitution. There is very little evidence to suggest that Gustav Adolf, now or at any other time, entertained any plan, or even much desire, to recast the Empire in another mould. The radicalism of William of Hesse and the old Palatine party had no attractions for him as such; and it was no concern of his to provide Germany with a better, or a different, form of government, if the present arrangements could be made to serve his ends. The quickest way to lose his most important —and most uncertain—ally would be to confront John George with bold schemes of constitutional reform. He had no wish, as he said at Nuremberg, to prescribe new laws for the Empire. But he could not admit that the cause for which he was fighting should be endangered, at present or in the future, by scruples and evasions based on legalistic objections which were convenient pretexts for doing nothing, rather than living constitutional principles. That was what he meant when he declared that Strassburg 'looked too much to *statum antiquum jmperii*, which in the present condition of the Empire . . . is no longer either advisable or possible'.[1] The war had begun, after all, as a constitutional issue between the Emperor and the princes; and even John George conceded that some change was necessary and possible. If God so ordered events 'that the Estates might attain *ad majorem libertatem*, as in Italy or the Netherlands, why then should they cast it from them?'[2] Adolf Frederick had declined the opportunity, no doubt; but he was at best, in Gustav Adolf's opinion, an obstinate and poor-spirited creature. It might well be that the end of the war would see some curtailment of imperial rights, some transference of sovereignty to the princes; but it would not therefore mean the destruction of the Empire. If Gustav Adolf had entertained grandiose schemes for a radical alteration of the political structure of Germany, he would hardly have been so precise in his insistence that he intended to hold Pomerania as an imperial fief. And the *corpus politicum* which he projected would not disrupt the ancient fabric either, any more than the Union and the League had disrupted it in former days. On the contrary, Gustav Adolf himself defined it as a '*corpus in corpore*, that is, a *corpus formatum evangelicorum per se subsistens, in ipso corpore jmperij Romani*'.[3] It is notable that the League of Heilbronn in 1633 specifically declared that it was not intended to violate the constitution of the Empire.[4] Gustav Adolf's league, it is true, would have had its own *parlamentum*; but this was nothing new in Germany. The relationship of the members of such a *corpus* to its head was nowhere clearly defined; but an earlier reference to Henry II of France suggests that the King may have envisaged it as no more than an imprecise protectorate, resting on the sanctions of war-time

[1] Breyer, p. 223.
[2] *ibid.*, p. 212.
[3] *ibid.*, p. 231.
[4] *AOSB*, I. VIII. 445-6.

jura superioritatis, and ultimately of Swedish military power. If his recommendation of the United Provinces as a model was seriously meant, it must be supposed that he would have been content with the relatively weak constitutional position occupied by Maurice and Frederick Henry. At all events, it seems very unlikely that he contemplated anything like a permanent feudal subordination to the Swedish crown.[1]

If, then, the imperial constitution were to continue, at least in its main features, what of the occupant of the imperial throne—that throne to which (as Oxenstierna later said) Gustav Adolf had given so unforgettable a shake?[2] At this moment, when at last the painful gropings of two years were bringing him towards the light of decision, when something like a clear-cut plan for the future was raising itself above the thickets of alternatives, contingencies and expedients—what was Gustav Adolf's attitude to the great question which all in Germany were asking? Did he wish to be Emperor, or no?

The answer to this question is, up to a point, easy: it is simply that we do not know. We know that Charnacé had dangled the idea before him as early as 1630.[3] We know that Gustav Adolf had deprecated John George's enthusiastic suggestion on the morrow of Breitenfeld. We know that not Germany only, but Europe, was canvassing the possibility; and that the Brandenburg council in May 1632 considered that he would accept election.[4] The matter was discussed among the King's confidential servants: Salvius wrote to Grubbe in October 1631 pointing out that Gustav Adolf's election would solve their difficulties in dealing with the German princes.[5] But as to Gustav Adolf himself, the evidence is slight and uncertain. In February 1632 he did indeed fling out, in exasperation, a famous sentence to Adolf Frederick of Mecklenburg: 'Were I to become Emperor, then would your grace be my prince'[6]—his only recorded remark on the subject. It is a remark, however, which proves only—what needed no proving—that he was not unaware that the possibility was being discussed. At Nuremberg, six months later, Sadler and

[1] For a review of the discussion, see Paul, III. 99-100 *note* 31; *Sv. Krig*, V 259-76.

[2] *RRP*, VII. 148.

[3] L. Weibull, *DF*, pp. 31, 58.

[4] Irmer, *VS*, I. 114; Koser, p. 450; *cf.* Dudík, p. 292; *Briefe und Akten*, II. 130.

[5] '*Si res regi Sveciae bene cesserint tum omnes principes non solum foederatos* but also *subditos habebit*, and consequently *omnes portus*': Boëthius, *NSK*, p. 207.

[6] Ahnlund, *Oxenstierna*, p. 668.

Chemnitz took it upon themselves to state that Gustav Adolf desired the imperial crown, but that he would not consent to be bound by any election capitulation.[1] But they said a good deal on this occasion which did not correspond with the King's own intentions as expressed on the following day. And he certainly displayed indifference when the Nurembergers offered to show him the imperial regalia, and did in fact decline to look at them.[2]

It may well be that Hjärne was right when he wrote that the idea that 'an imperial crown floated before his eyes as the final objective . . . is unprovable, and on the whole improbable'.[3] As to ambition, national pride forbade him to regard the Emperor as of higher rank than a King of Sweden: had not this same Empire once been overthrown by his Gothic ancestors? He was not so oblivious of his country's interests, moreover, as to be blind to the dangers to Sweden if he accepted such enormous commitments in Germany. A union of the crowns of Sweden and Russia he had once entertained, in younger and less sober days, and under pressure of a great national crisis; a union with Poland was still an element in his policy—though hardly a serious one; a union with Brandenburg was a conceivable method of dealing with a difficult dynastic problem. But the whole history of Germany spoke against an attempt to combine the responsibilities of empire with the kingship of a non-German country. His allies in Germany represented the cause not only of Protestantism but of princely particularism against imperial authority. It was inconceivable that they should remain his allies for long after he had ascended the imperial throne. (And indeed it was highly unlikely that he would find a legal majority in the electoral college to put him there: John George had long since repented his momentary exuberance.) His *corpus evangelicorum* had a real chance of survival only so long as it was a body concerned to resist the Emperor's attempts at arbitrary rule: its disintegration would have been an early consequence of Gustav Adolf's election. Another consequence, no less early, would have been the loss of the French alliance. Neither Germany nor Europe would welcome Totila sitting in the place of Caesar.[4] It is not, perhaps, too much to

[1] Breyer, p. 239.
[2] Ahnlund, *Oxenstierna*, p. 669.
[3] H. Hjärne, *Gustaf Adolf, Protestantismens förkämpe*, p. 98.
[4] For Gustav Adolf as Totila, *cf. RRP*, VII. 427, where Oxenstierna remarked: '*Gustavus neque Totilae neque Alarico neque alii regi secundus*, he swept over the land like a flood-tide, with *celeritate* like to that of Alexander *Magnus*'.

assume that Gustav Adolf was aware of these implications; but if he was not, Oxenstierna would doubtless take care that he became so, for he, at least, did not participate in the insubstantial fantasies of Salvius and Sadler.

Nevertheless, it was a possibility: an alternative to the *corpus evangelicorum* (since it could scarcely be combined with it); and of course he must have thought of it, especially when vexed by the intransigence of allies who refused to allow him to dragoon them. It was conceivable that things might come to such a pass that the assumption of the imperial title might offer the only way out of a maze of difficulties. But it was scarcely conceivable that he should take that way willingly and unconstrained. Better far the *corpus in corpore*, the Pomeranian fief, the rôle of leader of the opposition which his intended position as a German prince would open to him. For, after all, the German venture must end some day; and he had other tasks still before him. In 1635 the Polish truce would run out; and with Denmark there was a long score still unsettled. It was because he must be able at need to turn his back on Germany, able to devote himself to the prosecution of older, deeper-rooted, more national policies, without having always to look over his shoulder at central Europe, that the *corpus politicum* had been conceived. Even in the summer of 1632 he was not so wholly preoccupied with Germany as to forget his house's historic mission in the Baltic.

CHAPTER XI

THE LAST CAMPAIGN

(i) *Preliminaries*

In 1630 Gustav Adolf had celebrated Christmas by attacking Gartz and Greifenhagen. A year later he was able to keep the feast, secure and triumphant, in the historic capital of the Empire. In the winter of 1630-31 he had scarcely pushed beyond the perimeter of his beach-head; his army had been small, his supplies precarious, his monetary resources inadequate to the contentment of a half-mutinous soldiery. The end of the venture appeared distant: too distant for any precise planning of how the death-blow was to be delivered; and as to the terms of a peace settlement, it seemed profitless to speculate upon them. But now, in January 1632, the situation was utterly transformed. His swollen armies took their ease in the rich quarters of Franconia, and for the moment lacked for nothing; the burden of war finance had been almost wholly shifted from Sweden to Germany. Above all, the pattern of victory had arranged itself in the King's mind, the overthrow of the Habsburgs was timed to take place before the close of 1632, and the terms of a peace settlement were already under discussion.

The attack on Vienna was to be delivered not from the north but from the west; not up the line of the Elbe or the Oder, as in the plans of the 'twenties, but down the valley of the Danube. Bavaria was first to be crushed, Swabia occupied, the area between the Danube, the Lech and the Alps subjugated, the Alpine passes blocked to hostile debouchments; and then the Swedish armies would turn east for the final stroke at an isolated and friendless Austria. For such a plan to be successful, Gustav Adolf must be reasonably secure against blows in flank or in rear. A more or less continuous front, already stretching in an arc from Silesia to the Rhenish Palatinate, would be extended further to the frontiers of Switzerland and Italy. Behind that front, in the Lower Saxon and Westphalian Circles, there still lay a large pocket of imperialist-held territory: this must be sealed off and reduced, and Swedish control established even to the westernmost limits of Germany's North Sea coast. This was the more important, since this region was especially vulnerable to intervention from outside Germany. It presented obvious opportunities to Kristian IV; and it lay sufficiently close to the Netherlands to make collaboration between Spaniards and imperialists a possibility. Nor could the advance upon Vienna proceed with safety unless the Rhineland were firmly held, for a Spanish thrust down the Moselle might imperil Mainz; and the Spanish garrisons in the Palatinate might provide a nucleus for harassing and dangerous attacks in flank. Hence the insistence of Swedish diplomacy, throughout the winter, on retaining a grip upon the left bank of the Rhine; hence the vigorous military activity during these months, which pushed the Swedish control of the river far to the north and south of Mainz and culminated in the King's brilliant capture of Kreuznach in February.[1] And there was one other precondition for the success of Gustav Adolf's strategy. The right-handed blow which he intended to deliver could be dealt only if his strategic left flank held firm. Silesia and Saxony were to be the pivot upon which the active wing of his armies could freely swing. Here the campaign must be waged defensively and without risk, for here the essential was not to be victorious but to stand fast.

For a strategy of this sort much more was required than a single large field-army. Separate forces must hold the Rhineland and the Saxon bastion; others must complete the conquest of north-west Germany; and everywhere, throughout the whole vast and expanding area of conquest, there must be garrisons; garrisons to stem the tide of any counter-attack, garrisons to hold down ill-affectioned places, garrisons to give bite to the efforts of the civil authorities to drain the resources of Germany. Before the campaign ended there would be close on a hundred of them, and they would lock up many thousands of men.[2] Apart from the garrison troops, the field-armies would need to be of unprecedented dimensions if the war were to be finished off this year. Gustav Adolf reckoned with at least seven of them. The main army, under his own command, was destined to prosecute the offensive against Vienna; Horn with the Franconian

[1] The Rhinegrave Otto took Simmern, Bacharach and Boppard; the Landgrave William V of Hesse-Cassel took Wetzlar and Gelnhausen; Bernard of Saxe-Weimar took Kaiserslautern, Landau, Worms, Speyer and Mannheim; Horn took Mergentheim and Heilbronn. After the fall of Kreuznach only Frankenthal and Philipsburg, of all the Palatinate fortresses, remained in Spanish hands. For these operations, see *Sv. Krig*, V. 279-85; and for the capture of Kreuznach, *AOSB*, II. I. 752; Monro, II. 101.

[2] See the map and list in *Sv. Krig*, VI. 392-3.

army was to accompany him. The armies of Banér and William of Weimar were to guard the vital route through the Thuringian forest, and be available for action either in the Lower Saxon Circle or as a stiffening to John George. Tott with the Mecklenburg army was to operate against the Lower Saxon Circle from the north-east, the Landgrave with his Hessian forces from the south. Arnim's Saxon army was expected to hold the Bohemian frontier and to bar the Oder valley to any advance by Tiefenbach on that side.

It was clear, however, that strong forces would also have to be left in the Rhineland when Gustav Adolf moved away; and in fact the seven-army scheme was not only an indication of intended strategic dispositions, but also a device for the decentralization of recruiting. Gustav Adolf planned to raise fresh troops during the winter on the vastest scale. He hoped before the campaign opened to have added no less than 108,000 men to his armies. This would have brought the total allied strength to 210,000, of which 170,000 would have been directly under Gustav Adolf's command, and the remaining 40,000 under the command of John George.[1] These were numbers very much in excess of any that had been seen in this war before. They foreshadow the dramatic increase in the normal size of armies, which was to be one of the most important developments in the military art during the seventeenth century, and was to reach a climax in the armies of Louvois. But it was no megalomaniac passion for mere numbers that drove Gustav Adolf to set so high a target. His demands were based on a reasoned calculation of the forces required. He was faced with the simultaneous conduct of holding operations in Saxony and on the Rhine, mopping-up operations in the Lower Saxon Circle, and a decisive campaign in the main theatre. If his requirements were unprecedented, that was because his strategic conception was unprecedented too. No earlier commander had attempted so grandiose and complex a campaign, to be waged simultaneously on four different fronts; and none, certainly, had tried to combine such an enterprise with the task of effectively occupying and administering perhaps one-half of Germany. In the event, Gustav Adolf was forced to begin operations before his recruiting programme was within sight of completion. When he started for the Danube in March, he had no more than 120,000 men at his disposal (of whom only 13,000 were native

[1] *Arkiv*, I. 546-8, for these estimates; and see *AOSB*, I. VII. 63, II. I. 756, 769, 772; *Sv. Krig*, V. 219.

Swedes), and the Saxons only 20,000. Yet even these figures represent an increase of 42,000 upon the establishment as it stood at the close of 1631.[1] None of these additional troops came from Sweden. In the autumn of 1631 the King had indeed asked the *råd* to send him six regiments of foot and 1500 horse; but in deference to their remonstrances the number was reduced, and in the end none were sent. It was felt that the danger from Denmark made inadvisable any weakening of the forces at home.[2] An *utskrivning* was held, and produced a fairly satisfactory yield, but the recruits were not despatched to Germany: in 1632 a total of no less than 16,000 men were under arms to defend Sweden and the Baltic provinces. Gustav Adolf's new levies for Germany were mostly raised in Germany, and they were paid (in so far as they were paid at all) mostly from German resources. The outlay involved was indeed of a magnitude far exceeding Sweden's capacity to pay. The muster-money of the additional 42,000 men came to somewhere between 300,000 and 400,000 *rdr*., and their pay for the year would have greatly exceeded a million.[3] Even the contributions of conquered Germany and the plunder of Bavaria could scarcely be expected to provide such a sum in addition to what was being paid already. For lack of pay, discipline was bound to deteriorate. Purely financial considerations, therefore, made a final victory this year almost a necessity. No doubt the King knew this when he fixed his original target; and it may be that if that target had been attained the final victory would in fact have followed. Yet even as it was, Gustav Adolf's recruiting seems to have strained the mercenary-market: Maximilian protested (possibly with truth) that he could find no soldiers to enlist; and it is at all events certain that he was forced to swell his armies by the dubious expedient of calling up the militia.[4]

Gustav Adolf was not the only bidder against whom Maximilian had to compete. A formidable purchaser entered the market at the turn of the year in the person of Wallenstein. It was on 5 December 1631 that Wallenstein was reappointed to the command of the Emperor's armies, on terms which gave him virtually unlimited

[1] *Sv. Krig*, V. 298; and *cf. Arkiv*, II. 342, 348-50.
[2] *Arkiv*, I. 526, II. 357; *RRP*, II. 133; *AOSB*, II. III. 256; *Sv. Krig*, V. 342-65.
[3] *Arkiv*, I. 509, 511, 513, 541; *Sv. Krig*, V. 296, 299-300; P. Sörensson, *Ekonomi och krigföring*, p. 316.
[4] Hallwich, *Briefe und Akten*, II. 66, 153.

control of them; and though he affected to consider the appointment only as an interim measure, it was made definitive on 5 April.[1] He at once began vigorous efforts to form a great new army in Bohemia—an army which, until it was ready for action, he intended to keep disengaged from the fortunes of war in Germany.[2] His resumption of the command made it certain that Gustav Adolf would have to face, sooner or later, a general more formidable, and an army better organized, than any he had so far encountered. The location of that army in Bohemia made it a potential threat to one of the main props of his strategy. The return of Wallenstein had thus serious military implications; but also (at least potentially) political implications which were no less serious, and which in turn might well have grave military consequences. On both counts it involved the Saxon front—where stability was vital—in uncertainty, anxiety and peril.

Gustav Adolf had already gained some impressions of Wallenstein's personality at second hand, and was by this time disposed to distrust him, even had he not been in the Emperor's service. The history of their relations goes back to November 1630, when the King addressed to Wallenstein a letter which has not survived. Its contents are a matter of conjecture; but there is no reason to think that it was an attempt to seduce him from his allegiance, and some reason to suppose that it was of no particular consequence: it has been suggested that it may have concerned Wallenstein's estates in Mecklenburg.[3] However that may be, nothing came of it; and when, six months later, contact between them was renewed, the initiative did not come from Gustav Adolf, but from Wallenstein's brother-in-law, Adam Trčka. As early as February 1631 Trčka is said to have suggested an approach to the King.[4] The fall of Frankfurt-on-Oder, and the Swedish advance to Crossen, put Gustav Adolf within striking distance of Wallenstein's duchy of Sagan; and by April he perhaps thought it prudent to insure himself against further Swedish progress in this direction. Trčka belonged to the group of Bohemian patriots who aimed at the independence of their country,

[1] *ibid.*, I. 658-9, 673, II. 195; Dudík, pp. 171-85; Hallwich, *Wallenstein und Arnim im Frühjahre 1632*, pp. 150-1; Chemnitz, I. 270; *Sv. Krig*, V. 400; Pekař, *Wallenstein*, I. 182.

[2] See the very full study in *Sv. Krig*, V. 419-57.

[3] Pekař, I. 72-3; *Briefe und Akten*, I. 170; *Sv. Krig*, V. 384 *note* 3; Irmer, *VS*, I. xxiii; H. Schwarz, *Wallenstein und Gustav Adolf nach dem Kurfürstentag zu Regensburg*, pp. 32-3; A. Gaedeke, *Wallensteins Verhandlung mit Schweden und Sachsen*, p. 16; *cf.* Dudík, p. 13.

[4] Schwarz, p. 41 *seqq.*; Gaedeke, *op. cit.*, p. 14; *Sv. Krig*, V. 384-5.

and it is possible that Wallenstein shared his views; at all events, Trčka had no difficulty in making contact with the circle of Bohemian *émigrés* around Gustav Adolf, whose most conspicuous member was Henry Matthias, von Thurn. Since about 1628 a number of these exiles had drifted into the Swedish service, and they looked to Gustav Adolf to restore them to their fatherland.[1] The agent whom Trčka employed to approach Thurn was a certain Sezima Ražin; and towards the end of May 1631 Ražin and Thurn met Gustav Adolf at Spandau. Trčka had not authorized Ražin to give a message from Wallenstein himself, but it was indicated that his attitude to Sweden was friendly.[2] The King seems to have been taken completely by surprise[3]; but he could not afford, at this difficult moment, to neglect any possible ally. A revolt in Bohemia would be very convenient; and if Wallenstein were prepared to step forward in the unsuspected guise of a Czech patriot, so much the better. After a second interview with Ražin at Tangermünde on 27 June, the King empowered Thurn to enter into negotiations with Trčka, and may possibly have given Ražin a verbal promise of assistance if Wallenstein should rebel against the Emperor.[4] At all events, Wallenstein in mid-July sent to Gustav Adolf an explicit request for a force of 10,000-12,000 men, who were to be under Thurn's command—this last stipulation being no doubt intended to assure the King that they would really be used to support a patriot rising. At a further meeting at Alt-Brandenburg in August Gustav Adolf agreed to make these troops available, provided he emerged victorious from his impending clash with Tilly; and he seems also to have promised that Wallenstein should be his viceroy in Bohemia, pending the return of Frederick V. Soon after Breitenfeld, Thurn and Ražin came to him at Schleusingen to claim his promise. But Gustav Adolf refused to make good his word. He told them he could spare no more than 1500 men; he referred them to Arnim and John George for any further assistance; and he gave Thurn a commission to raise some five or six thousand troops, to aid a Bohemian revolt, provided the Saxons had no objection.[5]

It seems, then, that until the meeting at Tangermünde on 27

[1] P. M. Hebbe, *Svenskarne i Böhmen och Mähren*, pp. 1-5; E. Hildebrand, *Wallenstein och hans förbindelser med svenskarne*, p. 388; *cf. AOSB*, I. v. 728.

[2] *Sv. Krig*, V. 389-90; Schwarz, pp. 42-3.

[3] Pekař, I. 84; Schwarz, p. 43; Gaedeke, *op. cit.*, p. 15.

[4] *Schriftstücke*, pp. 205-6; Gaedeke, *op. cit.*, pp. 20-1; *Sv. Krig*, V. 390-1.

[5] Hebbe, p. 6; *Sv. Krig*, V. 392; Pekař, I. 93, 108; Gaedeke, *op. cit.*, pp. 22-3; *cf. Briefe und Akten*, II. 218-20.

June Gustav Adolf did not take the idea of co-operation with Wallenstein very seriously. The prospects for any solid alliance between them were not good. Gustav Adolf was committed to dispossessing Wallenstein of Mecklenburg; and any restoration of Frederick V to Bohemia might well deprive him of his Bohemian estates also. But before Breitenfeld promises were cheap; the exiles were excited and enthusiastic at the prospect of Wallenstein's support; and Gustav Adolf was not prepared to turn his back on such auxiliaries as presented themselves.

Wallenstein's motives and intentions are obscure: here begins a long historical controversy. It may be, as Pekař contended, that after the dismissal of 1630 the guiding motive in all he did was revenge upon the Emperor (though the proper object of his animus should surely have been Maximilian rather than Ferdinand), and that the cordial relations which had subsisted between himself and the court of Vienna during the eighteen months after his dismissal [1] were but an elaborate deception on his part. It may be that he later accepted the command-in-chief at the Emperor's hands, and fought the bloody battles of Nuremberg and Lützen, for no other purpose than the better to betray the Habsburgs at the appropriate moment. It may be so; but it strains credulity very far. It is perhaps unnecessary to seek for a single motive or a self-consistent policy in his actions. Whatever other views he may have held, whatever ideals he may have embraced, he was first of all the adventurer and the careerist, and his prime object was power. Power implied armed force to maintain it; and the easiest route to that goal lay through re-entry into the Emperor's service. It must have been clear to Wallenstein that Ferdinand looked forward to the day when he could venture once more to employ him, and that his own powerful friends in Vienna were working to that end. The death of the already aged Tilly, or a disaster to the armies under Tilly's command, might provide a suitable opportunity. Hence his fury at the news of Tilly's capture of Magdeburg [2]; hence his deliberate embarrassment of Tilly thereafter, by refusing to let him buy supplies.[3] In a Germany which at Regensburg had been almost united against him the imperial service still offered the likeliest prospects for his resurrection. Meanwhile, he needed an army of his own, to strengthen his hand

[1] See, *e.g.*, *Briefe und Akten*, I. 345, 373; Dudík, pp. 18, 21, 23, 27, 32-3, 76.
[2] Pekař, I. 87.
[3] A. Ernstberger, *Wallensteins Heeressabotage und der Breitenfelder Schlacht*, *passim*; Pekař, I. 75; Dudík, p. 45; contrast Schwarz, pp. 26-31.

against the moment when the Emperor should ask his aid again; and, more immediately, he needed security against disturbance by Gustav Adolf. Both considerations may have prompted the suggestion that Gustav Adolf should send him 12,000 men; and the request that Thurn should command them was the indispensable earnest of his good faith. Wallenstein may or may not have been a Czech patriot; it is at least clear that he saw how the patriot movement might be used to his own advantage, to induce Gustav Adolf to close with his proposals, and to serve as a bridge between the hostile camps.

Breitenfeld altered the position, both for him and for Gustav Adolf. The magnitude of the King's victory, the plain consequence that it made Wallenstein's aid no longer important to him, perhaps prompted Wallenstein's comment that it was 'a terrible thing'; the discredit of Tilly, and the feeling that it brought an eventual offer from Vienna appreciably nearer, were possibly reflected in his additional remark that the hand of God was in it.[1] He did not, however, abandon hope of his 12,000 men without another application; and when Gustav Adolf at Schleusingen refused to make good his word, Wallenstein took care to burn no boats unnecessarily: the King, he indicated, might still rest assured of his good affections.[2] But from this moment he thought no more of Gustav Adolf as the ladder by which he might climb back to his old position.

As for Gustav Adolf, he had no motive, after Breitenfeld, to make large promises to Wallenstein, and every inducement to go back on those he had already made. John George was now his ally; Bohemia was the allotted sphere for Saxon operations. If Gustav Adolf had really had much faith in Wallenstein's professions, he might perhaps have chosen the Bohemian theatre for himself; as it was, he could not saddle his ally with a Wallenstein who had 12,000 men at his disposal. John George was not the man to co-operate willingly with the usurper of Mecklenburg; and Gustav Adolf was careful to transmit to him the details of the negotiations that had passed between them. It was no doubt strictly true that at the time of the meeting at Schleusingen Gustav Adolf had few enough men to spare. It was equally true that he dared not gamble on Wallenstein at the expense of the Elector's newly acquired friendship. Nor could he venture to give unconditional backing to Thurn and the *émigrés*.

[1] Schwarz, p. 46.
[2] Gaedeke, *op. cit.*, p. 28; *cf.* Paul, III. 21-4.

John George had no wish to see a Calvinist Bohemia; nor had his view of the Bohemian rebels changed since 1618.[1] To refer Thurn to Arnim and John George, to make his levies subject to John George's consent, was virtually to write off the whole project. What Gustav Adolf did not perhaps foresee was that the negotiations with Wallenstein which he had broken off would be resumed, on imperial initiative, between Wallenstein and Arnim—this time for quite different ends.

On 26 September the Emperor's councillors had formally advised him to ask George of Hesse-Darmstadt to mediate, and the result had been those negotiations for a general peace which have already been noticed. But at the same time they advised that Wallenstein be asked to make an approach to Arnim; and two days later Questenberg duly conveyed this commission to him.[2] Immediately afterwards Wallenstein received news of Gustav Adolf's repudiation of his promises; and on 3 October the Emperor signed a safe-conduct for Arnim.[3] But Wallenstein was in no hurry to begin his negotiation; and before he had done anything in the matter the Saxons (on 22 October) had invaded Bohemia. Wallenstein waited a week for this event to make its full effect in Vienna, and then, on 29 October, notified his willingness to discuss the possibility of his resuming the command of the Emperor's armies.[4] The Saxons were meeting with no resistance in their advance; Wallenstein took care to let Arnim know that Prague was undefended [5]; and on 5 November the Saxon army arrived at the White Hill: Prague was occupied the same evening. On the 14th Wallenstein agreed to meet the Emperor's representatives at Znaim.[6] Not until 20 November did he act upon the Emperor's commission and meet Arnim at Kaunitz.[7] At that meeting he uttered his famous threat to be revenged upon the Habsburgs [8]; and there was some general talk of the need for peace

[1] Arnim replied to complaints about the excesses of returned *émigrés* in Prague by saying that 'sein Kurfürst habe bei Gott mit diesen Exulanten nichts gemeinsames': Pekař, I. 174; and *cf.* Irmer, *VS*, I. 82-3, where he complains of their 'calida consilia'.

[2] *Briefe und Akten*, I. 528; Gaedeke, *op. cit.*, pp. 26-7; *Sv. Krig*, V. 393-4.

[3] Pekař, I. 112.

[4] *ibid.*, I. 144; Schwarz, p. 57.

[5] Pekař, I. 149; *Sv. Krig*, V. 397.

[6] *Sv. Krig*, V. 399.

[7] Irmer, *VS*, I. 87-8; Pekař, I. 160-7, 177-80; Schwarz, pp. 57-62; Droysen, *Gustav Adolf*, II. 504-8; Gaedeke, *op. cit.*, pp. 34-6; Irmer, *Arnim*, pp. 148-54; Dudík, pp. 132-3, 150-1, 157-60.

[8] That 'der kayser mitt seinem gantzen hause soll schmerzlich sehen und empfinden, dass er einen cavallier affrontired hab': Irmer, *VS*, I. 87-8.

upon terms which would include the revocation of the Edict of Restitution; but the atmosphere seems to have been less than cordial. Nevertheless, the assumption of the command on 5 December did not interrupt negotiations with Arnim, which continued in secret throughout the early months of 1632, and included a meeting with Trčka at Aussig on 18 January as inconclusive as that which had preceded it.[1]

Gustav Adolf was informed by his representative in Dresden of what was said to have passed at Kaunitz, and he learned too of the Aussig interview; but for the rest he could only conjecture what might be hatching in Bohemia. Such facts as he knew were more than enough to give rise to anxiety. In a military aspect Arnim's invasion of Bohemia was in itself sufficiently disturbing. Gustav Adolf would have been willing enough, if John George had acquiesced, to leave Bohemia to be taken care of by the *émigrés*: the task of the Saxon army, as he saw it, was to stand firm in Lusatia and Silesia, blocking Tiefenbach's road to Frankfurt and Stettin. And at first Arnim seems to have agreed with him. Tiefenbach's invasion of Lusatia late in September was soon called off (on Wallenstein's advice) lest it make John George irreconcilably hostile [2]; but at first Arnim showed no great interest in any forward movement.[3] The decision to invade Bohemia was a sudden change of policy, undertaken without prior consultation of Gustav Adolf [4]; and it seems to have been dictated by considerations of purely local military convenience: it would enable the Saxon army to live on enemy resources, and would push the front further away from Dresden. But though there was something to be said for it from the purely Saxon point of view, it jeopardized the broader allied strategy; and when the advance was pushed on to the capture of Prague the position became highly precarious. Prague lay at the bottom of a deep salient, upon which imperialist armies could converge from three sides. As soon as the Emperor should have collected his forces it would become untenable; and when that happened Arnim would need all his skill to avert a major reverse. Thus, as a result of the Bohemian campaign, the whole right wing of the Swedish position,

[1] Ranke, *Wallenstein*, p. 171; Pekař, I. 183 *seqq.*; Irmer, *VS*, I. 107-8; *Sv. Krig*, VI. 127. Gaedeke, *Arnims Papieren*, pp. 288-9, for Thurn's report of the interview, in a letter to Arnim.

[2] *Sv. Krig*, V. 168-75; Dudík, p. 136.

[3] Irmer, *Arnim*, pp. 145-7; but *cf.* Gaedeke, *Wallensteins Verhandlungen*, p. 31.

[4] Gaedeke, *Arnims Papieren*, pp. 286-7, for Thurn's complaints to Arnim on this score; and *cf. ibid.*, p. 289.

which had been intended as a stable pivot, had become fluid, and in danger of dissolution and collapse within the near future. Tiefenbach did indeed send part of his forces into Bohemia, and Arnim's claim to have carried out a successful diversion had some basis [1]; but a Saxon defeat would leave the Oder uncovered, and John George, with characteristic pig-headedness, rejected George William's proposal, at Torgau in February, that they should collaborate to safeguard this front.[2]

Politically, these developments were not less disturbing. Lars Nilsson Tungel, the Swedish resident in Dresden from December onwards, suspected (wrongly, as it seems) that the invasion had been undertaken with Wallenstein's connivance.[3] It was remarked that Arnim left Bohemia and returned to Saxony at the end of the year—which, it was thought, he would hardly have dared to do without some assurance that he would not be attacked.[4] And Wallenstein's conduct could not fail to confirm Gustav Adolf's distrust of him. His motives in the intrigue with Arnim can only be conjectured; but it is not necessary to credit him with a suddenly developed idealist interest in the cause of peace and toleration on the one hand,[5] nor with an extraordinarily devious long-range plan of vengeance on the other.[6] Negotiation with Arnim offered opportunities to re-attach that officer to him, at a moment when he needed such coadjutors; and he had an inducement to offer in the shape of arrears of pay long due from the Emperor.[7] More generally, he may at first have felt that since the Emperor was determined on negotiations for a general peace, it would be better to take them into his own hands than to leave them solely in those of George of Hesse-Darmstadt. His profession of hostility to the Emperor at Kaunitz was necessary, in view of his recent negotiation with Gustav Adolf, if Arnim were to be induced to give any credit to his sincerity. If indeed the Kaunitz meeting showed that he had grown cooler to the idea of negotiation with Arnim, that may be explicable by his increasing irresolution, to be so marked in 1633, or by his conscious-

[1] Irmer, *VS*, I. 82. For the Bohemian campaign, see *Sv. Krig*, V. 176-85, 441 *seqq.*; Pekař, I. 114-20.

[2] Irmer, *VS*, I. 144-7; *cf. AOSB*, II. 1. 765-6.

[3] Gaedeke, *op. cit.*, pp. 30-1; Irmer, *VS*, I. 83.

[4] Pekař, I. 195.

[5] As Srbik did (*Wallensteins Ende*, pp. 38, 69, 81, 208); and as the authors of *Sv. Krig*, V: 'Wallenstein's dominant idea was now [in October 1631] undoubtedly to launch positive negotiations for a general peace' (p. 397). This explanation does not seem to accord very well with their contention that between the fall of Prague and the Kaunitz meeting Wallenstein's interest in making contact with Arnim had cooled.

[6] Pekař's view.

[7] Pekař, I. 69.

ness that by this time the offer of the imperial command on his own terms was virtually certain. As long as he was isolated and unemployed, the goodwill of John George might be worth cultivating; once in the saddle, he needed it the less. The encouragement of Arnim to occupy Prague was the last turn of the screw upon the Emperor to ensure that the command, when it was offered, would be offered unconditionally. And the negotiations with Arnim after his reappointment may be viewed (at least to begin with) as a continuation of the familiar imperialist tactics of attempting to detach Saxony from the Protestant cause. But whatever Wallenstein's motives, from Gustav Adolf's point of view he was now an enemy, and an enemy whose honour was more than suspect. And with that enemy Sweden's most important ally was secretly negotiating.

John George was still burning with indignation at the treatment he had received at the Emperor's hands [1]; but he was very ready to think of peace, provided that his Swedish ally had no hand in settling it; and he was therefore the more accessible to such overtures as Wallenstein might have to make to him. Gustav Adolf's negotiations with Richelieu filled him with alarm, for he feared that they might lead to the bringing in of another foreign army into Germany: he hated the French with a most lively hatred.[2] It was difficult for Gustav Adolf and Oxenstierna to form an estimate of the political prospects at Dresden: pro-Swedish and anti-Swedish factions at court struggled with varying success for the ear of the Elector, and one result of their contentions was the 'tardy and preposterous' conduct of affairs.[3] The balance of parties was fairly even; and Wallenstein's attempt to tilt it in the Emperor's favour by sending Francis Albert of Saxe-Lauenburg to work upon John George (he arrived in January) led to no significant result.[4] On the whole, Oxenstierna was inclined to think that the Elector, despite his mulishness and surly egotism, was fundamentally honest and loyal.[5]

[1] *Lars Nilsson Tungels efterlämnade papper*, pp. 10-22.

[2] He remarked that: 'es sei Alles auf einem guten Wege gewesen, nun hätte der Teufel den hässliche Franzosen dazugeführt, der die Karten verwirren und das Spiel gar verderben würde': Irmer, *VS*, I. lviii; and *cf.* Arnim's similar view, *ibid.*, 83, 98.

[3] 'Allt går långsampt och *praepostere* till': Irmer, *VS*, I. 86.

[4] Pekař, I. 188-91; Irmer, *VS*, I. 100, 105.

[5] Oxenstierna wrote to the *råd*, 21 March 1632: 'But what the attitude of the Elector is, and what his intentions are, I cannot at the moment say. There are queer stories . . . the Elector himself is all right, but he is not used to the devastations and dangers of war, and is for that reason irresolute': *AOSB*, I. vii. 73.

He could not be so easy about Arnim. Arnim was now the soul of the anti-Swedish group, as Hoë von Hoënegg was of its opponents [1]; and he seems to have cherished an obscure animus against Gustav Adolf personally. Now that Tilly was beaten, he had reverted to his earlier predilection for a third party in Germany, and his aim was a general peace. His negotiations with Wallenstein were entered into partly with this end in view: they were continued, after he had ceased to believe in Wallenstein's honesty, as a means of staving off an imperialist attack. Fortunately for Swedish policy, Arnim's relations with his master were anything but harmonious. The lack of organization, the deficiencies of supply, the indecision and woolly-mindedness of the Elector, goaded Arnim to uncontrollable irritation: he attempted to lay down his command in December; in March he threatened resignation in a letter of brutal and blistering criticism.[2] He would have agreed wholeheartedly with the Swedish complaint that John George made war 'neither offensively nor defensively'.[3] His dissatisfaction was indeed so notorious as to foster in Gustav Adolf the delusion that he was anxious to return to the Swedish service.[4] In reality, he was among the most dangerous of Sweden's enemies. If he were to persuade the Elector, and if Wallenstein were to cajole the Emperor, to a separate peace for Saxony, the military and political consequences might well be ruinous. And that was in effect the ultimate objective at which he aimed.

Gustav Adolf did what he could to preserve John George's attachment to the alliance. He was scrupulously careful to keep him informed of his military and diplomatic moves; he gave him reiterated assurances of speedy and effective aid if he should need it; he even congratulated him upon the advance into Bohemia and urged him to press home his advantage—no doubt upon the principle that since the mistake had been made it would be well to make the best of it. The Elector did not reciprocate.[5] And the suspicion provoked by Arnim's subterranean manœuvres, by the visit of Francis Albert, and by the intrigues of Kristian IV, together with the constant fear of a military or political collapse in Saxony, distorted the King's plans, clouded his judgment, reacted disastrously upon

[1] Knapp, *Hoë von Hoënegg*, pp. 42-3.
[2] Irmer, *Arnim*, p. 157; *Briefe und Akten*, II. 261-4: *cf.* Irmer, *VS*, I. 147.
[3] Droysen, *Universalfrieden*, p. 250.
[4] *AOSB*, II. I. 765-6.
[5] Irmer, *VS*, I. 99-100; *Schriftstücke*, pp. 54-6.

necessary operations elsewhere, and ultimately compromised the whole of the campaign of 1632.

Nowhere were the ill effects of the Saxon situation felt more keenly than in the Lower Saxon Circle.[1]

In the autumn of 1631 the imperialists were in a weak position in this area. After Tilly had re-formed his army and marched away south to Franconia, there remained a bare 5000 men to defend the Circle against a Swedish attack. There was virtually no field-army: the troops were dispersed to garrison the strong places of the region, of which the most important were Wolfenbüttel, Minden, Hameln, Höxter and Osnabrück. There were some troops in Bremen and Verden also; and to the south-east a considerable garrison bivouacked in the ruins of Magdeburg.

It was not to be expected that these forces would be capable of real resistance once Gustav Adolf applied himself to their subjugation. Had he pursued Tilly after Breitenfeld, he might have saved himself many anxieties in the future; but in the autumn of 1631 he did not doubt that the Lower Saxon Circle would shortly fall into his hands. His plan was for Tott's army to cross the lower Elbe as soon as the conquest of Mecklenburg should be completed; while William of Hesse was to strike northwards from Cassel and Ziegenhain: the imperialists would thus be caught between two fires.[2] Banér meanwhile was to recapture Magdeburg and occupy the surrounding country [3]; and William of Weimar at Erfurt would be available to help him, if help should be required. Between them, these four commanders could bring an overwhelming superiority of force to bear, and upon every reasonable calculation the conquest of the Circle, once seriously undertaken, might seem to be assured.

Yet the plan failed; the opportunity was lost; and the result was disastrous. Tott, ailing, querulous, selfish and slow,[4] made heavy weather of his Mecklenburg campaign. The siege of Wismar held him up for longer than had been expected. It did not capitulate until 7 January; his army did not cross the Elbe until a fortnight

[1] For the position and operations in the Lower Saxon Circle, see *Sv. Krig*, V. 127-68; Boëthius, *NSK*, p. 284 *seqq.*

[2] *Arkiv*, I. 497-500; *Handlingar rörande Skandinaviens Historia*, XXV. 112-15.

[3] *Arkiv*, I. 517-18.

[4] As early as December 1630 his dilatoriness had drawn upon him a severe rebuke from Gustav Adolf: *Arkiv*, I. 271. Tott was sensitive about it: *AOSB*, II. IX. 702. Hamilton was commenting on Tott's ill-health as early as November 1631: Hist. MSS. Comm., *Hamilton*, p. 74.

later; and even then he was diverted from his main objective by the need to rescue John Frederick of Bremen—who had risen in revolt in November, and was not making much of a success of the enterprise—and by the fear of possible intervention by Denmark.[1] The Landgrave of Hesse, on his side of the country, made for a time excellent progress: in November he captured Münden, Volkmarsen, Paderborn, Höxter and Warburg. But he was checked in full career by Gustav Adolf's summons to join him on the Main; and when he obeyed the call and withdrew his forces, the imperialists recovered much of what they had lost.[2] Banér found the raising of an adequate army more difficult than had been expected; he felt unequal to a regular siege of Magdeburg; and to the irritation of Hamilton (who had been attached to his army, his own having mostly perished)[3] he contented himself with a lame and half-hearted blockade—the more readily since the King's orders strictly enjoined him to take no risks.[4]

Thus for one reason or another virtually no progress had been made in the liquidation of this pocket of imperialist resistance by the end of 1631. And by the end of 1631 the best moment had already passed. It was on 16 November that Pappenheim received the welcome order to detach himself from Tilly's melancholy withdrawal to the Danube and to repair to the Lower Saxon Circle.[5] About 20 December he arrived at Hameln[6]; and his coming transformed the situation. It brought to this theatre of operations a commander far superior in daring, imagination and resource to any of the generals whom he had to meet.[7] Pappenheim utilized to the full the advantages afforded him by his ability to operate on the inner lines, by his command of the rivers, by his possession of convenient strong-points behind which he could retreat when hard pressed. He made a virtue of the very smallness of his forces, darting swiftly from point to point, dealing nimble blows which his stolider adversaries were powerless to parry. He was indeed a born guerrilla leader, as well as a great cavalry commander; but apart from his

[1] For the Mecklenburg campaign, see *Sv. Krig*, V. 109-27; *Arkiv*, I. 523.

[2] Boëthius, *NSK*, p. 281.

[3] Hist. MSS. Comm., *Hamilton*, pp. 75-6; *Briefe und Akten*, I. 708 *seqq.*

[4] *Sv. Krig*, V. 135-7; *Arkiv*, I. 515, 517-18. Banér's operations were not helped by a hail of contradictory orders from the King, who was usually ignorant of the real state of affairs.

[5] *Briefe und Akten*, I. 635, 707; Dudík, p. 203; *Sv. Krig*, V. 144.

[6] Boëthius, *NSK*, p. 284; *Sv. Krig*, V. 146.

[7] This was Banér's apprenticeship as a commander: he would have been equal to Pappenheim later.

GUSTAV ADOLF

Winter 1631-2

(The King is wearing his 'Polish Coat': see p. 556)

WALLENSTEIN

gifts as a tactician he had also a remarkable insight into the strategic possibilities presented by the Lower Saxon Circle. He perceived that if once the Circle passed under Swedish control Gustav Adolf would be able to throw almost the whole weight of his armies against Bavaria; and it was this which emboldened him (apart from his desire for an independent command) to ignore or disobey repeated instructions from Maximilian and Wallenstein to return to central Germany.[1] As long as he could keep imperialist resistance alive in the north, he was tying up Swedish forces very greatly in excess of his own. Moreover, from his strongholds on the Weser he was in a position to hold out a hand to Denmark, or to Spain; he could threaten the Swedish garrisons in Mecklenburg; and above all he could menace the rear of the long Swedish front at its most sensitive spot—the region of Erfurt and the Thuringian passes. A thrust in this direction might well scare John George into clamouring for assistance. In Gustav Adolf's mind the north-west was now an area of secondary importance: Pappenheim was determined to force him to treat it as a major theatre of operations. For such a plan the means at his disposal seemed almost ludicrously inadequate; but the difficulty was to be met by rapidity of movement, by daring, by reliance upon the effect of surprise, and by inducing his enemy to believe that his army was twice as numerous as it really was.

Such was Pappenheim's programme; and it was carried out with the brilliance of a virtuoso. His first operation was typical. The imperialists in Magdeburg at this time numbered about 4000 men—far too many for the intrinsic importance of the place, but potentially an invaluable reinforcement to Pappenheim's field-army. He determined, therefore, to break through the Swedish blockade, bring off the garrison, and decamp. For this enterprise he had at his disposal some 3000 foot and 1500 horse: against him, Banér had an army of not less than 11,000, with the possibility of powerful reinforcements at no great distance. His only hope lay in frightening Banér away. He accordingly caused it to be put about that his army numbered somewhere between 10,000 and 20,000 [2]; and such was the difficulty of obtaining accurate and speedy information in seventeenth-century warfare that Banér was quite unable to satisfy himself that this figure was not correct. He was bound by the King's orders not to hazard his army, and above all to avoid an unequal

[1] Riezler, V. 431; Dudík, p. 337.
[2] See, *e.g.*, his letter to Maximilian, in Dudík, p. 300.

encounter; he knew that an attack was impending; and though Louis of Anhalt warned him that Pappenheim's numbers were greatly exaggerated, he felt unable to neglect the latest report of his agents, which credited the imperialists with a force of 10,000. After a brief period of wavering, he made off on 1 January, and retired ignominiously behind the Saale to Calbe, to the disgust of many of his colleagues and subordinates. Pappenheim entered Magdeburg in triumph on 4 January. He made no effort to pursue his enemy, nor did he tarry longer in Magdeburg than was necessary to devastate the surrounding countryside and collect any portable supplies. By 8 January he had quitted the city and was on his way back to Hameln.[1]

The Swedish reaction to this exploit was no less typical than the exploit itself. Banér had appealed frantically for assistance to the other commanders in the area. Tott and John George absolutely refused it; William of Weimar sent promises; but only the Landgrave, with characteristic loyalty, did anything effective, and improvised a diversion in the hope of drawing Pappenheim off.[2] As for Gustav Adolf, he had been disinclined at first to take the threat to Magdeburg seriously. At the new year he changed his mind; and a concentration of forces to deal with Pappenheim was ordered to rally to Vacha.[3] William V was dragged away once more from his successful local offensive to join the King's army. Before he arrived, the news of Pappenheim's withdrawal reached Gustav Adolf at Gelnhausen. Confident that the commanders on the spot could now be left to deal with the situation, he cancelled the order to the Landgrave, whose operations had thus been interrupted to no purpose.[4] And the sequel was equally unfortunate. Banér remained nervous of Pappenheim, and did not venture to pursue him until reinforced by William of Weimar: the number of men at their disposal now totalled about 14,000. Yet when it was reported to them that Pappenheim had withdrawn behind the Weser, they forthwith developed doubts as to whether they ought to venture after him.

[1] Wallenstein, misconceiving the situation, complained because Pappenheim had retired from Magdeburg, adding that Calbe was 'kein Posto', since the Saale was there scarcely knee-deep (*Briefe und Akten*, II. 9-10). For the Magdeburg affair, see *Arkiv*, II. 337-8; *AOSB*, I. VII. 11, 15; B. Steckzén, *Johan Baner*, p. 121 *seqq.*; G. Björling, *Johan Banér*, I. 261-99; *Sv. Krig*, V. 147-53. Hamilton complained to Charles I of 'the extreme timerusnes of G.B. . . . who tuys or 3 allredi heaith taken the alarme tou hott': Hist. MSS. Comm., *Hamilton*, p. 79.

[2] *Arkiv*, II. 337-8; *Schriftstücke*, p. 170.

[3] *Schriftstücke*, pp. 54-5.

[4] *Arkiv*, II. 352; *Dagbok*, p. 36; *Sv. Krig*, V. 159, 286-8.

While they were debating the point, Lars Grubbe arrived, on 21 January, bearing detailed orders from Gustav Adolf.[1] The Lower Saxon Circle was to be cleaned up without delay—significantly enough, because of the King's uneasiness as to the situation on the Saxon front—and precise instructions were given to cover a variety of eventualities. But nothing was done to secure a unified command; and the King's emphatic orders to Banér to keep a vigilant eye on Brandenburg and Saxony provided sufficient ground for him to devote less than all his attention to Pappenheim. Nevertheless, Grubbe induced Banér and Weimar to agree upon an offensive to the west; William V was ready to do his share; consultations between him and Banér upon a plan of combined operations were on the point of beginning; when on 28 January there arrived further orders from headquarters which wrecked the whole enterprise.[2] These orders were prompted by Gustav Adolf's fear of an imminent collapse in Saxony. To safeguard himself against the consequences that would follow such a collapse, and if possible to prevent it, he now ordered William of Weimar back to Erfurt, while Banér was to retire to Magdeburg: both were to hold themselves ready to rush to the aid of John George. Pappenheim, after all, was in retreat; Tott and William V ought between them to be able to cope with him; George of Lüneburg and John Frederick of Bremen, each with his small army, could give additional assistance. The Landgrave protested at these orders; but though they were slightly modified in consequence, their effect was not substantially changed. All idea of an immediate blow at Pappenheim was abandoned; and that general was encouraged to think that it was possible to twist the tail of the Swedish lion with impunity. And when, early in February, large portions of the armies of Banér and William of Weimar were ordered to Franconia to accompany the King in his drive against Tilly,[3] it seemed as though the idea of annihilating Pappenheim had been abandoned, at least for the moment, and that the limit of Swedish ambition was now simply to contain him.

Gustav Adolf's view of the importance of the fighting in the Lower Saxon Circle was quite clear. He regarded the whole affair, as far as he was concerned, as a mopping-up operation. He recognized that Pappenheim's object was to distract him from his

[1] *Arkiv*, II. 346.
[2] *Schriftstücke*, pp. 172-3, 214-16; *Sv. Krig*, V. 161-8.
[3] *Schriftstücke*, pp. 175, 216-21: the orders were received 18-20 February; they did not actually move till March: *ibid.*, p. 181.

campaign against Maximilian. He did not propose to permit himself to be distracted. If he could reach a decision on the Danube, the '*motus*' in the north-west would collapse of itself.[1] It was surely not too much to expect that the Swedish generals in the area should be able to master any forces that Pappenheim could bring against them. In the middle of February 1632 Pappenheim had perhaps 8000 men under his command. William of Weimar had 9000; Banér was soon able to detach 6000 for service with the main army and still leave a substantial force behind him; the Landgrave, Tott, Kagg, George of Lüneburg and John Frederick of Bremen had between them certainly not less than 30,000.[2]

Numbers, however, were not everything. Apart from the personal talents of Pappenheim himself, one main factor in the situation was the lack of any effective co-ordination of the Swedish armies. For this the King himself was partly responsible. It is true that he more than once indicated that the Landgrave was to be considered as the commander-in-chief[3]; but he seems in practice to have tacitly acquiesced in the refusal of Tott and the others to subordinate themselves. The despatch of Grubbe to the Lower Saxon Circle on 6 February initiated a disastrous policy of trying to co-ordinate the efforts of the various generals by means of a civilian who was the King's personal representative.[4] The sequel was to show that neither Grubbe, nor Salvius, nor Erik Andersson Trana, was able to assert an effective authority over the arrogant, undisciplined and mutually jealous commanders.[5] If Gustav Adolf had sent Oxenstierna to Thuringia, as for a moment he thought of doing,[6] the chancellor might have been able to do what they could not do; but Oxenstierna's services were needed elsewhere, and the plan was abandoned. Moreover, the prospects of success were clouded by the King's habit of giving positive orders to his commanders when he was himself at a great distance from the scene of operations. Since they would not take proper measures themselves, he was driven to try to direct operations from Nuremberg or Munich, with results as unhappy upon occasion as in the case of Napoleon's interference in the campaigns in Spain. Regarding the

1 *Schriftstücke*, pp. 220-1.
2 *Sv. Krig*, V. 167-8.
3 *ibid.*, 125, 142-3; *Arkiv*, I. 530 *seqq.*, II. 389.
4 *Schriftstücke*, pp. 216-21.
5 The Landgrave was an honourable exception. As he once complained, he went to everybody's assistance, but nobody came to his: Rommel, VIII. 191.
6 *AOSB*, I. vii. 16; Ahnlund, *Oxenstierna*, p. 656.

Lower Saxon Circle as he did as a purely subordinate theatre, he did not hesitate suddenly to withdraw detachments of troops to his own army; and this too sometimes had unfortunate local consequences. The effect of these measures, or lack of measures, was that Pappenheim, so far from being contained, had the initiative almost permanently in his hands. The constant fear of disaster on the Saxon front influenced Gustav Adolf's judgment of the extent to which the generals should commit themselves in the Circle; and it helped to encourage in them a fatal cautiousness and passivity. Above all, the failure to annihilate Pappenheim exposed the whole Swedish system in Germany to danger at its weakest point. It is true that the Thirty Years' War was waged (particularly in the later stages of it) with a minimal concern for lines of communication; but it is true, too, that Gustav Adolf could not risk an enemy occupation of the main route home from central Germany to the Baltic—that which lay through the Thuringian passes. This route was already imperilled by the uncertain position in Bohemia: it was essential that it should not also be exposed to attack from the north-west. But the licence allowed to Pappenheim did so expose it; and it became a fragile bottleneck of increasing slenderness. Gustav Adolf saw the importance of this region plainly enough: in a letter to William of Weimar on 2 February he correctly pointed out that 'the Elbe, the Saale and the Mulde' were the bases upon which his campaign to south Germany must repose.[1] It is easy to see that he miscalculated as to the Lower Saxon Circle. But it was certainly a task of no ordinary difficulty to establish a correct order of priority for the claims which the various fronts made upon his resources of man-power. He could not commit himself to the Danubian campaign without taking troops from the armies arrayed against Pappenheim; he could not tell Tott to ignore the threat from Denmark; he could not allow the Spaniards a free hand on the Rhine and the Moselle; he dared not hazard anything on the continued resistance of the Saxons. Neither Gustav Adolf, nor any other commander, could in the circumstances of the time exercise an effective supervision and control of all these theatres of war; he could not inject his own spirit of enterprise and boldness into second-rate generals operating at a distance; and he failed even to ensure that they should work together in harmony. As it turned out, the best chance of crushing Pappenheim was lost in January; for then the competing claims of

[1] *Schriftstücke*, p. 175.

other fronts were less urgent than they were ever to be again. But how much better if the Lower Saxon Circle had after Breitenfeld been brought so solidly under Swedish control that no imperialist revival there would have been possible! In the event, Gustav Adolf set out for the south with the uncomfortable feeling that at any moment a crisis might blow up behind him; and the campaign of 1632 was hamstrung from the start by his anxiety for the Saxon front and for the Lower Saxon Circle. Steinberg hit the nail on the head when he wrote: 'as long as the King fails to purge the Weser and the Lower Saxon Circle, he makes but a gouty march of it'.[1]

(ii) *The Conquest of Bavaria*

The new campaign started with two main objectives. The first was to catch Tilly and beat him. The second was to establish a foothold in south Germany firm enough to ensure that a victory in the field should not prove ephemeral. The campaign was to be waged offensively, in that emancipated spirit of enterprise which had marked the King's operations since Breitenfeld; and his especial anxiety to be strong in cavalry was indication enough that he looked forward to swift movements and decisive engagements. Yet at the same time the policy of careful consolidation was not abandoned: as once he had 'conjoined Main and Rhine', so he intended to conjoin Rhine and Danube. Swabia was to be the new, the final, base area in the south, whose still-untapped resources would supply the wherewithal for a protracted effort. If things went ill, and the year closed without the victory for which he was hoping, the Swabian base would be the springboard from which the final campaign of 1633 might be launched. Thus, though the plan of operations reflected the increased confidence and vigour of the King's strategy, it revealed, too, that the fundamentals had not changed: the finale, after all, was designed only to be a variation, *vivacissimo*, upon a theme already familiar.[2]

The moment at which the offensive should be launched was not easy to determine. On the one hand, Gustav Adolf was concerned to collect the largest possible armies: commanders during the winter were warned not to waste men on enterprises of minor importance, and were reminded that their main object must be not to win battles

[1] Kretzschmar, *Der Heilbronner Bund*, I. 23.
[2] Tingsten, *Gustav Adolfs basering*, p. 326; Petri, II. 153; *Sv. Krig*, V. 292.

but to complete their quota of recruits.[1] From this point of view he would have wished to defer operations until his armies had been brought to the strength he had planned for them. But, on the other hand, he could not forget that Wallenstein, in the seclusion of the Bohemian quadrilateral, was similarly engaged in raising troops. It must be a matter of conjecture how long it would take him to put an effective army in the field; but that such an army would eventually intervene was certain, and it was likely to be a formidable force. It was thus important to beat Tilly quickly, before Wallenstein was ready to help him. It is impossible to say how Gustav Adolf would have resolved this dilemma; for, in the event, the decision was to some extent taken out of his hands. Tilly's operations pricked him into action at a time when he would certainly have preferred to lie quiet a little longer. When the advance began, he was still 90,000 men short of his estimates. The campaign of 1632 may almost be said to have gone off at half-cock.

That this was so is to be attributed to the indiscretion of Gustav Horn. Horn was among the very best of Gustav Adolf's generals, 'beloved of all men, very wise and silent',[2] the saviour of the day at Breitenfeld, and much more than the perfect subordinate that Monro thought him. He had been left behind at the post of danger in Franconia when Gustav Adolf moved on to Frankfort in November, and had been mildly astonished to find himself unmolested by Tilly.[3] Astonished, but perhaps encouraged; for he spent his winter in vigorously extending the area under his control. He paid less attention than he ought to have done to the armistice with the League: his attack on Hochstädt on 20 January was a clear violation of its terms; and he followed this up by the capture of Bamberg on 1 February. Gustav Adolf heard of these proceedings with misgivings, and indeed with disapproval: he warned Horn against provoking the enemy to attack; and reminded him that he—like Banér and William of Weimar—must keep himself free to send help to John George in the event of a crisis in Saxony.[4] To all this Horn paid not much attention; and in any case the warnings came too late. For Maximilian had reacted vigorously to the loss of Hochstädt and Bamberg. He feared for his garrison in Forchheim; he feared lest a Swedish advance into the Upper Palatinate, in the general direction of Nuremberg and Bayreuth, might cut off Wallenstein's

[1] Sörensson, *Ekonomi och krigföring*, p. 316.
[2] Monro, II. 143.
[3] *Arkiv*, II. 339-40.
[4] *Sv. Krig*, V. 283.

armies from the main theatre of war in Germany. Early in February Tilly was ordered to gather troops for a blow at Horn; Wallenstein was asked to send reinforcements, or at least to make a diversion towards Eger [1]; and on 13 February Tilly broke up from Nördlingen with 13,500 foot and 4500 horse. Wallenstein could spare no more than another 1000; but Gallas duly mounted the diversion, and had the Saxons entertained any notion of coming to Horn's assistance (which of course they did not), this would no doubt have been sufficient to deter them.[2] Against Tilly's advancing army Horn had only 8000 men at his disposal; and the fortifications of Bamberg were so decayed that not all his efforts since its capture had sufficed to make the place defensible against resolute attack.

On 28 February Tilly appeared before Bamberg. Though Horn had received warning of his approach, he allowed himself to be taken by surprise; and through a misunderstanding of his orders his troops engaged the enemy instead of withdrawing within the defences. They were routed; and in the resulting confusion the town was lost, the Swedes sustaining heavy casualties. Horn made an able retreat—to Hassfurt first, and then to Schweinfurt—but the affair was not one upon which he could look back with much satisfaction.[3]

The reverse at Bamberg was of no great consequence in a military point of view, for Tilly could hardly venture to push his advantage very far with the forces at his command; but it was felt as a sharp blow to Swedish prestige: Gustav Adolf considered it advisable to address a circular letter to the leading Protestant cities on 4 March in which he minimized his defeat and promised speedy retribution.[4] He had himself underestimated the danger to Bamberg until too late [5]; but he hoped to make good his error. Immediately after receipt of the news of Horn's defeat he took vigorous counter-measures. If Tilly lingered on the Main, it might be possible to crush him by a swift concentration of force before he realized his danger. William of Weimar and Banér were accordingly ordered to move at once on Würzburg [6]; the campaign in the Rhineland was

[1] *Briefe und Akten*, II. 179-80, 205, 216, 225; Dudík, *Waldsteins Correspondenz*, I. 26-7.

[2] *Briefe und Akten*, II. 211-13.

[3] *Arkiv*, II. 369-71, 371-6, 376-8; *Briefe und Akten*, II. 253; Chemnitz, I. 299-300.

[4] *Schriftstücke*, pp. 224-6.

[5] *AOSB*, I. VII. 29.

[6] *Schriftstücke*, pp. 178, 180-1; Huschke, *Wilhelm von Weimar*, pp. 39-40; *Sv. Krig*, V. 496-9.

broken off; and Gustav Adolf, leaving Oxenstierna in command of 10,000 men to guard Mainz, set out with an army of 13,000 in pursuit of the enemy. He failed to catch him; for Tilly, prompted by his own good sense, as well as by urgent orders of recall from Maximilian, withdrew in time to the south, and with his victorious army took the road for Ingolstadt.[1]

It was now for Gustav Adolf to decide whether Bamberg was to be regarded only as an episode, unsatisfactorily closed, or whether to treat it as the opening of the new campaign. He had certainly not intended serious operations so soon. The concentration at Würzburg had not occurred as planned: neither Weimar nor Banér could conform to the King's time-table. He lacked, therefore, the crushing superiority upon which he had counted. Moreover, Tilly had got the start of him. But Tilly might still be caught and brought to battle; and after 9 March (when Horn rejoined him at Kitzingen) the King had a marked advantage in cavalry. He believed, moreover, that a move to the Danube might serve as a diversion to draw Pappenheim from the Lower Saxon Circle: he was not the only commander to cherish this delusion.[2] After weighing all these considerations, he came to the conclusion that the chance of a battle was not to be missed. On 12 March he set out from Kitzingen, without waiting for Banér and Weimar. The campaign was thus launched as something of an improvisation: the attack on Bavaria had been started as it were by accident.

The prospect of catching Tilly north of the Danube soon vanished: the field-marshal had too long a lead. It made no difference to the military situation, therefore, that Gustav Adolf should have taken the opportunity to pay his first visit to Nuremberg. On 21 March he made a brilliant entry into the city. The burghers presented him with 'two silver Globes, one *Coelestiall*, the other *Terrestiall*: there were also . . . drinking *Credences* many, with some Antiquities that were rare'.[3] Gustav Adolf returned thanks in an impromptu speech of characteristic fluency and eloquence [4]; and at dinner that day his conversation was conducted in such loud tones that everyone in the hall could hear him—a delicate attention which gave great satisfaction

[1] Maximilian at first wished him to fall back on Bohemia, and so draw off Gustav Adolf from Bavaria; but Tilly dissuaded him: Chemnitz, I. 304; but *cf.* Dudík, *Waldsteins Correspondenz*, I. 51.

[2] *AOSB*, II. I. 768.

[3] Monro, II. III.

[4] Chemnitz, I. 305-6.

to the guests.[1] Of more immediate importance was the agreement concluded at the same time, which in effect gave him 2000 men for his army and 20,000 *rdr.* a month for his war-chest.[2] The visit to Nuremberg, indeed, so far from being a waste of time, was expedient on political and even on military grounds. By binding the city to him more firmly than before, he assured himself of a great munitions centre and a strong-point half-way between the Danube and the Main.[3] And the financial contribution was of real importance: in a year when the resources of Germany were to be strained to the uttermost to provide for Gustav Adolf's massive armies he could not afford to overlook the wealth of the great cities. This was a consideration which does much to explain the attention which he later paid to Augsburg and Munich.

The Swedish march was directed, not to Ingolstadt nor to Regensburg, but to Donauwörth. The route to Regensburg was perhaps rejected as lying too open to interference from Wallenstein; though it might have been expected that Gustav Adolf, since his declared object was battle, would have taken care to follow in Tilly's tracks. But the Danube crossing by this route was barred by the first-class modern fortress of Ingolstadt; and there seemed little chance that Tilly could be brought to action before he reached the security of its walls. And since Tilly had for the moment got away, the other half of Gustav Adolf's strategy must come into play. The route by Donauwörth, less formidably defended than that by Ingolstadt, crossed the Danube to the west of the point where it was joined by the Lech: it gave immediate access, therefore, to the projected Swabian base, that 'triangle bounded by the Lech, the Alps and the Danube' which the King had already destined to be the focus of his power in south Germany. As early as 16 March he had written to Oxenstierna that if he failed to force an engagement on Tilly he intended, after crossing the Danube, to make for Ulm.[4] From the beginning of the campaign, it is clear, Gustav Adolf swung freely between the two objectives of his strategy. If there were a chance of battle, he would take it; if the chance should not present

[1] Donaubauer, pp. 136-8.

[2] *Sverges traktater*, V. 745-8; Chemnitz, I. 307.

[3] For imperialist views of Nuremberg, see *Briefe und Akten*, II. 271-2. Tingsten's censure of the visit as a waste of precious time seems unjustified: it was already clear that he could hardly hope to catch Tilly: Tingsten, *Gustav II Adolfs politik och krigföring*, p. 129.

[4] *AOSB*, II. I. 768, and *cf. ibid.*, 775; I. VII. 73. Contrast Tingsten, *op. cit.*, p. 122, where he suggests that Gustav Adolf should have made for Regensburg.

itself, he would apply himself to elucidating the properties of his triangle.

It was before Donauwörth, therefore, that he made his appearance on 26 March. On that day Tilly was meeting Maximilian at Ingolstadt. The result of their deliberations was a determination to save Donauwörth if they could. But time, distance and the Swedish fury were against them. By 27 March the imperialist garrison of Donauwörth had decamped, and the Swedes were in the city; on the 28th Gustav Adolf's troops were across the Danube; on the 29th the arrival of the contingents of William of Weimar and Banér gave him a striking force of 22,500 infantry and 15,000 cavalry. Against this Maximilian and Tilly could put barely 22,000 men into the field.[1]

The merit of the capture of Donauwörth lay mainly with the Swedish artillery, commanded on this occasion by the greatest gunner of the age, Lennart Torstensson; and when the effect of its concentric fire was reinforced by a threat to cut off the way of escape over the river, the garrison—4000 men under Rudolf Maximilian of Saxe-Lauenburg—withdrew under cover of darkness. The Swedes entering the town cut down all found with arms, and many also who had none; orders to spare the citizens of this Protestant city were disobeyed; 'the Towne . . . was spoyled and quite plundered'; and 'the Iesuites and Monkes, that had escaped alongst the Bridge, being sent after were overtaken, and the most part cut off'.[2] Immediately afterwards, Gustav Adolf sent forces to secure the line of the river as far as Ulm; and so, before turning against Tilly, began the occupation of the triangle's apex. In this operation, as in the treatment of Donauwörth, the growing indiscipline of his armies began to appear, 'the *Swedens* . . . making great booty over all, where ever they came hanging the Papists by their purse, not sparing to torment their shinnes, as they [*sc.* the imperialists] did in *Pomeren* and in the Markes of *Brandenburg* to the Protestants, in exacting their monie, which they were made to repay againe, *Lege Talionis*'.[3] And the day was not distant when private enterprise in retaliation would receive official blessing.

The sudden irruption of the Swedish armies into the lands south of the Danube produced gloom and consternation in Bavaria. Maximilian sent urgent appeals to Wallenstein for aid; and predicted

[1] Huschke, p. 43; O. Norrman, *Övergången av Donau och Lech*, pp. 281-3.

[2] Monro, II. 114; contrast Chemnitz's glossing-over of these events: I. 309; a good account of the operations in *Dagbok*, pp. 38-40.

[3] Monro, II. 116.

that if it were not forthcoming, 'the Danube would go the way of the Rhine'.[1] But he was determined, while he waited an answer to these entreaties, to keep the enemy out of his electorate if he could. The western boundary of Bavaria was formed by the river Lech; and behind the Lech, between Rain and Augsburg, Maximilian and Tilly disposed their forces and stood to receive the Swedish attack.[2] Their position appeared a strong one. Through the broad flat valley, intersected with minor watercourses, the main stream of the Lech flowed swift, deep and turbulent from melting snows, northwards to its confluence with the Danube. All bridges had been broken, all boats removed from the river. The eastern bank, where Maximilian was posted, commanded the western; and thick woodlands screened the movements of the Bavarian army. By all contemporary canons of warfare the forcing of such an obstacle was impossible, and the attempting of it culpably rash. At a council of war held at Nordheim on 2 April most of the Swedish generals advised against the attempt, and dwelt upon the disastrous consequences of failure. But times had changed since Neu-Brandenburg. Gustav Adolf had tackled this kind of problem before, at Oppenheim; he correctly surmised that a considerable portion of Tilly's force consisted of raw recruits [3]; he had confidence in his own talent for improvisation; and he had confidence in his army. He rejected the advice of his generals, and decided to force the Lech. Two careful reconnaissances in person—in the course of the second of them he went so far forward as to be able to exchange badinage with Tilly's sentries [4]—informed him of the nature of the ground. Two days' incessant labour by army carpenters upon the house-timbers of the hamlet of Oberndorff produced a floating bridge so fashioned that its causeway lay almost flush with the surface of the water, and was thus the less vulnerable to gunfire. A massive barrage and a great show of force misled the enemy as to the point of attack, while the powder-smoke, made denser by the burning of damp straw, concealed the real preparations. On 5 April the lodgment on the further bank was effected; and when Tilly, too late aware of the real danger, tried to throw the Swedes back into the river, the stream of reinforcements over the floating

[1] *Briefe und Akten*, II. 328; Dudík, *Waldsteins Correspondenz*, II. 8, 22, 26, 27.

[2] For the passage of the Lech, see Norrman, *op. cit.*, pp. 283-6; Monro, II. 118; Hammarskiöld, *USAH*, p. 173 *seqq.*; Generalstaben, *Gustaf II Adolf*, pp. 344-6; *Sv. Krig*, Supp. Vol. II. 260; Krigsvetenskaps Akademiens Handlingar (1932), p. 68 *note* 2; Tingsten, *op. cit.*, p. 129.

[3] Riezler, V. 408.

[4] *Arkiv*, I. 781.

causeway enabled the bridgehead to hold firm until cavalry detachments, sent across the river above and below the crossing-point, converged inwards upon Tilly's flanks and forced him to withdraw. Aldringen had early been hit by a cannon-ball and forced to leave the field; and soon afterwards Tilly himself was severely wounded. The casualties in the Bavarian army had been heavy, not least from the flying splinters struck from the trees by the Swedish cannonade. By the morning of 6 April the whole Swedish army stood on Bavarian soil, Maximilian was leading his beaten troops back to Ingolstadt, and Gustav Adolf had won one of his most remarkable victories.

None, certainly, made a deeper impression upon contemporaries.[1] He had been helped, no doubt, by Tilly's mistakes; for the Bavarian position (as Clausewitz pointed out, and as Monro also saw)[2] was too close to the Lech: instead of defending the river with his army, he fell into the error of trying to defend his army with the river. Still, as a feat of arms the Lech was magnificent. But it was not the decisive victory the King was seeking. Bavaria indeed lay open to him; but the plunder of Bavaria, however useful, was not a main objective. The main objective had been the destruction of the Bavarian army; and this had by no means been achieved. The Emperor's ambassador at Rome might cry 'The curtain has fallen; all is over'[3]; but he was mistaken. The curtain was in fact just rising on the complex second act; and Urban VIII, if he had but known it, had no need for the present to alarm himself. A Gothic invasion of Italy was not in prospect, save in the haunted imaginations of Richelieu and his brethren in the Sacred College.[4]

While the Bavarian army, having recrossed the Danube, was making its way to Ingolstadt; while the aged Tilly fought his last long battle (he died in Ingolstadt on the 20th)[5]; Gustav Adolf

[1] When notifying George William of the victory, Gustav Adolf characteristically improved the occasion to press for more punctual payment of the Elector's monthly contribution: *Schriftstücke*, pp. 158-60.

[2] Clausewitz, p. 77; Monro, II. 118-19: 'But had Generall *Tilly* drawne up his Army out of reach of his Majesties Cannon, and resolved to suffer his Majesty to have set over his Army, the passe being so narrow, that scarce three men could march in Front, *Tillies* advantage had bin the greater to receive them as they came, who might have cut them off by divisions, which had bin more to his credit.'

[3] Droysen, *Gustaf Adolf*, II. 539.

[4] Leman, *Urbain VIII*, pp. 181-94, for Urban's alarms and Richelieu's intrigues.

[5] At Tilly's request Gustav Adolf sent a famous Ansbach surgeon to attend him: *AOSB*, II. IX. 741. Priorato, who was with Wallenstein at the time, narrates that at the news of Tilly's death 'à la cour de Walstein on étoit plus gai que triste': Priorato, p. 135.

consolidated his position on the Lech, which had now become the eastern fosse of his projected Swabian base. His immediate objective was Augsburg, the greatest and richest city of south Germany. For a pious Lutheran Augsburg had a strong sentimental appeal; for a strategist it had considerable importance; for an army paymaster it was irresistible. The population was predominantly Protestant; but Maximilian, in response to warnings from Wallenstein, had recently forced the burghers to admit a Bavarian garrison, 5000 strong; and though he remained pessimistic about the possibility of any prolonged resistance,[1] Augsburg was from the Swedish point of view a city in enemy hands. When Gustav Adolf arrived before its walls on 9 April, therefore, the guns opened fire upon the defences; and it was only the King's desire to spare the Protestant inhabitants (and to obtain possession of the town intact) which prevented a more serious cannonade.[2] The citizens sent out to parley; were reproached by Gustav Adolf for admitting the enemy, exhorted to extrude them, and professed their inability to do so; and on the 10th, these formalities being discharged, the basis of an agreement was reached whereby the garrison was allowed to leave the town and march off to Ingolstadt. On the 11th the King addressed the city's representatives in terms designed to be a tonic to their morale, which he evidently considered somewhat flaccid; and on the 14th he made his ceremonial entry.[3] The citizens appeared overjoyed; and at a festal *Te Deum* in St. Ann's church there was not a dry eye in the congregation.[4] The terms imposed upon the city, however, effectively precluded any protracted orgy of sentiment. They were to contribute 20,000 *rdr.* a month to the Swedish army, to accept a Swedish governor, and to take an exceptionally stringent oath of loyalty to the Swedish crown.[5] The oath shocked foreign opinion [6]; and though Gustav Adolf assured them, and the burghers subsequently asserted, that it did not affect their status as immediate vassals of the Emperor, it is to be explained only on the ground that Augsburg was considered to be a captured city. Moreover, the citizens were

[1] *Briefe und Akten*, II. 126, 287, 328; Dudík, pp. 306-7, 310, 351; *id.*, *Waldsteins Correspondenz*, I. 41, 56-7.

[2] *Briefe und Akten*, II. 348 *seqq.*

[3] For all this, see *Dagbok*, pp. 41-7; Chemnitz, I. 313-15; *Die Chronik des Jakob Wagner*, pp. 2-10; Droysen, *Gustaf Adolf*, II. 540-8.

[4] *AOSB*, II. IX. 741; Loenbom, I. 38. John George was sufficiently moved to order festal *Te Deums* too: Chemnitz, I. 315.

[5] *Sverges traktater*, V. 749-54.

[6] Söltl, III. 326; Droysen, II. 545 *note*; Boëthius, *NSK*, p. 362.

saddled with a comprehensive (and costly) scheme of refortification designed to turn Augsburg into a major stronghold of the most modern type. The new works were put in hand at once; trees were cut down and buildings razed—including even a church; and soon a labour force of 3000 men was working to the direction of Frans de Traytorrens.[1] The governor, Bengt Oxenstierna, proved rough and exacting.[2] The Roman Catholics, indeed, escaped more lightly than they had expected: though deprived of municipal offices, they otherwise enjoyed toleration, for Gustav Adolf was careful to observe the terms of Bärwalde. But the Lutheran citizens found a Swedish protectorate too astringent to be comfortable.

Having thus secured the Lech, Gustav Adolf turned towards Bavaria. His plan was to deny the crossing at Ingolstadt to the enemy, and to master the south bank of the Danube from Ingolstadt to Regensburg. Maximilian would thus be kept north of the river, shut out of his duchy; Wallenstein's intervention would be made more difficult; and the conquest of Bavaria could proceed without much interference. Or, if conquest proved impracticable, Bavaria 'could at least be devastated'.[3] The devastation had in fact already begun; and it continued, with ever-increasing ferocity, for so long as Gustav Adolf remained on Bavarian soil. Swedish sources speak of soldiers encumbered with a glut of booty, and of fields strewn with slaughtered peasants; Maximilian wrote in horror and despair of the fate of his country, and appealed to the French to use their influence to help him.[4] In vain: for the harrying was Gustav Adolf's deliberate policy. Its main purpose was the destruction of the hitherto untouched resources of the enemy's country, so that the area immediately to the east of his triangle should be incapable of sustaining a hostile army; but it is also clear that there was an appreciable admixture of the spirit of revenge. The sufferings of the Protestant north were to be repaid in kind; and Gustav Adolf's new armies were for once encouraged to emulate the worst excesses of Wallenstein's professionals. Retaliation bred retaliation: in October Maximilian was to order Pappenheim to do his worst in the lands of William of Weimar, in requital for William's conduct in Bavaria.[5]

On 19 April Gustav Adolf arrived before Ingolstadt. Maximilian had been lavishing money on the fortifications of Ingolstadt since

[1] Wagner, pp. 22-3.
[2] S. Hedin, *Resare-Bengt*, pp. 487-90.
[3] *AOSB*, II. I. 777-8.
[4] *Arkiv*, I. 780-1; *Briefe und Akten*, II. 349, 366, 415; Riezler V. 420-2.
[5] Huschke, p. 81.

the beginning of his reign,[1] and by 1632 it had become a formidable example of the most modern Italian methods of military architecture. It lay on the north bank of the Danube, with strong outworks—not quite finished—to the south of the river. Inside it was Maximilian himself, gloomily awaiting news of help from Wallenstein, and listening to the urgent advice of the dying Tilly to defend Ingolstadt and Regensburg at all hazards.[2] The Elector had his whole army with him; and with such strength to defend it Ingolstadt seemed impregnable. It was at least certain that it could not, like Frankfurt-on-Oder, be taken by a sudden attack. Gustav Adolf, in fact, intended no such thing. If he could prevent Maximilian from using the river-crossing, if he could pin him down in Ingolstadt, he might hope to take Regensburg before help could reach it. It was this calculation which prompted the violent Swedish cannonades of 19 and 20 April, in the course of which Gustav Adolf twice narrowly escaped with his life. But the calculations went astray; for on 21 April Maximilian moved out with the bulk of his forces and marched for Regensburg, leaving a strong garrison of 7000 regulars and 3500 militia behind him. The storm of one of the southern bastions, successfully carried out on the same day, was therefore a pointless gesture and a waste of Swedish lives.[3] And the hope of taking Regensburg soon vanished; for on 17 April the Bavarian garrison had overpowered the burghers. Maximilian was not confident about the town's ability to resist[4]; but a reconnaissance led by Horn returned with a discouraging report. The Ingolstadt-Regensburg operation had thus failed; and Gustav Adolf fell back on his alternative plan. For the moment he would advance no further, but would destroy or exploit the resources of Bavaria and seize the line of the Isar as a forward defence for the Lech.[5]

In the course of the demonstration against Ingolstadt there had arrived in the Swedish camp the French ambassador to Bavaria, St. Etienne; and in the intervals of Gustav Adolf's venturesome reconnaissances St. Etienne had had an interview with the King which cast a sharp light on the nature of Franco-Swedish relations. St. Etienne's purpose was to negotiate a peace between Sweden and

[1] Riezler, V. 410; *cf.* Priorato, p. 129.
[2] Riezler, V. 411.
[3] For Ingolstadt, see *Sv. Krig*, VI. 17-26; Monro, II. 120-2; *Dagbok*, p. 48; Wagner, p. 14. Gustav Adolf's horse was shot under him. As he picked himself up, covered with dust and blood, he is said to have remarked, 'The fruit is not yet ripe': Wahlström, p. 76.
[4] *Briefe und Akten*, II. 387.
[5] *Arkiv*, II. 427 *seqq.*

Bavaria. He seems to have acted entirely on his own initiative: Maximilian later denied any previous knowledge of his mission,[1] and his own government had not accredited him to Gustav Adolf. His action was no doubt in accordance with the spirit of Richelieu's policy; but it was vitiated from the start by St. Etienne's own incompetence.[2] He began the audience inauspiciously by trying to convince Gustav Adolf that Maximilian had not authorized, and had disapproved, Tilly's attack on Bamberg. It was easy to disprove this from intercepted letters; and when St. Etienne persisted, the King closed the discussion of the point with a cold '*je vous pardonne vostre ignorance*'. The ambassador then passed to a eulogy of Maximilian's private character which provoked the somewhat unworthy reply that no doubt even the louse was not devoid of the domestic virtues. St. Etienne, unabashed, permitted himself to address the King in a style which was resented as unduly familiar: he was magisterially rebuked, and informed that his mission was 'an impertinence and a French *légèreté*'. At this point he found it expedient to apologize. He then proceeded to importune the King to define the terms upon which he would be prepared to grant peace to Bavaria. Gustav Adolf, who can hardly have expected to be called upon to formulate conditions of peace on the spur of the moment, for some time refused; but at last, upon the ambassador's repeated solicitations, he told him that he would require the immediate disbandment of the Bavarian army, and a pledge by Maximilian not to engage in hostilities against Sweden for the next three years—or, alternatively, the handing over of the Danube crossing at Ingolstadt. Failing acceptance of one of these alternatives, he would 'harry Bavaria from end to end'. At this St. Etienne protested; and from protests proceeded to threats of French displeasure. Gustav Adolf retorted angrily that the feelings of France were a matter of the most perfect indifference to him: for all he cared, Louis XIII might send an army of 40,000 to Maximilian's assistance. St. Etienne retired, overwhelmed with royal objurgations, and mocked (we are told) by the very Frenchmen of his entourage; as he well deserved to be, for it would have been difficult to execute a task, in itself delicate and unhopeful, in a more tactless and blundering manner. He saved his self-esteem, at the expense of his veracity, by informing Maxi-

[1] *Briefe und Akten*, II. 413.

[2] For this episode, see *Briefe und Akten*, II. 372-3, 404-7; *Arkiv*, I. 431-2, 784; Fagniez, I. 591; Hanotaux, III. 431-2.

milian that Gustav Adolf was prepared to open negotiations upon certain conditions, and had empowered him to act as mediator. Maximilian's private comment to the Emperor was that if he did negotiate it would be simply in order to gain time—which was exactly what Gustav Adolf had suspected to be the purpose of St. Etienne's visit.[1]

The failure at Ingolstadt was in some ways the critical moment of the campaign of 1632. Gustav Adolf had supposed that the defeat of Tilly would be followed by the diversion of large portions of Wallenstein's army to reinforce the threatened front on the Danube. Even after Ingolstadt, he expected that as many as 15,000 men might be sent from Bohemia for this purpose.[2] His calculations were sound. Wallenstein was gravely concerned at the situation in Bavaria: he wrote to Colloredo on 20 April that Passau must be held at all costs, and that if Gustav Adolf's advance continued he would be forced to quit Bohemia.[3] At the moment of the demonstration against Ingolstadt, in fact, Gustav Adolf was still in the possession of the initiative; and if he had pushed on to attack Regensburg he might well have retained it. Despite the intelligence that reached him, Regensburg might have fallen to a swift attack; and even if it had held out, his advance would have distracted Wallenstein's attention from the Saxons. It would no doubt have been risky to leave the powerful garrison of Ingolstadt free to operate behind him; but it is possible that the risk was worth taking. For, as it proved, the failure to divert Wallenstein meant the failure of the campaign; the initiative passed to Wallenstein's hands; and henceforward, for some time to come, it was Wallenstein who imposed his will on Gustav Adolf.

This soon became apparent. From Ingolstadt Gustav Adolf turned south-east to the valley of the Isar. On 26 April he occupied Moosburg; and soon afterwards Horn took Landshut.[4] The King's intention was to move up the Isar and occupy Munich. But at Moosburg he received news which halted his advance and forced him to reconsider his position. The news concerned the situation in Saxony; and it was gravely disquieting.

For some time Lars Nilsson Tungel, the Swedish resident in

[1] *Briefe und Akten*, II. 413-15.
[2] *Sv. Krig*, VI. 35.
[3] *Briefe und Akten*, II. 362-3; and *cf. ibid.*, 377, 387; Dudík, *Waldsteins Correspondenz*, II. 40-1, 48.
[4] *AOSB*, II. VIII. 56.

Dresden, had been subjected to importunities from the Saxons, who complained that they were being left without aid from their ally to face the danger of a double attack from Wallenstein and Pappenheim.[1] The complaint was not unreasonable. It was clear that Wallenstein could drive Arnim out of Bohemia as soon as he felt ready to begin; Pappenheim's victory over the Hessians at Höxter on 14 March, and the obvious inability of the Swedish generals in the Lower Saxon Circle to contain him, made an attack on the Elbe from that side at least a possibility; while the withdrawal of Banér's and Weimar's armies to Bavaria meant that the Thuringian bottleneck was denuded of troops and John George deprived of the prospect of swift and effective assistance. Tungel's reports of Saxon dissatisfaction had already led Gustav Adolf to write to John George from Ingolstadt on 24 April.[2] He had reminded the Elector of his care for Saxony's safety in the foregoing months, had suggested that the Bavarian campaign would shortly relieve the danger to the electorate, and had urged an offensive in Bohemia. Two days later this letter was supplemented by the despatch of Grubbe once more to the Lower Saxon Circle, in the hope that he might be able to ensure that aid for John George should be available from that quarter if he should need it.[3]

Meanwhile Tungel had been reinforced in Dresden. Towards the end of March Philip Reinhard von Solms was instructed to go as envoy to the Elector, and on 8 April he arrived in the Saxon capital.[4] He found a confused domestic situation. Arnim was quarrelling with John George because of the Elector's failure to provide the army with an effective administration, and John George was engaged in a vain attempt to persuade Francis Albert of Saxe-Lauenburg to take over the command.[5] Arnim himself was once more in touch with Wallenstein, this time through Ernest George von Sparr, with whom he had had a meeting in Berlin at the end of March.[6] As a result of their talks Arnim had been able to inform John George on 14 April that Wallenstein had requested a further conference, at which he would himself be present.[7] The Elector, as usual, was taking his time about answering this invitation. Solms soon discovered that Arnim was in touch with the imperialists; but he was unaware that

[1] Irmer, *VS*, I. 151-2. [2] *Arkiv*, I. 595-6.
[3] *Sv. Krig*, VI. 36; *Arkiv*, I. 601 *seqq.*
[4] *AOSB*, I. VII. 73, II. I. 764; Irmer, *Arnim*, pp. 168-9; *Lars Nilsson Tungels efterlämnade papper*, p. 30.
[5] Irmer, *VS*, I. 167-9. [6] *Sv. Krig*, VI. 128. [7] *ibid.*, VI. 128.

the Elector was privy to the negotiations. He was not particularly alarmed at the military situation, for he had somehow formed the quite erroneous impression that the Saxon army numbered about 30,000 men, and he informed Gustav Adolf to this effect.[1] But he regarded Arnim as a dangerous enemy,[2] and was seriously afraid that his influence might push the Elector into a separate peace. He therefore exerted himself to unmask Arnim's machinations; and was able to get possession of a letter from Sparr in which he suggested a cessation of hostilities, to be masked by sham operations, pending the conclusion of a treaty of peace. On 30 April Solms confronted John George with this evidence, demanded an investigation and informed Gustav Adolf.[3]

It was this letter from Solms which Gustav Adolf received at Moosburg on 3 May. He had already written to Solms on 29 April, explaining his future plans.[4] Influenced, no doubt, by Solms's optimistic estimate of the strength of the Saxon army, he had rejected the idea of going to the Elector's assistance, at least for the present; had expressed the conviction that Arnim ought to be able to hold out against Wallenstein; and had made it clear that he still considered the main military objective to lie in Bavaria. But this latest news shook his confidence. He was still disposed to rely on the Elector personally [5]; but it seemed clear that Arnim was not to be trusted. If he should persuade John George to make a quick peace, the whole Swedish position in Germany might be imperilled. Moreover, there was an ominous absence of reliable information as to any large transference of troops from the army of Wallenstein to Bavaria; and this suggested that the advance beyond the Lech might have failed to ease the pressure on Saxony. Under the influence of these considerations, Gustav Adolf abruptly changed his plans. John George and Oxenstierna were informed that he intended to move northwards without delay. He would take 16,000 men with him,

[1] *Sv. Krig*, VI. 35.

[2] An opinion henceforward general in Swedish circles: in January 1633 Oxenstierna was calling Arnim 'eine Kreatur des Friedländers' (Irmer, *VS*, II. 43); and in 1637, when Arnim was a Swedish prisoner, the *råd* considered him as 'the leading and most pestilential intriguer in all Germany, and the main cause of all our misfortunes there, and especially of his late Majesty's death': *RRP*, VII. 27. Compare the Archduke Leopold's opinion that Arnim was 'ein böser Calvinist vnd vorher gahr ein grosser politicus': Dudík, p. 456.

[3] Irmer, *VS*, I. 170-90; *Briefe und Akten*, II. 396-9; *AOSB*, II. I. 786-7; Chemnitz, I. 332; Pekař, I. 207-9; Droysen, II. 565-7; Irmer, *Arnim*, pp. 172-4.

[4] Irmer, *VS*, I. 164-7.

[5] *AOSB*, II. I. 787.

leaving the remainder in Bavaria under Banér's command. He hoped to reach Nuremberg within a fortnight; and he suggested a junction with the Saxon army at Eger. John George was asked to bring as many guns as possible, since the speed of his intended march might make it impossible for the King to take much artillery with him. Horn would be sent to help Oxenstierna, since the intractability of Bernard of Weimar, and the threat from Spain, made the presence of a senior commander on that front desirable.[1]

Meanwhile in Dresden the investigation of the Arnim-Sparr affair had been a pure formality, and Solms had been excluded from the proceedings. John George and Arnim made up their differences; Solms was informed that Arnim had acted with the Elector's approval, and that negotiations with Wallenstein would continue [2]; and John George, in an immense maundering letter to Gustav Adolf, exonerated Arnim and offered shuffling explanations of his attitude.[3] On 3 May Wallenstein was informed that Arnim was prepared for another meeting; and on 7 May Arnim had talks with Sparr at Laun.[4] Wallenstein, fortified by the full powers to negotiate which he received from the Emperor on 10 April,[5] was baiting his hook with a choice array of specially selected lures: the cancellation of the Edict of Restitution, partial abolition of the Ecclesiastical Reservation, religious toleration, and even the restoration of Germany to the condition of 1618.[6] Arnim probably did not trust Wallenstein very far; but he considered that the desperate military situation made negotiations essential, as the only means of staving off an imperialist attack; and he was well aware that an attack was imminent.[7] On 11 May, therefore, he met Wallenstein at Smečno. The offers which Wallenstein put forward were now coupled with an ultimatum: he must have a clear decision from John George by 15 May. He obtained it; but *e silentio*. No answer came from Dresden. John George had no faith in Wallenstein's promises: the Papists were all rogues [8]; the offers they put forward were so much 'bacon in the mouse-trap' [9]; and he shrewdly enquired of George

[1] *Arkiv*, I. 603-4, 606-8; *AOSB*, II. I. 786-7; *Schriftstücke*, pp. 247-8; Irmer, *Arnim*, pp. 176-7.

[2] Pekař, I. 209-11; *Sv. Krig*, VI. 126.

[3] Irmer, *VS*, I. 181-8.

[4] Hallwich, *Wallenstein und Arnim*, p. 165.

[5] Ritter, III. 528.

[6] Irmer, *VS*, I. 193; Pekař, I. 216; Ranke, *Wallenstein*, p. 178.

[7] Hallwich, *Wallenstein und Arnim*, p. 159.

[8] Irmer, *Arnim*, p. 178: 'Die Pfaffen und ihre Knechte sind alle Schelme, sie suchen mich zu betrügen; ich will ihnen das Gleiche thun!'

[9] *Briefe und Akten*, II. 491: 'Da leit der speck, domit man die mausz fangen will'.

of Hesse-Darmstadt what concessions the ecclesiastical Electors would be willing to make in the interests of peace.[1] The negotiations were allowed to drop; and the expected military consequences were not slow to follow.

Gustav Adolf meanwhile was hastening to John George's assistance—by way of Munich. The decision to take Munich, rather than move directly from Moosburg to the Danube crossing at Donauwörth, is difficult to explain.[2] It may be that second thoughts suggested that it would be well to be certain that Wallenstein was committed in Bohemia before quitting Bavaria; it may be that the King wished to make sure of the massive financial contribution which he intended to extort from the city; it may be that purely human motives impelled him to the capture of his enemy's capital. At all events, Munich capitulated on 6 May; and Gustav Adolf and Frederick V made their triumphant entry on the following day. St. Etienne—at Maximilian's instance, this time—had approached Gustav Adolf with a plea that Munich be spared from plunder, and (whether because of his intercession or in despite of it) the city was in fact leniently treated. The Electress had fled to Salzburg as early as 29 March; but the Jesuits had stood their ground.[3] They were left undisturbed; and Gustav Adolf's insatiable curiosity led him to visit their quarters, where he chatted affably enough with the fathers, and even complimented them on the services they rendered to the Catholic cause. The Elector's Residence was relieved of some of its art treasures and curiosities—including 'all sorts of silver coins minted both before and after the birth of Christ, and a mountain out of which corals grow'—and 119 pieces of ordnance, hastily buried by Maximilian's orders, were satisfactorily located and disinterred (Gustav Adolf characteristically telling the workmen how to do it); but on the whole law and order prevailed, to the surprise and relief of the citizenry.[4] A swingeing fine of 300,000 *rdr.* was demanded; but only 163,000 *rdr.* was actually paid, the city protesting its inability to raise more. In view of the brisk bidding for booty

[1] Irmer, *VS*, I. 193: Pekař thought that John George broke off because he sensed that Wallenstein's aims were anti-imperialist: Pekař, I. 213-14.

[2] The explanation in *Sv. Krig*, VI. 40, seems unconvincing—namely that this was in fact the shortest way round. The route Freising-Augsburg was surely possible: Gustav Adolf had enough men to deal with any possible interference from Ingolstadt, and since he was taking only light guns with him the small streams intersecting the route should have presented little difficulty.

[3] L. Schaedel, *Gustav Adolf von Schweden in München*, p. 121.

[4] For events in Munich, see Schaedel, *op. cit.*, pp. 121-5; Monro, II. 124-6; *Dagbok*, pp. 49-50; Droysen, II. 557; Riezler, V. 414 *seqq.*; Loenbom, I. 40.

auctioned by the Swedish soldiers (in the course of which many burghers acquired choice pieces of Maximilian's property at bargain prices),[1] the validity of this excuse appears somewhat doubtful.

Gustav Adolf occupied himself in Munich in concerting plans for collaborating with Rohan to block the Splügen and the Bernina to Spanish troops, and perhaps to secure the Valtelline too [2]; and he spent some time which might have been better bestowed in listening to Des Hayes de Cormenin, who had come to Bavaria on behalf of Gaston of Orleans. Des Hayes's object was to enlist support for his master, and by way of preliminary he aspired to reconcile Gustav Adolf with the Emperor.[3] Nothing came of all this; but it cannot have been very agreeable to Richelieu to learn that his ally was receiving the agent of the most inveterate of his domestic enemies.[4] Gustav Adolf stayed in Munich till 16 May (by which date, according to his earlier programme, he should have been within sight of Nuremberg), when he moved with 15,000 men to Augsburg. From a letter to Oxenstierna of 10 May it is clear that he still adhered to his plan of marching to John George's assistance if Wallenstein were really threatening him.[5] But of this he could get no sure confirmation. His information service, so effective in north Germany, had become tardy and unreliable in the Catholic south. It might be, after all, that reinforcements were on their way from Bohemia to Maximilian: if so, he must stay in Bavaria in the hope of inflicting a decisive defeat upon them. For the first time he was irresolute, paralysed by lack of hard news. On 23 May came letters which helped him to a decision—John George's Resolution for Solms, and a report from Solms himself.[6] The material point in the Elector's Resolution was that he declared that Eger was impossible for him as a rendezvous, and instead suggested Leitmeritz, far to the

[1] Riezler, V. 419.

[2] L. Haas, *Schwedens Politik gegen der Eidgenossenschaft*, pp. 112-13; *cf. AOSB*, II. 1. 799; D. Veraguth, *Herzog Rohan und seine Mission in Graubünden und im Veltlin*, pp. 31-2.

[3] Richelieu, *Mémoires*, II. 414. Tongas alleges that Des Hayes's mission was to invite Gustav Adolf to mediate between Gaston and Louis XIII, and that the King promised to send an ambassador to France for this purpose. But since Tongas also puts the place of the meeting at Magdeburg, he may well be in error about the subject with which it was concerned: Tongas, *Des Hayes de Cormenin*, pp. 99-101.

[4] There was a story current among the imperialists that Gustav Adolf while at Munich asked to open negotiations with Maximilian, and expressed the hope that Maximilian would act as mediator with the Emperor; but there seems no confirmation of this: *Briefe und Akten*, II. 428-9; *cf.* Irmer, *VS*, I. lxxix.

[5] *AOSB*, II. 1. 789. Imperialist intelligence on 14 May reported him as already having reached Donauwörth on his way north: *Briefe und Akten*, II. 433.

[6] Irmer, *VS*, I. 191-2; *Arkiv*, II. 466-7; Chemnitz, I. 334.

east in central Bohemia. As for Solms, he painted a gloomy picture of the debauchery and demoralization of the Elector's court; he represented a separate peace as being distinctly possible; but he still estimated John George's army at 27,000 (of which 4400 were new levies) against Wallenstein's 30,000.

Gustav Adolf reached a decision at once. It represented a sharp reversal of his previous plans. He faced the possibility of a Saxon defection; but this time he discounted it to his own satisfaction. To John George himself he wrote simply that he had been delayed by operations in Bavaria, warned him to be careful in any negotiations with Wallenstein, and promised assistance if a real emergency should arise.[1] But to Oxenstierna he argued that it would not much matter if John George did make peace, provided the treaty ensured that Silesia were neutralized, and provided care were taken that troops disbanded from the Saxon service be made available to Sweden, and denied to the Emperor.[2] If John George were determined to withdraw from the war, the arrival of a Swedish contingent far inferior in strength to the Saxon army might present him with an opportunity to force peace upon Gustav Adolf too. The strength of the Elector's forces ought to be sufficient guarantee that he would be able to extort good terms from Wallenstein; but Gustav Adolf proposed to send a special envoy, in the person of the Palsgrave August, to put pressure on John George and to see to it that Swedish interests were safeguarded.

This reasoning was based on a false premiss: John George's army was barely half as numerous as Solms reported. But it was also fallacious in itself. The neutralization of Silesia would undoubtedly be a military advantage; but was there any reason to believe that John George would stand out for it as a condition of peace? Or, if such a provision were indeed inserted in a treaty, could Gustav Adolf be confident that it would be respected? He had not usually been so ready to accept the promises of papists. And in any case it was surely impossible to contemplate without misgiving the situation which would arise if Wallenstein's hands were freed by the defection of the Elector. Even if the road to Stettin were barred by treaty, a thrust by Wallenstein north-westwards might sever the Swedish lifeline at Erfurt and take the Lower Saxon Circle in the rear. There were, indeed, Swedish forces north of the Main more than sufficient, as far as numbers went, to meet such a threat; but if they proved

[1] *Schriftstücke*, pp. 57-60.

[2] *AOSB*, II. I. 797-800.

unable to deal with Pappenheim's 10,000, what hope had they of coping with an army thrice as numerous? They urgently needed strong leadership; but Gustav Horn—the only man other than the King himself who could have provided it—was destined for the Rhineland. The truth seems to be that Gustav Adolf was reluctant to leave south Germany. The main object for him was still the extension and consolidation of his system of bases, the 'conjunction of Rhine and Danube'; and in pursuit of it he closed his eyes to the dangers elsewhere. Swedish power in north Germany was in imminent danger; but he would not see the risks he was running: if the worst came to the worst, he told Oxenstierna, he could get back in time. Intent on a long-range combination which should infallibly checkmate his adversary, he thought too little of the threat to the very basis of his position.

His next move appears as an almost wilful step in the wrong direction. The subjugation of Swabia had been entrusted to Patrick Ruthven, Gustav Adolf's commandant in Ulm; and had at first made rapid progress. Latterly, however, Ruthven had had some trouble from the relatively small forces of Hareaucourt and Ossa, and from the local peasantry, which rose in rebellion against the Swedes, and were organized by Ossa to considerable effect.[1] It was to Swabia that Gustav Adolf now elected to go, using the steam-hammer of his main army to crack this egg of resistance. Nothing could more clearly demonstrate the obstinacy with which he clung to the plan of linking up the Rhenish and Bavarian Circles; and nothing could reveal more plainly that the original objective of the Bavarian campaign had not yet been attained. For Swabia was to be organized specifically to provide winter quarters[2]; a victory in 1632 was no longer expected.

To Swabia, accordingly, he went; and on 25 May arrived at Memmingen. And at Memmingen, on the following day, he received tidings from Saxony which he could ignore no longer.[3] Prague had fallen to Wallenstein on 15 May; Arnim was in full retreat from Bohemia. Rumour exaggerated the withdrawal into a major disaster; but the reality was bad enough. On the day after the fall of Prague Arnim once more resigned his command, in disgust at John George's failure to give him any precise orders. He did, indeed, half-rebuff another approach from Sparr, for he conformed loyally to his master's policy while he was in his service; but he did not conceal his opinion

[1] *Sv. Krig*, VI. 44-6. [2] *ibid.*, 49. [3] *ibid.*, 52, 134.

that only negotiation could avert a catastrophe.[1] John George, however, was now insistent that there must be no negotiation without Gustav Adolf (influenced, perhaps, by strong representations to that effect from George William)[2]; he met Arnim's demand for precise orders by directing him to take such steps as he thought proper[3]; and all the answer he returned to Sparr's initiative was that he would think of it.[4] Arnim, as had happened before, withdrew his resignation before it became effective; but there was little he could do to bar the progress of the imperialists if Wallenstein should push his offensive with vigour.

And now at last Gustav Adolf reacted swiftly to the situation. Horn was sent off to the Rhine, to infuse some spirit into the operations against the Spaniards; Grubbe was despatched yet again to animate and reconcile the generals of the Lower Saxon Circle; William of Weimar was ordered back to Erfurt to organize a new reserve army for the protection of the bottleneck; the instructions for the Palsgrave August were redrafted to meet the altered state of affairs; and the King himself prepared to march northwards with all convenient speed.[5] The decision in Bavaria was indefinitely postponed: postponed, as luck would have it, at the very moment when Wallenstein, deaf to the laments of Maximilian, inexorably recalled Aldringen and the imperialist contingent from the Bavarian army.[6] Gustav Adolf had hoped that his campaign on the Danube might, among other advantages, relieve Wallenstein's pressure on Saxony. As it fell out, Wallenstein's offensive had relieved Gustav Adolf's pressure on Bavaria.

(iii) *Nuremberg*

The decision of the last week of May marks a turning-point in Gustav Adolf's fortunes. For nearly a year events had moved steadily in his favour: every month had seen his military position grow stronger; every month had seen an increased assumption of political leadership and authority. Now, as it seemed quite suddenly,

[1] *Briefe und Akten*, II. 300-1, 467; Hallwich, *Wallenstein und Arnim*, pp. 169, 172-3. On 21 May Arnim informed John George that only 5150 foot and 4800 cavalry were available for field-operations.

[2] Irmer, *VS*, I. 194-6, 196-8; *cf. Arkiv*, II. 478-9; Chemnitz, I. 333.

[3] Hallwich, *Wallenstein und Arnim*, p. 172.

[4] *ibid.*, 175.

[5] *Sv. Krig*, VI. 134-7.

[6] *ibid.*, 52-3; *Briefe und Akten*, II. 442 *seqq.*

he found himself in the middle of a crisis: the brilliant successes in Bavaria were made to appear insubstantial; the entire Swedish position in north Germany was endangered. For the first time since the days of Magdeburg Gustav Adolf was thrown strategically on the defensive; the initiative passed into the hands of his enemy; and for almost the whole of the summer he was to be forced to concentrate his efforts upon parrying the blows that were aimed at him. Not until the very eve of Lützen was he again to be in a position to force his adversary to conform to his will.

The crisis was not, indeed, quite as sudden as it seemed to be: for some time now the storm-cones had been hoisted in the north, though the King, dazzled by the fair weather of Bavaria, had preferred not to notice them. But the emergency had now ceased to be a matter of opinion, and Gustav Adolf was at last awake to the full import of the danger to Saxony. In a letter to Oxenstierna of 2 June he wrote that the retention of Saxony was fundamental to the Swedish position in the south; and it was indicative of the gravity with which he viewed the military prospects that he urged the expediency of another *utskrivning* in Sweden, so that in the event of a disaster in Germany there might be an army at home to act as a last reserve.[1] On the previous day he had given Palsgrave August the instructions for his mission to Dresden.[2] On the one hand, August was to assure John George that Gustav Adolf was himself anxious for peace if proper safeguards could be obtained; and on the other, he was to try to induce the Elector to hold out by giving the clearest and most unequivocal pledge of immediate aid. Whether these assurances would reach John George in time seemed highly problematical. It was difficult to form any idea of the probabilities, for it was still impossible to get much news that could be relied on. Solms had met the King in Donauwörth on 31 May, with the information that no major collapse had so far occurred in Saxony [3]; but there was little further information to be had. For almost three weeks Gustav Adolf was forced to guess what was happening; and it is not surprising that his guesses at times were wrong. The imperialists, on their own ground, were better served: already by 11 June Aldringen could inform Wallenstein that Gustav Adolf was heading for Nuremberg.[4]

[1] *AOSB*, II. I. 806.
[2] Irmer, *VS*, I. 199-208; *Schriftstücke*, p. 66.
[3] *Sv. Krig*, VI. 137.
[4] *Briefe und Akten*, II. 513.

Aldringen's information, though it could not be called fresh, was at all events correct. On 4 June Gustav Adolf broke up from Donauwörth. He had with him only 10,000 infantry and 8500 cavalry; but he took no less than 70 guns, being perhaps justifiably sceptical as to whether John George could be relied upon to respond to his earlier appeal to bring artillery sufficient for them both. On 9 June he reached Nuremberg. News remained scanty. No tidings of disaster came in from Dresden, though it was now almost a month since the loss of Prague; and he began to wonder if he were not embarked upon a needless errand.[1] There was no lack of rumours as to Pappenheim's intentions and activities, and the King spent some energy in taking steps to counter them; but within a day or two the rumours would prove false and the counter-measures would be cancelled.[2] It was not until 10 June that he received definite and reliable information about enemy movements. On that day came news that Maximilian was on the march northwards from Regensburg, and was probably making for Eger. His army was reported to be small (in fact it numbered about 6000), and Gustav Adolf decided to try to intercept it and defeat it in the region of Amberg. For this purpose he made a dash eastwards from Nuremberg; and by 14 June had reached Sulzbach. Here he learned that he was too late: Maximilian had already passed by Amberg, and there was now no hope of catching him.[3] He accordingly made his way back to Hersbruck, where he stayed for a week, in the hope that the situation might clarify itself. In one respect it was clear enough already, though Gustav Adolf did not immediately perceive this. For if Maximilian intended to make his junction with Wallenstein somewhere in the region of Eger, it was a fair deduction that the objective of their combined forces was unlikely to be Saxony. And if it were not Saxony, it must be Gustav Adolf's army. Until 17 June, however, the King continued to believe that the imperialists' concentration threatened John George; and on this assumption he made plans for a diversion in Bavaria which, he hoped, would distract Maximilian's attention and force him to turn back to the Danube: Banér should besiege Ingolstadt; the King himself would march south to

[1] *Schriftstücke*, pp. 227-8.

[2] *e.g. AOSB*, II. I. 806-7, 810.

[3] As Alexander Hamilton unkindly put it, 'To relate in one word, all that we have done by this journey is the hastining of the enemyes joyning, and a hope to see shortly their intentions . . . How long we shall stay here, or which way take God knoweth, for oftener then once a day, there is just cause of changes': Hist. MSS. Comm., *Hamilton Supplementary*, p. 25.

Neumarkt.[1] On second thoughts he decided that he had better stay in Franconia; but for some days he clung to the idea of a demonstration against Ingolstadt.[2] He forgot that Maximilian, by leaving Bavaria at Banér's mercy, had already advertised his faith in Ingolstadt's ability to resist and signified his determination not to be diverted. It was not until 18 June that he became convinced that Wallenstein's moves were aimed not at Saxony but at himself; and on the following day his conviction was strengthened when his outposts at Hersbruck were attacked in force by advanced elements of Wallenstein's light cavalry.[3] It was now plain that his position was one of considerable danger: within a very few days he might find himself attacked by an overwhelmingly superior force. Gustav Adolf wasted no time in making up his mind what was to be done. On 18 June he called his staff together, and told them to get rid of the baggage-horses, since it was his intention to make a leaguer at Nuremberg.[4] On the following day he inspected the existing fortifications of the city, condemned them as unsatisfactory, and ordered the construction of a fortified camp outside the walls. Nuremberg was to be another and greater Werben; and behind the field-fortifications which he was throwing up he would sit still and await reinforcements. And when they had arrived in strength he would settle accounts with Wallenstein.[5]

Since the recovery of Prague, Wallenstein had made little effort to force the pace on the Bohemian front. He could without difficulty have swept into John George's dominions and driven the Elector from Dresden, for he had on his side great superiority in numbers, in organization and in genius. But though his troops did indeed invade Lusatia, he was careful to keep out of John George's hereditary dominions.[6] He continued to parley hopefully with Arnim, perhaps with a view to reconciling John George with the Emperor, perhaps

[1] *Schriftstücke*, pp. 61-4.

[2] *Arkiv*, I. 633; *AOSB*, II. i. 811.

[3] *Sv. Krig*, VI. 144.

[4] 'This day all the Coronells of foote hathe bene with him he hath desired them to put away all the waggon horses; telling them that he thinketh he will be forced to forme a Leaguer before Nuremberg to defend the Citie from the enemyes furie so as of provision either for the horses, waggon men or all other unnecessary charge he doeth intend to ease himself and the towne of . . .': Hist. MSS. Comm., *Hamilton Supplementary*, p. 24. As late as the 20th he still thought it just possible that the imperialists might turn back to Bavaria; and the situation did not become absolutely clear till the 23rd: *Schriftstücke*, pp. 65, 183-5, 229.

[5] There is an interesting discussion of Gustav Adolf's strategy at this time in Clausewitz, *op. cit.*, pp. 82-3.

[6] *Sv. Krig*, VI. 131.

from a private design to keep on terms with the leading exponent of the policy of a third party in Germany. His main aim, however, must be to destroy the army of Gustav Adolf; and it would be sufficient if his pressure upon John George forced the King to break off his campaign in Bavaria and return to central Germany. His expectations were realized; and it must have been with much satisfaction that he heard the news that Gustav Adolf had divided his forces and was marching northwards with one-half of his army. Wallenstein's object was now to thrust himself between the Swedes and the Saxons and prevent their junction. He was well placed for such a manœuvre. Since his resumption of the command he had taken particular care of the north-western corner of Bohemia.[1] He realized that it offered a good base for an advance towards Nuremberg, Bayreuth and the Thuringian defiles—an advance which might sever Swedish communications between Würzburg and Erfurt, and perhaps link up with Pappenheim's operations in the Lower Saxon Circle. In this area, therefore, he concentrated his forces: on 16 June he arrived in Eger; on 21 June his junction with Maximilian took place at Tirschenreuth.[2] He had now some 48,000 men under his command: Gustav Adolf had barely 20,000. It is true that many of the imperialists were new recruits whose training was incomplete; it is true, too, that Wallenstein was a cautious and methodical, rather than an enterprising and aggressive commander. But the opportunity was obvious; and Wallenstein was not blind to it. He marched against Gustav Adolf with the deliberate purpose of seeking battle. If he could force an engagement, victory seemed certain.[3]

It is not clear whether Gustav Adolf was accurately informed as to the size of the force which Wallenstein was bringing against him; but it was plain that he must decline to fight. Battle for him lay at the end of every strategic perspective—at least it did so after Breitenfeld—but until he could bring up powerful reinforcements battle must somehow be avoided. Yet at the same time Wallenstein must be 'amused', lest after all he turn aside to crush John George. The Nuremberg leaguer was his answer to this problem. Outside the city, and almost surrounding it, he caused to be constructed a continuous line of earthworks and redoubts. It linked up at either end with the existing defences; but for most of its course it was

[1] *Sv. Krig*, V. 446-7, 454.
[2] *ibid.*, VI. 149.
[3] See his explicit statement to Ernest Montecuccoli, 25 June 1632: *Briefe und Akten*, II. 573-4; and *cf. ibid.*, 588.

pushed so far out as to permit the comfortable accommodation of his army outside the city walls, and to afford ample room for manœuvre within the works. It was remarkable not merely for its frontal strength but for the provision of mutually supporting strong-points, with overlapping fields of fire; and it thus offered a less rigid barrier than was usual in contemporary defences, and presented some suggestion of defence in depth. The work was completed, under the King's personal direction, by his brilliant engineer Olof Hansson Örnehufvud; and it was pushed on with such speed that by the time Wallenstein arrived before Nuremberg it was virtually finished.[1]

The Nuremberg leaguer was in itself a reverse for Wallenstein. It robbed him of immediate victory, and it enforced upon him an abrupt change of plan. His reply to it was characteristic. He did not for a moment consider a direct assault upon the camp—as Gustav Adolf would certainly have done had the situation been reversed. He decided rather to starve the King out. The country to north, east and south of Nuremberg was more or less under his control, and he took care that it should be stripped of supplies as far as possible. To the south-west the road was still open; and here, at Zirndorf, on heights overlooking the Rednitz, Wallenstein proceeded to construct a leaguer of his own, not inferior in strength and engineering skill to that of his adversary. While the bulk of his army stayed quietly within its fortifications, his patrols would cut off the King's supplies and make the approach of reinforcements difficult. Before they could arrive, he hoped, the Swedes would be driven by hunger to a desperate sortie. But if, in spite of everything, the King should succeed in drawing together a large army at Nuremberg, that army would be faced with the uninviting alternatives of an attack on Wallenstein's position or a humiliating retreat. In supplies he believed he was at least as well off as Gustav Adolf; in patience he was certainly his superior. He felt he could afford to wait.

Before this situation had defined itself, Gustav Adolf had already begun to organize the collection of a relieving army. He was not greatly concerned at the threat of blockade: Nuremberg was well stocked with stores, and he thought that Wallenstein's commissariat difficulties might well prove greater than his own. But he was greatly concerned to assemble a force strong enough to permit an attack upon his enemy with some prospect of success. His chance of achieving this depended, of course, upon the state of affairs in the

[1] For the Nuremberg leaguer, see *Sv. Krig*, VI. 156 *seqq.*

subordinate theatres of war. How stood the account in these areas in July 1632? What hope was there of aid from Oxenstierna, from Banér, from the Lower Saxon Circle, or even from John George?

Oxenstierna had been left in command on the Rhine when the King set out for Bavaria in March. Apart from some weak imperialist forces under Ossa to the south of him, he had little immediate opposition to fear, and Gustav Adolf constantly urged him to a vigorous offensive. The chancellor, overwhelmed with work of all sorts, and a good deal harassed by the stream of not always practicable orders which came from his master, was further hampered by the quarrels of Bernard of Weimar and Christian of Birkenfeld, whom Gustav Adolf had left with him as military advisers. Little had been done to improve the Swedish position when, at the end of March, the long-impending Spanish offensive began on the Moselle. Starting from Trarbach, the Spaniards penetrated as far as the Rhine at Speyer; and Swedish prestige suffered a sharp shock when Hornec, the commander there, tamely surrendered the town after only a few days' siege. This, however, marked the culmination of the Spanish offensive: by mid-May it was clear that the Dutch were preparing for the siege of Maastricht, and the Spaniards began to think it was time to withdraw. Oxenstierna and his generals at last showed some enterprise. They drove hard against the retreating Spaniards; and only ill-luck, and an exceptionally skilful retreat by the enemy, deprived them of an important victory. At the end of May, Horn arrived to take over the command, under Oxenstierna; and his coming infused more vigour into the conduct of operations. On 21 June he took Coblenz; on 9 July he captured Trarbach. Apart from the possibility of an intervention by the ever-incalculable Pappenheim, the Swedish commanders on the Rhine had by July little to fear, and could safely detach a considerable force to Nuremberg.[1]

In Swabia and Bavaria, too, the war had continued to go in Sweden's favour. Here Banér had been left in command, with some 22,000 men, and with Bernard of Weimar (exchanged for Horn) to assist him. The imperialist forces with whom he had to contend were inconsiderable, but they were active and enterprising, and they

[1] For operations on the Rhine, see *Sv. Krig*, VI. 55-77; *AOSB*, I. VII. 37, 47, 119, 129-30, 150, 152, 180, 195, 225, 235, 237, 261, 306, 322, 340, 351, 373, 422, 444, 504, 522, II. I. 780, 783-4, 786, 790; *Briefe und Akten*, II. 477-8.

had some support from peasant guerrillas. The difficulty was not to defeat the enemy but to catch him. The towns could be garrisoned and held; but the countryside was still not entirely under control. And there was always the danger of reinforcements from over the Alps. Nevertheless, though the thorough subjugation of Swabia was desirable and even necessary in the future, Banér and Bernard did not doubt that it must be postponed to the requirements of the main theatre; and after one or two false starts they had no difficulty in bringing the bulk of their forces to the rendezvous.[1]

Far different was the state of the case in the Lower Saxon Circle. Here the position had gone from bad to worse. Between the armies of Tott, George of Lüneburg, John Frederick of Bremen and William V existed the very minimum of co-ordination; and in most of their commanders not much willingness to make personal sacrifices in the common cause. The departure of Banér and William of Weimar for Bavaria in March removed a useful link between the northern and southern forces, as well as exposing the area between Magdeburg and Erfurt to the risk of Pappenheim's attack. In these conditions Pappenheim, ably seconded by Gronsfeld, made good use of his opportunities. Tott's costive strategy and quarrelsome temper; the distractions of William V, liable at any moment to be summoned for assistance to Franconia on the one hand or the Rhine on the other; the intrigues of Kristian IV, which Pappenheim skilfully fostered, and which long paralysed any serious Swedish initiative in the north —all these played into Pappenheim's hands. Moving his small army swiftly on the interior lines, he appeared unexpectedly, now here, now there, striking sharp and damaging blows, and disappearing in a cloud of rumour before the lumbering Swedish generals could concentrate a force sufficiently large to satisfy their exaggerated caution. At the beginning of March he fell upon the Hessians near Höxter, and scattered them; in the following month he relieved Stade, which Tott had been blockading, and on 16-18 April inflicted upon him a severe defeat; on 17 June he routed a small Hessian army under Uslar at Volkmarsen.[2] By midsummer he was triumphantly in command of the situation: 'Pappenheim's shadow is everywhere dominant', wrote Grubbe [3]; 'there is such terror and lamentation', echoed Trana, 'that you might suppose the country

[1] For operations in this area, see *Sv. Krig*, VI. 170-9; *AOSB*, II. VI. 65-78.

[2] For these operations, see *Sv. Krig*, VI. 78-119; Boëthius, *NSK*, pp. 284-363; *Briefe und Akten*, II. 274-5, *AOSB*, II. VII. 331-3 (for Höxter); *Arkiv*, II. 502-3; *AOSB*, II. VII. 364-7 (for Volkmarsen).

[3] *Arkiv*, II. 446-7.

invaded by the Turks'[1]; and Oxenstierna told the King that 'he does exactly what he will, to the limits of his resources'.[2]

As Oxenstierna remarked, the main reasons for this state of affairs were the feebleness of the Swedish generals and the fact that they were not 'all under one hat'.[3] Faithful, too faithful, to the military maxims of the age,[4] they preferred to take no risks, and seized upon every passage in the King's orders which could afford them a pretext for doing nothing. They had a fatal *penchant* for councils of war which issued in agreements to wait and see; they were credulous of any report that could be considered discouraging; and their mutual jealousies caused them to divide their forces when they should at all costs have united them. William V, alone of them all, showed enterprise, moral courage and a real willingness to co-operate.[5] Tott was now really ill; he resented Gustav Adolf's sending of Salvius and Grubbe as his personal emissaries; and between himself and Salvius there developed a bitter animosity, sharpened by Tott's aristocratic contempt for the middle-class civil servant, whom he called 'an ink-slinger'.[6] Salvius revenged himself by writing damaging reports of Tott's personal habits.[7] Erik Andersson Trana, in charge of war supplies in the area, was at times on bad terms with Salvius too.[8] Grubbe had tact but no weight, and between George of Lüneburg, Baudissin and John Frederick of Bremen he could hardly hope to assert his authority. Repeated exhortations to unity by Oxenstierna, repeated orders by the King to work together, were met by the generals with explanations of altered circumstances or local difficulties; or, if they were obeyed, had but a transient effect.[9]

The result was not merely military failure, but general confusion

[1] *Arkiv*, II. 398.

[2] *AOSB*, I. VII. 104. So much did Pappenheim feel himself master of the field that he could write to Wallenstein (as early as 7 March): 'My main concern is still lest the Spaniards, if I should perchance draw the King of Sweden hither, should fail me, and content themselves with the recovery of the Rhine': *Briefe und Akten*, III. 273.

[3] *AOSB*, I. VII. 104.

[4] 'He that preserves an Armie', wrote Monro, 'will doubtlesse find a convenient time to fight': Monro, II. 204.

[5] See his letters to Oxenstierna: *AOSB*, II. VII. 333, 335, 343, 349-50, 353-7.

[6] 'Bläcksuddare': *Arkiv*, II. 488.

[7] During the winter, he wrote, Tott made no effort to reconnoitre Stade or Buxtehude, nor did he concern himself with quartering arrangements or supplies, 'but stayed *perpetuo* inside Hornburg, *a lecto in stabulam, e stabulo ad mensam, a mensa* to the hounds, *inde ad caenam, atque hinc rursus in lectum*': *ibid.*, 488-9, and *cf. ibid.*, 491-2.

[8] Lundgren, *Salvius*, p. 44.

[9] See, *e.g.*, *AOSB*, I. VII. 123, 156, 242, 243, 262, 281, 349-50, 370, 372, 384, II. I. 789; *Arkiv*, I. 570-3, 601.

and scandalous excesses. Discipline broke down, and the troops plundered the countryside indiscriminately.

> There is here such distraction, confusion and irregularity [wrote Trana] that it is a wonder that any peasant can live on the land, or any burgher in the towns. . . . I cannot, I may not describe what is carried on here. . . . Conditions are worse than they were in Novgorod, when we were, after all, concerned more with the preservation of our own power than with sparing the citizens. But here the case is otherwise: these are people of our religion; who have taken Y.M. (after God) as their guardian, and put themselves under your protection; and (finally) it is notorious to all the world, how much these poor folk have already had to endure from the imperialists.[1]

The King's regulations and articles of war were openly flouted; officers and even generals participated in the profits of extortion. The army of George of Lüneburg was especially notorious. Grubbe's reports bore out Trana's: 'Y.M. could not believe how things really are', he wrote [2]; 'indescribable disorders' occurred even as the troops were mustering [3]; the friends of Sweden were fast being alienated by the sufferings to which they were subjected. The only remedy, in the opinion of the outraged civil servants who were compelled to stand by while Swedish goodwill was thus being squandered, was the removal of the culpable generals and the appointment of a single supreme commander—preferably Gustav Adolf himself, or, failing him, Horn.[4] Salvius, Trana, Oxenstierna, Grubbe, they all harped on this string. In vain. There was a moment, at the end of March, when the danger from Denmark led the King to think of coming in person to the Lower Saxon Circle.[5] But the danger passed; and Bavaria, after all, was the main theatre of war. Horn, it seemed, could not be spared, for his presence was needed on the Rhine. This was an error of judgment: it would have been better for Gustav Adolf if he had left the Rhine to Christian of Birkenfeld and used Horn's talents to apply drastic cautery, even at this late date, to the gangrenous sore in the north-west. At the end of May there appeared to be some prospect of improvement, when Tott at last relinquished the command and betook himself in search of health from the hot water of the Lower Saxon Circle to the warm baths of some convenient spa.[6] The King sped him on his

[1] *Arkiv*, II. 410; *cf. ibid.*, 380-2.
[2] *ibid.*, II. 446-7.
[3] *ibid.*, II. 527.
[4] *ibid.*, II. 454-5.
[5] *AOSB*, II. I. 775-6; Boëthius, *NSK*, p. 343.
[6] *AOSB*, II. IX. 705.

way, and possibly retarded his convalescence, with a scarifying letter in which he accurately summed up his general's later performances as at once negligent and stupid.[1] But if he scolded Tott for flouting Salvius, he also scolded the civilians (very unfairly) for allowing themselves to be flouted.[2] Tott's successor was Baudissin, an ambitious cosmopolitan professional; but though possibly less cantankerous than Tott, he was scarcely more enterprising. In July he was presented with a great opportunity, when Pappenheim, tempted by the Infanta Isabella's offer of half a million *Reichsthaler*, allowed himself to be persuaded to attempt the relief of Maastricht, and was absent from the Lower Saxon Circle for several weeks. But even now nothing really effective was done; and Gronsfeld, left behind with an exiguous force, was able to hoodwink the Swedish generals into a heartbreaking prudence, as Pappenheim had so often done before him.[3]

Gustav Adolf's failure to deal firmly with the Lower Saxon Circle now brought its reward. When he called upon Baudissin to send aid to Nuremberg; when he summoned George of Lüneburg and his army to join the relieving force; he was met with excuses, protestations and refusal. Kagg's departure for Nuremberg, Baudissin explained, had weakened the forces available in the area; Pappenheim was said to be concentrating near Paderborn; Baudissin himself was in need of reinforcements.[4] There was some truth in this assessment of the situation: the King accepted Baudissin's arguments. But it was a pitiful upshot of six months' campaigning against greatly inferior forces. Of all the thousands of troops who had spent their time to such little purpose in the valleys of the Aller or Weser, none, apparently, could now be spared at this crisis of the King's fortunes. Only William V, somewhat restive now,[5] but still cooperative, was in a position to sacrifice local interests to the general welfare, and rally to Oxenstierna's army.

On 13 June the Palsgrave August arrived in Dresden, in company with Dr. Löffler.[6] They found less difficulty than had been expected in carrying out their task of persuading John George to

[1] *Arkiv*, I. 614-16.
[2] Kretzschmar, *Gustav Adolfs Pläne und Ziele*, pp. 115-16.
[3] *AOSB*, I. VII. 522, II. VIII. 68, II. IX. 809; Rommel, VIII. 198; Kretzschmar, *op. cit.*, pp. 122-38; Ritter, III. 540-1; *Sv. Krig*, VI. 228 *seqq.*
[4] *AOSB*, II. IX. 796, 799, 804; *Arkiv*, II. 520-1, 544-8; Kretzschmar, *op. cit.*, pp. 119-21.
[5] *AOSB*, II. VII. 340-2, 367-72; Rommel, VIII. 191.
[6] The journal of the embassy is printed in Irmer, *VS*, I. 209-31.

remain loyal to the Swedish alliance. The Elector had already virtually made up his mind to make no bargain with the imperialists; and the explicit assurances which the Palsgrave brought with him served to clinch his decision.[1] The negotiations between Arnim and Wallenstein continued in a desultory fashion: as late as 28 June Wallenstein was still expecting a reply to Sparr's offers; but the intrigue was now conducted with August's privity, and persisted in only in order to gain time for Arnim's military measures.[2]

Suspicion of John George nevertheless persisted. The Swedish agents well knew the vacillations of that *caput heteroclitum*.[3] The Elector's hatred of Calvinists led him to make a painful scene, on 24 June, when he insulted August at dinner because of his insistence that Frederick V's recovery of Bohemia must be a part of any peace-settlement.[4] Tungel scented bad faith in the slowness with which business was transacted; and reported the Elector as having said that, though he admitted his obligations to his ally, he had obligations still more binding to the Emperor.[5] Solms left Dresden on 23 June filled with doubts of Saxon fidelity. As ill-luck would have it, he met William of Weimar at Gera two days later, on his way with his army to a rendezvous with Oxenstierna. As a result of their conversation, William decided (without any orders from Gustav Adolf) to invade the electorate, in order to make sure of the Saxon army. He had actually crossed the border before he was stopped by orders from the King, who providentially learned of this mad enterprise in time to prevent serious consequences.[6]

The Elector took this scandalous affair very well: the King's apologies were accepted. This was fortunate; for Gustav Adolf was now needing his assistance. The danger to Saxony had by this time so far abated that it seemed reasonable to ask John George to send a contingent to Nuremberg; and August was instructed to press the Elector to agree to this.[7] By this time, however, John George had other calls upon his resources. At the end of June Arnim took advantage of the passivity of the imperialists to initiate a successful

[1] See above, p. 714.

[2] Hallwich, *Wallenstein und Arnim*, pp. 180-6; Irmer, *VS*, I. lxxii-lxxiii; *Briefe und Akten*, II. 489-91, 537, 589; Pekař, I. 217-20.

[3] Solms's expression: Irmer, *VS*, I. lxv.

[4] *ibid.*, I. 213, II. 30; *cf.* I. 228, 254-5.

[5] *ibid.*, I. 233, 243-4, 249-51.

[6] *ibid.*, I. 244-7; Huschke, pp. 60-3; Helbig, pp. 81-2; but *cf.* Söltl. III. 305.

[7] Irmer, *VS*, I. 211, 226; *Schriftstücke*, pp. 67-8, 230-2.

effort to recover Lusatia. From Lusatia he went on to the invasion of Silesia; and in July and August won brilliant victories on this front. He pointedly made Wallenstein's new principality of Glogau his first objective.[1] Glogau fell on 28 July; Breslau on 27 August. A diversionary attack by Holck on Saxony, ordered by Wallenstein as a measure of retaliation, failed to divert him, though the electorate was subjected to such terrible devastations that for the first time John George ordered the omission of the prayer for the Emperor from church services.[2] Arnim's campaign in Silesia represented, at long last, the conversion of Saxon strategists to the view which Gustav Adolf had always taken of the kind of enterprise which might properly be pursued on this wing of the allied front; but it necessarily engaged most of the Elector's forces. In these circumstances it was a real sign of his good faith that he should have consented to detach five regiments to join William of Weimar with the relieving army which Oxenstierna was assembling.[3]

For nearly two months Gustav Adolf and Wallenstein faced each other outside Nuremberg. From each camp patrols went out to gather forage and supplies, or to attack parties of the enemy similarly engaged, and a number of minor clashes resulted from these activities. On the Swedish side the most successful episode was an attack on Wallenstein's main supply depot at Freistadt, on the night of 31 July. The depot was destroyed, some booty captured, and among the prisoners taken was Wallenstein's negotiator with Arnim, von Sparr.[4] Neither side, despite these efforts, seems to have suffered serious commissariat difficulties. Gustav Adolf's main problem was a shortage of fodder rather than of food: the health of his army was good, rations were adequate (except in the article of salt), morale was high, and numbers were actually increasing as the result of local recruiting.[5] It was clear, nevertheless, that he

[1] Pekař, I. 222.

[2] Irmer, *VS*, I. 261-4. For the Silesian campaign, see *Sv. Krig*, VI. 267-85; Spannagel, *Burgsdorff*, pp. 33-6, 39-41; Pekař, I. 222-4; Irmer, *Arnim*, p. 192. The Elector is said to have resisted all suggestions to arm the peasants for the defence of his country: *Lars Nilsson Tungels efterlämnade papper*, p. 45; *cf. ibid.*, pp. 58, 62.

[3] *Schriftstücke*, p. 68.

[4] *AOSB*, II. 1. 830; *Briefe und Akten*, II. 719; *Dagbok*, p. 56.

[5] See the optimistic letters of the younger Camerarius in *Briefe und Akten*, II. 650-1, 700, 776; Söltl, III. 305-18; and *AOSB*, II. 1. 816; *Sv. Krig*, VI. 170-2. The burghers, on the other hand, suffered severely from hunger; and mortality among them from this cause, and from epidemics, was high: Droysen, II. 606-7.

could not keep his camp indefinitely without losing the greater part of his horses; and it was therefore a matter of some importance that the relieving army should make no avoidable delay. The organization of this force was a business of no ordinary difficulty. It was to be made up of separate contingents from north, west and south, which must meet at an agreed rendezvous and contrive to avoid being attacked and defeated in detail before their junction. The problem of timing and co-ordination was formidable, in view of the slowness and uncertainty of communications; and the problem of command was delicate, but also vital. It was solved by the appointment, on 28 June, of Oxenstierna to the command-in-chief of the whole operation [1]: no general, however ebullient, would be likely to contest his authority. Much of the planning and organization was done by Gustav Adolf himself. A stream of directives issued from Nuremberg. For the most part they were in the form of suggestions and advice rather than of positive orders; but they were perhaps more detailed than would have been the case had Oxenstierna been a soldier by profession. They made it plain, moreover, that the operation was not considered merely as an attempt to extricate the King from a difficulty; but aimed at the destruction of Wallenstein's army by the very means which Wallenstein himself was employing. The converging Swedish columns were to be the instruments of a counter-blockade; they were to sever, in the course of their advance, the routes by which Wallenstein received his supplies; they were systematically to destroy the resources upon which he would hope to draw.[2] The tables would then be turned; and Wallenstein would find himself, in the face of superior numbers, forced to quit his camp in order to preserve his army: as Gustav Adolf put it, '*hoc genus diabulorum* [*sic*] *optime exigitur praecatione et inedia*'.[3]

On receipt of Gustav Adolf's order of 28 June, Oxenstierna had left the Rhine, with a force of 6600 men, and made for Würzburg, which he reached on 13 July. Here he waited for William V and William of Weimar. The Landgrave, still somewhat shaken by Uslar's defeat at Volkmarsen, left Cassel on 1 July, and did not reach Würzburg till the 25th: he had with him about 4000 men. William of Weimar was delayed, partly by his escapade in Saxony, partly because he wanted to pick up the troops which John George was sending in response to Gustav Adolf's appeal for aid. When

[1] *AOSB*, II. 1. 815. [2] *ibid.*, II. 1. 821. [3] *ibid.*, *loc. cit.*

they had joined him, his army numbered 10,000; and with this force he entered Schweinfurt on 21 July. About the same time Banér and Bernard reached Dinkelsbühl on their march north from the Danube. They had taken a circuitous route in order to avoid any engagement with the enemy, and they had mercilessly devastated the country on either side of their line of march. Oxenstierna was now able to fix upon Windsheim as the place of rendezvous; and on 9 August the general junction of the northern and southern relieving forces occurred there. The united army now numbered 30,000. Three days later, Oxenstierna broke up from Windsheim; on 17 August he reached the Regnitz [1] at Bruck; and here the union with the King's army took place. The operation had been carried through, somewhat slowly indeed, but without a hitch; and it reflected the greatest credit on the chancellor.[2]

The arrival of the relieving army did not in itself solve Gustav Adolf's difficulties. The problem of supply was at once aggravated; and there was little sign that his counter-blockade was causing Wallenstein much inconvenience. It was true that he could now march away with impunity and leave such a garrison in Nuremberg as to secure the city from danger. But whither, in such a case, should he go? He could not return to the Danube; he could not leave Wallenstein's forces free to fall upon the Rhineland, or on the Lower Saxon Circle, or on Saxony itself: it was precisely to ease the pressure upon John George that he had come north. And in central and northern Germany there was no military objective with which it was worth his while to concern himself except Wallenstein's army. Horn, Baudissin, Arnim, either were or ought to be able to deal with all the enemies they had to face. The logic of the situation led to only one conclusion: an attack upon Wallenstein; and even if Wallenstein remained within his entrenchments the risk of an attack must be taken. The coming of Oxenstierna's army, so far from restoring Gustav Adolf's freedom of action, deprived him of any rational alternative. By merely sitting still, Wallenstein compelled the King to undertake the most difficult military enterprise of the war. For some time Gustav Adolf had foreseen how it must be,[3]

[1] The Pegnitz enters the Rednitz at Fürth, and below Fürth their united waters are called the Regnitz; which is not, of course, to be confused with the Recknitz, in Mecklenburg.

[2] For the progress of the relieving force, see *AOSB*, I. VII. 421, 449-51, 460, 464, 469-72, 474, 483, 486, 493, 499, 520, II. VI. 65-78, II. VII. 373-4; *Arkiv*, II. 531-2, 556-7; *Sv. Krig*, VI. 180-97.

[3] *AOSB*, II. I. 825-30, 834.

and had rather welcomed the prospect than otherwise, for he still sought the final victory which had escaped him at the Lech. He could not pass by the opportunity of bringing his only formidable adversary to battle when that opportunity was so plainly offered to him. But he was under no illusions as to the difficulty of the task that confronted him; and he had already begun to think of the measures to be taken in the event of a disaster.[1]

He might well approach the problem with more than ordinary concern. He was, indeed, now slightly superior to his adversary: he had 28,000 foot, 17,000 horse, and the large number of 175 guns, against Wallenstein's 32,000 infantry and 12,000 cavalry. But a frontal assault upon a position so long and carefully prepared was as violently unorthodox, by current standards, as the forcing of the Lech itself. Wallenstein's camp stretched from south to north along a ridge overlooking the Rednitz, and parallel to the valley of that river. It was most accessible on its southern and western faces; but attack here was made difficult or impossible for lack of roads practicable for artillery. To the east, on the side facing the river, the position was split into three by the narrow gullies of the Asbach and the Bibert, inconsiderable streams which here descended from the plateau to join the Rednitz. The Rednitz, with the swampy land around it, was itself an obstacle; and its banks were commanded by Wallenstein's artillery. The defences on the escarpment had been sited with great skill; and the prospects of repeating the manœuvre at Mewe[2] were anything but encouraging. To northwards of the Bibert the country rose gradually to a bluff hill, upon which stood an old fortification—the Alte Feste—which gave its name to the subsequent fighting, and which lay just beyond the limits of the camp. To the front of the perimeter on this side the ground fell away in rocky and woody slopes to the open country. The whole formed a most formidable position.

On 21 August Gustav Adolf drew out his army to face the southern sector of the eastern face of the camp, and on the following day began a cannonade which was probably intended to precede an attack across the Rednitz against the Asbach ravine.[3] After a short

[1] *ibid.*, II. I. 833-5.
[2] See above, p. 331.
[3] For what follows, see Monro, II. 147-52; *Schriftstücke*, pp. 69-72; *Dagbok*, pp. 59-61; Chemnitz, I. 401-4; *Sv. Krig*, VI. 198-217; Generalstaben, *Gustaf II Adolf*, pp. 366-74; D. W. Pickel, *Gustav Adolf und Wallenstein in der Schlacht an der Alten Veste, passim*; Petri, II. 162-6; Ericsson, *Olof Hansson Örnehufvud*, pp. 38-40; Hammarskiöld, *USAH*, p. 190.

while, however, Wallenstein drew his artillery back from the edge of the escarpment to a position in which they were out of range of the Swedish guns on the other side of the river, though they were still able to command the crossing-places. In the face of this manœuvre the King decided that it would be pointless to persist in an assault from this quarter. During the night of 22-23 August he moved his forces northwards to Fürth; crossed the river there; and proceeded to the construction of a new camp to the west of Fürth, facing the difficult northern approaches to Wallenstein's position. Wallenstein seems now to have expected an attack from the north-west or west. He marched the greater part of his army out of their fortifications and arrayed himself for battle in the open country to the west, behind the river Bibert. He thus presented Gustav Adolf with an opportunity for a pitched battle in more or less normal (though by no means easy) conditions. It was the opportunity he had long been seeking. By an improbable and unlucky accident, he missed it. The King's preference for personal reconnaissance, and the risks to which he exposed himself in search of information, were notorious to friend and foe. On this occasion he trusted to the eyes of others; and they deceived him.[1] His intelligence entirely failed to observe Wallenstein's battle-array; but reported, with disastrous plausibility, that the enemy was abandoning his works and in the act of decamping, leaving only a small rearguard to cover his retreat. This information seems to have reached Gustav Adolf before dawn on the 24th. If he were to catch Wallenstein and beat him, he must act quickly. He proceeded, with the minimum of delay, to improvise an assault. Most of the cavalry was sent far out to the west, to intercept and harry Wallenstein's supposedly retreating columns; and no more was heard of it that day. The rest of the army was hurled at the Alte Feste and the northern defences of the camp, in the expectation of an easy victory over weakened resistance. In two main battle-groups they advanced to the attack, over difficult broken country; and no sooner was the action well joined than it became clear to everybody that they had Wallenstein's whole army before

[1] *cf.* Monro's comment: 'Though a King leading an Army had *Argos* eyes, yet it is impossible he should looke unto all things himselfe. The fault of one here we see with the losse of many was irrecoverable, and he that before this day was the terrour of the Empire, by his former successe, being deceived with false intelligence, is thought to have overseene himselfe, the errour of another being imputed unto his Majesty in losing so many brave fellowes; which should teach others to be the more circumspect in recognoscing, before they should ingage men in bringing them upon the shamble-bankes': Monro, II. 151.

them. Bitter fighting raged all that day, and continued sporadically throughout the following night. The left wing, under the King's command, was held up by the Alte Feste, never succeeded in taking it, and never got near the main defences. The right, under Bernard of Weimar, battled its way to a commanding height outside the ramparts, from which it would have been possible to sweep the whole northern sector of the defences with gunfire. But by now it was getting dark; rain set in, and continued all night, so that the ground grew slippery and impracticable; and despite all efforts it proved impossible to get the guns up to the hill. Morning broke bleakly upon a situation as grey as the weather. A brief council of war sufficed to reach a decision to break off the action. The army withdrew in good order, and took up its quarters in the new camp near Fürth. The losses on the Swedish side had been heavy. Banér had been badly wounded on 21 August; Torstensson was captured as he fought 'within a paternoster' of the King [1]; the casualties in the infantry were over 1000 dead and 1400 wounded. The imperialists are said to have lost, in killed and wounded, only some 600 men.

It was a sharp reverse; and the news of it rang round Europe. 'The invincible *Gustavus*, the *Lyon* of the North' was invincible no longer [2]; the prodigy of Swedish success—beyond all calculations of the statesmen, and against all the apparent military probabilities—became of a sudden less prodigious. The King's prestige was shaken, with important military and political consequences. But the Alte Feste, significant though it seemed, might have proved of no permanent importance, and in a military sense might even have been retrieved. In itself it settled nothing; and Gustav Adolf was far from being discouraged: it is even possible that he at first believed that another attack upon the camp, better planned, and avoiding the mischances of the former, might be successful.[3] He was still at least equal in strength to his adversary. The real disaster for Gustav Adolf lay not in the repulse of 24 August; it lay rather in what happened during the fortnight that followed that repulse. The tactical reverse at the Alte Feste had been a casual setback; the strategic *débâcle* that followed it was calamitous.

After the Alte Feste, as before it, there were only two possible solutions to Gustav Adolf's difficulties. Either he might starve

[1] Ericsson, *Olof Hansson Örnehufvud*, p. 50.

[2] See Wallenstein's comments, Droysen, II. 622, and the Emperor's congratulations, *Briefe und Akten*, III. 81.

[3] *Sv. Krig*, VI. 307.

Wallenstein out, or he might attack and defeat him: any other course of action put the game in Wallenstein's hands. The first solution was not within sight: the imperialists were much better provided than Gustav Adolf supposed; and when at last Wallenstein marched off from Zirndorf, townsmen of Nuremberg who visited his camp found ample stores of provisions. His men were much worse plagued by the myriads of flies and the formidable sanitary conditions than by lack of food.[1] There remained the solution of a renewed assault. In the two catastrophic weeks that succeeded the fighting round the Alte Feste this solution was made utterly impossible. In the new camp at Fürth men were now crowded in much greater numbers than before; and the task of feeding them or their horses soon became impossible. The hungry troops began to slip away; and the severest measures proved unavailing to keep them to the colours. By 3 September deserters numbered 10,000; by 6 September there were 7000 of them in the cavalry alone, and 6000 horses were reported dead in Nuremberg. Epidemics broke out for the first time among the troops on a serious scale, and mortality was heavy.[2] Within a fortnight the army had lost one-third of its strength. By the end of the first week of September, Gustav Adolf could stay at Fürth no longer if he were to save the remnants of his army; nor could he now, with his weakened forces, renew the attack upon Wallenstein. His only course was to march away—it did not matter much whither.

On 8 September the King quitted his camp. Oxenstierna and 4500 men were left in Nuremberg, as a pledge to the anxious citizens that they were not to be deserted.[3] As a final gesture of defiance, Gustav Adolf drew up his forces for battle before Wallenstein's position; but that canny general felt no inclination to meet the challenge. He observed their '*bravade*' with composure; noting with professional approval that the enemy 'made a handsome *retirada*'.[4] He could afford to be phlegmatic; for the Swedish army had shrunk to 20,000 foot and 7000 horse, and it was not in good shape. Since Wallenstein was not to be tempted out, and there was no battle to be had, the King moved off to seek recruitment for his

[1] Wagner, p. 23; *Sv. Krig*, VI. 306 *note* 4.

[2] Spannagel, *Burgsdorff*, pp. 371-87; *Sv. Krig*, VI. 306; Bennedich, *Ur det gamla Gardets öden*, p. 83. On 6 September Wallenstein had captured a Swedish train of 152 waggons: *Briefe und Akten*, III. 111.

[3] For the agreement with Nuremberg, see *AOSB*, I. VII. 543-7.

[4] *Briefe und Akten*, III. 111; Förster, II. 245.

men at Neustadt-on-Aisch, where (as Monro tells us) 'we resolved to stay a few dayes, attending what the Emperiall Army would undertake, having still an eye in our necke-pole'.[1] The Nuremberg episode was over; and it needed an eye of no ordinary sharpness to spy a way through the uncertainties that it had left behind it.

(iv) *The Struggle for the Initiative* [2]

Gustav Adolf had broken off his campaign on the Danube at the beginning of June because he could not risk the consequences which might follow if Wallenstein were left with a free hand against Saxony. His object in moving northwards then had been to save John George from the consequences of his inept invasion of Bohemia and to prevent Sweden's most powerful ally from being constrained or cajoled into a peace. The Nuremberg campaign, however unfortunate in other respects, had succeeded in this, its main purpose. Arnim was now driving the imperialists before him in Silesia, and the defection of the Elector seemed perhaps less imminent at the end of August than at the end of May. But the cost of success had been heavy: heavy enough to affect future plans. It was far from easy to decide what those plans were to be. The objectives were clear enough: to safeguard the position between the Weser and the Oder; and to beat Wallenstein decisively in the field. But it was by no means clear what was to be done in the immediate future; and at Neustadt and Windsheim (whither he moved on 12 September) the King balanced alternative projects. Two courses seemed possible to him. Either he might move with the bulk of his army to Swabia, leaving William and Bernard of Weimar with the remainder to guard the line of the Main, observe Pappenheim and Wallenstein, and give aid to John George as he might require it; or he might himself with his whole army follow Wallenstein wherever he should go, detaching only a small force to complete the subjugation of the south-west. After weighing the arguments for each line of action, and after consultation with Oxenstierna, he finally decided to go south himself.[3]

[1] Monro, II. 153.

[2] For this particularly complex period, see, in general, G. Wittrock, *Gustaf II Adolfs krigföring i Tyskland efter striderna vid Nürnberg, passim*; *Sv. Krig*, VI. 303-98; Generalstaben, *Gustaf II Adolf*, p. 375 *seqq.*; Tingsten, *Gustav Adolfs politik och krigföring i Tyskland*, p. 160 *seqq.*; K. Deuticke, *Die Schlacht bei Lützen*, pp. 1-38; Petri, II. 166 *seqq.*

[3] *AOSB*, II. 1. 840-2; *Arkiv*, I. 658-9, 662; *Schriftstücke*, pp. 185-7, 236-7.

It was a fateful decision, and it turned out ill. Yet at the time there seemed good reasons for adopting it. It might have been supposed, in view of the King's anxiety about north Germany, that the most natural course after the repulse at the Alte Feste would have been either to fall back on the Lower Saxon Circle and take in hand the long-delayed stabilization of affairs in that quarter; or to unite with John George and try to force battle upon Wallenstein. The former alternative does not seem even to have been considered, though it had much to commend it; for the King had decided upon other measures to bring the situation on the Weser under control: at the beginning of September Oxenstierna was commissioned to go as plenipotentiary to the Lower Saxon Circle, and it was hoped that his authority would suffice.[1] But the idea of a junction with John George was considered long and carefully before it was finally rejected. It was rejected, in the first place, as unnecessary. Arnim, after all, was doing well; and by the general rule of these wars his army must have swollen as a result of his successes. Wallenstein's, on the other hand, must have diminished in his camp at Zirndorf. Gustav Adolf took an opportunity to view his adversary's cantonments after he had quitted them, and came to the erroneous conclusion that he had never had more than 22,000 men under his command.[2] He had since detached corps under Holck and Gallas. It was reckoned, therefore, that his main army could scarcely exceed 12,000.[3] If these calculations were correct, John George ought to be able to hold his own. Gustav Adolf believed that it could not be long before Wallenstein went into winter quarters; at the very worst the Elector should be able to hold out in Dresden and Wittenberg until then.[4] If this were so, it was better to leave him to his own devices. And in any case, since Wallenstein had moved to Forchheim on 13 September, a junction with the Saxon army might not be easy. Moreover, if Gustav Adolf went to Saxony, it must be with an army of only moderate size. His experience at Nuremberg had made him chary of large concentrations of force in a small area: it was too difficult to feed them—at least, it was becoming so in north Germany. But there were also objections to taking a small force—the same objections which he had felt three months earlier: if in a joint army

[1] *AOSB*, II. I. 842 *note*; Wittrock, *Gustaf Adolfs krigföring*, p. 8.
[2] *AOSB*, II. I. 844; *Schriftstücke*, p. 237.
[3] Irmer, *VS*, I. 268.
[4] *AOSB*, II. I. 841.

he were decidedly the inferior, he was afraid that the Elector might constrain him to accept an intolerable peace.[1] But if he were not to join John George, and if the Lower Saxon Circle were otherwise to be taken care of, what business had he in north Germany? He was not minded to stand passively by, waiting for Wallenstein's next move, following him two jumps behind, allowing him to 'drag him around in the dirt', as once he himself had dragged old Tilly. He believed that a move to south Germany would enable him once more to seize the initiative; for he argued (and Oxenstierna agreed with him) that a campaign across the Danube might well divert Wallenstein from Saxony.[2] Since early August a revolt had been brewing among the Protestant peasants in the Austrian hereditary lands beyond the Enns; and the leaders of this movement had already appealed to Gustav Adolf.[3] If he were to hold out a hand to them, he might cause the Emperor serious embarrassment. But, above all, he hoped to find in Swabia an unexhausted area to provide him with supplies and allow him to recruit his shattered army. He entertained great expectations of new levies to be obtained in Switzerland, or from Rohan. And really he was looking not to the immediate future but to next year. The campaign of 1632 was as good as finished: what interested him now was the campaign of 1633. For that campaign, as he planned it, Swabia was the long-designed base; and soon, he hoped, it would be solidly linked to the upper Rhine and Alsace by the victories of Gustav Horn.

This reasoning was not without its inconsequences. If John George's loyalty was so dubious that Gustav Adolf hesitated to join the Saxon army with an inferior force, was there any ground for supposing that it would stand the strain of Wallenstein's military onslaughts or diplomatic wiles when the King was at the other end of Germany? If Gustav Adolf could contemplate with vicarious stoicism the reduction of the Elector's grip upon his electorate to a point at which it had shrunk to the retention of only Dresden and Wittenberg, was he prepared to suffer with equal fortitude an

[1] *ibid.*, II. I. 798; *Sv. Krig*, VI. 312.

[2] Though the diversion-argument is subordinate in *AOSB*, II. I. 841, it is stressed in Gustav Adolf's instructions for Brandenstein as envoy to John George: 'den Feind von Ihrer Churfürstl. Durchl. Landen divertiren': Irmer, *VS*, I. 269. And *cf.* the King's somewhat disingenuous account of his motives in his letter to John George of 14 October: *Schriftstücke*, pp. 79-80.

[3] *AOSB*, I. VII. 559; *Briefe und Akten*, II. 742; *Schriftstücke*, pp. 233-5; Wittrock, *Gustaf Adolfs krigföring*, pp. 15-16: *cf. Arkiv*, II. 598; Riezler, V. 428 *seqq.*; and *cf. ibid.*, 292, 302, 312 for similar movements in 1626.

imperialist control of the Thuringian defiles, or face the prospect of Wallenstein's cantoning his troops in Saxony for the winter? Saxony was, after Swabia, perhaps the least ravaged part of Germany, which was one reason why Wallenstein desired it for winter quarters: was it really true that it could not have supported the united Swedish and Saxon armies? Gustav Adolf's anxiety not to burden the territories of his ally with the extortions of his own troops would have appeared more laudable if he had not been ready to see it burdened with the extortions of the enemy. Again, the calculation that Wallenstein could bring only 12,000 men against Saxony, even had it been sound, was based on the fact that some thousands had been detached to serve with Holck and Gallas. But it was precisely against Saxony that Holck and Gallas were now operating! Nor was the suggestion that a campaign on the Danube would act as a diversion a very happy one. For though Oxenstierna undoubtedly conceived Gustav Adolf's move as a threat to Bavaria, and perhaps to Austria—especially if aid were given to the Austrian peasants—the King thought of this only as a less preferable alternative. He marched south, not to besiege Ingolstadt or ravage Maximilian's lands, but to consolidate his position in Swabia. His objective (as his envoy told the Saxons, to their small comfort) [1] was Lake Constance, rather than Regensburg; and he can hardly have imagined that Wallenstein would relax his hold on north Germany and rush incontinent in pursuit in order to recover Memmingen or Lindau.

But even if the King were to strike a blow at Bavaria, it was doubtful at this time whether a campaign in this direction would serve as an effective diversion. Maximilian might indeed hurry home; but what cared Wallenstein for Bavaria? Even had the heart of the Habsburg monarchy been threatened, it may be questioned whether he would now have abandoned his advantages in the north. The loss of Vienna itself would decide nothing. Emperors had fled before, to Linz, to Innsbrück (and even to Villach); but mostly they had come back again: Gustav Adolf had not now (or not yet) the resources south of the Danube for a real conquest of the Habsburg lands. Whatever view be taken of Wallenstein's loyalty, it is unlikely that he would have concerned himself overmuch at Ferdinand's misfortunes at a moment when he had Saxon resources to live on, and when the vital nerve of Swedish power in Germany lay exposed to his sword. If it came to diversions, Wallenstein held

[1] Irmer, *VS*, I. 269.

all the trumps. He had only to ignore the King's efforts to distract him, and maintain his pressure upon Saxony, and sooner rather than later Gustav Adolf must forgo his plans: as he wrote to Pappenheim, 'if the Elector is lost, the King must be lost too'.[1] After Nuremberg it was open to him either to concentrate his attention on Gustav Adolf; or to ruin the Swedish position in north Germany as an end in itself; or to use the threat of doing so to force Gustav Adolf to do as he wished him to do. He failed, perhaps, to make the best of his opportunity; but he started with a clear advantage.

It is difficult to resist the impression that Gustav Adolf's decision at Windsheim was the product of self-deception and wishful thinking.[2] He assumed—because he wished it so—that Wallenstein would go into winter quarters early; that his numbers were no longer formidable; that John George would scrape through the autumn somehow or other. Clinging with habitual tenacity to his grand strategic plan, he persuaded himself (with Oxenstierna an ardent accessory) that the situation was not really serious, that the Lower Saxon Circle could be settled without him, that the 'conjunction of Rhine and Danube' was still the overriding consideration. The intoxication of Munich was still upon him, the waters of the Lech still potent in recollection, and he dreamed of what he would do in April next year. Perhaps he forgot that for his adversaries it was still only September.

At all events, he broke up from Windsheim on 17 September and headed for the Danube. Marching by Rothenburg and Dinkelsbühl, he reached Donauwörth on the 25th. Here he was met by the news of the imperialists' capture of Rain, feebly surrendered by its commandant after a brief siege.[3] With Rain in enemy hands, he could not feel his rear secure if he were now to turn west to Lake Constance; and its recovery was therefore a necessary preliminary to the prosecution of his plans. It proved to be a matter of no great difficulty. On 31 October the imperialist garrison, impressed by the speed and energy of the King's preparations for an assault, was glad to accept a capitulation which permitted them to withdraw to Ingolstadt. The way was thus cleared, and operations in Swabia could begin.

[1] *Briefe und Akten*, III. 257; *cf. ibid.*, 326.

[2] For the controversy over Gustav Adolf's move southwards, see Tingsten, *Gustav Adolfs politik och krigföring*, pp. 160-1, 181-3; *id.*, *Gustav Adolfs basering*, p. 336; Wittrock, *op. cit.*, pp. 1-4, 7-9; *Sv. Krig*, VI. 313-14; Paul, III. 119-21; Sörensson, *Ekonomi och krigföring*, p. 319.

[3] *AOSB*, II. 1. 847; Chemnitz, I. 424; Monro, II. 158-9; *Sv. Krig*, VI. 329-30. The commandant was subsequently beheaded by the King's order.

But already there were signs that Gustav Adolf was not to be allowed to pursue his design without interference. By 29 September tidings had reached him from the north which forced him to reconsider his position.[1] Wallenstein was reported to be at Bamberg; Pappenheim was said to be moving against Hesse. A junction between their forces seemed probable. If it took place, it might well portend a united attack on Saxony; or, alternatively, Wallenstein might move north across the Main and threaten the Thuringian passes or the Lower Saxon Circle. In a long letter to Oxenstierna on 29 September the King surveyed the implications of these moves and developed his argument upon the measures to be taken to meet them.[2] If Wallenstein struck northwards, Bernard was to reinforce the passes guarding the Main, and if necessary was to retire southwards on Rothenburg and Nördlingen: Gustav Adolf would advance to meet him, and their united army would then follow Wallenstein and try to bring him to battle. William of Weimar, meanwhile, was to defend Erfurt to the last man. But on the whole the King did not expect that Wallenstein would proceed on these lines. He expected him rather to make for Saxony, in search of comfortable winter quarters. And in that case he was prepared to let him go. Bernard might indeed follow, and might give John George such assistance as he thought proper; but Gustav Adolf himself would resume his progress towards Lake Constance. In the meantime, he would wait for further news.

News came soon enough in a letter from Oxenstierna dated 28 September.[3] Oxenstierna confirmed the reports of Wallenstein's move to Bamberg, and expressed the strong conviction that the enemy was above all anxious to distract Gustav Adolf's attention away from Bavaria and to fix the seat of war in Saxony or Franconia. In support of this view he retailed a story told to him by the French ambassador, La Grange aux Ormes. La Grange reported that he had been entreated by Küttner (a Bavarian diplomat at that time engaged in peace talks with Oxenstierna)[4] to use his influence to delay any Swedish invasion of Bavaria for six weeks, in order to give Wallenstein and Maximilian time to complete the conquest of Saxony. There was little enough in all this that was solid or new; but it seems to have influenced the King. It is possible that he had never been quite easy in his mind about the policy of leaving John George

[1] *Sv. Krig*, VI. 331.
[2] *AOSB*, II. I. 846-51.
[3] *ibid.*, I. VII. 561-3.
[4] See below, pp. 751-2.

to take care of himself. However that may be, the first two days of October saw an abrupt change of plan. Gustav Adolf turned his back on Swabia and advanced into Bavaria; siege guns and material were requisitioned from Augsburg—undoubtedly with a view to an attack on Ingolstadt [1]; and by 3 October he had reached Neuburg. The implication was plain: Saxony was now admitted to be in danger; Oxenstierna's thesis about Wallenstein's plans was endorsed. There was to be a real diversion after all.

If in the days after the Alte Feste Gustav Adolf had been groping for a policy and vacillating between alternatives, Wallenstein also had found a decision difficult. He appreciated, as well as Gustav Adolf, the strategic importance of Swabia for the campaign of 1633: at one moment, early in August, he had almost made up his mind to make it his objective, as soon as the struggle of attrition round Nuremberg should have ended in his favour.[2] But when Gustav Adolf moved off to Neustadt-on-Aisch Wallenstein was uncertain what to do. He was, indeed, confident: he considered Gustav Adolf's army as 'totally ruined'—as he had predicted that it would be—and that the King must necessarily stand on the defensive, since he was incapable of engaging in battle.[3] The end of the war seemed almost in sight: the only difficulty was how to clinch his advantage. He had summoned Pappenheim to join him, and for a moment hoped to squeeze the Swedish army between Pappenheim's and his own.[4] But Pappenheim was incorrigibly insubordinate, and to Wallenstein's intense indignation he preferred to pursue his successful private war for as long as he decently could, and perhaps longer.[5] Wallenstein, therefore, could not count on Pappenheim; and still less could he be certain of the movements of his enemy. In the three weeks after the breaking-up of the Nuremberg leaguers it is hardly too much to say that both sides lunged about blindly in the dark. As late as 27 September Wallenstein had no idea that Gustav Adolf had gone to the Danube: on the contrary, he supposed him to be moving northwards.[6] And information about Wallenstein's movements was

[1] *Sv. Krig*, VI. 334.
[2] *Briefe und Akten*, II. 645.
[3] *ibid.*, III. 245-7.
[4] *ibid.*, 82-3, 100, 104.
[5] Wallenstein wrote of Pappenheim on 14 October, '. . . denn Plätze succuriren kann man noch malamente excusiren; aber Plätze angreifen, das ist gar nicht zu excusiren' (Deuticke, pp. 35-6); and again: 'Ich bin des von Pappenheim sein guter Freund, aber dergleichen gefehrliche und weit aussehende indecenzen kan ich nicht aprobiren': *Sv. Krig*, VI. 358; *cf. ibid.*, 238, and *Briefe und Akten*, III. 375, where he complains that he does not know whether Pappenheim is alive or dead.
[6] Deuticke, p. 41; *Briefe und Akten*, III. 178.

almost equally slow in reaching Gustav Adolf. In this military fog Wallenstein had been making and revoking decisions about Saxony. On 9 September he had determined to invade the electorate in person; among other reasons, because he wished to distract Arnim from Silesia.[1] Soon afterwards he decided simply to send Gallas to reinforce the devastations of Holck. Finally, he ordered Gallas to refrain from devastations, since he had decided to use Saxony for his winter quarters.[2] Meanwhile he felt it necessary to bar Gustav Adolf's road to Leipzig; and it was upon the supposition that the King had struck north from Windsheim that Wallenstein moved, first to Bamberg and then to Coburg, which capitulated on 28 September. At Coburg he learned the truth about Gustav Adolf's movements; but he did not therefore alter his plans. He felt neither need nor obligation to follow the King to the Danube. He proposed to occupy Saxony forthwith, and he was reasonably confident that this would bring his enemy hurrying back from Bavaria.[3] He hoped to be ready for him when he came, for, as he wrote to Aldringen, 'once we have crushed the King, the others will fall of themselves' [4]; but he would be glad to delay his coming until the subjugation of Saxony had been completed. And it was probably for this reason that he permitted Maximilian (with whom his relations had latterly been strained) [5] to march off for Regensburg on 4 October. He took with him all the Bavarian troops, and two of Wallenstein's regiments for good measure; and in return left Pappenheim at Wallenstein's disposal. His task would be to keep Gustav Adolf engaged in Bavaria until Wallenstein had settled with John George.[6]

Gustav Adolf's diversion against Bavaria never really got under way. He had advanced no further than Neustadt, on his road to Ingolstadt, when the whole enterprise was abandoned as suddenly as it had been undertaken. On 5 October came yet another, and this time a decisive, change of plan. A letter to Oxenstierna informed the chancellor of the King's determination to march northwards again with half his army: he would be at Rothenburg in eight days; Oxenstierna was to meet him there with the Nuremberg garrison; the Swedish forces in central Germany were to concentrate at Erfurt.

[1] *Briefe und Akten*, III. 119-20.

[2] *ibid.*, III. 187; Wittrock, *op. cit.*, p. 14; *Sv. Krig*, VI. 318-26.

[3] Wittrock, p. 15: as Wallenstein put it, 'will der König sich nicht verlieren, so muss er dem Kurfürsten sekundieren': Irmer, *Arnim*, p. 193.

[4] Helbig, p. 88.

[5] But *cf.* Droysen, *Gustaf Adolf*, II. 632 and *note* 1.

[6] Wittrock, p. 15; *Sv. Krig*, VI. 326; Riezler, V. 428.

Christian of Birkenfeld would be left behind on the Danube, with the remainder of the forces in the south.[1]

This sudden reversal of policy seems to have been provoked by the receipt of a letter from Oxenstierna, dated 1 October.[2] In that letter the chancellor reported that Wallenstein was making for Coburg; that an early junction with Pappenheim seemed likely; and that their united army would probably invade Saxony. These tidings can hardly have been unexpected; and Oxenstierna was only echoing the King's earlier argument when he remarked that John George ought at least to be able to hold Dresden and Wittenberg, since Wallenstein would hardly embark on siege operations so late in the year.[3] But the move to Coburg was capable of another interpretation than that which Oxenstierna had put upon it: it might portend not an immediate attack on Saxony but a blow at Erfurt, at Thuringia, perhaps at the Lower Saxon Circle. And it is clear from the King's reply that this was the fear which preyed on his mind. He broke off his campaign on the Danube, not because Wallenstein was threatening Saxony, but because he saw with sudden clarity the danger to his life-line to Sweden. The problem of the Lower Saxon Circle, neglected, postponed, mismanaged, minimized, had claimed his attention at last. It could be ignored no longer: the hour of reckoning for former errors seemed now at hand.

Throughout the summer and early autumn the situation in this area had been slowly deteriorating. Baudissin was plainly no improvement on Tott; Grubbe's lamentations grew shriller with each month; the demands for the King's presence grew more urgent.[4] The opportunity afforded by Pappenheim's absence at Maastricht had been frittered away; and when he returned he found the opposition as feeble as ever. Baudissin was worsted near Höxter on 20 September, and subsequently threatened to throw up his command[5]; five days later, George of Lüneburg was driven ignominiously from a blockade of Wolfenbüttel which he had better never have undertaken. Well might the King remark that in the

[1] *AOSB*, II. I. 851-3.

[2] *ibid.*, I. VII. 566-71; *cf.* II. VII. 9-10.

[3] It is fair to record that Arnim used the same argument to justify his reluctance to return from Silesia: *Briefe und Akten*, III. 284.

[4] For operation in the Lower Saxon Circle, see *Sv. Krig*, VI. 219-54. For the complaints, *Arkiv*, II. 604, 614-15, 617, 624-6; *AOSB*, II. IX. 816; Rommel, VIII. 207.

[5] *Arkiv*, II. 624-6. On 7 October Oxenstierna reported that Baudissin's troops were 'a great part ruined and dissipated': *AOSB*, I. VII. 585.

Lower Saxon Circle 'the eagle's talons grip faster than the lion's claws'.[1] Oxenstierna's promised mission, which should put all right, was continuously deferred by the pressure of his other duties, though at the beginning of October it seemed as though he might really be going.[2] But now Gustav Adolf felt that half-measures would serve no longer: no subject, not even the chancellor with his unique authority and prestige, could be expected to transform the Swedish armies in the Circle into a united force capable of resisting Wallenstein. He must go himself, after all; and he must go at once.

His anxieties at Neuburg were not all military. The motives which prompted his decision were at least in equal degree political. There had been a disquieting hint in Oxenstierna's letter that Kristian IV might again be intriguing with Wallenstein. There were rumours of Danish recruitment in north Germany: already on 29 September the King had instructed Oxenstierna not to permit 'any king, prince or estate whatever' to raise troops in the Lower Saxon Circle.[3] And he suspected that Kristian was tampering with the fidelity of John George and William V.[4] The Landgrave had certainly gone home from Nuremberg in a huff because he was denied a command appropriate to his rank and his great services; he was annoyed because the King discouraged his family feud with George of Hesse-Darmstadt; and Gustav Adolf now feared that he was 'disgusted'.[5] Frederick V, too, was presuming to take a high line with his Swedish protector; and though his attitude provoked in Oxenstierna only contempt and indignation, Gustav Adolf was wounded by it.[6] As he brooded on the 'ingratitude' of those whom he had delivered, as he recalled the constant struggle to keep his allies staunch to the cause, he seems to have experienced a momentary revulsion of feeling, a sudden distaste for the whole baffling imbroglio. In his exaggerated and morbid anxiety he now believed

[1] *Arkiv*, II. 446.

[2] *AOSB*, I. VII. 571, 588-9, II. I. 849-50, II. VII. 376; Ahnlund, *Oxenstierna*, pp. 707-8, 713.

[3] *AOSB*, II. I. 850.

[4] *ibid.*, II. I. 854: the reference to an intrigue with William V is ambiguous: it may be intended for George of Hesse-Darmstadt. Gustav Adolf wrote, 'mit . . . dem Lanndtgrafenn zu Hessen . . . in verstäntdnus stehen', and since he had mentioned both William (as 'der Lanndtgraf') and George (as 'Lanndtgraf Georgen') in the preceding sentences, it might be either. Kristian IV did indeed send Detlev Reventlow on a secret mission to Wallenstein at this time: *Briefe und Akten*, III. 368.

[5] *AOSB*, II. I. 854; *Sv. Krig*, VI. 299; Kretzschmar, *Der Heilbronner Bund*, I. 36-7.

[6] *AOSB*, I. VII. 596, II. I. 854; Spannagel, pp. 371-87.

that he discerned the emergence of a new political alignment, a new third party—in Europe, this time, not in Germany—which would apply itself to holding the balance between Sweden and the Emperor: England, perhaps, and the Dutch, and of course the old enemy Denmark—Protestant powers all, engaged from selfish interests in an attempt to curb the deliverer of Protestants in Germany. He turned northwards at Neustadt in a fit of depression and weariness; and among the feelings that moved him was perhaps the simple longing to be nearer home.[1] The jungle of German politics was growing above his head; he must hack his way out, if only for a moment, to breathe a fresher northern air.

Whatever might be the case with Gustav Adolf, Oxenstierna was still buoyant. He might on occasion (as very lately) feel himself pushed to the limit of his endurance by the burden of work,[2] but he had no difficulty in maintaining his wonted imperturbability, and was rather inclined to optimism than otherwise. To him the situation appeared better, rather than worse, than at midsummer.[3] He was entirely convinced of the validity of a Bavarian diversion, and he felt so strongly the advantages of persisting in it that he ventured, in a succession of letters, to give his master advice about strategy which was not the less urgent and emphatic for being couched in terms of dutiful submission.[4] With all possible persuasiveness he conjured the King not to allow himself to be drawn away from the Danube by the fear of possible developments in the north. To go north would be to play the enemy's game. Difficulties in Bavaria could be overcome: if Ingolstadt could not be taken, it could be ignored, and Regensburg could be attacked instead. A blow at the Austrian lands would threaten Wallenstein's recruiting and supply area, and would bring him back from Saxony soon enough. Even if it did not, Oxenstierna was prepared to face the consequences. What matter if Gustav Adolf lost the two Saxon Circles, if he gained the Franconian, Rhenish and Swabian Circles in exchange, and fixed his *sedes belli* on Bavarian and Austrian soil? With astonishing coolness, Oxenstierna was prepared to leave north Germany for the moment to its fate, and to establish Swedish power firmly in the friendlier south; he was willing to plunge into the heart of Europe, and perhaps be cut off entirely from communications with Sweden, in the conviction

[1] *cf. AOSB*, I. VII. 628: I follow Ahnlund's interpretation in *Oxenstierna*, pp. 711-12.

[2] *AOSB*, I. VII. 509-10.

[3] *ibid.*, I. VII. 576-8.

[4] *ibid.*, I. VII. 566-78 (letters of 1, 2 and 4 October); *cf.* Irmer, *VS*, I. 289.

that when the Habsburgs had been conquered the north would be recovered easily enough. His financial and administrative experience enabled him to grasp the fact that, since the war had become self-supporting, what mattered was not so much the line of communication to the ports, and thence to a base at home, but control of those areas of Germany which could best furnish men, money and supplies. And those areas lay in the south-west, along the Main, the Rhine and the Danube, rather than in the devastated Lower Saxon Circle or the barren defiles of Thuringia. It was a heroic strategy, not unworthy of Karl XII; but it did not suit the King's present mood. He found objections: objections local, objections general. He could not take Ingolstadt[1]; he dared not ignore it; an advance into Upper Austria might end in disaster for lack of supplies. And he pointed out that if Wallenstein and Pappenheim had already effected their junction, Oxenstierna's diversion would not divert them now.[2] Under the pressure of his chancellor's arguments, the King had been driven at last to look reality in the face. The 'design you know of'—the 'conjunction of Rhine and Danube'—was not, indeed, abandoned: about this time there was drawn up a scheme, as grandiose in conception as it was precise in its detail, for the recruitment of four large new armies in south-west Germany, under Oxenstierna's supervision.[3] No, it was not abandoned. But it was to be postponed to a decision in the plains of Saxony. The King had his way, of course. Oxenstierna tactfully professed himself convinced by his master's arguments,[4] and loyally co-operated in the new policy. The decision of Neuburg stood; and without loss of time Gustav Adolf began to put it into effect.[5]

On 10 October the King reached Nördlingen; and there learned that Maximilian and Aldringen had separated from Wallenstein and were on their way to Bavaria. Holck and Gallas had been detached already; Pappenheim, by all accounts, had not yet arrived. If he could bring Wallenstein to battle while he was thus weakened, he might defeat him beyond hope of recovery. From this moment Gustav Adolf began to think of his operations not merely as a campaign to safeguard the Lower Saxon Circle but as the prelude to a decisive battle.[6] Pressing on now with all speed, he plunged

[1] Aldringen was of the same opinion: *Briefe und Akten*, III. 392.
[2] *AOSB*, II. I. 851-3.
[3] *ibid.*, II. I. 857-66; *Sv. Krig*, VI. 342-7.
[4] *AOSB*, I. VII. 591-4.
[5] *Schriftstücke*, pp. 187-8.
[6] *AOSB*, II. I. 856.

ahead of his army, and with only a small cavalry escort made a dash for Nuremberg. On his arrival he was met with the news that Maximilian's column was passing southwards, at no great distance to the east of him. He made a rapid cavalry sweep in that direction, and succeeded in scattering some enemy units at Lauf; but the main body of Maximilian's army had already got safely by, and the King was not now disposed to pursue them.[1] He left Nuremberg on 17 October, taking Oxenstierna and most of the garrison with him; and by 20 October had rejoined his army at Kitzingen.

It was in Nuremberg that he received the first definite information of Wallenstein's invasion of Saxony.[2] The news spurred him on to hasten his pace; and the army now moved by forced marches.[3] It confirmed him, too, in his determination to seek battle; for battle now seemed no longer merely desirable but also necessary, if John George were to be saved. So much hung upon the issue that he could not afford to take risks: if he engaged, he must do so with every man at his disposal; and when Bernard of Weimar, in response to John George's anguished appeals for help, proposed to go with his small army to the Elector's assistance, the King peremptorily forbade it.[4]

Everything now turned upon whether the Swedish army would find the Thuringian passes in friendly or hostile hands. If the defiles were closed to them, they had little chance of reaching John George in time. And it seemed for a day or two that this might happen; for Pappenheim was reported to be bearing down upon Erfurt. The situation was saved by Bernard, who had seen the danger and did not hesitate to act on his own initiative. By 21 September Bernard was in Arnstadt, waiting for the King; and the passes were securely in his hands. Two days later Gustav Adolf and the leading elements of the cavalry caught up with him. The King stopped two days in Arnstadt, to rest his wearied horses and give time for the straggling infantry to come up: they had covered something over 630 kilometres in seventeen days.[5] At Arnstadt he parted

[1] *ibid.*, I. VII. 594; *Sv. Krig*, VI. 364; Ahnlund, *Oxenstierna*, p. 716.

[2] *Briefe und Akten*, III. 231-3, 301-2.

[3] Monro, II. 160.

[4] *Arkiv*, I. 680; *Briefe und Akten*, III. 293-5, 327-8, 431. Bernard much resented this order.

[5] Deuticke, p. 46; *Schriftstücke*, pp. 81-2; Fleetwood, p. 5; Söltl, III. 319; Generalstaben, *Gustaf II Adolf*, p. 381; Droysen, II. 656. 'S'il [Pappenheim] couroit, les Suédois voloient, sentant de quelle importance il étoit pour eux d'arriver les premiers. Ils firent une diligence incroyable & des marches extraordinaires': Priorato, p. 205.

from Oxenstierna for the last time.[1] And at Erfurt, on the 28th, he had his last meeting with his troublesome, possessive, sentimental Queen, whose presence in Germany had for months placed an unnecessary additional burden upon Oxenstierna's shoulders.[2]

It was now of crucial importance to get possession of the line of the Saale; and it ought to have been one of Wallenstein's main concerns to prevent the King from doing so. But when the Swedish advance guard arrived before Naumburg on 29 October, they found the town, and the passage over the Saale which it commanded, defended by only a handful of musketeers, who were evicted with little difficulty. Wallenstein was just too late: the Swedes had scarcely ensconced themselves in Naumburg before imperialist reinforcements made their appearance beyond the river.[3] On 31 October the main body of the Swedish army came up. They crossed the Saale; they encamped upon the further bank. The King was waiting for reinforcements, and above all was waiting for news. The military fog still lay thick over Saxony. He had little or no accurate information of Wallenstein's position or movements. Of John George's whereabouts he had no inkling; and from William V had come no word. Baudissin, he knew, was too far away to be able to arrive in time for the battle which seemed to be impending, and the order to him to rally on Erfurt had consequently been cancelled. George of Lüneburg had vanished somewhere to the east of the lower Elbe; and it was only now, on 31 October, that word came that he was at Torgau, whither he had gone to give John George such help as he could.[4]

Since he must wait, the King resolved to wait securely. Naumburg lies in a crook of the Saale, in a situation not very different from that of Werben; and the similarity of topography produced a similar reaction. The Naumburg encampment became another Werben, constructed by Olof Hansson Örnehufvud with a skill enriched by the experience of Nuremberg.

While Gustav Adolf had been on the road north from Nördlingen, Wallenstein had been occupying his future winter quarters in Saxony. He met with little resistance.[5] The Saxon army was away in Silesia with Arnim, and Arnim paid no more attention than Pappenheim to

[1] Ahnlund, *Oxenstierna*, pp. 720-7.
[2] Geijer, III. 211.
[3] *Arkiv*, II. 635.
[4] *ibid.*, 628-9, 632-3; *Schriftstücke*, pp. 81, 83; *Sv. Krig*, VI. 375.
[5] Irmer, *VS*, I. 273-4; *id.*, *Arnim*, p. 193; *Sv. Krig*, VI. 357 *seqq.*

orders from his superiors. Wallenstein at first hoped (as John George most devoutly did) that his invasion of Saxony would force Arnim to return; but Arnim was reluctant to abandon his conquests and contemptuous of the Elector's panics.[1] It had been intended that the invasion of Saxony should take the form of a double-pronged drive to the Elbe, Wallenstein aiming at Meissen, Pappenheim at Torgau [2]; but Pappenheim's late arrival made this impossible, and Wallenstein was forced to advance alone. He took Leipzig on 22 September; but his move forward to the Elbe at Torgau was halted by the news of the King's approach from the south, with the result that he was presently compelled to face the prospect of an attack in the open country between Saale and Elbe, without having control of the passes over either of those rivers.[3]

At this conjuncture he received the news of Gustav Adolf's encampment at Naumburg. It became clear to him that his situation had become somewhat hazardous: Gustav Adolf was gathering strength to the front of him; from Torgau John George might be supposed to be threatening his rear; Arnim might sooner or later be expected from Silesia, to take him in flank. If he devoted all his attention to the Swedes, the Saxons might recover Leipzig. Gustav Adolf showed no immediate sign of obliging him by risking a battle prematurely; and he himself had no intention of battering his head against the breastworks of Naumburg.[4] But the weather already suggested that the campaigning season was drawing to a close; and he was disposed to hope that Gustav Adolf might have fixed on Naumburg for his winter quarters. If that were so, Wallenstein might solve his own immediate problem, and perhaps destroy his enemy too, by a recurrence to the strategy of Nuremberg. Against the King's fortified camp he would employ the weapon of attrition which had succeeded so well before. The supplies of the Swedes should be cut off, the surrounding countryside controlled by the imperialists, until a diminished enemy was goaded into a hopeless attack or forced to a disastrous withdrawal. Such a policy, moreover, promised other advantages. The scattering of Wallenstein's units, with a view to cutting the King's supply-routes, would ease his own commissariat problem; and it would enable him to keep an eye on

[1] Irmer, *VS*, I. 272-5; *Briefe und Akten*, III. 23-5, 209-11, 289-91; Irmer, *Arnim*, pp. 194-7; Helbig, p. 91.

[2] *Briefe und Akten*, III. 258.

[3] G. Jörlin, *Lützenoperationen*, p. 290; Deuticke, p. 43.

[4] But he took care to get the unanimous vote of a council of war against making the attempt.

John George and Arnim. In a longer view it might have even more important benefits. For Wallenstein seems to have hoped to be able to hold the whole of north Germany in his grip, from the Oder to the Weser—or even to the Rhine—with the help of new armies which he planned to raise during the winter in Westphalia and the Lower Saxon Circle. If all went well, he would be strong enough by spring to interpose an impassable barrier between Gustav Adolf and the Baltic.[1] In these bold calculations there was only one flaw: he mistook the intentions and character of his opponent.

On 4 November Gustav Adolf received the astounding tidings that Wallenstein, almost in presence of his enemy, was dispersing his forces and going into winter quarters. The fog had parted at last, to reveal a heaven-sent opportunity. 'Now in very truth I believe', the King is said to have exclaimed, 'that God has delivered him into my hands.'[2]

(v) *Gustav Adolf's Last Plans*

The repulse at the Alte Feste, and the apparent decline in military power which followed that repulse, reacted unfavourably on Gustav Adolf's political position. He could no longer venture to take such a high line with friends and allies; and towards enemies he was now constrained to appear less intransigent. The language of Mainz and Munich was inappropriate at Nuremberg. For purely tactical reasons some of the King's more controversial projects for Germany were perforce passed over for the moment in silence, until the opportunity to revive them should recur; and attention was concentrated rather upon short-term measures of a strictly practical nature. It became expedient to show an interest in the possibility of a peace; and Swedish diplomacy sent up a kite, or baited a hook, as the needs of the hour might require. For the first time since the landing, negotiation was used as a defensive weapon, to eke out purely military measures.

This certainly seems to have been the motive which prompted Gustav Adolf's surprising overtures to Wallenstein.[3] The oppor-

[1] G. Wittrock, *Fyra relationer om slaget vid Lützen*, p. 308; *Briefe und Akten*, III. 484-5; *Sv. Krig*, VI. 385-7; Deuticke, pp. 48-59; Jörlin, p. 291; Generalstaben, *Gustaf II Adolf*, pp. 383-5; Paul, III. 136-7.

[2] Hornborg, *Gustav Adolf*, p. 119.

[3] For this, see Pekař, I. 226-33; *Sv. Krig*, VI. 289; Schwarz, pp. 64-6; Spannagel, *Burgsdorff*, pp. 375-7; Struck, *Gustav Adolf und die schwedische Satisfaktion*, pp. 490-1; Ahnlund, *Oxenstierna*, pp. 701-2; Paul, III. 106-9.

tunity for an approach was provided by the capture of Wallenstein's intermediary with Arnim, Ernest George von Sparr, during the fighting round Nuremberg. Soon after he was taken prisoner, Sparr was sent to Wallenstein's camp with a suggestion for a meeting between the two commanders.[1] This was refused, Wallenstein explaining that he had no powers to treat [2]; but an outline of a peace settlement was sent to him, and by him was forwarded to Vienna. This draft [3] provided for the withdrawal of the Edict of Restitution; the renewal of the religious peace in terms designed to remove all doubts and ambiguities; toleration for Lutherans in Roman Catholic countries; and the retention by Protestant princes of all ecclesiastical lands secularized since the Peace of Passau. It sketched a large redistribution of territory within Germany: Sweden was to take Pomerania *jure perpetuo* as a fief of the Emperor, and the Emperor was to cede his somewhat shadowy rights in Livonia and Prussia; Brandenburg was to be given the dioceses of Magdeburg and Halberstadt, as compensation for the loss of claims to Pomerania; Saxony was to have Lusatia and the diocese of Bamberg; Hesse-Cassel was to have Fulda and Corvey (already donated to William V by Gustav Adolf); the Mecklenburg Dukes were to be restored to the legal ownership of their duchies; and Frederick V was to recover his electorate. On the other hand, the Elector of Mainz was also to be restored; and Maximilian was to be consoled for the loss of the Palatinate by being given Upper Austria. Finally, Wallenstein himself was to receive the rich diocese of Würzburg, in exchange for Mecklenburg, and the title of Duke of Franconia was proposed for him. It is possible that he was also given an assurance that Gustav Adolf would try to secure for him the crown of Bohemia.[4]

Terms such as these could not be acceptable in Vienna. Ferdinand was not unwilling to discuss a settlement (though he pointed out that the history of his negotiations with Protestants had been uniformly disillusioning); he was prepared to give Wallenstein powers to treat; but he had certain fundamental conditions of his own to put forward. Like Gustav Adolf, Ferdinand was concerned with the problem of post-war security—security against the abuse

[1] Sparr had been captured before, and had broken his parole not to fight the Swedes again. Gustav Adolf threatened to have him shot unless he promised to speak the truth: Droysen, II. 624-5; Rushworth, I. II. 168-9.

[2] Irmer, *VS*, II. 29.

[3] *AOSB*, I. I. 540 *seqq*.

[4] Gaedeke, *Wallensteins Verhandlung mit den Schweden und Sachsen*, p. 42.

of religious claims for political ends, security against Swedish aggression.[1] But the Emperor's reactions were really irrelevant to the prospects of the negotiation. The terms Gustav Adolf put forward were so plainly pointed against the Habsburgs, so obviously an attempt to detach Maximilian from the Emperor, and seduce Wallenstein from his duty, that it was scarcely worth while to send them to Vienna at all. Gustav Adolf was offering Wallenstein a considerable bribe; and he was propounding a religious settlement not very different from that which Wallenstein himself had recently outlined to Arnim. There seems little doubt that he hoped, if not to win Wallenstein over to his side, then at least to neutralize him; if not to neutralize him, then at least to lame his conduct of operations. It was the device which Arnim had used with such good effect in April and May.[2] Oxenstierna later expressed the opinion that an agreement would have been possible, if Wallenstein had wished it [3]; and this may well be true. Secret negotiations seem to have continued, in a desultory fashion, for some time, through Thurn and Bubna; and Ražin thought that they might have been resumed but for the battle of Lützen.[4] But Wallenstein's experience with Arnim had perhaps taught him the unwisdom of allowing his military measures to be affected by discussions of this sort; and whatever may have been his private ambitions, enlistment under Gustav Adolf's standard had no attractions for him now: as he himself said, 'you can't have two cocks on one dunghill'.[5] It suited him at present to be loyal; and he was careful to ask Philip IV for advice on how to deal with Swedish overtures.[6]

It would be vain, then, to look in these peace terms for a statement of Gustav Adolf's considered policy for Germany. They do, no doubt, contain something of what he wanted—many of the territorial changes reflect his real intentions—for it would have been pointless to put forward a plan which obviously did not square with what Sweden might be expected to ask. But the tacit abandonment of Frederick V's claim to Bohemia need not be significant—especially

[1] *Briefe und Akten,* III. 130, 151-4, 386-93; Irmer, *VS,* I. 275-6; Hallwich, *Wallenstein und Arnim,* p. 153.

[2] Gustav Adolf took care to keep John George informed of the progress of the negotiations: Droysen, *Gustaf Adolf,* II. 625.

[3] E. Hildebrand, *Wallenstein och hans förbindelser med svenskarne,* p. 395.

[4] *ibid.,* p. 398; *Arkiv,* II. 592-4.

[5] Gaedeke, p. 38. Hildebrand suggested, however, that Wallenstein may have dreamed of being Gustav Adolf's political heir: Hildebrand, *Kristina och Karl X Gustav,* p. 39.

[6] Lonchay, II. 667; *cf.* Günter, *Die Habsburger-Liga,* p. 126.

if the Bohemian crown was really held out as an inducement to Wallenstein. Still less can any conclusion be drawn from the failure to mention the *corpus evangelicorum*, or any guarantee for the stability of the peace. Gustav Adolf had neither abandoned nor forgotten them. On 6 September he outlined to the representatives of Nuremberg terms of peace which agreed closely with those propounded to Wallenstein; but this time with the addition of provisions for a Protestant *corpus* such as he had described to them in June.[1] The goal of his policy remained unaltered, despite tactical modifications to meet temporary needs; and he stuck to his political solution as obstinately as he adhered to his military plans.

Of a similar character to this approach to Wallenstein were some dim negotiations with Bavaria, begun about the same time. The impulse on this occasion came from France. In July Richelieu had sent La Grange aux Ormes and St. Etienne on simultaneous missions to Gustav Adolf and Maximilian, respectively, and empowered them to propose a suspension of arms for three months on the basis of *uti possidetis*.[2] In view of the military stalemate at Nuremberg, this was an enterprise less hopeless than most of those recently sponsored by Richelieu in Germany; and it seems that Gustav Adolf was prepared to consider an armistice of at all events one month.[3] Nothing came of this for the moment; but in September a Bavarian diplomat, Küttner by name, made his way to Nuremberg, ostensibly to treat with La Grange, but really, it appears, to negotiate with Oxenstierna. A draft of terms drawn by the chancellor survives, which he may have submitted to Küttner at this time[4]: if so, it is clear that what he contemplated was a short armistice upon terms very similar to those proposed to Bavaria in January. Küttner, however, though he held out prospects that an armistice might be considered, was more interested in the possibilities of a general peace. The situation by this time had become complex and not without difficulty: the French emissaries accused the Bavarians of betraying France; Maximilian was writing in acrimonious terms to the Cardinal-Nephew of French indifference to his sufferings, and was leaning more than ever towards the Habsburgs; Küttner and La Grange each strove to poison Oxenstierna's mind against the other;

[1] Irmer, *VS*, I. 265-6; Ahnlund, *Oxenstierna*, pp. 701-3.
[2] Avenel, IV. 321; *Briefe und Akten*, III. 20; Fagniez, I. 592; L. Weibull, *Gustaf Adolf och Richelieu*, p. 100.
[3] *Briefe und Akten*, III. 96-7; Söltl, III. 312.
[4] *AOSB*, I. VII. 555-6 *note* 2.

and Gustav Adolf was nervous lest the report of negotiations with Küttner should offend Wallenstein, whom he was still hopeful of seducing.[1] All in all, the discussions did not seem to afford much prospect of being useful; and Oxenstierna came to the conclusion that the negotiation had been set on foot with the privity of the Emperor, and was thus to be relegated to the class of 'Popish practices'. The King, still resentful of the breach of the truce in January, described Maximilian as 'that slippery eel'; Oxenstierna, while not dissenting from this verdict, opined that the imperialists were no better.[2] But if the Bavarians had been insincere, the Swedes had been equally so. In the following January Oxenstierna told the Brandenburg council frankly of the ideas which had inspired the peace talks with Maximilian [3]: 'The King sought thereby the *distractionem Ligae a Caesare et disarmationem*; for hitherto the *scopus* had not been to root them out entirely; but the *occasio* for that might have presented itself. Thus the object was so to clip his wings that we should be in a position to dictate *leges* to him.' Negotiations with Bavaria, whether at Mainz, Munich or Nuremberg, had one consistent aim: to detach Maximilian from Ferdinand, in order the better to deal severally with each. At Nuremberg the language of Oxenstierna might be less high, the asperities of Swedish diplomacy less galling; but the objective had not changed, nor the deep-ingrained suspicion of the good faith of papists. Sweden still sought, even after the Alte Feste, a peace dictated, a settlement imposed upon a prostrate enemy. Two envoys of Hesse-Darmstadt, who in October met Oxenstierna in the course of their pursuit of the Landgrave's favourite plan for a general peace, were left in no doubt of the chancellor's sentiments [4]:

> A blind man can see what sort of a peace it is that the papists are seeking. They long worked upon the Elector of Saxony, that they might part him from His Majesty—and Sparr was busy in that too—but they failed; and now they use other means. *In summa*, the King will trust them no more, but will fight them until he has them down with his knee on their neck and a dagger at their throat, and then he will say to them 'thus and thus shall you make peace'.

The same substratum of iron-hard determination, under a surface softened by a temporary thaw, is to be seen in Gustav Adolf's

[1] *AOSB*, I. VII. 500, 523, 552-5, 558-62, 574, II. I. 851; Riezler, V. 427; Günter, pp. 118-19.
[2] *AOSB*, I. VII. 574, II. I. 851.
[3] Irmer, *VS*, II. 40.
[4] *ibid.*, I. 290.

relations with John George. The mission of Palsgrave August and Dr. Löffler to Dresden had not been a success. Instead of obtaining the Elector's adhesion to the great plan for a permanent *corpus evangelicorum* they had found themselves, at the end of their talks with the Saxon councillors, side-tracked into discussions as to whether negotiations for a general peace ought to take place '*ex castris*', whether the interposition of non-belligerents was to be tolerated, and what reforms in the Aulic Council and the *Reichskammergericht* would afford adequate guarantees to German Protestants.[1] The Resolution which John George gave them upon their departure was vague, full of counsels of moderation, and zealous for a peace upon '*conditiones possibiles, tolerabiles et practicabiles*'—which meant, in fact, conditions which Gustav Adolf could not be expected to think safe.[2] However, the King was forced to face the fact that he could not afford to put further pressure on John George for the present. After the failure at the Alte Feste, indeed, the situation was such that he must take every means to conciliate him and bolster up his morale. It may have been consideration for the Elector's strong dislike of the prospect of a Palatine restoration in Bohemia which prompted the less benevolent tone adopted towards Frederick V at Nuremberg,[3] and the omission of any explicit mention of Bohemia in the plans for a peace which the King communicated to Wallenstein and the Nuremberg burghers. A desire to propitiate probably lay behind his letter to John George of 3 September, in which he accepted the Saxon view as to the type of peace negotiations, and declared his earnest desire to bring the war to a close. On *satisfactio*, however, he made no concessions at all. *Assecuratio*, on the other hand, was passed over in silence: all that he asked by way of guarantee for the future was 'real and eternal gratitude'.[4] And not only was he now anxious to please the Elector; he was also concerned to secure the support of the much-mistrusted Arnim. The instructions drawn for Count Brandenstein at the end of September, upon the occasion of his going as Swedish envoy to Dresden, enjoined him to promise Arnim the King's favour, and to hold out hope of military support, a larger army to command, and an elevation in rank.[5] It may be that Gustav Adolf was coming to take a more indulgent view of Saxon politics and politicians.[6] It is at all

[1] Irmer, *VS*, I. 230. [2] Droysen, *Gustaf Adolf*, II. 582; Chemnitz, I. 366-7.
[3] See above, p. 615. [4] *Schriftstücke*, pp. 73-8.
[5] *Arkiv*, I. 668-72; Irmer, *VS*, I. 271.
[6] As Oxenstierna was soon after to do: Irmer, *VS*, II. 32, 40; *AOSB*, I. VIII. 6.

events certain that his attitude to them altered markedly about the end of August; and it seems probable that the change was dictated by expediency rather than by conviction. For Gustav Adolf could abandon *assecuratio* only if he were prepared to wash his hands of the problems of German Protestantism and concentrate upon building up a bastion of conquered territory in north Germany which should serve as *satisfactio* and *assecuratio* too—only, in fact, if he were prepared to go back to the politics of eighteen months ago, as if the great victories had never been.

For this sacrifice he was not yet ready. He still believed in the possibility of total victory. And despite the need to humour John George, he still believed in the possibility of constructing a compact league of German states under his own direction which should be capable of winning the war and (if all went well) of not losing the peace. In the last weeks of his life he launched the most careful—and the most hopeful—plan for such a league that Germany had seen since the failure of the Leipzig Convention.

It was on 5 October, at the end of that letter in which the King informed Oxenstierna of his determination to abandon the campaign on the Danube, that he gave the first indication of having a plan for south-west Germany in contemplation.[1] Oxenstierna, he wrote, would be sent to Ulm to take command of the armies in that area, and to preside over a *consilium formatum* which was to be established there. The plan for this organization was drafted by Solms and Philip Horn, and reached its final form after discussions between King and chancellor at Arnstadt on 24-26 October.[2] It provided a military and civil organization for the Franconian, Swabian and Upper and Lower Rhenish Circles. On the military side, each Circle was to raise and maintain an army of fifteen regiments of foot and fifty companies of horse—a total of about 130,000 for the four. The commanders of these armies were to be subordinate to Oxenstierna, as the King's legate. Detailed provisions were made for quartering, garrisons, supplies and magazines. The primary purpose of the whole arrangement was to ensure not merely the raising but the supplying upon an orderly basis of the new armies which Gustav Adolf would need next year. But for this purpose a more regular civil administration than had so far been provided in occupied Germany was now to be created. Two councils were to

[1] *AOSB*, II. I. 853.
[2] *ibid.*, II. I. 857-65.

be set up: one, a *consilium formatum* over which Solms would preside, would deal with general policy, justice and the maintenance of discipline; the other would concern itself with finance. The revenues of the Circles were to be ascertained in advance, and properly collected; the Emperor's regalian dues were to be commandeered. Care was to be taken to reserve to Gustav Adolf any *jura superioritatis* to which he might be considered to have a colourable claim. Over the whole civil and military structure Oxenstierna would exercise the King's authority. He was to care for the religious liberties both of Lutherans and Calvinists, though without persecuting Roman Catholics; was to arrange for the appointment of a Superintendent and consistory in each Circle; and was to see to it that they took proper care of education. He was given a pretty free hand to deal with Sweden's allies in the region, and was to try to prevent dissensions between them. He was to keep a sharp eye on France. Offers of peace or truce from the enemy might be entertained; but he was to refer them to the King before committing himself. And finally, he was given a general discretionary power to deal with unforeseen emergencies.

In order that the new administration might be started with the greater prospect of success, it was also decided to summon a congress of the Estates of the four Circles to meet at Ulm in December.[1] Over this, too, Oxenstierna was to preside; and an instruction for his conduct was also prepared during his conferences with the King at Arnstadt. It was once more emphasized that the immediate object of the new arrangements was the restoration of military discipline through the provision of a regularly paid standing army; and Oxenstierna's first task would be to persuade the congress to accept the necessary financial measures: it was suggested that they be invited to agree to an excise on food and drink, to be let out on farm to the individual Estates (who might perhaps be induced to pay in advance). But matters more specifically political were not forgotten: Oxenstierna was to try to persuade the Estates not to recognize ('*agnoscere*') the Emperor henceforward; and, if he found them in a compliant humour, to propose a reform of the *Reichskammergericht* at Speyer, though for the time being he was not to press this point if it should meet with resistance.

Such was Gustav Adolf's programme for south Germany. He proceeded without delay to carry it out: summonses were at once

[1] *ibid.*, II. I. 866-8.

despatched calling the Estates to the congress at Ulm [1]; and Oxenstierna prepared to take up his new duties, although (as he complained privately to his brother) his powers and responsibilities were more extensive than he found agreeable.[2] It is highly significant that the King should have begun this experiment at the very moment when he was returning to north Germany. The extensive powers given to Oxenstierna suggest that he foresaw that the restoration of Swedish authority in the Saxon Circles might take a considerable time. But it is very plain that he had not modified his basic strategy. Upper Germany was selected for reorganization because (among other reasons) it was the base for the campaign which, next year, was to end the war. The political implications were perhaps less obvious, but they were hardly less important. The scheme meant a long step forward in the improvisation of a real Swedish administration for the occupied areas. But it meant much more than this. The south German states—for the most part small and weak—were to be bound together in a close collaboration; and this association for a specific military purpose would be effectively under Swedish control. For the first time Gustav Adolf would realize his wish to create a league of Protestant states; the policy of piecemeal alliances, pursued since the time of the *Norma futurarum actionum*, would be replaced in south-west Germany by something more highly integrated. True, it was a union only to provide armies [3]; but it was at least the *corpus bellicum* which Gustav Adolf had propounded at Nuremberg and Dresden. Oxenstierna was instructed, no doubt, to proceed with tact, and to humour the Estates as far as possible: there was to be no repetition of the shock tactics employed against Mecklenburg and the Welfs. But there was to be no yielding '*in realibus*': Swedish authority was to be enforced; with consent if possible, but if necessary without it. The attempt to persuade member-states to renounce the Emperor was to be made in order to deprive them of constitutional arguments and legal pretexts which might hinder efficiency; the projected reform of the *Reichskammergericht*—borrowed, perhaps, from John George, and adopted, possibly, because Speyer was after all in Swedish hands—was a guarantee that the lawyers should not cozen the states out of the fruits of victory.

[1] Irmer, *VS*, I. 284-6; *Arkiv*, I. 681-3; *Schriftstücke*, pp. 237-40.

[2] *AOSB*, I. VII. 625-6.

[3] *cf.* Oxenstierna's remarks on 30 January 1633: '*scopus* sei, des feindes *praeparatoriis* zu resistiren, *disciplinam* zu redressiren und wegen contentirung der soldatesca mit den ständen umb eine geldhülfe zu tractiren': Irmer, *VS*, II. 27.

No other guarantees than this were provided; but guarantees were surely implicit in the whole scheme. If the projected arrangements worked well, it was not very likely that they would long be confined purely to the organization and financing of the armed forces. The *corpus bellicum* would tend insensibly to develop into a *corpus politicum* too; and in south Germany at least, where the danger from Catholicism was greater than in the north, the states might be expected to welcome the continuance after the war of an organization which had proved its value. It would, no doubt, be something short of the *corpus evangelicorum* at which the King aimed, since it would embrace only a part of Germany. Yet, if it was not the *corpus evangelicorum*, it did provide a nucleus round which the larger body might grow. Experience had shown that there would be serious difficulties about starting such an organization in the north: the great Protestant Electors were difficult to manage; the Lower Saxon Circle was not yet fully under Swedish control. In the north, as Oxenstierna pointed out, Gustav Adolf was 'little attended to, and rather regarded with jealousy'[1]; in the south, his authority was firmer, and gratitude had not yet worn thin among Protestants whose case had but recently been so desperate that they had almost forgotten how to hope. When the southern association was in full working order, when the Lower Saxon Circle had at last been reduced to obedience, it might well prove possible to expand the Ulm congress to include the states north of the Main. Of this, it is true, there is no hint in the instructions drawn for Oxenstierna; but it would be mistaken to argue that Gustav Adolf had therefore abandoned his earlier plans for Germany. The probability is rather the other way. The plans still stood, strategic and political; but both awaited the issue in the north before they could be put into effect. Meanwhile the Ulm congress was an instalment; and the tone of moderation which the King now adopted, the willingness to proceed gradually which his instructions revealed, were better auguries than the Brunswick treaties for the eventual success of his grand design. From the moment when the German war had been decided on, Gustav Adolf's political projects had conformed flexibly to changing circumstances[2];

[1] *AOSB*, I. vii. 568.

[2] As Oxenstierna put it, at the end of January 1633: 'Der k. wurde sich geendert haben, nach dem, wie er gesehen, dass der feind sich gestellt, die zeiten sich angelassen und die freunde sich erwiesen haben würden. . . . *De futuris casibus* sei zwar auch wol ehr geredet, aber *magis obiter* und das werk nicht genugsamb gefasset': Irmer, *VS*, II. 27.

and they had always been intimately bound up with, and largely influenced by, purely military considerations. And so it was now. In November 1632 he could less than ever look very far beyond the imperious demands of the moment, less than ever do much more than steer events in a direction which was at least not irreconcilable with a broadly conceived final goal, less than ever define that goal with diamond clarity.

For there was no use blinking the fact that the King's situation had worsened sharply since the spring, whatever Oxenstierna might say. Among the broad masses of German Protestants his popularity was indeed undiminished, and even increased: in Nuremberg he was revered 'almost as a god'; on the last march north through Thuringia the people showed such extravagant enthusiasm that he was wholly unable to master his forebodings: God's chastening rod must surely await the object of such adulation.[1] His armies, whether German or Swedish, still gave him more devoted service than any other general could command: undisciplined they might be in their relations with the civilian population, but in the ranks morale was high. The extraordinary performances at the Lech, and still more at the Alte Feste in the face of heavy losses, bespoke an army inspired by devotion to a great personality; and the astonishing effort which was soon to turn defeat into victory at Lützen was in the nature of a supreme sacrifice to avenge the honour and placate the shade of a beloved leader. It was, indeed, the King's personality that forged that heterogeneous polygot collection of soldiers, part conscripts, part mercenaries, into a great army. Patriotism animated only a minority, as the Swedish element diminished; religion no doubt inspired not a few; but for most the only moral force was fidelity to Gustav Adolf. His death would deprive the greater part of them of all other sentiments than those of the hired soldier concerned mainly for pay and booty. It was highly significant that soon after Lützen Banér should have pressed upon Oxenstierna the expediency of collecting all purely Swedish forces into one army, in order that he might have at least one wholly reliable force at his disposal; and Oxenstierna lived to regret that he did not take this advice.[2] But if the living Gustav Adolf was idolized by his soldiers, among the princes and the politicians it was a very different story. Of all his allies in Germany, there were now only two—William V and William

[1] Monro, II. 162; Wahlström, p. 73; Paul, III. 134; Treitschke, p. 24.
[2] *AOSB*, II. vi. 81-3.

of Weimar—upon whom he felt himself able wholly to rely [1]; and both harboured grievances against him. John George was incalculable: blown hither by his fears, thither by his principles, pot-valiant in petty provocations, sullen with mediocrity's resentment of genius, jealous of a primacy usurped; while George William's new-found zeal was too obviously the result of his willingness to speculate in Swedish futures, and Gustav Adolf had no faith in him. The Welfs, the Mecklenburg Dukes, Christian of Bayreuth, had all been affronted. The Imperial Cities might well find their evangelical ardour grow cold when they thought of the terms imposed upon Augsburg, of the damage to the prosperity of Frankfort, of Gustav Adolf's obstinate attempts to force his copper coinage upon them. It was a sign of the times that Dr. Löffler, borrowed by Gustav Adolf from Württemberg, decisively refused a permanent post in the Swedish service.[2] The rigours of the fight for religious freedom involved such sacrifices of political liberty that the German states were becoming alarmed and resentful, and might soon be intractable; and imperialists found it easy to make sardonic comments.[3] And since this was the temper of Protestant Germany—at least in the north—it may well be questioned whether any comprehensive *corpus* had much hope of enduring. John George would never willingly join it; and without him it could never provide the security which Gustav Adolf desired: after his death Oxenstierna, recognizing this fact, debated whether it would not be better to aim at two such bodies, directed respectively by Saxony and Sweden.[4] In his attempt to obtain Protestant solidarity Gustav Adolf had already been driven to use violence or the threat of violence: would north Germany have entered his *corpus* without the application of similar pressures? Yet it was just these dictatorial methods which had done most to alienate the princes. He had indeed declared that none should be constrained to enter his league; but without constraint it could hardly fail to be defective, and with constraint it must inevitably be artificial, and therefore fragile and short-lived. It was already true that there were Protestant princes who wished the Swedes safely

[1] Breyer, p. 236. [2] *Sv. Krig*, VI. 300.

[3] Their tone can be gathered from the remarks of Trautmansdorf in 1639: 'Das haist die Teutsche freyheit per arma Suecia vindicirt wan man die fürsten von land und leut iagt, als Chur Brandenburg von Pomern, Mechlenburg von den seinigen. Mit solche eloquentz so dem factis zuwider ist muess man die baurn in Schweden'stilten, in Teutschland khent man die unwarheiten': H. F. Schwarz, *The Imperial Privy Council in the Seventeenth Century*, p. 91 *note* 14.

[4] Irmer, *VS*, II. 30.

back in Sweden: within a month of the King's death Salvius was writing to Oxenstierna of those who were intriguing to 'shovel us out of Germany by whatever means, or give us a crust for our pains and therewith usher us out'.[1]

Outside Germany, the isolation of Sweden was almost complete. France, indeed, was an ally; but there could be no illusions as to Richelieu's real sentiments. As long as Gustav Adolf seemed to serve France's interests, as long as the domestic situation in France remained disturbed, Richelieu would maintain a passive friendship, pending the day when he should be strong enough to intervene. But in September 1632 came the crushing of Gaston's rebellion, and Richelieu's definitive triumph; and the ending of internal embarrassments would certainly strengthen the Cardinal's hands. The time had not yet arrived when he was ready to stand on his own feet in Germany—he was to lament that Gustav Adolf died six months too soon—but it was fast approaching.[2] Gustav Adolf sensed this, perhaps: his instructions for Oxenstierna of 24-26 October reflect his distrust of French intentions; and the last letter he ever wrote to the chancellor was concerned with how to keep Richelieu's troops out of Germany.[3]

Failing France, there were no friends, even in appearance, and many potential enemies. In England, Sir Thomas Roe and his party had lost the battle, and sentiment at court (though not in the country) was rather adverse to Gustav Adolf than otherwise. Relations with Frederick Henry were worsening, and had latterly been marked by acrimonious wrangles about reciprocal aid.[4] The emergence of a European third party was not yet a fact, and perhaps Gustav Adolf was wrong to take the danger too seriously; but the will to create such a party was undeniably there: John George perhaps encouraged these ideas; and from Denmark Swedish agents

[1] *Arkiv*, II. 675-6.

[2] 'Si le roy de Suède eust attendu six mois à mourir, il y a apparence que les affaires de Vostre Majesté en eussent esté plus asseurées': Avenel, IV, 415. After Lützen Salvius foresaw the increased weight of France in European affairs: *Arkiv*, II. 671-3.

[3] *AOSB*, II. I. 870. As Oxenstierna put it, on 2 February 1633: 'Frankreich werde sonsten der päbstlichen *religioni* patrociniren und sein eigen interesse *contra domum Austriacam* unter das *publicum* stecken wollen. . . . Frankreich prätendirt, die Schweden seind seine guete Freunde; es ist auch ihm nöthig, sonderlich, wo der trefves in Niederland angehet. Gern were Frankreich am Rhein, was von Basel liegt bis an die Mosel, das hette er sehr gern': Irmer, *VS*, II. 44.

[4] Gustav Adolf feared, too, that the Dutch were on the point of a peace with Spain: Söltl, III. 299-302, 320, 323-41.

reported how Kristian Pentz, far gone in his cups, had shouted for 'Balance! Balance! Balance!' [1] No doubt could exist of the ill-will of Kristian IV, nor that he would seize any chance (unless his council restrained him) to reassert Denmark's primacy in the Baltic.[2] Further east, the prospects were not inspiriting. The truce of Altmark would run out in 1635; and even if a Russo-Polish war should still be raging at that time, some diversion of Swedish strength to the Düna and the Vistula would be necessary—to say nothing of the consequences of the ending of the Prussian tolls, which had been the great prize at Altmark. Before the Polish war was resumed, Gustav Adolf must if possible have settled the German problem.

But what hopes were there, in November 1632, of a speedy military and political decision in Germany? The King might, no doubt, emerge as victor from the coming battle, and if the victory were sufficiently overwhelming, it might enable him to reach his goal next year. But if it were not? Breitenfeld and the Lech had been notable victories; but the war dragged on. Gustav Adolf's objective for the winter was the subjugation of the Lower Saxon Circle and its real incorporation into Swedish-occupied Germany. His success would have entailed the detachment of still larger numbers of troops for garrison duty, in addition to the thousands already tied up in such service, and hence have necessitated an increase of his army. He aspired, in the last resort, to exploit and control, and if necessary administer, the whole of Germany, so that his enemies should be deprived of their sources of supply; he aimed also at a large concentration of force at the decisive moment of conflict. But the exhaustion of Germany was making it difficult to carry out both halves of this programme simultaneously, and soon would make it impossible. The vast armies of his imagination grew harder to raise, harder to maintain: Gustav Adolf himself began to see this, after Nuremberg. The day was coming when the war would be fought by smallish armies, preponderant in cavalry, moving swiftly from one undevastated area to the next, fighting battles which led nowhere, driving into the enemy's country in deep invasions which culminated

[1] Boëthius, *NSK*, pp. 360-3; Fridericia, *YPH*, I. 235. The younger Camerarius wrote to his father on 25 October: 'Wenn je, so muss man jetzt alle Handlungen Aller beobachten, der Generalstaaten, des Königs von Franckreich, da die Engländer mit dem Dänen, dieser mit den Hanseaten und diese auch mit dem Könige Böhmens ihren Frieden gemacht haben': Söltl, III. 324.

[2] K. Erslev, *Aktstykker og Oplysninger*, II. 340-3.

only to collapse for lack of supplies. This was the Thirty Years' War as Banér, Torstensson and Wrangel were to know it; and if fighting were to continue much longer it was an inevitable development. But it was very different from Gustav Adolf's grand strategic plan; and it seems likely that the time had almost gone by when conditions in Germany would permit such a plan to be carried out. In 1632 total victory was still perhaps possible; within a year or two it became a mirage.

Everything, therefore, seemed to point to the need to be quit of the German problem as soon as possible: military difficulties; political isolation; the prospect of trouble elsewhere; the nagging anxiety about the succession, reinforced by the King's repeated narrow escapes from death and the ominous accession of a virile and able Pretender to the Polish throne. Gustav Adolf himself was grown middle-aged and corpulent; a little weary, perhaps; at times embittered and disillusioned.[1] On the day before Lützen, Tönnes Langman overheard a curious monologue:

> H.M. began to bewail and lament, saying how well he had meant in the German business; but H.M. said that since he now understood that these German gentry little esteemed H.M.'s favour or good will, nor would they suffer H.M.'s authority over them, therefore (said H.M.) . . . 'I will prove it, so that every honest man shall esteem me for an honourable gentleman, let it go afterwards as God will. But those others, that have not heeded my orders, advice and exhortations, they shall be . . .' —what I do not venture to set down here.[2]

It was perhaps no more than a passing fit of depression or irritation. Yet it is difficult not to feel that there was much in the outlook to justify it. For if he were to obtain the victory he desired, and the only sort of peace which could make that victory worth the sacrifice that had purchased it, what other way remained open to him but to pursue the path he was treading—pursue it, though he might be conscious that the obstacles were growing greater at every step? He had not foreseen the anfractuous nature of the undertaking when he embarked two and a half years ago at Älvsnabben.[3] Yet he could not

[1] Ahnlund, *Oxenstierna*, p. 725. [2] *Ett par bref om slaget vid Lützen*, p. 160.

[3] As Oxenstierna put it on 30 January 1633, the King's aim 'sei ins gemein gewesen, des Feindes *conatus* zu brechen, dessen vorhaben, und was er durch die Ostseh thuen wollen, bekant. Haben also ihre maj. die meinung gehabet, ihr reich und die Ostsehe zu versichern und die bedrengte lande zu liberiren, hernach weiter zu gehen, oder zu stutzen, nachdem es sich schickete; hetten anfangs so weit zu kommen, nicht vermeinet. Hat wohl gesehen und verstanden, wie das weiter zu fuhren were, aber dem feind und den occasionen nachgehen müssen. Wo die gefahr am grössesten, da seint ihre maj. selbst gewesen. *Momenta temporum* weren allezeit das fundament gewesen': Irmer, *VS*, II. 26.

retrace his steps. He was not now willing to be content with a half-result and a botched achievement; to cut his losses, take his booty and decamp: it was not for booty that he had set out upon this venture. He had put too much spiritual capital into the affair to accept an easy composition, even had he believed in the integrity of those with whom he had to do. For Oxenstierna it might be different (and the event proved it so), but for him there was no alternative but to go on. He had been borne forward in the grip of circumstance to problems and predicaments not willed by him, and the hand of God had been upon him. 'He travels furthest who knows not whither he is going'; and he had at least this consolation, that the course plotted out by his reason had been approved by his faith. And for the moment, at all events, he had the anodyne of action. It would be time enough to take fresh bearings when Wallenstein's army was driven back into Bohemia, and Swedish authority established securely from the limits of Pomerania to the Dollart.

(vi) *Lützen*

Even before the news came that Wallenstein was dispersing his army, Gustav Adolf had made up his mind to fight. On 2 November he wrote to John George that he would have risked an engagement already, despite his inferiority in cavalry, had he not learnt that George of Lüneburg had reached Torgau [1]; for he hoped that George's 2000 horse might be able to join him, and he proposed to stay at Naumburg for their arrival. The position of the Saxon forces at Torgau, however, was by no means secure, nor was it as easy as the King imagined for George to make his way to Naumburg. He was ready enough to obey the King's summons; but John George feared that his departure might dangerously weaken the Elbe line, and Arnim, recalled from Silesia for consultation, urged that in any case he could hardly arrive in time. These arguments at last prevailed; and Gustav Adolf fought the battle of Lützen without George's assistance.[2] But the news that reached Naumburg on 4 November swept away all thought of waiting for reinforcements. A dazzling opportunity was now opened to crush the enemy by a surprise attack before he could recall the scattered elements of his

[1] *Schriftstücke*, pp. 84-6, 240-3; *Arkiv*, II. 632-3, 636-8; *Briefe und Akten*, III. 451, 470-2; Helbig, p. 91; Irmer, *Arnim*, pp. 194-7; Paul, III. 135; Deuticke, pp. 46-7.

[2] *Briefe und Akten*, III. 451; *Arkiv*, II. 638.

army. There could be little doubt that the King was superior in strength to the forces which remained with Wallenstein, and there was therefore no point in delay: the supreme need now was speed, and if possible secrecy.

On 5 November, at 4 o'clock on a black winter's morning, the Swedish army began to move out of Naumburg in the general direction of Wallenstein's camp.[1] Their first objective was Weissenfels; but as they neared it detailed information came in, giving the precise location of the main body of the imperialists, and establishing the fact that Pappenheim (who had at last joined Wallenstein on 27 September) had moved to Halle. It was accordingly decided to try to surprise the enemy in the course of the day, before Pappenheim should be able to return. The distance between the two armies was small; and Wallenstein was still quite unaware that the King was advancing against him. The defeat of the imperialists seemed virtually certain. But then occurred an accident which transformed the whole course of events. Ignorant as he was of the King's intentions, Wallenstein had nevertheless sent out Rudolf von Colloredo with a small force to strengthen the garrison in Weissenfels. On his way thither, Colloredo stumbled upon the Swedish army. He realized what was afoot, disengaged himself adroitly, and took up a defensive position behind the Rippach, a small stream which crossed the Swedish line of advance to Lützen. Gustav Adolf seems to have considerably overestimated the size of Colloredo's force; and it is clear that the imperialists defended the passage of the Rippach with courage and tenacity. The result was unfortunate for the Swedes. For two hours Gustav Adolf's army made heavy weather of the Rippach; and when at last Colloredo had been driven back, and the crossing made good, it was mid-afternoon. There could be no hope now of forcing a battle before dusk; and, what was worse, Wallenstein had been made aware of his danger. Even if all went as well as possible henceforward, if the battle could be joined early on the following morning, the imperialist commander

[1] For what follows, see K. Deuticke, *Die Schlacht bei Lützen*; *Sv. Krig*, VI. 408-55; Generalstaben, *Gustaf II Adolf*, pp. 375-98; G. Wittrock, *Die Schlacht bei Lützen*; Liv-Rustkammaren, *Gustav II Adolf vid Lützen*; *Det svenska svärdet*, p. 82 *seqq.*; G. Nordström, *Wallensteins stridsplan vid Lützen*; H. Kerchnawe, *Lützen*; H. R. von Srbik, *Zur Schlacht von Lützen und zu Gustav Adolfs Tod*; *Fyra relationer om slaget vid Lützen*; Fleetwood; *Arkiv*, II. 643-4; *Briefe und Akten*, III. 499-503; and lastly J. Seidler, *Untersuchungen über die Schlacht bei Lützen*, the most recent and most convincing (though not the most temperate) account of this highly controversial battle, which is mainly followed here.

would still have fifteen or sixteen hours to call in his troops from their scattered bivouacs. The obstinate delaying action at the Rippach had robbed the King of his most powerful ally—surprise.

When Wallenstein took the resolution to go into winter quarters on 4 November, it is clear that he did not think it probable that he would be attacked. But he did not wholly rule out the possibility, and his dispositions were calculated so as to enable him to meet it, if that should be necessary. He had his plans ready for going to Pappenheim's assistance if Gustav Adolf should turn against Halle; and there is reason to believe that he had already selected the Lützen position, against the eventuality of having to fight a holding action until help could arrive.[1] Nevertheless, Gustav Adolf's advance caught him unprepared. Fortunately for him, Colloredo lost no time in reporting his encounter with the Swedish army; and about the time that Gustav Adolf was beginning his attack on the Rippach three cannon-shots from the imperialist camp gave the signal to rally on Lützen. At that moment Wallenstein had no less than fifteen regiments dispersed over the countryside at various distances from his headquarters: six had gone off towards Torgau, Zwickau or Altenburg; nine were with Pappenheim at Halle. All were now ordered to return to Lützen without an instant's delay.[2] The order did not reach Pappenheim till midnight, and his infantry could not begin their march till six hours after that; but the cavalry seem to have moved off almost at once. The route they took to Lützen lay through Leipzig; and the distance they had to cover was something over 35 miles.

Meanwhile the two armies lay encamped, within four gun-shot lengths of each other. All that night the imperialists were feverishly busy, by the light of torches, in ordering their battle-line; and as the outlying units came in one by one throughout the hours of darkness they were directed by Holck to their allotted places on the field. The position Wallenstein had selected was a good one; as well adapted to a defensive action as was possible in that flat and open countryside. His line ran roughly east and west, and was protected in front by the high road from Lützen to Leipzig, which here was flanked by a considerable ditch. His right rested on Lützen itself, whose castle was in defensible shape, and whose gardens and tenements outside the walls formed an obstacle to easy advance on that side. A little inwards from the right flank stood a

[1] Seidler, pp. 21-2. [2] *Briefe und Akten*, III. 494.

group of windmills, with auxiliary buildings, and here Wallenstein concentrated the bulk of his artillery. The Lützen-windmills position was the anchor of the whole line; it was designed to hold fast to the last; and as long as it did so it would probably be possible to carry on the fight. The other wing was much less satisfactory. Some measure of protection was indeed afforded by a small stream, the Flossgraben, which after flowing north-easterly to the high road turned sharply north after it had crossed it, and formed a natural limit to the battlefield on the eastern side; but at this stage Wallenstein had not the men at his disposal to extend his line so far. When the battle opened, his left wing was very much in the air; and he is said to have mounted drivers and camp-followers on baggage-horses and stationed them on this wing in an effort to disguise its weakness.[1] It was here that Pappenheim's cavalry regiments were to take up their position; and until their arrival the imperialist left would always be in danger of being enveloped and crushed. Meanwhile, Wallenstein had 16,000 men, of which rather more than half were probably cavalry. Pappenheim was expected to bring some 3000 more. Against him Gustav Adolf (by the exact computations of the Swedish General Staff) had 12,800 foot and 6200 horse. The imperialists' superiority in cavalry was thus already considerable, and upon Pappenheim's arrival might well become decisive. The imperialists had also a slight advantage in field-guns (24 to 20); but this was balanced by a Swedish superiority in light regimental artillery.

Circumstances had not permitted the King to bring against his enemy the decisive concentration of force which he had hoped for. There were some Hessians and some Saxon units in his army; but neither John George nor William V was there. George of Lüneburg was at Torgau with his detachment; Baudissin was away in Westphalia with the Lower Saxon army; Horn was besieging Benfeld in Alsace; Christian of Birkenfeld was infesting western Bavaria. William of Weimar's forces were present at the battle, but William himself was absent, ill—a piece of good fortune, this, since it meant that his abler brother Bernard was second in command. Others of the King's more important generals were absent too: Banér, still suffering from the effects of his wound at Nuremberg; Torstensson, captured at the Alte Feste; Hepburn, resigned from the service in a huff.[2] The army which put all to the hazard at Lützen was weaker,

[1] Seidler, p. 39. [2] T. A. Fischer, *The Scots in Germany*, p. 75.

both in numbers and in leadership, than its commander could have wished.

Gustav Adolf's tactical problem could be simply stated. He had to dislodge Wallenstein from a defensive position chosen by himself, and somehow defeat him before Pappenheim's arrival. At latest, therefore, the affair must be settled by mid-afternoon; to be safe, rather earlier than that. Everything depended on speed of execution. Only one means of achieving this result seemed to offer itself: to turn the enemy's open left flank. Such a manœuvre, incidentally, would sever Wallenstein's line of retreat to Leipzig and Bohemia; for circumstances had forced him to choose a position in which (as in Tilly's case at Breitenfeld) his line of retreat led out of his left flank. From the beginning, therefore, Gustav Adolf made his right wing qualitatively the stronger: here he stationed his Swedish and Finnish horse—the *élite* of his army—and here he himself assumed the command. Wallenstein, it seems, had not foreseen so obvious a plan: he expected that the King, as at the Alte Feste, would attack at the strongest point rather than at the weakest, and the weight of the Swedish onslaught on his left came as something of a surprise.

Gustav Adolf made an early start. By 5 o'clock on the morning of 6 November his army was getting into order; his intention presumably being to attack as soon as there was light to distinguish friend from foe. But, as ill-luck would have it, the morning of 6 November was exceptionally dark, in consequence of a thick mist which hung over the plain. Not until between 7 and 8 could the army begin to move into battle-stations. The intolerable suspense was relieved by morning prayers, conducted by the court chaplain Fabricius; and the King himself took the opportunity to address his troops in Swedish and German.[1] At length the move from camp began. The army took its stations behind the Flossgraben; crossed it without interference from the enemy; and before 10 o'clock was in position for the attack. But once more the King's time-table was thrown out: at this moment the mist thickened again, and made any fighting impossible. The Swedish army stood to arms south of the high road for a whole invaluable hour; until towards 11 the sun at last began to break through and the fog slowly dispersed. Gustav Adolf was now already two or three hours behind his schedule.

But now at last the battle began. The Swedish right moved forward to the attack, and after a tough struggle with the musketeers

[1] Chemnitz, I. 462-3.

lining the ditch evicted them, crossed the high road, fell upon the imperialists' left wing, and drove it rapidly backwards. By about noon imperialist resistance on this side was collapsing, and Swedish cavalry was wheeling inwards to take the infantry of the centre in flank. At this crisis, in the very nick of time to save the situation, Pappenheim and his cavalry made their appearance on the battlefield. Without delay Pappenheim restored order on the left. He then organized two complementary attacks: one, by Croats and other light horsemen, was to swing round in a wide leftward arc and distract the Swedes by falling on their baggage; the other was to be a frontal attack on the victorious Swedish right wing, and this he led himself. He had hardly launched his onslaught before he was mortally wounded by a cannon-ball. He was borne from the field in a cart; and with his removal the fortunes of battle changed again. Pappenheim's troops were shaken by their leader's fall. Lieut.-Colonel von Hofkirchen, a Protestant with a brother serving in the Swedish army, and himself torn between military duty and religious sympathy, refused to charge, and led his men to the rear. The result of these things was an indescribable panic on the imperialist left, in the course of which whole regiments fled from the field—some of them so far to the rear as to shake the morale of Pappenheim's infantry, which was slowly making its way forward, several miles away. Wallenstein's left was now disintegrating; and about the same time the bitter struggle between the two infantry centres, which had swayed to and fro about the high road, began to go decisively in the Swedes' favour. The King's troops got across the ditch; they captured seven of the imperialists' guns, and turned them upon the enemy; and once again the Swedish cavalry began to take the imperialist centre in flank. The battle seemed as good as over.

At this supreme moment the mist came down once more, thicker than ever. It hid the mass-desertion on the imperialist left, it concealed from the Swedes the extent of their advantage, it blotted out the prospect of speedy victory. It did indeed give the Swedes some assistance too, for it threw a welcome veil over the disorder in their second line and rear which had been produced by the unexpected impact of the Croats; but this was no adequate compensation for the damage done elsewhere, for the Croat attack had at best a nuisance-value. The thickening of the mist was a piece of cruel ill-luck. And it was speedily followed by disaster.

On the Swedish left, where Bernard of Weimar was in command, the battle had not been going well. The foot of the left centre could make little headway, the cavalry of the left wing could barely hold its own. The smoke of burning Lützen was in their faces, the 14 guns concentrated near the windmills galled them severely, and they seemed in some danger of outright defeat by Wallenstein's powerful right. The news of their predicament seems to have reached the King just before Pappenheim's arrival, at a moment when success on his side of the field appeared to be assured. He determined, therefore, to go to Bernard's assistance; and taking the Småland regiment with him, he moved over towards the left.[1] He found the Green Brigade of his left centre struggling desperately against odds; and at once he led his cavalry to their assistance. Almost immediately, the King was hit: a ball from a musket shattered his left arm. His horse carried him away from most of his escort, and soon he was caught up helplessly in the *mêlée*. An imperialist horseman fired a pistol into his back; he fell heavily from the saddle, and with one foot still caught in a stirrup was dragged for some distance along the ground before he disengaged himself. As he lay there face downwards in the mud, a final shot through the head ended his life. The body lay where it fell, the escort being dispersed, wounded or captured, and the Småland regiment driven back from the charge; enemy plunderers took the King's ring, his watch, the chain which he habitually wore about his neck, and one of his spurs, until at last, stripped to the shirt, the corpse lay half naked and unregarded, while the King's horse careered riderless about the battlefield.

It happened that Fabricius, the court chaplain, was in this part of the field. He had seen the King ride off at the head of the Småland regiment, and watched him cross the ditch and vanish into the battle. Not long after, the Swedish horsemen came streaming back in flight; and to his enquiries as to where the King was Fabricius received no answer, until the pastor of a regiment called out to him as he passed, '*Rex vulneratus est*'. The King's death, and the repulse of the Småland regiment, had coincided with the thickening of the mist; and the Swedish cavalry, unable to see clearly what was happening, imagined themselves hotly pursued. A panic flight began to develop on this quarter of the field, and as they rode past Fabricius members

[1] The place and time of the King's death is perhaps the most hotly disputed point about the battle: the great bulk of expert opinion puts it on the Swedish right or right-centre. I have preferred to follow Seidler's account, though it is not without difficulties.

of the field chancery called to him (in the decent obscurity of a dead language): '*Fugiendum est. Ego autem respondebam, Standum est, alioqvin nostra fuga provocabimus omnes ad fugiendum*'.[1] The spirit of militant Protestantism rose to the emergency. Gathering a handful of men around him, Fabricius began to sing the psalm 'Sustain us by Thy mighty Word'; others gradually rallied to the sound of the singing; until at last Fabricius had some hundreds of men about him. Among them was George Fleetwood; and with Fleetwood's assistance Fabricius induced them to turn back to the battle. When one cried that the King was dead, Fabricius boldly denied it: the King was only wounded, he said; or, if perchance he was really dead, then it was their duty to avenge him: he himself, if need be, would be their leader.

Thanks to Fabricius, and to the now friendly mist, the panic was stopped in time, and before the air grew clear again discipline had been fully restored. The imperialists, meanwhile, had reorganized their shattered left wing; and Wallenstein had sent Piccolomini with reinforcements to take command there. The rumour of the King's death had spread through the imperialist army; and though Wallenstein and his officers scarcely believed it, a great shout went up all along their lines, so that Pappenheim, hearing it in his cart, was content to die, in the knowledge that his great adversary had preceded him. The right wing of the Swedish army as yet knew nothing of what had happened; and they had little leisure for speculation upon the cause of the enemy's jubilation. For now the mist was off again; and Piccolomini and his cuirassiers fell upon them in the most terrible onset of the day. In seven heavy attacks he restored the position on his wing. The Swedish right centre was driven back to the road; the seven lost imperialist guns were all retaken; the Swedish gains of the morning were all lost. Piccolomini had five horses shot under him, and six musket wounds in his body. Though von Hofkirchen again refused to fight, and took his regiment to what he imagined to be a quieter station on the opposite wing, the imperialist attacks continued with the utmost fury; and the losses among the Swedish foot, especially in the Blue and Yellow Brigades, were fearfully heavy. Any prospect of outflanking the imperialists on this wing had now vanished; and it was only with the greatest difficulty that the situation here was more or less stabilized.

By about 2 o'clock, therefore, the battle had turned clearly to the

[1] Fabricius's vivid narrative is in *Fyra relationer om slaget vid Lützen*, pp. 305-7.

Swedes' disadvantage: victory seemed doubtful, defeat more than likely. After the King's death the command had devolved upon Bernard of Saxe-Weimar, who seems to have been informed of the catastrophe very soon after it occurred. He consulted Knyphausen as to what was to be done; and Knyphausen advised him to break off the action. The advice was not taken. Bernard determined rather to make a last effort to retrieve the day on his own wing: if he could dislodge Wallenstein from his stronghold round the windmills, there was still a chance of victory. By this time the King's death seems to have been generally known on this wing; and Bernard counted on his men's eagerness to avenge it. He did not reckon in vain. Between 3 and 4 o'clock the Swedish left, supported by guns which had been moved to fresh positions, and fighting with frantic resolution, pushed forward once more across the road. After bloody fighting, the windmills were taken one by one; all the 14 imperialist guns passed into Swedish hands; and though for a time Wallenstein counter-attacked with limited success, the Swedes recovered and made good their ground. But the light was now failing fast; and when, soon after 5 o'clock, it grew too dark to see, the issue still appeared uncertain. Yet in effect it had been decided; for the key to Wallenstein's position was now in Bernard's hands; and every piece of artillery he possessed (except some guns coming up with Pappenheim's infantry) had been captured. Only the tenacity of the imperialist infantry had prevented a complete break-through. Fighting went on sporadically in the dusk, and near nightfall the arrival of the infantry from Halle made it possible that the combat might be resumed; but Wallenstein, tortured by gout, and physically and mentally exhausted, would fight no more. He believed that John George was marching against him from Torgau with 16,000 fresh troops, and he feared to be caught between two fires. He decided on a withdrawal; and no pleas could turn him from his resolution. By midnight he had arrived in Leipzig, though the last of his rear-guard did not come in till seven hours later; and the battlefield of Lützen was left to the Swedes, and to those marauding Croats who remained, like scum after the ebbing of the imperialist tide, to sabre the wounded and to rob the slain.

There was no pursuit. Wallenstein's withdrawal was carried out in exemplary order; and it was remarked that not one of the imperialists' mercenaries went over to the victors. Both sides were exhausted; and for many ammunition was exhausted too: in the final stages of the battle musketeers were reduced to clubbing each other with the butt. Bernard's troops were fought to a standstill; and in the supreme effort that gave him the victory he had thrown in his last reserves. The heaviness of the casualties bore witness to the ferocity of the fighting: the Swedes lost perhaps 5000 or 6000 men—nearly a third of their army; and though the losses of the imperialists were not computed, they are agreed to have been even heavier. Lützen, then, was a Swedish victory by all the contemporary criteria: Wallenstein quitted the battlefield, and he left his guns in his enemy's hands. But it was not a victory that was overwhelming or tactically decisive: the mist had cheated them of that. The military significance of Lützen lay rather in its strategic results. It smashed Wallenstein's plan for cutting off Gustav Adolf from the sea; it drove him to take the road to Bohemia, and once more to winter on imperial soil—a consequence which his enemies at Vienna were not slow to turn to his disadvantage.

But all balancing of purely military gain or loss was made insignificant in the face of the one great fact of the King's death. Upon contemporaries it made the profoundest impression. Elegies in verse poured from the pens of poets in half a dozen languages. The Danish chancellor, Kristian Friis, shut himself up for two days in his chamber to mourn the Protestant hero; while Władysław IV lamented the passing of the greatest of the Vasas. Richelieu, disconcerted, was divided between annoyance and relief; Madrid was proportionably jubilant; Urban VIII was credibly (but falsely) reported to have been plunged in grief for the enemy of the Habsburgs; while in Brussels they held a solemn service of thanksgiving in St. Gudule. Stout Protestant hearts in distant England refused to credit the news: as late as 12 December merchants in London were wagering that the report was false.[1] The King's frequent escapes from death had encouraged men to believe in his good fortune; but there were obstinate stories of treachery: Francis Albert of Lauenburg was long suspected of having murdered him in the heat of battle.

It was indeed a great event; for it was more than the end of a great man and a great reign. When Gustav Adolf perished, the last ideal element in the German wars perished too. Henceforward

[1] Fridericia, *YPH*, I. 78-9 (for Friis); Mommsen, p. 143; Hanotaux, III 432 (for Richelieu); S. Ehses, *Papst Urban VIII und Gustav Adolf*, pp. 336-41 (for Urban VIII); Lonchay, II. 664 (for the *Te Deum* in St. Gudule); *CSP Dom. 1631-33*, pp. 454, 457 (for English reactions).

Swedish interests, French interests, the particularist interests of German states, might combine, dissolve and combine again; but no leader now would be able to emulate the King's unselfconscious achievement; for no leader would be able to ennoble the aims of secular politics by identifying them with a deeply felt spiritual cause. The end of his life heralded the closing of an epoch: the epoch which had begun with the Reformation; and though England was still to produce, in Cromwell, Gustav Adolf's epigone, on the continent the influence of religion upon politics was waning fast. For Germany, in the immediate future, Lützen ushered in sixteen years of horror and gross darkness, before a peace of compromise and exhaustion gave surcease to misery; for Europe, in a wider view, it inaugurated a period of a century and a half when warfare would be divorced from idealism, and politics emptied of faith.[1]

[1] The question as to what the future of Germany might have been if Gustav Adolf had survived the battle of Lützen has in the past much exercised the speculative ingenuity of German historians. It is a somewhat barren and profitless question, differing in degree rather than in kind of interest from (for instance) the question as to what might have happened to France if Henry V had lived as long as Edward III; and as English historians do not as a rule concern themselves with the one problem, so a historian of Sweden may perhaps be excused from concerning himself with the other.

CHAPTER XII

THE KING AND THE REIGN

WHAT, then, of Sweden? What place does Gustav Adolf occupy in the long roll of Swedish kings; what significance has his reign in the broad perspectives of Swedish history?

It is obvious that in these two crowded decades the position of Sweden in Europe and Scandinavia underwent a portentous transformation: no reign in Swedish history had more striking immediate effects; and none, perhaps, had consequences more enduring. Both in the long and in the short run, Gustav Adolf changed the course of his country's development. At his accession Sweden's very existence as an independent nation was in jeopardy; at his death he left her a great power—more feared, perhaps, than any other in Europe. The treaties of Westphalia ratified his work. Henceforward Sweden was committed to participation in the general politics of the continent, to which her quasi-insular position might otherwise have rendered her comparatively indifferent. His heirs and successors henceforward asserted an equality with the Most Christian King; to the lively indignation of Louis XIV.[1] Like France, Sweden was a guarantor of the great political and religious settlement which was to provide one of the bases for international relations until the earthquakes of the last decade of the eighteenth century destroyed it. And Sweden was not merely a great power: she was—as Westphalia implicitly recognized—the pre-eminent Protestant power on the continent of Europe: the official champion of the Protestant cause whenever it should again be endangered. Cromwell's attitude to Karl X Gustav was in part determined by this fact. Karl XII was fully conscious of the obligations it entailed. As late as the Seven Years' War it was a factor in politics. The international position and obligations which sprang from Gustav Adolf's work thus provided the basis, or the impulse, for nearly a

[1] In April 1667 Louis XIV wrote to d'Estrades that 'Depuis que le roi Gustave Adolphe de Suède se mit en tête de prétendre l'égalité entre tous les rois, à cause du nom et du titre qu'ils ont égal, et qu'il fallut pour d'autres plus grands intérêts s'accommoder à son caprice et à cette injustice, tous les autres rois à son exemple ont prétendu la même chose': C.-G. Picavet, *La Diplomatie française au temps de Louis XIV* (1930), p. 151.

century of Swedish foreign policy. A new cycle of developments began to unfold itself which had little enough to do with Swedish interests as Gustav Vasa had conceived them, and still less with Swedish interests as they were to be interpreted by Oscar II.

Until Gustav Adolf's time, Sweden's natural spheres of action, the natural lines of force along which she exerted pressure, had lain to east and to west—against Muscovy, against Denmark. The quarrel with Denmark was a legacy of strife bequeathed upon the death-bed of the Kalmar Union; the enmity to Russia was sustained by an obscure but just appreciation of the danger to Sweden of Muscovite expansion to the west. No doubt it had been a political and economic necessity for Sweden to keep open her line of communication to north Germany, to resist the attempts of Danish kings to build up a broad belt of influence cutting athwart that line and stretching out eastwards from Copenhagen to the Gulf of Riga. But hitherto, save on rare occasions, Sweden had played no active part in north German politics. The dynastic struggle with Poland, and the intervention in Germany which in part grew out of it, turned Swedish energies towards quite new objectives, and for a time involved the partial neglect of the old. The rivalry with Denmark was put into cold storage for the sake of the Protestant cause. After Stolbova the Tsar was flattered and courted, that he might be available at need as an ally against the Polish Vasas. Thus the policy that reaped its reward at Westphalia lay outside the main current of Swedish history; it was an adventure excentric to the ordinary interests of the country, as they had been revealed by experience in the past. And even before the peace of Westphalia was made, Oxenstierna had returned—as Gustav Adolf had more than once been tempted to return—to the long-postponed duel with the Dane; and at Brömsebro in 1645 had taken the first step since 1613 towards the attainment of Sweden's natural frontiers. Until those limits had been reached, until at least one shore of the Sound was in Swedish hands, there could be no permanent peace with Denmark. Karl Gustav took up this task, for a moment dreaming of a united Scandinavia subjected to Sweden; and although the gains of Roskilde were in part lost at Copenhagen, he did enough to give Sweden all she really needed of Denmark, and all she was reasonably entitled to demand. After 1660 the secular enmity between them might well have withered away for lack of nutriment (as men such as Johan Gyllenstierna desired) had it not been for the unfortunate and unnecessary complication provided by the dynastic links with Gottorp. And if in regard to Denmark Karl Gustav was the vigorous reasserter of traditional policies which under Gustav Adolf had been at times obscured by vaster issues, he was so no less in regard to Sweden's eastern neighbour. Russia, rather than Poland, was for him the enemy; and the peace of Oliva, burying at long last the Vasa's dynastic hatchet, laid bare the truth which Karl Gustav had so shrewdly perceived, and left Sweden face to face with the Muscovite. One solution to this situation, though not perhaps the only one, was provided by the career of Karl XII.

But when Karl Gustav thus returned to a narrowly Swedish policy, he found himself confronted with difficulties which were to some degree the result of Gustav Adolf's divagations into other courses. His wars with Poland and with Denmark took on the appearance of a grand imperial design, a megalomaniac scheme of general Baltic domination, because they seemed to aim at completing that occupation of the southern coasts of the Baltic which Gustav Adolf had initiated. His invasion of Prussia entailed a clash with the Dutch, and made explicit the implicit rivalry of Brandenburg. The hostility of Brandenburg, which for three-quarters of a century was to be a more or less permanent feature of northern politics, was a direct legacy from Gustav Adolf. The loss, at Westphalia, of the most valuable part of Pomerania (and especially of Stettin), the fear of a revival of Gustav Adolf's designs upon the Vistula, drove Brandenburg into the camp of Sweden's enemies. Had Gustav Adolf's plan of a dynastic union with Brandenburg been realized, no doubt some of these inconveniences might have been avoided; and at least the task of policing Germany in the Protestant interest might have been transferred to Brandenburg's shoulders. But within a generation of Gustav Adolf's death it had already become clear that Protestant Germany was no longer in need of such protection. The War of the North would see Calvinist Brandenburg, Lutheran Denmark and Catholic Habsburg in league against Sweden: the guarantees which Gustav Adolf had so painfully striven for were no longer of any consequence; the desire of the German states for security found expression, not in the *corpus evangelicorum*, but in the League of the Rhine.

In these altered circumstances, the German provinces which Gustav Adolf had won could no longer be considered in the light of *assecuratio*; and though they had some value as *satisfactio*, it was a question whether the economic gain might not be offset by the political liabilities they brought with them. They constituted, no doubt, a bridge between the insular concerns of Scandinavia and the more important controversies of a wider world, as Hanover did for Britain a century later; but, like Hanover, they sometimes distorted and perverted policy too. The Baltic provinces were a very different matter: here Gustav Adolf's conquests long continued to make political sense. After 1648 Stralsund and Stettin were not perhaps much more beneficial to their possessor than Calais had been to England, or than Dunkirk was destined to be; but Riga and Reval were pillars of an intelligible, if not highly viable, political structure.

The Baltic empire of which Gustav Adolf was the most important architect was an empire which could be held together only by continuous and exhausting effort. Its scattered disposition, which rendered Sweden liable to involvement in the local controversies of widely dispersed areas; the length and vulnerability of its frontiers on the landward side; the difficulty or impossibility of maintaining continuous sea-communications with all parts of it when the ports were ice-bound—all this necessitated heavy expenditure on fortifications and garrisons. It has often enough been asserted that Sweden's resources, in men and money, were from the beginning inadequate to supporting the status of a great power; and the statement is in some respects true. It is true, at least, for the latter half of the seventeenth century. But it would be erroneous to assume that it is necessarily true for Gustav Adolf's lifetime, or for the closing period of the Thirty Years' War. The core of the Swedish army was, and remained, the native levies raised by *utskrivning*: at the close of that war they numbered no less than 74,000. Seven years later, on the eve of Karl Gustav's war against Poland, his army had only six mercenary regiments out of thirty-nine. The native standing army, as provided for in the Form of Government of 1634, was not a serious burden to the state; for the method of paying it which Gustav Adolf had developed—by the assigning of farms for its support—was probably more economical and effective than any other system in operation at that time. It is true that the German wars were fought increasingly by German mercenaries—the native armies were not risked in battle, but were used for garrison duty or home defence—and that this entailed the hiring of very large numbers of expensive professionals. But the burden of paying them did not fall on Sweden. It fell on Germany. War supported war, as Gustav Adolf had always contended that it should; and when Oxenstierna took over the direction of affairs in Germany after Lützen, he made it a cardinal point in his programme to ensure that this state of affairs should continue.[1] The strain of war was probably less severely felt between 1632 and 1648 than at any time in Gustav Adolf's reign; and in 1644 the real debt of the state is said not to have exceeded half a million *daler*. And the burden might well have been even less than it was had it not been for the alienation and sale of royal revenues; for the countervailing advantages which were expected from this policy failed, on the whole, to materialize, even after the abrogation of the nobility's exemption from customs dues in 1644.

There was thus no real reason to suppose that Sweden would be unequal to the military obligations entailed by her status as a great power, so long as those conditions with which Gustav Adolf had been familiar in Germany continued to obtain. But, as it happened, they were never to recur on the same scale. The age of the free mercenary-market and the independent military *entrepreneur* was drawing to a close; and armies, though they remained mercenary, were becoming state armies, bound by tighter conditions than of old. The peculiar circumstances of the Thirty Years' War, in which a very large area of rich and populous country was available for systematic plundering and quarter, proved to be unique. The enlistment of mercenaries upon the expectation of booty and a cash payment extorted from the surrounding countryside became less easy. A commander could no longer be confident that war would sustain war. Yet Sweden's new imperial responsibilities still demanded more men than *utskrivning* normally provided, even for purely defensive and precautionary purposes. When an international crisis impended, additional mercenaries had to be enlisted; and it was often a pretty problem how to pay them. The decline of Sweden's monopoly of copper after the middle of the century, the loss of the Prussian licences in 1635, deprived the country of those additional revenues which had helped Gustav Adolf to make ends meet, and no new source of income turned up to take their place: hence Karl Gustav's urgent need to conquer Prussia. It grew increasingly difficult to keep the straggling defensive system in a state of preparedness: every interval of peace saw a dangerous decline in the state of the fortifications which protected the overseas empire. Should a threatening situation arise, should it prove necessary from prudential motives to hire an un-

[1] *AOSB*, I. VIII. 162, 610.

usually large number of mercenary troops, the impossibility of paying them for more than a limited time might make it necessary to use them: this was among the factors which made for war in 1655, and made peace difficult in 1658. In short, though Sweden could have continued to fight indefinitely in the circumstances of 1632-48 (as Oxenstierna's obstinacy about the peace terms showed), in the absence of those abnormal and exceptional conditions Swedish statesmen were liable to be forced to choose between military unpreparedness and a financial burden which could be borne only (if at all) by a policy of apparent aggression.

The conclusion seems thus inescapable, that Gustav Adolf committed Sweden to a position which in the long run (though not immediately) she could not hope to sustain; and that—after 1626 at all events—his foreign policy represents a deviation from the main lines of Swedish interest. These were developments which may be regretted or applauded, according to the point of view. But they were not developments that could easily have been avoided. Whatever the consequences for Sweden, it does not seem likely that the King could have escaped the involvement, as things then stood. It may indeed be conceded that Gustav Adolf was by temperament inclined to an active, as Oxenstierna was perhaps inclined to a conservative, foreign policy. But it is not easy to point to a flaw in the chain of political logic which led him step by step to the landing at Peenemünde. It would have been possible, no doubt, by an abrogation of statesmanship, to pretend that the danger did not exist; it would have been possible, even, to embark upon a policy of appeasement, and emulate the ignominious (and discouraging) example of John George. In 1630, no doubt, there was a deliberate choice. But it was a choice so weighted by irrefutable arguments as to be scarcely a choice at all. Oxenstierna, a few years after Gustav Adolf's death, in a time of difficulty and depression, might regret that the German expedition had ever been undertaken [1]; but if he voiced any doubts before it set sail, little trace of them has survived in his correspondence. *Råd* and *riksdag* shared the King's purpose; since to responsible statesmen, to political realists, no other line of

[1] On 15 July 1636 he told the *råd*, 'I certainly advised his late Majesty not to betake himself with an army to German soil, as Grubbe can tell you; had his Majesty heeded my advice, he had become *arbiter totius Septentrionis*; but I can look on it no other way than this, that the King's going to Germany is a *fatum* and a *dispositio divina*, since God had destined his Majesty to be *oppressorem Caesaris*': *RRP*, VI. 394.

action seemed safe. The extension of the nation's commitments had increased upon them so gradually, they had been drawn by such clear necessities from one predicament to the next, that there was perhaps no one point of time at which a man might have cried halt to the process which was dooming Sweden to the strains and responsibilities of existence as a great power. If there was a moment at which it might have been conceivable to renounce what had come to appear as a manifest destiny, that moment fell after, and not before, the battle of Lützen. It was not by any deliberate act that Gustav Adolf twisted Swedish history out of its accustomed pattern: he would have been glad enough, had the press of events left him free, to dictate to Denmark a peace such as Brömsebro or Roskilde. It was not he that shaped the history of Germany in the 1620's: the truth is rather that the events in Germany imposed their dictate upon him. The destiny which dragged Sweden forward on the blood-drenched road from Altmark to Nystad may have been malign, but it was not the less destiny for that; in the sense that for the most part it was a close-meshed web of choices, each of which appeared so clear and inevitable in the context of the times that an intelligent statesman could hardly doubt what the choice must be.

Gustav Adolf was essentially an empirical statesman. He had no grandiose or cut-and-dried political plans. He dealt with situations as they arose, by successive expedients; or he prepared precautionary measures against menaces plainly impending. Some broad general aims he had: the security of his dynasty, the security of his country, the security of the Protestant religion; but on the whole his policy was the reaction to external pressures, and he himself would have considered it essentially defensive. Providence had not endowed him with a special gift of political divination, though he had, perhaps, a sufficiency of ordinary foresight. Security proved, as it has proved so often, a will o' the wisp, and the terms accepted by Sweden at Westphalia suggest that Gustav Adolf followed it too far. But security, not empire-building, was his real purpose; and he could not be expected to foresee that the territorial gains incidental to its pursuit might themselves one day be a source of weakness and danger.

Yet, whether the adventure of greatness must in the long run be deemed an aberration or no, it had effects which lasted far beyond the collapses of 1721 and 1809. It was not merely that the being great brought to Sweden Grotius and Descartes, Ehrenstrahl and

Tessin; that the intellectual pulse of the nation was quickened; that Swedish culture was stimulated by foreign influences and native patrons; that the treasures of Würzburg or Prague enriched a barren land: it was also that the Age of Greatness, brief as it was, set a mark upon the national character which the lapse of two and a half centuries has not been able to efface.

Gustav Adolf was the greatest of Swedish kings. Contemporaries were not sparing of their tributes; and by the generation that followed him he was called 'The Great' as a matter of course. His military exploits; his salvation of German Protestantism; his death, which the pious might esteem but one remove from martyrdom; combined to throw a radiance upon the monarchy, clothing it with a prestige which it had never before enjoyed, associating it unforgettably with the martial glories of the nation. But Breitenfeld was not merely a national, it was also a religious triumph: in its appeal comparable less to Agincourt than to the Boyne. Church and crown, after a century of relations at best uneasy, at worst openly hostile, sealed their union in the blood of the slaughtered *tercios* of the League. And the figure of the victor of that field was henceforward fixed unshakably, as no other Swedish king's, in the memories of all patriots. If to-day it is the portrait of Gustav Vasa—the founder of the realm, the wise economist on the throne—that stands on the Swedish banknotes, the image of Gustav Adolf lives as a national symbol in the popular consciousness. And every year still, in the murky slip-slop of a Stockholm November, the damp uniforms and dripping standards of the ceremonial parades evoke, with infinite melancholy, the fatal mists of Lützen. 'King Karl the youthful hero' is still—and will probably continue to be—an apple of discord among historians, a controversial figure fiercely fought over, a symbol around whom battle the champions of divergent outlooks on both past and present. But the voices raised against Gustav Adolf have been both few and feeble; and even the reaction against that school of historians which was anti-aristocratic and pro-monarchical has left his reputation virtually undisturbed.

It was not only upon Gustav Adolf's more heroic and spectacular achievements that the prestige of the monarchy was based. It was also the result of the profound impression produced by the King's character and personality. This is seen most clearly in the field of constitutional development. In the history of the legislature, of the judiciary and of the executive, Gustav Adolf's reign is of the first importance: the progress made was decisive. And it was made possible because for the last time for many years to come there was a practical measure of agreement upon the bases of the constitution, which was itself the outcome of the spirit of mutual trust prevailing between monarchy and aristocracy. In the age-long struggle of the two powerful forces which between them created the modern Swedish state, Gustav Adolf's reign is a period—perhaps the only period—of truce, each side observing a benevolent neutrality towards the other. Between 1612 and 1632 the intense concentration upon political theory which had marked the reigns of Sigismund and Karl IX dies away, the debate on fundamental law and the contractual basis of monarchy falls silent, only to burst out with increased vivacity as soon as Gustav Adolf is in his grave. The foundation-stones upon which the constitutional structure of the Age of Freedom was to rest had been rough-hewn by the generation of Erik Sparre; after 1632 his political heirs fell to work on them anew, and might fairly be said to have settled them firmly in the ground; but between the one period and the other was interposed a moveless interval, when this particular controversy was pushed into the background. And not this controversy only: for if Gustav Adolf's reign showed great constitutional advances, there is no doubt that towards its close progress was inhibited by the exercise of the royal will, and by the prestige of the occupant of the throne. Oxenstierna would be as little able to emulate his master's confident authority in the handling of the Estates as James I had been capable of repeating Elizabeth's successes with parliament; and the one technique had perhaps been as frustrating to constitutional advance as the other. With the coming of the regency, dissensions and resentments long unvented found free expression; the constitutional controversies revived, more vigorous than ever; the strife of classes, already implicit in the later 1620's, came into the open light of day. The national unity of which Gustav Adolf was the architect could be preserved, it seemed, only by him.

It was altogether appropriate that the monarch who had for a time reconciled the traditions of Karl IX and Hogenskild Bielke, and who had provided, in the intimate collaboration between himself and the greatest of aristocratic statesmen, the living example of that reconciliation—it was altogether appropriate that he should have bequeathed to his successors a Form of Government to which the upholders of either tradition might equally appeal. To the one school it appeared as a basis for contractual monarchy; to the other as an exposition of the theory of the division of power. Its phraseology echoed through Swedish history for more than a century and a half. Men looked back to it in 1719, across the constitutional desert of the absolutism, as a basis for the edification of a free government of the Estates; while half a century later Gustav III would find in it the justification for his abridgment of a liberty which had degenerated into licence.

The Form of Government was, indeed, a posthumous child; but it had been preceded by a long family of legislative enactments and administrative devices affecting every aspect of the national life, from education to mining, from religion to military discipline. For this was one of the great creative periods of Swedish history. The extraordinary activity developed by the King and his chancellor, especially after 1617; the ability, even under the stress of war and at moments of crisis, to find time for detailed attention to such matters as the provision of *stipendia* or the drafting of instructions for the Antiquary-Royal; the restless quest for information; the capacity for simultaneous *expertise* in widely divergent subjects—all this produces an almost Napoleonic impression. Had Gustav Adolf never commanded a squadron, nor won a battle, had he never added an acre to Sweden's dominions, he would still take rank among the great rulers; and not the less so since his domestic work was wrought in metal more durable than the trenchant steel of his sword.

The achievement was made possible because the King was able to find a band of subordinates and collaborators who could be relied upon to carry out his purposes, and to supply in their own fields an intelligent initiative. That this should have been so was in part the result of Gustav Adolf's reconciliation of the monarchy with that educated aristocracy which for long provided the skill and knowledge requisite for conducting the affairs of state; and in part it was the consequence of the King's gift for command—his capacity for inspiring his servants with his own enthusiasm and his own standards of public service. Sweden, unlike most European countries of that age, did not practise the sale of offices; and, on the whole, positions went to those who were fit to fill them. It seems, moreover, that this particular generation happened to produce an especially rich crop of talents. At all events, for whatever reason, Gustav Adolf was well served. Men such as Klas Fleming, Karl Bonde, Salvius, Skytte, Gabriel Gustavsson Oxenstierna, Per Brahe and John Casimir formed an administrative equipage of unusual quality; and Axel Oxenstierna was a statesman of the first rank.

The partnership of Gustav Adolf and Oxenstierna is one of the great historic collaborations. It was not, like the contemporary partnership of Richelieu and Louis XIII, the association of a dominant personality with another less forceful and more acquiescent, whose main contribution to the joint work was a dogged loyalty to a superior mind. King and chancellor were both men of strong character, widely different temperaments, conflicting historic traditions and very great abilities. Each recognized in the other the qualities complementary to his own defects: the King's choler was compensated by the chancellor's phlegm. Their association, continuing unbroken for over twenty years, was undisturbed by a single open clash. The history of the reign, for good or for evil, was their joint work: singly, neither could have compassed the measure of their combined achievement. Oxenstierna was eleven years older than his master—in 1611 he was twenty-eight, to the King's seventeen—but the passing of years narrowed the distance between them; and though in their correspondence neither for a moment forgot that the one was a subject and the other a sovereign, there developed between them not only complete frankness and trust, but a deep attachment and respect, which found expression in a moving letter from the King at the close of 1630.[1] Oxenstierna was endowed with high abilities: perhaps more generously equipped for the career of statesman than any other man of his century; Gustav Adolf, less variously developed, had the spark of genius Oxenstierna lacked. The difference in their approach to political problems was real, and even important; but it should not be exaggerated. The 'sense of space' which Geijer experienced in the contemplation of Gustav Adolf, and which has sometimes been contrasted with a certain narrow parochialism in Oxenstierna, was perhaps an impression produced by the King's ability to look beyond immediate objects and interests, to see Sweden's welfare in a larger context, to view her particular aims as an element in a broader ideal struggle—or, conversely, to recognize that struggle as the generalized expression of Sweden's own quarrel, and in consequence to nerve his people to sacrifices and deprivations, and to carry them with him in virtual unanimity along a road that was neither obvious nor easy. But there is little sign that Oxenstierna differed from his sovereign in his

[1] *AOSB*, II. I. 669-70; *ibid.*, I. VI. 61-6, for Oxenstierna's reply.

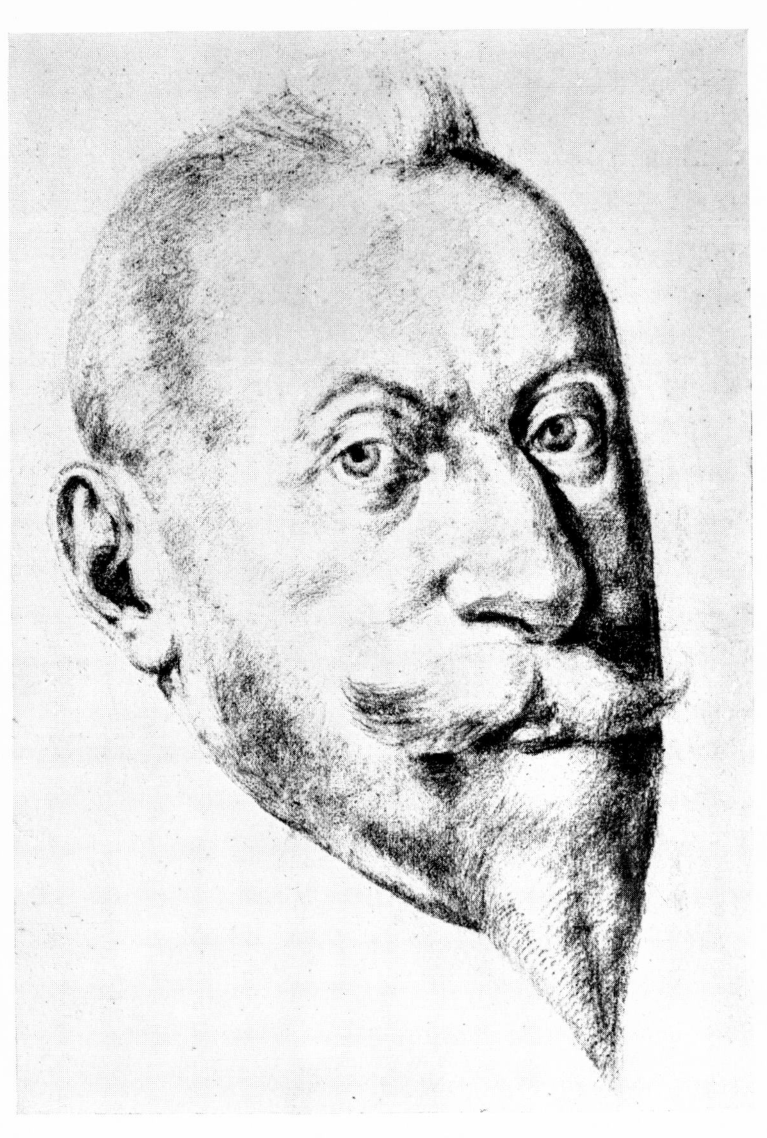

GUSTAV ADOLF
the last portrait

AXEL OXENSTIERNA
1633

appraisement of the issues at stake, though he had his own views on time and means. The antithesis between Gustav Adolf's idealism and Oxenstierna's nationalist realism is a little forced: the men differed more in temperament than in policy.

And certainly, when Gustav Adolf was dead, when it fell to Oxenstierna to be soldier and statesman too, and to take upon his single shoulders his master's burdens in addition to his own, he appeared as the constant custodian of Gustav Adolf's political inheritance.[1] Of all Gustav Adolf's ministers, he alone was of the stature to continue and uphold the King's work. He was the only one of them who never gave up, never lost his courage at the darkest moment, stoutly stood fast for what Gustav Adolf might have considered a reasonable *satisfactio*. After Nördlingen, *assecuratio* as Gustav Adolf had conceived it became more difficult; but until that disaster shook the Swedish position in Germany, Oxenstierna's League of Heilbronn could be considered as the fulfilment of the plans which Gustav Adolf had designed to launch at Ulm. Had it not been for the chancellor's feeling that he was the executor of Gustav Adolf's political testament, Swedish policy might conceivably have changed course as abruptly in 1632 as it was to do in 1660. It was his fortitude and determination, no less than the military gifts of Banér and Torstensson, that at last gave Sweden the peace which the King had desired. The great partnership that began in 1611 may in truth be said to have ended, not in 1632, but in 1648.

But Oxenstierna, for all his astonishing exertions, could never fill the King's place. Where Gustav Adolf had ordered, he must cajole. And he lacked not merely the authority of royalty: he lacked also that personal magic, which had nothing to do with rank, but which had been among the most important of Gustav Adolf's assets as a ruler. It was not that the King was an easy man to serve. His restless activity made him impatient of deliberate procedures, and intolerant of caution; and his itch to do things for himself, to know everything, to oversee everything, could at times try the patience of his subordinates, especially in the field. His quick mind leapt easily to conclusions, and sometimes he permitted himself hasty judgments whose severity afterwards proved to be unwarranted. A Brandenburg diplomat once ruefully observed that he had 'not the least inclination to middle courses' [2]; and his decisions were not seldom

[1] See his letter to Salvius, 14 November 1632: *AOSB*, I. VII. 651-2.
[2] Helbig, p. 25.

based on what Oxenstierna called an *impetus ingenii*. His temper was uncertain, and in anger he lost all judgment and measure: as Vane reported,

It is usual with the King to repent himself when the Blow is given; for he hath often told me, . . . That he would give all he had to be Master of his Passions; but that when he begins to be moved, he hath something rises in his Brain, that makes him forget what he saith or doth; that this he finds in himself, and the Inconveniencies that grow thereof, as soon as he is posed again; but yet he cannot get it mastered, though he hath often designed the same; and therefore he hopes God and all the World will forgive him.[1]

More than one of his officers had to endure treatment at his hands which they found intolerable; and one at least quitted his service in consequence.[2] Obstinate resistance to his will, the slighting of what he conceived to be his just claims, or the least failing in respect to his rank or to his country, could produce a formidable explosion, as many a crestfallen ambassador discovered for himself. '*Regum aures sua natura sunt tenerae*', as Oxenstierna reminded his colleagues at home after an exceptionally pungent rebuke from their master [3]; and Gustav Adolf's ears were perhaps a shade tenderer than most. He fell at times into a hectoring and bullying style, which for his reputation it had been better he had avoided; nor was he immune to the temptation to terrify and astonish. Of the sin of pride it is difficult to acquit him [4]; and of vanity he had at least a share, being prone to dwell beyond what was seemly upon his services to the Protestant cause, and the corporal hazards it had entailed upon him: it was neither tactful nor modest to invite Kristian IV to feel the Dirschau bullets. Though he held his course steady for as far ahead as he could see, his was not a mind untroubled by questionings or impervious to doubts. For he was not exempt from the strain of morbidity common to all the Vasas; and the suspiciousness which had destroyed the peace of mind of Karl IX, of Erik XIV and of Gustav Vasa did not leave him scathless.[5] He was as far as

[1] Rushworth, I. II. 169.

[2] For a selection of characteristic incidents, see Monro, II. 39; Hist. MSS. Comm., *Hamilton*, pp. 80-1; Spannagel, p. 382; Dahlgren, *Louis de Geer*, I. 99.

[3] *AOSB*, I. VI. 319-22.

[4] Compare Maximilian's allusion in April 1632 to his 'bekhandten unnd bei seinen progressen noch mehreres gewachszener hochmueth': *Briefe und Akten*, II. 365.

[5] Charnacé said of him that he was 'le plus aysé du monde à faire entrer en ombrage': L. Weibull, *Diplomatiska förbindelser mellan Sverige och Frankrike*, p. 71.

possible from being the ruthless conqueror, indifferent to the voice of conscience or the need for self-justification: a man, rather, who could not be easy without the absolution-in-advance of *råd* and secret committee, who kept Grotius in his knapsack, and wearied Oxenstierna, long after the die was cast, with otiose self-questionings and unseasonable qualms.[1]

But the ordinary observer saw little enough of all this. He learned, indeed, to fear the King's quick temper; but he knew, too, that these eruptions were as a rule followed swiftly by apologies and a spell of genial weather. To contemporaries the King seemed (as indeed on the whole he was) a man of sanguine temper, gay, sociable, garrulous and impulsive, 'ever *allegro* and *courage*'.[2] His affability was famous, and the Germans remarked that he was always laughing. He had a bubbling fount of high spirits; and the interlocutor who had but recently received a comminatory broadside might well find himself jollied afterwards at supper. At the close of a serious discussion, in which a relation of Hamilton's had been remonstrating on the Marquis's treatment at the King's hands, 'To act your [*sc.* Hamilton's] part he pulled my hatt out of my hand and put it on in such a huffing manner as I never sawe and then enquired whether this was a fitting for way you to use him, but [said] he, all is well and fell a-laughing'.[3] He loved the rough-and-tumble of battle; he loved hunting and horses and the outdoor life; but he entered with no less zest into urban pleasures, and danced indefatigably with the bourgeois wives of Frankfort. When he wished it, he could display a dazzling and irresistible charm, and many a man came from his first interview with the King feeling (as a Hessian envoy put it) that it was impossible not to love him.[4] His fair hair and prominent blue eyes, the backward poise of his head, the royal dignity of his massive thighs and swelling paunch, fixed themselves in the memories of those who beheld him; and the Italians called him '*il re d'oro*'. A careful education had implanted in him the tastes of a scholar, and some share of a scholar's attainments; and no trait in his character was more marked than that of intellectual curiosity.[5] The gift of tongues was not denied to him; and in Swedish or German his oratory was a powerful political weapon. In debate he was quick and keen; and

[1] *AOSB*, I. VI. 56-7; Ahnlund, *Oxenstierna*, p. 606.
[2] Fryxell, *Handlingar*, p. 43.
[3] Hist. MSS. Comm., *Hamilton Supplementary*, p. 21.
[4] Droysen, II. 367.
[5] See, *e.g.*, *Peder Galts Depescher*, p. 108.

Vosbergen recorded that he argued 'with very great dexterity'.[1] He applied himself not unsuccessfully, though in such fragmentary style as his preoccupations permitted, to the craft of authorship; and to music he was addicted, both as auditor and as performer.

In his personal habits he affected simplicity and frugality; and though the age was not disposed to censure intemperance—and the Swedes least of all—he practised a notable sobriety. He preferred to share the hardships of his soldiers, and in his desire to see everything imposed upon himself exertions above the ordinary. If for a time he maintained in his armies the best discipline in Europe, that was, as Roe remarked, in part 'because he is *commiles* with every man, and gives besydes excellent words and good usage as much as he hath'.[2] But his identification of himself with his men was not pressed so far as to persuade him to the morals of the camp: the episode of Margareta Slots was an isolated incident; and once his youthful heats were past he appears to have remained faithful to a wife whose failings he saw and regretted, and from whom he was separated for increasingly lengthy intervals by the obligations of command. His zeal for the Protestant cause was no mere partisan enthusiasm: it was an aspect, rather, of a profound personal piety, instant in prayer, and striving always (not without backslidings) to give to God the glory. He felt himself to be God's instrument, albeit unworthy; he believed that there was a work set apart for him to do; though he did not always find it easy to distinguish what that work might be. As he was almost wholly free from the weakness of superstition, so too he came to contemn the weakness of bigotry. Germany taught him not only the necessity for tolerance as between Lutherans and Calvinists; it taught him also that the faith of a Roman Catholic might be no less respectable than his own. Before his career ended he had reached the conclusion—which would have been inconceivable to him in 1617—that it is not the part of wisdom, nor the duty of the statesman, to seek to constrain men's consciences.[3]

No ruler of Sweden has shown a greater mastery of every branch of his *métier*; and none has been better acquainted with his dominions. The impress of his personality appears in almost all the great reforming and progressive measures of his reign: as Roe put it, he was 'both *caput* and *cor regni*'.[4] On his military qualities there

[1] Vosbergen, *Verbaal*, p. 113: 'deduceerende voorts met seer groote dexteriteyt.'

[2] Roe, pp. 49-50.

[3] Wagner, pp. 13-14, 20; Schaedel, pp. 122-5; *cf.* Urban VIII's remark, quoted in Söltl, III. 293.

[4] Roe, p. 81.

is no need to expatiate. The demonstrative grief of his subjects at the news of his death is the measure of his stature as a Swedish King; and the lamentations of those foreign soldiers of fortune who had enlisted under his standard provides the best evidence of the esteem in which they held him as a Protestant, a commander and a man. 'So are we', wrote Alexander Leslie, 'to our wnspeakable greife deprived of the best and most valorouse commaunder that evir any souldiours hade, and the church of God with hir good cause of the best instrument vnder God, we becaus we was not worthie of him, and she for the sinnes of hir children.' [1] And Robert Monro, looking back after an interval at the career of him whom he called 'the Captaine of Kings, and the King of Captaines', penned a succinct eulogium which may stand for all the rest: [2]

For though he had bin no King, he was a brave warriour, and which is more, a good man, magnificent, wise, just, meeke, indued with learning, and the gift of tongues, and as he had strength of body, and a manlike stature, he had also the ornaments of the minde, fitting a brave commander.

O would to GOD I had once such a Leader againe to fight such another day; in this old quarrell! . . . .

[1] Sanford Terry, *Leslie*, pp. 30-1. [2] Monro, II. 57, 70, 211.

BIBLIOGRAPHY

Part II

A few books which were listed in the subject-bibliographies to Volume I fall with equal or greater propriety under one or other of the headings below, and are therefore for convenience repeated here. It should be noted that general works appear in Sections C and D (Vol. I); and that printed primary material appears in Section B (Vol. I), with the exception of the short supplementary list of sources which is printed below.

B. Printed Primary Material

Dudík, B.: Waldsteins Correspondenz. Eine Nachlese aus dem K.K. Kriegsarchive in Wien, I-II. Vienna 1865-66.

Erslev, Kr.: Aktstykker og Oplysninger till Rigsraadets og Staendermødernes Historie i Kristian IVs Tid, II. Copenhagen 1887-1888. [Cited: Erslev.]

Gaedeke, A.: Aus den Papieren des kursächsischen Generalleutnants Hans Georg von Arnim 1631-1634. (*Neues Archiv für sächsische Geschichte und Altherthumskunde*, VII.) Dresden 1886.

Goetz, W.: Die Politik Maximilians I von Baiern und seine Verbündeten 1618-1651, IV. 2. Munich 1948.

Günter, H.: Die Habsburger-Liga 1625-1635. Briefe und Akten aus dem General-Archiv zu Simancas. Berlin 1908.

Hallwich, H.: Briefe und Akten zur Geschichte Wallensteins (1630-1634), I-III. (Fontes Rerum Austriacarum.) Vienna 1912. [Cited: *Briefe und Akten.*]

Irmer, G.: Die Verhandlungen Schwedens und seiner Verbündeten mit Wallenstein und dem Kaiser, von 1631 bis 1634, I-II. Leipzig 1888. [Cited: Irmer, *VS.*]

Kurtzer aber gegrundeter Bericht Warumb die Königl. Mayst. zu Schweden der Stadt Magdeburg nicht secundiren können. [? Hamburg 1631.]

Lonchay, H.; Cuvelier, J.; Lefevre, J.: Correspondance de la Cour d'Espagne sur les Affaires des Pays-Bas au XVIIe siècle. II. Précis de la correspondance de Philippe IV avec l'Infante Isabelle (1621-1633). Brussels 1927. [Cited: Lonchay.]

Lundorp, M. C. [continued by *Bellus, N.*]: Acta Publica, III. Frankfort 1640.

[*Richelieu*]: Testament politique du Cardinal de Richelieu, ed. L. André.

Rushworth, J.: Historical Collections, I. 2. London 1680.

[*Steinkallenfels, A. N. von*]: Reise in Schweden und Liefland (1615-1616) von Adolf Nicklass von Steinkallenfels, ed. C. Velten. (*Der Norden*, XXI.) Hamburg 1944.

Wittrock, G.: Fyra relationer om slaget vid Lützen. (Historisk Tidskrift, I. Series, 52.) Stockholm 1932.

J. Economic and Social History
(Chapters I and II)

Ahnlund, N.: Från medeltid och Vasatid. Stockholm 1933.

Ahnlund, N.: Sundsvalls historia, I. Sundsvall 1921.

Almqvist, C. J. L.: Svenska fattigdomens betydelse. [New edn.] Stockholm 1929.

Almquist, H.: Göteborgs historia, I. Göteborg 1929.

Almquist, J. A.: Den civila lokalförvaltningen i Sverige 1523-1630, I-III. Stockholm 1917-22.

Almquist, J. A.: Frälsegodsen i Sverige under storhetstiden, I. Stockholm 1931.

Almquist, J. E.: Om ärftlig besittningsrätt till jord före det sjuttonde seklets slut. En studie i romersk och svensk rätt. Uppsala and Stockholm 1929.

Ambrosiani, S.: Från de svenska skråämbetenas dagar. Stockholm 1920.

Ambrosiani, S.: Papperstillverkningen i Sverige intill 1800-talets mitt. Stockholm 1923.

Annerstedt, C.: Om samhällsklasser och lefnadssätt under förra hälften af 1600-talet. Stockholm 1896.

Barbour, V.: Dutch and English Merchant Shipping in the 17th Century. (*Economic History Review*, II.)

Beckman, *B.*: Dalupproret 1743 och andra samtida rörelser inom allmogen och bondeståndet. Göteborg 1930.

Berg, *G.*: Boskapsskötsel och jordbruk i det gamla Stockholm. (*Samfundet St. Eriks Årsbok* 1932.) Stockholm 1932.

Björkman, *R.*: Jönköpings historia, II. Jönköping 1918.

Boëthius, *B.*: art. 'Carl Bonde' in Svenskt Biografiskt Lexikon, V. Stockholm 1925.

Boëthius, *B.*: Dalafolkets herrarbete. (*Rig*, 16.) Stockholm 1933.

Boëthius, *B.*: Det treåriga Vadstenasmöret. (*Historisk Tidskrift*, II. Series, 12.) Stockholm 1949.

Boëthius, *B.*: Gruvornas, hyttornas och hamrarnas folk. Bergshanteringens arbetare från medeltiden till gustavianska tiden. Stockholm 1951.

Boëthius, *B.*: Review of F. Bothe, *Gustav Adolfs und seine Kanzlers wirtschaftspolitische Absichten auf Deutschland.* (*Historisk Tidskrift*, I. Series, 30.) Stockholm 1910.

Boëthius, *B.*: Rättsreception och folklig rättsvård. (*Svensk Tidskrift*, 17.) Stockholm 1927.

Boëthius, *B.*: Skogen och bygden. Stockholm 1939.

Boëthius, *B.*: Ur de stora skogarnas historia. [New edn.] Stockholm 1955.

Boëthius, *B.*; *Heckscher*, *E.*: Svensk handelsstatistik 1637-1737. Stockholm 1938.

Boëthius, *B.*; *Kromnow*, *Å.*: Jernkontorets historia, I. Stockholm 1947.

Bolin, *S.*: Erik XIV och 'säterifrihets uppkomst'. (Studier tillägnade Curt Weibull.) Göteborg 1946.

Bothe, *F.*: Gustav Adolfs und seine Kanzlers wirtschaftspolitische Absichten auf Deutschland. Frankfurt a. M. 1910.

Breedevelt-van Veen, *F.*: Louis de Geer, 1587-1652. Amsterdam 1935.

Brännman, *E.*: Frälseköpen under Gustav II Adolfs regering. Lund 1950.

Börjeson, *D. Hj. T.*: Stockholms segelsjöfart . . . Minneskrift 1732-1932. Stockholm 1932.

Carlborg, *H.*: Ur osmundsjärnets historia under 1600- och 1700-talen. (*Med hammare och fackla*, I.) Stockholm 1938.

Carlson, F. F.: Sveriges historia under konungarna af pfalziska huset, II. Stockholm 1856.

Carlsson, S.: Mellan Bolmen och Holaveden. (Meddelanden från Jönköpings läns hembygdsförbund, 1951.) Jönköping 1951.

Carlsson, S.: Svensk ståndscirkulation 1680-1950. Uppsala 1950.

Christensen, A. E.: Dutch Trade to the Baltic about 1600. Copenhagen 1941.

Clark, Sir G. N.: Science and Social Welfare in the Age of Newton. Oxford 1937.

Clason, S.: Till reduktionens förhistoria. Stockholm 1895.

Dahlberg, B. H.: Bidrag till svenska fattiglagstiftningens historia. Uppsala 1893.

Dahlgren, E. W.: De uppländska bruken Österby, Forsmark, Leufsta och Gimo under äldsta tider (intill 1627). (*Med hammare och fackla*, I.) Stockholm 1928.

Dahlgren, E. W.: Ett bidrag till Valloninvandringens historia. (En bergsbok till Carl Sahlin.) Stockholm 1921.

Dahlgren, E. W.: Järnvräkeri och järnstämpling. Stockholm 1930.

Dahlgren, E. W.: Louis de Geer, 1587-1652. Hans lif och verk, I-II. Uppsala 1923.

Danielsson, C.: 1500- och 1600-talens svenska tullpolitik. (*Statsvetenskapliga Tidskrift*, 27.) Lund 1924.

Davidson, J.; Gray, A.: The Scottish Staple at Veere. A Study in the Economic History of Scotland. London 1909.

Dietz, F. C.: English Public Finance 1558-1641. New York 1932.

Dillner, T. S.: Studier rörande Finlands handel under tidsrymden 1570-1622, I. Helsingfors 1897.

Dovring, F.: Agrarhistorien. (Det levande förflutna, 15.) Stockholm 1953.

Drummond, J. C.; Wilbraham, A.: The Englishman's Food. A History of Five Centuries of English Diet. London 1939.

Ejdestam, J.; Hedin, N.; Nygren, E.: Bilder ur lanthandelns historia. Västerås 1943.

Elgeskog, V.: Svensk torpbebyggelse från 1500-talet till laga skiftet. En agrarisk studie. Stockholm 1945.

Eriksson, M.: Järnräntor under 1500-talet. Stockholm 1940.

Erixon, S.: Skultuna bruks historia, I. Stockholm 1921.

Falk, E.: Finnarna i Värmland intill 1600-talets slut. (En bok om Värmland, III.) Uppsala 1921.

Falkman, L. B.: Om mått och vigt i Sverige, I-II. Stockholm 1884-85.

Forssell, H.: Anteckningar om Sveriges jordbruksnäring i sextonde seklet. Stockholm 1884.

Forssell, H.: Sverige år 1571. Försök till en administrativ-statistisk beskrifning öfver det egentliga Sverige, utan Finland och Estland. Stockholm 1872-73.

Forssell, N.: Borås stads historia, I. Borås 1952.

Forssell, N.: Svenska postverkets historia. Stockholm 1936.

Forsslund, K.-E.: Falu gruva och Stora Kopparbergs bergslag. Stockholm 1936.

Forsstrand, C.: En Stockholmsläkare under förra hälften av 1600-talet. Jakob Robertsson, livmedikus hos Gustaf II Adolf. (*Samfundet St. Eriks Årsbok*, 1925.) Stockholm 1925.

Franz, G.: Der dreissigjährige Krieg und das deutsche Volk. Jena 1943.

Fries, E.: Svenska kulturbilder ur 1600- och 1700-talens historia. Stockholm 1901.

Fries, E.: Teckningar ur svenska adelns familjelif i gamla tider, I-II. Stockholm 1895-1901.

Furuskog, J.: Det svenska järnet genom tiderna. Stockholm 1939.

Furuskog, J.: De värmländska järnbruken. Filipstad 1924.

Fyhrvall, O.: Om det bottniska handelstvånget. (*Historisk Tidskrift*, I. Series, 2.) Stockholm 1882.

Geijer, R.: Den värmländska järnhanteringen i forntid och nutid. (En bok om Värmland, II.) Uppsala 1918.

Gothe, R.: Från trolldomstro till Kristendom: studier rörande det kulturella tillståndet bland skogsfinnarna i Sverige under 16—1700-talen. Stockholm 1943.

Gothe, R.: Medelpads finnmarker. Kulturhistoriska undersökningar om finsk bosättning i mellersta Norrland under 15-, 16- och 1700-talen. Stockholm 1945.

Grill, E.: Jakob de la Gardie, affärsmannen och politikern, 1608-1636. Göteborg 1949.

Hamilton, E. J.: American Treasure and the Price Revolution in Spain, 1501-1650. Harvard 1934.

Hamilton, H.: The English Brass and Copper Industries to 1800. London 1926.

Hannerberg, D.: Närkes boskapsbestånd på 1620- och 1630-talen. Med en undersökning av källvärdet hos landskapets boskapslängder. Göteborg 1948.

Hannerberg, D.: Närkes landsbygd 1600-1820. Folkmängd och befolkningsrörelse, åkerbruk och spannmålsproduktion. Göteborg 1941.

Hansson, S.: Skråtidens gesäller. Stockholm 1930.

Hansson, S.: Ur skomakareyrkets historia. En studie över skråväsendet. Stockholm 1919.

Hauser, H.: La Pensée et l'Action économique du Cardinal de Richelieu. Paris 1944.

Heckscher, E. F.: De svenska penning-, vikt- och mått-systemen. Stockholm 1941.

Heckscher, E. F.: Den ekonomiska innebörden av 1500- och 1600-talens svenska stadsgrundningar. (*Historisk Tidskrift*, I. Series, 43.) Stockholm 1923.

Heckscher, E. F.: Det svenska penningväsendets öden. Stockholm 1942.

Heckscher, E. F.: Det äldre Vasakonungadömets ekonomiska politik och idéer. (Historiska studier tillägnade Ludvig Stavenow.) Stockholm 1924.

Heckscher, E. F.: Ekonomi och historia. Stockholm 1922.

Heckscher, E. F.: Historieuppfattning, materialistisk och annan. Stockholm 1944.

Heckscher, E. F.: Kopparen under Sveriges stormaktstid. (*Historisk Tidskrift*, I. Series, 57.) Stockholm 1937.

Heckscher, E. F.: Multilateralism, Baltic Trade, and the Mercantilists. (*Economic History Review*, II. Series, 3 [1950].)

Heckscher, E. F.: Natural and Money Economy as illustrated from Swedish History in the Sixteenth Century. (*Journal of Economic and Business History*, III.) Cambridge [Mass.] 1931.

Heckscher, E. F.: Svenskt arbete och liv. Stockholm 1941.

Heckscher, E. F.: Svenskt och utländskt under Sveriges stormaktstid. (Festskrift till Verner Söderberg.) Stockholm 1932.

Heckscher, E. F.: Sveriges ekonomiska historia från Gustav Vasa, I. 1-2. Stockholm 1935-6.

Heckscher, E. F.: 1600-tals kopparen än en gång. (*Historisk Tidskrift*, II. Series, 1.) Stockholm 1938.

Heckscher, E. F.: Un grand chapitre de l'histoire du fer: le monopole suèdois. (*Annales d'histoire économique et sociale.*) Paris 1932.

Heckscher, E. F.: Våra stadsgrundningars betydelse. (*Svenska Stadsförbundets Tidskrift*, 17.) Stockholm 1925.

Hedar, S.: Gustav Vasa och det saltgröna smöret. (*Historisk Tidskrift*, II. Series, 12.) Stockholm 1949.

Hedar, S.: Karl IX:s förmögenhetsbeskattningar. En undangömd källa till vår inre historia. (*Historisk Tidskrift*, I. Series, 57.) Stockholm 1937.

Hedenius, F.: Anteckningar rörande svenska bondeståndet under Gustaf II Adolfs regering. Uppsala 1863.

Hellberg, K.: Eskilstuna genom tiderna, I. Katrineholm 1935.

Hellberg, K.: Järnets och smedernas Eskilstuna, I. Katrineholm 1937.

Helmfrid, B.: Tiondelängderna som källa till ett byalags ekonomiska historia 1555-1753. Stockholm 1949.

Herdin, K. W.: Uppsala på 1600-talet, I-III. Uppsala 1926-9.

Hildebrand, E.: Den svenska diplomatiens organisation i Tyskland under 1600-talet. (*Historisk Tidskrift*, I. Series, 4.) Stockholm 1884.

Hildebrand, K.: Stockholms historia. Stockholm 1897.

Hildebrand, K.-G.: Falu stads historia till år 1687, I-II. Falun 1946.

Hughes, E.: Studies in Administration and Finance, 1558-1825, with special reference to the history of salt taxation in England. Manchester 1934.

Ingers, E.: Bonden i svensk historia, I. Stockholm 1943.

Jeannin, P.: Les Relations économiques des villes de la Baltique avec Anvers au XVIe siècle. (*Vierteljahrschrift für Sozial- und Wirtschaftsgeschichte*, 43.) Wiesbaden 1956.

Jenkins, Rhys: Notes on the Early History of Steel Making in England. (*Transactions of the Newcomen Society*, III.) London 1924.

Jenkins, Rhys: The Rise and Fall of the Sussex Iron Industry. (*Transactions of the Newcomen Society*, I.) London 1922.

Juhlin-Dannfelt, H.: Lantbrukets historia. Världshistorisk översikt av lantbrukets och lantmannalivets utveckling. Stockholm 1925.

Jägerskiöld, S.: Förvärv och förlust av frälse. (*Statsvetenskaplig Tidskrift*, 48.) Lund 1945.

Karlson, W.: Ebba Brahes hem. Ett herremansinventarium från 1600-talet. Lund 1943.

Karlson, W.: Kungligt, adligt, lärt och lekt. Lund 1941.

Kellenbenz, H.: Unternehmerkräfte im Hamburger Portugal- und Spanienhandel 1590-1625. Hamburg 1954.

Keyland, N.: Svensk allmogeskost, I-II. Stockholm 1919.

Kjellberg, C. M.: Norrtälje stad. 1622-1922. Norrtälje 1922.

Kjellberg, S. T.: Ull och ylle. Bidrag till den svenska yllemanufakturens historia. Lund 1943.

Klason, P.: Sveriges sockerhandel och sockerindustri, dess utveckling och nuvarande ståndpunkt. (*Kongl. Lantbruks-Akademiens Handlingar och Tidskrift*, 31.) Stockholm 1892.

Kolkert, W. J.: Nederland en het Zweedsche Imperialisme. Deventer 1908.

Kuylenstierna, C. W. U.: Om rekognitionsskogar och under bruk skatteköpta hemman, med särskild hänsyn till å desamma förbehållna enskilda rättigheter. Lund 1916.

Lagerroth, F.: Statsreglering och finansförvaltning i Sverige till och med frihetstidens ingång. Lund 1928.

Lagerstedt, T.: Livsmedel och livsmedelproduktion under stormaktstiden. (*Ymer*, 1946.) Stockholm 1946.

Lagerstedt, T.: Näringsliv och bygd i Seminghundra härad. Uppsala 1942.

Levander, L.: Fattigt folk och tiggare. Stockholm 1934.

Levander, L.: Landsväg, krog och marknad. Stockholm 1935.

Lewis, G. R.: The Stannaries. A study of the English tin miner. Boston [Mass.] 1908.

Ligtenberg, C.: Willem Usselinx. (*Utrechtsche bijdragen voor Letterkunde en Geschiedenis*, IX.) Utrecht 1915.

Lindberg, F.: Fogde, råd och menighet. Några drag i den svenska stadsförfattningens utveckling under medeltiden och 1500-talet. Stockholm 1941.

Lindberg, F.: Hantverkarna, I. Medeltid och äldre Vasatid. Stockholm 1947.

Lindberg, F.: Västerviks historia 1275-1718, I. Stockholm 1933.

Lindgren, G.: Falbygden och dess närmaste omgivning vid 1600-talets mitt. En kulturgeografisk studie. Uppsala 1936.

Lindroth, S.: Gruvbrytning och kopparhantering vid Stora Kopparberg intill 1800-talets början, I-II. Uppsala 1955.

Lindstedt, G.: Översikten af den svenska fattigvårdens historia. (Fattigvårdslagstiftningskommitténs betänkanden.) Stockholm 1915.

Lindström, H.: Näringsfrihetens utveckling i Sverige. Göteborg 1923.

Lubimenko, I.: The Struggle of the Dutch with the English for the Russian Market in the Seventeenth Century. (*TRHS*, IV. Series, 7.) London 1924.

Lund, Troels: Hälsobegrepp i Norden under sextonde århundradet [trans. *G. Geete*]. Stockholm 1901.

Lythe, S. G. E.: Scottish Trade with the Baltic 1550-1650. (Economic Essays in commemoration of the Dundee School of Economics 1931-1955.) Coupar Angus 1955.

Löfgren, A.: Det svenska tenngjutarehantverkets historia, I. 1. Stockholm 1925.

Lönborg, S.: Finnmarkerna i mellersta Skandinavien. (*Ymer*, 22.) Stockholm 1902.

Lövgren, B.: Ståndsstridens uppkomst. Uppsala 1915.

Malmsten, K.: Den svenska mässingsindustriens uppkomst. (*Med hammare och fackla*, X.) Stockholm 1939.

Malmsten, K.: En industriplanering under Vasatiden. (*Med hammare och fackla*, XII.) Stockholm 1943.

Mannerfelt, O.: Sjuhäradsbygden före 1622 och Borås stad 1622-1865. Borås 1922.

Matz, R.: Hur bestraffades landsköp på 1500-talet? (*Historisk Tidskrift*, II. Series, 15.) Stockholm 1952.

Meyerson, Å.: Vapenindustrierna i Arboga under äldre Vasatid. Stockholm 1939.

Munktell, H.: Till frågan om böndernas ställning vid 1600-talets mitt. (*Historisk Tidskrift*, II. Series, 6.) Stockholm 1943.

Nef, J. U.: Industry and Government in France and England 1540-1640. Philadelphia 1940.

Nelson, H.: Geografiska studier över de svenska städernas och stadslika orterna läge. Lund 1918.

Nilsson, S. A.: Kampen om de adliga privilegierna 1526-1594. Lund 1953.

Nilsson, S. A.: Reaktionen mot systemskiftet 1611. En linje i Gustav II Adolfs politik. (*Scandia*, XX.) Lund 1950.

Nilsson, S. A.: Review of E. Brännman, *Frälseköpen under Gustav II Adolfs regering.* (*Historisk Tidskrift*, II. Series, 15.) Stockholm 1952.

Nyström, P.: Avelgårdsprojektet 1555-6. Några anteckningar. (*Scandia*, IX.) Lund 1936.

Näsmark, J.: Sala stad. Ett bidrag till dess historia. Sala 1923.

Odén, B.: Rikets uppbörd och utgift. Statsfinanser och statsförvaltning under senare 1500-talet. Lund 1955.

Odhner, C. T.: Bidrag till svenska städernas och borgareståndets historia före 1635. Uppsala 1860.

Ohlsson, M. A.: Stormaktstidens privatpalats i Stockholm. Stockholm 1951.

Olan, E.: Svenska brännvinets historia. Göteborg 1922.

Olsen, A.: Kobberpolitik i den svenska Stormagtstid. (*Scandia*, X.) Lund 1937.

Olsen, A.: Kobberpolitik og Kritik. (*Scandia*, X.) Lund 1937.

Olsen, A.: Professor Eli Heckscher og det japanske Kobber. (*Scandia*, XI.) Lund 1938.

Petrén, S.: Lagläsarna. Ett bidrag till det svenska domstolväsendets historia. (*Rättshistoriska Studier*, II. Series, 1.) Lund 1951.

Posthumus, N. W.: Inquiry into the History of Prices in Holland, I. Leiden 1946.

Rebsomen, A.: Recherches historiques sur les relations commerciales entre la France et la Suède. Bordeaux 1921.

Rydberg, A.: Finnarna i Värmland. (*Historisk Tidskrift*, I. Series, 49.) Stockholm 1929.

Rydin, H. L.: P.M. angående det svenska skatteväsendets utveckling. Stockholm 1882.

Sahlin, C.: Svenskt stål före de stora götstålsprocessens införande. (*Med hammare och fackla*, III.) Stockholm 1931.

Schreiner, J.: Nederland og Norge 1625-1650. Trelastutførsel og handelspolitikk. Oslo 1933.

Schück, H.: Stockholm vid fjortonhundratalets slut. (2nd edn. ed. *T. O. Nordberg.*) Stockholm 1951.

Seebass, F.: Bergslagen. Versuch einer kulturgeographischen Beschreibung und Umgrenzung. Brunswick 1928.

Sepp, H.: Bidrag till Ingermanlands historia under 1600-talet. (*Svio-Estonica*, I.) Tartu 1934.

Smith, W.: Studier i svensk tulladministration, I. Från äldsta tid till omkring 1718. Stockholm 1950.

Soom, A.: De ingermanländska städerna och freden i Stolbova 1617. (*Svio-Estonica*, III.) Tartu 1936.

Staf, N.: Marknad och möte. Stockholm 1935.

Steckzén, B.: Luleå stads historia, 1621-1921. Uppsala 1921.

Steckzén, B.: Minneskrift till Piteå stads 300-års jubileum. Uppsala 1921.

Steckzén, B.: Om Söderhamns gevärsfaktori i äldre tider. (*Norrlands försvar*, 1923.) Stockholm 1923.

Steckzén, B.: Umeå stads historia 1588-1888. Umeå 1922.

Straker, E.: Wealden Iron. London 1931.

Styffe, C. G.: Om Sveriges kanalbyggnader intill medlet af adertonde seklet. Stockholm 1846.

Sundberg, H. G. F.: Den svenska stapelstadsrätten. Stockholm 1927.

Sundquist, S.: Finlands folkmängd och bebyggelse i början av 1600-talet. (Meddelanden från Generalstabens krigshistoriska avdelning, II.) Stockholm 1931.

Sundquist, S.: Sveriges folkmängd på Gustaf II Adolfs tid. Lund 1938.

Suolahti, G.: Finlands prästerskap på 1600- och 1700-talen [trans. *H. Gummerus.*] Stockholm 1927.

Svalenius, I.: Gustav Vasa. Stockholm 1950.

Swederus, M. B.: Bidrag till kännedomen om Sveriges bergshandtering 1612-1654. (*Jernkontorets Annaler*, 1909-10.) Stockholm 1909-10.

Swedlund, R.: Grev- och friherreskapen i Sverige och Finland. Donationerna och reduktionerna före 1680. Uppsala 1936.

Swenne, H.: Svenska adelns ekonomiska privilegier 1612-1651, med särskild hänsyn till Älvsborgs län. Göteborg 1933.

Söderberg, T.: Bergsmän och brukspatroner i svenskt samhällsliv. Stockholm 1948.

Söderberg, T.: Den namnlösa medelklassen. Socialgrupp två i det gamla svenska samhället. Stockholm 1956.

Söderberg, T.: Stora Kopparberget under medeltiden och Gustav Vasa. Stockholm 1932.

Söderberg, T.: Sveriges ekonomiska struktur och utveckling under Gustav Adolf. [Typescript in Krigsarkivet, Stockholm: *ca.* 1935.]

Söderlind, S.: Smöret i Vadstena. Ett diskussionsinlägg. (*Historisk Tidskrift*, II. Series, 13.) Stockholm 1950.

Tegengren, H.: Försök till saltproduktion i Sverige och Finland på 1500-, 1600- och 1700-talen. (*Historisk Tidskrift för Finland*, 19.) Helsingfors 1935.

Tegnér, E.: Svenska bilder från sextonhundratalet. Stockholm 1896.

Tham, W.: Lindesberg och Nora genom tiderna, I. Lindesberg 1943.

Thomson, A.: Grundskatterna i den politiska diskussionen 1809-1866. Lund 1923.

Thulin, G.: Om mantalet, I. Stockholm 1890.

Tunberg, S.: Stora Kopparbergets historia, I. Uppsala 1922.

Törne, P. O. von: Inverkningar av förläningsväsendet på jordbesittningsförhållandena före och efter reduktionen. Helsingfors 1917.

Uhr, G.: Om förhållandet mellan virkestillgång och virkeskonsumtion inom den norduppländska bergshantering en under 1600-talets första kvartsekel. (*Geographica*, XV.) Stockholm 1944.

Valentin, H.: Judarnas historia i Sverige. Stockholm 1924.

Vasar, J.: Utvecklingen av böndernas rättsläge i Estland till Karl XI. (*Svio-Estonica*, III.) Tartu 1936.

Vennberg, E.: art. 'Anders Bure' in Svenskt Biografiskt Lexikon, VI. Stockholm 1926.

Ward, C.: Svenskarna vid Delaware. Stockholm 1938.

Wendt, E.: Det svenska licentväsendet i Preussen 1627-1635. Uppsala 1933.

Wernstedt, F.: Ståthållaren Christoffer Wernstedt 1542-1627. Stockholm 1929.

Westin, G.: John Durie in Sweden 1636-1638. Uppsala 1936.

Wieselgren, S.: Sveriges fängelser och fångvård. Stockholm 1895.

Wieslander, G.: Skogsbristen i Sverige under 1600- och 1700-talen. (*Skogsvårdsföreningens Tidskrift*, 1936.) Stockholm 1936.

Wittrock, G.: Regering och allmoge under Kristinas egen styrelse. Riksdagen 1650. Uppsala 1953.

Wittrock, G.: Svenska handelskompaniet och kopparhandeln under Gustaf II Adolf. Uppsala 1919.

Wolontis, J.: Kopparmyntningen i Sverige 1624-1714. Helsingfors 1936.

Yernaux, J.: La Métallurgie liégeoise et son expansion au XVIIe siècle. Liége 1939.

Öhlander, C.: Bidrag till de adliga privilegiernas historia 1611-1626. Uppsala 1903.

K. The Army and Navy
(Chapters III and IV)

Adcock, F. E.: The Roman Art of War under the Republic. Cambridge [Mass.] 1940.

Alm, J.: Blanka vapen och skyddsvapen. Stockholm 1932.

Alm, J.: Eldhandvapen, I. Stockholm 1933.

Anderson, R. C.: Naval Wars in the Baltic during the Sailing-ship Epoch 1522-1850. London 1910.

André, L.: Michel Le Tellier et Louvois. Paris 1943.

Andrzejewski, S.: Military Organization and Society. London 1954.

Barkman, G. B. C:son: Gustaf II Adolf såsom härorganisatör och fältherre. (*Kungl. Krigsvetenskaps-Akademiens Handlingar och Tidskrift*, 9.) Stockholm 1932.

Barkman, G. B. C:son: Gustav II Adolfs militära gärning i den krigsvetenskapliga litteraturens belysning. (*Historisk Tidskrift*, I. Series, 52.) Stockholm 1932.

Barkman, G. B. C:son: Gustaf II Adolfs regementsorganisation vid det inhemska infanteriet. (Meddelanden från Generalstabens krigshistoriska avdelning, I.) Stockholm 1931.

Barkman, G. B. C:son: Kungl. Svea Livgardets historia, II. Stockholm 1938-39.

Belfrage, N.: Erik Soop och Västgöta ryttare, 1622-1631. Stockholm 1934.

Bennedich, C.: Ur det gamla Gardets öden. Stockholm 1926.

Bensow, E.: Kungl. Skaraborgs regementes historia, I. Göteborg 1931.

Broomé, B.: En polsk relation om sjöslaget utanför Danzig 1627. (*Forum navale*, X.) Uppsala 1951.

Brusiin, O.: Gustav II Adolfs krigsartiklar. (*Tidskrift utgiven av Juridiska Föreningen i Finland*, 79.) Helsingfors 1943.

Carman, W. Y.: A History of Firearms from the Earliest Times to 1914. London 1955.

Clausewitz, C. von: Strategische Beleuchtung mehrerer Feldzüge. (Hinterlassene Werke, vol. 9.) Berlin 1837.

Colin, J.: Les Transformations de la guerre. Paris 1933.

Colin, J.; Reboul, F.: Histoire militaire et navale, I. (Histoire de la Nation française [ed. *G. Hanotaux*], VIII.) Paris 1925.

Corbett, J. S.: Drake and the Tudor Navy. London 1899.

Corbett, J. S.: England in the Mediterranean 1603-1713, I. London 1917.

Corbett, J. S.: The Successors of Drake. London 1900.

Cruickshank, C. G.: Elizabeth's Army. Oxford 1946.

Czołowski, A.: Marynarka w Polsce. Szkic historyczny. Lwów 1922.

Davies, E.: The Art of War and Englands Traynings. London 1619.

Delbrück, H.: Geschichte der Kriegskunst im Rahmen der politischen Geschichte, IV. Berlin 1920.

Denison, G. T.: A History of Cavalry (2nd edn.). London 1913.

Deuticke, K.: Die Schlacht bei Lützen 1632. Giessen 1917.

Droysen, G.: Beiträge zur Geschichte des Militärwesens in Deutschland während der Epoche des dreissigjährigen Krieges. Hannover 1875.

Earle, E. M. [ed.]: Makers of Modern Strategy. Military Thought from Machiavelli to Hitler. Princeton 1944.

Ericsson, E.: Olof Hansson Örnehufvud och svenska fortifikationsväsendet. Till 300-årsminnet 1635-1935. Uppsala 1935.

Essén, R.: Sjömaktens och sjöfartens roll i Gustaf II Adolfs Sverige. (*Tidskrift i Sjöväsendet*, Jubileumshäfte.) Stockholm 1932.

Falls, C.: Elizabeth's Irish Wars. London 1950.

Firth, C. H.: Cromwell's Army. London 1905.

Frauenholz, E. von: Das Söldnertum in der Zeit des dreissigjährigen Krieges. Munich 1938.

Frauenholz, E. von: Die Landesdefension in der Zeit des dreissigjährigen Krieges. Munich 1939.

Frauenholz, E. von: Lazarus von Schwendi. Der erste deutsche Verkünder der allgemeinen Wehrpflicht. Hamburg 1929.

Führertum. 26 Lebensbilder von Feldherren aller Zeiten. [ed. Generalleutnant *von Cochenhausen*] (3rd edn.). Berlin 1937.

Fuller, J. F. C.: Armament and History. A Study of the Influence of Armament on History from the Dawn of Classical Warfare to the Second World War. London 1946.

Försvarsstabens krigshistoriska avdelning: Från Femern och Jankow till Westfaliska Freden. En minnesskrift år 1948. Stockholm 1948.

Försvarsstabens krigshistoriska avdelning: Slaget vid Jankow 1645-24/2-1945. Stockholm 1945.

Försvarsstabens krigshistoriska avdelning: Vägar och vägkunskap i Kellaneuropa under trettioåriga krigets sista skede. Stockholm 1948.

Gaya: Gaya's Traité des Armes 1678. Edited by *Charles ffoulkes*. Oxford 1911.

Generalstaben: Karl XII på slagfältet. Karolinsk slagledning sedd mot bakgrunden av taktikens utveckling från äldsta tider, I. Stockholm 1918.

Generalstabens krigshistoriska avdelning: Axtorna. En studie i organisation och taktik. (Meddelanden från Kungl. Krigsarkivet utgifna av Generalstabens krigshistoriska avdelning, IV.) Stockholm 1926.

Gierow, A.: Bidrag till det svenska militärkyrkoväsendets historia, I. Uppsala 1918.

Grönfors, K.: Ur det svenska militära rättegångsväsendets historia. (*Rättshistoriska Studier*, II. Series, 1.) Lund 1951.

Günther, R.: Die Entwicklung der Feuertaktik der Infanterie. Berlin 1902.

Hagedorn, B.: Die Entwicklung der wichtigsten Schiffstypen bis ins 19. Jahrhundert. (*Veröffentlichungen des Vereins für Hamburgische Geschichte*, I.) Berlin 1914.

Hahlweg, W.: Die Heeresreform der Oranier und die Antike. Berlin 1941.

Hall, A. R.: Ballistics in the Seventeenth Century. A Study in the Relations of Science and War with reference principally to England. Cambridge 1952.

Hamilton, H.: Afhandling om krigsmaktens och krigskonstens tillstånd i Sverige, under konung Gustaf II Adolfs regering. Stockholm 1846.

Hammarskiöld, L.: Artilleriöverstarna von Siegroth. (*Personhistorisk Tidskrift*, 36.) Stockholm 1935.

Hammarskiöld, L.: Gustav II Adolfs artilleri. (*Artilleri-Tidskrift*, 66.) Uppsala 1937.

Hammarskiöld, L.: Om svenskt artilleri i äldre tider. (*Historisk Tidskrift*, II. Series, 4.) Stockholm 1941.

Hammarskiöld, L.: Ur svenska artilleriets hävder. [This is a series of supplements, with separate and consecutive pagination, to various numbers of *Artilleri-Tidskrift*, 1941-44.] [Cited: Hammarskiöld, *USAH*.]

Heijkenskjöld, C.: Svensk styckegjutning och lodstöpning av järn under perioden 1540-1840. (*Artilleri-Tidskrift*, 64.) Uppsala 1935.

Heischman, E.: Die Anfänge des stehenden Heeres in Österreich. Vienna 1925.

Henderson, G. F. R.: The Science of War. London 1906.

Hornborg, E.: Kampen om Östersjön. Stockholm 1945.

Jähns, M.: Handbuch einer Geschichte des Kriegswesens von der Urzeit bis zur Renaissance. Leipzig 1880.

Jakobsson, T.: Über die Schussweiten der schwedischen Artilleri der Gustav-Adolfs-Zeit. (Pirmā Baltijas Vēsturnieku Konference 1937.) Riga 1938.

Jany, C.: Geschichte der Königlich Preussischen Armee, I. Berlin 1928.

Jonge, J. C. de: Het Nederlandsche Zeewezen, I. Haarlem 1858.

Jugannière, Le M. de la: Une Révolution dans la tactique au XVIIe siècle. (*Recueil des Publications de la Société Havraise d'Etudes diverses*, 1914.) Le Havre 1914.

Jörlin, G.: Lützenoperationen. (*Ny Militär Tidskrift*, V.) Stockholm 1932.

Kampen om Østersjøen, sett fra norsk, dansk, svensk og finsk synspunkt. [Symposium issued by Oslo Militaere Samfund.] Oslo 1935.

Kerchnawe, H.: Lützen. Zeitgemässe Betrachtung zum 16. November 1632. (*Militärwissenschaftliche Mitteilungen*, 63.) Vienna, 1932.

Knötel, R.; Knötel, H.; Sieg, J.: Handbuch der Uniformkunde. Die militärische Tracht in ihrer Entwicklung bis zur Gegenwart. Hamburg 1937.

Korhonen, A.: Om finska rytteriet under Gustaf II Adolf. (*Ny Militär Tidskrift*, IV.) Stockholm 1931.

Korzon, T.: Dzieje wojen i wojskowości w Polsce, II. Kraków, 1912.

Krusenstierna, H. von: Gustaf II Adolf och Sveriges försvar. (*Vår flotta*, 28.) Stockholm 1932.

Kukiel, M.: Zarys historji wojskowośce w Polsce. London 1949.

Kungl. Krigsvetenskaps-Akademiens Handlingar och Tidskrift, 9e häftet (Bihäfte 2). Stockholm 1932.

Kungl. Liv-Rustkammaren: Gustav II Adolf vid Lützen (ed. *R. Cederström*). Stockholm 1944.

La Bruyère, R.: La Marine de Richelieu. Maillé-Brézé. Paris 1945.

Laskowski, O.: Infantry Tactics and Firing Power in XVI Century. (*Teki historyczne*, IV.) London 1950.

Laskowski, O.: Uwagi na marginesie nowego wydanie Zarysu Historii Wojskowośce w Polsce Generała Mariana Kukiela. (*Teki historyczne*, V.) London 1951-52.

Lenk, T.: Le Cabinet royal des Armes (Kungl. Livrustkammaren). (*Révue internationale d'Histoire militaire*, 7.) Paris 1949.

Lenz, M.: Landgraf Moritz von Hessen (Kleine Historische Schriften, II). Munich and Berlin 1920.

Lewis, M.: The Navy of Britain. A Historical Portrait. London 1949.

Liddell Hart, B. H.: Great Captains Unveiled. London 1927.

Loewe, V.: Die Organisation und Verwaltung der Wallensteinischen Heere, I. Freiburg i. B. 1895.

Londoño, S. de: Discurso sobre la forma de reducir la Disciplina militar a mejor y antiguo estado. [New edn.] Madrid 1943.

Lorentzen, T.: Die schwedische Armee im dreissigjährigen Kriege. Leipzig 1894.

Mathisen, T.: Fra bondeoppbud til legdshaer. Oslo 1952.

Montecuccoli, R.: Mémoires de Montecuccoli, Généralissime des Troupes de l'Empereur. Strasbourg 1735.

Munthe, A.: Sjömaktens inflytande på Sveriges historia, I. Stockholm 1921.

Munthe, A.: Svenska sjöhjältar, V. Klas Fleming, Karl Gustaf Wrangel, Martin Thijsen Anckarhielm. Stockholm 1905.

Munthe, L. W.: Kongl. Fortifikationens historia, I. Stockholm 1902.

Nef, J. U.: War and Economic Progress 1540-1640. (*Economic History Review*, XII.)

Nef, J. U.: War and Human Progress. An essay on the rise of industrial civilization. London 1950.

Nordström, G.: Régiments Jaune, Bleu, Vert, Rouge et Blanc de l'ancienne Armée Suèdoise. (*Révue internationale d'Histoire militaire*, 8.) Paris 1950.

Nordström, G.: Wallensteins stridsplan vid Lützen (Krigshistoriska studier tillägnade Olof Ribbing). Stockholm 1950.

Norrman, O.: Övergången av Donau och Lech. (*Ny Militär Tidskrift*, V.) Stockholm 1932.

Odenrick, O. S. F.: Lantkrigskonstens utveckling sedd mot bakgrunden av den allmänna teknikens framåtskridande och stridsmedlens utveckling, II. Stockholm 1933.

Oestreich, G.: Der römische Stoizismus und die Oranische Heeresreform. (*Historische Zeitschrift*, 176.) Munich 1953.

Oman, Sir C.: A History of the Art of War in the Sixteenth Century. London 1937.

Petri, G.: Gustaf II Adolf och Sveriges försvarsväsendet (*Göteborgs försvar*). Göteborg 1932.

Petri, G.: Kungl. Första Livgrenadjärregements historia, I-II. Stockholm 1926.

[*Pett, P.*]: The Autobiography of Phineas Pett (ed. W. G. Perrin). (*Navy Records Society*, LI.) London 1918.

Pickel, D. W.: Gustaf Adolf und Wallenstein in der Schlacht an der Alten Veste. Nuremberg 1926.

Pieri, P.: Il Rinascimento e la crisi militare italiana. Turin 1952.

Pieri, P.: La Formazione dottrinale di Raimondo Montecuccoli. (*Révue Internationale d'Histoire Militaire*, 10.) Paris 1951.

Pihlström, A.: Kungl. Dalregementets Historia, I-II. Stockholm 1902-04.

Ribbing, O.: L'Art de Guerre nordique pendant la domination suèdoise sur la Baltique. (*Révue Internationale d'Histoire Militaire*, 7.) Paris 1949.

Ritter, M.: Das Kontributionssystem Wallensteins. (*Historische Zeitschrift*, 90 [N.F. 54].) Munich and Berlin 1903.

Robertson, F. L.: The Evolution of Naval Armament. London 1921.

Rockstroh, K. C.: Udviklingen af den nationale Haer i Danmark i det 17. og 18. Aarhundrede. I. Tiden 1614-1670. Copenhagen 1909.

Sander, E.: Zur Geschichte des Gleichschritts. (*Zeitschrift für Heeres- und Uniformkunde.*) Hamburg 1935.

Schmitthenner, P.: Europäische Geschichte und Söldnertum. (Schriften der Kriegsgeschichtlichen Abteilung im historischen Seminar der Friedrich-Wilhelms-Universität Berlin.) Berlin 1933.

Schmitthenner, P.: Krieg und Kriegführung im Wandel der Weltgeschichte. Potsdam 1930.

Seidler, J.: Untersuchungen über die Schlacht bei Lützen 1632. Memmingen 1954.

Seitz, H.: Bardisanen som svenskt drabant- och befälsvapen. Stockholm 1943.

Silberner, E.: La Guerre dans la pensée économique du XVIe au XVIIIe siècle. Paris 1939.

Sjöstrand, W.: Grunddragen av den militära undervisningens uppkomst- och utvecklingshistoria i Sverige till år 1792. Uppsala 1941.

Spens, E.: Flottan under Konung Gustaf II Adolfs regering. (*Kungl. Krigsvetenskaps-Akademiens Handlingar och Tidskrift*, 9.) Stockholm 1632.

Staszewski, J.: Review of G. MacMunn, *Le Lion du Nord* (*Baltic Countries*, II). Toruń 1936.

Steckzén, B.: Fältherren. (*Ny Militär Tidskrift*, V.) Stockholm 1932.

Steckzén, B.: Johan Baner. Stockholm 1939.

Stenbock, R.: Östgöta Kavalleriregimente 1618-1699. Stockholm 1927.

Stenbock, R.: Östgöta ryttare 1552-1617. Stockholm 1922.

Svenska Flottans Historia, I. Malmö 1942.

Det svenska svärdet. Tolv avgörande händelser i Sveriges historia (ed. *N. F. Holm*). Stockholm 1948.

Sveriges försvar (edd. *C. W. Kleen* and *E. H. K. Björn*). Stockholm 1927.

Sveriges Krig 1611-1632, I-VI, Supplementary vols. I-II. Stockholm 1936-39.

The Swedish Discipline, Religiovs, Civile and Military. London 1632.

Sörensson, P.: Adelns rusttjänst och adelsfanans organisation 1521-1680. (*Historisk Tidskrift*, I. Series, 42.) Stockholm 1922.

Sörensson, P.: Ekonomi och krigföring under Gustaf II Adolfs tyska fälttåg 1630-1632. (*Scandia*, V.) Stockholm 1932.

Sörensson, P.: Fältherrar, härorganisation och krigföring under trettioåriga krigets senare skede. En orientering. (*Scandia*, III.) Stockholm 1930.

Sörensson, P.: Krisen vid de svenska arméerna i Tyskland efter Banérs död. Stockholm 1931.

Terry, C. Sanford: The Life and Campaigns of Alexander Leslie, First Earl of Leven. London 1899.

Tingsten, L.: Fältmarskalkarna Johan Baner och Lennart Tortensson. Stockholm 1922.

Tingsten, L.: Gustav II Adolfs politik och krigföring i Tyskland 1630-1632. Stockholm 1927.

Tingsten, L.: Huvuddragen av medeltidens samt nya och nyare tidens krigskonst. Stockholm 1928.

Tingsten, L.: Några data angående Gustav II Adolfs basering och operationsplaner i Tyskland 1630-1632. (*Historisk Tidskrift*, I. Series, 48.) Stockholm 1928.

Turner, Sir J.: Memoirs of his own Life and Times. Edinburgh 1829.

Turner, Sir J.: Pallas Armata. Military Essayes of the Ancient Grecian, Roman, and Modern Art of War. Written in the Years 1670 and 1671. London 1683.

Törnbom, O.: Båtsmanshållets uppkomst. (*Forum navale*, IX.) Uppsala 1948.

Unger, G.: Illustrerad svensk sjökrigshistoria, I. Stockholm 1909.

Vagts, A.: A History of Militarism. Romance and Realities of a Profession. London 1938.

Wahlström, G.: Gustaf Adolf som befälhavare. En militärpsykologisk studie. (*Tidskrift i Sjöväsendet*, 1932.) Stockholm 1932.

Wallhausen, J. J.: Art militaire à Cheval. Francfort 1616.

Wallhausen, J. J.: L'Art militaire pour l'Infanterie. Oppenheim 1615.

Wendt, E.: Amiralitetskollegiets historia, I. Stockholm 1950.

Wendt, E.: Svenska örlogsflottan och handelsbeskattningen i Preussen under åren 1627-29. (*Tidskrift i Sjöväsendet*, Jubileumshäfte.) Stockholm 1932.

Weygand, General: Histoire de l'Armée française. Paris 1938.

Weygand, General: Turenne. Paris 1934.

Widén, A.: Underbefälets historia. Minnesskrift på uppdrag av Försvarsväsendets Underbefälsförbund. Stockholm 1938.

Wijn, *J. W.*: Het Krijgswezen in den Tijd van Prins Maurits. Utrecht 1934.

Wijn, *J. W.* [ed.]: Krijgskundige Aantekeningen van Johan den Middelste van Nassau. (Werken uitgegeven door het historisch Genootschap gevestigd te Utrecht, III. Series, 76.) Utrecht 1947.

Wittrock, *G.*: Die Schlacht bei Lützen. Quellenkritische Bemerkungen. (*Historische Vierteljahrschrift*, 25 [33].) Dresden 1931.

Zeeh, *E.*: Gustav II Adolf och den svenska västkustens försvar. (*Göteborgs försvar.*) Göteborg 1936.

Zeeh, *E.*: L'Influence française sur les méthodes de guerre en Suède du XVIe au XVIIe siècle. (*Révue Internationale d'Histoire Militaire*, 5.) Paris 1945.

Zettersten, *A.*: Svenska flottans historia, I. Stockholm 1890.

L. Political and Military History 1626-32

(Chapters V-XI)

(See also Sections C, D (Vol. I), and K, above)

Adler, *F.*: Die Belagerung Stralsunds 1628. Stralsund 1628.

Ahnlund, *N.*: Gustaf Adolf inför tyska kriget. Stockholm 1918.

Ahnlund, *N.*: Gustav Adolf och det evangeliska väsendet. (Festskrift till Verner Söderberg.) Stockholm 1932.

Ahnlund, *N.*: Gustaf II Adolf och tyska kriget 1620-5. (*Historisk Tidskrift*, I. Series, 37.) Stockholm 1917.

Ahnlund, *N.*: Gustaf II Adolfs första preussiska fälttåg och den europeiska krisen 1626. (*Historisk Tidskrift*, I. Series, 38.) Stockholm 1918.

Ahnlund, *N.*: 'Kejsardömet Skandinavien.' (*Historisk Tidskrift*, I. Series, 54.) Stockholm 1934.

Ahnlund, *N.*: Öfverläggningarna i riksrådet April 1629. (*Historisk Tidskrift*, I. Series, 35.) Stockholm 1915.

Ahnlund, *N.*: Öfverläggningar i riksrådet om tyska kriget 1628-1629. (*Historisk Tidskrift*, I. Series, 34.) Stockholm 1914.

Albertini, *R. von*: Das politische Denken in Frankreich zur Zeit Richelieus. Marburg 1951.

Altamira y Crevea, R.: Historia de España y de la Civilización española, III. Barcelona 1927.

Alvárez, M. F.: Don Gonzalo Fernández de Cordóba y la Guerra de Sucesión de Mantua y del Monferrato (1627-1629). Madrid 1955.

Angyal, D.: Gabriel Bethlen. (*Révue historique*, 158.) Paris 1928.

Armstedt, R.: Der schwedische Heiratsplan des Grossen Kurfürsten. Königsberg 1896.

Arnoldsson, S.: Krigspropagandan i Sverige före trettioåriga kriget. Göteborg 1941.

Arnoldsson, S.: Svensk-fransk krigs- och fredspolitik i Tyskland 1634-6. Göteborg 1937.

Bär, M.: Die Politik Pommerns während des dreissigjährigen Krieges. Leipzig 1896.

Batiffol, L.: Richelieu et la question d'Alsace. (*Révue historique*, 138.) Paris 1921.

Baur, J.: Philipp von Sötern, geistlicher Kurfürst zu Trier, und seine Politik während des dreissigjährigen Krieges, I. Speyer 1897.

Baur, J. B.: Die Kapuziner und die schwedische Generalität im dreissigjährigen Kriege. Brizen 1887.

Baustaedt, B.: Richelieu und Deutschland. Von der Schlacht bei Breitenfeld bis zum Tode Bernhards von Weimar. Berlin 1936.

Berggren, P. G.: Lars Grubbe, hans lif och verksamhet. Karlstad 1898.

Bierehe, J.: Gustav Adolf in Erfurt. Erfurt 1924.

Boehn, M. von: Wallenstein. (Menschen, Völker, Zeiten.) Vienna 1926.

Boëthius, A.: Romanus Nicephori och Gustaf Adolf. (*Historisk Tidskrift*, I. Series, 32.) Stockholm 1912.

Boëthius, B.: Aktstycken rörande Salvius' underhandlingar med Brandenburg i September 1631. (*Historisk Tidskrift*, I. Series, 33.) Stockholm 1913.

Boëthius, B.: Filip Reinhart von Solms och Gustaf Adolf före Leipzigkonventet. (*Historisk Tidskrift*, I. Series, 37.) Stockholm 1917.

Boëthius, *B.*: Filip Sadlers beskickning 1629-1630. (*Historisk Tidskrift*, I. Series, 37.) Stockholm 1917.

Boëthius, *B.*: Gustaf II Adolfs instruktion för Salvius den 30 juni 1630. (*Historisk Tidskrift*, I. Series, 33.) Stockholm 1913.

Boëthius, *B.*: 'Norma futurarum actionum.' (*Historisk Tidskrift*, I. Series, 31.) Stockholm 1911.

Boëthius, *B.*: Nyare undersökningar rörande Gustaf II Adolfs planer i Tyskland. (*Historisk Tidskrift*, I. Series, 28.) Stockholm 1908.

Boëthius, *B.*: Några Gustav Adolfs-forskningens problem. (*Svensk Tidskrift*, XVII.) Stockholm 1917.

Boëthius, *B.*: Salvius i den nedersaxiska kretsen, maj-december 1631. (*Historisk Tidskrift*, I. Series, 30.) Stockholm 1910.

Boëthius, *B.*: Svenskarne i de nedersachsiska och westfaliska kustländerna. Uppsala 1912. [Cited: Boethius, *NSK*.]

Brulin, *H.*: Stilleståndet i Altmark 1629. (Historiska studier tillägnade Harald Hjärne.) Stockholm 1908.

Bühring, *J.*: Venedig, Gustav Adolf und Rohan. Halle 1885.

Burnet, *G.*: The Memoires of the Lives and Actions of James and William, Dukes of Hamilton and Castleherald, etc. London 1677.

Carlsson, *W.*: Gustaf II Adolf och Stralsund. Uppsala 1912.

Carsten, *F. L.*: The Origins of Prussia. Oxford 1954.

Chemnitz, *B. F. von*: Königlichen Schwedischen in Teutschland geführten Krieg, I. Stettin 1648.

Cichocki, *M.*: Medjacja Francji w rozejmie altmarskim. Kraków 1928.

Dedouvres, *L.*: Le Père Joseph de Paris, Capucin. L'Eminence grise, I-II. Paris 1932.

Donaubauer, *S.*: Nürnberg um die Mitte des dreissigjährigen Krieges. Nüremberg 1893.

Droysen, *G.*: Brandenburgische Audienzen bei Gustaf Adolf. Berlin 1878.

Droysen, *G.*: Die niedersächsischen Kreisstände während des schwedisch-deutschen Krieges 1631 und 1632. n.d.

Droysen, G.: Die Verhandlungen über den Universalfrieden im Winter 1631-32. (*Archiv für die sächsische Geschichte*, N.S., 6.) Leipzig 1880. [Cited: Droysen, *Universalfrieden.*]

Dudík, B.: Waldstein von seiner Enthebung bis zur abermaligen Uebernahme des Armee-Ober-Commando. Vienna 1858.

Egelhaaf, G.: Gustav Adolf in Deutschland 1630-1632. Halle 1901.

Egelhaaf, G.: Gustav Adolf und die deutsche Reichsstände. (*Deutsche Rundschau*, CXI.) Berlin 1902.

Ehses, S.: Papst Urban VIII und Gustav Adolf. (*Historisches Jahrbuch*, XVI.) Munich 1895.

Endriss, J.: Ulms Beziehungen zu Gustav Adolf. Ulm 1932.

Ericsson, E.: Rosladin och Stralsunds belägring 1628. (*Kungl. Krigsvetenskapsakademiens Tidskrift*, 1932.) Stockholm 1932.

Ernstberger, A.: Wallensteins Heeressabotage und die Breitenfelder Schlacht (1631). (*Historische Zeitschrift*, 142.) Munich 1930.

Essen, A. van der: Le Cardinal-Infant, I. Brussels 1944.

Fagniez, G.: Le Père Joseph et Richelieu, I-II. Paris 1894.

Fagniez, G.: Richelieu et l'Allemagne. (*Révue historique*, 45.) Paris 1891.

Fäh, F.: Gustav Adolf und die Eidgenossen 1629-1632. Basel 1887.

Falk, E.: Sverige och Frankrike från Gustaf II Adolfs död till upplösningen af det svensk-franska förbundet 1632-1634. Uppsala 1911.

Fischer, T. A.: The Scots in Germany: being a contribution towards the History of the Scots abroad. Edinburgh 1902.

Flassan, de: Histoire générale et raisonnée de la Diplomatie française ou de la politique de la France, II-III. Paris 1811.

Forster, J.: Sir John Eliot: a biography, I-II. London 1865.

Frantz, J.: Ein englischer Bericht über den dreissigjährigen Krieg. (Beiträge zur Bücherkunde und Philologie August Wilmanns . . . gewidmet.) Leipzig 1903.

Fridericia, J. A.: Danmarks ydre politiske Historie i Tiden fra Freden i Lybek til Freden i Prag, I. Copenhagen 1876. [Cited: Fridericia, *YPH.*]

Fries, E.: Erik Oxenstierna. Biografisk Studie. Stockholm 1889.

Frohnhäuser, L.: Gustav Adolf und die Schweden in Mainz und am Rhein. Darmstadt 1894.

Gaedeke, A.: Wallensteins Verhandlung mit den Schweden und Sachsen 1631-1634. Frankfort 1885.

Gebauer, J.: Kurbrandenburg in der Krisis des Jahres 1627. Halle 1896.

Geyso, F. von: Die schwedenfreundliche Politik Hessens der Jahre 1631-34. Marburg 1923.

Gindely, A.: Beiträge zur Geschichte des dreissigjährigen Krieges. (*Archiv für österreichische Geschichte*, 98.) Vienna 1901.

Gindely, A.: Die Maritimen Pläne der Habsburger und die Antheilname Kaisers Ferdinand II am polnisch-schwedischen Krieg während der Jahre 1627-1629. (*Denkschriften der Kaiserlichen Akademie der Wissenschaften*, 39.) Vienna 1891-2.

Gindely, A.: Friedrich V von der Pfalz der ehemalige Winterkönig von Böhmen seit dem Regensburger Deputationstag vom Jahre 1622 bis zu seinem Tode. Prague 1885.

Grant, J.: Konung Gustaf Adolfs skottska krigare. Stockholm 1853.

Grauers, S.: Det pfalziska restitutionskravet. En rättsdiskussion från 30-åriga krigets dagar. Göteborg 1924.

Green, M. A. E.: Elizabeth Electress Palatine and Queen of Bohemia (revised by *S. C. Lomas*). London 1909.

[*Grotius*]: Hugonis Grotii de Jure belli ac pacis Libri Tres (ed. *W. Whewell*). Cambridge 1853.

Grönstedt, J.: Konung Gustaf II Adolphs död och likbegängelse. Stockholm 1912.

Gualdo-Priorato, G.: L'Histoire des dernières campagnes et négociations de Gustave-Adolphe en Allemagne. Avec des Notes . . . par M. l'Abbé de Francheville. Berlin 1772.

Haas, L.: Schwedens Politik gegenüber der Eidgenossenschaft während des dreissigjährigen Krieges. (*Schweizer Beiträge zur Allgemeinen Geschichte*, 9.) Bern 1951.

H[*allendorf*], *C. H.*: Review of J. Kretzschmar, *Gustav Adolfs Pläne und Ziele in Deutschland.* (*Historisk Tidskrift*, I. Series, 24.) Stockholm 1904.

Hallwich, H.: Fünf Bücher Geschichte Wallensteins, I-III. Leipzig 1910.

Hallwich, H.: Wallenstein und Arnim im Frühjahre 1632. (*Mittheilungen des Vereins für Geschichte der Deutschen in Böhmen*, 17.) Prague 1878.

[*Hamilton*]: De svenska ätterna Hamilton. En släktkrönika (ed. *J. A. W. Hamilton*), I. Stockholm 1936.

Hammarstrand, S. F.: Bidrag till historien om Konung Gustaf II Adolfs deltagande i trettioårige kriget. Uppsala 1859.

Hanotaux, G.; Duc de la Force: Histoire du Cardinal de Richelieu, II-IV. Paris.

Hart, W.: The History of the Life of Gustavus Adolphus, I-II. London 1767.

Hebbe, P. M.: Svenskarna i Böhmen och Mähren. Studier i tjeckiska folktradition och litteratur. Uppsala 1932.

Hedin, S.: Resare-Bengt. En levnadsteckning. Stockholm 1921.

Heimer, A.: De diplomatiska förbindelserna mellan Sverige och England 1633-54. Lund 1893.

Helbig, K. G.: Gustav Adolf und die Kurfürsten von Sachsen und Brandenburg. Leipzig 1854.

Hildebrand, E.: Wallenstein och hans förbindelser med svenskarne. (*Historisk Tidskrift*, I. Series, 3.) Stockholm 1883.

Hill, C. E.: The Danish Sound Dues and the Command of the Baltic. Durham, N.C. 1926.

Hoenig, B.: Memoiren englischer Officiere im Heere Gustav Adolfs und ihr Fortleben in der Literatur. (Beiträge zur neueren Philologie J. Schipper dargebracht.) Leipzig 1902.

Hoppe, I.: Israel Hoppe's Burggrafen zu Elbing Geschichte des ersten schwedisch-polnischen Krieges in Preussen, nebst Anhang (ed. *M. Toeppen*). Leipzig 1887.

Horn, C. C:son v.: Tilly och Wallenstein: ett försök till karakteristik. (*Ny Militär Tidskrift*, IV.) Stockholm 1931.

Huschke, W.: Herzog Wilhelm von Weimar als Statthalter Gustav Adolfs in Thüringen und schwedischer Generalleutnant 1631-1635. Jena 1936.

Irmer, G.: Hans Georg von Arnim. Leipzig 1894.

Jacob, K.: Strassburgische Politik vom Austritt aus der Union bis zum Bündniss mit Schweden (1621-1632). Strassburg 1899.

Jarring, G.: Gustaf II Adolf och tatarerna på Krim. (*Ny Militär Tidskrift*, V.) Stockholm 1932.

Jarrys von La Roche, C. du: Der dreissigjährige Krieg vom militärischen Standpunkte aus beleuchtet, II. Schaffhausen 1851.

Keller, R.: Die Friedensverhandlungen zwischen Frankreich und dem Kaiser auf dem Regensburger Kurfürstentag 1630. Bonn 1902.

Knapp, H.: Matthias Hoë von Hoënegg und sein Eingreifen in die Politik und Publizistik des dreissigjährigen Krieges. Halle 1902.

Koser, R.: Geschichte der brandenburgischen Politik bis zum westfälischen Frieden von 1648. Stuttgart and Berlin 1913.

Kötschke, R.; Kretzschmar, H.: Sächsische Geschichte. Werden und Wandlungen eines deutschen Stammes und seiner Heimat im Rahmen der deutschen Geschichte, I. Dresden 1935.

Kretzschmar, J.: Der Heilbronner Bund, I-II. Lübeck 1922.

Kretzschmar, J.: Die Allianzverhandlungen Gustav Adolfs mit Kurbrandenburg im Mai und Juni 1631. Berlin 1904.

Kretzschmar, J.: Gustav Adolfs Pläne und Ziele in Deutschland und die Herzöge zu Braunschweig und Lüneburg. Hannover and Leipzig 1904.

Leman, A.: Urbain VIII et la rivalité de la France et de la maison d'Autriche de 1631 à 1635. Paris 1920.

Lenz, M.: Schweden und Deutschland im 17. Jahrhundert. (Kleine Historische Schriften, III.) Munich and Berlin 1922.

Lundgren, S.: Johan Adler Salvius. Problem kring freden, krigsekonomien och maktkampen. Lund 1945.

Malmborg, G.: När Strumpebandsorden förlänades till Gustaf II Adolf och Karl XI. (Svenska Kulturbilder, V.) Stockholm 1931.

Mankell, J.: Om Gustaf II Adolfs politik. Stockholm 1881.

Mankell, J.: Om orsakerna till Gustaf II Adolfs deltagande i trettioåriga kriget. Stockholm 1878.

Mecenseffy, G.: Habsburger im 17. Jahrhundert. Die Beziehungen der Höfe von Wien und Madrid während des dreissigjährigen Krieges. Vienna 1955.

Messow, H. C.: Die Hansestädte und die Habsburgische Ostseepolitik im dreissigjährigen Kriege (1627-8). Berlin 1935.

Mommsen, W.: Kardinal Richelieu. Seine Politik im Elsass und in Lothringen. Berlin 1922.

Mommsen, W.: Richelieu als Staatsman. (*Historische Zeitschrift*, 127.) Munich and Berlin 1923.

Monro, R.: Monro His Expedition with the worthy Scots Regiment (called Mac-Keyes Regiment) levied in August 1626. London 1637.

Norrman, D.: Gustav II Adolf och Vladislav Vasa. (*Svio-Polonica*, 1.) Tartu 1939.

Norrman, D.: Gustav Adolfs politik mot Ryssland och Polen under tyska kriget (1630-1632). Uppsala 1943.

Odhner, C. T.: Om orsakerna till Gustaf II Adolfs deltagande i trettioåriga kriget. Kritisk belysning. (*Historisk bibliotek*, VI.) Stockholm 1879.

Oman, C.: Elizabeth of Bohemia. London 1938.

Opitz, W.: Die Schlacht bei Breitenfeld am 17. September 1631. Leipzig 1892.

Pekař, J.: Wallenstein 1630-1634. Tragödie einer Verschwörung. Berlin 1937.

Pfister, K.: Kurfürst Maximilian I von Bayern und sein Jahrhundert. Munich 1949.

Pickel, D. W.: Gustav Adolf und Wallenstein in der Schlacht an der Alten Veste bei Nürnberg 1632. Nuremberg 1926.

Ranke, L. von: Geschichte Wallensteins. Berlin, n.d. (Deutsche Bibliotek edn.).

Riezler, S.: Geschichte Baierns, V. Gotha 1903.

Rommel, C. von: Geschichte von Hessen, VIII (=Neuere Geschichte von Hessen, IV). Cassel 1843.

Rudel, —: Die Lage Pommerns vom Beginn des dreissigjährigen Krieges bis zum Eintreffen Gustav Adolfs (1620-1630). Stettin 1890.

Rydfors, A.: De diplomatiska förbindelserna mellan Sverige och England 1624-maj 1630. Uppsala 1890.

Sattler, C.: Reichsfreiherr Dodo zu Innhausen und Knyphausen, königl. schwedischen Feldmarschall. Norden 1891.

Schaedel, L.: Gustav Adolf von Schweden in München. (*Forschungen zur Geschichte Bayerns*, 16.) Munich 1908.

Scharold, C. G.: Geschichte der kön. schwedischen und herzogl. sachsenweimarischen Zwischenregierung im eroberten Fürstbisthume Würzburg i. J. 1631-1634, I-II. Würzburg 1844.

Schmitz, O.: Die maritime Politik der Habsburger in der Jahren 1625-1628. Bonn 1903.

Schott, T.: Württemberg und Gustav Adolf. (*Württembergische Vierteljahrshefte für Landesgeschichte*, N.S., 3.) Stuttgart 1894.

Schubert, F. H.: Ludwig Camerarius 1573-1651. Eine Biographie. Kallmünz 1956.

Schulze, R.: Das Projekt der Vermählung Friedrich Wilhelms von Brandenburg mit Christina von Schweden. Halle 1898.

Schwarz, H.: Wallenstein und Gustav Adolf nach dem Kurfürstentag zu Regensburg. Hamburg 1937.

Schybergson, M. G.: Sveriges och Hollands diplomatiska förbindelser 1621-1630. Helsingfors 1881.

Simson, P.: Danzig und Gustav Adolf. Danzig 1924.

Söltl, —: Der Religionskrieg in Deutschland, III. Denkwürdigkeiten aus den Zeiten des Religionskrieges in Deutschland. Hamburg 1842.

[*Spanheim, F.*]: Le Soldat svedois ov Histoire de ce qui s'est passé en Allemagne depuis l'entrée du Roy de Suede en l'année 1630 iusques apres sa mort. n.p. 1633.

Spannagel, K.: Konrad von Burgsdorff. Berlin 1903.

Srbik, H. R. von: Wallensteins Ende. Vienna 1920.

Srbik, H. R. von: Zur Schlacht von Lützen und zu Gustav Adolfs Tod. (*Mitteilungen des österreichischen Instituts für Geschichtsforschung*, XLI.) Vienna.

Struck, W.: Das Bündnis Wilhelms von Weimar mit Gustaf Adolf. Stralsund 1895.

Struck, W.: Gustav Adolf und die schwedische Satisfaktion. (*Historische Vierteljahrschrift*, 2.) 1899.

Szilágyi, A.: Georg Rákóczy I im dreissigjährigen Kriege 1630-1640. Mit Urkunden aus schwedischen und ungarischen Archiven. Budapest 1883.

Teitge, H.: Die Frage nach dem Urheber der Zerstörung Magdeburgs 1631. Halle 1904.

Tongas, A.: L'Ambassadeur Louis Deshayes de Cormenin. Paris 1937.

Treitschke, H. von: Gustav Adolf und Deutschlands Freiheit. Leipzig 1895.

Veraguth, D.: Herzog Rohan und seine Mission in Graubünden und im Veltlin. Biel 1892.

Waddington, A.: La République des Provinces-Unies, la France et les Pays-Bas espagnoles de 1630 à 1650, I. Paris 1895.

Watson, F.: Wallenstein, Soldier under Saturn. London 1938.

[*Watts, W.*]: The Swedish Intelligencer, I-IV. London 1632-33.

Weber, F.: Dietrich von Falkenberg, der Verteidiger Magdeburgs. Burg 1935.

Weibull, L.: De diplomatiska förbindelserna mellan Sverige och Frankrike 1629-1631. Ett bidrag till Gustaf II Adolfs och Kardinal Richelieus historia. Lund 1899. [Cited: L. Weibull, *DF.*]

Weibull, L.: Gustaf II Adolf och kardinal Richelieu. (*Scandia*, VI.) Lund 1933.

Wejle, C.: Sveriges politik mot Polen 1630-5. Uppsala 1901.

Westrin, T.: Philip Sadlers beskickning till Siebenbürgen 1626. (*Historisk Tidskrift*, I. Series, 10.) Stockholm 1890.

Wilmanns, E.: Der Lübecker Friede 1629. Bonn 1904.

Wissdorf, W.: Untersuchung über die Beziehungen Gustav Adolfs zu Frankreich vom schwedisch-polnischen Kriege des Jahres 1629 bis zum Vertrage von Bärwalde. Rostock 1904.

Wittich, K.: Magdeburg, Gustav Adolf und Tilly, I-II. Berlin 1874.

Wittrock, G.: Gustaf Adolfs krigföring i Tyskland efter striderna vid Nürnberg, 1632. Uppsala 1927.

Zeller, G.: La Réunion de Metz à la France (1552-1648), II. Paris 1926.

INDEX

DATE DUE
